The New Compact BIBLE DICTIONARY

A view of beautiful Mount Hermon across the Sea of Galilee. © *MPS*

The New Compact BIBLE DICTIONARY

Edited by T. Alton Bryant

Special Crusade Edition
The Billy Graham Evangelistic Association
Box 779, Minneapolis, Minnesota 55440

THE BILLY GRAHAM EVANGELISTIC ASSOCIATION

Box 779 (1300 Harmon Place), Minneapolis, Minnesota 55440
Box 841 (414 Graham Avenue), Winnipeg 1, Manitoba, Canada
Shirley House, 27 Camden Road, London, N.W. 1, England
820 Caltex House, Sydney, New South Wales, Australia
Box 870, Auckland, New Zealand
Decision, 102 Avenue des Champs-Elysees, Paris 8, France
Entscheidung, Postfach 16309, 6 Frankfurt/M, Germany
Casilla 5055, Buenos Aires, Argentina
Decimex, A.C. Bucareli #42-303 Apdo M. 10742 Mexico 1, D.F.
20 Samon Cho, Shinjuku Ku, Tokyo, Japan

Library of Congress Catalog Card Number 67-22682

Printed in the United States of America

Preface

The purpose of a Bible Dictionary is to place at the reader's fingertips a convenient and adequate explanation and definition of words and proper names which are used in the Bible, assisting in the better comprehension of the meaning and message of the Scripture passage, and to provide thorough and understandable data concerning the subject in which he is interested and with which he is concerned. That is the function of *The New Compact Bible Dictionary*. This book is designed with the lay reader, teacher, and minister, or Bible student in mind. Its definitions are concise yet thorough, and deal with persons, places, objects and events in the Bible. Its summaries of the various books of the Bible, alone, make it invaluable to the serious student.

One outstanding feature of this *Dictionary* is its extensive and up-to-date treatment of recent archaeological finds in the Holy Land, such as the Dead Sea Scrolls and related discoveries. These facts are heavily emphasized in the articles in which they appear, and form a backdrop for much of the recent scholarship evidenced in this reference work.

Another outstanding feature of this *Dictionary* is its extensive photo coverage of Bible places and objects. More than 250 illustrations from various sources have been used to graphically picture these places and events for the reader. The editor wishes to express his deepest appreciation to the following for permission to use photo and other illustrations from their sources: Mr. G. Eric Matson of Matson Photo Service, the Oriental Institute of the University of Chicago, the British Museum of London, the University Museum of Pennsylvania, the Radio Times Hulton Picture Library of London, the University of Michigan Library, Dr. John F. Walvoord, Dr. Siegfried H. Horn of Andrews University, and others.

Pronunciation follows the model of Webster's *New International Dictionary of the English Language*. All Hebrew and Greek names, as well as other names and terms, are followed by their English pronunciations in parentheses. A list of abbreviations follows this Preface.

It is the hope of editor and publisher that this reference work will be used widely and effectively among all who seriously study and revere the Word of God.

T. ALTON BRYANT

ENGLISH PRONUNCIATION

VOWELS		CONSONANTS	
ā	as in tāme, hāte, chā'ŏs, dāte	b	bed, dub
ă	as in hăt, ăsk, glăss, ădd, lăp	d	did, had
â	as in câre, bâre, râre	f	fall, off
ȧ	as in ȧh, ȧrm, fȧ'thêr, sō'fȧ	g	get, dog
		h	he, ahead
ē	as in ēve, hēre, ēvĕnt', mēēt	j	joy, jump
ĕ	as in ĕnd, sī'lĕnt, pĕt, ēvĕnt	k	kill, bake
êr	as in mākêr, ōvêr, ŭndêr, fȧthêr,	l	let, ball
	êrr	m	met, trim
		n	not, ton
ī	as in īce, bīte, mīle, fīne	p	put, tap
ĭ	as in ĭll, hĭt, hĭm, chârĭty	r	red, dear
î	as in bîrth, mîrth	s	sell, pass
		t	top, hat
ō	as in ōld, ōbey, gō, tōne, bōwl	v	vat, have
ŏ	as in ŏn, ŏdd, cŏnnĕct, lŏt, tŏp	w	will, always
ô	as in ôrb, sôft, hôrn, fôrk, nôr	y	yet, yard
o͞o	as in fo͞od, lo͞ot, tro͞op	z	zebra, haze
o͝o	as in fo͝ot, bo͝ok, ho͝ok	ch	chin, arch
		n	ring, drink
ū	as in tūne, rūde, ūnīte', ūse, cūte	sh	she, dash
ŭ	as in ŭs, ŭp, bŭt	th	thin, truth
û	as in ûrn, tûrn, fûr	*th*	then, father
		zh	azure, leisure

For other variations, also double vowels and consonants, we use simplified and phonetic spelling to indicate pronunciation:

â	for e in where, there, etc.	ĭ	for y in typical, hypnosis, etc.
â	for ei, ai, ea in their, fair, bear, etc.	oi	for oy, oi, in boy, boil, oil, foil
ā	for ai in hail, pail, etc.	ow	for ou in about, shout
aw	for au, ou in ought, caught, etc.	ū	for eu in neuter, etc.
ē	for ee, ea, in heed, meat, meal, dear, etc.	egs	for ex in example, etc.
ē	for i in machine, etc.	j	for soft g in giant, etc.
ē	for y in belly, fully, charity, etc.	k	for hard ch in character, etc.
ī	for ei in heil, etc.	s	for soft c in celestial, etc.
ī	for y in type, why, etc.	sh	for s in adhesion, etc.
		shun	for tion in attention, etc.
		z	for soft s in his, etc.

Picture Sources

As declared on the copyright page, the photos and other illustrations in this dictionary are used by special arrangement with the copyright owners and are not to be reproduced without specific permission from the original sources. These sources are indicated by initials (in caps) at the close of descriptive captions with each picture:

ABA	American Baptist Assembly, Green Lake, Wisconsin
ASOR	American Schools of Oriental Research, Jerusalem
BM	British Museum, London; courtesy of the Trustees of the British Museum
DV	J. DeVries' drawings from Bijbels Beeld Woordenboek, published by J. H. Kok, N.V., Kampen, Holland
EG	Ewing Galloway (photo agency), New York
JFW	Dr. John F. Walvoord, Dallas Theological Seminary
JG	John and J.B.E. Garstang, from *The Story of Jericho,* Marshall, Morgan, and Scott, Ltd., London
KC, FC	Kreigh Collins' drawings, from *Bible Days,* by Meindert DeJong, © Fideler Company, Grand Rapids, Mich.
LO	Mrs. Lowell Orth
MPS	Matson Photo Service, Los Angeles, Cal.
OICU	Oriental Institute of the University of Chicago
PAM	Palestine Archaeological Museum, Jerusalem
RTHPL	Radio Times Hulton Picture Library, British Broadcasting Corporation, London
SHH	Dr. S. H. Horn, Andrews University, Berrien Springs, Mich.
SPF	Standard Publishing Foundation, Cincinnati, Ohio. Drawings by Wilbur G. Adam from *Life and Customs in Jesus' Time,* by Joseph L. Gift, © 1957 SPF
UANT	Unger's *Archaeology and the New Testament*; drawings by Alan Marshall, courtesy Dr. Merrill F. Unger, Dallas Theological Seminary, © 1962 by Zondervan Publishing House.
UML	University of Michigan Library, Rare Book Department, Ann Arbor, Michigan
UMP	University Museum of the University of Pennsylvania, Philadelphia

The
New Compact
BIBLE
DICTIONARY

The "Hill of Aaron" in Sinai, close to Jebel Mousa, Mt. Sinai. © MPS

Aaron (âr'ŭn, meaning undetermined), the oldest son of Amram and Jochebed, of the tribe of Levi, and brother of Moses and Miriam (Num. 26:59; Exod. 6:20). Born during the captivity in Egypt, before Pharaoh's edict that all male infants should be destroyed, and three years older than Moses (Exod. 7:7). His name first appears in God's commission to Moses (Exod. 4:14). When Moses objected that he did not possess sufficient ability in public speaking to undertake the mission to Pharaoh, God replied: "Is not Aaron the Levite thy brother? Thou shalt speak unto him, and put words in his mouth: and I will be with thy mouth, and with his mouth, and will teach you what ye shall do. And he shall be thy spokesman unto the people: and he shall be, even he shall be to thee instead of a mouth, and thou shalt be to him instead of God" (Exod. 4:14-16). In accordance with this command he met Moses in "the mount of God" after forty years' separation, and took him back to the family home in Goshen. Aaron introduced him to the elders of the people, and persuaded them to accept him as their leader. Together Moses and Aaron proceeded to Pharaoh's court, where they carried on the negotiations that finally brought the end of the oppression of the Israelites and the exodus from Egypt.

During Moses' forty years in the wilderness Aaron had married Elisheba or Elizabeth, daughter of Amminadab, and sister of Naashon, a prince of the tribe of Judah (Exod. 6:23; I Chron. 2:10). They had four sons: Nadab, Abihu, Eleazar, and Ithamar.

Upon leaving Egypt, Aaron assisted his brother during the wandering in the wilderness. On the way to Sinai, in the battle with Amalek, Aaron and Hur held up Moses' hands (Exod. 17: 9-13) in which was the rod of God, and Israel consequently won the battle. With the establishment of the tabernacle, Aaron became high priest in charge of the national worship, and the head of the hereditary priesthood.

In character he was weak and occasionally jealous. He and Miriam criticized Moses for having married an Ethiopian (Cushite) woman, outside the nation of Israel, and complained that Moses was not God's sole spokesman (Num. 12:1, 2). When Moses went up onto Mt. Sinai to receive the tables of the law from God, Aaron acceded to the people's demand for a visible god that they could worship. Taking their personal jewelry, he melted it in a furnace and made a golden calf similar to the familiar bull-god of Egypt. The people hailed this image as the god who had brought them out of Egypt. Aaron did not remonstrate with them, but built an altar and proclaimed a feast to Jehovah on the morrow, which the people celebrated with revelry and debauchery (Exod. 32:1-6). When Moses returned from the mountain and rebuked Aaron for aiding this abuse, he made the naive answer: "They gave it (the gold) to me, and I threw it into the fire, and there came out this calf" (Exod. 32: 24). It may be that Aaron meant to restrain the people by a compromise, but he was wholly unsuccessful.

When the revelation of the pattern for worship in the Tabernacle was completed two months later, Aaron

The Tomb of Aaron on Mount Hor, near Petra. © *MPS*

and his sons were consecrated to the priesthood (Lev. 8:1-9:22).

At the end of the wilderness wandering Aaron was warned of his impending death. He and Moses went up onto Mt. Hor, where he was stripped of his priestly robes, which passed in succession to his son, Eleazar. He died at the age of 123, and was buried in the mountain (Num. 20:22-29; 33:38; Deut. 10:6; 32:50). The people mourned for him thirty days.

Aaronites (âr'ŭn-īts), descendants of Aaron who fought with David against Saul (I Chron. 12:27). They were distinguished from the general tribe of Levites (I Chron. 27:17).

Ab (ăb), the fifth month of the Hebrew year, coinciding approximately with early August (Num. 33:38).

Abaddon (ȧ-băd'ŭn, **ruin, perdition, destruction),** occurs six times in the OT (Job 26:6; 28:22; 31:12; Prov. 15:11; 27:20; Ps. 88:11). In Job 31:12 it has the general meaning of "ruin," "destruction." In three instances (Job 26:6; Prov. 15:11; 27:20) the word is parallel with Sheol, the abode of the dead. In Job 28:22 it means "death." In Ps. 88:11 it is synonymous with the grave. The word is found once in the New Testament (Rev. 9:11).

Abagtha (ȧ-băg'thȧ), one of the seven eunuchs who served King Ahasuerus as chamberlains (Esth. 1:10).

Abana (ȧ-băn'ȧ, KJV, ASV Abanah, m. Amanah, RSV Abana, m. Amana), the name of a river that flows through Damascus. Mentioned in the Bible only in II Kings 5:12.

Abarim (ăb'ȧ-rĭm, **those beyond,** or **on the other side**), either the region east of the Jordan or the name of a mountain range NW of Moab. The Israelites encamped here just before crossing the Jordan, and from one of its peaks Moses saw the Promised Land (Num. 27:12).

Abba (ăb'ȧ), Aramaic word for **father,** transliterated into Greek and thence into English. The corresponding Hebrew word is Ab. Found three times in the NT (Mark 14:36; Rom. 8:15; Gal. 4:6).

Abda (ăb'dȧ, probably **servant of God).** 1. The father of Adoniram (I Kings 4:6); 2. A Levite, the son of Shammua (Neh. 11:17), called "Obadiah the son of Shemaiah" (I Chron. 9:16).

Abdeel (ăb'dē-ĕl, **servant of God),** the father of Shelemiah, ordered by King Jehoiakim to arrest Jeremiah the prophet and his scribe Baruch (Jer. 36:26).

Abdi (ăb'dī, probably **servant of Jehovah).** 1. A Levite, father of Kishi or Kish; the grandfather of David's singer Ethan (I Chron. 6:44). It is uncertain whether the Abdi of II Chron. 29:12 is the same man.

2. One of the sons of Elam who in Ezra's time had married foreign wives (Ezra 10:26).

Abdiel (ăb'dĭ-ĕl, **servant of God),** a Gadite who lived in Gilead (I Chron. 5:15).

Abdon (ăb'dŏn, meaning uncertain; may be **servant, service,** or **servile**), 1. One of the judges of Israel — the eleventh one mentioned. Nothing is said about his rule except that he judged Israel for eight years (Judg. 12:13-15).

2. One of the sons of Shashak, a Benjamite, living in Jerusalem (I Chron. 8:23, 28).

3. The son of Jeiel of Gibeon (I Chron. 8:30; 9:35, 36).

4. An official of King Josiah, sent by him to Huldah the prophetess (II Chron. 34:20; called Achbor in II Kings 22:12).

Abdon (City), one of four Levitical cities in the tribe Asher (Josh. 21:30; I Chron. 6:74).

Abednego (ȧ-bĕd'nē-gō, **servant of Nego**), one of the three Hebrews (Shadrach, Meshach and Abednego) whom Daniel requested be appointed over the affairs of the province of Babylon.

Abel (ā'bĕl, etymology uncertain; several meanings have been suggested: **breath, transitoriness,** suggestive of his brief life; **shepherd, herdman,** and **son**). Adam's second son, murdered by his brother Cain (Gen. 4). "Abel was a keeper of sheep, but Cain was a tiller of ground" (Gen. 4:2). Abel is described as a righteous man (Matt. 23:35). He offered to God a lamb from his flock, which was accepted; while Cain's offer of the fruit of the ground was rejected. The reason for the divine preference is not given. It may be that God had made known that a sacrifice involving the shedding of blood would alone be acceptable to Him and that Cain had defiantly decided to disregard God's will. On the other hand, it may have been the disposition of the offerer, not the outward offering, that God regarded. We read that Cain's "works were evil, and his brother's righteous" (I John 3:12).

Abel (ā′bĕl, **a meadow**). 1. The name of a city involved in the rebellion of Sheba (II Sam. 20:14, 18); the same as Abel-beth-maacah (II Sam. 20:15). 2. In I Samuel 6:18 KJV, "the great stone of Abel" should probably be "stone."

Abel-beth-maacha (ā′bĕl-bĕth-mā′ȧ-kȧ), a town in Naphtali (II Sam. 20:15). Sheba fled there from King David (II Sam. 20:14-22). Benhadad later seized it (I Kings 15:20) and Tiglath-pileser captured it (II Kings 15:29).

Abel-cheramim (ā′bĕl-kĕr-ȧ-mĭm, **meadow of vineyards**), a place in Ammon, east of the Jordan, to which Jephthah pursued the Ammonites (Judg. 11:33).

Abel-maim (ā-bĕl-mā′ĭm, **meadow of waters**), a variant of Abel-beth-maacah (II Chron. 16:4).

Abel-meholah (ā′bĕl-mē-hō′lȧ, **meadow of dancing**), a town probably in the Jordan valley, where Elisha was born and lived.

Abel-mizraim (ā′bĕl-mĭz′rā-ĭm, **meadow** or **mourning of Egypt**), a place east of the Jordan at which the funeral cortege of Jacob stopped to mourn for seven days before entering Canaan to bury the patriarch (Gen. 50:11).

Abel-shittim (ā′bĕl-shĭt′ĭm, **acacia-meadow**), a place in Moab where Israel rested for the last time before crossing the Jordan (Num. 33:49).

Abel the Great, See second entry under Abel.

Abez (ā′bĕz). Used in KJV for Ebez. A town, mentioned in Joshua 19:20, found in Issachar.

Abi (ā′bī), the mother of King Hezekiah, spoken of also as the daughter of Zechariah. A contraction of Abijah (II Kings 18:2; II Chron. 29:1).

Abia (ȧ-bī′ȧ), a variant for Abijah.

Abiasaph (ȧ-bī′ă-săf, **the father gathers,** or **adds**), a descendant of Levi through Korah (Exod. 6:24).

Abiathar (ȧ-bī′ă-thar, **father of abundance**), the son of Ahimelech, the high priest, who with 84 priests was slain by Saul at Nob, on Doeg's telling the king that Ahimelech had inquired of the Lord for David and had given him the shewbread and the sword of Goliath (I Sam. 22). Abiathar escaped, bringing the ephod with him, and joined David (I Sam. 22:20-23).

Abiathar rendered David loyal service during Absalom's rebellion (II Sam. 15; 17:15; 19:11), but he joined Adonijah when the latter sought to seize the throne from Solomon (I Kings 1:7). Jesus refers to Abiathar in Mark 2:26.

Abib (ā′bĭb, **an ear of corn**), the pre-exilic name for the first month of the year (Exod. 13:4; 23:15; 34:18). After the exile the name was changed to Nisan. It fell about the time of our March and early April.

Abida (ȧ-bī′dȧ, **the father knows**), appears as Abidah in KJV (Gen. 25:4). A son of Midian and grandson of Abraham and Keturah (Gen. 25:4; I Chron. 1:33).

Abidan (ȧ-bī′dăn, **the father is judge**), a prince of the tribe of Benjamin chosen to represent his tribe in the wilderness of Sinai (Num. 1:11; 2:22). He was present at the dedication of the tabernacle (Num. 7:60, 65).

Abiel (ā′bĭ-ĕl, **the father is God,** or **God is father**).1. The grandfather of Saul and Abner (I Sam. 9:1; 14:51).

2. One of David's mighty men (I Chron. 11:32), also called Abi-Albon (II Sam. 23:31).

Abiezer (ā′bĭ-ē′zêr, **father of help**). 1. Head of a family in Manasseh (Judg. 6:11f). 2. One of David's mighty men (I Chron. 11:28).

Abigail (ăb′ĭ-gāl, **father is rejoicing**). 1. The wife of Nabal, and, after his death, of David (I Sam. 25:3, 14-44; 27:3; II Sam. 3:3), to whom she bore his second son, Chileab (II Sam. 3:3, or Daniel, as in I Chron. 3:1).

2. A sister of David, daughter of Nahash, and mother of Amasa, commander of David's army (I Chron. 2:16).

Abihail (ăb′ĭ-hāl, **the father is strength**). 1. A Levite, the father of Zuriel (Num. 3:25). 2. The wife of Abishur (I Chron. 2:29).

3. A Gadite who lived in Gilead of Bashan (I Chron. 5:14).

4. The wife of Rehoboam, king of Judah. A daughter of Eliab, David's eldest brother (II Chron. 11:18).

5. The father of Queen Esther (Esther 2:15; 9:29).

Abihu (ȧ-bī′hū, **the father is he**), second son of Aaron (Exod. 6:23). He and Nadab were slain by Jehovah when they offered strange fire (Lev. 10).

Abihud (ȧ-bī′hûd, **the father is majesty**), son of Bela, the eldest son of Benjamin (I Chron. 8:3).

Abijah (ȧ-bī′jȧ, **Jehovah is Father**). 1. The wife of Judah's grandson Hezron (I Chron. 2:24).

2. The seventh son of Becher the son of Benjamin (I Chron. 7:8).

3. The second son of the prophet Samuel. Appointed a judge by his father; he became corrupt (I Sam. 8:2; I Chron. 6:28).

4. A descendant of Aaron. The ancestral head of the eighth of the 24 groups into which David had divided the priests (I Chron. 24:10).

5. A son of Jeroboam I of Israel (I Kings 14:1-18). He died from illness when still a child, in fulfillment of a prediction by the prophet Ahijah.

6. King of Judah, the son and successor of Rehoboam. He made war on Jeroboam in an effort to recover the ten tribes of Israel. Prosperity tempted him to multiply wives and to follow the evil ways of his father. He reigned three years (II Chron. 12:16; 13; 14:1).

7. A priest of Nehemiah's time (Neh. 10:7; 12:4, 17).

8. The mother of Hezekiah (II Chron. 29:1), called Abi in II Kings 18:2.

9. A chief of the priests who returned from Babylon with Zerubbabel (Neh. 12:4, 7).

Abilene (ăb'ĭ-lēn, probably **meadow),** a tetrarchy near Anti-Lebanon. Luke 3:1 mentions it as the tetrarchy of Lysanias when John the Baptist began his ministry.

Abimael (ȧ-bĭm'ā-ĕl, **God is Father),** the ninth of the 13 sons or descendants of Joktan, who was descended from Shem (Gen. 10:28; I Chron. 1:22).

Abimelech (ȧ-bĭm'ĕ-lĕk, probably either **the father is king** or **the father of a king**). 1. A Philistine king of Gerar, near Gaza. It was at his court that Abraham tried to pass off Sarah as his sister. Struck by her beauty, Abimelech married her, but returned her to Abraham when he was warned by God in a dream (Gen. 20:1-18).

2. A second king of Gerar, probably the son of the one mentioned in 1, at whose court Isaac tried to pass off his wife Rebekah as his sister (Gen. 26:1-11).

3. The son of Gideon by a concubine (Judg. 8:31; 9:1-57). After the death of his father, aspiring to be king, he slew 70 sons of his father. Only one son, Jotham, escaped. He was then made king of Shechem. After a reign of three years, an insurrection broke out against him. He was severely wounded by a mill-stone dropped from a wall on his head by a woman, and ordered his armor-bearer to kill him with his sword, lest it be said to his shame that he was killed by a woman.

4. A Philistine king mentioned in the title of Psalm 34, who very likely is the same as Achish, king of Gath (I Sam. 21:10-22:1), with whom David sought refuge when he fled from Saul.

5. A priest in the days of David, a son of Abiathar (I Chron. 18:16); also called Ahimelech (LXX and in I Chron. 24:6).

Abinadab (ȧ-bĭn'ȧ-dăb, **father is generous).** 1. A Levite in whose home the ark was kept for a time (I Sam. 7: 1, 2; 17:13). 2. Son of Jesse (I Sam. 16:8). 3. Son of Saul (I Sam. 17:13; 31:2). 4. A relative of Solomon (I Kings 4:11).

Abinoam (ȧ-bĭn'o-ăm, **the father is pleasantness**), the father of Barak (Judg. 4:6; 5:12).

Abiram (ȧ-bī-răm, **the father is exalted**). 1. A Reubenite who with his brothers Dathan and Korah conspired against Moses and was destroyed by God (Num. 16).

2. The eldest son of Hiel the Beth-elite, who rebuilt Jericho (I Kings 16:34).

Abishag (ăb'ĭ-shăg, **the father wanders,** or **errs).** A Shunammite woman who nursed David in his old age (I Kings 1:3, 15). Adonijah's request to marry her after David's death caused Solomon to put him to death (I Kings 2:17ff.).

Abishai (ȧ-bĭsh'ā-ī). Son of David's sister Zeruiah, and brother of Joab and Asahel. Impetuous and courageous, cruel and hard to his foes; but always intensely loyal to David. He counselled David to kill the sleeping Saul (I Sam. 26:6-9). Late in David's life he rescued the king in the fight with Ishbibenob, the Philistine giant (II Sam. 21:17).

Abishalom (ȧ-bĭsh'ȧ-lŏm), a variant of Absalom.

Abishua (ȧ-bĭsh'ū-ȧ, perhaps **the father is salvation** or **noble).** 1. The son of Phinehas the priest (I Chron. 6:4, 5, 50; Ezra 4:5).

2. A Benjamite of the family of Bela (I Chron. 8:4).

Abishur (ȧ-bī'shêr, **the father is a wall),** a man of Judah, the son of Shammai (I Chron. 2:28, 29).

Abital (ȧ-bī'tăl, **the father is dew),** one of the wives of David (II Sam. 3:4; I Chron. 3:3).

Abitub (ȧ-bī'tûb, **the father is goodness**), a Benjamite, son of Shaharaim and Hushim (I Chron. 8:8-11).

Abiud (ȧ-bī-ûd, probably the Greek form of Abihud), the son of Zerubbabel. Mentioned only in the genealogy of Jesus (Matt. 1:13).

Ablution (See Washing)

Abner (ăb'nêr, **the father is a lamp).** The son of Ner, who was the brother of Kish, the father of King Saul. Abner and Saul were therefore cousins. During the reign of Saul, Abner was the commander-in-chief of his army (I Sam. 14:50). He accompanied Saul in his pursuit of David (I Sam. 26:5ff), and was rebuked by David for his failure to keep better watch over his master (I Sam. 15).

At Saul's death Abner had Ishbosheth, Saul's son, made king over Israel (II Sam. 2:8). Abner and his men met David's servants in combat by the pool of Gibeon and were defeated. During the retreat from this battle, Abner was pursued by Asahel, Joab's brother, and in self-defense, slew him (II Sam. 2:12-32).

Soon after, Abner and Ishbosheth had a quarrel. This resulted in Abner's joining David. David graciously received him; but when Joab heard of the affair, and believing or pretending to believe that Abner had come as a spy, Joab murdered him "for the blood of Asahel his brother."

David sincerely mourned the death of Abner. "Know ye not," he said, "that there is a prince and a great man fallen this day in Israel?" He left it to his successor to avenge Abner's death (I Kings 2:5).

Abomination of desolation, meaning **the abomination that desolates** or **appalls.** When Daniel, in prophecy, tried to describe an abomination so abhorrent and loathsome to all moral and religious decency as to leave its abode desolate, he used this term (Dan. 9:27; 11:31; 12:11).

Many scholars hold that Jesus' prophecy that His followers would see the abomination of desolation, spoken of by Daniel the prophet, standing in the Holy Place (Matt. 24:15) was fulfilled when Jerusalem was destroyed in the year A.D. 70.

Abraham (ā'brȧ-hăm, **the father is high).** The son of Terah and founder of the Hebrew nation. His family settled in Ur of the Chaldees. It appears that Terah was an idolater, for Joshua says of him that he "served other

Ancient Oak of Mamre. Here, near Hebron, Abram pitched his tent (Gen. 13:18). © MPS

gods" (Josh. 24:2). He had three sons — Abraham, Nahor, and Haran.

Abraham was married to his half sister, Sarah. After the death of his brother Nahor, Abraham and his family, including his nephew Lot and his father Terah, left Ur to go to the land of Canaan (Gen. 11:27-31). We are not told the reason for the migration. Stephen, however, says that God had appeared to Abraham before he dwelt in Haran and had told him to leave his country for another land (Acts 7:2-4).

After staying some time in Haran, Abraham, now 75 years old, departed for Canaan, probably by way of Damascus. Not more than a year later he arrived in Canaan, where the Lord assured him in a vision that this was the land his seed would inherit.

Abraham lived in the hill country at least 15 years. He strengthened his position with the local Amoritish chieftains by uniting with them in the rescue of Lot from an Elamite king. On his return he was blessed by Melchizedek, the priest-king of Salem, to whom he gave a tithe of his spoils.

God now renewed His promise of an heir to Abraham; but when no son came, his wife, despairing of having children of her own, suggested that he take as his concubine her maid Hagar. In the eighty-sixth year of his life Hagar bore him Ishmael (Gen. 16). Thirteen years later (Gen. 17:1), God revealed to him that the son of Sarah, and not Ishmael, should be his heir. God now appointed the rite of circumcision as a sign of the covenant made between Him and Abraham.

Tomb of Abraham (above) in the Mosque of Machpelah (below) built over the Cave of Machpelah in Hebron. © *MPS*

When Abraham was 100 years old, Isaac was born, an event soon followed by the expulsion of Ishmael (Gen. 21: 1-21). Abraham and Abimelech concluded a treaty at Beersheba. Abraham's faith in God's promise met one last severe test when God commanded him to sacrifice his only son. He was saved from doing so by God's gracious substitution of a ram (Gen. 22).

At the age of 175 years Abraham died and was buried beside Sarah (Gen. 25:7-10) in the Cave of Machpelah he had purchased from Ephon (Gen. 23).

Abraham's bosom was a Jewish symbol of blessedness after death (Luke 16:22, 23).

Abram (See Abraham).

Abrech (ăb′rĕk; Gen. 41:43) ASV margin, RSV margin, with note, **"Abrek,** probably an Egyptian word, similar in sound to the Hebrew word meaning **to kneel";** KJV "bow the knee." It was the cry with which Joseph was announced when he appeared in public as second to Pharaoh.

Absalom (ăb′sȧ-lŏm, **father (is) peace,** written Abishalom in I Kings 15:2, 10, meaning **my father (is) peace).** Third son of David, by Maacah, daughter of Talmai, king of Geshur, a small district NE of Lake Galilee (II Sam. 3:3; I Chron. 3:2). David's eldest son, Absalom's half-brother Amnon ravished Absalom's sister Tamar (II Sam. 13: 1-19), which greatly angered David, but Amnon was not punished (13:21). Absalom nursed his hatred for two years, then treacherously procured Amnon's assassination (13:22-29). Absalom fled to his grandfather and remained with him three years (13:37-39), while David "longed to go forth unto Absalom: for he was comforted concerning Amnon, seeing he was dead." At the end of that time Joab by stratagem induced David to recall Absalom, but David would not see him for two years more (14:1-24). Then Absalom by a trick of his own moved Joab to intercede with the king, and Absalom was restored to favor (14:28, 33).

Later, Absalom proclaimed himself king, and attracted the disaffected to his standard (II Sam. 15:7-14). David at once realized the seriousness of the rebellion and made hasty plans for immediate departure from Jerusalem (15:13-18). It was a sad as well as a hurried flight, marked by partings from friends, the defection of valued counselors such as Ahithophel, and the intense loyalty of men like Zadok and Abiathar the priests, whom David sent back to the capital, that with their sons as messengers they might keep David informed of events. Hushai the Archite also was asked to return and feign loyalty to Absalom, that he might "defeat the counsel of Ahithophel" (15:20-37).

Ahithophel advised Absalom to attack David at once, before he could gather a large following (17:1-4). Hushai advised delay until all the military power of the realm could be gathered under command of Absalom himself, to make sure of having a large enough force to defeat the warlike David and his loyal soldiers (17:5-14). Absalom actually followed a compromise plan. The armies met in the wood of Ephraim, where Absalom's men were disastrously defeated (18:1-8). Absalom, riding on a mule, was caught by his head in the branches of an oak, and the mule going on left him dangling helpless there, where Joab and his men killed him, though David had, in the hearing of the whole army, forbidden anyone to harm his son Absalom. It is thought that his luxuriant hair contributed to his downfall, by becoming entangled in the oak branches. Absalom was buried in a pit, covered with a heap of stones, in the wood where he fell (18:9-17). The title of Psalm 3 states that David wrote this psalm "when he fled from Absalom his son." The psalm breathes strong trust in God, to whom is ascribed the overthrow of David's enemies. There is no note of vindictiveness, but a sense of sorrow and resignation.

Abstinence (ăb'stĭ-nĕns). The noun occurs once in KJV, and means **abstinence from food** (Acts 27:21); the verb occurs six times, and means **to refrain from.** The Jerusalem Council (Acts 15:20, 29) commanded abstinence from "meats offered to idols, and from blood, and from things strangled, and from fornication." Abstinence was not commanded for its own sake, but was recommended to inculcate purity of diet and of life. Peter urged his friends to "abstain from fleshly lusts" (I Peter 2:11). God's people were told to abstain from idolatry (Exod. 34:15; Rom. 14:21; I Cor. 8:4-13).

Abyss (ȧ-bĭs), means, in the NT, **the nether world, prison of disobedient spirits** (Luke 8:31; Rev. 9:1, 2, 11; 11:7; 17:8; 20:1-3), or **the world of the dead** (Rom. 10:7). The word does not occur in the KJV, but is translated **bottomless pit** in Revelation, or **deep** in Luke.

Accad (ăk'ăd), one of the ancient cities of Babylonia, perhaps identical with Agade, where Sargon I, the Semitic conqueror of the Semitic Accadians, made his capital in 2475 B.C. The identification uncertain.

Accho (ăk'ō), a seacoast town of Palestine, identified with the Ptolemais of the NT (Acts 21:7) and the modern Akka or Acre, eight miles N of Mt. Carmel and 30 miles S of Tyre.

Aceldama (ȧ-sĕl'dȧ-mȧ), or Akeldama (a-kel'da-ma), **the field of blood,** the field purchased with the money which Judas received for betraying Christ (Acts 1:18, 19). It was so named because it was purchased with blood-money, or perhaps because Judas' gruesome death occurred there.

Achaia (ȧ-kā'yȧ). In NT times, a Roman province including the Peloponnesus and northern Greece south of Illyricum, Epirus and Thessaly, which were districts of Macedonia. Macedonia and Achaia generally mean all Greece (Acts 19:21; Rom. 15:26; II Cor. 1:1; I Thess. 1:7, 8). Other NT references to Achaia are II Corinthians 9:2 and 11:10.

Achaicus (ȧ-kā'ĭ-kŭs). A Corinthian Christian who visited Paul at Ephesus (I Cor. 16:17-19).

Achan (ā'kăn), an Israelite who took a garment, silver and gold, part of the spoil of Jericho. Joshua had devoted the metals to God (Josh. 6:17-19). All else was to be destroyed. Because of one man's disobedience Israel was defeated at Ai. God revealed the reason to Joshua. By a process of elimination Achan was found out. He confessed, and he and his family and possessions were brought down to the valley of Achor. The LXX reads, "and all Israel stoned him with stones. And they raised over him a great heap of stones."

Achar (ā'kȧr, **trouble).** The same as Achan (I Chron. 2:7).

Achaz (ā'kăz). The same as Ahaz.

Achbor (ăk'bôr, **mouse).** 1. Father of a king of Edom (Gen. 36:38, 39; I Chron. 1:49).

2. A messenger of King Josiah (II Kings 22:12, 14; called Abdon in II Chron. 34:20); father of Elnathan (Jer. 26:22; 36:12).

Achim (ā'kĭm, **Jehovah will establish).** A descendant of Zerubbabel (Matt. 1:14). One of the ancestors of Christ.

Achish (ā'kĭsh). Philistine king of Gath, to whom David fled for protection (I Sam. 21:10-15). David consented to join Achish against Israel, but the Philistine lords objected; so Achish sent David away (I Sam. 29:1-11).

Achmetha (ăk'mē-thȧ), ancient Ecbatana, modern Hamadân, capital of Media, where was found the decree of Cyrus authorizing the rebuilding of the Temple at Jerusalem (Ezra 6:2).

Achor (ā'kôr, **trouble).** Valley (Josh. 15:7) where Achan was stoned (Josh.

The Valley of Achor, near Jericho, where Achan was stoned. © MPS

7:24-26); subject of promises in Isaiah 65:10; Hosea 2:15.

Achsa (See Achsah)

Achsah (ăk′să, **anklet**), daughter of Caleb the son of Jephunneh, married to Othniel, son of Kenaz, Caleb's younger brother, in performance of a promise Caleb had made to give his daughter to him "that taketh Kirjath-sepher." The story is told in charming and picturesque detail in both Joshua 15:16-19 and Judges 1:12-15.

Achshaph (ăk′shăf), a city (Josh. 11:1) which Joshua captured with its king (Josh. 12:7, 20). It is named as being on the border of the lot assigned to Asher (Josh. 19:24, 25).

Achzib (ăk′zĭb, **a lie**). 1. A city of Judah (Josh. 15:44) perhaps Tell el-Beidâ, southwest of Adullam. Called Chezib (Gen. 38:5) and Chozeba (I Chron. 4:22). See Micah 1:14.

2. A town in Asher (Judg. 1:31; Josh. 19:29) on the coast north of Accho.

Acre (ā′kêr). The amount of land a yoke of oxen could plow in a day. In I Samuel 14:14, a field for plowing by a yoke of oxen.

Acropolis (ȧ-krŏp′ō-lĭs, from **ákros, highest**, and **pólis, city**), the upper or higher city, citadel or castle of a Greek municipality; especially the citadel of Athens, where the treasury and its first temple were.

Other NT cities — Corinth, Philippi, Samaria, etc. — each had its own Acropolis, which served as the town's civic and religious center.

Acrostic (ȧ-krôs′tĭc), a literary device by which the first letter of each line of poetry forms either a word or the successive letters of the alphabet. An outstanding example is the 119th psalm, in which each successive set of eight verses begins with a different letter of the Hebrew alphabet. The effect is not apparent in the English translation, but the Hebrew letters are given between the lines in order to preserve the construction.

Acts of the Apostles (ȧ-pŏs′'lz), the New Testament book which gives the history of early Christianity from the ascension of Christ to the end of two years of Paul's imprisonment in Rome.

I. Title of the book. An early MS has the title "Acts" (Greek **práxeis**, doings, transactions, achievements). Other early titles are "Acts of Apostles," "The Acts of the Apostles," "Acts of the Holy Apostles," etc. Acts narrates doings and speeches chiefly of Peter and Paul. There is some information about Judas (1:16-20), and the man chosen to succeed him (1:21-26); about John (3:1-4:31; 8:14-17); and James (12:12). The Twelve, except the betrayer, are listed in 1:13. Acts is not a history of all apostles, but a selection from the deeds and words of

The Acropolis, civic center of ancient Athens, crowned by the spectacular Parthenon and other temples. EG

some who illustrate the progress of first century Christianity in those phases which interested the author, as he was moved by the Holy Spirit. The title "Acts of the Holy Spirit" has often been suggested, and the contents of the book bear out the appropriateness of such a title.

II. Author. Not until A.D. 160-200 do we have positive statements as to the authorship of Acts. From that time onward all who mention the subject agree that the author of the two books dedicated to Theophilus, the Gospel according to Luke, and the Acts of the Apostles, are by "Luke the beloved physician."

III. Place. The place where Acts was written is not named, though the sudden ending of the book, while Paul is residing at Rome awaiting trial, makes Rome an appropriate place. The question of place is tied in with that of Luke's purpose in writing, and with the occasion for the publication of the book.

IV. Date. Allusions to the book in the Apostolic Fathers are too indefinite to compel the setting of a date much before the end of the first century A.D. Acts must have been finished after the latest date mentioned in the book, in 28:30. The abrupt close indicates that it was written at that time, c. A.D. 61 or 62. Luke's Gospel has an appropriate ending; Acts does not. We are not told how the trial of Paul came out. There is no hint of Paul's release or of his death.

V. Summary of the contents. Introduction, a. Summary of ground covered by the "former treatise," especially the resurrection ministry of Jesus, 1:1-11. b. The period of waiting; a ten days' prayer meeting in the upper room, 1:12-14. c. The choice of a successor to the betrayer as one of the Twelve, 1:15-26. 1. Pentecost, the birthday of the Church. a. the occasion and the event, 2:1-13. b. Peter's sermon, 2:14-36. c. The result: the beginning of the Church, 2:37-47. 2. Pictures of the first church in Jerusalem. 3. The Gospel spread to all Judea and Samaria, 8:1-25. 4. Three "continental" conversions. a. From the continent of Africa: the Ethiopian eunuch, 8:26-40. b. From Asia: Saul of Tarsus, 9:1-31. (Interlude: Peter in western Palestine, 9:32-43). c. From Europe: Cornelius of Italy, 10:1-48. 5. The Judean church accepts the mission to the Gentiles, 11:1-30. A further attempt to suppress the Christian movement frustrated by the miraculous escape of Peter from prison, 12:1-19. (Note: The death of Herod, 12:20-23). 6. Paul's first missionary journey (12:34 - 14:28). 7. The Church Council at Jerusalem: terms of admission of Gentile believers settled, 15:1-29. 8. Paul's second missionary journey, (15:30 - 18:20). 9. Paul's third missionary journey, (18:23 - 21:16). 10. Paul's arrest and voyage to Rome (24:17 - 28:31).

Adadah (ă-dā'dȧ), a city in Judah (Josh. 15: 22), not surely identified.

Adah (ā'dȧ, **ornament** or **morning).** 1. One of Lamech's two wives (Gen. 4:19, 20, 23), mother of Jabal and Jubal.

2. One of Esau's wives (Gen. 36:2, 4, 10, 12, 16), daughter of Elon the Hittite.

Adaiah (ȧ-dā'yȧ, **Jehovah hath adorned,** or **pleasing to Jehovah).** 1. A man of Boscath, father of Josiah's mother (II Kings 22:1).

2. A Levite descended from Gershom (I Chron. 6:41-43).

3. A son of Shimshi the Benjamite (I Chron. 8:1, 21).

4. A Levite of the family of Aaron, head of a family living in Jerusalem (I Chron. 9:10-12).

5. The father of Captain Maaseiah who helped Jehoiada put Joash on the throne of Judah (II Chron. 23:1).

6. A son of Bani who married a foreign wife during the exile (Ezra 10:29).

7. Another of a different Bani family who did the same (Ezra 10:34).

8. A descendant of Judah by Perez (Neh. 11:5).

9. A Levite of the family of Aaron. Most likely the same as 4 (Neh. 11:12).

Adalia (ăd-ā-lī'ȧ), the fifth of Haman's sons, all of whom were hanged with their father (Esth. 9:8).

Adam (ăd'ăm, **of the ground** or **taken out of the red earth),** the first human son of God (Luke 3:38; I Tim. 2:13-14; Jude 14), and God's masterpiece and crowning work of creation. The word occurs about 560 times in the OT, meaning **man** or **mankind,** sometimes clearly as a proper name (e.g., I Chron. 1:1), oftener as a common noun. In some cases it is hard to tell which the writer meant (e.g., Deut. 32:8); KJV "sons of Adam"; ASV "children of men"; RSV "sons of men."

I. Adam was a necessary complement to the divine plan. "There was not a man to till the ground" (Gen. 2:5). The accomplishment of God's plan required human instrumentality.

II. Adam was fashioned a creature of God, bearing the image of God and possessing God-like faculties (Gen. 1:27; Ps. 8:6; Eccl. 7:29).

III. Adam was created a tripartite being, having a spirit, soul and body (Gen. 2:7; I Thess. 5:23).

IV. Adam was alone and needed companionship to satisfy his created instincts (Gen. 2:18), thus Eve was formed.

V. Adam was enticed and sinned (Gen. 3:6).

VI. Adam received the promise of the Saviour. The first promise and prophecy of One able to deal with sin and Satan was given, not to Adam, but to the one responsible for Adam's transgression (Gen. 3:15), and in the coats of skins God provided to cover the discovered nakedness of Adam and Eve we have a type of the sacrifice of the Cross. In Adam we die, but in Christ we can be made alive.

The study of the life of Adam (Gen. 1:26-5:5) shows us the natural man in his original and intended glory, in the extremity of his fall, and in the possibilities which yet remain to him as man. The NT passages cited open before us the infinitely rich and eternal destiny awaiting and available to us through the perfect obedience unto death of the Second Adam, our Lord Jesus Christ.

Adam (ăd'ăm, **red,** or **made),** a city in the Jordan valley where the Israelites entered the promised land from east of Jordan (Josh. 3:16).

Adamah (ăd'á-má, **red ground),** a fenced city of Naphtali (Josh. 19:36). Location disputed.

Adamant (ăd'á-mănt), a stone harder than flint (Ezek. 3:9; Zech. 7:12). The Heb. word is translated "diamond" in Jeremiah 17:1, "briers" in Isaiah 5:6; 7:23-25; 9:18; 10:17; 27:4; 32:13.

Adami (ăd'ă-mī, **earthy),** a place on the border of Naphtali (Josh. 19:33), united with "Nekeb" and forming "Adami-nekeb."

Adar (ā'dár), a place on the south border of Judah (Josh. 15:3 KJV). In ASV and RSV, Addar.

Adar (á-dár', ā'dár), the 12th month of the Babylonian calendar.

Adbeel (ăd'bē-ĕl, **languishing for God),** the third son of Ishmael and grandson of Abraham (Gen. 25:13; I Chron. 1:29).

Addan (ăd'ăn, Ezra 2:59; **'āddôn** in Neh. 7:61), one of the places in Babylonia from which the people named in Ezra 2:60-63 and Nehemiah 7:62-65 returned to Jerusalem after the exile.

Addar (ăd'ár, **threshing floor).** 1. Son of Bela, grandson of Benjamin (I Chron. 8:3). Called Ard in Genesis 46:21 and Numbers 36:40; counted as a son of Benjamin and head of a family in the tribe.

2. In ASV and RSV for Adar of KJV.

Adder (See Animals—Reptiles)

Addi (ăd'ī, **my witness,** or **adorned),** an ancestor of Joseph, the husband of Mary, our Lord's mother (Luke 3:28).

Addon (ăd'ŏn), the same place as Addan (Neh. 7:61; compare Ezra 2:59).

Ader (ā'dêr, **a flock),** a son of Beriah, grandson of Shaharaim, a Benjaminite (I Chron. 8:15).

Adiel (ā'dĭ-ĕl, **ornament of God).** 1. A descendant of Simeon (I Chron. 4:36). 2. A priest, son of Jahzerah (I Chron. 9:12). 3. Father of Azmaveth, who was supervisor of David's treasuries (I Chron. 27:25). Perhaps the same as No. 2.

Adin (ā'dĭn, **delicate,** or **ornament).** 1. One whose family returned from exile with Zerubbabel (Ezra 2:15; Neh. 7:20).

2. One whose posterity came back with Ezra (Ezra 8:6).

3. The name of a family sealing the covenant (Neh. 10:16).

Adina (ăd'ĭ-ná, **ornament),** one of David's military officers (I Chron. 11:42).

Adino (ăd'ĭ-nō, á-dī'nō, **his adorned one).** A Tachmonite (II Sam. 23:8 KJV).

Adithaim (ăd-ĭ-thā'ĭm, **double ornaments),** one of "the uttermost cities of . . . Judah" (KJV), (Josh. 15).

Adjuration (ăj-ōō-rā'shŭn). The noun does not occur in the Bible, but the verb "adjure" is often found in both Testaments (I Sam. 14:24; I Kings 22:16; Mark 5:7). In every case, an appeal in the most impressive manner is meant.

Adlai (ăd'lā-ī, **justice of Jehovah,** or **weary),** father of Shaphat, who was overseer of David's cattle in the lowlands (I Chron. 27:29).

Admah (ăd'mȧ, **red earth),** a city near Gomorrah and Zeboiim (Gen. 10:19) with a king (Gen. 14:2, 8), destroyed with Sodom and Gomorrah (Deut. 29:23 with Gen. 19:24-28; see Hos. 11:8).

Admatha (ăd'mȧ-thȧ, **unrestrained),** a prince of Persia and Media (Esth. 1:14).

Adna (ăd'nȧ, **pleasure).** 1. A son of Pahath-moab who had married a foreign wife during the exile (Ezra 10:30).

2. A priest, head of his father's house in the days of Joiakim (Neh. 12:12-15).

Adnah (ăd'nȧ, **pleasure).** 1. A Manassite who joined David at Ziklag (I Chron. 12:20).

2. A man of Judah who held high military rank under Jehoshaphat (II Chron. 17:14).

Adoni-Bezek (ȧ-dō'nī-bē'zĕk, **lord of lightning,** or **of the city of Bezek),** a king of Bezek, captured by the men of Judah and Simeon and taken to Jerusalem, where he was mutilated (Judg. 1:5-7; Gal. 6:5).

Adonijah (ăd'ō-nī'jȧ, **my Lord is Jehovah),** the fourth son of David, by Haggith, born at Hebron (II Sam. 3: 2-4; I Chron. 3:2). Amnon and Absalom, David's first and third sons, had died; the second, Chileab, had not been mentioned since his birth, and might have died also. Adonijah, as the eldest living son, aspired to the throne. The story of his attempt and failure to seize the crown is told in I Kings 1:5-2:25. See under **Abishag.**

2. A Levite, sent by Jehoshaphat to teach the law (II Chron. 17:8).

3. A chieftain who with Nehemiah sealed the covenant (Neh. 10:14-16).

Adonikam (ăd-ō-nī'kăm, **my Lord has arisen),** the ancestor of a family, 666 of whom returned from exile with Zerubbabel (Ezra 2:13). Among the chiefs of the people who returned with Ezra are three sons and 60 males of this family (Ezra 8:13). In the list of exiles whose genealogy proved them Israelites are 667 of this family (Neh. 7:18).

Adoniram (ăd-ō-nī'răm, **my Lord is exalted),** first appears by the name Adoram as an officer of David "over the tribute" (II Sam. 20:24). He continues under Solomon (I Kings 4:6); "over the levy" of laborers in Lebanon (I Kings 5:14). Rehoboam sends Adoram to compel the obedience of the rebels, but "all Israel stoned him . . . that he died" (I Kings 12:18). Both Adoram and Hadoram (II Chron. 10: 18) are shortened forms of Adoniram.

Adoni-Zedek, Adoni-Zedec (KJV) (ȧ-dō'nī-zē'dĕk, **lord of righteousness,** or **my lord is righteous),** Amorite king of Jerusalem (Josh. 10:1-27) who with four other Amorite kings attack Gibeon. Joshua came to the aid of Gibeon. This was the day when Joshua called on the sun and moon to stand still until the people had avenged themselves upon their enemies. The kings hid in a cave, which Joshua sealed with great stones. Victory complete, Joshua ordered the kings brought out and slew them. An earlier king of Jerusalem (Salem) bore a name, Melchizedek, meaning "king of righteousness" (Gen. 14:18-20).

Adoption (ȧ-dŏp'shŭn). The word occurs five times in the NT. The practice of adoption is exemplified in the OT: Pharaoh's daughter adopted Moses (Exod. 2:10) as her son. Hadad the Edomite married the sister of the Egyptian queen, and their son Genubath was brought up "among the sons of Pharaoh," whether formally adopted or not (I Kings 11:20). Esther was adopted by Mordecai (Esth. 2:7, 15). These cases were outside Palestine, in Egypt or Persia. Whether adoption was practiced in the Hebrews' own land is not clear.

But none of the OT instances have a direct bearing on the NT usage of the term. Paul is the only writer to employ it, and with him it is a metaphor derived from Hellenistic usage and Roman law. The legal situation of a son in early Roman times was little better than that of a slave, though in practice its rigor would vary with the disposition of the father. The son was the property of his father, who was entitled to his earnings; who could transfer ownership of him by adoption or by a true sale; who could, under certain circumstances, even put him to death. An adopted son was considered like a son born in the family. He could no longer inherit from his natural father. He was no longer liable for old debts (a loophole eventually closed). So far as his former family was concerned, he was dead. Modifications of the rigor of sonship were at intervals introduced into Roman law, and a more liberal Hellenistic view was doubtless in the mind of Paul.

In Galatians 4:1-3 Paul states accurately the Roman law of sonship. In verse 4 he says that God sent His Son to be born into the human condition under law, and in verse 5 the purpose of God in so doing: "to redeem them that were under the law, that we might receive the adoption of sons." The adoption brought us from slavery to sonship and heirship (verse 7).

The same thought appears in Romans 8:15. Verses 1-14 demonstrate that the adoption is more than a matter of position or status; when God adopted us, He put His Spirit within us, and we became subject to His control. This involves chastisement (Heb. 12:5-11) as well as inheritance (Rom. 8:16-18).

In Romans 8:23 "the adoption" is spoken of as future, in the sense that its full effects are to be consummated at the time of "the redemption of our body."

In Romans 9:4 Paul begins with enumeration of the privileges of Israelites with "the adoption." Though God said, "Israel is my son, my first-born" (Exod. 4:22); and, "When Israel was a child, then I loved him, and called my child out of Egypt" (Hos. 11:1); and Moses expressed the relationship, "Ye are the children of the Lord your God" (Deut. 14:1); yet Israel's sonship was not the natural relationship by creation, but a peculiar one by a covenant of promise, a spiritual relationship by faith, under the sovereign grace of God, as Paul goes on to explain in Romans 9-11. Thus a clear distinction is drawn between the "offspring" of God by creation (Acts 17:28) and the children of God by adoption into the obedience of faith.

With utmost compression of language Paul expresses, in Ephesians 1:4, 5, God's action which resulted in His adoption of us; and enumerates its effects in verses 6-12.

Adoption is a serious matter under any system of law. As a figure of speech expressing spiritual truth it emphasizes the sovereign and gracious character of the act of God in our salvation; our solemn obligation as adopted sons of our adopting Parent; the newness of the family relationship established; its climate of intimate trust and love; and the immensity of an inheritance which eternity alone can reveal to us.

Adoraim (ăd′ō-rām), a fortress built by Rehoboam in Judah (II Chron. 11:9). Probably now Dûra, a large village on rising ground W of Hebron.

Adoram (ȧ-dō′răm), the same as Adoniram.

Adoration (ăd-ō-rā′shŭn), "to kiss the hand with the mouth" in homage (Job 31:26, 27). Laying the hand on the mouth expressed deep reverence and submission (Job 40:4). So "kiss the Son," i.e. adore Him (Ps. 2:12). Falling down prostrate was the worship paid to Babylonian idols (Dan. 3:5, 6). Worship is due to God only, and was rejected by angels and saints when offered to them (Luke 4:8; Acts 10:25, 26; Rev. 19:10; 22:8, 9).

Adore (See Adoration)

Adrammelech (ăd-răm′ĕ-lĕk, **Adar is king).** 1. The name which the author of II Kings 17:31 gives to Adar, the god the Sepharvites brought to Samaria when the king of Assyria settled them there, and in the worship of whom children were burnt in fire. It was a time of syncretism, when Israelites and Assyrian colonists both paid service to God and to heathen deities alike (II Kings 17:24-41).

2. A son of Sennacherib, who, with his brother Sharezer, slew their father in the temple of Nisroch (II Kings 19:37; Isa. 37-38).

Adramyttium (ăd′rȧ-mĭt′ĭ-ŭm), an old port city of Mysia, in the Roman province of Asia, near Edremit. Paul sailed in a ship of Adramyttium along the coast from Caesarea in Palestine to Myra in Lycia, where an Alexandrian ship bound for Italy took him on board (Acts 27:2-6).

Adria (ā′drĭ-ȧ), originally that part of the gulf between Italy and the Dalmatian coast near the mouth of the Po River, named for the town of Adria. Later, it was extended to include what is now the Adriatic Sea; and, in NT times, also that part of the Mediterranean between Crete and the Peloponnesus on the east and Sicily and Malta on the west. This extended meaning appears in Acts 27:27, where Paul's ship is "driven up and down in Adria."

Adriel (ā′drĭ-ĕl), son of Barzillai the Meholathite, to whom Merab, Saul's daughter, was given in marriage, although she had been promised to David (I Sam. 18:19).

Adullam (ȧ-dŭl′ăm, **retreat, refuge),** a city in the Shephelah or low country, between the hill country of Judah and the sea, 13 miles SW of Bethlehem; very ancient (Gen. 38:1,

12, 20; Josh. 15:35); the seat of one of the 31 petty kings smitten by Joshua (Josh. 12:15). Fortified by Rehoboam (II Chron. 11:7). Called for its beauty "the glory of Israel" (Mic. 1: 15). Reoccupied on the return from the Babylonian exile (Neh. 11:30).

David hid in one of the many limestone caves near the city, with his family and about 400 men (I Sam. 22: 1, 2) at times when Saul sought his life.

Adullamite (ȧ-dŭl′ăm-īt, **belonging to Adullum**), used of Hirah, Judah's friend (Gen. 38:1, 12, 20).

Adultery (ȧ-dŭl′têr-ē). In the OT, sexual intercourse, usually of a man, married or unmarried, always with the wife of another. One of the Ten Commandments forbids it (Exod. 20: 14; Deut. 5:18). The punishment for both man and woman was death (Lev. 20:20; 18:20), probably by stoning (Deut. 22:22-24; John 8:3-7). The OT uses adultery as a figure for idolatrous worship.

While fornication (the wider term for sexual offenses) is frequently and severely condemned in the OT, special solemnity attaches to the reproof of adultery, either in the relations of individual men and women, or figuratively, in the relations of the covenant people Israel, conceived of as a wife, with God, their spiritual husband. Isaiah, Jeremiah and Ezekiel use the figure. Hosea develops from personal experience with an adulterous wife an allegory of God's love for His unfaithful people.

The NT treatment of adultery, following the implications of the OT concept, supports marriage as a lifelong monogamous union. Adultery is a special and aggravated case of fornication. In the teaching of Jesus and the apostles in the NT, all sexual impurity is sin against God, against self, and against others. Spiritual adultery (unfaithfulness to God) violates the union between Christ and His own.

Adummim (ȧ-dŭm′ĭm, **red spots**), a pass (Josh. 15:7; 18:17), on the road between Jerusalem and Jericho. On the north border of Judah and the south border of Benjamin. Convincingly held to be the scene of Jesus' parable of the Good Samaritan (Luke 10:30-35).

Advent (See Eschatology)

Adversary (ăd′vêr-sâr′ē), an enemy, personal, national, or supernatural (Exod. 23:22; Matt. 5:25).

The Caves of Adullam, near Bethlehem, where David took refuge from Saul. © MPS

Advocate (ăd′vō-kāt, **supporter, backer, helper, Paraclete**), Jesus Christ (I John 2:1). Also Jesus speaks of the Holy Spirit as "another Comforter" (John 14:16), using the same Greek word, thereby implying that He Himself is a "Comforter." The Holy Spirit is the Advocate of the Father with us, therefore our Comforter (John 14: 16, 26; 15:26; 16:7, where RSV translates "Counselor"). As applied to the Holy Spirit, the Greek word is so rich in meaning that adequate translation by any one English word is impossible. Comforter is as satisfactory as any, taken in the fullest sense of one who not only consoles but strengthens, helps, counsels, with such authority as a legal advocate has for his client. Applied to Christ, the meaning is narrowed to that of Advocate with the Father (I John 2:1, 2).

Aeneas (ē-nē′ăs), a paralytic, healed at Lydda by Peter (Acts 9:32-35).

Aenon (ē′nŏn; in Aramaic means **springs**), a place near Salim, where John the Baptist was baptizing at the time Jesus was baptizing in Judea (John 3:22, 23). The site of Aenon is unknown.

Aeon (ē′ŏn). The word "aeon" does not occur in the English Bible, but is variously translated. Its original meaning is "relative time duration, limited or unlimited," i.e., a period of time, or eternity. A common translation in the NT is "world" (RSV often "age"). Frequently it occurs in phrases meaning "forever" (e.g., Matt. 6:13). KJV has "ages" twice (Eph. 2:7; Col. 1:26).

The "Tree of Agony" in the Garden of Gethsemane. © MPS

When aeon is the word translated "world," its duration in time is involved, though aeon is sometimes synonymous with Greek **kósmos,** world-order (e.g., Mark 4:19; I Cor. 1:20; 2:6; 3:19). Good examples of aeon meaning a period of time are Hebrews 9:26, where "the end of the world" is the period ushered in by the first coming of Christ; and Matthew 24:3; 28:20, where "the end of the world" is its culmination at His second coming. We live during the period between (I Cor. 10:11). "This present age (time)" and "the age (world) to come" are distinguished (e.g., Mark 10:30; Matt. 12:32). "This (present) age (world)" (e.g., Rom. 12:2; II Tim. 4:10; Titus 2:12) implies the existence of another world. In Ephesians 1:21 "this world" precedes "that which is to come." Hebrews 6:5 speaks of "the powers of the world (RSV "age") to come," which believers already experience.

Agabus (ăg′à-bŭs), a prophet living in Jerusalem who prophesied a world-wide famine (Acts 11:27-30) and warned Paul he would be arrested in Jerusalem (Acts 21:10, 11).

Agag (ā′găg, perhaps meaning **violent).** 1. An important king of Amalek, (Num. 24:7), of whom Balaam prophesied that a king of Jacob (Israel) would surpass him.

2. The king of the Amalekites, whom Saul captured alive, though God had through the prophet Samuel ordered him to destroy them entirely (I Sam. 15:8, 9). Samuel, as judge, pronounced sentence of death upon him for all his cruel deeds, "and Samuel hewed Agag in pieces before the Lord" (I Sam. 15:32, 33).

Agagite (ăg′à-gĭt, ā′găg-īt), an epithet applied to Haman as enemy of the Jews (Esth. 3:1, 10; 8:5; 9:24).

Agape (ăg′à-pā), the more frequent of two NT words for love, connoting the preciousness or worthiness of the one loved. It is used in Jude 12 (KJV "feasts of charity," ASV, RSV "love-feasts") of common meals which bore that name because they cultivated brotherly love among Christians. I Corinthians 11:20-34 rebukes abuses which had crept into the love-feasts, and which marred the Lord's Supper. The Lord's Supper properly followed, but was distinct from the love-feast.

Agar (ā′gâr), the Greek name of Sarai's handmaid (Gal. 4:24, 25).

Agate (See Minerals)

Age (See Aeon)

Age, Old, called the reward of filial obedience, according to the commandment (Exod. 20:12). The Mosaic legislation spelled out the respect to be shown the aged (Lev. 19:32). Younger men waited till they had spoken (Job 32:4). God promised Abraham "a good old age" (Gen. 15:15). When Pharaoh received him, Jacob lamented that he had not lived as long as his ancestors (Gen. 47:7-9). Official position went to older men (elders, e.g., Exod. 3:16; Matt. 21:23). Elders were ordained for the early Christian churches (e.g., Acts 14:23). Aged men and women are given sound advice in Titus 2:2-5. There is a fine picture of old age in Ecclesiastes 12:1-7.

Agony (ă′gō-nē, **agony, anguish).** Occurs only in Luke 22:44, of Jesus' agony in Gethsemane. The word is derived from the Gr. **agon,** "contest," "struggle," and depicts severe conflict and pain. Luke tells us that Christ's agony was such that "His sweat was as it were great drops of blood falling down to the ground."

Agora (ă′gō-rà, **market place).** In ancient cities the town meeting place, where the public met for the exchange of merchandise, information and ideas. As centers where people congregated, the agorae of Galilee and Judea were the scenes for many of the healing miracles of Christ (Mark 6:56). In Athens, Paul's daily disputations in the agora led directly to his famed message before the Areopagus (Acts 17:17ff), which court met on Mars Hill, west of the Acropolis.

Agrapha (ăg′rȧ-fȧ, **unwritten things**), sayings ascribed to Jesus transmitted to us outside of the canonical Gospels. The number is not large, and most are obviously apocryphal or spurious. They are found in the NT outside the Gospels, ancient manuscripts of the NT, patristic literature, papyri, and apocryphal gospels.

Agriculture (ăg′rĭ-kŭl-chûr). Not a Bible word; husbandry and husbandman are used for the activity and the man who practices it. In the form of horticulture, it is as old as Adam (Gen. 2:5, 8-15). Caring for the garden of Eden became labor after the curse (Gen. 3:17-19). Nomad and farmer began to differentiate with Abel and Cain (Gen. 4:2-4), with the herdsman gaining favor with God. As animal husbandry took its place along with tillage as part of the agricultural economy, the farmer gained in social status. Yet as late as shortly before the Babylonian exile, nomads still felt a sense of superiority over the settled agricultural people (Jer. 35:1-11, the Rechabites). "Noah began to be an husbandman, and he planted a vineyard" (Gen. 9:20). Abraham and his descendants were nomad herdsmen in Canaan, though Isaac and Jacob at times tilled the soil (Gen. 26:12; 37:7). Recurrent famines and the sojourn in Egypt taught the Israelites to depend more on agriculture, so that the report of the spies regarding the lush growth in Canaan interested them (Num. 13:23; Deut. 8:8). Agriculture became the basis of the Mosaic commonwealth, whose land legislation is suited to an agricultural rather than a pastoral economy.

Viticulture is pictured in Isaiah 5:1-7, and Matthew 21:33-41. Some farming procedures are described in Isaiah 28:24-28. The plough was light, and drawn by yokes of oxen (I Kings 19:19). Fallow ground was broken and cleared early in the year (Jer. 4:3; Hos. 10:12). Seed was scattered broadcast, as in the parable of the sower (Matt. 13:1-8), and ploughed in afterward, the stubble of the preceding crop becoming manure by decay. In irrigated fields the seed was trodden in by cattle (Isa. 32:20). The contrast between the exclusive dependence on irrigation in Egypt and the larger dependence on rain in Palestine is drawn in Deuteronomy 11:10-12.

We have glimpses of the relations of farm laborers, steward (manager or overseer) and owner, in the book of Ruth, in Matthew 20:1-16, and Luke 17:7-9.

Agriculture was beset with pests: locust, cankerworm, caterpillar and palmerworm (Joel 2:25): God calls them "my great army," as destructive as an invasion by human enemies. Haggai speaks (2:17) of blasting, mildew and hail. See Farming, Occupations.

Agrippa I (ȧ-grĭp′ȧ), known in history as King Herod Agrippa I, and in the NT, where he is mentioned in Acts 12, as Herod. He was the son of Aristobulus and Bernice and grandson of Herod the Great. Through friendship with the emperors Caligula and Claudius he gained the rulership first of Iturea and Trachonitis, then of Galilee and Perea, and ultimately of Judea and Samaria. He ruled over the thus reunited domain of Herod the Great from A.D. 40 until his death in A.D. 44 at the age of 54. While owing his position to the favor of Rome, he recognized the importance of exer-

A shepherd and his flock in the Shepherds Fields near Bethlehem (visible on the distant hills). © *MPS*

Ahab's Well near Jezreel. © MPS

cising great tact in his contacts with the Jews. Thus it was that his natural humanity gave way to expediency in the severe conflict between Judaism and the growing Christian movement. He slew James "to please the Jews" and imprisoned Peter with the intention of bringing him before the people for execution after the passover (Acts 12:2-4). Agrippa's sudden death shortly thereafter, noted in Acts 12:20-23, is fully recorded by Josephus (**Ant.** XIX, 8).

Agrippa II (á-grĭp'á), known in history as King Herod Agrippa II and in the NT as Agrippa. He was the son of Agrippa I, and ruled over only a small part of his father's territory. His consort was his sister, Bernice. Paul appeared before him and Festus, as recorded in Acts 25:23-26:32. He died in A.D. 100.

Ague (See Diseases, Malaria)

Agur (ā-gûr, **gatherer**), the author or "collector" of the wise sayings in Proverbs 30. He is named as the son of Jakeh (Prov. 30:1). His words are called "the prophecy," but better "the weighty utterance" (Heb. **massa'**). Cf. ASV mg. which reads, "Jakeh, of Massa." If this is the true reading, a connection might possibly be made between Agur and the tribe of Ishmael (Gen. 25:14).

Ahab (ā'hăb, **father's brother**). 1. Son of Omri and seventh king of the northern kingdom of Israel. He reigned 22 years, 873-851 B.C. Politically, Ahab was one of the strongest of the kings of Israel. In his days Israel was at peace with Judah and maintained her dominion over Moab, which paid a considerable tribute (II Kings 3:4). He went into battle on three different occasions in later years against Benhadad, king of Syria. While he had great success in the first two campaigns, he was defeated and mortally wounded in the third.

Ahab owes his prominence in the OT to the religious apostasy which occurred in Israel during his reign. Of him it is said, he "did evil in the sight of the Lord above all that were before him" (I Kings 16:30). His marriage to Jezebel, daughter of the king of the Zidonians, while politically advantageous, was religiously disastrous. Jezebel introduced the idolatrous worship of Baal into Israel as well as the licentious orgies of the goddess Ashtoreth. She also instituted a severe persecution against the followers of Jehovah and killed all the prophets of the Lord with the sword, except the one hundred who were hidden by Obadiah (I Kings 18:4; cf. 19:14). At this critical period in the history of Israel, God raised up Elijah, whose faithful ministry culminated in the conflict with the prophets of Baal on Mount Carmel (I Kings 18). Ahab's religious corruption was equaled by his love of material wealth and display. Not content with what he had, however, he coveted the vineyard of Naboth, which adjoined his palace at Jezreel. Jezebel had false witnesses testify against Naboth and he was stoned to death, following which Ahab took possession of the vineyard. This crime sealed the doom not only of Ahab, but of his family as well. The judgment of the Lord was that all of his posterity would be cut off (I Kings 21:21), even as had been the case with the two previous dynasties, those of Jeroboam and Baasha. The ringing condemnatory sentence given by Elijah, "In the place where dogs licked Naboth's blood, shall dogs lick thy blood," was fulfilled to the letter on Joram, his son (II Kings 9:24-26), and in part on Ahab himself (I Kings 22:38). Execution of this sentence was delayed owing to Ahab's partial and temporary repentance (I Kings 21:27-29). Ahab sinned also in failing to kiil Benhadad, king of Syria, in their second battle (I Kings 20:20-43). This disobedience, as Saul's in the case of

Agag, king of the Amalekites, was prompted by practical considerations which took precedence in Ahab's mind over God's will. For this sin, Ahab, as Saul before him, was told that he would pay with his life. Three years later he went into battle accompanied by Jehoshaphat, king of Judah, in the attempt to recover Ramoth-Gilead from the Syrians. He was mortally wounded by an arrow shot by one who "drew a bow at a venture" (I Kings 22:34). Ahab's character is succinctly summarized by the historian: "There was none like unto Ahab, which did sell himself to work wickedness in the sight of the Lord, whom Jezebel his wife stirred up" (I Kings 21:25). See also Jezebel and Elisha.

2. A false prophet who deceived the Jews in Babylon. Joining with Zedekiah, another false prophet, Ahab predicted an early return to Jerusalem. For this sin and for their immoral conduct, Jeremiah prophesied that they would be burned to death by the king of Babylon and that their names would become a byword (Jer. 29:21-23).

Aharah (ȧ-hâr'ȧh), the third son of Benjamin, probably the founder of a family (I Chron.. 8:1).

Aharhel (ȧ-hȧr'hĕl), a son of Harum, founder of a family enrolled in the tribe of Judah (I Chron. 4:8).

Ahasai (ȧ-hā'sī, **my protector**), a priest who lived in Jerusalem (Neh. 11:13).

Ahasbai (ȧ-hăs'bī), the father of Eliphelet, one of David's heroes (II Sam. 23:34).

Ahasuerus (ȧ-hăz'ū-ē'rŭs). 1. The father of Darius the Mede. Mentioned in Daniel 9:1.

2. King of Persia, mentioned in the book of Esther. There seems to be little doubt that he is to be identified with the well-known Xerxes, who reigned from 486 to 465 B.C. The Ahasuerus of Ezra 4:6, to whom were written accusations against the Jews of Jerusalem, is in all probability this same Xerxes, although sometimes identified with Cambyses, son of Cyrus. See Esther.

Ahava (ȧ-hā'vȧ), a river in Babylonia named after a place by which it flowed (Ezra 8:15, 21), where Ezra assembled the Jewish exiles to seek God's guidance and protection for the long dangerous journey to Jerusalem.

Ahaz (ā'hăz, **he has grasped**). 1. The 12th king of Judah in the divided monarchy; son of Jotham. He ruled from 735 to 715 B.C. Ahaz ascended the throne at the age of 20 (II Kings 16:2), ruling as co-regent with his father for four years and as sole monarch for 16. The critical period of his reign began when Rezin, king of Damascus, and Pekah, king of Israel, made a league against Judah. As the moment of attack approached, the prophet Isaiah was sent by God to deliver a comforting message to Ahaz (Isa. 7:1-9). After having promised that God would spare the city, Isaiah told Ahaz to ask a sign of God. Ahaz hypocritically refused to "tempt the Lord" by asking one, whereupon Isaiah cried out, "The Lord himself shall give you a sign: Behold, a virgin shall conceive and bear a son and shall call his name Immanuel" (Isa. 7:14). In the invasion, Pekah slew 120,000 men of Judah in one day; Zichri of Ephraim slew the king's son, Maaseiah, as well as Azrikam, the governor of his house, and Elkanah, who was second to the king. The Israelites carried 200,000 men, women and children captive to Samaria along with much spoil. Oded, the prophet, however, persuaded them to release the captives (II Chron. 28:6-15). Rezin also took many captives (II Chron. 28:5) and captured Elath (II Kings 16:6). Following this disastrous defeat, Judah was invaded by the Edomites from the E and the Philistines from the S and W (II Chron. 28:17, 18). In his distress, Ahaz asked assistance of Tiglath-pileser, king of Assyria, but this otherwise added to the difficulties of Ahaz. For "Tiglath-pileser king of Assyria came unto him, and distressed him, but strengthened him not" (II Chron. 28:20). The contact with Tiglath-pileser confirmed Ahaz in his religious apostasy (II Kings 16:3, 4). Following his meeting with Tiglath-pileser in Damascus, Ahaz "sacrificed unto the gods of Damascus" (II Chron. 28:23). He cut the temple vessels in pieces, closed the doors of the temple, made altars in every corner of Jerusalem, and made high places to burn incense to other gods in the cities of Judah (II Chron. 28:24, 25). After the death of Ahaz, his body was "not brought into the sepulchres of the kings" (II Chron. 28:27) because of his great wickedness.

2. A great-grandson of Jonathan,

son of King Saul; one of four sons of Micah and the father of Jehoadah (I Chron. 8:35,36).

Ahaziah (ā'hȧ-zī'ȧ, **Jehovah hath grasped**). 1. Son of Ahab and Jezebel; eighth king of Israel. He reigned only briefly, 851-850 B.C. Ahaziah was a worshiper of Jeroboam's calves and of his mother's idols, Baal and Ashtoreth. The most notable event of his reign was the revolt of the Moabites, who had been giving a yearly tribute of 100,000 lambs and 100,000 rams (II Kings 1:1; 3:4, 5). Ahaziah was prevented from trying to put down the revolt by a fall through a lattice in his palace at Samaria. Injured severely, he sent messengers to inquire of Baalzebub, god of Ekron, whether he would recover. Elijah the prophet was sent by God to intercept the messengers and proclaimed to them that Ahaziah would die. The king in anger tried to capture the prophet, but two groups of 50 men were consumed by fire from heaven in making the attempt. A third contingent was sent to seize the prophet but instead prayed Elijah to deliver them from the fate of their predecessors (II Kings 1:13, 14). Elijah then went down to Samaria and gave the message directly to the king, who died shortly afterwards. He was succeeded by his brother Jehoram (II Kings 1:17; cf 8:16).

2. Son of Jehoram and Athaliah. He was the 6th king of Judah in the divided monarchy and reigned only one year, 843 B.C. (II Chron. 22:2). He walked in all the idolatries of the house of Ahab (II Chron. 21:5-20).

Ahban (ȧ-băn), a man of Judah, of the house of Jerahmeel (I Chron. 2:29).

Aher (ā-hêr), a Benjamite (I Chron. 7:12).

Ahi (ā'hī). 1. Chief of the Gadites in Gilead (I Chron. 5:15).

2. A man of Asher, son of Shamer (I Chron. 7:34).

Ahiah (See Ahijah)

Ahiam (ā-hī'ăm, **mother's brother**), one of David's 30 heroes (II Sam. 23:33).

Ahian (ȧ-hī'ăn), a Manassite of the family of Shemida (I Chron. 7:19).

Ahiezer (ā-hī-ē'zêr). 1. The head of the tribe of Dan in the wilderness (Num. 1:12; 2:25; 7:66).

2. A Gibeonite who joined David at Ziklag (I Chron. 12:3).

Ahihud (ȧ-hī'hŭd, **brother is majesty**). 1. Prince of the tribe of Asher; selected by Moses to help divide the land of Canaan (Num. 34:27).

2. A son of Ehud (I Chron. 8:7).

Ahijah (ȧ-hī'jȧ, **brother of Jehovah**).

1. One of the sons of Jerahmeel, a great-grandson of Judah and brother of Caleb (I Chron. 2:25).

2. A descendant of Benjamin, mentioned in connection with an intra-family conflict (I Chron. 8:7).

3. Son of Ahitub, the brother of Ichabod and son of Phinehas, the son of Eli. He served as priest in Shiloh, "wearing an ephod," in the days of Saul (I Sam. 14:3).

4. The Pelonite, one of the valiant men of David's armies (I Chron. 11:36).

5. A Levite who was in charge of the treasures of the house of God in David's reign (I Chron. 26:20).

6. Son of Shisha and brother of Elihoreph. He was a scribe of Solomon (I Kings 4:3).

7. A prophet of Shiloh who met Jeroboam as he was going out of Jerusalem and foretold the transfer of ten tribes to him from Solomon by the symbolic action of rending his garment into twelve pieces, ten of which he gave to Jeroboam. He told him further that God would build him a "sure house" such as He had built for David if Jeroboam would walk in God's ways (I Kings 11:29-39). His other recorded prophecy was given to Jeroboam's wife, who in disguise consulted him as to her son Abijah's recovery. The prophet foretold not only the death of the son but also the extermination of the house of Jeroboam because he "had done evil above all that were before" him in making idols and in provoking God to anger (I Kings 14:1-16).

8. The father of Baasha, King of Israel, of the tribe of Issachar (I Kings 15:27).

9. One of the men who set their seal to the covenant drawn up before the Lord in the days of Nehemiah (Neh. 10:26).

Ahikam (ȧ-hī'kăm, **my brother has risen up**), son of Shaphan the scribe, and sent by Josiah to ask the meaning of the Book of the Law that was found (II Kings 22:12). Later, he successfully pleaded before the princes and elders that Jeremiah should not be put to death for his warnings of impending doom (Jer. 26:24). After the deportation to Babylon, Ahikam's son Gedaliah became governor over the remnant who remained in the cities of Judah (II Kings 25:22; Jer. 40:5).

Ahilud (ȧ-hī′lŭd, **a child's brother**), father of Jehoshaphat the recorder (II Sam. 8:16; 20:24; I Kings 4:3; I Chron. 18:15).

Ahimaaz (ȧ-hĭm′ā-ăz, **brother of anger**). 1. The father of Ahinoam, wife of King Saul (I Sam. 14:50).

2. Son of Zadok the high priest (I Chron. 6:8). With Jonathan, son of Abiathar, he served as messenger in Absalom's rebellion, carrying tidings from Hushai, David's counselor and spy, and also the king of Absalom's death.

3. One of Solomon's 12 commissary officers (I Kings 4:15). He married Basemath, the daughter of Solomon. Some suggest that he should be identified with the son of Zadok.

Ahiman (ȧ-hī′măn, **my brother is a gift**). 1. One of the three giant sons of Anak seen in Mount Hebron by the spies (Num. 13:22). The three sons, Sheshai, Ahiman, and Talmai, were driven by Caleb from Hebron (Josh. 15:14) and killed (Judg. 1:10).

2. A Levite gatekeeper (I Chron. 9:17).

Ahimelech (ȧ-hĭm′-ĕ-lĕk, **brother of a king**). 1. Saul's high priest who helped David by giving him the shewbread and Goliath's sword. Upon hearing this, Saul ordered the death of Ahimelech and the other priests with him (I Sam. 21-22). Abiathar, son of Ahimelech, escaped.

2. Son of Abiathar, and grandson of Ahimelech (II Sam. 8:17; I Chron. 18:16; 24:6).

3. A Hittite who, with Abishai, was asked to accompany David to Saul's camp (I Sam. 26:6).

Ahimoth (ȧ-hī′-mŏth, **brother of death**), son of Elkanah (I Chron. 6:25), descendant of Kohath and a Levite.

Ahinadab (ȧ-hĭn′-ȧ-dăb), a commissary officer of Solomon (I Kings 4:14).

Ahinoam (ȧ-hĭn′-ō-ăm, **my brother is delight**). 1. Wife of King Saul (I Sam. 14:50).

2. One of David's wives, a Jezreelitess (I Sam. 25:43), who lived with him at Gath (27:3). She and Abigail were captured by the Amalekites at Ziklag (30:5), but rescued by David (30:18). Ahinoam bore Amnon, David's first son (3:2).

Ahio (ȧ-hī′ō, **brotherly**). 1. Son of Abinadab. He and his brother Uzzah accompanied the ark of God from Gibeah on David's first attempt to remove it to Jerusalem (II Sam. 6:1-11; I Chron. 13:1-14).

2. A Benjamite (I Chron. 8:14).

3. A Gibeonite, son of Jehiel (I Chron. 8:31; 9:37).

Ahira (ȧ-hī′rȧ, **brother of evil**), prince captain of the tribe of Naphtali (Num. 1:15; 2:29; 7:78, 83; 10:27).

Ahiram (ȧ-hī′răm, **brother of height, exalted brother**), son of Benjamin (Num. 26:38).

Ahiramite (ȧ-hī′-rȧ-mīt, **of the family of Ahiram**), Num. 26:38.

Ahisamach (ȧ-hĭs′-ȧ-măk, **my brother supports**), a Danite, the father of Aholiab (Exod. 31:6; 35:34; 38:23).

Ahishahar (ȧ-hĭsh′ȧ-hȧr, **brother of dawn**), a descendant of Benjamin through Jediael and Bilhan (I Chron. 7:10).

Ahishar (ȧ-hī′shȧr, **my brother has sung**), an official over Solomon's household (I Kings 4:6).

Ahithophel (ȧ-hĭth′ō-fĕl, **brother of folly**), David's counselor who joined the conspiracy of Absalom. His main motivation would appear to be ambition for personal power. When his advice to Absalom that he pursue David immediately was disregarded, he went home and hanged himself (II Sam. 17:1-23).

Ahitub (ȧ-hī′tŭb, **brother of goodness**). 1. The brother of Ichabod and son of Phinehas the son of Eli; father of Ahiah (I Sam. 14:3) and Ahimelech (22:9, 11, 20)..

2. Son of Amariah and father of Zadok the high priest (II Sam. 8:17; I Chron. 6:7, 8). He appears as grandfather of Zadok in I Chronicles 9:11; Nehemiah 11:11. A descendant of Aaron through Eleazar, he is to be distinguished from Ahitub 1. who descended through Ithamar (I Chron. 24).

3. Son of another Amariah and father of another Zadok (I Chron. 6:11, 12). Cf. list in Ezra 7:1-5. Due to compression of names or copyist's error, 3. may be the same as 2.

Ahlab (ȧ′lăb, **fat** or **fruitful**), a town of Asher from which the Israelites were not able to drive the inhabitants.

Ahlai (ȧ′lī, **O would that!**). 1. The father of Zabad, one of David's soldiers.(I Chron. 11:41).

2. A daughter of Sheshan who married her father's Egyptian slave

Jarha. They had a son Attai (I Chron. 2:31-35).

Ahoah (ȧ-hō'ȧ, **brotherly),** a son of Bela (I Chron. 8:4), from whom is derived the term "Ahohite" (II Sam. 23: 9, 28; I Chron. 11:12).

Ahohite (ȧ-hō'hīt), a patronymic given to the descendants of Ahoah: Dodo (II Sam. 23:9), Zalmon (23:28), and Ilai (I Chron. 11:29).

Ahola (See Aholah)

Aholah (ȧ-hō'-lȧ, **tent-woman).** In God's parable to Ezekiel (Ezek. 23) is a woman who represents Samaria, capital of the Northern Kingdom. Her sister Aholibah **(my tent is in her)** is a symbol of Jerusalem (v. 4), capital of Judah whose worship was appointed by God. These "women" had been unfaithful to Jehovah their true husband (Isa. 54:5) by their lewdness with Egypt in their youth (i.e. adopting the ways of the world). Later, Aholah (Israel) was spiritually adulterous by her coalition with Egypt and Assyria and by imitating their luxury and idolatry. For these "whoredoms" God punished her with captivity by the very agent of her sin (Ezek. 23:9, 10). See also Aholibah.

Aholiab (ȧ-hō'-lĭ-ăb, **father's tent),** a man who was divinely endowed with artistic skill to construct the tabernacle (Exod. 31:6).

Aholibah (See Aholah)

Aholibamah (ȧ-hŏl'ĭ-bā'mȧ, **tent of the high place).** 1. One of Esau's three wives (Gen. 36:2, 18, 25). Also called Judith the daughter of Beeri (Gen. 26:34).

2. An Edomite duke (Gen. 36:41; I Chron. 1:52), probably so named from the district of his possession.

Ahumai (ȧ-hŭ'mī), a descendant of Judah (I Chron. 4:2).

Ahura Mazda (ȧ'hōō-ră măzdȧ), the all wise spirit in the dualistic system of Zoroastrianism.

Ahuzam (ȧ-hŭ-zăm, **possessor),** a man of the tribe of Judah, one of four sons born to Ashur by his wife Naarah (I Chron. 4:6).

Ahuzzath (ȧ-hŭz'ăth, **possession),** a "friend" of Abimelech, who made a peace treaty with Isaac at Beersheba after they saw that the Lord had blessed him (Gen. 26:23-33).

Ai (ā'ī, **ruin).** 1. A city of central Palestine, E of Bethel. Abraham pitched his tent between Ai and Bethel when he arrived in Canaan (Gen. 12:8). Ai figures most prominently in the account of the conquest of the land; it was the second Canaanite city taken by the forces under Joshua (Josh. 7, 8).

2. A city of Ammon, near Heshbon (Jer. 49:3).

Aiah (ā'yȧ, **falcon).** 1. A Horite (Gen. 36:24; I Chron. 1:40).

2. The father of Rizpah, Saul's concubine (II Sam. 3:7; 21:8).

Aiath (ā'yăth), feminine form of the city Ai (Isa. 10:28).

Aija (ā-ī'-jȧ), another form of the city Ai (Neh. 11:31).

Aijalon (See Ajalon)

Aijeleth Shahar (ā'-jĕ-lĕth shā'hȧr, **the hind of the morning),** title of Psalm 22. Some explain it as the name of a hunting tune to which the psalm was sung. More likely it alludes to its subject, the lovely and innocent hind symbolizing one who is persecuted unjustly (vss. 12, 13, 16).

Ain (ȧ'ēn, **eye, fountain).** 1. A landmark on the eastern border of the Promised Land; west of Riblah (Num. 34:11). It is usually thought to be the modern **Ain el' Azy,** the main source of the Orontes river.

2. A southern city of Judah (Josh. 15:32), afterwards of Simeon (Josh. 19:7), then assigned to the priests (Josh. 21:16).

Ain Feshka, oasis on the western side of the Dead Sea, S of Khirbet Qumran. Remains of buildings found in 1956 suggest that this was another center of the Qumran community.

Ain Karem. A Hebrew phrase found in the Song of Solomon 1:14, meaning "the vineyards of Engedi." Engedi was a town on the W coast of the Dead Sea, about 35 miles from Jerusalem.

Ain Karim (ȧ'ēn kâr'ĭm), a village in the hill country of Judea, five miles W of Jerusalem, and the traditional home of Zacharias and Elizabeth, parents of John the Baptist.

Ajah (ā'jȧ, **falcon),** a Horite (Gen. 36:24).

Ajalon, Aijalon (ā'jȧ-lŏn, **place of gazelles).** 1. A city of Dan (Josh. 19:42), assigned to the Levite sons of Kohath (I Chron. 6:69). It is mentioned most notably in the memorable words of Joshua, "Sun, stand thou still upon Gibeon, and thou moon, in the valley of Ajalon" (Josh. 10:12).

2. The burial place of the judge Elon, in Zebulun (Judg. 12:12).

Akan (ā'-kăn, **twisted),** a descendant or branch of the Horites of Mount Seir (Gen. 36:27).

Akeldama (See Aceldama)

Akhenaton (ȧ'kĕn-ȧ't'n, **he who is beneficial to Aton),** the name chosen by Amenhotep IV (1377-1360 B.C.), ruler in the Eighteenth Dynasty of Egypt, when he changed the religion of his country, demanding that all worship only the sun god under the name Aton.

Akkad (See Accad)

Akkub (ăk'-ŭb, **pursuer).** 1. Son of Elioenai (I Chron. 3:24).

2. A Levite who founded a family of Temple porters (I Chron. 9:17).

3. The head of a family of the Nethinim (Ezra 2:45).

4. A Levite who helped expound the Law (Neh. 8:7).

Akrabbim (ăk-răb'ĭm, **scorpions),** always found with **Ma'ăleh** (Mā'-a-la), meaning "the going up to," "ascent of," or "pass." So the "ascent of the Scorpions," rising between the SW corner of the Dead Sea and Zin, was the southern boundary between Judah and Edom (Num. 34:4; Josh. 15:3), and was the boundary of the Amorites (Judg. 1:36).

Alabaster (ăl'-ȧ-băs'têr), not today's softer gypsum or sulphate of lime often called alabaster, but the harder oriental alabaster, a carbonate of lime. Sometimes called onyx or onyx marble. Popular for making perfume vases and boxes for precious ointments.

Alameth (ȧl'ă-mĕth, **concealment).** 1. A son of Becher and grandson of Benjamin (I Chron. 7:8).

2. Variant of Alemeth (KJV, ASV), son of Jehoadah or Jarah (I Chron. 8:36; 9:42).

Alammelech (ȧ-lăm'ĕ-lĕk, **oak of a king),** a town of Asher (Josh. 19:26).

Alamoth (ăl'ȧ-mŏth, **maidens, virgins),** a musical term (Ps. 46:1; I Chron. 15:20) which may indicate a women's choir, musical instruments set in a high pitch, or instruments played by virgins.

Alemeth or **Almon** (ăl'ĕ-mĕth, ăl'mŏn, **hidden),** a priests' city (I Chron. 6:60; Josh. 21:18). Now modern Almit.

Aleph (á'lĕf, **ox),** first letter of the Hebrew alphabet (. .). Although a consonant, it is the forerunner of the Gr. **alpha** and our English "a."

Alexander, The Great (ăl'ĕg-zăn'dêr, **man-defending),** son of Philip, King of Macedon, and Olympias, an Epirote princess; born 356 B.C. Although not named in the Bible, he is described prophetically in Daniel, the "he goat" from the West with a notable horn between his eyes. He came against the ram with two horns which was standing before the river, defeated the ram, and became very great until the great horn was broken and four notable ones came up from it (Dan. 8:5-8). The prophecy identifies the ram as the kings of Media and Persia, the goat as the king of Greece, the great horn being the first king. When he fell, four kings arose in his place (Dan. 8:18-22). The historical fulfillment is striking: Alexander led the Greek armies across the Hellespont into Asia Minor in 334 B.C. and defeated the Persian forces at the river Granicus. Moving with amazing rapidity (the he goat "touched not the ground," Dan. 8:5), he again met and defeated the Persians at Issus. Turning south, he moved down the Syrian coast, advancing to Egypt, which fell to him without a blow. Turning again to the East, he met the armies of Darius for the last time, defeating them in the battle of Arbela, E of the Tigris River. Rapidly he occupied Babylon, then Susa and Persepolis, the capitals of Persia. He later marched his armies eastward as far as India where they won a great battle. The army, however, refused to advance farther, and Alexander was forced to return to Persepolis. While still making plans for further conquests, he contracted a fever. Weakened by the strenuous campaign and increasing dissipation, he was unable to throw off the fever and died in Babylon in 323 B.C. at the age of 32. His empire was then divided among four of his generals.

Alexandra (ăl'ĕg-zăn'drȧ, wife of Aristobulus, King of the Jews (105-104 B.C.)

Alexandria (ăl'ĕg-zăn'drĭ-ȧ), founded by Alexander the Great, 332 B.C.; successively the Ptolemaic, Roman and Christian capital of Lower Egypt. Its harbors, formed by the island Pharos and the headland Lochias, were suitable alike for commerce and war. It was the chief grain port for Rome. Its merchant ships, the largest and finest of the day, usually sailed directly to Puteoli, but at times, because of the severity of the weather, sailed under the coast of Asia Minor, as did the vessel which carried Paul (Acts 27:6). Alexandria was also an important cultural center, boasting an excellent university. In different eras it was reported as possessing from

400,000 to 900,000 books and rolls. The population of Alexandria had three prominent elements: Jews, Greeks and Egyptians. The Jews enjoyed equal privileges with the Greeks, so that they became fixed there. At Alexandria the OT revelation was brought into contact with Greek philosophy. The consequent synthesis became of great importance in subsequent religious thought. The influence of Alexandrian philosophy on the thought of the writers of the NT is debatable, but its impact on later theological and Biblical studies in the Christian church was great. According to tradition, Mark the evangelist first carried the Gospel to Alexandria and established the first church there. From this city, Christianity reached out into all Egypt and the surrounding countries. A theological school flourished here as early as the second century. Among its great teachers were Clement and Origen, pioneers in Biblical scholarship and Christian philosophy.

Algum (See Plants of the Bible)

Aliah (See Alvah)

Alian (See Alvan)

Allegory (Gr. **allegoreúein,** from **állos, other,** and **agoreúein, to speak in the assembly).** Used but once (Gal. 4:24), in reference to Hagar and Sarah, and Ishmael and Isaac; the literary device is used extensively in Scripture, for example in Isaiah 5:1-7 and in the Song of Songs. To speak allegorically is to set forth one thing in the image of another, the principal subject being inferred from the figure rather than by direct statement. Clarity of inference differentiates between allegory and parable, because the latter usually requires an interpretation for the teaching which it parallels. Allegorizing (to be distinguished from the drawing out of spiritual truths from factual presentations) has had broad application in Bible teaching.

Alleluia (ăl-lē-lū'yȧ, **praise ye Jehovah),** a word used by the writers of various psalms to invite all to join them in praising God (104:35; 105:45; 106:1, 48; 111:1; 112:1; 113:1, 9; 115:18; 116:19; 117:2; 135:1, 21; first and last vs. of Psalms 146 to 150). The term Alleluia in Revelation 19:1, 3, 4, 6 is borrowed from these psalms.

Alliances, Bible: **affinity, confederacy, conspiracy, covenant, join, testament.** In this article **covenant** and **testament** are omitted when associated with God. In Genesis 21:27-32 Abraham and Abimelech "made a covenant" (Heb. **kārath bĕrith, cut a covenant).** To **cut a covenant** is a formal term basic to alliance and covenant making. The cutting up and arranging the pieces of the sacrificial victim in pact-making was common among nations of antiquity and a regular practice of the Israelites. Jeremiah 34:18-20 refers to the practice of contracting parties passing between the pieces of flesh. Such cutting up and arrangement is understood variously: threat of similar treatment to covenant-breakers, animals representative of contracting parties, new unity by contractors passing between the pieces, association of divine witness in consecration of the sacrifice. In the NT **diathekē** is a "covenant" or "testament," between men (Gal. 3:15), or with God.

Allon (ăl'ŏn, **oak).** 1. Prince of Simeon (I Chron. 4:37). 2. Or Elon, a town, or **"the oak** in Zaanannim," a southern boundary point in Naphtali (Josh. 19:33 cf. Judg. 4:11).

3. **Allon Bachuth,** "the oak of weeping," a tree marking the burial place of Deborah, the nurse of Rebekah (Gen. 35:8).

Allon Bachuth (See Allon 3).

Almighty (awl-mīt'ē, meaning uncertain). LXX **pantokrátor, all powerful.** Used 57 times with **'ēl, Kúrios, Theós,** for identification (Gen. 17:1), invocation (Gen. 28:3), description (Ezek. 10:5), praise (Rev. 4:8).

Almodad (ăl-mō'-dăd, **the beloved),** first-mentioned of Joktan's 13 sons (Gen. 10:26; I Chron. 1:20).

Almon (ăl'mŏn, **hidden),** a Levitical city in Benjamin (Josh. 21:18). The same as "Alemeth" KJV and "Allemeth" ASV (I Chron. 6:60).

Almon-diblathaim (ăl'mŏn-dĭb-lȧ-thā'ĭm, **Almon of two cakes of figs),** one of the last stops of the Israelites on their journey from Egypt to the Jordan.

Almon Tree (See Plants)

Alms (ȧhms), kind deeds arising out of compassion, mercy, pity for the unfortunate. Word found 14 times, in Matthew, Luke and Acts only.

In later Judaism the righteousness of almsgiving becomes somewhat legalistic and professional. The lame man at the Gate Beautiful exemplifies professional begging in that daily he "sat for alms," and would "ask for alms," being well known to the people (Acts 3:1ff.). Almsgiving was of two kinds: "alms of the dish," food and money received daily for distribution; and "alms of the chest," coins received on the sabbath for widows, orphans, strangers and the poor. Practice of the NT Church is foreshadowed in the admonition of Jesus, "give alms of such things as ye have" (Luke 11:41, cf. I Cor. 16:2); and "sell that ye have, and give alms" (Luke 12:33, cf. II Cor. 8:3). Alms in the NT Church, not named as such, are seen in the church of Macedonia in "their deep poverty . . . beyond their power . . . willing of themselves . . . ministering to the saints" (II Cor. 8:1-5).

Almug (See Plants of the Bible)

Aloe (See Plants of the Bible)

Aloth (ā'-lŏth), a town or district mentioned with Asher and of which Baanah was Solomon's commissary (I Kings 4:16) ASV has Bealoth.

Alpha (ăl'fȧ), first letter of the Gr. alphabet, (A). **Alphabet,** a list of elementary sounds in any language, comes from the first two Gr. letters, Alpha and Beta. In contrast is Omega, the last letter of the Gr. alphabet. Combined with Alpha, it signifies completeness, as "from A to Z" in modern usage. So God is the Alpha and Omega, the First and the Last, the Beginning and the End (Rev. 1:8), as is also Christ (Rev. 21:6; 22:13). Compare Isaiah 41:4; 44:6.

Alphabet (See Writing)

Alphaeus (ăl-fē'-ŭs). 1. Father of Levi (Mark 2:14). 2. Father of James the apostle (Matt. 10:3; Mark 3:18; Luke 6:15; Acts 1:13).

3. Possibly Cleophas, husband of the Mary at the cross (John 19:25 cf. Mark 15:40), as **Cleophas** and **Alphaeus** are of Semitic derivation. Unlikely the Cleopas of the Emmaus road (Luke 24:18) since **Cleopas** was a common Greek name.

Altar (awl'têr, **place of slaughter).** Altars in Old Testament times were many and varied. Their importance is seen in that the word "altar" is used 433 times in the Bible (KJV).

Some of the early ones were crude elevations, usually of earth or stone, though other materials were sometimes employed. The shape and size varied with the kind of materials used. For instance, in I Kings 18:31 one is noted that was simply a pile of stones, while another was made of one single stone (I Sam. 14:33-35). Later on, altars were made of a great variety of materials such as bronze, horns, ashes, wood, marble, brick and alabaster.

The first Hebrew altar we read about (Gen. 8:20) was the one erected by Noah after leaving the ark. Subsequently altars are spoken of as being built by Abraham (Gen. 12:7-8; 13:4, 18; 22:9), Isaac (Gen. 26:25), Jacob (Gen. 35:1-7), Moses (Exod. 17:15), and Joshua (Josh. 8:30-31). Some of these must have been very simple in structure as the context of Genesis 22:9 would indicate. Most of the altars were built for sacrificial purposes, but some seem to have been largely memorial in character (Exod. 17:15-16; Josh. 22:26-27). Sometimes God stated just how the altar was to be built and of what materials.

With the erection of the tabernacle, altars were constructed by the Hebrews for two chief purposes, the offering of sacrifices and the burning of incense.

Certain brass utensils were made in connection with the altar. There were plans to hold the ashes, shovels for removing the ashes, basins to receive the blood and to convey it to the varied places for sprinkling, three-pronged flesh hooks with which to remove the flesh, and censers for carrying coals from the altar (Exod. 27:3). Once the fire on this altar was kindled, it was required that it burn continually (Lev. 6:13).

In addition to the altar for sacrifice, Moses was also commanded by God to make "an altar of incense" (Exod. 30:1), sometimes called a "golden altar" (Exod. 39:38; Num. 4:11). This altar was to be located before the veil that separated the holy place from the holy of holies, midway between the walls (Exod. 30:6; 40:5). Because of its special location, it was referred to as "the altar before the Lord" (Lev. 16:12).

There are no altars recognized in the New Testament Church. While Hebrews 13:10 is sometimes used to prove the contrary, a careful study of this passage in its context is fatal to this idea. The idea in this passage is that Jesus Christ is the true altar of each believer. Paul mentions in Acts 17:23 the inscription "the altar to the unknown God," that had been placed over the altar erected in Athens. Such inscriptions were common in heathendom and are referred to by a number of early writers (see Augustine, **The City of God** 3:12).

There is good reason to feel that the need for altars was revealed to man very early as basic in approaching God. It played a leading role in all OT worship of the true God, and is seen both in and outside the Bible as playing a prominent part in most heathen religions. The altar looked to the great sacrifice that the Son of God was to make on the cross. The altar of sacrifice, being the first thing visible as one approached the tabernacle, spoke loudly to man that without the shedding of blood there would be no access to God and no forgiveness of sin (Heb. 9:9, 22). Most writers feel the brass or copper speaks of divine judgment.

Altaschith (ăl-tăs′chĭth, **destroy not**), a title notation in Psalms 57, 58, 59, 75. Same form found in prayer of Moses, "O Lord God **destroy not** thy people" (Deut. 9:26).

Alush (ā′lŭsh), a desert campsite of the Israelites between Dophkah and Rephidim (Num. 33:13, 14). Meaning: "crowding" (Rabbis).

Alvah, Aliah (ăl′vȧ), a duke of Edom (Gen. 36:40) called "Aliah" in I Chron. 1:51.

Alvan, Alian, (ăl′văn, **tall**), a son of Shobal the Horite (Gen. 36:23; I Chron. 1:40).

Amad (ā′măd), a town of the tribe of Asher (Josh. 19:26).

Amal (ā′măl), an Asherite (I Chron. 7:35).

Amalek (ăm′ȧ-lĕk), son of Eliphaz (eldest son of Esau) by his concubine Timna (Gen. 36:12; I Chron. 1:36). Duke of Edom (Gen. 36:16).

Amalekites (ă-măl′ĕk-īts), an ancient and nomadic marauding people dwelling mainly in the Negeb from the times of Abraham to Hezekiah, c. 2000-700 B.C. They are frequently mentioned in the history of Israel (Exod. 17:8ff.; Num. 14:45; I Sam. 15).

Amam (ā′-măm), an unidentified southern town belonging to Judah (Josh. 15:26).

Amana, Amanah (See Abana)

Amana (ă-mā′nȧ, **constant** (?)), a mountain near Lebanon (S of Sol. 4:8), whence flow the Amana springs (II Kings 5:12, marg.).

Amaranthine (ăm-ȧ-răn′thĭne, **fadeth not away**), an inheritance (I Pet. 1:4), glory (I Pet. 5:4). From **amaranth,** a flower which when picked does not wither; the unfading flower of the poets.

Amariah (ăm′ȧ-rī′ah). 1. Levite, and ancestor of Ezra (I Chron. 6:7, 11, 52; Ezra 7:3).

2. Levite serving in house of the Lord under David (I Chron. 23:19; 24:23).

3. Chief priest under Jehoshaphat (II Chron. 19:11).

4. Levite under Hezekiah (II Chron. 31:15).

5. One guilty of intermarrying (Ezra 10:42).

6. Covenant signer (Neh. 10:3).

7. Levite under Zerubbabel (Neh. 12:2).

8. Son of Hezekiah and great-grandfather of Zephaniah (Zeph. 1:1). See also Nehemiah 11:4 and 12:13.

Amarna, Tell El (ȧ-mär′nȧ, tĕl ĕl, **the hill amarna**), the modern name for the ancient capital of Amenhotep IV (c. 1387-1366 B.C.), where in 1887 a large number of clay tablets containing the private correspondence between the ruling Egyptian Pharaohs and the political leaders in Palestine were discovered.

Amasa (ă-mā′sȧ). 1. Captain of the rebel forces under Absalom. He was later killed by Joab (II Sam. 17:25; 20:4-12). 2. Prince of Ephraim (II Chron. 28:12f).

Amasai (ȧ-măs′ā-ī). 1. An officer who assured David of his loyalty to him (I Chron. 12:18). 2. A trumpeter (I Chron. 15:24). 3. Levite in the time of Hezekiah (II Chron. 29:12).

Amashai (ȧ-măsh′ā-ī), priest in Nehemiah's time (Neh. 11:13).

Amasiah (ăm′ȧ-sī′ȧ), a captain under Jehoshaphat (II Chron. 17:16).

Amaziah (ăm-ȧ-zī′ȧ, **whom Jehovah strengthens**). 1. Ninth king of Judah; coregent with his father Joash for at least a year; ruled for 29 years. The account of his life is found chiefly in II Kings 14 and II Chronicles 25. He was killed in a conspiracy. 2. Priest of Bethel in the reign of Jeroboam II (Amos 7:10-17). 3. A Simeonite (I Chron. 4:34, 43). 4. Levite in the time of David (I Chron. 6:45, 48).

Ambassador, an envoy or messenger. Usually men of high rank, as Sennacherib's field-marshal, Tartan; chief eunuch, Rabsaris; and chief officer, Rabshakeh, met by Hezekiah's housemaster, scribe and recorder (II Kings 18:17f). Note: Joshua 9:4, ". . . made as if they had been ambassadors . . ." may be read ". . . supplied themselves with provisions. . ." "We are ambassadors for Christ" (II Cor. 5: 20) and, "I am an ambassador in bonds" (Eph. 6:20), are both from **presbeuein,** "to be, work or travel as an envoy or ambassador." The concept of ambassador as personal representative of sovereign and state, in foreign residence, is likely foreign to the Biblical concept of messenger as ambassador.

Amber (ăm′bêr, **unknown),** only in description of color of divine glory (Ezek. 1:4, 27; 8:2).

Amen (ā-mĕn), English and Greek both transliterations of Hebrew, from root meaning "confirm" or "support." General sense "so let it be," "truly," "indeed."

Amethyst (See Minerals)

Ami or **Amon** (ā′mī), a servant of Solomon (Ezra 2:57), called Amon in Neh. 7:59.

Aminadab (See Amminidab)

Amittai (ȧ-mĭt′ī, **faithful),** father of Jonah (II Kings 14:25; Jonah 1:1).

Ammah (ăm′ȧ, **mother,** or **beginning),** a hill facing Giah by way of the wilderness of Gibeon, where Joab and Abishai stopped in their pursuit of Abner after Asahel's death (II Sam. 2:24).

Ammi (ăm′ī, **my people),** a symbolic name given to Israel (Hos. 2:1) predictive of God's reconciliation to them, in contrast to sinful Israel represented by Hosea's son Lo-ammi, "not my people" (Hos. 1:9). See Rom. 9:25, 26.

Ammiel (ăm′ĭ-ĕl, **my kinsman is God).** 1. The son of Gemali and spy sent out by Moses (Num. 13:12).

2. The father of Machir, of Lodebar (II Sam. 9:4, 5; 17:27).

3. The father of Bath-sheba, one of David's wives (I Chron. 3:5).

4. The sixth son of Obed-edom who, with his family, was associated with the Tabernacle porters (I Chron. 26:5).

Ammihud (ă-mī′hŭd, **my kinsman is glorious).** 1. The father of Elishama, chief of Ephraim (Num. 1:10; 2:18; 7:48, 53).

2. A man of Simeon and father of Shemuel (Num. 34:20).

3. A Naphtalite whose son, Pedahel, also assisted in the division of the land (Num. 34:28).

4. Father of Talmai and king of Geshur. Absalom fled to Talmai after he slew his brother Amnon (II Sam. 13:37).

5. Son of Omri, father of Uthai (I Chron. 9:4).

Amminadab (ă-mĭn′ȧ-dăb, **my people is willing** or **my kinsman is generous).** 1. A Levite. Aaron's father-in-law (Exod. 6:23).

2. A prince of Judah (Num. 1:7; 2:3; 7:12, 17; 10:14; Ruth 4:19, 20; I Chron. 2:10).

3. A son of Kohath, son of Levi (I Chron. 6:22). Perhaps the same as No. 1.

4. A Kohathite who assisted in the return of the Ark from the house of Obed-edom (I Chron. 15:10, 11).

Ammishaddai (ăm-ĭ-shăd′ī, **an ally is the Almighty),** father of Abiezer, captain of the tribe of Dan in Moses' time (Num. 1:12; 2:25; 7:66, 71; 10:25).

Ammizabad (ȧ-mĭz′a-băd, **my kinsman hath endowed,** made a present), son of Benaiah, third of David's captains (I Chron. 27:6).

Ammon (ăm′ŏn, **a people).** Ammon or Ben-ammi is the name of one of the sons of Lot born to him by his youngest daughter in the neighborhood of Zoar (Gen. 19:38).

Ammonites (ăm′ŏn-īts), the name given to the descendants of Ben-ammi or Ammon (Gen. 19:38). They were related to the Moabites by ancestry (Gen. 19:38) and often appear in the Scriptures in united effort. Because by ancestry they were related to Israel, reflected in the name by which they are often called in the OT, Ben-ammi "children of my people," the Israelites were told by the Lord not to enter into the battle with them as they journeyed toward the land of Canaan (Deut. 2:19). The Ammonites made war with Israel in order to extend her borders farther west. Though this land never really belonged to the Ammonites, they claimed it, and gave this as a reason for their aggression (Judg. 11:13).

The people were fierce in nature, rebellious against Israel and idolatrous in their religious practices. They thrust out the right eye of all in Jabesh Gilead (I Sam. 11:2). They were given to brutish murder (Jer. 40:14; 41:5-7; Amos 1:14). Though related to Israel, they refused to help them when asked (Deut. 23:4) and they joined with Moab in securing Balaam to curse them (Deut. 23:3-4).

Because of their sins and especially because they constantly opposed Israel, Ezekiel predicted their complete destruction (Ezek. 25:1-7). Their last stand seems to have been against Judas Maccabeus (I Macc. 5:6).

Amnon (ăm′nŏn). 1. Son of David

Ruins of Tekoah, birthplace of the prophet Amos. © MPS

by Ahinoam. By trickery, he forced his half-sister Tamar as she tended him during a pretended sickness. For this he was later murdered by Tamar's brother Absalom.

2. A son of Shimon, of Judah (I Chron. 4:20).

Amok (ā'mŏk), chief of priests who returned with Zerubbabel from exile (Neh. 12:7, 20).

Amon (ā'mŏn), the successor and son of king Manasseh and the father of the illustrious king Josiah.

2. The governor of Samaria to whom Micaiah the prophet was committed by Ahab the king of Israel because he had predicted the king's death (I Kings 22:15-28).

3. One of Solomon's servants (Neh. 7:57-59) though sometimes he is called Ami (Ezra 2:57).

Amon (ā'mon), a city thought by most scholars to be the same as No (Jer. 46:25; Ezek. 30:14-15, 16; Nah. 3:8), and as No-Amon. Thebes is the Greek name of this old capital of Upper Egypt. It was called "No Amon" meaning "city of Amon," because this was the name of its chief deity. It has a number of famous temples and tombs. Perhaps the most famous tomb, discovered in 1922, was the tomb of Tutankhamen, with all of its equipment still intact.

Amos (ā'mŏs, **burden-bearer**), was one of the colorful personalities in an era which saw the rise of several towering prophetic figures. His ministry occurred in the reign of Jeroboam II (c. 786-746 B.C.), the son of king Jehoash of the Jehu dynasty. His forty-year reign was one of great prosperity for the northern kingdom, approaching in character the "golden age" of David and Solomon. With the threat of war removed, a cultural, social and economic revival took place. The expansion of trade and commerce resulted in a steady drift from country to city, and the small towns in the northern kingdom gradually became overcrowded. But prosperity was accompanied by an almost unprecedented degree of social corruption (Amos 2:6-8; 5:11-12).

Archaeological discoveries in Palestine have furnished a dramatic picture of the extent to which this depraved, immoral religion exerted its corrupting influences over the Israelites. Characteristic of the ritual observances were drunkenness, violence, gross sensuality and idolatrous worship. The effect of this demoralizing religion upon Hebrew society was seen in the corruption of justice, in wanton and luxurious living, and in the decay of social unity.

To this perilous situation Amos brought a message of stern denunciation. Although he was not an inhabitant of the northern kingdom he was painfully aware of its moral, social and religious shortcomings. Amos lived in the small mountain village of Tekoa, which lay to the south of Jerusalem on the borders of the extensive upland pastures of Judah. By trade he was a herdsman of sheep and goats (7:14), and was also engaged in dressing the sycamore-fig tree, whose fruit needs to be incised about four days before the harvest to hasten the ripening process. His background was of a strictly agricultural nature, and his work afforded him ample time for meditating upon

God's laws and their meaning for wayward Israel.

On receiving his call, Amos protested vigorously against the luxurious and careless living characteristic of Samaria, castigated the elaborate offerings made at the shrines of Beersheba and Gilgal, and stated flatly that ritual could never form an acceptable substitute for righteousness. He asserted the moral jurisdiction of God over all nations (1:3, 6, 9, 11; 2:1, 4, 6) and warned the Israelites that unless they repented of their idolatry, and following a renewed spiritual relationship with God, commenced to redress social inequalities, they would fall victim to the invader from the East. So great was the impact of this vigorous personality that Amos was accused of sedition by Amaziah, the idolatrous high priest of Bethel (7:10 seq.).

The style of his book, though simple, is picturesque, being marked by striking illustrations taken from his rural surroundings. His work as a herdsman was clearly not incompatible either with a knowledge of history (9:7) or with an ability to assess the significance of contemporary political and religious trends. The integrity of his book has suffered little at the hands of modern critical scholars. Analysis:

1-2. The indictment of foreign nations including Judah and Israel.

3:1-5:17. The condemnation of wicked Samaria.

5:18-6:14. False security exposed; judgment foretold.

7:1-9:10. Five visions illustrate Divine forbearance and justice; Amos' reception at Bethel (7.10-17).

9:11-15. Epilogue promising restoration and prosperity.

Amoz (ā'mŏz), the father of the prophet Isaiah (II Kings 19:2, 20; Isa. 1:1; etc.).

Amphipolis (ăm-fĭp'ō-lĭs, **a city pressed on all sides**), a city of Macedonia, situated on a bend of the river Strymon, founded by the Athenians in the fifth century B.C. and under the Romans, the capital of one of the four districts into which Macedonia was divided.

Amplias (ăm'plĭ-ăs) **ASV, RSV, Ampliatus** (ăm'plĭ-ā-tŭs) **a Christian to** whom Paul sent a greeting (Rom. 16:8).

Amram (ăm'răm, **people exalted**). 1. A descendant of Levi and of Kohath, and father of Aaron, Moses and Miriam (Exod. 6:18, 20; Num. 26:59; I Chron. 6:3). 2. A son of Bani, who married a foreign wife during the exile (Ezra 10:34).

3. A son of Dishon, descendant of Anah (I Chron. 1:41). ASV, RSV have Hamran.

Amraphel (ăm'rȧ-fĕl), king of Shinar, one of four kings, led by Chedorlaomer, king of Elam, who invaded Palestine to crush a rebellion (Gen. 14). After pillaging Sodom and Gomorrah, they took Lot and his goods and departed.

Amulet (ăm'ŭ-let), occurs once in ASV, RSV, (Isa. 3:20), never in KJV. It translates the plural of Heb. **lāhash,** meaning "serpent-charmer" as shown by KJV of Jeremiah 8:17, and ASV, RSV of Ecclesiastes 10:11; Isaiah 3:3, etc. Amulets have been worn from earliest times to ward off harm from snake-bites, diseases and other dangers. They were commonly stones, gems, or clay figurines, representing animals or gods, or scrolls inscribed with sacred words and were worn usually suspended from the neck.

Amun (See Amon)

Amzi (ăm'zī). 1. A descendant of Merari and of Levi, and progenitor of Ethan, whom David set over the service of song (I Chron. 6:44-46). 2. Ancestor of Adaiah, a priest in the second Temple (Neh. 11:12).

Anab (ā'năb, **grapes**), a city of the Anakim, taken by Joshua (Josh. 11:21). It fell to Judah (Josh. 15:50). SE of Debir, SW of Hebron. It retains its ancient name.

Anah (ā'nȧ). 1. Daughter of Zibeon and mother of Aholibamah, Esau's wife (Gen. 36:2, 14, 25). 2. Son of Seir, duke of Edom (Gen. 36:20, 29; I Chron. 1:38). 3. Son of Zibeon (Gen. 36:24; I Chron. 1:40, 41).

Anaharath (ȧ'nā'hȧ-răth), a town in the territory of Issachar, in the valley of Jezreel, near Shunem, Nain, and Endor. Modern en-Naura (Josh 19:19).

Anaiah (ȧ-nī'ȧh, **Jehovah has answered**). 1. A prince or priest who assisted in the reading of the law to the people (Neh. 8:4).

2. A Jew who, with Nehemiah, sealed the covenant (Neh. 10:22). Nos. 1 and 2 may be the same person.

Anak (ā'năk, **long necked**), descendant of Arba (Josh. 15:13) and ancestor of the Anakim (Num. 13: 22, 28, 33).

Anakim (ăn'ȧ-kĭm), also called "sons (children) of Anak" or "of the Anakim." The spies compared them to the giants of Genesis 6:4 (ASV, RSV, Nephilim); also they were reckoned among the Rephaim (Deut. 2:11, ASV, RSV). Three chiefs of the Anakim were in Hebron (Num. 13:22) from the time of the spies till Caleb took it (Josh. 15:13, 14). Remnants of them remained in Gaza, Gath and Ashdod (Josh. 11:21, 22).

Anamim (ăn'ȧ-mĭm), a people descended from Mizraim (Gen. 10:13; I Chron. 1:11) of whom nothing further is known.

Anammelech (ȧ-năm'ĕ-lĕk), one of the gods worshipped by the heathen people settled in Samaria by the king of Assyria (II Kings 17:31).

Anan (ā'năn, **cloud**), a returned exile who sealed the covenant with Nehemiah (Neh. 10:26).

Anani (ȧ-nā'nī), a son of Elioenai, of the family of David (I Chron. 3:24).

Ananiah (ăn'ȧ-nī'ȧh, **Jehovah is a protector**). 1. The father of Maaseiah and grandfather of Azariah (Neh. 3: 23).

2. A town of Benjamin (Neh. 11:32).

Ananias (ăn'ȧ-nī'ăs, **Jehovah has been gracious**). 1. Husband of Sapphira (Acts 5:1-11). He and his wife pretended to give to the church all they received from a sale of property, but kept back part. When Peter denounced his deceit, Ananias fell down dead. The generosity of others (Acts 4:32-37) accentuates the meanness of Ananias. Yet lying to the Holy Spirit, rather than greed, was the sin for which he was punished. Peter rather prophesied than decreed his death, which was a penalty God inflicted.

2. A disciple of Damascus, who, obeying a vision, was the means of healing the sight of Saul of Tarsus, and of introducing him to the Christians of Damascus (Acts 9:10-19).

3. A high priest before whom Paul was tried in Jerusalem (Acts 23:1-5).

Anat (ā'năt) or **Anu**, Babylonian-Assyrian god of the sky, first named in a triad with Bel and Ea.

Anath (ā'năth), father of Shamgar, third judge after Joshua (Judg. 3:31; 5:6).

Anathema (ȧ-năth'-ĕ-mȧ, **anything devoted**). A thing devoted to God becomes His and is therefore irrevocably withdrawn from common use.

Anathema Maranatha (ȧ-năth'ĕ-mȧ mâr'-ȧ-năth'ȧ). The words were formerly interpreted as a double imprecation, but are now believed to have no necessary connection.

Anathoth (ăn'ȧ-thŏth, probably the plural of "Anath," a **goddess**). 1. A city of Benjamin assigned to the priests (Josh. 21:18), the native place of Abiathar the high priest (I Kings 2:26) and Jeremiah the prophet (Jer. 1:1). Two of David's distinguished soldiers, Abiezer (II Sam. 23:27) and Jehu (I Chron. 12:3), also lived there.

2. A Benjamite, the son of Becher (I Chron. 7:8).

3. A leader of the men of Anathoth who sealed the covenant to worship Jehovah (Neh. 10:19).

Anchor. An appliance for holding a ship in a particular spot by mooring it to the bottom of the sea (Acts 27: 29, 30, 40; Heb. 6:19).

Ancient of Days. In Daniel 7:9, 13, 22, God, as He appeared in a vision to the Prophet.

Ancients (ān'shĕnts) This word (except in one instance — I Sam. 24:13) renders a Hebrew word which should always be translated "old men" or "elders."

Andrew (ăn'drōō, **manly**), the brother of Simon Peter, and son of Jonas, of Bethsaida on the Sea of Galilee (John 1:44). He was a fisherman, like his

Aerial view of the village of Anathoth, home of the prophet Jeremiah. © *MPS*

Andrew was a fisherman like one of these, on the sea of Galilee. © *MPS*

brother, with whom he lived at Capernaum (Mark 1:29). In the lists of the apostles his name always appears next to that of Phillip, who was also from Bethsaida, and with whom he is associated at the feeding of the 5,000. According to tradition, he preached in Scythia and suffered martyrdom in Achaia, being crucified on an X-shaped cross, now called a St. Andrew's cross.

Andronicus (ăn'drō-nī'kŭs), a Jewish believer, once a fellow-prisoner of Paul, to whom the apostle sent a greeting (Rom. 16:7).

Anem (ā'nĕm), a city of Issachar, set aside for the Levites (I Chron. 6:73). Omitted in the parallel list in Joshua 21:29.

Aner (ā'nêr). 1. A brother of Mamre the Amorite, Abraham's ally in battle (Gen. 14:13, 24).

2. A Levitical city in Manasseh (I Chron. 6:70).

Angel (Messenger), a supernatural or heavenly being a little higher in dignity than man. Angels are created beings (Ps. 148:2-5; Col. 1:16). Scripture does not tell us the time of their creation, but it was certainly before the creation of man (Job 38:7). They are described as "spirits" (Heb. 1:14). Although without a bodily organism, they have often revealed themselves in bodily form to man. Jesus said that they do not marry and do not die (Luke 20:34-36). They therefore constitute a company, not a race developed from one original pair. Scripture describes them as personal beings, not mere personifications of abstract good and evil. Although possessed of superhuman intelligence, they are not omniscient (Matt. 24:36; I Peter 1:12); and although stronger than men, they are not omnipotent (Ps. 103:20; II Peter 2:11; II Thess. 1:7). They are not glorified human beings, but are distinct from man (I Cor. 6:3; Heb. 1:14). They are of various ranks and endowments (Col. 1:16), but only one — Michael — is expressly called an archangel in Scripture (Jude 9). This great host of angels, both good and bad, is highly organized (Rom. 8:38; Eph. 1:21; 3:10; Col. 1:16; 2:15).

Angels were created holy (Gen. 1:31; Jude 6), but after a period of probation some fell from their state of innocence (II Peter 2:4; Jude 6). Scripture is silent regarding the time and cause of their fall, but it is clear that it occurred before the fall of man (for Satan deceived Eve in the Garden of Eden) and that it was due to a deliberate, self-determined rebellion against God.

The work of the angels is varied. Good angels stand in the presence of God and worship Him (Matt. 18:10; Rev. 5:11; Heb. 1:6). They assist, protect, and deliver God's people (Gen. 19:11; Ps. 91:11; Dan. 3:28; 6:22; Acts 5:19).

Angels had an important place in the life and ministry of Christ. They made their appearance in connection with His birth to Mary, Joseph, and the shepherds. After the wilderness temptation of Christ they ministered to Him (Matt. 4:11); an angel strengthed Him in the Garden (Luke 22:43); an angel rolled away the stone from the tomb (Matt. 28:2-7); and angels were with Him at the ascension (Acts 1:11).

Scripture shows that good angels will continue in the service of God in the future age, while evil angels will have their part in the lake of fire (Matt. 25:41).

Angel of the Lord. In the OT we find the oft-recurring phrase, "the angel of the Lord," in which, in almost every case, this messenger is regarded as deity and yet is distinguished from Jehovah (Gen. 16:7-14; Gen. 22:11-18; Gen. 31:11, 13; Exod. 3:2-5; Num. 22:22-35; Judg. 6:11-23; 13:2-25; I Chron. 21:15-17; I Kings 19:5-7). There is good reason for thinking that He is the pre-incarnate Logos, His appearance in angelic or human form foreshadowing His coming in the flesh.

Anger, used of both the anger of man and of God. The early Hebrews sometimes used the expression "his nose burned" for "he became angry" (Gen. 30:2; Exod. 4:14). God's anger differs from man's in that it is a holy wrath against sin.

Aniam (ȧ-nī'ăm, **lament of the people**), a son of Shemidah, a Manassehite (I Chron. 7:19).

Anim (ā'nĭm), a city in the southern hill country of Judah (Josh. 15:50).

Animals of the Bible. As there are far more references to mammals in the Bible than to any other animal forms, with the possible exceptions of insects and birds, the first part of this section treats of mammals, listing them alphabetically.

Apes. King Solomon sent ships once every three years to Tarshish to obtain gold, silver, apes and other treasures. Although the identity of Tarshish is uncertain, it seems probable that the rhesus monkey of India, the one so popular in present-day zoos, was the animal meant. The term ape is now more restricted in meaning and would exclude the monkey.

Ass. More than 150 verses in the Bible refer to the ass. Along with zebras and horses they constitute the horse family, **Equidae.** The domesticated ass or donkey has served man for thousands of years, and is believed to have been derived from the still-existing Abyssinian or Somali Wild Ass. The ass is better at carrying loads, and is more sure-footed on mountain trails than the horse.

Abraham is believed to have owned asses that he took into Egypt, and Egyptians used them in monument building in 3000 B.C. The number of asses an Old Testament worthy owned was an indication of his wealth. Heavy farm work was done by them and they were also used as saddle animals, being preferred by rulers and great men for peaceful journeys. Horses were reserved for war. Jesus entered Jerusalem on the colt of an ass. Balaam rode a she-ass that was given the power of speech by the Lord in order to rebuke him. On one occasion the Israelites captured 61,000 asses from the Midianites.

Badger. The badger as we know it, is not found in Bible lands. Where it is referred to in the OT, the goat is probably meant, and this is the translation of the RSV.

Bats. Although bats are mammals they are named along with birds in the Scriptures. The bats of Palestine according to Wiley are mostly insectivorous but this statement has been questioned by one who has more recently lived for a considerable period in the Bible Lands. Among the approximately two thousand kinds throughout the world are fruit, meat, fish, nectar, and blood eaters. All are equipped with a natural "radar" system; most are social and nocturnal. The Bible classified them as unclean.

Bears. Fourteen references to bears occur. The "Syrian Brown Bear" **Ursus syriacus,** is the bear of the Old Testament. The prophets Isaiah and Daniel, and John all had visions in which the bear figured prominently.

Behemoth. The hippopotamus is thought by some to be the animal Job had in mind. Known as the "River horses of Africa," they are bulky, ungainly, short-legged creatures weighing up to four tons. They sleep by day, blow and snort at night, and can swim, float, or sink and run along on the bottom.

The elephant has also been named as the animal meant by "Behemoth." The fact that the Arabs traded extensively in ivory, that the elephant has a larger tail than a hippo's, and the manner of visibly taking copious draughts of water, all are presented as evidence that the animal that "moveth his tail like a cedar" and "drinketh up a river, and hasteth not" was surely an elephant (Job 40:17, 23).

Boar. In Psalm 80:13 the wild "boar from the forest" is said to destroy the vine, but other references imply domesticated swine. Although the meat of swine was forbidden as food for the Israelites, in one instance a herd of two thousand was found in the country of the Gadarenes (Mark 5:11-13). The prodigal's degradation led to the feeding of swine (Luke 15: 15, 16). Warning was given not to cast pearls before swine.

Camel. The Bible is reported to contain sixty-six references to the camel. These animals are very hardy, can endure privation, can withstand temperature extremes very well, and have a life span of forty to fifty years. They are cud-chewing vegetarians with a three-chambered stomach that can store a three days' water supply. In their hump a reserve supply of food is stored in the form of fat.

Camel's hair is used in cloth making. Their flesh and milk are esteemed by natives in certain areas.

As beasts of burden the two-humped Bactrian camel can carry about four hundred pounds and in caravans covers about thirty miles per day. The one-humped camel or dromedary has longer legs, travels faster, and in a twenty-four hour day may cover more than 150 miles, and more often is the one used for riding and for carrying mail.

Cattle. Cattle of today are descendants of wild forms such as the Aurochs, or Urus, **Bos taurus primigenius,** that occurred in parts of Europe and Northern Africa. These, like other members of the family **Bovidae,** are true ruminents with cloven hoofs and hence a very important item of food. As ruminants they have the four-chambered stomach enabling them to masticate their food leisurely and thoroughly.

Cattle are mentioned in the first chapter of the Bible and constituted much of the wealth of Abraham and his descendants. Cattle figure prominently in the account of Joseph, Pharaoh, and the Egyptians. While wandering forty years the Israelites killed very few animals for food and consequently lusted for flesh. Heavy judgments upon the Egyptians in the time of Moses, and upon the Israelites in later times included the destruction or loss of their cattle.

The products which gave cattle much of their value are milk, butter, cheese, and leather. To describe Canaan as a place of prosperity it was called "a land flowing with milk and honey."

Oxen provided not only food and animals for sacrifice, but they also were important as draft animals. A number of commands were given pertaining to the care of these animals, and property rights associated therewith. When Elijah found him, Elisha was plowing with twenty-four oxen. They were partly responsible for Saul's decline when he spared the oxen after routing the Amalekites. Nebuchadnezzar was reduced to eating grass as the oxen. Ezekiel's vision of four creatures included the ox.

Chamois. In Deuteronomy 14:4-6 the chamois is listed among those animals that could be eaten. "Mountain sheep" is the name used in the RSV. It was probably the mountain sheep of Egypt and Arabia known as the Barbary Sheep or Aoudad.

Coney. The coney is similar to a rabbit except for its short legs and ears, and the absence of a tail. They are also called "little cousins of the elephant" and "drassies." As rock dwellers they are timid but very active. Conies occur from Africa north through Arabia to Asia.

Dogs. Dogs were possibly the first animal domesticated, being derived from wolf stock of Europe and Asia. Job spoke of the dogs that guarded his flocks (Job. 30:1). In Bible times they were generally despised outcasts known for their ravenous and ruthless nature, and given to prowling and filthy habits (Prov. 26:11). The Syrophenician woman spoke of dogs that ate the children's crumbs (Matt. 15: 26, 27). Approximately forty Bible references are made to these unclean animals.

Dragons. Thirty-five references to "dragons" appear in the KJV. In those instances where the word is derived from the Hebrew word "tannin" a long serpent-like, symbolical animal is meant. Examples of this sort are found in Psalm 74:13; Ezekiel 32:2; and the Revelation. John uses the word "dragon" for Satan. Where "tannim," the plural of the Hebrew "tan" occurs, literal animals are understood. In some of these instances the crocodile is meant and elsewhere jackals were intended.

Dromedary. See Camel.

Elephant. In the RSV the word "behemoth" is rendered "hippopotamus" in the footnote, whereas it is given as "elephant" in the margin of KJV (Job 40:15). Repeated references to elephants being used in warfare occur in the first and second books of Maccabees.

In a dozen or more instances ivory is mentioned in the Bible. For example, Solomon overlaid his ivory throne with gold thereby giving an indication of the relative values of these materials (I Kings 10:18). Where the doom of Tyre and Babylon is foretold reference is made to the extensive use they had made of ivory.

Fallow Deer. This term is changed to roebuck, q.v., the male of the roe deer, in the RSV (Deut. 14:5; I Kings 4:22, 23).

Fox. In nine verses this animal is named, where it refers to the common fox of Palestine, **Vulpes vulgaris,** that resembles the common fox of Europe and the red fox of America. It is a member of the dog family, and in a number of ways resembles the dog. It is carnivorous, wary, quick-sensed, and swift. It is believed that the word fox in Scripture referred to jackals, for example, "that spoiled the vines." Samson could have more readily secured jackals in such numbers so that three hundred could be used in burning the fields of the Philistines (Judg. 15:14). It is thought that the animals were tied in pairs with a firebrand connected by a cord to their tails, thereby spreading fire far and wide as they raced away in terror.

The fox's craftiness was attested to by the fact that Jesus likened Herod's conduct to that of a fox.

Gazelle. The RSV employs the term "gazelle" in a dozen or more verses. They are small, swift antelopes found in hot, arid, barren wilderness areas of the Old World.

Goats. Goats and sheep in the wild are inhabitants of the mountains. Both are cud-chewing, have hairy coats, and hollow horns. Wild goats are more sure-footed and adventurous. Both sheep and goats were domesticated as early as 3000 B.C. Milk, butter, cheese, and meat are obtained from goats. Goats were much used for sacrifice and for feasts. Their hair was made into clothing. Containers for water and wine were made from goatskins in Bible times. The Bible has more than 130 referencs to goats and approximately fifty references to kids.

Greyhound. Proverbs 30:31 lists the "greyhound" among those things that Solomon said are "comely in going." An alternate translation given in the footnote of the ASV is "war-horse," whereas it is translated "strutting cock" in the RSV. Early Egyptian monuments carry pictures of this ancient breed of dog that is known to attain speeds up to forty miles per hour.

Hare. Baby hares are born with a good coat of hair and good eyesight whereas rabbits are born naked and blind. No native rabbits occur in Palestine but at least two species of hares are numerous. Hares are classified as unclean because they lack the divided hoof. Their jaw action resembles cud-chewing but they lack the ruminant's stomach.

In two instances where hares are mentioned in the Bible they are named by Moses (Lev. 11:4, 6; Deut. 14:7).

Hart. Harts were apparently rather plentiful since they are mentioned as part of the daily fare at Solomon's table. The former is similar to the American elk but somewhat smaller. Harts are stags or male deer whereas hinds are female deer. A single hart may weight as much as three hundred pounds. The habitat of the hart differs from that of the gazelle as the former must have more water. This requirement is alluded to in Psalm 42:1, where the hart is said to long for flowing streams and its need of pasture is implied in Lamentations 1:6. The leaping of the hart is referred to in Isaiah 35:6.

Hind. See Hart. These female red deer are mentioned a number of times in the poetical books of the KJV, but are not listed as an item of food. Their fleetness is referred to by both Habakkuk and David who, almost four hundred years apart, used very similar expressions. "He maketh my feet like hinds" in speaking of swiftly escaping their enemies (Ps. 18:33; Hab. 3:19).

Horse. At least four thousand years ago in central Asia some type of wild horse was tamed and domesticated. Babylonians began using them to draw war chariots around 1700 B.C. Without horses, conquests on a large scale would have been impossible for Alexander the Great and for Genghis Khan. Herodotus reported the use of swift horses by the Persians for their postal system at least three thousand years ago.

The first of more than 150 verses referring to horses is found in Genesis 47:17 where Joseph in Egypt bought horses by giving bread to the people during a famine.

Under Moses, God warned the people not to multiply horses. Saul was later killed in a battle with the Amalekites who were outfitted with chariots and horses. David captured chariots and horses from the Syrians and destroyed most of them but reserved a hundred chariots. Solomon greatly increased their numbers and depended heavily on them as he strengthened the defenses of his land.

In most instances horses were employed in warfare; however, Isaiah connected them with agriculture (Isa. 28:24-29). They were also used in idolatrous processions (II Kings 23:5, 11). Their use for riding is mentioned in II Kings 9:14-37 and Esther 6:8, 10, 11. In prophecy horses play a role as in Joel 2:4, 5, and Revelation 9:7, 9 and 6:1-8, where four horses of different colors are associated with singular disasters.

Hyena. Curiously, the word for hyena does not occur in the Bible although hyenas were abundant in Palestine. The word "Zeboim" in I Samuel 13:17-18 comes from a Hebrew word that is generally considered to refer to hyenas, and basically the same word is translated "speckled bird" in Jeremiah 12:7-9.

Ibex. See Pygarg.

Jackal. In both the ASV and RSV the word "jackals" in Job 30:29, is substituted for the word "dragons" of the KJV. The same change has been made in Psalm 44:19 and Isaiah 13:22; 34:13. In other instances where the word "dragon" is applied literally, that is, to mammals inhabiting desert places, one finds "jackals" in the newer versions.

Jackals are the wild dogs of warmer parts of the Old World. They hunt in small packs in a stealthy manner at night, and their role as scavengers is important. See Fox.

Lamb. See Sheep.

Leopard. The word "leopard" is used in the same eight verses in the RSV as in the KJV. A leopard (panther) is more savage and malevolent than a lion. In Solomon's time leopards lived in parts of Palestine and in mountainous regions of Lebanon in Syria. Isaiah suggested the improbable by referring to a leopard lying down with a kid; Jeremiah spoke of the impossibility of the leopard changing its spots; Daniel and John used it in a figurative sense.

Leviathan. Both the ASV and RSV employ "leviathan" in Job 3:8 and 41:1. In footnotes for the latter verse both versions give the crocodile as an alternative meaning; however crocodiles are not caught with fishhooks. Some fabulous creature may be meant in Job 3:8 and also in Psalm 74:14 where breaking or crushing "the heads of Leviathan" is mentioned. It has been suggested that the latter reference was telling of the removing of the crocodiles so that the Israelites could safely cross the Red Sea.

Lion. Lions by their size and majestic bearing have won the title, "King of Beasts." Usually they are friendly, travel in small groups, share prey peaceably, and kill only what they intend to consume. Few are man-killers. However, once a lion eats a man it is a threat thereafter.

The Hebrew people were very familiar with lions and many books in the Bible mention them. The lion's strength is often referred to in the Scriptures. The Lord Jesus Christ is called the Lion of the tribe of Judah. The traits of lions are used to foreshadow those of the "King of Kings." Jacob compared three of his sons, Judah, Dan, and Gad, to lions. Throughout the Bible lions are either treated as natural animals or they are used as symbols of might.

Daniel's experience in the lions' den illustrates the use Oriental monarchs made of them as executioners. A man occasionally killed a lion in a single-handed encounter (Judg. 14:5-18 and I Sam. 17:36, 37).

God's judgment was visited upon the disobedient by the actual use of lions, and its severity predicted by likening the character of attacking nations to the ferocity of a lion.

Symbolically, Daniel described Babylon as a winged lion. Peter represented the devil as a destroying lion.

Mouse. The terms "mouse" and "mice" occur in both the RSV and KJV in references found in Leviticus, I Samuel, and Isaiah, and probably include a number of small rodents. Evidently the Jews had followed heathen practices of eating swine's flesh and mice, and perhaps even hamsters, rats and jerboas, as the Arabs and Syrians did. After taking the ark from the Israelites, the Philistines were ravaged by a scourge of mice.

Mole. Where "mole" occurs in Leviticus 11:29, 30 in the KJV, it is rendered "chameieon" in the RSV. Isaiah (Isa. 2:20) probably meant the blind rat or mole rat of Southeastern Europe rather than our true mole of America.

Monster. In place of "sea monsters" the ASV and RSV use "jackals" in Lamentations 4:3. From the facts that monsters are usually large, powerful animals, and that in this instance no difficulty was experienced in nursing their young during a time of severe famine, it seems probable that whales are meant. Where the KJV in Genesis 1:21 speaks of "great whale," the RSV uses "Sea monsters."

Mule. A mule is a cross between a male donkey and a female horse. Mules have been bred since earliest times and are almost always sterile. Breeding them was forbidden to Israelites (Lev. 19:19), but they were imported into Palestine. The finest were usd by kings and officers, King David apparently having initiated their use for riding purposes.

The fat-tailed sheep of Palestine. DV

Pygarg. The word "pygarg" means white-rumped and hence has been said to apply to some antelope such as the addax, one species of which is a native of desert regions of Northern Africa and the Egyptian Sudan. The RSV translates it ibex, meaning a type of bearded wild goat.

Roe. This word is used in nearly a dozen verses in the KJV but does not appear in the RSV. In most instances, both the RSV and ASV use the word "gazelle."

Satyr. Both the KJV and RSV use "satyr" in Isaiah 13:21 and 34:14, but the ASV used "wild goat." Monsters supposedly half man and half goat were worshiped in both Egypt and Greece. The same word is translated "devils" in Leviticus 17:7 and II Chronicles 11:15, where idolatrous practices are denounced.

Sheep. If sheep ever existed in the wild state they were certainly domesticated before 3000 B.C., and probably before cattle. Sheep receive more attention in the Bible than any other animal. They were important in the domestic, civic, and religious life of the Israelites. Even today the Arabs depend heavily upon them. Earliest mention of sheep is in Genesis 4:2 where it is said that "Abel was a keeper of sheep."

Sheep were kept for their milk more than for their flesh. The common breed could store a vast amount of fat in the tail and this was used as food. They also provided wool, and horns, used either for carrying oil or wine, or as trumpets for summoning the people and in religious rites. The skins of rams were used in making the covering of the tabernacle.

The reason why so much attention is given to sheep in the Bible is doubtless because they were used so much in sacrifice. Offerings consisted not only of lambs but also of ewes and rams. Where a prescribed service was intended, the type of animal was usually named. The ultimate and final sacrifice was the Lamb of God who in many respects was foreshadowed by the way in which lambs had served as sacrifices.

Swine. Although the names of "hog" and "pig" are not named in the Bible, "swine" are referred to a number of times. Members of the family Suidae, swine are unclean although they have the divided hoof. Solomon declared that "a beautiful woman without discretion" is "like a gold ring in a swine's snout" (Prov. 11:22, RSV). Jesus warned against casting pearls before swine (Matt. 7:6). Peter spoke of a washed sow wallowing in mire (II Pet. 2:22). The prodigal son was degraded to the place where he was forced to feed swine.

Unicorn. Wiley enumerates characteristics of this creature which may be pieced together from the eight passages where it is mentioned: it is exceptionally powerful, a voracious eater, has a pair of strong horns, was well known to people of Old Testament lands, was untamable, impossible to use for agriculture, very active while young, and fit for sacrifice. Instead of "unicorn" the ASV and RSV use "wild ox." This was possibly the auroch that stood six feet at the shoulder and was once plentiful in Palestine. Seen in profile it appeared to have but a single horn, hence the name unicorn.

Weasel. The weasel is listed along with the mouse and tortoise as an unclean animal (Lev. 11:29). These important rodent killers seem to kill for the sake of killing, and are found in almost all parts of the world.

Whale. "Whale" is retained in the RSV in the account found in Matthew 12:40. In Jonah 1:17 the RSV uses "great fish," and in Genesis 1:21 and Job 7:12 it is rendered "sea monsters" or "sea monster." Goodwin maintains that among whales, only the sperm whale has a throat structure capable of swallowing a man.

Wolf. Wolves, dogs, and jackals are members of a family of carnivores. Wolves were very widely distributed across Europe and North America. Unprovoked attacks upon man are questioned unless the animal is famished. They are mentioned twelve times. Benjamin, a tribe, was likened to a wolf. Jesus repeatedly likened false prophets and teachers to wolves. Isaiah foretold that the wolf and lamb will feed together in the Messianic Kingdom (Isa. 11:6; 65:25).

Non-Mammalian Animals

Sponges. Sponges have served many purposes since earliest times. Ancient Greeks used them for padding their shields and armor as well as for bathing and scrubbing floors and furniture. They were used as mops and paint brushes by the Romans, and at one time were used as drinking cups, the user squeezing their contents into his upturned mouth. At the crucifixion a bystander used a sponge fastened to a reed to lift vinegar to the lips of Jesus.

Corals. The central and western Mediterranean has a red coral, **Corallium nobile,** that has varied greatly in commercial value through the years. Slender twigs from its branching colonies are extensively used in making jewelry. Coral is mentioned by both Job and Ezekiel (Job 28:18; Ezek. 27:16).

Mollusks. The occurrence of mollusks is implied by numerous Old Testament references to the use of purple cloth. A dye, "Tyrian purple," was obtained from a glandular fluid secreted by several members of the genera Murex and Purpua. Pearls are mentioned in several instances in the New Testament. They are produced by certain bivalve mollusks such as the clam and oyster and have always been highly esteemed.

Fishes. Many references to fish occur in both Old and New Testaments, but in no instance is a particular species implied in any way. They are mentioned in all five books of the Pentateuch.

The use of line and hook is referred to in the Old Testament and the use of the net is mentioned in both Old and New Testaments. The numerous references to fish and to fishing in the Gospels give clear indication of their commercial importance in Palestine.

Amphibians. Two species of frogs and three of toads are reported from Egypt. One frog, **Rana esculenta,** is found all over Europe, in Syria and in Palestine, as well as in Egypt. One of the plagues visited on Pharaoh was a horde of frogs.

Reptiles. The Northern Viper or Adder, **Vipera berus,** is common in Europe and members of the same genus are found in Africa. In any case, the context in which the word "adder" occurs clearly implies a poisonous reptile. Because this English word is used for several different Hebrew words it is difficult to determine present-day species to which it applied.

Asp. Four times the word "asp" is used in such a manner as to indicate a poisonous reptile. There is general agreement that the Egyptian Cobra, **Naja haje,** is meant. This reptile was used by Pharaoh Tutankhamen as his imperial symbol. It attains a length of at least eight and a half feet, prefers warm, dry regions with water available, and is found along the north and east coasts of Africa.

Chameleon. A family of large lizards, the Varanidae, are represented by species in Africa and Asia. The Nile Monitor, **Varanus niloticus** is the largest four-footed reptile in Africa with the exception of the crocodile, and attains a length of six feet. Nile monitors eat a wide variety of food, and deposit their eggs in termite nests.

Cockatrice. Some dreaded reptile is evidently meant in Isaiah 11:8 and 59:5, and Jeremiah 8:17. Although basilisks have been suggested, they are harmless despite myths to the contrary.

Gecko. The word "ferret" of Leviticus 11:30 is translated "gecko" in the RSV and ASV.

Lizard. Mentioned once in the Bible (Lev. 11:30), this animal may refer to the commonest lizard of Palestine, the **Agama stellio,** belonging to a family of dragon-lizards. These animals are diurnal, possess crests and dewlaps, and somewhat resemble the iguanids.

Serpent. The Bible has many references to serpents which imply poisonous qualities. No single species can be identified with certainty. The serpent is commonly used as a symbol of evil and Satan was called a serpent.

Tortoise. This unclean animal of Leviticus 11:29 is rendered "great lizard" in the RSV. The Arabian thorny-tailed, color-changing lizard (**Uromastix spinipes**) is common in Egypt, and members of the same genus occur in Syria and Arabia.

Viper. Poisonous serpents of several varieties are probably meant where this term is used.

Anise (See Plants of the Bible)

Anklet, an ornament for the ankles, consisting of metal or glass spangles, worn by women. Sometimes anklets were linked together by an ankle chain. See Dress.

Anna (ăn′ȧ, **grace),** daughter of Phanuel of the tribe of Asher. Widowed after seven years of marriage, she became a prophetess, and at the age of 84, when the infant Jesus was brought into the Temple to be dedicated, she recognized and proclaimed Him as the Messiah (Luke 2:36-38).

Annas (ăn′ȧs, **gracious),** high priest from A.D. 6 to about 15. Five of his sons and his son-in-law Caiaphas were also high priests. He is referred to as high priest in Luke 3:2 and Acts 4:6, but that is probably because as head of the family he was the most influential priest and still bore the title.

Anoint. A practice common in the East, anointing was of three kinds: ordinary—after bathing, as a mark of respect (Luke 7:46), for burial (Mark 14:8; 16:1), for shields; sacred — both things and people, such as prophets (I Kings 19:16), priests (Exod. 28:41), and kings (I Sam. 9:16); and medical —for the sick and wounded (Isa. 1:6; Luke 10:34). The words "Messiah" and "Christ" mean "the anointed one."

Antelope (See Animals, Gazelles)

Antichrist (against or **instead of Christ).** The word antichrist may mean either an enemy of Christ or one who usurps Christ's name and rights. The word is found only in I John 2:18, 22; 4:3; II John 7, but the idea conveyed by the word appears throughout Scripture. It is evident from the way John and Paul refer to the Antichrist that they took for granted a tradition well known at the time (I John 4:3 "ye have heard," II Thess. 2:6 "ye know").

The OT gives evidence of a general Jewish belief in a hostile person or power who in the end time would bring an attack against God's people —an attack which would be crushed by Jehovah or His Messiah. Psalm 2 gives a picture of the rebellion of the world kingdoms "against the Lord and against his anointed." The same sort of contest is described in Ezekiel 38, 39 and in Zechariah 12-14. In the Book of Daniel there are vivid descriptions of the Antichrist which find their echo in the writings of the apostles (cf., e.g., II Thess. 2:4 with Daniel 11:36f, and Rev. 13:1-8 with Daniel 7:8, 20f; 8:24; 11:28, 30).

In His eschatological discourse Christ warns against "the false Christs" and "the false prophets" who would lead astray, if possible, even the elect (Matt. 24:24; Mark 13:22). In Matthew 24:15 He refers to "the abomination of desolation" spoken of by Daniel.

Paul gives us, in II Thessalonians 2:1-12, a very full description of the working of Antichrist, under the name of the "man of sin," in which he draws on the language and imagery of the OT.

In I John 2:18 John shows that the coming of the Antichrist was an event generally expected by the Church. It is apparent, however, that he is more concerned about directing the attention of Christians to antichristian forces already at work ("even now are there many antichrists"). He says that teachers of erroneous views of the person of Christ (evidently Gnostic and Ebonite) are antichrists (I John 2:22; 4:3; II John 7).

In the Book of Revelation the Beast of Revelation 17:8 recalls the horned Beast of Daniel 7, 8. He claims and is accorded divine homage, and makes war on God's people. With his defeat the contest of Good and evil comes to its final decision.

Anti-Lebanon (See Lebanon)

Antioch (ăn′tĭ-ŏk). 1. Antioch in Syria, the capital of Syria, built in 301 B.C. by Seleucus Nicator, the founder of the Seleucid Empire, which had been the Asiatic part of the vast empire of Alexander the Great. It was the greatest of 16 Antiochs he founded in honor of his father, Antiochus. In 65 B.C. the Romans took the city and made it the capital of the Roman province of Syria. Seleucid kings and early Roman emperors extended and adorned the city until it became the third largest in the Roman Empire (after Rome and Alexandria), with a population, in the first century A.D., of about 500,000. A cosmopolitan city from its foundation, its inhabitants included many Jews, who were given privileges similar to those of the Greeks.

Antioch is important in the early history of Christianity. One of the original deacons of the Apostolic church was Nicolas, a proselyte of Antioch (Acts 6:5). The first Gentile church, the mother of all the others, was founded there. Many fugitive Christians scattered at the death of Stephen went to Antioch, where they inaugurated a new era by preaching not only to Hellenist Jews but to "the Greeks also" (Acts 11:20). The Jerusalem church sent Barnabas to assist in the work, and he, after laboring there for a while, summoned Paul from Tarsus to assist him. After working there for a year, they were sent with relief to the famine-stricken saints in Jerusalem. The disciples were called Christians first in Antioch (Acts 11:19-26), a designation probably coming from the populace, who were well-known for their invention of nicknames. The church at Antioch sent Paul and his companions out on his three missionary journeys (Acts 13:1ff; 15:3ff; 18:23), and he reported to it on his return from the first two (Acts 14:26ff; 18:22).

Antioch gave rise to a school of thought distinguished by literal interpretation of the Scriptures. Between 252 and 380 ten Councils were held there. The city was taken and destroyed in A.D. 538 by the Persians, rebuilt by the Roman emperor Justinian shortly afterward, and in A.D. 635 was taken by the Moslems, by whom it has since, except for a brief period, been held.

2. Antioch near Pisidia, a town in southern Asia Minor, founded by Seleucus Nicator, and named in honor of his father, Antiochus. It was situated in Phrygia, not far from Pisidia, and was therefore called Antioch toward Pisidia and Pisidian Antioch to distinguish it from the other cities of the same name. In 25 B.C. it became a part of the Roman province of Galatia. The Romans made it a strong garrison center to hold down the surrounding wild tribes. Paul and Barnabas preached in the synagogue there on their first missionary journey, but the Jews, jealous of the many Gentile converts that were made, drove the misisonaries from the city to Iconium, and followed them even to Lystra (Acts 13:14-14:19). On Paul's return journey he revisited Antioch to establish the disciples. He must have visited Antioch on his second journey (Acts 16:6), and on his third (Acts 18:23).

Antiochus (ăn-tī'ŏkŭs, **withstander).** 1. Antiochus III, the Great (223-187 B.C.), king of Syria and sixth ruler of the Seleucid dynasty. By his victory over the Egyptians in 198 B.C. Syria gained control of Palestine. He was decisively defeated by the Romans in 190 and later murdered by a mob while plundering a temple.

2. Antiochus IV (Epiphanes), son of Antiochus III and eighth ruler of the Seleucid dynasty, 175-163 B.C. (I Macc. 1:10; 6:16). In his attempt to Hellenize the Jews he had a pig sacrificed on the altar in Jerusalem, forbade circumcision, and destroyed all the OT books he could find. These outrages involved him in the Maccabean war in which the Syrian armies were repeatedly defeated by the brilliant Judas Maccabeus.

3. Antiochus V (Eupator), son of the above. He reigned as a minor for two years and then was slain.

Antipas (ăn'tĭ pȧs), a contraction of Antipater. 1. An early Christian martyr of Pergamum (Rev. 2:13).

2. Herod Antipas, son of Herod the Great, and brother of Philip the tetrarch and of Archelaus. See Herod.

Antipater. (See Herod)

Antipatris (ăn-tĭp'ȧ-trĭs, **belonging to Antipater),** a city built (or rebuilt) by Herod the Great, and named after his father Antipater. It lay on the road between Jerusalem and Caesarea. There is only one reference to it in Scripture, in connection with Paul's being taken, following his arrest in Jerusalem, from that city to Caesarea (Acts 23:31). It marked the NW limit of Judea.

Antitype. By a type, in a Biblical sense, is meant a picture or object lesson by which God taught His people concerning His grace and redemptive power. An antitype is that which is represented by the type.

Antonia, Tower of, a castle connected with the Temple of Jerusalem, rebuilt by Herod the Great and named by him in honor of Mark Anthony, his patron. When Paul was seized in the Temple by the Jews, he was carried to this castle, from the stairs of which he addressed the people (Acts 21:30ff).

Antothijah (ăn'tō-thī'jȧ), a son of Shashak, a Benjamite (I Chron. 8:24, 25).

Antothite (ăn'tŏth-īt), inhabitant of Anathoth; ASV, "Anathothite"; RSV, "of Anathoth" (I Chron. 11:28; 12:3).

Ants (See Insects)

Anub (ā'nŭb), a son of Coz, descendant of Judah (I Chron. 4:8).

Anvil (ăn'vĭl). The Heb. **pa'am** originally meant strike, hit. The word occurs in several senses in the OT; only once with the meaning "anvil," Isaiah 41:7.

Apelles (ȧ-pĕl'ēz), an approved Christian at Rome to whom Paul sent a greeting (Rom. 16:10).

Apes (See Animals)

Apharsathchites (ăf'ȧr-săth'kīts), Ezra 4:9; **Apharsakites** (ȧ-fȧr'săk-īts), Ezra 5:6; 6:6, people in Samaria who protested to Darius against the rebuilding of the Temple in Jerusalem. RSV translates "governors."

Apharsites (ȧ-fȧr'sīts), Ezra 4:9, people in Samaria who protested against the rebuilding of the Temple in Jerusalem. RSV translates "Persians."

Aphek (ā'fĕk, **strength, fortress).** 1. A city NE of Beirut, identified with Afqa (Josh. 13:4).

2. A city in the territory of Asher, never wrested from its Canaanite inhabitants (Josh. 19:30; Judges 1:31).

3. A town in the Plain of Sharon (Josh. 12:18), probably within 25 miles of Shiloh (I Sam. 4:1, 12).

4. A town W of the Jordan in the Plain of Jezreel. The Philistines used it as a base in two important campaigns against Israel (I Sam. 1:4; 29:1).

Aphekah (ȧ-fē'kȧ), a city in the hill country of Judah (Josh. 15:33) whose location is unknown.

Aphiah (ȧ-fī'ȧ), one of Saul's ancestors (I Sam. 9:1).

Aphik (See Aphek)

Aphrah (ăf'rȧ). "The house of Aphrah" is named in parallelism with Gath in Micah 1:10. ASV, RSV have "Beth-le-aphrah."

Aphses (ăf'sēz), a Levite chief of the 18th of the 24 courses in the service of the Temple (I Chron. 24:15). ASV, RSV, Happizzez.

Apocalypse (See Apocalyptic Literature)

Apocalyptic Literature. There are two types, canonical and uncanonical. The first includes Daniel and Revelation which give revelations of the secret purposes of God, the end of the world, and the establishment of God's Kingdom on earth. The second appeared between c. 200 B.C. and A.D. 200 and also purports to give revelations of the last judgment, and the hereafter. Outstanding apocalypses are I Enoch, Jubilees, Assumption of Moses, Second Esdras, Apocalypse of Baruch, Second Enoch. The Testaments of the Twelve Prophets, the Psalms of Solomon (17th and 18th), and the Sibylline Oracles are also usually included in a discussion of apocalyptic literature. Certain characteristics mark them. They deal with the future; imitate the visions of the prophets; are written under the names of OT worthies; use symbolism; are Messianic.

Apocrypha (ȧ-pŏk'rĭ-fȧ, **hidden, spurious).** Books and chapters interspersed among the canonical books of the OT in the Vulgate, but not found in the Hebrew OT. The Roman Catholic Church received as canonical at the Council of Trent (1546) all of these books except I and II Esdras and the Prayer of Manasseh. From the time of Luther Protestants have rejected their canonicity. They include: I and II Esdras, Tobit, Judith, Additions to the Book of Esther, The Wisdom of Solomon, Ecclesiasticus, Baruch, Epistle of Jeremiah, The Prayer of Azariah and the Song of the Three Young Men, Susanna, Bel and the Dragon, The Prayer of Manasseh, I and II Maccabees.

Apollonia (ăp'-ŏ-lō'nĭ-ȧ, **pertaining to Apollo),** a town of Macedonia, 28 miles W of Amphipolis and 38 miles E of Thessalonica (Acts 17:1).

Apollos (ȧ-pŏl'ŏs, **belonging to Apollo),** a learned Alexandrian Jew, instructed in the Christian faith by Aquila and Priscilla at Ephesus, subsequently went to Corinth where he became a mighty preacher of the gospel. Before long an Apollos party arose which was a rival to the Pauline party, but there does not appear to have been any feeling of rivalry between Paul and Apollos. (Acts 18:26-28; I Cor. 3:4; I Cor. 16:12; Titus 3:13.)

Apollyon (See Abaddon)

Apostasy (ȧ-pŏs'tȧ-sē, **a falling away).** There are many warnings against apostasy in the Bible (II Thess. 2:3; Jude). Among apostates in the Bible are Saul (I Sam. 15:11); Hymenaeus and Alexander (I Tim. 1:19, 20); Demas (II Tim. 4:10).

Apostle (ȧ-pŏs'l, **one sent forth, a messenger),** one chosen and sent with a special commission as the fully authorized representative of the sender.

In the NT the word appears in a twofold sense, as the official name of those 12 disciples whom Jesus chose to be with Him during the course of His ministry on earth, to see Him after His resurrection, and to lay the foundations of His Church; and in a broader, non-official sense, to designate Christian messengers commissioned by a community — like Barnabas, who was sent forth as a missionary by the church at Antioch (Acts 13:3). Once in the NT Jesus is called an apostle (Heb. 3:1), obviously in the sense referred to by Him in John 17:18. The Twelve were chosen by Jesus early in His Galilean ministry. Some had previously been disciples of John the Baptist (John 1:35-42). Four, at least, were fishermen (Luke 5:1-11) and one, a tax-collector (Matt. 9:9-13). Their names are given by each of the Synoptists (Matt. 10:2-4; Mark 3:14-19; Luke 6:13-16) and by the author of Acts (1:13).

In the Gospels they are usually called disciples, because as long as Jesus was with them they were still learners; after that, they are invariably referred to as apostles. Jesus gave much attention to their spiritual training; yet to the time of His resurrection, they failed to understand His mission, thinking that He was going to set up a temporal kingdom (Matt. 20:20-28; Mark 10:35-45). All were on an equal footing, although three of them — Peter, James the son of Zebedee, and John — seem to have been somewhat closer to Jesus than the others; and Peter, by force of personal character, usually took the place of leadership. Peter, however, is nowhere in Scripture accorded a position of superiority or primacy. John is called the disciple whom Jesus loved (John 19:26; 20:2; 21:7, 20). Judas betrayed the Lord into the hands of His enemies and then committed suicide. His place was later taken by Matthias (Acts 1:15-26). When finally they saw Him arrested and crucified, as He had often foretold He would be, they all forsook Him and fled (Matt. 26:56). It is plain that they did not expect His resurrection, which Jesus had also frequently foretold. It was only when this became undeniable, that light entered their minds and they saw Him for what He is, the Saviour of the world. Between the resurrection and the ascension Jesus spent much time opening their minds to understand the Scriptures (Luke 24:45; Acts 1:2).

The experience of Pentecost, ten days after the Lord's ascension, made them altogether different men, so that henceforth they fearlessly gave witness with power to the life, death, and resurrection of Jesus.

The number of the Twelve was increased when Paul, the chief persecutor of the Christians, was miraculously converted and called to be an apostle. With the transfer of the center of church activity from Jerusalem to Antioch, where an active church consisting of Jews and Gentiles was built up, Paul became the leading figure in the Church, and most of the remaining narrative of the Acts is occupied with his missionary activity to the Gentiles. When we leave him a prisoner in Rome, the Gospel witness has spread through all the Mediterranean world.

Of the missionary work of the other apostles we know almost nothing from Scripture. Tradition tells us a little, but not much that is trustworthy. The majority, it seems, died martyr's deaths. In the early Church they consistently claimed to possess and exercised a unique authority, given them by Christ, to lay the foundations of the Church. They spoke, wrote, and acted with a consciousness that they were specially commissioned to represent their Lord and to give to needy men the message of redemption. Their office was not, and could not be, passed on to others. It was unique.

Apostolic Age, the period in the history of the Christian Church when the Apostles were alive, beginning with the Day of Pentecost and ending with the death of the Apostle John near the end of the first century.

Apothecary (ȧ-pŏth′ĕ-kâ-rē), a word found in Exodus 30:25, 35; 37:29; II Chronicles 16:14; Nehemiah 3:8; Ecclesiastes 10:1 in the KJV, although the Hebrew word it renders is more accurately translated "perfumer," as it usually is in the RV; for the reference is not to the selling of drugs, but to the making of perfumes.

Appaim (ăp′ā-ĭm), son of Nadab (I Chron. 2:30, 31).

Apparel (See Dress)

Appeal (ȧ-pēl′). No provision is made in the OT for the reconsideration from a lower to a higher court of a case already tried. Exodus 18:26 shows, however, that Moses provided for lower and higher courts.

In NT times the Roman government allowed each synagogue to exercise discipline over Jews, but only the Romans had the power of life and death. A Roman citizen, could, however, claim exemption from trial by the Jews and appeal to be tried by a Roman court. Paul did this when he

The Appian Way in Rome (road is now paved for modern travel). © MPS

said, "I appeal unto Caesar" (Acts 25:11).

Appearing (See Eschatology)

Appellatio (ăp′ĕ-lȧ′tĭō), the judicial process to which Paul resorted in Festus' court (Acts 25:1-12), was the act by which a litigant disputes a judgment, with the effect that the matter in dispute is automatically referred to a higher magistrate, in Paul's case, the appeal to Caesar.

Apphia (ăf′ĭ-ȧ, ăp′fĭ-ȧ), called "our beloved" in KJV, "our sister" in ASV, RSV, following a different text. A Christian of Colossae, by many believed to be the wife of Philemon and mother of Archippus (Philem. 2).

Appian Way (ăp′ĭ-ăn), ancient Roman road which originally ran from Rome to Capua and was later extended to Brundisium. Parts of the road are still in use. Paul must have traveled by it from Puteoli to Rome (Acts 28: 13-16).

Appii Forum (ăp′ĭ-ī fō′rŭm), a town on the Appian Way, 40 miles from Rome toward Naples, where Paul was met by Christian brethren from Rome (Acts 28:15).

Appius, Market of (See Appii Forum)

Apple (See Plants)

"Apple of the Eye," the eyeball, or the pupil in its center, protected by the eyelids. A symbol of that which is precious and protected.

Apron (See Dress)

Aqabah, Gulf of (ȧ′kȧ-bȧ), the eastern arm of the Red Sea, between the Sinai Peninsula on the W and Midian on the E. Solomon's seaport of Eziongeber is located at its head.

Aqueduct (ăk′wĕ-dŭkt), a channel made of stone to convey water to places where the water is to be used. Many fine Roman aqueducts survive.

Aquila (ăk′wĭ-lȧ, Latin for "eagle"), a Jew whom Paul found at Corinth on his arrival from Athens (Acts 18:2, 18, 26; Rom. 16:3, 4; I Cor. 16:19; II Tim. 4:19). A characteristic feature of Aquila and his wife Priscilla is that their names are always mentioned together. One in their interest in Christ, all that they accomplished was the result of that unity of spiritual nature and purpose. Having been expelled from Rome, they opened a tent-making business in Corinth. Because Paul followed the same trade, he lived and worked with them. By their spiritual insight Apollos and many others were helped. Aquila and Priscilla had a "church in their house."

Ar (ȧr), a city or district of Moab, referred to in Numbers 21:15; Deuteronomy 2:9, 18, 29 and Isaiah 15:1.

Ara (ā′rȧ), son of Jether, of the tribe of Asher (I Chron. 7:38).

Arab (ăr′ăb), a city in the hill country of Judah, probably er-Râbiyeh, south of Hebron (Josh. 15:52).

Arabah (ăr′ȧ-bȧ, **desert plain),** name applying to the rift running from Mt. Hermon to the Gulf of Aqabah. It is a narrow valley of varying breadth and productivity. The Israelites made stops there in their wilderness wanderings, and Solomon got iron and copper from its mines. (Deut. 1:1, 7; 11:30; Josh. 3:16; I Sam. 23:24; Jer. 39:4).

Arabia (ȧ-rā′bĭ-ȧ, **steppe).** Originally the N part of the peninsula between the Red Sea and the Persian Gulf (Isa. 21:13; Ezek. 27:21), but later the entire peninsula (Neh. 2:19; Acts 2:11; Gal. 1:17; 4:25). Its ill-defined border, proximity, and plundering population made it a major factor conditioning the history of Israel.

Arad (ā'răd). 1. A descendant of Benjamin (I Chron. 8:15).

2. A city in the Negev, about 17 miles south of Hebron.

Arah (ā'rȧ, **wayfarer**). 1. A son of Ulla, an Asherite (I Chron. 7:39).

2. The father of a family that returned from exile (Ezra 2:5; Neh. 7:10). Perhaps the same as No. 1.

3. A Jew whose granddaughter became the wife of Tobiah the Ammonite (Neh. 6:18).

Aram (ā'răm). 1. Son of Shem (Gen. 10:22, 23). 2. Son of Kemuel, Abraham's nephew (Gen. 22:21). 3. An Asherite (I Chron. 7:34). 4. In KJV, for the Greek form of Ram (Matt. 1:3, 4, ASV, RSV), called Arni in ASV, RSV of Luke 3:33. 5. Place in Gilead (I Chron. 2:23). 6. The name of Syria (Num. 23:7), and usually so designated (II Sam. 8:5; I Kings 20:20; Amos 1:5). The Aramaean people spread from Phoenicia to the Fertile Crescent, and were closely related to Israel, with whom their history was intertwined.

Aramaic (âr'ȧ-mā'ĭk), a West Semitic language, closely related to Hebrew, which developed various dialects. Genesis 31:47 calls attention to Laban's use of Aramaic in contrast to Jacob's use of Hebrew. That Aramaic had become the language of Assyrian diplomacy is clear from II Kings 18:26; Isaiah 36:11 (see RSV); also that Aramaic and Hebrew were so different that the people of Jerusalem did not understand the former. Some Aramaic places and personal names occur in the OT, as Tabrimmon and Hazael. There are several Aramaic words and phrases in the NT, such as **Talitha cumi** (Mark 5:41); **Ephphatha,** (Mark 7:34); **Eloi, Eloi, lama sabachthani** (Mark 15:34; Matt. 27:46); **Maranatha** (I Cor. 16:22); **Abba,** Father (Mark 14:36; Rom. 8:15; Gal. 4:6), and many others. It is probably safe to assert that our Lord habitually spoke Aramaic and occasionally Greek, and read and could speak Hebrew.

Typical desert scene in the Arabah. © MPS.

Mount Ararat, in eastern Armenia, now Turkey. RTHPL

Aran (ā'răn), one of the two sons of Dishan (Gen. 26:28; I Chron. 1:42).

Ararat (âr'ȧ-răt), a country in eastern Armenia, a mountainous tableland from which flow the Tigris, Euphrates, Aras (Araxes) and Choruk rivers. Its mountains rise to as much as 17,000 feet, the height of the extinct volcano which in modern times is called Mt. Ararat, and on which the ark is supposed to have rested, though Genesis 8:4 in indefinite: "upon the mountains of Ararat" (plural). The region is now a part of Turkey.

Aratus (âr'ȧ-tŭs), Greek poet from Paul's native province, Cilicia. Flourished about 270 B.C. From his **Phaenomena** Paul quotes (Acts 17:28).

Araunah (ȧ-rô'nȧ), the Jebusite who owned a threshing floor on Mount Moriah, which David purchased in order to erect an altar.

Arba (âr'bȧ), giant ancestor of Anak, founder of the city which bore his name, Kirjatharba or Hebron (Josh. 14:15; 15:31; 21:11).

Ruins of the city walls of ancient Jericho.
© MPS

Arbathite (ȧr′bȧ-thīt), one of David's 30 heroes.
Arbite (ȧr′bīt), one of David's mighty men, in II Samuel 23:35, Parai.
Arch (See Architecture)
Archaeology (är-kē-ŏl′ŏ-jĭ). Study of the material remains of the past by excavating ancient buried cities and examining their remains, deciphering inscriptions, and evaluating the language, literature, art, architecture, monuments, and other aspects of human life and achievement. Biblical archaeology is concerned with Palestine and the countries with which the Hebrews and early Christians came into contact. Modern archaeology began with Napoleon's expedition to Egypt, on which many scholars accompanied him to study Egyptian monuments (1798), and with the work of Edward Robinson in Palestine (1838, 1852). Discoveries of great importance which throw much light upon the Patriarchal Period are the Mari Tablets, the Nuzi Tablets, the Tell-el Amarna Tablets, and the Ras Shamra Tablets. The discovery of the Dead Sea Scrolls and the excavation of Qumran are the most recent archaeological finds of importance. Archaeology is of great help in better understanding the Bible, in dealing with critical questions regarding the Bible, and in gaining an appreciation of the ancient world.
Archangel (See Angel)
Archelaus (ȧr′kĕ-lā′ŭs), son of Herod the Great, ruled Idumea, Samaria and Judea in 4 B.C. Deposed by the Roman government in A.D. 6 (Matt. 2:22).
Archers (ȧr′cherz), hunters or warriors with bow and arrow, weapons universally used in ancient times (Gen. 21:20; Judg. 5:11; I Sam. 20:17-42; Isa. 21:17). "Arrow" is often used figuratively (Job 6:4; Jer. 9:8), as is also "bow" (Pss. 7:12; 64:3).
Archevites (ar′kē-vīts), colonists in Samaria who complained to Artaxerxes about the Jews' rebuilding Jerusalem (Ezra 4:9).
Archi (ȧr′kī), probably the name of a clan which possessed Ataroth in Ephraim.
Archippus (ȧr-kĭp′ŭs, **master of the horse**), a Christian at Colossae, conspicuous as a champion of the Gospel, a close friend (or perhaps son) of Philemon (Col. 4:17; Philem. 2).
Archite (ȧr′kīt), a member of the clan of Ataroth in Ephraim (Josh. 16:2; I Chron. 27:33).
Architecture, may be defined as the art or science of building. The materials of architecture in antiquity were wood, clay, brick and stone. Clay bricks seem to have been invented by the Obeid people in Persia before they descended to the Mesopotamian plain early in the fourth millennium B.C. In Egypt, early builders not only experimented with clay and brick, but also with wood, and then they made a

remarkable transition to stone masonry.

One of the early problems to be faced in building was the construction of the roof, and the solutions led to two main forms of architecture; trabeated and arcuated. The trabeated form is designed and constructed using horizontal beams supported by vertical posts, commonly called "post and lintel." The arcuated form makes use of various modifications of the arch.

Unusual styles of architecture include the pyramid-shaped building. The Ziggurat in Mesopotamia is generally believed to be the representative of a mountain; it was built of clay brick with exterior staircases, or a sloping ramp, and probably a shrine at the top.

Among the Israelites, architecture does not seem to have been developed as an art or a skill; rather, Phoenician craftsmen were brought in to build Solomon's palace and temple. Phoenician elements seem to be present also in the building of subsequent Israelite periods; it is difficult to classify these, however, for the Phoenicians seem to have made use of many techniques and styles, some of which can be traced to Cyprus and Egypt. Their use of metalwork in architecture, (e.g., the columns in front of Solomon's temple) was possibly derived from Asia Minor.

The supreme achievement in architecture is admittedly the Periclean architecture of Greece (460-400 B.C.). Roman architecture owed much to the Greeks but adopted some elements from the Etruscans; among the latter is principally the arch. In general we may say that Roman is not as subtle as Greek architecture but at the same time it is more utilitarian. The Greeks had developed the skill of masonry to a high degree of perfection and fit marble blocks together with remarkable accuracy without mortar or cement. The Romans, on the other hand, developed the use of pozzolana, a volcanic earth which was mixed with lime to make a hydraulic cement. Using this as mortar, they were able to bond courses of stone without exact precision in masonry, increase the span in arches, and build two-story structures. Roman architecture even more so than Greek included memorial arches and columns, amphitheaters, theaters, the

A view of Athens from Areopagus Hill (Mars Hill) as Paul probably saw it. JFW

forum (or market place), and many other forms familiar to us from the numerous remains of the Roman world to be found all over the Middle East.

Ard (ȧrd), listed as a son of Benjamin in Genesis 46:21, but as a son of Bela, son of Benjamin, in Numbers 26:40; called Addar (with the consonants transposed) in I Chronicles 8:3.

Ardite (ȧr'dīt), a descendant of Ard (Num. 26:40).

Ardon (ar'dŏn), a son of Caleb (I Chron. 2:18).

Areli (ȧ-rē'lī), a son of Gad and founder of the tribal family, the Arelites (Gen. 46:16; Num. 26:17).

Areopagite (âr'ē-ŏp'ȧ-jīt, -gīt), Dionysius (Acts 17:34), a member of the court of Areopagus which had jurisdiction of manners, morals and teaching in Athens.

Areopagus (âr'ē-ŏp'ȧ-gŭs), the rocky hill of the god Ares, or Mars.

Areopagus is also the name of the council which met on Mars' hill, a court dating back to legendary times, in NT days still charged with questions of morals and the rights of teachers who lectured in public. Its importance was enhanced under the Romans. Paul was brought to the Areopagus (Acts 17:19) to be examined regarding his teaching.

Aretas (ār'ē-tăs, **pleasing** or **virtuous**), a Nabatean king, father-in-law of Herod, whose deputy sought to apprehend Paul at Damascus (II Cor. 11:32, see Acts 9:24).

Relief, showing structure on wheels, representing the Ark of the Covenant, found in the ruins at Capernaum. © MPS

Argob (ár′gŏb, **heap,** or **region of clods**). 1. A well-defined region of Bashan, identified with the kingdom of Og in Deuteronomy 3:4, 13, 14, and I Kings 4:13. This land of 60 strong, fortified cities was taken by the Israelites under Moses (Deut. 3:4).

2. II Kings 15:25 refers to either a place or a person. If a place, probably where one of the king's houses was located. If a person, he may have been either a follower of Pekahiah, killed with him; or a follower of Pekah who took part in the murder of Pekehiah.

Aridai (ȧ-rĭd′ā-ī, ȧ-rĭd′ī), one of Haman's ten sons (Esth. 9:9).

Aridatha (ȧ-rĭd′ȧ-thȧ, ăr-ĭ-dā′thȧ), another son of Haman (Esth. 9:8).

Arieh (ȧ-rī′ĕ, ār′ĭ-ĕ), named with Argob in II Kings 15:25 KJV, ASV, either as places or as persons.

Ariel (âr′ĭ-ĕl, **lion of God).** 1. One of an embassy sent by Ezra to bring "ministers for the house of our God" to the returning exiles from Babylonia (Ezra 8:16, 17).

2. In II Samuel 23:20 and I Chronicles 11:22, KJV has "two lionlike men of Moab."

3. A poetic name, "lioness of God," given to Jerusalem (Isa. 29:1, 2, 7).

Arimathea (âr′ĭ-mȧ-thē′ȧ), the city of the Joseph who buried the body of Jesus in his own new tomb near Jerusalem (Matt. 25:57; Mark 15:43; Luke 23:51; John 19:38). The location of Arimathea is in doubt, but is conjectured to be Ramathaim-zophim, the Ramah of Samuel's residence, in the hill-country of Ephraim.

Arioch (ăr′ĭ-ŏk). 1. The king of Ellasar in Syria (Gen. 14:1, 4, 9).

2. Captain of the king's guard at Babylon under Nebuchadnezzar (Dan. 2:14-25).

Arisai (ȧ-rĭs′ā-ī, ăr′ĭ-sī), a son of Haman who was killed by the Jews (Esth. 9:9).

Aristarchus (ăr′ĭs-tȧr′kŭs, **the best ruler**), a Macedonian of Thessalonica, one of Paul's travel-companions (Acts 19:29; 20:4; 27:2; Col. 4:10; Philem. 24).

Aristobulus (ȧ-rĭs′tō-bū′lŭs, **the best counselor**), a Christian in Rome, whose household Paul greeted.

Ark (árk) of Noah; meaning 1. **a chest;** 2. **a vessel to float.** It is used of the vessel which God directed Noah to build (Gen. 6:14-16). God told Noah what to bring into it (Gen. 6:18-21), and Noah obeyed (Gen. 6:22-7:10). The ark floated during the Flood (Gen. 7:11-8:3), then came to rest "upon the mountains of Ararat" (Gen. 8:4). After Noah abandoned the ark (Gen. 8:18, 19), what happened to it is unknown.

The ark of Noah is referred to in Matthew 24:38; Luke 17:27 in a warning of coming judgment; in Hebrews 11:7 as an example of faith; and the same Hebrew word is used of the basket of bulrushes in which Moses was cast out to float upon the Nile (Exod. 2:2-5).

Ark, of the covenant or **of the testimony; chest of the covenant.** The word **'ărôn** is used of the coffin (mummy-case) of Joseph (Gen. 50:26); elsewhere of the chest containing the tables of the law, resting in the tabernacle or in the temple. God told Moses (Exod. 25:10-22; Deut. 10:2-5) how to make it.

It went before Israel in the wilderness journeys "to search out a resting-place for them" (Num. 10:33). It was instrumental in the crossing of Jordan on dry land under Joshua (Josh. 3), and in the capture of Jericho (Josh. 4:7-11). Joshua prayed before the ark after the defeat at Ai (Josh. 7:6) and after the subsequent victory, at Mt. Ebal, the ark being present (Josh. 8:33). In the days of Eli the ark was in the tabernacle at Shiloh (I Sam. 3:3). It was captured by the Philistines and held until a plague convinced them that the ark was too dangerous to keep, and it was ceremoniously sent back (I Sam. 5:1-6:15).

David brought the ark to Jerusalem (II Sam. 6; I Chron. 13 and 15). After the destruction of the first temple, there is no evidence as to what happened to the ark, but only highly speculative tradition and conjecture. Synagogues, from our earliest knowledge of them to the present, have had arks in the side wall toward Jerusalem; therein the scrolls of the Law are stored behind a curtain.

Arkites (ȧr′kīts), people of Arka, a Phoenician town a few miles NE of Tripoli.

Arm, used as a figure for might, of God (Isa. 53:1). "Break the arm," i.e., the power (Ezek. 30:25).

Armageddon (ȧr-mȧ-gĕd′ŏn), a word found only in Revelation 16:16, for the final battleground between the forces of good and evil. The Valley of Jezreel and the Plain of Esdraelon at the foot of Mount Megiddo were the scene of many decisive battles in the history of Israel. The town of Megiddo guarded the pass which formed the easiest caravan route between the Plain of Sharon and the Valley of Jezreel, and the low mountains around were silent witnesses of perhaps more bloody encounters than any other spot on earth, continuing down to recent times. Hence the appropriateness of this place for the vast conflict pictured in Revelation 16.

Armenia (ȧr-mē′nĭ-ȧ), a mountainous country N of Assyria.

Armlet, Bracelet (ȧrm′lĕt; -lĭt; brās′-lĕt; -lĭt), an ornament usually for the upper arm, worn by both men and women. The Heb. original uses several different words, the precise meaning of which is uncertain.

Armoni (ȧr-mō′nī, **belonging to the palace),** a son of Saul by his concubine Rizpah, slain by the Gibeonites to satisfy justice (II Sam. 21:8-11).

Armor-Bearer, bearer of weapons. Abimelech (Judg. 9:54), Saul (I Sam. 31:4), Jonathan (I Sam. 14:12) and Joab (II Sam. 23:37) had one. Cf. Goliath (I Sam. 17:7, 41).

Armory. Three Hebrew words: (Jer. 50:25) figurative for the "Lord's means of judgment"; rendered also "treasure," "treasury," store-house," "store-house for valuables and arms"; used figuratively for "beauty" in S. of Sol. 4:4.

Arms, Armor (ȧrms, ȧr′mẽr), mentioned often in the Bible, both literally and as illustrative of spiritual conflicts. Here only hand weapons and chariots or machines used in sieges.

Roman and Greek soldiers in armor.

A. Offensive weapons. 1. **Sword** is the first mentioned in the Bible; "a flaming sword which turned every way, to keep the way of the tree of life" (Gen. 3:24). A weapon for smiting is the common sword (Gen. 27:40; Exod. 17:13); a sword for punishment is ascribed to God (Exod. 5:3; 22:24). Figurative and literal are united in "the sword of the Lord and of Gideon" (Judg 7:20). 2. **Rod,** a stick loaded at one end, which could be for reassurance (Ps. 23:4); used to count sheep (Lev. 27:32); or a weapon (Ps. 2:9). 3. **Sling,** a band of leather, wide in the middle to receive a stone. 4. **Bow,** sometimes of steel (II Sam. 22:35; Job 20:24; Ps. 18:34) and **arrows.** First mentioned (Gen. 27:3) as used in hunting, except the "bow in the cloud" (Gen. 9:13-16, rainbow). 5. **Spear, lance, javelin** or **dart,** sharp-pointed instruments to be thrust or thrown (Josh. 8:18; Judg. 5:8; I Sam. 17:7; 18:11; Ps. 68:30, different Heb. words).

B. Defensive armor. 1. **Shields** were both large and small, round. 2. **Helmet,** (I Sam. 17:5; Isa. 59:17), sometimes of brass (I Sam. 17:38), surrounding the head (Eph. 6:17; I Thess. 5:8). 3. **Coat of mail,** only in I Samuel 17:5, 38, called "breastplate" in Isaiah 59:17. In the NT, Greek **thorax** (Eph. 6:14; I Thess. 5:8, figuratively; Rev. 9:9, 17, symbolic). 4. **Greaves,** for the legs, only in I Samuel 17:6. 5. **Girdle,** or belt from which the sword hung (II Sam. 20:8).

Army, a collection of men armed and organized for warfare. The armies of Israel, when directed of God and led by Him, were uniformly successful (Josh. 1:3; 5:14), but when like Amaziah (II Chron. 25:14) and, earlier, Saul (I Sam. 15) the king refused to listen to God, defeat and death followed. "Army" most frequently implies infantry, which has been the

Gorge of the River Arnon, where it enters the Dead Sea. © MPS

backbone of the army. For some reason, God did not want Israel to use or to depend upon cavalry.

God's arrangement for His people and His army in the wilderness journey made for perfect order. They encamped with the tabernacle at the center (Num. 2), the three families of the Levites and the priests closely surrounding it, then the other 12 tribes at a slightly greater distance. Three tribes were grouped on each side of the tabernacle under the banners of the leading tribes.

Numbers 1 contains a military census of Israel at Sinai just after the exodus, and Numbers 26 a second census taken 40 years later in the plains of Moab. According to the plain sense of the English versions, the number of military men was immense: over 603,000 at the exodus and nearly as many at the Jordan, and these figures imply a total population of something like three million men, women, and children, accompanied by herds and flocks.

Israel, on condition of obedience (Deut. 28:1-7) could have become the paramount power of the earth, but when she had gone into hopeless apostasy, God began to raise up great universal world powers (Dan. 2) and to overturn (Ezek. 21:27) Israel, preparing for the coming of our Lord. The Babylonians with their hordes were overthrown by the Persians, originally a hardy race whose armies were mostly cavalry; but when Xerxes, the "Ahasuerus" of Esther 1, attempted to invade Europe, he was defeated.

Esther 1 tells of his great "feast" of six months, which was really a military council preparing for his invasion of Greece in 480 B.C. The eastern army was defeated by the Greeks with their phalanxes of heavy armed infantry, arranged closely in ranks and files. The Greek armies, in turn, were conquered by the Romans. The Romans had a genius for government and for military organization, and the various NT references mention their "chief captains" (Acts 21:31), whom we would call colonels, their centurions (Acts 10:1), etc., implying their organization into legions and armies. Our Lord (Matt. 26:53) hints at a possible angelic army divided like the Roman into legions. The smallest group of soldiers mentioned in the Bible is the quaternion (Acts 12:4), composed of only four soldiers.

Arnan (ăr′năn), head of a noble Jewish family about 500 B.C. (I Chron. 3:21).

Arnon (ăr′nŏn), the swift "roaring stream" and the valley of the same name which empty into the E side of the Dead Sea a little N of its center. It arises in the hills of northern Arabia and flows a little W of N and then turns westward to descend into the Sea, emptying at about the lowest point on the earth's surface. It now flows through the kingdom of Jordan.

Arod (ā′rŏd), a son of Gad (Gen. 46:16), where he is called Arodi, head of the family of Arodites in the time of Moses (Num. 26:17).

Aroer (ȧ-rō′êr, **poor, naked, helpless**). The same word is rendered "heath" in Jeremiah 17:6; 48:6. 1. A town on a branch of the brook Jabbok, fortified early by the tribe of Gad (Num. 32:34). A camping place of Joab (II Sam. 24:5) when taking a census in the days of David. Isaiah speaks of it (Isa. 17:2) as being deserted in his time.

2. Reubenite town on the Arnon (Josh. 13:9). Hazael, king of Syria, took it from Israel in the days of Jehu (II Kings 10:33).

3. A town in the southern part of Judah (I Sam. 30:28).

Arpad (ăr′păd), a town and its surrounding region in the northern part of Syria near Hamath (modern Hamah), with which it is associated in all six biblical references.

Arphaxad (ăr-făk′săd), third son of Shem, c. 2479 B.C., the first birth recorded after the Flood. He lived 438 years, and was the ancestor of Abraham and of many Arab tribes. (Gen. 10:22-11:13). Also possibly a region of Assyria.

Arrow (See Arms)

Art. The six major arts are music, the dance, architecture, sculpture, painting, and literature. They can be classified as spatial (architecture, sculpture, painting) and temporal (music, literature), with the dance extending over both categories. Because of the commandment against representational art (Exod. 20:4), Israel did little with painting and sculptoring. Phoenician craftsmen helped Israel in its major architectural works. Dancing was practiced. Music reached a high development; but Israel's literature was not surpassed in all antiquity.

Artaxerxes (är-tȧ-zûrk′sēz), a proper name or possibly title, for several kings of Persia. Two, or possibly three, Persian kings are so named in the OT: the pseudo-Smerdis of Ezra 4:7-23; "Longimanus," who granted the requests of Ezra (7:6) and Nehemiah (2:1-8) to go to Jerusalem; and possibly another king who reigned before 516 B.C. (Ezra 6:14).

Artemas (är′tē-măs), a companion of Paul at Nicopolis (Titus 3:12).

Artemis (är′tē-mĭs), the Greek goddess of hunting, corresponding to the Roman Diana. Her largest and most famous temple was at Ephesus; it was regarded as one of the wonders of the ancient world (Acts 19:23-41).

Artificer (See Occupations)

Artillery (är-til′ēr-ē), used only in I Samuel 20:40, where it refers to Jonathan's bow and arrows. The RV has "weapons."

Aruboth (ȧ-rŭb′ŏth), a region of the Shephelah in Judah assigned to Benhesed to provide food for Solomon's court (I Kings 4:10).

Arumah (ȧ-rōō′mȧ), a place near Shechem in Ephraim where Abimelech dwelt (Judg. 9:41).

Arvad (är′-văd), a small island off the coast of Syria about 40 miles north of Tripoli. Its people were descendants of Ham through Canaan (Gen. 10:18). The name seems to mean "a place of fugitives."

Asa (ā′sȧ, **healer**). 1. Third king of Judah, reigning from 964-923 B.C. (I Kings 15:9-24; II Chron. 14-16). He was the first of the five kings of Judah (Asa, Jehoshaphat, Joash, Hezekiah, Josiah) who were outstanding for godliness. Asa began his reign by deposing his wicked and powerful grandmother and by destroying a fearful, impure image that she had set up. He then drove out the Sodomites, and destroyed idols that his fathers had worshiped (15:12), commanding Judah to seek the Lord God of their fathers (II Chron. 14:4).

In the early peaceful days of his reign, he gathered into the house of the Lord the dedicated things which his father and he had vowed to the Lord (I Kings 15:15). In the 39th year of his reign Asa was taken with a severe disease of the feet. By this time his faith had deteriorated and because he trusted his physicians rather than the Lord, he died (II Chron. 16:11-14).

2. A Levite among those who had returned from captivity (I Chron. 9:16).

Asadiah (ă-să-dī′ȧ), the son of Chelcias and father of Sedecias, in the ancestry of Baruch, according to the apocryphal book (Baruch 1:1).

Asahel (ăs′ȧ-hĕl, **whom God made**). 1. Youngest son of Zeruiah, David's sister; and brother of Joab and Abishai. These three were among the mighty men of David.

2. A teaching Levite under Jehoshaphat (II Chron. 17:8).

3. A Levite in Hezekiah's reign (II Chron. 31:13).

4. Father of a certain Jonathan (Ezra 10:15).

Asahiah (ăs′ȧ-hī′ȧ, **whom Jehovah made**), one of Josiah's officers whom he sent to inquire of the Lord concerning the words of the law which Shaphan had read to the king (II Kings 22:12-14).

Asaiah (ȧ-sā′yȧ, **whom Jehovah made**). 1. A Simeonite, c. 800 B.C. (I Chron. 4:36).

2. A Levite of the family of Merari in the time of David (I Chron. 6:30).

3. A Shilonite, one of the first after the captivity to dwell in Jerusalem (I Chron. 9:5).

4. One of the chief Levites of the family of Merari in David's day (I Chron. 15:6, 11). This may be the same as 2 above. He seems to have been the leader of about 220 Levites who assisted in bringing the ark from the house of Obed-edom to Jerusalem.

Asaph (ā′săf), a Levite of the Gershonite family, appointed over the service of praise in the time of David and Solomon (I Chron. 16:5; II Chron. 5:12). He led the singing and sounded cymbals before the ark, and apparently set up a school of music (Neh. 7:44). There are 12 psalms credited to Asaph (50, 78-83); and it seems as though there must have been two Asaphs, centuries apart, who wrote psalms. Psalms 50, 73, 76, 78 certainly, and perhaps 75, 77, 82, could have been written in David's time; but 74, 79, and perhaps 83 belong to the Captivity.

2. Father of Hezekiah's recorder (II Kings 18:18).

3. An official under Artaxerxes Longimanus, king of Persia (Neh. 2:8).

4. In I Chronicles 26:1 read Ebiasaph (cf. ch. 9:19).

Asareel (ȧ-sā'rē-ĕl), a descendant of Judah and a son of Jehallelel (I Chron. 4:16).

Asarelah (ăs'ȧ-rē'lȧ), a Levite singer of the sons of Asaph in David's time (I Chron. 25:2). Called Jesharelah in v. 14.

Ascension of Christ (See Acts 1:6-11; Mark 16:19; Luke 24:50-52). The ascension of our Lord Jesus Christ necessarily came between His earthly and His heavenly ministry. His ascension was predicted in the OT (Ps. 68:18, cf. Eph. 4:8) and by our Lord Himself (John 20:17), and has been accepted as a central doctrine by all Christians since Pentecost.

Asenath (ăs'ĕn-ăth), a daughter of Poti-pherah, priest of On, the modern Heliopolis, near Cairo, Egypt. Pharaoh gave her to Joseph as wife (Gen. 41:45-50), and she bore to him Manasseh ("causing to forget") and Ephraim ("doubly fruitful").

Aser (ā'sêr), Greek form of Asher **(q.v.).**

Ashan (ā'shăn), a town in the tribe of Judah, later given to Simeon because Judah's territory was too large; then made a city of refuge and given to the priests (Josh. 15:42; 19:7; I Chron. 4:32; 6:59).

Ashbea (ăsh'bē-ȧ), head of a family in Judah which worked in fine linen (I Chron. 4:21).

Ashbel (ăsh'bĕl), the second son of Benjamin, son of Jacob. (I Chron. 8:1).

Ashchenaz (See Ashkenaz)

Ashdod (ăsh'dŏd, **stronghold),** one of the five chief cities of the Philistines (Josh. 13:3). Center of Dagon (fish-god) worship; ark taken there but returned (I Sam. 5:1-7); conquered by Uzziah (II Chron. 26:6); destruction predicted by Amos (1:8); captured by Sargon II of Assyria (Isa. 20:1); tried to hinder Jews in Nehemiah's time (Neh. 4:7-9; 13:23, 24). Called Azotus in LXX and NT (Acts 8:40).

Ashdodites (people of Ashdod).

Ashdoth Pisgah (ăsh'dŏth-pĭz'gȧ), the slopes or the springs of Pisgah, a mountain range just E of the northern end of the Dead Sea.

Asher, or **Aser** (ăsh'êr, ā'sêr, **happy,** Aser in KJV of NT). 1. The second son of Zilpah, the hand-maid whom Laban gave to Leah his daughter.

2. The tribe descended from Asher (Josh. 19:24-31) was given the territory along the Mediterranean in the NW corner of Palestine. By David's time Asher seems to have become insignificant, for this tribe is omitted in the list of David's chief ruler (I Chron. 27:16-22). In NT and LXX "Aser" **(q.v.).**

Asherah (ȧ-shē'rȧ). 1. A goddess of the Phoenicians and Syrians. 2. The images supposed to represent this goddess. Her worship was lewd and associated with that of Baal (Ex. 34:13; I Kings 16:29-33).

Ashes. The expression "dust and ashes" (Gen. 18:27, etc.), is a play on words **("aphar"** and **"epher")** and signifies man's origin, as to his body, from the ordinary chemical elements. It contrasts the lowliness of man with the dignity of God.

The lovely expression "beauty for ashes" (Isa. 61:3) is also a play on words. Another word for ashes, **deshen,** is used for the remains of the burnt offering (Lev. 6:10, 11, etc.).

Ashima (ȧ-shī'mȧ), god of the Hamathites, whose worship was brought to Samaria by the king of Assyria c. 715 B.C. (II Kings 17:30).

Ashkelon, Askelon, Ascalon (ăsh'kĕ-lŏn, ăs'kĕ-lŏn), one of the 5 chief cities of the Philistines, 12 miles N of Gaza; taken by tribe of Judah (Judg. 1:18), but retaken by Philistines, who held it through most of OT period; denounced by Amos (1:6-8), Zephaniah (2:4,7) and Zechariah (9:5). Destroyed A.D. 1270.

Ashkenas (See Ashkenaz)

Ashkenaz (ăsh'kĕ-năz). 1. Descendant of Noah (Gen. 10:3; I Chron. 1:6). 2. People associated with Ararat mentioned in Jer. 51:27.

Ashnah (ăsh'nȧ), two towns of Judah (Josh. 15:33; 15:43).

Ashpenaz (ăsh'pē-năz), prince of the eunuchs in the court of Nebuchadnezzar, who gave to Daniel and his companions their new heathen names: Belteshazzar, etc. (Dan. 1:3, 7).

Ashtaroth or Astaroth (ăsh′tȧ-rŏth) city in Bashan, where king Og dwelt. Probably so named from its having a temple to the goddess Ashtoreth **(q.v.).** Given in Joshua's time to the children of Gershon, of the tribe of Levi (Josh. 21:27—here called "Beeshterah").

Ashtaroth (ăsh′tȧ-rŏth), **Astarte** (ăs-tär′tē). Ashtaroth is plural of Ashtoreth, name of any of the fertility goddesses of the ancient Near East; Babylonian **Ishtar,** Greek **Astarte;** in Canaan a consort of El (Baal) (Judg. 2:13; I Kings 11:5, 33; II Kings 23:13). The plural Ashtaroth refers to the many local goddesses (Judg. 10:13; I Sam. 7:3, 4; 12:10; 31:10); also to the city of Og, king of Bashan (Deut. 1:4; Josh. 9:10; 12:4; 13:12, 31).

Ashteroth - Karnaim (ăsh′tē-rŏth-kȧr-nā′ĭm), region of the Rephaim in Abram's time (Gen. 14:5). Exact site unknown.

Ashtoreth (ăsh′tō-rĕth), a goddess of the Canaanites, worshiped all along the seacoast from Ras Shamra (Ugarit) southward through Phoenicia and Philistia. The plural Ashtaroth is found commonly and refers to the idols representing her. Her male consort was apparently Baal, and the two were worshiped with lewd rites. In Judges 2:11-23 we are told that Israel forsook their God, and served Baal and Ashtaroth. The prophet Samuel brought about a great revival, but before Israel could be saved from the Philistines, they had to give up Ashtoreth and turn to Jehovah (I Sam. 7:3, 4). Gesenius related the name Ashtoreth to the Persian word "sitarah" or "star" and connects it with Venus, the goddess of love.

Ashur (ăsh′ẽr), great grandson of Judah through Pharez and Hezron (I Chron. 2:24; 4:5).

Ashurbanipal (ä-shōōr-bä′nē-päl, **Ashur creates a son),** king of Assyria. He was grandson of the famous Sennacherib **(q.v.)** who reigned from 704 to 681 B.C. and son of Esar-Haddon, who reigned from 681-668 B.C. Ashurbanipal was a lover of learning and collected a great library of cuneiform tablets (over 22,000 in number) which have given to us most of what we know of Babylonian and Assyrian literature.

Ashurites (ăsh′ûr-īts) a people belonging to Ishbosheth, son of Saul (II Sam. 2:9).

Ashurnasirpal II (ä-shōōr-näs′ĭr-päl), ruthless and mighty king of Assyria late in the tenth or early in the ninth century B.C.

Ivory carving from Nimrud, of the "woman at the window," possibly the goddess Ashtoreth, or Astarte. BM

Ashvath (ăsh′văth), a descendant of Asher (I Chron. 7:33).

Asia (ā′zhȧ). 1. The great continent E of Europe and Africa.

2. Asia Minor, otherwise Anatolia, the great western promontory of Asia partially bounded by the three seas, Black, Aegean and Mediterranean.

3. Proconsular Asia, the Roman province in NT times, which contained the SW part of Asia Minor, and in particular "the seven churches of Asia" addressed in the first three chapters of Revelation.

Asiarchs (ā′shĭ-ȧrk, "chief of Asia"), found once in ASV as a transliteration of the Greek title, but is rendered "chief of Asia" (Acts 19:31) in KJV. Civil and priestly officials of the province of Asia chosen yearly to preside over the national games and theatrical displays. These patriotic pageants were financed by the Asiarchs, and so only rich men could afford to enjoy the honor.

Asiel (ā′sĭ-ĕl, **God is maker),** a Simeonite, mentioned only in I Chronicles 4:35.

Asnah (ăs′nȧ), head of a family of temple servants ("Nethinim") who returned from the captivity with Zerubbabel, 536 B.C. (Ezra 2:50).

Asnapper (ăs-năp′ẽr), mentioned only in Ezra 4:10 as "the great and noble Asnapper" who had brought over and set in Samaria people of various nations previous to the time of Zerubbabel. It was he who colonized Samaria and other regions by wholesale deportations of conquered peoples.

Asp (See Animals)

Aspatha (ăs-pā′thȧ), third son of Haman, (Esth. 9:7).

Asriel (ăs′rĭ-ĕl). KJV once **Ashriel.** 1. Grandson of Manasseh and son of Gilead (Num. 26:31; Josh. 17:2).

2. A son of Manasseh (I Chron. 7:14).

Ass (See Animals)

Assir (ăs′ēr, **captive).** 1. A cousin of Moses (Exod. 6:24).

2. Great grandson of the former (I Chron. 6:23).

3. In KJV apparently a son of Jeconiah (I Chron. 3:17), but it should read "Jeconiah the captive." Cf. ASV.

Assos (ăs′ŏs), modern Behramkoy, seaport of Mysia in Asia Minor (Acts 20: 13, 14). The ship, with Luke and others, sailed from Troas around Cape Lectum, while Paul walked the shorter way (20 Roman miles) overland to Assos, where he reached the ship in time for her to arrive that evening at Mitylene, a port on the SE coast of Lesbos.

Assur, Asshur (ăs′ûr, ăsh′ûr), the god of the Assyrians; their reputed human founder; the ancient capital of the country; often the nation Assyria. Asshur is the builder of Nineveh and nearby cities (Gen. 10:11). He comes from the kingdom of Nimrod, a descendant of Ham, but may not be of his race. For most occurrences of the Heb. word, KJV has Assyria, which is the probable meaning in every instance.

Assurance (ă-shōōr′ăns), OT teaching clearly is that assurance, though under other names, is open to those who are righteous before God in any age (Ps. 37:1-7, 25; Prov. 3:5, 6). As in the OT, much NT teaching fosters assurance without using the word (John 14-17; I John 5:13, 20). Interpretations by theologians of the nature and extent of assurance differ widely from one confessional group to another. The Biblical basis remains for the Christian to explore and appropriate.

Assyria (ȧ-sĭr′ĭ-ȧ), originally a land between the upper Tigris and Zab rivers. First mentioned in the Bible in Genesis 2:14, Assyria and the Assyrians are frequently named, sometimes as Asshur or Assur. In the tenth century began a powerful and systematic advance. Under Shalmaneser III, the Assyrians turned toward Palestine, and in 853 were defeated at Karkar, but claimed a victory over Ben-hadad of Damascus and a coalition including Ahab, king of Israel. They failed to follow up their effort.

After the religious revival under Elijah and Elisha, the coalition of Israel with Syria broke up, at the accession of Jehu as king (II Kings 9, 10). Internal difficulties kept Assyria from further Palestinian inroads for nearly a century, when, shortly after the middle of the eighth century B.C., Tiglath-pileser III invaded the West. In 733-732 B.C. he conquered Galilee, the plain of Sharon and Gilead from Israel, and made Israel and Judah pay tribute (II Kings 15:29; 16:9). Isaiah prophesied that this attempt to subjugate Judah would eventually fail. Shalmaneser V besieged Samaria for three years. He died during the siege, and his successor Sargon II (now called Sargon III) took the city in 721 B.C. and carried its more prosperous citizens into exile, replacing them with colonists from other provinces of his empire (II Kings 17:6-41).

For nearly a century thereafter, Assyria was troubled from all sides, from Babylon, Elam, the Medes, Phrygia and Egypt. Yet Sennacherib nearly captured Jerusalem in 701-700 B.C. (II Kings 18:13-19:37; Isaiah 36, 37), the danger ending only when "the angel of the Lord went out and smote in the camp of the Assyrians" 185,000, followed by the assassination of Sennacherib. Manasseh, king of Judah, paid tribute, except during a short rebellion for which he was carried to Babylon, but released after he sought the Lord (II Chron. 33:11-13). The last quarter of the seventh century B.C. saw the decline of the Assyrian empire and its subjugation by the Chaldean conquerors of Babylonia, with the Medes. Ninevah was taken in 612 B.C. For a short time Babylonia replaced Assyria as the great power. The prophets Elijah, Elisha and Isaiah are largely concerned with Assyria, and several other prophets, Jeremiah, Ezekiel, Hosea, Micah, Nahum, Zephaniah and Zechariah refer to it. Jonah was actually sent to prophesy to Nineveh, and the revival he unwillingly promoted saved the city from destruction for a long period of time.

Assyrian kings who reigned during the centuries of closest contact with Israel and Judah, with approximate dates from the list found at Khorsabad in Mesopotamia (all B.C.):

Shalmaneser III	858-824
Shamshi-Adad V	823-811
Adad-Nirari III	810-783
Shalmaneser IV	782-773
Ashur-dan III	772-755
Ashur-Nirari V	754-745
Tiglath-pileser III	744-727
Shalmaneser V	726-722
Sargon III (formerly called Sargon II)	721-705
Sennacherib	704-681
Esarhaddon	680-669
Ashurbanipal	668-633
Ashur-eti-ilani	632-629
Sin-shum-lishir	———
Sin-shar-ishkum	623-612
Ashur-uballit	611-608

Astarte (See Ashtaroth, Ashtoreth)

Astrologers (ăs-trŏl′ō-jêrz), in Daniel 2:10, 27; 4:7; 5:7; 11, 15, singular; 1:20, 2:22, plural; means "conjurer, necromancer." RSV translates uniformly "enchanter," but has "astrologer" for KJV "soothsayer." It is difficult to distinguish the various sorts of practicers of magical arts. Seeking information from the stars was widely practiced from earliest times, but with all other forms of superstition was forbidden to the Chosen People, who were to seek their God directly.

Astrology (ăs-trŏl′ō-jē), the art practiced by astrologers.

Astronomy. While the word astronomy is not found in the Bible, there are many passages in the Scriptures which refer to some aspect of the subject. God is recognized as the maker of the stars (Gen. 1:16) as well as the one who knows their number and names (Ps. 147:4). In the 19th Psalm there is a beautiful poem telling how the heavenly bodies (referring to the stars) show forth the glory of their Creator. Here there is reference made to the sun as another of the heavenly bodies.

In the Bible there are hundreds of references to stars, sun, moon, and planets. When God wished to tell Abraham how numerous his descendants would be, He took him out and showed him the stars. Then God said, "Look toward heaven and number the stars, if you are able to number them" (Gen. 15:5). Later on God compared the number of Abraham's descendants not only with the stars, but also with the sand on the seashore (Gen. 22:17). For many years it was not clear that this was a fair comparison. Before the invention of the astronomical telescope it was not at all certain that the number of stars was as great as the number of grains of sand on the seashore.

It appears that the Biblical writers were aware that the stars differ greatly from each other. Paul, writing to the church at Corinth, says, "There is one glory of the sun, and another glory of the moon, and another glory of the stars; for star differs from star in glory" (I Cor. 15:41). This has been verified by the astronomers. Not only do stars have different colors, but they also differ widely in size, in density, in temperature, and in total amount of light emitted. The sun, about which the earth revolves, is an average star. While it is over one million times as large as the earth, there are some stars which are one million times as large as the sun.

While there is little evidence in the Bible that the Hebrew people had indulged much in the study of astronomy, it is abundantly clear that they recognized a sublime order in the movements of the heavenly bodies. They observed carefully the daily ris-

The Great Milky Way — "stars without number." EG

ing of the sun, its majestic movement across the meridian, and its final setting in the west. This is vividly portrayed in the story of the battle with the Amorites as recorded in the tenth chapter of Joshua. Here it is recorded that the sun stood still in the midst of the heaven. This expression undoubtedly refers to the meridian, the great arc connecting the zenith with the north and south points.

There are a number of allusions in the Bible to eclipses of the sun and of the moon. In Isaiah 13:10 it is stated that, "the sun will be dark at its rising," while in Joel 2:31 we have the statement, "the sun shall be turned to darkness, and the moon to blood." These two descriptions accord quite well with observations of eclipses of the sun and of the moon.

Calculated eclipses of the sun which occurred during Old Testament times are as follows: July 31, 1063 B.C.; Aug. 15, 831 B.C.; June 15, 763 B.C.; May 18, 603 B.C.; May 28, 585 B.C. Very likely the prophets Amos and Joel witnessed the eclipse of Aug. 15, 831 B.C. Such an eclipse is vividly described by Amos, "I will make the sun go down at noon, and darken the earth in broad daylight" (Amos 8:9).

The subject of astrology has been connected with astronomy since early times. The reference in Judges 5:20 no doubt refers to the influence of the stars in the lives of men. The writer states, "From heaven fought the stars, from their courses they fought against Sisera." However, the Hebrew people seemed to have had little to do with the subject. In the book of Daniel there are repeated statements made concerning the astrologers. It is to be noted that Daniel and his three friends, though closely associated with astrologers, are always mentioned as keeping themselves separate and undefiled. Again and again when the magicians and the astrologers were unable to perform a task, it was Daniel who was able to do important things for the king. Thus it is apparent that the Bible condemns the pseudo-science of astrology.

Probably the most fascinating part of Biblical astronomy concerns the star of Bethlehem in the second chapter of Matthew. What kind of a star can continually guide men to a definite point on the earth? Many answers have been proposed, but none is final or authoritative.

Evidently we have here another of the many Bible miracles which modern science is unable to explain. Undoubtedly this miraculous appearance, which is called a star, aroused the curiosity of the wise men to such an extent that they followed it for many miles until finally it pointed out the exact place where they wished to go.

There is abundant evidence in the Bible that many of the constellations were known to the writers. The Lord asked Job many questions. Among these is the following: "Can you bind the chains of the Pleiades, or loose the cords of Orion?" (Job 38:31). One constellation has a special significance to the Christians. It is Cygnus, the flying swan or the Northern Cross. It really has the appearance of a huge cross in the summer sky. Six bright stars form a Roman Cross. It is about the size of the Big Dipper.

In the last book of the Bible and in the last chapter of that book, the Lord Jesus is called "the bright and morning star" (Rev. 22:16). Evidently the writer, the apostle John, had frequently waited for the morning light and had watched for the bright morning star, which is usually a planet. Its beauty had greatly inspired him, so he uses this apt figure by referring to the Lord Jesus Christ as the bright morning star.

Asuppim (ȧ-sŭp'ĭm), a Heb. word meaning "collectors," left untranslated in KJV (I Chron. 26:15, 17); in ASV, RSV, "storehouses." The same word (Neh. 12:25) in KJV is "thresholds," ASV, RSV, "storehouses."

Asyncritus (ȧ-sĭng'krĭ-tŭs, **incomparable**), a Christian in Rome whom Paul greeted (Rom. 16:14).

Atad (ā'tăd, **thorn**), name of a place, "the threshing floor of Atad," E of Jordan, where the Children of Israel mourned for Joseph.

Atarah (ăt'ȧ-rȧ), a wife of Jerahmeel and mother of Onam (I Chron. 2:26).

Ataroth (ăt'ȧ-rŏth, -rōth, **crowns**). 1. Modern Khirbet-at-tārûs, E of Jordan in the territory of Reuben (Num. 32: 3, 34).

2. On the border between Ephraim and Benjamin, to the W (Josh. 16:2), probably the same as Ataroth-addar (Josh. 16:5; 18:13).

3. On the eastern border of Ephraim (Josh. 16:7).

4. Near Bethlehem (I Chron. 2:54). The locations of the last three are uncertain.

Ater (ā'têr). 1. The ancestor of an exiled family (Ezra 2:16; Neh. 7:21).

2. Ancestor of a family of gatekeepers who returned from exile with Zerubbabel (Ezra 2:42; Neh. 7:45).

3. The chief of the people who, with Nehemiah, sealed the covenant (Neh. 10:17).

Athach (ā'thăk), a city of Judah, probably near Ziklag. David sent to it from Ziklag some of the spoil taken from the Amalekites (I Sam. 30:30).

Athaiah (ȧ-thī'ȧ, **Jehovah is helper),** the son of Uzziah a Judahite in Nehemiah's time (Neh. 11:4).

Athaliah (ăth'ȧ-lī'ȧ). 1. The only woman who ever reigned over Judah. Her story is told in II Kings 8:18, 25-28; 11:1-20, and in fuller detail in II Chronicles 22:1-23:21; 24:7. She was the daughter of Ahab and Jezebel.

2. A son of Jeroham, a Benjamite (I Chron. 8:26, 27).

3. The father of Jeshiah, a returned exile (Ezra 8:7).

Athens (ăth'ĕnz), in ancient times the famous capital of Attica, one of the Greek states, now the capital of Greece. The city was named after its patron goddess Athene. It centered around a rocky hill called Acropolis, and was 4½ miles from the sea.

In ancient times Athens had a population of at least a quarter of a million. It was the seat of Greek art, science and philosophy, and was the most important university city in the ancient world. Although politically conquered, it conquered its conquerors with its learning and culture.

Paul visited the city on his second misisonary journey, and spoke to an interested but somewhat disdainful audience on Mars Hill (Acts 17).

Athlai (ăth'lȧ-ī), a man of Israel who in the days of Ezra (c. 456 B.C.) divorced his foreign wife (Ezra 10:28).

Atonement (ă-tōn'mĕnt, **to cover, cancel),** satisfactory reparation for an offense or injury; that which produces reconciliation (Exod. 30:16). In the Bible it means the covering of man's sins through the shedding of blood; in the OT, the blood of sacrificed animals; in the NT, the blood of man's Redeemer, Jesus Christ.

Atonement, Day of, a Hebrew festival, instituted by Moses, and held on the 10th day of the 7th month, involving abstinence from labor, fasting, penitence and sacrifice for sin. The day marked the only entry of the high priest into the Holy of Holies (Lev. 16).

Augustus Caesar. JHK

Atroth (ăt'rŏth). A town built and fortified by the tribe of Gad, E of Jordan (Num. 32:35).

Attai (ăt'ȧ-ī). 1. Half-Egyptian member of the tribe of Judah (I Chron. 2:35-36).

2. Mighty man of Gad who joined David (1 Chron. 12:11).

3. Younger brother of Abijah (II Chron. 11:20).

Attalia (ăt'ȧ-lī'ȧ), a seaport of Pamphylia near Perga, in S. Asia Minor, mentioned in Acts 14:25.

Attire (See Dress)

Augustus Caesar (ô-gŭs'tŭs sē'zêr). Gaius Octavius, whose male ancestors for four generations had the same name, was born in Rome, Sept. 23 63 B.C. and early became influential through his great-uncle, Julius Caesar. He was studying quietly in Illyria when he heard of Caesar's murder, March 15, 44 B.C. and then, hastening to Italy he learned that Caesar had adopted him and made him his heir. Thus, in his early manhood, by skillful manipulation of his friends he conquered his rival, Antony, at Actium. The beginning of the Roman Empire may be reckoned from this date, Sept. 2, 31 B.C. By his adoption he had become "Caesar," and now, in 31 B.C., the Roman senate added the title "Augustus." Jesus was born during his reign. He reigned till A.D. 14. In the NT, Augustus Caesar is mentioned just once (Luke 2:1).

Aul (ôl), an obsolete variant of awl. A sharp, piercing tool (Exod. 21:6; Deut. 15:17).

Authorized Version (See Bible, Translations of)

Ava (ā′vȧ). A region in Assyria from which Sargon brought men to populate devastated Samaria (II Kings 17: 24).

Aven (ā′vĕn, **vanity**). 1. City of Heliopolis in Egypt (Ezek. 30:17). 2. Places of idolatry in Bethel (Hosea 10:5, 8). 3. Place in Syria dedicated to heathen worship; perhaps Baalbek (Amos 1:5).

Avenger (ȧ-vĕn′jêr). If a man was killed, his nearest of kin was made the avenger of blood (Num. 35:11-34). A distinct difference was made between murder and manslaughter. The same Hebrew word is rendered "kinsman" (Ruth 4:1) and "redeemer" (Job 19: 25).

Avim, Avims, Avites (ā′vĭm, ā′vĭmz, ā′vīts). 1. Ancient inhabitants of Gaza before the time of Moses (Deut. 2:23). 2. A city in the tribe of Benjamin (Josh. 18:23).

Avith (ā′vĭth), capital city of Hadad, the fourth king of Edom (Gen. 36:35).

Awl (See Aul)

Ax, chopping instrument, represented by a number of Heb. and Gr. words (I Kings 6:7; Ps. 74:6; II Sam. 12:31; Jer. 10:3; Matt. 3:10).

Ayin (ā′yēn), "an eye," "a spring or fountain." 1. The 16th letter of the Hebrew alphabet, probably so named because originally in outline an eye. 2. A place on the N boundary line of Palestine (Num. 34:11). 3. A town in Judah near Rimmon (Josh. 15:32; I Chron. 4:32).

Azal (See Azel)

Azaliah (ăz′ȧ-lī′ȧ, probably **Jehovah has set aside,** or **Jehovah has shown himself distinguished),** a son of Meshullam and father of Shaphan the scribe (II Kings 22:3).

Azaniah (ăz′ȧ-nī′ȧ, **Jehovah has set aside,** or **Jehovah has given ear),** a son of Jeshua, a Levite who signed the covenant (Neh. 10:9).

Azareel, Azarael (ȧ-zā′rē-ĕl, **God is helper).** 1. A Levite who entered the army of David at Ziklag (I Chron. 12: 6). 2. A musician in the temple in David's time (I Chron. 25:18). 3. A captain in the service of David (I Chron. 27:22). 4. A man Ezra persuaded to divorce his foreign wife (Ezra 10:41). 5. A priest who lived in Jerusalem after the exile (Neh. 11:13). 6. A musician who played in the procession when the wall was dedicated (Neh. 12:36).

Azarel (Same as Azareel)

Azariah (ăz′ȧ-rī′a, **Jehovah hath helped).** 1. King of Judah. See Uzziah. 2. A man of Judah of the house of Ethan the Wise (I Chron. 2:8). 3. The son of Jehu, descended from an Egyptian through the daughter of Sheshan (I Chron. 2:38). 4. A son of Ahimaaz (I Chron. 6:9). 5. A Levite of the family of Kohath (I Chron. 6:36). 6. A son of Zadok the high priest, under Solomon (I Kings 4:2). 7. A high priest and son of Johanan (I Chron. 6:10). 8. Son of Nathan, an officer at Solomon's court (I Kings 4:5). 9. A prophet, son of Obed, in the reign of King Asa (II Chron. 15:1-8). 10. Two sons of King Jehoshaphat; probably half brothers. 11. A son of Jehoram (II Chron. 22:6, called Ahaziah in verse 1). 12. Son of Jeroham, who helped to overthrow Athaliah (II Chron. 23:1). 13. Son of Johanan who helped in getting the captives of Judah released (II Chron. 28:12). 14. A Levite who assisted in purifying the Temple in Hezekiah's reign (II Chron. 29:12). 15. A high priest who rebuked Uzziah's attempt to assume priestly functions (II Chron. 26:16-20). 16. A son of Hilkiah; a high priest not long before the Exile (I Chron. 6:13, 14). 17. A man of Judah who bitterly opposed Jeremiah (Jer. 43:2). 18. One of the captives taken to Babylon, whose name was changed to Abed-nego (Daniel 1:7). 19. The son of Maaseiah, who helped repair the walls of Jerusalem (Neh. 3:23 f). 20. A Levite who assisted Ezra in explaining the Law (Neh. 8:7). 21. A priest who sealed the covenant (Neh. 10:2). 22. A prince of Judah (Neh. 12:32, 33).

Azaz (ā′zăz, **strong),** a Reubenite, the son of Shema or Shemaiah (I Chron. 5:8).

Azazel (ȧ-zā′zĕl, **KJV, scapegoat).** Word of uncertain meaning found only in Lev. 16:8, 10, 26 in connection with one of the goats chosen for the service of the Day of Atonement. It has been interpreted both personally and impersonally as meaning 1) an evil spirit, 2) removal, 3) devil.

Azaziah (ăz′ȧ-zī′ȧ, **Jehovah is strong).** 1. A harper during the reign of David (I Chron. 15:21). 2. Father of the prince of Ephraim (I Chron. 27:20). 3. A Levite overseer of the Temple (II Chron. 31:13).

Azbuk (ăz′bŭk), father of a Nehemiah (Neh. 3:16).

Azekah (ȧ-zē′kȧ), a town in NW Judah. It is mentioned as a place to which Joshua pursued the kings at the battle of Gibeon (Josh 10:10, 11; Josh. 15:35; I Sam. 17:1; II Chron. 11:9; Jer. 34:7; Neh. 11:30).

Azel (ā′zĕl). 1. A descendant of Jonathan, son of Saul (I Chron. 8:37f.; 9:43 f). 2. A place near Jerusalem (Zech. 14:5).

Azgad (ăz′găd, **Gad is strong,** or **fate is hard),** the ancestral head of a family of postexilic Jews (Ezra 2:12; 8:12; Neh. 7:17; 10:15).

Aziel (ē′zĭ-ĕl, **God is my strength),** a Levite musician (I Chron. 15:20, Jaaziel in verse 18, and Jeiel in 16:5).

Aziza (ȧ-zī′zȧ, **strong),** a man in the time of Ezra who divorced his foreign wife (Ezra 10:27).

Azmaveth (ăz-mā′vĕth, **death is strong).** 1. One of David's heroes (II Sam. 23:31). 2. A Benjamite, one of whose sons followed David (I Chron. 12:3) 3. A man in charge of David's treasures (I Chron. 27:25). 4. A descendant of Jonathan, Saul's son (I Chron. 8:36). 5. A place north of Anathoth to which some exiles returned (Ezra 2:24; Neh. 12:29).

Azmon (ăz′mŏn, **strong),** a town on the south border of Judah (Num. 34:4, 5; Josh. 15:4, RV).

Aznoth - Tabor (ăz′nŏth-tā′bôr, **tavor, the ears,** i.e., slopes of Tabor), a place near Mt. Tabor on the border of Naphtali (Josh. 19:34).

Azor (ā′zôr), a post-exilic ancestor of Christ (Matt. 1:13, 14).

Azotus (See Ashdod)

Azriel (ăz′rĭ-ĕl, **God is help).** 1. A chieftain of the half tribe of Manasseh (I Chron. 5:24). 2. A Naphtalite (I Chron. 27:19). 3. The father of Seraiah (Jer. 36:26).

Azrikam (ăz′rĭ-kăm, **my help has arisen).** 1. A son of Neariah (I Chron. 3:23). 2. A descendant of Saul (I Chron. 8:38; 9:44). 3. A Levite, descended from Merari (I Chron. 9:14). 4. An officer of Ahaz (II Chron. 28:7).

Azubah (ȧ-zū′bȧ, **forsaken).** 1. A wife of Caleb (I Chron. 2:18, 19). 2. The mother of Jehoshaphat (I Kings 22:42).

Azur (See Azzur)

Azzah (See Gaza)

Azzan (ăz′ăn, **strong),** the father of Paltiel (Num. 34:26).

Azzur (ăz′êr, **helped,** in KJV twice **Azur).** 1. Father of Hananiah the false prophet (Jer. 28:1). 2. Father of Jaazaniah (Ezek. 11:1). 3. One of the signers of the covenant in the days of Nehemiah (Neh. 10:17).

–B–

Baal (bā′ăl, **lord, possessor, husband).** 1. Appears in the OT with a variety of meanings: "master" or "owner" (Exod. 21:28, 34; Judg. 19:22), "husband" (Exod. 21:3; II Sam. 11:26). 2. Usually, however, it refers to farm god of the Phoenicians and Canaanites, responsible for crops, flocks, fecund farm families. Each locality had its own Baal. The Baalim were worshiped on high places with lascivious rites, self-torture, and human sacrifice. Altars to Baal were built in Palestine; Jezebel in Israel and Athaliah in Judah championed Baal worship (I Kings 16:31, 32; II Chron. 17:3). 3. Descendant of Reuben (I Chron. 5:5). 4. Benjamite (I Chron. 8:30). 5. In composition it is often the name of a man and not of Baal, e.g. Baal-hanan (I Chron. 1:49).

Baalbek (bāl′bêk, **city of Baal),** a city of Coele-Syria, about 40 miles NW of Damascus, celebrated for its magnificence in the first centuries of the Christian era, and famous since then for its ruins.

Baale of Judah (bā′ăl-jōō′dȧ), a town on the N border of Judah, the same as Baalah and Kiriath-baal and Kiriath-jearim (II Sam. 6:2; I Chron. 13:6).

Baal-Gad (bā′ăl-găd, **Gad is Baal),** a place in the valley of Lebanon, at the foot of Mount Hermon (Josh. 11:17; 12:7; 13:5). Its site is uncertain.

Baal-Hamon (bā′ăl-hā′mŏn, **Baal of Hamon**), a place where Solomon had a vineyard (S. of Sol. 8:11). Its location is unknown.

Baal-Hanan (bā′ăl-hā′năn, **Baal is gracious**), 1. The son of Achbor and king of Edom (Gen. 36:38; I Chron. 1:49). 2. An official under David (I Chron. 27:28).

Baal-Hazor (bā′ăl-hā′zôr, **Baal of Hazor),** where Absalom had a sheep-range and where he brought about the death of Amnon in revenge for the outrage upon his sister (II Sam. 13: 23).

Baal-Hermon (bā′ăl-hûr′mŏn, **Baal of Hermon**), a town or place near Mt. Hermon (Judg. 3:3; I Chron. 5:23).

Baali (bā′ă-lī, **my lord, my master).** The common name for all local gods, as well as "Jehovah." Hosea demands that this degradation cease and that Jehovah be no longer called "my Baal," but "Ishi" (my husband) (Hos. 2:16). The Israelites later abandoned the use of "Baal" for "Jehovah."

Baalis (bā′ȧ-lĭs), a king of the Ammonites.

Baal-Meon (bā′ăl-mē′ŏn, **Baal of Meon**), an old city on the frontiers of Moab.

Baal-Peor (bā′ăl-pē′ôr, **Baal of Peor),** a Moabite deity, probably Chemosh, the national deity of the Moabites.

Baal-Perazim (bā′ăl-pē-rā′zĭm, **Baal of the breaking through**), a place near the valley of Rephaim where David obtained a great victory over the Philistines (II Sam. 5:18-20; I Chron. 14:9-11).

Baal-Shalisha (bā′ăl-shăl′ĭ-shȧ, **Baal of Shalisha**), a place in Ephraim from which bread and corn were brought to Elisha at Gilgal (II Kings 4:42-44).

Baal-Tamar (bā′ăl-tā′mȧr, **Baal of the palm tree**), a place in Benjamin, near Gibeah and Bethel (Judg. 20:33).

Baal-Zebub (bā′ăl-zē′bŭb, **Baal,** or **lord of flies),** name under which Baal was worshiped by the Philistines of Ekron (II Kings 1:2, 3, 6, 16). Ahaziah consulted him to find out whether he should recover from his illness, and was therefore rebuked by Elijah. There can be little doubt that Beelzebub is the same name as Baalzebub. The Greek text, however, has Beelzebul. Just how these changes in spelling took place is a matter of conjecture. Beelzebub is the prince of the demons (Matt. 10:25; 12:24; Mark 3: 22; Luke 11:15, 18, 19). Jesus identifies him with Satan (Matt. 12:26; Mark 3:23; Luke 11:18). Beelzebul signifies "lord of the dwelling"; this is pertinent to the argument in Matthew 10:25; 12:29; Mark 3:27.

Baal-Zephon (bā′ăl-zē′fŏn, **lord of the north**), a place near which the Israelites encamped just before they crossed the Red Sea (Exod. 14:2, 9; Num. 33: 7). The site is unknown.

Baana (bā′ȧ-nȧ, **son of oppression).** 1. Two officers in the service of Solomon (I Kings 4:12; 4:16; A. V. "Baanah"). 2. The father of Zadok, one of those who helped in rebuilding the wall in Nehemiah's time (Neh. 3:4).

Baanah (bā′ȧ-nȧ, **son of oppression).** 1. A captain in the army of Ish-bosheth who with his brother murdered Ish-bosheth (II Sam. 4). 2. The father of Heleb, one of David's warriors (II Sam. 23:29; I Chron. 11:30). 3. A Jew who returned from Babylon with

Zerubbabel (Ezra 2:2; Neh. 7:7; 10:27).

Baara (bā'ȧ-rȧ, **the burning one**), a wife of Shaharaim, a Benjamite (I Chron. 8:8).

Baaseiah (bā'ȧ-sē'yȧ, **the Lord is bold**), an ancestor of Asaph, the musician (I Chron. 6:40).

Baasha (bā'ȧ-shȧ, **boldness**), the son of Ahijah, of the tribe of Issachar. He became the third king of Israel by assassinating Nadab, the son of Jeroboam. He ascended the throne in the third year of Asa, king of Judah (I Kings 15, 16) and carried on a long war with him. Baasha continued the calf worship begun by Jeroboam, and the Prophet Jehu threatened him and his house with a worse fate than Jeroboam's. After a reign of 24 years he died a natural death and was succeeded by his son, Elah, who was killed, along with every member of the house of Baasha, by Zimri (I Kings 15, 16).

Babel, Tower of (bā'bêl, **gate of God**), an expression is not found in the OT, but used popularly for the structure built in the plain of Shinar, as the story is told in Genesis 11:1-9.

Babylon (băb'ĭ-lŏn, Greek form of "Babel"; name of city and country of which it was the capital. First mentioned in Gen. 10:10; Hammurabi became ruler in 18th cent.; reached height of power under Nebuchadnezzar II (605-562 B.C.); conquered by Cyrus of Persia, 539 B.C.; often mentioned in prophecy (Isa. 13:1, 19; 14:22; 21; 46; 47; Jer. 50; 51), famous for hanging gardens, temples, palace; ruins remain. In NT the symbol of opposition to God (I Pet. 5:13; Rev. 14:8).

Among the ruins of the great palaces of Babylon. © MPS

Although remaining as an inhabited site, Babylon declined still further in importance under the Parthians (c. 125 B.C.), and was last mentioned on a Babylonian clay tablet dated about 10 B.C. At the present time the Baghdad to Bassorah railway line passes within a few yards of the mound that was once the most splendid city of the world.

Baca (bā'kȧ, **balsam tree**), in KJV in Psalm 84:6, where RV has "the Valley of weeping," with a marginal variant, "the valley of the balsam-trees." The tree is called a weeper probably because it exudes tears of gum. The phrase refers figuratively to an experience of sorrow turned into joy.

Bachrites (băk'rīts), a family of Ephraim, called Becherites in ASV, RSV (Num. 26:35), descendants of Becher (called Bered in I Chron. 7:20).

Badger (See Animals)

Ruins of the so-called Tower of Babel at Birs-Nimrud in Babylonia. © MPS

Bag, sack or pouch made for holding anything. Many kinds are mentioned in Scripture (Deut. 25:13; II Kings 5:23; Matt. 10:10 "scrip").

Bahurim (bȧ-hū′rĭm, a place in Benjamin which lay on the road from Jerusalem to Jericho, not far from the Mount of Olives. It is frequently mentioned in the history of David.

Bajith (bā′jĭth, **house),** found only in Isaiah 15:2. **Bayith** may be textual error for **bath,** "daughter."

Bakbakkar (băk-băk′êr, **investigator),** a Levite (I Chron. 9:15).

Bakbuk (băk-bŭk, **bottle),** the founder of a family of Nethinim who returned from the Captivity with Zerubbabel (Ezra 2:51; Neh. 7:53).

Bakbukiah (băk′bū-kī′ȧ, **flask,** or perhaps, **the Lord pours out**), a name occuring three times in Nehemiah (11:17; 12:9, 25), a Levite in high office in Jerusalem right after the Exile.

Baker (See Occupations and Professions)

Balaam (bā′lăm, perhaps **devourer),** son of Beor from Pethor on the Euphrates (Deut. 23:4), a diviner employed by king Balak to curse Israel, but God caused him to bless instead (Num. 22-24); tried to turn Israelites from Jehovah (Num. 31), and was killed by them. In NT he is held up as an example of the pernicious influence of hypocritical teachers who attempt to lead God's people astray (Jude 11; II Peter 2:15).

Balah (bā′lȧ), a town in SW Palestine (Josh. 19:3), Bilhah in I Chronicles 4:29.

Balak (bā′lăk, **devastator),** a king of Moab in Moses' day who hired Balaam to pronounce a curse on the Israelites (Num. 22-24; Judg. 11:25; Micah 6:5; Rev. 2:14). Instead of cursings, he heard blessings; but he achieved his end in an indirect way when he followed Balaam's advice to seduce men of Israel to idolatry.

Balance (băl′ăns), "having two scales." The balances of the Hebrews consisted of a horizontal bar, either suspended from a cord that was held in the hand, or pivoted on a perpendicular rod. Weighing with such balances could be accurately done, but the system was liable to fraud, so that in the OT there is much denunciation of "wicked balances" (Micah 6:11).

Bald Locust (See Insects)

Baldness (bôld′nĕs). Natural baldness is seldom mentioned in the Bible. It was believed to result from hard work (Ezek. 29:18) or disease (Isa. 3:17, 24). Baldness produced by shaving the head, however, is frequently referred to and forbidden. It was done as a mark of mourning for the dead (Lev. 21:5; Isa. 15:2; 22:12; Micah 1:16). When a Nazarite completed his vow, the shaven hair was offered as a sacrifice to Jehovah (Num. 6:18; cf. Acts 18:18; 21:24).

Balm (bȧm, an odoriferous resin (Gen. 37:25; Jer. 8:22; 46:11) used as an ointment for healing wounds (Jer. 51:8).

Bamah (bȧ′mȧ, **high place).** Ezekiel (Ezek. 20:29) plays upon two syllables **ba** (go) and **mah** (what), with evident contempt for the high place to which the word refers.

Bamoth-Baal (bā′mŏth-bā′ăl, **high places of Baal**), a place N of the Arnon, to which Balak took Balaam (Num. 21:19; 22:41).

Band. That which holds together or binds, and a company of men. Both meanings are found in Scripture. In the NT reference is made to the "Italian Band," a cohort of Roman soldiers stationed at Caesarea (Acts 10:1), and the "Augustan Band," a cohort to which the Roman centurion Julius, who had charge of Paul on his voyage to Rome, belonged (Acts 27:1).

Bani (bā′nī, **posterity).** 1. A Gadite, one of David's heroes (II Sam. 23:36). 2. A Levite of David's time (I Chron. 6:46). 3. A descendant of Judah whose son lived in Jerusalem after the Captivity (I Chron. 9:4). 4. A Levite and builder (Neh. 3:17). 5. A Levite (Neh. 9:4). 6. A Levite who lived before the return from exile (Neh. 11:22). 7. A Levite who sealed the covenant (Neh. 10:13). 8. A leader who also signed the covenant (Neh. 10:14). 9. Founder of a family some of whom returned from Babylonia with Zerubbabel (Ezra 2:10). Some took foreign wives (Ezra 10:29). 10. Founder of a house (Ezra 10:34), a descendant of whom was also named Bani (Ezra 10:38).

Bank (băngk). Banking of a primitive kind was known in ancient times, among both Jews and Gentiles. Money was received on deposit, loaned out, exchanged for smaller denominations or for foreign money. Israelites could not charge each other interest (Exod. 22:25), but could lend on interest to Gentiles (Deut. 23:20).

Banner (băn′êr, **ensign, standard).** Used in ancient times for military, national, and ecclesiastical purposes much as they are today. The word occurs frequently in the figurative sense of a rallying point for God's people (Isa. 5:26; 11:10; Jer. 4:21).

Banquet (băng'kwĕt). The Hebrews were very fond of social feasting. There were three great religious feasts. Sacrifices were accompanied by a feast (Exod. 34:15; Judg. 16:23-25). There were feasts on birthdays (Gen. 40:20; Job 1:4; Matt. 14:6), marriages (Gen. 29:22; Matt. 22:2), funerals (II Sam. 3:35; Jer. 16:7), laying of foundations (Prov. 9:1-5), vintage (Judg. 9:27), sheep-shearing (I Sam. 25:2, 36), and on other occasions. At a large banquet a second invitation was often sent on the day of the feast, or a servant brought the guests to the feast (Luke 14:17; Matt. 22:2ff). The host provided robes for the guests, and they were worn in his honor and were a token of his regard. Guests were welcomed by the host with a kiss (Luke 7:45), and their feet were washed (Gen. 18:4; Judg. 19:21; Luke 7:44). A great banquet sometimes lasted seven days, but excess in eating and drinking was condemned by the sacred writers (Eccl. 10:16f; Isa. 5:11f).

Baptism (băp'tĭzm). The word **baptizo** in Jewish usage first appears in the Mosaic laws of purification (Exod. 30:17-21; Lev. 11:25), where it means washing or cleansing. Jews baptized proselytes. John's baptism was connected with repentance so that Jews might be spiritually prepared to recognize and receive the Messiah, and it differed from the baptism of Jesus (Luke 3:16; John 1:26). Christian baptism symbolizes union with Christ (Gal. 3:26, 27), remission of sins (Acts 2:38), identification with Christ in His death to sin and resurrection to new life (Rom. 6:3-5), and becoming a member of the body of Christ (I Cor. 12:13). The blessings of baptism are received by faith (Rom. 6:8-11).

Bar- (bȧr), an Aramaic word meaning "son." In the NT it is used as a prefix to the names of persons, e.g., Bar-Jonah, "son of Jonah" (Matt. 16:17), etc.

Barabbas (bȧr-ăb'ăs, **son of the father,** or **teacher**), a criminal chosen by the Jerusalem mob, at the instigation of the chief priests, in preference to Christ, to be released by Pilate on the feast of the Passover. Matthew calls him a notorious prisoner, and the other evangelists say he was arrested with others for robbery, sedition and murder (Matt. 27:16; Mark 15:15; Luke 23:18; John 18:40).

A baptism scene at the River Jordan. © MPS

Barachel (băr'ȧ-kĕl, **God blesses),** a Buzite, whose son Elihu was the last of Job's friends to reason with him (Job 32:2, 6).

Barachias (băr'ȧ-kī'ăs), the father of Zachariah, who was slain between the Temple and the altar (Matt. 23:35).

Barak (bâr'ăk, **lightning).** He was summoned by Deborah the judge and prophetess to lead the Israelites to war against the Canaanites under the leadership of Sisera, the commander in chief of Jaban, king of Canaan. The army of Israel routed Jabin. Sisera abandoned his chariot and ran away on foot. Barak pursued him and found him slain by Jael in her tent. A peace of 40 years was secured (Judg. 4, 5). In Hebrews 11:32 Barak's name appears among those who achieved great things through faith.

Barbarian (bȧr-bâr'ĭ-ăn). Originally anyone who did not speak Greek (Rom. 1:14); later, one who was not a part of the Graeco-Roman culture (Col. 3:11).

Barber (See Occupations and Professions)

Bar-Jesus (bȧr'jē'sŭs, **son of Jesus),** a Jewish magician and false prophet in the court of Sergius Paulus, struck blind for interfering with Paul's work (Acts 13:6-12).

Bar-Jona (bȧr'jō'nȧ, probably **son of Jonah**, or **son of John**), a surname of the Apostle Peter (Matt. 16:17).

Barkos (bȧr'kŏs), founder of a family that returned with Zerubbabel to Jerusalem (Ezra 2:53; Neh. 7:55).

Barley (See Plants)

Barnabas (bår′nȧ-băs, **son of exhortation** or **consolation**), Levite from Cyprus (Acts 4:36); early friend and co-worker of Paul (Acts 9:27); worked with Paul at Antioch (Acts 11:22-26) and on Paul's 1st missionary journey (Acts 13-14); went to Jerusalem council with Paul (Acts 15); left Paul because he would not take Mark on 2nd missionary journey (Acts 15:36-41). Paul speaks highly of him in epistles (I Cor. 9:6; Gal. 2:1, 9, 13; Col. 4:10).

Barrel (băr′el). A large earthenware water jar.

Barsabas (bår-săb′ăs, **son of Sabbas,** or perhaps, **son of,** i.e., **born on, the Sabbath**). 1. The surname of the Joseph who with Matthias was nominated by the apostles as the successor of Judas (Acts 1:23). 2. The surname of Judas, a prophet of the Jerusalem church, sent with Silas to Antioch with the decree of the Jerusalem council (Acts 15:22).

Bartholomew (bår-thŏl′ŏ-mū, **son of Tolmai** or **Talmai,** one of the twelve apostles. He is mentioned in all four of the lists of the apostles in the NT (Mark 3:18; Matt. 10:3; Luke 6:14; Acts 1:13). There is no further reference to him in the NT.

Bartimaeus (bår′tĭ-mē′ŭs, **son of Timaeus**), a blind man healed by Jesus as He went out from Jericho on His way to Jerusalem shortly before Passion Week. A similar account is given by Luke (18:35-43), except that the miracle occurred as Jesus drew near to Jericho, and the blind man's name is not given. Matthew (20:29-34) tells of Jesus healing **two** blind men on the way out of Jericho.

Baruch (bâr′ŭk, **blessed).** 1. Son of Neriah and brother of Seraiah (Jer. 36:32). The trusted friend (Jer. 32:12) and amanuensis (Jer. 36:4ff) of the prophet Jeremiah. A man of unusual acquirements, he might have risen to a high position if he had not thrown in his lot with Jeremiah (Jer. 45:5). Jeremiah dictated his prophecies to Baruch, who read them to the people (Jer. 36). In the reign of Zedekiah, during the final siege of Jerusalem, Jeremiah bought his ancestral estate in Anathoth, and since he was at that time a prisoner, placed the deed in Baruch's hands, and testified that Israel would again possess the land (Jer. 32). The high regard in which Baruch was held is shown by the large number of spurious writings that were attributed to him, among them **The Apocalypse of Baruch,** the **Book of Baruch;** the **Rest of the Words of Baruch;** the **Gnostic Book of Baruch,** and others. 2. A man who helped Nehemiah in rebuilding the walls of Jerusalem (Neh. 3:20). 3. A priest who signed the covenant with Nehemiah (Neh. 10:6). 4. The son of Colhozeh, a descendant of Perez (Neh. 11:5).

Baruch, Book of, one of the Apocryphal books, standing between Jeremiah and Lamentations in the LXX. It is based on the tradition which represents Baruch, the son of Neriah, as spending his last years in Babylon. Although some modern Roman Catholic scholars hold that it is the work of Jeremiah's friend and amanuensis, the book in its present form is usually thought to belong to the latter half of the first century of our era.

Barzillai (bår-zĭl′ā-ī, **made of iron).** 1. A wealthy Gileadite of Rogelim, E of the Jordan, who brought provisions to David and his army when the king fled from Absalom (II Sam. 17:27-29). David before his death charged Solomon to "show kindness unto the sons of Barzillai" (I Kings 2:7). 2. One of the returning exiles living in Ezra's time (Ezra 2:61, 62). 3. A Meholathite, whose son Adriel married Saul's daughter, either Michal (II Sam. 21:8) or Merab (I Sam. 18:19).

Basemath (băs′ĕ-măth, **fragrant),** see Bashemath.

Bashan (bā′shăn, **smooth, fertile land),** the broad, fertile region E of the Sea of Galilee. In the days of Abraham it was occupied by a people called the Rephaim (Gen. 14:5). The Nabataens held it in the second century B.C. It was included in the kingdom of Herod the Great, and then belonged to Philip, Herod's son.

Bashan-havoth-jair (bā′shăn-hă′vŏth-jā′ĭr, **encampments of Jair in Bashan),** a group of 60 unwalled towns in the NW part of Bashan (Deut. 3:14).

Bashemath (băsh′ĕ-măth, **fragrant,** "Basemath" in RV). 1. One of Esau's wives (Gen. 26:34). She is called Adah in the genealogy of Edom (Gen. 36: 2, 3). 2. Ishmael's daughter and sister of Nebaioth, the last of Esau's three wives, according to the genealogy in Genesis 36:3, 4, 13, 17. In Genesis 28:9 she is called Mahalath. 3. Solomon's daughter, married to Ahimaaz, Solomon's tax collector for Naphtali (I Kings 4:15).

Basin (bā′sĭn, the ARV has "basin," the KJV and ERV "bason"), a wide hollow vessel for holding water for washing and other purposes (John

13:5). 1. Also a small vessel used for wine and other liquids (Exod. 24:6). 2. A shallow vessel used to receive the blood of sacrifices in the Temple (Exod. 12:22) and for domestic purposes. 3. A large bowl used in the Temple for various purposes, especially at the great altar (Zech. 9:15).

Basket (băs′ket), four kinds of baskets mentioned in the OT. Made of various materials — leaves, reeds, rushes, twigs, or ropes, they had various shapes and sizes. Some were small enough to be carried in the hands; others had to be carried on the shoulder or head or borne upon a pole between two men. Used for a variety of purposes: carrying fruit (Deut. 26:2); carrying bread, cake, and flesh (Gen. 40: 17; Exod. 29:2, 3); carrying clay to make bricks, and earth for embankments (Ps. 81:6). In the NT two kinds of baskets are referred to. The **kóphinos** (Matt. 14:20; Mark 6:43; John 6:13) was a relatively small basket that could be carried on the back to hold provisions. Twelve of these baskets were used to gather the food that remained after the feeding of the 5,000. The **spuris** was considerably larger, as we may be sure from its being used in letting Paul down from the wall at Damascus (Acts 9:25). Seven of these were used to gather the food that was left after the feeding of the 4,000 (Matt. 16:9, 10).

Basmath (băs′măth), in the KJV, with this spelling, appears only in I Kings 4:15. Elsewhere it is spelled Bashemath. See Bashemath.

Bastard (băs′têrd, specifically, **child of incest),** appears only three times in Scripture, twice in the OT, once in the NT. In Deut. 23:2 it probably means a "child of incest," not simply an illegitimate child. Such were excluded from the assembly of the Lord. Zech. 9:6, "And a bastard shall dwell in Ashdod." The RVm has "a bastard race." Brown, Driver, and Briggs suggest this means a "mixed population." In Hebrews 12:8 the word is used in its proper sense of "born out of wedlock." Bastards had no claim to paternal care or the usual privileges and discipline of legitimate children.

Bat (See Animals)

Bath (See Weights and Measures)

Bath, Bathing, Bathe. The average Hebrew had neither the water nor the inclination for bathing. In most cases where "bathe" occurs in the KJV, partial washing is meant. Bathing in the Bible stands chiefly for ritual acts — purification from ceremonial defilement because of contact with the dead, defiled persons or things, or things under the ban. Priests washed their hands and feet before entering the sanctuary or making an offering on the altar (Exod. 30:19-21). The high priest bathed on the day of the atonement before each act of expiation (Lev. 16:4, 24). In the time of Christ, the Jews washed their hands before eating (Mark 7:3, 4).

Bathrabbim (băth′răb′ĭm, **daughter of multitudes**), the name of a gate of Heshbon (S. of Sol. 7:4). Near it were two pools which are compared to the Shulammite's eyes.

Bath-sheba (băth-shē′bȧ, **daughter of Sheba**). The wife of Uriah the Hittite, a soldier in David's army, during whose absence in the wars David forced her to commit adultery with him (II Sam. 11). Uriah was then treacherously killed by the order of David (II Sam. 11:6ff). She became David's wife and lived with him in the palace. Four sons, including Solomon, were the result of this marriage (II Sam. 5:14; I Chron. 3:5), after the first child had died (II Sam. 12:14ff). Her sons Nathan and Solomon were both ancestors of Jesus Christ (Matt. 1:6; Luke 3:31).

Bath-shua (băth′shōōȧ, **daughter of opulence,** or **daughter of Shua).** 1. In Genesis 38:2 and I Chronicles 2:3, where the name is translated "Shua's daughter." 2. In I Chronicles 3:5, the mother of Solomon, probably a scribal error for Bath-sheba.

Battering Ram (See War, Warfare)

Battle. In ancient times a trumpet-signal by the commander opened each battle (Judg. 7:18). Priests accompanied the army into war to ascertain the Divine will (I Sam. 14:8ff; Judg. 6:36ff). To make Jehovah's help in battle more certain, the Ark was taken along. Military science was relatively simple. A force was usually divided into two attacking divisions, the one in the rear serving as a reserve or as a means of escape for the leader, in case of defeat. Spearmen probably formed the first line, bowmen or archers the second, and slingers the third. Horses and chariots were not used by Israel until quite late. Most of the fighting was done by footmen. Sometimes the battle was preceded by duels between individuals, and these on occasions determined the outcome

The traditional Mount of Beatitudes (Hattin), probably the scene of the Sermon on the Mount. © MPS

of the battle (I Sam. 17:3ff; II Sam. 2:14ff).

Battle-Ax (See Arms and Armor)

Battle-Bow (See Arms and Armor)

Battlement, a parapet surmounting ancient fortified buildings and city walls. From the openings, stones, lances, and arrows were hurled upon attacking soldiers below. In Deuteronomy 22:8 we read that battlements should be provided for the roofs of houses to keep people from falling from them.

Bavai (băv′ā-ī), a man who helped in the rebuilding of the wall of Jerusalem (Neh. 3:18).

Baytree (See Plants)

Bazlith (băz′lĭth, **stripping),** the ancestor of a family of Nethinim (Ezra 2:52; Neh. 7:54).

Bazluth (băz′lŭth), the same as Bazlith, see above. Spelled Bazluth in Ezra 2:52 and Bazlith in Nehemiah 7:54.

Bdellium (dĕl′ĭ-ŭm), a substance variously taken to be a gum or resin, a precious stone, or a pearl.

Bealiah (bē′ȧ-lī′ȧ, **Jehovah is Lord),** a Benjamite soldier who joined David at Ziklag (I Chron. 12:5).

Bealoth (bē′ȧ-lŏth). 1. A town in Judah (Josh. 15:24). 2. A locality in north Israel (I Kings 4:16, Aloth KJV).

Beam (bēm), used in the OT to refer to beams used in constructing the upper floors and roofs of buildings (I Kings 7:3) and to the beam of a weaver's loom (Judg. 16:14). Jesus uses the term in a figurative sense in Matthew 7:3 and Luke 6:41.

Bean (See Plants)

Bear (See Animals)

Beard (bērd), a badge of manly dignity. As a sign of mourning, it was the custom to pluck it out or cut it off. The Israelites were forbidden to shave off the corners of their beards, probably because it was regarded as a heathenish sign (Lev. 19:27).

Beast (bēst). 1. A mammal, not man, distinguished from birds and fishes, and sometimes also from reptiles (Gen. 1:29, 30). 2. A wild, as distinguished from a domesticated animal (Lev. 26:22; Isa. 13:21, 22; 34:14; Mark 1:13). 3. Any of the inferior animals, as distinguished from man (Ps. 147:9; Eccl. 3:19; Acts 28:5). 4. An Apocalyptic symbol of brute force — sensual, lawless, and God-opposing.

Beatitudes (bé-ăt′ĭ-tūds, **blessedness),** a word not found in the English Bible, but meaning either (1) the joys of heaven, or (2) a declaration of blessedness. Beatitudes occur frequently in the OT (Pss. 32:1, 2; 41:1). The Gospels contain isolated beatitudes by Christ (Matt. 11:6; 13:16; John 20:29), but the word is most commonly used of those in Matt. 5:3-11 and Luke 6:20-22, which set forth the qualities that should characterize His disciples.

Bebai (bē′bā-ī). 1. Ancestor of a family that returned from the captivity (Ezra 2:11; 8:11; Neh. 7:16; 10:15). 2. One of this family.

Becher (bē′kêr, **first born,** or **young camel).** 1. Second son of Benjamin (Gen. 46:21; I Chron. 7:6). 2. A son of Ephraim, and founder of a family (Num. 26: 35, Bachrites in KJV). But in I Chronicles 7:20 we read "Bered," which may be the correct form.

Bechorath (bē-kō′răth, **the first birth),** an ancestor of Saul of the tribe of Benjamin (I Sam. 9:1).

Bed. In ancient times the poor generally slept on the ground, their outer garment serving as both mattress and blanket. Sometimes a rug or a mat was used as a bed. Bedsteads were early known (Deut. 3:11); and the wealthy had elaborate beds (Amos 6:4; Esther 1:6).

Bedad (bē′dăd, **alone),** the father of

Beersheba, near the southern boundary of Judah. © MPS

Hadad, king of Edom (Gen. 36:35; I Chron. 1:46).

Bedan (bē′dăn, perhaps **son of judgment**). 1. A Hebrew judge who is mentioned as a deliverer of the nation (I Sam. 12:11). 2. A son of Ulam of the house of Manasseh (I Chron. 7:17).

Bedeiah (bē-dē′yȧ, **servant of Jehovah**), a son of Bani who had taken a foreign wife (Ezra 10:35).

Bee (See Insects)

Beeliada (bē′ē-lī′ȧ-dȧ, **the Lord knows**), a son of King David (I Chron. 14:7); called Eliada in II Samuel 5:16 and I Chronicles 3:8.

Beelzebub (See Baalzebub)

Beelzebul (See Baalzebub)

Beer (bē′êr, **a well**). **1.** Encampment of Israel (Num. 21:16; Isa. 15:8). 2. Place to which Jotham fled (Judg. 9:21).

Beera (bē-ê′rȧ, **a well**), a descendant of Asher (I Chron. 7:37).

Beerah (bē-ê′rȧ, **a well**), a Reubenite prince whom Tiglath-pileser carried away captive (I Chron. 5:6).

Bedtime in a Palestinian home of Bible times. © SPF

Beer-elim (bē′êr-ē′lĭm, **well of Elim**), a village of Moab (Isa. 15:8). See Beer 1.

Beeri (bē-ê′rī, **belonging to the well**). 1. A Hittite, father of Judith, one of Esau's wives (Gen. 26:34). 2. The father of the prophet Hosea (Hos. 1:1).

Beer-la-hai-roi (bē′êr-lȧ-hī′roi, **the well of the living one who sees me**), a well, probably near Kadesh, where the Lord appeared to Hagar (Gen. 16:7, 14) and where Isaac lived for some time (Gen. 24:62; 25:11).

Beeroth (bē-ē′rŏth, **wells**), a Canaanite town whose inhabitants succeeded in deceiving Israel by making a covenant with them (Josh 9:3 ff). When the deceit was discovered, they were made slaves by the Israelites (Josh. 9).

Beersheba (bē′êr-shē′bȧ, **well of seven**, or **the seventh well**).

Location: The most southerly town in the kingdom of Judah; hence, its practical boundary line. The familiar expression "from Dan to Beersheba" is employed to designate the northern and southern extremities of the nation of Israel (II Sam. 3:10; 17:11; 24:2, et. al).

The religious and historical background: Hagar wandered in the wilderness of Beersheba as she fled from before her mistress, Sarah (Gen. 21:14). Abraham made the covenant with the Philistine princess here (Gen. 21:32) and made this his residence after the "offering up" of Isaac (Gen. 22:19). God appeared here to Jacob on his way down into Egypt to be reunited to his son Joseph (Gen. 46:1). Elijah, the prophet, sought refuge in Beersheba from wicked Queen Jezebel (I Kings 19:3). The prophet Amos was constrained to rebuke the idolatrous tendencies which he saw infiltrating into the religious life of Beersheba from Bethel and from Dan (Amos 8:14). The modern name of Beersheba is Bir Es Seba.

Beetle (See Insects)

Beggar (bĕg′ȧr). Professional beggars were unknown in Mosaic times, since the law made ample provision for the poor. Later it became more prevalent; and in the NT beggars appear more frequently (Mark 10:46-52; Luke 16: 19-31; John 9:8, 9; Acts 3:1-11).

Behemoth (See Animals)

Bekah (See Weights & Measures)

Bel (Bāl), the Baal of the Babylonians (Isaiah 46:1; Jeremiah 50:2; 51:44. See Baal).

Bela (bē′lȧ, **destruction),** a neighboring city of Sodom and Gomorrah, in the vicinity of the Dead Sea (Gen. 19: 23-30), later known as Zoar. According to Deuteronomy 34:3, Moses is said to have viewed the southern sector of the Promised Land from Jericho, the city of palm trees, unto Zoar. For all practical purposes this places its situation at the S end of the Dead Sea.

Belah (bē′lȧ). 1. The son of Beor, an Edomite king, previous to the kings of Israel (Gen. 36:32 ff; I Chron. 1:43). 2. First-born son of Benjamin (I Chron. 7:6; 8:1). Head of the family of the Belaites (Num. 26:40). 3. Son of Azaz, a Reubenite, an exceptionally wealthy man (I Chron. 5:8, 9).

Belial (bē′lĭ-ăl), not a proper noun in the OT, but a word meaning "worthlessness," "wickedness," "lawlessness" (Deut. 13:13; Judg. 19:22; I Sam. 25: 25). Personified in II Cor. 6:15.

Bell. Attached to the hem of the sacerdotal robes worn by Aaron and his descendants as they performed priestly service in the Tabernacle (Exodus 28: 33-35; 39:35). The bell was not used in Biblical times for the purpose of religious convocation as today. The use of the bell to summon the worshipers is a distinctively Christian practice dating back to the end of the fourth century, A.D.

Bellows (bĕl′ōs), device made of skins for blowing fire (Jer. 6:29).

Belshazzar (bĕl-shăz′ȧr, **may Bel protect the king),** son of Nabonidus, grandson of Nebuchadnezzar, last king of the Neo-Babylonian Empire. During a drunken feast Daniel told him that God had found him wanting; and shortly thereafter Babylon fell to the Medo-Persians and Belshazzar was slain (Dan. 5:1-30).

Belteshazzar (bĕl′tē-shăz-ȧr, **may Bel protect his life).** The name given to the Hebrew Prophet Daniel by Nebuchadnezzar's steward (Dan. 1:7; 2:26; 4:8; 5:12). Not to be confused with Belshazzar (Dan 5:1 ff).

Ben. 1. In Semite usage, a term employed to designate a male descendant. Also employed in connection with a clan; in plural only, as in the children of (sons of) Israel; children of (sons of) Ammon, etc. Also used in prefixes of proper names, as BENjamin, BENhadad, etc. Likewise connotes a class, as "Sons of the prophets" (II Kings 2:15). 2. A Levite appointed by David to serve in a musical capacity before the Ark of the Lord (I Chron. 15:18).

Benaiah (bē-nā′yȧ, **Jehovah has built),** the son of Jehoiada, the priest (I Chron. 27:5). Appointed over David's personal body-guard, the Cherethites and the Pelethites (I Kings 1:38). A man of exceptional prowess and bravery.

Some 12 men bear this designation. 1. One of David's ('valiant 30," the Pirathonite, tribe of Ephraim (II Sam. 23:30). 2. A prince from the tribe of Simeon, who drove out the Amalekites (I Chron. 4:39 f). 3. A Levite who played with the psaltery "upon alamoth" at the return of the Ark to Jerusalem (I Chron. 15:18). 4. A priest appointed to blow the trumpet upon the same occasion (I Chron. 15:24). 5. Ancestor of Jahaziel the prophet who prophesied for Moab and Ammon in the days of Jehoshaphat (II Chron. 20: 14). 6. One of the overseers for the offerings in the Temple in the days of Hezekiah (II Chron. 31:13). 7. A man who had taken a foreign wife in the time of Ezra (Ezra 10:25). Four different men are called Benaiah in Ezra (Ezra 10:25, 30, 35, 43). 8. Father of Pelatiah who died as a judgment for teaching falsity in the days of Ezekiel (Ezek. 11:13).

Ben-Ammi (bĕn′ăm′ī, **son of my people),** son of the younger daughter of Lot (Gen. 19:38) whom she conceived through her own father following the destruction of Sodom. The progenitor of the Ammonites. Moab shares a like origin through the older sister (Gen. 19:37).

Bene-berak (bĕn′ĕ-bē′răk, **sons of lightning),** a town allotted to the tribe of Dan (Josh. 19:45).

Bene-Jaakan (bĕn′ē-jā′ȧ′kăn), a desert encampment of the Israelites on their journey, placed immediately before Mosera, the site of Aaron's demise in Deuteronomy 10:6.

Benevolence, Due (bĕn-ĕv′ō-lĕns), so rendered by the KJV, I Corinthians 7:3. Paul uses it to refer to obligation in the marriage bed. A euphemism for sex relations.

Benhadad (bĕn-hā′dăd), the name is titular, as opposed to a proper name (like Pharaoh) for Syrian rulers. Benhadad I was a contemporary with Asa, king of Judah (I Kings 15:18). It is plausible that he is to be identified with Rezon, the founder of the kingdom of Damascus (I Kings 11:23-25). Asa was sternly reprimanded for his unfortunate alliance with Benhadad I (II Chron. 16:7 ff).

Benhadad II was in all probability the son of Benhadad I. He is the Hadadezer of the monuments, contemporary with Ahab of Israel, against whom he waged war, laying siege to the newly constructed capital, Samaria. Ahab refused to capitulate. With divine aid, he was able utterly to rout the Syrian army at the battle of Aphek (I Kings 20:26 ff). He spared the life of Benhadad, thus never fully realizing the victory which otherwise would have been his.

Benhadad III was son of the usurper Hazael, hence not in direct line. A contemporary of Amaziah, king of Judah, and Jehoahaz of Israel, he reduced the fighting personnel of the nation till it was like the dust of the threshing (II Kings 13:7). God raised up to Israel a deliverer, most likely Ramman-Mirari III, as shown from an inscription. Joash was able to defeat Benhadad on three different occasions and to recover the cities of Israel (II Kings 13:25).

Benhail (bĕn′hā′ĭl, **son of strength),** one of the princes sent out by Jehoshaphat on a "teaching-mission" to the cities of Judah (II Chron. 17:7).

Ben-Hanan (bĕn′hā′năn, **son of grace),** a son of Shimon of the tribe of Judah (I Chron. 4:20).

Beninu (bĕ-nī′nū, **our son),** a Levite in post-exilic days, one of the co-signers of the covenant with Nehemiah (Neh. 10:13).

Benjamin (Bĕn′jȧ-mĭn, **son of my right hand,** Gen. 35:17ff), the youngest son of the patriarch Jacob whom his wife Rachel bore to him in her dying agony; named Benoni ("son of my sorrow") by Rachel, his mother, but renamed Benjamin ("son of my right hand") by his father Jacob. 2. A great-grandson of Benjamin, son of Jacob (I Chron. 7:10). 3. One of those who had married a foreign wife (Ezra 10:32).

Benjamin, Tribe of, named for Jacob's youngest son. On the basis of the first census taken after the exodus, the tribe numbered 35,400; at the second census, it numbered 45,600 (Num. 1:37; 26:41).

In the division of territory by Joshua among the 12 tribes, the portion for the tribe of Benjamin was assigned between Judah on the S and Ephraim on the N (Josh. 11:18 ff). Benjamin thus occupied a strategic position commercially and militarily.

Saul, son of Kish, came from this tribe (I Sam. 9:1 ff). At the time of the schism, after the death of Solomon, however, the Benjamites threw in their lot with the tribe of Judah, and followed the Davidic house as represented by Rehoboam, as against Jeroboam, the son of Nebat, to the north. Benjamin was included in the restoration. Saul of Tarsus (Paul) was a member of the tribe of Benjamin (Phil. 3:5).

Beno (bē′nō, **his son),** a Levite, the son of Jaaziah (I Chron. 24:26, 27).

Ben-oni (bĕn′ō′nī, **son of my sorrow),** the other name given to Benjamin by his expiring mother Rachel (Gen. 35:18). See Benjamin.

Ben-zoheth (bĕn′zō′hĕth, probably **to be strong),** son (or perhaps grandson) of Ishi of the tribe of Judah (I Chron. 4:20).

Beon (bē′ŏn, Num. 32:3, known also as Baal-Meon), a town built by the tribe of Reuben. See Baal-Meon.

Beor (See Balaam)

Bera (bē′rȧ, **gift),** king of Sodom, defeated by Chedorlaomer in the days of Abraham (Gen. 14:2, 8).

Berachah (bêr′ȧ-kȧ, **a blessing),** one of the 30 volunteers who came to the aid of David at Ziklag when he fled from Saul (I Chron. 12:3).

Berachah, Valley of (bêr′ȧ-kȧ, **valley of blessing),** the location where Jehoshaphat assembled his forces to offer praise to God for victory over the Ammonites and Moabites (II Chron. 20:26). Between Bethlehem and Hebron.

Berachiah (bêr-ȧ kī′ȧ, **Jehovah blesses)** sometimes Berechiah. 1. One of David's descendants (I Chron. 3:20). 2. Father of Asaph (I Chron. 6:39). 3. A Levite dwelling in Jerusalem (I Chron.

Ruins of the home of Mary and Martha in Bethany. © MPS

9:16). 4. A custodian of the Ark (I Chron. 15:23). 5. An Ephraimite who protested the sale of Hebrews to their fellows (II Chron. 28:12). 6. The father of Meshullam, a builder during the days of Nehemiah (Neh. 3:4, 30; 6:18). 7. The father of Zechariah, a prophet of the restoration (Zech. 1:1, 7).

Beraiah (bêr′ā-ī′à), a son of Shimei of the house of Benjamin (I Chron. 8:21).

Berea or **Beroea** (bêr-ē′à), city in SW Macedonia (Acts 17:10-14; 20:4); church founded there by Paul on 2nd missionary journey.

Bered (bē′red, **to be cold**). Between Kadesh and Bered was the well-known well, Beer-la-hai-roi (Gen. 16:14).

Beri (bê′rī, **wisdom**), a descendant of Asher (I Chron. 7:36).

Beriah (bē-rī′à, meaning uncertain, perhaps **gift** or **evil**). 1. This name is given to a son of Asher the father of Heber and Malchiel (Gen. 46:17; I Chron. 7:30). 2. Ephraim called one of his sons Beriah "because it went evil with his house" (I Chron. 7:23). 3. One of the descendants of Benjamin (I Chron. 8:13, 16). 4. A Levite, the son of Shimei of the Gershonites (I Chron 23:7-11).

Beriites (bē-rī′īts), a people mentioned only once in the Bible (Num. 26:44). Descended from Beriah, who, in turn, was from the tribe of Asher (Gen. 46: 17).

Berites (bē′rīts, **choice young men**), mentioned only in II Samuel 20:14. During the revolt of Sheba, responding to his call, these people followed him.

Bernice (bêr-nī′sē, **victorious**). Herod Agrippa's eldest daughter (Acts 12:1; 25:13, 23; 26:30), a very wicked woman who lived an incestuous life. According to Josephus, she was first married to Marcus. After his death she became the wife of Herod of Chalcis, her own uncle (Josephus, **Ant.** 19:5; 1; 20:7; 1-3). After Herod's death she had evil relations with Agrippa, her own brother, and with him listened Paul's noble defense at Caesarea. Later she was married to King Ptolemy of Sicily. This marriage was of short duration, as she returned to Agrippa. She was later the mistress of Vespasian and Titus, who finally cast her aside.

Berodach - Baladan (bē-rō′dăk-băl′à-dăn, **Marduk has given a son**), a king of Babylon, called also Merodach-baladan, and referred to in Isaiah 39:1.

Berothah, Berothai (bē-rō′thà, bē-rō′thī, **well or wells**), a town situated between Hamath and Damascus (Ezek. 47:16).

Beryl (bêr′ĭl, **yellow jasper**), a stone mentioned several times in the OT and once in the NT (Rev. 21:20). Brown, Driver and Briggs feel this was a yellow or gold-covered stone. One of the precious stones in the high priest's breastplate (Exod. 28:20; 39:13). Daniel uses it to describe the man in his vision (Dan. 10:6). Our modern beryl is beryllium aluminum silicate, but of the true nature of this ancient stone, little is known.

Besai (bē′sī, **down-trodden**), the founder of a family which returned to Jerusalem from Babylon under Zerubbabel (Ezra 2:49; Neh. 7:52).

Besodeiah (bĕs′ō-dē′yà, **in the counsel of Jehovah**), the father of Meshullam, a builder under Nehemiah (Neh. 3:6).

Besom (bē′zŭm, **broom**), a word signifying the punishment that was to be meted out to Babylon (Isa. 14:23).

Besor (bē′sôr), a brook five miles S of Gaza where David left 200 of his men who were too faint to assist in pursuing the Amalekites (I Sam. 30:9, 10, 21).

Betah (bē′tà, **confidence**), a city of Syria which David captured and from which he took much brass.

Beten (bē′tĕn, **hollow**), a city on Asher's border (Josh. 19:25).

Beth (bĕth, **house**), the name by which the second letter of the Hebrew alphabet is known. The Hebrew uses it also for the number two. It is the most common OT word for house.

Bethabara (bĕth′ăb′à-rà, **house of the ford**), a place on the E bank of the Jordan where John baptized (John 1: 28).

Bethanath (bĕth′ā′năth, **the temple of Anath**), a city near Naphtali (Josh. 19: 38; Judg 1:33).

Beth-Anoth (bĕth′a′nŏth, **house of Anoth**), a town in the hill country of Judea (Josh. 15:59).

Bethany (bĕth′à-nē, **house of unripe dates or figs**). 1. Bethabara of John 1: 28 (KJV) is in the best MSS. rendered "Bethany." From the best authorities we learn that nothing certain is known of its location except that it is beyond the Jordan where John was accomplishing his work (John 1:28). 2. Another city of this name, the home of Mary, Martha and Lazarus, situated about two miles SE of Jerusalem (John 11:18) on the eastern slope of Mount Olivet.

The village of Bethel. © MPS

Beth-Arabah (bĕth'ăr'ȧ-bȧ, **house of the desert**), a town known also as Arabah (Josh. 18:18), probably located at the northern end of the Dead Sea.

Betharam (bĕth'ā'răm), a town belonging to Gad, E of the Jordan (Josh. 13:27). Called "Bethharam" (Num. 32:36).

Betharabel (bĕth'ȧr'bĕl, **house of Arbel**), town destroyed by Shalmaneser, perhaps in Naphtali (Hos. 10:14).

Bethaven (bĕth'ā'vĕn, **house of vanity**), town in N Benjamin (Josh. 18:12). The word is used figuratively by Hosea (4:15; 10:5).

Bethazmaveth (bĕth'ăz-mā'vĕth, **house of the strong one of death**), a village belonging to Benjamin mentioned in Nehemiah 7:28.

Beth Baal Meon (bĕth bā'ȧl mē'ŏn, **house of Baal-meon**), a place in the territory assigned to Reuben, E of the Jordan (Josh. 13:17). This is the same as Baal-meon (Num. 32:38) and Beon (Num. 32:3). Jeremiah speaks of it as belonging to Moab (Jer. 48:23).

Bethbarah (bĕth'bâr'ȧ, **house of the ford**), one of the important fords across the Jordan. The Midianites were expected to use this as they escaped from Gideon. This is the reason for Gideon's instruction to his messengers to "take before them the waters unto Beth-barah" (Judg. 7:24). Here Jephtha slew the Ephraimites (Judg. 12:4) and perhaps it is the place where Jacob crossed (Gen. 32:22).

Beth-Birei (bĕth'bĭr'ī, **house of my creator**), a town of Simeon (I Chron. 4:31) in the southern part of Judah. Joshua refers to this place as Beth-lebaoth "abode of lions" (Josh. 19:6) and as Lebaoth (Josh. 15:32).

Bethcar (bĕth'kȧr, **house of sheep**), a place W of Mizpah to which Israel pursued the Philistines (I Sam. 7:11).

Beth Dagon (bĕth'dā'gŏn, **house of Dagon**), a town located in the shephelah of Judah, mentioned in Joshua 15:41. Also used of a town on the border of Asher (Josh. 19:27).

Beth-Diblathaim (bĕth' dĭb'lȧ-thā'ĭm, **house of a double cake of figs**), a Moabitish town known also as Almondiblathaim (Num. 33:46) and Diblath (Ezek. 6:14). Jeremiah speaks of it (Jer. 48:22) and it is mentioned on the Moabite Stone.

Bethel (bĕth'ĕl, **house of God**). 1. Town 12 miles N of Jerusalem, originally known as "Luz" (Gen. 28:19). Abraham encamped near it (Gen. 12:8; 13:3); God met Jacob there (Gen. 28:10-22) and Jacob built an altar there, calling the place "El-bethel" (Gen. 35:7). Assigned to Benjamin (Josh. 18:21, 22); captured by Joseph's descendants (Judg. 1:22-26); ark abode there (Judg. 20:26-28). Jeroboam set up golden calf there (I Kings 12:26-30). Amos and Hosea denounced it (Amos 3:14; called Beth-aven, "house of idols," Hos. 4:15). Josiah restored worship of Jehovah (II Kings 23:15-23). 2. City in S Judah (I Sam. 30:27). "Bethul" in Josh. 19:4.

Bethel is mentioned in the apocryphal books as being fortified by Bacchides (I Macc. 9:50).

Bethemek (bĕth'ē'mĕk, **house of the valley**), a city mentioned in Joshua 19:27 in the valley of Jiphthahel on the edge of Asher's territory.

Bether (bē'thêr, **separation**), a range of mountains mentioned in the Song of Solomon (2:17).

Bethesda (bĕ-thĕs'dȧ, **house of grace**), a spring-fed pool at Jerusalem, surrounded by five porches (John 5:1-16). Sick folk waited to step down into these waters which were thought to have healing properties.

Bethezel (bĕth'ē'zĕl, **a house adjoining**), a town in southern Judea in the Philistine plain (Mic. 1:11).

Bethgader (bĕth'gā'dêr, **house of the wall**), place in the tribe of Judah (I Chron. 2:51).

Bethgamul (bĕth'gā'mŭl, **house of recompense**), a Moabitish city (Jer. 48:23).

Beth-Gilgal (bĕth'gĭl'găl, **house of Gilgal**), probably the same as Gilgal (Neh. 12:27-29).

Bethhaccerem (bĕth'hă-kē'rĕm, **house of the vineyard**), a Judean town (Neh. 3:14), ruled by Malchiah. Jeremiah notes it as a vantage site for signaling in time of danger (Jer. 6:1).

Beth-Haran (bĕth'hā'răn, **house of the mountaineer**), a fenced city E of the Jordan (Num. 32:36). The same as Bethharam.

Beth-Hoglah (bĕth'hŏg'lȧ, **house of a partridge**), a village of Benjamin lying between Jericho and the Jordan (Josh. 15:6; 18:19, 21).

Bethhoron (bĕth'hō'rŏn, **place of a hollow**), two towns, the upper and the lower (Josh. 16:3, 5; I Chron. 7:24;

Typical street scene in old Bethlehem. © MPS

The Pool of Bethesda. © MPS

II Chron. 8:5), separated by a few miles. Beit Ur el foka ("the upper") is 800 ft. higher than Beit Ur el tahta ("the lower"). Built by Sherah, a granddaughter of Ephraim (I Chron. 7:24), Bethhoron lay on the boundary line between Benjamin and Ephraim (Josh 16:3, 5), on the road from Gibeon to Azekah (Josh. 10:10, 11). It was assigned to Ephraim and given to the Kohathites (Josh. 21:22). It was in this valley that Joshua commanded the sun and moon to stand still.

Beth-Le-Aphrah (bĕth'lē-ăf'rȧ, **house of dust**), a town, site unknown; "in the house of Aphrah roll thyself in the dust" (Mic. 1:10).

Bethlebaoth (bĕth'lē-bā'ŏth, **house of lionesses**), a town of Simeon (Josh. 19: 6), called Beth-birei in I Chronicles 4: 31).

Bethlehem (bĕth'lē-hĕm, **house of bread**). 1. Town 5 miles SW of Jerusalem. Called Ephrath in Jacob's time; after conquest of Canaan called Bethlehem-judah (Ruth 1:1) to distinguish it from Bethlehem of Zebulun. Burial place of Rachel (Gen. 35:16, 19); home of Ibzan (Judg. 12:8-10), Elimelech (Ruth 1:1, 2) and Boaz (Ruth 2:1, 4). David anointed there (I Sam. 16:13); known as "city of David" (Luke 2:4, 11). Jesus born there (Matt. 2:1; Luke 2:15-18). 2 Town of Zebulun (Josh. 19:15).

Beth-Lehem-Judah (See Bethlehem)

Bethphage, in foreground with Bethany behind it. © MPS

Beth-Le-Jeshimoth or **Bethjesimoth** (bĕth′jĕsh′ĭ-mŏth, **place of deserts),** a town E of the mouth of the Jordan, next to the last camp of the Israelites (Num. 33:49), assigned to Reuben (Josh. 13:20).

Beth-Maachah (bĕth′mā′ȧ-kȧ), a town to which Joab pursued Sheba (II Sam. 20:14, 15).

Bethmarcaboth (bĕth′mȧr′kȧ-bŏth, **the house of chariots),** a town of Simeon in the extreme S of Judah (Josh 19:5; I Chron. 4:31). Possibly one of the cities which Solomon built for his chariots (I Kings 9:19).

Beth-Meon (bĕth′mē′ōn), a city of Moab (Jer. 48:23), same as Beth-baal-meon (Josh. 13:17).

Bethnimrah (bĕth′nĭm′rȧ, **house of leopard),** a fenced city of Gad E of the Jordan (Num. 32:3, 36). Some identify this with Bethabara in the NT (John 1:28).

Bethpalet or **Beth-Phelet** (bĕth′pā′lĕt or bĕth′fē′lĕt, **house of escape),** a town in the S of Judah (Josh. 15:27; Neh. 11:26).

Bethpazzez (bĕth′păz′ĕz), a town of Issachar (Josh. 19:21).

Bethpeor (bĕth′pē′ôr, **house of Peor),** one of Israel's last camp sites (Deut. 3:29; 4:46). Here Moses was buried (Deut. 34:6). A possession of Reuben (Josh. 13:20).

Bethphage (bĕth′fȧ-jē, **house of unripe figs),** a village on the mount of Olives.

Bethrapha (bĕth′rā′fȧ), son of Eshton in the genealogy of Judah (I Chron. 4:12).

Bethrehob. (bĕth′rē′hŏb, **house of Rechob),** an Aramean town and district near Laish or Dan (Judg 18:28).

Bethsaida (bĕth′sā′ĭ-dȧ, **house of fishing).** 1. A village close to the W side of the Sea of Tiberias, in the land of Gennesaret, where Jesus sent His disciples by boat after He had fed the 5000 (Mark 6:45-53). Along with Chorazin and Capernaum, Jesus upbraided Bethsaida for unbelief (Matt. 11:20-23; Luke 10:13-15). 2. Another Bethsaida, NE of the sea of Tiberias and scene of the feeding of the 5000 (Luke 9:10). Jesus restored sight to a blind man in this Bethsaida (Mark 8: 22), which is on the E side of the lake.

Bethshan or **Bethshean** (bĕth′shăn or bĕth′shē′ăn, **house of quiet),** a city of Manasseh in the territory of Issachar, but one out of which the Canaanites could not be driven (Josh. 17:11, 12; Judg. 1:27). It lay 14 miles S of the Sea of Galilee, overlooking the plain of Esdraelon in the valley of Jezreel.

Fishing boats on the Sea of Galilee at Bethsaida. © MPS

After Saul died in Mount Gilboa, the Philistines fastened his body to the wall of Bethshan and put his armor in the temple of Ashtaroth as trophies of their victory (I Sam. 31:8-12). Later, the men of Jabesh-gilead stole the bones of Saul and his sons from the street of Bethshan, but David recovered them and gave them a proper burial (II Sam. 21:12-14).

Bethshemesh (bĕth′shē′mĕsh, **house of the sun**). 1. A town of NW Judah near the Philistine border (Josh. 15:10; I Sam 6:12). It was a priests' city given by Judah to the Levites (Josh. 21:16; I Chron. 6:59).

Bethshemesh was in a commissary district of Solomon (I Kings 4:9). Here Joash king of Israel encountered Amaziah of Judah and took him prisoner (II Kings 14:11-13; II Chron. 25:21-23). 2. A city of Issachar (Josh. 19:22). 3. A city of Naphtali (Josh. 19:38; Judg. 1:33) from which the Canaanites were not driven. 4. An idol city in Egypt (Jer. 43:13).

Bethshitta (bĕth′shĭt′ȧ, **house of the acacia**), a town in Zererath near Jordan to which the Midianites fled after their overthrow by Gideon (Judg. 7:22).

Bethtappua (bĕth′tăp′ū-ȧ, **house of apples**), a town in the hill part of Judah (Josh. 15:53).

Bethuel or **Bethul** (bē-thū′ĕl or bĕth′ŭl, **abode of God**). 1. Son of Nahor and Milcah, nephew of Abraham, and father of Rebekah and Laban (Gen. 22:22, 23; 24:15, 24, 47; 28:2). 2. A town in the S of Simeon (Josh. 19:4; I Chron. 4:30) and same as Chesil (Josh. 15:30).

Bethul (See Bethuel)

Bethzur (bĕth′zûr, **house of rock**), one of Judea's strongest natural fortresses in the mountains of Judah, near Halhul and Gedor (Josh. 15:58). It was fortified by Rehoboam (II Chron. 11:7). Nehemiah, son of Azbuk and ruler of half of Beth-zur, helped to repair the wall of Jerusalem (Neh. 3:16). Known as Bethsura in Maccabean times, it was an important military stronghold, where Judas Maccabeus defeated the Greek army under Lysias (I Macc. 4:28-34). It is now Beit Sur, four miles N of Hebron.

Betonim (bĕt′ō-nĭm), a town of Gad, E of the Jordan (Josh. 13:26).

Beulah (bwū′lȧ, **married**), a poetic name for the land of Israel in its future restored condition (Isa. 62:4).

Bezai (bē′zā-ī). 1. Head of a family of 323 men who returned with Zerubbabel (Ezra 2:17; Num. 7:23). 2. Probably a member of the same family a century later (Neh. 10:18).

Bethshemesh near the Philistine Border, © *MPS*

Bezaleel (bē-zăl′ē-ĕl, **in the shadow of God**). 1. Son of Uri, son of Hur of the tribe of Judah, whom the Lord called by name (Exod. 31:2; 35:30) and by his Spirit empowered to work in metals, wood, and stone for the tabernacle. 2. A descendant of Pahath-moab, an official of Moab, who in the days of Ezra and Nehemiah was compelled to give up his foreign wife (Ezra 10:30).

Bezek (bē′zĕk, **scattering, sowing**). 1. A town in the territory of Judah taken for Israel under Joshua from the Canaanites and Perizzites of whom more than 10,000 had congregated there. Its king had either the name or more probably the title "Adonibezek" (i.e. lord of Bezek). 2. The place where Saul numbered his forces before going to relieve Jabesh-gilead (I Sam. 11:8), about 14 miles NE of Samaria.

Bezer (bē′zêr, **strong**). 1. A city in the wilderness plateau E of the Dead Sea and in the tribe of Reuben, set apart as a city of refuge (Deut. 4:43). 2. One of the mighty men of the tribe of Asher (I Chron. 7:37).

Bible. The collection of books recognized and used by the Christian Church as the inspired record of God's revelation of Himself and of His will to mankind.

1. Names. The word "Bible" is from Gr. **biblia, pl. of biblion,** diminutive of **biblos** (book), **from byblos** (papyrus). In ancient times papyrus was used in making the paper from which books were manufactured. The words **biblion** and **bibila** are used in the OT (LXX) and the Apocrypha for the

Scriptures (Dan. 9:2; I Macc. 1:56; 3:48; 12:9). By about the fifth century the Greek Church Fathers applied the term **biblia** to the whole Christian Scriptures. Later the word passed into the western church, and although it is really a plural neuter noun, it came to be used in the Latin as a feminine singular. Thus "The Books" became by common consent "The Book."

In the NT the OT is usually referred to as "the scriptures" (Matt. 21:42; 22:29; Luke 24:32; John 5:39; Acts 18:24). Other terms used are "scripture" (Acts 8:32; Gal. 3:22), the "holy scriptures" (Rom. 1:2; II Tim. 3:15, KJV), and "sacred writings" (II Tim. 3:15, RV).

The names "Old" and "New Testament" have been used since the close of the second century to distinguish the Jewish and Christian Scriptures. "Testament" is used in the NT (KJV) to render the Greek word **diatheke** (Latin **testamentum),** which in classical usage meant "a will," but in the LXX and in the NT was used to translate the Hebrew word **berith,** "a covenant." Strictly, therefore, "Old" and "New Testament" mean "Old" and "New Covenant," the reference being to the covenants God made with His elect people in the two dispensations.

2. Languages. Most of the OT is written in Hebrew, the language spoken by the Israelites in Canaan before the Babylonian Captivity, but after the "Return" giving way to Aramaic, a related dialect generally spoken throughout SW Asia. A few parts of the OT are in Aramaic (Ezra 4:8-7:18; 7:12-26; Jer. 10:11; Dan. 2:4-7:28). The ancient Hebrew text consisted only of consonants, since the Hebrew alphabet had no written vowels. Vowel signs were invented by the Jewish Masoretic scholars in the sixth century and later. Except for a few words and sentences, the NT was composed in Greek, the language of ordinary intercourse in the Hellenistic world.

3. Compass and Divisions. The Protestant Bible in general use today contains 66 books, 39 in the OT and 27 in the NT. The 39 OT books are the same as those recognized by the Palestinian Jews in NT times.

In the Hebrew Bible the books are arranged in three groups, the Law, the Prophets, and the Writings. The Law comprises the Pentateuch. The Prophets include the Former Prophets: Joshua, Judges, Samuel, and Kings; and the Latter Prophets: Isaiah, Jeremiah, Ezekiel, and the Minor Prophets. The Writings take in the remaining books: Psalms, Proverbs, Job, Canticles, Ruth, Lamentations, Ecclesiastes, Esther, Daniel, Ezra-Nehemiah, and Chronicles. The total is traditionally reckoned as 24, but these correspond to the Protestant 39, since in the latter reckoning the minor prophets are counted as 12 books, and Samuel, Kings, Chronicles, and Ezra-Nehemiah as two each.

All branches of the Christian Church are agreed on the NT canon. The grouping of the books is a natural one: first the four Gospels; then the one historical book of the NT, the Acts of the Apostles; after that the Epistles, first the Epistles of Paul and then the General Epistles; and finally the Revelation.

4. Text. Although the Bible was written over a period of approximately 1,400 years, from the time of Moses to the end of the first century A.D., its text has come to us in a remarkable state of preservation. It is of course not identical with the text that left the hands of the original writers. Scribal errors have necessarily crept in. Until the invention of printing in the middle of the 15th century, all copies of the Scriptures were made by hand. There is evidence that the ancient Jewish scribes copied the books of the OT with extreme care. The recently discovered Dead Sea Scrolls, some going as far back as the second and third centuries B.C., contain either whole books or fragments of all but one (Esther) of the OT books; and they bear witness to a text remarkably like the Hebrew text left by the Masoretes. The Greek translation of the OT, the Septuagint, begun about 250 B.C. and completed about 100 years later, although it differs in places from the Hebrew text current today, is also a valuable witness to the accuracy of the OT text.

In the NT the evidence for the reliability of the text is almost embarrassingly large, and includes about 4500 Greek manuscripts, dating from about A.D. 125 to the invention of printing; versions, the Old Latin and Syriac going back to about A.D. 150; and quotations of Scripture in the writings of the Church Fathers, beginning with the end of the first century.

5. Chapters and Verses. The books of the Bible originally had no chapters or verses. For convenience of reference, Jews of pre-Talmudic times divided the OT into sections corresponding to our chapters and verses. The chapter divisions we use today were made by Stephen Langton, archbishop of Canterbury, who died in 1228. The division of the NT into its present verses is found for the first time in an edition of the Greek NT published in 1551 by the Paris printer, Robert Stephens, who also, in 1555, brought out an edition of the Vulgate which was the first edition of the Bible to appear with our present chapters and verses. The first English Bible to be so divided was the Genevan edition of 1560.

6. Translations. The Old and New Testaments appeared very early in translations. The OT was translated into Greek (the LXX) between 250-150 B.C., and other translations in Greek appeared soon after the beginning of the Christian era. Parts, at least, of the OT were rendered into Syriac as early as the first century; and a Coptic translation appeared probably in the third century. The NT was translated into Latin and Syriac c. 150 and into Coptic c. 200. In subsequent centuries versions appeared in the Armenian, Gothic, Ethiopic, Georgian, Arabic, Persian, and Slavonic languages. The Bible, in whole or in part, is now available in more than 1100 different languages and dialects.

7. Message. Although the Bible consists of many different books written over a long period of time by a great variety of writers, it has an organic unity that can be explained only by assuming, as the book itself claims, that its writers were inspired by the Holy Spirit to give God's message to man. The theme of this message is the same in both Testaments, the redemption of man. The OT tells about the origin of man's sin and the preparation God made for the solution of this problem through His own Son the Messiah. The NT describes the fulfilment of God's redemptive plan; the four Gospels telling about the Messiah's coming; the Acts of the Apostles describing the origin and growth of the Church, God's redeemed people; the Epistles giving the meaning and implication of the Incarnatian; and the Revelation showing how some day all of history will be consummated in Christ.

See also: Texts and Versions, Old Testament, New Testament.

Bible, English Versions. In the earliest days of English Christianity the only known Bible was the Latin Vulgate, made by Jerome between A.D. 383 and 405. This could be read only by the clergy and by monks, who alone were familiar with the language. There was no thought as yet of providing ordinary layfolk with the Bible in their own tongue. It was Wycliffe who first entertained this revolutionary idea. And it was Wycliffe who first made the whole Bible available in English.

John Wycliffe. Born in Yorkshire about the year 1320, Wycliffe stands out as one of the most illustrious figures of the 14th century. The outstanding Oxford theologian of his day and an ardent ecclesiastical reformer, he is called the "Morning-star of the Reformation." He was convinced that the surest way of defeating Rome was to put the Bible into the hands of the common people, and therefore decided to make such a translation available. Under his auspices, the NT came out in 1380, and the OT two years later.

William Tyndale. William Tyndale, the next great figure in the history of the English Bible, was born about the year 1494, and spent ten years studying at Oxford and Cambridge. In his projected translation he tried to get the support of the Bishop of London, but without success. A wealthy London cloth-merchant finally came to his support, but after six months, in 1524, Tyndale left for the Continent because, he said, "there was no place to do it (translate the Bible) in all England, as experience doth now openly declare." Never able to return to England, he seems to have visited Luther at Wittenberg, and then went to Cologne, where he found a printer for his New Testament. A priest discovered his plan, and Tyndale was obliged to flee. In Worms he found another printer, and there, in 1525, 3000 copies of the first printed English NT were published. By 1530 six editions, numbering about 15,000 copies, were published. They were all smuggled into England—hidden in bales of cotton, sacks of flour, and bundles of flax.

So well did Tyndale do his work that the KJV reproduces about 90 per cent of Tyndale in the NT. After the completion of the NT, Tyndale started to bring out a translation of the OT

William Tyndale translating the Bible (painting by Alexander Johnstone). © *RTHPL*

Sir George Harvey's historic painting of the first reading from the Chained Bible in the crypt of old St. Paul's Church in London, 1540. © *RTHPL*

from the Hebrew text, but he lived only to complete the Pentateuch, Jonah, and probably the historical books from Joshua to II Chronicles. After ten years on the Continent, mostly in hiding, he was betrayed in Antwerp by an English Roman Catholic, and was condemned to death for being a heretic. He was strangled, and his body burned at the stake. His last words were a prayer, "Lord, open the King of England's eyes." But Tyndale won his battle. Although his NT was burned in large quantities by the Church, it contributed greatly towards creating an appetite for the Bible in English. The government, moreover, began to see the wisdom and necessity of providing the Bible in English for common use. The break with the papacy in 1534 helped greatly in this.

Miles Coverdale. While Tyndale was incarcerated in Belgium, an English Bible suddenly appeared in England. This was in 1535. It had come from the Continent. The title-page stated that it had been translated out of the German and Latin into English. This Bible was the rendering of Miles Coverdale, although in the NT and in those parts of the OT done by Tyndale, it was no more than a slight revision of the latter's work. It was the first complete printed Bible in the English language. It was not made from the Hebrew and Greek, for in the dedication (to Henry VIII) Coverdale says that he used the work of five different translators. His version of the Psalms still appears in the Book of Common Prayer, used daily in the ritual of the Church of England. Two new editions of Coverdale's Bible appeared in 1537, with the significant word on the title page, "Set forth with the King's most gracious license." So within a year of Tyndale's death, the entire Bible was translated, printed, and distributed, apparently with royal approval.

Thomas Matthew. In 1537 another Bible appeared in England, this one by Thomas Matthew (a pen-name for John Rogers, a former associate of Tyndale's) who was burned at the stake by Queen Mary in 1555. The whole of the NT and about half of the OT are Tyndale's, while the remainder is Coverdale's. It bore on its title-page the words, "Set forth with the king's most gracious license." This Bible has the distinction of being the first edition of the whole English Bible actually to be printed in England.

The Great Bible. The next Bible to appear was a revision of the Matthew Bible, by Coverdale. The printing of this was begun in Paris, but the Inquisition stepped in and the work was completed in England. It appeared in 1539 and was called the Great Bible because of its large size and sumptuousness.

In the brief reign of Edward VI, who succeeded his father Henry VIII on the latter's death in 1547, no new translation work was done, but great encouragement was given to the reading of the Bible and to the printing of existing versions, and injunctions were repromulgated that a copy of the Great Bible be placed in every parish church.

The Genevan Bible. With the accession of Mary in 1553, hundreds of Protestants lost their lives, among them some men closely associated with Bible translation, like John Rogers and Thomas Cranmer. Coverdale escaped martyrdom by fleeing to the Continent. Some of the English Reformers escaped to Geneva, where the leading figure was John Calvin. One of their number, William Wittingham, who had married Calvin's sister, produced in 1557 a revision of the English NT printed in roman type and with the text divided into verses. He and his associates then undertook the revision of the whole Bible. This appeared in 1560 and is known as the Genevan Bible, or more familiarly as the Breeches Bible from its rendering of Genesis 3:7, "They sewed fig-tree leaves together, and made themselves breeches." It enjoyed a long popularity, going through 160 editions, 60 of them during the reign of Queen Elizabeth alone, and continued to be printed even after the publication of the KJV in 1611.

The Bishops' Bible. Queen Elizabeth, who succeeded Mary Tudor after the latter's three years and nine months' reign, restored the arrangements of Edward VI. The Great Bible was again placed in every church, and people were encouraged to read the Scriptures. The excellence of the Genevan Bible made obvious the deficiencies of the Great Bible, but some of its renderings and the marginal notes made it unacceptable to many of the clergy. Archbishop Parker, aided by eight bishops and some other scholars, therefore made a revision of the Great Bible, which was completed and published in 1568 and came to be known as the Bishops' Bible. It gained considerable circulation, but the Genevan Bible was far more popular and was used more widely.

Rheims and Douai Version. This came from the Church of Rome, and is the work of Gregory Martin, who with a number of other English Romanists left England at the beginning of Elizabeth's reign and settled in the NE of France, where in 1568 they founded a college. The NT was published in 1582, and was done while the college was at Rheims, and hence is known as the Rheims New Testament, but the OT was not published until 1609-10, after the college had moved to Douai, and hence it is called the Douai Old Testament. The Rheims-Douay Bible in use today is not the same as the one made by Gregory Martin, but is a thorough revision of it between 1749 and 1763 by Bishop Richard Challoner. It was first authorized for use by American Roman Catholics in 1810.

King James Version. When Elizabeth died, in 1603, the crown passed to James I, who had been king of Scotland for 37 years as James VI. Several months after he ascended the throne of England he authorized a new translation of the Bible to replace the Bishops' Bible.

Forty-seven of the best Hebrew and Greek scholars of the day were divided into six groups: three for the OT, two for the New, and one for the Apocrypha. Two of the groups met at Oxford, two at Cambridge, and two at Westminster. When a group had completed its task, its work was submitted to 12 men, two from each panel. Final differences of opinion were settled at a general meeting of each company. In cases of special difficulty, learned men outside the board of revisers were consulted. Marginal notes were used only to explain Hebrew and Greek words to draw attention to parallel passages. Italics were used for words not found in the original but necessary to complete the sense.

The revisers, who received no financial remuneration for their work, completed their task in two years; and nine more months were devoted to a revision of their work by a special committee consisting of two members from each group. In 1611 the new version was published. It did not win immediate universal acceptance, taking almost 50 years to displace the Genevan Bible in popular favor. In the course of time slight alterations were made, especially in spelling, to conform to changing usage, but these were all done piecemeal by private enterprise. Its excellence is shown by the fact that after 350 years it is still used in preference to any other version in the English-speaking Protestant world, for both public and private use.

English Revised Version. This version was made necessary for a number of reasons: in the course of time the language of the KJV had become obsolete; a number of Greek manuscripts were discovered that were far superior to those available to the KJV translators; and improvement in the knowledge of Hebrew made possible a more accurate rendering of the OT. It had its origin in 1870 with the Convocation of Canterbury of the Church of England. Eventually two companies were formed, each of 27 men, one for the OT, the other for the NT. American scholars were also invited to cooperate, and they formed two companies corresponding to the British. It was agreed that American suggestions not accepted by the British revisers were to be recorded in an appendix to the published volume, and that the American revisers were to give their moral support to the new Bible and were not to issue an edition of their own for a term of 14 years. The revisers were guided by a number of rules, the most important being that they were to make as few alterations as possible into the text of the KJV consistently with faithfulness.

Altogether, the Greek text underlying the revised NT differed from that used by the KJV translators in 5,788 readings, only about one fourth of these making any material difference in the substance of the text, although none so seriously as to affect the doctrines of the faith. In the English text of the NT there are about 36,000 changes. The new Bible differed from its predecessors in printing poetical passages in the OT as poetry and in grouping verses into paragraphs according to sense-units.

The NT was published in 1881, and the OT in 1885. The revisers gave their time and labor without charge. When they completed their work, they disbanded. Although the new version received acceptance unprecedented in the history of the Bible, so that three

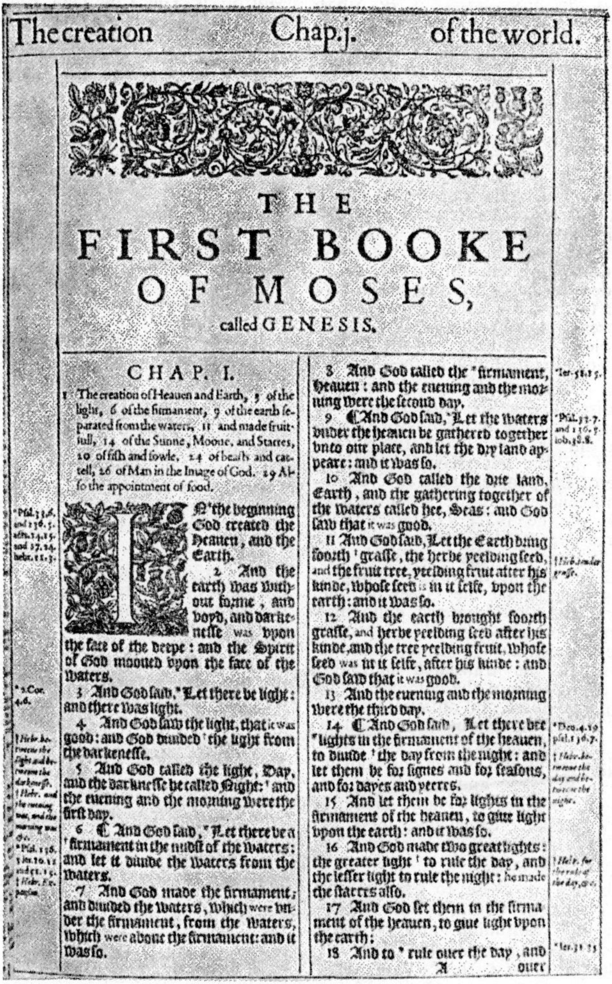

The creation Chap.j. of the world.

THE
FIRST BOOKE
OF MOSES,
called GENESIS.

CHAP. I.

1 The creation of Heauen and Earth, 3 of the light, 6 of the firmament, 9 of the earth separated from the waters, 11 and made fruitfull, 14 of the Sunne, Moone, and Starres, 20 of fish and fowle, 24 of beasts and cattell, 26 of Man in the Image of God. 29 Also the appointment of food.

IN the *beginning
God created the
Heauen, and the
Earth.
2 And the
earth was with-
out forme, and
voyd, and darke-
nesse was vpon
the face of the deepe: and the Spirit
of God mooued vpon the face of the
waters.
3 And God said, *Let there be light:
and there was light.
4 And God saw the light, that it was
good: and God diuided †the light from
the darkenesse.
5 And God called the light, Day,
and the darknesse he called Night: †and
the euening and the morning were the
first day.
6 ¶ And God said, *Let there be a
†firmament in the midst of the waters:
and let it diuide the waters from the
waters.
7 And God made the firmament;
and diuided the waters, which were vnder the firmament, from the waters,
which were aboue the firmament: and it
was so.
8 And God called the *firmament,
Heauen: and the euening and the morning were the second day.
9 ¶ And God said, *Let the waters
vnder the heauen be gathered together
vnto one place, and let the dry land ap-
peare: and it was so.
10 And God called the drie land,
Earth, and the gathering together of
the waters called hee, Seas: and God
saw that it was good.
11 And God said, Let the Earth bring
foorth †grasse, the herbe yeelding seed,
and the fruit tree, yeelding fruit after his
kinde, whose seed is in it selfe, vpon the
earth: and it was so.
12 And the earth brought foorth
grasse, and herbe yeelding seed after his
kinde, and the tree yeelding fruit, whose
seed was in it selfe, after his kinde: and
God saw that it was good.
13 And the euening and the morning
were the third day.
14 ¶ And God said, Let there bee
*lights in the firmament of the heauen,
to diuide †the day from the night: and
let them be for signes and for seasons,
and for dayes and yeeres.
15 And let them be for lights in the
firmament of the heauen, to giue light
vpon the earth: and it was so.
16 And God made two great lights:
the greater light †to rule the day, and
the lesser light to rule the night: he made
the starres also.
17 And God set them in the firmament of the heauen, to giue light vpon
the earth:
18 And to *rule ouer the day, and
A ouer

*Psal. 33.6. and 136.5. acts. 14.15. and 17.24. hebr. 11.3.
*2.Cor. 4.6.
†Hebr. betweene the light and betweene the darkenesse.
†Hebr. and the euening was, and the morning was &c.
*Psal. 136.5. Ier. 10.12 and 51.15.
†Hebr. Expansion.
*Ier. 51.15.
*Psal. 33.7. and 136.9. iob. 38.8.
†Heb. tender grasse.
*Deu. 4.19 psal. 136.7.
†Hebr. betweene the day and betweene the night.
†Hebr. for the rule of the day, &c.
*Ier. 31.35

The opening verses of the book of Genesis from the first edition of the Authorized (King James) version, 1611. BM

million copies were sold within the first year, it did not meet with immediate approval, nor has it in the years since then won for itself a place of undisputed supremacy.

American Standard Version. The American scholars who cooperated with the English revisers on the ERV were not entirely satisfied with it. For one thing, the suggested changes printed in the Appendix represented only a part of the changes they wanted made; and for another thing, the English revisers retained a large number of words and phrases whose meanings and spelling were regarded as antiquated, and words that are English but not American in meaning. For these and other reasons they did not disband when the ERV was published, but their revision of the ERV was not published until 1901. It is regarded as being on the whole superior to the ERV, at least for American uses, but it has its defects, as for example, the substitution of "Jehovah" for "Lord," especially in the Psalter.

Other Twentieth Century Versions. The discovery, at the end of the 19th century, of many thousands of Greek papyri in the sands of Egypt, all written in the everyday Greek language of the people, had a revolutionary influence upon the study of the Greek of the NT. NT Greek had hitherto presented a vexing problem, since it is neither classical Greek nor the Greek of the Septuagint. Now it was shown to be the Greek of the papyri, and therefore the colloquial language of Greek-speaking people in the first century. It was felt that the NT should be translated into the everyday speech of the common man, and not in stilted and antiquated English. These developments created a keen interest in bringing out fresh translations of the NT in the spoken English of today; and in the next 45 years a number of new modern-speech versions came out, most of them by individuals, but a few by groups of scholars.

The first of these to appear was **The Twentieth Century New Testament: A Translation into Modern English Made from the Original Greek. (Westcott & Hort's Text).** This was published in 1902 (reprinted 1961) and was the work of about 20 translators whose names were not given. In 1903 R. F. Weymouth brought out **The New Testament in Modern Speech;** it was thoroughly revised in 1924 by J. A. Robertson. James Moffatt, the well-known Scottish NT scholar, brought out **The Bible: A New Translation** in 1913, 14. The American counterpart of Moffatt is **The Complete Bible: An American Translation** (1927, revised 1935). The NT part first appeared in 1923 and was the work of E. J. Goodspeed; while four scholars, headed by J. M. Powis Smith, did the OT. **The New Testament. A Translation in the Language of the People,** by C. B. Williams, came out in 1937. **The New Testament in Modern English** (1958, by J. B. Phillips, is one of the most readable of the modern-speech translations. **The Amplified New Testament** (1958), which gives variant shades of meaning in the original, was followed in 1961 by **The Amplified Old Testament.** Part Two (Job-Malachi), balance of OT followed in 1964. It is the work of Frances E. Siewert and unnamed assistants. **The Holy Bible: The Berkeley Version in Modern English** (1959) is the work of Gerrit Verkuyl in the NT and of 20 American scholars in the OT. Kenneth Wuest's **The New Testament — An Expanded Translation** appeared complete in 1961. Also in 1961 appeared **The Simplified New Testament,** a new translation by Olaf M. Norlie.

During this period the Roman Catholic Church brought out a number of new versions: **The New Testament of Our Lord and Savior Jesus Christ** (1941), a revision of the Rheims-Challoner NT sponsored by the Episcopal Committee of the Confraternity of Christian Doctrine; the **Westminster Version of the Sacred Scriptures,** under the general editorship of Cuthbert Lattey, of which only the NT (1935) and parts of the OT have thus far appeared; and the translation from the Latin Vulgate made by Ronald A. Knox, the NT in 1945 and the OT in 1949.

Revised Standard Version. This is a revision of the ASV (1901), the NT appearing in 1946 and the OT in 1952. It was sponsored by the International Council of Religious Education, and is the work of 32 American scholars who worked in two sections, one dealing with the OT, the other with the NT. It was designed for use in public and private worship. In this version the language is modernized; direct speech is regularly indicated by the use of quotation marks; and the policy is followed (as in the KJV) of using a variety of synonyms to translate the Greek words where it is thought to be advisable.

New English Bible. The discovery of thousands of Greek papyri in the sands of Egypt revealed that the NT was written in the everyday language of the people, and this has resulted in bringing out many translations in the spoken English of today, among which those of Weymouth (1903), Moffatt (1913, 1914), Goodspeed (1923), and Phillips (1958) have been the most popular. The Revised Standard Version, which is a revision of the ASV, appeared in 1946 (NT) and 1952 (OT); and the NT part of the New English Bible in 1961.

Bichri (bĭk′rī, **first-born**), the father of Sheba, who made insurrection against David (II Sam. 20:1).

Bidkar (bĭd′kȧr), a military officer of Israel who joined Jehu in his revolt and was made his captain (II Kings 9:25).

Bigtha (bĭg′thȧ), one of the seven chamberlains of Ahasuerus, i.e.: Xerxes (Esth. 1:10).

Bigthan or **Bigthana** (bĭg′thăn or bĭg′thā′nȧ), one of the chamberlains of king Ahasuerus, i.e. Xerxes, who with another, Teresh, had plotted to slay the king. Mordecai heard of the plot, and through Esther warned the king, who had the two men hanged (Esth. 2:21-23; 6-2).

Bigvai (bĭg′vā-ī, **fortunate**). 1. Man who returned from the captivity (Ezra 2:2; Neh. 7:19). 2. Ancestor of family that returned from the captivity (Ezra 2:14; Neh. 7:19). 3. Probably the same as 2 (Ezra 8:14).

Bildad (bĭl′dăd), one of Job's three "comforters" (cf. Job 2:11-13 with 42:7-10) who made three speeches (Job 8, 18, 25), a "traditionalist" (8: 8-10).

Bileam (bĭl′ē-ăm), a town in the western half of Manasseh (I Chron. 6:70), perhaps the same as the Ibleam of Joshua 17:11; Judges 1:27, and II Kings 9:27.

Bilgah (bĭl′gȧ, **cheerfulness**). 1. Head of the 15th course of priests in David's time (I Chron. 24:14). 2. A priest who returned with Zerubbabel in 536 B.C. (Neh. 12:5).

Bilgai (bĭl′gā-ī), a priest in Nehemiah's time, 444 B.C. (Neh. 10:8).

Bilhah (bĭl′hȧ, **foolish**). 1. Rachel's maid-servant; Jacob's concubine; mother of Dan and Naphtali (Gen. 29:29; 30:1-8). 2. Town of Simeon (I Chron. 4:29). Balah in Josh. 19:3.

Bilhan (bĭl′hăn, **foolish**). 1. Horite; son of Ezer (Gen. 36:27; I Chron. 1:42). 2. Early Benjamite (I Chron. 7:10).

Bilshan (bĭl′shăn), Jewish leader who returned from the captivity (Ezra 2: 2; Neh. 7:7).

Bimhal (bĭm′hăl), Asherite (I Chron. 7:33).

Binding and Loosing. The carrying of a key or keys was a symbol of the delegated power of opening and closing. The apostles were given power to bind and to loose. Peter loosed the feet of the lame man at the Gate Beautiful (Acts 3:1-10) and Paul bound the sight of Bar-Jesus (Acts 13:8-11).

Binnui (bĭn′ū-ī). 1. Levite (Ezra 8:33). 2. Man who divorced his foreign wife (Ezra 10:30). 3. Another who divorced his foreign wife (Ezra 10:38). 4. Alternate spelling of Bani (cf Ezra 2:10; Neh. 7:15). 5. Rebuilder of Jerusalem (Neh. 3:24; 10:9). 6. Levite (Neh. 12: 8).

Birds. 360-400 different kinds are found in Palestine, and of these, 26 are found only there. The Bible lists about 50 classifying them as clean and unclean (Lev. 11:13-19; Deut. 14:11-19). Birds are mentioned in all but 21 books of the Bible. The following birds are specifically noted: bittern, chicken, cock, cormorant, crane, crow, cuckoo, cuckow (KJV name for cuckoo), dove, eagle, falcon, fowl (used of all flying birds), gier eagle, glede, great owl, hawk, hen, heron, hoopoe (same as lapwing), kite (same as falcon), lapwing, little owl, nighthawk, ospray, ossifrage, ostrich, owl, partridge, peacock, pelican, pigeon, quail, raven, screech owl, sea mew (same as cuckoo), sparrow, stork, swallow, swan, turtledove, vulture.

Birsha (bîr′shȧ), king of Gomorrah (Gen. 14:2, 10).

Birth. The Hebrew ceremonies connected with childbirth are given in Leviticus 12. The permission to the poor to offer "a pair of turtledoves or two young pigeons" in place of a lamb (Luke 2:24) gives touching testimony to the comparative poverty of Mary, the mother of Jesus. Our Lord, in John 3:3-6, makes a clear distinction between the first and second births of a regenerate person.

Birthright. Among the Israelites God had a special claim on the firstborn, at least from the time of Exodus, when He destroyed the firstborn of Egypt, and claimed those of Israel by right of redemption (Exod. 13:2, 12-16). The birthright included a double portion of the inheritance (Deut. 21:15-17), and the privilege of priesthood; but in Israel God later set apart the tribe of Levi instead of the firstborn for that service. (Note Numbers 3:38-51, where the Levites are about the same in number as the firstborn of Israel). Esau lost his birthright by selling it to Jacob for a mess of pottage (See Gen. 25:27-34; Heb. 12:6 and compare the destinies of Israel and of Edom, Obad. 17, 18). In Israel, Reuben lost his birthright through sin, and his next brothers Simeon and Levi lost theirs through violence; and so the blessing came to Judah (Gen. 49:3-10).

Birzavith (bîr-zā′vĭth), an Asherite (I Chron. 7:31), or a village of Asher.

Bishlam (bĭsh′lăm), an officer of Cambyses ("Artaxerxes") (Ezra 4:7).

Bishop (bĭsh′ŭp, **overseer**), originally the principal officer of the local church, the other being the deacon or deacons (I Tim. 3:1-7). The title "elder" or "presbyter" generally applied to the same man; "elder" referring to his age and dignity, and "bishop" to his work of superintendence.

Bithiah (bĭ-thī′ȧ, **daughter of Jehovah**), the name suggests that she was a convert to Judaism, though she is called a daughter of Pharaoh. Wife of Mered of the tribe of Judah (I Chron. 4:18).

Bithron (bĭth′rŏn, **rough country**), a region in Gad between the Jordon and Mahanaim (II Sam. 2:29).

Bithynia (bĭ-thĭn′ĭ-ȧ), a region in N. Asia Minor fronting on the Black Sea, the Bosphorus and the Sea of Marmora. Paul and his companions desired to enter Bithynia with the Gospel (Acts 16:6-10) but the Holy Spirit was leading toward Europe, and so they could not enter. However, there were Christians there in the first century (I Pet. 1:1).

Bitter Herbs. A Passover lamb (whose blood had been sprinkled for their salvation) was to be eaten by the Israelites with unleavened bread (because of the haste of their departure), and bitter herbs (as symbolic of the bitterness of their servitude, Exod. 12:8; Num. 9:11). Similar to horseradish. See Plants.

Bittern (See Birds)

Bitumen (bĭ-tū′mĕn), a mineral pitch widely scattered over the earth, and one of the best waterproofing substances known. It was used with slime (or perhaps as "slime and pitch") to cover the ark of bulrushes (Exod. 2:3) and to waterproof Noah's ark (Gen. 6:14), for mortar in the tower of Babel (Gen. 11:3), and as a curse upon Edom (Isa. 34:9). There were great deposits near the Dead Sea, and at different places in Mesopotamia.

Bizjothjah (bĭz-jŏth′jȧ, **contempt of Jehovah,** (ASV Biziothiah), a town in the south of Judah (Josh. 15:28).

Bizthah (bĭz′thȧ), one of the seven chamberlains in the court of Xerxes ("Ahasuerus") who were commanded to bring out Queen Vashti for exhibition.

Blains (See Diseases)

Blasphemy (blăs′fē-mē). To reproach or to bring a railing accusation against any one is bad enough (Jude 9), but to speak lightly or carelessly of God is a mortal sin. In Israel the punishment for blasphemy was death by stoning (see Lev. 24:10-16). Our Lord (Matt. 9:3, etc.) and Stephen (Acts 6:11) were falsely accused of blasphemy. What our Lord said would have been blasphemy were it not true.

Blastus (blăs′tŭs), a chamberlain of King Agrippa (Acts 12:20).

Bless, Blessing. 1. God blesses nature (Gen. 1:22), mankind (Gen. 1:28), the Sabbath (Gen. 2:3), nations (Ps. 33:12), classes of men (Ps. 1:1-3) and individuals (Gen. 24:1, etc.). 2. Godly men should "bless" God; i.e. they should adore Him, worship Him and praise Him (Ps. 103:1, 2, etc.). 3. Godly men can bestow blessings on others (Matt. 5:44; I Pet. 3:9). 4. In Bible times, godly men under inspiration bestowed prophetic blessings on their progeny, e.g. (Gen. 9:26, 27; 27:27-29, 39, 40, 49; Deut. 33). 5. We can bless things when we set them apart for sacred use (I Cor. 10:16).

Blessing, The Cup of. In the "communion" service, the church (i.e. the assembly of believers) blesses the cup when it is set apart for the Lord's Supper (I Cor. 10:16).

Blindness (See Diseases)

Blood. The word occurs over 400

times in the Scriptures, being especially frequent in Leviticus, which deals with Hebrew worship and the way to holiness; in Ezekiel, which has much to say about God's judgments; and in the letter to the Hebrews, which is the divine commen tary on Leviticus.

The blood contains the vital principle or the essence of animal and human life (Gen. 9:4 — "But flesh with the life thereof which is the blood thereof, shall ye not eat"). Because of the sacredness of life, that energy which only God can give, the Israelites were enjoined from eating the blood, or even flesh from which the blood had not carefully been removed. This prohibition is at the basis of the Jewish usages referred to as "kosher," which prevents the orthodox Jew from buying or eating meat which has not been slaughtered and drained of blood under the supervision of a rabbi.

Because of the sacredness of God's law and of His demand of holiness in His creature, man, from the beginning this principle has held — that "the wages of sin is death" (Rom. 6:23a); but "God is love," and so, in His infinite wisdom, He has provided an escape for the sinner. Though it is true that "without the shedding of blood, there is no remission" (Heb. 9:22), He has been pleased to accept the blood of our Lord Jesus Christ in lieu of ours, but only on condition of our belief in Him. "Christ was once offered to bear the sins of many" (Heb. 9:28) and this could take place only once, and so the Old Testament offerings were provided, not to take away sin, but to point forward to the supreme sacrifice upon Calvary.

Blood, Avenger or **Revenger of.** In the law of Moses, it was recognized that the nearest of kin would pursue a killer, and so cities of refuge were provided for those guilty of manslaughter, but not of murder (Num. 35:6). The Hebrew word for "avenger" is **go'el** and this word means also "kinsman" and "redeemer." This indicates that the executioner would ordinarily be a kinsman. In the book of Ruth, Boaz was the kinsman, who also performed the duty of a redeemer in Ruth's behalf (Ruth 4:1-8; Deut. 25:5-10). The word **go'el** had a twofold application to Boaz, who was both kinsman and redeemer to Ruth, but in the case of our Lord it is threefold. As Son of man He is our kinsman, He was our Redeemer (I Pet. 1:18, 19), and He will be the Avenger of blood (Isa. 63:1-6; Rev. 14:14-20; 19:11-21).

Blood, Issue of (See Diseases)

Bloody Sweat (See Diseases)

Boanerges (bō'ă-nûr'jēz, **sons of thunder**), a title bestowed by our Lord upon two brothers James and John, the sons of Zebedee (Mark 3:17), probably because of their temperamental violence (cf. Luke 9:54-56).

Boar (See Animals)

Boaz (bō'ăz), a well-to-do Bethlehemite in the days of the judges who became an ancestor of our Lord by marrying Ruth, the Moabitess, widow of one of the sons of Elimelech, his kinsman (Ruth 2, 3, 4). This was in accordance with the levirate law of

Harvesting in the fields of Boaz near Bethlehem (reminiscent of Ruth 2:5). © MPS

Ancient Hebrew scrolls in a synagogue in the old city of Jerusalem. © *MPS*

Deuteronomy 25:5-10; Boaz could marry Ruth only after the nearer kinsman (Ruth 3:12; 4:1-8) had refused the privilege, or the duty. The other refused because if he had married Ruth and had had a son, a portion of his property would have gone to the credit of Elimelech's posterity, instead of his own by a former marriage.

Boaz and Jachin (See Temple)

Bocheru (bō′kĕ-rōō), a distant descendant of Saul (I Chron. 8:38). One of the six sons of Azel.

Bochim (bō′kĭm, **weepers),** the place where the Angel of Jehovah appeared and rebuked the children of Israel because of their failure to drive out the heathen and to destroy their places of worship (Judg. 2:1-5).

Bohan (bō′hăn), a descendant of Reuben after whom a boundary stone was named (Josh. 15:6; 18:17).

Boil (See Diseases)

Bolster, a head-rest, or pillow (Gen. 28:11, 18; I Sam. 19:13; 26: 11, 16).

Bondmaid, Bondman (See Occupations)

Bone. Bones form the strong framework, and the connotation is one of strength. "Bone of my bones and flesh of my flesh" (Gen. 2:23) was spoken in a literal sense of Eve; but almost the same words (Gen. 29:14), spoken by Laban to Jacob, are figurative and show only kinship. Strong chastening is thought of as a bone-breaking experience (Ps. 51:8), and the terrible writhing on the cross of Calvary literally threw bones out of joint (Ps. 22:14). Dry bones form a picture of hopeless death (Ezek. 37: 1-12). The paschal lamb, without a broken bone (Exod. 12:46) was a type of the Lamb of God (John 19:36).

Book. In ancient Assyria and Babylonia most books were written on soft clay which was then baked. In Egypt papyrus was used several thousand years before the time of Christ. C. 200 B.C. skins of animals began to be used. Books made of papyrus and parchment were in roll form. The codex (book with pages) was invented in the 2nd cent. A.D. Israel used papyrus and parchment.

Booth, a temporary shelter generally made of tree-branches (Gen. 33:17) (Cf Isa. 1:8 ARV).

Booty. Spoils of war. Property and persons were sometimes preserved, and sometimes completely destroyed (Josh. 6:18-21; Deut. 20:14, 16-18). Abraham gave a tenth (Gen. 14:20); David ordered that booty be shared with baggage guards (I Sam. 30:21-25).

Booz (See Boaz)

Borrow, Borrowing. The law of Moses gives careful directions concerning the responsibility of those who borrow, or who hold property in trust, or who are criminally careless in regard to the property of another (Exod. 22: 1-15). Among the blessings promised Israel on condition of obedience is that they would be lenders and not borrowers (Deut. 28:12).

Boscath (See Bozkath)

Bosom (bōōz′ŭm). Although in English the word means the part of the body between the arms, in Scripture it is generally used in an affectionate sense, e.g. "the Son, who is in the bosom of the Father" (John 1:18), carrying the lambs in His bosom (Isa. 40:11), John leaning on the bosom of Jesus (John 13:23), or Lazarus in Abraham's bosom (Luke 16:22, 23). It can be almost synonymous with "heart" as the center of one's life, as in Ecclesiastes 7:9, "anger resteth in the bosom of fools," or Psalm 35:13, "my prayer returned unto mine own bosom."

Bosor (Same as Beor, See Balaam)

Bosses, the convex projection in the center of a shield (Job 15:26).

Botch (See Diseases)

Bottle. 1. Container made of goatskin, sewed up with the hair outside and used for carrying water (Gen. 21:14-19), for storing wine (Josh. 9:4, 13), for fermenting milk into "leben" or "yogurt" (Judg. 4:19, etc.). 2. Container made of baked clay, and hence very fragile (Jer. 19:1-11). 3. Beautifully designed glass bottles often found in Egyptian tombs, were used originally for burying some of the tears of the mourners with the deceased. See Psalm 56:8. 4. The word rendered "bottles" in Hosea 7:5 could better be translated "heat" or "fury." 5. Figuratively, the clouds as the source of rain (Job 38:37).

Bottomless Pit (See Abyss)

Boundary Stones. Our God is a God of order and not of confusion; and so in the matter of property, He not only set careful bounds to the land of His people (Josh. 13-21), but provided a curse for those who removed their neighbors' landmarks (Deut. 27:17; cf. 19:14). Figuratively, this implies a decent regard for ancient institutions (Prov. 22:28; 23:10).

Bow (See Arms and Armor)

Bow (See Rainbow)

Bowels, the word is used to translate a number of Heb. words. 1. Literally (II Chron. 21:15-19). 2. Generative parts of the body (Gen. 15:4; Ps. 71:6). 3. Seat of the emotions, "heart" (See Lam. 1:20; Phil. 1:8).

Water carriers using goatskin "bottles." © *MPS*

Bowl (bōl), a vessel, usually hemispherically shaped, to hold liquids (Amos 6:6; Zech. 4:3).

Box, Box Tree (See Plants)

Bozez (bō'zez), a rocky crag near Gibeah (I Sam. 14:4).

Bozkath or **Boscath** (bŏz'kăth), a city of S Judah (Josh. 15:39).

Bozrah (bŏz'ra̤, **sheepfold).** 1. City of Edom (Gen. 36:33; Jer. 49:13, 22). 2. City of Moab c. 75 miles S of Damascus (Jer. 48:24).

Bracelet, properly a circlet for the wrist, but the word translates in the KJV five different Hebrew nouns. In II Samuel 1:10 the word probably means "armlet" as a mark of royalty; in Exodus 35:22 it could be "brooches," as in ASV, or "clasps"; in Genesis 38:18, 25 it represents the cords about the neck from which the signet ring was suspended (see ASV in loc); in Genesis 24:22, etc., it is properly "bracelet," from the root meaning, "something bound on," and so in Ezekiel 16:11 and 23:42, and in Isaiah 3:19, in the interesting inventory of 21 items of feminine adornment, it could be rendered "twisted chains."

Bramble (See Plants)

Branch, a title applied to the Messiah as the offspring of David (Jer. 23:5; 33:15; Zech. 3:8; 6:12). Symbol of prospering (Gen. 49:22).

Brass, next to silver and gold, the most frequently mentioned metal in Scripture. KJV usually uses "brass" (an alloy of copper and zinc) when it should be "copper" or "bronze" (an alloy of copper and tin). Gen. 4:22; II Sam. 22:35; Job 28:2; Dan. 2:31-39.

Bray. 1. The ass brays when hungry (Job 6:5), and some low-grade people are described contemptuously as braying (Job 30:7). 2. To pound or "bray" as in a mortar (Prov. 27:22).

Brazen Sea. In II Kings 25:13; I Chronicles 18:8, and Jeremiah 52:17, we read of the great "sea of brass," a rather exaggerated figure for the immense laver which Solomon placed in front of the temple.

Brazen Serpent. In Numbers 21:4-9 the people of Israel complained against God, who in judgment sent fiery serpents against them. When the people confessed their sin, Moses made a "serpent of brass," set it upon a pole and in effect said, "Look and live"; and whosoever looked recovered. This brazen serpent later was worshiped, but Hezekiah contemptuously called it "a piece of brass" (II Kings 18:4) and destroyed it. This brazen serpent was a type of our Lord bearing our sins on the cross (John 3:14-16).

Bread, the universal staff of life. Wheat was generally used, but barley was a substitute among the poor. Flour was ground by hand between two stones. Flour, yeast, salt, olive oil and water or milk were the ingredients. Some bread was made without yeast, such as the "unleavened bread" of The Passover (Exod. 12:15-20). Dough placed in the oven was only about ¼ inch thick, and was therefore quickly baked. "Bread" is often used figuratively for food in general (Gen. 3:19; Matt. 6:11). In the Tabernacle the loaves of shewbread indicated the presence of the Lord among His people.

Bread, Shew (See Bread)

Breeches (See Dress; Inner Tunic)

Brick, building material made of clay dried in the sun. The earliest mention of brick in the Bible (Gen. 11:3) shows that the molding of clay into brick and its thorough burning were known

Grinding meal and baking bread. © SPF

when the tower of Babel was built, not more than a century after the Flood; and the finding of potsherds **under** the Flood deposits at Ur and Kish shows that the allied art of making clay into pottery was known before the Flood. The ancient bricks were generally square instead of oblong, and were much larger than ours; something like 13x13x3½ inches, and often were stamped before baking with the name of the monarch: e.g. Sargon or Nebuchadnezzar. Much of the ancient brick-work was of bricks merely baked in the sun, especially in Egypt, but at Babylon the bricks were thoroughly burned.

Bride, Bridegroom (See Wedding)

Bridechamber (See Wedding)

Bridge. The word is not found in the English Bible. Bridges were hardly known among the Israelites, who generally crossed streams by a ford (Gen. 32:22) or a ferry (II Sam. 19:18).

Bridle, the word appears in a literal and figurative sense (Prov. 26:3; Ps. 32:9; James 1:26; 3:2; Rev. 14:20).

Brier (See Plants)

Brimstone, properly "sulphur" (Gen. 19:24). Also used figuratively for punishment and destruction (Job 18:15; Ps. 11:6; Rev. 21:8).

Bronze, an alloy of copper and tin. The word is not found in Scripture, but probably the "steel" used for making metallic bows was really bronze (II Sam. 22:35; Job 20:24). (See Brass).

Brook, a small stream, usually one which flows only during the rainy season (Deut. 2:13; I Kings 18:40; II Sam. 15:23).

Brother. 1. Kinsman of same parents (Gen. 27:6), or the same father (Gen. 28:2), or the same mother (Judg. 8:19). 2. A man of the same country (Exod. 2:11; Acts 3:22). 3. Member of the same tribe (II Sam. 19:12). 4. An ally (Amos 1:9). 5. One of a kindred people (Num. 20:14). 6. Co-religionist (Acts 9:17; Rom. 1:13). 7. Fellow office-bearer (Ezra 3:2). 8. Someone of equal rank or office (I Kings 9:13). 9. Any member of the human race (Matt. 7:3-5; Heb. 2:17). 10. Someone greatly beloved (II Sam. 1:26). 11. Relative (Gen. 14:16; Matt. 12:46).

Brothers of Our Lord. James, Joses, Simon, and Judas are called the Lord's brothers (Matt. 13:55); He also had sisters (Matt. 13:56); John 7:1-10 states that His brothers did not believe in Him. There are differences of opinion as to whether the "brothers" were full brothers, cousins, or children of Joseph by a former marriage.

Bucket or **Pail,** the word is used figuratively in Isa. 40:15 and Num. 24:7.

Bukki (bŭk'ī). 1. Prince of the tribe of Dan (Num. 34:22). 2. High priest of Israel (I Chron. 6:5, 51; Ezra 7:4).

Bukkiah (bŭ-kī'ȧ), Levite (I Chron. 25:4, 13).

Bul (bōōl), 8th month of Jewish ecclesiastical year (I Kings 6:38).

Bull (See Animals: Cattle).

Bullock (See Animals: Cattle).

Bulrush (See Plants).

Bunah (bū'nȧ), descendant of Judah (I Chron. 2:25).

Bunni (bŭn'ī), 3 Levites mentioned in Nehemiah had this name (9:4; 10:15; 11:15).

Burden, that which is laid upon one in order to be carried. The word translates eight different words in the OT and three in the NT. When it is literally used, it is easily understood and needs no special comment. Figuratively, it is used in the sense of "responsibility" (Num. 11:11; Matt. 11:30) or of a "sorrow" (Ps. 55:22), but by far the most frequent use in the OT is "oracle" (Isa. 15:1; 19:1; 22:1, etc.). These are generally "dooms," though in Zechariah 12:1 and in Malachi 1:1 the word is used simply for a "message."

Burial. Partly because of God's word, "Dust thou art and to dust thou shalt return" (Gen. 3:19), the people of Israel almost always buried their dead; and because the land of Canaan had so many caves, these places were very frequently used as places of burial. In Canaan, in ancient times, and in the more primitive parts of the land even today, there was (and is) no embalmment in most cases, but immediate burial to avoid unpleasant odors (Acts 5:5-10) and ceremonial uncleanness (Num. 19:11-22). In the time of Christ, men's bodies were wrapped in clean linen (Matt. 27:57-60) and spices and ointments were prepared (Luke 23:56).

Burning. God's judgments have often been accompanied with fire, e.g. Sodom and Gomorrah (Gen. 19:24-28), Nadab and Abihu (Lev. 10:1-6), the 250 rebels in the wilderness (Num. 16:2, 35).

Burning Bush, a thorny bush which Moses saw burning and from which he heard Jehovah speak (Exod. 3:2, 3; Deut. 33:16; Mark 12:26).

Burnt Offering (See Offerings)

Bush (See Plants)

Bushel (See Weights & Measures)

Business (See Trade and Travel)

Butler (See Occupations and Professions)

Butter. It is mentioned eleven times in the OT, of which three are figurative uses: (Job 20:17, "the brooks of honey and butter"; 29:6, "when I washed my steps with butter"; and Psalm 55:21, "the words of his mouth were smoother than butter, but war was in his heart"). In the other cases, where the word is used literally, e.g. Gen. 18:8, it implies good eating.

Buz (bŭz). 1. A nephew of Abraham, second son of Nahor (Gen. 22:21). 2. Head of a family in the tribe of Gad (I Chron. 5:14).

Buzi (bū'zī), Ezekiel's father (Ezek. 1:3).

Byblos (See Gebal)

Byways, literally "crooked paths" traveled to avoid danger (Judges 5:6).

A view of Caesarea Philippi on the slopes of Mount Hermon. © *MPS*

Cab (căb, **a hollow vessel,** ASV "kab"), a measure of capacity, a little less than two quarts; mentioned only in II Kings 6:25.

Cabbon (kăb′ŏn), a town in Judah, taken by Israel from the Amorites (Josh. 15:40).

Cabul (kā′bŭl). 1. A city of Galilee, mentioned in Joshua 19:27 as a border city of the tribe of Asher in the NE of Palestine. 2. A name given by Hiram of Tyre to a district in N Galilee, including twenty cities, which Solomon ceded to him (I Kings 9:13).

Caesar (sē′zêr). 1. The name of a Roman family prominent from the third century B.C., of whom Caius Julius Caesar (c. 102 — Mar. 15,44 B.C.) was by far the most prominent. 2. The title taken by each of the Roman emperors: e.g. Augustus Caesar who reigned when our Lord was born (Luke 2:1); his successor Tiberius Caesar who reigned 14-37 A.D. (Luke 3:1); Claudius Caesar, 41-54 (Acts 11:28; 18:2). Nero, under whom Peter and Paul were martyred, 54-68 (Philip. 4:22). Domitian was "Caesar" from 81-96 and it was under him that John was exiled to Patmos. "Caesar" is mentioned by our Lord (Luke 20:22-25) both literally as referring to Tiberius, and figuratively as meaning any earthly ruler.

Caesarea (sĕs′ȧ-rē′ȧ), a city built between 25-13 B.C. by Herod "the Great" at a vast cost and named in honor of his patron Augustus Caesar. On the coast of the Mediterranean about 25 miles NW of Samaria. Herod intended it as the port of his capital, and a splendid harbor was constructed. It was the home of Cornelius in whose house Peter first preached to the Gentiles (Acts 10). It was the place of residence of Philip, the evangelist, with his four unmarried prophesying daughters (Acts 8:40; 21:8, 9).

Caesarea Philippi (sĕs′ȧ-rē′ȧ fĭ-lĭp′ī **Caesarea of Philip),** a town at the extreme northern boundary of Palestine, about 30 miles inland from Tyre and 50 miles SW of Damascus. Augustus Caesar presented it, with the surrounding country, to Herod the Great, who built a temple there in honor of the emperor. Herod's son, Philip the tetrarch, enlarged the town and named it Caesarea Philippi to distinguish it from the other Caesarea. It was at a secluded spot near here that the Lord began to prepare His disciples for His approaching sufferings and death and resurrection, and that Peter made his famous confession (Matt. 16:13-17).

Cage, so-called when used by the fowler to keep his live birds, but "basket" when used for fruit (Jer. 5:27; Amos 8:1, 2). Cf. Revelation 18:2 KJV.

Caiaphas, Joseph (kā′yȧ-făs). In the century from 168 B.C. when Antiochus Epiphanes desecrated the temple, to 66 B.C. when the Romans took over, the high-priesthood was almost a political office, the priests still coming from the descendants of Aaron but being generally appointed for worldly consideration.

Annas, the father-in-law of Caiaphas (John 18:13) had been high-priest by appointment of the Roman governor from A.D. 7 to 14 (see Luke 3:2) and though three of his sons succeeded for a short period, Caiaphas held the office from A.D. 18-36, with Annas still a sort of "high-priest emeritus." After our Lord had raised Lazarus from the dead (John 11) many of the Jews believed in Him (11:45, 46), but some through jealousy reported the matter to the Pharisees, who with the chief priests gathered a council, fearing, or pretending to fear, that if Jesus were let alone many would accept Him, and the Romans would destroy what was left of Jewish autonomy.

Caesarea on the Mediterranean. Ruins of the ancient seafront from which Paul set sail for Rome and where Peter preached to Cornelius. © MPS

Then Caiaphas (John 11:41-53) declared that it would be better for Jesus to die than that the nation be destroyed. When, a little later, our Lord was betrayed into the hands of His enemies, the Roman soldiers and the Jewish officers took Him first to the house of Annas, where by night He was given the pretense of a trial (John 18:12-23). Then Annas sent Him bound to Caiaphas before whom the "trial" continued (John 18:24-27). Thence He was delivered to Pilate, because the Jews could not legally execute Him.

Cain (kān). 1. The first son of Adam and Eve, and a farmer by occupation. As an offering to God, he brought some of the fruits of the ground, while his brother brought an animal sacrifice. Angry that his offering was not received (Heb. 11:4 shows that this was because of the lack of a right disposition toward God), he slew his brother. He added to his guilt before God by denying his guilt and giving no evidence of repentance. 2. The progenitor of the Kenites (Josh. 15:57). 3. A village in Judah (Josh. 15:57).

Cainan (kā-ī'năn). 1. In ASV "Kenan," the fourth from Adam in the Messianic line (Gen. 5:12-14; I Chron. 1:2; Luke 3:37). 2. A son of Arphaxad (Luke 3:36).

Calah (kā'lȧ), an ancient city of Assyria on the upper reaches of the Tigris, built originally by Nimrod, who is listed in Genesis 10:6-12 as a grandson of Ham. The city was apparently rebuilt by Shalmanezer I (reigned c. 1456-1436 B.C.), then later abandoned for many centuries till Ashurnasir-pal who is pictured as "Ruthlessness Incarnate" (reigned c. 926-902 B.C.) restored it.

Calcol (See Chalcol)

Caldron, a large pot or vessel in which meat is to be boiled (Jer. 52:18, 19 [ASV "pots"]; Ezek. 11:3, 7, 11).

Caleb (kā'leb, **dog).** 1. The son of Jephunneh, the Kenezite; the prince of Judah who represented his tribe among the twelve chief men whom Moses sent from the wilderness to Paran to spy out the land (Num. 13:6). Most of the spies brought back a pessimistic report. Their names are almost forgotten, but two heroes of faith, Caleb and Joshua, who encouraged the people to go up and take the land are still remembered. Caleb was 40 years old when the spies were sent (Josh. 14:7). At the age of 85, at the distribution of the land of Canaan, he asked for Hebron and the hill country where lived the fearful Anakim who had terrorized ten of the spies, and Joshua gave it to him. Later he became father-in-law of Othniel, the first of the "judges" (Judg. 1:12-15, 20). 2. A son of Hezron, son of Judah (I Chron. 2:18, 19, 42).

Caleb - Ephratah (kā'lĕb-ĕf'rȧ-tȧ), named in I Chronicles 2:24 as the place where Hezron died. The Hebrew and LXX texts differ here; and many scholars prefer the LXX reading, "after the death of Hezron, Caleb came unto Ephrath, the wife of Hezron, his father." When a son took his father's wife, it signified that he was claiming his father's possessions.

Calendar. During the Bible period time was reckoned solely on astronomical observations. Days, months, and years were determined by the sun and moon. 1. Days of the week were not named by the Jews, but were designated by ordinal numbers. The Jewish day began in the evening with the appearance of the first stars. Days were subdivided into hours and watches. The Hebrews divided nights into three watches (Exod. 14:24; Judg. 7:19; Lam. 2:19). 2. The seven-day week is of Semitic origin. Egyptians had a week of 10 days. The Jewish week had its origin in the Creation account, and ran consecutively irrespective of lunar or solar cycles. This was done for man's physical and spiritual welfare. The Biblical records are silent regarding the observance of the Sabbath day from creation to the time of Moses. Sabbath observance was either revived or given special emphasis by Moses (Exod. 16:23; 20:8). 3. The Hebrew month began with the new moon. Before the exile months were designated by numbers. After the exile names adopted from the Babylonians were used. Synchronized Jewish sacred calendar: 1. Nisan (March-April) (7). 2. Iyyar (April-May) (8). 3. Sivan (May-June) (9). 4. Tammuz (June-July) (10). 5. Ab (July-August) (11). 6. Elul (August-September) (12). 7. Tishri (September-October) (1). 8. Heshvan (October-November) (2). 9. Kislev (November-December) (3). 10. Tabeth (December-January) (4). 11. Shebat (January-February) (5). 12. Adar (February-March) (6). 4. The Jewish calendar had two concurrent years, the sacred year, beginning in the spring with the month

Nisan, and the civic year, beginning with Tishri, numbered in parentheses above. The sacred year was instituted by Moses, and consisted of lunar months of 29½ days each, with an intercalary month, called Adah Sheni, every 3 years. Every 7th year was a sabbatical year for the Jews — a year of solemn rest for landlords, slaves, beasts of burden, and land, and freedom for Hebrew slaves. Every 50th year was a Jubilee year, observed by family reunions, canceled mortgages, and return of lands to original owners (Lev. 25:8-17).

Calf, a young bull or cow. Calves were used for food and for sacrifice.

Calf, Golden (See Calf Worship)

Calf Worship was a part of the religious worship of almost all ancient Semitic peoples. At least as early as the Exodus, living bulls were worshiped in Egypt. Bulls symbolized strength, vigor, and endurance.

Aaron made a golden calf in order that the people might worship Jehovah under this form (Exod. 32:4). After the division of the kingdom, Jeroboam set up two golden calves in his kingdom, one at Bethel and one at Dan (I Kings 12:28, 29). In time, these images, at first recognized as symbols, came to be regarded as common idols (I Kings 12:30; Hos. 13:2).

Calker, one who makes a boat waterproof (Ezek. 27:9, 27).

Call (calling), one of the most common verbs in the Bible, used principally with one or another of four different meanings: 1. To speak out in the way of prayer (Jer. 33:3). 2. To summon or appoint (Jer. 1:15). 3. To name a person or thing (Gen. 1:5). 4. To invite men to accept salvation through Christ. This last is a call by God through the Holy Spirit, and is heavenly (Heb. 3:1) and holy (II Tim. 1:9).

Calneh (kăl'nĕ), one of the four cities, including also Babel, Erech (whence "Iraq"), and Akkad which were founded by Nimrod in the third generation after the Flood (Gen. 10:10).

Calno (kăl'nō), a city named in Isaiah 10:9 in a list of the Assyrians' victories.

Calvary (kăl'vȧ-rē, **skull),** a place not far from the walls of Jerusalem where Christ was crucified and near which He was buried (Luke 23:33). The Latin **calvaria** is a rendering of the Greek **kranion,** skull, which renders the Hebrew **Gulgoleth** and the Aramaic **Gulgulta.** The common explanation is that

The bronze bull-calf of the god Apis of Egypt, after which the Israelites may have patterned the golden calf of the wilderness. © BM

the name was due to the cranial shape of the hill.

Camel, draught animal of Semitic peoples (II Kings 8:9); source of wealth; regarded as unclean by Israelites (Lev. 11:4); hair used for cloth (II Kings 1:8 RSV; Matt. 3:4).

Camel's Hair, mentioned only in Matt. 3:4 and Mark 1:6, where it is said that John the Baptist wore a garment of camel's hair. Such garments are still used in the Near East.

Camon or **Kamon** (cā'mŏn), town in Gilead near Mazareth (Judg 10:5).

Camp, Encampment, a group of tents intended for traveling or for temporary residence as in case of war. Israel in the wilderness was given precise instructions as to the order and arrangements of its camp, both at rest and in traveling (Num. 2, 3).

Camphire (kăm'fīr), an Asiatic thorny shrub with fragrant white flowers (S. of Sol. 1:14; 4:13). "Henna-flowers" in ASV.

Cana of Galilee (kā'nȧ of găl'ĭ-lē), mentioned four times in the Gospel of John (2:1-11; 4:36-54; 21:2) and nowhere else in Scripture. It was in the highlands of Galilee, as one had to go **down** from there to Capernaum; but opinions differ as to its exact location.

Canaan, Canaanites (kā′năn, kā′năn-īts). 1. Canaan was the son of Ham in the genealogical lists in Genesis 9, 10. His descendants occupied Canaan and took their name from that country (Gen. 9:18, 22; 10:6). 2. Canaan was one of the old names for Palestine, the land of the Canaanites dispossessed by the Israelites. The etymology of the name is unknown, as is also the earliest history of the name; but Egyptian inscriptions of c. 1800 B.C. use it for the coastland between Egypt and Asia Minor. The Canaanites were of Semitic stock, and were part of a large migration of Semites (Phoenicians, Amorites, Canaanites) from NE Arabia in the third millennium B.C. They came under Egyptian control c. 1500 B.C. The Israelites were never able completely to exterminate them.

Canaanite, Simon the, so-called in Matthew 10:4 KJV, but in ASV "the Cannanaean" (margin "or Zealot"); one of the original twelve apostles.

Cananaean (kā′nȧ-nē′ăn), the description of Simon "the Zealot" in Matthew 10:4 ASV, but "Canaanite" by mistake in KJV. Probably "zealot" (Luke 6:15) from an Aramaic word is the correct description.

Candace (kăn′dȧ-sē), the Queen of Ethiopia mentioned only in Acts 8:27. The name seems to have been a general designation of Ethiopian queens (like "Pharaoh" for Egyptian kings, and "Caesar" for Roman emperors).

Candlestick. The Hebrew word **menôrâh,** always rendered "candlestick" in KJV, occurs 43 times in the OT, but could more accurately be rendered "lampstand," because the "lights" were not candles at all, but olive-oil lamps.

Candy, a word that does not occur in the Bible, but the Jews had "confections" (Exod. 30:35) and the children chewed sugar cane when they could.

Cane, probably the sweet calamus (in KJV Isa. 43:24; Jer. 6:20 only; but cf. Exod. 30:23, where it is listed among the "chief spices").

Canker (kăn′kêr, **gangrene),** a word that occurs once in Scripture, II Timothy 2:17. It may mean cancer. See Diseases.

Cankerworm, the name given to a larval stage of the locust (Joel 1:4; 2:25; Nah. 3:15, 16). It was very voracious (Nah. 3:15). See Insects.

Canneh (kăn′ē), mentioned only in Ezekiel 27:23 among the towns and regions with which Tyre traded. Some identify it with Calneh, **q.v.**

Canonicity. By the canon is meant the list of the books of the Bible accepted by the Christian Church as genuine and inspired. The Protestant canon includes 39 books in the OT and 27 in the New. The Roman Catholic canon has 7 more books and some additional pieces in the OT. The Jews have the same OT canon as the Protestants. The OT canon was formed before the time of Christ, as is evident from Josephus (Against Apion 1:8), who wrote c. A.D. 90. We know very little of the history of the acceptance of the OT books as canonical. There is much more documentary evidence regarding the formation of the NT canon. The Muratorian Canon (c. A.D. 170), which survives only as a fragment, lists most of the NT books. Some of the books were questioned for a time for various reasons, usually uncertainty of authorship, but by the end of the 4th century our present canon was almost universally accepted, and this was done not by arbitrary decree of bishops, but by the general concensus of the church.

Capernaum (kȧ-pûr′nā-ŭm, **village of Nahum),** a town on the NW shore of the Sea of Galilee where Jesus made His headquarters during His ministry in Galilee (Matt. 4:13; Mark 2:1). In Scripture it is mentioned only in the

Ruins of the ancient synagogue at Capernaum. © MPS

Gospels, and perhaps did not arise until after the Captivity. Jesus performed many striking miracles there, among them the healing of the centurion's palsied servant (Matt. 8:5-13), the man sick of the palsy borne by four (Mark 2:1-13), and a nobleman's son (John 4:46-54). It was there that He called Matthew to the apostleship as he was sitting at the receipt of custom (Matt. 9:9-13). The discourse on the Bread of Life, which followed the feeding of the 5,000, and many other addresses were delivered there (Mark 9:33-50). In spite of Jesus' striking works and teachings, the people did not repent, and Jesus predicted the complete ruin of the place (Matt. 11: 23, 24; Luke 10:15). His prophecy was so completely fulfilled that the town has disappeared and its very site is a matter of debate.

Caph (kȧf), the 11th letter of the Hebrew alphabet corresponding to our "k." As a numeral it is eleven.

Caphtor (kăf′tôr), place from which the Philistines originally came (Amos 9:7), probably from the island of Crete.

Cappadocia (kăp′ȧ-dō′shĭ-ȧ), province in E part of Asia Minor; its people were Aryans (Acts 2:9; I Peter 1:1).

Captain, a title usually expressing leadership, not necessarily military as the "captain of the temple" (Acts 4:1). The term does not refer to specific grades or ranks in a military organization.

Captivity. The term Captivity has reference to the captivity of the Ten Tribes in 722 B.C. and to the captivity of Judah in 586 B.C. Both came in stages. After a series of invasions by the Assyrian kings Tiglath-pileser (II Kings 15:29; I Chron. 5:26) and Shalmaneser (II Kings 17:3, 5), Sargon II (II Kings 17:6, 7) took the Ten Tribes captive, and Esarhaddon and Ashurbanipal imported to the region of Samaria some conquered peoples from the East (Ezra 4:2, 10). The Southern Kingdom was taken into captivity by the Babylonian king, Nebuchadnezzar, over a period of years. In 605 B.C. he took to Babylon some members of the nobility, including Daniel the prophet (II Chron. 36:2-7; Jer. 45:1; Dan. 1: 1-3); in 597 B.C. he carried off King Jehoiachin and thousands of the nobility and leading people (II Kings 24: 14-16), among them the prophet Ezekiel; in 586 B.C. he destroyed Jerusalem and deported into Babylonia all but the poorest of the land (II Kings 25:2-21); 5 years later still another group was taken into Babylonia. Ezra and Nehemiah describe the return of the captives, which took place in 538 B.C., when Cyrus king of Persia, to whom Babylonia fell the year before, issued a decree permitting the return of the Jews (Ezra 1:1-4), of whom 43,-000 returned with Zerubbabel (Ezra 2:64). In 458 B.C. 1800 returned with Ezra.

Caravan, company of travelers united together for a common purpose or for mutual protection and generally equipped for a long journey, especially in desert country or through foreign and presumably hostile territory (Gen. 32, 33; I Sam. 30:1-20).

Carbuncle, a word occurring four times in KJV but rendering three different Hebrew words, all representing something bright and glittering. Both ruby and emerald have been suggested as equivalents. Used in the high priest's breastplate (Exod. 28:17; 39:10). See Minerals.

Carcas (kȧr′kăs), a eunuch in the service of Xerxes ("Ahasuerus") (Esth. 1:10).

Carcase (ASV and modern English, **carcass**), the dead body of a man or beast. The word is a translation of six different words in Scripture with root ideas of something fallen, faded, exhausted; or just the bare idea of body, as in Judges 14:8, 9.

Carchemish (kȧr′kē-mĭsh), an ancient city of the Hittites located on the W bank of the Euphrates 63 miles NE of Aleppo.

Careah (kȧ-rē′ȧ), or generally and more properly Kareah. The father of Johanan and Jonathan who tried to save Gedaliah from assassination (Jer. 40:8-43:7), but later wickedly went to Egypt to dwell there.

Carmel (kȧr′mĕl, **garden**). **1.** The mountainous promontory jutting into the Mediterranean Sea just S of the modern city Haifa and straight W of the Sea of Galilee. At Carmel Elijah stood against 850 heathen prophets and defeated them (I Kings 18). Carmel was visited by Elisha (II Kings 2:25; 4:25). 2. A very ancient town of Judah about seven miles nearly S of Hebron. First mentioned in Joshua 15: 55, it is best known as the residence of the very churlish Nabal (I Sam. 25: 2-40).

Sunset scene at M. Carmel on Mediterranean coast. © MPS

Carmelite (kȧr′mĕl-īt), a native of Judaean Carmel: applied to David's wife Abigail who had first married Nabal (I Sam. 27:3, etc.) and to Hezro, one of David's mighty men (I Chron. 11. 37, etc.).

Carmi (kȧr′mē). 1. One of the sons of Reuben, eldest son of Jacob (Gen. 46: 9; Num. 26:6, etc.). 2. An early descendant of Judah (probably great-grandson) and father of Achan (Josh. 7:1).

Carnal (kȧr′nȧl). Fleshly, of or pertaining to the body as the seat of the desires and appetites; usually employed in Scripture in the bad sense, as opposed to spiritual.

Carpenter (See Occupations, Professions)

Carpus (kȧr′pŭs), friend of Paul (II Tim. 4:13).

Carriage, baggage (I Sam. 17:22; Isa. 10:28).

Carshena (kȧr′ shē-nȧ), Medo-Persian prince (Esth. 1:14).

Carts, light, small, usually two-wheeled vehicles for carrying people or freight (I Sam. 6:7-16; Amos 2:13).

Casiphia (cā-sĭf′ĭ-ȧ), place where exiled Levites lived (Ezra 8:17).

Casluhim (kăs′lū-hĭm), people descended from Mizraim (Gen. 10:13, 14; I Chron. 1:11, 12).

Cassia (See Plants)

Castle, fortified building or stronghold (Neh. 7:2—KJV has "palace"). Where KJV has "castles," ASV sometimes, more correctly, uses encampments (I Chron. 6:54).

Castor and Pollux (kȧs′têr, pŏl′ŭks, **sons of Zeus),** sons of Zeus by Leda; considered tutelary deities favorable to sailors (Acts 28:11).

Catacombs, subterranean burial places used by the early church. Most are in Rome, where they extend for 600 miles.

Caterpillar (See Insects)

Catholic Epistles, term applied to the Epistles of James, Peter, John, and Jude, probably because most of them are not addressed to individual churches or persons, but to the universal church.

Cattle (See Animals)

Cauda (kow′dȧ), a small island lying about 25 miles to the S of Crete (Acts 27:16 in KJV "Clauda").

Caul. 1. The chief meaning is a deep fold above the liver, the omentum, which is loaded with fat and which with the kidneys was used in several of the Levitical offerings (Lev. 3:4; 4: 9, etc.) 2. The pericardium or the breast as a whole (Hos. 13:8). 3. Bag or purse (Isa. 3:18). See also Dress.

Cave, hollowed-out place in the earth, usually in limestone, used as dwellings, places of refuge, burial, storehouses, cisterns, stables for cattle (Gen. 19:30; I Kings 19:9; Judg. 6:2; Matt. 27:60; John 11:38).

Cedar (See Plants)

Cedron (sē′drŏn, in ASV more properly "Kidron"), a ravine which in winter contains the brook of the same name, flowing southward between Jerusalem and Mt. of Olives on the E of the city.

Ceiling (KJV and ERV "cieling"), appears only in I Kings 6:15. The reference here is not to the upper surface of a room, but to the inner walls. The word "ceiled" appears several times, but it usually means to panel the walls of a building.

Cellar, a place for storage of wine (I Chron. 27: 27) or oil (v. 28). Not a room under a house, but a place of storage.

Cenchrea (sĕn′krē-ȧ, **Cenchreae** in ASV), the eastern harbor of Corinth, and the little town on the harbor.

Censer, a vessel, probably shaped like a saucepan, for holding incense while it is being burned (Num. 16:6, 7, 39).

Census, a numbering and registration of a people. The Bible tells of a number of censuses (Exod. 38:26; Num. 1:2, 3; 26:51; I Chron. 21:1-6; 27:24; I Kings 5:15; II Chron. 2:17, 18; Ezra 2; Luke 2:1).

Centurion (cĕn-tū′rĭ-ŏn, Lat. **centum,** 100), commander of a hundred soldiers in the Roman army. The one first mentioned is the centurion of Capernaum whose beloved servant was sick unto death (Matt. 8:15-13; Luke 7:2-

10). The next is Cornelius (Acts 10) "a devout man, and one that feared God with all his house." Another was Julius, of the Augustan band (Acts 27:1-43) whose duty it was to take Paul to Rome. He saved Paul's life when the soldiers wished to kill all the prisoners, and Paul, by his presence and counsel, saved the centurion with all the ship's company. Other centurions are mentioned elsewhere (Matt. 27:54; Acts 22:25; 23:17).

Cephas (sē'făs, **rock,** or **stone).** A name given by Jesus to the Apostle Peter (John 1:42). See Peter.

Chaff, refuse of grain which has been winnowed (Job. 21:18; Ps. 1:4; Isa. 17:13; Hos. 13:3; Zeph. 2:2); also dry grass (Isa. 5:24) and straw (Jer. 23:28). Often used figuratively for something worthless (Ps. 1:4; Matt. 3:12).

Chain, used as mark of distinction (Gen. 41:42; Dan 5:7, 16, 29), for ornaments in the tabernacle (Exod. 28:14, 22; 39:15, 17, 18), for fetters (Pss. 68:6; 149:8; Isa. 45:14); also used figuratively for oppression (Lam. 3:7; Pss. 73:6; 149:8).

Chalcedony (kăl-sĕd'ō-nē, kăl-sĕ-dō'nē), the precious stone adorning the third foundation of the New Jerusalem (Rev. 21:19).

Chalcol (kăl'kŏl), descendant of Mahol (I Kings 4:31). Solomon was wiser than he. Calcol, a descendant of Zerah (I Chron. 2:6). Since four of the same names occur in both passages as brothers, Chalcol and Calcol are probably the same person. ASV, RSV have Calcol in both places.

Chaldaea or **Chaldea** (kăl-dē'ȧ), the country of which Babylon was the capital, and which conquered Judah and carried its inhabitants into captivity.

Chaldean (kăl-dē'ăn), coming from Chaldaea.

Chaldean Astrologers (See Wise Men)

Chaldees (kăl-dēz, kăl'dēz), the people of Chaldea; the Chaldeans.

Chambering (chām'bêr-ĭng), illicit intercourse (Rom. 13:13).

Chamberlain (chām'bêr-lĭn). In the OT the eunuch in charge of a king's harem (Esth. 1:10, 12, 15; 2:3, 14, 15, 21). In Acts 12:20 the chamberlain is an attendant on a lord in his bedchamber. In Rom. 16:23 he is a steward.

Chambers of Imagery, rooms in the temple where seventy elders of Israel worshiped idols with incense.

Chameleon (See Animals)

Chamois (See Animals)

Chanaan (See Canaan)

A Jewish money-changer in Jerusalem. © *MPS*

Chancellor (Chȧn'sĕ-lêr, RSV **commander),** a Persian official in Palestine (Ezra 4:8, 9, 17).

Changers of Money, men who exchanged one currency for another at a premium. Coins issued by many governments circulated in Palestine; also Jews must convert their currency into shekels for the temple-tax. It was not the trade but the place where they plied it which led Christ to drive them out of the temple court (Matt. 21:12; Mark 11:15; John 2:14, 15).

Chapman (chăp'măn), a peddler (II Chron. 9:14).

Charashim (kăr'ă-shĭm, **craftsmen),** Valley of, E. of Joppa between Ono to the N and Lod (Lydda) to the S (I Chron. 4:14).

Charchemish, Carchemish (kȧr'kē mĭsh, kȧr-kē'mĭsh), Hittite capital on the Euphrates. See Carchemish.

Charger, a dish or platter given as an offering for the tabernacle (Num. 7:13-85); called "dishes" in Exodus 25:29; 37:16.

Chariot (chăr'ĭ-ŭt), a two-wheeled vehicle for war, racing, processions, etc. (Gen. 41:43; 46:29; I Kings 18:44; II Kings 5:9; Acts 8:28). Used by enemies of Israel (Exod. 14:7-15:19; I Sam. 13:5, but not by Israel until time of David (II Sam. 8:4; I Kings 9:19; 10:26).

Charity (chăr'ĭ-tē). Charity in the Bible never means giving to the poor, but always a God-inspired love which includes respect for, and concern for the welfare of the loved one. The inspired description is found in I Cor. 13.

Charran (See Haran)

Chaste, Chastity (chāst, chăs′tĭ-tē, originally meaning **pure** in a ritual sense, **tabu, consecrated;** it developed a moral sense as the Greeks gained higher conceptions of deity. Derivatives are translated "pure," "pureness," "purity," "purify," "purification," "sincerely," and in the LXX they are used for Heb. words of kindred meanings. Chastity in the relations of men and women is the NT norm; the standard for all forms of purity.

Chastisement (chăs′tīz-mĕnt, discipline [the moral nature]. Translated by many English words, exhibiting shades of meaning derived from the central concept; the widest sense (Deut. 11:2); **punishment** (Jer. 30:14); **discipline** (Heb. 12:8); in Isaiah 53:5 the whole range of meaning is exhibited in the substitution of the sinless Servant of Jehovah for His guilty people. Chastisement is the process by which God provides a Substitute to bear our sins, brings men to put their trust in Him, trains those whom He has received till they reach maturity.

Chebar (kē′bȧr), a river or canal beside which Ezekiel saw visions (Ezek. 1:1; 3:23; 10:15, 20, 22; 43:3).

Checker Work (chĕk′êr-wûrk), ornamentation for the capitals of two pillars in Solomon's temple (I Kings 7: 17).

Chedorlaomer (kĕd′ŏr-lā-ō′mûr), king (Gen. 14:1, 4, 5, 9, 17) of Elam, S of Media and E of Babylonia; named by Semites (Gen. 10:22). Chedorlaomer and his allies conquered the country they traversed, and met the king of Sodom and his allies on the same battleground (the value of Siddim or the Salt Sea) where Chedorlaomer had defeated them 14 years earlier. The bitumen pits of the region were the undoing of the local defenders. But Abram the Hebrew in a swift night raid with 318 retainers recovered the spoil of Sodom, and pursued the invaders to a point near Damascus. The story is told fully (Gen. 14) because it involved Abram and his brother's son Lot.

Cheese. Milk of kine, goats or sheep was stored in skins. In a warm climate, without refrigeration, it would soon curdle and become cheese.

Chelal (kē′lăl), a man of Palath-moab who put away his foreign wife (Ezra 10:30).

Chelluh (kĕl′ū), one of the sons of Bani who married a foreign wife (Ezra 10:35).

Chelub (kē′lŭb, another form of **Caleb).** 1. A brother of Shuah, a Judahite (I Chron. 4:11). 2. Father of Ezri, and superintendent of the tillers of the ground in David's time (I Chron. 27: 26).

Chelubai (kē-lōō′bī), son of Hezron, elsewhere called Caleb (I Chron. 2:9).

Chemarim (kĕm′ȧ-rĭm). Idolatrous priests (II Kings 23:5; Hos. 10:5).

Chemosh (kē′mŏsh), the god of Moab (Num. 21:29, alluded to in Jer. 48:7, 13, 46). Solomon introduced the worship of Chemosh into Jerusalem to please a foreign wife, though thereby he displeased his God (I Kings 11:7, 33). Josiah put an end to its use as a place of worship (II Kings 23:13).

Chenaanah (kē-nā′ȧ-nȧ). 1. The father of the false prophet Zedekiah who smote Micaiah (I Kings 22:11, 24; II Chron 18:10, 23). 2. The brother of Ehud (I Chron. 7:10).

Chenani (kē-nā′nī, kĕn′ȧ-nī), a Levite who helped bring the returned exiles into agreement about the covenant worship of God (Neh. 9:4).

Chenaniah (kĕn′ȧ-nī′ȧ). 1. A chief Levite who brought up the ark from the house of Obededom (I Chron. 15:22, 27). 2. An Izharite, an officer of David's (I Chron. 26:29).

Chephar-haammoni (kē′fȧr-hă-ăm′ō-nī, ASV, RSV Chephar-ammoni, Josh. 18:24), an Ammonite town in the territory of Benjamin.

Chephirah (kē-fī′rȧ), a Hivite town which, with Gibeon, by deceit gained the protection of the Israelites (Josh. 9:17); in the territory of Benjamin (Josh. 18:26); some of whose citizens returned after the Exile (Ezra 2:25; Neh. 7:29).

Cheran (kērăn), son of Dishon, the son of Seir the Horite (Gen. 36:26; I Chron. 1:41).

Cherethim, Cherethites (kĕr′ĕ-thim, kĕr′ĕ-thīts), a Philistine tribe in southern Palestine (I Sam. 30:14; Ezek. 25: 16; Zeph. 2:5), from whom David drew his bodyguard, commanded by Benaiah (II Sam. 8:18; 15:18; 20:7, 23; I Kings 1:38, 44; I Chron. 18:17).

Cherith (kē′rĭth), the brook where, at God's command, Elijah hid himself during the first part of the famine he had predicted (I Kings 17:1-5).

Cherub (chĕr′ŭb), pl., **Cherubim** (cher′ŭ-bĭm), KJV has cherubims. Outside the Bible, the English plural is cherubs. Cherubim are living heavenly creatures in winged human-animal form with the faces of lion, ox, man, and eagle. Guardians of Eden (Gen. 3:24); two golden cherubim were placed on the mercy seat above the ark (Exod. 25:18-22; curtains of the tabernacle were embroidered with cherubim (Exod. 26:1); God dwelt between cherubim (Num. 7:89; I Sam. 4:4) and rides on them (II Sam. 22:11); Solomon placed 2 cherubim in Holy of Holies (I Kings 6:23-28; 8:7). See Rev. 4:6, 9.

Cherub (kē′rŭb), unknown place in Babylonia from which exiles returned (Ezra 2:59).

Chesalon (kĕs′ȧ-lŏn), landmark on N border of Judah, W of Jerusalem (Josh. 15:10).

Chesed (kē′sĕd, kĕs′ĕd), son of Nahor, and nephew of Abraham (Gen. 22:22).

Chesil (kē′sĭl, kĕ′sĭl), a town in the S of Judah, near Hormah and Ziklag Josh. 15:30).

Chest. 1. Receptacles for money to repair the temple (II Kings 12:9, 10; II Chron. 24:8, 10, 11). 2. "Chests of rich apparel, bound with cords, and made of cedar," of the merchandise of Tyre (Ezek. 27:24).

Chestnut Tree (See Plants)

Chesulloth (kē-sŭl′ŏth), a town in Issachar (Josh. 19:18).

Chezib (kē′zĭb), the town where Shelah was born to Judah and Shuah (Gen. 38:5).

Chicken (See Birds)

Chidon (kī′dŏn), threshing floor of, (I Chron. 13:9), where Uzza died for touching the ark.

Childbearing, an expression found only in I Tim. 2:15, a verse of uncertain meaning.

Child, Children, (chīld, chĭl′drĕn). Among the people of the Bible, both OT and NT, as in most other cultures, children, especially male, were greatly desired (Gen. 15:2; 30:1; I Sam. 1:11, 20; Pss. 127:3; 128:3; Luke 1:7, 28). Among the Hebrews all the firstborn belonged to God and must be redeemed (Num. 3:40-51). Children were sometimes dedicated to God for special service (Judg. 13:2-7; I Sam. 1:11; Luke 1:13-17, 76-79). Discipline was to be firm, with corporal punishment (Prov. 22:15; 23:13; 29:15). Much was expected of children (Prov. 20:11). Obedience and respect to parents were commanded (Exod. 21:17; Eph. 6:1-3; Col. 3:20; I Tim. 3:4, 12; Tit. 1:6). Affection for children is strikingly portrayed in many instances, as in David's love for a child who died (II Sam. 12:15-23); and in the raising of children to life by Elijah (I Kings 17:17-24), by Elisha (II Kings 4:18-37) and by Jesus (Matt. 9:23-26; Mark 5: 35-43; Luke 8:49-56). Jesus' love and concern for children is seen in Matthew 18:1-14; 19:13-15; Mark 9:35-37; 10:13-16; Luke 9:46-48; 18:15-17. Jesus recognized children's play (Matt. 11:16). Many attractive pictures of childhood occur; e.g. Moses (Exod. 2:1-10), Samuel (I Sam. 1:20-3:19), Jesus (Luke 2:7-40), Timothy (II Tim. 1:5; 3:14, 15).

Children of God. 1. Angelic beings (Job 1:6, 2:1; 38:7). 2. Men, by creation (Luke 3:38; Isa. 64:8). 3. Israel in covenant relation to God (Exod. 4:22). 4. Individual Israelites (Hos. 1:10). 5. Gentiles (Isa. 19:25). 6. Jesus (Matt. 3:17; 17:5; Luke 1:35). 7. God's redeemed ones (John 1:12; 14:6).

Children of Israel (See Israel)

Chileab (kĭl′ē-ăb), son of David (II Sam. 3:3).

Chilion (kĭl′ĭ-ŏn), son of Elimelech and Naomi; married Orpah (Ruth 1:2-5; 4:9, 10).

Chilmad (kĭl′măd), place (site unknown) which traded with Tyre (Ezek. 27:23).

Chimham (kĭm′hăm), Gileadite friend of David (II Sam. 19:37-40).

Chinnereth, Chinneroth (kĭn′ē-rĕth, rŏth). 1. A fortified city on the NW shore of the Sea of Galilee (Josh. 19: 35). 2. District in Galilee (I Kings 15: 20). 3. The sea later known as Gennesaret or Galilee (Num. 34:11; Deut. 3:17; Josh. 11:2; 12:3; 13:27).

Chios (kī′ŏs), an island in the Mediterranean Sea (Acts 20:15).

Chislev (kĭz′lev, KJV Chisleu), the ninth month of the Hebrew ritual year (Neh. 1:1; Zech. 7:1).

Chislon (kĭz′lŏn), the father of Elidad, the prince of Benjamin in Moses' time (Num. 34:21).

Chisloth-Tabor (kĭs′lŏth-tā′bêr), the same place as Chesulloth (Josh. 19: 12).

Chittim, Kittim (kĭt′ĭm), descendants of Javan (Gen. 10:4; 1 Chron. 1:7, Kittim); Cyprus and its inhabitants, and eventually also the islands and coasts of the Mediterranean (Isa. 23: 12; Jer. 2:10; Ezek. 27:6).

Chiun (kī′ŭn), the god Saturn (Amos 5:26). Probably same as Rephan.

Chloe (klō′ē), a woman whose people informed Paul of contentions in the

Bethlehem in Judaea. © *MPS*

Corinthian church. She was well-known to the Corinthian Christians by her personal name (I Cor. 1:11).

Chorashan (kŏr′ăsh′ăn), a place in the S of Judah (I Sam. 30:30).

Chorazin (kō-rā′zĭn), modern **Khirbet Kerâzeh,** ruins about two miles N of Capernaum. Mentioned only in the woes Christ pronounced upon it (Matt. 11:21; Luke 10:13).

Chozeba (kō-zē′bȧ), a town of Judah (I Chron. 4:22).

Christ, Jesus (krīst, jē′zŭs, Gr. **Iesous,** for Heb. **Jeshua, Jehoshua, Joshua, Jehovah is salvation;** Heb. **mashiah,** Gr. **Christos, anointed).** Christ signifies Anointed One (Acts 10:38); Jesus signifies Saviour (Matt. 1:21, 25; Luke 1:31).

I. Comprehensive Life and Work. The Scriptures teach the pre-existence of Jesus (John 1:1). All things have been created and are maintained in existence by Him (Col. 1). Moses and the prophets spoke of Him in OT times (John 5:46; Luke 24:27, 44). In OT times He appeared as the Angel of Jehovah (Gen. 18:1-19; Judg. 13). By His incarnation He took on human nature to reveal God more fully (John 1:14, 18) and to redeem men (Mark 10:45). He is still the God-man, and in heaven He represents the saints before God (I John 2:1; Heb. 7:25). Some day He will return for His people, judge all men, and usher in His eternal kingdom, where there will be no sin and death.

II. The Earthly Ministry. The Messiah foretold in the OT came in the fulness of time (Gal. 4:4). God providentially supplied the proper background for His appearing and mission. The hand of God may be seen in using Augustus to make possible the birth of Jesus in the place appointed by prophetic announcement (Luke 2:1-7; Mic. 5:2). The shepherds and the Magi from the East illustrate the joy of humble folk in seeing the Saviour and the desire of Gentiles to share in the benefits of the incarnation. Christ was not simply a messenger from God like an OT prophet, but the eternal Son of God taking on human nature, yet free from any taint of sin. He had a divine and a human nature united in one person. The boy Jesus grew up in a normal way, developing in body and advancing in knowledge and wisdom. He performed no miracles until after He began His public ministry. At His baptism the Holy Spirit anointed Him to enable Him to fulfill His ministry. Immediately following His baptism Satan tempted Him to break His dependence on the Father and rely upon special consideration as the Son of God. His ministry was a brief one, about 2-½ or 3-½ years. The Gospel of John supplements the Synoptic Gospels in telling about the place of Jesus' ministry. A large part of his Gospel reports His ministry in Judea, whereas the Synoptic Gospels stress His ministry in Galilee, although there are also notices of visits to Tyre and Sidon (Matt. 15:21-28), Caesarea-Philippi (Matt. 16:13ff), the Decapolis (Mark 7:31), Samaria (Luke 9:51-56), and Perea (Mark 10:1). During His Galilean ministry Jesus made Capernaum His headquarters. From there He went forth to the surrounding country healing the sick, casting out demons, and preaching the coming of the kingdom of God. By the kingdom of God is meant the rule of God over His willing creatures. The kingdom is both a present and a future reality. Entrance into the present aspect of the kingdom comes through faith in the Son of God. The final phase will be inaugurated when Jesus comes again in power and glory. A characteristic teaching method of Jesus was the parable. This He used to veil the truth from His enemies, who were hoping to hear Him say something incriminating so they could arrest Him, and to reveal the truth to His friends more clearly. During the earlier phase of His ministry Jesus ministered mainly to the multitude. He was popular with it until He refused to be made king after the feeding of the 5,000 and made clear that He was not the political redeemer they were looking for, but was Bread from heaven. The multitude then abandoned Him, and He spent a large part of His remaining ministry teaching the Twelve, chiefly about His coming death and resurrection. Somehow even those closest to Him could not see the necessity of His death, even when they recognized Him as Messiah and the son of the living God, as Peter did at Caesarea Philippi. His chief opponents were the scribes and Pharisees, who resented His rejection of the traditions they kept so carefully and who were shocked when He claimed to be deity and declared men's sins forgiven. They made common cause with their opponents, the Sadducees, and with the Herodians to destroy Jesus. From the days of the transfiguration on, He moved steadily toward Jerusalem to fulfill His mission at the cross. At least a quarter of the Gospel material is devoted to Passion Week and the resurrection story, showing that for the early church the events of this period were of supreme importance. Christ came to die; but His resurrection was the Father's attestation to the truth of the claims Christ made about Himself.

III. Names, Titles, and Offices. The name Jesus means Saviour (Matt. 1:21) and is the same as the Hebrew name Joshua. It is usually joined with other terms; when it stands alone it is doubtless for the purpose of emphasizing His humanity. **Christ,** meaning "anointed one," is the Greek equivalent of the Hebrew word **Messiah.** Often it is used with the definite article, which gives it the force of "the promised Christ." Sometimes Jesus forbade people to make Him known as the Messiah (Matt. 16:20). Jesus knew that if this title should be used freely of Him among the Jews, it would excite the populace to expect in Him a political Messiah. Since this was not the purpose of Jesus He suppressed the use of the term except among the apostles (Matt. 16:16). The name **Emmanuel** occurs only once (Matt. 1:23), and means "God with us." Because of the years He spent in Nazareth Jesus was often called the Nazarene (Luke 24:19). When Jesus referred to Himself His most usual method of identification was to use the title **Son of Man.** This may occasionally lay stress on Jesus' humanity, but in the main it serves to point to His transcendence as a

The traditional Mount of Temptation. © MPS

heavenly figure (Dan. 7:13). The designation **Son of God** sets off the uniqueness of this particular Son. It is to be noticed that whenever Jesus spoke of the Father He recognized a unique relationship to Him, one that human beings cannot share. The title **Son of David** (Matt. 21:9; Luke 18:38) is a distinctly Messianic title pointing to Him as the one who fulfilled the Davidic covenant. A few passages proclaim outright that Jesus is **God** (John 1:1, 18; 20:28; Rom. 9:5; Titus 2:13; Heb. 1:8). The term **Lord** (Acts 2:36; 10:36; Rom. 10:9; I Cor. 8:6; Phil. 2:11) denotes the sovereignty of Christ, His headship over the individual believer, the church as a body, and all things. The title **Word** (John 1:1, 14; I John 1:1) points to Jesus as the revealer of God. The designation **Servant** (Phil. 2:7) illustrates that the early church regarded Jesus as fulfilling the Servant of Jehovah role in Himself (see Matt. 12:17-21). The name Saviour suggests the reason for Jesus coming into the world (Luke 2:11; John 4:42). Jesus' saving mission is also declared in the expression, **Lamb of God** (John 1:29, 36). Jesus is referred to as **High Priest** in Hebrews and **Mediator** between God and man in I Tim. 2:5. Paul uses the title **Last Adam** (I Cor. 15:45) in contrast to the first Adam, suggesting the undoing of the consequences of sin brought on by Adam's transgression.

Nazareth, a view from ancient road leading east to the Lake of Galilee. © *MPS*

IV. Character. To describe Jesus in all the perfections of His character would be impossible. Certain perfections deserve special mention, but it cannot be said that He was noted for these above others. He had integrity. He was truth incarnate. He had courage — both physical courage and the courage of conviction. He had **compassion** as He dealt with people. He clothed Himself with **humility.** His character was crowned with **sinlessness** — not simply the absence of sin, but a positive holiness in all that He said and did.

V. Influence. The influence of Jesus, in spite of the brevity of His life, is seen in the NT, where every book centers in Him. When He comes into a human life, He brings to it a new point of reference and a new set of values. Sinners are transformed by Him. He is the conscience of the world. He has mightily effected society in its organized state. He has taught the world the dignity of human life, improved the status of women, brought about the abolition of slavery, stimulated interest in social work. The arts owe their sublimest achievements to the desire to honor Him. Even moralists and philosophers who do not acknowledge His deity nevertheless acknowledge the excellence of His moral teaching.

Bibliography: Eric F. F. Bishop, **Jesus of Palestine,** London: Lutterworth Press, 1955; Otto Borchert, **The Original Jesus,** London: Lutterworth Press, 1933; E. Digges La Touche, **The Person of Christ in Modern Thought,** London: James Clarke and Co., 1912; T. W. Manson, **The Servant-Messiah,** Cambridge: The University Press, 1953; A. E. J. Rawlinson, **Christ in the Gospels,** London: Oxford University Press, 1944; Wilbur Moorehead Smith, **The Supernaturalness of Christ,** Boston: W. A. Wilde Co., 1943; Maisie Spens, **Concerning Himself,** London: Hodder and Stoughton, 1937; James S. Stewart, **The Life and Teaching of Jesus Christ,** London: SCM Press Limited, 1933; Vincent Taylor, **The Names of Jesus,** London: Macmillan and Co., 1953.

Christian. The Biblical meaning is "adherent of Christ." The disciples were formally called Christians first in Antioch (Acts 11:26). Agrippa recognized that to believe what Paul preached would make him a Christian (Acts 26:28). Peter accepted the name as in itself basis for persecution (I Pet. 4:16). The apostles wrote of themselves as servants (slaves) of Christ (Rom. 1:1; James 1:1; II Pet. 1:1; Jude 1:1; Rev. 1:1). The NT calls the followers of Christ **brethren** (Acts 14:2); **disciples** (Acts 6:1, 2); **saints** (Acts 9:13; Rom. 1:7; I Cor. 1:2); **believers** (I Tim. 4:12); **the church of God** (Acts 20:28); **those that call upon the name of the Lord** (Acts 9:14; Rom. 10:12, 13).

Christianity. The name was made by Christians to designate all that which Jesus Christ brought to them of faith, life and salvation. Its character is summed up in the words of Jesus, "I am the way, the truth, and the life: no man cometh unto the Father but by me" (John 14:6); "I am come that they might have life, and that they might have it more abundantly" (John 10:10). The classic summary of its doctrines is in the words of Paul in I Corinthians 15:1-4. It is all "according to the scriptures": OT and NT together form the authoritative revelation of what Christianity is.

Christmas, the anniversary of the birth of Christ, and its observance; celebrated by most Protestants and by Roman Catholics on December 25; by Eastern Orthodox churches on January 6; and by the Armenian church on January 19. The first mention of its observance on December 25 is in the time of Constantine, about A. D. 325. The date of the birth of Christ is not known. The word Christmas is formed of Christ plus Mass, meaning a mass of religious service in commemoration of the birth of Christ. A commemoration of the birth of

Christ in harmonious keeping with the events surrounding that birth (Luke 2:1-20; Matt. 1:18-2:12) is a natural and normal expression of love and reverence for Jesus Christ.

Chronicles, I and II, contains no statements about its own authorship or date. The last event it records is the decree of Cyrus in 538 B.C., which permitted the Jews to return from their Babylonian captivity (II Chron. 36:22), and its genealogies extend to approximately 500 B.C., as far, that is, as to Pelatiah and Jeshaiah (I Chron. 3:21), two grandsons of Zerubbabel, the prince who led in the return from exile. The language, however, and the contents of Chronicles closely parallel that of the book of Ezra, which continues the history of the Jews from the decree of Cyrus down to 457 B.C. Both documents are marked by lists and genealogies, by an interest in priestly ritual, and by devotion to the law of Moses. The closing verses, moreover, of Chronicles (II 36:22-23) are repeated as the opening verses of Ezra (1:1-3a). Ancient Hebrew tradition and the modern scholarship of Wm. F. Albright (JBL 40 [1921], pp. 104-124) therefore unite in suggesting that Ezra may have been the author of both volumes. His complete work would then have been finished some time around 450 B.C. (See Cyrus)

The occasion for the writing of Chronicles appears to be that of Ezra's crusade to bring post-exilic Judah back into conformity with the law of Moses (Ezra 7:10). From 458 B.C. and onward Ezra sought to restore the temple worship (7:19-23, 27; 8:33-34), to eliminate the mixed marriages of Jews with their pagan neighbors (9-10), and to strengthen Jerusalem by rebuilding its walls (4:8-16). Chronicles, accordingly, consists of these four parts: genealogies, to enable the Jews to establish their lines of family descent (I Chron. 1-9); the kingdom of David, as a pattern for the ideal theocratic state (I Chron. 10-29); the glory of Solomon, with an emphasis upon the temple and its worship (II Chron. 1-9); and the history of the southern kingdom, stressing in particular the religious reforms and military victories of Judah's more pious rulers (II Chron. 10-36).

As compared with the parallel histories in Samuel and Kings, the priestly annals of Chronicles lay a greater emphasis upon the structure of the temple (I Chron. 22) and upon Israel's ark, the Levites, and the singers (I Chron. 13, 15-16). The chronicler foregoes discussion of David's disputed inauguration and later shame (II Sam. 1-4, 11-21), of Solomon's failures (I Kings 11), and of the whole inglorious history of Saul (I Sam. 8-30, except his death, 31) and of the northern kingdom of Israel: the disillusioned, impoverished Jews of 450 B.C. knew enough of sin and defeat; but they needed an encouraging reminder of their former, God-given victories (as II Chron. 13, 14, 20, 25).

Chronology, New Testament. In ancient times historians were not accustomed to record history under exact dates, but were satisfied when some specific event was related to the reign of a noted ruler or a famous contemporary. Our method of dating events in reference to the birth of Christ was started by Dionysius Exiguus, a monk who lived in the 6th century. The birth of Christ may be dated in the latter part of the year 5 B.C., as it is known that Herod the Great died in 4 B.C., and according to the Gospels Jesus was born some time before the death of the king. Luke gives the age of Jesus at His baptism as "about thirty years" (3:23). This would bring the baptism at c. A.D. 26 or 27. Since Herod began the reconstruction of the temple in 20 B.C., the "forty and six years" mentioned by the Jews during the first Passover of Jesus' public ministry (John 2:13-22) brings us to A.D. 27 for this first Passover. The ministry of John the Baptist began about the middle of A.D. 26. The time of the crucifixion is determined by the length of the ministry of Jesus. Mark's Gospel seems to require at least 2 years. John's Gospel explicitly mentions 3 Passovers (2:23; 6:4; 11:55). If the feast of 5:1 is also a Passover, as seems probable, then the length of the ministry of Jesus was full three years and a little over. This places the crucifixion at the Passover of A.D. 30. As for the Apostolic Age the chronological data are very limited and uncertain. The death of Herod Agrippa I, one of the fixed dates of the NT, is known to have taken place in A.D. 44. This was the year of Peter's arrest and miraculous escape from prison. The proconsulship of Gallio was between 51 and 53, and this would bring the beginning of Paul's ministry at

Corinth to c. A.D. 50. The accession of Festus as governor, under whom Paul was sent to Rome, probably took place c. 59, 60.

The following chronological table is regarded as approximately correct:

Birth of Jesus	5 B.C.
Baptism of Jesus	— late A. D. 26 or early 27
First Passover of Ministry	27
Crucifixion of Jesus	30
Conversion of Saul	34 or 35
Death of Herod Agrippa I	44
Epistle of James	before 50
First Missionary journey	48-49
Jerusalem Conference	49 or 50
Second Missionary journey	begun spring 50
Paul at Corinth	50-52
I & II Thessalonians from Corinth	51
Galatians from Corinth (?)	early 52
Arrival of Gallio as Proconsul	May 52
Third Missionary journey	begun 54
Paul at Ephesus	54-57
I Corinthians from Ephesus -	spring 57
II Corinthians from Macedonia	fall 57
Romans from Corinth	winter 57-58
Paul's arrest at Jerusalem	Pentecost 58
Imprisonment at Caesarea	58-60
On Island of Malta	winter 60-61
Arrival at Rome	spring 61
Roman Imprisonment	61-63
Colossians, Philemon, Ephesians	summer 62
Philippians	spring 63
Paul's release and further work	63-65
I Timothy and Titus	63
Epistle to the Hebrews	64
Synoptic Gospels and Acts	before 67
I & II Peter from Rome	64-65
Peter's death at Rome	65
Paul's second Roman imprisonment	66
II Timothy	66
Death at Rome	late 66 or early 67
Epistle of Jude	67-68
Writings of John	before 100
Death of John	98-100

Chronology, Old Testament. The chronology of the OT presents many complex and difficult problems. Often the data are completely lacking, and where they exist, they are not adequate or plain. Even where the data are abundant, the exact meaning is not immediately clear, and there are therefore many interpretations possible. For the period from the creation to the Deluge the only Biblical data are the ages of the patriarchs in the genealogical tables of Genesis 5 and 7:11. Extra-Biblical sources for this period are almost completely lacking. For the period from the Deluge to Abraham we are again dependent upon the genealogical data in the Bible. The numbers vary in the Masoretic text, the LXX, and the Samaritan Pentateuch. The construction of an absolute chronology from Adam to Abraham is not now possible on the basis of the available data. The patriarchs may be dated c. 2100-1875; the Exodus c. 1445 B.C.; the beginning of the conquest of Canaan c. 1405. An accurate chronology of the period of the judges is impossible, as the length of the period is unknown, and a number of the judges undoubtedly exercised control at the same time. The United Monarchy began c. 1050 B.C.; the Divided Monarchy in 931 B.C. The kingdom of Israel went into the Assyrian captivity c. 722 B.C.; and the kingdom of Judah into the Babylonian captivity in 586 B.C. Judah returned from the Babylonian captivity in 538 B.C. Nehemiah returned to Babylon in 433 B.C.

Bibliography: W. F. Albright, "The Chronology of the Divided Monarchy of Israel," **Bulletin of the American Schools of Oriental Research,** No. 100 (December, 1945), pp. 16-22. S. H. Horn and L. H. Wood, "The Fifth-Century Jewish Calendar at Elephantine," **Journal of Near Eastern Studies,** XIII (January, 1954), pp. 1-20. A. Malamat, "A New Record of Nebuchadnezzar's Palestinian Campaigns," **Israel Exploration Journal**, Vol. 6, No. 4 (1956), pp. 246-256; "The Kingdom of David & Solomon in its Contact with Egypt and Aram Naharaim," **The Biblical Archaeologist,** XXI (December, 1958), pp. 96-102. P. Van der Meer, **The Ancient Chronology of Western Asia and Egypt,** Leiden: E. J. Brill, 1955. James A. Montgomery, Henry Snyder Gehman (ed.), **A Critical and Exegetical Commentary on the Books of Kings,** "The International Critical Commentary," New York: Charles Scribner's Sons, 1951, pp. 45-64. Richard A. Parker and Waldo H. Dubberstein, **Babylonian Chronology** 626 B.C.-A.D. 75, Providence: Brown University Press, 1956. John Rea, **The Historical Setting of the Exodus and the Conquest,** Winona Lake, Indiana: Grace Theological Seminary, 1959, (mimeographed). Hayim Tadmor, "Chronology of the

Last Kings of Judah," **Journal of Near Eastern Studies,** XV (October, 1956), pp. 226-230; "The Campaigns of Sargon II of Assur; A Chronological-Historical Study," **Journal of Cuneiform Studies,** XII 1 (1958), pp. 22-24. Edwin R. Thiele, "A Comparison of the Chronological Data of Israel and Judah," **Vetus Testamentum,** IV (April, 1954), pp 185-195; "New Evidence on the Chronology of the Last Kings of Judah," **Bulletin of the American Schools of Oriental Research,** No. 143 (October, 1956), pp. 22-27; "The Chronology of the Kings of Judah and Israel," **Journal of Near Eastern Studies,** III (July, 1944), pp. 137-186; **The Mysterious Numbers of the Hebrew Kings,** Chicago: The University of Chicago Press, 1955; "The Question of Coregencies Among the Hebrew Kings," **A Stubborn Faith,** ed. Edward C. Hobbs, Dallas: Southern Methodist University Press, 1956, pp. 39-52. John C. Whitcomb, Jr. **Bible Chronology, 640-400 B.C.,** Winona Lake, Indiana: Grace Theological Seminary, 1958, (mimeographed).

Chub (kŭb) an ally of Egypt.

Chun (kŭn), Aramean city taken by David (I Chron. 18:8).

Church. The English "church" derives from the Greek **kuriakós** (belonging to the Lord), but it stands for another Greek word **ekklesia** (whence "ecclesiastical"), denoting an assembly.

In the Gospels the term is found only in Matthew 16:18 and 18:17. This paucity is perhaps explained by the fact that both these verses seem to envisage a situation still future. Only after the saving work of Christ is effected will the Old Testament Church be reconstituted as that of the New. Yet the verses show that Christ has this reconstitution in view, that the Church thus reconstituted will rest on the apostolic confession, and that it will take up the ministry of reconciliation.

When we turn to Acts, the situation changes. The saving work has been fulfilled, and the New Testament form of the Church can thus have its birthday at Pentecost. The term is now used regularly to describe local groups of believers. Thus we read of the churches at Jerusalem in Acts 5:11, Antioch in 13:1, and Caesarea in 18:22. At the same time the word is used for all believers in universal fellowship, as is possibly the case in 9:31. From the outset the Church has both a local and a general significance, denoting both the individual assembly and the world-wide community.

This twofold usage is also seen in Paul. He addresses his epistles to specific churches, e.g., Corinth (I Cor. 1:2) or Thessalonica (I Thess. 1:1) or groups within the one city (cf. Rom. 16:5). Yet Paul also develops more fully the conception of a Church of all believers embracing the local churches, as in I Corinthians 10:32 and I Timothy 3:15, and with an even grander sweep in Colossians 1:18 and especially Ephesians.

This leads us to the further consideration that the Church is not primarily a human structure like a political, social or economic organism. It is basically the Church of Jesus Christ ("my church" Matt. 16:18), or of the living God (I Tim. 3:15). The various Biblical descriptions all emphasize this. It is a building of which Jesus Christ is the chief corner-stone or foundation, "an holy temple in the Lord," "an habitation of God through the Spirit" (Eph. 2:20f). It is the fellowship of saints or people of God (cf. I Pet. 2:9). It is the bride of Jesus Christ, saved and sanctified by Him for union with Himself (Eph. 5:25f). Indeed, it is the body of Jesus Christ, He being the head or whole body, and Christians the members (Rom. 12:5; I Cor. 12:12f; Eph. 4:4, 12, 16f). As the body, it is the fullness of Christ, who Himself fills all in all (Eph. 1:23).

This brings us to the means of the Church's life, and its continuing function. It draws its life from Jesus Christ by the Holy Spirit, but it does so through the Word of which it is begotten (James 1:18), and by which it is nourished and sanctified (Eph. 5:26; I Pet. 2:2). Receiving life by the Word, it also receives its function, namely, to pass on the Word that others may also be quickened and cleansed. It is to preach the Gospel (Mark 16:15), to take up the ministry of reconciliation (II Cor. 5:19), to dispense the mysteries of God (I Cor. 4:1). Necessarily, therefore, it is the Church of the divine Word and sacraments first received by believers and then passed on to others; hence the Reformation insistence that the marks of the visible Church are preaching of the Word and administration of the Gospel sacraments.

Finally, the Church's work is not

merely for man's salvation, but to the praise of God's glory (Eph. 1:6; 2:7). Hence neither the Church nor its function ceases with the completion of its earthly task. There is ground, therefore, for the old distinction between the Church triumphant and the Church militant. All the Church is triumphant in its true reality. But the warring and wayfaring church is still engaged in conflict between the old reality and the new. Its destiny, however, is to be brought into full conformity to the Lord (I John 3:2) with all the saints.

Chushan Rishathaim (kū'shăn rĭsh'ȧ-thā'ĭm), a Mesopotamian king who held Israel captive for eight years.

Chuza (kū'zȧ), the steward of Herod Antipas whose wife Joanna "and Susanna, and many others," ministered to Christ (Luke 8:3).

Cilicia (sĭ-lĭsh'ĭ-ȧ), country in SE Asia Minor. Its chief city was Tarsus, birthplace of Paul (Acts 21:39; 22:3; 23:34). It became a Roman province in 100 B.C. The gospel reached it early (Acts 15:23), probably through Paul (Acts 9:30; Gal. 1:21), who confirmed the churches established there (Acts 15:41).

Cinnamon (See Plants).

Circumcision (sĭr-kŭm-sĭ'shŭn, **a cutting around**), the cutting off of the foreskin, a rite instituted by God as the sign of the covenant between Him and Abraham and his descendants (Gen. 17:10) that He would be their God, and they were to belong to Him, worshiping and obeying only Him. It was made a legal institution in the wilderness by Moses (Lev. 12:3; John 7:22, 23). Every male child was circumcised on the 8th day after its birth. Other nations also practiced the rite (Egyptians, Arabians, etc.). The Christian Church refused to force Gentiles to be circumcised (Acts 15:5; Gal. 5:2).

Cistern (sĭs'têrn), an artificial tank or reservoir dug in the earth or rock for the collection and storage of rainwater, or, sometimes, of spring water brought from a distance by a conduit. Where the substratum of the soil was earth and not rock, cisterns of masonry were built. Some of these were large and had vaulted roofs supported by pillars. Besides the large public cisterns, there were many smaller private ones. Ancient sites are honeycombed with them. All cisterns had one or more openings for drawing water to

A covered well, or cistern, near the entrance to the Church of the Nativity in Bethlehem. © *MPS*

the surface. They needed periodic cleaning because of the impurities washed in from the outside. Empty cisterns were sometimes used as prisons. Joseph was cast into one (Gen. 37:22), and Jeremiah the prophet was let down into one with a miry bottom (Jer. 38:6).

Cities of Refuge, six cities set apart by Moses and Joshua as places of asylum for those who had accidentally committed manslaughter. There they remained until a fair trial could be held. If proved innocent of willful murder, they had to remain in the city of refuge until the death of the high priest (Num. 35; Deut. 19:1-13; Josh. 20).

Cities of the Plain (circle of the Jordan), cities near the Dead Sea, includ-

Southern end of the Dead Sea, site of the Cities of the Plain mentioned in Genesis. © *MPS*

ing Sodom, Gomorrah, Admah, Zeboiim, and Zoar. Lot lived in Sodom (Gen. 13:10-12). They were destroyed because of their wickedness (Gen. 19). They were probably at the S end of the Dead Sea, and it is believed that the sea covers the site.

Citizenship (commonwealth). In the NT the word for citizen often means nothing more than the inhabitant of a country (Luke 15:15; 19:14). Among the ancient Jews emphasis was placed on Israel as a religious organization. Thus, the good citizen was the good Israelite.

Among the Romans, citizenship brought the right to be considered as equal to natives of the city of Rome. Emperors sometimes granted it to whole provinces and cities, and also to single individuals, for services rendered to the state or to the imperial family, or even for a certain sum of money. Roman citizens were exempted from shameful punishments, such as scourging and crucifixion, and they had the right of appeal to the emperor with certain limitations.

Paul says he had become a Roman citizen by birth. Either his father or some other ancestor had acquired the right and had transmitted it to his son.

City. In ancient times cities owed their origin not to organized manufacture, but to agriculture. Usually they were built on the side of a mountain or the top of a hill, and where a sufficient supply of water was assured. Cities always had walls, many of them 20-30 ft. thick, which were protected sometimes with moats and towers. Gates of the city were closed at night (Josh. 2:5, 7). Within the walls, the important features of a city were the Tower or Stronghold; a High Place, where sacrifices were offered and feasts held; the Broad Place by the Gate, an open area just inside the city gate serving the purpose of social intercourse in general; and the streets, which were narrow, winding, unpaved alleys, rarely cleaned, and never lighted. Little is known about the way city government was administered.

City of David. 1. Jebusite stronghold of Zion captured by David and made by him his royal residence (II Sam. 5:6-9). 2. Bethlehem, the home of David (Luke 2:4).

Clauda (klô'dȧ), a small island off the SW coast of Crete. Paul's ship was driven under its lee by a storm on his way to Rome (Acts 27:16.)

Claudia (klô'dĭ-ȧ), a member of the Christian Church at Rome (II Tim. 4:21).

Claudius (klô'dĭ-ŭs) the fourth Roman emperor (41-54). Claudius gave to the Jews the right to religious worship, but later he banished all Jews from Rome (Acts 18:2; cf. Suet. **Claud.** 25). The famine foretold by Agabus took place in the reign of Claudius (Acts 11:28). Ancient writers say that from various causes his reign was a period of distress over the whole Mediterranean world.

Claudius Lysias (klô'dĭ-ŭs lĭs'ĭ-ăs), a chief captain who rescued Paul from fanatical Jewish rioters at Jerusalem (Acts 21:31; 24:22). He was a chiliarch (i.e. leader of 1,000 men), in charge of the Roman garrison at Jerusalem, stationed in the Castle of Antonia, adjoining the temple. To protect Paul he sent him to Caesarea.

Clay. Was widely used in OT times for the making of brick, mortar, and pottery, and, in some countries, for the making of tablets on which inscriptions were impressed. As a building material, clay has been used from very ancient times. Babylon was made wholly of brick, either baked or dried in the sun. Nineveh, the capital of Assyria, was made mostly of brick. The villages of Egypt were constructed of sun-dried clay.

Clay Tablets. In ancient times writing was done on papyrus, parchment, potsherds, and clay tablets. Clay tablets were made of clean-washed, smooth clay. While still wet, the clay had wedge-shaped letters (now called "cuneiform" from the Latin **cuneus,** meaning "wedge") imprinted on it with a stylus, and then was kiln-fired or sun-dried. Tablets were made of various shapes — cone-shaped, drum-shaped, and flat. They were often placed in a clay envelope. Some tell the story of the Creation, the Fall, and the Deluge. They do much to verify the truthfulness of the Biblical record.

Cleanthes (klē-ăn'thēz), son of Phanius of Assos and head of the Stoic school from 263 to 232 B.C.

Clement (klĕm'ĕnt), a Christian who labored with Paul at Philippi (Phil. 4:3).

Cleopas (klē'ō-păs), one of the two disciples to whom the Lord appeared on the afternoon of the resurrection day.

Cleophas (klē'ō-făs), mentioned in John 19:25 as the husband of Mary, one of the women who stood beside the cross. Not the same as the Cleopas who walked with Jesus to Emmaus (Luke 24:18).

Clerk (See Occupations, Professions)

Cloak (See Dress)

Closet, found in Matthew 6:6 and Luke 12:3, and referring most probably to a special storage closet. Our Lord advised that it be used for private prayer.

Cloth, Clothes, Clothing (See Dress)

Cloud. Most references to clouds in the Bible are metaphoric or figurative, symbolizing calamity (Ezek. 30:3), danger (Isa. 44:22), mystery (Job 3:5), presence of God (Isa. 19:1), etc.

Cloud, Pillar of, symbol of the presence and guidance of God in the wilderness journeys of the Israelites (Exod. 13:21, 22).

Clout (See Dress)

Cnidus (nī'dŭs), a city of Carial, at the SW corner of Asia Minor, past which Paul sailed on his journey to Rome (Acts 27:7).

Coal. The Bible never refers to true mineral coal, which has not been found in Palestine proper. The references are always either to charcoal or to live embers of any kind. Hebrews usually used charcoal for warmth or cooking (Isa. 47:14; John 18:18; 21:9).

Coat (See Dress)

Cock (See Birds)

Cockatrice (See Animals)

Cock Crowing, when referring to time, is between 12 and 3 a.m. (Matt. 26:34; Mark 13:35).

Cockle (See Plants)

Coele Syria (sēl'ē-sēr'ĭ-à), in KJV Celosyria, **hollow Syria),** the name for that part of Syria that lay between the Lebanon and Anti-Lebanon Mountains.

Coffer (kŏf'êr), a word occurring only in I Samuel 6:8, 11, 15, and probably referring to a small box in which the Philistines put their golden mice and other offerings when they returned to the Ark.

Coffin, used only in Genesis 50:26. Probably box, in this case may mean "mummy-case." Coffins were unknown among the Israelites, who were carried to the grave upon a bier, a simple flat board. In Egypt, where Joseph died, the dead were embalmed and put in a mummy-case.

Coin (See Money)

Col-hozeh (kŏl-hō'ze, **all-seeing one),** a Judahite whose son Shallum rebuilt the fountain gate of Jerusalem (Neh. 3:15; 11:5).

Collar (See Dress: 4, Cloak, Mantle, Robe)

College, denotes the second quarter of the city of Jerusalem, which was not far from the Fish-Gate.

Collop (kŏl'ŭp), an old English word meaning a **slice of meat** or **fat.** Used only in Job 15:27.

Colony, a transliteration of the Latin **colonus, farmer),** in the only occurrence of the word in the NT, Acts 16:12, it says that Philippi was a colony. A colony was a settlement of Roman citizens, authorized by the government, in conquered territory. Such colonies had the rights of Italian cities: municipal self-government and exemption from poll and land taxes.

Colossae (kŏ-lŏs'ē), an ancient city of Phrygia, situated on the S bank of the Lycus river about 11 miles from Laodicea and 13 from Hierapolis. Colossae stood on the most important trade route from Ephesus to the Euphrates. The church at Colossae was established on Paul's third missionary journey, during his three years in Ephesus, not by Paul himself (Col. 2:1), but by Epaphras (Col. 1:7, 12, 13).

Colossians, Book of (kŏ-lŏsh'ănz), an epistle written by the Apostle Paul when he was a prisoner (Col. 4:3, 10, 18), about the year 62, probably during his first imprisonment in Rome (Acts 28:30, 31), although Caesarea (Acts 23:35; 24:27) and Ephesus have also been suggested. The external and internal evidence for its genuineness is all that can be desired. The church was very likely founded during Paul's three year stay in Ephesus on his third missionary journey. It appears from Colossians 2:1 that Paul himself had never preached in Colossae. Epaphras, a native of Colossae (Col. 4:12), was

Colossae in Phrygia (Asia Minor). SHH

The Plain of the Law at the foot of Mt. Sinai. © *MPS*

probably converted under Paul's ministry at Ephesus, and was then sent by the apostle to preach in his native city (Col. 1:7).

In the few years since Paul had been in the province of Asia an insidious error had crept into the church at Colossae. Who the false teachers were we do not know; but it is clear that the trouble was different from that faced by Paul at Galatia, where Judaizers had tried to undermine his work. The teaching attacked by Paul is described in 2:8, 16-23. It was, at least in part, Judaistic (2:11; 2:14; 2:16; 3:11). There was also in it a strong ascetic element. Special self-denying rules were given (2:16, 20, 21, 23). Some sort of worship of angels was practiced — a worship which continued for several centuries, as we know from the fact that in the fourth century the Council of Laodicea in one of its canons condemned it, and in the fifth century Theodoret said that the archangel Michael was worshiped in the area. Some find this teaching in Essenism; others in incipient Gnosticism or in contemporary Judaism with a syncretistic admixture of local Phrygian ideas.

Paul met these errors, not by controversy of personal authority, but by presenting the counter truth that Jesus Christ is the image of the invisible God (1:15), in whom are hid all the treasures of wisdom and knowledge and in whom the fulness of the divine perfections find their perfect embodiment (1:19). He is the creator of all, and all power is from Him. On the cross He revealed the impotence of all the powers that had tried to thwart His purposes (2:15). Freedom from the corruption of human nature is found in the newness of life which the death and resurrection of Christ provide. The epistle may be divided into four parts: 1. The salutation and thanksgiving (1:1-8); 2. The doctrinal section (1:9-2:5); 3. Practical exhortations (2:6-4:6); 4. Concluding salutations (4:7-18).

Colt (See Animals; Ass)

Comforter, The (See Holy Spirit)

Commandment, used in the English Bible to translate a number of Heb. and Gr. words meaning law, ordinance, statute, word, judgment, precept, saying, charge, etc.

Commandments, Ten. In Heb. the Ten Commandments are called the ten words (Exod. 34:28; Deut. 4:13) or the words (Exod. 20:1; Deut. 5:22). They are God's precepts given to Moses on Mt. Sinai. The Bible contains 2 accounts of how they were given (Exod. 20:1-17; Deut. 5:6-21). They were written on 2 tables of stone (Exod. 31:18; 32:15-19; 34:1-4, 27-29; Deut. 10:1-5). There is uncertainty as to how they are to be numbered and how they were divided between the two tables. They were not intended to be a "yoke of bondage" to the Israelites, but a wise provision for God's people to enable them to enter a life of joyful fellowship with their God. The first four deal with man's relationship to God; the others, with his relationship to other people. All except the 4th are repeated in the NT and are expected to be obeyed by Christians. Indeed, Jesus shows that God's interpretation is stricter than that of the Jews. Except as the NT deepens and extends its principles, the Decalogue represents the high-water level of morality. Jesus says that love is the fulfillment of the law (Matt. 22:35-40).

Compel, as used by Jesus in Luke 14:23 does not mean physical force, but zeal and moral urgency.

Conaniah (cŏn′ȧ-nī′ȧ, **Jehovah has founded).** 1. Levite (II Chron. 31:12, 13). 2. Another Levite (II Chron. 35:9).

Concision (cŏn-sĭzh′ŭn, **mutilation, cutting),** circumcision that is wholly ceremonial and without regard for its spiritual significance (Phil. 3:2).

Concubine, a woman lawfully united in marriage to a man in a relation inferior to that of the regular wife (Gen. 16:1; 22:24; Judg. 8:31; II Sam. 3:7; 5:13). Law of Moses allowed it (Exod. 21:7-11; Deut. 21:10-14). A number of prominent OT figures had concubines —Abraham (Gen. 25:6), Jacob (Gen. 35:22), Gideon (Judg. 8:31), David (II Sam. 5:13), Solomon (I Kings 11:3), Rehoboam (II Chron. 11:21).

Concupiscence (kŏn-kū′pĭ-sĕns), intense longing for what God would not have us to have (Rom. 7:8; Col. 3:5; I Thess. 4:5).

Conduit (kŏn′dū-ĭt), a channel for conveying water from its source to the place where it was delivered (II Kings 20:20; Isa. 7:3).

Coney (See Animals)

Confection, a compound of perfume or medicine (not sweetmeats) (Exod. 30:35).

Confectionary, a perfumer, found only in I Sam. 8:13.

Confectioner (See Occupations, Professions).

Confession, to acknowledge one's faith in anything, as in the existence and authority of God, or the sins of which one has been guilty. Occasionally it also means to concede or allow (John 1:20; Acts 24:14; Heb. 11:13), or to praise God by thankfully acknowledging Him (Rom. 14:11; Heb. 13:15). In the Bible confession of sin before God is recognized as a condition of forgiveness.

Congregation, the Hebrew people viewed in their collective capacity as Gods' people or as an assembly of the people summoned for a definite purpose (I Kings 8:65). Sometimes it refers to an assembly of the whole people, sometimes to a part (Num. 16:3; Exod. 12:6; 35:1; Lev. 4:13).

Coniah (kō-nī′a, **Jehovah is creating).** A form of the name Jehoiachin, found in Jeremiah 22:24, 28; 37:1. See Jehoiachin.

Conscience, awareness that an action conforms to or is contrary to one's standard of right and wrong (Acts 23: 1; I Tim. 1:5; Heb. 13:18). Important NT pasasges that deal with it are Rom. 2:14, 15 and I Cor. 8:10. The NT stresses the need of having a good conscience toward God.

Consecration, an act by a person or thing dedicated to the service and worship of God, like Levites (Exod. 13:2; Num. 3:12), objects (Josh. 6:19), nations (Exod. 19:6).

Conversation, a word often used in the KJV to render various terms signifying conduct or manner of life, especially with respect to morals. In Philippians 1:27 and 3:20, "civil life" or "citizenship," Paul means that we should live like citizens of heaven.

Conversion (kŏn-vêr′zhŭn, **a turning),** a turning, which may be literal or figurative, ethical or religious, either from God, or, more frequently, to God. It implies a turning from and a turning to something, and is therefore associated with repentance (Acts 3:19; 26:20) and faith (Acts 11:21). On its negative side it is turning from sin, and on its positive side it is faith in Christ (Acts 20:21). Although it is an act of man, it is done by the power of God (Acts 3:26). In the process of salvation, it is the first step in the transition from sin to God.

Conviction (kŏn-vĭk′shŭn, **to convince** or **prove guilty).** Although the word "conviction" is never used in the KJV, both Testaments give many illustrations of the experience. In the OT one of the most notable is found in Psalm 51, where David, realizing he has sinned against God, is overwhelmed with sorrow for his transgression and cries out to God for forgiveness and cleansing. In the NT the central passage bearing on this theme is John 16:7-11.

Convocation (kŭn-vō-kā′shŏn), used in the expression "Holy Convocation," but it is sometimes used alone (Num. 10:2; Isa. 1:13; 4:5). A convocation was a religious festival during which no work could be done.

Coos (Kō′ôs, **summit),** a long, narrow island off the coast of Caria in S Asia Minor, mentioned in connection with Paul's third missionary journey (Acts 21:1).

Coping (kōp′ĭng), a parapet on Oriental house roofs.

Coppersmith (kŏp′êr-smĭth), found in the NT only in II Timothy 4:14. The word should be rendered "worker in brass."

Cor (See Weights and Measures)

Coral (kŏr′ăl), ranked by Hebrews with precious stones (Job. 28:18; Ezek. 27:16).

Corban (kôr′băn, **an offering),** occurs in the Hebrew text of the OT and refers to an offering or sacrifice, whether bloody or unbloody, made to God (Lev. 1:2, 3; 2:1, 3:1; Num. 7:12-17). It is found in the NT in Mark 7:11, where it has reference to money dedicated to God.

Cord (kôrd). In ancient times ropes and cords were made of goat's or camel's hair spun into threads and then plaited or twisted into the larger and stronger form. Sometimes they were made of strips of skin from goats and cows twisted together. Ropes for temporary fastenings were sometimes made from vines twisted together, and also from the bark of branches of the mulberry tree. Frequently the word is used in a figurative sense (Job 36:8; Prov. 5:22; Ps. 2:3; 129:4; 140:5; Eccl. 4:12; Isa. 5:18; 54:2).

Coriander, (See Plants)

Corinth (côr'ĭnth, **ornament),** Greek city on isthmus between the Peloponnesus and the mainland; destroyed by Romans in 146 B.C. and rebuilt in 46 B.C.; capital of the Roman province of Achaia. Paul founded a church there (Acts 18:1; 20:2, 3); wrote two epistles to it.

Corinthians (kô-rĭn'thĭ-ănz), First and Second Epistles. I Corinthians was written by the Apostle Paul in Ephesus on his 3rd missionary journey (Acts 19; I Cor. 16:8, 19), probably in 56 or 57. He had previously written a letter to the Corinthians which has not come down to us (I Cor. 5:9), and in reply had received a letter in which he was asked a number of questions. Paul had also heard of factions in the church from the servants of Chloe (1: 11). These circumstances led to the writing of I Corinthians. Outline: 1. Factions in the church (1-4). 2. Incestuous marriage (5). 3. Disputes of Christians brought before heathen courts (6). 4. Phases of the subject of marriage (7). 5. Meat offered to idols (8-10). 6. Head coverings for women; proper observance of the Lord's Supper (11). 7. Spiritual gifts (12-14). 8. Resurrection of the body (15). 9. Collection for the poor of Jerusalem; closing remarks (16).

II Corinthians was written by Paul somewhere in Macedonia on his 3rd misisonary journey as a result of a report concerning the church brought to him by Titus. Outline: 1. Some thoughts on the crisis through which the church has just passed (1-7). 2. Collection for the poor (8, 9). 3. Defense of Paul's ministry against the attacks of his enemies and a vindication of his apostleship (10-13).

Ruins of the Forum at Corinth. SHH

Cormorant (See Birds)

Corn (See Plants, Wheat)

Cornelius (kôr-nēl'yŭs, **of a horn),** Roman centurion stationed at Caesarea, and the first Gentile convert (Acts 10, 11).

Cornerstone, foundation stone upon which a building is started. The word is used in both a literal and a figurative sense in Scripture (Ps. 118:22; Job 38:6; Isa. 28:16; Zech. 10:4, etc.). Christ is the Cornerstone of the Church (Matt. 21:42; Eph. 2:20; I Peter 2:5-7).

Cornet, a wind instrument with a curved horn, the sound being a dull monotone (I Chron. 15:28; Ps. 98:6; Dan. 3:5, 10, 15; Hos. 5:8).

Cos, Coos (kŏs), island in Aegean Sea; mentioned in connection with Paul's 3rd missionary journey (Acts 21:1).

Cosam (kō'săm), ancestor of Christ (Luke 3:28).

Cosmetics, any of the various preparations used for beautifying the hair and skin (II Kings 9:30; Jer. 4:30; Ezek. 23:40).

Cotton. Imported to Palestine shortly after the Captivity. Cotton was spun into cloth by weavers in Egypt. The mummies of Egypt were wrapped in this material. It is mentioned but once in the Bible (Esth. 1:5, 6) where the word "green" should be rendered "cotton," as in the RSV. See Plants.

Couch, a piece of furniture for reclining. The couch became so ornate that Amos rebuked the rich for the costly display of their couches (Amos 6:4).

Coulter (kōl'têr), a plowshare (I Sam. 13:19-21).

Council (koun'sĕl). 1. Group of people gathered for deliberation (Gen. 49:6; II Kings 9:5). 2. The Jewish Sanhedrin (Matt. 26:59; Acts 5:34) and lesser courts (Matt. 10:17; Mark 13:9).

Counsellor (koun′sĕ-lêr), one who gives counsel; a member of the Sanhedrin (Mark 15:43; Luke 23:50).

Course of Priests and Levites. David divided the priests and Levites into 24 groups, called courses in Luke 1:8; each with its own head (I Chron. 24: 1 ff). Each course officiated a week at a time.

Court. 1. Enclosed yard of a building (II Sam. 17:18; II Kings 20:4; Jer. 32:2). 2. System of courts was set up by Moses and his successors (Exod. 18:25, 26).

Covenant, a mutual agreement between 2 or more persons to do or refrain from doing certain acts; sometimes the undertaking of one of the parties. In the Bible God is regarded as the witness of this pact (Gen. 31: 50; I Sam. 20:8). In the OT there are 3 different types of covenant. 1. A two-sided covenant between human parties, both of which voluntarily accept the terms of the agreement (I Sam. 18:3, 4; Mal. 2:14; Obad. 7). 2. A one-sided disposition imposed by a superior party (Ezek. 17:13, 14). In this God "commands" a covenant which man, the servant, is to obey (Josh. 23:16). 3. God's self-imposed obligation, for the reconciliation of sinners to Himself (Deut. 7:6-8; Ps. 89:3, 4). Covenants of God: 1. Edenic, God's promise of redemption (Gen. 3:15). 2. Noachian, for the preservation of the race (Gen. 9:9). 3. Abrahamic, granting blessings through Abram's family (Gen. 15:18). 4. Sinaitic, designating Israel as God's chosen people (Exod. 19:5, 6). 5. Levitical, making reconciliation through priestly atonement (Num. 25:12, 13). 6. Davidic, Messianic salvation promised through David's dynasty (II Sam. 23: 5). The prophets foretold a New Covenant (Jer. 31:31-34) which would center in a person (Isa. 42:6; 49:8). In the New Covenant man is placed in right relationship to God through Christ (Heb. 7:22; 8:6-13; II Cor. 3:6-18).

Covering the Head, mentioned only in I Corinthians 11:15. At that time in Greece only immoral women were seen with their heads uncovered. Paul means that Christian women cannot afford to disregard social convention; it would hurt their testimony. In giving them long hair, a natural veil, nature teaches the lesson that women should not be unveiled in public assemblies.

Covetousness (kŭv′ĕt-ŭs-nĕs), has various shades of meaning: 1. The desire to have something (I Cor. 12:31; 14: 39). 2. The inordinate desire to have something (Luke 12:15 ff; Eph. 5:5; Col. 3:5). 3. Excessive desire of what belongs to another (Exod. 20:17; Rom. 7:7). Outstanding examples of covetousness are: Achan (Josh. 7); Saul (I Sam. 15:9, 19); Ananias and Sapphira Acts 5:1-11).

Cow (See Animals: Cattle)

Coz (kōz), a man of the tribe of Judah (I Chron. 4:8).

Cozbi (kŏz′bī), a Midianite woman slain by Phineas, Aaron's grandson (Num. 25:16-18).

Cracknel, a light, crisp biscuit, of a curved or hollowed shape (I Kings 14: 3).

Craft, Craftsman (See Occupations, Professions)

Craftiness, Crafty, guile, cunning (Dan. 8:25; Luke 20:23).

Crane (See Birds)

Creation. The Bible clearly teaches that the universe, and all matter, had a beginning, and came into existence through the will of the eternal God (Gen. 1, 2). The Bible gives no information as to how long the original creation of matter occurred, or the first day of creation began, or the sixth day ended. It appears that God ceased His creative activity after the 6th day and now rests from His labors. The Bible does not support the view that everything now existing has come into its present condition as a result of natural development. God determined that plants and animals were to reproduce "after their kind." The Scriptures do not say how large a "kind" is, and nothing in the Bible denies the possibility of change and development within the limits of a particular "kind." The two creation accounts in Gen. 1, 2 supplement each other. Gen. 1 describes the creation of the universe as a whole, while Gen. 2 gives a more detailed account of the creation of man and says nothing about the creation of matter, light, heavenly bodies, plants and animals, except to refer to the creation of animals as having taken place at an earlier time.

Creature, in the NT the word denotes that which has been created (Rom. 1:25; 8:39; Heb. 4:13). Sometimes used with adjective **kaine** in the sense of the new creation (II Cor. 5:17) or in contrast to the old man versus the new man (Gal. 6:15).

Creature, Living, a symbolical figure presented first in Ezekiel's vision (Ezek. 1:5 ff), and again in Revelation 4:6-9; 5:6, 8, 11; 6:1, 3, 5-7. In Ezekiel's vision there are four living creatures. They had the general appearance of a man, but each had four faces and four wings, and the feet of an ox. Under their wings they had human hands. The front face was that of a man; to the right and left of this were the faces of a lion and of an ox, and in the back was the face of an eagle. Fire gleamed from their midst. Later they are called "cherubim" (Ezek. 10:1 ff). The living creatures in Revelation are somewhat modified from those in Ezekiel's vision.

Creed, a succinct statement of faith epitomizing the basic tenets of religious faith. Such passages as Matt. 16: 16 and I Tim. 3:16 give the Biblical foundation for the Christian creed. There are 3 ancient creeds: the Apostles' Creed, the Nicene Creed, and the Athanasian Creed. The Reformers also prepared creeds.

Creek, modern translations use "bay" for the KJV "creek" in Acts 27:39, identified as St. Paul's Bay, c. 8 miles NW of the town of Zaletta on the island of Malta.

Creeping Thing (See Animals, Insects)

Crescens (krĕs′ĕnz, **increasing),** companion of Paul (II Tim. 4:10).

Crete, Cretan (krēt, krē′tăn), an island in the Mediterranean, 165 miles long, 6-35 miles wide, forming a natural bridge between Europe and Asia Minor. It was the legendary birthplace of Zeus. Paul and Titus founded a church there (Titus 1:5-14). The Cretans in the OT are called Cherethites (I Sam. 30:14; Ezek. 25:16). Cretans were in Jerusalem on the Day of Pentecost (Acts 2:11). According to Paul they were not of a high moral character (Titus 1:12).

Crib, rack for the feeding of domestic livestock (Job 39:9; Prov. 14:4; Isa. 1:3; Luke 2:7).

Crimson, brilliant red dye obtained from a bug (II Chron. 2:7, 14; Jer. 4: 30; Isa. 1:18).

Crisping Pin, pin for curling the hair (Isa. 3:22).

Crispus (krĭs′pŭs), former ruler of Jewish synagogue at Corinth, converted by Paul (Acts 18:8; I Cor. 1:14).

Crop, pouch-like enlargement in gullet of many birds in which food is partially prepared for digestion (Lev. 1:16).

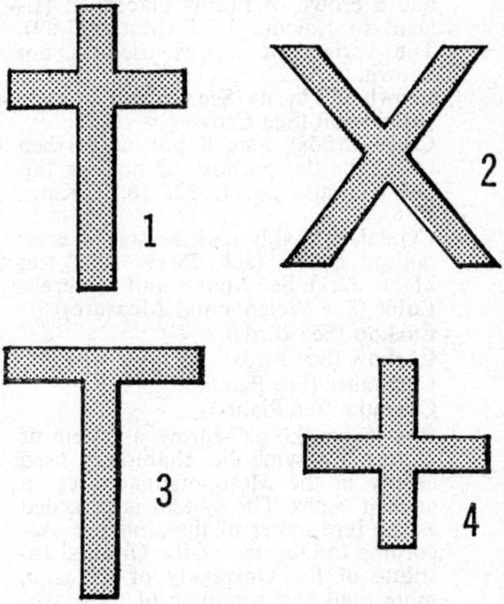

Four forms of the Cross.

Cross. The cross existed in 4 different forms: 1. The Latin, with the cross beam near the upper part of the upright beam. 2. St. Andrew's, in the shape of an "X." 3. St. Anthony's, in the form of the letter "T." 4. The Greek, with the cross beams of equal length. Sometimes the cross was a simple upright. Crucifixion was practiced, especially in times of war, by the Phoenicians, Carthaginians, Egyptians, and the Romans. Before he was crucified a prisoner was scourged with a lash. Crucifixion was by tying or nailing. Death by crucifixion resulted not from loss of blood but from heart failure. Victims did not usually succumb for 2 or 3 days. Death was hastened by the breaking of the legs. Sometimes a fire was built beneath the cross that its fumes might suffocate the sufferer. The word cross is often used figuratively to represent the gospel (Gal. 6:14) or suffering (Eph. 2:16).

Crow (See Birds)

Crown, a band encircling the head to designate honor, worn by priests, kings, queens (Exod. 28:36-38; II Chron. 23:11; Esther 2:17). In the NT two Gr. words for crown are used: **stephanos** and **diadema,** the first referring to a garland or chaplet such as was worn by a victorious athlete (II Tim. 4:8; Rev. 2:10), the other crown was worn by kings (Rev. 19:12). Jesus had a crown of thorns placed on His head to ridicule Him (Matt. 27-29). The variety of thorns used is not known.

Crown of Thorns (See Crown)

Crucifixion (See Cross)

Cruse (krōōs), a small, porous, earthen vessel for the purpose of holding liquids (I Sam. 26:11, 12, 16; I Kings 19:6).

Crystal, probably rock crystal or crystallized quartz (Job 28:17; Rev. 4:6; 21:11; 22:1). See Metals and Minerals.

Cubit (See Weights and Measures)

Cuckoo (See Birds)

Cuckow (See Birds)

Cucumber (See Plants)

Cummin (See Plants)

Cuneiform (kū-nē'ĭ-fôrm), a system of writing by symbolic characters used chiefly in the Mesopotamian area in ancient times. The system is regarded as the forerunner of the alphabet. According to Olmsted of the Oriental Institute of the University of Chicago, more than half a million of these tablets are yet to be deciphered.

Cup, a term used in a literal and figurative sense. Cups were of various forms and designs, and made of a variety of materials: gold, silver, earthenware, copper, bronze, etc. The word **cup** may also signify a laver (Exod. 24:6) or goblet (S. of Sol. 7:2; I Chron. 28:17). The cup is used as a symbol of prosperity or of Jehovah's blessing and, in reverse, of Jehovah's malediction upon the wicked (Pss. 11:6; 16:5; 23:5), and other illicit pleasures (Prov. 23:31; 51:7; Rev. 17:4; 18:6). "Cup of consolation" (Jer. 16:7), "Cup of Salvation" (Ps. 116:13), "Cup of blessing" (I Cor. 10:16), or "Cup of the Lord" (verse 21). Paul here refers to the communion cup, over which the blessing is said prior to the feast which commemorates the Lord's death and burial. At the communion service, the cup is sacred to the name of the Redeemer who instituted its practice (Matt. 26:27; Mark 14:23, 24; Luke 22:20). The "cup of trembling" literally, cup of intoxication (Isa. 51:17, 22; Zech. 12:2); "Cup of astonishment, desolation" (Ezek. 23:33); "Cup of fury" (Isa. 51:17-22); "Cup of indignation" (Rev. 14:10).

Cupbearer, (one giving drink), a palace official who served wine at a king's table. Cupbearers were men of confidence and trust (Gen. 40:1 ff; I Kings 10:5; II Chron. 9:4; Neh. 1:11).

Curse, the reverse of "to bless." On the human level, to wish harm or catastrophe. On the divine, to impose judgment. The cursing of one's parents is sternly prohibited by Mosaic regulations. Christ commanded those who would be His disciples to bless and curse not (Luke 6:28). When Peter, at Christ's trial, denied that he knew Him, he invited a curse upon himself (Matt. 26:74). This passage is often misunderstood by Western readers. Paul represents the curse of the law as borne by Christ upon the cross for the believer (Gal. 3:13). The modern Western practice of cursing, i.e., using profane language, is never referred to in the Scriptures. See Blasphemy.

Curtains. 1. The curtains of fine linen and goats' hair which covered the tabernacle (Exod. 26:1 ff; 38:9 ff). 2. Employed figuratively by Isaiah (40:22), referring to the heavens.

Cush (kūsh). 1. The oldest son of Ham, one of the three sons of Noah (Gen. 10:6-8; I Chron. 1:8-10). 2. "Cush, the Benjamite," the title for Psalm 7, viewed as referring to King Saul, the Benjamite. 3. Cush, the country. The name of the territory through which the Gihon flowed (Gen. 2:13).

Cushi (kū'shī), a member of the Cushite people. 1. The man sent by Joab to inform David that Absalom's rebellion was quelled (II Sam. 18:21-32). 2. A contemporary of Jeremiah (Jer. 36:14). 3. The father of the Prophet Zephaniah) Zeph. 1:1).

Custom, when not referring to a tax, usually means "manner," "way," or "statute" (Gen. 31:35; Judg. 11:39; Jer. 32:11). In the NT it means "manner," "usage" (Luke 1:9; Acts 6:14) and "religious practices."

Custom, Receipt of (RV "place of toll"), from which Matthew (Levi) was called to follow Christ (Matt. 9:9). In post-exilic days the tribute was usually in terms of a road toll. Tax collectors or publicans were despised because of their notorious dishonesty and willingness to work for a foreign power.

Cutha or **Cuth** (kū'thȧ, kŭth), the longer form preferable, one of the cities from which Sargon, king of Assyria, brought immigrants to repopulate the area of Samaria which he had sacked in 720 B.C. (II Kings 17:24-30). Because of their numerical predominance, the inhabitants of Samaria were henceforth referred to as Cutheans. As a result of mixture, a synthesis between Mosaism and heathenism arose. This is one of the explanations for the deep antipathy existing between the Jews and the Samaritans down into the days of the NT (John 4:9).

Cuttings (cuttings in the flesh), a heathen practice, usually done in mourning for the dead, which was forbidden to the children of Israel (Lev. 19:28). This cruel practice, extending from the cutting of the hair or beard to self-mutilation, was widespread among the heathen nations. In Elijah's day, the priests of Baal cut themselves till the blood ran in a vain attempt to make Baal answer (I Kings 18:28). Tattooing as a mark of allegiance to a deity, or as soldiers to their commander was also explicitly forbidden (Lev. 19:28). The holiness code of Israel reads, "Ye are the children of the Lord your God: ye shall not cut yourselves" (Deut. 14:1). The LXX adds the phrase, "in your flesh for the dead." The only cutting in the flesh allowed in Israel is that of circumcision at the command of God (Gen. 21:4).

Cylinder Seals, a cylindrical disc measuring from 1½ to 3 inches long—sometimes made of terra cotta, other times of precious stones, on which was printed different descriptions.

Cypress (See Plants)

Cyprus (sī′prŭs, **"copper"),** an island in the eastern part of the Mediterranean directly off the coast of Syria and Cilicia, 148 miles long and about 40 miles across. Rich in copper deposits. In the pre-Christian era, a large colony of Jews settled there, who later formed the nucleus of the Christian Church ministered to by Paul and company. During the Roman rule, the Jews were expelled from Cyprus in the days of Hadrian.

Cyrene, Cyrenian (sīrē′nĭ, **wall),** a Libyan city in N. Africa, W of Egypt from which it was separated by a part of the Libyan Desert. It was situated some 2,000 feet above the Mediterranean from which it was ten miles distant. The coastline afforded a natural shelter from the heat of the Sahara. It is protected by steps of descending ranges about 80 miles to the S. The fertility and climate of the city are delightful and productive.

Cyrene is not mentioned in the OT but becomes important in the NT. A native of Cyrene, Simon by name, was impressed by the Roman soldiers into carrying the cross of Jesus (Luke 23:26). Thus Simon immortalized his city. There were also representatives of this city present in Jerusalem upon the day of Pentecost (Acts 2:10). Its Jewish population warranted a synagogue (Acts 6:9). Lucius of Cyrene receives mention in Acts 11:19, 20.

The cylinder of Cyrus, telling of his capture of Babylon and his liberation of its captives. BM

Cyrenius (sī-rē′nĭ-ŭs, KJV, better Quirinius, RV) mentioned but once in the NT (Luke 2:2). (See Quirinius)

Cyrus (sī′rŭs). With the rise of Cyrus began the renowned Persian Empire which was to continue until the coming of Alexander the Great. Cyrus himself announced his genealogy: "I am Cyrus, king of the hosts, the great king, king of Babylon, king of Sumer and Akkad . . . son of Cambyses, the king, king of Anshan; the grandson of Cyrus . . . the great-grandson of Teispes . . . king of Anshan . . ." In this same inscription, Cyrus proceeds to relate how the city of Babylon opened its gates to him without resistance, thus confirming the Biblical account recorded in Daniel 5 when Darius, acting as vice-regent for Cyrus, took the city of Babylon in the name of Cyrus the Great.

Cyrus entered Babylon on October 29, 539 B.C. and presented himself in the role of the liberator of the people. He allowed the images of the gods to be transported back to their original cities, and instituted a kindly policy of repatriation for captive peoples. His policies of moderation naturally extended to the Hebrews, whom he encouraged to return to Judea to rebuild their temple (II Chron. 36:22, 23; Ezra 1:1-6; etc.). Isaiah refers to Cyrus as the "Anointed One" (Isa. 44:27, 28; 45:1-5).

Gateway to Straight Street. © *MPS*

-D-

Dabareh (dăb′ȧ-rĕ), erroneous spelling of Daberath (Josh. 21:28).

Dabbasheth (dăb′ȧ-shĕth), hill town on W. of Zebulun (Josh. 19:10).

Daberath (dăb′ĕ-răth), a town on border of Issachar given to the Levites (Josh. 19:12; I Chron. 6:72). The probable site of the defeat of Sisera by Barak (Judg. 4:14-22).

Dagon (dā′gŏn, **fish?,**) pagan deity with body of fish, head and hands of man. Probably god of agriculture. Worshiped in Mesopotamia and Canaan; temples in Ashdod (I Sam. 5:1-7), Gaza (Judg. 16:21-30), and in Israel (I Chron. 10:10). Samson destroyed the temple in Gaza (Judg. 16:30).

Dalaiah (dăl′ā-ī′ȧ). 1. Descendant of David (I Chron. 3:1-24). 2. A priest of Aaron's line (I Chron. 24:18). 3. A prince who pleaded with King Jehoiakim not to destroy Jeremiah's scroll (Jer. 36:12, 25). 4. The founder of a returned family (Ezra 2:60; Neh. 7:62). 5. The father of Shemaiah (Nah. 6:10).

Dale, the Kings. 1. Where Abram met Melchizedek (Gen. 14:17). 2. Absalom's memorial (II Sam. 18:18).

Dalmanutha (dăl-mȧ-nū′thȧ), a village on the W coast of the Sea of Galilee, adjoining Magdala (Matt. 15:39). Landing place of Jesus after feeding the multitude (Mark 8:10).

Dalmatia (dăl-mā′shȧ, **deceitful**), a mountainous province on the E shore of the Adriatic Sea. Christianity, implanted under Titus (II Tim. 4:10), continues until today. Ruled by Rome as early as A.D. 160. Paul may have visited in the province (Rom. 15:19); in his time it was regarded as part of Illyricum.

Dalphon (dăl′fŏn), one of Haman's sons who were slain and hanged after Esther became queen (Esth. 9:6-13).

Damaris (dăm′ȧ-rĭs), a convert of Paul at Mars Hill (Acts 17:34).

Damascus (dȧ-măs′kŭs), ancient city of Syria, more than 4000 years old; 2000 feet above sea level; watered by Abana and Pharpar rivers (II Kings 5:12); at E foot of Anti-Lebanon mts. Played an important part in Biblical history. David conquered it (II Sam. 8:5, 6; I Chron. 18:3-6). Rulers who played prominent part in history of Israel and Judah: Rezon (I Kings 11:23-25), Ben-hadad (I Kings 15:16-21), Hazael (II Kings 8:15; 13:22-25), Ben-hadad II (II Kings 13:24, 25). During NT times Damascus was ruled by Arabia under Aretas (II Cor. 11:32). Paul converted near Damascus (Acts 9:1-18) and preached there (Acts 9:22). Captured by Moslems in A.D. 635 and made the seat of the Mohammedan world.

The "Street called Straight" in Damascus. © *MPS*

Damnation, when referring to the future it means primarily eternal separation from God with accompanying awful punishments (Matt. 5:29; 10:28; 23:33; 24:51). The severity of the punishment is determined by the degree of sin (Luke 12:36-48), and is eternal (Mark 3:29; II Thess. 1:9; Isa. 33:14; 66:24; Jude 6, 7).

Dan (City), northernmost city of Palestine; originally Leshem (Josh. 19:47; Judg. 18:29); captured by Danites and renamed Dan (Judg. 18). "From Dan to Beersheba" (Judg. 20:1; I Sam. 3:20) means the whole length of Palestine.

Dan (Tribe of), the tribe to which Dan the fifth son of Jacob gave origin, and the territory allotted it in Canaan. The tribe acted as rear guard during the Exodus (Num. 10:25). They were given a fertile area lying between Judah and the Mediterranean Sea (Josh. 13:3). Failure to conquer Philistia made the Danites move northward where, by a bit of strategy, they conquered Leshem (Laish of Judg. 18:29), and renamed it Dan (Josh. 19:47; Judg. 18: 1-29). Aholiab and Samson were Danites (Exod. 31:6; Judg. 13:2, 24). Jeroboam, Solomon's servant, set up a golden calf in Dan and put high places throughout Israel (I Kings 12: 25-33). Pul overran Israel and took many Danites into captivity (I Chron. 5:26).

Dancing has formed a part of religious rites and has been associated with war and hunting, with marriage, birth, and other occasions since the records of man began to be written. It grew out of three basic human reactions: 1, the desire to imitate movements of beasts, birds, even the sun and moon; 2, the desire to express emotions by gestures; 3, gregarious impulses.

Throughout past ages dancing has been associated with worship. Closely related to religious praises was the sacramental dance in which worshipers sought to express through bodily movements praise or penitence, worship or prayer. Percussion and other noise-making instruments seem to be native to the dance (Judg. 11:34; Ps. 68:25).

The Hebrew people developed their own type of dancing, associated in the main with worship. Basically, it was more like modern religious shouting by individuals, or processions of exuberant groups. Three things characterized it: 1, the sexes never intermingled in it, except where pagan influences had crept in (cf. Exod. 32:19); 2, usually dancing was done by women, with one leading, as in the case of Miriam (Exod. 15:20, 21). 3. Dancing usually took place out of doors. For women dancers, see Exodus 15:20; Judges 21:19 ff; I Samuel 18:6; Psalm 68:25. Men danced solo, as in the case of David before the Ark (II Sam. 6: 14-16), and in groups, as when Israel celebrated the victory over the Amalekites (I Sam. 30:16). The Romans introduced the Greek dance to Palestine. Primitive Christian churches allowed the dance, but it soon caused degeneracy and was banned, as is indicated by many of the early Christian writers.

Daniel (dănyĕl, **God is my judge**). 1. David's second son (I Chron. 3:1;—Chileab, II Sam. 3:3). 2. A post-exilic priest (Ezra 8:2; Neh. 10:6). 3. The exilic seer of the book of Daniel. The prophet was born into an unidentified family of Judean nobility at the time of Josiah's reformation (621 B.C.). He was taken to Babylon by Nebuchadnezzar in 605 B.C., the third year of king Jehoiakim (Dan. 1:1, 3).

For three years Daniel was trained in all the wisdom of the Chaldeans (Dan. 1:4-5) and was assigned the Babylonian name Belteshazzar, "Protect his life!", thereby invoking a pagan deity (4:8). Daniel and his companions, however, remained true to their ancestral faith, courteously refusing "the king's dainties" (1:8, tainted with idolatry and contrary to the Levitical purity-laws). God rewarded them with unsurpassed learning (1:20), qualifying them as official "wise-men" (cf. 2:13). Upon Daniel, moreover, He bestowed the gift of visions and of interpreting dreams (1: 17; cf. Daniel's wisdom in the Apocryphal stories of **Susanna** and **Bel and the Dragon**).

Near the close of his second year (602 B.C.) Nebuchadnezzar required his fellow-Chaldeans to identify and interpret an undisclosed dream that had troubled him the preceding evening (2:5, 8, ASVmg). The hoax of spiritism and astrology was duly exposed, but when judgment was pronounced upon the enchanters Daniel and his companions were included under the death-sentence. But the "God in heaven that revealeth secrets" (2:28, cf. 2:11) answered Daniel's prayer for illumination (2:18-19). Daniel revealed both the dream, depicting a fourfold image, and its import of four world empires (Babylon, Persia, Greece, and Rome) that should introduce God's Messianic kingdom (2:44; see Daniel, Book of). Nebuchadnezzar forthwith elevated him to be chief over the wise-men (2:48 does not, however, state that he became a pagan priest, as inferred by those who would discredit Daniel's historicity). He further offered him the governorship of the province of Babylon, though Daniel committed this latter appointment to his three friends (2:49; see Shadrach, Furnace).

In the latter years of Nebuchadnezzar's reign (604-562 B.C.), Daniel's courage was demonstrated (4:19, cf. 4:7) when he interpreted the king's dream of the fallen tree. Tactfully informing his despotic master that for seven "times" (months? cf. 4:33) pride would reduce him to beast-like madness, he reiterated "that the Most High ruleth in the kingdom of men" (4:24-25; cf. its historical fulfillment twelve months later, 4:28-33).

The Lion monument in the ruins of Babylon supposedly marking the site of Daniel's den of lions. © *MPS*

In 552 B.C., after the retirement of king Nabonidus to Arabian Teima and the accession of his son Belshazzar to the royal dignity (ICC, p. 67), Daniel was granted his vision of the four great beasts (Dan. 7), which parallels Nebuchadnezzar's earlier dream of the composite image. Then in 550, at the time of Cyrus' amalgamation of the Median and Persian states and of the growing eclipse of Babylon, Daniel received the prophecy of the ram and the he-goat, concerning Persia and Greece (8:20-21) down to Antiochus IV (8:25). On Oct. 12, 539 B.C., Cyrus' general Gobryas, after having routed the Chaldean armies, occupied the city of Babylon. During the profane revelries of Belshazzar's court that immediately preceded the end, Daniel was summoned to interpret God's "handwriting on the wall"; and the prophet fearlessly condemned the desperate prince (5:22-23). He predicted Medo-Persian victory (v. 28), and that very night the citadel fell and Belshazzar was slain.

When Darius the Mede was made king of Babylon by Cyrus (5:31; 9:1), he at once sought out Daniel as one of his three "presidents" (6:2), because of his excellency, and was considering him for the post of chief administrator (6:3). Daniel's jealous colleagues, failing to uncover valid charges of corruption (6:4), proceeded to contrive his downfall through a royal edict prohibiting for thirty days all prayers or petitions, save to Darius himself. Daniel was promptly apprehended in prayer to God; and Darius had no recourse but to cast him into a den of lions, as had been prescribed. God, however, intervened on behalf of His faithful servant (cf. 6:16) and shut the lions' mouths, though they subsequently devoured his accusers, when condemned to a similar fate.

The last known event in the life of Daniel took place in the third year of Cyrus (536 B.C.), when he was granted an overpowering vision of the course of world history and God's final judgment (11:40-12:4). The vision concluded with the assurance that though Daniel would come to his grave prior to these events he would yet receive his appointed reward in the consummation (12:13). Thus in his mid-eighties, after completing his inspired autobiography and apocalyptic oracles, he finished his honored course.

Daniel, Book of, a prophetic book which stands among the "writings" in the Hebrew OT (which consists of "the law, prophets, and writings") because while he had the gift of a prophet (Matt. 24:15), his position was that of a governmental official. The book is apocalyptic in character and abounds in symbolic and figurative language, and as a result it has been subject to many different interpretations. The first half of the book (chs. 1-6) consists of six narratives on the life of Daniel and his friends: their education, his revelation of Nebuchadnezzar's dream-image, the trial by a fiery furnace, his prediction of Nebuchadnezzar's madness, his interpretation of the handwriting on the wall, and his ordeal in the lion's den. The second half (7-12) consists of four apocalyptic visions, predicting the course of world history. There are references to the book in the NT (Matt. 24:15; Luke 1: 19, 26; Heb. 11:33, 34). Chs. 2:4b-7: 28 are composed in Aramaic; the rest is in Hebrew. His book was designed to inspire Jewish exiles with confidence in Jehovah (4:34-37).

Dan-Jaan (dăn′jā′ăn) a town, probably in Dan, covered by David's census (II Sam. 24:6).

Dannah (dăn′ȧ), a mountain town given by Caleb as part of the heritage of Judah (Josh. 15: 49).

Dara, Darda (dăr′ȧ, dȧr′dă), a member of a noted family of wise men. Either a son of Mahol (I Kings 4:31) or Zerah (I Chron. 2:6).

Daric (dăr′ĭk), a Persian gold coin used in Palestine after the return from captivity (Ezra 2:69; Neh. 7:70-72 ASV). Worth about $5.00. See Money.

Darius (dă-rī′ŭs), a common name for Medo-Persian rulers. 1. Darius the Mede (Gubaru), son of Ahasuerus (Dan. 5:31; 9:1); made governor of Babylon by Cyrus, but he seems to have ruled for only a brief time (Dan. 10:1; 11:1); prominent in the Book of Daniel (6:1, 6, 9, 25, 28; 11:1). 2. Darius Hystaspes, 4th and greatest of the Persian rulers (521-486 B.C.); reorganized government into satrapies and extended boundaries of empire; great builder; defeated by Greeks at Marathon 490 B.C.; renewed edict of Cyrus and helped rebuild the temple (Ezra 4:5; 24; 5:5-7; 6:1-12; Hag. 1:1; 2:1, 10, 18; Zech. 1:1, 7; 7:1). Died in 486 B.C. and was succeeded by Xerxes, grandson of Cyrus the Great. 3. Darius, the Persian, last king of Persia (336-330 B.C.); defeated by Alexander the Great in 330 B.C. (Neh. 12: 22). Some scholars identify him with Darius II (Nothus), who ruled Persia and Babylon (423-408 B.C.).

Darkness, used in the Old and the New Testament both in a literal and in a figurative sense. Associated with evil, danger, crime; it has also been the metaphor whereby mystery is described and the place of eternal punishment has been pictured. Several uses of the term are found in the Scriptures: 1. To denote the absence of light (Gen. 1:2, 3; Isa. 45:7; Job 34:22). 2. To depict the mysterious (Exod. 20:21; I Kings 8:12; Ps. 97:2; Isa. 8:22; II Sam. 22:10; Matt. 10:27). 3. As ignorance, especially about God (Job 37:19; Prov. 2:13; Eccl. 2:15; John 12:35; I Thess. 5:1-8). 4. To describe the seat of evil (Prov. 4:19; Matt. 6:23; Luke 11:34; 22:53; John 8:12; Rom. 13:12; I Cor. 4:5; Eph. 5:11). 5. Presenting supernatural events (Gen. 15:12; Exod. 10: 21; Matt. 27:45; Rev. 8:12; 16:10). 6. A sign of the Lord's return (Joel 2:2; Amos 5:8; Isa. 60:2; Matt. 24:29). 7. An agency of eternal punishment (Matt. 22:13; II Pet. 2:4, 17; Jude 6, 7; see also Job 2:1-5; 20:20). 8. Spiritual blindness (Isa. 9:2; John 1:5; I John 1:5; 2:8; Eph. 5:8), sorrow and distress (Isa. 8:22; 13:10; Ps. 23:4).

Darkon (dȧr′kŏn), descendant of Solomon's servant, Jaala, who returned with Zerubbabel from exile (Ezra 2: 56).

Dathan (dā′thăn), a great-grandson of Reuben (Num. 16:1). He, with his brothers, Abiram and Korah, rebelled against Moses (Num. 16:2-15), for which sin they were swallowed by the earth (Num. 16:31-35; see also Num. 26).

Daughter, a word of various uses in the Bible, it refers to both persons

Bethlehem, the City of David. © *MPS*

and things, often without regard to kinship or sex. 1. Daughter (Gen. 11:29) or female descendant (Gen. 28:48). 2. Women in general (Gen. 28:6; Num. 25:1). 3. Worshipers of the true God (Ps. 45:10; Isa. 62:11; Matt. 21:5; John 12:15). 4. City (Isa. 37:22). 5. Citizens (Zech. 2:10).

David (dā'vĭd, **beloved** or, as in ancient Mari, **chieftain),** Israel's greatest and most loved king, described in I Sam. 16 through I Kings 2:11 (I Chron. 11-29), plus many of the Psalms. Born in 1040 B.C. (II Sam. 5:4), the youngest son of Jesse of Bethlehem (I Sam. 16:10, 11); took care of his father's sheep (I Sam. 16:11; 17:34-36); anointed king by Samuel (I Sam. 16:13); played harp for Saul (I Sam. 16:18, 23); killed Goliath (I Sam. 17:45-51); became loved friend of Jonathan (I Sam. 18:1-3); Saul, jealous, tried to take his life (I Sam 18:13-16, 28-19:1); driven into outlawry by Saul (I Sam. 19:11; 21:10); fled to Philistine Gath (I Sam. 21) and lived in wilderness cave of Adullam (I Sam. 22); joined by Abiathar and a variety of malcontents (I Sam. 22:2); pursued by Saul (I Sam. 23; Ps. 7:4; I Sam. 26); after the death of Saul at Mt. Gilboa in 1010 B.C. he was declared king over Judah (II Sam. 2-4). In 1003 B.C. all Israel acclaimed him king (II Sam. 5:1-5; I Chron. 11:10; 12:38). After the defeat of the Philistines (II Sam. 5:18-25) he captured the Jebusite stronghold of Jerusalem and made it his religious capital by bringing the ark to Jerusalem (II Sam. 6; I Chron. 13; 15:1-3); organized worship (I Chron. 15, 16); expanded kingdom on all sides (II Sam. 8:10; 12:26-31); planned temple (II Sam. 7; I Chron. 17; 22:7-10); had family problems (II Sam. 12-19; I Kings 1); sinned with Bathsheba (II Sam. 11:1-12:23; Ps. 51); fought Philistines (II Sam. 21:15-22); made Solomon his successor (I Kings 1, 2); died after reigning 40 years (II Sam. 2:11; 5:4; I Chron. 29:27). Wrote 73 psalms; ancestor of Jesus (Matt. 1:1; 22:41-45).

David, City of, a part of the Jerusalem plateau, 2500 feet above sea-level. Solomon enlarged Jerusalem beyond the City of David to include Mt. Moriah, for the temple and other buildings, on the N (I Kings 8:1) and probably part of the western plateau opposite Ophel. In the eighth century, Hezekiah seems to have extended the City of David southward to include the new Pool of Siloam, for his water tunnel from Gihon (II Chron. 32:4-5, 30; II Kings

Sketch of the High Priest in the Holy of Holies on the Day of Atonement, after DeVries. JHK

20:20; Isa. 22:9-11). By the time of Josiah, 621 B.C., Jerusalem also included the **mishneh** or "second quarter." After A.D. 70 the original City of David was abandoned and now lies outside the walls of Jerusalem. In Luke 2:11, the Christmas angels identified David's native town of Bethlehem as "the city of David."

Day, a word having various meanings in the Bible, denoting time from sunrise to sunset (Ps. 74:16), time in general (Judg. 18:30; Obad. 12; Job 18:20), length of life (Gen. 5:4), the time of opportunity (John 9:4), etc.

Day of Atonement, an annual Hebrew feast when the high priest offered sacrifices for the sins of the nation (Lev. 23:27; 25:9). It was the only fast period required by Mosaic law (Lev. 16:29; 23:31). It was observed on the 10th day of the 7th month, a day of great solemnity and strictest conformity to the law.

Day of Christ, a term used in the NT to indicate the redemptive ministry of Jesus, both while in the flesh and upon His return. Sometimes it is called "that day" (Matt. 7:22) and "the day" (I Cor. 3:13). It refers to the return of Jesus for His own and for the judgment of unbelievers (I Cor. 1:8; 5:5; II Cor. 1:14; Phil. 1:6, 10; 2:16; II Thess. 2:2, 3).

Day of the Lord, an eschatological term referring to the consummation of God's kingdom and triumph over His foes and deliverance of His people. It begins at the second coming and will include the final judgment. It will remove class distinction (Isa. 2:12-21), abolish sins (II Pet. 3:11-13) and will be accompanied by social calamities and physical cataclysms (Matt. 24; Luke 21:7-33). It will include the millennial judgment (Rev. 4:1-19:6) and culminate in the new heaven and the new earth (Isa. 65:17; 66:22; Rev. 21:1).

Daysman (dāz′măn, **to act as umpire),** a mediator or arbitrator — one who has set a day for hearing a dispute. As used in Job 9:33, the word means an umpire or referee who hears two parties and decides the merits of the case. Job means that no human being is worthy of acting as a judge of God.

Dayspring (dā′sprĭng, **to break forth),** a poetic name for dawn (Job 38:12). It describes the advent of Messiah (Luke 1:78).

Daystar (light-giving), the planet Venus, seen as a morning star, heralding the dawn (Isa. 14:12; in RV daystar) (Rev. 22:16; II Peter 1:19).

Deacon, Deaconess (dē′kŭn, dē′kŭn-es, **servant**), in the KJV the word "deacon" appears only in Phil. 1:1 and four times in I Tim. 3; but the Greek word so rendered occurs c. 30 times in the NT. In most cases there is no technical meaning relating to a specialized function in the church. The word means basically a servant. Paul uses the word of himself and of Epaphras (Col. 1:7, 23, 25). The word in the NT is usually connected with the supply of material needs and service (Rom. 15:25; II Cor. 8:4). The diaconate, as a church office, is based by inference upon Acts 6:1-8; but at least two of the seven men were evangelists. Qualifications given in I Timothy 3 show that they were not considered ordinary lay members of the church. This is evident in Phil. 1:1. It does not appear from the NT that deaconesses were ever church officers. See Rom. 16:1.

Dead Sea, called in Scripture the Salt Sea (Gen. 14:3), Sea of the Arabah or East Sea (Joel 2:20; Zech. 14:8). It measures 47 by 10 miles and occupies a geologic fault that extends from Syria through the Red Sea into Africa. It is 1300 feet below sea level, and in its deepest place is 1300 feet deep. Has no outlet; therefore its salt concentration is four times that of ocean water; is slowly expanding; is often mentioned in the Bible (Num. 34:12; I Chron. 18:12; II Chron. 20: 1, 2; Ezek. 47:18).

Dead Sea Scrolls, discovered, in 1947, by Arabic Bedouin, in caves a mile or so W of the NW corner of the Dead Sea, at Qumran. So far MSS have been found in 11 caves, and they are mostly dated as coming from the last century B.C. and the first century A. D. At least 382 MSS are represented by the fragments of Cave Four alone, c. 100 of which are Biblical MSS. These include fragments of every book of the Hebrew Bible except Esther. Some of the books are represented in many copies. Not all the MSS are in fragments; some are complete or nearly complete. In addition to Biblical books, fragments of apocryphal and apocalyptic books, commentaries, Thanksgiving Psalms, and sectarian literature have been found. Near the caves are the remains of a monastery of huge size, the headquarters of a monastic sect of Jews called the Essenes. The discoveries at Qumran are important for Biblical studies in general. They are of great importance for a study of the OT text, both Hebrew and the LXX. They are also of importance in relation to the NT, as they furnish the background to the preaching of John the Baptist and Jesus. There is no evidence that either John the Baptist or Jesus was a member of the group.

Bibliography: F. F. Bruce, **Second Thoughts on the Dead Sea Scrolls.** Millar Burrows, **The Dead Sea Scrolls; More Light on the Dead Sea Scrolls.** William Sanford LaSor, **Amazing Dead Sea Scrolls and the Christian Faith; A Bibliography of the Dead Sea Scrolls, 1948-1957.**

Death, refers to cessation of natural life: Abraham (Gen. 25:11), Aaron's wicked sons (Lev. 16:1), Moses (Deut. 34:5), a woman in travail (I Sam. 4: 20), a father (Matt. 8:22), David's child (II Sam. 12:23), a thief (Mark 15:27), even the son of Man (Mark 15:37). Pictured as the departure of the spirit from the body (II Tim. 4: 6), as being inevitable (Josh. 23:14), as laying aside the body (II Cor. 5:1), as the return to the former natural state (Eccl. 3:20; 12:7), as a sleep (Jer. 51:39; Dan. 12:2; John 11:11; Acts 7:60), a state in which God is not seen (Isa. 38:11; Job 35:14), nor praised (Ps. 6:5; Isa. 38:18). It is the result of sin (Gen. 2:17; Rom. 5:21; 6:23; I Cor. 15:56; Heb. 2:14; James 1:15). In the spiritual sense death is a separation from God, or spiritual night (Luke 1:79; I John 3:14; Rom. 5:12; 6:23; John 3:36; Eph. 2:1, 5; Rev. 2:11). The righteous and wicked go on forever, the righteous to everlasting good (Isa. 35:10; 45:17; Dan. 7:14; 12:2; Rev. 7:17), the evil to eternal torment (Jer. 20:11; Dan. 12: 2; Matt. 25:46; Mark 3:29; II Thess. 1:9; Jude 7). The Bible does not teach the annihilation of the wicked. Jesus has conquered death and removed its sting (John 5:24; I Cor. 15:53-57; I John 5:12; Rev. 1:18). The second death is final separation from God (Rev. 20:6, 14).

Debir (dē'bĕr). 1. City of Judah, c. 10 miles SW of Hebron; captured by Joshua from the Anakim (Josh. 10: 38, 39); later became a Levitical city (Josh. 21:15; I Chron. 6:58). 2. King of Eglon; defeated by Joshua at Gibeon (Josh. 10:1-11). 3. Town E of Jordan on border of Gad (Josh. 13: 24-26). 4. Town on road between Jerusalem and Jericho (Josh. 15:7).

Deborah (dĕb'ō-rȧ, **bee**). 1. Rebekah's nurse (Gen. 24:59; 35:8), who accompanied her to Palestine. 2. The fourth and greatest (with Gideon) of Israel's judges, a prophetess, a wife of Lappidoth (Judg. 4-5).

Summoning Barak of Naphtali, she prophesied that an offensive from Mt. Tabor at the northeastern limit of Esdraelon would lure Sisera and Jabin's army to annihilation on the plains below (4:6-7). Barak agreed, provided Deborah's inspiring presence should accompany the troops, though Deborah predicted Sisera's death by a woman (4:8-9). Deborah accomplished Israel's first united action since the conquest, 175 years before.

Sisera was slain in single flight, by the woman Jael at Kedesh (4:11, 17-

22); Jabin was destroyed (4:24); and the land rested 40 years (5:31), corresponding to the reign of Rameses III, the last great Pharaoh of Egypt's XXth dynasty. After the battle, Deborah and Barak sang Deborah's song of victory (5:2-31, cf. v. 7).

Deborah's insight into her fearless and unsolicited devotion to God's people renders her "blessed above women" (5:24).

Debt (a sum owed, an obligation), under Mosaic law Jews were not allowed to exact interest from other Jews (Exod. 22:25). The poor were protected against usurers by special laws (Exod. 22:25-27). Debtors unable to pay could have their property, family, and even person seized (Lev. 25:25-41), and could be thrown into prison (Matt. 18:21-26). The word also has reference to moral obligation (Matt. 6:12; Rom. 8:12).

Decalogue (dĕk′à-lŏg, **ten words),** the Ten Commandments given by God to Moses at Mt. Sinai (Exod. 20) and inscribed on tablets of stone (Deut. 4:13). Jesus approved the law (Matt. 5:18; 22:40), fulfilled it (Matt. 5:27-48; 23:23), and became the end of the law for righteousness to all who believe (Rom. 10:4; 8:1-4).

Decapolis (dē-kăp′ô-lĭs, **ten cities), a** region E of Jordan that had been given to the tribe of Manasseh (Num. 32:33-42). A league of ten cities, consisting of Greeks who had come in the wake of Alexander's conquest, was established after the Romans occupied the area (65 B.C.). According to Ptolemy, the number was later increased to 18. They had their own coinage, courts, and army (Jos. XIV: 4:4).

Decision, Valley of, where God will some day gather all nations for judgment (Joel 3:2, 12). It is called the Valley of Jehoshaphat **(Jehovah judges),** and has been identified by some with the Valley of Kidron, but this is only conjecture.

Decree, an official ruling or law. In Esther 1:20, Daniel 3:10, Jonah 3:7, the word refers to laws governing special occasions. In Acts 16:4 the Greek **dogma** means rules for Christian living. God's decree is His settled plan and purpose (Ps. 2:7-10; Dan. 4:24; see also Exod. 32:32; Rev. 13: 8).

Dedan (dē′dăn). 1. An Arabian people descended from Noah (Gen. 10:6, 7); lived in NW part of the Persian Gulf. 2. A descendant of Abraham by Keturah (Gen. 25:3).

Dedication (to sanctify, to consecrate), an expression denoting dedication of persons, but usually of the setting apart of things for God's use. Consecration of the tabernacle (Num. 7) was an elaborate ceremony, as was that of the temple (I Kings 8). Among various dedicated things were: the city wall (Neh. 12:27), private dwellings (Deut. 20:5), the temple treasure (I Chron. 28:12), the child (Exod. 13:2), people (Exod. 19:14; I Sam. 16:5), and booty of war (II Sam. 8: 10, 11).

Dedication, Feast of, an annual festival of the Jews held throughout the country for eight days, celebrating the restoration of the temple following its desecration at the hands of the Syrians under Antiochus Epiphanes (I Macc. IV; 52-59; II Macc. X:5), of which Josephus gives a graphic picture (Ant. XII:5:4). The feast came on the 25th of Kislev (December). Josephus called it the "Feast of Lights." It was at this feast that Jesus delivered the discourse recorded in John 10:24ff.

Deep, the ocean (Neh. 9:11), chaos (Gen. 1:2), deepest part of sea (Gen. 49:25), abyss (Luke 8:31; Rev. 9:1; 11:7).

Defile (dē-fīl′), **to profane, pollute, render unclean.** In the OT, defilement was physical (S. of Sol. 5:3), sexual (Lev. 18:20), ethical (Isa. 59:3; Ezek. 37:23), ceremonial (Lev. 11:24; 17:15; etc.), and religious (Num. 25:33; Jer. 3:1). In the NT it is ethical or religious (Mark 7:19; Acts 10:15; Rom. 14:20), the idea of ceremonial or ritual defilement does not exist.

Degree (dē-grē, **a going up** or **ascent, low**). The word **degrees** occurs in the titles of 15 psalms, Psalms 120 to 134, which are called Songs of Degrees. The word is also used in II Kings 20:9, 10, and in a secondary sense of rank or order (I Chron. 15:18; 17:17; Ps. 62:9; Luke 1:52; James 1:9).

Degrees, Songs of, the title given Psalms 120-134. Uncertainty exists as to the origin of the title. Some Jewish authorities attributed it to the use made of fifteen steps leading from the court of men to the court of women in the temple. Some scholars attribute the title to the way in which the thought advances from step to step, as seen in 121:4, 5; 124:1, 2, 3, 4, but all these songs do not do this. The most logical explanation is that the title was given the series of hymns because they were used by pilgrims during the annual journeys to the three required feasts in Jerusalem.

Dekar (dē′kär), the father of one of Solomon's twelve purveyors (I Kings 4:7-9).

Delaiah (dē-lā′yȧ, **raised** or **freed by Jehovah**). 1. A descendant of David (I Chron. 3:1, 24). 2. A priest of David's time (I Chron. 24:18). 3. A prince who tried to save Jeremiah's roll (Jer. 36:12, 25). 4. Head of a tribe that returned under Zerubbabel from captivity (Ezra 2:60; Neh. 7:62). 5. The father of Shemaiah (Neh. 6: 10).

Delilah (dē-lī′lȧ, **dainty one),** a Philistine woman from the valley of Sorek who lured Samson to his ruin (Judg. 16:4-20).

Deluge (See Flood)

Demas (dē′măs, **popular),** a faithful helper of Paul during his imprisonment in Rome (Col. 4:14). Paul called him a "fellow laborer" (Philem. 24). He was probably a citizen of Thessalonica to which place he went upon deserting Paul (II Tim. 4:10).

Demetrius (dĕ-mē′trĭ-ŭs, **belonging to Demeter).** 1. The disciple whom John praised in his letter to Gaius (III John 12). 2. The jeweler of Ephesus who raised a mob against Paul because his preaching had resulted in damage to his lucrative business of making silver images of the goddess Diana (Acts 19:23-27).

Demons, evil spirits (Matt. 8:16; Luke 10:17, 20); invisible, incorporeal; form hierarchy (Eph. 6:10-12); have superhuman intelligence; are opposed to God; take possession of people, bringing upon them such evils as blindness (Matt. 12:22), insanity (Luke 8:26-36), dumbness (Matt. 9:32, 33), and suicidal mania (Mark 9:22). Two classes: those who are free (Eph. 2:2; 6:11, 12) and those who are imprisoned in the abyss (Luke 8:31; Rev. 9:1-11; 20:1-3).

Denarius (See Money)

Depravity (dē-prăv′ĭ-tē) the loss of original righteousness and love for God. Positively, it means that man's moral nature has become corrupted, and that he has an irresistible bias toward evil. The depraved man can do nothing perfectly pleasing to God. He cannot, no matter how hard he tries, love God with all his heart or his neighbor as himself; nor can he change his supreme preference for himself, or so radically transform his character that he can live according to God's law. Without the saving grace of God no salvation is possible.

Deputy (dĕp′ū-tē), one appointed to rule under a higher authority, as a regent in place of a king (I Kings 22: 47) or a Roman consul or proconsul (Acts 13:7; 18:12; 19:38).

Derbe (dûr′bē), a city in the SE corner of Lycaonia, in Asia Minor. **In** Acts 14:20 it is called **Dérbe;** in 20:4, **Derbaíos.** Paul visited it on the first journey after being stoned at Lystra (Acts 14:20), also on his second tour (Acts 16:1), and probably on the third. Gaius, who accompanied Paul to Jerusalem, was from there (Acts 20:4).

Desert, a waste, desolate, uncultivated, and often arid, place (Deut. 32:10; Job 24:5).

Desire of all Nations, some expositors refer the prophecy to Christ's first advent; others, to the second advent; still others deny a Messianic application altogether and hold it means the precious gifts of all nations (Hag. 2:7).

Desolation, Abomination of (See Abomination of Desolation)

Deuel (dū′ĕl), a Gadite, father of Eliasaph, prince of Gad in the wilderness just after the Exodus from Egypt (Num. 1:14; 7:47; 10:20).

Deuteronomy (dū′têr-ŏn′ō-mē, **second law**), the Jewish name for it is "words," from the opening expression, "These are the words which Moses spake." Mosaic authorship is claimed in 31:9, 24, 26. The book contains three farewell addresses of Moses, given by him in sight of Canaan, which he was forbidden to enter, and a renewal of Israel's covenant with God. Outline: 1. First discourse (1-4). 2. Second discourse (5-26). 3. Third discourse (27-30). 4. Last counsels; parting blessings (31-34).

Deuteronomy is the Bible's full-scale exposition of the covenant concept and demonstrates that, far from being a contract between two parties, God's covenant with His people is a proclamation of His sovereignty and an instrument for binding His elect to Himself in a commitment of absolute allegiance.

Israel is confronted with the demands of God's governmental omnipotence, redemptive grace, and consuming jealousy. By the covenant oath Israel came under both the curses and the blessings which were to be meted out according to God's righteous judgment. The covenant relation bestowed, called still to responsible decision: "I call heaven and earth to witness against you this day, that I have set before you life and death, blessing and curse; therefore choose life, that both you and your seed may live: that you may love the Lord your God . . . for that is your life" (30:19, 20a).

Devil (slanderer), one of the principal titles of Satan, the arch-enemy of God and of man. It is not known how he originated, unless Isa. 14:12-20 and Ezek. 28:12-19 give us a clue, but it is certain that he was not created evil. He rebelled against God when in a state of holiness and apparently led other angels into rebellion with him (Jude 6; II Peter 2:4). He is a being of superhuman power and wisdom, but not omnipotent or omniscient. He tries to frustrate God's plans and purposes for human beings. His principal method of attack is by temptation. His power is limited and he can go only as far as God permits. On the Judgment Day he will be cast into hell to remain there forever.

Devoted Thing, that which is set apart unto the Lord. A sacrifice or offering is a voluntary gift from the owner, and can at any time previous to the ceremony be recalled, but not so a devoted thing. Achan's sin at Jericho (Josh. 6:17-19) was considered far more serious than mere stealing, for he had taken of the devoted thing.

Dew, in the dry summers and autumns of Palestine dew was a great blessing to the land (Gen. 27:28; Judg. 6:37-40), while the absence of it was regarded as a misfortune (II Sam. 1:21; I Kings 17:1). Often used as a symbol of blessing (Gen. 27:28) and of refreshment (Deut. 32:2; Job. 29:19; Ps. 133:3; Isa. 18:4).

Diadem, the Hebrew word is usually rendered "mitre" and refers to the turban of the chief priest (Zech. 3:5), a royal diadem (Isa. 62:3), or a turban (Job 29:14). In the NT, the word does not occur in the KJV but is used three times in Rev. (12:3; 13:1; 19:12) as an emblem of absolute power. Our Lord, too, will wear the diadem (Rev. 19:12).

Dial, a graduated arc intended to mark the time of day by the shadow of a style or gnomon falling upon it. The word occurs only twice in the Bible (II Kings 20:11; Isa. 38:8) referring to the "sun-dial of Ahaz." The Hebrew **ma'ălâh** here rendered "dial" is generally "degrees" or steps, from the root meaning "to go up." It would seem from this that the time of day was found by the men of Hezekiah's time by the shadow of a pillar as it ascended or descended the steps leading to the palace. The miracle recorded in connection with the dial can be compared with the "long day" in Joshua's time (Josh. 10:12-14) and is equally inexplicable on natural grounds.

Diana (dī-ăn'à), the Roman goddess of the moon; identified with Artemis, her Greek counterpart; usually represented as a virgin huntress. The Diana of the Ephesians (Acts 19:24-35) was a combination of the Greek Artemis and the Semitic goddess Ashtoreth, the patroness of the sexual instinct. Her images were lascivious. Her special worship was centered in the great temple at Ephesus.

Diana of the Ephesians (Artemis). JHK

Diaspora (dī-ăs'pô-rȧ, **that which is sown**), the name applied to the Jews living outside of Palestine and maintaining their religious faith among the Gentiles. God had warned the Jews through Moses that dispersion among other nations would be their lot if they departed from the Mosaic Law (Deut. 4:27; 28:64-68). These prophecies were largely fulfilled in the two captivities, by Assyria and Babylonia, but there were other captivities which helped scatter the Israelites. By the time of Christ the diaspora must have been several times the population of Palestine. Paul invariably contacted the people in every city he visited.

Diblaim (dĭb-lā'ĭm), father-in-law of Hosea, the prophet (Hos. 1:3).

Diblath (dĭb'lăth) occurs in Ezekiel 6:14; in the RV it is "Diblah," which seems to have been an early copyist's error for Riblah, **q.v.** It was a town about 50 miles S of Hamath.

Dibon, Dibon-Gad (dī'bŏn). 1. A place in the high plain of Moab about ten miles E of the Dead Sea. It was one of the stations of Israel in its journey toward the Promised Land (Num. 33:45, 46). Moses apparently gave it to Reuben (Josh. 13-17). 2. A town in Judah (Neh. 11:25).

Dibri (dĭb'rē), a Danite, whose grandson fought with an Israelite in the camp, cursed, and then was stoned for his blasphemy (Lev. 24:11-16).

Didrachma (See Money)

Didymus (dĭd'ĭ-mŭs, **a twin**), surname of Thomas (John 11:16; 20:24; 21:2).

Diklah (dĭk lȧ), son of Joktan, and his descendants who probably lived in Arabia (Gen. 10:27; I Chron. 1:21).

Dilean (dĭl'ē-ăn), a town in the lowlands of Judah (Josh. 15:38).

Dimnah (dĭm'nȧ), a town in Zebulun, bestowed upon the Merarite Levites (Josh. 21:35). Rimmon (I Chron. 6:77) may be the same place.

Dimon (dīmŏn), a town in Moab, generally called "Dibon" (**q.v.**), but in Isaiah 15:9 twice written Dimon, about four miles N of Aroer.

Dimonah (dī-mŏ'nȧ), a town in the S of Judah (Josh. 15:22), probably the same as the "Dibon" of Neh. 11:25.

Dinah (dī'nȧ), a daughter of Jacob and Leah (Gen. 30:21), and so far as is recorded, his only daughter (Gen. 34). Shechem, the prince, violated her.

Dinaite (dī'nȧ-īt), a member of the tribe of Dinaites whom Ashurbanipal had brought from Assyria to colonize Samaria (cf. II Kings 17:24 with Ezra 4:7-10).

Dinhabah (dĭn'hȧ-bȧ), the city of Bela, the first known king of Edom (Gen. 36:32).

Dionysius, The Areopagite (dī-ŏnĭsh'ĭ-ŭs, the ăr'ē-ŏp'ȧ-gīt), a member of the Areopagus, the Athenian supreme court; one of Paul's converts at Athens (Acts 17:34).

Dioscuri (dī-ŏs'kŭ-rē, **sons of Zeus**). In mythology, they were twin sons of Zeus by Leda, named Castor and Pollux (Acts 28:11).

Diotrephes (dī-ŏt'rē-fēz, **nurtured by Zeus**), a leading member, perhaps the bishop, of the church to which Gaius belonged, to whom John the beloved apostle wrote his third epistle. His domineering attitude made him an obstacle to the progress of the church.

Discerning of Spirits, the ability which the Holy Spirit gives to some Christians to discern between those who spoke by the Spirit of God and those who were moved by false spirits (I Cor. 12:10).

Disciple (a learner), a pupil of some teacher. The word implies the acceptance in mind and life of the views and practices of the teacher. Usually, however, it refers to the adherents of Jesus. Sometimes it refers to the Twelve Apostles (Matt. 10:1; 11:1; etc.); but, more often, simply to Christians (Acts 6:1, 2, 7; 9:36).

Diseases to which the Bible refers appear to have been mostly diseases that now exist. I. Diseases with primary manifestations in skin were of two kinds, those which were believed to require isolation and those not requiring isolation. A. Those requiring isolation: leprosy (Exod. 4:6), syphilis (Prov. 7:22, 23), smallpox (perhaps Job's boils), boil or carbuncle (Hezekiah's — II Kings 20:7), anthrax (Exod. 9:3), scabies (Deut. 28:27). B. Skin diseases not requiring isolation: inflammation (Lev. 22:22). II. Diseases with primary internal manifestations. A. Plague - bubonic (I Sam. 5:9; 6:5) and pneumonic (II Kings 19:35). B. Consumption: tuberculosis (Lev. 21:20), typhoid fever, malaria (Lev. 26:16; Deut. 28:22), diarrhea, dysentery, and cholera (Acts 28:8). III. Diseases caused by worms and snakes: intestinal roundworm infection (Acts 12:21-23), guinea worm, snake-bite (Acts 28:3, 6). IV. Diseases of the eyes: epidemic blindness (II Kings 6:18), infirmity (Gal. 4:13). V. Nervous and mental diseases. Miscellaneous medical disorders and therapy: excessive menstrual flow (Luke 8:43, 44), gangrene (II

Tim. 2:17), dropsy (Luke 14:2), dumbness (Luke 1:20-22, 64), coronary occlusion (II Sam. 24:10), cretinism (Lev. 21:20), lameness (Luke 14:21), palsy or paralysis (Matt. 9:2). Physicians mentioned in the NT; Matt. 9:12; Luke 4:23; Col. 4:14.

Bibliography: Short, A.R. **The Bible and Modern Medicine.** Paternoster Press, London, 1953; Strong, R. P. **Stitt's Diagnosis, Prevention and Treatment of Tropical Diseases.** 7th Edition. Blakiston Co., Philadelphia, 1944; Spinka, H. M. "Leprosy in Ancient Hebraic Times," **Journal of the American Scientific Affiliation** 11:17-20 (March) 1959; Hobart, W. K. **Medical Language of Luke.** Baker Book House, Grand Rapids, Mich., 1954.

Dish, a receptacle for food, generally made of baked clay, or else of metal. Orientals ate from a central platter or dish, generally using a thin piece of bread for a spoon and handling the food quite daintily (Matt. 26:23). See Pottery.

Dishan (dī'shăn), son of Seir (Gen. 36:21, etc.).

Dishon (dī'shŏn). 1. A chief among the Horites (Gen. 36:21). 2. A great-grandson of Seir the Horite (Gen. 36: 25). The two may, however, be the same.

Dispensation (dĭs-pĕn-sā'shŭn, **law or arrangement of a house**), a word that appears in the Bible four times, all of them in the NT: I Corinthians 9:17; Ephesians 1:10; 3:2; Colossians 1:25. In the first two and the fourth it means "stewardship," "office," "commission" — words involving the idea of administration. In Ephesians 1:10, a linguistically difficult passage, the word dispensation refers to God's plan of salvation. The NT therefore uses the word in a twofold sense: with respect to one in authority, it means an arrangement or plan; with respect to one under authority, it means a stewardship or administration.

Dispersion (See Diaspora)

Dives (dī'vēz, **rich**), a name applied to the rich man in the parable of the rich man and Lazarus (Luke 16:19-31) in the Vulgate.

Divination (dĭv-ĭ-nā'shŭn), the practice of foreseeing or foretelling future events or discovering hidden knowledge; forbidden to Jews (Lev. 19:26; Deut. 18:10; Isa. 19:3; Acts 16:16). Various means were used: reading omens, dreams, the use of the lot, astrology, necromancy, and others.

Dizahab (dī'zȧ-hăb), a place located in the region of Sinai, or possibly farther north where Moses gave his farewell address (Deut. 1:1).

Doctor (teacher). Usually rendered **master** or **teacher,** whether referring to Jesus or other teachers.

Dodai (dō'dī), David's captain over 24,000 men (I Chron. 27:4).

Dodanim (dō'dȧ-nĭm), fourth son of Javan, the son of Japheth (Gen. 10:4).

Dodavah (dō'dȧ-vȧ), father of Eliezer (II Chron. 20:37).

Dodo (dō'dō). 1. Grandfather of Tola (Judg. 10:1). 2. Son of Ahohi (II Sam. 23:9). 3. Man whose son Elhanan was one of David's mighty men (II Sam. 23:24).

Doeg (dō'ĕg), Edomite herdsman of Saul who reported to the king that Ahimelech the priest had helped David. In revenge Saul had Doeg slay Ahimelech and the inhabitants of Nob (I Sam. 22:11-23).

Dog (See Animals)

Door. Doors in ancient times turned on pivots turning in sockets above and below, and were frequently two-leaved. The word is often used in the NT in a figurative sense, many times referring to Christ (John 10:2, 7; Rev. 3:20); but also to opportunity (Matt. 25:10; Acts 14:27; I Cor. 16:9), and freedom and power (Col. 4:3).

Doorkeeper. Keeper of doors and gates in public buildings, temples and walled cities (Ps. 84:10; John 18:16, 17). Generally in the English Bible the word is "porter," e.g. II Sam. 18:26, "the watchman called unto the porter."

Dophkah (dŏf'kȧ), a station of the Israelites, between the Red Sea and Sinai (Num. 33:12).

Dor (dôr), a Canaanite city on the coast of Palestine, about eight miles north of Caesarea (Joshua 11:12; 12: 23).

Dorcas (dôr'kăs, a **gazelle),** an early Christian disciple living at Joppa, who was well known for her works of charity. Peter raised her from the dead (Acts 9:36-43).

Dothan (dō'thăn, **two wells),** place c. 13 miles N of Shechem where Joseph was sold (Gen. 37:17) and Elisha saw vision of angels (II Kings 6:13-23).

Dough, the soft mass of moistened flour or meal which after baking becomes bread or cake (Exod. 12:34, 39; Jer. 7:18; Hos. 7:4).

Dove (See Birds)

Dove Cote, referring to the opening of pigeonhouses (Isa. 60:8).

Dove's Dung, food to which the famished people of Samaria were reduced (II Kings 6:25). See Plants.

Dowry (dou'rē), the price paid by the suitor to the parents of the prospective bride; also the portion which the bride brought to her husband. Genesis 30:20; 34:12; Exodus 22:17, and I Samuel 18:25 illustrate various uses of the word.

Drachma (See Money)

Dragon. An imaginary creature of great size and frightening aspect. A number of passages in the KJV rendered "dragon" are more correctly translated "jackal" in the RV (Job 30:29; Ps. 44:19; Isa. 13:22; etc). In the NT, Satan is portrayed in the Book of Revelation by means of dragon imagery (12:9; 20:2).

Dram (See Weights and Measures)

Draught House, a privy or water-closet (II Kings 10:27).

Drawer of Water. One who brought water from a well or a spring to the house (Deut. 29:11; Josh. 9:23-27).

Dream. There are numerous instances in the OT of God revealing something to people by means of dreams (Gen. 20:3; 28:12; 37:5-11; 40:5; Dan. 2; 4; Matt. 1:20). Some of these dreams were given to persons outside the chosen family, e.g. Abimelech of Gerar (Gen. 20:3), Laban (Gen. 31:24), Pharaoh (Gen. 41:1-36). God gave to some men the gift of interpreting dreams (Gen. 40:5-23; Dan. 4:19-27). Dreams may lead people astray (Deut. 13:1-3).

Dress. Knowledge of the kind of clothing worn by the people of Biblical times comes from Scriptural statements; from representations of the people and their clothing we find on monuments, reliefs, seals, plaques, and tomb-paintings; and from graves and tomb remains.

All these, coupled with the traditions and usages extant among the present Bedouin Arab tribes, lead to the conclusion that at a very early period of man's existence he learned the art of spinning and weaving cloth of hair, wool, cotton, flax, and eventually silk (Gen. 14:23; 31:18, 19; 37:3; 38:28; Job 7:6; Ezek. 16:10, 13), and from these established certain simple styles which were continued from generation to generation, then carried by Esau and Ishmael and their descendants into Arabia, where the Arab continued them through the centuries — always with a feeling that it was decidedly wrong to change.

The clothing worn by the Hebrew people of Biblical times was graceful, modest, and exceedingly significant. They were considered so much a part of those who wore them that they not only told who and what they were, but were intended as external symbols of the individual's innermost feelings and deepest desires, and his moral urge to represent God aright. With certain

The Hill of Dothan. © MPS

Arab peasants still wearing clothing very similar to that worn in Bible days. © MPS

kinds of cloth and with astonishingly vivid colors of white, purple, scarlet, blue, yellow, and black, they represented the state of their minds and emotions. When joyful and ready to enter into festive occasions, they donned their clothing of brightest array, and when they mourned or humbled themselves, they put on sackcloth — literally cloth from which sacks were made — which was considered the very poorest kind of dress, and quite indicative of their lowly feelings (I Kings 20:31, 32; Job 16:15; Isa. 15:3; Jer. 4:8; 6:26; Lam. 2:10; Ezek. 7:18; Dan. 9:3; Joel 1:8).

The basic garments in general used among the men of Biblical times, seem to have consisted of the inner-tunic, the tunic-coat, the girdle, and the cloak. Added to this was the head-dress, and the shoes or sandals.

The word "skirt," found a number of times in the Bible (KJV), usually refers to an article of male, not female, clothing, and has a number of meanings: (1) "extremity" (Ruth 3:9), (2) "corner" (I Sam. 24:4ff), (3) "hem" (Exod. 28:33), (4) "collar" (Ps. 133:2).

The **headdress** was chiefly worn as a protection against the sun and a finish to a completed costume. It varied from time to time according to rank, sex, and nationality. In the main, however, there were three known types that were worn by the male members of the Hebrew and surrounding nations; the **cap**, the **turban**, and the **headscarf.**

The ordinary brimless cotton or woolen cap, corresponding somewhat to our skull-cap, was sometimes worn by men of poorer circumstances. Captives are seen wearing these as they are depicted on the Behistun Rock. The turban (hood, RV in Isa. 3:23) was made of thick linen material and formed by winding a scarf or sash about the head in artistic style and neatly concealing the ends. That of the high priest was called a **mitre** (Exod. 28).

Shoes and **sandals** were considered the lowliest articles that went to make up the wearing apparel of the people of Bible Lands (Mark 1:7). In the Bible, and in secular sources, they were mentioned at a very early period, and are seen in considerable variety on the Egyptian, Babylonian, Assyrian, and Persian monuments.

Shoes were of soft leather, while sandals were of a harder leather. The sandals were worn for rougher wear. According to some authorities, the sole was of wood, cane, or sometimes bark of the palm tree and was fastened to the leather by nails. They were tied about the feet with thongs, or **shoelatchets** (Gen. 14:23; Neh. 1:7). It was customary to have two pairs, especially on a journey.

Women's Dress. Among the Hebrews neither sex was permitted by Mosaic law to wear the same form of clothing as was used by the other (Deut. 22:5). A few articles of female clothing carried somewhat the same name and basic pattern, yet there was always sufficient difference in embossing, embroidery, and needlework so that in appearance the line of demarcation between men and women could be readily detected.

The women wore long garments reaching almost to the feet, with a girdle of silk or wool, many times having all the colors of the rainbow. Often such a garment would have a fringe hanging from the waist nearly to the ankles. The ladies' head-dress, for example, usually included some kind of a **kaffiyeh** or cloth for covering the head, yet the material that was in that covering was of a different quality, kind, or color from that worn by the men.

Women often added to their adornment by an elaborate "plaiting" of the hair. I Peter 3:3 finds it necessary to warn Christian women against relying upon such adorning to make themselves attractive. In the OT there are a number of references to painting the eyes in order to enhance their beauty, but it is always spoken of as a meretricious device, unworthy of good women. Jezebel painted her eyes (II Kings 9:30).

In ancient times women especially were much given to various kinds of ornaments. Earrings and nose-rings were especially common. On account of their drop-like shape, earrings are called "pendants" (Isa. 3:19), "chains" (Isa. 3:19 KJV), and "collars" (Judg. 8:26). Men also wore such earrings (Gen. 35:4; Judg. 8:24). The nose-ring, or nose-jewel made necessary the piercing of the nostrils. Rings were worn by both men and women. All ancient Israelites wore signet-rings (Gen. 38:18). Rings were often worn on the toes; anklets (spangles) on the ankles (Isa. 3:18); bracelets on the arms and wrists (Gen. 24:22; Ezek. 16:11).

Making clothing in the home. © *SPF*

Beginning about the second century B.C., all male Jews were expected to wear at morning prayers, except on sabbaths, and festivals two **phylacteries,** one on the forehead, called a **frontlet,** the other on the left arm. They consisted of small leather cases containing four passages of Scripture from the OT; Exodus 13:1-10, 11-16; Deuteronomy 6:4-9; 11:3-21.

Drink. The most common beverage of the Jews was water.

Wine was also widely used, both in the form of new wine, called must, and fermented wine. Because of the hot climate, fresh milk soon became sour, but it was very effective for quenching thirst.

Drink Offering, an offering of oil and wine made to God accompanying many of the sacrifices (Exod. 29:40, 41). See Offerings.

Dromedary (See Animals)

Dropsy (See Diseases)

Dross, refuse metals separated by melting, when the dross rises to the top and may be skimmed off. Used figuratively of what is worthless (Isa. 1:22, 25; Ezek. 22:18, 19; Ps. 119:119).

Drunkenness, a major vice in antiquity, even among the Hebrews, but more so among the wealthy. Drunkenness is forbidden by the Scriptures (Lev. 10:9; Deut. 21:20; Prov. 23:21; I Cor. 5:11; 6:10; Gal. 5:21). Among drunken people in the OT are Noah (Gen. 9:21), Lot (Gen. 19:33, 35), Nabel (I Sam. 25:36), Uriah (II Sam. 11:13). Sometimes used figuratively (Isa. 29:9).

Drusilla (drōō-sĭl'ȧ), youngest daughter of Herod Agrippa I. At the age of 14 she married Azizus, king of Emesa, but left him for Felix, procurator of Judea. They had one son, Agrippa, who died in an eruption of Mount Vesuvius. When Paul unsparingly preached before Felix and Drusilla of righteousness, temperance, and judgment, Felix trembled (Acts 24:24, 25). See Herod.

Duke. In general, a leader of a clan or a tribal chief. See Genesis 36:15 ff; Exodus 15:15; I Chronicles 1:51 ff; Joshua 13:21.

Dumah (dū'mȧ, **silence**). 1. One of the twelve sons of Ishmael (Gen. 25:14-16). 2. A place (unknown) connected with Seir or Edom (Isa. 21:11-12). The designation may be symbolic. 3. A village in the S of Judah (Josh. 15: 52-54).

Dumbness (See Diseases)

Prayer time in the home. Note phylacteries on the men's arms and forehead. © *SPF*

Dung, laws were made regarding excrement of human beings and animals used in sacrifice (Deut. 23:12-14; Exod. 29:14; Lev. 8:17). Dry dung was often used as fuel (Ezek. 4:12-15); also fertilizer (Isa. 25:10; Luke 13:8).

Dung Gate, one of the eleven gates of Jerusalem (See Neh. 3, especially v. 14), used for the disposal of rubbish, garbage and dung. It led out to the valley of Hinnom.

Dura (dū'rȧ), a plain in Babylon, where Nebuchadnezzar set up his image (Dan. 3:1).

Dwarf (thin, small, withered), an abnormally small person, but in Leviticus 21:20 one of those twelve sorts of unfortunate people who could not officiate at the altar, but who could eat the bread of their God. See Diseases.

Dyers, Dyeing (See Occupations)

Ear (physical organ of hearing). In Biblical times people spoke to each other's ears; instead of listening they "inclined their ears." When they prayed, God "bowed down His ear" to hear them. The ear was sanctified by blood in the consecration of Aaron and his sons to the priesthood (Exod. 29:20; Lev. 8:24) and at the cleansing of a leper (Lev. 14:14). The piercing of the ear of a slave denoted permanent servitude (Exod. 21:6; Deut. 15: 17).

Earing (ēr′ing, **ploughing time**), translated "earing" in KJV, the RV rendering is **blowing** (Gen. 45:6; Exod. 34: 21).

Earnest (êr′nĕst), a legal term denoting the payment of a sum of money to make a contract binding, guaranteeing a further payment to fulfill the contract. Thus the significance of the apostle Paul's use of this word in regard to the Holy Spirit may be understood (II Cor. 1:22; 5:5; Eph. 1:14). The gift of the Holy Spirit to believers is the assurance that their redemption will be fully carried out.

Earring (ēr′rĭng, **hoop**), worn by men and women either on the nose or on the ears: a nose-ring in the following passages (Gen. 24:47; Isa. 3:21; Ezek. 16:12), and earrings in these references (Gen. 35:4; Exod. 32:2, 3; Ezek. 16: 12). In the rest of the passages where such rings or hoops are mentioned they may be either nose rings or earrings (Exod. 35:22; Num. 31:50; Judg. 8:24-26; Job 42:11; Prov. 11:22; 25: 12; Hosea 2:13).

Earth, a word with a variety of meanings: as a material substance (Gen. 2:7), territory (Gen. 28:15), whole earth (Gen. 12:3), country (Gen. 13: 10; 45:18). inhabitants of world (Gen. 6:11), world (Gen. 1:1).

Earthquake. Four actual earthquakes are recorded in Scripture: the one which occurred at Mt. Horeb for Elijah's benefit (I Kings 19:11); that referred to by Amos (1:1) and Zechariah (14:5); the one which happened at the resurrection of Christ (Matt. 28:2); and the one which freed Paul and Silas from prison (Acts 16:26). An earthquake is mentioned in Isaiah 29:6 as a form of judgment from the Lord on the enemies of His people.

East (place of the sunrise), a significant direction for the Hebrews. The gate of the tabernacle was on the east side (Exod. 38:13; 14).

The phrase "children of the East" occurs frequently in the OT. It refers to the inhabitants of the lands E of Palestine, on the edge of the desert. Job was such a one (Job 1:3). The Wise Men came from the East, and said they had seen the star of the King of the Jews in the East (Matt. 2:1, 2).

Easter (passover), rendered **Easter** in Acts 12:4 KJV, but correctly translated **Passover** in ASV. The day on which the Church celebrates the resurrection of Jesus Christ.

Easter is celebrated on the first Sunday after the full moon following the vernal equinox, the date of Easter varying between March 22 and April 25.

East Sea, or the Dead Sea, formed part of the eastern boundary of Canaan proper.

East Wind. Winds of the E came to Palestine over the desert; therefore it was a hot, dry, wind in the wilderness (Jer. 4:11). An E wind brought the plague of locusts on Egypt (Exod. 10:13), and dried up the sea so the Israelites could cross over on dry land (Exod. 14:21). Many references mention the destructive results of the E wind (Gen. 41:6; Ps. 48:7; Ezek. 27:26; Ezek. 17:10; Hosea 13:15; Jonah 4:8). The E wind was used as a means of judgment by God (Isa. 27:8; Jer. 18:17).

Ebal (ē′băl). 1. A son of Shobal (Gen. 36:23; I Chron. 1:40). 2. A mountain 3077 feet high, one of the highest points in the land of Samaria. At its foot was Jacob's well (see John 4:20), and the city of Shechem was located near by. When the Israelites first entered the land, Moses commanded them to erect on Mt. Ebal a monument of stones on which the law was inscribed, and a stone altar. The law, with its blessings and curses was recited by the people antiphonally, the blessings from Mt. Gerizim, and the curses from Mt. Ebal (Deut. 27:4-26). 3. One of the sons of Joktan (I Chron. 1:22).

Ebed (ĕ′bĕd, **servant**). 1. Father of Gaal (Judg. 9:26-45). 2. Son of Jonathan (Ezra 8:6).

Ebed-Melech (ē'bĕd-mē-lĕk, **servant of the king**), an Ethiopian eunuch who drew Jeremiah up out of that dungeon (Jer. 38:7-13). The Lord gave Jeremiah a message for Ebed-Melech, assuring him of safety and protection in the coming destruction of the city (Jer. 39:15-18).

Eben-Ezer (ĕb'ĕn-ē'zêr, **stone of help).** A town of Ephraim near Aphek by which the Israelites encamped before fighting a losing battle with the Philistines (I Sam. 4:1). 2. Later God gave them victory over the Philistines. Samuel then set up a memorial stone calling it **Eben-ezer,** "the stone of help" (I Sam. 7:12).

Eber (ē'bêr). 1. Son of Shelah, a grandson of Shem (Gen. 10:24; 11:14; I Chron. 1:18). 2. The head of a family of Gad (I Chron. 5:13). 3. The oldest son of Elpaal, a Benjamite (I Chron. 8:12). 4. A son of Shemei, a Benjamite (I Chron. 8:22). 5. Head of a priestly family (Neh. 12:20).

Ebiasaph (ē-bī'ȧ-săph, **my father has gathered),** a son of Elkanah (Exod. 6: 24; I Chron. 6:23; 9:19).

Ebronah (ē-brō'-nȧh), the encampment of the Hebrews just before they arrived at Ezion-geber (Num. 33:34).

Ecbatana (ĕk-băt'ă-nȧ). It is mentioned in the Bible only in Ezra 6:2 as **Achmetha,** denoting the location of the palace in which the decree of Cyrus authorizing the building of the Jewish temple was found.

Ecclesiastes (ĕ-klē-zĭ-ăs'-tēz, **preacher).** This is one of the most perplexing books in the Bible. The Solomonic authorship, now generally rejected, can still be maintained on the following grounds: 1. The one who calls himself "the Preacher" is described as David's son and as king in Jerusalem (1:1, 12). 2. This same person designates himself as a collector of proverbs (12:9), a description that obviously fits Solomon (cf. I Kings 4:32). 3. The reference to the author's great wisdom (1:16; 2:9) accords with Solomon's ability (cf. I Kings 4:30f). 4. The author's description of the splendor of Jerusalem during his reign (2:4-9) points unmistakably to Solomon (cf. I Chron. 29:25). 5. Several rather subtle references to characteristics of his life (e.g., 4:13; 7:26, 28; 10:6, 16) point plainly to Solomon. 6. The close parallel between this book and Proverbs is best explained by unity of authorship.

This book, properly understood, is a negative preparation for the Gospel; for, using a man especially endowed with knowledge and experience, the Spirit of God shows in this book how far such a man can go "under the sun." Here we have natural revelation at its best; for, let us note, there is nothing in this book that contradicts the rest of Scripture. In fact, the author's final conclusion (12:1, 13) leads him to the very door of the kingdom of God.

Ecumenicism (ĕcū-mĕn'ĭ-cĭsm), derives from the Greek **oikouméne,** the whole inhabited world. An older adjectival derivative is **ecumenical.** Thus the first world-wide councils from Nicea (A.D. 325) were described as ecumenical.

More recently, the term ecumenical has come into Protestant usage to describe a movement among Christian religious groups — Protestant, Eastern Orthodox, Roman Catholic — to bring about a closer unity in work and organization. The word is not found in the Bible, but Biblical backing for the movement is found in John 17 where Jesus prays for the unity of His Church.

Edar (ē'dār, **flock),** tower near which Jacob encamped on his way back to Canaan (Gen. 35:21).

Eden (ē'd'n, **delight).** 1. Place where God planted a garden in which He put Adam and Eve. They lived there until they sinned by eating the forbidden fruit and were expelled from it (Gen. 2-3). Later Scripture writers mention Eden as an illustration of a delightful place (Isa. 51:3; Ezek. 28: 13; 31:9, 16, 18; 36:35; Joel 2:3). 2. An Eden is mentioned by the Assyrians as conquered by them (II Kings 19:12; Isa. 37:12). Ezekiel 27:23 also mentions this region. The house of Eden, or Beth-Eden (Amos 1:5), was probably near Damascus. 3. A Gershonite who lived in Hezekiah's time (II Chron. 29:12; 31:15).

Eder (ē'dêr, **floods).** 1. A city in S Judah near Edom (Josh. 15:21). 2. A son of Mushi (I Chron. 23:23; 24: 30).

Edom, Edomites (ē'dŏm, ē'dŏmīts, **red**), the nation and its people who were the descendants of Esau. He founded the country, so his name is equated with Edom (Gen. 25:30; 36: 1, 8). The country was also called Seir, or Mt. Seir, which was the name of the territory in which the Edomites lived.

The kingdom of Edom was founded during the 13th century B.C., according to archaeological evidence. In the process of about four centuries the government of Edom changed from one under tribal chiefs to a monarchy. Saul fought against the Edomites (I Sam. 14:47), but David conquered them and put garrisons throughout the whole land (II Sam. 8:14).

Judah lost Edom in the reign of Jehoram when she revolted against him about 847 B.C. (II Kings 8:20, 22). About 50 years later Amaziah, king of Judah, inflicted a severe defeat on the Edomites (II Kings 14:7). About 735 B.C., Rezin, king of Syria, at war with Judah, captured Eloth and drove the Jews out (II Kings 16:6). When Jerusalem was destroyed and Judah depopulated by the Babylonians in 586 B.C., the Edomites rejoiced over the affliction of the Judeans and began to take over the southern part of Palestine. Eventually they penetrated as far N as Hebron. This action intensified the already smoldering hatred between the Jews and Edomites (see Ps. 137:7; Ezek. 25:12-14; Amos 1:11; Obadiah 10-14).

The Assyrians came in contact with Edom as early as the seventh century B.C. When her kings began to penetrate as far south as Palestine, Edom, along with Judah, and her other neighbors, paid tribute to Assyria for many years. She is mentioned many times in the inscription of the kings of Assyria beginning with Adad-Nirari III 800 B.C. to Ashurbanipal (686-633).

Edom figures prominently **in** the prophetic Scriptures as the scene of great future judgments (see notably Isa. 34:5, 6; 63:1). She is the only neighbor of the Israelites who was not given any promise of mercy from God.

Edrei (ĕd′rē-ī, **strong).** 1. A chief city of Og, king of Bashan (Deut. 1:4; Josh. 12:4) where he fought with the Israelites (Num. 21:33; Deut. 3:1). They defeated him and took his country with its cities, including Edrei (Deut. 3:10). This town was assigned to Manasseh (Josh. 13:12, 31). Located near the southern source of the Yarmuk river, about ten miles NE of Ramoth-Gilead, and about 30 miles E and a little S of the Sea of Galilee. 2. A fortified city of Naphtali (Josh. 19:37).

Education (See Schools)

Egg (whiteness), appears only in the plural form, **bêtsîm** (Deut. 22:6; Job 39:14; Isa. 10:14; 59:5).

Eglah (ĕg′lȧh, **heifer),** one of David's wives who was the mother of his sixth son, Ithream (II Sam. 3:5; I Chron. 3:3).

Eglaim (ĕg′lā-ĭm), a place in Moab (Isa. 15:8).

Eglon (ĕg-lŏn). 1. A city of Canaan located between Gaza and Lachish. Joshua captured the city (10:36, 37; 12:12). It was assigned to Judah (Josh. 15:39). 2. A king of Moab who captured Jericho (Judg. 3:12, 13). The Israelites served him for 18 years (3:14). Then he was killed by Ehud, whom the Lord had raised up to save Israel (3:21).

Egypt (ē′jipt), country NE of Africa; also called country of Ham (Ps. 105:23, 27); watered by Nile, the longest river in the world (4000 miles), the annual overflow of which is of the greatest importance to the country because of the almost complete absence of rain. Country divided into Upper and Lower Egypt, Lower Egypt including the delta area. Nile valley and delta bounded by desert. Called Mizraim by Israelites. Ruler called Pharaoh. Religion polytheistic; gods: Ptah, Ra, Thum, Amon. History begins c. 3000 B.C. Powerful empire in OT times; granary of Roman empire and cultural center in NT times. Held Israel in bondage for centuries until appearance of Moses (Exod. 1-14). Often in contact with Israel (I Kings 3:1; 14:25, 26).

Egypt, River of, the dividing line between Canaan and Egypt (Gen. 15:18; Num. 34:5), the southern boundary of Judah (Josh. 15:4, 47). It is not really an Egyptian river at all, but a **wady** (a stream and its valley) of the desert near the border of Egypt.

Ehi (e′hī), a son of Benjamin (Gen. 46:21).

Ehud (ē′hŭd, **union).** 1. A descendant of Benjamin (I Chron. 7:10; 8:6). 2. A judge of the Israelites, who killed Eglon, the king of Moab, who had captured Jericho and extracted tribute from Israel from there. Ehud rallied the Israelites and led them against the Moabites. They subdued these enemies and the land had peace for 80 years until Ehud died (Judg. 3:15-30).

Eker (ē′kêr, **root),** son of Ram (I Chron. 2:27).

The Nile River at ancient Cairo, showing a typical sailboat, the Felucca.

The temple of Rameses III at Karnak.
© MPS

A list of slaves, including Hebrews, from Egypt about the time of Joseph, 1700 B.C. BP

Ekron (ĕk′rŏn, **eradication**), the most northern of the five chief cities of the Philistines (see I Sam. 6:17). Located on the boundary between Judah and Dan (Josh. 15:11; 19:43), assigned to Judah (Josh. 15:45). After the captured ark of God was sent by the Philistines from Ekron to escape the wrath of God (I Sam. 6), the Israelites regained possession of Ekron and other cities (I Sam. 7:14). Following David's victory over Goliath the Israelites drove the Philistines back to Ekron (I Sam. 17:52).

El (ĕl, **God**), the primitive, generic word for God in the Semitic languages. A plural term, **'elohim**, was the Hebrews' regular name for God.

The Canaanite god El was the father of men and of gods. He was an immoral and debased character. It is a tribute to the high quality of the character of the God of Israel that when the Hebrews took over this name and applied it to Him, it lost all its evil connotations.

Ela (ē′lȧ), father of commissary officer of Solomon (I Kings 4:18 RSV).

Eladah (ĕl′ȧ-dȧh), descendant of Ephraim (I Chron. 7:20).

Elah (ē′lȧh, **terebinth**). 1. Chief of Edom (Gen. 36:41). 2. Valley in which David killed Goliath (I Sam. 17:2, 19; 21:9). 3. King of Israel, son of Baasha; killed by Zimri (I Kings 16:8-10). 4. Father of Hoshea, the last king of Israel (II Kings 15:30; 17:1; 18:1, 9). 5. Son of Caleb (I Chron. 4:15). 6. Benjamite (I Chron. 9:8).

Elam (ē′lăm). 1. A son of Shem (Gen. 10:22; I Chron. 1:17). 2. A son of Shashach (I Chron. 8:24). 3. Son of Meshelemiah (I Chron. 26:3). 4. Ancestor of family of 1254 members which returned from exile under Zerubbabel (Ezra 2:7; Neh. 7:12). 5. Another forefather of a returned family with the same number of members (Ezra 2:31; Neh. 7:34). 6. The father of two sons who returned from exile with Ezra (Ezra 8:7). 7. An ancestor of a man who married a foreign woman. Evidently this ancestor was either No. 4, 5, or 6 (Ezra 10:2, 26). 8. Chief who sealed the covenant with Nehemiah (Neh. 10:14). 9. Priest who took part in the dedication of the wall (Neh. 12:42).

Elam (ē′lăm), a country situated on the E side of the Tigris river opposite Babylonia. Its population was made up of a variety of tribes. Elam was one of the earliest civilizations. Elam was one of the nations forced to drink the cup of God's wrath (Jer. 25:25), and doomed to judgment (Jer. 49:34-39). Ezra 4:9, 10 refers to Elamites as among the peoples brought over to Samaria by the Assyrians. Acts 2:9 includes Elamite as one of the tongues being spoken by visitors at Jerusalem.

Elasah (ĕl′ȧ-sȧh, **God has made**). 1. One of the sons of Pashur who was guilty of marrying foreign women (Ezra 10:22). 2. Son of Shaphan, with whom Jeremiah sent from Jerusalem a letter to the exiles in Babylon (Jer. 29:3).

Elath, Eloth (ē′lăth, ēlŏth, **lofty trees**), a town situated at the head of the Gulf of Aqabah in Edom. It was located very near to Ezion-geber, Solomon's seaport (I Kings 9:26). The Israelites passed by the area on the way to the promised land (Deut. 2:8).

El-Bethel (ĕl-bĕth′ēl, **the God of the house of God**), the name Jacob gave to Luz because there God revealed Himself to him (Gen. 35:7).

Eldaah (ĕl-dā′ah, **God has called**), a son of Midian (Gen. 25:4).

Eldad (ĕl′dăd, **God has loved**), one of the 70 elders selected by Moses gathered around the Tabernacle to receive the gift of prophecy (Num. 11:24-29).

Elder (ĕld′êr). The older men of a community who governed the community and made all major decisions (Exod. 3:29; 12:21; 24:9; Num. 11:25). Each town had its group of elders, as Bethlehem did (I Sam. 16:4), "the elders of every city" (Ezra 10:14). After the return from exile the elders made up the Sanhedrin, the governing council of the Jews.

The elders joined the priests and scribes against Jesus (Matt. 27:12). When churches came into being, elders were appointed for each congregation (Acts 14:23). The terms "elders" and "bishops" are used interchangeably in the NT. The "elders" of Acts 20:17 are called "bishops" in verse 28. In Titus 1:5, "elders" in the Cretan churches are mentioned. In listing qualifications for such an office, Paul calls them "bishops" in verse 7. These men were required to be blameless in their lives and obedient to the truth in their faith (I Tim. 3:1-7; Titus 1:6-9).

Elead (ĕ′lē-ăd, **God has testified**), an Ephraimite slain by men of Gath while stealing cattle (I Chron. 7:21).

Eleadah (See Eladah)

Elealeh (ē′lē-ā′lĕ, **God doth ascend**), a town always mentioned with Heshon, being located about a mile N of that place, in the tribe of Reuben (Num. 32:3, 37; Isa. 15:4; 16:9; Jer. 48:34).

Eleasah (ĕ′lē-ā-săh, **God has made**). 1. A Hezronite (I Chron. 2:39, 40). 2. A Benjamite (I Chron. 8:37; 9:43).

Eleazar (ĕ-lē-ā′-zăr, **God has helped**). 1. The third son of Aaron (Exod. 6: 23). After the death of the two elder sons, Nadab and Abihu (Lev. 10:1, 2), Eleazar was designated to be chief priest (Num. 3:22; 20:28). He assisted Moses in numbering the people (Num. 26:1, 2); in dividing the spoil from the slaughter of the Midianites (Num. 31:13-54); and in assigning to the 2½ tribes land E of the Jordan River (Num. 32:28). He helped Joshua divide the promised land among the tribes (Num. 34:17). 2. The son of Abinadab (I Sam. 7:1). 3. Son of Dodai, one of the three mightiest men of David who wrought a great victory over the Philistines (II Sam. 23:9, 10; I Chron. 11:12-14). 4. A childless son of Mahli (I Chron. 23: 21, 22; 24:28). 5. Son of Phineas (Ezra 8:32-34). 6. A priest (Neh. 12:42). 7. An ancestor of Joseph, the husband of Mary (Matt. 1:15).

Elect (ē-lĕct′, **chosen**), In the OT Moses is called "the chosen of God" (Ps. 106:23). The nation of Israel is 6 times noted as God's chosen people (I Chron. 16:13; Pss. 105:6, 43; 106:5; Isa. 43:20; 45:4). King Saul is once so designated (II Sam. 21:6). David is once called God's chosen one (Ps. 89:3). In prophecy Christ is set forth as God's "elect one" (Isa. 42:1). The redeemed Israelites of the future will be "God's elect" (Isa. 65:9, 15, 22).

In the NT those who have received Christ as Saviour are called "the elect" 20 times. Twice Jesus is designated as "God's chosen" (Luke 9:35; 23:35). Once angels are called "elect" (I Tim. 5:21).

Election (choice, selection). God's eternal and immutable decree to choose from sinners those whom He will save, providing the source of their salvation in grace through Christ, and the means through the instrumentality of the Holy Spirit's regenerative work.

The sovereign decree of God to **choose out (ek,** from **lego,** to pick out) is the basic idea in election. This concept is applied in at least five ways: to elect those who are to be saved, to elect the means of their salvation in Christ, to elect the means in the redeeming activity of the Holy Spirit, to elect the results in the implantation of Christ's righteous nature to those who are saved, and to elect the destiny of eternal fellowship with God.

Much attention has been given to the relation between God's sovereign choice in election and the foreknowledge of God, since the two concepts are related in Romans 8:27-30, and I Peter 1:1, 2. Erroneous interpretations have implied that election was based on a foreknowledge by God of the choice which man would make, using foreknowledge, "prior" knowledge. This interpretation not only contradicts the idea of sovereignty, but ignores the basic meaning of the word foreknow.

When election refers to salvation, its objects are individual men. The concept of universal election is foreign to Scriptures; rather, particular election only is taught (Matt. 22:14; John 15:19; Rom. 8:29; 9:13, 15, 18, 22; I Thess. 5:9).

Bibliography: G. C. Berkouwer, **The Providence of God** (Grand Rapids: Eerdmans) 1952; **Divine Election** (Grand Rapids: Eerdmans) 1957; C. H. Hodge, **Commentary on Romans;** Pierre Maury, **Predestination and other Papers** (Richmond: John Knox) 1960; John Murray, **Redemption: Accomplished and Applied** (Grand Rapids: Eerdmans) 1955; B. B. Warfield, **Biblical Studies.**

El-Elohe-Israel (ĕl′ē-lō′hĕ-ĭz′ră-ĕl), an altar erected by Jacob when he settled near Shechem. The name means "God, the God of Israel" (Gen. 32:24-32).

Elements (ĕl′ĕ-mĕnts, **rows, series, alphabet, first principles of a science, physical elements, primary constituents of the universe, heavenly bodies, planets, personal cosmic powers**). In Hebrews 5:12 **first principles.** Galatians 4:3, 9 refer to heathen deities and practices. Colossians 2:8, 20, translated **rudiments,** indicate a more philosophical concept of the elements. II Peter 3:10, 12 refer to heavenly bodies or physical elements.

Eleph (ē′lĕf), a town of Benjamin, near Jerusalem (Josh. 18:28).

Elephant (See Animals)

Eleusis (ĕl′ū-sĭs), the shrine of Demeter, or the Earth-Goddess, into whose "mystery cult" freeborn Athenians were annually initiated. Little is known about the ceremony, but it seems clear that part of the ritual was the elevation of an ear of corn (wheat), the symbol of death and re-birth. This is perhaps the explanation of the imagery of Christ's remark at John 12:24.

Eleven, The, the eleven apostles (Acts 1:26) or disciples (Matt. 28:16) remaining after the death of Judas (Mark 16:14; Luke 24:9, 33; Acts 2: 14).

Elhanan (ĕl-hā'năn). 1. Son of Jaare-oregim (called also Jair), who slew Lahmi, the brother of Goliath (II Sam. 21:19; I Chron. 20:5). 2. One of David's 30 heroes (II Sam. 23:24; I Chron. 11:26).

Eli (ē'lī), of the family of Ithamar, fourth son of Aaron, who acted as both judge and high priest in Israel. He lived at Shiloh in a dwelling adjoining the Tabernacle (I Sam. 1-4; 14:3; I Kings 2:27). Little is known about him until he was well advanced in age, when Hannah came to pray for a son. His sins so shocked the people that they "abhorred the offering of the Lord." While Eli warned them of their shameful ways, he did not rebuke with the severity their deeds merited. An old man of ninety, almost blind, Eli waited to hear the result of the battle between the Israelites and the Philistines. When the messenger came with the news of the slaughter of his sons and of the taking of the ark, Eli fell off his seat and died of a broken neck. A good and pure man, Eli was weak and indecisive.

Eli, Eli, Lama Sabachtani (ā'lēē, ā'lēē, làmà sà-bàk'tà-nēē, **my God, my God, why hast Thou forsaken me**), one of the seven cries of Jesus from the cross (Matt. 27:46; Mark 15:34).

Eliab (ē-lī'ăb). 1. A leader of the tribe of Zebulun when the census was taken (Num. 1:9; 2:7; 7:24, 29; 10:16). 2. A Reubenite and father of Nathan and Abiram (Num. 16:1, 12; 26:8, 9; Deut. 11:6). 3. The eldest son of Jesse and brother of David (I Sam. 16:6; 17:13, 28). 4. A Levite in David's time (I Chron. 15:18, 20; 16:5). 5. A Gadite warrior who joined David at Ziklag (I Chron. 12:9). 6. A Levite ancestor of Samuel the phophet (I Chron. 6:27).

Eliada (ē-lī'à-dà). 1. One of David's sons (II Sam. 5:16; I Chron. 3:8). 2. A Benjamite who led 200,000 of his tribe to the army of Jehoshaphat (II Chron. 17:17). 3. The father of Rezon, captain of a roving band that annoyed Solomon (I Kings 11:23).

Eliah (ē-lī'à). 1. A son of Jeroham (I Chron. 8:27). 2. Israelite who divorced a foreign wife (Ezra 10:26).

Eliahba (ē-lī'à-bà), a member of David's famous guard (II Sam. 23: 32; I Chron. 11:33).

Eliakim (ē-lī'ă-kĭm, **God sets up**). 1. Master of Hezekiah's household (Isa. 22:15-25). Spokesman for the delegation from Hezekiah, king of Judah, which attempted to negotiate with the representatives of Sennacherib, king of Assyria who was besieging Jerusalem (II Kings 18:17-37; Isa. 36:1-22). Headed the delegation sent to implore the help of Isaiah the prophet (II Kings 19:2; Isa. 37:2). 2. The original name of King Jehoiakim (II Kings 23: 34; II Chron. 36:4). 3. A priest (Neh. 12:41). 4. An ancestor of Jesus (Matt. 1:13). 5. Another and earlier ancestor of Jesus (Luke 3:30).

Eliam (ē-lī'ăm). 1. Father of Bathsheba, wife of David (II Sam. 11:3). Called Ammiel in I Chronicles 3:5. 2. Son of Ahithophel the Gilonite (II Sam. 23:34).

Elias (ē-lī'ăs), the Greek form of the name Elijah, used in KJV in all occurences in the NT. See Elijah.

Eliasaph (ē-lī'à-săf). 1. Head of the Gadites in the wilderness (Num. 1:14; 2:14; 7:42, 47; 10:20). 2. A son of Lael (Num. 3:24).

Eliashib (ē-lī'à-shĭb, **God restores**). **1.** Head of 11th priestly course (I Chron. 24:12) 2. Judahite (I Chron. 3:24). 3. High priest (Neh. 3:1, 20, 21; 13:4, 7, 28). 4. Levite who put away his foreign wife (Ezra 10:24). 5. Man who married a foreign wife (Ezra 10:27). 6. Another man who married a foreign wife (Ezra 10:36). 7. Ancestor of man who helped Ezra (Ezra 10:6; Neh. 12:10, 22, 23).

Eliathah (ē-lī'à-thà), musician in David's reign (I Chron. 25:4, 27).

Elidad (ē-lī'dăd), a Benjamite prince (Num. 34:21).

Eliel (ē'lī-ĕl, ē-lī'ĕl, **God is God**). **1.** Ancestor of Samuel the prophet (I Chron. 6:34). Called Eliab in 6:27. 2. Chief man of the half tribe of Manasseh (I Chron. 5:24). 3. A son of Shimhi (I Chron. 8:20). 4. A son of Shashak (I Chron. 8:22). 5. A captain in David's army (I Chron. 11:46). 6. Another of David's heroes (I Chron. 11:47). 7. Gadite (I Chron. 12:11). Perhaps same person as No. 5 or 6. 8. A chief of Judah (I Chron. 15:9). Perhaps same as No. 5. 9. A chief Levite (I Chron. 15:11). 10. A Levite overseer in Hezekiah's reign (II Chron. 31:13).

Elienai (ĕl'ĭ-ē'nī), a Benjamite (I Chron. 8:20).

Eliezer (ĕl-ĭ-ē-zĕr, **God is help).** 1. Steward of Abraham (Gen. 15:2). Perhaps same as servant mentioned in Gen. 24. 2. Son of Moses and Zipporah (Exod. 18:4; I Chron. 23:15, 17; 26:25). 3. Grandson of Benjamin (I Chron. 7:8). 4. Priest (I Chron. 15: 24). 5. Reubenite chief (I Chron. 27: 16). 6. Prophet who rebuked Jehoshaphat (II Chron. 20:37). 7. Chieftain sent to induce Israelites to return to Jerusalem (Ezra 8:16). 8. Priest who put away foreign wife (Ezra 10:18). 9. Levite who did the same (Ezra 10: 23). 10. Son of Harim who did the same (Ezra 10:31). 11. Ancestor of Jesus (Luke 3:29).

Elihoenai (ĕl'ĭ-hō-ē'nī, **to Jehovah are my eyes.** See also Elioenai). 1. A man who returned with Ezra in Artaxerxes' time (Ezra 8:4). 2. A Korahite doorkeeper of the tabernacle in David's reign (I Chron. 26:3).

Elihoreph (ĕl'ĭ-hō'ref), one of Solomon's scribes (I Kings 4:3).

Elihu (ē-lī'hū, **He is my God).** The great-grandfather of Samuel the prophet (I Sam. 1:1). Called Eliel in I Chronicles 6:34. 2. A Manassehite who joined David at Ziklag (I Chron. 12:20). 3. A tabernacle porter (I Chron. 26:7). 4. A brother of David (I Chron. 27:18). 5. The youngest of Job's friends (Job 32:2-6; 34:1; 35:1; 36:1).

Elijah (ē-lī'jȧ, **Jehovah is God).** See also Elias. 1. Benjamite (I Chron. 8: 27 ASV, RSV; called Eliah in KJV). 2. Son of Harim (Ezra 10:21). 3. Man who put away his foreign wife (Ezra 10:26 ASV, RSV; called Eliah in KJV). 4. Tishbite. Predicts to Ahab that there will be a drought; he is fed by ravens, and then taken care of by a widow at Zarephath (I Kings 17:17-24). After three years he proposes to Ahab a test as to whether the Canaanite Baal or the Israelite Jehovah is the true God (18:17-40). On Mt. Carmel the god Baal is thoroughly discredited and 450 prophets of Baal are slain. Jezebel vows vengeance on the prophet (19:1-8) and he flees into the wilderness, where he hears the still, small voice of the Lord. He anoints Elisha to succeed him as prophet. He rebukes Ahab for the murder of Naboth (21:27-29). He tells Ahab's son, Ahaziah, that he will die (II Kings 1). He is taken up to heaven in a whirlwind (II Kings 2:1-15). John the Baptist is called Elijah (Matt. 11:14; 17: 10-13; Luke 1:17). Elijah appears to Jesus on the Mt. of Transfiguration (Matt. 17:3, 4; Mark 9:4, 5; Luke 9: 30-33).

Traditional site of Elijah's victorious sacrifice on Mt. Carmel. © MPS

A view of ancient Elim, an oasis in the Sinai Peninsula. © *MPS*

Elika (ē-lī'kȧ), one of David's mighty men (II Sam. 23:25).

Elim (ē'lĭm, **terebinths),** the second stopping-place of the Israelites during the exodus (Exod. 15:27; 16:1; Num. 33:9, 10).

Elimelech (ē-lĭm'ĕ-lĕk, **my God is king**), husband of Naomi who emigrated to Moab during a famine in Judah (Ruth 1:2, 3; 2:1, 3; 4:3, 9). He is remembered because his daughter-in-law Ruth was faithful to his widow Naomi.

Elioenai (ĕl'ĭ-ō-ē'nī, **to Jehovah are my eyes**). See also Elihoenai. 1. A son of Neariah (I Chron. 3:23, 24). 2. Simeonite prince (I Chron. 4:36). 3. A Benjaminite (I Chron. 7:8). 4. A priest who put away his foreign wife (Ezra 10:22). 5. A man who divorced a foreign wife (Ezra 10:27). 6. A priest, perhaps the same as 4 (Neh. 12:41).

Eliphal (ē-lī'făl, ĕl'ĭ-făl, **God has judged),** son of Ur, one of David's mighty men (I Chron. 11:35).

Eliphalet (ē-lĭf'ă-lĕt), the last of David's sons, born at Jerusalem (II Sam. 5:16; I Chron. 14:7).

Eliphaz (ĕl'ĭ-făz, possibly **God is fine gold**). 1. A son of Esau (Gen. 36:4-16; I Chron. 1:35, 36). 2. The chief of Job's three friends (Job 2:11). In his first speech (Job 4, 5) Eliphaz traces all affliction to sin, and admonishes Job to make his peace with God. In his second address (Job 15) he shows irritation at Job's sarcasm. In his third address (Job 22) Eliphaz definitely charges Job with sin. In Job 42:7-9 God commands him to make sacrifice in expiation of fault in wrongly accusing Job.

Elipheleh (ē-lĭf'ĕ-lĕh), a Levite singer and harpist (I Chron. 15:18, 21).

Eliphelet (ē-lĭf'ĕ-lĕt). 1. The last of David's sons (I Chron. 3:8). See Eliphalet. 2. Another son of David (I Chron. 3:6). 3. A son of Ahasbai, one of David's heroes (II Sam. 23:34). 4. A Benjamite (I Chron. 8:39). 5. Leader who returned with Ezra (Ezra 8:13). 6. Man who put away his foreign wife (Ezra 10:33).

Elisabeth (See Elizabeth)

Elisha (ē-lī'shȧ, **God is salvation).** At Horeb God directed Elijah to anoint Elisha as his successor (I Kings 19:16-21). Elisha was the son of Shaphat of Abelmeholah (I Kings 19:16). Elijah cast his mantle upon Elisha, who understood the significance of the act as the choice of himself to succeed the older prophet. Elisha next appeared in connection with the translation of Elijah (II Kings 2). He persisted in following Elijah till the latter was carried up to heaven. Because he saw him go, a double portion of Elijah's spirit was given him. Taking the mantle of Elijah, he used it to make a dry path over Jordan, as his master had done.

Elisha had a long ministry and performed many miracles during the reigns of Jehoram, Jehu, Jehoahaz and Joash, kings of Israel. He saved a poor widow from financial distress by miraculous multiplication of her oil supply (II Kings 4:1-7). He brought a child back to life (II Kings 4:8-37). At Gilgal during a famine (II Kings 4:38-41), Elisha saved a school of the prophets from death because of eating poisonous vegetables. When a present of food was given him, Elisha set it before 100 men, and the Lord increased the supply to satisfy them (II Kings 4:24-44). Elisha healed the Syrian captain Naaman of leprosy (II Kings 5). He gave timely warning, repeatedly saving Israel from defeat by the Syrians (II Kings 6:8-23).

Elisha's ministry was filled with miracles, many relieving private needs, some related to affairs of state. Elisha's prophetic insight and wise counsel made him a valuable though not always appreciated adviser to kings. He finished the work of Elijah, destroying the system of Baal worship, completed the tasks assigned to Elijah of anointing Hazael and Jehu, and saw the final ruin of the house of Ahab and Jezebel. The mention of the cleansing of Naaman, the Syrian, from leprosy in Luke 4:27 perhaps indicates this as the crowning achievement of his career, giving Elisha an influence with the Syrian king which enabled him to help Israel.

Elishah (ē-lī'shȧ, **God saves**), the eldest son of Javan, grandson of Noah and founder of a tribal family (Gen. 10:4; I Chron. 1:7).

Elishama (ē-lĭsh'ȧmȧ, **God has heard**). 1. Grandfather of Joshua (Num. 1:10; 2:18; 7:48, 53; 10:22; I Chron. 7:26). 2. A son of David (II Sam. 5:16; I Chron. 3:8). 3. Another son of David, who is also called Elishua (I Chron. 3:6; cf. II Sam. 5:15). 4. A son of Jekaniah (I Chron. 2:41). 5. Father of Nethaniah and grandfather of Ishmael (II Kings 25:25; Jer. 41:1). Nos. 4 and 5 may be the same person. 6. A scribe to Jehoiakim (Jer. 36:12, 20, 21). 7. A priest (II Chron. 17:8).

Elishaphat (ē-lĭsh'ȧ-făt), a captain who supported Jehoiada in the revolt against Athaliah (II Chron. 23:1).

Elisheba (ē-lĭsh'ēbȧ), wife of Aaron (Exod. 6:23).

Elishua (ĕl'ĭ-shū'ȧ), a son of David born in Jerusalem (II Sam. 5:15; I Chron. 14:5). Called Elishama in I Chronicles 3:6.

Eliud (ē-lī'ŭd), ancestor of Christ (Matt. 1:14, 15).

Elizabeth (ē-lĭz'ȧ-bĕth, **God is [my] oath,** KJV Elisabeth), the wife of Zacharias (Luke 1:5-57). In fulfillment of God's promise, she in her old age bore a son, John the Baptist. She was a woman of unusual piety, faith, and spiritual gifts, whose relationship to Mary must have been an incomparable encouragement.

Elizaphan (ĕl'ĭ-zā'făn, ē-lĭz'ȧfăn, **God has concealed).** 1. Son of Uzziel, (Num. 3:30; I Chron. 15:8; II Chron. 29:13), called Elzaphan in Exodus 6:22 and Leviticus 10:4. 2. Prince of the tribe of Zebulun (Num. 34:25).

Elizur (ē-lī'zėr), prince of the Reubenites, who helped in the census Moses took (Num. 1:5; 2:10; 7:30-35; 10:18).

Elkanah (ĕl-kā'nȧ, **God has possessed).** 1. The father of Samuel (I Sam. 1:1-2:21). He is called an Ephraimite from Ramathaim-zophim, in the hill country of Ephraim, but he appears to have been a Levite, descendant of Kohath (I Chron. 6:22, 23, 27, 33, 34). 2 Son of Korah (Exod. 6:23, 24; I Chron. 6:24). 3. Officer of King Ahaz (II Chron. 28:7). 4. Warrior of David (I Chron. 12:6). 5. In addition, several Levites bear the name Elkanah (I Chron. 6:22-28, 33-38; 9:16).

Elkosh (ĕl'kŏsh), Nahum 1:1, birthplace of Nahum. (KJV, ASV, the Elkoshite; RSV, of Elkosh).

Ellasar (ĕl-lā'sȧr), one of the city-states whose king, Arioch (Eri-aku), invaded Palestine in the time of Abraham (Gen. 14:1, 9).

Elmodam (ĕl-mō'dăm), Elmadam in ASV, RSV), ancestor of Joseph, Mary's husband (Luke 3:28).

Elnaam (ĕl-nā'ăm), the father of David's guard, Jeribai and Joshaviah (I Chron. 11:46).

Elnathan (ĕl-nā'thăn, **God has given).** 1. Grandfather of Jehoiachin (II Kings 24:8). 2. The son of Achbor (Jer. 26:22). (He may be the same person as No. 1). 3. Levites sent on an embassy by Ezra (Ezra 8:16).

Elohim (ĕ-lō'hĭm), the most frequent Hebrew word for God (over 2,500 times in the OT). Plural in form, but singular in construction (used with a singular verb or adjective). When applied to the one true God, the plural is due to the Hebrew idiom of a plural of magnitude or majesty (Gen. 1:

1, etc.). When used of heathen gods (Exod. 18:11; 20:3; Gen. 35:2; Josh. 24:20, etc.) or of angels (Pss. 8:5; 97:7; Job 1:6, etc.) or judges (Exod. 21:6; I Sam. 2:25, etc.) as representatives of God, Elohim is plural in sense as well as form. Means either "be strong," or "be in front," suiting the power and preëminence of God. Jesus is quoted as using a form of the name from the cross (Matt. 27:46, Eli; Mark 15:34, Eloi). See articles **Eli, Eli, lama sabachthani.**

Eloi (See Elohim)

Elon (ē′lŏn). 1. Hittite whose daughter (Gen. 36:2) Esau married. 2. Son of Zebulon (Gen. 46:14; Num. 26:26). 3. A judge (Judg. 12:11, 12).

Elon. 1. Town of Dan (Josh. 19:43). 2. Elon-beth-hanan, a town (I Kings 4:9).

Elpaal (ĕl-pā′ăl), a Benjamite (I Chron. 8:11, 12, 18).

Elpalet (ĕl-pā′lĕt, ĕl′pȧ-lĕt). See Eliphalet (I Chron. 3:6).

El Shaddai (ĕl shăd′ȧ-ī, -shăd′ī), probably "Almighty God," the name by which, according to Exodus 6:3, He appeared to Abraham, Isaac, and Jacob. As to Abraham, this is borne out by Genesis 17:1; as to Jacob, by Genesis 28:3; 35:11; 43:14; 48:3.

Eltekeh (ĕl′tē-kē), a city of Dan (Josh. 19:44).

Eltekon (ĕl′tē-kŏn), one of six cities in the hill country of Judah (Josh. 15:59).

Eltolad (ĕl-tō′lăd), a city in S. Judah (Josh. 15:30), assigned to Simeon (Josh. 19:4). Also (I Chron. 4:29) called Tolad.

Elul (ĕ-lōōl′), sixth month of the Hebrew year, approximately August-September (Neh. 6:15). See Calendar.

Eluzai (ē-lū′zā-ī), a Benjamite (I Chron. 12:5).

Elymas (ĕl′ĭmăs), a Jew, Bar-jesus (meaning **son of Jesus** or **Joshua**), a sorcerer who was with Sergius Paulus, the proconsul of Cyprus. He became blind following Paul's curse, in consequence of which the proconsul believed in the Lord (Acts 13:4-13).

Elzabad (ĕl-zā′băd, ĕl′zȧ-băd). 1. A Gadite (I Chron. 12:12). 2. A Levite (I Chron. 26:7).

Embalm (ĕm-bȧm), to prepare a dead body with oil and spices to preserve it from decay. Embalming was of Egyptian origin. The only clear instances of it in the Bible were in the cases of Jacob and Joseph (Gen. 50:2, 3; 50:26). The purpose of the Egyptians in embalming was to preserve the body for the use of the soul in a future life: the purpose of the Hebrews was to preserve the bodies of Jacob and Joseph for a long journey to their resting place with Abraham (Gen. 50:13).

Embroidery; artistic needlework and fine weaving were highly prized by the Hebrews and their neighbors (Judg. 5:30; Josh. 7:20). The hangings of the temple and the robes of the priests were decorated with embroidery (Exod. 26:37; 27:16; 28:33, 39; 39:29).

Emim (ē′mĭm), the original inhabitants of Moab (Deut. 2:10, 11). They were a great people, that is, powerful and of advanced civilization; numerous; and tall of stature.

Emmanuel (ĕ-măn′ū-ĕl, **God with us**), name of child which virgin would bear (Isa. 7:14) and at whose birth salvation would be near. Micah 5:2 takes Him to be the Messiah.

Emmaus (ĕ-mā′ŭs), the village to which two disciples were going on the day of Jesus' resurrection, when He met and was recognized by them as He broke the bread at supper (Luke 24:7-35). It was about 60 furlongs or stadia (RSV, seven miles) from Jerusalem, in what direction is not stated.

Emmor (ĕm′êr), the father of Sychem (Acts 7:16). Same as Hamor.

Enam (ē′năm), city in lowland of Judah, possibly translated "open place" (Gen. 38:14, 21). Not identified.

Enan (ē′năn), father of Ahira (Num. 1:15; 2:29).

Encampment (ĕn-kămp′mĕnt). The children of Israel encamped at many places on their way from Egypt to Canaan (Exod. 13:20; 14:2, 9; 15:27; Num. 33:10-46; Josh. 4:19; 5:10). References to encampments of soldiers, of Israel or of other nations, assembled for war, occur (Josh. 10:5, 31, 34; Judg. 6:4; 9:50; 10:17; 20:19; I Sam. 11:1; 13:16; II Sam. 11:11; 12:28; I Kings 16:15, 16; I Chron. 11:15; II Chron. 32:1).

Enchantment (ĕn-chȧnt′mĕnt), the use of any form of magic, including divination. Forbidden God's people (Deut. 18:10; Acts 8:9, 11; 13:8, 10; 19:19).

Endor (ĕn′dôr, **spring of habitation**), a village about seven miles SE of Nazareth, home town of the "witch of Endor," the spiritist medium Saul visited before his last battle with the Philistines (I Sam. 28:8-25).

The village of Emmaus. © MPS

Upper spring of En-gedi, a place where David found refuge from Saul.
© MPS

En-Eglaim (ĕn-ĕg′lā-ĭm), a place by the Dead Sea (Ezek. 47:10). Site unknown.

En-Gannim (ĕn-găn′ĭm, **fountain, spring of gardens**). 1. A town in the lowland of Judah (Josh. 15:34). 2. A town in the territory of Issachar, assigned to the Gershonite Levites (Josh. 19:21; 21:29).

En-Gedi (ĕn-gē′dī, **spring or fountain of the kid or wild goat**), an oasis on the W coast of the Dead Sea about midway of its length, in the territory of Judah (Josh. 15:62). Here David fortified a refuge from Saul (I Sam. 23:29; 24:1). En-gedi is identified with Hazazon-tamar, occupied by Ammorites, which Chedorlaomer invaded in the days of Abraham (Gen. 14:7).

Engraver. The OT and archaeology reveal a knowledge of engraving or carving among the Israelites, although developed neither to the extent nor skill as among neighboring countries. This may have been due to the warnings against "graven images" (Exod. 20:4). See also Occupations.

En-Haddah (ĕn-hăd′ȧ, **swift fountain**), a town on border of Issachar (Josh. 19:21).

En-Hakkore (ĕn-hăk′-ō-rē, **fountain of him who cried**), a spring which burst out from Ramath-lehi ("hill of the jawbone") at Samson's cry (Judg. 15:19).

En-Hazor (ĕn-hā′zôr, **fountain of the village**), a fenced city in Naphtali (Josh. 19:37).

En-Mishpat (ĕn-mĭsh′-păt, **fountain of judgment**), the older name for Kadesh (Gen. 14:7).

Enoch (ē′nŭk, **consecrated**). 1. Cain's eldest son (Gen. 4:17, 18). 2. Son of Jared (Gen. 5:18) and father of Methuselah (Gen. 5:21-22; Luke 3:37). Abram walked "before God" (Gen. 17:1), but of Enoch and Noah alone it is written that they walked **"with God"** (Gen. 5:24; 6:9). The secret of his walk with God was "faith"; faith was the ground of his "pleasing God"; his pleasing God was the ground of his being "translated that he should not see death" (Heb. 11:5, 6). After the monotonous repetition of the patriarchs who "lived ... begat ... and died" (Gen. 5), the account of Enoch's walk with God and translation without death stands forth in bright relief.

Enoch, Books of, apocalyptic literature written by various authors and circulated under the name of Enoch. I Enoch was written by the Chasidim or by the Pharisees between 163-63 B.C. It is the best source for the development of Jewish doctrine in the last two pre-Christian centuries. II Enoch was written A.D. 1-50.

Enos (ĕ'nŏs, **mortal),** son of Seth and grandson of Adam (Gen. 4:26; 5:6-11; Luke 3:38).

Enosh (ĕ'nŏsh, **mortal),** a more acceptable way of Anglicizing the name of Seth's son (I Chron. 1:1; ERV Gen. 4:26; 5:6-11; Luke 3:38).

En-Rimmon (ĕn-rĭm'ŏn, **fountain of a pomegranate**), a place S of Jerusalem (Zech. 14:10), 11 miles NE of Beersheba. "Ain and Rimmon" (Josh. 15:32; Josh. 19:7; I Chron. 4:32).

En-Rogel (ĕn-rō'gel, **fountain of feet),** so-called because fullers trod their cloth with their feet there. It was on the border between Benjamin and Judah (Josh. 15:7; 18:16), below Jerusalem near the junction of the valley of Hinnom and the valley of Jehoshaphat. Here Jonathan and Ahimaaz hid to receive intelligence for David from within the walls (II Sam. 17:17).

Entappuah (ĕn-tăp'ū-ȧ, **spring of apple**), a town on the eastern border of Manasseh in the land of Tappuah (Josh. 17:7, 8).

Epaenetus (ēp-ē'nē-tŭs, **praised), a** Christian at Rome greeted by Paul as "my well-beloved, who is the firstfruits of Asia (better MS reading) unto Christ" (Rom. 16:5).

Epaphras (ĕp'ȧ-frăs), a contraction of Epaphroditus, but not the same NT character. He was Paul's "dear fellowservant" and minister to the church at Colosse, perhaps its founder (Col. 1:7). Paul also called him "my fellowprisoner." This may mean that he voluntarily shared the apostle's imprisonment; or he may have been apprehended for his zeal in the Gospel.

Epaphroditus (ē-păf-rō-dī'tŭs, **lovely),** the messenger delegated by the church at Philippi to bring their gifts to Paul while he was in prison in Rome.

Ephai (ē'fī, **gloomy),** Netophathite; sons warned Gedaliah (Jer. 40:8-16; 41:3).

Epher (ē'fēr, **calf).** 1. Son of Midian and grandson of Abraham (Gen. 25:4, I Chron. 1:33). 2. Son of Ezra of the tribe of Judah (I Chron. 4:17). 3. A family head in the half-tribe of Manasseh (I Chron. 5:23, 24).

Ephesdammim (ē-fĕs-dăm'ĭm, **boundary of blood**), a place so-called from the bloody battles fought there between Israel and the Philistines. Lying between Shocoh and Azekah in Judah, it was the Philistine encampment when David slew Goliath (I Sam. 17:1).

Ephesians, Epistle to the, generally acknowledged to be one of the richest and most profound of the NT epistles. The depth and grandeur of its concepts, the richness and fullness of its message, and the majesty and dignity of its contents have made it precious to believers in all ages and in all places.

Ephesians explicity claims Pauline authorship (1:1; 3:1) and its entire tenor is eminently Pauline. The early Christian Church uniformly received and treasured it as from Paul. Only within the modern era have liberal critics raised doubts as to its Pauline origin. The attacks are based solely on internal arguments drawn from the style, vocabulary, and theology of the epistle. These arguments are subjective and inconclusive and offer no compelling reasons for rejecting the undeviating evidence of text and tradition. If the Pauline authorship is rejected, the epistle must be ascribed to someone who was fully Paul's equal, but the literature of the first two centuries reveals no traces of anyone capable of producing such a writing.

Ephesians was written while Paul was a prisoner (3:1; 4:1; 6:20). The prevailing view has been that it was written from Rome during Paul's first Roman imprisonment (Acts 28:30-31). The letter was transmitted to its destination by Tychicus (6:21-22), being dispatched together with Colossians and Philemon (Col. 4:7-8; Philem. 9, 13, 17). Thus all three were sent to the Roman province of Asia.

Its contents offer no clear indication as to the occasion for the writing of Ephesians. Its affinity to Colossians in time of origin and contents suggests an occasion closely related to the writing of that epistle. Ephesians seems to be the after-effect of the controversy that caused the writing of Colossians. Colossians has in it the intensity, rush, and roar of the battle field, while Ephesians has a calm atmosphere suggestive of a survey of the field after the victory.

Ephesians sets forth the wealth of the believer in union with Christ. It portrays the glories of our salvation and emphasizes the nature of the Church as the Body of Christ. As indicated by the doxology in 3:20-21, its contents fall into two parts, the first doctrinal (1-3), the second practical and hortatory (4-6). An outline may suggest some of its riches.

The Salutation. 1:1-2. I. Doctrinal: The Believer's Standing in Christ. 1:3-3:21. 1. The thanksgiving for our redemption. 1:3-14. 2. The prayer for spiritual illumination. 1:15-23. 3. The power of God manifested in our salvation. 2:1-10. 4. The union of Jew and Gentile in one Body in Christ. 2:11-22. 5. The apostle as the messenger of this mystery. 3:1-13. 6. The prayer for the realization of these blessings. 3:14-19. 7. The doxology of praise. 3:20-21. II. Practical: The Believers' Life in Christ. 4:1-6:20. 1. Their walk as God's saints. 4:1-5:21. (a) The worthy walk, in inward realization of Christian unity. 4:1-16. (b) The different walk, in outward manifestation of a changed position. 4:17-32. (c) The loving walk, in upward imitation of our Father. 5:1-17. (d) The summary of the Spirit-filled life. 5:18-21. 2. Their duties as God's family. 5:22-6:9. 3. Their warfare as God's soldiers. 6:10-20. The Conclusion. 6:21-24.

Ephesus (ĕf'ĕ-sŭs, **desirable),** an old Ionian foundation at the mouth of the Cayster. Built near the shrine of an old Anatolian fertility goddess, Ephesus became the seat of an oriental cult. The Anatolian deity had been taken over by the Greeks under the name of Artemis, the Diana of the Romans. Grotesquely represented with turreted head and many breasts, the goddess and her cult found expression in the famous temple, served, like that of Aphrodite at Corinth, by a host of priestess courtesans.

Round the cult clustered much trade. Ephesus became a place of pilgrimage for tourist-worshipers, all eager to carry away talisman and souvenir, hence the prosperous guild of the silversmiths whose livelihood was the manufacture of silver shrines and images of the meteoric stone which was said to be Diana's image "fallen from heaven." Ephesus leaned more and more on the trade which followed the cult as commerce declined in her silting harbor. Twenty miles of reedy marshland now separate the old harbor works from the sea and even in Paul's day the process was under way. Tacitus tells us that an attempt was made to improve the seaway in A.D. 65, but the task proved too great. Ephesus in the first century was a dying city, given to parasite pursuits, living, like Athens, on a reputation, a curious meeting place of old and new religions, of East and West. Acts 19 gives a peculiarly vivid picture of her unnatural life.

Ephlal (ĕf'lăl, **judge),** son of Zabad of the tribe of Judah (I Chron. 2:37).

Ephod (ĕf'-ŏd). 1. A sacred vestment originally worn by the high priest and made of "gold, blue, purple, scarlet, and fine twined linen, with cunning work" (Exod. 28:4ff; 39:2ff). Attached

High Priest clothed in the Ephod. DV

to the ephod by chains of pure gold was a breastplate containing 12 precious stones. Beneath the ephod was worn the blue robe of the ephod, having a hole for the head and extending to the feet with a hem alternating with gold bells and pomegranates of blue, purple, and scarlet (Exod. 28:31-35; 39: 22-26).

Later, persons other than the high priest wore ephods. Samuel wore a linen ephod while ministering before the Lord (I Sam. 2:18) which was characteristic of the ordinary priests (2:28; 14:3; 22:18). David wore a linen ephod while he danced before the Lord after bringing the ark to Jerusalem (II Sam. 6:14).

2. Prince of Manasseh (Num. 34: 23).

Ephphatha (ĕf′à-thȧ, **be thou opened),** occurs only in Mark 7:34. Uttered by Jesus as He was healing a deaf man.

Ephraim (ē′frâ-ĭm, **double fruit),** the younger of two sons of Joseph and his Egyptian wife Asenath (Gen. 41: 50-52). The aged Jacob, when he blessed his grandsons Manasseh and Ephraim, adopted them as his own sons. Despite Joseph's protest, Jacob gave the preferential blessing (signified by the right hand) to Ephraim (Gen. 48:1-22). When Jacob blessed his own sons, he did not mention Ephraim and Manasseh, but gave a special blessing to their father Joseph (Gen. 49:22-26).

Ephraim was the progenitor of the tribe called by his name, as was also Manasseh. This brought the number of the Hebrew tribes to 13, but the original number 12 (derived from the 12 sons of Jacob, of whom Joseph was one) continued to be referred to. The separation of the tribe of Levi from the others for the Tabernacle service, and its failure to receive a separate territory in which to live, helped to perpetuate the concept of "The Twelve Tribes of Israel."

At the division of the land among the tribes the children of Joseph (except half of Manasseh which settled E of the Jordan, Num. 32:33; 39-42) received the central hill country of Palestine, sometimes called Mt. Ephraim. The Joseph tribes were not able to occupy this land completely for a long time, being forced up into the heavily wooded hill country (Josh. 17:14-18) by the Canaanites and Philistines who occupied the good bottom lands and who by their superior civilization and power (Judg. 1:27-29) kept the Hebrews subservient until the time of David. Ephraim and Manasseh seem to have been bitter rivals (Isa. 9:20, 21), Manasseh being the larger group (Gen. 49:22) but Ephraim asserting the more vigorous leadership. Although they seem to have held their land in common for a time (Josh. 17:14-18) it was presently devided between them. Ephraim's portion was well defined and very fruitful, its soil fertile and its rainfall more plentiful than Judah's to the S (Deut. 33:13-16).

Ephraim is also the name of a city N of Jerusalem, mentioned in II Sam. 13:23 and John 11:54.

Ephraim, Woods of, place in Gilead where David defeated forces of Absalom (II Sam. 18:6).

Ephraimite (ē′frȧ-ĭm-īt), member of tribe of Ephraim (Josh. 16:10; Judg. 12).

Ephrain (ē′frȧ-ĭn), town taken from Jeroboam by Abijah (II Chron. 13:19).

Ephrath (ĕf′răth, **fruitful land),** 1. A shorter form of Ephrathah, KJV Ephratah, the place where Rachel was buried. (Gen. 35:16). 2. Second wife of Caleb (I Chron. 2:19, 20). 3. Ancient name of Bethlehem or the district around it (Mic. 5:2).

Ephron (ē′frôn, **fawn).** 1. A Hittite who sold Abraham the field of Machpelah which contained a cave in which he buried Sarah, his wife (Gen. 23:8, 9). 2. A mountain about six miles NW of Jerusalem (Josh. 15:9). 3. A city taken from Jeroboam by Ahijah (II Chron. 13:19).

Epicureans (ĕp-ĭ-kū-rē′ănz). 1. The followers of Epicurus, the Greek philosopher (341-270 B.C.). He taught that the chief purpose of man is to achieve happiness. For the philosopher the highest joy is found in mental and intellectual pursuits, but for lesser souls lower goals of sensual satisfaction fulfill the greatest pleasure. Thus the high standards of the founder were not maintained and the philosophy gained a bad reputation. It was widely held at the time of Christ. Paul met it at Athens when he encountered its philosophers (Acts 17:16-33). They were not impressed by his teaching of creation, judgment and resurrection, since all these doctrines were denied by the Epicurean philosophy.

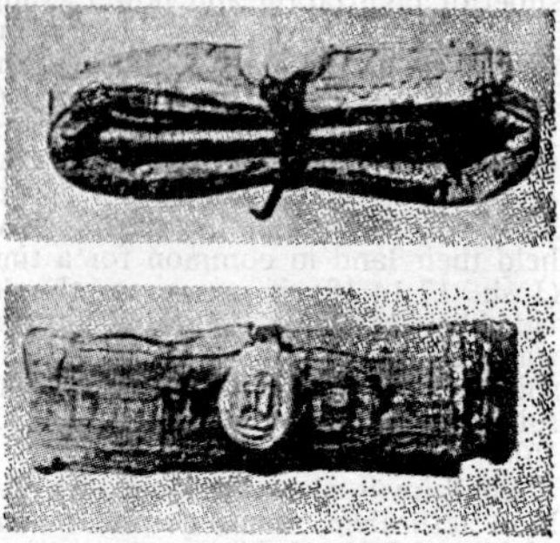

Sealed letter, or epistles, sheets of papyrus rolled, tied and sealed. JHK

Epistle (ē-pis'l, **letter, epistle**). Written correspondence, whether personal or official, has been common to all ages. The OT abounds with evidences of widespread written letters (II Sam. 11:14, 15; I Kings 21:8, 9; II Kings 19:14).

The term is, however, almost a technical one, referring particularly to the 21 epistles of the NT. The NT epistles were written by 4 (possibly 5) writers: Peter, Paul, John, Jude, and the author of Hebrews. Paul wrote 13 (or 14, if Hebrews is by him); Peter, 2; John, 3; and Jude, 1. According to the custom of the time, they usually begin with the name or title of the writer and that of the addressee or addressees; then follow words of greeting, the message of the epistle; and at the end the author usually gives his name. It was Paul's usual practice to employ an amanuensis to write from dictation. The epistles were written to individual churches or groups of churches (almost always given by name) and to individuals. Seven are called General Epistles, because they were written to the church at large.

It is not to be supposed that all of the epistles of the apostles have survived. Paul in I Corinthians 5:9 refers to a letter he had written to the Corinthians prior to our I Corinthians; and in Colossians 4:6 he speaks of an epistle to the Laodicean church.

Er (ûr, **watchful**). Son of Judah (Gen. 38:3, 6, 7). 2. Son of Shelah (I Chron. 4:21). 3. Ancestor of Jesus in the maternal line (Luke 3:28).

Eran (ē'răn, **watcher**). Grandson of Ephraim (Num. 26:36).

Erastus (ē-răs'tŭs, **beloved**), a name which occurs three times, each time denoting a friend of Paul: 1. Acts 19:22 "And having sent into Macedonia two of them that ministered under him, Timothy and Erastus," Paul stayed in Asia. 2. The treasurer of the city of Corinth (Rom. 16:23).

Erech (ē'rĕk), a city of ancient Babylonia mentioned in Genesis 10:10 as the second city founded by Nimrod. The Babylonian form of the name is **Uruk.** Archaeology has found that this city was one of the oldest of Babylonia, being founded before 4000 B.C., and continued to flourish until after 300 B.C.

Eri (ē'rī, **my watcher**), son of Gad (Gen. 46:16).

Esaias (See Isaiah)

Esar-Haddon (ē'sár-hăd'ŏn, **Ashur has given a brother**), son and successor of Sennacherib (II Kings 19:36, 37; II Chron. 32:21; Isa. 37:37, 38). Reigned from 681-669 B.C. He restored the city of Babylon which his father had destroyed, and fought campaigns against the Cimmerians and other barbaric hordes from beyond the Caucasus. His greatest accomplishment was the conquest of Egypt, Assyria's competitor for world domination. According to Ezra 4:2, Esarhaddon brought deportees into Samaria, which had already been colonized with pagans by Sargon when he destroyed it in 722 B. C. After Sidon's fall, 12 kings along the Mediterranean seacoast submitted to the Assyrians. Manasseh's summons to appear before an Assyrian king, mentioned in II Chronicles 33:11-13, probably took place in the reign of Esar-haddon's successor, Assurbanipal.

Esau (ē'saw, **hairy**), firstborn of twin brothers, Esau and Jacob, sons of Isaac and Rebecca (Gen. 25:24, 25); sold his birthright for a mess of pottage to his brother (Gen. 25:30-34); married two Hittite women (Gen. 26:34); sought to kill Jacob for tricking him out of Isaac's blessing (Gen. 27); later reconciled to Jacob (Gen. 32:7-33:15). Scripture sometimes uses Esau as the name of the land of Edom in which his descendants lived (Gen. 36:8).

Eschatology (ĕs-kȧ-tŏl'ō-gē), a division of systematic theology dealing with the doctrine of last things such as death, resurrection, the second coming of

Christ, the end of the age, divine judgment, and the future state. It properly includes all that was prophetic of future events when recorded in Scripture. Biblical eschatology assumes that the Scriptures predict future events with infallible accuracy and constitute a divine disclosure of the future.

Though conservatives agree on essential doctrines, three types of interpretations have arisen. The early church adopted the point of view of premillennialism or chiliasm, anticipating a literal return of Christ to the earth, the establishment of His kingdom on the earth for one thousand years, and the beginning of the eternal state thereafter. The Alexandrian school of theology (third century), interpreting prophecy in a nonliteral or allegorical way, viewed the millennial kingdom as having already begun with the first coming of Christ, to be consummated in His second coming, and to be followed immediately by the eternal state. This view was championed by Augustine (354-430) and was adopted by the Roman Catholic Church and the Protestant Reformers such as Calvin and Luther. A variation of amillennialism known as postmillennialism was introduced by Daniel Whitby (1638-1725) who taught that the last one thousand years of the present age would fulfill promises of peace and righteousness on earth and be a crowning triumph of the Gospel. The world conflicts of the first half of the 20th century and a realistic appraisal of the world situation have caused a general abandonment of postmillennialism and a return to either Augustinian amillennialism or premillennialism.

Differing interpretations of eschatology result from the literal or nonliteral interpretation of prophecy, the more literal leading to premillennialism, the less literal to the amillennial view. Approaches also vary on the question of the central purpose of God in eschatology. Amillennialism tends to emphasize soteriology or the salvation of the elect as the dominating factor, whereas premillennialism usually adopts the principle that the manifestation of the glory of God is the supreme purpose in divine dealing with men in successive ages, and distinguishes God's program in eschatology for Israel from that of His program for the world as a whole or His program for the Church.

Though eschatology is not the main theme of the early books of the OT, eschatological considerations are constantly applied. Individual eschatology, concerned with life, death, resurrection, and reward or punishment, is set in a context of general eschatology or prediction of the movement of history. In the OT this concerns principally the nation Israel, beginning with Genesis 12 and the divine covenant with Abraham. Abraham was promised not only personal reward, but that his seed should possess the Holy Land. Amillenarians and postmillenarians interpret these prophecies as largely fulfilled in the Church, and have not attempted literal explanation of the details. Many premillenarians assert the promise of future possession of the Holy Land to Israel as valid and to be fulfilled literally in the coming millennial kingdom of Christ on earth following His second advent. Promises given to Israel are distinguished from promises addressed to saints in general or to the Church in the present age.

The OT abounds also in prophecies relating to Gentiles or those outside the seed of Abraham. Many predictions were given of individual judgments, already largely fulfilled. To Daniel was revealed the larger picture of the divine program for the nations of the world as embodied in the four empires of his vision (Dan. 2, 7).

Though sometimes distinguished sharply from OT eschatology, it is reasonable to assume that the NT continues, interprets, enlarges, and completes the OT eschatology. The fulfillment of prophecies in the NT which are related to the first advent of Christ, involving hundreds of OT Scriptures, is obvious proof of the principle that prophecy will have actual fulfillment in specific events. Looming large in eschatology are the teachings of Christ related to the kingdom of God. A comprehensive prophetic picture presenting moral and spiritual aspects of the kingdom of God is given in the Sermon on the Mount (Matt. 5-7), the character of divine spiritual government in the present age (Matt. 13), and the consummating events climaxing in the second advent of Christ to set up His earthly kingdom (Matt. 24-25). In recognition of the age between the

The valley of Eschol, near Hebron. © *MPS*

first and second advents, Christ gave extensive teaching on the spiritual qualities of the present age (John 13-16.) This is subsequently enlarged in the epistles and recorded in part historically in Acts. The present age is characterized as a time in which the Church is formed, composed of Jews and Gentiles alike, who believe in Christ. Premillenarians find also in the NT, and especially in Revelation 20, anticipation of a future mediatorial kingdom of Christ in which He reigns over the entire earth for one thousand years.

Eschatology is not designed to satisfy curiosity but to provide an intelligent comprehension of the future as a guide for a present program, and a sure ground for hope. The superlative and distinctive character of Biblical eschatology becomes immediately apparent when compared to the fragmentary and fantastic eschatologies offered in heathen religions.

Esdraelon (ĕs′drā-ē′lŏn), the great plain which breaks the central range of Palestine in two. In the OT it is known as the plain, or valley, of Jezreel. It affords a direct connection between the maritime plain and the Jordan valley. It lies between Galilee on the N and Samaria on the S.

Esdraelon was the scene of some of the most important battles in Bible history: the victory of Barak over Sisera (Judg. 4) and of the Philistines over Saul and his sons (I Sam. 31). Here the Egyptians mortally wounded Josiah, king of Judah, when he went out to intercept the army of Pharaoh Necho (II Kings 23:29).

Esdras, Books of (See Apocrypha)

Esek (ē′sĕk, **contention),** well which Isaac's servants dug in the valley of Gerar and which the herdsmen of Gerar demanded (Gen. 26:20).

Esh-Baal (ĕsh′bā′ăl, **man of Baal),** son of Saul (I Chron. 8:33 and 9:39). Called Ishbosheth in II Samuel 2:8, 10, 12, etc.

Eshban (ĕsh′băn, **man of understanding),** descendant of Seir (Gen. 36:26; I Chron. 1:41).

Eschol (ĕsh′kŏl, **cluster).** 1. An Amorite who helped Abram defeat King Chedorlaomer (Gen. 14:13, 24). 2. A valley near Hebron where Moses' spies found a cluster of large grapes (Num. 13:23, 24).

Eshean (ĕsh′ē-ăn), a city near Hebron (Josh. 15:52).

Eshek (ē′shĕk, **oppression**), descendant of Jonathan. His grandsons were mighty men of valor in the tribe of Benjamin (I Chron. 8:38-40).

Eshtaol (ĕsh′tā-ŏl), town 13 miles NW of Jerusalem (Josh. 15:33), assigned to Dan (Josh. 19:41); scene of Samson's exploits (Judg. 13:24, 25; 16:31).

Eshtemoa (ĕsh′tē-mō-ȧ). 1. A city eight miles S of Hebron assigned to the Levites (Josh. 21:14). This city, among others, received from David a share of the spoil of his victory over the Amalekites (I Sam. 30:28). 2. Son of Ishbah (I Chron. 4:17). 3. A Maacathite (I Chron. 4:19).

Eshtemoh (ĕsh′tē-mō), a city located in the hill country of Judah (Josh. 15:50). The same as Eshtemoa above.

Eshton (ĕsh′tŏn, perhaps **effeminate**), a descendant of Judah (I Chron. 4:11, 12).

Esli (ĕs′lī), ancestor of Christ (Luke 3:25).

Esrom (ĕs′rŏm), son of Perez (Matt. 1:3; Luke 3:33).

Essenes (ĕ-sēnz′). A sect of the Jews in Palestine during the time of Christ, not mentioned in the NT. Josephus and Philo (first century) and Pliny the Elder and Hippolytus (second century) describe them.

The Essenes lived a simple life of sharing everything in common, practicing strict rules of conduct. Mostly unmarried, they were reported to number 4,000. The majority of them lived together in settlements, but some resided in the cities of the Jews. Apparently they kept their ranks filled by the adoption of other people's children. They did not participate in the temple worship, but had their own purification rites. They observed the sabbath day very strictly and greatly venerated Moses. They would take no oaths; but new members, after going through a three-year probationary period, were required to swear a series of strong oaths that they would cooperate in every way with the organization and would never reveal to outsiders anything about the sect.

The Essenes have come into public attention in late years because of the study of the Dead Sea scrolls, and the excavation of the monastery called Khirbet Qumran where the scrolls were written. This literature and building give evidence of an organization very similar to what is known about the Essenes.

Many Essenes perished in the wars against the Romans. Some of the survivors probably became Christians.

Esther (ĕs′tēr, **Ishtar,** Babylonian Goddess, **star**), a Jewish orphan maiden in the city of Shushan, who became queen of Persia. Her Hebrew name was Hadassah (myrtle). Her cousin, Mordecai, who was a minor official of the palace, reared her as his own daughter. Xerxes, the Persian king, had divorced his wife, and when he sought a new queen from among the maidens of the realm he chose Esther. When the Jews in the empire were faced with destruction she was able to save them. In honor to her the book which bears her name is read every year at the Feast of Purim.

Esther, Book of, last of historical books of the OT; author unknown; probably written c. 400 B.C. Peculiar features of book: no mention of the name of God; no mention of prayer. Tells of Jewish girl Esther who became queen of Persia and saved her people from destruction. Outline. 1. Esther becomes queen (1-2:17). 2. Jewish danger (2:18-3:15). 3. Jews saved (4-10). In the LXX there are several interpolations scattered through the story.

Etam (ē′tăm). 1. A town and clan in Judah between Bethlehem and Tekoa (I Chron. 4:3). 2. A village in Simeon (I Chron. 4:32). 3. The rock where Samson lived after a slaughter of Philistines (Judg. 15:8, 11).

Eternal Life. Not merely age-long, after which it ceases to be, it is endless in duration, having its beginning in the mind of the eternal God (Eph. 1:4), and eternal in quality, that is, like the life of God as revealed in His Son Jesus Christ (I John 5:11, 12). Though our eternal life thus has an eternal past in the purposes of God, our experience of it begins with the new birth (John 3; Tit. 3:4-7), when we believe in Jesus Christ who truly is our eternal life (John 17:2, 3; Gal. 2: 20). Eternal or everlasting life is most prominent in John's Gospel (3:15, 16, 36; 4:14, 36; 5:24, 39; 6:27, 40, 47, 54, 68; 10:28; 12:25, 50; 17:2, 3) and in I John (1:2; 2:25; 3:15; 5:11, 13, 20) but is not absent from the Synoptics (Matt. 19:16, 29; 25:46; Mark 10:17, 30; Luke 10:25; 18:18, 30), nor from Acts (13: 46, 48) or the Epistles (Rom. 2:7; 5: 21; 6:22, 23; Gal. 6:8; I Tim. 1:16; 6: 12; Tit. 1:2; Jude 21). John 3 describes the beginning of eternal life; John 6 its continuance; I John 1:1-4 its rootage in Christ. The references in the Synoptic Gospels show that eternal life was a concept independent of, though related to, the kingdom of God; not peculiarly Johannine.

Eternity. Refers to the endless past, the unending future, or to God's present experience of all time; one of the attributes of God (Jer. 1:5; Ps. 90).

Etham (ē′thăm), an uncertain site on the journey of Israel out of Egypt (Exod. 13:20; Num. 33:6-8). Appears to have been a wilderness district on both sides of the N end of the Red Sea.

Ethan (ē′thăn). 1. Wise man of Solomon's time (I Kings 4:31; Ps. 89 title). 2. A son of Zerah (I Chron. 2:6, 8). 3. A descendant of Gershon (I Chron. 6:39-43). 4. A singer (I Chron. 6:44; 15:17, 19).

Ethbaal (ĕth′bā′ăl), a king of Sidon whose daughter Jezebel became the wife of Ahab, king of Israel (I Kings 16:31).

Ether (ē′thêr), a town in Judah named between Libnah and Ashan (Josh. 15:42); Khirbet 'Ater; perhaps the same assigned to Simeon named between En-rimmon and Ashan (Josh. 19:7, 9).

Ethiopia (ē′thĭ-ō′pĭ-ȧ), a country extending S of Egypt from the first cataract of the Nile indefinitely, including Nubia, Sudan and northern if not southern modern Ethiopia. Cush, son of Ham (Gen. 10:6-8; I Chron. 1:8-10), from whom descended the most southern peoples known to the Hebrews, in Arabia and N Africa. Ethiopia (Gen. 2:13 ASV, RSV Cush) may be anywhere in this general direction. Job 28:19 mentions the topaz of Ethiopia. Moses married an Ethiopian woman (Num. 12:1 RSV Cushite). In the reign of Rehoboam, Ethiopians came against Judah with the king of Egypt (II Chron. 12:3); and in the reign of Asa (II Chron. 14:9-13; 16:7-9) Zerah, the Ethiopian with a million men, was defeated in Judah. "The Arabians, that were near the Ethiopians" (II Chron. 21:16) indicates the lands on both sides of the Red Sea, in the Arabian peninsula and in Africa, sometimes under the same rule.

The Ethiopians had skin of different appearance (Jer. 13:23); the Greek name **Aithiops**, burnt-face, shows the color to have been dark. Pictures on monuments show that they were a mixed race, some Negro, some Semitic, some Caucasian. Ethiopia enters Bible history most prominently when Tirhakah, an Ethiopian king of a dynasty which had conquered Egypt, came against Judah in the days of Hezekiah, and was only driven away by the superior force of Assyria (II Kings 19:9; Isa. 37:9). Henceforth the ultimate ruin of Ethiopia is a theme of prophecy (Isa. 11:11; 18:1; 20:3-5; 43:3; 45:14; Jer. 46:9; Ezek. 29:10; 30:4, 5; 38:5; Zeph. 3:10; Nah. 3:9). The English versions vary between "Ethiopia" and "Cush." Echoes are in Psalms 68:31; 87:4. Ethiopia is the western limit of the Persian empire of Ahasuerus (Esth. 1:1; 8:9). Ethiopia in NT times was ruled by a queen whose name or title was Candace (Acts 8:27). Ethiopia was a sparsely populated land traversed by the Blue and White Nile and their tributaries, a reservoir of hardy manpower for ambitious rulers (Isa. 18:1; 2 ASV, RSV).

Ethiopian Eunuch (ē′thĭ-ō′pĭ-ăn ū′nŭk), treasurer of Candace, queen of the Ethiopians (Acts 8:26-39). He was a mighty man or nobleman. As a eunuch he could not be a full member of the Jewish community (Deut. 23:1), but he had been worshiping in Jerusalem and was reading aloud the book of Isaiah when Philip, sent by the Holy Spirit from Samaria to help him, met his chariot. From Isaiah 53, Philip led the African to faith in Christ, so that he asked for and received baptism and went on his way toward Gaza rejoicing.

Ethnan (ĕth′năn), a son of Helah, wife of Ashur, a Judahite (I Chron.4:7).

Ethni (ĕth′nī), a Gershonite Levite and an ancestor of Asaph whom David set over the service of song (I Chron. 6:41). Likely the same person named Jeaterai in I Chronicles 6:21.

Eubulus (ū-bū′lŭs), a Christian disciple at Rome who, with others, saluted Timothy (II Tim. 4:21).

Euergetes (ū-ûr′jē-tēz), "benefactors," a title of honor often voted by Greek states to public men. Our Lord alludes to the title (Luke 22:25).

Eunice (ū′nĭs, ū-nī′sē), the Jewish wife of a Greek; daughter of Lois and mother of Timothy (Acts 16:1; II Tim. 1:5). They lived at Lystra, where the two women and Timothy were converted, probably on Paul's first visit (Acts 14:6-20), since Timothy knew of Paul's persecution there (II Tim. 3:11). She brought up her son to know the OT Scriptures (II Tim. 3:15).

Eunuch (ū′nŭk), a castrated male. From the employment of such men as custodians of royal harems the term came to designate an officer, whether physically a eunuch or not. Heb. **sarîs** is translated **officer** 12 times (e.g., Gen. 37:36; 39:1, **a married man); chamberlain** 13 times (e.g., II Kings 23:11); **eunuch** 17 times (II Kings 9:32, Jezebel's attendants; Jer. 29:2; 34:19; 38:7; 41:16; in 52:25 ASV, RSV **Officer,** of the last kings of Judah; II Kings 20:18; Isa. 39:7; Dan. 1:3-18, in the service of heathen kings). The Mosaic law forbade those blemished by castration to enter the congregation (Deut. 23:1), but Isaiah prophesied of a day when this disability would be removed and their loss compensated (Isa. 56:3-5). Eng. eunuch is a transliteration of Greek **eunoûchos.** The Ethiopian (Acts 8:27-39) was a queen's treasurer in whom Isaiah's prophecy may well have encouraged a new hope. Our Lord uses the term and its cognate verb four times in Matthew 19:12; those born eunuchs and those made eunuchs by men are physically incapable of begetting children; those who "have made themselves eunuchs for the kingdom of heaven's sake" are they whom continence has kept chaste and celibate that they may concentrate their lives on promoting the kingdom of heaven. Jesus Himself was the prime example. Such are the men referred to as "virgins" (RSV chaste) in Revelation 14:4. The eminent though erratic Christian scholar Origen, late in life regretted having taken Matthew 19:12 literally.

Euodias, properly **Euodia** (ū-ŏ'dĭ-à, **prosperous journey** or **fragrance),** a Christian woman at Philippi. She is mentioned in Philippians 4:2 where Paul beseeches Euodia and Syntyche that they be of the same mind in the Lord.

Euphrates (ū-frā'tēz, from a root meaning **"to break forth,"** the longest and most important river of Western Asia, frequently in the OT called "the river," "the great river," as being the largest with which Israel was acquainted, in contrast to the soon drying up torrents of Palestine (Isa. 8:7; Gen. 15:18; Deut. 1:7). It rises from two sources in the Armenian mountains whose branches join after having run 400 and 270 miles, respectively. The united river runs SW and S through the Taurus mountains towards the Mediterranean; but the ranges N of Lebanon prevent its reaching that sea; it turns SE and flows 1000 miles to the Persian

A view of the Euphrates River near ancient Babylon. © MPS

Gulf. The whole course is 1780 miles; for 1200 it is navigable for small vessels. The melting of the snows in the Armenian mountains causes the river to flood each spring. Nebuchadnezzar controlled the floods by turning the water through sluices into channels for distribution over the whole country. The promise to Abraham that his seed's inheritance should reach the Euphrates (Gen. 15:18; Deut. 1:7; Josh. 1:4) received a partial fulfillment in Reuben's pastoral possessions (I Chron. 5:9, 10); a fuller accomplishment under David and Solomon, when an annual tribute was paid by subject petty kingdoms in that area (I Chron. 18:3; II Sam. 8:3-8; I Kings 4:21; II Chron. 9:26). The Euphrates was the boundary between Assyria and the Hittite country after Solomon's time, according to inscriptions.

Euroclydon (ū-rŏk′lĭ-dŏn) **an east wind raising mighty waves,** found only in Acts 27:14. An ENE wind, just that which is best suited to the facts. It came down from the island of Crete, S of which Paul was sailing. It would be extremely dangerous to a ship with large sails, threatening either to capsize her or to drive her onto the quicksands (vs. 17).

Eutychus (ū′tĭ-kŭs, **fortunate),** a youth of Troas mentioned in Acts 20: 9 who, while listening to Paul preach, was overcome with sleep and fell out of the third story window to his death. Paul restored him to life.

Evangelist (ē-văn′jĕ-lĭst, **one who announces good news),** used in a general sense of anyone who proclaims the Gospel of Jesus Christ. Sometimes in the NT, however, it designates a particular class of ministry, as in Ephesians 4:11. The evangelist was not confined in service to one spot, but moved about in different localities, preaching the good news concerning Jesus Christ to those who had not heard the message before. Apostles (Acts 8:25; 14: 7; I Cor. 1:17) did the work of an evangelist, as did also bishops (II Tim. 4:2-5). Philip, who had been set apart as one of the seven deacons (Acts 6: 5) was also called "the evangelist" (Acts 21:8). Evangelist in the sense of "inspired writer of one of the four Gospels," was a later usage.

Eve (life, living), the first woman, formed by God out of Adam's side. Both the way in which Eve was created and the designation "woman" serve to emphasize the intimacy, sacredness and inseparability of the marital state, transcending even that relationship which exists between children and parents (Gen. 2:24). The name "Eve" was given to her after the fall and implies both her being the mother of all living and her being the mother of the promised Seed who should give life to the human race now subjected to death. Her greater weakness and susceptibility to temptation are juxtaposed with Adam's willful act of disobedience in Gen. 3. Deceived by Satan, she ate of the fruit. Enamored of his wife, Adam chose to leave God for the one He had given him. Paul twice refers to her in his epistles (II Cor. 11: 3; I Tim. 2:13).

Evening Sacrifice, one of the two daily offerings of a lamb prescribed in the Mosaic ritual (Exod. 29:38-42; Num. 28:3-8).

Evi (ē′vī), one of the five kings of Midian slain by the Israelites during their encampment in the plains of Moab (Num. 31:8).

Evil, that which is not in harmony with the divine order, both moral and physical. The reconciliation of the existence of evil with the goodness and holiness of a God infinite in His wisdom and power is one of the great problems of theism. The Scriptures indicate that evil has been permitted by God in order that His justice might be manifested in its punishment and His grace in its forgiveness (Rom. 9:22, 23). Moral evil, or sin, is any lack of conformity to the moral law of God. According to the Bible, it is the cause of the existence of physical or natural evil in this world. Adam and Eve, the first humans, enjoyed perfect fellowship with God until they fell under God's condemnation and were banished from the garden. The ground was then cursed for man's sake, and from that time forward man has been forced to gain his sustenance through arduous, sorrowful toil, even as woman has borne children only through suffering and labor (Gen. 3:16-19). In the NT the relationship between moral and natural evil is indicated by Paul in Romans 8:18-22.

Evil-Merodach (ē′vil-mĕ-rō′dăk), a king of Babylon who reigned two years (561-560 B.C.). Murdered by his brother-in-law, Neriglissar (the Nergal-Sharezer of Jer. 39:3), a prince who usurped the throne. References to him as lawless and indecent indicate the probable reasons for the coup which cut short his reign.

Evil-Merodach released Jehoiachin, king of Judah, from his 37-year Babylonian imprisonment, and gave him a position of prominence among the captive kings and daily allowance of food for the rest of his life (II Kings 25:27-30; Jer. 52:31-34).

Evil Spirits (See Demons)

Ewe (ū), a female sheep.

Excommunication, disciplinary exclusion from church fellowship. The Jews had two forms of excommunication: temporary and permanent (Luke 6:22; John 9:34, 35). Christian excommunication is commanded by Christ (Matt. 18:15-18), and apostolic practice (I Tim. 1:20) and precept (I Cor. 5:11; Titus 3:10) are in agreement. Paul's infallible authority when inspired gives no warrant for uninspired ministers claiming the same right to direct the church to excommunicate as they will (II Cor. 2:7-9).

Executioner, commander of the bodyguard who executed the king's sentence. Potiphar (Gen. 37:36, marg.) was the "chief of the executioners." Nebuzaradan (Jer. 39:9, marg.) and Arioch (Dan. 2:14, marg.) held this office.

Exile usually refers to the period of time during which the Southern Kingdom (Judah) was forcibly detained in Babylon. It began with a series of deportations during the reigns of the Judaean kings, Jehoiakim (609-598 B.C.), Jehoiachin (598 B.C.), and Zedekiah (598-587 B.C.). After the destruction of Jerusalem by Nebuchadnezzar (587 B.C.) the kingdom of Judah ceased to exist as a political entity. Although there were settlements in Egypt, it was the exiles in Babylon who maintained the historic Jewish faith and provided the nucleus which returned to Judea subsequent to the Decree of Cyrus (536 B.C.). The Northern Kingdom (Israel) was earlier exiled to Assyria (722 B.C.). It was the policy of the Assyrian conquerors to move the populations of captured cities, with the result that Israelites were scattered in various parts of the empire, and other captives were brought to the region around Samaria (II Kings 17:24). Subsequent history knows these people as the Samaritans. Although men from the Northern Kingdom doubtless returned with the Judaean exiles, no organized return took place from the Assyrian captivity.

The exile worked great hardships on a people who were forcibly removed from their homeland and settled in new territory. The Babylonians permitted the Jews to congregate in their own settlements. One of these, known as Tel Abib, was the scene of Ezekiel's prophetic ministry. Tel Abib was located near Nippur on the River Chebar, also known as the Grand Canal. The Prophets Ezekiel and Daniel ministered in Babylon during the exile. Jeremiah, who had urged Zedekiah to make peace with Nebuchadnezzar, was permitted to remain in Judah after the destruction of Jerusalem. The murder of Gedaliah, appointed by Nebuchadnezzar as governor of Judah, precipitated a move on the part of the remaining Jews to migrate to Egypt. Although tradition suggests that he subsequently went to Babylon, Jeremiah's actual prophetic ministry ends among the Jews in Egypt.

Babylonian chronicle 4605-599 B.C. describing the removal of King Jehoiachin and other Jewish prisoners in Babylonia. BM

The sacred books of the Jews assumed great importance during the period of the exile. The law, which had been lost prior to Josiah's reign (II Kings 22:8), became the subject of careful study. By the time of the return from Babylon, the institution of the scribe was established. Scribes not only made copies of the law, but they also served as interpreters. Ezra is regarded as the first scribe (Neh. 8:1 ff).

Although the exile ended the political independence of Judaea, it served to emphasize the fact that God was in no sense confined to Palestine. He accompanied His people to Babylon and providentially cared for them there. In an idolatrous environment, the Jew stressed his monotheistic faith, having seen the errors of idolatry which brought on the exile. Although many Jews returned to their homeland following the decree of Cyrus, others remained in the Persian Empire with the result that Judaism became international in scope.

Exodus (ĕk′sō-dŭs, **a going out),** the event which terminated the sojourn of Israel in Egypt, the departure of Israel from Egypt under Moses.

The Biblical record (Exod. 13:17) states that Israel did not take the direct route through the Philistine country to Canaan. Had she done so

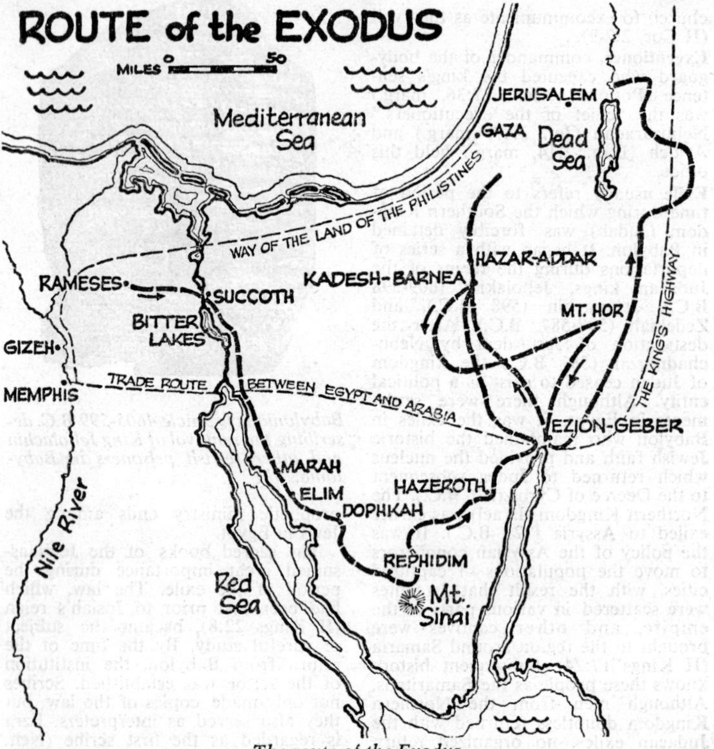

The route of the Exodus.

Israel would have had to pass the Egyptian wall (Biblical Shur) which protected the northeastern highways out of Egypt. This wall was guarded and could be passed only with great difficulty. If she successfully crossed the border, further opposition could be anticipated from the Philistines. The discipline of the wilderness was a part of God's preparation for His people before they were to come into open conflict with formidable foes. Leaving Rameses (Exod. 12:37), in the eastern delta, the Israelites journeyed southeastward to Succoth **(Tell el-Mashkutah).** They then moved on to Etham "in the edge of the wilderness" where they were conscious of God's guidance in the pillar of cloud and pillar of fire (Exod. 13: 21-22). The Exodus from Egypt was made possible by the direct intervention of God, who "caused the sea to go back by a strong east wind" (Exod. 14:21). Israel was thus able to cross from Egypt to the Sinai Peninsula. When the armies of Pharaoh attempted to pursue the Israelites, the Egyptians were destroyed by the waters which returned to their normal course.

The Bible states that 600,000 men took part in the Exodus (Exod. 12: 37). A year later the number of male Israelites over the age of 20 was 603,550 (Num. 1:46). During the years of Israel's sojourn in Egypt, the population multiplied to the point where Pharaoh was alarmed lest Israel side with an enemy in the event of war (Exod. 1:7-10). It was this very fear that brought about the oppression.

The Exodus period was one of the great epochs of Biblical miracles. The first nine plagues may have been related to the natural phenomena of

Egypt, but their timing and intensification were clearly supernatural. The last plague — the death of the firstborn — signaled the beginning of the Exodus. Israel ate the Passover meal in haste, ready to depart from Egypt. The opening of the Red Sea by the "strong east wind" was the means by which God brought His people out of Egypt into the wilderness where, for a period of 40 years, they were miraculously sustained.

Exodus, Book of, the second book of the Bible. The name is a transliteration of the Greek word meaning "a going out," referring to the departure of Israel from Egypt. The Hebrews called the book "and these are the names," which are the opening words of 1:1. The book may be conveniently divided into three main sections: **1. Israel in Egypt** (1:1 - 12:36), describing the multiplication of Israel and their sufferings; the birth, preparation, and commission of Moses; the ministry of Moses and Aaron to Israel and to Pharaoh; and the ten plagues upon the Egyptians, climaxed by the Passover and the death of the firstborn. **2. The Journey to Sinai** (12:37 - 19:2), which tells of the hasty flight of Israel from Egypt; the importance of the Passover and the consecration of the firstborn; the destruction of Pharaoh's army; the Song of Moses and Miriam; the waters of Marah; the miracle of the quails and the manna; the waters of Massah and Meribah; the war with Amalek; and the counsel of Jethro. **3. Israel at Sinai** (19:3 - 40:38) deals with Jehovah's manifestation at Mount Sinai: the Ten Commandments; the civil law; instructions for building the tabernacle and its furniture and for making the priests' garments; sacrifices for the consecration of Aaron and his sons; the episode of the golden calf; the renewing of the two tables; the shining of Moses' face; the construction of the tabernacle; and the filling of the tabernacle with the glory of Jehovah.

Whereas the Book of Genesis sets forth the origin of the nation of Israel, the Book of Exodus describes the process whereby God molded it into a full-grown theocratic nation, redeemed and set apart for His purposes in the earth. In this book is recorded the fulfillment of three great prophecies of Genesis: 1. that Israel would become a great nation in Egypt (Gen. 46:3); 2. that they would be afflicted there 400 years (Gen. 15:13); and 3. that God would finally judge Egypt and bring Israel out with great substance (Gen. 15:14). Joseph emphasized the hope of Exodus on his deathbed (Gen. 50:24-25), and during the centuries that followed, this promise must have served as "a more sure word of prophecy . . . a light that shineth in a dark place" (II Pet. 1:19).

Exorcism (ĕk'sôr-sĭzm, **to adjure),** the expelling of demons by means of magic charms, spells, and incantations. In Acts 19:13-16, the profane use of Jesus' name as a mere spell was punished by the demon's turning on the would-be exorcists. Christ, however, implies that some Jews actually cast out demons (Matt. 12:27), probably by demoniacal help; others, in the name of Jesus, without saving faith in Him (Matt. 7:22).

Expiation (ĕx'pĭ-ā'shŭn), the act or means of making amends or reparation for sin. The word is to be distinguished from its correlative term, "propitiation." From the Bible viewpoint sin is looked upon as a failure to meet obligations, a failure for which satisfaction must be provided. "Expiation" speaks of this satisfaction. See Propitiation.

Eye, the organ of sight. The literal sense is that which is most frequently found in the Scriptures, where the eye is recognized as among the most valued of the members of the body. Frequently "eye" speaks of spiritual perception and understanding. Thus the Word of God enlightens the eyes (Ps. 19:8). Growth in spiritual knowledge comes through the eyes of the understanding being enlightened (Eph. 1:18). Other expressions speak of the eye as indicative of character. The good man has a "bountiful eye (Prov. 22:9). High or lofty eyes (Ps. 131:1) describe the proud man. The envious man is one with an evil eye (Matt. 20:15).

Eyes, Painting of, to enhance the beauty of the feminine face (Jer. 4:30, marg.; Ezek. 23:40). Thus Jezebel "put her eyes in painting" (II Kings 9:30, marg.). To this day Oriental women paint the eyelids with antimony or **kohl** to make them look full and sparkling.

Eyesalve, a preparation compounded of various ingredients used either by simple application or by reduction to a powder to be smeared on the eye (Rev. 3:18).

Ezbai (ĕz'bā-ī), father of Naari, one

of David's valiant men (I Chron. 11: 37).

Ezbon (ĕz'bŏn). 1. One of the sons of Gad (Gen. 46:16). 2. Son of Bela, a son of Benjamin (I Chron. 7:7).

Ezekiel (ē-zēk'yĕl, **God strengthens**), a Hebrew prophet of the Exile. A play is made on this name in connection with the prophet's call (3:7, 8, 14). Of a priestly family (1:3), Ezekiel grew up in Judah during the last years of Hebrew independence and was deported to Babylon with Jehoiachin in 597 B.C., probably early in life. He was thus a younger contemporary of the Prophet Jeremiah and of Daniel, who, also as a young man was taken to Babylon in 605 B.C. Ezekiel lived with the Jewish exiles by the irrigation canal Chebar (1:1, 3; 3:15) which connected the Tigris River with the Euphrates above Babylon; Daniel carried out his quite different work in the Babylonian court. We know little more about Ezekiel, except that he was married (24:18).

Ezekiel was called to be a prophet in the fifth year of his captivity (1:1, 2); the last date mentioned is the 27th year (29:17); his ministry therefore lasted at least 22 years, from about 593-571 B.C.

When Jerusalem was finally destroyed, some ten years after he arrived in Babylon, Ezekiel entered into the sufferings of his people. On the day on which the final siege began, the prophet's wife became suddenly sick and died. In this he became a sign to the people and was not allowed to go through the customary period of mourning, doubtless to emphasize to them the greater sorrow now coming upon the nation.

Ezekiel was a powerful preacher. Possessing a deeply introspective and religious nature, he used allegory, vivid figures and symbolic actions to clothe his message. His favorite expression to denote the divine inspiration, "The hand of the Lord was upon me" (1:3; 3:14, 22, **et al**) shows how strongly he felt impelled to communicate the message given him.

The prophet's ministry was divided into two periods. The first ends with the siege of Jerusalem in 587 B.C. (24:1, 27). It was a message of approaching destruction for Jerusalem and of condemnation of her sin. The second period begins with the reception of the news of Jerusalem's fall, some two years later (33:21, 22). Now the prophet's message emphasized comfort and looked forward to the coming of the Kingdom of God. It would appear that during the two years between, Ezekiel ceased all public ministry.

Ezekiel, Book of. The book is divided into three parts: 1. Denunciation of Judah and Israel, 1-24, dated 593-588 B.C. 2. Oracles against foreign nations, 25-32, dated 587-571 B.C. 3. The future restoration of Israel, 33-48, dated 585-573 B.C.

The prophecies of the first section (1-24) were uttered before the fall of Jerusalem. Ezekiel's call to the prophetic work is described in chapters 1-3. Here occurs his vision of the divine glory — God's throne borne by an unearthly chariot of cherubim and wheels (1:4-21). The prophet eats the scroll upon which his sad message is written (2:8 - 3:3) and he is commanded to be the Lord's watchman, his own life to be forfeit if he does not cry the alarm (3:16-21; cf. 33:1-9). Ezekiel then predicts the destruction of Jerusalem by symbolic acts (4-7), such as laying siege to a replica of the city (4:1-8) and by rationing food and drink (4:9-17). Next follows the famous vision of Jerusalem's iniquity, for which Ezekiel is raptured in spirit to Jerusalem (8-11), and sees all kinds of loathsome idolatry being practiced in the temple courts. While he watches the desecration of the House of the Lord, he beholds the divine glory which had been manifested in the holy of holies (8:4) leave the temple and city (9:3; 10:4, 19; 11:22, 23) symbolizing God's abandonment of His apostate people. At that moment Ezekiel returns in spirit to Babylon. The rest of the first section (12-24) records symbolic actions and sermons of the prophet predicting the fall of Jerusalem. He enacts the departure into exile (12:1-7), preaches against false prophets (13) and in two deeply moving oracles (16, 23) depicts the ungrateful people's apostasy. His statement of the individual's responsibility before God (18) is famous. Finally he announces the beginning of the siege of Jerusalem, and in the evening of the same day his wife dies and he becomes dumb until the fall of the city (24).

After the prophecies of judgment against foreign nations (25-32) comes the climax of the prophet's vision, written after the fall of Jerusalem —

the restoration of Israel (33-48). God will bring back the people to their land, send the Son of David to reign over them, and give them a new heart (34, 36). The vision of the valley of dry bones (37) is a figurative statement of this regathering of the nation. Then follows Israel's defeat of the Gentile powers, Gog and Magog (38, 39). Finally a great restored temple is pictured (40-43), its holy services (44-46), the river of life running from it (47) and the people of Israel living in their places around the city called "The Lord is there" (48) to which the glory of the Lord has returned (43:2, 4, 5; 44:4).

Ezel (ē'zĕl, **departure**), stone marking the final meeting of David and Jonathan (I Sam. 20:19).

Ezem (ē'zĕm or Azem, **mighty**), a town near Edom assigned to Simeon (Josh. 15:29; 19:3; I Chron. 4:29).

Ezer (ē'zêr, **help**). 1. Horite chief (Gen. 36:21; I Chron. 1:38). 2. Descendent of Hur (I Chron. 4:4). 3. An Ephraimite slain by men of Gath (I Chron. 7:21). 4. Gadite warrior who joined David in Ziglag (I Chron. 12: 9). 5. Helped repair a section of the wall of Jerusalem (Neh. 3:19). 6. Levite singer (Neh. 12:42).

Ezion-Geber (ē'zĭ-ŏn-gē'bêr), a city near Elath on the Gulf of Aqabah. It was the last stopping place of the Israelites in their wilderness wanderings before Kadesh (Num. 33:35, 36). The city's period of greatest prosperity was in the time of Solomon, who there built a fleet of ships which sailed between Ezion-Geber and Ophir, a source of gold (I Kings 9:26ff; II Chron. 8:17, 18).

Eznite (ĕz'nīt), designation of Adino, one of David's chief captains (II Sam. 23:8).

Ezra (ĕz'rȧ, **help**). 1. A man of Judah (I Chron. 4:17). 2. Priest who returned from Babylon to Jerusalem with Zerubbabel (Neh. 12:1). 3. The famous Jewish priest and scribe who is the main character of the Book of Ezra and the co-worker of Nehemiah.

Ezra was a lineal descendant from Eleazar, the son of Aaron, the high priest, and from Seraiah, the chief priest put to death at Riblah by order of Nebuchadnezzar (II Kings 25:18-21). All that is really known of Ezra is what is told in Ezra 7-10 and Nehemiah 8-10.

In the seventh year of the reign of Artaxerxes Longimanus, king of Persia (458 B.C.), Ezra received permission from the king to return to Jerusalem to carry out a religious reform. Following the return from the Babylonian captivity, the temple had been rebuilt in 516 B.C., in spite of much powerful and vexatious opposition from the Samaritans; but after a brief period of religious zeal, the nation drifted into apostasy once more. Many of the Jews intermarried with their heathen neighbors (Mal. 2:11); the temple services and sacrifices were neglected (Mal. 1:6-14) and oppression and immorality were prevalent (Mal. 3:5). Just how Ezra acquired his influence over the king does not appear, but he received a royal edict granting him authority to carry out his purpose. Eighteen hundred Jews left Babylon with him. Four months later they reached the Holy City, having made a journey of 900 miles. The treasures were delivered into the custody of the Levites, burnt-offerings were offered to the Lord, the king's commissions were handed to the governors and viceroys, and help was given to the people and the ministers of the temple.

When he had discharged the various trusts committed to him, Ezra entered on his great work of reform. A divorce court, consisting of Ezra and some others, was set up to attend to the matter of the foreign wives; and after three months, in spite of some opposition, the work of the court was finished and the strange wives were put away.

The Book of Ezra ends with this important transaction, and nothing more is heard of Ezra till 13 years later, in the 20th year of Artaxerxes (446 B.C.), he appears again at Jerusalem, when Nehemiah, a Babylonian Jew and the favored cupbearer of Artaxerxes, returned to Jerusalem as governor of Palestine with the king's permission to repair the ruined walls of the city. It is uncertain whether Ezra remained in Jerusalem after he had effected the above-named reformation, or whether he had returned to the king of Persia and now came back with Nehemiah, or perhaps shortly after the arrival of the latter. Since he is not mentioned in Nehemiah's narrative till after the completion of the wall (Neh. 8:1), it is probable that Nehemiah sent for him to aid in his work. Under Nehemiah's government his functions were entirely of a priestly and ecclesiastical character. He read and interpreted the law of Moses before the assembled congregation during the eight days of the feast of Tabernacles, assisted at the dedication of the wall, and helped Nehemiah in bringing about a religious reformation. In all this he took a chief place. His name is repeatedly coupled with Nehemiah's, while the high priest is not mentioned as taking any part in the reformation at all. Ezra is not again mentioned after Nehemiah's departure for Babylon. It may be that he had himself returned to Babylon before that year.

According to Jewish tradition, Ezra is the author of the Book of Ezra and of I and II Chronicles. Many modern scholars hold that he wrote the Book of Nehemiah as well.

Ezra made a lasting impression upon the Jewish people. His influence shaped Jewish life and thought in a way from which they never altogether departed.

Ezra, Book of, so named because Ezra is the principal person mentioned in it; possibly also because he may be its author. It does not in its entirety claim to be the work of Ezra, but Jewish tradition says it is by him. Supporting this view is the fact that chs. 7-10 are written in the first person singular, while events in which he did not take part are described in the third person.

The Book of Ezra continues the narrative after Chronicles, and tells the story of the return from Babylon and the rebuilding of the temple. The purpose of the author is to show how God fulfilled His promise given through prophets to restore His exiled people to their own land through heathen monarchs, and raised up such great men as Zerubbabel, Haggai, Zechariah, and Ezra to rebuild the temple, re-establish the old forms of worship, and put a stop to compromise with heathenism. All material which does not contribute to his purpose he stringently excludes.

The period covered is from 536 B.C., when the Jews returned to Jerusalem, to 458 B.C., when Ezra came to Jerusalem to carry out his religious reforms. It thus covers a period of about 78 years, although the 15 years between 535 and 520 and the 58 years between 516 and 458 are practically a blank; so that we have a description of selected incidents, and not a continuous record of the period.

The Book of Ezra consists of two parts. The first (chs. 1-6) is a narrative of the return of the Jews from Babylonia under Zerubbabel and the restoration of worship in the rebuilt temple; while the second (7-10), tells the story of a second group of exiles returning with Ezra, and of Ezra's religious reforms.

Ezrahite (ĕz'rȧ-hīt, **designation**), of Ethan and Heman (I Kings 4:31; titles of Pss. 88, 89).

Ezri (ĕz'rī, **my help**), son of Chelub and overseer for David (**I Chron. 27:26**).

The Behistun Rock, northeast of Babylon, dated 516 B.C., engraved by order of Darius the Great, under whose authority the temple at Jerusalem was rebuilt, as recounted by Ezra. UMP

— F —

Fable, a narrative in which animals and inanimate objects of nature are made to act and speak as if they were human beings. The OT has two fables: Judges 9:7-15 and II Kings 14:9. In the NT "fable" is found as the translation of **múthos** ("myth") in I Timothy 1:4; 4:7; II Timothy 4:4; Titus 1:14; II Peter 1:16. In II Peter 1:16 it has the general meaning of **fiction,** that is, a story having no connection with reality.

Face, the word is used literally, figuratively and idiomatically. Often "my face" is nothing more than an oriental idiomatic way of saying "I." Sometimes it means **presence,** and sometimes **favor.** The averted face was the equivalent of disapproval or rejection (Pss. 13:1; 27:9). To spit in the face was an expression of contempt and aversion (Num. 12:14). To harden the face means to harden one's self against any sort of appeal (Prov. 21:29). Falling on the face symbolized prostration before man or God (Gen. 50:18). Setting the face signified determination (Luke 9:51). To cover the face expressed mourning (Exod. 3:6).

Fair, has the meaning of beautiful, attractive (Acts 7:20); unspotted (Zech. 3:5); persuasive (Prov. 7:21); making a fine display (Gal. 6:12); good (of weather) (Job 37:22). No reference to complexion.

Fair Havens, a small bay on the S coast of Crete, about 5 miles E of Cape Matala. Paul stayed there for a time on his way to Rome (Acts 27:8-12).

Fairs, a word found in KJV only in Ezekiel (27:12, 14, 16, 19, 27). The RV more accurately renders it "wares," the commodities bartered in Oriental markets.

Faith, has both an active and a passive sense; in the former, meaning "fidelity," "trustworthiness"; in the latter, "trust," "reliance." An example of the first is found in Romans 3:3, where "the faith of God" means His fidelity to promise. In the overwhelming majority of cases it has the meaning of reliance and trust.

In the OT (KJV) the word "faith" occurs only twice (Deut. 32:20; Hab. 2:4), and even the verb form, "to believe," is far from common, appearing less than 30 times. What we find in the OT is not so much a doctrine of faith, as examples of it.

In contrast with the extreme rarity with which the terms "faith" and "believe" are used in the OT, they occur with great frequency in the NT — almost 500 times. A principal reason for this is that the NT makes the claim that the promised Messiah had finally come, and, to the bewilderment of many, the form of the fulfillment did not obviously correspond to the Messianic promise. It required a real act of faith to believe that Jesus of Nazareth was the promised Messiah. It was not long before "to believe" meant to become a Christian. In the NT, faith therefore becomes supreme of all human acts and experiences.

It is in Paul's epistles that the meaning of faith is most clearly and fully set forth. Faith is trust in the person of Jesus, the truth of His teaching, and the redemptive work He accomplished at Calvary. Faith is not to be confused with a mere intellectual assent to the doctrinal teachings of Christianity, though that is obviously necessary. It includes a radical and total commitment to Him as the Lord of one's life.

Unbelief, or lack of faith in the Christian Gospel, appears everywhere in the NT as the supreme evil. Not to make a decisive response to God's offer in Christ means that the individual remains in his sin and is eternally lost. Faith alone can save him.

Faithfulness, an attribute both of God and man, implying loyalty, constancy, and freedom from arbitrariness or fickleness (II Cor. 1:18; Gal. 5:22; II Tim. 2:2).

Falcon (See Birds)

Fall, The. The fall of man as related in Genesis 3 is a historical fact, not a myth. It stands in a context of historical facts. Though not alluded to again in the OT, it is regarded as historical in the Apocrypha (Wis. 2:24) and in the NT (Rom. 5:12 f.; I Cor. 15:22). Some philosophers and theologians think the story is an allegory describing the awakening of man from a brute state of self-consciousness and personality — a fall upward, rather than downward, but such an explanation conflicts radically with Biblical teaching. There is no doubt that Paul takes the story literally and sees in the fall the origin of sin in the human race. The Scriptural view of sin and of redemption takes the fall for granted.

The effect of the fall, as the rest of the Bible explicity and implicitly brings out, was not merely immediate alienation from God for Adam and Eve, but guilt and depravity for all their posterity and the cursing of the earth.

Redemption from the effects of the fall is accomplished through the second man Adam, Jesus Christ (Rom. 5: 12-21; I Cor. 15:21, 22, 25-49).

Fallow Deer (See Animals)

Fallow Ground (untilled), is used in the sense of untilled ground (Jer. 4:3; Hos. 10:12).

False Christs. Jesus warned His disciples that false Christs and false prophets would arise and that they would with great signs and wonders try to lead astray even the elect (Matt. 24:5, 11; 23:25; Mark 13:6, 21-23; Luke 21:8).

False Prophet, The, is referred to only in the book of Revelation (16:13; 19:20; 20:10), but is usually identified with the two-horned beast of Revelation 13:1-18. In Revelation 16:13 we are told that three unclean spirits like frogs came out of the mouths of the dragon, beast, and false prophet. In Revelation 19:20 the beast (apparently the one with seven heads) and the false prophet, who is described as having performed deceiving miracles and killed those who refused to worship the image of the beast, are cast into a lake burning with brimstone (Rev. 20:10). Christian opinion is divided upon the interpretation of the two-horned beast.

Familiar Spirit. Generally used to refer to the spirit of a dead person which professed mediums claimed they could summon for consultation (Deut. 18:11). The word "familiar" has the sense of the Latin **familiaris,** belonging to one's family, and hence ready to serve one as a servant. Such a spirit was thought to be able to reveal the future (Isa. 8:9; I Sam. 28: 7). Israelites were forbidden to consult familiar spirits (Lev. 19:31; Isa. 8:19). This was regarded as apostasy so serious that those who consulted them were put to death (Lev. 20:6). Saul put away mediums early in his reign, but consulted the witch of Endor, who "had a familiar spirit," when he became apostate just before his death (I Sam. 28:3-25; 1 Chron. 10:13).

Family. The concept of the family in the Bible differs from the modern institution. The Hebrew family was larger than families today, including the father of the household, his parents, if living, his wife or wives and children, his daughters and sons-in-law, slaves, guests and foreigners under his protection. Marriage was arranged by the father of the groom and the family of the bride, for whom a dowry, or purchase money was paid to her father (Gen. 24). Polygamy and concubinage were practiced, though not favored by God. The husband could divorce the wife, but she could not divorce him.

The father of a family had the power of life and death over his children. To dishonor a parent was punishable by death (Exod. 21:15, 17). The NT concept followed that of the OT. Parents and children, husbands and wives, masters and slaves were enjoined to live together in harmony and love (Eph. 5:22 - 6:9).

Famine (hunger, want of food). In ancient times, in Palestine and Egypt, famines were frequent, produced by (1) want of rainfall in due season, (2) destructive hail storms and rain out of season, (3) destruction of crops by locusts and caterpillars, and (4) the cutting off of food supplies by a siege. Famines are sometimes said to be sent as punishments, and sometimes they are threatened as such (Lev. 26:19 f; Deut. 28:49-51; II Kings 8:1; Isa. 14: 30; 51:19; Jer. 14:12, 15; Ezek. 5:16). A special mark of God's favor and power is to be preserved in time of famine (Job. 5:20; Pss. 33:19; 37:19). Sometimes the word "famine" is used in a figurative sense, as when Amos says that God will send a famine "of hearing the words of the Lord" (Amos 8:11).

Fan, a fork with two or more prongs used to throw grain into the air after it had been threshed, so that the chaff might be blown away.

Farming. Was the chief occupation of Israel after the conquest of Canaan. Agriculture was the background for all the legislation of Israel. At the time of the conquest every family probably received a piece of land, marked off by stones that could not be removed lawfully (Deut. 19:14; 27:17; Hos. 5: 10). The soil of Palestine was generally fertile. Fertilizing was almost unknown. To maintain the fertility of the land, the law required that farms, vineyards, and olive orchards were to

Palestine peasant plowing with primitive plough, in a field before the Hill of Samaria. © *MPS*

Winnowing on the threshing floor. © *MPS*

Traditional method of sowing seed. © *SPF*

lie fallow in the seventh year (Exod. 23:10). On the year of jubilee those who had lost their ancestral estates recovered possession of them. Terracing was necessary to make use of soil on the hillsides. Irrigation was not required, since there was usually sufficient rainfall.

Plowing to prepare the land for sowing was done in autumn, when the early rains softened the ground that had become stone-hard in the summer sun. This was done with a crude wooden plough drawn by oxen; or, if the soil was thin, with a mattock. With such implements the surface of the ground was hardly more than scratched — perhaps three or four inches. Little harrowing was done, and was probably unknown in Palestine in early times.

The summer grain was sown between the end of January and the end of February. Usually the seed was scattered broadcast from a basket, but careful farmers put it in furrows in rows (Isa. 28:25). The time of harvest varied somewhat according to the climatic condition of each region, but usually began about the middle of April with the coming of the dry season. The grain was threshed in the open air, a custom made possible because the harvest season was free from rain (I Sam. 21:16 ff.). During the threshing-time the grain was guarded by harvesters who spent the nights upon the threshing floor (Ruth 3:6). The threshing floor was constructed in an exposed position in the fields, preferably on a slight elevation, so as to get the full benefit of the winds.

Of the large number of crops the Israelites cultivated, wheat and barley were the most important. Among other crops they raised were rye, mulet, flax and a variety of vegetables. See also Agriculture.

Farthing (See Money)

Fasting or abstinence from food and drink for a longer or shorter period, is frequently mentioned in the Scriptures. The only fast required was that of the Day of Atonement. Before the Babylonian Captivity it was the one regular fast (Lev. 16:29, 31; 23:27-32; Num. 29:7; Jer. 36:6). During this period there are many examples of fasts on special occasions, held because of transgression or to ward off present or impending calamity. Samuel called for such a fast (I Sam. 7:6). We read of individuals who were moved to fast — for example, David, when his child became ill (II Sam. 12:16, 21-23).

Religious fasting was observed as a sign of mourning for sin. The prophets often condemn the abuse of the custom, for Israelites superstitiously thought that it had value even when dissevered from purity and righteousness of life (Isa. 58:3-7; Jer. 14:10-12; Zech. 7, 8). Fasts were not necessarily religious in nature. They were commonplace when someone near and dear died, as when the inhabitants of Jabesh fasted after they had buried Saul and Jonathan (I Sam. 31:13).

There are few references to fasting in the Gospels, but what is said shows that frequent fasts were customary with those Jews who desired to lead a specially religious life. We are told that Anna "served God with fastings and prayers night and day" (Luke 2:37). Again, the Pharisee in the parable says, "I fast twice in the week" (Luke 18:12). Jesus fasted for forty days in the wilderness.

There are in the NT only four indisputable references to voluntary fasting for religious purposes, two by our Lord in the Gospels, and two in the Acts of the Apostles. Jesus does not disapprove of the practice, but says nothing to commend it. The apostolic church practiced it, but perhaps only as a carry-over from Judaism, since most of the early disciples were Jews.

Fat. 1. The layer of fat around the kidneys and other viscera, which, like the blood, was forbidden by the Mosaic law to be used for food, but was burned as an offering to Jehovah, for a sweet savor unto Him (Lev. 4:31) to teach the Israelite that his best belonged to God. Long before the Mosaic law was given, Abel brought the fat of the firstlings of his flock to Jehovah; and we read that the Lord had respect unto Abel and to his offering. (Gen. 4:4). 2. Sometimes used in the KJV to refer to a wine vat (Joel 2:24; Isa. 63:2).

Father, has various meanings in the Bible: 1. Immediate male progenitor (Gen. 42:13). In the Hebrew family the father had absolute rights over his children. He could sell them into slavery and have them put to death; 2. An ancestor, immediate or remote. Abraham is called Jacob's father (Gen. 28:13), and God tells him he will be the "father of many nations" (Gen. 17:4); 3. A spiritual ancestor, whether good or bad, as Abraham, "the father of all them that believe" (Rom. 4:11); and the devil, "Ye are of your father the devil" (John 8:44); 4. The originator of a mode of life ("Jabal: he was the father of such as dwell in tents, and of such as have cattle" — Gen. 4:20); 5. One who exhibits paternal kindness to another: "be unto me a father and a priest" (Judg. 17:10); 6. A revered superior (I Sam. 10:12; I John 2:13); 7. Royal advisors and prime ministers: "God hath made me a father to Pharaoh" (Gen. 45:8); 8. Early Christians who have died: "since the fathers fell asleep" (II Peter 3:4); 9. A source: "Hath the rain a father?" (Job 38:28); 10. God is Father: as Creator of the universe, "the Father of lights" (James 1:17); as Creator of the human race."

Fathom (See Weights and Measures)

Fatling. A clean animal (calf, lamb, kid, etc.) fattened for offering to God. See Psalm 66:15, II Samuel 6:13, etc.

Fear. May be either that apprehension of evil which normally leads one either to flee or to fight or that awe and reverence which a man of sense feels in the presence of God, and to a less extent in the presence of a king or other dread authority. For the two senses in the OT, contrast Psalm 31:13, "fear was upon every side," with Proverbs 9:10, "the fear of the Lord is the beginning of wisdom."

Feasts were the sacred festivals of Judaism which were occasions of public worship. There were seven in all. The Passover, or Feast of Unleavened Bread was established before the giving of the Law to celebrate the Exodus from Egypt. It began on the 14th day of Nisan, and continued for a week (Lev. 23:5-8). Attendance was required of all male Jews (Deut. 16: 16).

The Feast of Pentecost or Feast of Weeks was celebrated fifty days after

A Samaritan chief priest exposing the Scroll of the Law before the congregation on Mt. Gerizim, during the Passover celebration. © *MPS*

the Passover. The feast lasted one day, and marked the completion of the wheat harvest, at which two loaves of bread made from the new grain were offered to God (Deut. 16:9-12).

The Feast of Trumpets or New Moon was held on the first day of the seventh month (October), and began the civil year of the Jews (Lev. 23:23).

The Day of Atonement was observed ten days later as a day of national penitence and mourning. The high priest confessed the sins of the community, and entered into the Most Holy Place with the blood of the offering to make atonement for the people (Lev. 23:26-32).

The Feast of Tabernacles was the last of the feasts prescribed by the Law. It began five days after the Day of Atonement (Lev. 23:34; Deut. 16: 13), and lasted eight days. It commemorated the entrance into the Promised Land after the wandering in the wilderness.

The Feast of Lights originated with the cleansing of the Temple under the Maccabees, and was observed for eight days beginning with the 25th day of Kislev (December).

The Feast of Purim was a memorial to the deliverance of the Jews by Esther from the plot of Haman (Esther 9:1-10).

Felix was the Roman procurator of Judea from A.D. 52 to 60, under whose administration Paul was imprisoned (Acts 23:24-24:27). Tacitus said of him that "he revelled in cruelty and lust, and wielded the power of a king with the mind of a slave." He began his career as procurator of Judea by seducing Drusilla, the sister of Agrippa II, and wife of the king of Emesa (modern Homs), and marrying her. Because she was Jewish (at least on one side) he learned much of Jewish life and customs. Felix appears in the Biblical account only in Acts 23:24-25:14. He was susceptible to flattery, as the speech of Tertullus shows, and also to conviction of sin, as is shown by his terror when Paul reasoned before him of "righteousness, temperance and judgment to come." His conviction faded; he procrastinated; and then held Paul for about two years (c. 58-60), hoping that Paul would buy his freedom. He was then replaced by Festus, a far better man.

Felloes (fĕl′oz), the exterior parts of the rim of a wheel which unite the outer ends of the spokes (I Kings 7: 33).

Fellow, a contemptuous name for an unnamed person (Judg. 18:25), or a friend or equal (Heb. 1:9).

Fellowship (that which is in common). 1. Partnership or union with others in the bonds of a business partnership, a social or fraternal organization. 2. Membership in a local Christian church or in **the** Church (Acts 2:42). 3. Partnership in the support of the Gospel and in the charitable work of the Church (II Cor. 8:4). 4. That love which fills (or should fill) the hearts of believers one for another and for God.

Fenced City. All of the six Hebrew words which are used for fenced cities are from the one root, **batsar,** which means to **restrain, withhold,** or **to make inaccessible.** Owing to the usual insecurity in the East, most of the towns and even many of the small villages are enclosed in walls. Figuratively, the word is used to show God's protection of Jeremiah — "I will make thee unto this people a fenced brazen wall . . . for I am with thee to save thee and to deliver thee, saith the Lord" (Jer. 15:20).

Fertile Crescent. A modern description of the territory which may roughly be described as reaching NW from the Persian Gulf through Mesopotamia, then W to the N of Syria, then SW through Syria and Palestine. In this crescent the land is mostly rich and fertile, and is watered by the Tigris, the Euphrates, the Orontes and the Jordan, besides numerous rivers descending the west side of Lebanon, and in most of the region irrigation has long been employed.

Festivals (See Feasts)

Festus, Porcius (festal, joyful), the Roman governor who succeeded Felix in the province of Judea (Acts 24:27). Of the life of Festus before his appointment of Nero as procurator of Judea almost nothing is known, and he appears in the Bible (Acts 24:27-26:32) principally in his relationship with the apostle Paul, whom he sent to Rome. Festus was apparently a far better and more efficient man than his predecessor. Festus evidently knew that Paul was a good man (Acts 25: 25), but he was unable to understand Paul's reasoning with King Agrippa, and thought that Paul had gone mad with much study (Acts 26:24). Festus died at his post, and was followed, c. A.D. 62, by Albinus.

Fetters, bonds, chains or shackles, generally for the feet of prisoners and made of brass or of iron (Judg. 16:21; Pss. 105:18; 149:8).

Fever (See Diseases)

Field. The Biblical "field" was generally not enclosed, but was marked off from its neighbors by stone markers. Because they were unenclosed, and because of the usually unsettled condition, a watchman was ordinarily employed. The word is used also in a larger sense for "territory," as in Genesis 36:35, where "the field of Moab" is any place in Moabite territory; and as in the parable of the tares (Matt. 13:38), where "the field is the world."

Fig (See Plants)

Fillets (Ex. 27:10, 11 and 38:10-19) were the rods between the columns that supported the hangings of the Tabernacle. In Jeremiah 52:21 the word means a cord for measuring.

Fining-Pot is the crucible in which silver or gold is melted to be purified from dross (Prov. 17:3; 27:21).

Fir (See Plants)

Fire. An emblem of the presence of God (Ezek. 1:27) and a means of judgment (Gen. 19:24). The offerings of the Tabernacle were consumed by fire (Lev. 9:24); "strange fire" was forbidden (10:1, 2). Fire was used for cooking (John 21:9), for warmth (18: 18), and for the disposal of rubbish (15:6). Fire was an emblem of testing (I Cor. 3:12-15) and of judgment (Rev. 1:14).

Firebrand, from three Hebrew words: (1) a stick for stirring fire (Isa. 7:4; Amos 4:11), (2) brands, sparks (Prov. 26:18), and (3) a torch, as in Judges 15:4 and Judges 7:16. Job 12:5 has the same word, meaning a lamp that is burnt out.

Firepan, a vessel used for carrying live coals, as in Exodus 27:3. The Hebrew word is rendered "censer" 15 times, as in Leviticus 10:1, and "snuff dish" three times, as in Exodus 25:38.

Firkin (See Weights and Measures)

Firmament, the expanse of sky surrounding the earth, made to divide the waters from the waters (Gen. 1:6). The Hebrew word **(raqia)** does not denote a solid substance, but thinness or expanse.

First-Begotten, a term applied to the Lord Jesus Christ in Hebrews 1:6 and in Revelation 1:5.

Firstborn. The Hebrew word is used chiefly of men, but is used also of animals (Exod. 11:5). Because the firstborn of the Israelites were preserved at the time of the first Passover, every firstborn male of man and beast became consecrated to Jehovah (Exod. 13:2; 34:19). The beasts were sacrificed, while the men were redeemed (Exod. 13:13, 15; 34:20; cf. Lev. 27:6).

Among the Israelites the firstborn son succeeded his father as the head of the house and received as his share of the inheritance a double portion.

First Day of the Week (See Sunday)

First Fruits, that portion of the fruits that ripened first, these being looked upon as an earnest of the coming harvest. The offering of the first fruits was made both on behalf of the nation (Lev. 23:10, 17) and by individuals (Exod. 23:19; Deut. 26:1-11). These first fruits went for the support of the priesthood.

Fish (See Animals)

Fish Gate, an ancient gate on the E side of the wall of Jerusalem, where in the days of Nehemiah, men of Tyre congregated to sell fish and various wares on the sabbath (II Chron. 33:14; Neh. 13:16).

Fishing (See Occupations and Professions)

Fishhook, a metal hook used to catch fish as is done today, but also to keep them, at least for a time (cf. Amos 4:2 with Job 41:1, 2). Peter generally used a net, but see Matthew 17:27, where the Lord told him to cast a hook.

Fish Pool (See Song of Solomon 7:4).

Fitch (See Plants)

Flag See Plants)

Flagon, a large container for wine (Isa. 22:24), elsewhere "bottle." In II Samuel 6:19 and other places in KJV word should be "cakes of raisins" as in ASV.

Flax (See Plants)

Fleas (See Insects)

Fleece, the shorn wool of a sheep. The first of the shearing was to be given to the priesthood (Deut. 18:4). Gideon's experience (Judg. 6:37-40) has given rise to the custom of "putting out a fleece" in seeking God's guidance.

Flesh 1. Literally, the soft part of the bodies of men and animals. 2. All animals, as in Gen. 6:19. 3. Mankind in general, as in Numbers 16:22, "the God of the spirits of all flesh." 4. Our ordinary human constitution as opposed to our mental and moral qualities as in Matthew 26:41, "the spirit indeed is willing but the flesh is weak." 5. Human nature deprived of the Spirit of God and dominated by sin (Rom. 7:14; I Cor. 3:1, 3; Col. 2:18; I John 2:16).

Flesh-Hook, a metal implement with one or more teeth, used for handling large pieces of flesh, especially around the sacrificial altar (Exod. 27:3; 38:3; I Chron. 28:17; I Sam. 2:13, 14).

Flies (See Insects)

Flint (See Minerals)

Flock, a collection of sheep under the care of a shepherd, sometimes including goats as well (Gen. 27:9). Figuratively both Israel and the Church are counted as flocks, and God is the Good Shepherd (Isa. 40:11; Matt. 26:31; Luke 12:32; I Pet. 5:2, 3).

Flood, Deluge. The Noahic Flood has been a subject for discussion among scientists and theologians for many centuries. As a result, many interpretations of the meaning and physical characteristics of the Flood have been suggested, modified, abandoned, and sometimes reproposed. The reality of the Flood can hardly be questioned, however, because of the many references to it in both the Old and New Testament. Among these are chapters 6, 7, and 8 of Genesis, Genesis 9:11, 28; 10:1, 32; Matt. 24:38, 39; Luke 17:27; II Peter 2:5.

An important aspect of the deluge is that God preserved some men, for Noah and his family were saved from destruction by going into an ark which Noah made according to God's specifications, and in which he gathered animals and birds preserved to replenish the earth.

It is apparent from Gen. 6:5-7 and other passages such as II Peter 2:5, 6 that the Flood was brought upon the earth as a judgment on the sins of the people. Man had become so sinful that "it repented the Lord that He had

A pre-flood tablet, with pictographic inscriptions, found under the flood deposit at Kish in Babylonia. BM

made man on the earth" (Gen. 6:6 KJV). In Scripture the reference to the Flood is linked with the judgment at the second coming of the Lord (Matt. 24:39). It is also mentioned in relation to the destruction of Sodom and Gomorrah (Luke 17:27-29; II Peter 2:5, 6).

Despite all attempts at scientific explanation of the minute details of the Flood, there seems to be no doubt that God worked a miracle in causing the Flood. In II Peter 3:5, 6, the Flood is compared with the creation of the world and is a miracle of the same order. In the same passage, II Peter 3:7ff, the final destruction of the world is given the same miraculous explanation as the Noahic Flood.

The length of the Flood is generally agreed upon within a few days. The Hebrews used a solar calendar in contrast to the Babylonian lunar month and the Egyptian arbitrary 365 day year. Most authorities would put the number of days from the time the rain started (Gen. 7:11) to the time Noah left the ark (Gen. 8:14) between 371 and 376 days.

One of the great differences of opinion in describing the Flood concerns its extent. Traditionally most Biblical interpreters considered the submergence to be universal; that is, that it covered the entire globe including the highest mountains. The reasons proposed to defend this viewpoint include the fact that in the Genesis account universal terms are used (Gen. 7:19, 21). It has been pointed out that if the Flood were local there would be no need for an ark to preserve Noah, for God could have directed him to move with the animals to an area that was not to be submerged. The fact that many civilizations have flood traditions has been cited as evidence for a universal flood. The same evidence could be used to argue for a local flood because the accounts of floods in other parts of the world are less like the Hebrew tradition than those of the Assyrians and Babylonians who lived in the same areas as the Hebrews.

Today many conservative scholars defend a local flood. The crux of their argument seems to center in the covenant relation of God to man. He deals with certain groups, such as the children of Israel. The reasoning in regard to Noah is that Noah was not a preacher of righteousness to peoples of other areas but was concerned with the culture from which Abraham eventually came. Physical arguments have also been raised against a universal flood. It seems, therefore, that a person can advocate either a local or a universal concept of the Flood and find evidence to support his view.

Tabulated Chronology of the Flood. 1. The making of the ark (Gen. 6:14). 2. Collection of the animals (Gen. 7:9). 3. Fountains of the great deep were broken up and the windows of heaven were opened. 4. Rain (Gen. 7:12). 5. All the high hills covered (Gen. 7:19). 6. Water prevailed upon the earth (Gen. 7:24). 7. Water returned from off the earth (Gen. 8:3). 8. Ark rested upon the mountains of Ararat (Gen. 8:4). 9. Waters decreased (Gen. 8:4). 10. Tops of mountains seen (Gen. 8:5). 11. Noah waited (Gen. 8:6). 12. Noah sent forth raven and a dove; dove returned (Gen. 8:7-9). 13. Noah waited (Gen. 8:10). 14. Noah sent forth dove again (Gen. 8:10); dove returned with olive branch (Gen. 8:11). 15. Noah waited (Gen. 8:12). 16. Noah sent forth dove which did not return (Gen. 8:12). 17. Noah removed covering; face of the ground was dry (Gen. 8:13). 18. Earth dried; Noah left ark (Gen. 8:14).

Flour, fine-crushed and sifted grain, generally wheat or rye or barley (Judg. 6:19). Eastern flour was not quite as fine or as white as ours, and as a result, the bread was more wholesome. The "meat" offerings, were of flour. "Meat" here should be "meal." (Cf. Lev. 6:15 in KJV and ASV.)

Flower (See Plants)

Flute (See Music)

Fly (See Insects)

Foal (See Animals)

Fodder, the mixed food of cattle, generally from several kinds of grain sown together (Job 6:5; Job 24:6 "corn" in ASV; Isa. 30:24).

Food. Various kinds of food were used in Bible times. The staple of diet was bread made from wheat, barley, or rye. Vegetables such as beans, lentils,

Cooking in a peasant home (cf. Psalm 58:9). © MPS

The ford of the Jabbok River, near where Jacob wrestled with the angel.
© MPS

onions, cucumbers, and gourds were eaten freely. Fruits abounded; grapes, melons, figs, pomegranates are mentioned frequently (Deut. 23:24; Num. 13:23). Fish and meat were included in the Jewish diet with certain restrictions: beef and lamb or goat were "clean," camel, rabbit, and pork were forbidden, together with shellfish and eels, carnivorous birds, and reptiles of all kinds. Insects were forbidden, except for certain types of grasshoppers or locusts (Lev. 11:1-45). Honey, spices and salt were included in daily diet. Milk and cheese were the chief dairy products (Deut. 32:14; I Sam. 17:18).

Fool, in modern usage, a dolt or a simpleton, but in Scripture generally impiety or lack of moral good sense is implied as well. "The fool hath said in his heart, There is no God" (Pss. 14:1; 53:1). Solomon in his writings, Proverbs and Ecclesiastes, makes about 80 statements about fools. The Lord called the scribes and Pharisees fools; not implying intellectual stupidity, but spiritual blindness (Matt. 23:17).

Foot, the part of the body on which men and animals walk, or that part of furniture on which it stands. The base of the laver is several times called its foot (Exod. 30:18; 35:16, etc). To humiliate an enemy utterly, one sometimes put his foot upon the captives' necks as Joshua's captains did (Josh. 10:24).

Footman. A member of the infantry or a runner, a messenger, one of the king's bodyguards (I Sam. 22:17).

Footstool, a word is used in Scripture both literally (II Chron. 9:18; James 2:3) and figuratively: of the earth (Isa. 66:1; Matt. 5:35), of the Temple (Lam. 2:1), of the ark (Ps. 99:5), and of subjection, especially of heathen enemies by the Messianic king (Ps. 110:1; Matt. 22:44; Acts 2:35).

Ford, a shallow place in a stream where men and animals can cross on foot (Gen. 32:22; Isa. 16:2). The Jordan, a strong and rapid stream, has few fording places. When Israel crossed, God miraculously stopped the waters upstream by a landslide. John the Baptist baptized at Bethabara

(John 1:28 KJV), which name indicates that a ford was there. Joshua's spies (Josh. 2:7) evidently forded the Jordan, and Ehud (Judg. 3:28) took the same place to prevent Moabites from crossing there. Jephthah (Judg. 12:5, 6) made his famous "Shibboleth test" at a ford of the Jordan.

Forehead, the part of the face above the eyes, often revealing the character of the person: shamelessness (Jer. 3:3), courage (Ezek. 3:9), or godliness (Rev. 7:3).

Foreigner (sojourner, stranger). Among the Jewish people, anyone outside the nation was regarded as inferior (Gen. 31:15), and possessed restricted rights. He could not eat the Passover (Exod. 12:43), enter the sanctuary (Ezek. 44: 9), become king (Deut. 17:15), or intermarry on equal terms (Exod. 34:12-16). They could be included in the nation by accepting the Law and its requirements. In the NT the word is applied to those who are not members of God's kingdom (Eph. 2:19).

Foreknowledge (See Election)

Foreordination (See Election)

Forerunner. John the Baptist was the forerunner, the advance agent, of our Lord (Isa. 40:3; Luke 3:4-6). The word "forerunner" is used of Jesus, who has preceded us into the visible presence of God to insure our personal access to God (Heb. 6:20).

Foreskin, the fold of skin cut off in the operation of circumcision. In Deuteronomy 10:16 the word is used figuratively meaning submission to God's law. In Habakkuk 2:16 it refers to the indecent exhibitionism of a drunken man.

Forest. In ancient times, most of the hills of Palestine were covered with trees. The forest of Lebanon yielded the cedar and fir lumber which Hiram of Tyre sold to Solomon (I Kings 5: 8-10).

Forgiveness is the giving up of resentment or claim to requital on account of an offense. The offense may be a deprivation of a person's property, rights, or honor; or it may be a violation of moral law. Forgiveness is conditioned on repentance and the willingness to make reparation, or atonement; and the effect of forgiveness is the restoration of both parties to the former state of relationship. The ground of forgiveness by God of man's sins is the atoning death of Christ. Christ's atonement was retroactive in its effect (Heb. 11:40). God's forgiveness seems, however, to be limited. Christ speaks of the unpardonable sin (Matt. 12:31, 32), and John speaks of the sin unto death (I John 5:16). The deity of Christ is evidenced by His claim to the power to forgive sins (Mark 2:7; Luke 5:21; 7:49).

Fork, probably the ancient type of our modern pitchfork (I Sam. 13:21).

Fornication, unlawful sexual intercourse of an unwed person (I Cor. 6: 9, 18). It was commonly associated with heathen worship (Jer. 2:20; 3:6), and was used as a figure of disloyalty to God (Ezek. 16:3-22).

Fort, Fortress. Every city in ancient times was fortified by a wall and its citadel. The KJV often speaks of such cities as "fenced," and other terms are also used by the KJV and the RV. Jerusalem was so well fortified that it was not until the time of David that the city was captured from the Jebusites. Usually a city was built on a hill, and the fortifications followed the natural contour of the hill. The walls were built of brick and stone, many feet thick.

Fortunatus (fôr-tū-nā'tŭs, **blessed, fortunate**), a Corinthian Christian who came with two others to bring gifts to Paul when he was about to leave Ephesus in A.D. 59 (I Cor. 16:17).

Forum Appii, (Acts 28:15), "The Market of Appius," a place 43 miles SE of Rome, where Paul was met by friends.

Foundation, the footing or wall on which a building is erected. Used figuratively of the foundation of faith (I Cor. 3:10, 11) or of the church (Eph. 2:20).

Fountain, a spring of water issuing from the earth, of great importance in a land like Palestine. The word is used both literally and figuratively, both pleasantly and unpleasantly. Figuratively, it refers to the source of hemorrhages (Lev. 20:18; Mark 5:29). In Proverbs, compare "a troubled fountain and a corrupt spring" (25:26) with "a fountain of life" (13:14; 14: 27). In the Bridegroom's praise of his pure bride (S. of Sol. 4:12, 15) she is first "a fountain sealed" then "a fountain of gardens." In the curse of Ephraim (Hos. 13:15), "his fountain shall be dried up" as a terrible punishment; but on the pleasant side, David speaks (Ps. 36:9) of "the fountain of life" as being with the Lord. In the Lord's conversation with the woman at the well (John 4:14), He told

The Virgin's Fountain at Nazareth. © *MPS*

her of "a well of water springing up into everlasting life."

Fountain Gate, the gate at the SE corner of the walls of ancient Jerusalem (Neh. 2:14; 3:15; 12:37).

Fowl (See Birds)

Fowler, a bird-catcher who caught their prey by trickery. Used to describe those who try to ensnare the unwary and bring them to ruin (Pss. 91:3; 124:7; Hos. 9:8).

Fox (See Animals)

Frankincense, a resin obtained from certain trees of the **Boswellia** genus and the family of balsams. Has been used as a perfume, as a medicine, and by Egyptains and Hebrews in their religious rites. It is spoken of as coming from Arabia (Isa. 60:6; Jer. 6:20) and perhaps from Palestine (S. of Sol. 4:6, 14). Soon after the birth of Jesus, the wise men presented to Him gifts of gold, of frankincense and myrrh (Matt. 2:11, 15). See Plants.

Freeman, refers to a slave who has received his freedom, although in I Cor. 7:22 the reference is to one who has received spiritual freedom from the Lord. In Gal. 4:22, 23, 30 and Rev. 6:15 it means a free man as opposed to a slave.

Freewill Offering (See Offerings)

Fret 1. To fret is to be vexed, chafed, irritated, or to be angry; and the godly man is not to fret himself (Ps. 37:1, 7, 8). 2. A painful type of leprosy (Lev. 13:51, 52).

Fringe, the tassel of twisted cords fastened to the outer garments of Israelites to remind them of their obligations as Israelites to be loyal to Jehovah (Num. 15:38, 39; Deut. 22:12).

Frog (See Plagues)

Frontlet (to bind), anything bound on the forehead, particularly phylacteries, which were worn on the forehead and on the arms. Phylacteries were prayer bands which were put in small leather cases and fastened to the forehead and the left arm, worn by all male Jews during the time of morning prayer, except on the sabbath and festivals.

Frost, usual in winter on the hills and high plains in Bible lands. Frost is an evidence of God's power (Job 37:10; 38:29).

Fruit. The fruits most often mentioned in Scripture are the grape, pomegranate, fig, olive, apple. The word "fruit" is often used metaphorically: (Deut. 7:13; cf. 28:11; Prov. 1:31; John 4:36 etc.). The fruit of the Holy Spirit consists of all the Christian virtues (Gal. 5:22, 23).

Frying Pan, properly a pot or saucepan in which things are boiled or baked (Lev. 2:7 and 7:9).

Fuel. Wood, charcoal, various kinds of thorn bushes, dried grass, and the dung of camels and cattle was used as fuel (Isa. 9:5, 19; Ezek. 4:12, 15; 15:4, 6; 21:32).

Fuller (See Occupations and Professions)

Fuller's Field, a field, just outside of Jerusalem, where fullers washed the cloth material they were processing. A highway and a conduit for water passed through it (Isa. 7:3; 36:2).

Fuller's Soap, an alkali prepared from the ashes of certain plants and used for cleansing and fulling new cloth (Mal. 3:2).

Funeral, the ceremonies used in disposing of a dead human body; whether by burying, cremation, or otherwise. The word does not occur in the Bible. The rites differed with the place, the religion, and the times; except for royal burials in Egypt, the elaborate ceremonies that are used with us today were not held.

In Palestine, as a general thing, there was no embalmment and the body was buried a few hours after death; sometimes in a tomb, but more often in a cave. Coffins were unknown. The body was washed and often anointed with aromatic spices (John 12:7; 19:39). In Egypt, the bodies were embalmed so skillfully that many of them are recognizable today after the lapse of thousands of years.

Furlong (See Weights and Measures)

Furnace. Furnaces for central heating are not mentioned in the Bible nor are they much used today in Bible lands. The burning fiery furnace of Daniel 3 was probably a smelting furnace and used only incidentally for the punishment of men. The most common word "tannur" could be and often is more properly rendered oven (cf. Gen. 15:17 with Lev. 2:4; Hos. 7:4-7). Furnaces were used for melting gold (Prov. 17:3), silver (Ezek. 22:22), brass or bronze (Ezek. 22:18) and including also tin, iron and lead and for baking bread (Neh. 3:11; Isa. 31:9). Often used figuratively, as in Deuteronomy 4:20 where it means Egypt and in Matthew 13:42, which refers to the punishment of the wicked at the end of the world.

Furniture. The principle reference to furniture in the Bible concerns the articles in the Tabernacle and Temple. Common people had little furniture; kings had bed-steads (Deut. 3:11) and tables (Judg. 1:7).

Future Life (See Immortality, Eschatology).

A funeral procession in Bible days. © SPF

–G–

Gaal (gā′ăl, **loathing**), a son of Ebed (Judg. 9:26-41), who led the Shechemites to rebel against Abimelech, the son of Gideon.

Gaash (gā′ăsh, **quaking**), a hill near Mount Ephraim, where Joshua was buried (Judg. 2:9).

Gaba (gā′-bȧ), a Benjamite city (Josh. 18:24). Same as Geba (21:17; I Kings 15:22).

Gabbai (**găb′-ā-ī, collector**), a Benjaminite (Neh. 11:8).

Gabbatha (**găb′**ȧ-thȧ, **height, ridge**), the place called the "Pavement" (John 19:13) where Jesus was tried before Pilate.

Gabriel (**gā′brĭ-ēl, man of God**), an angel mentioned four times in Scripture, each time bearing a momentous message (Dan. 8:16; 9:21f; Luke 1:11-20; Luke 1:26-38).

Gad (găd, **fortune**). 1. Jacob's seventh son; firstborn of Zilpah, Leah's handmaid (Gen. 30:9-11). Of his personal life nothing is known except that he had seven sons at the time of the descent into Egypt (46:16). The Gadites numbered 45,650 adult males (Num. 1:24, 25), but at the second census their number had fallen to 40,500 (26:18).

The territory of Gad, difficult to define, was formerly ruled by Sihon, king of the Amorites. It lay chiefly in the center of the land E of Jordan, with the half-tribe of Manasseh on the N and Reuben to the S.

Genesis 49:19 seems to describe the military prowess of the Gadites: "Gad, a troop shall overcome him: but he shall overcome at the last" ("press upon their heel," ASV) meaning that they would put their enemies to retreat. Gad finally was carried captive by Assyria (II Kings 15:29; I Chron. 5:26) and Ammon seized their land and cities (Jer. 49:1).

2. The seer or prophet of King David. Gad assisted in arranging the musical services of the temple (II Chron. 29:25) and recorded the acts of David in a book (I Chron. 29:29).

3. A Canaanite god of fortune, seen in compound names such as Baal-gad (Josh. 11:17; 12:7; 13:5) and Migdal-gad (Josh. 15:37).

Gadara, Gadarenes (găd′ȧrȧ, găd-ȧ-rēnz), one of the cities of the Decapolis

The country of the Gadarenes, as viewed from the Lake of Galilee. *© MPS*

near the SE end of the Sea of Galilee, near which the demoniacs lived whom Jesus healed (Mark 5:1; Luke 8:26, 37; Matt. 8:28, Gr. text).

Gaddi (găd'ī), Manassah's representative among the twelve spies (Num. 13:11).

Gaddiel (găd'ĭ-ĕl), Zebulun's representative among the twelve spies (Num. 13:10).

Gadi (gā'dī), father of Menahem who usurped the throne of Israel (II Kings 15:14-20).

Gaham (gā'hăm), a son of Nahor, brother of Abraham, by his concubine Reumah (Gen. 22:24).

Gahar (gā'hȧr), a family of the Nethinim who returned with Zerubbabel to Jerusalem (Ezra 2:47).

Gaius (gā'yŭs). 1. A Macedonian who traveled with Paul on his third missionary journey (Acts 19:29). 2. A man of Derbe who accompanied Paul from Macedonia to Asia (Acts 20:4). 3. A Corinthian whom Paul baptized (I Cor. 1:14). 4. The addressee of III John. A convert of John (III John 5-8).

Galal (gā'lăl), the name of two Levites mentioned in I Chronicles 9:15, 16; Nehemiah 11:17.

Galatia (gȧ-lā'shĭ-ȧ), originally a territory in north-central Asia Minor where the Gauls settled; later the name of a Roman province in central Asia Minor, organized in 25 B.C. The cities of Antioch of Pisidia, Iconium, Lystra, and Derbe belonged within this province. Paul's use of the term (I Cor. 16: 1; Gal. 1:2; II Tim. 4:10) and Peter's allusion (I Pet. 1:1) probably refer to the province as a whole.

Galatians, Epistle to the, is a short but important letter of Paul, containing a protest against legalism and a clear statement of the gospel of God's grace. It was written shortly after the close of the first missionary journey to the churches of Galatia (Gal. 1:1) to counteract the propaganda of certain Jewish teachers who insisted that to faith in Christ must be added circumcision and obedience to the Mosaic Law (2:16; 3:2-3; 4:10, 21; 5:2-4; 6:12).

The contents of Galatians make evident Paul's purpose in writing. The first two chapters show that he was compelled to vindicate his apostolic authority. The Judaizers, in order to establish their own position which contradicted Paul's teaching, had attempted to discredit his authority. Having vindicated his apostolic call and authority, Paul next sets forth the doctrine of justification in refutation of the teaching of the Judaizers. A reasoned, comprehensive exposition of the doctrine of justification by faith exposed the errors of legalism. Since the Judaizers asserted that to remove the believer from under the law opened the floodgates to immorality, Paul concluded his presentation with an elaboration of the true effect of liberty upon the Christian life, showing that the truth of justification by faith logically leads to a life of good works. The epistle may be outlined as follows:

The Introduction. 1:1-10
- 1. The salutation. 1-5
- 2. The rebuke. 6-10

I. The Vindication of His Apostolic Authority. 1:11 - 2:21
- 1. The reception of his Gospel by revelation. 1:11-24
- 2. The confirmation of his Gospel by the apostles at Jerusalem. 2:1-10
- 3. The illustration of his independence. 2:11-21

II. The Exposition of Justification by Faith. 3:1 - 4:31
- 1. The elaboration of the doctrine. 3:1 - 4:7
  - a. The nature of justification by faith. 3:1-14
  - b. The limitations of the law and its relations to faith. 3:15 - 4:7
- 2. The appeal to drop all legalism. 4:8-31

III. The Nature of the Life of Christian Liberty. 5:1 - 6:10
- 1. The call to maintain their liberty. 5:1
- 2. The peril of Christian liberty. 5:2-12
- 3. The life of liberty. 5:13 - 6:10

The Conclusion. 6:11-17
The Benediction. 6:18

Galbanum (gal'bȧ-nŭm), a gum resin used in the sacred incense to increase and retain its fragrance longer (Exod. 30:34).

Galeed (găl'ē-ĕd, **a heap of witnesses**), the name given by Jacob to the heap of stones which he and Laban raised on Mount Gilead as a memorial of their compact (Gen. 31:47, 48).

Galilean (găl'ĭ-lē'ăn), a native or resident of Galilee (Matt. 26:69; John 4: 45; Acts 1:11; 5:37).

Galilee (găl'ĭ-lē, **the ring or circuit**), the most northerly of the three prov-

The north end of the Sea of Galilee showing inflow of the Jordan River. © *MPS*

Fishing on the Sea of Galilee. © *MPS*

inces of Palestine (Galilee, Samaria, Judea). Measuring approximately 50 miles N to S and 30 miles E to W, it was bounded on the W by the plain of Akka to the foot of Mt. Carmel. The land was luxurious and productive, a rugged mountainous country of oaks and terebinths interrupted by fertile plains. It was said of Asher, in the west, that he would eat fat for bread and yield royal dainties and dip his feet in oil (Gen. 49:20; Deut. 33:24, 25). The olive oil of Galilee has long been esteemed as of the highest quality. Lower Galilee was largely the heritage of Zebulun and Issachar. Less hilly and of a milder climate than Upper Galilee, it included the rich plain of Esdraelon (or Jezreel) and was a "pleasant" land (Gen. 49:15) that would yield "treasures in the sand" (Deut. 33:19). The sand of these coasts was especially valuable for making glass.

Jesus preached His first public sermon in the synagogue at Nazareth, in Lower Galilee, where He had been brought up (Luke 4:16-30). His disciples came from Galilee (Matt. 4:18; John 1:43, 44; Acts 1:11; 2:7); in Cana of Galilee He performed His first miracle (John 2:11). Capernaum in Galilee, the home of His manhood (Matt. 4:13; 9:1), is where the first three Gospels present His major ministry. Galilee's debasement made some of its people feel their need of the Saviour. This and its comparative freedom from priestly and pharisaical prejudice may have been additional reasons for receiving the larger share of the Lord's ministry.

Galilee, Sea of, so-called from its washing the E side of Galilee. It is also called "the Sea of Gennesaret" (Luke 5:1), since the fertile Plain of Gennesaret lies on the NW (Matt. 14:34). The OT calls it "the Sea of Chinnereth" (Heb. "harp-shaped," the shape of the sea, Num. 34:11; Deut. 3:17; Josh. 13:27) or "Chinneroth" (Josh. 12:3; I Kings 15:20), from the town so named on its shore (Josh. 19:35). "The Sea of Tiberias" is another designation (John 6:1; 21:1), associated with the capital of Herod Antipas.

Located some 60 miles N of Jerusalem, its bed is but a lower depression of the Jordan valley. The lake is 13 miles long and 8 miles wide, filled with sweet and clear water, and full of fish. Because it was located in a pocket in the hills, it was subject to sudden violent storms.

Gall. 1. From a Heb. root meaning **bitter,** the human gall (Job 16:13; 20:25); the poison of serpents (20:14). 2. A bitter and poisonous herb (Deut. 29:18; Jer. 8:14; 9:15; Hos. 10:4, "hemlock") to deaden pain.

Gallery, three terraced passageways or balconies running round the chambers in the temple of Ezekiel's vision (Ezek. 41:16; 42:3, 5, 6).

Galley (See Ship)

Gallim (găl'ĭm, **heaps),** a town of Benjamin (Isa. 10:30).

Gallio (gal'ĭ-ō), Junius Annaeus Gallio, the Roman proconsul (AV, "deputy") of Achaia when Paul was in Corinth (A.D. 51). Of his amiable character Seneca said, "No mortal was ever so sweet to one as Gallio was to all," and, his brother adds, "to love him to the utmost was to love all too little." How exactly this independent testimony coincides with Acts 18:12-17! Alarmed over the inroads that the Gospel was making, the Jews in Corinth brought Paul before the judgment seat of Gallio. He refused to hear any accusations against Paul, and discharged him as innocent (Acts 18:12-17).

Gallows, a pole for executing and exhibiting a victim by impalement. Made 75 feet high by Haman for Mordecai (Esth. 5:14; 6:4).

Gamaliel (gà-mā'lĭ-ĕl, **reward of God).** 1. Chief of the tribe of Manasseh (Num. 1:10; 2:20; 7:54, 59; 10:23). 2. A Pharisee and eminent doctor of the law. Paul was one of his pupils (Acts 22:3). When the enraged Sanhedrin sought to slay the Apostles for their bold testimony to Christ, Gamaliel urged caution (Acts 5:34-39).

Games. Little is known of the amusements of the Hebrews. There are references to dancing (Jer. 31:13; Luke 15:25), and the play of children is mentioned in Scripture (Zech. 8:5; Matt. 11:16, 17; Luke 7:32). Paul alludes to athletic contests (I Cor. 9:24, 25; Eph. 6:12) and the author of Hebrews speaks of the race (Heb. 12:1, 2).

Gammadim (gă'mà-dĭm, probably **valiant men**), the garrison in the watchtowers of Tyre (Ezek. 27:11).

Gamul (gā'-mŭl), the head of the twenty-second course of priests (I Chron. 24:17).

Garden, a cultivated piece of ground, usually in the suburbs, planted with flowers, vegetables, shrubs, or trees, fenced with a mud or stone wall (Prov. 24:31) or thorny hedges (Isa. 5:5) and

A corner of the Garden of Gethsemane. © MPS

guarded (whence "garden") by a watchman in a lodge (Isa. 1:8) or tower (Mark 12:1) to drive away wild beasts and robbers.

The Hebrews used gardens as burial places. The field of Machpelah, Abraham's burial ground, was a garden with trees in and around it (Gen. 23: 17). Manasseh and Amon were buried in Uzza's garden (II Kings 21:18, 26). The garden of Gethsemane was a favorite resort of Jesus for meditation and prayer (Matt. 26:36; John 18: 1, 2).

Spiritually, the believer is a garden watered by the Holy Spirit (Jer. 2:13; 17:7, 8; John 4:13, 14; 7:37-39). The righteous "shall be like a tree planted by the rivers of water, that bringeth forth his fruit in his season" (Ps. 1:3). "A well watered garden" expresses abundant happiness and prosperity (Isa. 58:11; Jer. 31:12) just as "a garden that hath no water" (Isa. 1:30) expresses spiritual, national and individual barrenness and misery.

Gardener (See Occupations & Professions)

Gareb (gā'rĕb, **scabby).** 1. One of David's mighty men (II Sam. 23:38; I Chron. 11:40). 2. A hill near Jerusalem to which the city would expand, as foreseen by Jeremiah (31:39).

Garlick, Garlic (See Plants)

Garments (See Dress)

Garmite (gȧr'mīt), a name applied to Keilah (I Chron. 4:19).

Garner (gȧr'nêr), **a barn** or **storehouse** (Ps. 144:13; II Chron. 32:27; Joel 1: 17). A barn used as a granary (Matt. 3:12; 6:26; Luke 3:17; 12:18, 24).

Garrison, a fortress manned by soldiers (II Chron. 17:2). Chiefly for occupation of a conquered country (I Sam. 10:5; 13:3; 14:1, 6). David put garrisons in Syria and Edom when he subjugated those people (II Sam. 8: 6, 14).

Gashmu (găsh'mū, Neh. 6:6), a form of Geshem (2:19; 6:1, 2), an Arabian who opposed Nehemiah's restoration of Jerusalem.

Gatam (gā'tăm), grandson of Esau; an Edomite chief (Gen. 36:11, 16; I Chron. 1:36).

Gate, the entrance to enclosed buildings, grounds, or cities. The gates of a city were the place where the Oriental resorted for legal business, conversation, bargaining, and news. Usually consisted of double doors plated with metal (Ps. 107:16; Isa. 45: 2). Wooden doors without iron plating were easily set on fire (Judg. 9: 52; Neh. 2:3, 17). Some gates were made out of brass, as was "the Beautiful Gate" of Herod's temple (Acts 3:2).

Typical scene at a city gate. © SPF

Markets were held at the gate, and the main item sold there gave its name to the gate ("sheep gate," Neh. 3:1; "fish gate," Neh. 3:3; "horse gate," Neh. 3:28). The gate was the place where people met to hear an important announcement (II Chron. 32: 6; Jer. 7:2; 17:19-27) or the reading of the law (Neh. 8:1, 3) or where the elders transacted legal business (Deut. 16:18; 21:18-20; Josh. 20:4; Ruth 4: 1, 2, 11). To sit at the gate meant the attainment of eminence (Prov. 32:33).

Figuratively, gates refer to the glory of a city (Isa. 3:26; 14:31; Jer. 14:2) or to the city itself (Pss. 87:2; 122:2). In Matthew 16:18, the "gates of Hades" not prevailing against the Church may refer to infernal powers assaulting the Church or to the

Church's greater power in retaining her members than the grave has for its victims.

Gath (găth, **winepress),** one of the five great Philistine cities (Ashdod, Gaza, Askelon, Gath, and Ekron, Josh. 13:3; I Sam. 6:17). Its people were the Gittites, of whom were Goliath (I Sam. 17:4) and other giants (II Sam. 21:19-22). It was one of the five cities to which the Philistines carried the ark of God and thereby brought on the people God's heavy visitation with tumors (I Sam. 5:8, 9). David fled from Saul to Gath where he feigned madness to save his life (I Sam. 21:10-15).

Gath-Hepher (găth-hē′fêr, **winepress of the well**), a town on Zebulun's border (Josh. 19:12, 13, ASV). Birthplace of Jonah the prophet (II Kings 14:25).

Gath-Rimmon (găth-rĭm′ŭn, **winepress of Rimmon**). 1. A city of Dan on the Philistine plain (Josh. 19:45; 21:24; I Chron. 6:69). 2. A town of Manasseh, W of Jordan, assigned to the Levites (Josh. 19:25).

Gaulanitis (gôl-ăn-ī′-tís), a province NE of the Sea of Galilee ruled by Herod Antipas.

Gaza (gā′zȧ, **strong),** one of the five chief Philistine cities, and the most southwesterly toward Egypt. It was an important stop on the caravan route. Originally a Canaanite city (Gen. 10:19) Gaza was assigned bv Joshua to Judah (Josh. 15:47), and was occupied later (Judg. 1:18). It was captured by the Philistines (Judg. 13:1) and controlled by them until the time of Hezekiah (II Kings 18:8). Samson was imprisoned and died in Gaza (Judg. 16:1, 21). It is mentioned once in the NT in connection with Philip's ministry to the Ethiopian eunuch (Acts 8:26).

Gazelle (See Animals)

Gazer (See Gezer)

Gazez (gā′zĕz). 1. Son of Ephah. 2. Grandson of Ephah, Caleb's concubine (I Chron. 2:46).

Gazzam (găz′ăm), one of the Nethinim, whose descendants returned from exile (Ezra 2:48; Neh. 7:51).

Geba (gē′bȧ, **hill),** a town in the territory of Benjamin (Josh. 18:24 ASV, RSV; Gaba in KJV), assigned to the Levites (Josh. 21:17; I Chron. 6:60; 8:6). Jonathan defeated the Philistines at Geba (I Sam. 13:3). Asa fortified Geba (I Kings 15:22). In the time of Hezekiah Geba was the northernmost city of the kingdom of Judah, as Beersheba its southernmost (II Kings 23:8; II Chron. 16:6). Men from Geba returned after the exile (Ezra 2:26; Neh. 7:30).

Gebal (gē′băl, **border).** 1. A seaport of Phoenicia, between Sidon and Tripolis; modern Jebeil, 25 miles N of Beirut. Joshua 13:5, 6 refers to the land of the Giblites or Gebalites, the land of Lebanon at the foot of Mt. Hermon, as part of the land God gave to the children of Israel. Expert stonemasonry was among the industries of Gebal. Shipbuilding was another, for Ezekiel 27:9 tells us that caulkers from Gebal worked on ships at Tyre. 2. A land between the Dead Sea and Petra (Ps. 83:6-8).

Geber (gē′bêr). 1. One of Solomon's twelve purveyors for S. Gilead (I Kings 4:13). 2. The son of Uri (I Kings 4:19).

Gebim (gē′bĭm), a place near Anathoth (Isa. 10:31).

Gecko (See Animals)

Gedaliah (gĕd′ȧ-lī′ȧ). 1. Son of Shaphan, governor of Mizpah, and friend of Jeremiah (II Kings 25:22-25; Jer. 40:5-16), assassinated by Ishmael, son of Nethaniah (Jer. 41:1-3). 2. A priest of the sons of Jeshua (Ezra 10:16). 3. Grandfather of Zephaniah (Zeph. 1:1). 4. One of the six sons of Jeduthun (I Chron. 25:8, 9). 5. A son of Pashur (Jer. 38:1-6).

Geder (gē′dêr), Canaanite city near Debir, taken by Joshua (Josh. 12:13).

Gederah (gĕ-dē′rȧ, **wall),** the modern Jedireh on the heights between the valleys of Sorek and Aijalon in the hills of Judah (Josh. 15:36, 41).

Gedor (gē′dôr, **wall).** 1. A city in the hill country of Judah (Josh. 15:58). 2. Town where Jeroham lived, whose sons were among the Benjamites who came to David at Ziklag (I Chron. 12:7). 3. A descendant of Benjamin (I Chron. 8:31; 9:37). 4. Descendants of Judah (I Chron. 4:4). 5. In the time of Hezekiah, princes of Simeon went to Gedor to find pasture for their flocks, and finding it so good, they drove out the inhabitants and settled there.

Gehazi (gē-hā′zī, **valley of vision),** the servant of Elisha. He first appears when Elisha sought to reward the Shunamite woman for her hospitality (II Kings 4:8-37). When she declined to ask any reward, Gehazi answered, "Verily she hath no child, and her husband is old." Elisha promised her that she should bear a child, which came to pass. "When the child was grown," he died of sunstroke. The woman went with her sorrow to Elisha. He sent Gehazi with instructions to lay Elisha's staff upon the face of the child; but "the child is not awaked." Elisha then came himself and restored the child to life. Elisha had Gehazi call the woman to receive her son. Gehazi next appears when Naaman is healed (II Kings 5:1-27). Elisha refused any reward. After Naaman left, Gehazi determined to run after Naaman and ask something. Naaman gave him more than he asked. Gehazi hid his booty before he reached home, but Elisha knew what had happened, and rebuked Gehazi by invoking upon him the leprosy of which Naaman had been cured.

Gehenna (gē-hĕn'à, **valley of Hinnom),** a valley on the W and SW of Jerusalem, which formed part of the border between Judah and Benjamin (Josh. 15:8; 18:16; Neh. 11:30, 31). Here Ahaz (II Chron. 28:3; see II Kings 16:3) and Manasseh (II Chron. 33:6; see II Kings 21:6) sacrificed their sons to Molech (Jer. 32:35). For this reason Josiah defiled the place (II Kings 23: 10). After referring to the idolatrous barbarities (Jer. 7:31, 32) Jeremiah prophesies a great slaughter of the people there, and in the siege of Jerusalem (Jer. 19:1-13). After the OT period, Jewish apocalyptic writers began to call the Valley of Hinnom the entrance to hell, later hell itself. The word occurs 12 times in the NT, always translated "hell" ASV, RSV margin "Gehenna." Eleven times it is on the lips of Jesus; as the final punishment for calling one's brother a fool (Matt. 5:22); for adultery, when the severest measures have not been taken to prevent commission of this offense (Matt. 5:29, 30); and others (Matt. 18:9; Mark 9:43, 45, 47). See Hades, Hell.

Gehenna, the valley of Hinnom, which was a place for dumping and burning refuse. © MPS

Geliloth (gē-lĭ'lŏth). A place on the border of Benjamin with Judah, E of Jerusalem (Josh. 18:17).

Gemalli (gē-măl'ī, **camel owner** or **rider**), the father of Ammiel, and one of the twelve spies sent out to explore the land (Num. 13:12).

Gemariah (gĕm'à-rī'à, **Jehovah hath fulfilled** or **accomplishment of the Lord**). 1. A prince, son of Shaphan the scribe and friend of Jeremiah (Jer. 36:10-25). 2. A son of Hilkiah, sent by King Zedekiah as ambassador to Nebuchadnezzar (Jer. 29:3).

Genealogy (jĕn'ē-ăl'ō-jē), a list of ancestors or descendants, or the study of lines of descent. The genealogies of the Bible show biological descent, the right of inheritance, succession to an office, or ethnic and geographical relationships. There are numerous genealogical lists in Genesis (5:1-32; 10:1-32; 11:10-32; 35:22-39; 36:1-43; 46:8-27) and in I Chronicles 1-9. Some family genealogies of the Restoration are given in Ezra (2:1-63; 8:1-20) and in Nehemiah (7:7-63). In the NT "genealogies" seems to refer to an excessive concern for pagan or Gnostic series of angelic beings (I Tim. 1:4; Titus 3:9).

Genealogy of Jesus Christ. Two genealogies are given in the NT; in Matthew 1:1-17, and in Luke 3:23-38. Matthew traces the descent of Jesus from Abraham and David, and divides it into three sets of fourteen generations each. Matthew omits three generations after Poram, namely Ahaziah, Joash and Amaziah (I Chron. 3:11, 12). Contrary to Heb. practice, he names five women: Tamar, Rahab, Ruth, Bathsheba (the wife of Uriah), and Mary, each name evoking associations, dark or bright, with the history of the chosen people. Matthew carefully excludes the physical paternity of Joseph by saying "Joseph the husband of Mary, of whom" (feminine singular in Greek) "was born Jesus" (1:16). The sense of "begat" in Heb. genealogies was not exact: it indicated immediate or remote descent, an adoptive relation, or legal heirship, as well as procreation.

Luke's genealogy moves from Jesus to Adam. Between Abraham and Adam it is the same as in I Chronicles 1:1-7, 24-28, or the more detailed genealogies in Genesis; making allowance for the different spelling of names in transliteration from Heb. or Greek. From David to Abraham Luke agrees with OT genealogies and with Matthew. Between Jesus and David Luke's list differs from Matthew's. Perhaps Matthew gives the line of legal heirship, while Luke gives the line of physical descent. Matthew's genealogy establishes the legal claim to the throne of David through his foster-father Joseph; Luke's establishes His actual descent from David through Mary. Isaiah 11:1 indicates that Messiah is to be physically a descendant of David's father Jesse. The genealogies must be seen in the light of this fact. (Compare Matt. 22:41-46 and parallels with the answer in Rom. 1:4.)

Generation (jĕn'ĕr-ā'shŭn), in the OT, the translation of two Heb. words: (1) **tôledhôth,** from a root **yalad,** to beget, used always in the plural, refers to lines of descent from an ancestor, and occurs in the phrase "these are the generations of," (Gen. 2:4; 5:1; 6:9; Ruth 4:18). (2) **dôr, a period of time** (e.g., Deut. 32:7, past; Exod. 3:15, future; Ps. 102:24, both); **all the men living in a given period** (e.g., Gen. 7:1; Judg. 3:2); **a class of men characterized by a certain quality** (e.g., Deut. 32:5; Ps. 14:5); **a dwelling place or habitation** (Isa. 58:12; Ps. 49:19).

In the NT **generation** translates four Greek words, all having reference to descent: (1) **genea,** for lines of descent from an ancestor (Matt. 1:17); or all the men living in a given period (Matt. 11:16); or a class of men having a certain quality (Matt. 12:39); or a period of time (Acts 13:36); (2) **genesis,** meaning **genealogy** (Matt 2:17); (3) **gennema,** meaning brood or offspring (Matt. 3:7; 12:34; 23:33); (4) **genes,** clan, race, kind, nation (I Pet. 2:9).

Genesis (jĕn'ĕ-sĭs), the first book of the Bible. The name is derived from a Greek word meaning "origin" or "beginning," which is the title given to the book in the Greek Septuagint. The Hebrew name for the book is **bereshîth,** from Genesis 1:1 ("in the beginning"). The special phrase, "These are the generations of" divides the book into eleven sections (2:4; 5:1; 6:9; 10:1; 11:10; 11:27; 25:2; 25:19; 36:1, and 37:2), and serves as a superscription to the section that follows it. These sections do not describe the origin of the person mentioned in the superscription (or of "the heavens and earth" in the case of 2:4), but rather

Fragment of a creation tablet, from Nineveh, with an account of creation. **BM**

The "Adam and Eve Seal" found near Nineveh in 1932 by Dr. E. A. Spiser, who dated it about 3500 B.C. UMP

the further history of the one whose origin has already been described, plus that of his immediate offspring. A broader outline divides the book into two unequal sections. Genesis 1:1 through 11:26 describes the creation of the heavens, the earth, plants, animals, and man; the Fall and the Edenic curse; the antediluvian age and the great Flood; and the descendants of Noah down to Terah. Genesis 11:27 through 50:26 traces the history of Abraham and Lot; Ishmael and Isaac; Jacob and Esau; and Joseph and his brethren in Egypt. Genesis reveals that God created the heavens and the earth as a dynamic, functioning entity. Thus, even as Adam was created instantly as a grown man, so also the earth and its living creatures were created fully "grown" within six days, with the oceans already containing the salts and chemicals necessary for sustaining marine life (1:2, 10, 20), the dry land equipped with a mantle of soil for plants and trees (1:11), the light rays from distant stars already performing their God-intended function of shining upon the earth (1:14-19), and the animals and plants created after their kinds (1:11, 12, 20-25). The "grown creation" doctrine is simply the Biblical doctrine of creation rightly understood, and is illustrated in the NT by the miracle of the changing of water to wine (John 2:1-11). Genesis 11:27 through 50:26 traces the history of Abraham and Lot; Ishmael and Isaac; Jacob and Esau; and Joseph and his brethren in Egypt.

Gennesaret (gĕ-nĕs′ȧ-rĕt). 1. "The land of Gennesaret" (Matt. 14:34; Mark 6:53) is a plain on the northwest shore of the Sea of Galilee, extending about a mile inland. 2. "The Lake of Gennesaret" (Luke 5:1), elsewhere in Luke simply "the lake" (5:2; 8:22, 23, 33); the same as the Sea of Galilee (Matt. 4:18; 15:29; Mark 1:16; 7:31; John 6:1); or the OT "Sea of Chinnereth." See Galilee, Lake of.

The Plain of Gennesaret and the Sea of Galillee as viewed from Bethsaida. © MPS

Gentiles (jĕn′tīlz, **nation, people**). Usually it means a non-Israelite people (Judge. 4:2; Isa. 11:10; 42:1; Mal. 1:11).

Under conditions of peace, considerate treatment was accorded Gentiles by the Israelites under OT law (e.g., Deut. 10:19; 24:14, 15; Num. 35:15; Ezek. 47:22). Men of Israel often married Gentile women, of whom Rahab, Ruth and Bathsheba are notable examples, but the practice was frowned upon after the return from exile (Ezra 9:12; 10:2-44; Neh. 10:30; 13:23-31). Separation between Jew and Gentile became more strict, until in the NT period the hostility is complete. Persecution embittered the Jew, and he retaliated by hatred of everything Gentile, and by avoidance, so far as was possible, of contact with Gentiles. The intensity of this feeling varied, and gave way before unusual kindness (Luke 7:4, 5).

While the teachings of Jesus ultimately broke down "the middle wall of partition" between Jew and Gentile, as is seen in the writings of Paul (Rom. 1:16; I Cor. 1:24; Gal. 3:28; Eph. 2: 14; Col. 3:11) and in Acts, yet Jesus limited His ministry to Jews, with rare exceptions (the half-Jewish Samaritans, John 4:1-42, the Syrophoenician woman, Matt. 15:21-28; Mark 7: 24-30; the Greeks in John 12:20-36). He instructed His twelve disciples, "Go not into the way of the Gentiles, and into any city of the Samaritans enter ye not" (Matt. 10:5); but did not repeat this injunction when He sent out the Seventy (Luke 10:1-16). Jesus' mission was first to "his own" (John 1:11), the Chosen People of God; but ultimately to "as many as received him" (John 1:12).

In Acts, from the appointment of Paul as the apostle to the Gentiles (9: 15), the Gentiles become increasingly prominent. Even the letters addressed particularly to Jewish Christians (James; I Pet.; Heb.; Rom. 9-11) are relevant to Gentiles also. The division of all mankind into two classes, Jew and Gentile, emphasizes the importance of the Jews as the people through whom God made salvation available to all people.

Gentiles, Court of the, the outer part of the temple, which Gentiles might enter. See Temple.

Genubath (gē-nū′băth, **theft),** a son of Hadad the Edomite (I Kings 11:20).

Gera (gē′rȧ, **grain),** a name common in the tribe of Benjamin. 1. A son of Benjamin (Gen. 46:21). 2. A grandson of Benjamin (I Chron. 8:3, 5). 3. Father of Ehud (Judg. 3:15). 4. A son of Ehud (I Chron. 8:7). 5. Father of Shimei (II Sam. 16:5; 19:16, 18; I Kings 2:8).

Gerah (See Weights and Measures)

Gerar (gē′rȧr, **circle, region),** a town in the Negev, near the Mediterranean coast south of Gaza, on a protected inland caravan route from Palestine to Egypt (Gen. 10:19). Here Abraham sojourned with Abimelech (Gen. 20: 1, 2); and later Isaac (Gen. 26:1-33) had similar and more extended experiences with the king and people of the region.

Gerasa (gē-rȧ′sȧ), a city E of the Jordan midway between the Sea of Galilee and the Dead Sea. The name does not occur in the Bible, but the adjective Gerasenes occurs in Mark 5:1 ASV, RSV, and the margin of Matthew 8: 28 RSV and Luke 8:26, 37 RSV. The MSS vary in all these passages between Gadarenes, Gerasenes and Gergesenes; and all the above occurrences relate to the region where Jesus healed a demoniac.

Gergesa (gûr-gē′sȧ), a place probably midway of the eastern shore of Lake Galilee, where the bank is steep. The adjective Gergesenes occurs in Matthew 8:28 KJV and RSV margin; Mark 5:1 RSV margin; and Luke 8:26, 37 ASV, RSV margins. See Gadara.

Gerizim (gĕ-rī′zĭm), a mountain of Samaria, Jebel et-Tôr, 2,849 feet high, SW of Mt. Ebal. Of military importance. Moses commanded that when the Israelites came into the Promised Land, the blessing for keeping the law should be spoken from Mt. Gerizim (Deut. 11:29; 27:4-26). After the Israelites, returning from Babylonian exile, refused to let the mixed races of Samaria help rebuild Jerusalem (Ezra 4:1-4; Neh. 2:19, 20; 13:28), the Samaritans built themselves a temple on Mt. Gerizim (John 4:20, 21).

Gershom (gûr′shŏm, **to cast out stranger,** Exod. 2:22; 18:3). 1. The first son of Moses and Zipporah (Exod 2:22; 18:3; I Chron. 23:15, 16; 26:24). 2. The eldest son of Levi (I Chron. 6:16, 17, 20, 43, 62, 71; 15:7). 3. One of the "heads of houses" who returned with Ezra from Babylon (Ezra 8:2). 4. Father of the Levite who became priest to the Danites in Laish (Judg. 18:30).

General view of the Garden of Gethsemane, lying beneath the east city wall of Jerusalem. © *MPS*

Gershon (gûr′shŏn), firstborn of the three sons of Levi (Gen. 46:11). The work of his descendants (Num. 3:23-26) during the wilderness wanderings is described in Numbers 3:23-25; 4:21-28; for which functions two wagons and four oxen were deemed sufficient (Num. 7:7). They continued prominent in the service of the Temple of Solomon, and in that of Zerubbabel, especially as singers. See also Gershom 2.

Gerzites (gûr′zīts), **Gizrites** (gĭz′rīts), or **Gerizzites** (gĕ-rĭz′īts, gĕr′ĭ-zīts), a tribe named with the Geshurites and the Amalekites (I Sam. 27:8), They are called the ancient inhabitants of the land, on the way to Shur, toward Egypt.

Gesham (gē′shăm), a son of Jahdai and descendant of Caleb (I Chron. 2:47).

Geshem (gē′shĕm), the Arabian who along with Sanballat and Tobiah, opposed the building of the wall by Nehemiah (Neh. 2:19; 6:1, 2). The same as Gashnu (Neh. 6:6).

Geshur (gē′shûr, **bridge**). 1. A country in Syria (II Sam. 15:8) on the western border of Og's kingdom of Bashan E of the Jordan (Josh. 12:5). Jair of Manasseh conquered Bashan up to Geshur (Deut. 3:14). Although in the territory of Israel, the Geshurites were not driven out (Josh. 13:11, 13). David made alliance with their King Talmai by marrying his daughter Maacah (II Sam. 3:3; I Chron. 3:2). Her son Absalom, after he murdered Amnon, sought refuge with her father (II Sam. 13:37, 38), whence Joab brought Absalom back (II Sam. 14:23, 32; 15:8). 2. A district between southern Palestine and Sinai, near Philistine territory (Josh. 13:2).

Gether (gē′thêr), third son of Aram (Gen. 10:23; I Chron. 1:17).

Gethsemane (gĕth-sĕm′à-nē, probably Aramaic for "oil-press"), the place of Jesus' agony and arrest (Matt. 26:36-56; Mark 14:32-52; Luke 22:39-54; John 18:1-12 — John tells of the arrest only). In Matthew 26:36; Mark 14:32 it is called "a place"; Luke does not give the name, says that the place was one to which Jesus customarily resorted, and that it was on the Mount of Olives; John 18:1, also without naming it, explains that it was a garden across the Cedron (Kidron) valley from Jerusalem. The sufferings of Christ as His hour approached, portrayed by Matthew, Mark and Luke, and the humiliation of His arrest, told by all four evangelists, concentrate the reverent thought and feeling of believers, so that the very name Gethsemane evokes the love and adoration due to the Saviour who prayed here.

Geuel (gē-ū′ĕl), a representative of the Gadite tribe sent out to explore Canaan (Num. 13:15).

Gezer (gē′zêr, **portion**), a fortified place 18 miles NW of Jerusalem. The Egyptians captured Gezer about 1500 B.C. The king of Gezer is listed (Josh. 12:12) among those whom Joshua defeated. David smote the Philistines as far as Gezer (I Chron. 20:4; also Gazer, KJV, Gezer in ASV, RSV, in II Sam. 5:25; I Chron. 14:16), but it remained for Solomon to reduce the people of Gezer to forced labor, and to rebuild the city, which the pharaoh of Egypt had taken and burnt and given to Solomon as a dowry with his daughter (I Kings 9:15-17).

Ghor, The (gôr), the upper level of the Jordan valley.

Ghost (gōst), the human spirit as distinguished from the body. To "give up the ghost" means to breathe one's last, to die (Job 11:20; Gen. 25:8; 35:29; 49:33; Matt. 27:50; John 19:30). "Holy Ghost" in KJV is translated "Holy Spirit" in ASV, RSV. Unlike modern usage, it does not refer to an apparition.

Giah (gī′à), an unknown place near Hebron, where Joab overtook Abner (II Sam. 2:24).

Giants. The first mention of giants in the Bible is in Genesis 6:4, where ASV, RSV have **Nephilim,** a Heb. word of uncertain etymology. Nephilim were found in Canaan when the spies went through the land (Num. 13:33; KJV giants). Once (Job 16:14) "giant" translates Heb. **gibbôr,** which RSV text renders "warrior, ASV margin "mighty man," its usual meaning. The other Heb. words translated "giant" are **rāphā, rāphâh,** and the plural **rephāîm,** of uncertain etymology. The giants whom the Israelites met when they attempted to enter Canaan through Moab (Deut. 2:11, 20), are called Rephaim in ASV, RSV. They were tall, large-framed and powerful. The last of this race was Og, king of Bashan, whose iron bedstead, nine cubits long, was famous (Deut. 2:11; Josh. 12:4; 13:12). The land of the giants (Rephaim) is referred to in Joshua 17:15; the valley of the giants or Rephaim, located southwest of Jerusalem, in Joshua 15:8; 18:16. The

Rephaim are named in Genesis 14:5; 15:20; the valley of Rephaim in II Samuel 5:18, 22; 23:13; I Chronicles 11:15; 14:9; Isaiah 17:5. The best known giant of all, Goliath of Gath, champion of the Philistines, whom David as a youth slew (I Sam. 17), though described as of huge stature and great strength, is not called a giant on that account. Giants terrorized the Israelites from their entry into Canaan until the time of David.

Gibbar (gĭb′ȧr), a man whose children returned from captivity with Zerubbabel (Ezra 2:20).

Gibbethon (gĭb′ē-thŏn), a city W of Gezer in the territory of Dan (Josh. 19:44), allotted to the Kohathite Levites (Josh. 21:23). Baasha killed King Nadab at Gibbethon while Israel was besieging the city, which was now in the hands of the Philistines (I Kings 15:27).

Gibea (gĭb′ē-ȧ), a grandson of Caleb (I Chron. 2:49).

Gibeah (gĭb′ē-ȧ). 1. A city in the hill country of Judah (Josh. 15:57). 2. A city of Benjamin (Josh. 18:28), on the E side of the N-S road a few miles north of Jerusalem where excavation has uncovered the strong fortress-palace of Saul (I Sam. 10:26; 11:4; 13:2, 15, 16; 14:2, (ASV, RSV have Geba); 14:16; 15:34; 22:6; 23:19; 26:1. 3. Also ASV margin has Gibeah instead of "the hill," referring to the place where stood the house of Abinadab to which the ark of God was brought when it was returned by the Philistines (I Sam. 7:1). Here seven of Saul's descendants were hanged to satisfy the vengeance of the Gibeonites (II Sam. 21:6; RSV has Gibeon). One of David's mighty men was from Gibeah of Benjamin (II Sam. 23:29; I Chron. 11:31).

Gibeath (gĭb′ē-ăth, Josh. 18:28), probably the same as Gibeah of Saul, which see. RSV text has Gibeah; margin Heb. Gibeath.

Gibeon (gĭb′ē-ŏn, **pertaining to a hill**), a city of Benjamin (Josh. 18:25) NW of Jerusalem; it was given to the priests (Josh. 21:17). At the time of the Conquest, Joshua, without consulting the Lord, was deceived by the ambassadors of Gibeon into making a treaty with them (Josh. 9). David smote the Philistines from Gibeon on the north to Gezer on the south (I Chron. 14:16). Solomon, at the outset of his reign, came to Gibeon to sacrifice, and to dream—to good purpose (I Kings 3:3-15; II Chron. 1:2-13). Again Solomon received a message from the Lord here (I Kings 9:1-9).

Gibeonites (gĭb′ē-ŏn-īts), the inhabitants of Gibeon; Hivites (Josh. 9:3, 7), Hurrians or Horites (Gen. 36:20; Deut. 2:12). Because of the deceitful manner in which they gained the favor of Joshua, they were made slave-laborers for menial tasks such as chopping wood and drawing water (Josh. 9). A Gibeonite was leader of David's thirty mighty men (I Chron. 12:4). Gibeonites helped repair the walls of Jerusalem (Neh. 3:7).

Giblites (gĭb′līts), the inhabitants of Gebal or Byblos (Josh. 13:5; ASV, RSV Gebalites). See Gebal.

Giddalti (gĭ-dăl′tī), a leader of music (I Chron. 25:4, 29).

Giddel (gĭd′ĕl). 1. One of the Nethinim who returned from exile with Zerubbabel (Ezra 2:47; Neh. 7:49). 2. Sons of Giddel (Ezra 5:26; Neh. 7:58).

Gideon (gĭd′ē-ŏn, **feller** or **hewer**), the son of Joash, an Abiezrite (Judg. 6:11), who lived in Ophrah, not far from Mt. Gerizim. When he is first mentioned he was a mature man (8:20). Gideon had already become a noted warrior (6:12), perhaps by waging "underground" warfare against the marauding Midianites. The extent to which the people had been enslaved is shown by the fact that Gideon had to hide in a winepress to do the threshing (6:11). That the messenger who called Gideon to lead Israel was from God was attested to by supernatural fire which consumed a sacrifice which he had placed upon a rock (6:17-23).

Gideon responded to the call and, with the help of some friends, overthrew the altar of Baal and cut down the sacred grove around it. For his daring feat the followers of Baal wanted to slay him, but his father intervened. Instead of death he was given a new name, Jerubbaal, or "Contender with Baal" (6:28-32). Later the name was changed to Jerubbesheth, "Contender with the Idol," evidently to eliminate any recognition of Baal (II Sam 11:21). Gideon then issued a call to adjoining tribesmen to war against the Midianites. Having gathered a formidable host, he sought to know the surety of his faith and so put forth the famous test of the fleece (6:36-40). As further assurance, he was instructed to slip into the enemy's camp, and there he overheard one soldier tell another of a dream and interpret it as meaning that Gideon's smaller army would win the battle (7:9-14). To prevent human boasting over victory, God instructed Gideon to reduce his force to 300 picked men by (1) letting the faint-hearted go home; and (2) by choosing only such men as were cautious enough to dip their drinking water while passing over a stream (7:1-8). Thus came the famous army of 300.

After his country was delivered all the way to the Jordan (7:22, 23; 8:1-21), his people would have made him king. Gideon refused. Gideon's ability and statesmanship are shown in his long and fruitful ministry of forty years as judge (8:28). During his life he begat 71 sons, one, Abimelech, by a concubine of Shechem. After Gideon's death idolatry returned (8:32-35), Abimelech seized an opportune time, engaged mercenaries, invaded the land of Gideon, and destroyed all the seventy sons except Jotham who escaped by a bit of strategy (9:1-6).

Gideoni (gĭd'ē-ō'nī, **cutter down),** a prince of Benjamin's tribe (Num. 7:60).

Gidom (gī'dŏm, **desolation).** An isolated place east of Bethel, to which the routed Benjamites fled from angry brethren (Judg. 20:45).

Gier Eagle (See Birds)

Gift, Giving. At least fifteen words in the Bible are used for it: **eshkār,** a reward (Ps. 72:10); **minhâh,** an offering to a superior (Judg. 3:15); **mattān,** that given to gain a favor (Gen. 34:12), or as an act of submission (Ps. 68:29); **mattenā** and **mattānâh,** an offering (Gen. 25:6; Dan. 2:6; **shōhadh,** a bribe (Deut. 16:19). In the NT, **dósis** and **dóron,** anything given (Luke 21:1; James 1:17); **dóma,** a present (Matt. 7:11); **cháris,** and **chárisma,** special enduement (Rom. 1:11; I Tim. 4:14); to be cherished (I Cor. 12:31).

Gifts, Spiritual (Gr. **charismata), a** theological term meaning any endowment that comes through the grace of God (Rom. 1:11). Paul discussed at length in I Corinthians 12 the enduements for special tasks in and through the churches (Rom. 6:23; II Cor. 1:11; I Pet. 4:10). They are found in ability to speak an unlearned tongue (I Cor. 14:1-33); power to drive out evil spirits (Matt. 8:16; Acts 13:7-12); special ability in healing the sick (I Cor. 12:9); prophecy (Rom. 12:6); keenness of discernment (wisdom) and knowledge (I Cor. 12:4-8). These gifts are to be sought diligently (I Cor. 12:31), but never at the risk of neglecting the "more excellent way" of pursuing faith, hope and love, of which love is the greatest gift (I Cor. 13:13). Fruits of the Spirit are given in Galatians 5:22-23. Everyone is accountable for any gift bestowed upon him (I Pet. 4:10; I Cor. 4:7).

Gihon (gī'hŏn, **burst forth).** 1. One of the four rivers in Eden (Gen. 2:8-14). Since Eden was probably in the Tigris-Euphrates Valley, it is possible that Gihon was a small stream in that region. 2. Gihon is also the name of a noted spring near Jerusalem. Solomon was anointed there to succeed David (I Kings 1:32-40).

Gilalai (gĭl'ȧ-lī), a musician who assisted in the dedication of the wall of Jerusalem (Neh. 12:36).

Gilboa (gĭl-bō'ȧ, **bubbling).** A range of barren hills on the eastern side of the Plain of Esdraelon, named from a noted spring. The mean elevation of the hills is about 1,600 feet. Saul gathered his forces here to await an attack by the Philistines. During the battle he was wounded; his forces were routed; and he committed suicide (I Chron. 10:1-8).

Gilead (gĭl'ē-ăd, **rugged).** The land owned by Israel E of the Jordan River, extending from the lower end of the Sea of Galilee to the northern end of the Dead Sea, and from the Jordan eastward to the desert, a plateau of some 2,000 feet elevation. At the time of Moses it was a lush region with goodly forests, rich grazing lands, and abundant moisture. Jacob camped at Gilead when fleeing from Laban (Gen. 31:7-43). Overtaken at that place, he made a covenant with Laban which was confirmed by a pile of stones which Jacob named **Galeed,** "Heap of Witness" (Gen. 31:47 marg.). During succeeding years it came to be applied to the entire region which included Mount Gilead (Gen. 31:25), the land of Gilead (Num. 32:1), and Gilead (Gen. 37:25).

When Canaan was allocated to the Israelites, Gilead fell to the Reubenites, Gadites and to half the tribe of Manasseh (Deut. 3:13). An account of the conquest of the region is found in Deuteronomy 2 and 3. Moses was permitted to see the goodly plain before his death (Deut. 34:1). After the land was conquered a great altar was erected beside the Jordan that true worship might not be forgotten (Josh. 22:10).

Gilead became famous because of

Site of ancient Gilgal, one of the first camping sites of Joshua's army in the Promised Land. © *MPS*

some of its products. Balm was exported to Tyre (Ezek. 27:17); Jeremiah knew of its curative power (8:22; 46:11; 51:8). Absalom gathered his forces in Gilead when he rebelled against David (II Sam. 15:13-23). The Gileadites finally fell into gross idolatry (Hos. 6:8; 12:11), were overcome by Hazael (II Kings 10:32-34), and led into captivity by Tiglath-pileser (II Kings 15:27-29).

Gilgal (gĭl′găl, **circle of stones),** the first camp of Israel after crossing the Jordan (Josh. 4:19, 20). According to Josephus, Gilgal was about ten miles from the Jordan and two miles or more from Jericho.

It was to Gilgal that Saul was sent by Samuel to be confirmed as king over Israel (I Sam. 11:15). There Saul later grew restless because of the delay in the coming of Samuel and offended Jehovah by presuming to act as priest and make his own sacrifice (I Sam. 13:1-10). Judah gathered at Gilgal to meet David when he returned from defeating the rebels under Absalom (II Sam. 19).

Gilgal is not mentioned in the NT and its location is not known. The town from which Elijah ascended was not this Gilgal (II Kings 2:1). Gilgal furnished singers who had part in the dedication of the wall of Jerusalem (Neh. 12:27-43).

Giloh (gī′lō), home of Ahithophel, one of David's counsellors (II Sam. 15:12), also a town of Judah (Josh. 15:51).

Gimzo (gĭm′zō, **place of lush sycamores),** a town some three miles southwest of Lydda, off the Jerusalem highway, captured by Philistines during the reign of Ahaz (II Chron. 28:18).

Gin, a trap to ensnare game (Amos 3:5) or to deceive and destroy (Pss. 140:5; 141:9); a pitfall (Job 18:9) or an offense (Isa. 8:14).

Ginath (gī′năth, **protector),** the father of Tibni (I Kings 16:21).

Ginnetho (See Ginnethon)

Ginnethon (gĭn′ē-thon), a priest who returned to Jerusalem with Zerubbabel (Neh. 10:6; 12:4).

Girdle (See Dress)

Girgashites (gûr′gȧ-shītes), a Hamitic tribe of Canaan conquered by Joshua (Deut. 7:1).

Gispa (gĭs′pȧ, **listener),** an overseer of the Nethinims, in Nehemiah's time (Neh. 11:21).

Gittah-Hepher (See Gath-hepher)

Gittaim (gĭt′ā-ĭm, perhaps **two wine presses),** a town of Benjamin to which the Beerothites fled (Neh. 11:31, 33). Exact site unknown.

Gittites (gĭt′īt, **of Gath),** natives of Gath, unconquered at the time of Joshua's death (Josh. 13:1-3). The Ark was deposited in a Gittite home (II Sam. 6:8-11). David's guard included 600 men of Gath (II Sam. 15:18). Goliath was a Gittite (II Sam. 21:19).

Gittith (gĭt′ĭth), a word found in the titles of Psalms 8, 81, 84. It may denote some musical instrument made in Gath, or a tune popular in Gath.

Gizonite (gī′zō-nīt). Hashem, one of David's valiant men, was a Gizonite (I Chron. 11:34).

Glass, although a product known and used by man for ages, where its manufacture first arose is unknown. The fact that glass does not seem to have been used to any degree by the Hebrews may be accounted for by their hatred of Egyptian products (Lev. 18:3), or else it was cheaper for them to produce pottery. Mirrors (Exod. 38:8) were made of polished bronze. The only direct reference in the OT to glass is Job 28:17, where gold and crystal (glass RSV) are compared with wisdom. The glass mentioned by Paul (II Cor. 3:18), and that to which James referred (1:23, 24) was evidently the customary mirror of polished bronze, as the Gr. word used, meant such. By the time of Christ the people of Palestine were familiar with glass. The figurative expressions, revealing the transparent nature of the Holy City, pictured by John in Revelation 21:18, 21, refer to crystal glass.

Glean, the Hebrew custom of allowing the poor to follow the reapers and gather the grain that was left behind or the grapes which remained after the vintage (Judg. 8:2; Ruth 2:2, 16; Isa. 17:6).

Glede (See Birds)

Glory. Concerning God, it is the display of His divine attributes and perfections. Concerning man, it is the manifestation of his commendable qualities, such as wisdom, righteousness, self-control, ability, etc. A connotation of splendor is included, such as "the glory of the moon and the stars" (I Cor. 15:41). In both Testaments there are references to the Shekinah glory of God, although not by name, for the word occurs in the Targums, not in the Bible. To avoid anthropomorphisms (ascription of physical characteristics to God) which might lead to erroneous doctrine, the Targum writers spoke of the glory of the Shekinah. This was actually the physical manifestation of the presence of God, as seen in the pillars of cloud and fire. NT references to the Shekinah glory are seen in John 1:4 and Romans 9:4. Glory culminates in the changing of the bodies of the saints to the likeness of their glorified Lord (Phil. 3:20).

Gnash (năsh). In the OT the expression "to gnash with the teeth" represents for the most part rage, anger, or hatred (Job 16:9; Pss. 35:16; 37:12; 112:10). In the NT it expresses disappointment rather than anger (Matt. 8:12; 13:42, 50; 22:13; 24:51; 25:30; Luke 13:28).

Gnat (See Insects: Flies)

Goad (gōd), an eight-foot wooden pole shod at one end with a spade used for removing mud from the plow and at the other with a sharp point for prodding oxen. It was a formidable weapon in the hands of Shamgar (Judg. 3:31).

Goat (See Animals)

Goath (gō′ăth), a place **(RV has Goah)** the site of which is unknown, but apparently W of Jerusalem. Mentioned only once, in Jeremiah 31:39.

Gob (gŏb, **pit, cistern),** a place mentioned in II Samuel 21:18 as the scene of two of David's battles with the Philistines.

God. Although the Bible does not contain a formal definition of the word "God," yet His being and attributes are displayed on every page. The greatest definition of the word in the history of Christendom, that is, in the culture in which the Bible has been a prevailing influence, is the definition found in the Westminster Shorter Catechism (Q.4): "God is a Spirit, infinite, eternal, and unchangeable, in his being, wisdom, power, holiness, justice, goodness, and truth." It is fair to say that this definition faithfully sets forth what the Bible constantly assumes and declares concerning God.

"God is a Spirit." These words mean that God is a non-material personal being, self-conscious and self-determining.

"Infinite in His being." This doctrine is intended to teach that God is everywhere. The omnipresence of God is vividly brought out in such Scriptures as Psalm 139. He is **"infinite in His wisdom."** This phrase designates God's omniscience. The Bible throughout regards His omniscience as all-inclusive.

The words **"Infinite in His power"** point to His omnipotence, His ability to do with power all that power can do, His controlling all the power that is or can be. **"Infinite in His holiness, justice and goodness,"** signify God's moral attributes.

"Infinite in His truth," designates the basis of all logic and rationality. The axioms of logic and mathematics, and all the laws of reason, are not laws apart from God, to which God must be subject. They are attributes of His own character. When the Bible says that "it is impossible for God to lie" (Heb. 6:18; Titus 1:2) there is no contradiction of omnipotence. How much power would it take to make two times two equal five? Truth is not an object of power. **"Eternal"** in the Bible means, without temporal beginning or ending; or in a figurative sense, "eternal" may designate (as in the words "eternal life") a quality of being suitable for eternity. **"Unchangeable,"** in Bible language, points up the perfect self-consistency of God's character throughout all eternity.

God is known by His acts. Supremely, "God has spoken in his Son" (Heb. 1:1ff). Further, His "invisible" being, that is, His "eternal power and divine character **[theiotes** as distinguished from **theotes]**" are "known" and "clearly seen" by "the things He has made" (Rom. 1:20). "The heavens declare the glory of God" (Ps. 19; Rom. 10:18).

God is known in fellowship. That by faith God is known, beyond the mere cognitive sense, in fellowship with His people, is one of the most prominent themes throughout the Bible. Moses, leading His people in the exodus, was assured, "My presence shall go with thee, and I will give thee rest." And Moses replied, "If thy presence go not with me, carry us not up hence" (Exod. 33:14f). The Bible abounds in invitations to seek and find fellowship with God. See Psalm 27, Isaiah 55, and many similar gracious invitations.

Other gods are referred to in the Bible as false gods (Judg. 6:31; I Kings 18:27; I Cor. 8:4-6), or as demonic (I Cor. 10:19-22).

Godliness, the piety toward God and rectitude of conduct which springs from a proper relationship with Him. It is not right action which is done from a sense of duty, but is that spontaneous virtue that comes from the indwelling Christ, and which reflects Him.

Golan (gō'lăn), a city in the territory of the half tribe of Manasseh in Bashan, E of the Jordan. It was one of the three cities of refuge, and assigned to the Gershonite Levites (Deut. 4:43).

Gold (See Minerals)

Goldsmith (See Occupations and Professions: Artificer)

Golgotha (gŏl'gō-thȧ, **skull),** the place of our Lord's crucifixion. From the Heb. **gulgoleth,** which implies a **bald, round, skull-like mound** or **hillock.** The Latin name, **Calvarius (bald skull)** has been retained in the form **Calvary** (Luke 23:33). In the RV, it is simply, "the skull." Two explanations of the name are found: (1) It was a place of execution, and therefore abounded in skulls; (2) The place had the appearance of a skull when viewed from a short distance. Both Matthew (27:33) and Mark (15:22) locate it outside the city, but close to it (John 19:20) on the public highway, which was the type of location usually chosen by the Romans for executions.

Goliath (gō-lī'ăth, **exile),** a gigantic warrior of the Philistine army, probably one of the Anakim (Num. 13:33; Josh. 11:22). Goliath's size was extraordinary. If a cubit is 21 inches, he was over eleven feet in height; if about 18 inches, he was over nine feet. The only mention made of Goliath is his appearance as a champion of the Philistines (I Sam. 17). When David heard Goliath's challenge, he inquired its meaning. Upon being told, he went to face Goliath, armed only with a sling and five stones. Hit in the forehead, Goliath fell, and David cut off his head. When the Philistines saw that

Traditional site of Golgotha, called Gordon's Calvary. JFW

their champion was dead, they fled, pursued by victorious Israel. The Goliath of II Samuel 21:19 was probably the son of the giant whom David killed. He was slain by Elhanan, one of David's men.

Gomorrah (gō-mŏr'ȧ, **submersion**), one of the five "cities of the plain" located in the Vale of Siddim at the S end of the Dead Sea. Zoar alone escaped the destruction by fire from heaven in the time of Abraham and Lot.

Gopher Wood (gō'fer wōōd), the wood from which Noah's ark was made (Gen. 6:14), probably some resinous wood, like pine, cedar, or cypress.

Goshen (gō'shĕn, **mound of earth**). 1. The NE section of the Nile delta region is usually termed "the land of Goshen." Here the Israelites under Jacob settled, while Joseph was prime minister (Gen. 46). 2. A district of S Palestine, lying between Gaza and Gibeon (Josh. 10:41). 3. A town in the SW part of the mountains of Judah (Josh. 15:51).

Gospel (gŏs'pĕl, **good news**). The English word Gospel is derived from the Anglo-Saxon **godspell**, which meant "good tidings" and, later, the "story concerning God." As now used, the word describes the message of Christianity and the books in which the story of Christ's life and teaching is found. In the NT the word Gospel never means a book (one of the four Gospels); but always the good tidings which Christ and the apostles announced. It is called "the gospel of God" (Rom. 1:1; I Thess. 2:2, 9); "the gospel of Christ" (Mark 1:1; Rom. 1:16; 15:19); "the gospel of the grace of God" (Acts 20:24); "the gospel of peace" (Eph. 6:15); "the gospel of your salvation" (Eph. 1:13); and "the glorious gospel" (II Cor. 4:4). The Gospel has to do entirely with Christ.

Gospels, The Four. Because they contain the basic facts of Jesus' life, the writings of Matthew, Mark, Luke, and John are called the Gospels. The first three are called "Synoptic" because they "see the whole together," and present similar views of the life and teaching of Christ. Matthew presents Christ as the Messiah; Mark emphasizes His activity and the popular reaction to Him; Luke stresses His humanitarian interests; and John's Gospel is a collection of selected memoirs, carefully organized to induce belief (John 20:30, 31).

Reduced to writing, the gospel message constitutes a new type of literature. Although it is framed in history, it is not pure history, for the allusions to contemporary events are incidental, and the Gospels do not attempt to develop them. They contain biographical material, but they cannot be called biography in the modern sense of the word, since they do not present a complete summary of the life of Jesus. The chief purpose of the Gospels is to create faith in Christ on the part of their readers, who may or may not be believers.

The existence of the oral Gospel is attested by Papias, one of the earliest of the church fathers, who lived at the close of the first century.

A clue to the transition from oral preaching to written record is provided by explanatory statements in the Gospels of Luke and John. In the introduction to his Gospel, Luke asserts that he was undertaking to confirm by manuscript what his friend Theophilus had already learned by word of mouth (Luke 1:1-4). He spoke of facts which were taken for granted among believers, and indicated that there had already been numerous attempts to arrange them in orderly narratives. Since his use of the word "narrative" implies an extended account, there must have been a number of "gospels" in circulation which he considered to be either inaccessible or else unsatisfactory.

Luke affirmed that he had derived his facts from those who "from the beginning were eye-witnesses and ministers of the word" (1:2). Not only had his informants shared in the events of which they spoke, but also they had been so affected that they became propagandists of the new faith. Luke had been a contemporary of these witnesses, and had investigated personally the truth of their claims, that he might produce an orderly and accurate record of the work of Christ.

John also committed his Gospel to writing that he might inculcate faith in Christ as the Son of God (John 20: 30, 31). He did not profess to give an exhaustive account of Jesus' activities, but took for granted that many of them would be familiar to his readers. The selective process that he employed was determined by his evangelistic purpose and theological viewpoint.

Although Matthew and Mark are less explicit concerning their origins, the same general principles obtain. The introduction of Matthew, "The book of the generation of Jesus Christ, the son of David, the son of Abraham" (Matt. 1:1), duplicates the phraseology of Genesis (Gen. 5:1) to convey the impression that, like Genesis, it is giving a significant chapter in the history of God's dealing with man. Mark's terse opening line, "The beginning of the Gospel of Jesus Christ, the Son of God," is a title, labeling the following text as a summary of current preaching. Neither of these two offers any reason for its publication, but one may deduce fairly that all of the Gospels began in an attempt to preserve for posterity what had hitherto existed in the minds of the primitive witnesses and in their public addresses.

Where and when these documents were first given to the public is uncertain. The earliest quotations from the Gospel material appear in the letters of Ignatius, in the **Epistle of Barnabas, the Teaching of the Twelve Apostles,** and the **Epistle of Polycarp.** All of these are related to Antioch of Syria, and their quotations or allusions bear a stronger resemblance to the text of Matthew than to that of any other Gospel. If, as Papias said, Matthew was first written for the Hebrew or Aramaic church in Jerusalem, it may have been the basis for a Greek edition issued from Antioch during the development of the Gentile church in that city. It would, therefore, have been put into circulation some time after A.D. 50, and before the destruction of Jerusalem in A.D. 70.

The Gospel of Luke may have been a private document, sent first of all to Luke's friend and patron, Theophilus. It can hardly have been written later than A.D. 62, since it must have preceded Acts, which was written about the end of Paul's first imprisonment.

The last chapter of John's Gospel attempts to correct a rumor that he would never die. Obviously the rumor would have no basis unless he had attained an advanced age at the time when the concluding chapter was written. It is possible that it can be dated before A.D. 50, but most conservative scholars place it about A.D. 85. Traditionally it has been ascribed to the apostle John, who ministered at Ephesus in the closing years of the first century.

The Gospels were among the first writings to be quoted as sacred and authoritative. Growing intercommunication between the churches and the need for strengthening their defenses against heresy and the attacks of pagan critics promoted their interest in a canon of the Gospels. By A.D. 170 the four Gospels were securely established as the sole authorities. Eusebius (c. A.D. 350) and the fathers following him exclude all other Gospels from their official list, leaving these four the undisputed supreme authorities for knowledge of the life and work of

Christ. See Matthew, Gospel of; Mark, Gospel of; Luke, Gospel of; John, Gospel of; Canon, N.T.

Bibliography:

Bruce, F. F. **Are the New Testament Documents Reliable?** London: The Inter-Varsity Fellowship of Evangelical Unions, 1943.

Grant, R. M. **The Secret Sayings of Jesus.** Garden City, New York: Doubleday & Co., Inc., 1960.

Nineham, D. E., Ed. **Studies in the Gospels.** Oxford: Basil Blackwell, 1955.

Redlich, Edwin Basil. **Form Criticism: Its Value and Limitations.** New York: Charles Scribner's Sons. 1839.

Scroggie, W. Graham. **A Guide to the Gospels.** London: Pickering and Inglis, Ltd., 1948.

Stonehouse, Ned B. **Origins of the Synoptic Gospels.** Grand Rapids, Mich.; Wm. B. Eerdmans Pub. Co., 1963.

Streeter, Burnet H. **The Four Gospels.** Fifth Impression, **Revised.** London: Macmillan & Co., Ltd., 1936.

Zahn, Theodor. **Introduction to the New Testament.** Ed. M. W. Jacobus. Three volumes. Edinburgh: T. & T. Clark, 1909. See II, pp. 307-617; III, pp. 1-354.

Gourd (See Plants)

Governor (gŭv'êr-nôr), a word applied to an official who rules a land on behalf of a king or emperor to whom he is subordinate. The term is applied to Joseph (Gen. 42:6), Gedaliah (Jer. 40:5), and in the NT to the Roman procurators of Judea, Pilate, Felix, Festus (Matt. 27:2; Acts 23:24; 26:30).

Gozan (gō'zăn), a city located in NE Mesopotamia, on the Harbor River, a tributary of the Euphrates. Here the Israelites were deported by the Assyrians following the fall of Samaria, the capital of the northern kingdom (II Kings 17:6; 18:11; 19:12; II Chron. 5:26).

Grace, a term employed by the Biblical writers with a considerable variety of meaning: (1) Properly speaking, that which affords joy, pleasure, delight, charm, sweetness, loveliness; (2) Good will, loving-kindness, mercy, etc; (3) The kindness of a master toward a slave. Thus by analogy, it has come to signify the kindness of God to man (Luke 1:30). The NT writers, at the end of their various epistles, frequently invoke God's gracious favor upon their readers (Rom. 16:20, 24; Phil. 4:23; Col. 1:19; I Thess. 5:28; **et. al.**). In addition, the word "grace" is frequently used to express the concept of kindness bestowed upon someone undeserving thereof. Hence, undeserved favor, especially that kind or degree of favor bestowed upon sinners through Jesus Christ.

The relationship between law and grace is one of the major themes of the Pauline writings (Rom. 5:1, 15-17; 8:1, 2; Eph. 2:8, 9; Gal. 5:4, 5). Grace is likewise without equivocation identified as the medium or instrument through which God has effected the salvation of all believers (Titus 2:11). Grace is also regarded as the sustaining influence enabling the believer to persevere in the Christian life (Acts 11:23; 20:32; II Cor. 9:14). Thus, it is not merely the initiatory act of God in grace which secures the believers' eternal salvation, but also that which maintains it throughout the entirety of the Christian life. It is also used as a token or proof of salvation (II Cor. 1:5, RV "benefit"). A special gift of grace is imparted to the humble (I Pet. 5:5; James 4:6). Grace can also refer to the capacity for the reception of divine life (I Pet. 1:10). There are likewise several secondary senses in which "grace" is used: a gift of knowledge (I Cor. 1:4); thanksgiving or gratitude expressed for favor (I Cor. 10:30; I Tim. 1:1, 2). Grace is employed at least once in the sense of "reward or recompense" (Luke 6:32), for which Matthew substitutes the term **misthos,** or **wages** (Matt. 5:46).

Graff, Graft, a horticultural process by which the branches of the wild olive tree in eastern lands are cut back so that branches from a cultivated olivé may be inserted and grafting take place. Paul makes use of this practice in reverse (Rom. 11:17-24) where the opposite process is envisioned as happening; **i.e.,** the wild branches, the Gentiles, are thought of as "grafted in" to the good stock of the parent tree, the children of Israel.

Grain (See Plants)

Granary (grăn'êrē, derived from a Hebrew word meaning **to gather** [Ps. 144:15], or **storehouse** [Joel 1:17]). In the NT the term is sometimes rendered **barn,** and sometimes **garner** (Matt. 3:12; Luke 3:17).

Grape (See Plants)

Grass. There are a great many species of true grasses in Palestine, but actual turf is virtually unknown. The word

One of the Tombs of the Kings in Jerusalem, showing a rolling stone at the opening. © *MPS*

"grass" is used in a somewhat comprehensive sense in the English version and is the rendering of a number of Hebrew terms and one Greek term (Gen. 1:11, 12). The word is used in a figurative sense, too, as when man's brief exile is compared to grass (Ps. 103:15, 16; Matt. 6:30; Luke 12:28).

Grasshopper (See Insects)

Grate, a copper network, moved by a copper ring at each corner and placed under the top of the great altar (Exod. 27:4; 35:16; 38:4, 5) to catch the ashes from the burning sacrifices.

Grave, a place for the interment of the dead; a tomb, a sepulchre. Graves and accompanying burial customs differed in Biblical times from country to country. The pyramids were used for burial of members of the royal house. The Egyptians were meticulous in the construction of their graves because of their ardent belief in a future life. The rich were buried in a **mastaba,** or a rectangular structure of brick placed above the grave itself. In the neighborhood of Gizeh near the pyramids and at Saqqarah a number of these mastabas have been discovered. The very poor were interred clothesless and coffinless in the dry, sandy soil of Egypt. Among the Hebrews, graves were sometimes mere holes in the earth (Gen. 35:8; I Sam. 31:13); natural caves or grottos; or artificial tombs hewn out of the rock (Luke 7:12; John 11:30). In such a sepulchre, provided through the kindness of Joseph of Arimathea, the body of Jesus was laid. Whitewashed flat stones were placed upon the graves as markers to warn passers-by that they should not contract ceremonial defilement by unwittingly trespassing.

Grave Clothes. Preparatory to burial, the body was washed, and frequently anointed with spices, then stretched out on a bier until it was ready to be buried (Acts 5:7). After the washing and anointing, the corpse was wrapped in a linen winding sheet, the hands and feet were bound with grave-bands, and the face covered with a napkin (John 11:44; 19:40).

Graven Image, an image of wood, stone, or metal, shaped with a sharp cutting instrument as distinguished from one cast in a mold (Isa. 20:22; 44:16, 17; 45:20).

Great Owl (See Birds)

Greaves (See Arms, Armor)

Greece (grecia, grecians), Grecia is Greece, the home of the Hellenes. Greeks and Grecians, however, are to be distinguished. Greeks are generally those of Hellenic race (e.g. Acts 16:1; 18:4 and probably John 12:20), but the word may be used to indicate non-Jews, foreigners and aliens (Rom. 1: 16). Grecians were Greek-speaking Jews, folk of the Dispersion, from areas predominantly Greek (Acts 6:1; 9:29). Greece and its associated island groups form the SE end of southern Europe's mountain system, a rugged peninsula and archipelago, not rich in fertile or arable land, which was the terminus of the southward movement of the Indo-European-speaking tribes who became the Greek people. These tribes, or their predecessors, had established ordered life in the peninsula and islands by the twelfth century before Christ. Their civilization vanished before the end of the second millennium, in a dark age of destruction and invasion occasioned by further waves of wandering tribes, just as Celt, Roman, Saxon, Dane, Norman, ripples of the same folk-movement of related peoples, made a succession of construction and destruction in Britain. Out of four centuries of chaos emerged the complex of peoples on island and mainland who are called the Greeks. Their own generic name was Hellenes, but Graecia was a portion of the land which, lying in the NW, naturally came first into the ken of Rome. After the common fashion of popular nomenclature (see under "Palestine"), the name of the part which first claimed attention was extended to include the whole. Mediated through Rome, the term Greece was applied to all Hellas, and all Hellenes were called Greeks by western Europe.

To reason, question, speculate, was a habit with the Greeks. Hence the logical mind of Greek-speaking Paul of Tarsus, heir of both Hellenism and Judaism. Hence the "Grecians" of the NT, Stephen, for example, and Philip, who sweep fresh, bold, and vigorous into the story of the early Church, ready to reform, and to rethink old concepts. Paul needed his Greek education, as he needed the Judaism of Gamaliel. Paul's synthesis of the covenants, so compelling in its logic, so fundamental in Christian theology, was the work of a Greek Jew.

Greek Language was a major branch of the Indo-European language which is the presumed parent of all the languages of Europe except Basque, Finnish and Hungarian, and of Sanskrit and the languages which derive from the Sanskrit stock in India. Attic Greek was one of the major achievements of the human mind. The richness and subtlety of its syntax, its flexibility, the delicacy of its particles, these and other linguistic features make Attic the most expressive medium ever developed for human thought. The dialects passed with the city states and the unification of Greece, and were followed by a basic Greek which developed in the form of a simplified Attic. This, spread by Alexander's conquests throughout the eastern end of the Mediterranean, was called the **Koine** or Common Dialect. It was the speech of the LXX and the NT, and the major influence in bringing the contributions of Palestine, Greece, and Rome into that partnership which determined the form and shape of the NT, the global Gospel of Paul of Tarsus, the Christian Church, and modern Europe. Greek was widely spoken in Palestine, and became the chief language of the early church (Acts 21:37).

Greek Versions. 1. The first and most famous of the Greek Versions of the OT, and the only one to survive in its entirety, is the Septuagint or "Version of the Seventy." The Septuagint was published in the time of Ptolemy II Philadelphus (295-247 B.C.), the Golden Age of Greek Alexandria. It is written in the common dialect, but tinged by Hebraisms. 2. The acceptance of the Septuagint as the Bible of Greek-speaking Christianity, prompted orthodox Jewry to produce its own version distinct from it. Hence the version of Aquila of Hadrian's day (A.D. 117-138). 3. Theodotian, an Ephesian of the second century, and an Ebionite Christian, produced a version which could be described as a RV of the Septuagint. It found favor with the Christian community. 4. Symmachus, of unknown date, produced, perhaps at the end of the second century, a Greek version which appears to have been the best of all the translations, a rendering into idiomatic Greek.

Greyhound (See Animals)

Grind, the grinding of grain into flour when pulverized between two heavy stones (Matt. 24:41; Luke 17:35).

Grove, a mistranslation of the Hebrew **asherah,** emblem of the goddess of fertility, symbolized by the trunk of a tree. The reforming kings of Judah destroyed these idolatrous emblems (I Kings 15:13; II Kings 17:10; 21:3; 23:4).

Guard, the rendering of a number of Heb. and Gr. words: 1. **tabbāh, slaughterer,** used of Potiphar (Gen. 37:36, etc.), Nebuzaradan (II Kings 25:8, etc.; Jer. 39:9, etc.), and Arioch (Dan. 2:14). 2. **rûts, runner,** trusted foot soldiers of a king, who performed various functions (I Kings 14:27, 28; II Kings 10:25). 3. **mishmār, watch** Neh. 4:22). 4. **mishma'ath, guard** (II Sam. 23:23). 5. **spekoulátor, guard, a spy** (Mark 6:27). 6. **koustodía, watch** (Matt. 27:65).

Gudgodah (**gŭd-gō′dȧ, cleft, division**), a place in the wilderness journeys of the children of Israel (Deut. 10:7), location still uncertain.

Guest Chamber (Heb. **lishkâh,** in I Sam. 9:22 of KJV "parlor," **katáluma, inn, room in which to eat**). The **lishkâh** may have been a room in which the sacrificial feasts were held. **Katáluma** often means "inn," but in Mark 14:14 and Luke 22:11 it means a room in which to eat.

Guilt is the deserving of punishment because of the violation of a law or a breach of conduct. In the OT law the conception of guilt is largely ritualistic and legalistic. A person could be guilty as the result of unwitting sin (Lev. 5:17). Israel, moreover, is viewed as an organic whole, so that what one does affects all. There is collective responsibility for sin, as when Achan sinned and all Israel suffered. With the prophets, the ethical and personal aspects of sin and of guilt are stressed. God is less interested in ritual correctness than in moral obedience.

In the NT Jesus stressed the importance of right heart attitude as over against outwardly correct acts, and taught that there are degrees of guilt, depending upon a person's knowledge

A fragment from the Septuagint, the Sinaitic manuscript, photographed from one of the scraps found by Dr. Tischendorf at Mt. Sinai. © MPS

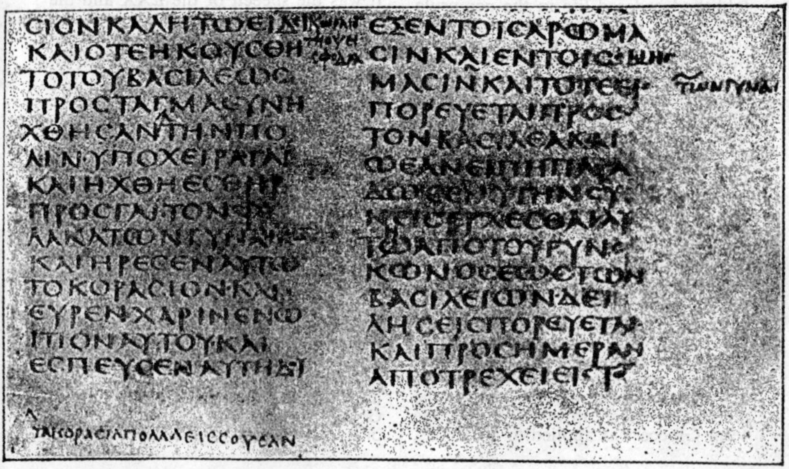

and motive (Luke 11:29-32; 12:47, 48; 23:34). Paul also recognized differences of degree in guilt (Acts 17:30; Eph. 4:18; Rom. 3:19).

Guni (gū'nī). 1. The name of a family of Naphtali (Gen. 46:24; Num. 26:48; I Chron. 7:13). 2. The head of a Gadite family (I Chron. 5:15).

Gunite (gū'nīt), the family of Guni (Num. 26:48).

Gur (gûr). The place where Ahaziah received his mortal wound while fleeing from Jehu (II Kings 9:27).

Gur-Baal (gûr'bā'ăl, **sojourn of Baal**), a town of Arabs, against whom Uzziah of Judah was given divine aid (II Chron. 26:7); perhaps S of Beer-sheba.

Gutter (gŭt'têr, **pipe, spout, conduit**), the channel or tunnel (AV gutter) through which David's soldiers are inferred to have marched to wrest the city of Jerusalem from Jebusite rule (II Sam. 5:8). Hezekiah constructed (II Kings 20:20) a tunnel connecting the spring at Gihon with the pool of Siloam. It was 1800 ft. long and 6 ft. high, dug out as a far sighted measure so that the city's water supply would not be imperiled during the impending siege at the hands of Sennacherib of Assyria.

A view in the Siloam Tunnel, built by Hezekiah in the eighth century B.C., also known as Hezekiah's Tunnel or the Gutter. © *MPS*

–H–

Haahashtari, Haashtari (hā′ȧ-hăsh′tȧ-rī, hā-ăsh′tȧ-rī, **the Ahashtarite**) a man of Judah (I Chron. 4:6).

Habaiah (hȧ-bā′yȧ, **Jehovah has hidden**), ancestor of some priests in Zerubbabel's time (Ezra 2:61).

Habakkuk (hȧ-băk′ŭk, **embrace**), the name of a prophet and of the eighth book of the Minor Prophets, which is entitled "The oracle which Habakkuk the prophet saw" (1:1). Of the man Habakkuk nothing is known outside of the book which bears his name. The musical references in Chapter 3 have led some to believe that he was a member of a Levitical musical guild.

Most traditional scholars believe the book to be a unity, the work of Habakkuk, produced in Judah during the Chaldean period. The reasons for this view are found in the book itself. The temple still stands (2:20; 3:19) and the rise of the Chaldean power is predicted (1:5, 6). The argument here depends upon the understanding of the Hebrew word **kasdîm,** translated Chaldeans.

The prophecy of Habakkuk could hardly have been given before 605 B.C. Jerusalem fell to Nebuchadnezzar in 587 B.C. The book must be placed somewhere between these dates, probably during the reign of the Judean king Jehoiakim.

Chapters 1 and 2 set forth Habakkuk's prophetic oracle or burden. Twice the prophet is perplexed and asks divine enlightenment; twice he is answered. First he is concerned over the violence and sin of his people, the Judeans. Why are these wicked men not punished (1:2-4)? God answers that He is about to send the Chaldeans to judge Judah (1:5-11). This answer plunges Habakkuk into a greater perplexity: How can a righteous God use the wicked Chaldeans to punish Judah, which, although it has become

A fragment of the Habbakuk commentary from the Dead Sea Scrolls. © Shrine of the Book, Jerusalem. MPS

apostate, is still better than the Chaldeans (1:12-17)? God's answer is that the proud conquerors will themselves be punished (2:1-20). The righteous will live by His faithfulness, i.e., by His constancy, abiding in God although all of the helps given to the OT believers (the nation, the temple and its ritual) are swept away (2:4). This statement naturally becomes important to the NT writers and is quoted in Rom. 1:17; Gal. 3:11; and Heb. 10:38. The second answer to Habakkuk concludes with a series of woes against the Chaldeans (2:5-20).

Chapter 3 is called "a prayer of Habakkuk the prophet" (3:1). In a moving lyric poem the prophet records his final response to God's message of judgment. (3:2-19).

Habaziniah (hab'ȧ-zĭ-nī'ȧ), ancestor of the Rechabites of the time of Jeremiah (35:3).

Habergeon (hăb'êr-jŭn), a jacket of mail to defend the breast and neck (II Chron. 26:14; Neh. 4:16).

Habiru (hȧ-bī'rū), a people first made known in the Amarna letters (15th century B.C.), where they are mentioned among those who are intruders of Palestine. Since then the name has appeared in Babylonian texts and documents from Mari (18th century B.C.), the Hittite records from Boghaz-keui and the Hurrian texts from Nuzi (14th century B.C.). The fundamental meaning of Habiru seems to be "wanderers." It is not an ethnic designation, for the Habiru of these various texts are of mixed racial origin, including both Semites and non-Semites. The name Habiru therefore has a wider connotation than the people known as Hebrews, although it became associated with them particularly. The patriarchal movements of Genesis appear to be parts of a larger movement of peoples known as the Habiru, with the Hebrew conquest of Canaan as only one of these. The connection, if any, of the Hebrews with the Habiru still remains obscure.

Habor (hā'bôr), a river of Gozan, the region in the northern part of Mesopotamia to which Shalmanezer, king of Assyria, banished the northern tribes of Israel after Hoshea, the last king, had rebelled against him (II Kings 17:6; 18:11).

Hachaliah (hăk'ȧ-lī'ȧ), the father of Nehemiah (Neh. 1:1; 10:1).

Hachilah (hȧ-kī'lȧ), a hill in the wilderness SE of Hebron, near Ziph and Maon (I Sam. 23:19; 26:1, 3), where David hid from Saul.

Hachmoni (hăk'mō-nī, **wise),** father of Jehiel (I Chron. 27:32) and Jashobeam, one of David's mighty men (I Chron. 11:11).

Hadad (hā'dăd, **sharpness, fierceness).** 1. Grandson of Abraham (Gen. 25:15; Hadar in KJV; I Chron. 1:30). 2. An early king of Edom (I Chron. 1:50). 3. An earlier king of Edom, a son of Bedad, (Gen. 36:35; I Chron. 1:46). 4. An Edomite prince who became an adversary to Solomon (I Kings 11:14-25). 5. The supreme God of Syria.

Hadadezer, Hadarezer (hăd'ăd-ē'zêr, hăd'ăr-ē'zêr, **Hadad is a help),** a king of Zobah, defeated by David (II Sam. 8:3ff; 10:1-19; I Chron. 18:3ff).

Hadad-Rimmon (hā'dăd-rĭm'ŏn, **Hadad and Rimmon, two Syrian divinities),** a place in the valley of Megiddo, where Josiah, king of Judah, was mortally wounded (II Kings 23:29, 30).

Hadar (hā'dȧr). 1. A son of Ishmael (Gen. 25:15). 2. The last of the ancient kings of Edom (Gen. 36:39). See Hadad.

Hadashah (hȧ-dăsh'ȧ, **new),** a town of Judah in the low plain in Joshua's time (Josh. 15:37).

Hadassah (hȧ-dăs'ȧ, **a myrtle),** Esther, queen of Xerxes, i.e. Ahasuerus (Esth. 2:7, 15).

Hadattah (hȧ-dăt'ȧ, **new),** a town in the S of Judah.

Hades (hā'dēz, **not to be seen),** the place or state of the dead, the equivalent of the Hebrew Sheol, which is variously rendered "grave," "hell," "pit." (See Sheol). The NT word, generally translated "hell," does not necessarily imply a place of torment, but connotes the grim and cheerless aspect of death (Acts 2:27; Rev. 1:18; 6:8; 20:13, 14). It may include the idea of retribution (Luke 16:23).

Hadid (hā'dĭd, **sharp),** a village in Benjamin (Ezra 2:33; Neh. 7:37; 11:34) about three miles E of Lydda.

Hadlai (hăd'lī, **ceasing, forbearing),** the father of Amasa (II Chron. 28:12).

Hadoram (hȧ-dō'răm). 1. A son of Joktan (Gen. 10:27; I Chron. 1:21). 2. Son of the king of Hamath (I Chron. 18:9-11). 3. Rehoboam's superintendent of the men under taskwork (II Chron. 10:18).

Hadrach (hā'drăk), Syrian country that lay E of Damascus (Zech. 9:1).

Hagab (hā'găb, **locust),** ancestor of

The Lahai-Roi Spring at Mount Seir, the spot where Hagar and her son Ishmael obtained water. © MPS

temple servants who returned with Zerubbabel (Ezra 2:46).

Hagar (hā′gȧr, **emigration, flight**), an Egyptian handmaid to Sarai, wife of Abram (Gen. 12:10-20). Sarai gave Hagar to her husband as her substitute (Gen. 16:1-16). Hagar was driven out, but the angel of the Lord appeared to her and sent her back to her mistress (Gen. 16:7-14). When Ishmael, her son, was 14 years old, his father 100 and Sarah 90, Isaac was born. At a great feast held in connection with Isaac's weaning, Ishmael scoffed at the proceedings (Gen. 21:9), and as a result Sarah insisted that Hagar and her son be cast out, which Abraham unwillingly did. God told Abraham that Ishmael's descendants would become a nation. Hagar is last seen taking for her son a wife out of the land of Egypt, her own land (Gen. 21:1-21). Paul made the story of Hagar an allegory of the difference between law and grace (Gal. 4:21-5:1).

Hagarenes, Hagarites (hā′gȧr-ēnz, hā′-gȧr-īts), descendants of Ishmael with whom Saul made war (I Chron. 5:10, 18-22; 27:31).

Haggai (hăg′ā-ī, **festal**), prophet of the Lord to the Jews in 520 B.C. Little is known of his personal history. He lived soon after the Captivity, and was contemporary with Zechariah (cf. Hag. 1:1 with Zech 1:1).

After the return from the Captivity the Israelites set up the altar upon its base, established daily worship, and laid the foundation for the second temple; then they were compelled to cease building for some years. However, though times were hard they were able to build fine ceiled houses for themselves (Hag. 1:4). Meanwhile kings succeeded one another in Persia. Cyrus, favored of God and friend of the Jews (Isa. 44:28; II Chron. 36:22) passed away in 529 B.C.; then his son Cambyses (the "Ahasuerus" of Ezra 4:6) reigned 529-522 B.C., followed for only seven months in 522 by the Pseudo-Smerdis (a usurper); then arose Darius Hystaspes (Ezra 4-6; Hag., Zech. 1-6), who helped and encouraged the Jews to go ahead, and who commanded the hinderers to desist. In the second year of Darius (520 B.C.) Haggai fulfilled his brilliant mission of rebuking and encouraging the Jews. The five short messages which make up his books are all dated, occupying only three months and 23 days; and in those few weeks the whole situation changed from defeat and discouragement to victory. Zechariah assisted Haggai in the last month of his recorded ministry (Zech. 1:1-6). Outline. 1. Call and encouragement to build (1). 2. The Messianic hope (2).

Haggeri (hăg'ē-rĭ, **wanderer**), the father of Mibhar (I Chron. 11:38).

Haggi (hăg'ī, **festal**), a son of Gad, and grandson of Jacob (Gen. 46:16; Num. 26:15).

Haggiah (hă-gī'ȧ, **a festival of Jehovah**), a Levite of the family of Merari (I Chron. 6:30).

Haggith (hăg'ĭth, **festal**), wife of David (II Sam. 3:4) and mother of Adonijah (I Kings 1:5-31).

Hagiographa (hăg'ĭ-ŏg'rȧ-fȧ, **holy writings**), the third division of the OT by the Jews, the other two being the Law and the Prophets. Sometimes called the "Writings," they comprise 11 books, in the following order: Psalms, Proverbs, Job, Song of Solomon, Ruth, Lamentations, Ecclesiastes, Esther, Daniel, Ezra, Nehemiah, I and II Chronicles.

Hai (hā'ī, **the heap**). 1. A town E of Bethel and near Beth-aven (Gen. 12:8; 13:3). 2. A city of the Ammonites (Jer. 49:3).

Hail. 1. Hail storms sometimes take place in the Near East in the spring and summer and do considerable damage to crops, sometimes even injuring property and endangering life. Plagues of hail are mentioned in Exodus 9:23, 24 and Joshua 10:11. The prophets speak of hail as a means of punishing the wicked (Isa. 28:2; Ezek. 38:22; Rev. 8:7; 11:19). 2. A greeting (Matt. 26:49).

Hair, regarded by Jews as a mark of beauty and sometimes of pride; baldness was despised (II Kings 2:23; Isa. 3:24; Jer. 47:5). Nazarites and women wore hair long (Num. 6:5; Luke 7:38). Israelites could not cut the corners of their beards (Lev. 19:27).

Hakkatan (hăk'ȧ-tăn, **the little one**), father of Johanan who returned with Ezra (Ezra 8:12).

Hakkoz (hăk'ŏz, **the nimble,** KJV sometimes has Koz, once Coz). 1. A descendant of Aaron whose descendants returned with Zerubbabel (I Chron. 24:10; Ezra 2:61; Neh. 3:4, 21). 2. A man of Judah (I Chron. 4:8).

Hakupha (hȧ-kū'fȧ, **bent, bowed**), father of some of the Nethinim (Ezra 2:51; Neh. 7:53).

Halah (hā'lȧ), a district in Media to which many of the captive Israelites were taken (II Kings 17:6; 18:11; I Chron. 5:26).

Halak (hā'lăk, **smooth**), mountain that marked the S limit of the conquests of Joshua (Josh. 11:17; 12:7).

Halhul (hăl'hŭl), a town in Judah (Josh. 15;58) about four miles N of Hebron.

Hali (hā'lī, **ornament**), a town of Asher (Josh. 19:25).

Hall. (1) The court of the high priest's palace (Luke 22:55); (2) the official residence of a Roman provincial governor (Matt. 27:27; Mark 15:16).

Hallel (hă-lāl, **praise**). Psalms 113-118 were called the "Egyptian Hallel"; Psalm 136 is an antiphonal Psalm of praise and is sometimes called "the Hallel." Psalms 120-136 are often called the "Great Hallel."

Hallelujah (hăl'ē-lōō'yȧ, **praise ye Jehovah**), liturgical ejaculation urging all to praise Jehovah. Occurs at the beginning of Psalms 106, 111-113, 117, 135, 146-150 and at the close of 104-106, 113, 115-117, 135, 146-150.

Hallohesh (hă-lō'hĕsh, **the whisperer**), in Neh. 3:12, father of Shallum, a ruler, and in Neh. 10:24 one of the covenanters, perhaps the same man.

Hallow (hăl'ō, **to render or treat as holy**). To set apart a person or a thing for sacred use; to hold sacred; reverence as holy.

Ham (hăm, **perhaps hot**). 1. The youngest son of Noah, born probably about 96 years before the Flood; and one of eight persons to live through the Flood. He became the progenitor of the dark races; not the Negroes, but the Egyptians, Ethiopians, Libyans and Canaanites (Gen. 10:6-20). His indecency, when his father lay drunken, brought a curse upon Canaan (Gen.

9:20-27). 2. City E of the Jordan (Gen. 14:5). 3. The descendants of the original Ham (Pss. 78:51; 105:23; 106:22). In these passages "Ham" is used as another name for Egypt as representing Ham's principal descendants.

Haman (hā'măn), the great enemy of the Jews in the days of Esther. "Ahasuerus" or Xerxes, as he is known in secular history, had promoted Haman to a high position in the court, but Mordecai, the noble Jew, refused to do him obeisance, and so Haman plotted to destroy the Jewish race, but God intervened. Esther foiled Haman's plot (Esth. 7) and Haman died on the gallows he had made for Mordecai.

Hamath (hā'măth, **fortification),** a very old city on the Orontes in Syria (Gen. 10:18; Num. 13:21; I Kings 8:65); now called Hama.

Hamath-zobah (hā'măth-zō'bȧ), a place mentioned in II Chron. 8:3.

Hammath (hăm'ăth, **hot spring).** 1. One of the fortified cities assigned to the tribe of Naphtali in the division of the land under Joshua (Josh. 19:35). It lay close to the shore of the Sea of Galilee, only a mile or so S of the city of Tiberias. Gesenius thinks that it is probably the same as the Hammoth-dor of Joshua 21:32, and Hammon of I Chronicles 6:76. 2. The founder of the house of Rechab (I Chron. 2:55).

Hammedatha (hăm'ē-dā-thȧ), father of Haman the Agagite (Esth. 3:1, etc.).

Hammelech (hăm'ĕ-lĕk, **the king),** father of Jerahmeel and Malchiah (Jer. 36:26; 38:6). The KJV wrongly translates it as a proper name; it should be rendered "the king," as in ARV.

Hammer. A tool for smoothing metals and for breaking rocks (Isa. 41:7; Jer. 23:29), and a mallet to drive tent-pins into the ground (Judg. 4:21; I Kings 6:7), for building and for making idols (Isa. 44:12; Jer. 10:4). Sometimes used figuratively for any crushing power (Jer. 23:29; 50:23).

Hammoleketh (hă-mŏl'ē-keth, **the queen),** a sister of Gilead (I Chron. 7:18).

Hammon (hăm'ŏn, **hot spring).** 1. A place in Asher about 10 miles S of Tyre (Josh. 19:28). 2. A city of Naphtali (I Chron. 6:76). See Hammath, which may be the same place (Josh. 19:35).

Hammoth-dor (hăm'ŏth-dôr, **warm springs of Dor),** a city in Naphtali, appointed as a city of refuge (Josh. 21:32). See Hammath.

Hammurabi (hȧm'ōō-rȧ'bē), the king (1728-1686 B.C.) of Babylon who brought that city to its century-and-a-half rule over southern Mesopotamia known as the Old Babylonian Kingdom. He was an Amorite, the name given to a Semitic group which invaded the Fertile Crescent about 2000 B.C., destroying its civilization and establishing their own Semitic culture.

Hammurabi began the first golden age of Babylon — the second being that of Nebuchadnezzar, over a thousand years later. He systematically unified all of the old world of Sumer and Akkad (southern Mesopotamia) under his strongly centralized government.

By far his most famous claim to fame is Hammurabi's law code.

It is now known that Hammurabi's was not the first attempt to systematize the laws of Babylonia. Fragments of several previous law codes have been found. Uh-nammu of Ur and Lipit-Ishtar of Isin both promulgated earlier codes and another was known in Eshnunna. But Hammurabi's is the most complete expression of early Babylonian law, and undoubtedly incorporates many laws and customs which go back to far earlier times. Hammurabi did not invent these laws; he codified them.

The law code itself included nearly 300 paragraphs of legal provisions touching commercial, social, domestic and moral life.

Students of the Bible are especially interested in the comparison of Hammurabi's code with the Mosaic legislation of the Bible. There are many similarities. In both a false witness is to be punished with the penalty he had thought to bring upon the other man. Kidnapping and house-breaking were capital offenses in both. The Biblical law of divorce permits a man to put away his wife, but does not extend to her the same right as did Hammurabi. Both codes agree in prescribing the death penalty for adultery. The principle of retaliation upon which a number of Hammurabi's laws were based is vividly stated in Exodus 21:23-25.

Hamonah (hȧ-mō'nȧ, **multitude,** prophetic name of a city near which Gog is defeated (Ezek. 39:16).

Hamon-Gog, Valley of (hā'mŏn-gŏg, **multitude of God),** a place E of the Dead Sea which will be set apart for the burial of the "multitude of God" (Ezek. 39:11-15).

Hamor (hā'môr, **an ass),** father of Shechem who criminally assaulted Dinah, a daughter of Jacob (Gen. 34:1-31).

Hamuel (hăm′ū-ĕl, **warmth of God**), a Simeonite mentioned only in I Chronicles 4:26.

Hamul (hā′mŭl, **pitied, spared**), a son of Perez (Gen. 46:12), head of the Hamulites.

Hamutal (hȧ-mū′tal, **father-in-law is dew**), wife of Josiah, mother of two kings of Judah, Jehoahaz (II Kings 23:31) and Zedekiah (24:18).

Hanameel (hăn′ȧ-mĕl), a cousin of Jeremiah the prophet (Jer. 32:7-12).

Hanan (hā′năn, **gracious**). 1. A Benjamite (I Chron. 8:23). 2. A son of Azel (I Chron. 9:44). 3. One of David's mighty men (I Chron. 11:43). 4. A temple-servant who returned with Zerubbabel (Ezra 2:46; Neh. 7:49). 5. An interpreter of the Law (Neh. 8:7). 6. Three covenanters with Nehemiah (Neh. 10:10, 22, 26). 7. An influential Jew in Jerusalem (Jer. 35:4).

Hananeel (hȧ-năn′ē-ĕl, **God is gracious**), a tower in the wall of Jerusalem (Jer. 31:38; Zech. 14:10).

Hanani (hȧ-nā′nī, **gracious**). 1. A son of Heman (I Chron. 25:4, 25). 2. Seer who rebuked Asa and was imprisoned (II Chron. 16:7-10). 3. A priest who had married a foreigner (Ezra 10:20). 4. A brother of Nehemiah (Neh. 1:2; 7:2). 5. Musical priest (Neh. 12:36).

Hananiah (hăn′ȧ-nī′ȧ, **Jehovah is gracious**). 1. A son of Heman, David's seer (I Chron. 25:4, 23). 2. A captain of Uzziah's army (II Chron. 26:11). 3. Father of Zedekiah (Jer. 36:12). 4. The grandfather of Irijah (Jer. 37:13). 5. A Benjamite household (I Chron. 8:24). 6. The Heb. name of Shadrach, one of the three who survived the furnace of fire (Dan. 1:6, 7). 7. A son of Zerubbabel (I Chron. 3:19, 21). 8. A returner with Ezra (Ezra 10:28). 9. A perfumer in the time of Nehemiah (Neh. 3:8). 10. Another repairer of the wall (Neh. 3:30). 11. A governor of the castle in Jerusalem (Neh. 7:2). 12. One of the chief covenanters, perhaps the same as the preceding (Neh. 10:23). 13. Head of a priestly house in the days of the high priest Joiakim (Neh. 12:12, 41). 14. A false prophet of Gibeon in the days of Zedekiah, the last king of Judah (Jer. 28).

Hand, one of the most frequently used words in Scripture, occurring over 1,600 times. Besides its literal use, it occurs in many figurative senses as well. It very often stands for power, as in Gen. 9:2, 5. To "put one's hand under the thigh" as in Gen. 24:2, 9; 47:29 meant to take a solemn oath; to "put one's hand upon the head" meant blessing as in Gen. 48:14, and signifies ordination, as in I Tim. 4:14 and II Tim. 1:6. To "kiss one's own hand" can be a mark of adoration, as in Job 31:27; while to kiss the hand of another is one of the usual marks of respect in the East, though this custom is not mentioned in Scripture.

Handicraft, a trade requiring manual skill, the art of using one's hands gainfully. Among some rich and decadent nations, the crafts and trades were left to slaves, but the Jews trained every boy to a trade; so Paul was a tent-maker (Acts 18:3) and even our Lord learned the art of carpentry (Mark 6:3).

Handkerchief. Handkerchiefs were brought from Paul's body for healing purposes (Acts 19:12); the wicked servant (Luke 19:20-23) kept his lord's money in a napkin; the face of dead Lazarus was enclosed in a napkin — the same word — (John 11:44), as was also the face of our Lord (John 20:7).

Handle, door knob (Song of Sol. 5:5).

Handmaid or **Handmaiden,** a female slave or servant. When used of one's self, it indicates humility, as Ruth, speaking to Boaz (Ruth 3:9); Hannah praying to the Lord (I Sam. 1:11) and speaking to Eli (1:16); Mary speaking to Gabriel (Luke 1:38) and singing (Luke 1:48).

Hands, Imposition of, a ceremony having the idea of transference, identification, and devotion to God (Exod. 29:10, 15, 19; Lev. 16:21; Acts 8:14-17; II Tim. 1:6).

Handstaff, a rod carried in the hand (Ezek. 39:9).

Hanes (hā′nēz), a place in Egypt (Isa. 30:4).

Hanging, or death by strangulation, was not a form of capital punishment employed in Bible times. Where the word is used in Scripture, except in the two cases of suicide by hanging (Ahithophel, II Sam. 7:23; Judas, Matt. 27:5), it refers to the suspension of a body from a tree or post after the criminal had been put to death.

Hangings, those parts of the tabernacle and its court which were so hung as to preserve the privacy and the sacredness of that which was within, and the curtains of the tent itself (Exod. 26:1-14; 27:9-19).

Haniel (hăn′ĭ-ĕl, **grace of God**). 1. A prince of Manasseh (I Chron. 34:23). 2. An Asherite (I Chron. 7:39).

Hannah (hăn′ȧ, **grace, favor),** one of the two wives of Elkanah, a Levite who lived at Ramathaim-zophim, a village of Ephraim. It was otherwise known as Ramah (cf. I Sam. 1:1 with 1:19). Peninnah, the other wife of Elkanah (I Sam 1:2), had children, but Hannah was for a long time barren, and as is common in polygamous households, "her rival provoked her sore" (1:6). The fact that Elkanah loved Hannah and gave her a double portion (1:5) only increased the hatred and jealousy in Peninnah's heart. But Hannah was a godly woman and she prayed for a son and vowed to give him to the Lord as a perpetual Nazirite. Eli saw Hannah's lips moving in silent prayer, and rebuked her for what he thought was drunkenness. She replied very humbly and Eli apologized; the family returned home; she conceived and became the mother of Samuel the great prophet of Israel and the last of the judges. Hannah's praise (2:1-10) shows that she was a deeply spiritual woman.

Hannathon (hăn′nȧ-thŏn, **gracious), a** city on the northern boundary of Zebulon (Josh. 19:14).

Hanniel (han′ĭ-ĕl, **the favor of God).** 1. A prince of Manasseh (Num. 34:23). 2. Son of Ulla, and a descendant of Asher (I Chron. 7:39).

Hanoch (hān′nŏk, **initiation).** 1. A grandson of Abraham by Keturah (Gen. 25:4; I Chron. 1:33).

2. Eldest son of Reuben (Gen. 46:9; Exod. 6:14; I Chron. 5:3).

Hanun (hā′nŭn, **favored).** 1. King of Ammon who provoked David to war (II Sam. 10; and I Chron. 19). 2. A man who built the valley gate in the wall of Jerusalem (Neh. 3:13). 3. Son of Zalaph who helped repair the wall of Jerusalem (Neh. 3:30).

Haphraim (hăph-rā′ĭm, **two pits),** a city near Shunem in Issachar (Josh. 19:19).

Hara (ha′rȧ), mountain country, probably a place named in I Chron. 5:26 as the destination of the tribes of Reuben and Gad and the half-tribe of Manasseh when they were exiled by the Assyrians.

Haradah (hȧr-ā′da, **terror),** one of Israel's encampments in the wilderness wanderings (Num. 33:24).

Haran (hā′răn, **mountaineer).** 1. Youngest brother of Abram and father of Lot (Gen. 11:27, 28). 2. A son of Caleb (I Chron. 2:46). 3. A Gershonite Levite (I Chron. 23:9).

Haran or **Charran** (hā′răn, chăr′ăn), a city in Mesopotamia, on the Balikh river, a branch of the Euphrates, to which Terah, the father of Abram, emigrated with his family (Gen. 11:31). After his father's death Abram departed from this city to go into the land of Canaan (Gen. 12:4). Abraham later sent his servant to find a wife for his son Isaac among his relatives there (Gen. 24:4). After that Jacob, at the request of his father, Isaac, came to this same area in search of a wife (Gen. 29:4, 5). Ezekiel mentions this city as one of those which carried on trade with Tyre (Ezek. 27:23).

Hararite (hā′rȧ-rīte, **mountain dweller),** an area in the hill country of either Judah or Ephraim (II Sam. 23:11, 33; I Chron. 11:34; 35).

Harbona, Harbonah (hȧr-bō′nȧ, hăr-bō′nȧ, **ass driver),** one of the seven chamberlains of Ahasuerus (Esth. 1:10; 7:9).

Hare (See Animals)

Hareph (hā′rĕf, **scornful),** son of Caleb, and father of Bethgader (I Chron. 2:51).

Hareth, Hereth (hā′rĕth), forest in Judah where David stayed (I Sam. 22:5).

Harhaiah (hȧr-hā′ja, meaning unknown), father of Uzziel, a goldsmith (Neh. 3:8).

Harhas (hȧr′hăs, meaning uncertain), grandfather of Shallum, husband of Hulda the prophetess (II Kings 22:14).

Harhur (hȧr′hûr, **fever),** head of family which returned from exile with Zerubbabel (Ezra 2:51; Neh. 7:53).

Harim (hā′rĭm, **consecrated or slitnosed).** 1. A priest in David's time (I Chron. 24:8). 2. A family which returned from Babylon with Zerubbabel (Ezra 2:2; Neh. 7:35). 3. A family of priests which returned from exile with Zerubbabel (Ezra 2:32; Neh. 7:35). 4. A family who married foreign wives (Ezra 10:31). 5. Father of Malchijah, a worker on the wall (Neh. 3:11). 6. Another man who covenanted with the Lord under Nehemiah (Neh. 10:27).

Hariph (hā′rĭf, **autumn),** a family which returned to Judah from Babylon with Zerubbabel (Neh. 7:24). A man of this name was among those sealed in the covenant with God (Neh. 10:19).

Harlot, both common and religious harlotry very prevalent in ancient times; both kinds were forbidden to the Israelites (Lev. 19:29; 21:7, 9, 14;

Deut. 23:18). Paul warned against fornication with harlots (I Cor. 6:15, 16).

Harnepher (hàr′nĕ-fêr), a son of Zophal in the tribe of Asher (I Chron. 7:36).

Harod (hā′rŏd, **trembling),** a spring, or well, beside which Gideon and his men encamped one morning. The Lord reduced his army there to 300 men with whom he routed the Midianites that night (Judg. 7:1). It was located in the Mount Gilboa area about four miles SE of the city of Jezreel.

Harodite (hā′rŏd-īt, **belonging to Herod),** patronymic of two of David's mighty men, Shammah and Elika (II Sam. 23:25).

Haroeh (hȧ-rō′ĕ, **the seer),** a grandson of Caleb (I Chron. 2:52).

Harosheth of the Gentiles (hā-rō′shĕth), a town near the Kishon river in N. Palestine. The home of Sisera, the captain of the army of Jabin, king of Canaan (Judg. 4:2, 13, 16).

Harp (See Music)

Harrow (hăr′rō), occurs three times, always as a verb. Job 39:10 translated "harrow." In Isaiah 28:24 and Hosea 10:11 it is rendered "break up the clods." From the root meaning of the word it seems to mean dragging or leveling off a field.

Harrows, a sharp instrument made of iron with which David cut conquered peoples (II Sam. 12:31; I Chron. 20:3).

Harsha (hàr′shȧ, **dumb, silent),** the head of family of the Nethinim which returned under Zerubbabel (Ezra 2:52; Neh. 7:54).

Hart (See Animals)

Harum (hā′rŭm, **made high),** a descendant of Judah (I Chron. 4:8).

Harumaph (hȧ-rōō′maf, perhaps **slit-nosed),** the father of Jedaiah (Neh. 3:10).

Haruphite (hȧ-rōō′fīt). Shephatiah, one of the men who joined David's forces in Ziklag, was called the Haruphite or the Hariphite (I Chron. 12:5).

Haruz (hā′rŭz, **diligent),** father-in-law of Manasseh, king of Judah (II Kings 21:19).

Harvest (hàr-vĕst). The economy of the Israelites was strictly agricultural. Harvest time was a very significant event for them. They had three each year. The barley reaping (Ruth 1:22) came in April-May; the wheat harvest (Gen. 30:14) was about six weeks later in June-July, and the ingathering of the fruits of tree or vine took place in September-October.

The Lord fitted the three main religious feasts which He prescribed for the people into this agricultural economy. The Passover came in the season of the barley harvest (Exod. 23:16). Seven weeks later at time of the wheat harvest occurred the feast of Pentecost (Exod. 34:22). The feast of Tabernacles was observed the seventh month, which was the period of the fruit harvest (Exod. 34:22).

In the New Testament, most of the time the term harvest is used figuratively for the gathering in of the redeemed saints at the end of the age (Matt. 13:39).

Hasadiah (hă-sȧ-dī′a, **Jehovah is kind),** a son of Zerubbabel (I Chron. 3:20).

Hasenuah (hăs-ē-nū′ȧ). 1. A Benjamite (I Chron. 9:7). 2. The father of Judah, the assistant overseer of Jerusalem in Nehemiah's time (Neh. 11:9).

Hashabiah (hăsh-ȧ-bī′ȧ, **whom Jehovah esteems).** 1. An ancestor of Ethan, a Levite and temple singer in David's time (I Chron. 6:45). 2. An ancestor of Shemaiah (I Chron. 9:14; Neh. 11:15). 3. A son of Jeduthun (I Chron. 25:3). 4. A civil official in David's time (I Chron. 26: 30). 5. Overseer of the tribe of Levi (I Chron. 27:17). 6. A chief of the Levites in Josiah's time (II Chron. 35:9). 7. A Levite teacher whom Ezra brought with him (Ezra 8:19). 8. A chief priest in Ezra's company (Ezra 8:24). 9. Ruler of the half tribe of Keilah, a worker on the wall (Neh. 3:17). 10. Head of the family of Hilkiah (Neh. 12:21). 11. An ancestor of Uzzi (Neh. 11:22). 12. A chief of the Levites (Neh. 3:17; 12:24).

Hashabnah (hȧ-shăb′nȧh), man who sealed the covenant with Nehemiah (Neh. 10:25).

Hashabniah (hăsh′ăb-nē-ī′ȧ). 1. The father of Hattush, a worker on the wall (Neh. 3:10).

2. One of the Levites who prayed at the confession of sin (Neh. 9:5).

Hashbadana (hăsh-băd′ȧ-nȧ), a man who stood by Ezra as he read the law to the people (Neh. 8:4).

Hashem (hā′shĕm), a man whose sons were among David's mighty men (I Chron. 11:34).

Hashmannim (hăsh′-măn-nĭm), a Hebrew word that occurs only in Psalm 68:33 and is translated **heaven of heavens.**

Hashmonah (hăsh-mō′nȧ), a station where the Israelites encamped in the wilderness (Num. 33:29, 30).

Hashub (See Hasshub)

Hashubah (hȧ-shōō′bȧ, **consideration**), a son of Zerubbabel (I Chron. 3:20).

Hashum (hā′-shŭm). 1. A family that returned from exile under Zerubbabel (Ezra 2:19; 10:33; Neh. 7:22). 2. A priest who stood by Ezra as he read the law to the people (Neh. 8:4). 3. A chief of the people who sealed the covenant (Neh. 10:18). Maybe the same as 2.

Hashupha (hȧ-shōō′fȧ), a family that returned from exile under Zerubbabel (Ezra 2:43; Neh. 7:46).

Hasmonaeans (See Maccabees)

Hasrah (hăs′rȧ), grandfather of Shallum, the husband of Hulda the prophetess (II Chron. 34:22). Harhas in II Kings 22:14.

Hassenaah (hăs-ē-nā′ȧ). Father of the men who built the fish gate in the wall of Jerusalem (Neh. 3:3).

Hasshub (hăsh′ŭb, **considerate**). 1. The father of Shemaiah, a Levite who returned from exile (I Chron. 9:14). 2. A worker on the wall of Jerusalem (Neh. 3:11). 3. Another worker on the wall (Neh. 3:23). 4. One who sealed the covenant (Neh. 10:23). KJV Hashub. May be identical with 2 or 3.

Hasupha (See Hashupha)

Hat (See Dress)

Hatach (hā′tăk), a chamberlain of the king of Persia appointed to attend Esther (Esth. 4:5-10).

Hathath (hā′-thăth, **terror**), a son of Othniel, the first judge of Israel (I Chron. 4:13).

Hatipha (hȧ-tī′fȧ), head of family of the Nethinim which returned from exile under Zerubbabel (Ezra 2:54; Neh. 7:56).

Hatita (hȧ-tī′tȧ, **exploring**), an ancestor of a family of Levitical porters which returned from exile (Ezra 2:42; Neh. 7:45).

Hatsi Ham Menuchoth (hă-tsī-hăm-mĕn-ū′-kōth, **half of the Menuhoth**), a marginal reading on I Chronicles 2:54 in KJV which is eliminated in ASV.

Hattil (hăt′-ĭl, **waving**), a family which returned from exile (Ezra 2:57; Neh. 7:59).

Hattin, Horns of (hăt′tēn, **hollows**), a peculiar form of a hill near the village of Hattin, which tradition dating from the 13th century holds as the scene of Christ's Sermon on the Mount. May denote the "mountain" of Matthew 5:1.

Hattush (hăt′ŭsh, meaning unknown). 1. A descendant in the royal line of Judah (I Chron. 3:22). 2. A descendant of David who returned from Babylon with Ezra (Ezra 8:2). 3. A worker on the wall (Neh. 3:10), may be the same as 2. 4. Man who sealed the covenant (Neh. 10:4), may be the same as 2 or 3. 5. A priest who returned with Zerubbabel (Neh. 12:2).

Hauran (hȧ′ōō-rȧn, probably **black** or **black land**), the modern name of a great plain situated on a plateau 2000 feet high E of the Jordan river and N of the land of Gilead. In ancient times it was called Bashan. Its soil is of volcanic origin and is very rich, making the region famous for its wheat crops. The name Hauran is mentioned only by Ezekiel in his description of the boundaries of the land of Israel in the Millennial age (47:16, 18). In the time of the Romans it was known as Auranitis. Today Hauran is an integral part of Syria.

Havilah (hăv′ĭ-lȧ, **sand-land**). 1. A son of Cush (Gen. 10:7; I Chron. 1:9). 2. A son of Joktan, a descendant of Shem (Gen. 10:29; I Chron. 1:23). 3. A land encompassed by the river Pishon which flowed from a source in the Garden of Eden (Gen. 2:11, 12). 4. A land mentioned as one of the boundaries of the Ishmaelites (I Sam. 15:7).

Havoth-Jair (hā-vŏth-jā′îr, **villages of Jair**), a group of 30 villages which Jair, son of Manasseh, took (Num. 32:41). The word **hawwah** means a village of tents; it is used only in connection with these towns of Jair.

Hawk (See Birds)

Hazael (hăz′ā-ĕl, **God sees**), a high official of Benhadad, king of Syria, whom, when the king was sick, he sent to inquire of the prophet Elisha concerning his recovery from this illness. Elisha told Hazael the king would certainly recover, but he would surely die. Previously God had instructed Elijah to anoint Hazael king of Syria (I Kings 19:15). Hazael pretended to be surprised by Elisha's statement that he would become king. He returned and suffocated Benhadad, and seized the throne for himself (II Kings 8:7-15).

Hazael greatly punished Israel, as Elisha had foreseen (II Kings 8:12). He wounded Jehoram, son of Ahab, at Ramoth-gilead (II Kings 8:29). During the reign of Jehu, Hazael took all the territory E of the Jordan valley from Israel (II Kings 10:32). While Joash was ruling in Judah, Hazael captured Gath and threatened Jerusalem, but Joash induced him to retire by paying tribute (II Kings 12:17, 18). He continually raided Israel during the reign of Jehoahaz (II Kings 13:3). He oppressed Israel all the days of this king (II Kings 13:22).

Hazaiah (hȧ-zā'yȧ, **Jehovah sees),** member of a family of Shiloh whose great-grandson lived in Jerusalem 444 B.C. (Neh. 11:5).

Hazar (hā'zȧr, **a settlement),** often the first element in Heb. place names.

Hazar-Addar (hā'zȧr-ăd'ȧr), a place on the southern boundary of Judah, W of Kadesh-barnea and E of Azmon (Num. 34:4). In Joshua 15:3 it is called simply Addar (KJV Adar).

Hazar-Enan (hā'zȧr-ē'năn, **village of fountains),** the NE corner of the land of Canaan as promised of the Lord to the people of Israel (Num. 34:9, 10; cf. Ezek. 47:17).

Hazar-Gaddah (hā'zȧr-găd'ȧ, **village of good fortune),** a town in the S of Judah, near Simeon (Josh. 15:27).

Hazar-Hatticon (hā'zȧr-hăt'ĭ-kŏn, **middle-village),** a place near Damascus and on the border of Hauran (Ezek. 47:16).

Hazarmaveth (hā'zȧr-mā'vĕth, **village of death),** (Gen. 10:26 and I Chron. 1: 20); apparently a son of Joktan, but probably representing the people or the district of modern Hadramut.

Hazar-Shual (hā'zȧr-shōō'ăl, **village of the jackal),** a town in the south of Judah (Josh. 15:28; 19:3; I Chron. 4:28; Neh. 11:27).

Hazar-Susah (hā'zȧr-sū'sȧ, **village of a mare),** a town given to Simeon out of Judah (Josh. 19:5).

Hazazon-Tamar (hăz'ȧ-zŏn-tā'mer, **Hazazon of the palm trees),** a town on the W coast of the Dead Sea (Gen. 14: 7). KJV has Hazezon-tamar.

Hazel (hā'z'l), KJV renders the Heb. **luz,** which the RV better translates "almond tree" (Gen. 30:37).

Hazelelponi, Zelelponi (hăz'ĕ-lĕl-pō'nī, zĕlĕl-pō'nī, ASV Hazzelelponi), a Jewish woman (I Chron. 4:3).

Hazerim (hȧ-zē'rīm, **villages),** should be "villagers" (Deut. 2:23).

Hazeroth (hȧ-zē'rŏth, **courts** or **villages),** a station on Israel's journeys in the wilderness, about 40-45 miles from Mt. Sinai, northeastward toward the Gulf of Akabah (Num. 11:35; 12).

Hazezon-tamar (hăz'e-zŏn-tā'mēr) another spelling for Hazazon-tamar, **q.v.**

Haziel (hā'zī-ĕl, **God sees),** a Gershonite Levite in David's day (I Chron. 23:9).

Hazo hā'zō), son of Nahor (Gen. 22:22).

Hazor (hā'zôr, **enclosed place).** 1. City c. 5 miles W of waters of Merom, ruled by Jabin (Josh. 11:1, 10); conquered by Joshua and, later by Debor-

The site of Hazor, the chief city of Canaan. © MPS

ah and Barak (Judg. 4; I Sam. 12:9); fortified by Solomon (I Kings 9:15); its inhabitants taken into exile by Assyria (II Kings 15:29). 2. Town in S of Judah (Josh. 15:23). 3. Another town in S Judah (Josh. 15:25). 4. Town N of Jerusalem (Neh. 11:33). 5. Region in S Arabia (Jer. 49:28-33).

Hazor-hadattah (hā'zôr-hȧ-dăt'ȧ, **new Hazor),** town in S Judah (Josh. 15:25).

He (hā), the fifth letter of the Hebrew alphabet, pronounced like English **h.** Also used for the number 5.

Head (hĕd). The word "head" occurs about 433 times in Scripture and the Hebrew word for "head" occurs 592 times. There are many figurative uses: "the hoary head" (Prov. 16:31), expressing old age; "heads over the people" (Exod. 18:25); "heads of the people" (Num. 25:4, probably meaning "chiefs"; Cf. ASV); "his blood shall be upon his head" (Josh. 2:19, meaning "we shall not be responsible for his life"); "yet will I not lift up my head" (Job 10:15, i.e. "yet will I not be self-assertive"); "his head reached unto the clouds" (Job 20:6, i.e. "he be highly exalted"), etc.

Headband, Headdress (See Dress)

Head of the Church. In the NT Christ is described as "the head of the church" (Eph. 1:22; 5:23), and "head of the body, the church" (Col. 1:18; cf. Eph. 4:15). This figure speaks of the preeminence of Christ, His authority, and the complete dependence of the Church upon Christ. In Colossians 1:18 the headship of Christ over the body denotes His priority of rank.

Headstone (See Cornerstone)

Heart. In the Bible the "heart" is regarded as being the seat of the intellect, the feelings and the will; e.g., "every imagination of the thoughts of his heart" (Gen. 6:5) would imply intellect; "comfort ye your hearts" (Gen. 18:5; or "strengthen your heart" as in ASV) would imply feeling; while "that seeking him with the whole heart" (Ps. 119:2) means the will. It is often used to signify the innermost being, i.e., "It grieved him at his heart" (Gen. 6:6). In modern usage, "heart" is used to imply affection, as "I have you in my heart," as found in Psalm 62:10. Often the word "heart" implies the whole moral nature of fallen man, e.g. "The heart is deceitful above all things, and desperately wicked" (Jer. 17:9).

Hearth. Brand (Ps. 102:3), fire pan (Zech. 12:6), hearth on altar (Lev. 6:9), brazier (Jer. 36:22, 23), burning mass (Isa. 30:14).

Heath, a shrub with very small, narrow, rigid leaves growing on the W slopes of Lebanon. (See Jer. 17:6; 48:6.)

Heathen (hē̄'th'n, **people, nation).** Usually used for a non-Israelitish people, and thus has the meaning of "Gentiles."

The differentiation between Israelites and Gentiles was more sharply accentuated in NT times than in OT times, the reason for this being chiefly that the Jews had suffered so much from Gentile hands. Gentiles were looked upon with aversion and hatred. This is evident in the NT (John 18:28; Acts 10:28; 11:3).

God's interest in and concern for the heathen is seen in the OT, especially in the Book of Jonah. In the NT Jesus commanded the apostles to preach the Gospel to all the world; and we find them proclaiming it to Gentile nations throughout the Mediterranean world.

Heaven. 1. One of the two great divisions of the universe, the earth and the heavens (Gen. 1:1; 14:19; etc.); or one of the three — heaven, earth, and the waters under the earth (Exod. 20:4). In the visible heavens are the stars and planets (Gen. 1:14-17; Ezek. 32:7, 8). The term "heaven of heavens" (Deut. 10:14; I Kings 8:27; Ps. 148:4) probably means the "height of heaven." 2. The abode of God (Gen. 28:17; Ps. 80:14; Isa. 66:1; Matt. 5:12) and of the good angels (Matt. 24:36); where the redeemed shall some day be (Matt. 5:12; 6:20; Eph. 3:15). 3. The inhabitants of heaven (Luke 15:18; Rev. 18:20).

Heave Offering (See Offerings)

Heave Shoulder (See Offerings)

Heaving and Waving (See Offerings)

Heber (hē'bẽr, **associate).** 1. A great-grandson of Jacob (Gen. 46:17). 2. The Kenite whose wife Jael killed Sisera (Judg. 4:11-21). 3. A son of Ezrah (KJV "Ezra") (I Chron. 4:18). 4. A Benjamite (I Chron. 8:17). 5. A Gadite (I Chron. 5:13). 6. A Benjamite, son of Shashak (I Chron. 8:22). 7. One mentioned in Christ's genealogy (Luke 3:35 KJV), father of Peleg and Joktan. See Eber, Hebrews.

Hebrew of the Hebrews. When Paul in Philippians 3:4-6 so described himself, he meant that he was a pure-blooded Hebrew who had retained the language and customs of his fathers.

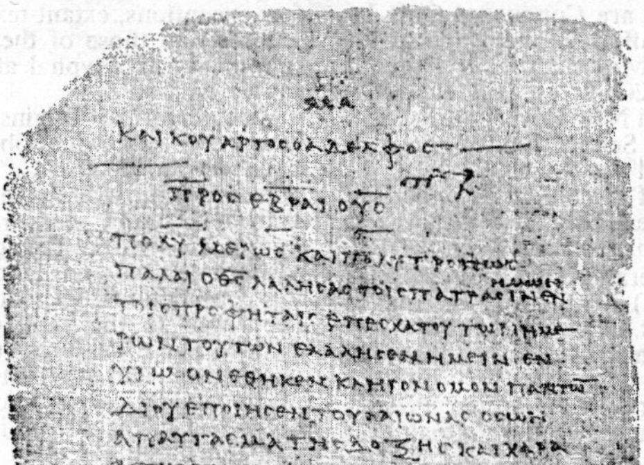

Beginning of the Epistle to the Hebrews (with ending of Romans) on a leaf (P[46]) from the Michigan papyri (Beatty-Michigan Ms.) in the University of Michigan Library. UML

Hebrews, Epistle to the. Authorship uncertain; authors suggested: Paul, Timothy, Barnabas, Apollos; place of writing also uncertain; written to Christians in danger of lapsing from faith.

Although absolute certainty cannot be reached, it seems best to regard the original readers as being located somewhere in Italy. Many roads led to Rome. These believers may have been in one of the cities nearer or farther from the capital. Paul himself spent seven days with the brothers in Puteoli (Acts 28:13-14). They could have been in Rome or its suburbs. As the writer pens this letter, Timothy has departed [from him] and is absent (perfect tense) — very likely on some tour of churches. As soon as he appears (or if he comes soon), the writer and Timothy together will visit the readers (Heb. 13:23).

Outline and Summary of Content— An outline shows the centrality of Jesus Christ in the book of Hebrews.

Prologue: Course and Climax of Divine Revelation (1:1-3)

I. Pre-eminence of Christ Himself (1:4-4:13). (A). Superiority of Christ to Angels (1:4-14). (B.) Warning: Peril of Indifference to These Truths (2:1-14). (C.) Reason Christ Became Human (2:5-18). (D.) Christ's Position is Greater than That of Moses (3:1-6). (E.) Warning: Unbelief Brings Temporal and Eternal Effects (3:7-4:13).

II. Priesthood of Jesus Christ (4:14-10:18). (A.) Importance of His Priesthood for a Believer's Conduct (4:14-16). (B.) Qualifications of a High Priest (5:1-10). (C.) Warning: Immaturity and Apostasy are Conquered Only by Faith, Longsuffering, and Hope (5:11-6:20a). (D.) Melchizedek's Eternal Successor (6:20b-7:28). (E.) Heavenly Sanctuary and New Covenant (8:1-13). (F.) Priestly Service under the Old Covenant and the New (9:1-28). (G.) Inadequacy of the Sacrifices under the Law contrasted with the Efficacy and Finality of Christ's Sacrifice (10:1-18).

III. Perseverance of Christians (10:19-12:29). (A.) Attitudes to be Sought and Attitudes to be Shunned (10:19-38). (B.) Faith in Action — Illustrious Examples from the Past (11:1-40). (C.) Incentives for Action in the Present Scene and in the Future Goal (12:1-29).

Postscript: Exhortations, Personal Concerns, Benediction (13:1-25).

Although more space is devoted to Christ, the letter has a fully developed set of teachings about God the Father. Much is said about Christ. He is fully God and fully man. He is active in creation. The atonement of Christ, as both priest and sacrificial victim, is developed in detail. In the role of a priest, He is a leader and guide. He also is the revealer of God. Great depth is achieved in all of these teachings about Christ's person and work. Very little is said about the Holy Spirit in Hebrews.

The Old and New Covenants are compared and reasons for the superiority of the New or Eternal Covenant are given.

The doctrine of sin in Hebrews focuses attention on unbelief and the failure to go on with God to the eternal city.

Hebrew, Hebrews, designation for Abraham and descendants, the equivalent of Israelites. Abraham is first in OT to be called Hebrew (Gen. 14:13). Origin of word uncertain; may be same as Habiru of Amarna tablets; may come from "Eber," the father of Peleg and Joktan (Gen. 10: 24, 25), or from a Heb. root meaning "to pass over" (from the crossing of the Euphrates by Abraham).

Hebrew Language. With the exception of Aramaic in Ezra 4:8-6:18; 7:12-26; Daniel 2:4-7:28 and Jeremiah 10:11, Hebrew is the language of the OT. With close affinity to Ugaritic, Phoenician, Moabitic and the Canaanite dialects, Hebrew represents the northwest branch of the Semitic language family. Its sister languages include Arabic, Akkadian and Aramaic. With few exceptions, extant texts of Ancient Hebrew are those of the OT and certain of the apocryphal and pseudepigraphic works.

The historical origins of the language are somewhat obscure but go back beyond 2000 B.C. The OT literature, written over a period of more than a thousand years, reveals a minimum of stylistic changes. With its short sentences and simple coordinating conjunctions, ancient Hebrew lent itself well to the vivid expression of events. These features, together with parallelism and rhythm and special meanings and constructions made Hebrew poetry, as found in the Psalms and to a large extent in the Prophets, most expressive and strikingly effective.

Hebron (hē'brŏn, **league, confederacy**). 1. One of the oldest cities of the world, located 19 miles SW of Jerusalem on the main road to Beer-sheba, and has one of the longest records for continuous occupation. It was early a camping place for Abram (Gen. 13:18). At the partition of Canaan after the partial conquest, Hebron and its environs were given to Caleb to conquer (Josh. 14:6-15), which he did (15:14-19); but later the city itself was given to the Kohathite Levites (I Chron. 6:55, 56), though Caleb's descendants kept the suburban fields and villages. When David was king over Judah, but not yet over all Israel, his capital city was Hebron for seven and a half years. 2. Third son of Kohath, and so an uncle of Moses, Aaron and Miriam (Exod. 6:18). 3. A town in Asher (Josh. 19: 28 KJV). 4. A descendant of Caleb (I Chron. 2:42, 43).

Hedge, loose stone walls without mortar, or cut thorn branches or thorny bushes, common as "hedges" and "fences" in Palestine. The word can be rendered, **fence, wall** or **hedge** (Ps. 80:12; Ezek. 13:5; Mark 12:1; Luke 14:23).

Hegai or **Hege** (hĕg'ā-ī, hē'gē), eunuch who was keeper of the women in the king's harem (Esth. 2:3, 8, 15).

Heifer, a young cow (Gen. 15:9; Deut. 21:3; I Sam. 16:2).

Heifer, Red (See Animals)

Heir (See Inheritance)

Helah (hē'lȧ), wife of Ashur (I Chron. 4:5, 7).

Helam (hē'lăm), a place in the Syrian desert E of the Jordan where David defeated the forces of Hadarezer, king of Aram-zobah (II Sam. 10:16, 17).

A general view of Hebron. Mosque in center is built over Cave of Machpelah, tomb of Abraham and Sarah. © *MPS*

Helbah (hĕl′bȧ, **a fertile region),** a town of Asher (Judg. 1:31).

Helbon (hĕl′bŏn, **fertile),** a city of northern Syria (Ezek. 27:18).

Heldai (hĕl′dā-ī). 1. The captain over 24,000 men under David (I Chron. 27:15). 2. Returned Jewish exile who brought gold and silver from Babylon (Zech. 6:9-15). Spelled "Helem" in 6:14.

Heleb (hē′lĕb), one of David's valiant men of war (II Sam. 23:29). See Heled and Heldai.

Heled (hē′lĕd), a mighty man of David's army (I Chron. 11:30). See Heleb and Heldai.

Helek (hē′lĕk), son of Gilead (Num. 26:30; Josh. 17:2).

Helem (hē′lĕm, **health).** 1. A man of the tribe of Asher (I Chron. 7:35). 2. An ambassador (Zech. 6:14); but also certainly the same person as Heldai (Zech. 6:10).

Heleph (hē′lĕf, **change),** an ancient village on the border of Naphtali (Josh. 19:33).

Helez (hē′lĕz). 1. A man of Judah (I Chron. 2:39). 2. One of David's mighty leaders (II Sam. 23:26; I Chron. 11: 27; 27:10).

Heli (hē′lī), father of Joseph, the husband of Mary (Luke 3:23); or perhaps the father of Mary, the mother of Jesus.

Heliopolis (hē-lĭ-ŏp′ō-lĭs, **city of the sun),** a city near the S end of the Delta of the Nile, the site of a temple to the sun built by Amenophis I (Gen. 41: 45; 46:20).

Helkai (hĕl′kā-ī, perhaps an abbr. of **Helkiah),** a priest in the days of Joiakim (Neh. 12:15).

Helkath (hĕl′kăth, **a field),** a town in Asher (Josh. 19:25). Later called Hukok (I Chron. 6:75).

Helkath Hazzurim (hĕl′kăth hăz′ū-rĭm, **the field of the sharp knives),** a place near the pool of Gibeon where the men of Joab fought with the men of Abner (II Sam. 2:12-16).

Hell, place and condition of retribution for unredeemed man; eternal (Matt. 18:8, 9); unquenchable (Matt. 3:12; Mark 9:44) fire; lake of fire (Rev. 20:14); fire and worm (Mark 9:48); place of torment (Rev. 14:10); place of outer darkness (Matt. 8:12; 22:13; 25:30).

Hellenists (hĕl′ĕn-ĭsts), Jews who made Greek their tongue, and with it often adopted Greek ideas and practices (Acts 6:1; 9:29).

Helmet (See Arms, Armor)

Helon (hē′lôn, **valorous),** father of Eliah, a leading man of Zebulun (Num. 1:9).

Helpmeet, a helper, generally a wife; but in Genesis 2:18 it is two words. "I will make him a help meet for him," i.e., suitable for or answering to him.

Helps, one of the gifts of the Spirit, probably the ability to perform helpful works in a gracious manner (I Cor. 12:7-11, 28-31).

Hemam (hē'măm), a grandson of Seir the Horite (Gen. 36:22). "Homam" in I Chronicles 1:39.

Heman (hē'măn, **faithful).** 1. A grandson of Judah (I Chron. 2:6). 2. Levite musican of David (I Chron. 6:33; 25: 5). 3. Ps. 88 is attributed to Heman the Ezrahite, who may be the same as 1. above.

Hemath (hē'măth). In Amos 6:14 "Hemath" should be "Hamath" as in A SV. In I Chronicles 2:55 "Hemath" should be "Hammath" as in ASV. He was the father of Rechabites (Jer. 35: 2-18). See Hamath.

Hemdan (hĕm'dăn, **pleasant),** an early Horite in the land of Seir (Gen. 36:26).

Hemlock (See Plants)

Hem of a Garment, fringes or tassels on the borders of the Jewish outer garment (Num. 15:38, 39; Exod. 28: 33, 34).

Hen (favor), son of Zephaniah (Zech. 6:14).

Hen, a general term for "bird," "fowl," etc. (Matt. 23:37; Luke 13:34).

Hena (hēn'ȧ), city on the S bank of the Euphrates, about 180 miles NW of ancient Babylon (II Kings 18:34; 19: 13; Isa. 37:13).

Henadad (hĕn'ȧ-dăd, **favor of Hadad),** Levite whose descendents helped Zerubbabel (Ezra 3:9), and Nehemiah in building (Neh. 3:18, 24).

Henoch (See Enoch)

Hepher (hē'fēr, **pit, well).** 1. Head of the family of the Hepherites (Num. 26:32; 27:1-8; 36:1-9). 2. A son of Ashhur (KJV Ashur), the founder of Tekoa (I Chron. 4:5, 6). 3. One of David's mighty men (I Chron. 11:36). 4. A royal city in Canaan which Joshua conquered (Josh. 12:17). The land of Hepher (I Kings 4:10) was SW of Jerusalem.

Hephzibah (hĕf'zĭ-bȧ, **my delight is in her).** 1. Wife of Hezekiah (II Kings 21:1). 2. A symbolical name given to Zion (Isa. 62:4).

Herb (See Plants)

Herd. Consisted of the larger animals (Job 1:3 or 42:12), as contrasted with the flocks of sheep, goats, etc. The cattle were used in plowing and threshing, and for sacrifice, but were not commonly fattened for food, though in contrast, see Ezekiel 39:18.

Herdman, person in charge of cattle (Gen. 13:7) or pigs (Matt. 8:33); despised in Egypt (Gen. 46:34), but honored in Israel (Gen. 47:6; I Chron. 27:29).

Heres (he'rez, **sun).** 1. A district around Aijalon (Judg. 1:35). 2. A place E of the Jordan from which Gideon returned after his defeat of Zebah and Zalmunna (Judg. 8:13). 3. An Egyptian city (Isa. 19:18).

Heresh (hē'resh, **dumb, silent),** a Levite who early returned from captivity (I Chron. 9:15).

Heresy (hâr'ĕ-sē, **to choose).** 1. A sect or faction, not necessarily representing a departure from orthodox doctrine as "sect of Sadducees" (Acts 5: 17; 24:5; 26:5). Christianity is called a heresy in Acts 24:14; 28:22. 2. A doctrine or sect representing a departure from sound doctrine (II Pet. 2:1).

Hermas (hûr'măs), a Roman Christian (Rom. 16:14).

Hermes (hûr'mēz). 1. The Greek god rendered "Mercury" in Acts 14:12. 2. One to whom Paul sends greetings in Romans 16:14.

Hermogenes (hûr'mŏj'ē-nēz, **born of Hermes),** professed Christian in Asia (probably at Ephesus) who deserted Paul (II Tim. 1:15).

Hermon (hûr'mŏn, **sacred mountain),** mt. marking S terminus of Anti-Lebanon range; 30 miles SW of Damascus; 9,000 ft. above sea level; marks N boundary of Palestine; has three peaks. Has borne several names: "Shenir" or "Senir" (Deut. 3:9), "Sirion" (Deut. 3:9), "Sion" (Deut. 4:48). Probably mt. of Transfiguration (Matt. 17:1). Seat of Baal worship (Judg. 3:3). Modern Jebelesh Sheikh.

Herod (hĕr'ŭd). Idumean rulers of Palestine (47 B.C.-A.D. 79). Line started with Antipater, whom Julius Caesar made procurator of Judaea in 47 B.C. 1. Herod the Great, first procurator of Galilee,, then king of the Jews (37-4 B.C.); built Caesarea, temple at Jerusalem; slaughtered children at Bethlehem (Matt. 2:1-18). At his death his kingdom was divided among his three sons: Archelaus, Herod Antipas, and Philip. 2. Archelaus ruled over Judaea, Samaria, and Idumea (4 B.C.-A.D. 6), and was removed from office by the Romans (Matt. 2: 22). 3. Herod Antipas ruled over Galilee and Perea (4 B.C.-A.D. 39); killed John the Baptist (Matt. 14:1-12); called "fox" by Jesus (Luke 13:32). 4. Philip, tetrarch of Batanaea, Trachonitis, Gaulanitis, and parts of Jamnia

A view of beautiful Mount Hermon across the Sea of Galilee. © MPS

(4 B.C.-A.D. 34). Best of the Herods. 5. Herod Agrippa I; grandson of Herod the Great; tetrarch of Galilee; king of Palestine (A.D. 41-44); killed James the apostle (Acts 12:1-23). 6. Herod Agrippa II. King of territory E of Galilee (c. A.D. 53-70); Paul appeared before him (Acts 25:13-26:32).

Herodians (hĕ-rō′dĭ-ănz), a party mentioned in the NT only twice (Matt. 22: 16; Mark 12:13; 3:6) as joining with the Pharisees to oppose Jesus. Jews who supported the dynasty of Herod, and therefore the rule of Rome (Matt. 22:16).

Herodias (hĕ-rō′dĭ-ăs), wicked granddaughter of Herod the Great who put to death John the Baptist (Luke 3: 19, 20; Matt. 14:3-12; Mark 6:14-29). Later her husband Antipas was banished to Spain. Herodias accompanied him, and died there.

Herodion (hĕ-rō′dĭ-ŏn), a Christian kinsman of Paul (Rom. 16:11).

Heron (hĕr′ŏn), a bird mentioned only in Leviticus 11:19 and Deuteronomy 14:18, where they are listed among the birds Israelites could not eat. They were of three kinds — white, blue, and brown. Their wing-sweep was from 3½ to 5 feet. They lived principally on fish and reptiles.

Hesed (hē′sĕd, **mercy**), father of one of Solomon's officers (I Kings 4:10).

Heshbon (hĕsh′bŏn, **reckoning**), Moabite city lying nearly 20 miles E of the Jordan. Sihon, king of the Amorites in the days of Moses took this and the surrounding country from the Moabites, and Israel in turn took it from Sihon (Num. 21:21-31). The tribe of Reuben asked Moses for this land as it was suitable for cattle, and Moses granted their request; so, three hundred years later (1260 B.C.) when the Ammonites made war against Israel, Jephthah taunted them (Judg. 11:12-28) with the fact that their god Chemosh was not able to stand against Israel for all those centuries. Heshbon and its suburbs were given to the Levites (I Chron. 6:81).

Heshmon (hĕsh′mŏn), a town on the S boundary of Judah (Josh. 15:25).

Heth (hĕth), great-grandson of Noah (Gen. 10:15) and progenitor of the great Hittite people (Gen. 23:3; 27:46). See Hittites.

Hethlon (hĕth′lŏn), a place just N of Mt. Lebanon from which one passes into the great plain of Coelo-Syria (Ezek. 47:15; 48:1).

Hexateuch (hĕk′sȧ-tūk), a term invented to include the book of Joshua with the Pentateuch in a literary unit, on the assumption that its component parts were combined by a common editor.

Hezeki (hĕz′ē-kī), a Benjamite (I Chron. 8:17).

Hezekiah (hĕz′ē-kī′ȧ, **Jehovah has strengthened**), king of Judah for 29 years, from c. 724 to 695 B.C. (II Kings 18-20; II Chron. 29-32, and Isa. 36-39). Hezekiah's father Ahaz reigned at Jerusalem (735-715 B.C.) when Hezekiah was a child, and though he was in some ways a good king, he allowed the people to sacrifice and burn incense in the high places. Because of Judah's growing apostasy, Jehovah permitted the Syrians and the Northern Kingdom to trouble Jerusalem. Ahaz went so far as to follow the abominable rites of the Moabites by burning children in the fire (II Chron. 28:3). For a while Hezekiah was associated in the government with his father, but because of his father's incapacitation he was made active ruler. He began his reign, at the age of 25, in troublous times. One of the first acts of Hezekiah was the cleansing and reopening of the temple, which his father had left closed and desecrated.

From the fourth to the sixth year of Hezekiah's reign the Northern Kingdom was in trouble. Shalmanezer finally destroyed Samaria and deported the people to Assyria. According to an Assyrian account, Sennacherib subjugated Judah (c. 715 B.C.). Hezekiah became ill, probably from a carbuncle, and almost died, but God granted him 15 years' extension of life (II Kings 20:1-11). After his recovery, Merodach-Baladan of Babylon sent an embassy ostensibly to congratulate him, but actually to persuade him to join a secret confederacy against the Assyrian power. Hezekiah, flattered by the attention he was being shown by the Babylonian ambassador, displayed to him his wealth, and was soundly rebuked by Isaiah (II Kings 20:12-19). Assyria compelled Judah to pay heavy tribute. Shortly after, Assyria decided to destroy Jerusalem, but God saved the city by sending a sudden plague which in one night killed 185,000 Assyrian soldiers. After Hezekiah's death, his son Manasseh succeeded him (II Kings 20:21).

Hezion (hē′zĭ-ŏn, **vision**), grandfather of Benhadad, king of Syria (I Kings 15:18).

Hezir (hē′zēr, **swine**). 1. A priest in the 17th course of Aaronic priests (I Chron. 24:15). 2. One of the covenanters with Nehemiah (Neh. 10:20).

Hezrai (hēz′rā-ī) Carmelite hero (II Sam. 23:35; RV has Hezro).

Hezro (See Hezrai)

Hezron (hĕz′rŏn, **enclosure**). 1. A grandson of Judah (Gen. 46:12, etc). 2. A son of Reuben (Gen. 46:9). 3. A place on the S border of Judah (Josh. 15:3). Cf. Hazor (3) which is the same place.

Hiddai (hĭd′ā-ī), one of David's heroes (II Sam. 23:30). Same as Hurai of I Chron. 11:32.

Hiddekel (hĭd′ē-kĕl), Hebrew name of the Tigris river, one of the four rivers of Genesis 2:11-14.

Hiel (hī′ĕl, probably, **God liveth**), man who rebuilt Jericho and thereby brought upon himself and his sons God's curse (I Kings 16:34; cf. Josh. 6:26).

Hierapolis (hī′ĕr-ăp′ō-lĭs, **sacred city**), a city mentioned only in Colossians 4:13, in the territory of ancient Phrygia near Colossae but in the NT period a part of the Roman province of Asia.

Hieroglyphics (See Writing)

Higgaion (hĭ-gā′yŏn), a musical term (Ps. 9:16), probably referring to the "solemn sound" of harp music that was to be played at that point (Ps. 92:3).

High Places (elevation). From earliest times men have tended to choose high places for their worship, whether of God, or of the false gods which men have invented. In Canaan these high places had become the scenes of orgies and human sacrifice connected with the idolatrous worship of these imaginary gods; and so, when Israel entered thc Promised Land they were told to be iconoclasts as well as conquerors. "Then ye shall drive out all the inhabitants of the land from before you, and destroy all their figured stones (KJV 'pictures') and destroy all their molten images, and demolish all their high places" (Num. 33:52). In Judges 1:19-35 we read of the failures of eight different tribes to drive out the people of the land, and though "the people served Jehovah all the days of Joshua, and all the days of the elders" who outlived Joshua (Josh. 24:31; Judg. 2:7), they soon relapsed into idolatry, used the high places for the worship of Baalim, and "provoked Jehovah to anger."

Before God would use Gideon to drive out the Midianites (Judg. 6:25) Gideon had to throw down his father's altar to Baal and the image (**Asherah**) which was beside it. Before Solomon built the temple, there was a mixed condition of worship. Solomon went to the high place at Gibeon to offer sacrifice, and there God heard his prayer and granted him surpassing wisdom (II Chron. 1:1-13). Later some godly kings like Hezekiah (II Chron. 31:1) destroyed the high places, while others like Manasseh relapsed and rebuilt them (II Chron. 33:3). After Manasseh had been punished and had repented, he was restored to his throne, and resumed the temple worship, but the people "sacrificed still in the high places, but only unto Jehovah their God" (II Chron. 33:17). Through Manasseh's early influence, the people had gone so far into apostasy that they could not repent, but through the godliness of Josiah, especially after he had heard the law read (II Kings 22:8-20), the judgment was delayed till after the death of Josiah. His great "housecleaning" is described in II Kings 23:1-25. God's attitude toward the godly kings and toward the wicked ones like Ahab in the north and Ahaz and Manasseh in the south depended largely upon their attitude towards the high places.

High Priest (See Priest)

Hilen (hī′lĕn), a city of Judah assigned to the Levites (I Chron. 6:58).

Hilkiah (hĭl-kī′ȧ, **the portion of Jehovah**), the name of seven persons mostly priests in Israel: 1. The father of Eliakim (II Kings 18:18). 2. A Merarite Levite (I Chron. 6:45). 3. Another Merarite (I Chron. 26:11). 4. The high priest in the days of Josiah, who found the book of the Law while cleaning the temple (thought by many to have been the book of Deuteronomy) and sent it to Josiah (II Kings 22, 23; II Chron. 34). 5. A priest who returned to Jerusalem with Zerubbabel 536 B.C. (Neh. 12:7). 6. The father of Jeremiah (Jer. 1:1). 7. Father of Gemariah (Jer. 29:3).

Hill Country, any region of hills and valleys which could not quite be called mountainous, but in Scripture it generally applies to the higher part of Judaea (Luke 1:39, 65) and in the OT to the southern part of Lebanon E of Sidon (Josh. 13:6).

Looking westward up the valley of Hinnom, from the Hill of Offense above Siloam. © *MPS*

Hillel (hĭl'ĕl, **he has praised**), the father of Abdon who judged Israel.

Hin (See Weights and Measures)

Hind (See Animals)

Hinge, a contrivance which enables a movable part such as a door or a window to swing in its place, often used figuratively for something of cardinal importance. Ancient heavy doors swung upon "ball and socket" joints (I Kings 7:50).

Hinnom, Valley of (hĭn'ŏm). A dumping ground and a place for burning SW and S of Jerusalem. Here was Topheth (II Kings 23:10) where human sacrifices had been offered to Molech, and so it was later to be called "the valley of slaughter" (Jer. 19:6). The Hebrew name, transliterated into Greek **geenna** (or **gehenna)** becomes the word for "hell," used 11 times by our Lord and once by James (3:6).

Hip and Thigh, used only in Judges 15:8 to denote the thoroughness with which Samson slew the Philistines.

Hirah (hī'rȧ), a "friend" of Judah, living at Adullam (Gen. 38:1, 12, 20) SW of Bethlehem.

Hiram (hī'răm). 1. King of Tyre in reigns of David and Solomon. First mentioned in II Sam. 5:11, almost at the beginning of his reign, when he sent messengers to David with cedar-trees, carpenters and masons who built David a house. After David's death he sent an embassy to Solomon (I Kings 5:1), of which Solomon promptly took advantage and arranged that Hiram should send him timber of cedar and fir from Lebanon.

When Solomon had finished building the temple (seven years) and his own palace (thirteen years), Hiram journeyed to Galilee and was greatly dissatisfied when he surveyed the cities, and he nicknamed them "Cabul," a term of uncertain origin. No definite record is found of his death. He had a daughter who became one of Solomon's "seven hundred" (I Kings 11: 1, 3). 2. A worker in brass whom Solomon brought from Tyre to assist in the building of the temple (I Kings 7:13, 14, 40-45; II Chron. 2:13, 14; 4:11-16).

Hireling, laborer who works for his wages (Deut. 24:15). Cf. (Matt. 20: 1-6).

Hittites (hĭt'īts), (II Kings 7:6) one of the three great powers confronting early Israel. The original Hittites, or "Hattians," sprang from Ham, through Canaan's second son Heth (Gen. 10: 15; I Chron. 1:13).

They were "the people of the land" (Gen. 23:7), especially in the central hills (Num. 13:29; Josh. 11:3). At Hebron, in 2029 B.C., Abraham purchased Machpelah from the Hittites (Gen. 23:3-20; 49:29-32; 50:13); 60 years later, Esau married Hittite (or Hurrian-Hivite) wives (26:34; 36:2), to the distress of Rebekah (27:46); with Israel's conquest of Canaan, despite the Mosaic ban (Deut. 20:17) Hittite unions became common (Judg. 3:5-6); and from Solomon to Ezra (I Kings 11:1; Ezra 9:1) such intermarriage continued. Ezekiel thus condemned his people's morals and race, by exclaiming, "Your mother was a Hittite, and your father an Amorite" (16:3, 45).

Hittite culture survived for another half-millennium in the city-states of Syria to the S. King Toi of Hamath 1000 B.C., supported David (II Sam. 8:9-10); and Hittite warriors served among his heroes (I Sam. 28:6; II Sam. 11:3; 23:39). Solomon reduced the Palestinian Hittites to bondservice (I Kings 9:20). In the service of their depraved mother-goddess of fertility, "Diana of the Ephesians" (Acts 19: 24-35), the Hittites became guilty of "a bestiality of which we would gladly think them innocent" and which corrupted God's people Israel (Ezek. 16: 44-45).

Hivites (hī'vīts), one of the seven nations of Canaan conquered by Joshua (Josh. 24:11); often mentioned in the OT (Josh. 11:3; Judg. 3:3; II Sam. 24: 7); last referred to when Solomon raised a levy from their remnants to do task work for him (II Chron. 8:7). Some scholars think they may be the same as the Horites.

Hizkiah, Hizkijah (hĭz-kī'ȧ, hĭz-kī'jȧ), found twice in KJV but in each case should be Hezekiah as in ASV. 1. The great-great-grandfather of Zephaniah (Zeph. 1:1). 2. Covenanter with Nehemiah (Neh. 10:17).

Hobab (hō'băb, **beloved),** a person who is named only twice in the Bible. In Numbers 10:29 he is called "the son of Reuel, the Midianite, Moses' father-in-law" which would seem quite clearly to make him a brother of Zipporah (Exod. 18:2) and brother-in-law of Moses. In Judges 4:11 KJV speaks of "Hobab, the father-in-law of Moses" while ASV with more deference to logic reads "Hobab, the brother-in-law of Moses."

Hobah (hō'bȧ), place N of Damascus to which Abram pursued the captors of Lot (Gen. 14:15).

Hod (hŏd, **majesty),** a man of Asher (I Chron. 7:37).

Hodaiah (hō-dā'yȧ), a descendant of David (I Chron. 3:24). ASV, RSV, Hodaviah.

Hodaviah (hō'dȧ-vī'ȧ). 1. Chief of the half tribe of Manasseh, E of Jordan (I Chron. 5:24). 2. Benjamite (I Chron. 9:7). 3. A Levite whose family returned with Zerubbabel (Ezra 2:40). Also called Hodevah (Neh. 7:43) and Judah (Ezra 3:9).

Hodesh (hō'dĕsh), a wife of Shaharaim, a Benjamite (I Chron. 8:9).

Hodevah (See Hodaviah)

Hodiah (hō-dī'ȧ), a man who married the sister of Naham, and who was reckoned in the tribe of Judah (I Chron. 4:19). See Hodijah.

Hodijah (hō-dī'jȧ). 1. A Levite (Neh. 8:7; 9:5; 10:10, 13). 2. A chief under Nehemiah (Neh. 10:18).

Hoglah (hŏg'lȧ), one of the five daughters of Zelophehad, a Manassite (Num. 26:33; 27:1-11; 36:1-12; Josh. 17:3, 4).

Hoham (hō'hăm), Amorite king of Hebron, who entered into league with other kings against Joshua (Josh. 10: 3).

Holiness, Holy, usually translate words derived from a Heb. root meaning **separateness, withdrawal.** It is first applied to God, and is early associated with ideas of purity and righteousness. The words "holiness, holy" do not occur in Genesis, though implied in the dread which the presence of God inspires (Gen. 28:16, 17), but from Exodus 3:5 on, where God reveals His name and nature, holiness is constantly stressed. A few of the many Biblical references: God is "glorious in holiness" (Exod. 15:11); He acts with "his holy arm" (Isa. 52:10); His words and promises are holy (Jer. 23: 9; Ps. 105:42); His name is holy (Lev. 20:3; I Chron. 29:16); His Spirit is holy (Isa. 63:10, 11; Ps. 51:10, see separate article, Holy Spirit). Persons connected with holy places and holy services were holy: priests (Lev. 21:1-6) and their garments (Exod. 28:2, 4); Israel as a nation (Jer. 2:3); individually (Deut. 33:3); many things connected with Israel (I Chron. 16:29). Times given to worship were holy (Exod. 16: 23; 20:8; 12:16; Isa. 58:13).

The holiness of Jesus Christ is specifically stressed. Evil spirits recognized Him as "the holy one of God" who has come to destroy them (Mark 1:24; Luke 4:34). Jesus is holy because of His wondrous birth (Luke 1:35). The Father "hath sanctified" Him, declared Him and made Him holy (John 10: 36). He is "holy and true" (Rev. 3:7).

The holiness of the Church is developed in the NT. As in the OT, Jerusalem is holy (Matt. 4:5; 27:53; Rev. 11:2), so is the temple (Matt. 24: 15; Acts 6:13) and the new temple, the church; collectively (Eph. 2:21, 22) and individually (I Cor. 3:16, 17). The Scriptures are holy (Rom. 1:2; II Tim. 3:15). The law is holy (Rom. 7: 12). Since the earthly holy place, priests, cult apparatus, sacrifices and services were holy, much more are the heavenly (Heb. 8:5). The Church is a holy nation (I Pet. 2:9; 1:16). Christ died for the Church in order to make it holy (Eph. 5:26; I Cor. 1:2, sanctified in Christ Jesus, I Cor. 6:11). Gentile Christians are now "no more strangers" and foreigners, but fellow-citizens with the Jewish Christian "saints" (holy ones, Eph. 2:19). Thus the Church as a whole, the local churches, and individual Christians, are holy, "called . . . saints" (Rom. 1: 7; I Cor. 1:2; II Cor. 1:1; Eph. 1:1; Phil 1:1; Col. 1:2; "saints" translating **hagioi,** holy. The life of the individual Christian is to be a living, holy sacrifice (Rom. 12:1), not only through death (Phil. 2:17), but through life itself (Phil. 1:21-26).

Summary: the idea of holiness originates in the revealed character of God, and is communicated to things, places, times and persons engaged in His service. Its ethical nature grows clearer as revelation unfolds, until the holiness of God the Father, Son and Holy Spirit, of the Church as a body, and of individual members of that body, fills the NT horizon. Holiness is interwoven with righteousness and purity. To seek holiness apart from the other qualities of a Christlike life, is to wander from the way of holiness itself.

Holon (hō'lŏn). 1. A Levitical city in the hill country of Judah (Josh. 15: 51) (called Hilen [hī'lĕn], in I Chron. 6:58). 2. A Moabite town (Jer. 48:21).

Holy of Holies (See Tabernacle)

Holy Ghost (See Holy Spirit)

Holy Place (See Tabernacle)

Holy Spirit, the Third Person of the

Triune Godhead (Matt. 28:19; II Cor. 13:14).

That the Holy Spirit is a power, an influence, is plain from Acts 1:8; that He is a Person, the NT makes clear in detail: He dwells with us (John 14:17), teaches and brings to remembrance (14:26), bears witness (15:26), convinces of sin (16:8), guides, speaks, declares (16:13, 15), inspires the Scriptures and speaks through them (Acts 1:16; II Pet. 1:21), spoke to Philip (Acts 8:29), calls ministers (13:2), sends out workers (13:4), forbids certain actions (16:6, 7), intercedes (Rom. 8:26), etc. He has the attributes of personality: will (I Cor. 12:11), mind (Rom. 8:27), thought, knowledge, words (I Cor. 2:10-13), love (Rom. 15:30). The Holy Spirit can be treated as a Person: lied to and tempted (Acts 5:3, 4, 9), resisted (Acts 7:51), grieved (Eph. 4:30), outraged (Heb. 10:29 RSV), blasphemed against (Matt. 12:31). The Holy Spirit is God; equated with the Father and the Son (Matt. 28:19; II Cor. 13:14). Jesus speaks of Him as of His other self (John 14:16, 17) whose presence with the disciples will be of greater advantage than His own (John 16:7). To have the Spirit of God is to have Christ (Rom. 8:9-12). God is Spirit (John 4:24) in essential nature, and sends His Holy Spirit to live and work in men (John 14:26; 16:7).

At Pentecost a new phase of the revelation of God to men began (Acts 2); as new as that when the Word became flesh in the birth of Jesus. With the rushing of a mighty wind and the appearing of cloven tongues like fire, the disciples were all filled with the Holy Spirit, and spoke in foreign languages (listed in 2:9-11). The excitement drew a crowd of visitors to the feast, to whom Peter explained that the prophecy of Joel 2:28-32 was being fulfilled, in accordance with the salvation which Jesus of Nazareth had wrought in dying on the cross. Three thousand souls were added by baptism to the 120 disciples, and thus began the fellowship of apostolic teaching, of breaking of bread and of prayer, which is the Church. When the first crisis which threatened the extinction of the early church was passed, again "they were all filled with the Holy Ghost" (Acts 4:31) binding them more closely together. When the first Gentiles were converted, the Holy Spirit was poured out on them and they spoke in tongues (Acts 10:44-48); likewise when Paul met a group of John the Baptist's disciples (Acts 19:1-7).

The NT is full of the work of the Holy Spirit in the lives of believers (Rom. 8:1-27): e.g., His gifts (I Cor. 12-14); that our "body is the temple of the Holy Ghost" (I Cor. 6:19); "the fruit of the Spirit" (Gal. 5:22, 23). Being "filled with the Spirit" (Eph. 5:18) we shall experience Christ living within us (Rom. 8:9, 10). As the heavenly Father is God, and His Son Jesus Christ is God, so the Holy Spirit is God. The Holy Spirit as well as the Son was active in creation; on occasion acts in His own Person in OT times; more intensively in the gospels; and in Acts and the epistles becomes the resident divine Agent in the Church and in its members. Teaching concerning the Holy Spirit has been both neglected and distorted, but the subject deserves careful attention as one reads the NT.

Homam (hō'măm), son of Lotan and grandson of Seir (I Chron. 1:39). Also called Hemam (Gen. 36:22 KJV; Heman in ASV, RSV).

Homer (See Weights and Measures)

Honey, at first rare (Gen. 43:11), found wild in clefts of the rocks (Deut. 32:13; Ps. 81:16), in the comb on the ground (I Sam. 14:25-43). Job 20:17 speaks of brooks of honey and butter, indicating abundance due to domestication of bees. Canaan is "a land flowing with milk and honey" (from Exod. 3:8 to Ezek. 20:15). Samson ate wild honey found in the carcass of a lion (Judg. 14:8-18). Honey became a common food (II Sam. 17:29) even in times of scarcity (Isa. 7:15, 22). Honey as food is recognized and recommended, but in moderation (Ezek. 16:13, 19; Prov. 24:13; 25:16, 27; 27:7). Honey is a standard of comparison for pleasant things, good or bad (S. of Sol. 4:11; 5:1; Prov. 16:24; 5:3; Ezek. 3:3; Rev. 10:9). John the Baptist ate honey (Matt. 3:4; Mark 1:6).

Hood (See Dress: Headdress)

Hook, used for fishing (Job. 41:1; Matt. 17:27), hanging curtains (Exod. 26:32, 37; 27:10, 17), pruning (Joel 3:10; Mic. 4:3), hanging meat (Ezek. 40:43).

Hoopoe (See Birds)

Hope, a gift of the Holy Spirit which abides, an essential characteristic of the Christian (I Cor. 13:8, 13). Not mere expectation and desire, as in Greek literature, but includes trust, confidence, refuge in God, the God

Mount Hor (Jebal Harun) near Petra. © *MPS*

of hope (Rom. 15:13). Christ in you is the hope of glory (Col. 1:27). Christ Jesus is our hope (I Tim. 1:1 RSV). Hope of eternal life is bound up with "that blessed hope, and the glorious appearing of . . . Jesus Christ" (Tit. 1: 2; 2:13), which motivates purity (I John 3:3). Hope is linked with faith (Heb. 11:1). It depends on the resurrection of Christ (I Cor. 15:19). In the OT "hope" translates a variety of Heb. words in KJV, which mean "confidence, trust, safety," etc., and are so translated in ASV, RSV. NT hope has deep roots in the OT.

Hophni (hŏf′nī), an unworthy son of Eli (I Sam. 1:3; 2:34; 4:4, 17). Hophni is always associated with his brother Phinehas. The two were partners in evil practices and brought a curse upon their heads (I Sam. 2:34; 3:14). Both were slain at the battle of Aphek and this, coupled with the loss of the Ark, caused the death of Eli (I Sam. 4:17, 18).

Hor (hôr, **mountain**). 1. Mountain where Aaron died and was buried (Num. 20:22-29; 33:37-41; Deut. 32: 50). 2. A mountain on the N border of the land given to the Israelites, between the Great Sea (Mediterranean) and the entrance of Hamath (Num. 34:7, 8).

Horam (hō′răm), a king of Gezer (Josh. 10:33).

Horeb (hō′rĕb, **drought, desert**), the mountain where Moses received his commission (Exod. 3:1); where he brought water out of the rock (Exod. 17:6); where the people stripped off their ornaments in token of repentance (Exod. 33:6); Elijah fled here (I Kings 19:8). It is geographically indistinguishable from Sinai.

Horem (hō′rĕm, **consecrated**), a fortified city in Naphtali, near Iron (Josh. 19:38).

Hor-Hagidgad (hôr′hă-gĭd′găd, **hollow** or **cavern of Gilgad**), an Israelite camp in the wilderness (Num. 33:32, 33), called Gudgodah in Deuteronomy 10:7. See Gudgodah.

Hori (hō′rī, **cave-dweller**). 1. A son of Seir (Gen. 36:22, 29, 30; I Chron. 1:39). 2. A Simeonite whose son Shaphat was one of the spies (Num. 13:5).

Horim (See Horites)

Horite, Horim (hō′rīt, hō′rĭm), a people found in Mount Seir as early as the time of Abraham, and conquered by Chedorlaomer and his allies (Gen. 14:6); the early inhabitants, before the Edomites dispossessed them and intermarried with them (Gen. 36:20-30; Deut. 2:12, 22). Esau married the daughter of one of their chieftains, also called a Hivite (Gen. 36:2). The Hivites are thought to be identical with, or else confused with, the Horites (Gen. 34:2; Josh. 9:7), in which case the Horites lived as far N as Gibeon and Shechem in the time of Jacob's sons, and till the conquest under Joshua. The LXX makes this identification.

Hormah (hôr′mȧ, **a devoted place**), about midway between Gaza and Beersheba. Here the disobedient Israelites were defeated by Amalekites and Canaanites (Num. 14:45; Deut. 1:44). Judges 1:17 relates that it was Judah and Simeon who subdued Zephath and renamed it Hormah.

Horn, first made of animal horns, later of metal (Num. 10:2); for giving signals (Josh. 6:5) and containers (I Sam. 16:1). Projections of corners of altar were called "horns of the altar" (Exod. 27:2; I Kings 1:50). A symbol of strength and honor (Ps. 18:2; Dan. 7:7; Luke 1:69).

Hornet (See Insects)

Horonaim (hôr-ŏ-nā′ĭm, **two hollows, caves** or **ravines**), a place in Moab, (Isa. 15:5; Jer. 48:3, 5, 34).

Horonite (hôr′ō-nīt), a designation of Sanballat (Neh. 2:10, 19; 13:28).

Horse (See Animals)

Horse Gate, gate of Jerusalem, between the Water Gate and the Sheep Gate; probably near the SE corner of the city (Neh. 3:28-32; Jer. 31:38-40).

Horse Leech, a bloodsucking worm which clings to the flesh (Prov. 30:15).

Hosah (hō′sȧ, **refuge**). 1. A town on the N border of Asher, (Josh. 19:29). 2. A Levite porter (I Chron. 16:38; 26:10, 11, 16).

Hosanna (hō-zăn′ȧ, **save now**), originally a prayer, "Save, now, pray" (Ps. 118:25), which had lost its primary meaning and became an exclamation of praise (Matt. 21:9, 15; Mark 11:9, 10; John 12:13). That it is transliterated instead of translated in three of the Gospels (Luke omits it) is evidence of the change of meaning. In its application to God the Father and to Jesus, Hosanna was concerned with the Messianic salvation.

Hosea (hō-zē′ȧ, **salvation**). This notable eighth century B.C. prophet lived during a period of great national anxiety. Born during the reign of Jeroboam II (c. 786-746 B.C.), (1:1) he exercised his prophetic ministry in Israel when Uzziah (c. 783-743 B.C.), Jotham (c. 742-735 B.C.), Ahaz (c. 735-715 B.C.) and Hezekiah (c. 715-686 B.C.) reigned in Judah.

The time of Hosea was marked by great material prosperity. Under Jeroboam II the northern kingdom experienced a degree of economic and commercial development unknown since the early days of the united kingdom.

While there is no reference to the occupation of Beeri, father of Hosea, he may well have been a middle-class merchant, perhaps a baker. Hosea himself was an educated person, and probably hailed from a town in Ephraim or Manasseh. A man of profound spiritual vision, he was gifted with intellectual qualities which enabled him to comprehend the significance of those unhappy events which marked his domestic life and interpret them as a timely reminder of Divine love toward a wayward, sinful Israel.

Hosea saw that their form of worship was the exact opposite of what God desired of His people. The emphasis of the Sinaitic covenant was upon the exclusive worship of Jehovah by a nation holy unto the Lord. However, the religious life of the covenant people had degenerated to the point of becoming identified with the shameless immoral worship of the pagan Canaanite deities. The emphasis upon unbridled sexual activity coupled with excessive indulgence in alcohol was sapping the vitality not only of the Canaanites but also of Israel. All this, carried out against a background of magic and pagan mythology, was vastly removed from the purity of worship contemplated in the Sinai covenant.

It was Hosea's primary duty to recall wayward Israel to its obligations under the agreement made at Sinai. On that occasion Israel had voluntarily made a pact with God which involved surrender, loyalty and obedience. As a result Israel had become God's son (11:1; cf. Exod. 4:22) by adoption and Divine grace. Of necessity the initiative had come from God. But Hosea saw that it was important to emphasize the free co-operative acceptance of that relationship by the Israelites. Hence he stressed that Israel was really God's bride (2:7, 16, 19) and employed the marriage metaphor to demonstrate the voluntary association of the Bride with her Divine Lover.

His own marital experience (chapters 1-3) was made a parable for all to see. He was commanded to marry a woman who would subsequently be unfaithful, to have children by her, and to give them symbolic names indicating Divine displeasure with Israel. After Gomer has pursued her paramours she was to be brought back and with patient love readmitted to his home, there to await in penitence and grief the time of restoration to full favor. This was a clear picture of wayward Israel in its relationship with God, and showed the unending faithfulness of the Almighty.

Analysis:

- 1-3 Hosea's unhappy marriage and its results.
- 4 The priests condone immorality.
- 5 Israel's sin will be punished unless she repents.
- 6 Israel's sin is thoroughgoing; her repentance halfhearted.
- 7 Inner depravity and outward decay.
- 8 The nearness of judgment.
- 9 The impending calamity.
- 10 Israel's guilt and punishment.
- 11 God pursues Israel with love.
- 12-14 An exhortation of repentance, with promised restoration.

Hoshaiah (hō-shā'yȧ, **Jehovah has saved).** Man who assisted at the dedication of the wall (Neh. 12:32).

2. The father of Jezaniah (Jer. 42:1) or Azariah (Jer. 43:2), who opposed Jeremiah after the fall of Jerusalem (Jer. 42:1-43:7, see ASV, RSV).

Hoshama (hŏsh'ȧ-mȧ), a son of Jeconiah or Jehoiachin, captive king of Judah (I Chron. 3:18).

Hoshea (hō-shē'ȧ, **salvation).** 1. Joshua's earlier name, changed by Moses (Num. 13:8, 16 ASV RSV; Deut. 32:44 RSV Joshua). 2. The son of Azaziah and prince of Ephraim (I Chron. 27:20). 3. A son of Elah; the last king of the northern kingdom (II

"Given to hospitality." © *SPF*

Kings 15:30; 17:1-6; 18:1-10). 4. A chief ruler under Nehemiah (Neh. 10:23).

Hospitality, commanded in Mosaic law (Lev. 19:34); illustrations: Gen. 14:17-19; 18; 19; 24:15-28; 29:1-14; 43:15-34; Exod. 2:15-22; Judg. 13:2-23; Matt. 14:15-21; Luke 10:38-42.

Host. Army (Gen. 21:22); angels (Ps. 103:21; Josh. 5:14); heavenly bodies (Deut. 4:19); creation (Gen. 2:1); God of hosts (I Sam. 17:45). Host occurs but four times in the NT: 1. **army** (Luke 2:13 **angels;** Acts 7:42 **heavenly bodies as objects of worship); 2. guest,** also **host** (Rom. 16:23); 3. **one who receives all comers** (Luke 10:35 RSV **inkeeper). Hostage (son of pledges).** Jehoash (Joash), king of Israel, took hostages after his victory over Judah.

Hotham (hō'thăm) An Asherite (I Chron. 7:32). See also Hothan.

Hothan (hō'thăn), an Aroerite, whose two sons Shama and Jehiel were among David's heroes (I Chron. 11:44; ASV, RSV have Hotham).

Hothir (hō'thẽr), son of Henan, David's seer and singer. A Kohathite (I Chron. 25:4, 28).

Hough (hŏk, **to hamstring an animal)** (Gen. 49:6; Josh. 11:6, 9; II Sam. 8:4; I Chron. 18:4). A cruel practice, justified only by extreme military necessity.

Hour, may be a point of time (Matt. 8:13), or a period (Rev. 17:12). Israelites reckoned days from sunset to sunset; Romans reckoned hours from midnight to noon, as we do.

House. In OT oftenest Heb. and Aramaic **bayith, a dwelling place** (Gen. 12:15), usually of solid materials (Exod. 12:7); or its inhabitants (Gen. 12:17); or the family or race wherever dwelling (Exod. 2:1), often translated "household" or "family"; the tabernacle (Exod. 23:19; 34:26), or temple (I Kings 5:3-7:1) as the house of God; a temple of heathen gods (Judg. 16:23-30; I Sam. 31:9, 10). It might be a nomad tent (Gen. 14:13, 14, cf. 18:1) or a building (Gen. 19:2-11) in a city. God contrasts tent with house in II Samuel 7:6.

After the conquest under Joshua, the Israelites came increasingly to live in houses in the cities and towns of Canaan; though some, like the Rechabites (Jer. 35:7, 10) continued to live

The housetop was a popular place in Bible days. © SPF

in tents; and some took refuge in caves in times of uncertainty (I Kings 19:9). House walls were often of rough stones as much as three feet thick; of unburned clay brick (Job 4:19), sometimes protected with a casing of stone slabs. In large buildings the stones were squared, smoothed and pointed. The floor might be leveled rock surface, more often beaten clay. The rich might have a stone slab floor. Solomon's temple had a floor of cypress boards (I Kings 6:15). For doors there were square openings in the wall with a stone or wood lintel, doorposts (Exod. 12:22, 23; I Kings 6:31) and a stone threshold. Roofs had beams with transverse rafters, covered with brushwood and overlaid with mud mixed with chopped straw. They were flat, and were beaten and rolled. The roof was used for worship (II Kings 23:12; Jer. 19:13; 32:29; Acts 10:9). Absalom pitched his tent on the roof for publicity (II Sam. 16:22). Three thousand Philistines used the roof of their temple as bleachers (Judg. 16:27), illustrating its strength, while its weakness was demonstrated when Samson pushed apart the middle pillars on which the structure depended. There were outside stairs leading to the roof and its "upper chamber." In some cases the "upper room" may have been inside the house. In the living room a raised brick platform ran across one side of the room (in the Hellenistic period at least), sometimes with ducts to heat it, and on this the family spread their bedding by night, or sat by day. In cold weather the cattle might be admitted to the lower part of the living room of a poor family.

Palaces were much more elaborate (I Kings 7:1-12). There is a sharp contrast between the humble homes of the common people and the luxurious dwellings of kings and the very rich, in Egypt, Mesopotamia, Palestine under the Hebrew monarchy and after, in Greece and Rome of the Hellenistic period. But a Christian community, many of whose members were slaves, would be familiar with the lavish contents of great houses (II Tim. 2:20). While Christians at first continued to worship in temple and synagogue, from the beginning they met also in private homes (Acts 1:13; 2:2, 46). "The church in their house" is a well-established pattern in Paul's ministry (Rom. 16:5; I Cor. 16:19; Col. 4:15; Philem. 2). Special buildings for Christian churches do not appear in the NT. The family had been the religious unit from the beginning of creation (Gen. 2:8); worship centered in the house, from tent to palace. Tabernacle and temple were "the house of God" and of the larger family of God, the Chosen People. So in the NT the house where a Christian family lived welcomed other Christian brothers and sisters besides its own members to worship together, and when the temple was destroyed and the synagogue closed to Christians, the church in the home became the sole refuge of the believer, until special buildings were erected. Thus to all the human associations of home which permeate a house are added the sanctifying influences of the spiritual life.

Hukkok (hŭk'ŏk), a border town of Naphtali (Josh. 19:34).

Hukok (See Helkath)

Hul (hŭl), son of Aram and grandson of Shem (Gen. 10:23). Also called son of Shem (I Chron. 1:17).

Huldah (hŭl'dȧ, **weasel**), a prophetess in the reign of Josiah (II Kings 22:14-20; II Chron. 34:22-28). When Hilkiah the priest found the book of the law in the temple, Josiah sent messengers to Huldah. She attested the genuineness of the book and prophesied ruin because of desertion of the law.

Humanity of Christ (See Christ)

Humility, freedom from pride, lowliness, meekness, modesty, mildness. There is a false humility (Col. 2:18, 23), properly rendered "self-abasement" in RSV. God humbles men to bring them to obedience (Deut. 8:2). To humble ourselves is a condition of God's favor (II Chron. 7:14). Humility is enjoined (Prov. 15:33; 18:12; 22:4). To the Greeks humility was weak and despicable, but Jesus made it the cornerstone of character (Matt. 5:3, 5; 18:4; 23:12; Luke 14:11; 18:14). Jesus by His humility drew men to Himself (Matt. 11:28-30; John 13:1-20; Rev. 3:20). Paul emphasized the humility of Jesus (Phil. 2:1-11; II Cor. 8:9); commanded us to be humble toward one another (Phil. 2:3, 4; Rom. 12:10; I Cor. 13:4-6) and spoke of himself as an example (Acts 20:19). Peter exhorted to humility toward the brethren and toward God (I Pet. 5:5, 6).

Humtah (hŭm'tȧ), a town in the hill country of Judah near Hebron (Josh. 15:54).

Hupham (hū'făm), a son of Benjamin and founder of the Huphamites (Num. 26:39).

Huphamites (See Hupham)

Huppah (hŭp'ȧ), a priest in David's time (I Chron. 24:13).

Huppim (hŭp'ĭm, **coast people**), probably the same as Hupham, but the references leave his descent uncertain (Gen. 46:21; I Chron. 7:12, 15).

Hur (hûr, **whiteness**). 1. One who, with Aaron, held up Moses' hands during a battle against Amalek, bringing victory to Israel (Exod. 17:10, 12). 2. Grandfather of Bezaleel, chief workman in the tabernacle (Exod. 31:2; 35:30; 38:22; II Chron. 1:5). 3. Midianite king killed with Balaam (Num. 31:1-8); a leader of Midian and a prince of Sihon the Amorite king (Josh. 13:21). 4. In KJV, the father of one of 12 officers who supplied food for Solomon's household (I Kings 4:8); ASV, RSV treat "son of" (Heb. **bēn**) as part of a proper name, Ben-hur. 5. Father of Rephaiah (Neh. 3:9).

Hurai (hū'rā-ī), one of David's heroes (I Chron. 11:32). Also called Hiddai (II Sam. 23:30).

Huram (hū'răm, **noble-born**). 1. A Benjamite (I Chron. 8:5). See Hupham 2. The king of Tyre (II Chron. 2:3, 11, 12). Usually called Hiram. 3. A Tyrian artificer sent to Solomon by No. 2 (II Chron. 2:13; 4:11, 16).

Huri (hū'rī), a Gadite (I Chron. 5:14).

Hurrians (See Horites)

Husbandman (hŭz'bănd-măn), a farmer, whether owner or tenant. The term is retained in ASV except Zechariah 13:5, "tiller of the ground," where Zechariah asserts that he is a farmer, not a professional prophet. The Heb. words mean "farmer, plowman, tiller of the soil," and RSV uses all three translations in the OT.

Husbandry (See Occupations & Professions: Farmer)

Hushah (hū'shȧ), son of Ezer (I Chron. 4:4).

Hushai (hū'shī, hū'shā-ī), the friend and counselor of David who overthrew the counsels of Ahithophel (II Sam. 15:32, 37; 16:16-18; 17:5-15; I Chron. 27:33).

Husham (hū'shăm), a king of Edom, who succeeded Jobab (Gen. 36:34, 35; I Chron. 1:45, 46).

Hushathite, The (hū'shăth-īt), the patronymic of Sibbecai, one of David's 30 heroes (II Sam. 21:18; I Chron. 11:29; 20:4; 27:11).

Hushim (hū'shĭm). 1. The sons of Dan (Gen. 46:23). 2. The sons of Aher (I Chron. 7:12). 3. Wife of Shaharaim (I Chron. 8:8, 11).

Husks, Luke 15:16, the pods of the carob tree.

Huz (hŭz), the eldest son of Nahor and Milcah (Gen. 22:21; ASV, RSV Uz).

Huzzab (hŭz'ăb). It is disputed whether the word in Nahum 2:7 is to be taken as a noun or as a verb. If a noun (KJV; ASV margin), it may be an epithet of Nineveh or of its queen (and so RSV "its mistress").

Hyacinth (hī'ȧ-sĭnth). 1. A color, deep purple (Rev. 9:17); KJV has "jacinth." 2. A precious stone (Rev. 21:20); RV has "sapphire."

Hyena (See Animals)

Hyksos (hĭk'sōs), a West Semitic (Canaanite, Amorite) people who ruled an empire embracing Syria and Palestine; called the Shepherd Kings by the Egyptian historian Manetho. Around 1700 B.C. their use of a new weapon, the horse-drawn chariot, enabled them to conquer Egypt, where they ruled till about 1550 B.C. During their rule, which was more friendly to foreigners than were native Egyptian dynasties, Joseph came to Egypt and rose to be prime minister.

Hymenaeus (hī'mĕ-nē'ŭs, **apostate pertaining to Hymen, the god of marriage**), Christian who was excommunicated by Paul (I Tim. 1:19, 20; II Tim. 2:16-18).

Hymn (See Music)

Hypocrisy (hĭ-pŏk'rĭ-sē). Hpyocrite or hypocritical, in the OT, render words from the Heb. correctly translated "profane, godless" in ASV, RSV (Isa. 32:6; 9:17; 10:6; 33:14; Job 8:13; 13:16; 15:34; 17:8; 20:5; 27:8; 34:30; 36:13; Prov. 11:9; Ps. 35:16). The LXX used Greek **hypokrínomai, act a part in a play; hypókrisis, hypocrisy; hypokritḗs, hypocrite,** which occur in the NT and are taken over in English (Matt. 6:2, 5, 16; 7:5; 15:7; 22:18; 23:13, 15, 23, 25, 27, 28, 29; 24:51; Mark 7:6; 12:15; Luke 12:1, 56; 13:15). In Galatians 2:13 KJV, ASV have "dissimulated . . . dissimulation," RSV "acted insincerely . . . insincerity." **Anypókritos, without hypocrisy** (Rom. 12:9; II Cor. 6:6; I Tim. 1:5; II Tim. 1:5; I Pet. 1:22 is usually rendered "sincere, genuine" in RSV. In Luke 20:20 the verb is translated "feign themselves." The thought in the NT lies close to the literal meaning "play-acting," with special reference to religion (II Tim. 3:5; Matt. 6:1-18; 23:13-36).

Hyssop (See Plants)

–I–

Ibhar (ĭb′här, **he chooses),** one of David's sons (II Sam. 5:15; I Chron. 14:5).

Ibleam (ĭb′lē-ăm), a town in the territory of Issachar, given to the tribe of Manasseh (Josh. 17:11). Ahaziah, king of Judah, was slain near there (II Kings 9:27). Zechariah, king of Israel, was killed there (II Kings 15:10, text of Lucian).

Ibneiah (ĭb-nī′yȧ, **Jehovah builds),** a Benjamite (I Chron. 9:8).

Ibnijah (ĭb-nī′jȧ, **Jehovah builds up),** a Benjamite, father of Reuel (I Chron. 9:8).

Ibri (ĭb′rī, **a Hebrew),** a Merarite Levite, son of Jaaziah (I Chron. 24:27).

Ibzan (ĭb′zăn), tenth judge of Israel, who ruled for seven years. He had 30 sons and 30 daughters (Judg. 12:8-10).

Ichabod (ĭk′ȧ-bŏd, **inglorious),** son of Phinehas, Eli's son, slain by the Philistines at the battle of Aphek when the ark was taken. Ichabod was born after his father's death, and was given this name by his mother on her deathbed because she felt that the "glory (had) departed from Israel" (I Sam. 4:19ff).

Iconium (ī-cō′nĭ-ŭm), a city in S. Central part of Asia Minor, visited by Paul and Barnabas on Paul's first missionary journey (Acts 13:51ff). On his second missionary journey, Paul with Silas stopped off at Iconium to read the letter sent out by the Jerusalem Council on the Judaizing question, and at nearby Lystra he took young Timothy with him as his associate (Acts 16:1-5). In II Timothy 3:11 Paul alludes to persecutions endured by him at Antioch, Iconium, and Lystra. In the first century it was one of the chief cities in the southern part of the Roman province of Galatia.

Coins from Iconium (1st Century B.C.). Above, shows Zeus with sceptre and thunderbolt; below, Athena Polias, goddess of the city, holding a serpent entwined spear. UANT

Idbash (ĭd′băsh, **honey-sweet),** a man of Judah (I Chron. 4:3).

Iddo (ĭd′ō), the English equivalent of several Jewish names: 1. (a) Son of Zechariah, and a captain under David (I Chron. 27:21). (b) One who had taken a foreign wife at the time of Ezra (Ezra 10:43). 2. The head of a community of Nethinim (Ezra 8:17). 3. (a) A Levite descended from Gershom; ancestor of Asaph (I Chron. 6:21). (b) A seer and prophet (II Chron. 9:29; 12:15; 13:22). (c) Father of Abinadab (I Kings 4:14). (d) Grandfather of the prophet Zechariah (Zech. 1:1, 7; Ezra 5:1; 6:14).

Idol (See Idolatry)

Idolatry (ī-dŏl′ȧ-trē), All the nations surrounding ancient Israel were idolatrous, although their idolatry assumed different forms. The early Semites of Mesopotamia worshiped mountains, springs, trees, and blocks of stone, in which the deity was supposed to be in some sense incarnate (Judg. 6:25-32). The religion of the Egyptians centered mostly about the veneration of the sun and of the Nile, as sources of life. They also had a number of sacred animals: the bull, cow, cat, baboon, crocodile, etc. Some of the deities had human bodies and animal heads. Among the Canaanites, religion took on a very barbarous character. The chief gods were personifications of life and fertility. The gods had no moral character whatsoever, and worship of them carried with it demoralizing practices, including child sacrifice, prostitution, and snake-worship. Human and animal images of the deities were worshiped. The Israelites, on succeeding to the land, were commanded to destroy these idols (Exod. 23:24; 34:13; Num. 33:52; Deut. 7:5).

The first clear case of idolatry in the Bible is the account of Rachel's stealing her father's teraphim, which were images of household gods (Gen. 31: 19). They were used in Babylonia. The Second Commandment, forbidding man to make and bow down to images of any kind, was directed against idolatry (Exod. 20:4, 5; Deut. 5:8, 9). This sin seems to have been shunned until the period of the judges, when the nation was caught in its toils again.

The whole of Judges tells of successive apostasies, judgments, and repentances. The story of Micah in Judges 17, 18 is an illustration of how idolatry was often combined with outward worship of Jehovah. It is significant that Jonathan, a Levite and a grandson of Moses, assumed the office of priest to the images of Micah, and that later he allowed himself to be persuaded by some Danites, who had stolen Micah's idol, to go with them as the priest of their tribe. He became the first of a line of priests to officiate at the shrine of the stolen idols all the time that the tabernacle was at Shiloh.

The prophet Samuel persuaded the people to repent of their sin and to renounce idolatry; but in Solomon's reign the king himself made compromises that affected disastrously the whole future of the kingdom. His wives brought their own heathen gods with them, and openly worshiped them.

In the southern kingdom things went somewhat better. Hezekiah restored the temple services, which had been abandoned during his father's reign, but the change was only outward (II Chron. 28, 29; Isa. 29:13). Not long before the destruction of Jerusalem by Babylonia, Josiah made a final effort to bring about a purer worship, but it did not last (II Chron. 34).

In the NT, references to idolatry are understandably few. The Maccabean war resulted in the Jews becoming fanatically opposed to the crass idolatry of OT times. The Jews were never again tempted to worship images of gods other than Jehovah. Jesus, however, warned that to make possessions central in life is also idolatry, and said, "Ye cannot serve God and mammon" (Matt. 6:24). Paul, in Romans 1:18-25, teaches that idolatry is not the first stage of religion, from which man by an evolutionary process emerges to monotheism, but is the result of deliberate religious apostasy. The OT conception of idolatry is widened to include anything that leads to the dethronement of God from the heart, as, for example, covetousness (Eph. 5: 5; Col. 3:5).

Idumaea (ĭ′ū-mē-ȧ, **pertaining to Edom),** Greek and Roman name for Edom (Mark 3:8; 34:5, 6). See Edom.

Igal (ī′găl, **God redeems).** 1. One of the 12 spies sent by Moses (Num. 13: 7). 2. One of David's heroes (II Sam. 23:36). 3. A son of Shemaiah (I Chron. 3:22).

Igdaliah (ĭg′dȧ-lī′ȧ, **Jehovah is great),** father of the prophet Hanan (Jer. 35: 4).

Igeal (ī′ge-ăl, **God redeems),** a son of Shemaiah (I Chron. 3:22, RV Igal).

Iim (ī′ĭm, **heaps, ruins).** 1. A town in Judah near Edom (Josh. 15:29). 2. A town E of the Jordan (Num. 33:45).

Ije-Abarim (ī′jē-ăb′ȧ-rĭm, **ruins of Abarim),** a halting place in the journeyings of Israel, "in the border of Moab" (Num. 33:44).

Ijon (ī′jŏn, **a ruin),** a town in the territory of Naphtali, captured by Benhadad, king of Syria, at the instigation of Asa (I Kings 15:20; II Chron. 16: 4).

Ikkesh (ĭk′ĕsh, **crooked),** father of Ira, one of David's heroes (II Sam. 23:26; I Chron. 11:28).

Ilai (ī′lā-ī), one of David's mighty men (I Chron. 11:29); called Zalmon in II Samuel 23:28).

Illyricum (ĭl-ĭr′ĭ-kŭm), Roman province on E coast of Adriatic. Paul preached there (Rom. 15:19). Now part of Yugoslavia.

Image (See Idolatry)

Image, Nebuchadnezzar's. Nebuchadnezzar in his second year had a dream which none of his wise men could describe or interpret for him except Daniel, to whom God had revealed the secret of the dream in a night vision. The king's dream was of a huge image with a head of gold, the breast and arms of silver, the belly and thighs of brass, the legs of iron, and the feet of iron mixed with clay. A stone cut without hands fell on the feet and broke them in pieces, and then became a mountain, filling the whole earth. Each of the four principal parts of the image is interpreted to represent one of four successive empires. The head of gold represented Nebuchadnezzar's empire. Among the various identifications for the second empire that have been proposed are the Grecian, the Median, and the Medo-Persian. The third has been referred to Medo-Persia, Persia, Alexander, Greece, and Rome. The fourth has been thought to be Nabonidus and Belshazzar, Mohammed, Greece, Syria, the successors of Alexander, and Rome. The stone cut without hands represents the kingdom of God smiting and destroying the anti-theocratic powers of the world. The central truth of this chapter (Daniel 2) is that some day the kingdom of God will supersede all human empires.

Image of God. Two fundamental truths about man taught in Scripture are that he is created by God and that God made him in His own image. The passages in which it is expressly stated that man is made in God's image are Genesis 1:26, 27; 5:1, 3; 9:6; I Corinthians 11:7; Ephesians 4:24; Colossians 3:10 and James 3:9. The Scriptures do not specifically describe the nature of the image; consequently theologians differ in their views regarding it. Among the principal views are the following: God has a bodily form, and this serves as the pattern for the body of man; it consists in simple lordship over the animals; it refers to man's moral nature; it is his personality. Since it is unlikely that it consists in bodily form, for God is a spirit, it can only refer to spiritual qualities, in man's mental and moral attributes as a rational, self-conscious, self-determining creature, capable of obedience to moral law, and intended by God for fellowship with Himself. All this, of course, makes possible dominion over the animal world. The image of God is restored in the redemption of Christ (Eph. 4:24; Col. 3:10).

Image Worship (See Idol

Imlah (ĭm'lȧ, **fulness**), the father of the prophet Micaiah (I Kings 22:8, 9; II Chron. 18:7, 8).

Immanuel (ĭ-măn'ū-ĕl, **God is with us**), a child borne by a maiden whose birth was foretold by Isaiah, and who was to be a sign to Ahaz (Isa. 7:14); at his birth salvation would be near. Many prophecies cluster around this child (Isa. 8:9, 10; 9:6; 7; 11:1; Micah 5: 2, 3; Matt. 1:22, 23).

Isaiah's words have led to much controversy and have been variously interpreted, chiefly because of the indefinite terms of the prediction and the fact that there is no record of their fulfillment in any contemporary event. 1. The traditional Christian interpretation is that the emphasis should be laid upon the virgin birth of Immanuel, as Matthew does when he relates the birth of Jesus (1:22, 23). Difficulties with this view are that the idea of a virgin birth is not unambiguously expressed and such an event could not serve the purpose of a sign to Ahaz, who expected a miracle to be performed in the immediate future. 2. Another explanation is that the event of the birth of the child is intended as a sign to Ahaz and nothing more. At the time of Judah's deliverance from Syria and Ephraim, some young mothers who then give birth to sons will spontaneously name them "Immanuel." Children bearing this name will be a sign to Ahaz of the truth of Isaiah's words concerning deliverance and judgment. 3. A third view, somewhat similar to the preceding one, is that Isaiah has a certain child in mind, the **almah** being his own wife, or one of Ahaz's wives, or perhaps someone else. Before its birth it will have experienced a great deliverance (vs. 14); before he has emerged from infancy, Syria and Ephraim will be no more (vs. 16); and later in his life Judah will be a country fit only for the pastoral life (vs. 15). 4. There are semi-Messianic interpretations, which apply the prophecy to a child of Isaiah's time and also to Jesus Christ. 5. Perhaps the most widely-held view in evangelical circles is that Isaiah has in mind the Messiah. When the prophet learns of the king's cowardice, God for the first time gives to him a revelation of the true King, who would share the poverty and affliction of His people and whose character and work would entitle Him to the great names of Isaiah 9:6. In this interpretation the essential fact is that in the coming of Immanuel men will recognize the truth of the prophet's words. He would be Israel's deliverer and the government would rest upon His shoulder (9:6). II Samuel 7:12 and Micah 5:3 show that the Messianic idea was prevalent in Judah at this time.

Immer (ĭm'ẽr). 1. The ancestral head of the 16th course of priests (I Chron. 24:14; Ezra 2:37; 10:20; Neh. 3:29; 7:40; 11:13). 2. A priest in Jeremiah's time (Jer. 20:1). 3. A place in Babylonia (Ezra 2:59).

Immortality (ĭm-ŏr-tăl'ĭ-tē). The Biblical concept of immortality is not simply the survival of the soul after bodily death — the bare continued existence of the soul — **but** the self-conscious continuance of the whole person, body and soul together, in a state of blessedness, due to the redemption of Christ and the possession of "eternal life."

The **OT** teaches immortality, **but** not with the clarity of the NT, chiefly because God's revelation in Scripture is progressive and gradually increases in clearness. 1. Unlike animals, man is composed of body and soul, and is made in the image of God. He is constantly reminded that he is constituted for fellowship with God and that he is only a pilgrim on this earth. God has set eternity in his heart (Eccl. 3:11). 2. The dead in the OT descend into **Sheol (Hades,** in the Greek), a word which may be rendered in a number of ways, depending on the context: grave, state of death, underworld, or hell. In **Sheol** they are in a state of conscious existence. 3. Belief in immortality by OT Jews is obvious from the practice of necromancy, or consulting the dead, against which there are frequent warnings in the OT (Lev. 19:31; 20:27; Deut. 18:11; Isa. 8:19; 29:4). 4. Jesus points out to the Sadducees that the doctrine of the resurrection of the dead is implicity taught in the statement in Exodus 3:6, "I am the God of . . . Abraham, the God of Isaac, and the God of Jacob." It is explicitly taught in such passages as Job 19:23-27; Psalms 16:9-11; 17:15; 49:15; 73:24; Isaiah 26:19; Daniel 12:2; Hosea 13:14. 5. Some OT passages speak confidently of enjoying communion with God after death (Job 19:25-27; Pss. 16:9-11; 17:15; 73:23, 24, 26).

The doctrine of immortality is found everywhere in the NT. 1. A future state for both righteous and wicked is clearly taught (Matt. 10:28; Luke 23:43; John 11:25f; 14:3; II Cor. 5:1; Matt. 11:21-24; 12:41; Rom. 2:5-11; II Cor. 5:10). 2. The bodily resurrection of believers is taught in Luke 20:35, 36; John 5:25-29; I Cor. 15; I Thess. 4:16; Phil. 3:21; and of unbelievers, in John 5:29; Acts 24:15; Rev. 20:12-15. 3. The condition of believers in their state of immortality is not a bare endless existence, but a communion with God in eternal satisfaction and blessedness.

Immutability (í-mū-tȧ-bĭl'ĭ-tē, **unchangeableness),** the perfection of God by which He is devoid of all change in essence, attributes, consciousness, will, and promises. No change is possible in God, because all change must be to better or worse, and God is absolute perfection. No cause for change in God exists, either in Himself or outside of Him. The immutability of God is clearly taught in such passages of Scripture (Mal. 3:6; James 1:17; Pss. 33:11; 102:26).

Imna (ĭm'nȧ, **He — God — keeps off,** i.e., **defends),** the ancestral head of a family of Asher (I Chron. 7:35).

Imnah (ĭm'nȧ, **right hand,** or, **good fortune).** 1. Son of Asher (Num. 26:44; I Chron. 7:30; Gen. 46:17). 2. A Levite (II Chron. 31:14).

Imprecatory Psalms. A number of OT Psalms, especially Nos. 2, 37, 69, 79, 109, 139, and 143, contain expressions of an apparent vengeful attitude towards enemies which, for some people, constitute one of the "moral difficulties" of the OT. It is thought that the spirit of the imprecatory Psalms is morally not justifiable by the standard of the ethics of the NT. Such passages may cause less difficulty when it is observed that they are not dictated merely by private vindictiveness, but spring ultimately from zeal for God's cause, with which the psalmist identifies himself, and they show a willingness to leave vengeance in the hands of God. They show a spirit of righteous indignation, and spring from an aroused sense of justice.

Imputation (See Impute)

Impute (ĭm-pūt), to attribute something to a person, or reckon something to the account of another. Aspects of the doctrine found in the NT: the imputation of Adam's sin to his posterity; the imputation of the sin of man to Christ; the imputation of Christ's righteousness to the believer (Gen. 2:3; I Pet. 2:24; Rom. 3:24; 5:15; Gal. 5:4; Titus 3:7).

Imrah (ĭm'rȧ, **He [God] resists),** a descendant of Asher (I Chron. 7:36).

Imri (ĭm'rī, contraction of **Amariah).** 1. A man of Judah (I Chron. 9:4). 2. The father of Zaccur, who helped in the rebuilding of the wall of Jerusalem (Neh. 3:2).

Incarnation. The doctrine of the incarnation is taught or assumed throughout the Bible, and comes to explicit statement in such passages as John 1:14, "The word became flesh and dwelt among us" (cf. I Tim. 3:16; Rom. 8:3). The doctrine of the incarnation teaches that the eternal Son of God (see Trinity) became human, and that He did so without in any manner or degree diminishing His divine nature.

The virgin birth is necessary for our understanding of the incarnation. In the process of ordinary birth, a new personality begins. Jesus Christ did not begin to be when He was born. He is the eternal Son. The virgin birth was a miracle, wrought by the Holy Spirit, whereby the eternal Son of God "became flesh," i.e. took to Himself a genuine human nature, in addition to His eternal divine nature. It was a **virgin** birth, a miracle. The Holy Spirit has never been thought of as the father of Jesus. Jesus was not half man and half god like the Greek mythological heroes. He was fully God, the Second Person of the Trinity. "In Him dwells all the fullness of the Godhead in bodily form" (Col. 2:9). At the same time He became genuinely a man. To deny His genuine humanity is "the spirit of the Antichrist" (I John 4: 2, 3).

The Biblical data on the incarnation came to permanent doctrinal formulation at the council of Chalcedon, A.D. 451. That council declared that Christ was "born of the virgin Mary" and is "to be acknowledged in two natures, inconfusedly, unchangeably, indivisibly, inseparably . . . the property of each nature being preserved, and concurring in one Person . . ." This doctrine is concisely stated in the Westminster Shorter Catechism, Q. 21. "The only Redeemer of God's elect is the Lord Jesus Christ, who, being the eternal Son of God, became man, and so was, and continueth to be, God and man, in two distinct natures and one Person for ever."

But we need an **understanding of the words** of our doctrine, not just a formula to repeat. First, the emphasis upon the unity of His personality means that He was, in Himself, in His **ego,** His nonmaterial self, the same numerical identity, the same person. The person who was God and with God "in the beginning" before the created universe, is the same person who sat wearily at the well of Sychar, the same person who said, "Father, forgive them," on the cross. Secondly, the distinction of His natures means, and has always meant to the Church, that Jesus is just as truly God as the Father and the Spirit are God, and at the same time, without confusion or contradiction, He is just as truly man as we are men. (His humanity as the "last Adam" is perfectly sinless, yet genuinely human as was Adam before the fall.)

Since man is made in the image of God (see Jesus' argument in John 10: 34-38 as discussed in the article on Trinity) it follows that for God the Son, without diminution of His divine attributes, to assume a genuine human complex of attributes, including a normal human body, involves no contradiction.

Incense (ĭn′sĕns), an aromatic substance made of gums and spices to be burned, especially in religious worship. It was compounded according to a definite prescription of stacte, onycha, galbanum, and pure frankincense in equal proportions, and was tempered with salt (Exod. 30:23f). It could not be made for ordinary purposes (Exod. 30:34-38; Lev. 10:1-7). Incense not properly compounded was rejected as "strange increase" (Exod. 30:9). The offering of incense was common in the religious ceremonies of nearly all ancient nations (Egyptians, Babylonians, Assyrians, Phoenicians, etc), and was extensively used in the ritual of Israel.

A small incense altar from Megiddo, about 1000 B.C. OIUC

Incense was symbolical of the ascending prayer of the officiating high priest. The psalmist prayed, "Let my prayer be set forth before thee as incense" (Ps. 141:2). In Revelation 8:3-5 an angel burns incense on the golden altar, and smoke ascends with the prayer of saints.

India (ĭn′dĭ-ȧ). The name occurs in the Bible only in Esther 1:1; 8:9, of the country which marked the eastern limit of the territory of Ahasuerus. The Hebrew word comes from the name of the Indus, **Hondu,** and refers not to the peninsula of Hindostan, but to the country adjoining the Indus, i.e. the Punjab, and perhaps also Scinde. Some have thought that this country is the Havilah of Genesis 2:11 and that the Indus is the Pishon.

Inflammation (See Diseases)

Inheritance (ĭn-hĕr′ĭ-tăns). The English word, in the OT, is a common term for something inherited, an estate, a portion. A fundamental principle of Hebrew society was that real, as distinguished from personal, property belonged to the family rather than to the individual. This came from the idea that the land was given by God to His children, the people of Israel, and must remain in the family. The Mosaic Law directed that only the sons of a legal wife had the right of inheritance. The first-born son possessed the birthright, i.e., the right to a double portion of the father's possession; and to him belonged the duty of maintaining the females of the family (Deut. 21:15-17). The other sons received equal shares. If there were no sons, the property went to the daughters (Num. 27:8), on the condition that they did not marry out of their own tribe (Num. 36:6ff). If the widow was left without children, the nearest of kin on her husband's side had the right of marrying her; and if he refused, the next of kin (Ruth 3:12, 13). If no one married her, the inheritance remained with her until her death, and then reverted to the next of kin (Num. 27:9-11).

"Inheritance" is not used in Scripture only to refer to inherited property. It is also used with a definitely theological significance. In the OT, at first it refers to the inheritance promised by God to Abraham and his descendants — the land of Canaan, "thy land, which thou hast given to thy people for an inheritance" (I Kings 8:36; cf. Num. 34:2; Deut. 4:21, 38; 12:9f; 15:4; Pss. 105:9-11; 47:4).

The idea finds a further expansion and spiritualization along two other directions. Israelites came to learn that Jehovah Himself was the inheritance of His people (Jer. 10:16) and of the individual believer (Pss. 16:5f; 73:26; 142:5), and that His inheritance is His elect, brought "out of Egypt to be unto him a people of inheritance" (Deut. 4:20). "For the Lord's portion is his people; Jacob is the lot of his inheritance" (Deut. 32:9). This conception was later broadened until Jehovah's inheritance is seen to include the Gentiles also (Isa. 19:25; 47:6; 63:17; Ps. 2:8).

The conception of inheritance is very prominent in the NT too, but now it is connected with the person and work of Christ, who is the heir by virtue of His being the Son (Mark 12:7; Heb. 1:2). Through Christ's redemptive work believers are sons of God by adoption and fellow-heirs with Christ (Rom. 8:17; Gal. 4:7). As a guarantee of this "eternal inheritance" (Heb. 9:15), Christ has given to them the Holy Spirit (Eph. 1:14). The Epistle to the Hebrews shows that as Israel in the Old Covenant received her inheritance from God, so in the New Covenant the New Israel receives an inheritance, only a better one. This inheritance, moreover, is not for Jews alone, but includes all true believers, including Gentiles (Eph. 3:6). The inheritance is the kingdom of God with all its blessings (Matt. 25:34; I Cor. 6:9; Gal. 5:21), both present and eschatological (Rom. 8:17-23; I Cor. 15:50; Heb. 11:13; I Pet. 1:3, 4). It is wholly the gift of God's sovereign grace.

Ink, any liquid used with pen or brush to form written characters. Mentioned once in the OT (Jer. 36:18), where Baruch says he wrote Jeremiah's prophecies "with ink." Hebrew ink was probably a lamp-black and gum, as is suggested by the "blotting out" of Exodus 32:33 and Numbers 5:23; but it is possible that in the course of Jewish history various inks were used. The word occurs three times in the NT (II Cor. 3:3; II John 12; III John 13).

Inn. The Heb. word **mălôn** means a "night resting-place," and can apply to any place where there is encampment for the night, whether by caravans, individuals, or even armies. The presence of a building is not implied.

An inn with lodging for travelers (above) and stables for animals (below). DV

It was originally probably only a piece of level ground near a spring where carriers of merchandise could, with their animals, pass the night. Inns in the modern sense were not very necessary in primitive times, since travelers found hospitality the rule (Exod. 2:20; Judg. 19:15-21; II Kings 4:8; Acts 28:7; Heb. 13:2). We do not know when buildings were first used, but they would be needed early in the history of trade as a protection from inclement weather and in dangerous times and places. The "lodging place of wayfaring men" of Jeremiah 9:2 may have been such an establishment. An Oriental inn bore little resemblance to a hotel today. It was a mere shelter for man and beast.

Innkeepers in ancient times had a very bad reputation, and this, together with the Semitic spirit of hospitality, led Jews and Christians to recommend hospitality for the entertainment of strangers. The "upper room" where the Last Supper was held (Mark 14: 14), and of the place in Bethlehem that turned away Joseph and Mary (Luke 2:7), was probably a room in a private house rather than in a public inn. The vast numbers who went to Jerusalem to attend the annual feasts were allowed to use such guest-chambers; and for this no payment was taken.

Innocents, Slaughter of, the murder, by Herod the Great, of all the male children in Bethlehem two years old and under, when the wise men failed to return and tell him where they found the infant Jesus (Matt. 2:16-18).

I.N.R.I., the initials of the Latin superscription which Pilate had placed above the cross of Jesus in three languages (Greek, Hebrew, Latin). The Latin reads: Iesus Nazarenus, Rex Iudaeorum, **Jesus of Nazareth, King of the Jews** (Matt. 27:37; Mark 15:26; Luke 23:38; John 19:19).

Insects of the Bible. Through the centuries, insects have been an important factor in the life and well-being of man. Over 600,000 described species of insects are known and there are many hundred thousand more undescribed species. The frequent mention of insects in Bible references indicates their prevalence throughout Bible lands and times. This article discusses the various insects with the references, identification wherever possible, influence upon human welfare, and brief pertinent life history details.

I. Grasshoppers, Locusts, and Crickets. The grasshopper is the most frequently mentioned insect of Scripture with many Hebrew words used. Edible locusts are listed in Leviticus 11:21, 22 as the locust **chargol,** bald locust **sal'am** or edible winged leaper or consumer, the grasshopper, and the beetle which is a misnomer for cricket. In the East locusts are still eaten by the poor. "The heads, legs and wings being removed, they are boiled, stewed or roasted and sometimes dressed in butter. They are eaten both fresh, and dried, or salted" (John A. Broadus, **Commentary on the Gospel of Matthew,** American Baptist Publication Society, 1886, p. 37). The insects John the Baptist ate were locusts (Mark 1:6).

The bristling locust, **yeleq,** is designated the palmerworm in Joel 1:4, and is also listed in Joel 2:25; Nahum 3:15, 16; Psalm 105:34; Jeremiah 51: 14, 27 and other references. The name, grasshopper, **chāgāb,** the "coverer" is listed in Leviticus 11:22; Numbers 13: 33; Ecclesiastes 12:5 and Isaiah 40: 22. The term, locust, **'arbeh,** is the edible winged leaper mentioned in Exodus 10:4, 12, 13, 14; Leviticus 11:22; II Chronicles 6:28, and many other references. The Hebrew words, **ts'lātsāl,** of Deuteronomy 28:42, and **gāzām** of Joel 1:4; 2:25; and Amos 4:9 also refer to locust. **Gāzām** in the latter reference is more properly translated "cutting locust" RSV rather than "palmerworm," KJV.

Most species of locusts are non-migratory, but some which are small in size and countless in number "migrate in vast swarms, short or long distances, settling in grainfields, orchards, and other cultivated areas and often devastating everything before them" (E. O. Essig, **Insects of Western North America,** Macmillan, New York, 1926, p. 72). They are omnivorous feeders on all kinds of vegetable matter and become cannibalistic and carnivorous when natural food is lacking.

Jerome in his commentary on Joel describes his own observation of locusts. "Even in our time we have seen troops of locusts cover the land of Judah. Then, when the shores of both seas were filled with heaps of dead locusts, which the waters had cast forth, their decay and stench became harmful to the extent of infecting the air and engendering disease for both animals and men" (Jerome: **Commentary on Joel,** II, col. 25, col. 970).

II. Scale insects. The scarlet color often mentioned in Scripture was made from the dried bodies of scale insects belonging to the order **Homoptera.** This order includes the cicadas, leafhoppers, aphids, scale bugs, tree-hoppers, white flies, and others. The scale insects are indirectly mentioned in the Bible. The two Hebrew words, **argvan** and **hokkinos** are translated "scarlet." **Argvan** occurs in Genesis 38:28, 30; Exodus 25:4f; Leviticus 14:4, 6, 51, 52; Joshua 2:18, 21. **Hokkinos** occurs in II Samuel 1:24; Proverbs 31:21; Song of Solomon 4:3. New Testament references also of interest include Matthew 27:28; Hebrews 9:19 and Revelation 17:3, 4.

The scale insect of Scripture is **Coccus ilicis,** the host of which is the oak **Quercus coccifera,** common in Syria. It is called **kirmi** (Sanskrit), **kermes** (Arabic), and **karmil** (Hebrew) hence **carmin.** Many of the worst horticultural pests are of this family. The female is wingless and remains attached to the leaf. The young are deposited in a waxy material. The female dies and the body dries into a concave shell under which the young develop. These dried bodies when made into a powder produce the red dye.

The Cochineal Coccids have been cultivated in India, Spain and elsewhere for the purpose of gathering the females which are dried and ground into powder for dye. Aniline dyes now largely replace the insect dyes.

The lac-insect, **Tachardia lacca,** excretes a resinous substance useful as a source of shell-lac or shellac. The bodies are then used for lac-dye.

III. Moths and Butterflies. The order **Lepidoptera** includes two groups of insects, moths and butterflies. Moths commonly called "millers" are nocturnal, with wings wrapped around the body or spread horizontally and usually thread-like antennae. Butterflies are daytime insects most of which fold wings vertically, and have clubbed antennae.

The moth of Scripture is usually the familiar clothes moth of the large family, **Tineidae.** The moth ash is mentioned in Job 4:19; 13:28; 27:18; Psalm 39:11; Isaiah 50:9; 51:8; Hosea 5:12 and Matthew 6:19. From ancient times, the clothes moth has been a most destructive pest of valued fabrics and the symbol of the perishable.

Above, a fig tree at Jerusalem in full leaf, before invasion of locust. Below, the same tree fifteen minutes later completely denuded of every leaf by a locusts' swarm. © *MPS*

Scripture also mentions sik garments (Prov. 31:22; Ezek. 16:10, 13; Rev. 18:12). Silk is reeled from the cocoons of the silk worm pupae. Essig states that the Chinese or mulberry silkworm, **Bombyx mori Linn.,** is by far the most important commercial member of the insect world. The silkworm is native to Asia and has been domesticated so long as to require human care. It is the basis of large industries in Asiatic and European countries.

The worm of Jonah 4:7 may have been a Lepidopterous larva. Such larvae are often voracious feeders, becoming very large before pupating and emerging as adults. Most of the references to worms in the Bible refer to the larvae of flies familiarly known as maggots.

IV. Flies. All insects properly termed flies are included in the order **Diptera.** Comstock states that true flies are distinguished by a single pair of wings and a pair of halteres, thread-like clubbed appendages which are the second pair of wings and bear sense organs. This large order has 8,000 described species in North America distributed in over one thousand genera.

All types of crops are attacked by flies. Many species attack humans with most serious results. Malaria, yellow fever and filariasis are transmitted by flies.

Flies figured prominently in the plagues of Egypt. The third judgment of Exodus 8:16-19 termed "lice" **(kinnim)** was probably a sandfly capable of inflicting a painful sting, though identification is not certain. The fourth judgment of Exodus 8:20-32 termed "flies" is considered by many to be the mosquito from the Hebrew **arob,** meaning to suck.

Another fly not mentioned in the Bible but probably the cause of losses to olive crops is the olive fly. Frequent references are made to such losses (Deut. 28:40; Amos 4:9; Mic. 6:16; Hab. 3:17). The olive fly is a very serious pest to ripe olives in the Mediterranean region and also occurs in Northwest India on wild olives. The adult fly deposits eggs beneath the skin of ripening olives. A maggot hatches from the egg destroying the fruit.

In Acts 12:23 Herod is described as dying the horrible death of being eaten of worms. The screwworm is capable of such ravages. The adult female fly lays eggs on decaying animal matter and also in wounds, sores, nostrils and ears of men and cattle causing serious diseases.

Several Bible verses speak of worms on dead bodies (Job 7:5; 17:14; 21:26; Isa. 14:11; 66:24). Mark 9:43-48 probably conveys the same repulsive phenomenon. The flesh-flies of the family **Sarcophagidae** lay eggs in the bodies of dead animals which hatch into maggots. They serve the beneficial purpose of assisting in the decomposition of dead bodies.

V. Fleas. Two Bible verses speak of the flea (I Sam. 24:14; 26:20). The flea **(par'osh),** belongs to the order **Siphonaptera.** The description given by Comstock is that of a small, wingless insect with body greatly laterally compressed. In I Samuel 24:14, David's reference to the flea is to indicate insignificance. The second reference seems to indicate the agility of the insect and difficulty of catching it. The flea illustrates this faculty with its body surface hard and smooth and its legs highly developed for jumping.

There are over 500 species of fleas and their distribution is very wide. They are abundant and offensive in the Orient and common in Palestine and Arabia. The bite is very irritating.

Bubonic plague of history is a flea-borne disease. It is spread by rats infected through fleas. In the 14th century, 25,000,000 deaths were caused by this disease. The simultaneous death of rats led to a study which proved the disease to be primarily a rodent disease conveyed to man by fleas. In 1665 the plague accounted for 68,596 deaths in London.

Eggs of fleas are scattered on floors of dwellings and sleeping-places of infested animals. Larvae are slender, worm-like creatures which feed on decaying particles of animal and vegetable matter. Fleas are parasitic only in the adult stage.

VI. Ants and bees. Ants. Two Bible verses speak of the ant (Prov. 6:6; 30:25). The industry and foresight of the ant are here eulogized. Studies of their habits reveal these characteristics dramatically true. Some ants raid other ant nests, carrying away captives for slaves. Over 100 kinds of ants raise fungi for food. In large numbers they climb trees cutting leaves which they drop to the ground for the "ground crew" to gather and drag to the colony for fungi-growing medium. Ants tending root-feeding aphids carry them to protective galleries, convey them to food sources, collect and store their eggs for winter, and in the spring take them to their food. Some ants tend aphids for the honeydew secreted. The honey-ants **Myrmecocystus,** are so called from the characteristic of individual workers serving as reservoirs for storing honey-dew gathered by other ants of the colony. These are called "repletes." They swallow sufficient honey-dew gathered by the others to distend their abdomens to a pea-sized sphere. Now incapable of locomotion, they remain quiet in the colony disgorging their honey-dew supply for nourishment to the others in time of need.

Typical ants belong to the subfamily **Formicinae,** including the carpenter ant, mound-building ant, blood-red slave-maker, harvesting ants, and many others. Most harvesting ants are found in arid regions of scant food supply and are therefore compelled to feed on seeds. Solomon's ants mentioned in Proverbs 6:6 and 30:25 are harvester ants. Species of harvester ants include the small harvester ant, acrobat ant, black harvester ant, agricultural ant, and the mound-building prairie ant. The prairie ant lives in large colonies surrounded by a cleared area 6 to 15 feet in diameter with mounds 4 to 12 inches high and 2 to 3 feet in diameter. Tunnels in the soil below the surface reach a depth of 9 feet.

Ants are all social insects. There are three castes: males, female or queen, and workers. Comstock states that the most important work on the subject is that of Professor W. M. Wheeler, **Ants, Their Structure, Development and Behavior,** 1910.

Bees. Hornets and yellow jackets belong to the family **Vespidae.** In Exodus 23:28; Deuteronomy 7:20 and Joshua 24:12 the hornet is mentioned as the means used by God to drive out the enemies of Israel. Hornets are medium-sized insects, mostly yellow and black in color, and build large and small paper nests mostly above ground, but also below. They feed on flies and are beneficial insects. They possess a severe sting, a pugnacious spirit, and fast flight thus making them a formidable opponent from which to flee.

Several references in Scripture speak of bees (Deut. 1:44; Ps. 118:12; Isa. 7:18). Enemies are likened unto bees in their pursuing tactics and large numbers. Bees are very common in Palestine where the warm climate and abundance of flowers favor their increase.

The mention of a swarm of bees and honey in Judges 14:8 may refer to the honey-bee of commerce today. There is no evidence that the Hebrews cultivated honey-bees. The honey-bee is a highly social insect living in colonies varying from 20,000 to 50,000 individuals. The phrase "bee hive of activity" is a graphic picture, for the hive is the residence of these many thousands of individuals each with responsible activity. Within the hive is found the nursery for rearing larvae, the place of wax production for food storage, the processing of nectar for honey, the preparation of pollen for food and plant waxes for plastering. A continuing stream of bees depart and return throughout sunny daylight hours in ceaseless work for the hive. Food gathered in the hive includes honey which is made from nectar brought from flowers and elaborated in the honey sac of the workers and stored in the wax cells of the comb. Bee bread is also a food material for larvae consisting of pollen gathered from flowers and mixed with honey. Royal jelly is a highly nutritious material secreted mostly by young adult workers and fed to all very young larvae. It is the entire food of larvae destined to become queens, for the production of queens is a voluntary activity of the workers controlled by the use of this food material exclusively.

Periodically the old queen and a large number of workers and drones leave the hive in a swarm to establish a new hive leaving ample "personnel" to maintain the old hive. (The location of the new hive varies widely.)

Inspiration, the special influence of the Holy Spirit guiding certain persons to speak and write what God wanted communicated to others, without suspending their individual activity or personality (I Cor. 2:13; II Tim. 3:16; I Peter 1:10, 11; II Peter 1:19-21).

Because of the character of the God of truth who "inspired" (or produced) the Holy Scriptures, the result of "inspiration" is to constitute it as fully trustworthy and authoritative. Indeed, this absolute divine authority of Scripture, rather than its inspiration, is the great burden of Scriptural teaching about its own nature (see Pss. 19:7-14; and 119:89, 97, 113, 160; Zech. 7:12; Matt. 5:17-19; Luke 16:17; John 10: 34 and 35; I Thess. 2:13). Besides those passages directly teaching the authority of Scripture, such phrases as "It is written" (Luke 4:4, 8, 10; Matt. 21: 13). "It (or He) says" (Rom. 9:15; Gal. 3:16), and "Scripture says" (Gal. 3:8; Rom. 9:17) — all clearly imply an absolute authority for the Scriptures.

These passages teaching the authority of Scripture indicate also the extent of inspiration. If the authority and trustworthiness of Scripture are complete, inspiration itself must also extend to all of Scripture. This completeness of inspiration and consequent authority of all Scripture is made explicit in such passages as Luke 24:25: "O fools, and slow of heart to believe all that the prophets have spoken" (see also Matt. 5:17-19; Luke 16:17; and John 10:34 and 35).

The inerrant and infallible inspiration of Scripture, though not exactly synonymous terms, are nevertheless both correctly applied to Scripture in order to indicate that inspiration and authority are complete. The word **inerrant** suggests that the Scriptures do not wander from the truth. **Infallible** is stronger, suggesting an incapability of wandering from the truth ("Do ye not therefore err, because ye know not the Scriptures?" (Mark 12:24).

Biblical inspiration must be complemented by an interior illumination of the Holy Spirit (I Cor. 2:14ff) in order to make that which God has given in the past really become His living, revealing Word today in the heart and mind of the believer. It is in this sense that the word **inspiration** is used in the Authorized translation of Job 32:8. In traditional theological terminology this latter work is generally referred to as the **illumination** of the Holy Spirit.

In summary, Biblical inspiration (as distinguished from illumination) may be defined as the work of the Holy Spirit by which, through the instrumentality of the personality and literary talents of its human authors, He constituted the words of the Bible in all of its several parts as His written word to men and therefore of divine authority and without error in the autographs.

Interest. The law of Moses forbade lending at interest to a fellow Israelite (Exod. 22:25), but permitted charging interest to a foreigner (Deut. 23:20). A needy Israelite might sell himself as a servant (Lev. 25:39; II Kings 4:1). The prophets condemn the taking of interest as a heinous sin (Ezek. 18:8, 13, 17; Jer. 15:10). In the NT, references to interest occur in two parables — of the Pounds (Luke 19:23) and of the Talents (Matt. 25:27), and it is distinctly encouraged.

Intermediate State. The life of man is represented in Scripture as falling into three stages: first, the period from birth until death, which is life in the present world and in the natural body; second, life in the intermediate state, between death and the resurrection, which is life without the body; and, third, life in the resurrection body, which is the final and eternal state.

The Bible does not have a great deal to say regarding the intermediate state.

For the righteous the intermediate state is a time of rest and blessedness, holiness and happiness. The NT sometimes represents the state of death as a "sleeping" and the act of dying as a "falling asleep" (Matt. 9:24; John 9:4; 11:11; I Thess. 4:13, 15; II Pet. 3:4), but this does not mean that the soul is unconscious until the resurrection, but that the dead person is like one asleep in not being alive to his surroundings. The story of the rich man and Lazarus represents the latter as conscious and blessed in Abraham's bosom (Luke 16:19-31). On the cross Jesus said to the penitent thief, "Today shalt thou be with me in Paradise" (Luke 23:43). John says, "Blessed are the dead which die in the Lord from henceforth: yea, saith the Spirit, that they may rest from their labors; and their works follow them" (Rev. 14:13). Paul says to the Corinthians that he is "willing rather to be absent from the body, and to be at home with the Lord" (II Cor. 5:8); and to the Philippians he writes that he has a "desire to depart and to be with Christ" (Phil. 1:23). But while the intermediate state is for believers a time of freedom from sin and pain, it is nevertheless also one of imperfection, or incompleteness. This is because the soul is without a body, which for man is an abnormal condition, and because Christ's rewards to His people for the labors of this life will not be given until His second coming. The blessings of the intermediate state are, as it were, only an earnest of the good things to come.

That the intermediate state involves conscious suffering for the unregenerate, is shown by the story of the rich man and Lazarus, in which the rich man finds himself in torment immediately upon dying, with his brothers still on earth (Luke 16:19-31).

Iphedeiah (ĭf-ē-dē'yȧ, **Jehovah redeems),** a descendant of Benjamin (I Chron. 8: 25).

Ir (ĭr, **watcher),** a Benjamite (I Chron. 7:7, 12).

Ira (ī'rȧ). 1. A chief minister of David (II Sam. 20:26). 2. One of David's mighty men (II Sam. 23:26; I Chron. 11:28). 3. One of David's heroes (II Sam. 23:38; I Chron. 11:40).

Irad (ī'răd), son of Enoch (Gen. 4:18).

Iram (ī'răm), a chief of Edom (Gen. 36:43; I Chron. 1:54).

Ir-ha-heres (ĭr-hă-hĕ'rĕz), a city of Egypt mentioned only in Isa. 19:18 as "the city of destruction."

Iri (ī'rī), a Benjamite (I Chron. 7:7, 12).

Irijah (ī-rī'jȧ, **Jehovah sees),** a captain who arrested Jeremiah (Jer. 37:13).

Ir-Nahash (ĭr-nā'hăsh), a town of Judah founded by Tehinnah (I Chron. 4:12).

Iron. Tubal-cain, of the race of Cain, is described as "an instructor of every artificer in brass and iron" (Gen. 4:22). Modern archaeology shows that there was a knowledge of iron as early as the third millennium B.C. Remains of an iron blade dating c. 2700 B.C. have been found by the Oriental Institute at the University of Chicago at a site about 50 miles NE of Baghdad. Lack of iron for farming implements, nails, and weapons for war kept the Israelites comparatively poor through the period of the judges. They could not drive the Canaanites out of the plains because the latter had chariots and weapons of iron (Josh. 17:18; Judg. 1:19; 4:2, 3). Even in the time of Saul, his army had no swords or spears for battle, he and Jonathan alone possessing them (I Sam. 13:22). When the power of the Philistines was broken by Saul and David, the iron-smelting formula became public property, and the metal came to be widely used in Israel.

Iron was used in Bible times much as it is used today. Out of iron, blacksmiths in the Mosaic period made axes and other implements (Num. 35: 16). In the time of Joshua and of the judges vessels were made of metal (Josh. 6:19, 24). Later, of iron were made threshing instruments (Amos 1: 3), harrows (II Sam. 12:31), axes (II Sam. 12:31; II Kings 6:6), other tools (I Kings 6:7), weapons (Num. 35:16; Job 20:24), armor (II Sam. 23:7), horns (I Kings 22:11), fetters (Ps. 105: 18), chariots (Josh. 17:16), yokes (Jer. 28:14), chisels (Job 19:24; Jer. 17:1), sheets or plates (Ezek. 4:3), gods (Dan. 5:4), weights (I Sam. 17:7). Iron was among the materials gathered by David for the building of the temple (I Chron. 22:14, 16; 29:2, 7). There are allusions to iron gates (Acts 12:10), prison bars (Ps. 107:10, 16; Isa. 10:34), nails or bolts (I Chron. 22:3). We read that when David captured the city of Rabbah, he set the inhabitants to laboring with saws, iron picks, and iron axes (II Sam. 12:31). There is a description of a smith at work in Ecclesiasticus 38:28.

The word **iron** is often used figuratively in Scripture. It is made to represent barrenness (Deut. 23:23), slavery ("yoke of iron," Deut. 28:48), captivity (Ps. 107:10), moral deterioration (Jer. 6:28), political strength (Dan. 2:33), fortitude ("iron pillar," Jer. 1: 18), strength "bars of iron," Job 40: 18), severity ("rod of iron," Ps. 2:9), destructive power ("iron teeth," Dan. 7:7), and affliction ("iron furnace," Deut. 4:20; Ezek. 22: 18-22). See Minerals and Metals.

Iron (ī'rŏn), a fortified city in the territory of Naphtali (Josh 19:38).

Irpeel (ĭr'pī-ĕl, **God heals),** a city of Benjamin (Josh. 18:27).

Irrigation (ĭr-ĭ-gā'shŭn), a word for which there is no Hebrew or Greek equivalent in the Bible, although the use of irrigation for watering plants and trees is frequently implied (Eccl. 2:5, 6; Isa. 58:11) in Palestine and Egypt.

Ir-Shemesh (ĭr-shē'mĕsh, **city of the sun),** a city of Dan (Josh. 19:41).

Iru (ī'roo), son of Caleb (I Chron. 4:15).

Isaac (ī'zȧk, **one laughs),** the only son of Abraham by Sarah, and the second of three Hebrew patriarchs who were the progenitors of the Jewish race. He was born in the south country, probably Beer-sheba (Gen. 21:14, 31), when Abraham was 100 and Sarah 90 years

The site of ancient Gerar, the birthplace of Isaac. © *MPS*

old (Gen. 17:17; 21:5). He was named Isaac because both Abraham and Sarah had laughed incredulously at the thought of having a child at their age (Gen. 17:17-19; 18:9-15; 21:6). His birth must be regarded as a miracle. It was 25 years after God had promised the childless Abraham and Sarah a son, that the promise was fulfilled. He is thus rightly called the child of promise, in contrast with Ishmael, who was born of Hagar, Sarah's maid, and Abraham. When he was eight days old, he was circumcised (Gen. 21:4).

God commanded Abraham to offer Isaac as a sacrifice on a mountain in the land of Moriah (Gen. 22). His exact age then is not stated, but he is described as a "lad," able to carry up the mountainside the wood for the burnt-offering. Bound upon the altar and about to be slain, he was spared when an angel of the Lord interposed and substituted for him a ram, which was offered up in his stead.

Sarah died at Hebron when Isaac was 36 years old (Gen. 23:1). At the age of 40 he married Rebekah, a kinswoman from Mesopotamia (Gen. 24), but he and his wife were childless until, in answer to prayer, twin sons, Esau and Jacob, were born to them when he was 60 (Gen. 25:20, 26).

The last prominent event in the life of Isaac is the blessing of his sons (Gen. 27). Esau, the elder, was his father's favorite, even though God had told him that the elder would serve the younger, while Rebekah's favorite was Jacob (Gen. 25:28). When he was over 100 years old, and dim of sight, and perhaps thinking that his end was near, he desired to bestow his last blessing upon his elder son; but through Rebekah's cunning and guile, Jacob the younger supplanted his brother, and the blessing of the birthright was bestowed upon him. To save Jacob from the murderous wrath of Esau, who determined to kill him after his father's death, Rebekah induced Isaac to send Jacob into Mesopotamia, that, after his own example, his son might take a wife from among his own kindred, and not imitate Esau by marriage with Canaanite women. Isaac invoked another blessing upon the head of Jacob and sent him away to Laban in Padan-aram (Gen. 27-28:5).

Isaac is mentioned only once more, when 20 years later, Jacob returned from his sojourn in Mesopotamia, having, agreeable to his father's command, married into Laban's family. Jacob found the old man at Mamre in Hebron, and there Isaac died, 180 years old, and his two sons, Esau and Jacob, buried him (Gen. 35:27-29).

The NT refers to Isaac almost a score of times. His sacrifice by Abraham is twice mentioned, in Hebrews 11:17, 18 and James 2:21, but while the submission of Isaac is referred to, the stress is upon the triumph of Abraham's faith.

Of the three patriarchs, Isaac was the least conspicuous, traveled the least, had the fewest extraordinary adventures, and lived the longest. He was free from violent passions; quiet, gentle, dutiful; less a man of action than of thought and suffering. His name is always joined in equal honor with Abraham and Jacob.

Isaiah. Little is known about the Prophet Isaiah except what his own words reveal. His name Isaiah **(Salvation of Jehovah)** is almost identical in meaning with Joshua **(Jehovah is salvation)** which appears in the NT as Jesus, the name of the Messiah whom Isaiah heralded. That his name played a formative role in his life is not improbable since it expresses the great theme of his prophetic ministry.

Isaiah prophesied in four reigns, from Uzziah to Hezekiah (1:1). The first date given is the year of Uzziah's death (6:1), which probably occurred about 740 B.C. or several years later. The last historical event referred to is the death of Sennacherib (37:38) which occurred in 681 B.C. The most important events are the Syro-Ephraimitic war in the days of Ahaz (7:1-9), which Isaiah treated, despite its devastation (II Chron. 28:5-15), as almost insignificant compared with the far greater scourge. Assyria, which was so soon to follow (vss. 17-25). Assyria is the great enemy with which much of chapters 7-39 deals; and beyond it looms an even mightier foe, Babylon, whose downfall is foretold in chapters 13-14 and is the great theme of 40-48. Over against these terrible instruments of divine judgment Isaiah pictures the Messianic hope, first in counseling unbelieving Ahaz, and repeatedly thereafter.

The complete scroll of Isaiah, from the Dead Sea Scrolls, opened to chapter 40. The entire scroll consists of 17 sheets of parchment, sewn together, and measures 24 feet in length. ASOR

Analysis. The structure of Isaiah is, in its broad outlines, a simple one, but in its details it raises many problems. It may be briefly analyzed as follows:

I. Chapters 1-5, Introductory. Like so many of Isaiah's utterances, it combines dire threatenings with urgent calls to repentance and gracious offers of forgiveness and blessing. It is followed by the promise of world redemption (2:1-5). Then come a series of threatening passages, including a detailed description of the finery of the women of Jerusalem as illustrating the sinful frivolity of the people as a whole. The land is likened to an unfruitful vineyard, which will soon become desolate. It concludes with a series of six woes which end in gloom: "and the light is darkened in the heavens thereof."

II. Chapter 6, The Temple Vision. Whether this represents the initial call of Isaiah has been much debated. The question must remain unsettled. It is a vision of the Holy God; and "Holy One of Israel" becomes one of Isaiah's favorite titles for the Deity in whose name he speaks.

III. Chapters 7-12, the Book of Immanuel. This group of chapters belongs to the period of the Syro-Ephraimitic war (II Kings 16:1-20; II Chron. 28). In the midst of this time of peril, Isaiah utters the great prophecies regarding Immanuel (7:14-16; 9: 6f.; 11:1-10).

IV. Chapters 13-23, Prophecies against the Nations. These are ten "burdens," i.e., weighty, solemn, and grievous utterances (Jer.23:33f.) against nations which were or would be a menace to God's people: Babylon (13-14:27), Philistia (14:28-32), Moab (15-16), Damascus (17-18), Egypt (19-20), Babylon (21:1-10), Dumah (vss. 11-12), Arabia (vss. 13-17), Jerusalem (22), Tyre (23). Here prophecies regarding the near future (16:14; 21:16:cf.22:20 with 37:2) appear along with others which refer to a more distant (23:17) or a quite remote time.

V. Chapter 24 looks far into the future. It is world-embracing and may be called an **apocalypse.** The world judgment will be followed by songs of thanksgiving for divine blessing (24-26). A prophecy against Egypt follows (27). Then there are again six woes (28-34), the last being a frightful curse on Edom. This group also closes with a beautiful prophetic picture of future blessedness (35).

IV. Chapters 36-39, Historical (comp. parallel passages in Kings and Chronicles). They describe the blasphemous threats of Sennacherib against Jerusalem, Hezekiah's appeal to Isaiah who ridicules the invader, the flight and death of the blasphemer (36-37) — one of the most thrilling stories in the whole Bible. Probably Hezeziah's illness and the embassage of Merodach Baladan (38-39) took place during the reign of Sargon. If so, the arrangement is topical and intended to prepare for the prophecies of consolation which follow.

Chapters 40-46 have been called the **Book of Consolation.** The words "Comfort ye, comfort ye my people" are clearly intended to give Israel a comfort and hope not to be gathered from Hezekiah's words, which they immediately follow. These chapters fall into three parts as is suggested by the refrain-like words, "There is no peace, saith the Lord, unto the wicked" (48:22; compare 57:21) which have their terrible echo in Isaiah's final words (66:24).

Isaiah is preeminently the prophet of redemption. The greatness and majesty of God, His holiness and hatred of sin and the folly of idolatry, His grace and mercy and love, and the blessed rewards of obedience are constantly recurring themes. No wonder that the NT writers quote so often from Isaiah and that so much of Handel's **Messiah** is taken from it. Redeemer and saviour (save, salvation) are among his favorite words. It is significant that the words which describe the character of the promised Messiah (9:6) are frequently on his lips: wonderful (25:1; 28:29; 29:14), counsellor (19:17; 25:1; 28:29; 40:13f; 40:10), mighty God (30:29; 33:13; 40: 17f, 26; 42:13; 49:20-26; 60:16), everlasting father (26:4; 40:28; 45:17; 55: 3; 57:15; 60:19f.; 63:16; 64:8), a prince of peace (26:12; 45:7; 52:7; 53:5; 55: 12; 57:19; 66:12). Isaiah has a deep appreciation of beauty and wonder of the world of nature (e.g., chap. 35). A striking figure which he uses repeatedly is the "highway" (11:16; 19:23; 33: 8; 35:8; 36:2; 40:3; 49:11; 57: 14; 62:10). All the barriers which separate nation from nation and delay the coming of the King to His kingdom will be removed and "the glory of the Lord shall be revealed and all flesh shall see it together" (40:5).

The importance of the book is indicated by the frequency with which it is quoted in the NT. Isaiah is quoted by name 21 times, slightly more than all the other writing prophets taken together; and there are many more allusions and quotations where his name is not given. He has been called the evangelist of the OT and many of the most precious verses in the Bible come to us from his lips. The fact that the Lord began His public ministry at Nazareth by reading from Chapter 61 and applying its prophetic words to Himself is significant of the place which this book has ever held in the Christian Church.

Iscah (ĭs'kȧ), a daughter of Haran and sister of Milcah (Gen. 11:29).

Ishbah (ĭsh'bă), a member of the tribe of Judah (I Chron. 4:17).

Ishbak (ĭsh'băk), a name in the list of sons of Abraham by Keturah (Gen. 25:2).

Ishbi-Benob (ĭsh'bī-bē'nŏb), a giant slain by Abishai as he was about to kill David (II Sam. 21:16, 17).

Ish-Bosheth (îsh'bō'shĕth, **man of shame),** the fourth son of Saul (II Sam. 2:8), originally called Eshbaal, "man of Baal," but for some reason subsequently changed. After the death of Saul and his three elder sons at the battle of Gilboa, where the Philistines won an overwhelming victory, he was proclaimed king over Israel by Abner, the captain of Saul's army, at Mahanaim (II Sam. 2:8ff.), while Judah proclaimed David as its king. Ish-bosheth was then about 40 years old, and reigned two years (II Sam. 2:8-10). He was not successful in the war which he waged with David to rule over all 12 tribes, but the war did not come to a close until Abner transferred his allegiance to David because of a serious charge made against him by Ish-bosheth (II Sam. 3:6ff.). Abner fulfilled David's condition to return to him Michal, his wife, before peace could be made. It was not, however, until Abner was murdered at Hebron that Ish-bosheth lost heart and gave up hope of retaining his power (II Sam. 4). Soon after, Ish-bosheth was murdered by his own captains, but David had the assassins put to death for their crime and buried Ish-bosheth in the grave of Abner at Hebron. Ish-bosheth's death ended the dynasty of Saul.

Ishi (ĭsh'ī, **my husband),** a symbolic term, expressive of the ideal relation between Jehovah and Israel (Hos. 2:16).

Ishi (salutary). 1. A man of Judah (I Chron. 2:31). 2. Another man of Judah (I Chron. 4:20). 3. A descendant of Simeon (I Chron. 4:42). 4. The head of a family of Manasseh (I Chron. 5:24).

Ishiah (ī-shī'ȧ, **Jehovah forgets).** 1. A man of Issachar (I Chron. 7:3). 2. Head of a Levite family (I Chron. 24:21). 3. Another Levite (I Chron. 23:20, Jesiah in KJV). 4. One of David's men at Ziklag (I Chron. 12:6).

Ishijah (ī-shī'jȧ), a son of Harim, one of those induced by Ezra to put away their foreign wives (Ezra 10:31).

Ishma (ĭsh'mȧ), the head of a clan of Judah (I Chron. 4:3, 4).

Ishmael (ĭsh'mā-ĕl, **God hears).** 1. The son of Abraham by Hagar, the Egyptian maid of his wife Sarah. Sarah was barren (Gen. 16:1); and in accordance with the custom of the age she gave to Abraham her handmaid Hagar, an Egyptian, as his concubine, hoping that he might obtain a family by her. Abraham was then 86 years old, and had been in Canaan for ten years (Gen. 16:3.) When Hagar saw that she had conceived, she began to despise her mistress, so that Sarah complained bitterly to Abraham, who told her that since Hagar was her slave, she could do anything she wanted with her. Sarah made things so difficult for her that she fled, and somewhere on the road to Egypt the angel of Jehovah met her and told her to return to her mistress and submit herself to her hands, and He encouaged her by the promise of a numerous seed. Ishmael was circumcised when he was 13 (Gen. 17:25). Abraham loved him, and even after God had promised him a son by Sarah, he fervently exclaimed, "O that Ishmael might live before thee!" (Gen. 17:18).

At the weaning of Isaac, the customary feast was made, when Ishmael, now a boy of 16, was seen by Sarah to be mocking. Jealous, and probably fearing future trouble if the boys were brought up together, Sarah tried to get Abraham to cast out Ishmael and his slave-mother, but this he was unwilling to do until he was encouraged to do so by God. Sent away with bread and a bottle of water, Ishmael and his mother wandered about in the wilderness of Beersheba near death. For the second time in her life, the angel of the Lord appeared to her. He directed her to some water and renewed His former promise of Ishmael's future greatness (Gen. 21:19, 20). Ishmael grew up and became famous as an archer in the wilderness of Paran. He was married by his mother to an Egyptian wife. When Abraham died, he returned from exile to help Isaac to bury their father (Gen. 25:9). He became the father of 12 sons and a daughter, whom Esau took for his wife. He died at the age of 137 (Gen. 25:17). 2. A descendant of Jonathan (I Chron. 8:38; 9:44). 3. The father of Zebadiah (II Chron. 19:11). 4. The son of Jehohanan (II Chron. 23:1). 5. The son of Nethaniah, a member of the royal house of David. After the capture of Palestine, Nebuchadnezzar left behind as governor of Judah a Jew called Gedaliah. About two months after the destruction of Jerusalem, Gedaliah and others with him were murdered at a banquet held in honor of Ishmael, who then attempted to flee. While his captives were recovered, he and a few of his men succeeded in escaping to the king of Ammon (II Kings 25:25; Jer. 40:7-16; 41:1-18).

Ishmaelite (ĭsh′mā-ĕl-īt), a descendant of Ishmael, the son of Abraham and Hagar (Gen. 21:14-21). The 12 sons of Ishmael, and his Egyptian wife, became princes and progenitors of as

An Ishmaelite caravan at Dovan, reminiscent of Genesis 27:25-28. © MPS

many tribes. They lived in camps in the desert of Northern Arabia, although occasionally some of them settled down, as the Nabateans. Mostly, however, they lived like Ishmael, "a wild man" of the desert (Gen. 16:12), and also like him they were famous for their skill with the bow. Joseph was sold by his brothers to some Ishmaelites (Gen. 37:25-28).

The word is apparently used in the OT in a wider sense, referring to the nomadic tribes of Northern Arabia generally (Gen. 37:28, 36; Judg 8:24). All Arabs, following Mohammed's example, claim descent from Ishmael.

Ishmaiah (ĭsh-mā′yȧ, **Jehovah hears).** 1. A Gibeonite who joined David (I Chron. 12:4). 2. Chief of the Zebulunites (I Chron. 27:19).

Ishmeelite (See Ishmaelite)

Ishmerai (ĭsh′mē-rī, **Jehovah keeps),** a Benjamite (I Chron. 8:18).

Ishod (ī′shŏd, **man of majesty),** a man from Manasseh (I Chron. 7:18).

Ishpan (ĭsh′păn, **he will hide),** a Benjamite, son of Shashak (I Chron. 8:22).

Ishtar (ĭsh′tăr), a Semitic goddess worshiped in Phoenicia, Canaan, Assyria, and Babylonia. Her name is spelled in various ways — Ashtoreth, Astarte, Ashtartu (in the Amarna letters), Ishtar (in Babylonia), etc. The name and cult of the goddess were derived from Babylonia, where she was the goddess of love and war. Prostitution was practiced in her name by bands of men and women. In Assyria the warlike side of the goddess was stressed. In Canaan her warlike attributes were dropped, and she became a moon-goddess and the consort of Baal. The Philistines worshiped her and built a temple for her at Ascalon. As early as the times of Judges her cult had spread to the Hebrews (Judg. 2:13; 10:6). Solomon supported her worship (I Kings 11:5; II Kings 23:13), and the Hebrew women in Jeremiah's day gave her a high place in their worship (Jer. 44:17f).

Ishtob (ĭsh′tŏb, **the men of Tob),** a place in Palestine which supplied at least 12,000 soldiers to the Ammonites in their war with David (II Sam. 10:6, 8).

Ishuah (ĭsh′ū-ȧ, **he will level),** son of Asher (Gen. 46:17; I Chron. 7:30).

Ishuai (ĭsh′ū-ī, **level).** 1. Son of Asher and founder of a tribal family (Num. 26:44, Jesuai in KJV). 2. Son of Saul (I Sam. 14:49, Ishui in KJV).

Ishui (ĭsh′ū-ī). See Ishuai, of which Ishui is another spelling in the KJV.

Island, Isle. The Hebrew word has a much wider significance than the English words. Its root-meaning is supposed to be habitable land. 1. Dry land, as opposed to water (Isa. 42:15). 2. An island as usually understood (Jer. 2:10). 3. A coastland (Isa. 20:6; Gen. 10:5). 4. The farthest regions of the earth (Isa. 41:5; Zeph. 2:11). John was banished to the isle of Patmos for the sake of the Word of God. (Rev. 1:9).

Ismachiah (ĭs′mȧ-kī′ȧ, **Jehovah sustains),** temple overseer in the reign of Hezekiah (II Chron. 31:13).

Ismaiah (ĭs-mā′yȧ, **Jehovah hears).** 1. A Gibeonite who joined David (I Chron. 12:4). 2. A Zebulunite chief (I Chron. 27:19).

Ispah (ĭs′pȧ, **firm),** a Benjamite, son of Beriah (I Chron. 8:16).

Israel (ĭz′rā-ĕl) is used in Scripture to designate: (a) an individual man, the son of Isaac (see Jacob); or (b) his descendants, the twelve tribes of the Hebrews; or (c) the ten northern tribes, led by Ephraim, as opposed to the southern, under Judah.

Before the year 2100 B.C., the God who directs all history chose the patriarch Abraham and called him out of Ur of the Chaldees (Gen. 11:31; Neh. 9:7). The Lord's redemptive purpose was to bring Abraham and his descendants into a saving (covenant) relationship with Himself (Gen. 17:7) and also to make of Abraham's seed a nation in Palestine (vs. 2) through which He would some day bring salvation to the entire world (12:3; 22:18). God accordingly blessed Abraham's grandson Jacob with many children. Furthermore, upon Jacob's return to Palestine in 1909 B.C., God "wrestled" with him and brought him to a point of total submission (32:25; Hos. 12:4). By thus yielding his life to God's purpose, Jacob achieved victory; and God changed his name to Israel, which means, "He strives with God (and prevails)" (Gen. 32:28; 35:10). Jacob's twelve sons were thus, literally, the children of "Israel" (42:5; 45:21). Israel, however, was aware that God would build each of them into a numerous tribe (49:7, 16). The term "children of Israel" came therefore to signify the whole body of God's chosen and saved people (32:32; 34:7). It included Jacob's grandchildren and all subsequent members of the household, as they proceeded to Egypt for a sojourn of 430 years, 1876-1446 B. C. (46:8; Exod. 1:7).

In the space of approximately ten generations, God increased Israel from a clan of several hundred (Gen. 14: 14; 46:27) to a nation of almost 3,-000,000 souls (Exod. 12:37; Num. 1: 46), equipped with all the material and cultural advantages of Egypt (Exod. 2:10; 12:36; Acts 7:22). Their very increase, however, seems to have a-roused the envy and fear, first of the land's foreign "Hyksos" rulers (Dynasties XV-XVI, about 1730-1580 B. C.) and then of the native Egyptian Empire that followed (Dyn. XVIII), Exodus 1:8-10. Israel was thus enslaved and compelled to erect certain Hyksos store-cities in the region of the eastern Delta (1:11; compare Gen. 15:13) and was threatened with total national destruction under the anti-Semitic policy of the Empire (Exod. 1:16). Moses (born 1527) was befriended by an Egyptian princess, but even he was forced to flee Egypt during the reign of the great conqueror and oppressor, Thothmes III (dated 1501-1447 B.C.).

God, however, still remembered His covenant promises with Abraham (Exod. 2:24-25). At the death of the great Pharaoh (vs. 23) He appeared to Moses in a burning bush on Mt. Sinai and commissioned him to deliver the enslaved people (3:10). Only after a series of ten miraculous plagues, climaxing in the death of all the first-born of Egypt (see Passover), was the hard-hearted Pharaoh compelled to yield to the Lord (12:31).

In the spring of 1446 B.C. the nation of Israel achieved their exodus from Egypt (12:37-40). Scripture is explicit in placing the Exodus in the 480th year before the beginning of Solomon's Temple in 966 B. C. (I Kings 6:1); and the 15th century date is then confirmed by other Scriptural testimonies (compare Judg. 11:26; Acts 13:19 ASV). Israel marched eastward from Goshen toward the Red Sea. But when Pharaoh pursued after the seemingly entrapped Hebrews (Exod. 14: 3), the Lord sent a strong east wind that blew back the waters of the Sea (vs. 21). Israel crossed, and then the Lord caused the waters to return so that the Egyptians were destroyed to the last man (Exod. 14:28; excepting the Pharaoh, who is not mentioned after vs. 10).

Israel reached Mt. Sinai at the commencement of summer, 1446 (19:1). At this point God extended the covenant

A "Moses' eye-view" of the Promised Land, looking westward as seen from Mount Nebo-Mount Pisgah. The Jerusalem area is on the horizon, just right of center. Below, in the foreground, is the northern end of the Dead Sea. © MPS

offer of reconciliation that He had made with Abraham and Israel (Jacob, Gen. 28:13-15) so as to embrace the whole nation of Israel. In May of 1445 B.C. Israel broke up camp (Num. 10:11) and marched northeast to Kadesh, on the southern border of the promised land of Canaan. But after taking 40 days to spy out the land, all the tribal representatives except Caleb and Joshua reported unfavorably on attempting any conquest of Canaan (13:28). Impetuous Israel thereupon refused to advance into the promised land and prayed for a return to Egypt (14:4). Moses' intercession did save them from immediate divine wrath; but the Lord still condemned them to wander for 40 years in the wilderness, one year for each day of spying, until that entire generation should fall by the way (14:32-34).

During the last month of Moses' life, God's great servant conducted a "numbering" or census of the people, which indicated a figure of over 600,000 fighting men, only slightly less than had taken part in the Exodus 40 years before (Num. 26:51, compare 1:46). Moses then acceded to the request of the tribes of Reuben, Gad, and half of Manasseh to settle in the conquered lands of Transjordan (Num. 32); and he provided for the division of western Canaan among the remaining tribes (33-34). At this time Balaam, who had been employed by the Moabites to curse Israel, uttered his famous blessings. Moses then anointed Joshua as his successor (27:23), spoke his final two addresses, that constitute most of the book of Deuteronomy, Chapters 1-4 and 5-30, and ascended Mt. Pisgah to view the promised land. There Moses died and was buried by God's own hand (Deut. 34:5-6).

At Joshua's accession, the land of Canaan lay providentially prepared for conquest by the Hebrews. In the spring of 1406 the Jordan was in its annual flood-stage (Josh. 3:15). But Joshua anticipated a miracle of divine intervention (vs. 13), and the Lord did indeed open a gateway into Canaan (vs. 16). Israel thus marched across the relatively dry river bed (compare 4:18), led by the ark of God's testament (3:16).

Joshua's war of conquest developed in three major campaigns: in central, southern, and northern Canaan. His first objective was the city of Jericho. Within six years of the fall of Jericho (compare 14:10) all Canaan had come to lie at Joshua's feet (11:16). "So Jehovah gave unto Israel all the land which He sware unto their fathers... all came to pass" (21:43, 45). The Canaanites had not yet lost their potential for resistance; and, indeed, what the Lord had sworn to Israel had been a gradual occupation of the land (Exod. 23-28-30; Deut. 7:22). Much still remained to be possessed (Josh. 13:1), but at this point Joshua was compelled by advancing age to divide the land among the 12 Hebrew tribes (Chapters 13-22). He then charged his people with faithfulness to Jehovah (24:15) and died.

Moses had ordered the "devotion" (extermination) of the Canaanites (Deut. 7:2), both because of their long-standing immoralities (9:5; compare Gen. 9:22, 25; 15:16) and because of their debasing religious influence upon God's people (Deut. 7:4; 12:31). In the years immediately following Joshua's death, Judah accordingly accomplished an initial capture of Jerusalem (Judg. 1:8; though the city was not held, vs. 21); and Ephraim and west-Manasseh slew the men of Bethel (vs. 25), which city had begun to reassert itself. But then came failure: Israel ceased to eradicate the Canaanites; no more cities were taken (vss. 27-34); and the tribe of Dan actually suffered eviction themselves (vs. 34). Tolerance of evil had to be rectified by national chastening (2:3).

The next three and one-half centuries were thus used of God to impress upon His people three major lessons. 1. The Lord's wrath at sin. For when Israel yielded to temptation, God would "deliver them over into the hands of their enemies round about, so that they could not any longer stand" (2:14). 2. God's mercy upon repentance. For the Lord would then "raise them up judges and save them out of the hand of their enemies" (2:18). 3. Man's total depravity. For "it came to pass, when the judge was dead, that they turned back and dealt more corruptly than their fathers" (2:19). The period of the 14 judges (12 in Judges, plus Eli and Samuel in I Samuel) thus demonstrates a repeated cycle of human sin, of servitude, or supplication, and then of salvation.

The United Kingdom of Israel was precipitated by the demand of the people themselves. King Saul's accession proceeded in three steps. He was first privately anointed by Samuel and filled with God's Spirit (10:10), then publicly selected at Mizpah (vs. 24), and at last popularly confirmed at Gilgal, after having delivered the town of Jabesh-gilead from Ammonite attack (Chapter 11). The primary concern of his 40 year reign (1050-1010 B.C., compare Acts 13:21) was the Philistines. These oppressors had already occupied much of his territory, and open war was provoked in 1048 (I Sam. 13:1 ASV) when one of their garrisons was destroyed by Saul's son Jonathan (vs. 3). In the ensuing battle at Michmash, Jonathan's personal bravery (14:14), plus the Philistines' own superstitious reaction to a heaven-sent earthquake (vss. 15, 20), brought about their total defeat. Saul thus terminated the oppression but, by his failure to submit to Samuel (13:8-9), suffered the rejection of his dynasty from the throne of Israel (vs. 14).

Samuel then privately anointed David, a son of Jesse of Judah, as king over Israel (16:13). David was about 15 at the time (compare II Sam. 5:4); but, by God's providence, he gained rapid promotion at court, first as a minstrel (vss. 21-23) and then by his victory over the Philistine champion Goliath (Chapter 17). Even Saul's growing jealousy, which removed David from court to the dangers of battle, augmented the latter's popularity (vss. 27-30). Saul's overt hostility finally drove David and his followers into exile, first as outlaws in Judah (I Sam. 20-26) and then as vassals to the Philistine king of Gath (27-30). But while Saul was diverting his resources in the futile pursuit of David, the Philistines prepared for a third, all-out attack on Israel, (1010 B.C.). David barely escaped engaging in war against his own people (29:4, compare vs. 8); and Saul, routed at Mt. Gilboa, committed suicide rather than suffer capture (31:4). Israel's sinful demand for a king had brought about its own punishment.

Having learned of the death of Saul, David moved to Hebron and was there proclaimed king over his own tribe of Judah (II Sam. 2:4). But despite David's diplomacy, the supporters of Saul set up his son, Ish-bosheth, over the northern and eastern tribes (vss. 7-8). Civil war followed, but David increasingly gained the upper hand (3:1). Finally, after the death of Ish-bosheth, the tribal representatives assembled to Hebron and anointed David as king over all Israel (1003 B.C.). The Philistines now realized that their vassal had gotten out of hand and that their own future depended upon prompt action. David, however, after an initial flight to his former outlaw retreat (5:17), rallied his devoted forces (compare 23:13-17); and, by two brilliant victories in the vicinity of Jerusalem (5:9-25), not simply terminated the last Philistine oppression but eventually incorporated Gath into his own territory and subdued the remaining Philistine states (I Chron. 18:1).

The time was ripe for the rise of a Hebrew empire. The Hittites had succumbed to barbarian invasion; the Twenty-first Dynasty of Egypt stagnated under the alternating rule of priests and merchants (1100 B.C. on); and Assyria, after having weakened others, was itself restrained by inactive kings. With Philistia broken, Israel remained free from foreign threat for 150 years. David's first strategic move was to capture Jerusalem from the Canaanites. Militarily, Mt. Zion constituted a splendid fortress (II Sam. 5:6, 9); politically, the city afforded David a neutral capital between the recently hostile areas of Judah and northern Israel; and religiously, Zion's possession of the ark of God's testament (6:17) centered the people's spiritual hopes within its walls (Ps. 87). From about 1002 to 995 B.C. David then extended his power on every side. At his death in 970 B.C. David was able to commit to his son Solomon an empire that marked the peak of Israel's power.

Solomon, after a bloody accession (I Kings 2:25, 34, 36), reigned in peace, culture, and luxury, experiencing only one military campaign in 40 years (II Chron. 8:3). His greatest undertaking was the Jerusalem temple, erected from 966 to 959 B.C. (I Kings 6) out of materials lavishly provided by David (I Chron. 22). Like the tabernacle before it, the temple symbolized the abiding presence of God with His people (I Kings 8:11).

But Solomon also engaged in a number of luxurious building projects of his own (7:1-12), so that despite his great commercial revenues (9:26-28; 10:14-15) indebtedness forced him to surrender territory (9:11-12) and to engage in excessive taxation and labor-conscription. Unrest grew throughout the empire; and, while the tribute continued during his lifetime (4:21), surrounding subject countries, such as Edom and Damascus, became increasingly independent (11:14, 23). More serious was Solomon's spiritual failure, induced by wanton polygamy (vss. 1-8). "And Jehovah was angry . . . and said unto Solomon, 'Forasmuch as thou hast not kept My covenant, I will surely rend the kingdom from thee and will give it to thy servant . . . out of the hand of thy son' " (vss. 9-12).

Early in 930 B.C. Solomon died and his son Rehoboam went to Shechem to be confirmed as king. The people, however, were led by Jeroboam of Ephraim to demand relief from Solomon's tyranny (I Kings 12:4); and when Rehoboam spurned their pleas, the ten northern tribes seceded to form an independent kingdom of Israel and Israel was never again united. Here is a brief summary:

1. Name given to Jacob (Gen. 32:28; 35:10). 2. Name given collectively to 12 tribes of Israel (Exod. 3:16). 3. Name given to N kingdom after revolt of 10 tribes (I Sam. 11:8; I Kings 14:19, 29). 4. Name given to all who have faith of Abraham (Ps. 73:1; Isa. 45:17; John 1:47; Rom. 11:13-36; Gal. 6:15, 16).

Israelite (See Israel)

Issachar (ĭs′ȧ-kȧr). 1. Son of Jacob and Leah (Gen. 30:17, 18; 35:23). He had four sons, and with them went down with Jacob into Egypt (Gen. 46:13; Exod. 1:3). There he died and was buried. His descendants formed a tribe, consisting of five great tribal families (Num. 26:23, 24). 2. A Korahite doorkeeper in the reign of David (I Chron. 26:5).

Isshiah (ĭs′shī′ȧ, **Jehovah exists**). 1. A man of Issachar (I Chron. 7:3, Ishiah in KJV). 2. One of those who came to David at Ziklag (I Chron. 12:6, Jesiah in KJV). 3. A Levite (I Chron. 24:21). 4. Another Levite (I Chron. 23:20; 24:25).

Isuah (See Ishuah)

Issue (See Diseases: Miscellaneous Medical Disorders)

Isui (See Ishui)

Italian Band. A cohort of Roman soldiers stationed in Caesarea when Peter preached to Cornelius (Acts 10:1).

Italy (ĭt′ȧ-lĭ), the geographical term for the country between the Alps and Messina of which Rome was the capital. 2. It is mentioned in Acts 27:1 as Paul's destination when he had appealed to Caesar. 3. In Heb. 13:24 Christians from Italy send their greetings. 4. In Acts 10:1 it is mentioned as the country that gave its name to the cohort stationed at Caesarea, of which Cornelius was the centurion.

Itch (See Diseases)

Ithai (ĭth′ā-ī), a Benjamite (I Chron. 11:31) called Ittai in II Sam. 23:29.

Ithamar (ĭth′ȧ-mȧr), youngest son of Aaron; founded priestly family (Exod. 6:23; I Chron. 6:3; 24:1).

Ithiel (ĭth′ĭ-ĕl, **God is**). 1. Friend of Agur (Prov. 30:1). 2. A Benjamite (Neh. 11:7).

Ithmah (ĭth′mȧ, **purity**), Moabite hero (I Chron. 11:46).

Ithnan (ĭth′năn), town in the S of Judah (Josh. 15:23).

Ithra (ĭth′rȧ, **abundance**), the father of Amasa, commander of Absalom's rebel army (I Chron. 2:17, Jether in KJV).

Ithran (ĭth′răn, **excellent**). 1. A Horite (Gen. 36:26; I Chron. 1:41). 2. An Asherite (I Chron. 7:37).

Ithream (ĭth′rē-ăm), son of David by Eglah (II Sam. 3:5; I Chron. 3:3).

Ithrite (ĭth′rīt, **excellence**), a family from which two of David's heroes came (II Sam. 23:38; I Chron. 11:40).

Ittah-Kazin (ĭt′ȧ-kā′zĭn), a place on the border of Zebulun (Josh. 19:13). Site unknown.

Ittai (ĭt′ȧ-ī). 1. One of David's heroes (II Sam. 23:29; I Chron. 11:31). 2. Gathite who became a loyal follower of David (II Sam. 15:18-22; 18:2, 5).

Ituraea (ĭt′ū-rē′ȧ, **pertaining to Jetur**). This word is found only once in Scripture, in the description of Philip's territory (Luke 3:1). It was a region NE of Palestine, beyond the Jordan, and cannot now be exactly located. The Ituraeans were descended from Ishmael (Gen. 25:15), who had a son named Jetur, from whom the name Ituraea is derived. The Ituraeans were semi-nomads and famous archers, a lawless and predatory people.

Ivah (ī′vȧ), a city, probably in Syria, captured by the Assyrians (II Kings 18:34; 19:13; Isa. 37:13).

Ivory (ī′vō-rĭ). Ivory was brought to Palestine by both ship and caravan, and came from India. Solomon's throne was made of ivory (I Kings 10:18); and he imported large quantities of it. Amos denounces Israel for its luxuries, among them the use of ivory (Amos 3:15; 6:4). Even houses were overlaid with it (I Kings 22:39; Ps. 45:8).

Izchar (See Izhar)

Izhar (iz'hâr, **the shining one).** 1. A Levite (Exod. 6:18, 19; Num. 3:19; I Chron. 6:18, 38). 2. A descendant of Judah (I Chron. 4:7).

Izrahiah (ĭz'rȧ-hī'ȧ, **Jehovah arises** or **shines),** a chief of the tribe of Issachar (I Chron. 7:3).

Izrahite (iz'ra-hīt, **rising, shining).** Shamhuth, the captain of the fifth monthly course, is called an Izrahite (I Chron. 27:8). The name may be a corruption of "Zerahite," a descendant of Zerah of Judah.

Izri (ĭz-rī, **creator, former),** a man of the "sons of Jeduthun," chief of one of the Levitical choirs (I Chron. 25:11). Called Zeri in verse 3.

A scene in the gorge of the Jabbok River. SHH

-J-

Jaakan (jā'ȧ-kăn), a descendant of Esau (I Chron. 1:35-42, spelled **Jakan).** He was the son of Ezer, who was a Horite (Gen. 36:20-27, spelled **Akan).**

Jaakobah (jā'ȧ-kō'bȧ), a Simeonite prince (I Chron. 4:36).

Jaala, Jaalah (jā'ȧ-lȧ, jā'ȧ-lȧ), a servant of Solomon whose children returned from Babylon (Ezra 2:56).

Jaalam (jā'ȧ-lăm), a son of Esau, a duke in Edom (Gen. 36:2, 5, 18).

Jaanai (jā'ȧ-nī), a son of Gad (I Chron. 5:11, 12).

Jaare-Oregim (jā'ȧ-rē-ôr'ē-jĭm), the father of Elhanan, who slew the giant brother of Goliath (II Sam. 21:19).

Jaasau (jā'ā-sāū), man who divorced foreign wife (Ezra 10:37).

Jaasiel, Jasiel (jā-ā'sĭ-ĕl, jā'sĭ-ĕl, **God makes),** a son of Abner, a leader of Benjamites (I Chron. 27:21) and valiant warrior (I Chron. 11:47).

Jaazaniah (jā-ăz'ȧ-nī'ȧ, **Jehovah hears),** also called Azariah (Jer. 43:2). 1. Manassehite who slew Gedaliah and led Israelites into Egypt (Jer. 43:1-7). Jeremiah calls him Jezaniah (40:8; 42:1) and Azariah (43:2). 2. Son of Jeremiah (not prophet) (Jer. 35:1-11). 3. Leader in idolatrous worship (Ezek. 8:10-12). 4. Prince denounced by Ezekiel (Ezek. 11:1-3).

Jaazer, Jazer (jā'ȧ-zêr, jā'zêr, **helpful),** Ammonite stronghold E of the Jordan, probably c. 14 miles N of Heshbon; assigned to Gad (Josh. 13:24, 25); later given to Levites (Josh. 21: 39).

Jaaziah (jā'ȧz-ī'ȧ, **Jehovah strengthens)** a Levite temple musician (I Chron. 24:20, 26).

Jaaziel (jā-ā'zĭ-ĕl, **God strengthens),** a temple musician (I Chron. 15:18), called Aziel in v. 20.

Jabal (jā'băl), a son of Lamech, who was the great-grandson of Cain (Gen. 4:19, 20). He and his brothers, Jubal and Tubal, are credited with the origin of civilized society (Gen. 4:21, 22).

Jabbok (jăb'ŏk, **flowing),** an important river E of the Jordan about halfway between the Dead Sea and the Sea of Galilee. It was the northern border of the Amorite king, Sihon (Josh. 12:2) and was captured by the Hebrews after Sihon refused to let them cross his land (Num. 21:21-25). It was also the southern border of the kingdom of Og (Josh. 12:5). At a ford on the Jabbok, Jacob had his encounter with the angel, which resulted in his being given a new name (Gen. 32:22-30).

Jabesh (jā'bĕsh, **dry).** 1. Father of Shallum (II Kings 15:8-13). 2. A short term for Jabesh-Gilead (I Chron. 10:12), a town. See Jabesh-Gilead.

Jabesh-Gilead (jā'bĕsh-gĭl'ē-ăd, **dry),** city E of the Jordan, 10 miles SE of Bethshan in area of Manasseh (Num. 32:33). Its men were killed when they refused to attend the sacred assembly at Mizpeh (Judg. 21:8-15); its people buried the remains of Saul and Jonathan (I Sam. 31:1-13).

Jabez (jā'bēz, **to grieve).** 1. The head of a family in Judah (I Chron. 4:9). His offspring are listed as scribes and as Kenites (I Chron. 2:55). He was more honorable than his brethren (I Chron. 4:9). He made an earnest appeal for a blessing and it was granted (I Chron. 4:10). 2. A town in Judah (I Chron. 2:55).

Jabin (jā'bĭn, **able to discern).** 1. King of Hazor; defeated and slain by Joshua (Josh. 11). 2. Another king of Hazor; defeated by Barak (Judg. 4; I Sam. 12:9; Ps. 83:9).

Jabneel (jăb'nē-ĕl, **God causes to build).** 1. A town in the northern border of Judah, just S of Joppa (Josh. 15:11), modern Jabna. It is called Jabneh in II Chron. 26:6. Later called Jamnia. 2. A frontier town of Naphtali (Josh. 19:33).

Jabneh (jăb'nĕ), the same as Jebneel 1.

Jachan (jā'kăn), a descendant of Gad (I Chron. 5:13).

Jachin, Jachin and Boaz (jā'kĭn, **he will set up).** 1. Son of Simeon (Gen. 46:10, Jarib in I Chron. 4:24). Founder of the tribe of Jachanites (Num. 26:12). 2. One of the priests in Jerusalem during the captivity (Neh. 11:10). During David's reign he was leader of the twenty-first course of priests (I Chron. 24:17). 3. Jachin and Boaz were the names of two symbolic pillars in the porch of Solomon's temple (I Kings 7:13-22; II Chron. 3:15-17).

Jacinth (jā'sĭnth, **hyacinth),** one of the precious stones in the foundation of New Jerusalem (Rev. 21:20). Hyacinth in RV. See Minerals.

Jackal (See Animals)

Jacob (jā'kūb, **supplanter).** 1. Son of Isaac and Rebekah; younger twin brother of Esau (Gen. 25:21-26) from whom he secured the birthright by giving him a bowl of soup (Gen. 25:29-34); got Isaac's blessing through fraud (Gen. 27:1-41); fled to Haran and on way had vision of ladder (Gen. 27:42-28:22); served Laban for many years and married his daughters, Leah and Rachel (Gen. 29:1-30); had 12 sons and a daughter by his wives and their maids, Zilpah and Bilhah (Gen. 29-31); fled from Laban (Gen. 31); wrestled with angel of the Lord at Peniel (Gen. 32:24-32); friendship with Esau restored (Gen. 33); went to Egypt during time of famine (Gen. 42-46) and died there (Gen. 49). 2. Patronymic of Israelites (Num. 23:10; Ps. 59:13). 3. Father of Joseph, husband of Mary (Matt. 1:15, 16).

Jacob's Well. The well mentioned in John 4:6 as the well of Jacob, where Jesus talked to the Samaritan woman. For more than 23 centuries Samaritans have believed that this is true. Jews likewise have believed the same in spite of the location of the well in Samaria. The ground mentioned by John had been purchased by Jacob (Gen. 33:19). The area was later wrested by force from the Amorites (Gen. 48:22). The well is near the base of Mt. Gerizim, whose bluffs may have inspired Jesus to say "this mountain" (John 4:21).

Jada (jā'dȧ, **a wise one),** Judahite, a son of Onam (I Chron. 2:26, 28).

Jadau (jā'dō), Israelite who married an alien woman during the captivity (Ezra 10:43).

Jaddua (jā-dū'ȧ, **known).** 1. An Israelite prince who had part in making the covenant (Neh. 10:21). 2. Son of Jonathan and great-grandson of Eliashib. Priest who returned with Zerubbabel from Babylon (Neh. 12:11).

Jadon (jā'dŏn, he will plead), one who helped rebuild the wall of Jerusalem (Neh. 3:7).

Jael (jā'ĕl, wild goat), the wife of Heber the Kenite (Judg. 4). Being a woman she could not meet Sisera in combat, so resorted to cunning, slaying him with a weapon she had long since learned to use, a tent peg. That Deborah approved of her act (Judg. 5:24) only shows to what extremes a harassed people can be driven by a brutal foe. Jael's deed was considered an act of Israel, hence the manner in which Deborah gloated over it. No question is raised in the record about the moral nature of Jael's deed, nor is it attributed to divine leading, although the victory over Sisera was (Judg. 5:20).

Jagur (jā'gêr), a town in the S of Judah (Josh. 15:21).

Jah (jȧ), a contraction of **Jahweh.** It is found in poetry, as in Psalms 68:4; 118:14, RSV marg., and is seen in compound words like Isaiah, **Jah is saviour.**

Jahath (jā'hăth). 1. A grandson of Judah (I Chron. 4:1, 2). 2. A great-grandson of Levi (I Chron. 6:16-20). 3. A Gershonite Levite chief (I Chron. 23:10, 11). 4. Another Levite (I Chron. 24:22). 5. An overseer of construction during the restoration of the temple under Josiah (II Chron. 34:8-12).

Jahaz (jā'hăz), **Jahaza** (jȧ-hā'zȧ), **Jahazah** (jȧ-hā'zȧ), a city in Reuben's heritage (Josh. 13:18) in the land given to the Merarites (Josh. 21:34-36, Jahazah). Later Israel captured the city, conquered Sihon and took the region (Num. 21:21-25). It was once a stronghold N of the Arnon river.

Jahaziah (jȧ-hā'zī-ȧ, **God sees),** one of four who opposed Ezra's plan to divorce alien wives married during the captivity (Ezra 10:15).

Jahaziel (jȧ-hā'zĭ-ĕl, **God sees).** 1. One of a band of ambidextrous warriors who aided David at Ziklag (I Chron. 12:1-4). 2. A priest who sounded the trumpet before the ark (I Chron. 16:6). 3. One called by David to help build the temple (I Chron. 23:2-20). 4. Levite prophet. In a time of great peril he was led by the Holy Spirit to announce a victory when defeat seemed certain (II Chron. 20:14ff). 5 An ancestor of one of the families of the restoration (Ezra 8:5).

Jahdai (jȧ'dā-ī, a descendant of Caleb (I Chron. 2:46, 47).

Jahdiel (jȧ'dĭ-ĕl, **God gives joy),** head of a Manassite clan (I Chron. 5:24).

Jahdo (jȧ'dō), a Gadite (I Chron. 5:14).

Jahleel (jȧ'lē-ĕl), son of Zebulun (Gen. 46:14); founder of Jahleel clan (Num. 26:26).

Jahmai (jȧ'mā-ī), a grandson of Issachar, a chieftain in his tribe (I Chron. 7:1, 2).

Jahweh (See God)

Jahzah (jȧ'zȧ), a town given to Reuben (I Chron. 6:78).

Jahzeel (jȧ'zē-ĕl), **Jahziel** (jȧ'zĭ-ĕl), a son of Naphthali (Gen. 46:24); Jaziel in I Chronicles 7:13.

Jahzerah (jȧ′zĕ-rȧ), priest (I Chron. 9: 12).

Jair (jā′ĕr, **he enlightens).** 1. A son of Manasseh and a leading warrior in the conquest of Gilead by Moses (Num. 32:40, 41). 2. One of the judges (Judg. 10:3, 4). 3. Father of Elhanan who slew Goliath the Gittite (II Sam. 21:19 marg.). 4. The father of Mordecai (Esth. 2:5).

Jairus (jā′ĭ-rŭs), a synagogue ruler whose child Jesus raised from death (Mark 5:22; Luke 8:41).

Jakan (jā′kăn), a Horite (I Chron. 1: 42). The same as **Akan** in Genesis 36: 27, and **Jaakan** in Genesis 36:20, 21, 27; Deuteronomy 2:12, etc.

Jakeh (jā′kĕ, **very religious),** the father of Agur, a writer of proverbs (Prov. 30).

Jakim (jā′kĭm, **God lifts).** 1. A Benjamite (I Chron. 8:12, 19). 2. Head of 12th course of priests (I Chron. 24: 12).

Jalon (jā′lŏn), a son of Ezra (I Chron. 4:17).

Jambres (jăm′brēz), magician who opposed Moses before Pharaoh (II Tim. 3:8).

James (jāmz). 1. Son of Zebedee and Salome (Matt. 27:56; Mark 1:19; 15: 40); elder brother of Apostle John (Matt. 17:1; Mark 3:17; 5:37); one of the apostles (Matt. 17:1); may have been cousin of Jesus; fisherman (Luke 5:10, 11); with Jesus at transfiguration (Matt. 17:1-8) and in Gethsemane (Matt. 26:36-46); with John given surname Boanerges (Mark 3:17); angered other apostles (Mark 10:41); killed by Herod Agrippa I (Acts 12:2). 2. James the Less; apostle (Matt. 10:3; Acts 1:13); son of Alphaeus. 3. James, the Lord's brother (Matt. 13:55; Mark 6:3; Gal. 1:19); did not accept Jesus' claims during His ministry (John 7: 5), but did after the resurrection (I Cor. 15:7); head of church in Jerusalem (Acts 12:17; 21:18; Gal. 1:19; 2:9, 12); presided at Jerusalem council (Acts 15:13; 21:18); gave advice to Paul (Acts 21); Josephus says he was martyred by Jewish High Priest (c. A. D. 62). 4. Father of Apostle Judas (not Iscariot) (Luke 6:16; Acts 1:13).

James The Less (See James)

James, Epistle of. The author of the epistle refers to himself as "James, a servant of God and of the Lord Jesus Christ" (1:1). The NT mentions four who bore the name of James: (1) the father of Judas the Apostle, not Iscariot (Luke 6:16), (2) the apostle, James the son of Alphaeus (Matt. 10:3), (3) the apostle, James the son of Zebedee and the brother of John (Matt. 4:21), (4) the brother of our Lord (Matt. 13:55; Gal. 1:19). The father of Judas the apostle is entirely unknown except for the mention of his relation to the apostle, and nothing is said of James the son of Alphaeus except that he was an apostle, so it is unlikely that either of these two men could have written the epistle. James the son of Zebedee was martyred about A.D. 44 (Acts 12:2), so he cannot be the author; and besides, the author of this epistle does not call himself an apostle, but describes himself merely as a servant. Tradition attributes the authorship of the epistle to James the brother of the Lord, who was favored with a special appearance of the risen Christ (I Cor. 15:7) and who from a very early date occupied a leading position in the church at Jerusalem (Acts 12:17; Gal. 1:19). Paul names him first among the three pillars of the church in Jerusalem he saw on his second visit there after his conversion (Gal. 2:9), and in Acts 15 he is described as the leader and chief spokesman of the Apostolic Council. All that is known of him shows that he was highly esteemed not only by Christians but by unbelieving Jews. According to Josephus he was put to death by the High Priest in the interregnum between the death of Festus and the arrival of his successor Albinus in A.D. 62.

All the characteristics of the epistle support the traditional attribution of it to James the brother of the Lord. The author speaks with the authority of one who knew he did not need to justify or defend his position. There is no more Jewish book in the NT than this epistle; and this is to be expected from a man whom both tradition and the rest of the NT show was distinguished by a greater attachment to the law of Moses than Paul. The whole of the epistle, moreover, bears a striking resemblance to the Sermon on the Mount both in the loftiness of its morality and in the simple grandeur of its expression.

The letter is addressed to "the twelve tribes which are scattered abroad." This ambiguous expression may be interpreted in a number of ways. 1. The Jews of the Diaspora in general, who were living throughout the Mediterranean world outside Palestine. This meaning is impossible, for the writer is addressing Christians (1: 18, 25; 2:1, 12; 5:7-9). 2. The Jewish Christians of the Diaspora. 3. The Christian Church as the new people of God living far from their heavenly homeland. Early Christians regarded themselves as the true Israel (Gal. 6: 16), the true circumcision (Phil. 3:3), and the seed of Abraham (Gal. 3:29; Rom. 4:16), so it would not be surprising if they also thought of themselves as "the twelve tribes." There is no doubt, however, that the epistle is intended for Jewish Christians, although its message is applicable to all Christians. Those to whom the author writes worship in synagogues (2:2), and the faults he attacks were characteristic of Jews: misuse of the tongue (3:2-12; 4:2, 11), unkind judgments of one's neighbor (3:14; 4:11), the making of rash oaths (5:12), undue regard for wealth (2:1-13), etc. Outline: 1. Comfort (1). 2. Warnings against specific sins of which they are guilty, such as pride, favoring the rich, misuse of the tongue, believing in faith without works (2-4). 3. Exhortation to patience in suffering and prayer (5).

Jamin (jā'mĭn, **right hand).** 1. A son of Simeon (Gen. 46:10). 2. A Judahite (I Chron. 2:3, 27). 3. A teacher of the law under Ezra (Neh. 8:7).

Jamlech (jăm'-lĕch, **whom God makes king),** a prince of the tribe of Simeon (I Chron. 4:34).

Janna (jăn'à), an ancestor of Jesus, fifth in line before Joseph (Luke 3: 23, 24).

Jannes (jăn'ēz), a magician who withstood Moses and Aaron by duplicating some of their miracles. Paul, who was familiar with rabbinical traditions, named him along with Jambres as types of evil men of the last days (II Tim. 3:8).

Janoah (jȧ-nō'ȧ), **Janohah** (jȧ-nō'hȧ), in KJV of Joshua. 1. A town of Naphthali (II Kings 15:29). 2. A town on the boundary of Ephraim (Josh. 16: 6, 7).

Janum (jā'nŭm), a town in Judah; part of heritage of Judah (Josh. 15: 53).

Japheth (jā'fĕth, **God will enlarge),** son of Noah (Gen. 5:32; 6:10; 7:13; 10:21); had seven sons (Gen. 10:2); descendants occupied "isles of Gentiles" (Gen. 10:5); blessed by Noah (Gen. 9:20-27).

Japhia (jȧ-fī'ȧ, **tall** or **may God make bright).** 1. A ruler of Lachish who joined a coalition against Joshua (Josh. 10:1-5). Later Joshua had the kings executed and buried in the cave (vss. 22-27). 2. A son of David (II Sam. 5: 15; I Chron. 3:7). 3. A small city on the eastern border of Zebulun (Josh. 19:12).

Japhlet (jăf'lĕt), Asherite (I Chron. 7: 32).

Japhleti (jăf'lē-tī), clan on the western border of Joseph's heritage (Josh. 16: 1-3).

Japho (jā'fō), Hebrew form of Joppa, a border town in Dan (Josh. 19:46). See Joppa.

Jarah (jā'rȧ, **honeycomb),** a descendant of Gibeon (I Chron. 9:42), called Jehoaddah in 8:36.

Jareb (jā'rĕb, **contender),** an Assyrian king to whom Ephraim went for help (Hos. 5:13).

Jared (jā'rĕd), the father of Enoch (Gen. 5:18-20).

Jaresiah (jăr'ē-sī'ȧ), a son of Jerohan (I Chron. 8:27), of the tribe of Benjamin.

Jarha (jȧr'hȧ), an Egyptian slave of Sheshan (I Chron. 2:34, 35). Since Sheshan had no son, he gave Jarha his freedom so he could marry a daughter.

Jarib (jā'rīb, **he strives).** 1. A son of Simeon, also called Jachin (I Chron. 4:24; Gen. 46:10 marg.). 2. A chief of returning captives (Ezra 8:15-20). 3. Man who divorced foreign wife (Ezra 10:18).

Jarmuth (jȧr'mŭth). 1. City of Judah 16 miles W by S of Jerusalem (Josh. 15:35); identified with Yarmuk. 2. Levite city of Issachar (Josh. 21:28, 29). Ramoth in I Chron. 6:73; Remeth in Josh. 19:21.

Jaroah (jȧ-rō'ȧ), a chieftain of the tribe of Dan, living in land of Bashan (I Chron. 5:14).

Jashen (jā'shĕn, **brilliant),** father of some of David's heroes (II Sam. 23: 32).

Jasher, Book of (jā'shêr, Jashar in RSV), quoted in Josh. 10:13; II Sam. 1: 18, and in LXX of I Kings 8:53. This ancient book is thought to have been a collection of poetry, probably odes and psalms in praise of Israel's heroes and exploits. Many ideas about the book have been advanced: 1. It continued the Song of Deborah (Judg. 5). 2. It contained the book of the law. 3. It vanished during the Babylonian captivity. It was certainly a well-known bit of Hebrew literature.

Jashobeam (jȧ-shō′bē-ăm, **the people return).** 1. Hero who joined David at Ziklag (I Chron. 12:6). A Korahite. 2. One of David's chieftains (I Chron. 11:11, or 800, II Sam. 23:8). The LXX usually gives the name as Ishbaal. Adino in II Samuel 23:8, Jashebassebet in margin. Supposed to have been one of the three who brought David water from the well of Bethlehem (I Chron. 11:15-19). 3. One who commanded a division of 24,000 men of Israel (I Chron. 27:2, 3).

Jashub (jā′shŭb, **he returns).** 1. A son or clan descended from Issachar (Num. 26:24). 2. Shear-Jashub, a son of Isaiah (Isa. 7:3). 3. One who married a foreign wife (Ezra 10:29).

Jashubi-Lehem (jȧ-shōō′bī-lē′hĕm), a word of doubtful meaning. Probably a member of the tribe of Judah (I Chron. 4:22, 23).

Jason (jā′sŭn, **to heal),** a believer who sheltered Paul and Silas in Thessalonica (Acts 17:5-9). One who sent greetings from Corinth to Rome (Rom. 16: 21).

Jathniel (jăth′nĭ-ĕl), a son of Meshelemiah, a temple porter (I Chron. 26:2); also a gate (threshold) guard (9:19).

Jattir (jăt′êr), a large town in the hills of Judah (Josh. 15:20, 48), given to the Levites (I Chron. 6:57).

Javan (jā′văn, **Ionian),** a region settled by one of the sons of Japheth (Gen. 10:2). Javan was the name of this country to Ezekiel (27:11f), who saw it as an important trade center. So Javan (Greek, Ionia) came to be the name of Greece to the Hebrews. During the period 700-630 B.C. the Ionians carried on extensive trade in the Near East, hence all people of Greece were called Javan.

Javelin (See Arms, Armor)

Jazer, Jaazer (jā′zêr), a Gadite city in Gilead E of the Jordan, having dependent villages (Num. 21:31, 32). David found mighty men among her citizens (I Chron. 26:31).

Jaziz (jā′zĭz), an overseer of the flocks of David (I Chron. 27:31).

Jealousy, Water of, the name given holy water which was used in determining the guilt or innocence of a wife accused by her husband of being untrue (Num. 5:11-25).

Jearim (jē′ȧ-rĭm), a hill on the N border of Judah's heritage, with Chesalon, a village, on it (Josh. 15:10).

Jeaterai (jē-ăt′ē-rī), a Gershonite Levite, grandson of Iddo (I Chron. 6:21). RV has Jeatherai.

Jeberechiah (jē-bĕr′ē-kī′ȧ), the father of Zechariah, a trusted scribe (Isa. 8:2).

Jebus (jē′bŭs), the name by which Jerusalem was known when it was in the possession of the Jebusites (Josh. 15:63; Judg. 19:10; I Chron. 11:4). Jebus was small in area compared with the size of Jerusalem in Solomon's time.

Jebusites (jĕb′ū-zīts), a Canaanite tribe, descended from Canaan according to the table of nations in Genesis 10, and dwelling in the land before the Israelite conquest (Gen. 10:15, 16; 15:21; Exod. 3:8, 17; 13:5; 23:23; 33:2; Deut. 7:1; 20:17; Josh. 3:10; 10:1-5; 12:8; 18:16; Judg. 1:8). Their king, Adonizedek, was one of the five who conspired against Gibeon and was slain by Joshua.

Jecamiah, Jekamiah (jĕk′ȧ-mī′ȧ). 1. A descendant of Sheshan by a freed slave (I Chron. 2:34-41). 2. A son of a king named Jeconiah (I Chron. 3:17, 18).

Jecoliah, Jecholiah (jĕk-ō-lī′ȧ), mother of King Uzziah (II Chron. 26:3; II Kings 15:2).

Jeconiah (jĕk′ō-nī′ȧ), a variant of Jehoiachin. Son of Jehoiakim and grandson of Josiah (I Chron. 3:15, 17) who began to reign at 18 years of age, but after 3 months was captured by Nebuchadnezzar (II Kings 24:1-12). Contracted to Coniah (Jer. 22:24, 28; 37:1).

Jedaiah (jĕ-dā′yȧ, **Jehovah knows).** 1. A descendant of Simeon and the father of a prince (I Chron. 4:37, 38). 2. A priest who returned with Zerubbabel (Neh. 3:10; 12:6, 19). 3. One of the priests whose names were entered in the book of the kings which held the genealogy of the Hebrew captives in Babylon (I Chron. 9:1-10). By the time of the return from Babylon his family had grown to be very large (Ezra 2:1, 36; Neh. 7:39). 4. Another priest among the captives, commissioned by Nehemiah to have part in the prophetic coronation of Joshua (Zech. 6:9-15).

Jediael (jĕ-dī′ā-ĕl, **known of God).** 1. A son of Benjamin who became head of a mighty clan (I Chron. 7:6, 11). 2. Another valiant man in David's band (I Chron. 11:45), probably the same as No. 1. 3. A temple doorkeeper (I Chron. 26:1, 2).

Jedidah (jĕ-dī′dȧ, **beloved),** mother of King Josiah (II Kings 22:1).

Jedidiah (jĕd-ĭ-dī′ȧ, **beloved of Jeho-**

vah), name that Nathan gave to Solomon (II Sam. 12:24, 25).

Jeduthun (jĕ-dū′thŭn, **praise),** Levite whom David set over the service of praise in the tabernacle (I Chron. 25: 1-3). They with their children were to give thanks and sing, with harps and cymbals accompanying. Psalm 39 by David is dedicated to Jeduthun and Psalms 62 and 77 are "after the manner of Jeduthun."

Jeezer (jĕ-ē′zêr), head of a family in the tribe of Manasseh (Num. 26:30; Josh. 17:2; Judg. 6:11ff).

Jegar-Sahadutha (jē′gȧr-sā′hȧ-dū′thȧ, **heap of witness),** the name given by Laban to the "cairn of witness," called by Jacob **Galeed** (Gen. 31:47).

Jehaleleel, Jehalelel (jē-hăl′ē-lĕl). 1. A descendant of Judah (I Chron. 4:16). 2. A Merarite Levite (II Chron. 29:12).

Jehdeiah (jĕ-dē′yȧ, **Jehovah will be glad).** 1. A direct descendant of Moses through Gershom (I Chron. 24:20). 2. A Zebulunite (I Chron. 27:30).

Jehezekel (jē-hĕz′ē-kĕl, **God will strengthen),** a priest in David's time (I Chron. 24:16).

Jehiah (jē-hī′ȧ, **Jehovah lives),** doorkeeper of the ark in David's time (I Chron. 15:24).

Jehiel (jē-hī′ĕl, **God lives).** 1. Levite musician (I Chron. 15:18, 20; 16:5). 2. A Gershonite Levite treasurer (I Chron. 23:8; 29:8). 3. Son of Hachmoni "the wise" who was with David's sons, probably as tutor (I Chron. 27: 32). 4. A son of Jehoshaphat (II Chron. 21:2). 5. A descendant of Heman the singer in Hezekiah's time (II Chron. 29:14). 6. One of the overseers of the offerings under Hezekiah (II Chron. 31:13). 7. Temple ruler in Josiah's time (II Chron 35:8). 8. Father of Obadiah (Ezra 8:9). 9. Father of Shecaniah (Ezra 10:2). 10. Priest who confessed to having married a "strange" wife (Ezra 10:21).

Jehieli (jē-hī′ĕ-lī), a Gershonite Levite in David's day (I Chron. 26:21, 22).

Jehizkiah (jē′hĭz-kī′ȧ, **Jehovah strengthens),** an Israelite chief in the days of Ahaz (II Chron. 28:12).

Jehoadah (jē-hō′ȧ-dȧ), a descendant of King Saul through Jonathan (I Chron. 8:36). In I Chronicles 9:42 he is called "Jarah."

Jehoaddan (jē′hō-ăd′ăn), wife of King Joash of Judah and mother of Amaziah (II Chron. 25:1). In II Kings 14: 2 ASV has Jehoaddin.

Jehoahaz (jē-hō′ȧ-hăz, **Jehovah has grasped).** 1. The son and successor of Jehu, and 11th king of Israel. Reigned 17 years, c. 815-800 B.C. (II Kings 10: 35; 13:1). Like his father, he maintained the calf-worship begun by Jeroboam; God permitted the Syrians to inflict heavy defeats upon his armed forces, until he had almost none left. His kingdom became involved in such awful straits that he in desperation called upon Jehovah for help. God answered his prayers after his death in the persons of his two successors, Jehoash and Jeroboam II (II Kings 13:2-9, 22-25), through whom Israel's ancient boundaries were restored. The life of Elisha extended through his reign. 2. King of Judah 608 B.C., son of Josiah. Succeeded to the throne, but reigned only three months, and was then deposed and taken in chains into Egypt by Pharaoh Necho, who had defeated Josiah in battle. The throne was given to Jehoahaz's elder brother (II Kings 23:30-45). Jehoahaz is also called Shallum (I Chron. 3:15; Jer. 22:10-12). He died in Egypt. 3. A variant form of the name of Ahaziah, king of Judah (II Chron. 21:17; cf. ch. 22:1). 4. Full name of Ahaz, king of Judah.

Jehoash, Joash (jĕ-hō′ăsh, jō′ăsh). 1. Grandson of Benjamin (I Chron. 7:8). 2. Descendant of Judah (I Chron. 4: 22). 3. Father of Gideon, (Judg. 6:12). 4. Keeper of David's cellars of oil (I Chron. 27:28). 5. Israelite who joined David at Ziklag (I Chron. 12:3). 6. Son of King Ahab (I Kings 22:26). 7. King of Judah from 884-848 B.C. (II Kings 11-13; II Chron. 24, 25). 8. King of Israel from 848-832 B.C. (II Kings 13:10-13; 14:8-16; II Chron. 25:17-24).

Jehohanan (jē′hō-hā′năn, **Jehovah is gracious).** 1. Doorkeeper of the tabernacle in David's time (I Chron. 26: 3). 2. Officer of Jehoshaphat (II Chron. 17:15). 3. Father of Ishmael who assisted Jehoiada (II Chron. 23:1). 4. Man who married a foreign wife (Ezra 10:28). 5. A priest under Joiakim the high priest (Neh. 12:13). 6. A priestly singer at the dedication of the new wall of Jerusalem (Neh. 12:42).

Jehoiachin (jĕ-hoi′ȧ-kĭn, **Jehovah establishes),** son and successor of King Jehoiakim; next to last king of Judah; reigned three months in 597 B.C. (II Chron. 36:9); also called Coniah (Jer. 22:24, 28; 37:1), Jeconiah and Jechonias (Matt. 1:11, 12); burned prophecies of Jeremiah (Jer. 36:23, 32); deported to Babylon (II Chron. 36:10), where after 37 years of captivity he was released by Evil-merodach (II Kings 25:27).

Jehoiada (jē-hoi'ȧ-dȧ, **Jehovah knows**). 1. Father of Benaiah, one of David's most faithful officers (II Sam. 23:22; I Kings 4:4). 2. Grandson of the preceding (I Chron. 27:34). 3. Descendant of Aaron who aided David at Ziklag (I Chron. 12:27). 4. High priest; wife hid Joash; plotted overthrow of Queen Athaliah (II Chron. 23; II Kings 11).

Jehoiakim (jē-hoi'ȧ-kĭm, **Jehovah sets up**), son of Josiah, godly king of Judah; originally named "Eliakim," but name changed to Jehoiakim by Pharaoh Necho by whom he was made king and to whom he paid tribute; rebelled three years later; died ignoble death (II Kings 23:34-37; 24:1-6; II Chron. 36:4-8).

Jehoiarib, Joiarib (jē-hoi'ȧ-rĭb, joi'ȧ-rĭb). 1. Priest in days of David (I Chron. 24:7). 2. Priest who returned from exile (I Chron. 9:10). 3. Man who helped Ezra (Ezra 8:16, 17). 4. Judahite (Neh. 11:5). 5. Priest (Neh. 11:10; 12:6).

Jehonadab (jē-hŏn'ȧ-dăb). 1. Son of David's brother Shimeah (II Sam. 13:3). 2. Kenite who helped Jehu abolish Baal-worship in Samaria (II Kings 10:15f). See also Jonadab.

Jehonathan (jē-hŏn'ȧ-thăn). 1. Overseer of David's property (I Chron. 27:25). 2. Levite (II Chron. 17:8). 3. Priest (Neh. 12:18).

Jehoram (jē-hō'răm, **Jehovah is exalted**), often contracted to **Joram.** 1. Jehoram was associated with his father in the kingship for the last four or five years of Jehoshaphat's reign and took complete charge at his father's death in 849 B.C. When Jehoram became the sole ruler, he slew his own brothers with the sword. As soon as his father died (900 B.C.) Jehoram began to slip into the idolatrous ways of the northern kingdom; but because of God's covenant with David (II Kings 8:19) and no doubt because of Jehoshaphat's goodness, God did not remove the kingdom from Jehoram's hand, but God did cause him to have real troubles. Edom revolted from under the rule of Judah. Libnah in Judah, a Levitical city far enough from Jerusalem to be somewhat independent, showed its abhorrence of Jehoram's deeds by revolting at the same time (II Kings 8:22). Meanwhile, the great prophet Elijah sent to Jehoram a letter of denunciation for his wickedness. God sent a plague upon Judah, especially upon the family of Jehoram. He suffered and died unlamented from a horrible disease. The Arabians or their associated forces slew all of Jehoram's sons (II Chron. 21:17) except Ahaziah, the youngest, who succeeded his father at his death.

2. Second son of Ahab and Jezebel, he succeeded his brother Ahaziah, who died childless, as king of Israel. He reigned for 12 years (853-840 B.C.). Jehoram came to his end, with all his family, at the hand of Jehu (II Kings 9) and Jehu succeeded to the throne. 3. A priest in the days of Jehoshaphat whom the king sent with a group of learned Levites to go through Judah and to teach the people the law of the Lord (II Chron. 17:8).

Jehoshabeath (jē'hō-shăb'ē-ăth, **the oath of Jehovah**), the name of Jehosheba (q.v.) in II Chronicles 22:11.

Jehoshaphat (jē-hŏsh'ȧ-făt, **Jehovah is judge**). 1. Priest who blew trumpet before the ark of the Lord in David's time (I Chron. 15:24). 2. Son of Ahilud (II Sam. 8:16, etc.). 3. Son of Paruah, appointed by Solomon as officer of the commissariat over the tribe of Issachar (I Kings 4:17). 4. 4th king of Judah; son and successor of King

The Tomb of Jehoshaphat in the valley of Jehoshaphat, otherwise known as Kedron valley, outside of Jerusalem. © *MPS*

Asa; reigned 25 years, beginning c. 871 B.C. (II Chron. 17-20); took away high places and taught people law of the Lord; rebuked for joint enterprises with Ahab and Ahaziah; died c. 850 B.C. and his son Jehoram succeeded to throne. 5. Father of Jehu who destroyed house of Ahab (II Kings 9:2, 14).

Jehoshaphat, Valley of (jē-hŏsh′ȧ-făt, **Jehovah judgeth),** a name used in Joel 3:2, 12 as the scene where all nations shall be gathered by Jehovah for judgment.

Jehosheba (jē-hŏsh′ē-bȧ, **Jehovah is an oath),** sister of King Ahaziah (II Kings 11:2) and daughter of King Jehoram and his wicked consort Athaliah. She married the high priest Jehoiada. When Athaliah usurped the throne and slew the seed royal, Jehosheba (called Jehoshebeath in II Chron. 22:11), rescued the baby Joash, hid him with his nurse in a bedchamber in the temple, and preserved the Messianic line.

Jehoshua, Jehoshuah (jē-hosh′ū-ȧ, **Jehovah saves),** a variant spelling for Joshua (Num. 13:16; I Chron. 7:27 KJV).

Jehovah (jē-hō′vȧ), the English rendering of the Hebrew tetragram **Yhwh,** one of the names of God (Exod. 17:15). Its original pronunciation is unknown. The Jews took seriously the third commandment "Thou shalt not take the name of Jehovah thy God in vain; for Jehovah will not hold him guiltless that taketh his name in vain" (Exod. 20:7) and so, to keep from speaking the holy name carelessly, around 300 B.C. they decided not to pronounce it at all; but whenever in reading they came to it they spoke the word **adhonai** which means "Lord." This usage was carried into the LXX where the sacred name is rendered "Kurios," i.e. Lord. Consequently in the KJV, Lord occurs instead of Jehovah, whereas ASV renders the name "Jehovah." When the vowel points were added to the Hebrew consonantal text, the Massoretes (Jewish scribes) inserted into the Hebrew consonantal text the vowels for **adhonai.** The sacred name is derived from the verb "to be," and so implies that God is eternal ("Before Abraham was, I AM") and that He is the Absolute, i.e. the Uncaused One. The name "Jehovah" belongs especially to Him when He is dealing with His own, while "God" is used more when dealing with the Gentiles. See for instance II Chronicles 18:31 where "Jehoshaphat cried out and Jehovah helped him; and God moved them to depart from him."

There are ten combinations of the word "Jehovah" in the OT. Besides the five with which succeeding articles deal, are **Jehovah-ropheka,** "Jehovah that healeth thee" (Exod. 15:26); **Jehovah-meqaddeshkem,** "Jehovah who sanctifieth you" (Exod. 31:13); **Jehovah-tsabaoth,** "Jehovah of hosts" (I Sam. 1:3); **Jehovah-elyon,** "Jehovah Most High" (Ps. 7:17); and **Jehovah-roi,** "Jehovah, my Shepherd" (Ps. 23:1).

Jehovah-Jireh (jē-hō′vȧ-jī′rĕ, **Jehovah will provide),** name given by Abraham to place where he was ready to sacrifice Isaac (Gen. 22:14).

Jehovah-Nissi (jē-hō′vȧ-nĭs′ī, **Jehovah is my banner),** name given by Moses to altar he built as memorial of victory over Amalekites (Exod. 17:15).

Jehovah-shalom (jē-hō′vȧ-shā′lŏm, **Jehovah is peace),** name Gideon gave to altar at Ophra (Judg. 6:24).

Jehovah-shammah (jē-hō′vȧ-shă′mȧ, **Jehovah is there),** name given to heavenly Jerusalem in Ezekiel's vision (Ezek. 48:35m).

Jehovah-tsidkenu (jē-hō′vȧ-tsĭd-kē′nū, **Jehovah is our righteousness),** name given king who is to rule over Israel (Jer. 23:6) and his city (Jer. 33:16).

Jehozabad (jē-hŏz′ȧ-băd, **Jehovah has bestowed).** 1. Man who conspired against King Joash (II Chron. 24:26). 2. One of the eight sons of Obed-edom, a doorkeeper of the tabernacle in the days of David (I Chron. 26:4). 3. A Benjamite (II Chron. 17:18), commander of 180,000 soldiers prepared for war.

Jehozadak (jē-hōz′ȧ-dăk, **Jehovah is righteous),** high priest at time of Babylonian captivity (I Chron. 6:14, 15; Neh. 12:26); **Josedech** in Haggai and Zechariah; **Jozadak** in Ezra and Nehemiah.

Jehu (jē′hū). 1. Judahite (I Chron. 2:38). 2. Simeonite (I Chron. 4:35). 3. Benjamite (I Chron. 12:3). 4. Prophet; rebuked Baasha (I Kings 16:1, 7, 12) and Jehoshaphat (II Chron. 19:1-3). 5. 10th king of Israel; son of Jehoshaphat; slew Joram (II Kings 9:24-26), Ahaziah, king of Judah, and Jezebel, also worshipers of Baal; began dynasty which lasted more than 100 years.

Jehubbah (jē-hŭb′ȧ), an Asherite (I Chron. 7:34).

Jehucal (jē-hū′kăl, probably **Jehovah is able**), one whom King Zedekiah sent to Jeremiah, asking for prayers (Jer. 37:3).

Jehud (jē′hŭd), a town in the tribe of Dan, about seven miles nearly E of Joppa and near the modern Tel-Aviv (Josh 19:45).

Jehudi (jē-hū′dī, **a Jew**), one who sat with the princes in Jehoiakim's court and who secured from Baruch the prophecies of Jeremiah and read them to the king (Jer. 36:14, 21).

Jehudijah (jē′hū-dī′jă, **Jewess**), in I Chron. 4:18 this word is written as a proper name, but in the Hebrew it has the definite article, and ASV properly translates it "the Jewess" to distinguish her from Bithiah, the Egyptian princess, who was the other wife of Mered.

Jehush (jē′hŭsh), a Benjamite (I Chron. 8:39).

Jeiel (jē-ī′ĕl, probably **God has gathered**). 1. A Reubenite (I Chron. 5:7). 2. A Benjamite (I Chron. 9:35). 3. One of David's mighty men (I Chron. 11:44). 4. A harpist for King David (I Chron. 15:18, 21). 5. A Levite (II Chron. 20:14). 6. A scribe under Uzziah (II Chron. 26:11). 7. Levite chief under Josiah (II Chron. 35:9). 8. Man with a foreign wife (Ezra 10:43).

Jekabzeel (jē-kăb′zē-ĕl, **God gathers**), place re-inhabited by the men of Judah (Neh. 11:25).

Jekameam (jĕk′ă-mē-ăm, **the kinsman will raise up**), the head of a Levitical house (I Chron. 23:19; 24:23).

Jekamiah (jĕk′ȧ-mī′ȧ, **may Jehovah establish**). 1. Judahite (I Chron. 2:41).

2. Son of King Jeconiah (Jehoiachin); in AV Jecamiah (I Chron. 3:18).

Jekuthiel (jē-kū′thĭ-ĕl, **God will nourish**), a man of Judah, father of the inhabitants of Zanoah (I Chron. 4:18).

Jemima (jē-mī′mȧ, **a dove**), the first of the three daughters born to Job after his affliction.

Jemuel (jē-mū′ĕl, meaning unknown), a son of Simeon (Gen. 46:10; Exod. 6:15).

Jephthah (jĕf′thȧ, **he opens**), 9th judge of Israelites; history given in Judg. 11:1-12:7; driven from home by brothers because of his illegitimacy, but called back by Israel to fight Amorites, whom he defeated; sacrificed daughter because of rash promise. KJV has Jephthae in Heb. 11:32, where he is listed among the heroes of faith.

Jephunneh (jē-fŭn′ĕ, **it will be prepared**). 1. The father of Caleb (Num. 13:6). 2. A son of Jether, an Asherite (I Chron. 7:38).

Jerah (jē′rȧ, **moon**), an Arabian tribe (Gen. 10:26; I Chron. 1:20).

Jerahmeel (jē-rȧ′mē-ĕl, **may God have compassion**, or **God pities**). 1. A descendant of Judah (I Chron. 2:9, 25-27, 33, 42). 2. A Merarite Levite (I Chron. 24:29). 3. One of the three officers sent by King Jehoiakim to arrest Jeremiah and Baruch (Jer. 36:26).

Jerash (See Gerasa)

Jered (jē′rĕd, **descent**). 1. Son of Mahalaleel (I Chron. 1:2). 2. A Judahite (I Chron. 4:18).

Jeremiah (jĕr′ē-mī′ȧ, **Jehovah founds**, or perhaps, **exalts**), in KJV of NT "Jeremy" and "Jeremias" (Matt. 2:17; 16:14).

Jeremiah was one of the greatest Hebrew prophets. He was born into a priestly family of Anathoth, a Benjamite town two and one-half miles NE of Jerusalem. His father was Hilkiah (1:1), not to be confused with the high priest Hilkiah mentioned in II Kings 22, 23. Because of the autobiographical nature of his book, it is possible to understand his life, character and times better than those of any other Hebrew prophet.

Jeremiah was called to prophesy in the 13th year of King Josiah (626 B.C.), five years after the great revival of religion described in II Kings 23. This was a time of decision, great with both hope and foreboding. Looking back, we can know it as the last religious awakening in a series which only slowed down the idolatry and apostasy of the Hebrews, which apostasy finally plunged the nation into destruction. It was the time of the revival of the Babylonian empire.

Jeremiah's call is described in Chapter 1. The young priest pleads his youth (1:6) but God assures him that he will be strengthened for his task. Undoubtedly Jeremiah supported Josiah's reform (11:1-8; 17:19-27), but as time went on he realized its inadequacy to stave off national disaster (3:10). Upon Josiah's unhappy death (609 B.C.) Jeremiah mourned Judah's last good king (II Chron. 35:25) and life became more difficult for him. Jehoahaz, son of Josiah, reigned only three months before he was deported to Egypt. Jehoiakim, the brother of Jehoahaz, succeeded him and reigned 11 years. A strong ruler and a very wicked man, he tried to do away with the prophet, and failing that, to silence him. In Jehoiakim's fourth year Jeremiah dictated the first edition of his prophecies to Baruch, which the king promptly destroyed (36). During this reign Jeremiah preached his great temple discourse (7-10), which led to a plot to kill him, from which he was saved only by the intervention of friendly nobles who were a remnant of Josiah's administration (26). Judah was brought into the Babylonian orbit when Jerusalem fell to Nebuchadnezzar in 605 B.C. and a few Hebrews (Daniel among them) were deported to Babylon. Jehoiakim later rebelled against Babylon. Jeremiah opposed this strong-willed despot all his reign and predicted a violent death for him (22:13-19). It has been supposed that he fell in a palace coup.

The birthplace of Jeremiah, the little village of Anathoth, northeast of Jerusalem. © *MPS*

Jehoiachin, son of Jehoiakim, succeeded him to the throne. Jeremiah called this king Coniah and Jeconiah (24:1; 27:20; 29:2). After he had reigned only three months, the Babylonians attacked Jerusalem and carried off Jehoiachin to Babylon (597 B.C.) as Jeremiah had predicted (22: 24-30), together with many artisans and other important Jews.

For the events in Judah after the destruction of Jerusalem we are dependent almost exclusively on Jeremiah (40-45). The captors treated Jeremiah with kindness, giving him the choice of going to Babylon or remaining in Judah. He chose to stay behind with some of the common people who had been left in Judah when most of the Jews were deported. Gedaliah was made puppet governor over this little group. After civil unrest, in which Gedaliah was assassinated, the Jews fled to Egypt, forcing Jeremiah to accompany them. In Egypt, a very old man, he died.

Because his book is full of autobiographical sections—Jeremiah's "Confessions"—Jeremiah's personality can be understood more clearly than that of any other prophet. These outpourings of the human spirit are some of the most poignant and pathetic statements of the tension of a man under divine imperative to be found anywhere in Scripture. The most important are listed below:

10:23, 24	17:9-11, 14-18
11:18-12:6	18:18-23
15:10-21	20:7-18

Jeremiah's penetrating understanding of the religious condition of his people is seen in his emphasis on the inner spiritual character of true religion. The old covenant had failed; a new and better one will take its place and then God's law will be written on men's hearts (31:31-34). God will give His renewed people a heart to know Him (24:7). In this doctrine of the "new heart" Jeremiah unfolds the depth of human sin and predicts the intervention of divine grace (Heb. 8:1-9:28).

Six other Jeremiahs are briefly mentioned in the OT: a Benjamite and two Gadites who joined David at Ziklag (I Chron. 12:4, 10, 13), the head of a family in Manasseh (I Chron. 5:24), a native of Libnah and the father of Hamutal, wife of King Josiah and mother of Jehoahaz (II Kings 23:30, 31), and the son of Habaziniah, a Rechabite (Jer. 35:3).

Jeremiah, Book of. Jeremiah is a book of prophetic oracles, or sermons, together with much autobiographical and historical material which gives the background of these oracles.

The material contained in Jeremiah's book is not arranged in chronological order. The outline given below indicates what seems to have been the purpose of the present arrangement—to set forth a group of oracles against the Jewish nation, then to record selected events in the prophet's ministry, then to give certain preachments of Jeremiah against foreign nations, and finally to tell the story of the fall of Jerusalem. The record of Jerusalem's fall had been given in Chapter 39; the somewhat different account at the end of the book (chap. 52) is practically identical with II Kings 24, 25 and may have been added from that source to give a climactic conclusion to Jeremiah's oracles.

I. Jeremiah's oracles against the theocracy, 1:1-25:38.
  - A. The prophet's call, 1:1-19.
  - B. Reproofs and admonitions, mostly from the time of Josiah, 2:1-20:18.
  - C. Later prophecies, 21:1-25:38.

II. Events in the life of Jeremiah, 26:1-45:5.
  - A. The temple sermon and Jeremiah's arrest, 26:1-24.
  - B. The yoke of Babylon, 27:1-29:32.
  - C. The book of consolation, 30:1-33:26.
  - D. Some of Jeremiah's experiences before Jerusalem fell, 34:1-36:32.
  - E. Jeremiah during the siege and destruction of Jerusalem, 37:1-39:18.
  - F. The last years of Jeremiah, 40:1-45:5.

III. Jeremiah's oracles against foreign nations 46:1-51:64.
  - A. Against Egypt, 46:1-28.
  - B. Against the Philistines, 47:1-7.
  - C. Against Moab, 48:1-47.
  - D. Against the Ammonites, 49:1-6.
  - E. Against Edom, 49:7-22.
  - F. Against Damascus, 49:23-27.
  - G. Against Kedar and Hazor, 49:28-33.
  - H. Against Elam, 49:34-39.
  - I. Against Babylon, 50:1-51:64.

IV. Appendix: The fall of Jerusalem and related events, 52:1-34.

Jeremoth (jĕr'ē-mŏth, **swollen, thick).** 1. A Benjamite (I Chron. 7:8). 2. An-

An aerial view of the mound of ancient Jericho (foreground) in the Plain of Jericho, looking southward over the modern city. © MPS

other Benjamite (I Chron. 8:14). 3. A Levite (I Chron. 23:23; 24:30). 4. The head of the 15th course of musicians for David (I Chron. 25:4, 22). 5. A prince of Naphtali (I Chron. 27:19). 6. Three men who consented to put away their foreign wives (Ezra 10:26, 27, 29).

Jeriah (jē-rī'ȧ, **Jehovah sees),** head of a Levitical house (I Chron. 23:19; 24: 23; 26:31).

Jeribai (jĕr'ĭ-bī, **Jehovah pleads),** a son of Elnaam, and one of David's mighty men (I Chron. 11:46).

Jericho (jĕr'ĭ-kō, **moon city), city** 5 miles W of the Jordan and 7 miles N of Dead Sea, c. 800 feet below sea level; an oasis with tropical climate. There are three Jerichos: the OT city, the NT city, and a modern town, all near each other. Probably the oldest city in the world; strategically located to control ancient trade route from the E to Palestine; destroyed by Joshua (Josh. 6); given to Benjamin (Josh. 18: 21); rebuilt by Hiel (I Kings 16:34). OT Jericho excavated by John Garstang and Kathleen Kenyon.

Jerimoth (jĕr'ĭ-mŏth, **thick, swollen). 1.** A Benjamite (I Chron. 7:7). 2. A Benjamite who joined David at Ziklag (I Chron. 12:5). 3. Son of David (II Chron. 11:18). 4. Temple overseer (II Chron. 31:13). 5. A Levite musician (I Chron. 25:4). 6. A Merarite (I Chron. 24:30).

Jerioth (jĕr'ĭ-ŏth, **tent curtains),** one of Caleb's wives (I Chron. 2:18).

Jeroboam I (jĕr'ō-bō'ăm, **the people become numerous),** 1st king of Israel after division of kingdom, overseer of public works under Solomon (I Kings 11:28); told by the prophet Ahijah that he would become king of 10 tribes (I Kings 11:29-40); fled to Egypt because Solomon sought to kill him (I Kings 11:40); became king with Shechem as capital (I Kings 12:1-25); built centers of worship with golden calves at Dan and Bethel (I Kings 12:25-33); downfall foretold by the prophet Ahijah (I Kings 13, 14).

Jeroboam II (jĕr'ō-bō'ăm), 13th king of Israel (c. 785-754 B.C.); son and successor of Jehoash, king of Israel; successful in war with adjacent nations, and extended territory of Israel; moral corruption and idolatry prevalent during his reign; contemporary prophets: Hosea, Joel, Jonah, Amos; succeeded by son Zechariah (II Kings 14:23-29).

Jeroham (jē-rō'hăm, **may he be compassionate,** or **be pitied** (by God). **1.** Grandfather of Samuel (I Sam. 1:1; I Chron. 6:27, 34). 2. A Benjamite (I Chron. 8:27). 3. Another Benjamite (I Chron. 9:8), may be same as following. 4. Priest (I Chron. 9:12; Neh. 11: 12). 5. Father of two of David's recruits at Ziklag (I Chron. 12:7). **6.** Father of Azarel (I Chron. 27:22). 7. Father of Azariah who helped to put Joash on the throne of Judah (II Chron. 23:1).

Jerubbaal (See Gideon)

Jerubbesheth (See Gideon)

Jeruel (jē-rōō'ĕl, **founded by God),** a wilderness in Judah, in the vicinity of En-gedi (II Chron. 20:16).

Jerusalem was the royal city, the capital of the only kingdom God has (thus far) established among men; here the temple was erected, and here alone, during the kingdom age, were sacrifices legitimately offered. This was the city of the prophets, as well as the kings of David's line. Here occurred the death, resurrection, and ascension of Jesus Christ, David's greater Son. Upon an assembled group in this city the Holy Spirit descended at Pentecost, giving birth to the Christian Church, and here the first great Church Council was held. This city has been the preeminent objective of the pilgrimages of devout men and women for over 2,000 years.

While the word **Jerusalem** is Semitic, it apparently was not a name given to the city for the first time by the Hebrew people. Far back in the time of the Tell-el-Amarna (1400 B.C.) letters, it was called **U-ru-sa-lim,** that is, a city of Salim, generally taken to mean "city of peace."

The Rabbis say there are 60 different names for Jerusalem in the Bible, a characteristic exaggeration, but truly there are a great number. Jerusalem itself occurs about 600 times in the OT, though it is not found in Job, Hosea, Jonah, Nahum, Habakkuk, and Haggai.

Jerusalem appears in the NT after the close of the Book of Acts rather infrequently, four times near the conclusion of the epistle to the Romans (15:17, 25, 26, 31), once at the close of the first letter to the Corinthians (16: 3), and again in the Galatian epistle (1:17, 18 and 2:1). The most frequently used name for this city, apart from Jerusalem, of course, is **Zion,** which

A first glimpse of Jerusalem from the belfry of the Church of the Holy Sepulchre, looking out over the Dome of the Rock (mosque) in the Mount of Olives. © *MPS*

occurs over 100 times in the OT, beginning as early as II Kings 19:21, and found most frequently in the Book of Psalms and the prophecy of Isaiah (1:8; 4:4, 5; 62:11). Zion appears in the NT in some very interesting passages. Twice on the lips of our Lord (Matt. 21:5; John 12:15); twice in the epistle to the Romans, with spiritual significance (9:33 and 11:36); and similarly in I Peter 2:6 and Revelation 14:1. Jerusalem is often called in the historical books and once in the prophetical writings, "the city of David" (II Sam. 5:7, 9; 6:10-16; Neh. 3:15 and 12:37; Isa. 22:9, etc.). This title is later, on one occasion, applied to Bethlehem (Luke 2:4, 11).

The greatest group of titles for this city are those which identify it as **the city of God.** It is called exactly this in the Psalms, as well as in the NT (Pss. 46:4; 48:1, 8; 87:3; Heb. 12:22; Rev. 3:12). It is also called the city of Jehovah (Isa. 60:14); the mountain of the Lord (Isa. 2:3 and 30:39); the mountain of Jehovah of hosts (Zech. 8:3); the holy mountain of Jehovah (Isa. 27:13; 66:20); Zion of the Holy One of Israel (Isa. 60:13). The Lord Himself refers to it, and to no other place, as "my city" (Isa. 45:13), or more often, "my holy mountain" (Isa. 11:9; 56:7; 57:13; 65:11, 25; 66:20). Because it is the city of God, where He has put His name, it is often referred to as the Holy City (Isa. 48:2; 52:1; Neh. 11:1-18), a title twice used by Matthew (in 4:5 and 27:53) and once of a future event by St. John (Rev. 11:2), and used in referring to our eternal heavenly home at the close of the Scriptures (Rev. 21:2; 22:19). Generally, the phrase, "the holy mountain," refers to this city (Ps. 48:1; Isa. 11:9; Dan. 11:45, etc.). Once it is given the beautiful name of Hephzibah, meaning "My delight is in her" (Isa. 62:4).

Nothing is known of the history of Jerusalem, either from Biblical or non-Biblical writings, from the time of Joshua's death until the capture of this city by David (II Sam. 5:6-10; prob. 998 B.C.). No doubt the fortress which David took is that which later came to be called Zion, located on the SE hill, and outside of the present walls of the city. Kraeling estimates that the population of this city during David's time did not exceed 1,230, estimating it as 250 people per acre. Later David purchased "the threshing floor of Araunah, the Jebusite" (II Sam. 24:18; I Chron. 21:18-28) on which site the great Temple of Solomon later was erected. (See Temple.) Upon finishing the temple, Solomon then built a magnificent palace to the N of it, of which there is not the slightest vestige today.

With the death of Solomon, the glory of Israel, and so also the glory of Jerusalem, began to dim. In the fifth year of Rehoboam, 917 B.C., Shishak, king of Egypt, without any struggle whatever, coming up to Jerusalem, "took away the treasures of the house of Jehovah, and the treasures of the king's house; he even took away all: and he took away all the shields of gold which Solomon had made" (I Kings 14:26; II Chron. 12:9). This is the first of eight different plunderings of the Jerusalem Temple occurring within a little more than 300 years.

Entire books have been written, of course, on the single subject of Jesus and the city of Jerusalem. Here we can only summarize the relevant data. One is safe in saying that of the four Gospel writers, it is Luke who, though a Gentile, seems to have had the greatest interest in this city, so that the opening events of our Lord's life occurring here are exclusively in the third Gospel and many of the concluding events are here also alone recorded. We begin with the annunciation to Zacharias, a priest in the temple (Luke 1:5-22). Our Lord, when a babe, was taken up to Jerusalem for what is called His presentation (Luke 2:22-38). Luke alone records our Lord's visit to the city at the age of 12. The principal episodes down to the last year of our Lord's life are given exclusively by John. If we place the death of our Lord in A.D. 30, then in April A.D. 27, we have the first cleansing of the temple (John 2:13-25); on April 28 the healing of the man at the pool of Bethesda (John 5:1-47); on October 29 He goes up to Jerusalem at the time of the Feast of Tabernacles where we have a detailed record (John 7:2; 10:21); on December 29, He is in Jerusalem for the Feast of Dedication (Luke 10:38-42). Of course, as all know, the final week of our Lord's life was spent in and near the city (Matt. 27:1-27:66; Mark 11:1-15:47; Luke 19:29-23:56; John 12:12-19:42). Of the five appearances of our Lord on Easter Sunday, four of them are found only in Luke's Gospel (chap. 24). The sixth appearance in Jerusalem a week later is recorded only by John (20:26-29). In Jerusalem our Lord appeared to all the disciples (Acts 1:1-8 and Luke 24:49), and from the Mount of Olives nearby He ascended (Luke 24:50-53).

Our Lord made four principal statements about the city, all of them with a note of sadness. First of all, in stating that He must go up to Jerusalem He declared, "It cannot be that a prophet perish out of Jerusalem" (Luke 13:33). On Tuesday of Holy Week, He cried out, "O Jerusalem, Jerusalem, that killeth the prophets, and stoneth them that are sent unto her! how oft would I have gathered thy children together, even as a hen gathereth her chickens under her wings, and ye would not!" (Matt. 23:37). We are told by Luke that as He wept over the city, He said sadly, "If thou hadst known in this day, even thou, the things which belong unto peace! but now they are hid from thine eyes" (Luke 19:42). Finally, our Lord declared that the buildings of that city, and their very walls, would be thrown down, and that Jerusalem would be trodden down of the Gentiles until the times of the Gentiles are fulfilled (Matt. 24:2; Mark 13:2; Luke 21:24).

The Book of Acts opens with a group of the followers of Jesus meeting together in an Upper Room in Jerusalem, probably where the Lord's Supper was held, waiting for the fulfillment of the promise of Christ, that they might be endued with power from on high. The Church is born in Jerusalem on the Day of Pentecost (Acts 2). The early persecutions occurred in that city toward these initial be-

A section of the east city wall of Jerusalem — on the right, a part of the old Herodian wall, and to the left, the closed Golden Gate. © MPS

lievers, and the Sanhedrin that condemned Christ was now confronted with the phenomenon of a growing company of the faithful of the crucified and risen Lord. In this city, the first great crisis of the Church was successfully faced in the first Council, deciding forever the question of salvation wholly by grace, apart from works (Acts 15). Years later in this same city, the Apostle Paul was arrested, mobbed in the temple and falsely accused (Acts 21 and 22).

The destruction of the city, after a siege of 143 days by Roman armies, under the leadership of Titus, while predicted in the Gospels, is not, strange to say, actually recorded anywhere in the NT. Before this dreadful event concluded, 600,000 Jews were slain and thousands more were led away into captivity. "Jerusalem has no history for 60 years after its destruction" (C. R. Conder).

Passing over the next several hundred years, we come down to the first World War. General Allenby of the British forces entered the city on foot, December 9, 1917, and on October 31 of the next year, the armistice was signed, when 400 years of Turkish misrule came to an end. "Thus again, after more than seven centuries, was Jerusalem entered by a Christian conqueror. Not a stone of the city had been injured. Not a soldier was allowed to enter the city except on duty, until all sacred spots had been placed under guards consisting of men of the religions to which such spots were respectively sacred" (H. O. Lock: **The Conquerors of Palestine,** London, 1920, p. 108).

On April 24, 1920, the mandate for Palestine and Transjordan was assigned to Great Britain, and for nearly 30 years she suffered one reverse after another in her attempt to rule this country. On May 14, 1948, the British mandate terminated, and the National Council at Tel-Aviv proclaimed the State of Israel. There followed the bitter, often brutal war for Palestine, as a result of which nearly a million Arabs were driven from their homes. At this time there were about 100,000 Jews in the city of Jerusalem, about ten per cent of all that there were in Palestine. By the spring of the next year, Israel was recognized by 45 governments.

Until Israel's war for independence, the city within the walls for centuries had been divided into nearly four equal quarters: on the SE the Jewish quarter, on the SW the Armenian, in the NE, the largest of the four areas, was the Moslem quarter, and in the NW the Christian quarter. There are, of course, no Jews living within the walls of Jerusalem today.

In 1830 it was said by those visiting the city that there were not 100 Jews living within the walls. In 1838, there were but 3,000 Jews in Jerusalem, and only 11,000 in all Palestine. In 1872 there was a slight proportionate gain — of 21,000 in all of Palestine, 10,600 were in Jerusalem. By 1900 there was further gain — of a population in the city of 46,500, there were 29,000 Jews, 8,500 Moslems and 9,000 Christians. In 1915 there were 50,000 Jews in the Holy City. Israel's War for Independence has radically altered this entire matter — in 1957, the old city, Jerusalem proper, had a population of 80,000, of whom **none** were Jews. The city of Jerusalem, Israel, to the N and W of the old city, in March, 1959, had a population of 156,000, with Tel Aviv-Jaffa far ahead, with 380,000. At that time the total population of Israel was 2,054,434.

Though there are scores of prophecies in the Bible relating to cities, rivers, and nations, no Bible encyclopedia ever includes these matters in its articles on such geographical terms. Here it is possible to give only a bare summary of those pertaining to Jerusalem.

1. In Deuteronomy 12, though no name is mentioned, six times reference is made to the future place of the sanctuary, "the place which Jehovah your God shall choose" (See also I Kings 8:29, 48).

2. The promise that Sennacherib's attempt to capture the city would fail (Isa. 29:7; 30:19; 31:4, 5; II Kings 19:32-34).

3. Of the destruction of the city by Nebuchadnezzar (II Kings 22:16, 17; 23:7; II Chron. 34:24, 25; Isa. 4:3-5; 10:11, 12; 22:9-11; 32:13-15; 34:8; 39:6; 64:10, 11; Jer. 4:1-6, 22, 23; 7:14, 32, 34; 9:11, 19; 11:6, 11-13; 13:9; 13, 27; 15:5; 16:1-21; 17:24-27; 19:8, etc.; 21:5, 6, 9, 10; 22:4-9; 35:17; 38:2, 17-23; Ezek. 8:9; 24, etc.).

4. The desecration of the city by Antiochus Epiphanes (Dan. 8:11-14; 11:30-32).

5. The destruction of the city by the Romans, under Titus (Dan. 9:26;

The Ecce Homo Arch on the Via Dolorosa, traditional site of Pilate's declaration, "Behold, the Man." © *MPS*

The reading of General Allenby's proclamation, ending 400 years of Turkish rule, December 11, 1917. At the entrance to the tower of David, General Allenby just to the right of the gate in the front row. © *MPS*

Luke 13:33-35; 19:41-44; 21:6, 20, 24; Matt. 24:2; Mark 13:2).

6. A prophecy concerning this city during the present age (Dan. 9:26; Zech. 12:3; Luke 21:24).

(A very remarkable passage).

7. The Jewish people at the end of this age will return to Palestine, and this, of course, includes Jerusalem sometimes specifically designated (Joel 3:1; Isa. 49:22, 23 [probably]). This includes the erection of some kind of temple in the Holy City (Dan. 9:27; 12:11; Jer. 31:8, 9; Isa. 55:11; 60:1-3; Matt. 24:15; Mark 13:14; II Thess. 2:3, 4).

8. The episode of the two witnesses (Rev. 11).

9. A final assault upon this city by the nations of the earth (Joel 3:9-12; Isa. 29:1-7, 31-34; Zech. 14:1-3).

10. A cleansing of the city (Isa. 1: 25, 26; 4:3, 4; Joel 3:17; Zech. 14:20, 21).

11. A city that will ultimately know, and permanently, the presence of the glory of God (Ezek. 43:1, 2; Isa. 62: 2); peace (Ps. 122:6-9; Isa. 60:17; 66: 12); and joy (Ps. 53:6; Isa. 5:11).

12. To this city the nations of the earth will come for instruction and blessing (Isa. 2:2-4; Ps. 102:21, 22).

There is no doubt about it that even in the OT, Jerusalem, especially when referred to as Zion, sometimes was used to express spiritual rather than geographical or historical ideas. In the NT such interpretations are twice recognized by the Apostle Paul, who in that enigmatical passage speaks of "Jerusalem that is above is free, which is our mother" (Gal. 5:26), and the writer of the Epistle to the Hebrews, in a passage that is also fraught with difficulties, tells these Hebrew Christians that they have already "Come unto Mount Zion, and unto the city of the living God, the heavenly Jerusalem" (12:22). The exalted conception of the yet-to-come New Jerusalem, as set forth in the Apocalypse, is well known to everyone (Rev. 3:12; 21:2 ff.).

Jerusalem, New, city of God referred to in Rev. 3:12 and Rev. 21:2 as coming down out of heaven from God. Gal. 4:26 describes the New Jerusalem as the mother of believers.

Jerusha, Jerushah (jē-rōō'shȧ, **possessed, i.e., married),** the wife of Uzziah, king of Judah, and mother of Jotham, his successor (II Kings 15:33; II Chron. 27:1).

Jesaiah, Jeshaiah (jē-sā′yȧ, jē-shā′yȧ, **Jehovah saves).** 1. A son of Jeduthun, and a musician in David's reign (I Chron. 25:3, 15). 2. A Levite, one of David's treasurers (I Chron. 26:25). 3. Grandson of Zerubbabel (I Chron. 3:21). 4. One who returned from Babylon with Ezra (Ezra 8:7). 5. A descendant of Merari (Ezra 8:19). 6. A Benjamite (Neh. 11:7).

Jeshanah (jĕsh′ȧ-nȧ or jē-shā′na, **old),** a town near Bethel, in Ephraim, captured by Abijah from the Northern Kingdom (II Chron. 13:19).

Jesharelah (jĕsh′ȧ-rē′lȧ, meaning doubtful), the ancestral head of the seventh course of musicians (I Chron. 25:14), called Asarelah in Verse 2.

Jeshebeab (jē-shĕb′ē-ăb), the ancestral head of the 14th course of priests (I Chron. 24:13).

Jesher (jē′shēr, **uprightness),** a son of Caleb (I Chron. 2:18).

Jeshimon (jē-shī′mŏn, **a waste, a desert).** The word is often used as a common noun to refer to the desert of Sinai (Deut. 32:10; Pss. 78:40; 106:14; Isa. 43:19, etc.), and is usually translated "desert." Sometimes it is used as a geographical term, and probably refers to two different districts. 1. The "desert" in the Jordan Valley, NE of the Dead Sea, which was overlooked from Pisgah (Num. 21:20; 23:28). 2. The sterile plateau into which David retreated before Saul, near Ziph and Maon, SE of Hebron (I Sam. 23:19, 24; 26:1, 3).

Jeshishai (jē-shĭsh′ā-ī, **aged),** a Gadite (I Chron. 5:14).

Jeshohaiah (jĕsh-ō-hā′yȧ), a prince in Simeon (I Chron. 4:36).

Jeshua, Jeshuah (jĕsh′ū-ȧ, another form of Joshua, **Jehovah is salvation).** 1. A name used once for Joshua (Neh. 8:17). 2. A priest (I Chron. 24:11). 3. A family which returned with Zerubbabel from Babylon to Jerusalem (Ezra 2:6; Neh. 7:11). 4. A Levite in charge of the distribution of tithes in Hezekiah's time (II Chron. 31:15). 5. The high priest who returned with Zerubbabel (Ezra 2:2; Neh. 7:7, called "Joshua" in Haggai 1:1 and in Zech. 3:1ff). 6. A leading Levitical family (Ezra 2:40; 3:9; Neh. 7:43; 8:7; 9:4; 10:9). From the last passage, it appears that Jeshua was the son of Azaniah. 7. A post-Exilic town in the S of Judah (Neh. 11:26).

Jeshurun, Jesurun (jĕsh′ū-rŭn, jĕs′ū-rŭn, **upright one),** a poetical or ideal title of Israel. Except in Deuteronomy 32:15, where it is used in reproach of Israel, it is always used as a title of honor (Deut. 33:5, 26; Isa. 44:2).

Jesiah (jē-sī′ȧ). I Chronicles 23:20. See Isshiah.

Jesimiel (jē-sĭm′ĭ-ĕl, **God establishes),** a prince of Simeon (I Chron. 4:36).

Jesse (jĕs′ē), son of Obed. Grandson of Boaz, whose wife was Ruth the Moabitess (Ruth 4:18-22). From his descent and from the fact that when Saul pursued David he entrusted his parents to the care of the king of Moab (I Sam. 22:3, 4), we can assume that he was the chief man of his village. He had eight sons, of whom the youngest was David (I Sam. 17:12-14), and two daughters, the latter being by a different wife from David's mother (I Chron. 2:16; cf. II Sam. 17:25). Jesse lived at Bethlehem, and probably had land outside the town wall, like Boaz. When Samuel went to Jesse to anoint a king from among his sons, neither of them at first discerned God's choice. Jesse had not even thought it worth while to call his youngest son to the feast (I Sam. 16:11). He is almost always mentioned in connection with his son David.

Jesui (jĕs′ū-ī). 1. A son of Asher (Gen. 46:17; Num. 26:44; I Chron. 7:30). 2. A son of Saul (I Sam. 14:49).

Jesus, Jesus Christ (See Christ)

Jether (jē′thēr, **abundance, excellence).** 1. In Exodus 4:18 for Jethro, father-in-law of Moses (see KJVm). 2. Gideon's eldest son (Judg. 8:20, 21) 3. The father of Amasa, Abaslom's commander-in-chief (I Kings 2:5). 4. A descendant of Judah (I Chron. 2:32). 5. A Judahite (I Chron. 4:17). 6. A man of Asher, apparently the same as Ithran, son of Zophah (cf. I Chron. 7:37 with vs. 38).

Jetheth (jē′thĕth), Edomite chieftan (Gen. 36:40; I Chron. 1:51).

Jethlah (jĕth′lȧ, **a hanging** or **lofty place),** a town of Dan (Josh. 19:42).

Jethro (jĕth′rō, **excellence),** a priest of Midian and father-in-law of Moses (Exod. 3:1). Reuel, which means friend of God, seems to have been his personal name (Exod. 2:18; 3:1), and Jethro, his honorary title. When Moses fled from Egypt to Midian, he was welcomed into the household of Jethro. After the deliverance from Egypt, before the Israelites reached Sinai, Jethro came to see Moses, bringing his daughter Zipporah, David's wife,

The Valley of Jethro, or Jethro's Pass, below Mount Sinai. © *MPS*

and her two sons (Exod. 18:1-7). We are told that he "rejoiced for all the goodness which Jehovah had done to Israel," and offered a burnt offering to Jehovah. When he saw how occupied Moses was in deciding disputes among his people, he suggested the appointment of judges of various grades to help him dispose of cases of minor importance. Moses acted on his advice. Jethro then returned to his own country.

Jetur (jē′têr), a people descended from Ishmael (Gen. 25:15; I Chron. 1:31; 5:18f). The Itureans of NT times.

Jeuel (jē-ū′ĕl). 1. A man of Judah who with 690 of his clan lived at Jerusalem (I Chron. 9:6). 2. A Levite under Hezekiah (II Chron. 29:13). 3. A leader of Ezra's company (Ezra 8:13, Jeiel in KJV).

Jeush (jē′ŭsh, **he comes to help).** 1. A son of Esau (Gen. 36:5). 2. A Benjamite (I Chron. 7:10). 3. A Gershonite Levite (I Chron. 23:10, 11). 4. A descendant of Jonathan (I Chron. 8:39, Jehush KJV). 5. A son of Rehoboam (II Chron. 11:19).

Jeuz (jē′ŭz, **he counsels),** a Benjamite (I Chron. 8:10).

Jew. Originally it denoted one belonging to the tribe of Judah or to the two tribes of the Southern Kingdom (II Kings 16:6; 25:25), but later its meaning was extended, and it was applied to anyone of the Hebrew race who returned from the Captivity. As most of the exiles came from Judah, and as they were the main historical representatives of ancient Israel, the term Jew came finally to comprehend all of the Hebrew race throughout the world (Esth. 2:5; Matt. 2:2). As early as the days of Hezekiah the language of Judah was called Jewish. In the OT the adjective applies only to the Jews' language or speech (II Kings 18:26, 28; Neh. 13:24; Isa. 36:11, 13). In the Gospels "Jews" (always pl.) is the usual term for Israelites; and in the NT Jews (Israelites) and Gentiles are sometimes contrasted (Mark 7:3; John 2:6; Acts 10:28). Paul warns against "Jewish fables" in Titus 1:14, and speaks of the "Jews' religion" in Galatians 1:13, 14.

Jewel, Jewelry. Articles of jewelry in OT times: diadems, bracelets, necklaces, anklets, rings for fingers, gold nets for hair, pendants, head-tire gems, amulets and pendants with magical meanings, jeweled perfume and ointment boxes, crescents for camels; used for personal adornment and utility and for religious festivals. Not much said about jewelry in NT; most condemnatory (I Tim. 2:9; James 2:2). The New Jerusalem is adorned with jewels (Rev. 21:19).

Jezaniah (jĕz-ȧ-nī'ȧ, probably **Jehovah hears**), a Maacathite captain at the fall of Jerusalem (II Kings 25:23; Jer. 40:7, 8; 42:1).

Jezebel (jĕz'ĕ-bel). 1. Daughter of Ethbaal, king of the Zidonians, and queen of Ahab, king of Israel (c. 874-853 B.C.). To please her, Ahab built a temple and an altar to Baal in Samaria (I Kings 16:32). Four hundred fifty prophets of Baal ate at her table (I Kings 18:19). She slew all the prophets of Jehovah on whom she could lay her hands (I Kings 18:4-13). When she was told of the slaughter of the prophets of Baal by Elijah, she threatened his life, and he was obliged to flee. In II Kings 9:7 we are told that the slaying of Ahab's family was a punishment for the persecution of the prophets of Jehovah by Jezebel. Later, she secured Naboth's vineyard for Ahab by causing its owner to be judicially murdered (I Kings 21). When Elijah heard of this crime, he told Ahab that God's vengeance would fall upon him and that dogs would eat Jezebel's body by the wall of Jezreel. The prophecy was fulfilled when, 11 years after the death of Ahab, Jehu executed pitiless vengeance upon the royal household. (II Kings 9:7, 30-37). See Jezreel. 2. Rev. 2:20 mentions "the woman Jezebel, who calleth herself a prophetess," and led some members of the Christian Church there to commit spiritual fornication. This may be a symbolic name, given because of a resemblance between her and the idolatrous wife of Ahab.

Jezer (jē'zẽr, **form, purpose**), a son of Naphtali (Gen. 46:24; Num. 26:49; I Chron. 7:13).

Jeziah (jē-zī'ȧ, **Jehovah unites**), a man who put away his foreign wife (Ezra 10:25).

Jeziel (jē'zĭ-ĕl), a Benjamite who became one of David's recruits at Ziklag (I Chron. 12:3).

Jezliah (jĕz-lī'ȧ, **Jehovah delivers**), a Benjamite (I Chron. 8:18).

Jezoar (jē-zō'ẽr, **the shining one**), an Ashurite (I Chron. 4:5-7).

Jezrahiah (jĕz-rȧ-hī'ȧ, **Jehovah appears or shines**). 1. A descendant of Issachar, (I Chron. 7:3). 2. A musician (Neh. 12:42).

Jezreel (jĕz'rē-ĕl, jez'rēl, **God soweth**). 1. A city on the border of the territory of Issachar (Josh. 19:18), not far from Mount Gilboa. Jehu ordered that the heads of Ahab's 70 sons be placed in heaps at the gate of Jezreel (II Kings 10:1-11). Jezebel met her death by being thrown from a window of the palace in Jezreel, and it was there that her body was eaten by dogs (II Kings 9:30-35). Jezreel was the scene of the meetings between Elijah and Ahab (I Kings 21:17ff). 2. A town in the hill country of Judah from which David obtained his wife Ahinoam (I Sam. 25:43; 27:3). 3. A descendant of Judah (I Chron. 4:3). 4. A son of the prophet Hosea, so called because God had declared that He would avenge the blood of Jezreel on the house of Jehu (Hos. 1:4, 5).

Jibsam (jĭb'săm, **fragrant**), a descendant of Issachar (I Chron. 7:2).

Jidlaph (jĭd'lăf), son of Nahor and Milcah (Gen. 22:22).

Jimna (jĭm'nȧ), son of Asher (Num. 26:44).

Jiphtah (jĭf'tȧ), an unidentified town in the Shephelah of Judah (Josh. 15:43).

Jiphthah-el (jĭf'thȧ-ĕl), a valley on the N border of Zebulun (Josh. 19:14, 27).

Joab (jō'ăb, **Jehovah is father**). 1. Son of Zeruiah, the half-sister of David (II Sam. 2:18); brother of Asahel and Abishai (I Chron. 2:16); slew Abner (II Sam. 3:22-39); became David's commander-in-chief (I Chron. 11:4-

The so-called Tower of Jezebel in the village of Jezreel on the Plain of Esdraelon. © *MPS*

9); defeated Syria, Edom, Ammon (II Sam. 10-12); brought about murder of Uriah (II Sam. 11); killed Absalom (II Sam. 18:9-15) and Amasa (II Sam. 20:4-13); supported Adonijah (I Kings 1); killed at order of Solomon (I Kings 2:28-34). 2. Judahite (I Chron. 4:14). 3. Founder of family of returned exiles (Ezra 2:6; 8:9; Neh. 7:11). 4. Village, apparently in Judah (I Chron. 2:54). In KJV name is "Ataroth, the house of Joab."

Joah (jō′ȧ, **Jehovah is brother).** 1. A son of Obed-edom (I Chron. 26:4). 2. A Levite (I Chron. 6:21). 3. Son of Asaph and recorder under King Hezekiah (II Kings 18:18, 26; Isa. 36:3, 11, 22). 4. Son of Joahaz and recorder under King Josiah (II Chron. 34:8).

Joahaz (jō′ȧ-hăz, **Jehovah has grasped)** father of Joah, the recorder of King Josiah (II Chron. 34:8).

Joanna (jō-ăn′ȧ). 1. The wife of Chuza, Herod's steward. She was one of the women who ministered to Jesus and His disciples of their substance during His Galilean ministry (Luke 8:2, 3) and went to the tomb with the intention of embalming the body of Jesus (Luke 23:55, 56; 24:10). 2. An ancestor of Christ mentioned in Luke's genealogy (3:27). He lived about 500 B.C.

Joash, I (jō′ăsh, **Jehovah has given),** a shorter form of "Jehoash." 1. Father of Gideon (Judg. 6:11, 15). Although Gideon says that the family was the poorest in Manasseh, Joash was undoubtedly a man of substance, as Gideon was able to command ten servants to destroy the altar of Baal and the Asherah (Judg. 6:27, 34). 2. A son of Ahab (I Kings 22:26; II Chron. 18:25). 3. A Benjamite who joined David's recruits at Ziklag (I Chron. 12:3). 4. A man of Judah (I Chron. 4:22). 5. Son of Ahaziah, king of Judah. When Joash was an infant, his father was murdered, and he too would have been slain with the rest of the royal family, had not the late king's sister hidden him in the temple. In the seventh year he was brought out and crowned king. He reigned for 40 years. He led his people into idolatry and when Zechariah, the son of Jehoiada, denounced his apostasy, Joash had him murdered. After a long illness, he was slain in his bed by his servants for the murder of Zechariah (II Kings 12:20; II Chron. 24:25). 6. Son of Jehoahaz, king of Israel. He began to reign c. 800 B.C., and reigned 16 years. Friend to Elijah. He was succeeded by his son, Jeroboam II.

Joash, II (jō′ăsh, **Jehovah has come to help).** 1. A Benjamite (I Chron. 7:8). 2. One of David's officers (I Chron. 27:28).

Joatham (jō′ȧ-thăm), the KJV for RV "Jotham" (Matt. 1:9). King of Judah, the son of Uzziah.

Job (jōb, meaning **uncertain),** chief character of Book of Job, one of the wisdom books of the OT and great literary masterpiece, written in form of poetry; author unknown and date unknown, but many scholars favor Solomonic age; deals with justice of God in His dealings with human beings. Outline —

I. Desolation: The Trial of Job's Wisdom. 1:1-2:10.
II. Complaint: The Way of Wisdom Lost. 2:11-3:26
III. Judgment: The Way of Wisdom Darkened and Illuminated. 4:1-41:34.
   A. The Verdicts of Men. 4:1-37:24.
      1. First Cycle of Debate. 4:1-14:22.
      2. Second Cycle of Debate. 15:1-21:34.
      3. Third Cycle of Debate. 22:1-31:40.
      4. Ministry of Elihu. 32:1-37:24.
   B. The Voice of God. 38:1-41:34.
IV. Confession: The Way of Wisdom Regained. 42:1-6.
V. Restoration: The Triumph of Job's Wisdom. 42:7-17.

The Book of Job identifies the way of the covenant with the way of wisdom (cf. 28:28) and so brings philosophy under the authority of divine revelation.

No comprehensive answer is given to the problem of suffering since theodicy is not the book's major theme; nevertheless, considerable light is afforded. In addition to the prologue's contribution is that of Elihu, who traces the mystery to the principle of divine grace; sufferings are a sovereign gift, calling to repentance and life. Moreover, impressive assurance is given that God as a just and omnipotent Lord will ultimately visit both the curses and blessings of the covenant on His subjects according to righteousness. Especially significant are the insights Job himself attains into the role

God will play as his heavenly vindicator. Job utters in raw faith what progressive revelation elaborates in the doctrines of the eschatological theophany, resurrection of the dead, and final redemptive judgment. This vision does not reveal the why of the particular sufferings of Job or any other believer, but it does present the servants of God with a framework for hope.

Jobab (jō'băb, **to call loudly, howl**). 1. An Arabian tribe descended from Joktan (Gen. 10:29; I Chron. 1:23).

2. The second king of Edom (Gen. 36:33; I Chron. 1:44, 45).

3. A king of Madon who joined the northern confederacy against Joshua (Josh. 11:1; 12:19).

4. A Benjamite (I Chron. 8:9).

5. A Benjamite (I Chron. 8:18).

Jochebed (jŏk'ĕ-bĕd, **Jehovah is glory**), daughter of Levi, wife of Amram and mother of Moses (Exod. 6:20; Num. 26:59).

Joed (jō'ĕd, **Jehovah is witness**), a Benjamite (Neh. 11:7).

Joel (jō'ĕl, **Jehovah is God**). 1. Joel the son of Pethuel is the author of the second of the Minor Prophets books. Concerning the man, his life and times we know nothing. His name, meaning "The Lord (Yahweh) is God," was a common one, for a dozen other persons mentioned in the OT bear it (see below). 2. Samuel's firstborn son (I Sam. 8:2; I Chron. 6:33). 3. A Simeonite prince (I Chron. 4:35). 4. A Reubenite chief (I Chron. 5:4, 8). 5. A Gadite chief (I Chron. 5:12). 6. An ancestor of Samuel (I Chron. 6:36). 7. A chief of Issachar (I Chron. 7:3). 8. One of David's mighty men (I Chron. 11:38). 9. A Levite (I Chron. 15:7, 11, 17; probably also mentioned in I Chron. 23:8; 26:22). 10. David's officer over half of Manasseh (I Chron. 27:20) 11. A Levite of Hezekiah's time (II Chron. 29:12). 12. A Jew who had married a foreign wife (Ezra 10:43). 13. A Benjamite overseer (Neh. 11:9).

Joel, Book of (jō'ĕl). Dates suggested range from c. 830 to 350 B.C.; no clear indication in book of time of writing; background of book a locust plague, regarded by prophet as pun-

A vineyard stripped of every leaf, the branches left bare and white, within a matter of minutes during a locust plague. A similar devastation was part of the background in the book of Joel. © *MPS*

ishment for sin, causes him to urge nation to repent of its sins and predict a worse visitation, the future Day of the Lord. Outline: 1. Locust plague and its removal (1:1-2:27). 2. Future day of the Lord (2:28-3:21). a. Spirit of God to be poured out (2:28-32); b. judgment of the nations (3:1-17); c. blessing upon Israel following judgment (3:18-21).

Joel's greatest contribution to Christian thought is his teaching of the outpouring of the Holy Spirit "on all flesh" (2:28). This prophecy is quoted by Peter in his Pentecostal sermon (Acts 2:14-21). The Holy Spirit came upon men in OT times to enable them to serve God acceptably (Judg. 6:34; I Sam. 16:13) and certainly He was in the world and dwelling in the saints then as now, although they had very little consciousness of this fact. But in a special way the new age was to be one of the Spirit (Isa. 32:15; Zech. 12:10; John 7:39). All of God's people would now be priests and prophets, for the ideal stated when the law was given but never achieved would now become actual (Exod. 19:5, 6; I Pet. 2:9, 10).

Joelah (jō-ē'lȧ, perhaps **let him help**), one of David's recruits at Ziklag (I Chron. 12:7).

Joezer (jō-ē'zẽr, **Jehovah is help**), one of David's recruits at Ziklag (I Chron. 12:6).

Jogbehah (jŏg'bē-ȧ, **lofty**), a city in Gilead assigned to Gad (Num. 32:35; Judg. 8:11).

Jogli (jŏg'lī, **led into exile**), father of Bukki (Num. 34:22).

Joha (jō'hȧ). 1. A Benjamite, son of Beriah (I Chron. 8:16). 2. One of David's mighty men (I Chron. 11:45).

Johanan (jō'hā'năn, **Jehovah has been gracious**). 1. Jewish leader who tried to save Gedaliah from plot to murder him (Jer. 40:13, 14); took Jews, including Jeremiah, to Egypt (Jer. 40-43). 2. Son of King Josiah (I Chron. 3:15). 3. Son of Elioenai (I Chron. 3:24). 4. Father of Azariah, high priest in Solomon's time (I Chron. 6:9, 10). 5. Benjamite; joined David at Ziklag (I Chron. 12:4). 6. Gadite; captain in David's army (I Chron. 12:12, 14). 7. Ephraimite chief (II Chron. 28:12). 8. One of those who left Babylon with Ezra (Ezra 8:12). 9. Son of Tobiah, who married a Jewess in days of Nehemiah (Neh. 6:18). 10. Son of Eliashib (Ezra 10:6). 11. High priest, grandson of Eliashib (Neh. 12:22).

John (jŏn, **Jehovah has been gracious**). 1. John the Baptist (q.v.). 2. The apostle, the son of Zebedee, and brother of James. (See **John, the Apostle**). 3. John Mark (q.v.). 4. Father of Simon Peter (John 1:42; 21:15, 17, called Jonas in KJV). 5. Jewish religious dignitary who called Peter and John to account for their preaching about Jesus (Acts 4:6). 6. Father of Mattathias (I Macc. 2:1). 7. Eldest son of Mattathias (I Macc. 9:36). 8. Father of Eupolemus (I Macc. 8:17; II Macc. 4:11). 9. John Hyrcanus, son of Simon (I Macc. 13:53; 16:1). 10. Jewish envoy (II Macc. 11:17).

John, the Apostle. Son of Zebedee and Salome, and brother of James (Matt. 4:21; 27:56; Mark 15:40; Acts 12:1, 2); lived in Galilee, probably in Bethsaida (Luke 5:10; John 1:44); fisherman (Mark 1:19, 20); became disciple of Jesus through John the Baptist (John 1:35); called as apostle (Mark 1:19, 20; Luke 5:10); one of three apostles closest to Jesus (others, Peter and James); at raising of Jairus' daughter (Mark 5:37; Luke 8:51); transfiguration (Matt. 17:1; Mark 9:2; Luke 9:28); Gethsemane (Matt. 26:37; Mark 14:33); asked Jesus to call fire down on Samaritans, and given name Boanerges (sons of thunder) (Mark 3:17; Luke 9:54); mother requested that John and James be given places of special honor in coming kingdom (Mark 10:35); helped Peter prepare Passover (Luke 22:8); lay close to Jesus' breast at Last Supper (John 13:25); present at trial of Jesus (John 18:15, 16); witnessed crucifixion of Jesus (John 19:26, 27); recognized Jesus at Sea of Galilee (John 21:1-7); active with Peter in Apostolic church (Acts 3:1-4:22; 8:14-17). Lived to old age; 4th Gospel, three epistles, and Revelation attributed to him.

John the Baptist (jŏn băp'tĭst), forerunner of Jesus; son of Zacharias and Elizabeth, both of priestly descent (Luke 1:5-25, 56-58); lived as Nazirite in desert (Luke 1:15; Matt. 11:12-14, 18); began ministry beyond Jordan in 15th year of Tiberias Caesar (Luke 3:1-3); preached baptism of repentance in preparation of coming of Messiah (Luke 3:4-14); baptized Jesus (Matt. 3:13-17; Mark 1:9, 10; Luke 3:21; John 1:32); bore witness to Jesus as Messiah (John 1:24-42); imprisoned

The birthplace of John the Baptist Ain Karim in the hill country of Judaea. © *MPS*

and put to death by Herod Antipas (Matt. 14:6-12; Mark 6:17-28); praised by Jesus (Matt. 11:7-14; Luke 7:24-28); disciples loyal to him long after his death (Acts 18:25).

John, Epistles of. The First Epistle of John. Evidently written by author of 4th Gospel; date uncertain, but apparently late in 1st century; purpose: to warn readers against false teachers (Gnostic) and exhort them to hold fast to Christian faith and fulfill Christian duties, especially love; false teachers called anti-Christs (2:18, 22; 4:3); plan of Epistle is difficult to follow, but thoughts repeated often are the necessity of doing righteousness as an evidence of divine sonship, the necessity of love for the brethren, and believing that Jesus is the Christ come in the flesh.

The Second Epistle of John. Written to exhort readers to hold fast to the commandments which they had received, to warn against false teachers who deny that Christ is come in the flesh, and to tell them that he will soon visit them. "Elect lady" may be woman or church.

The Third Epistle of John. Addressed to Gaius to commend him for his Christian life and hospitality to evangelists sent by John and to censure Diotrephes for his bad conduct.

John, The Gospel of. Early tradition and internal evidence of the Gospel show that this book was written by the apostle John. Early tradition also places the book sometime toward the close of the 1st century A.D., in Asia Minor. The author states his purpose in 20:30, 31: to show that Jesus is the Christ, the Son of God, and that those believing this might have life in His name. Some of the characteristics which distinguish the Gospel from the others are: an emphasis on the deity of Christ; stress upon the King rather than upon the kingdom; non-parabolic teaching; emphasis upon the coming and work of the Holy Spirit.

Outline: Jesus, the Christ, the Son of God:

I. During His Public Ministry
   A. Revealing Himself to ever-widening circles, **rejected.** (Chaps. 1-6)
   B. Making His tender appeal to sinners, **bitterly resisted** (Chaps. 7-10).
   C. Manifesting Himself as the Messiah by two mighty deeds, **repulsed** (Chaps. 11, 12).

II. During His Private Ministry
   A. Issuing and illustrating His new commandment (Chap. 13).
   B. Tenderly instructing His disciples and committing them to the Father's care (Chaps. 14-17).
   C. Dying as a substitute for His people (Chaps. 18, 19).
   D. Triumphing gloriously (Chaps. 20, 21).

John Mark (See Mark)

Joiada (joi'ȧ-dȧ, **Jehovah knows).** 1. Man who repaired the walls of Jerusalem (Neh. 3:6; in KJV Jehoiada). 2. Son of Eliashib the high priest (Neh. 12:10; 13:28).

Joiakim (joi'ȧ-kĭm, **Jehovah raises up),** father of Eliashib, the high priest (Neh. 12:10, 12, 26).

Joiarib (joi'ȧ-rĭb, **Jehovah pleads).** 1. A "teacher" of Ezra's time (Ezra 8:16). 2. A Judahite (Neh. 11:5). 3. A chief of the priests who returned with Zerubbabel (Neh. 12:6, 7).

Jokdeam (jŏk'dē-ăm), a town in Judah, probably S of Hebron (Josh. 15:56).

Jokim (jō'kĭm, **Jehovah raises up),** a man of Judah (I Chron. 4:22).

Jokmeam (jŏk'mē-ām, **let the people arise**), a town of Ephraim (I Chron. 6:68).

Jokneam (jŏk'nē-ăm), a town on or near Mt. Carmel (Josh. 12:22) assigned to the Merarite Levites (Josh. 21:34).

Jokshan (jŏk'shăn), son of Abraham and Keturah (Gen. 25:2, 3). From him descended Sheba and Dedan.

Joktan (jŏk'tăn), a tribe descended from Shem through Eber and from whom 13 tribes of Arabia descended (Gen. 10:25, 26, 29; I Chron. 1:19, 20, 23).

Joktheel (jŏk'thē-ĕl), 1. A town in Judah. Site unknown (Josh. 15:33, 38). 2. A place in Edom (II Kings 14:7), probably Petra, the capital of Edom.

Jona (See Jonah, Jonas)

Jonadab (jŏn'ȧ-dăb, **Jehovah is bounteous).** 1. Son of David's brother Shimeah (II Sam. 13:3). He planned for Ammon the sin against Tamar. 2. Son of Rechab (II Kings 10:15ff). He helped Jehu abolish Baal-worship in Samaria.

Jonah (jō'nȧ, **dove).** 1. A prophet of Israel, the son of Amittai, and of the town of Gath-hepher in the tribe of Zebulun (II Kings 14:25). He predicted the restoration of the land of Israel to its ancient boundaries through the efforts of Jeroboam II.

The identity of the prophet with the

prophet of the Book of Jonah can not reasonably be doubted. Jonah 1:1 reads, "Now the word of the Lord came to Jonah the son of Amittai, saying." It is extremely unlikely that there were two prophets with the same name. While the author of the Book of Jonah does not identify himself, the likelihood is that he is the same as the book bearing his name. It is sometimes objected that he writes in the third person; but this is true of the OT prophets in general. In all probability the book was written not long after the events recorded, in the latter part of Jeroboam's reign.

The spirit and teaching of the Book of Jonah rank with the highest of the OT prophetical books. Not as much can be said for the prophet himself, who ranks low in the catalog of OT prophets. He was a proud, self-centered egotist: willful, pouting, jealous, blood-thirsty; a good patriot and lover of Israel; without proper respect for God or love for his enemies.

2. Father of Simon Peter (Matt. 16:17; John 1:42; 21:15).

Jonah, Book of, fifth in the order of the Minor Prophets. It differs from them in that while they for the most part contain prophetic discourses, with a minimum of narrative material, the Book of Jonah is mainly occupied with a story, and the prophetic message in it is almost incidental. The chapter divisions mark the natural divisions of the book: Chapter 1, Jonah's disobedience; Chapter 2, Jonah's prayer; Chapter 3, Jonah's preaching to the Ninevites; Chapter 4, Jonah's complaints.

The purpose of the book is primarily to teach that God's gracious purposes are not limited to Israel, but extend to the Gentile world. The author wishes to enlarge the sympathies of Israel, so that as God's missionaries they will lead the Gentiles to repentance and to God. The ready response of the Ninevites shows that the heathen are capable of genuine repentance. The Book of Jonah may be regarded as a great work on foreign missions. It anticipates the catholicity of the Gospel program of Jesus, and is the OT counterpart of John 3:16, "For God so loved the world."

The traditional view, that Jonah is the author and the story historically true, is supported by a number of considerations. 1. The book is written as a simple narrative, and was so regarded by both Jews and Christians until about a century ago. 2. There seems no doubt that our Lord thought of the story as history and taught it as such. On three different occasions He referred to Jonah (Matt. 12:38-41; 16:4; Luke 11:29-32), saying that as Jonah was three days and three nights in the body of the fish, so should the Son of Man be three days and three nights in the heart of the earth, and that the men of Nineveh repented at the preaching of Jonah, while His own contemporaries for the most part rejected His message. Some critics, taking refuge in the doctrine of the Kenosis (Phil. 2:5-8), set aside the teaching of Jesus on this point as erroneous; while others, holding to a doctrine of accommodation, think that Jesus did not consider it worth while to correct the wrong views of His contemporaries; but neither of these explanations harmonizes with a Biblical view of the person of Christ.

Most modern critical scholars in the last hundred years have regarded the book as a work of the imagination. Some call it a myth; others an allegory; others a parable; others a didactic story; etc. This interpretation avoids the miraculous elements in the story, which the critics find it impossible to accept; but it does not do justice to the fact that our Lord very evidently held to the historicity of the book.

Jonan (jō'năn), an ancestor of Jesus mentioned in the genealogy of Luke (3:30).

Jonas (jō'nȧs). 1. The name given to the OT prophet Jonah (Matt. 12:39-41; 16:4; Luke 11:29-32 KJV). 2. The name given in John 21:15, 16 KJV to the father of the Apostle Peter. In John 1:42 KJV he is called Jona.

Jonath Elem Rechokim, Upon (jō'năth ē'lĕm rē-hō'kĭm, **the silent dove of them that are afar off**), probably the tune to the melody to which Psalm 56 was written.

Jonathan (jŏn'ȧ-thăn, **Jehovah has given**). 1. Levite; became priest of Micah in Ephraim, and later of Danites (Judg. 17, 18). 2. Son of King Saul. See separate article, following. 3. Son of high priest Abiathar (II Sam. 15:27, 36; 17:17, 20; I Kings 1:42, 43). 4. Son of Shimea (II Sam. 21:21). 5. One of David's mighty men (II Sam. 23:32). 6. Son of Uzziah (I Chron. 27:25). 7. Jerahmeelite (I Chron. 2:32, 33). 8. David's "uncle" (I Chron. 27:

The gorge at Michmash, showing the rocks over which Jonathan and his armorbearer climbed, "upon hands and feet," (during the war against the Philistines) I Samuel 14:4, 5, 13. © MPS

32). 9. Father of Ebed (Ezra 8:6). 10. Son of Asahel (Ezra 10:15). 11. Priest (Neh. 12:11). 12. Priest (Neh. 2:14). 13. Levite (Neh. 12:35). 14. Scribe (Jer. 37:15, 20). 15. Son of Kareah (Jer. 40:8). 16. Son of Mattathias (I Macc. 2:5; 9-13). 17. Son of Absalom (I Macc. 13:11). 18. Priest (II Macc. 1: 23).

Jonathan, the eldest son of Saul, the first king of Israel (I Sam. 14:49). He first comes upon the scene soon after his father was crowned king and gained an important victory over the Ammonites, who had been harassing the Israelites. Saul's army numbered 3000 men, a third of whom he placed under the command of Jonathan at Gibeah, while the rest he retained at his headquarters at Michmash.

Great as were Jonathan's military qualities, he is best remembered as the friend of David. He exemplified all that is noblest in friendship — warmth of affection, unselfishness, helpfulness, and loyalty. His love for David began the day the two first met after the slaying of Goliath (I Sam. 18:1-4), and it remained steadfast despite Saul's suggestion that David would some day be king in their stead (I Sam. 20:31). When Jonathan first realized his father's animosity towards David, he interceded for his friend (I Sam. 19: 1-7); and later, more than once, he risked his life for him. Once, Saul, angered by what he regarded as unfilial conduct, threw a javelin at him, as he had done several times at David. The last meeting of the two friends took place in the desert of Ziph, where Jonathan strengthened his friend in God (I Sam. 23:16). He could not take part in the proceedings of his father against his friend, who was forced to live in hiding and from whom he was separated for many years. His disinterestedness and willingness to surrender all claims to the throne for the sake of his friend gives evidence of a character that is unsurpassed. While always holding to his own opinion of David, he conformed as much as he could to his father's views and wishes, and presents a noble example of filial piety. There was one temporary estrangement between Saul and Jonathan, provoked when Saul impugned the honor of Jonathan's mother. Jonathan fell with Saul and his brothers on Mt. Gilboa in battle against the Philistines (I Sam. 31:2). Their bodies were hung on the walls of Beth-shan, but under cover of night the men of Jabesh-gilead, out of gratitude for what Saul had done for them at the beginning of his career, removed them and gave them honorable burial.

Joppa (jŏp′pȧ), once in KJV Japho (Josh. 19:46); ancient walled town on coast of Palestine, c. 35 miles NW of Jerusalem; assigned to Dan; mentioned in Amarna letters; seaport for Jerusalem. In NT times Peter there raised Dorcas to life (Acts 9:36f) and received vision of sheet filled with animals (Acts 10:1ff; 11:5ff). Now called Jaffa.

Jorah (jō′rȧ), a family which returned with Zerubbabel (Ezra 2:18).

Jorai (jō′rā-ī, **whom Jehovah teaches),** head of a Gadite family (I Chron. 5: 13).

Joram (jō′răm, **Jehovah is exalted).** 1. A son of king of Hamath (II Sam. 8: 10). 2. A Levite (I Chron. 26:25). 3. Son of Ahab, king of Israel. The name is the same as Jehoram (II Kings 8: 29). 4. Same as Jehoram, king of Judah (II Kings 8:21-24; 11:2; I Chron. 3:11; Matt. 1:8). 5. A priest sent by Jehoshaphat to instruct the people (II Chron. 17:8).

Jordan River, the only large flowing body of water in Palestine and, as such, it played a significant part in the history of Israel, as well as in the earlier days of our Lord's ministry. The word **Jordan** derives from a Hebrew word, **hayyardēn,** meaning "flowing downward," or "the descender," and one with any knowledge of its course can easily see the appropriateness of the name.

By far the most important single event relating to the Jordan River in the entire history of Israel is the crossing on the part of the Israelites, after the death of Moses. Actually, this crossing is referred to, in anticipation, by Moses in the book of Deuteronomy 3:20, 25, 27. In reality, while the Jordan River is now and then referred to as a boundary, it was **not** a boundary for Israel, or even for the specific tribes, for Manasseh occupied a huge territory on both sides of the river. Nevertheless, Israel was told that until this river was crossed, and the territory on the western side possessed, she would not be occupying the land flowing with milk and honey (Num. 35:10; Deut. 3:20; 11:31; 31:13; Josh. 12, etc). One might say that the Prom-

A peaceful view of the Jordan, near the traditional site where John the Baptist carried on his ministry and baptized his converts. © *MPS*

The well at Dothan known as Joseph's Well. © *MPS*

Joseph's Tomb at the foot of Mount Ebal, on the "parcel of ground that Jacob gave to his son Joseph." © *MPS*

ised Land more generally refers to the territory on the western side of the Jordan than to all of the land occupied by Israel. The story of the crossing of the Jordan is given in detail in the third and fourth chapters of Joshua.

The Jordan is important in only one particular in the New Testament. It was here that John the Baptist carried on his ministry (Matt. 3:6; Mark 1:5; John 1:28 and 3:26), and thus in this river Jesus Himself was baptized (Matt. 3:13; Mark 1:9; Luke 4:1). No other event occurs in the New Testament directly relating to the Jordan River. (References to our Lord's ministry on the far side of the Jordan [Matt. 19:1; Mark 10:1] only imply that the Lord did cross the river.) In the statement relating to the closing days of our Lord's ministry, when escaping from those who would make Him King, He "resorted once more to the place beyond the Jordan, where John first baptized, and there He stayed" (John 10:40, Berkeley Version).

Jorim (jō′rĭm), an ancestor of Jesus (Luke 3:29).

Jorkeam (jôr′kē-ăm), a place inhabited by members of the family of Hezron and house of Caleb (I Chron. 2:44).

Josabad, Jozabad (jŏs′á-băd, jŏz′á-băd, **Jehovah has bestowed).** 1. One of David's recruits at Ziklag (I Chron. 12:4). 2. Two Manassites who joined David at Ziklag (I Chron. 12:20). 3. A Levite overseer (II Chron. 31:13). 4. Son of Jeshua (Ezra 8:33). 5. Priest who put away his foreign wife (Ezra 10:22).

Josaphat (jŏs′á-făt), KJV for Jehoshaphat in Matthew 1:8, the genealogy of Christ. An ancestor of Jesus.

Jose (jō′sé), KJV form for Jesus in Luke's genealogy (3:29).

Josedech (jŏs′ĕ-dĕk, **Jehovah is righteous),** father of Jeshua the high priest (Ezra 3:2, 8) who went into captivity under Nebuchadnezzar.

Joseph (jō′zĕf, **may God add).** 1. The eleventh of Jacob's 12 sons, and the firstborn son of Rachel, who said when he was born, "The Lord shall add to me another son," and therefore called his name Joseph (Gen. 30:24). He became the ancestor of the two northern tribes, Manasseh and Ephraim. The story of his birth is told in Genesis 30:22-24 and the story of the rest of his life in Genesis 37-50. He presents a noble ideal of character, remarkable for his gentleness, faithfulness to duty, magnanimity, and forgiving spirit, so that he is often regarded as an OT type of Christ. 2. The father of Igal of Issachar, one of the 12 spies (Num. 13:7). 3. A son of Asaph (I Chron. 25:2, 9). 4. A son of Bani (Ezra 10:42). 5. A priest of the family of Shebaniah in the days of the high priest Joiakim (Neh. 12:14). 6. The name of three ancestors of Jesus according to the KJV (Luke 3:24, 26, 30). 7. Son of Zacharias (I Macc. 5:18, 55-62). 8. The husband of Mary, the mother of Jesus (Matt. 1:16; Luke 3:23). He was a carpenter (Matt. 13:55) living in Nazareth (Luke 2:4), was of Davidic descent (Matt. 1:20; Luke 2:4), the son of Heli (Luke 3:23) or Jacob (Matt. 1:16), and the supposed father of Jesus (Matt. 13:55; Luke 3:23; 4:22; John 1:45; 6:42). After learning that Mary was with child before marriage, he was minded to put her away "privily," but an angel assured him in a dream that the child to be born was conceived by the Holy Spirit, and he thereupon made her his wife (Matt. 1:18-25). When the emperor Augustus decreed that all the world should be enrolled in their ancestral homes, Joseph went with Mary to Bethlehem, and there Jesus was born. He was with Mary when the shepherds came to do homage to Jesus (Luke 2:8-20), and when, 40 days after His birth, Jesus was presented in the temple. Warned by the Lord in a dream that Herod was plotting the murder of the child, he fled with Mary and Jesus to Egypt (Matt. 2:13-19), returning to Nazareth after the death of Herod. Every year, at the Passover, he attended the feast in Jerusalem (Luke 2:41); and when Jesus was 12, he too went with Joseph and Mary. He undoubtedly taught Jesus the carpenter trade (Mark 6:3). It is likely that he was alive after the ministry of Jesus had well begun (Matt. 13:55), but as we do not hear of him in connection with the crucifixion, and as Jesus commended Mary to John at the crucifixion (John 19:26, 27), it may be inferred that he had died prior to that event. 9. One of the brethren of Jesus (Matt. 13:55). KJV has "Joses." 10. Jew of Arimathaea; member of Sanhedrin (Matt. 27:57; Mark 15:43); secret disciple of Jesus (John 19:38);

had Jesus buried in his own tomb (Matt. 25:57-60; Luke 23:50-53; John 19:38). 11. Christian considered by apostles to replace Judas Iscariot (Acts 1:21, 23, 26). 12. Personal name of Barnabas (Acts 4:36; in KJV Joses).

Joseph Barsabas (jō′sĕf bȧr-sȧb′ăs), an early disciple of Christ who became a candidate for the apostleship against Matthias (Acts 1:21, 26), in order to fill the vacancy produced by the apostasy of Judas. Matthias was chosen.

Joses (jō′sĕz). 1. One of the brothers of Jesus (Mark 6:3). In Matthew 13:55 the Gr. is **Joseph.** 2. A name of Barnabas, for a time a co-worker of Paul (Acts 4:36).

Joshah (jō′shȧ, **Jehovah's gift),** a descendant of Simeon (I Chron. 4:34).

Joshaphat (jŏsh′ȧ-făt, **Jehovah has judged).** 1. One of David's mighty men (I Chron. 11:43). 2. A priest and trumpeter in David's time (I Chron. 15:24, in KJV Jehoshaphat).

Joshaviah (jŏsh′ȧ-vī′ȧ), son of Alnaam, one of David's mighty men (I Chron. 11:46).

Joshbekashah (jŏsh′bē-kā′shȧ), a leader in music (I Chron. 25:4, 24).

Josheb-Bassebet (jō′shĕb-bă′sē-bĕt, **he that sitteth in the seat)** (II Sam. 23:8). One of David's mighty men. In ASV Josheb-basshebeth.

Joshua (jŏsh′ū-ȧ, **Lord is salvation.** Later **Jeshua, Jesus).** 1. Ephraimite, son of Nun (I Chron. 7:27); assistant of Moses; repulsed Amalekite attack (Exod. 17:9); one of 12 spies (Num. 13:8); succeeded Moses (Deut. 31; Josh. 1); entered, conquered, and apportioned Canaan (Joshua); buried at Timnath-serah (Josh. 24:29). KJV has Jesus in Acts 7:45; Heb. 4:8. 2. Native of Bethshemesh (I Sam. 6:14). 3. Governor of Jerusalem (II Kings 23:8). 4. High priest who returned with Zerubbabel, called Jeshua (Ezra 2:2; 3:2-9; Neh. 7:7).

Joshua, Book of, 6th book of Bible; first of "historical books" in English, but first of prophets in Heb. OT. Tells how Joshua, Moses' successor, conquered Canaan, as promised by God (Josh. 1:1; 24:31). Author not named; date uncertain, but probably prior to 1200 B.C. Outline: 1. Conquest of Canaan (1-12). 2. Apportionment of territory to tribes (13-22). 3. Joshua's farewell address (22-24).

Josiah (jō-zī′ȧ, **Jehovah supports him),** son of Amon and Jedidah and the grandson of Manasseh, the son of Hezekiah. Josiah's reign on the Davidic throne for 31 years was the last surge of political independence and religious revival before the disintegration of the Southern Kingdom which ended with the destruction of Jerusalem in 586 B.C. In the eighth year of his reign (c. 632 B.C.) he began to seek after God and four years later initiated reforms. Images, altars, and all manner of idolatrous practices were destroyed not only in Jerusalem and Judah but in the cities of Manasseh, Ephraim, Simeon, and as far north as Naphtali. At the same time offerings and contributions were collected throughout the nation for the restoration of the temple in Jerusalem which had been neglected for such a long period.

In the course of renovating the temple (622 B.C.) the book of the law was recovered. The reformation movement consequently was stimulated anew by the reading of this "book of the Law given by Moses." With the king himself leading the reformation movement, changes in personnel occurred. Priests serving by royal appointment of former kings and dedicated to idol worship were removed from office. The religious climate established by Josiah must have provided favorable conditions for Jeremiah's ministry during the first 18 years of his ministry (627-609 B.C.). In 609 B.C. Josiah's leadership was abruptly ended. In an effort to interfere with Necho's plans to aid the Assyrians Josiah was fatally wounded at Megiddo. National and religious hopes vanished with the funeral of this 39-year-old king so that all Judah had reason to join Jeremiah in lamenting for Josiah.

Josibiah (jŏs′ĭ-bī′ȧ), a Simeonite (I Chron. 4:35).

Josiphiah (jŏs′ĭ-fī′ȧ, **Jehovah will increase),** ancestor of 160 men who returned with Ezra (Ezra 8:10).

Jot (jŏt), the smallest letter in the Hebrew alphabet and almost identical with our apostrophe sign,'. Used figuratively, the "jot" signifies something of apparently small moment. See Matt. 5:17, 18.

Jotbah (jŏt′bȧ, **pleasantness),** a Levitical city in Judah, just S of Hebron (II Kings 21:19), the home of the father-in-law of Jotham, king of Judah.

Jotbath (jŏt′băth), Deuteronomy 10:7; see Jotbathah.

Jotbathah (jŏt′bȧ-thȧ, **pleasantness),** a place in the Wilderness of Paran in the peninsula of Sinai where Israel encamped (Num. 33:33, 34; Deut. 10: 7).

Jotham (jō′thăm, **Jehovah is perfect).** 1. Youngest of the 70 sons of Gideon, and the speaker of the first Bible parable (Judg. 9:5-57). After the death of Gideon, Abimelech, an illegitimate son, got the men of Shechem behind him and desired to make himself a king over Israel. To that end he slew his half-brothers, all but Jotham, the youngest, who hid himself, and so escaped. 2. A man of the tribe of Judah (I Chron. 2:47). 3. A son of Uzziah, king of Judah. Uzziah had been for the most part a good and a powerful king, but his successes turned his head and he intruded into the priest's office (II Chron. 26:16). As a result, he was struck with leprosy, and Jotham acted as regent. Jotham began to reign just about the time when Isaiah began his great ministry (Isa. 6:1) and was probably influenced by that godly man (II Kings 15:32-38 and II Chron. 27).

Journey, Sabbath Day's, 3,000 feet (Acts 1:12).

Joy. In the Word of God, joy is an attribute of Deity (Ps. 104:31), and is an important part of that ninefold "fruit of the Spirit" (Gal. 5:22, 23) which He imparts to believers (Gal. 5:24). Joy is often equated with happiness, but the two are quite distinct. Happiness depends largely upon happenings: good health, congenial company, pleasant surroundings, etc. Happiness and unhappiness do not exist together; but joy and sorrow can and do. Our Lord was "a man of sorrows and acquainted with grief" (Isa. 53:3) but "for the joy that was set before him, endured the cross, despiring the shame, and is set down at the right hand of the throne of God" (Heb. 12: 2). Paul and Silas experienced it in prison (Acts 16:23-33).

Jozabad (jŏz′ȧ-băd, **Jehovah endows).** 1. A man from Gederah who joined David at Ziklag (I Chron. 12:4 but "Josabad" in KJV). 2. Two Manassites who also joined David (I Chron. 12:20). 3. Levites overseer (II Chron. 31:13). 4. A chief Levite in the time of Josiah (II Chron. 35:9). 5. A Levite who assisted Ezra (Ezra 8:33). 6. A priest who put away foreign wife (Ezra 10:22). 7. A Levite who did the same (Ezra 10:23). 8. A Levite who translated the law from the Hebrew as it was read into the Aramaic (Neh. 8:7). 9. A chief Levite who helped oversee the outward business of the temple (Neh. 11:16).

Jozachar (jŏz′ȧ-kȧr, **whom Jehovah has remembered),** one of the two assassins of Joash, king of Judah (II Kings 12:20, 21; II Chron. 24:26).

Jozadak (jŏz′ȧ-dăk, **Jehovah is righteous),** father of Jeshua the priest who returned with Zerubbabel (Ezra 3:2, etc). Called Josedech in Haggai and Zechariah.

Jubal (jōō′băl), son of Lamech, and the inventor of the harp and pipe (Gen. 4:21).

Jubilee (jōō′bĭ-lē, **ram's horn, trumpet).** According to Leviticus 25, every 50th year in Israel was to be announced as a jubilee year. Three essential features characterized this year. First, liberty was proclaimed to all Israelites who were in bondage to any of their countrymen. The law provided that the price of slaves was to vary according to the proximity of the Jubilee Year. Second, there was to be a return of ancestral possessions to those who had been compelled to sell them because of proverty. This, of course, excluded the possibility of selling a piece of land permanently. Provision was made that the price of real property was to vary according to the proximity of the Jubilee Year. The third feature of this year was that it was to be a year of rest for the land. The land was to remain fallow, even though it had been so in the previous sabbatical year. The people were to live simply, on what the fields had produced in the sixth year and whatever grew spontaneously.

Jubilees, Book of, a Jewish apocalyptic book written in the inter-testamental period. It gives a history of the world from the creation to the giving of the law, and defends Pharisaical views as against liberal Hellenistic tendencies.

Jucal (jōō′kăl, **Jehovah is able),** one of the evil princes of Judah who put Jeremiah into prison for his prophecies (Jer. 38:1).

Juda (See Judah)

Judaea (See Judea)

Judah (jōō′dȧ, **praised).** 1. The fourth son of Jacob; his mother was Leah (Gen. 29:35). Few details of his life are known. He saved Joseph's life by persuading his brothers to sell him to the Midianites at Dothan (Gen. 37:

26-28). His disgraceful actions recorded in Genesis 38 left a stain upon his memory. He gradually appears to have achieved leadership among his brothers (Gen. 43:3; 46:28; 49:8-12). Through his son Perez, Judah became an ancestor of David (Ruth 4: 18-22) and of Jesus Christ (Matt. 1: 3-16). The blessing of dying Jacob to Judah (Gen. 49:9, 10) is usually understood as being a Messianic prophecy.

2. Also the name of the Hebrew tribe descended from the man Judah described above. Caleb, a hero among the Hebrew spies and captors of Canaan, was a member of this tribe (Num. 13:6; 34:19). Judah was one of the tribes which stood on Mt. Gerizim to bless the people at the ceremony of covenant renewal at Shechem (Deut. 27:12). After Joshua's death, this tribe seems to have been first in occupying its allotted territory in the southern hill country of Canaan, even to occupying temporarily the city of Jerusalem (Judg. 1:1-20). Upon settling in Canaan, the tribe of Judah occupied the territory extending from the extreme southern point of the Dead Sea eastward to the Mediterranean, lying S of Kadesh Barnea.

During the period of the rule of the judges, Judah tended to be separated from the rest of the Hebrew tribes, which lived to the N, by pagan people dwelling between them (Gibeonites, Josh. 9; Jebusites, Judg. 19:10-13), and also by rough and wild land, with deep east-west valleys to the N of Judah. The Simeonites, who lived in southern Judean cities tended to become assimilated into Judah and thus to lose their tribal identity.

Othniel, the judge who delivered the people from the domination of Mesopotamia, was a Judean (Judg. 3:8-11). The Philistine threat must have been especially troublesome to this tribe, for the Philistine plain, as it came to be called, was actually Judah's coastal plain land. The story of Ruth and Boaz, which centers in Bethlehem, occurs during the time of the judges and first brings the country town of Bethlehem into prominence in Hebrew history. Saul, whose reign brings the judges' period to an end, ruled over Judah, and it was the Judeans who first anointed their fellow tribesman, David, king at Hebron (II Sam. 2:1-4).

3. Judah is also the name of five individuals who are mentioned in Ezra-Nehemiah. Three were Levites (Ezra 3:9; Neh. 12:8; Ezra 10:23), one a Benjamite (Neh. 11:9) and the fifth probably a prince of Judah (Neh. 12: 34).

Judah, Kingdom of, began when 10 N tribes withdrew from Rehoboam (c. 912) and lasted until Jerusalem fell in 587 B.C.; 50 years later Cyrus, king of Persia, permitted the Jews to return (I Kings 12-22; II Kings; II Chron. 11-36; Ezra; Nehemiah). Consisted of tribes of Judah and Benjamin. One dynasty ruled throughout. Great importance is attached to Judah for it was from this tribe that Jesus, according to the flesh, came (Rev. 5:5).

Judaism (jōō'dā-ĭz'm), the religious system held by the Jews. Its teachings come from the OT, especially from Exodus 20 through Deuteronomy; but also from the traditions of the elders (Mark 7:3-13), some of which our Lord condemned.

Judas, Juda (jōō'dȧs, jōō'dȧ, **praised).** 1. An ancestor of our Lord (Luke 3: 30 ASV). 2. A Galilean insurrectionist (Acts 5:37). 3. One of the brothers of our Lord (Matt. 13:55). 4. An apostle of Jesus (Luke 6:16). 5. One who apparently had a guest-house or hostel in the street which was called Straight in the city of Damascus and with whom Paul lodged (Acts 9:11). 6. One of the leading brethren in the church at Jerusalem at the Council of Jerusalem (Acts 15:6-35).

Judas Iscariot, the arch-traitor, who betrayed our Lord. He and his father Simon were both surnamed "Iscariot" (see John 6:71 in Greek and in ASV). "Iscariot" is commonly thought to be from the Hebrew **Ish Kerioth,** i.e. "a man of Kerioth," and Kerioth is almost certainly in the south of Judah (Josh. 15:25). He was appointed treasurer for the disciples (John 12:6; 13: 29), but his hopes for a high place in an earthly kingdom of Jesus were dashed (John 6:66) and he became a thief. His indignation when Jesus was anointed at Bethany was hypocritical. His pretended zeal for the poor was really covetousness, and is so interpreted by John (12:6). Jesus, however, was not deceived (John 6:64), but knew from the beginning who should betray Him (Mark 14:10). He sold the Lord for thirty pieces of silver, betrayed him with a kiss, then in remorse threw down the money before the chief priests and elders (Matt. 27:3-10) and went out and committed suicide. Matthew (27:5) says he hanged himself, and Acts (1:18) says that falling headlong, he burst asunder.

Judas Barsabas (See Judas)

Judas of Galilee (See Judas)

Jude (jōōd), writer of the last of the epistles in the NT. Both James and Jude in the opening of their epistles show their Christian humility and their faith in the deity of Jesus by referring to themselves as "bond-servants" of Jesus Christ, rather than His brothers in the flesh. Beyond this we know of him from Scripture only that, like his brothers, he did not believe in Jesus during His earthly life (John 7:5), but became His follower after the resurrection (Acts 1:14).

Jude, Epistle of. The author of the epistle gives his name as Jude or Judas, and calls himself a bondservant of Jesus Christ and brother of James (vs. 1). There is good evidence for believing that Jude and James were brothers of the Lord (Matt. 13:55; Mark 6:3), although neither refers to himself as such in his epistle. They were not apostles, and did not believe in Him until after the resurrection. Its destination is quite general: "To them that are called, beloved in God the Father, and kept for Jesus Christ" (vs. 1). It is not clear where he was when he wrote or precisely when he wrote.

The occasion for the writing of the epistle was the appearance among Jude's readers of an alarming heresy with immoral tendencies, perhaps the Gnosticism rebuked elsewhere in the NT, and its aim was to save them from its inroads. How he had received information about this is not told, but it is obvious that he was deeply disturbed about it. A striking feature of the book is the use made of apocalyptic literature. There is an almost exact quotation from the Book of Enoch (1:9) in Verses 14 and 15, and Verse 9 apparently refers to something recorded in the Assumption of Moses. The epistle also has echoes from the Testament of Moses.

After the introduction and the reason given for the writing of the epistle in Verses 1-4, Jude announces the condemnation in store for the false teachers (vss. 5-16). He then explains the duty of Christans in the circumstances (vss. 17-23), and ends with a doxology (vss. 24, 25).

Judea, Judaea (jōō-dē'ȧ), a geographical term that first appears in the Bible in Ezra 5:8, where it designates a province of the Persian Empire. The land of Judea is also mentioned in the apocryphal books I Esdras (1:30) and I Maccabees (5:45; 7:10). Since most of the exiles who returned from the Babylonian exile belonged to the tribe of Judah, they came to be called Jews and their land Judea.

Under the Persian empire, Judea was a district administered by a governor who was usually a Jew (Hag. 1:14; 2:2). With the banishment of Archelaus, Judea became annexed to the Roman province of Syria; but its governors were procurators appointed by the Roman emperor.

Judge, a civil magistrate; Moses organized judiciary of Israel (Exod. 18:13-26; Deut. 1:9-17); prophets complained about courts corrupted by bribery (Isa. 1:23; Amos 5:12; Micah 3:11).

Judges, The. Heads of families ("patriarch") and elders of the tribes were the judges (Gen. 38:24) and their authority was based on custom.

After the Exodus from Egypt, Moses, upon the advice of Jethro (Exod. 18:13-26), organized the nation into groups of thousands, hundreds, fifties and tens, within each tribe. Over each unit a qualified man was placed as judge, and only the most important cases were brought before Moses (Deut. 1:12-18; 21:2). Upon entering Canaan, a similar plan of local government was followed (Deut. 16:18-20; 17:2-13; 19:15-20; Josh. 8:33; 23:2; 24:1; I Sam. 8:1). During the period of the judges the office assumed a very different character; this will be treated below.

When the monarchy was instituted, the king himself tried important cases (II Sam. 15:2; I Kings 3:9, 28; 7:7; Prov. 20:8). David assigned Levites to the judicial office, and appointed 6000 as officers and judges (I Chron. 23:4; 26:29). According to II Chronicles 19:5-8, Jehoshaphat enlarged the judicial system of Judah with a kind of supreme court, made up of Levites, priests and heads of fathers' houses, at Jerusalem.

The prophets often complained bitterly that justice was corrupted by bribery and false witness (Isa. 1:23;

5:23; 10:1; Amos 5:12; 6:12; Mic. 3: 11; 7:3). Kings were often unjust (I Kings 22:26; II Kings 21:16; Jer. 36: 26) and the case of Ahab's seizure of Naboth's vineyard (I Kings 21:1-13) shows how far a king could go in getting his own way, in flagrant contradiction of law and custom, at least in the northern kingdom of Israel.

From the time of the death of Joshua to the reign of Saul, Israel's first king, the principal leaders of the people were called judges. These men and their times are described in the book of Judges and in I Samuel 1-7. They were charismatic leaders; that is, they were raised up to be Israel's "saviors" by a special endowment of the Spirit of God. It is clear that they were judges only in the broadest sense of that term. In reality, they were principally military deliverers, raised up to save the people of Israel from oppressing foreign powers.

The first judge mentioned in detail is Ehud, son of Gera (Judg. 3:12-30). A Benjamite, he is said to have been lefthanded, a serious defect in those superstitious times. Few if any of the judges are pictured as ideal individuals. The occasion of the raising up of Ehud was an oppression by Eglon, king of Moab, who with the Ammonites and Amalekites (all Transjordan herdsmen or nomads), occupied the region of Jericho ("the city of palm trees," 3:13). After 18 years of oppression, Ehud led a revolt by killing Eglon when he presented the tribute. The gory details of the deed fit well this violent period. With Ephraimite help Eglon took the fords of the Jordan and slew the Moabites as they sought to flee homeward. There followed an 80-year period of peace.

In the second detailed deliverance story (Judg. 4, 5), the scene shifts from the lower Jordan valley to the valley of Jezreel and the Galilee hill country in northern Palestine. The oppressor is Jabin, king of Canaan, who reigned in Hazor, whose 900 chariots of iron must have struck terror into the Hebrew tribes still in the stone age (I Sam. 13:19-22). The recent excavation of Hazor by Israeli scholars has underscored the importance of this Canaanite stronghold, probably the largest city in ancient Palestine. The deliverers were Deborah "the prophetess," surely the actual leader of the uprising, and Barak, son of Abinoam, a fearful man (4:8) who led the Hebrew army at Deborah's urging. The tribes of the Galilee hill country united for this battle, which was fought in the valley of Jezreel by the brook Kishon. Evidently a cloudburst upstream caused the Kishon to overflow onto the plains through which it flows, thus immobilizing the Canaanite chariots, upon which they depended (4:15; 5:20-22). The army of Jabin defeated, his general Sisera fled, only to be killed ignominiously by the woman Jael (4:17-22). Deborah's warlike song of praise (Judg. 5) is believed to be one of the oldest poems of the Bible, and is noted for its rough primitive vigor. A 40-year rest followed this deliverance.

The third great judge was Gideon (chaps. 6-8), the location of whose village of Ophrah is a matter of uncertainty. The oppressing Midianites, desert Bedouin from the Transjordan region, had crossed the Jordan, because of the internal weakness of the land, and were raiding in Palestine proper. Gideon is commonly remembered for his doubt and reluctance to take action (6:15, 17, 36-40; 7:10) but it should be noted that once he assumed command he proved a steady and effective soldier (6:25-27; 7:15-24). His ruse, carried out by a mere 300 companions, frightened the disorganized Bedouin from the valley of Jezreel into full retreat across the Jordan. Gideon promptly called the Ephraimites to take Jordan fords, by doing which they destroyed the Midianites. Gideon appears to have established some form of regular rule over at least the region of the Jezreel valley during his lifetime. His importance can be gauged by his rather large domestic establishment (8:30). Adhering to the ancient ideal of charismatic leadership, he rejected the idea of setting up a dynasty (8:22, 23). His rule is said to have lasted 40 years.

The story of Gideon's son Abimelech and his violent rule over the Shechem area in the central hill country is told in Judges 9. Abimelech is not called a judge and he appears more as a brigand or political-military adventurer than as a deliverer of Israel from an oppressing enemy. He died as he lived—his head crushed by a millstone; and finally killed by his armorbearer.

Jephthah, a Transjordan chieftain, next appears (Judg. 11, 12), as the deliverer of Gilead and Manasseh (northern Transjordan) from the oppression of the Ammonites—a pastoral people who pressured Manasseh from the south. He is chiefly remembered for his thoughtless vow (11:30, 31).

The last of the great judges was Samson (Judg. 13-16) with whom the scene shifts to a different part of Palestine—the Philistine Plain. Samson lived in the Shephelah area which bordered that plain. He was dedicated to a life of Nazirite obedience before his birth. His life was the tragedy of one whose great potential was vitiated through the lack of self discipline.

Hardly a very religious person, Samson was known for his great strength. He thus became the Hebrews' champion against the Philistines, doubtless as the Philistine Goliath later did against the Hebrews. His failure to discipline his sensuous nature led him into three liaisons with Philistine women. Doubtless each was an instrument of the Philistine lords in their effort to subdue Samson.

We do not know that Samson ever led a Hebrew army against the Philistines. Rather, he made single-handed exploits in Philistine territory, a number of which are described (14:19; 15: 4, 5, 8, 15; 16:3). The story of Samson's subduing at the hand of Delilah is well known. Killing in his death more Philistines than he killed in his life (16:30), he became at the last a tragic figure. He had judged Israel 20 years.

Eli (I Sam. 1-4) and Samuel (I Sam. 2:12) are also called judges. Although they did do some of the work of the judges described above, it would seem better to regard them as priest and prophet respectively—transitional figures preparing the way for the monarchy.

Judges, Book of. The seventh book of the OT takes its name from the title of the men who ruled Israel during the period from Joshua to Samuel. They are called judges (**shōphetîm,** Judg. 2: 16), their principal function being that of military deliverers to the oppressed Hebrews.

The purposes of the book of Judges are: 1. To bridge in some manner the historical gap between the death of Joshua and the inauguration of the monarchy. 2. To show the moral and political degradation of a people who neglected their religious heritage and compromised their faith with the surrounding paganism. 3. To show the need of the people for the unity and leadership by a strong central government in the person of a king.

In its structure, the book falls into three easily recognizable parts: (1) Introduction: the state of things at the death of Joshua, 1:1-2:10; (2) Main body: the judges' cycles, 2:11-16:31; (3) Appendix: life in Israel in the days of the judges, 17-21.

The judges, and that part of Israel which they served (when that can be known), are here listed. For a discussion of the principal judges, see article **Judges, The.**

1. Othniel (3:7-11).
2. Ehud (3:12-30): Central Palestine and Transjordan.
3. Shamgar (3:31): Philistine plain.
4. Deborah and Barak (4, 5): Central Palestine and Galilee.
5. Gideon (6-8): Central Palestine and Transjordan.
6. Abimelech (9): Central Palestine. Abimelech is considered by many as merely an outlaw and not a judge.
7. Tola (10:1, 2): Central Palestine.
8. Jair (10:3-5): Transjordan.
9. Jephthah (10:6-12:7): Transjordan.
10. Ibzan (12:8-10): Southern Palestine.
11. Elon (12:11, 12): Northern Palestine.
12. Abdon (12:13-15): Central Palestine.
13. Samson (13-16): Philistine plain.

The remaining chapters form a kind of appendix containing incidents describing the near-pagan period of the Judges. We have the account of the idolatrous Levite priest whose actions were alien to the priesthood under the Mosaic Law (17-18)—the migration of the Danites (18)—the story of brutality and beastliness in connection with the Levite's concubine (19).

The cruelty and paganism of the stories of Judges are often a stumbling block to readers. It should not be imagined that the writer is approving of everything which he records. Rather, the book should be viewed as a story of the tragic judgment of God upon a people who failed to keep their heritage of true religious faith by assimilating far too much of their surrounding culture. The story of the Judges has been called "The struggle between faith and culture." In this struggle, faith lost.

All this should not close our eyes to the beauty of the book of Judges as literature. Many of the stories would rank high in any collection of the short stories of the world. Even in the most brutal passages there is an austere dignity. Sin is never reveled in; it is always held up to the gaze of horror. In the pungent words of Jotham (9:7-15), Judges has preserved almost the only fable in ancient Hebrew literature. The song of Deborah, much studied by recent scholars, has a sonorous quality and vivid narrative power. The narratives of the book are amazingly brief. The Hebrew literary artist was at his best when he crammed action and emotion into a few sentences.

Judgment (jŭj′mĕnt), referring in Bible sometimes to the pronouncing of a formal opinion or decision by men, but more often to a calamity regarded as sent by God, by way of punishment, or a sentence of God as the judge of all. The history of Israel is the story of a succession of judgments upon enemies of God's people and upon His covenant nation when they flouted His will. "Day of Jehovah," a day of punishment for all the unjust, even those who boast of belonging to the people of the covenant (Isa. 2:12; Amos 5:18; Hos. 5:8, 9); purpose of judgment of God's people is their purification, not destruction. Jesus warns against uncharitable judgments (Matt. 7:1); so also Paul (Rom. 14; I Cor. 8-10). Final Judgment referred to in Matt. 11:20-24; 25:31-46; John 16:11; present world will be shaken and destroyed (Matt. 24:29-35); entrusted to Christ (Matt. 3:11, 12; John 5:22; Rom. 2:16).

Judgment, Day of (See Judgment)

Judgment Hall, originally the tent or building where the general or governor held council. In John 18:28—19:9 KJV renders it "hall of judgment" or "judgment hall," whereas ASV uses the Latin term **praetorium,** but with "palace" in the margin. The term comes in again in the story of Paul at Caesarea (Acts 23:35), where it refers to the palace of Herod, used as the official residence of the propraetors Felix and Festus in their day. In Matthew 27:27 KJV renders the word "common hall"; and in Philippians 1:13 KJV has "palace," and ASV "praetorian guard," but with "praetorium" in the margin.

Judgment Seat (platform), bench or seat where a judge sits to hear arguments and pleas and delivers sentence (Matt. 27:19; John 19:13; Acts 18:12). Also refers to judgment seat of Christ before which all believers will stand (Rom. 14:10; II Cor. 5:10).

Judgment Seat of Christ (See Judgment)

Judgment, The Last (See Judgment)

Judgments, The (See Judgment)

Judgments of God (See Judgment)

Judith (jōō′dĭth, **Judean, Jew).** 1. One of the wives of Esau (Gen. 26:34). 2. Heroine of the apocryphal book of Judith.

Julia (jōōl′ya), an early Christian at Rome to whom Paul sent greetings (Rom. 16:15).

Julius (jōōl′yŭs), a Roman centurion of the Augustan band in whose care Paul was placed for the journey to Rome (Acts 27:1, 3). He with his soldiers saved Paul's life by frustrating the sailors' plot near Malta.

Junia, Junias (jōō′nĭ-ȧ, jōō′nĭ-ăs, a kinsman and fellow prisoner of Paul (Rom. 16:7). He had become a Christian before Paul's conversion (Rom. 16:7).

Juniper (See Plants)

Jupiter (jōō′pĭ-têr), the chief of the Roman gods. The Greeks called him "Zeus." The people of Lystra called Barnabas "Jupiter" and Paul "Mercury" (Acts 14:12, 13).

Jushab-hesed (jōō′shăb-hē′sĕd, **mercy has returned),** a son of Zerubbabel (I Chron. 3:20).

Justification (jŭs′tĭ-fĭ-kā′shŭn, **to make valid, to absolve, to vindicate, to set right).** Justification may be defined as, "that judicial act of God, by which, on the basis of the meritorious work of Christ, imputed to the sinner and received by him through faith, He declares the sinner absolved from his sin, released from its penalty, and restored as righteous."

See Acts 13:38, 39; Romans 3:24-26 and Romans 4:5-8.

As a reversal of God's attitude toward the sinner because of his new relation in Christ, justification is: a **declarative** act, by which the sinner is **declared** to be free from guilt and the consequences of sin (Rom. 4:6-8; 5:18-19; 8:33-34; II Cor. 5:19-21); a **ju-**

dicial act in which the idea of judgment and salvation are combined to represent Christ fulfilling the law on behalf of the sinner (Rom. 3:26; 8:3; Gal. 3:13; II Cor. 5:21; I Pet. 3:18; Matt. 10:41 and I Tim. 1:9); a **remissive** act in which God actually remits the sin of man unto forgiveness (Rom. 4:5 and 6:7); and, a **restorative** act by which the forgiven sinner is restored to favor through the imputation of Christ's righteousness (Rom. 5:11; Gal. 3:6; I Cor. 1:30).

Four basic essentials in the act of justification are taught by Scripture:

1. Remission of punishment, in which the justified believer is declared to be free of the demands of the law since they have been satisfied in Christ (Rom. 4:5) and is no longer exposed to the penalty of the law (Rom. 6:7). It is more than a pardon from sin, but a declaration by God that the sinner, though guilty, has had the fact of his guilt remitted in Christ.

2. Restoration to favor, in which the justified believer is declared to be personally righteous in Christ, and therefore accepted as being in Christ's righteousness. Justification goes further than acquittal in that it implies that God's treatment of the sinner is as if he had never sinned since he is now regarded as being personally righteous in Christ (Gal. 3:6), not only pardon, but promotion.

3. Imputed righteousness of God, which is granted the justified believer through Christ's presence in him. His salvation in Christ imparts the quality and character of Christ's righteousness to him (Rom. 3:25, 26). Christ is made the Justifier through whom a new life is inaugurated in the believer (I Cor. 1:30).

4. New legal standing before God in which, instead of being under the condemnation of sin, the justified believer stands before God in Christ (Gal. 3:15; II Cor. 5:21; Rom. 3:25; Gal. 4:5).

The instrumental cause of justification is faith, as the response of the soul to God's redeeming grace (Rom. 3:28). Faith is the condition of justification not in that it is considered meritorious, but only as the condition by which the meritorious work of Christ is apprehended by man. The final ground of justification is the completed, finished, sufficient work of Christ atoning for man in His redeeming work upon the cross.

Justus (jŭs′tŭs, **just).** 1. The surname of Joseph Barsabas, one of the two whom the "brethren" appointed as candidates for Judas' place among the Twelve (Acts 1:23-26). 2. The surname of Titus, of Corinth, with whom Paul lodged for a time (Acts 18:7). 3. The surname of Jesus, an early Hebrew Christian at Rome, evidently known to the Christians at Colosse (Col. 4:11).

Juttah (jŭt′ȧ, **extended),** a town of the tribe of Judah, about five miles S of Hebron in the hill-country (Josh. 15:55; 21:16).

–K–

Kabzeel (kăb′zē-ĕl, **[whom] God gathers)**, a city in the south of Judah near the border of Edom (Josh. 15:21). It was the home of Benaiah (II Sam. 23:20), one of David's mighty men.

Kadesh (kā′dĕsh, **be holy)**, also known as En-mishpat (Gen. 14:7), place c. 70 miles E of Hebron, in vicinity of which Israel wandered for 37 years (Deut. 1:46; Num. 33:37, 38; Deut. 2:14); Miriam died there (Num. 20:1); Moses sent spies to Palestine from there (Num. 13:21-26; Deut. 1:19-25); Moses displeased God there by striking instead of speaking to rock (Num. 20:2-13). Often called Kadesh-barnea (Num. 32:8; Deut. 2:14).

Kadesh-Barnea (See Kadesh)

Kadmiel (kăd′mĭ-ĕl, **God is in front)**, head of a family of Levites who returned with Zerubbabel (Ezra 2:40; Neh. 7:43). One of his family sealed the covenant (Nah. 10:9).

Kadmonites (kăd′mŏn-īts, **children of the East)**, a very ancient tribe, one of the ten whose possessions God gave to the seed of Abraham (Gen. 15:18-21).

Kain (kān, **smith)**. 1. A town in Judah, in KJV spelled Cain (Josh. 15:57). 2. A tribal name; KJV has "the Kenite" (Num. 24:22; Judg. 4:11). See Kenites.

Kallai (kăl′ā-ī, **swift)**, a high priest in the days of Joiakim (Neh. 12:20).

Kamon (See Camon)

Kanah (kā′na, **reeds)**. 1. A brook running from S of Shechem westward to the Mediterranean Sea (Josh. 16:8; 17:9). 2. A city near the boundary of the tribes of Asher (Josh. 19:28).

Kareah (kȧ-rē′ȧ, **bald)**, father of Jonathan and Johanan, who warned Gedaliah the Babylonian governor of Judah of his danger (II Kings 25:23, where KJV has Careah; Jer. 40:8-43:5).

Karka (kȧr′kȧ, **ground)**, a place on the southern boundary of Judah (Josh. 15:3). KJV has Karkaa.

Karkor (kȧr′kôr), a place in the territory of the Ammonites where Zebah and Zalmunna were resting with the remains of the great army of the Midianites, and where Gideon overtook them and destroyed them (Judg. 8:10).

Kartah (kȧr′tȧ, **city)**, a city in Zebulun given to the Merarite Levites (Josh. 21: 34).

Kartan (kȧr′tăn), a city in Naphtali given to the Gershonite Levites (Josh. 21:32).

Kattath (kăt′ăth), a town in Galilee given to Zebulun (Josh. 19:15).

Kedar (kē′dêr, probably either **mighty** or **dark)**. 1. One of the 12 sons of Ishmael, son of Abram by Hagar (Gen. 25:13). 2. The tribe which descended from him, and their territory. They were for the most part nomads (Ps. 120:5, S. of Sol. 1:5), raising sheep (Isa. 60:7), but sometimes intruding into villages (Isa. 42:11). Their territory was in the northern part of the Arabian desert.

Kedemah (kĕd′ē-mȧ, **eastward)**, son of Ishmael, head of a clan (Gen. 25:15).

Kedemoth (kĕd′ē-mŏth, **eastern parts)**, a place E of the Jordan given to the tribe of Reuben (Num. 21:21-32; Deut. 2:26).

Kedesh (kē′dĕsh, **sacred place)**. 1. A city of the Canaanites conquered by Joshua in his northern campaign (Josh. 12:22), later given to the tribe of Naphtali (Josh. 19:37), appointed as a city of refuge (Josh. 20:7; 21:32) and bestowed upon the Gershonite Levites. Here Barak and Deborah assembled the hosts of Israel to fight against Sisera of the Canaanites (Judg. 4:6-10). 2. A city in the tribe of Issachar, given to the Gershonite Levites (I Chron. 6:72). 3. A city in the very southern part of Judah near the border of Edom (Josh. 15:23).

Kedesh Naphtali (See Kedesh)

Kedron (See Kidron)

Kehelathah (kē′hē-lā′thȧ, **gathering)**, a station in the wilderness of Paran where Israel encamped (Num. 33:22, 23).

Keilah (kē-ī′lȧ). 1. A city lying in the Shephelah (Josh. 15:44) threatened by the Philistines, but David rescued it (I Sam. 23:1-13). 2. A descendent of Caleb (I Chron. 4:19).

Kelaiah (kē-lā′yȧ), also Kelita, a Levite who divorced a foreign wife (Ezra 10:23).

Kelita (See Kelaiah)

Kemuel (kĕm′ū-ĕl). 1. Son of Nahor, uncle of Laban and Rebekah (Gen. 22:21); had a son Aram. 2. A prince of the tribe of Ephraim appointed by Moses to help divide the land of Canaan (Num. 34:24). 3. Father of Hashabiah, a leading Levite in the days of David (I Chron. 27:17).

Possible site of Kadesh, or Kadesh-barnea, in the Negev north of Sinai.
© *MPS.*

Kenan (kē'năn), great-grandson of Adam (I Chron. 1:2). In KJV of Gen. 5:9-14 Cainan.

Kenath (kē'năth, **possession),** a city of the Amorites in the region of Bashan in the kingdom of Og (Num. 32:42; I Chron. 2:22, 23).

Kenaz (kē'năz, **hunting).** 1. A grandson of Esau (Gen. 36:11, 15). Called "duke" in KJV and "chief" in ASV, but the Arab title "sheikh" would give a truer picture. 2. Father of Othniel (Josh. 15:17; Judg. 1:13; 3:9-11). 3. A grandson of Caleb (I Chron. 4:15).

Kenezite, Kenizzite (kē'nĕz-īt, kē'nĭz-īt), a patronymic name derived from Kenaz, one of the ten tribes of Canaan in the days of Abram (Gen. 15:19). No one knows who was the "Kenaz" from whom these Kenizzites were descended; and the tribe disappears from history with this mention.

Kenites (kē'nīts, **smith).** 1. One of the ten tribes of Canaan in the time of Abraham (Gen. 15:19). 2. The descendants of Hobab, the brother-in-law of Moses (Judg. 4:11). Hobab visited Israel as they left Sinai and Moses invited him to come along with Israel and to act as a pathfinder (Num. 10:29-32), which he did. His descendants were friendly with Israel; they went with Judah from Jericho (Judg. 1:16) and amalgamated with the tribe of Judah. Heber was the Kenite (Judg. 4:11). Heber's wife Jael, slew Sisera the Canaanite general, and so fulfilled Deborah's prophecy to Barak that a woman would get the honor for his victory (read Judg. 4).

Kenizzites (See Kenezite)

Kenosis (kē-nō'sĭs, **emptying** Phil. 2:7). A term applied to what Christ did when He became man. In Philippians 2:6-8 Paul pictures Christ as existing in the form of God. He says that Christ did not count the being on an equality with God a prize to be taken advantage of or to be profited by. Rather, "he made himself of no reputation" (KJV), "he emptied himself" (ASV, RSV). Christ did not cease to be a God when He deprived Himself of divine glory. Neither has Christ ceased to be man because He is free from the humiliation of the servant. In depriving Himself of His pre-incarnate manner of living, Christ made clear His complete awareness of all that redemption costs. Such a self-deprivation is described further in Philippians as a humbling of Himself (2:8), a becoming obedient even to the point of death. This is followed by God's exaltation of Christ with every being confessing that Jesus Christ is Lord to the glory of God the Father (Phil. 2:11).

Kerchief (See Dress)

Keren-Happuch (kĕr'ĕn-hăp'ŭk, **horn of antimony, i.e. beautifier),** the youngest daughter of Job, born to him after his release from the torments of Satan (Job 42:14, 15).

Kerioth (kĕr'ĭ-ŏth, **cities).** 1. Kerioth-hezron (not "Kerioth and Hezron" as in KJV), a city in the south of Judah (Josh. 15:25); otherwise "Hazor." 2. A city of Moab (Amos 2:1-3), probably its capital in the eighth century B.C. In "the judgment of Moab" (Jer. 48) Moab is pictured as ruined because of its idolatry (vs. 13) and its pride (vs. 29).

Keros (kē'rŏs), one of the Nethinim (temple servants) whose descendants returned with Zerubbabel (Ezra 2:44; Neh. 7:47).

Kettle (a cooking vessel), mentioned with pan, pot and caldron, and elsewhere translated by all these terms. Also a basket for carrying clay or bricks (I Sam. 2:14).

Keturah (kĕ-tū'rȧ), Abraham's second wife (Gen. 25:1), married probably after the death of Sarah and marriage of Isaac (Gen. 24:67; I Chron. 1:32; cf. Gen. 25:6). She was the mother of six sons, ancestors of Arabian tribes (Gen. 25:2-6; I Chron. 1:33).

Key, an Oriental key was made of wood, with nails or wooden pegs to fit corresponding holes in the bolt which held the door fast (Judg. 3:25). Figuratively, a symbol of authority (Isa. 22:20-22; Matt. 16:19; Rev. 1:18; 3:7; 9:1).

Kezia, Keziah (kĕ-zī'ȧ), the second of three daughters of Job born after his great trial (Job 42:14).

Keziz (kē'zĭz), a valley near Beth-hoglah in Benjamin, KJV; a city, Emek-keziz (Josh. 18:21 ASV, RSV).

Kibroth-hattaavah (kĭb'rŏth-hă-tā'ȧ-vȧ **the graves of lust or greed),** the next encampment of the Israelites after they left the wilderness of Sinai. Here they gorged themselves on the quails God sent, dying of the resulting sickness. This explains the name (Num. 11:34, 35; 33:16, 17; Deut. 9:22).

Kibzaim (kĭb-zā'ĭm), a town in Ephraim, assigned to the Kohathite Levites (Josh. 21:22). Jokmean appears in its place in I Chron. 6:68.

Kid (See Animals: Goats)

Kidney (kĭd′nē). This organ, being surrounded by pure fat, was adapted to burning in sacrifice, when the whole animal was not burned (Exod. 29:13, 22; Lev. 3:4, 10, 15; 4:9; 7:4; 8:16, 25; 9:10, 19). Regarded as the seat of the emotions; KJV, ASV margin, **reins,** usually "heart" in ASV, RSV text (Job 19:27; Ps. 7:9; Jer. 11:20, etc.).

Kidron (kĭd′rŏn), valley along E side of Jerusalem, joins Valley of Hinnom, and extends 20 miles to Dead Sea; burial ground (II Kings 23:6); dumping place for idols and their altars (I Kings 15:13; II Chron. 29:16; 30:14); David crossed it when he fled Absalom (II Sam. 15:23); Jesus crossed it on way to Gethsemane (John 18:1, KJV Cedron).

Kinah (kī′nȧ), a city in the S of Judah, near the border of Edom (Josh. 15: 21, 22).

Kine (See Animals: Cattle)

King. The earliest king mentioned in the Bible is Nimrod (Gen. 10:8-12). Israel contacted many kings in their wanderings (Num. 20:14-33:40; Deut. 1:4-4:47; 7:24; 29:7; 31:4) and in Canaan (Josh. 2:2-24:12; Judg. 1:7-11:25; I Sam. 14:47; 15:8, 20, 32, Agag; 21: 10, 12; 22:4). These varied in power from headmen of towns to rulers of large areas.

It is reiterated that in the time of the judges there was no king in Israel (Judg. 17:6; 18:1; 19:1; 21:25); every man did that which was right in his

Aerial view of the Kidron Valley, looking northward, with the Garden of Gethsemane between the road at the center and the northeast portion of the Jerusalem city wall at left. © MPS

own eyes. Moses had forseen that the people would demand a king as a strong human ruler (Deut. 17:14, 15; 28:36), not content with theocracy, but the direct rule of God over them (Deut. 33:5). Hannah looked forward to a time when there would be a God-appointed and anointed king of Israel (I Sam. 2:10). Israel, however, toward the end of Samuel's judgeship, was unwilling to wait for a Messianic King, and demanded one like all the nations (I Sam. 8:5, 22; 19:19, 24; 12:1-25; cf. Hos. 13:10). Samuel duly warned the people what to expect of a king, then selected Saul, whose choice they ratified. The reigns of Israelite kings are chronicled; Saul (I Sam. 12-31; I Chron. 10); David (II Sam.; I Kings 1; I Chron. 11-29); Solomon (I Kings 1-11; I Chron. 28-II Chron. 9); later kings of Israel and Judah (I Kings 12-II Kings 25; II Chron. 10:36). Ezra, Nehemiah and Esther deal with kings of Persia.

The prophets (especially Isa. 1-31; 36:1-39:7; Jer.; Lam.; Ezek.; Dan.) refer to kings of Judah and other nations. Isaiah develops the concept of a messianic King (Isa. 32:1; 33:17) identified with the Lord (33:22; 42:21; 43:15; 44:6). Jeremiah refers to God as King (Jer. 8:19; 10:7, 10; 46:18; 48: 15; 51:57) and to the messianic King (23:5). Ezekiel 37:22, 24 refers to the Davidic king of restored Israel whom the context shows to be messianic. The messianic King enters Jerusalem riding on a colt (Zech. 9:9); and God is King (Zech. 14:9, 16, 17; Mal. 1:14). Nebuchadnezzar praises the King of heaven (Dan. 4:37).

The Gospels speak of kings in general (Matt. 10:18; 11:8; 17:25; 18:23; 22:2, 7, 11, 13; Mark 13:9; Luke 10:24; 14:31; 21:12; 22:25); Herod the Great (Matt. 2:1, 3, 9; Luke 1:5); Herod Antipas (Matt. 14:9; Mark 6:14, 22-27); David (Matt. 1:6); the messianic King of the Jews (Matt. 2:2; 21:5; 25:34, 40; 27:11, 29, 37, 42; Mark 15: 2, 9, 12, 18, 26, 32; Luke 19:38; 23: 2, 3, 37, 38; John 1:49; 6:15; 12:13, 15; 18:37, 39; 19:3-21); and God (Matt. 5:35). References in Acts are to earthly kings except 17:7, Jesus. A few references in the Epistles are to earthly kings; one is to God (I Tim. 1:17, cf. 6:15). In Revelation, besides earthly kings, reigning and prophesied, Jesus Christ is introduced as prince (ruler) of the kings of the earth (1:5), who made us kings (1:6; 5:10, ASV, RSV a kingdom; cf. I Pet. 2:9). Among God's chosen people a rightful king was designated by God and anointed by His representative (I Sam. 9:15, 16; 16:1-13) with the approval of the people. He ruled by virtue of a covenant between God and His people, to which the king was a party (II Sam. 7). This covenant was extended and renewed as the basis of the NT kingdom of God or of heaven, of which Jesus is sovereign until at the resurrection He delivers the Kingdom to His Father (I Cor. 15:24-28).

Kingdom of God. The word "kingdom" is capable of three different meanings: 1. the realm over which a monarch reigns; 2. the people over whom he reigns; 3. the actual reign or rule itself. In English, the third use of the word is archaic and therefore is not always given its rightful place in discussion of the term; but in Greek and Hebrew, this is the primary meaning.

All three meanings are found in the New Testament. 1. The Kingdom of God is sometimes the people of the Kingdom. In Revelation 5:10, the redeemed are a kingdom, not, however, because they are the people over whom God reigns but because they will share His reign. The same usage appears in Revelation 1:6.

2. The Kingdom of God is the realm in which God's reign is experienced. This realm is sometimes something present, sometimes future. It is a realm introduced after the ministry of John the Baptist into which men entered with violent determination (Luke 16: 16). John did not stand within this new realm but only on its threshold; but so great are the blessings of God's Kingdom that the least in it is greater than John (Matt. 11:11). Jesus offered the Kingdom to Israel, for they were its proper heirs (Matt. 8:12); but the religious leaders, followed by most of the people, not only refused to enter its blessings but tried to prevent others from entering (Matt. 23:13). Nevertheless, many tax-collectors and harlots did enter the Kingdom (Matt. 21:31; see also Col. 1:13). In all of these verses, the Kingdom is a present realm where men may enjoy the blessings of God's rule.

Elsewhere the Kingdom is a future realm inaugurated by the return of Christ. The righteous will inherit this Kingdom (Matt. 25:34) and will shine like the sun in God's Kingdom (Matt.

13:43). Entrance into this future Kingdom is synonymous with entering the eternal life of the Age to Come (Matt. 19:16, 23-30; Mark 10:30).

3. The kingdom is also God's reign or rule. Only those who "receive the kingdom of God," i.e., accept God's rule here and now, enter into the realm of its blessings in the future (Mark 10:15). When we seek God's Kingdom and righteousness, we seek for God's rule in our lives (Matt. 6:33).

However, God's Kingdom is not merely an abstract rule. The Kingdom is God's rule **dynamically** active to defeat evil and redeem sinners (I Cor. 15:24-26).

The New Testament pictures three stages in the victory of God's Kingdom. Death is not finally destroyed until the end of the millennial reign of Christ (Rev. 20:14). Yet Christ has already destroyed **(katargeo)** death and brought life and immortality to light (II Tim. 1:10) through His death and resurrection.

The Kingdom of God — His redemptive rule — has come into history in the person of Christ to break the power of death and Satan; it will come in power and glory with the return of Christ to complete the destruction of these enemies. Because of this present victory of God's Kingdom, we may enter the realm of its blessings in the present yet look forward to greater blessings when Christ comes again.

We may now define the Kingdom of God as the sovereign rule of God manifested in Christ to defeat His enemies, creating a people over whom He reigns, and issuing in a realm or realms in which the power of His reign is experienced. May be summerized: Entrance into the kingdom is by the new birth (John 3:3-5); two stages in the kingdom of God: present and future in an eschatological sense; Jesus said that His ability to cast out demons was evidence that the kingdom of God had come among men (Matt. 12:28); the term "kingdom of heaven" is used synonymously with "kingdom of God" in the Bible.

Kingdom of Heaven (See Kingdom of God)

Kingdom of Israel (See Israel)

Kingdom of Judah (See Judah)

Kings, I and II, Books of. These are named in English by subject-matter: four centuries of kings of Israel, from David (his death in 930 B.C.) to Jehoiachin (in Babylon, after 561); provide a sequel to books of Samuel, which embrace the reigns of Saul and David; the two books were originally written as a unit, which was divided in two at the time of the LXX translation; shows how God rewards the good and punishes the wicked. Outline: 1. Solomon's reign (I Kings 1-11). 2. Kings of Israel and Judah (I Kings 12-II Kings 18). 3. Kings of Judah to exile (II Kings 18-25).

King's Garden, near the Pool of Siloam (II Kings 25:4; Jer. 39:4; 52:7; Neh. 3:15).

King's Highway, the ancient N and S road E of the Jordan through Edom and Moab (Num. 20:17; 21:22). Still in use.

King's Vale, or Dale, the Valley of Shaveh E of Jerusalem, where Abram met Melchizedek (Gen. 14:17); and Absalom set up his pillar (II Sam. 18: 18).

Kinsman (kĭnz′măn, **near relative, one who has the right to redeem).** Boaz exercised such a right by marrying Ruth and purchasing the property of her first husband's father, a near relative (Ruth 2:20-4:14). In the NT, Greek **suggenés, of the same race** (Luke 14: 12; John 18:26; Acts 10:24; Rom. 9: 3; 16:7, 11, 21; in Mark 6:4, kin). The NT meaning is always the broad one of undefined relationship. In the OT, kinsman translates Heb. words with three distinct ideas: one who has a right to redeem or avenge; one too closely related for marriage; a neighbor, friend or acquaintance.

Kir (kûr, kĭr, **inclosure, wall),** a place to which the Assyrians carried the inhabitants of Damascus captive (II Kings 16:9; Amos 1:5; 9:7; Isaiah 15: 1; 22:6).

Kir of Moab (See Kir)

Kir-Harasheth (kŭr-hăr′á-sĕth). The capital of Moab when Jehoram, king of Israel, made war on Mesha, king of Moab (II Kings 3:4-25) and devastated the country except for this city, which he besieged. When Mesha offered his son as a sacrifice on the wall, the siege was raised (25-27). Its later destruction is a subject for serious lamentation (Isa. 15:1; 16:7, 11; Jer. 48:31, 36).

Kiriath, Kirjath (kĭr′ĭ-ăth, kĭr′jăth, **a city).** The word occurs alone (Josh. 18: 28 KJV, ASV) where Kiriath-jearim (so RSV) is meant, and as part of other names identified with the same i.e.: Kiriath-arim (Ezra 2:25); Kiriath-baal

Abu Gosh, the likely site of ancient Kirjath-jearim, once a Canaanite high place and center of Baal worship. © *MPS*

(Josh. 15:60; 18:14); Kiriath-arba, Hebron (Gen. 23:2, etc.).

Kiriathaim, Kirjathaim (kĭr'ĭ-á-thā'im, **double city).** 1. A city in the uplands of Moab, given to Reuben (Num. 32:37; Josh. 13:19). 2. A city of the Gershonite Levites in Naphtali (I Chron. 6:76); Kartan (Josh. 21:32). In N Galilee, SE or Tyre, el-Qureiyeh.

Kiriath-Sepher (See Kiriath)

Kirioth (See Kiriath)

Kirjath (See Keriath)

Kirjath-Arba (See Kiriath)

Kirjath-Arim (See Keriath)

Kirjath-Baal (See Kiriath)

Kirjath-Huzoth (See Kiriath)

Kirjath-Jearim (kĭr'jăth-jē'á-rĭm, **city of woods).** With Gibeon, Chephirah, and Beeroth, one of four Gibeonite towns (Josh. 9:17), same as Baalah (15:9) and Kirjath-baal (15:60); a Canaanite high-place and center of Baal-worship, first assigned to Judah (15:60); at the SW corner of the boundary with Benjamin, to which it was later assigned (18:14, 15, 28). Men of Kirjath-jearim were listed in the genealogies (I Chron. 2:50-53). The prophet Urijah, son of Shemaiah, came from Kirjath-jearim. It is thought to be Tell-el-Azhar; by others Abû Ghôsh. Its location must be sought with reference to the other places mentioned, and it must be a high elevation. The name means "city of thickets or of forests," probably sacred groves.

Kirjath-Sannah (See Kiriath)

Kish (kĭsh, **bow, power).** 1. A Benjamite, a son of Abiel and father of Saul (I Sam. 9:1, 3; 10: 11, 21). Called Cis in KJV of Acts 13:21. 2. A Benjamite (I Chron. 8:30; 9:36). 3. A Levite in David's time (I Chron. 23:21, 22; 24:29). 4. A Levite who assisted in the cleansing of the temple in Hezekiah's time (II Chron. 29:12). 5. Ancestor of Mordecai, the cousin of Queen Esther (Esth. 2:5). 6. A city in Mesopotamia, a few miles E of Babylon.

Kishi (kĭsh'ī), a Merarite Levite, ancestor of Ethan (I Chron. 6:44).

Kishion (kĭsh'ĭ-ŏn, kĭsh'yŏn), a city in the tribe of Issachar, given to the Gershonite Levites (Josh. 19:20; 21:28 KJV Kishon; in I Chron. 6:72 called Kedesh).

Kishon, Kison (kī'shŏn, kī'sŏn, **curving),** stream which flows from Mt. Tabor and Mt. Gilboa westward through Plain of Esdraelon and enters Bay of Acre N of Mt. Carmel (Josh. 19:11; I Kings 18:40; Ps. 83:9).

The Kishon River, before Mount Carmel. © *MPS*

Kishon River (See Kishon)

Kiss, a common greeting among male relatives (Gen. 29:13; 33:4; 45:15; Exod. 4:27; 18:7; II Sam. 14:33); male and female relatives (Gen. 29: 11; 31:28); in farewell (Gen. 31:55; Ruth 1:9, 14) and before death (Gen. 50:1). The kiss had a more formal character in connection with a blessing (Gen. 27:26, 27; 48:10) or the anointing of a king (I Sam. 10:1). The kiss was generally given on the cheek, forehead or beard, though a kiss on the lips is indicated (Prov. 24:26) and is probable (in S. of Sol. 1:2; 8:1). Once Jesus' host did not give Him this customary greeting, but a sinful woman kissed His feet (Luke 7:38, 45). The father kissed the returning prodigal (Luke 15:20). Judas kissed Jesus as a sign to the temple police (Matt. 26:48, 49; Mark 14:44, 45; Luke 22:47, 48). The Ephesian elders kissed Paul in farewell (Acts 20:37). The kiss was adopted as a formal greeting among believers; the holy kiss (Rom. 16:16; I Cor. 16:20; II Cor. 13: 12; I Thess. 5:26) or kiss of charity or love (I Pet. 5:14); given by men to men and by women to women.

Kite (See Birds)

Kithlish (kĭth'lĭsh), a town in the lowland of Judah (Josh. 15:40); ASV, RSV, Chitlish (chĭt'lĭsh).

Kitron (kĭt'rŏn), a town in Zebulun, whose inhabitants that tribe did not drive out (Judg. 1:30).

Kittim (kĭt'ĭm). 1. Descendants of Javan (Gen. 10:4; I Chron. 1:7). 2. KJV Chittim, ASV Kittim. Where RSV has Cyprus, that island is probably meant (Isa. 23:1, 12; Jer. 2:10; Ezek. 27:6).

Kneading Trough, a shallow dish in which dough was prepared to be made into bread. The plague of frogs infested them in Egypt (Exod. 8:3). The Israelites bound them, dough and all, in the bundles of clothing on their backs, when they escaped from Egypt (Exod. 12:34). Called "kneading bowls" in RSV.

Knee. The first references are to taking on the knees in token of adoption (Gen. 30:3; 48:12; 50:23). The knees are equivalent to the lap (Judg. 16:19; Job 3:12; II Kings 4:20). Their strength or weakness is commented on (Job 4:14; Ps. 109:24; Heb. 12:12). To bow the knee to Baal identified one as his worshiper (I Kings 19:18; Rom. 11:4). Kneeling expressed homage or worship (II Kings 1:13, to Elisha; Matt. 17:14; Mark 1:40; 10:17; Luke 5:8, to Jesus; I Kings 8:54; II Chron. 6:13; Ezra 9: 3; Rom. 14:11 quoting Isa. 45:23; Eph. 3:14; Phil. 2:10; Acts 7:60; 9:40; 20: 36; 21:5, to God in prayer; notably Luke 22:41, Jesus in Gethsemane; Dan 6:10 shows that kneeling in prayer was already a customary practice). Kneeling in mockery, Mark 15:19.

Knife, a sharp-edged cutting instrument. Made of **flint** (Josh. 5:2, 3), kept for religious purposes. Priests of Baal cut themselves with knives in their contest with Elijah (I Kings 18:28); **a sword** (ASV, RSV) **used as a razor** (Ezek. 5:1, 2). Used to carve sacrifices (Gen. 22:6, 10; Judg. 19:29; figuratively, Prov. 30:14). A temple vessel taken from Jerusalem as spoils, and returned after the Exile, "29 knives" (KJV, ASV) which RSV calls "censers." A penknife (Jer. 36:23) was used to sharpen reed pens. Knives were not used to eat with, meat being cut in small pieces before serving, and bread broken at the table. The Philistines had metal knives long before they came into general use in Israel (see I Sam. 13:19, 22).

Knop (nŏp). 1. Knob ornamenting candlestick in tabernacle (Exod. 25: 31-36; 37:17-22). 2. Ornaments carved on walls of Solomon's Temple (I Kings 6:18).

Koa (kō'ȧ), a people E of the Tigris, between Elam and Media, named with others as about to invade Judah (Ezek. 23:23).

Kohath, Kohathites (kō'hăth, īts), second son of Levi (Gen. 46:11), ancestor of Moses (Exod. 6:16-20; Num. 3:17, 19; I Chron. 6:1-3). His descendants, the Kohathites, one of three divisions of the Levites, comprised four families (Num. 3:17-20, 27-31). Joshua allotted them 23 cities (Josh. 21:4, 5). Under the monarchy they are prominent (I Chron. 23:13-20; 24:20-25), especially Heman in the service of song (I Chron. 6:33ff; 16:41ff; 25:1ff). They took part in the religious service the day before Jehoshaphat's victory over his allied enemies (II Chron. 20:19); and in Hezekiah's cleansing of the temple (II Chron. 29:12-19).

Kolaiah (kō-lā'yȧ, **voice of Jehovah**). 1. A Benjamite who settled in Jerusalem after the Captivity (Neh. 11:7). 2. The father of the false prophet Ahab (Jer. 29:21).

Korah, Korahite (kō'rȧ, īt). 1. A son of Esau (Gen. 36:5, 14, 18; I Chron. 1:35). 2. A grandson of Esau (Gen. 36:16). 3. A descendant of Caleb (I Chron. 2:43). 4. A Levite from whom descended the Korahites, doorkeepers and musicians of tabernacle and temple (Exod. 6:24; I Chron. 6:22). 5. A son of Izhar and grandson of Kohath (Exod. 6:21, 24; I Chron. 6:37; 9:19) who led a rebellion (Num. 16; 26:9-11; 27:3; Jude 11 KJV Core). Korah, with two companions, resisted the civil authority of Moses. For refusing to appear before him as commanded, Korah, Dathan and Abiram and their followers were swallowed up by the earth (Num. 26:11).

Kore (kō'rē). 1. A Korahite whose son, Shallum, was a tabernacle gatekeeper (I Chron. 9:19; 26:1, 19). 2. A Levite set over the free will offerings in Hezekiah's time (II Chron. 31:14).

Koz (kŏz). 1. A priest whose descendants returned from exile with Zerubbabel (Ezra 2:61; Neh. 7:63 ASV, RSV Hakkoz). 2. Ancestor of Meremoth, who helped in the repair of the wall (Neh. 3:4, 21 ASV, RSV Hakkoz).

Kushaiah (kū-shā'yȧ), a Levite of the family of Merari (I Chron. 15:17). Called Kishi in I Chronicles 6:44.

–L–

Laadah (lā′ȧ-dȧ), a man of Judah, of the family of Shelah (I Chron. 4:21).

Laadan (lā′ȧ-dăn), Ladan in RV. 1. An ancestor of Joshua (I Chron. 7:26). 2. A Levite of the family of Gershon (I Chron. 23:7-9; 26:21), called Libni in I Chronicles 6:17.

Laban (lā′băn, **white).** 1. The nephew of Abraham who lived in Haran. He belonged to that branch of the family of Terah (Abraham's father) which was derived from Abraham's brother Nahor and his niece Milcah (Gen. 22: 20-24), and is first mentioned when Rebekah is introduced, as Rebekah's brother (Gen. 24:29). Laban takes a prominent place in the story of Rebekah's leaving for Canaan to be Isaac's bride. His grasping nature is hinted at in Genesis 24:30, 31.

Laban's later history is interwoven with Jacob's **(q.v.).** When Jacob fled from the anger of his brother Esau, he settled in his uncle Laban's house in Haran and stayed there 20 years. The relationship between Laban and his nephew is an interesting one. Both appear as resourceful, often grasping men, each eager to best the other in every transaction. Even in the circumstances surrounding the marriage of Jacob to Laban's daughters Rachel and Leah (Gen. 29) this competition is evident.

At the end of 20 years, Jacob quietly stole away from Laban, taking his now large family with him to Canaan (Gen. 31). Pursuing him, Laban overtook him in Gilead. After mutual protestations and incriminations, uncle and nephew parted, after erecting a "heap of witness"—a kind of dividing line—between them.

2. A place in the Plains of Moab, or perhaps in the Sinai peninsula. (Deut. 1:1).

Labor. Bible refers to labor as honorable (Ps. 128:2; Prov. 21:25; I Thess. 4:11); laborers protected by laws (Deut. 24:14). Creative work of God described as labor (Gen. 2:2). Onerous labor the result of the curse (Gen. 3: 17-19).

Lace, mentioned in the English Bible four times (Exod. 28:28, 37; 39:21, 31), always a translation of the Hebrew **pāthol** ("thread" or "cord"), the "lace of blue" used to bind the high priest's breastplate to the ephod.

Lachish (lā′kĭsh, perhaps meaning "rough"), a Canaanitish royal city and Judean border fortress, that occupied a strategic valley 25 miles SW of Jerusalem, the southernmost of the five that transect the Palestinian Shephelah, or piedmont, and communicate between Judah's central ridge and the coastal highway leading into Egypt. Its king, Japhia, joined with Adonizedek of Jerusalem in a confederacy against Joshua, 1406 B.C. (Josh. 10:3), only to be defeated and executed (10:23-26; 12:11). In Joshua's subsequent sweep through the southwest, Israel captured Lachish (reinforced by Gezer) and annihilated its inhabitants, in accordance with Moses' ban (10:31-33; Deut. 7:2). Scripture contains no record, however, of its destruction (cf. Josh. 11:13).

Lachish was fortified by Rehoboam, shortly after the division of the Hebrew kingdom in 930 B.C. (II Chron. 11:9); and it witnessed the murder of King Amaziah in 767 (25:27). The Prophet Micah condemned Lachish's chariots as "the beginning of Zion's sin," perhaps because of the city's use as a staging point for the extravagant importation of Egyptian horses (1:13; cf. I Kings 10:28-29; Deut. 17:16). In any event, Lachish was successfully besieged by Sennacherib in 701 (II Chron. 32:9); thither Hezekiah directed his submission (II Kings 18:14); and from it the Rabshakeh's troops marched against Jerusalem (18:17; 19: 9). Finally, in Nehemiah's day a resettled Lachish (Neh. 11:30) achieved the construction of a palace and Persian sun temple that are among the finest of the period.

Ladder, mentioned only once in the English Bible—Jacob's ladder between heaven and earth, seen in his Bethel dream (Gen. 28:12).

Lael (lā′ĕl), a member of the family of Gershon, father of Eliasaph (Num. 3: 24). Meaning "belonging to God," the name is almost unique in the OT.

Lahad (lā′hăd), a Judahite family name (I Chron. 4:2).

Lahai-Roi (See Beer-Lahai-Roi)

Lahmam (lȧ′măm), a town in the Judean Shephelah (Josh. 15:40).

Lahmi (lȧ′mī), the brother of Goliath from Gath, who was slain by a certain Elhanan (1 Chron. 20:5).

Above, the Mount at Lachish (Tell Ed-Duweir), the north and northeast sides of the Tell. Below, excavation work in progress on the Mound at Lachish. © *MPS*

Laish (lā'ĭsh). 1. A city in the upper Jordan valley, captured by the Danites and renamed Dan (Judg. 18:7, 14, 27, 29). It is called Leshem in Joshua 19: 47. Laish in Isaiah 10:30 (KJV) should be rendered Laishah (RSV) and is a town a little N of Jerusalem. 2. The father of Phalti or Phaltiel, a Benjamite, to whom Michal, David's wife, was given by Saul (I Sam. 25:44; II Sam. 3:15).

Lakum, Lakkum (lā'kŭm, lăk'ŭm), a town of Naphtali (Josh. 19:33).

Lamb, a translation of several Hebrew words in the English Bible, most of them meaning the young of the sheep. One however (sheh, used in Exod. 12: 3-6), refers to the young of either sheep or goats (cf. Exod. 12:5) and seems to include adult specimens at times.

The meat of lambs was considered a delicacy among the ancient Hebrews (Deut. 32:14; Amos 6:4; II Sam. 12:3-6). Meat was scarce among them, and the killing of a lamb would mark an important occasion. Lambs were used for sacrifices from the earliest times (Gen. 4:4; 22:7; Exod. 29:38-42 etc.).

Lamb of God, Jesus was called the Lamb of God by John the Baptist (John 1:29, 36). The expression certainly emphasizes the redemptive character of the work of Christ. More than a score of times in the Revelation the lamb is used as a symbol of Christ.

The OT is full of the lamb as a sacrificial victim (see lamb). Of special interest is the Passover lamb (Exod. 12: 3-6) with the sacrifice of which deliverance from Egypt was achieved (a picture of redemption from sin, Luke 9: 31; I Cor. 5:7).

Lame (See Diseases)

Lamech (lā'mĕk), the name of two men in the antediluvian records: 1. A son of Methusael (Gen. 4:18-24), a descendant of Cain, he had two wives, Adah and Zillah. Lamech's sons by Adah, Tubal and Jubal, founded the nomadic life and the musical arts; Lamech's son by Zillah, Tubal-cain, invented metalcrafts and instruments of war; Lamech also had a daughter Naamah, by Zillah. As far as the record reveals, this man was the first poet. His song (Gen. 4:23f) expresses every feature of Hebrew poetry (parallelism, poetic diction, etc.).

2. The son of Methuselah (Gen. 5: 28-31). A descendant of Seth, he became the father of Noah. His faith is attested by the name he gave his son (Noah, meaning "rest"), and by the hope of "comfort" (Gen. 5:29) that he anticipated in his son's life.

Lamentations, Book of. Author not stated, but ancient authorities ascribe it to Jeremiah. LXX, Vulgate, and English Bible place it after Jeremiah, but in Heb. Bible it appears between Ruth and Ecclesiastes. Title accurately designates contents; the book bewails the seige and destruction of Jerusalem, and sorrows over the sufferings of the inhabitants during this time; makes poignant confession of sin on behalf of the people and their leaders, acknowledges complete submission to the divine will, and prays that God will once again favor and restore His people. Five poems (the first four consisting of acrostics based on Heb. alphabet) make up the five chapters.

Lamp. Archaeology has recovered many specimens in a great variety of forms from the early simple shallow, saucer-like bowl with one side slightly pointed for the lighted wick, to the later closed bowl with only a hole on top to pour in the oil, a spout for the wick, and a handle to carry it. Lamps for domestic use were generally of terra-cotta or of bronze.

The KJV often uses "candle" and "candlestick" where "lamp" and "lampstand" would be more literal.

The use of lamps is mentioned in connection with the golden candlestick in the tabernacle and the ten golden candlesticks in the temple (Exod. 25: 37; I Kings 7:49; II Chron. 4:20; 13: 11; Zech. 4:2). As shown from their usage, the "lamps" of Gideon's soldiers were doubtless torches. The common NT mention of lamps is in connection with their household usage (Matt. 5:15; Mark 4:21; Luke 8:16; 11:33; 15:8). The use of oil-fed lamps in a marriage procession is mentioned in Matthew 25:1. Since such lamps contained only a few spoonfuls of oil, a reserve supply would be a necessity. The lighted lamp is also mentioned metaphorically to symbolize (1) God's Word (Ps. 119: 105; II Pet. 1:19); (2) God's guidance (II Sam. 22:29; Ps. 18:28); (3) God's salvation (Isa. 62:1); (4) man's spirit (Prov. 20:27); (5) outward prosperity (Prov. 13:9); (6) a son as successor (I Kings 11:36; 15:4).

Lance (See Arms, Armor)

Landmark, an object (stone or post) used to mark the boundary of a field. Removal of landmarks was prohibited

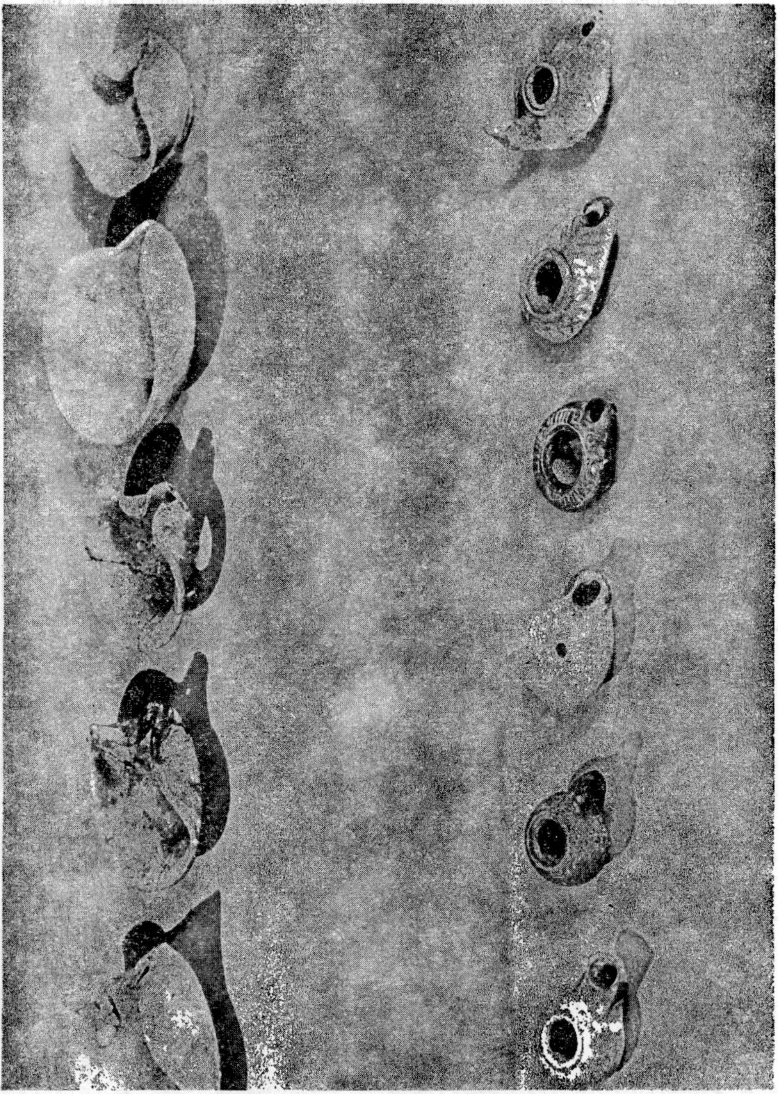

Lamps of Palestine in series, from patriarchal times to the New Testament era. Note the progression from simple open dish types (lefthand column) to "slipper" types (righthand column). © Andrews University.

by the Mosaic law (Deut. 19:14; 27: 17). Hebrew piety denounced the act (Prov. 22:28; 23:10) and it was considered equal to theft (Job 24:2).

Lane, alley of a city (Luke 14:21).

Languages. Many different languages spoken in OT times. Israelites spoke Hebrew when they entered Palestine and at least as late as the time of Nehemiah, and it remained the literary language permanently. In colloquial use it was replaced by Aramaic. The chief languages in NT Palestine: Aramaic (Hebrew), Greek, Latin (John 19:20).

Laodicea (lā-ŏd'ĭ-sē'ȧ), a wealthy city in Asia Minor founded by Antiochus II (261-246 B.C.) on one of the great Asian trade routes. She was "rich and increased with goods" and had "need of nothing" (Rev. 3:17). The scornful imagery of the apocalyptic letter to Laodicea is obviously based on these facts (Rev. 3:14-22).

Laodicea, Church at (See Laodicea)

Laodiceans, Epistle to, mentioned by Paul in Colossians 4:16. Could be: 1. The spurious "Epistle to the Laodiceans" found among the Pauline epistles

Ruins of Phrygian city of Laodicea. © SHH

in some Latin Mss. from the sixth to the 15th centuries. 2. A Pauline letter to the Laodiceans now lost. 3. Our Ephesians. This view is very probable if the encyclical view of Ephesians is accepted, and accounts for Marcion's title of it as "the epistle to the Laodiceans."

Lapped, Lappeth (lăpt, lăp'ĕth, **to lap, lick).** The Hebrew verb is used (1) to indicate alertness and alacrity (in the test of Gideon's army; Judg. 7:5, 6, 7); (2) to indicate disgust and loathsomeness (in the comparison between Naboth's death and Ahab's death; I Kings 21:19; 22:38).

Lappidoth (lăp'ĭ-dŏth, **torches or lightning flashes),** the husband of Deborah (Judg. 4:4).

Lapwing (See Birds)

Lasciviousness (lă-sĭv'ĭ-ŭs-nĕs). (Mark 7:22; II Cor. 12:21; Gal. 5:19; Eph. 4: 19; I Pet. 4:3; II Pet. 2:18; Jude 4), shameful immorality "lascivious" (II Pet. 2:7), "lascivious doings" (II Pet. 2:2), "wantonness" (Rom. 13:13).

Lasea (lȧ-sē'ȧ), seaport town on the S coast of Crete, listed by Luke (Acts 27: 8) in the log of Paul's voyage to Rome.

Lasha (lā'shȧ), a place near Sodom and Gomorrah mentioned in Gen. 10: 19.

Lasharon (lă-shā'rŏn), a royal Canaanite town whose king was slain by Joshua (Josh. 12:18).

Latchet (lăch'ĕt;-ĭt, **[sandal-]thong),** the thong or strap, usually made of leather, by which the sandal was fastened to the foot. It is used figuratively to describe (1) the most insignificant possession (Gen. 14:23); (2) the efficiency of an invading army (Isa. 5:27); (3) the most menial kind of service (Mark 1:7; Luke 3:16; John 1:27; cf. Acts 13:25).

Latin (lăt'ĭn), the language of the Romans in Palestine (Luke 23:38; John 19:20).

Lattice (lăt'ĭs). Latticework, made by crossing laths or other material across an opening, served a threefold purpose: (1) privacy; (2) ventilation; (3) decoration (Judg. 5:28; Prov. 7:6; II Kings 1:2).

Laughter (lȧf'têr). 1. Laughter's limitations: it cannot satisfy (Prov. 14: 13; Eccl. 2:2; 7:3, 6; 10:19). 2. God's laughter at His enemies (Pss. 2:4; 37: 13; 59:8). 3. The believers' laughter (Gen. 17:17; 18:12-15; 21:6; Ps. 126:2; Luke 6:21; Job 22:19; Ps. 52:6; Isa. 37:22). 4. The unbelievers' laughter (Ps. 22:7; Matt. 9:24; Neh. 2:19; Job 12:4; Ps. 80:6; II Chron. 30:10; Prov. 1:26; Luke 6:25; James 4:9).

Laver (lā'vêr, **pot, basin),** a vessel containing water, located between the altar and the door of the tabernacle, at which Jewish priests washed their hands and feet before ministering (Exod. 30:17-22). Had typical meaning, signifying: (1) baptism as a cleansing from sin (cf. Acts 2:38; 22:16; I Cor. 6:11; Eph. 5:26; Titus 3:5; Heb. 10:22; I Pet. 3:20f); (2) the need of daily purification before approaching the Lord (cf. Ps. 24:3f; John 13:2-10; I John 1:7ff).

Law. 1. Ten Commandments given to Moses (Exod. 20:3-17; Deut. 5:6-21), summarized God's requirements of man. 2. Torah, first five books of OT (Matt. 5:17; Luke 16:16). 3. OT (John 10:34; 12:34). 4. God's will in words, acts, precepts (Exod. 20:1-17; Ps. 19). OT Jews manifested their faith in Jehovah by observing the law. Christ fulfilled the law; respected, loved it, and showed its deeper significance (Matt. 5:17-48). Purpose of OT law to prepare way for coming of Christ (Gal. 3:24). Law shows man's sinfulness, but cannot bring victory over sin (Rom. 3-8; Gal.). Jesus' summary of the law: it demands perfect love for God and for one's neighbor comparable to that which one has for himself (Matt. 22: 35-40).

Law of Moses (See Law)

Lawgiver, (Gen. 49:10; Num. 21:18; Deut. 33:21; Pss. 60:7; 108:8; Isa. 33: 22; James 4:12). God is the only absolute lawgiver (James 4:12). Instrumentally, Moses bears this description (John 1:17; 7:19).

Lawyer, a professional interpreter of the written and oral law; also called scribe (Matt. 22:35; Luke 10:25).

Laying on of Hands. An act symbolizing (1) the parental bestowal of inheritance-rights (Gen. 48:14-20); (2) the gifts and rights of an office (Num. 27:18, 23; Deut. 34:9); and (3) substitution, of an animal for one's guilt (Exod. 29:10, 15, 19; Lev. 1:4; 3:2, 8, 13; 4:4, 15, 24, 29, 33; 8:14, 18, 22; 16:21; cf. Gen. 22:9-13), of a tribe for the firstborn of other tribes (Num. 8: 10-13), of one's innocency for another's guilt (Lev. 24:13-16; Deut. 13: 9; 17:7). In the NT the act symbolizes (1) the bestowal of blessings and benediction (Matt. 19:13, 15; cf. Luke 24: 50); (2) the restoration of health (Matt. 9:18; Acts 9:12, 17); (3) the reception of the Holy Spirit in baptism (Acts 8:

17, 19; 19:6); (4) the gifts and rights of an office (Acts 6:6; 13:3; I Tim. 4: 14; II Tim. 1:6).

Lazarus (lăz'á-rŭs, **God has helped).** 1. Lazarus, the brother of Martha and Mary, who lived in Bethany. He died; Christ, after some delay, returned and raised Lazarus from death (John 11:1-12:19).

This miracle (1) illustrates Christ's sympathy (John 11:5, 11, 34f) and power (John 11:40ff); (2) manifests the purposiveness of His miracles (John 11:4, 40; 20:31); (3) gives concreteness to Luke 16:30f; (4) affords opportunity for eschatological teaching (John 11: 23-25); (5) precipitates the crucifixion (John 11:45-53; 12:9-19).

Leaf, used in a threefold manner in the Bible. 1. Leaf of a tree (Dan. 4:12, 14, 21; Ezek. 17:9 etc.). 2. Leaf of a door (I Kings 6:34; Ezek. 41:24). 3. Leaf of a book (Jer. 36:23).

Leah (lē'á), Laban's daughter and Jacob's first (though not preferred) wife (Gen. 29:21-30); mother of Reuben, Simeon, Levi, Judah, Issachar, Zebulun, and Dinah (Gen. 29:31-35; 30:17-21). Two of her sons (Levi and Judah) became progenitors of prominent tribes in Israel; and through Judah, Jesus Christ came (Gen. 49:10; Mic. 5:2; Matt. 2:6; Heb. 7:14; Rev. 5:5; cf. Ruth 4:11).

Leasing (lēz'ĭng, **lie, falsehood),** now obsolete (Pss. 4:2; 5:6). RSV has "falsehood" and "lies."

Leather (lĕth'êr, **made of skin),** designates the skin of certain animals after it has been tanned (Acts 10:32). Leather was a common article of clothing (Lev. 13:48; Heb. 11:37). Leather was also used for armor, shoes, containers, and writing material.

Traditional tomb of Lazarus at Bethany. JFW

Terrain of Lebanon, showing the town of Bshirre in the valley and the road to the cedars. © *MPS*

Leaven (lĕv′ĕn) substance used to make dough rise (Exod. 12:15, 20); could not be used in meal offerings (Lev. 2:11) or in Passover (Lev. 2:11; Exod. 12); symbol of moral influence, whether good or bad (Matt. 13:33; 16:6).

Lebanon (lĕb′á-nŭn, **white**), mt. range extending in a NE direction for 100 miles along the Syrian coast, from Tyre to Arvad, and the country which bears its name. Between the Lebanon and Anti-Lebanon ranges there is a valley known as Coele (hollow) Syria. Some peaks reach 10,000 feet. Mt. Herman (9383 ft.) is southernmost spur of Anti-Lebanons. Formed N boundary of Palestine (Deut. 1:7). Heavily wooded; known especially for cedars (Judg. 9:15; I Kings 5:6).

Lebaoth (lē-bā′ŏth, **lionesses**), a town in S part of Judah (Josh. 15:32) also called Beth-lebaoth (Josh. 19:6) and (probably) Beth-birei (I Chron. 4:31).

Lebbaeus (lĕ-bē′ŭs, **hearty**), one of Christ's apostles who is also called Thaddaeus (Matt. 10:3; Mark 3:18) and Judas (Luke 6:16; Acts 1:13).

Lebonah (lē-bō′nȧ, **frankincense**), a town (Judg. 21:19), N of Bethel on the highway between Shiloh and Shechem.

Lecah (lē'ka, **walking**), son of Er (I Chron. 4:21).

Leeks (See Plants)

Lees (lēz, **something preserved**), that undisturbed and thick portion of wine that naturally falls to the bottom of the vat. The word is used figuratively throughout to express (1) the blessings of Messianic times (Isa. 25:6; cf. Isa. 55:1). (2) the spiritual lethargy and decadence of Moab (Jer. 48:11); (3) the indifference of Israelites to spiritual realities (Zeph. 1:12); (4) the bitterness and inevitability of God's wrath upon the wicked (Ps. 75:8—"dregs").

Left, has a variety of connotations in the Bible: (1) simple direction (II King 23:8; Neh. 8:4); (2) geographic North (Gen. 14:15; Ezek. 16:46, RSV); (3) all directions (with "right") (Job 23:9); (4) the lesser blessing (Gen. 48: 13-19); (5) weakness (Judg. 3:15, 21), immaturity (Jonah 4:11), perversity (Eccl. 10:2), or evil (Matt. 25:33, 41); (6) completion (with "right") (Ezek. 4:4, 6); (7) special ability (I Chron. 12:2); (8) a woman's preference (S. of Sol. 2:6; 8:3).

Legion (lē'jŭn). 1. The largest single unit in the Roman army (about 6,000 Roman soldiers). 2. The term "legion" in the NT represents a vast number (Matt. 26:53; Mark 5:9, 15; Luke 8: 30).

Lehabim (lē-hā'bĭm), the third son of Mizraim (Gen. 10:13; I Chron. 1:11). Libyans (Jer. 46:9; Dan. 11:43) or the inhabitants of Libya (Ezek. 30:5; 38: 5; Acts 2:10), represent the same ethnic group. Descendants of Ham, they occupied the N coast of Africa W of Egypt.

Lehi (lē'hī, **jawbone, cheek**), a place in Judah between the cliff Etam and Philistia, where Samson killed 1,000 Philistines with a jawbone (Judg. 15: 9, 14).

Lemuel (lĕm'ū-ĕl, **devoted to God**), a king, otherwise unknown, to whom his mother taught the maxims in Proverbs 31:2-9. Probably Solomon (Prov. 31:1).

Lentile, Lentil (See Plants)

Leopard (See Animals)

Leper (See Diseases)

Leprosy (See Diseases)

Leshem (lē'shĕm, **gem**), the original of Dan (Josh. 19:47), a city at extreme N of Palestine (I Sam. 3:20); variant of Laish.

Letter. In general, "letter" designates (1) an alphabetical symbol (Gal. 6:11, ASV); (2) rudimentary education (John 7:15); (3) a written communication; (4) the external (Rom. 2:27, 29); (5) Jewish legalism (Rom. 7:6; II Cor. 3:6).

Lettushim, Letushim lĕ-tū'shĭm, **sharpened**), the second son of Dedan, who was the grandson of Abraham by Keturah (Gen. 25:3).

Leummim (lē-ŭm'ĭm, **peoples, nations**), third son of Dedan (Gen. 25:3), who was a grandson of Abraham by Keturah.

Levi (lē'vī, **joined**). 1. Jacob's third son by Leah (Gen. 29:34; 35:23). Born in Haran, he accompanied his father on his return to Canaan. He joined his brothers in sinister plots against Joseph (Gen. 37:4, 28); and, with them, eventually bowed before Joseph (Gen. 42:6). Levi died in Egypt at age 137 (Exod. 6:16). His three sons, Gershon, Kohath and Merari (Gen. 46:11), later became heads of families. (See Levites.) Levi's curse became a blessing (Deut. 33:8-11) to his descendants.

2 and 3. Ancestors of Jesus (Luke 3: 24, 29). 4. See Matthew.

Leviathan (See Animals)

Levirate Marriage (lĕv'ĭ-rāt, lē'vĭ-, **a husband's brother**), an ancient custom, sanctioned by practice (Gen. 38:8ff) and by law (Deut. 25:5-10, which does not contradict Lev. 18:16; 20:21, where the participants are all alive), whereby a deceased man's brother or nearest male kin was required to marry his bother's widow and raise up seed in his brother's name. Ruth's marriage to Boaz recognized this law (Ruth 4:1-17). It also underlies the argument of the Sadducees in Matthew 22:23-33.

Levites (lē'vīts), name given to descendants of Levi through his sons Gershon, Kohath, Merari (Exod. 6:16-25; Lev. 25:32); became substitutes for fellow-Israelites in duties pertaining to God (Num. 3:11-13; 8:16); three-fold organization: top echelon occupied by Aaron and his sons, and they alone were priests in the restricted sense; middle echelon consisted of some Levites not of Aaron's family, who had the privilege of bearing the tabernacle (Num. 3:27-32); bottom echelon, comprised all members of the families of Gershon and Merari, who had lesser duties in the tabernacle (Num. 3:21-26, 33-37). Priests were Levites belonging to Aaron's family, but Levites were not necessarily priests. Levites received no tribal territory; 48 cities were assigned to them (Num. 35), and they were supported by tithes (Lev. 27:30-33; Num. 18:21-24).

Levitical Cities. The plan set forth in Numbers 35:1-8 (fulfilled in Joshua 21) gave the Levites 48 cities. This plan involved a threefold purpose: (1) Such cities caused the Levites to be "scattered" in Israel and thus fulfilled Jacob's dying prophecy (Gen. 49:7); (2) thus "scattered," they could carry out their teaching ministry better (Deut. 33:10); (3) since six of their cities were to be "cities of refuge" (Num. 35:6), they would thereby become more accessible to those seeking legal protection (Deut. 19:1-3, 7-10, 17ff).

Leviticus (lĕ-vĭt'ĭ-kŭs, **relating to the Levites**). The book is closely associated with Exodus and Numbers in historical continuity, but differs from them in that the purely historical element is subordinate to legal and ritual considerations. Although the emphasis in Leviticus is more on priests than Levites, the English title is not inappropriate, since the Jewish priesthood was essentially Levitical (cf. Heb. 7:11).

Leviticus contains much that is technical in nature and meant for the direction of the priesthood in the conduct of worship and the regulating of social life. Thus it is distinct from Deuteronomy which is in effect a popular exposition of Levitical law.

The first seven chapters of Leviticus give the detailed sacrificial procedures showing how the various kinds of burnt offerings, the meal offering, the sin and guilt offerings and other sacrifices avail for the removal of sin and defilement under the covenant. A subsequent liturgical section (8:1-10:20) described the consecration of Aaron and the priesthood, being followed by the designation of clean and unclean beasts and certain rules of hygiene (11:1-15:33). The ritual of the Day of Atonement occurs in Chapter 16, followed by a section (17:1-20:27) treating of sacrificial blood, ethical laws and penalties for transgressors. The theme of 21:1-24:33 is priestly holiness and the consecration of seasons, while the following chapter deals with the legislation surrounding the sabbatical and jubilee years. A concluding chapter outlines promises and threats (26:1-46), while an appendix (27:1-34) treats of vows. Man as sinner, substitutionary atonement and divine holiness are prominent throughout Leviticus.

Levy (lĕv'ē, **tribute**), a tax or tribute. It is used of the 30,000 free Israelites conscripted by Solomon for four months service a year in Lebanon (I Kings 5:13-14); also of the tribute labor imposed upon the surviving Canaanites (I Kings 9:21).

Libation, the pouring out of liquids, such as wine, water, oil, etc., but generally wine, as an offering to a deity. Libations were common among the heathen nations (Deut. 32:38). Drink-offerings accompanied many OT sacrifices (Exod. 29:40-41; Lev. 23:13, 18, 37; Num. 15:4-10, 24; 28:7-10). In II Tim. 4:6; Philippians 2:17 Paul pictures his death as a drink-offering.

Libertines, captive Jews brought to Rome by Pompey in 63 B.C., liberated subsequently, and repatriated to Palestine, where, presumably they built a synagogue still occupied by their descendants a century after Pompey's Palestinian campaign (Acts 6:9). These people would be Roman citizens.

Liberty, freedom, the opposite of servitude or bondage, whether physical, moral, or spiritual. The term is used of slaves or captives being set free from physical servitude or imprisonment (Lev. 25:10; Jer. 34:8, 15-17; Acts 26:23; Heb. 13:23), or the granting of certain privileges while in imprisonment (Acts 24:23; 27:3). In Ezekiel 46:17 reference is made to "the year of liberty," the year of jubilee. The term has a legal and moral tone in I Corinthians 7:39 in asserting the right of a widow to remarry. The special concern of Christianity is the spiritual liberty of believers in Christ. Found in union with Christ, it carries with it freedom from the ceremonial law (Gal. 5:1; 2:4) and must be valued and guarded. The essence of Christian liberty lies not in external freedom but in deliverance from the bondage of sin and its consequent inner corruption (John 8:34-36; Rom. 6:20-22).

Spiritual liberty is the result of the Spirit's regenerating work, for His presence and work within produces liberty (II Cor. 3:17), giving a sense of freedom through a filial relation with God (Rom. 8:15-16). Godly men of the OT knew a measure of this spiritual liberty (Psa. 119:45), but the Gospel reveals and offers it in its fulness (Luke 4:18; Rom. 6:18-22; Gal. 5:13; I Pet. 2:16; II Pet. 2:19; James 2:12).

Libnah (lĭb'nȧ, **whiteness**). 1. A desert camp of Israel, after leaving Sinai (Num. 33:20-21). 2. A Canaanite city, near Lachish, captured by Joshua (Josh. 10:29-32; 12:15) and named at the head of a group of nine cities in the lowland (15:42-44).

Libni (lĭb'nī, **white**). 1. The first-named of the two sons of Gershon, the son of Levi (Exod. 6:17; Num. 3:17; I Chron. 6:17, 20). Also Laadan or Ladan (I Chron. 23:7; 26:21). 2. A Levite (I Chron. 6:29).

Libnites (lĭb'nītes), the descendants of Libni, the son of Gershon (Num. 3:21; 26:58).

Libraries. Libraries, both public and private, were not uncommon in ancient times in the Oriental, Greek, and Roman worlds. The Dead Sea Scrolls is one example of an ancient library that has survived to modern times.

Libya (lĭb'ĭ-ȧ), the ancient Greek name for northern Africa W of Egypt (Ezek. 30:5; 38:5; Jer. 46:9; Dan. 11:43). Cyrene was one of its cities (Acts 2:10).

Lice (See Insects)

Lieutenants, the official title of satraps or viceroys governing large provinces of the Persian empire as representatives of the sovereign. KJV has "lieutenants" in Ezra 8:36; Esther 3:12; 8:9; 9:3 and "princes" in Daniel 3:2, 3, 27; 6:1-7; "satraps" in ASV.

Life, a complex concept with varied shades of meaning, rendering several Heb. and Gr. terms. It may denote **physical** or natural life, whether animal (Gen. 1:20; 6:17; Rev. 8:9) or human (Lev. 17:14; Matt. 2:20; Luke 12:22, etc). It is the vital principle, or breath of life, which God imparted to man, making him a living soul (Gen. 2:7). But the primary concern of the Scriptures is **spiritual** or **eternal life** for man. It is the gift of God, mediated through faith in Jesus Christ (John 3:36; 5:24; Rom. 5:10; 6:23; I John 5:12; etc). It is not synonymous with endless existence, which is also true of the unsaved. It is qualitative, involving the importation of a new nature (II Pet. 1:3-4). It is communicated to the believer in this life, resulting in fellowship with God in Christ, and is not interrupted by physical death (I Thess. 5:10). It will find its perfection and full reality of blessedness with God in the life to come (Rom. 2:7; II Cor. 5:4).

Life, The Book of, a figurative expression denoting God's record of those who inherit eternal life (Phil. 4:3; Rev. 3:5; 21:27).

Light, denotes natural light; also used figuratively. Scripture pictures the coming into existence of natural light through the sublime command of God ("let there be light" Gen. 1:3) as the initial step in the preparation of the world for vegetable and animal life. The origin and nature of light find their explanation in the nature and purpose of God Himself (I John 1:5). The possession of light is one of the most remarkable and valuable blessings of this earthly sphere, without which life as we know it could not exist.

Since darkness is the symbol of sin, by contrast light is the figure of holiness and purity (Isa. 5:20; Rom. 13:12; I John 1:6-7; 2:9-11). It is also a general figure for that which tends to cheer or renders prosperous (Esth. 8:16; Job 30:26), hence especially of spiritual joy (Pss. 27:1; 97:11). The Word of God is symbolized as light (Ps. 119:105; Isa. 8:20). The figure is also applied to believers generally (Matt. 5:14; Eph. 5:8; Phil. 2:15), or to individuals like John the Baptist (John 5:35). Finally, the figure is applied to the bliss of the heavenly state (Isa. 60:19; Col. 1:12; Rev. 21:23-24; 22:5).

Lightning, a visible electric discharge between rain clouds or between a rain cloud and the earth, producing a thunderclap. The Scriptures mention lightning as a manifestation of God's power, symbolizing His command of the forces of nature (Job 28:26; 38:35; Ps. 135:7; Zech. 10:1); lightnings are His instruments in bringing about the destruction of His opponents (Pss. 18:14; 144:6; Zech. 9:14-15). Lightning is used as a symbol of speed (Ezek. 1:14; Nah. 2:4; Zech. 9:14) and of dazzling brightness (Dan. 10:6; Matt. 28:3).

Lign-Aloes (See Plants)

Ligure (See Minerals)

Likhi (lĭk'hī), a Manassite (I Chron. 7:19).

Lily (See Plants)

Line. Usually the meaning is **a measuring line** (II Sam. 8:2; Ps. 78:55; Isa. 34:17; Jer. 31:39; Ezek. 47:3; Zech. 1:16; 2:1), or a cord or thread (Josh. 2:18, 21; Ezek. 40:3), "pencil" (ASV) or a cutting instrument (Isa. 44:13); "portion" (Ps. 16:6); the sound made by a musical chord (Ps. 16:6; cf. Rom. 10:18). In II Corinthians 10:16 "line" means a "province" or sphere worked by another.

Linen, thread or cloth, prepared from the fiber of flax. Used as far back as the Stone Age. Flax was cultivated in Mesopotamia, Assyria, and Egypt, and linen was well known in the ancient Biblical world. Ancient Egypt was noted for its fine linen and carried on a thriving export with neighboring nations. Flax was being cultivated in the tropical climate around Jericho at the time of the conquest (Josh. 2:6). Having learned the art in Egypt (Exod. 35:25). Hebrew women practiced the spinning and weaving of flax (Prov. 31:13, 19, etc.). Linen was especially used for apparel of priests, Levites, and royal personages (Exod. 28:5-42; II Chron. 5:12; II Sam. 6:14); the temple veil was made of it (II Chron. 3:14); it was the symbol of wealth (Luke 16:19); purity (Rev. 19:8, 14).

Lintel, the horizontal beam, of stone or wood, forming the upper part of a doorway (Exod. 12:22, 23, vs. 7 "the upper door post" "lintel" ASV), to be marked by the blood of the paschal lamb at the first Passover.

Linus (lī'nŭs), a Christian in Rome joining Paul in sending salutations to Timothy in II Timothy 4:21.

Lion (See Animals)

Litter, a portable couch or sedan, borne by men or animals (Isa. 66:20).

Little Owl (See Birds)

Liver, considered center of life and feeling (Prov. 7:23); used especially for sacrifice (Exod. 29:13) and divination (Ezek. 21:21).

Living Creatures, mentioned in Ezekiel 1:5-22; 3:13; 10:15-20 and Revelation 4:6-9 (KJV "beasts") and apparently identical with the cherubim.

Lizard (See Animals)

Lo-Ammi (lō-ăm'ī, **not my people**), the symbolic name given to Hosea's third child; it is transliterated "Lo-ammi" in Hosea 1:9a, but translated "not my people" in Hosea 1:9b, 10; 2:23.

Lock, Locks. 1. A mechanical device for fastening a city gate or a door. The primitive locks used to fasten city gates consisted simply of heavy beams of wood, the ends of which were dropped into slots cut into the masonry of the gate (Neh. 3:3-15; ASV "the bolts and bars"; cf. Deut. 3:5; I Sam. 23:7; etc.). Used figuratively, their strengthening spoke of divine protection (Ps. 147:13), their burning of a country's invasion (Jer. 51:30; Nah. 3:13). To strengthen them, iron bars were used (I Kings 4:13; Isa. 45:2). When used to lock house doors (Judg. 3:23, 24) they were reduced in size and became flat bolts.

2. In Numbers 6:5 the term indicates the unshorn and disheveled locks of the Nazarite; in Judges 16:13, 19 the braided locks of the Nazarite Samson; in Ezekiel 8:3 a forelock of the prophet's hair; in Song of Solomon 5:2, 11 the luxuriant locks of the Hebrew youth.

Locust (See Insects)

Lod (lŏd), a town of Benjamin (I Chron. 8:12); located in the shephelah or low hills in SW Palestine, the Lydda of the NT.

Lo-Debar (lō'dē'bår, **probably without pasture**), a town in Gilead E of the Jordan, where Mephibosheth, Saul's grandson, lived in the house of Machir until summoned by David to eat at his table (II Sam. 9:1-13).

Lodge, a temporary shelter erected in a garden for a watchman guarding the ripening fruit (Isa. 1:8). In relation to travelers, "a lodging" is a temporary place of sojourn for strangers (Acts 28:23; Philem. 22).

Loft, the upper chamber or story of a building (I Kings 17:9 and Acts 20:9).

Logia, the Greek word for the non-Biblical sayings of Christ, the latest collection of which is the so-called Gospel of Thomas discovered in 1945, and first made public in 1959. The Church has always been aware of sayings of Christ not included in the Gospels. Paul speaks of "the words of the Lord Jesus, how He said, It is more blessed to give than to receive" (Acts 20:35).

Logos, a philosophical and theological term and concept; a dynamic principle of reason operating in the world, and forming a medium of communion between God and man.

In the New Testament the Logos appears principally in Johannine contexts (John 1:1ff; I John 1:1; Rev. 19:13), though Pauline references and the Epistle to the Hebrews might be added. Logos is imperfectly rendered by "Word," and it is not easy to apprehend the full content of the idea in its Judaeo-Hellenistic context.

Loin, the part of the body between the ribs and the hip bones. It is the place where the girdle was worn (Exod. 12:11; II Kings 1:8; Jer. 13:1; Matt. 3:4; etc.), and the sword was fastened (II Sam. 20:8). Pain and terror were reflected in weakness and shaking of the loins (Pss. 38:7; 66:11; 69:23; Jer. 30:6). Girding the loins with sackcloth was the sign of mourning (I Kings 20:32; Isa. 32:11; Jer. 48:37). To have the loins girded with truth signified

The Church of the Lord's Prayer on the Mount of Olives. © *MPS*

strength in attachment to truth (Eph. 6:14; Isa. 11:5).

Lois (lō'ĭs), the maternal grandmother of Timothy, commended by Paul for her faith (II Tim. 1:5).

Looking-Glass (See Mirror)

Lord, applied to both men and God and expresses varied degrees of honor, dignity, and majesty. It is frequently used of God (Matt. 1:22; Mark 5:19; Acts 7:33; etc.) as well as of Jesus as Messiah who by His resurrection and ascension was exalted to lordship (Acts 2:36; Phil. 2:9-11; Rom. 1:4; 14:8). At times it is difficult to determine whether by "the Lord" the Father or the Son is meant (Acts 1:24; 9:31; 16:14; Rom. 14:11; I Cor. 4:19; II Thess. 3:16; etc.).

Lord's Day, the day especially associated with the Lord Jesus Christ, the first day of the week on which Christ arose. It was the resurrection victory on that day which marked it as distinct and sacred to the Christian Church. The Gospel emphasis upon "the first day of the week" as the day of resurrection stresses its distinctiveness. On that day the risen Christ rerepeatedly appeared to His disciples (Luke 24:13-49; John 20:1-25), and again a week later (John 20:26). The day was set aside for worship (Acts 20:7).

Lord's Prayer, The, properly "the Disciples' Prayer," since not prayed with but taught to them by Jesus (Matt. 6: 9-13; Luke 11:2-4). In Luke, Jesus, at the request of a disciple, gives a modified form of His earlier spontaneous presentation in the Sermon on the Mount. The earlier form is fuller and is commonly used. As a pattern prayer it is unsurpassed for conciseness and fullness, delineating the proper approach and order in prayer.

Lord's Supper. The meaning of the Lord's Supper may be gained by viewing its origin and theological significance.

Its historical significance arises out of the context of its institution by Christ on the night of His betrayal (Matt. 26:26-28; Mark 14:22-24; Luke 22:19-20). Its theological significance arises out of the interpretation placed on it by the apostle Paul (I Cor. 10: 16-17 and I Cor. 11:23-28). Both the historical and theological significance constitute it as the basis of fellowship by which the assembled church commemorates the death and ressurrection of Christ as its source of spiritual life.

The table of the Lord is known in Scripture by many names, each of which is descriptive of an aspect of its nature. It is called the body and blood of Christ (Matt. 24:26, 28); the communion of the body and blood of Christ (I Cor. 10:16); the bread and cup of the Lord (I Cor. 11:27); the breaking of bread (Acts 2:42 and 20: 7) and as the Lord's Supper (I Cor. 11:20).

The symbolism arises out of its application to the Christian life. It symbolizes the death of Christ for our sins, and our death to sin in Christ (I Cor. 11:26 and Rom. 6:1-13); the extension of Christ's death as the means of our righteousness (I Cor. 5:7); our participation in the death of Christ (I Cor. 10:16); the union between ourselves and Christ through His death (Rom. 6:4); and our expectant hope in Christ until He comes again (I Cor. 11:26).

The elements used suggest the symbolism. Bread, as a symbol of the body of Christ, suggests the staff of life, the very basis of life itself. The breaking of the bread suggests the breaking of Christ's life in redemptive sacrifice. Wine, as a symbol of the blood of Christ, suggests the pressing out of Christ's life, the bruising by divine wrath. Together they symbolize the sacrifice of the very life of Christ.

Its greatest significance, however, lies in its nature as a memorial feast. It is here that the believer interacts inwardly and spiritually with the grace of God displayed in the death of Christ. As he receives the elements, symbolic in their nature, he submits himself again to receive the merits of Christ's death, not as if it needs to be renewed periodically, but as a continual commemoration of the time when God's mercy drew him into grace and imparted Christ's righteousness to him. As a memorial to Christ's death is a renewal of obedience to Christ's will — an acknowledgment again that his salvation is solely through the broken body and shed blood of Christ.

Two requirements for participating in the Lord's Supper are specified in Scripture: that the communicant be regenerated by grace, and that he be walking a life consistent with commemorating the death of Christ.

Since the Supper symbolizes the inward experience of grace, only such persons as have participated in Christ's

The Last Supper, as portrayed by Leonardo da Vinci. EG

meritorious death can memorialize His death. Each communicant is required to examine his faith before participating (I Cor. 11:27-29).

Furthermore, the communicant must be living a life of obedience, refraining from deliberate sin, and intent upon a more intimate fellowship in Christ when he comes to the table, discerning the full meaning of his act in commemorating Christ's death in his life (I Cor. 11:28).

Though there is no saving grace in the ordinance, there are some concomitant relationships existing in it. It depicts the total work of Christ in man's behalf, and captures in one act man's total response to this work. When the believer receives the elements he receives spiritual blessings in proportion to the faith he exercises in Christ. The commemorative aspect of the ordinance lies not in its nature, but within the heart of the believer. It is here that faith must be exercised, and here that the efficacy of the Lord's table lies.

Lo-Ruhamah (lō-rōō-hȧ'mȧ, **not pitied),** the symbolic name given to Hosea's daughter; it is transliterated "Lo-ruhamah" in Hosea 1:6, 8, but transliterated "not have mercy" in Hosea 2:4, 23.

Lot (lŏt, covering). 1. A means of deciding an issue or of determining the divine will in a matter; often used in ancient times, both by heathens and Jews (Esth. 3:7; Jonah 1:7). 2. That which is assigned by lot, as a share or inheritance (Deut. 32:9; Josh. 15:1).

Lot (lŏt, envelope, covering), son of Haran and nephew of Abraham (Gen. 11:31; 12:5); went with Abraham to Canaan (Gen. 11:27-32; 12:4, 10; 13:1); settled near Sodom (Gen. 13:5-13); rescued by Abraham (Gen. 14:1-12); left Sodom (Gen. 19); ancestor of Moab and Ammon (Gen. 19:36-38).

Lot's life illustrates many spiritual truths: (1) the degenerating influence of a selfish choice (Gen. 13:11f); (2) the effect of a wicked environment on one's family (Gen. 19); (3) retribution in one's children (Gen. 19:8, 31ff); (4) God, the only true judge of a man's real state (II Pet. 2:7ff).

Lotan (lō'tăn, a wrapping up), the son of Seir, father of Hori and Heman (Homan), (Gen. 36:20, 22, 29; I Chron. 1:38, 39).

Love, presented in Scripture as the very nature of God (I John 4:8, 16) and the greatest of the Christian virtues (I Cor. 13:13). It receives definition in Scripture only by a listing of its attributes (I Cor. 13:4-7). It lies at the very heart of Christianity, being essential to man's relations to God and man (Matt. 22:37-40; Mark 12:28-31; John 13:34-35; Rom. 13:8-10). Love found its supreme expression in the self-sacrifice on Calvary (I John 4:10).

All human love, whether Godward or manward, has its source in God. Love in its true reality and power is seen only in the light of Calvary (I John 4:7-10). It is created in the believer by the Holy Spirit (Rom. 5:5; Gal. 5:22), prompting him to love both God and man (II Cor. 5:14-15; I

A pillar of salt on Jebel Usdum (Hill of Sodom), the mountain of salt on the western shore of the Dead Sea. This pillar of salt is known as "Lot's Wife." © *MPS*

John 4:20-21). Love finds its expression in service to our fellow-men (Gal. 5:13) and is the chief test of Christian discipleship (John 13:35; Luke 14:26; I John 3:14). The Christian must love God supremely and his neighbor as himself (Matt. 22:37-39). He must love his enemy as well as his brother (Matt. 5:43-48; Rom. 12:19-20; I John 3:14). Our love must be "without hypocrisy" (Rom. 12:9 ASV) and be "in deed and truth" (I John 3:18). Love is the bond uniting all the Christian virtues (Col. 3:14).

Love Feast, a common meal eaten by early Christians in connection with the Lord's Supper to express and deepen brotherly love. (I Cor. 11:18-22, 33, 34; Jude 12).

Loving-Kindness, the kindness and mercy of God toward man in the OT. This term does not occur in the NT, but the concept of "grace" covers about the same area of meaning.

Lubim (lū'bĭm, probably the Libyans who inhabited the area directly W of Egypt along the northern coast of Africa (II Chron. 12:3; 16:8; Nah. 3:9).

Lucas (lū'căs), same as Luke (Philem. 24). See Luke.

Lucifer (See Satan, Devil)

Lucius (lū'shĭ-ŭs). 1. A Christian from Cyrene in the church at Antioch (Acts 13:1). 2. A kinsman of Paul (Rom. 16:21).

Lud, Ludim (lŭd, lū'dĭm), either one or two nations of antiquity. Lud was the son of Shem (Gen. 10:22; I Chron. 1:17). It is generally agreed that Lud was the kingdom of Lydia in Asia Minor. Ludim was the son of Mizraim (Egypt) (Gen. 10:13; I Chron. 1:11), which indicates an African country. Other Bible references are: Isa. 66:19; Jer. 46:9; Ezek. 27:10; 30:5).

Luhith (lū'hĭth), a town of Moab (Isa. 15:5; Jer. 48:5).

Luke (lūk), the writer of the Third Gospel, and the Acts of the Apostles. From the latter book his association with Paul is established (16:10-17; 20:5-15; 21:1-18; 27:1-28:16). These so-called "we-sections" constitute the major portion of the extant biographical material on Luke. Apart from this he is mentioned three times in the NT (Col. 4:14; Philem. 24; II Tim. 4:11). From the first reference it is evident that Luke was a physician; from the last, that he was with Paul some time after he disappears from view at the end of Acts of the Apostles. The context of the Colossians reference also suggests that Luke was a Gentile and a proselyte.

It appears from Luke's own writings that he was a man of education and culture. He is an accurate and able historian, and has left some of the most powerful descriptive writing in the NT. His medical knowledge and his interest in seafaring are apparent from his writings. Beyond this is tradition and conjecture. Luke must have been a person of singular sweetness of character to earn the apostle's adjective "beloved" (Col. 4:14). He was obviously a man of outstanding loyalty, of unusual capacity for research, and the scholar's ability to strip away the irrelevant and dispensable detail. A bare tradition states that he suffered martyrdom in Greece.

Luke, Gospel of. Third book of NT, written, according to tradition, by Luke the beloved physician and co-worker of Paul. Preface to Acts shows that the Gospel was written before it, somewhere c. A.D. 58-60; both books were done by the same person, as tradition and internal evidence show. The author states in the preface (1:2) that he collected his material from eye-witnesses. Outline: 1. Thirty years of private life (1-4:13). 2. Galilean ministry of Jesus (4:14-9:50). 3. Journey from Galilee to Jerusalem (9:51-19:44). 4. Last days of Jesus in Jerusalem, His crucifixion and burial (19:45-23:56). 5. Resurrection and appearances of the risen Lord and His ascension (24:1-53).

Lunatic (See Diseases)

Lute (See Musical Instruments)

Luz (lŭz, **turning aside**). 1. A town on the N boundary of Benjamin (Josh. 16:2; 18:13). To this place Jacob came when fleeing from home. 2. A Hittite town (Judg. 1:26).

Lycaonia (lĭk'ā-ō'nĭ-à), a district in the central plain of Asia N of the Taurus range, in early Roman days a division (or **conuentus**) of the province of Cilicia (Acts 14:6).

Lycia (lĭsh'ĭ-à), a district on the coast of the southern bulge of western Asia Minor, forming the western shore of the Gulf of Adalia. After the Roman overthrow of Syria, Lycia was placed briefly under Rhodes, a situation which was bitterly resented. Freed in 169 B.C., the region enjoyed comparative

The village of Lydda, with the church of St. George at left. © *MPS*

independence in the imperial system until Vespasian. Even then the forms of local administration were retained (see I Macc. 15:23; Acts 21:1, 2; 27:5).

Lydda (lĭd′ȧ), or Lod, lies some 30 miles NW of Jerusalem at the mouth of the Vale of Ajalon and at the head of the valley which runs down to Joppa, an old highway called the Valley of the Smiths in recollection of ancient Philistine supremacy in iron (I Sam. 13:19). On the edge of the Maritime Plain, Lydda was of some commercial importance, "a village not less than a city" in Josephus' phrase. After the Exile, the settlements of the returning Jews reached this point before meeting the resistance of the occupants of the plain (Ezra 2:33; Neh. 7:37).

Lydia (lĭd′ĭ-ȧ), Paul's first convert in Europe. She resided in Philippi as a seller of the purple garments for which Thyatira, her native city, was famous. She was evidently well-to-do as she owned her house and had servants. She was "one who worshipped God," meaning a proselyte. She and other women, probably also proselytes, resorted to a place by a river for prayer. She came into contact with the Gospel when Paul and his company came there and spoke to these women, and she became a believer. After she and her household had been baptized, she constrained the group to come to her home to stay, which they did (Acts 16: 14, 15). Her home thus became the first church in Philippi (v. 40).

Lyre (See Musical Instruments)

Lysanias (lī-sā′nĭ-ăs), tetrarch of Abilene mentioned by Luke (3:1). The tetrarchy is a small region in the Lebanon.

Lysias (lĭs′ĭ-ăs). Claudius Lysias, of the Jerusalem garrison, tribune by rank, was probably one of the career men of the days of Pallas and Narcissus, the powerful freedmen and executive officers of the Emperor Claudius. Lysias was a Greek, as his second name shows. His first name was assumed when he secured Roman citizenship "at a great price" (Acts 22:28).

Lystra (lĭs′trȧ), a Roman colony of Augustus' foundation, with an aristocratic core of citizens with franchise, a group likely to honor the similar status of Paul (Acts 14:13). Timothy was a native of Lystra (Acts 16:1).

-M-

Maacah, Maachah (mā'ā-kā, **oppression).** 1. Son of Nahor, brother of Abraham (Gen. 22:24). 2. A wife of David; the mother of Absalom (II Sam. 3:3; I Chron. 3:2). 3. The father of Achish, king of Gath, (I Kings 2:39). 4. The favorite wife of Rehoboam, and the mother of Abijam (II Chron. 11:20-22). 5. A concubine of Caleb, son of Hezron (I Chron. 2:48). 6. Wife of Machir, the son of Manasseh (I Chron. 7:14-16). 7. Wife of Jeiel, the founder of Gibeon (I Chron. 8:29; 9:35). 8. Father of Hanan, one of David's mighty men (I Chron. 11:43). 9. Father of Shephatiah, the overseer of the tribe of Simeon in David's reign (I Chron. 27:16).

Maachah (mā'ā-kā, **oppression),** a small country on the edge of the Syrian desert N of Gilead (ASV Maachah. The Ammonites hired a thousand men of this nation to assist them in fighting against David (II Sam. 10:6-19).

Maachathi, Maachathites, (mā-ăk'a-thī, mā-ăk'ā-thīts), the people of the nation of Maachah, in the region of Bashan. The Israelites did not drive out the Maacathites or Geshurites, but dwelt with them (Deut. 3:14; Josh. 12:5; 13:11; II Sam. 23:34; I Chron. 4:19).

Maadai (mā'ā-dā'ī, **ornaments),** son of Bani, one of the Israelites who married foreign women (Ezra 10:34).

Maadiah (mā-ā-dī'ā, **Jehovah is ornament),** priest who returned from exile with Zerubbabel (Neh. 12:5).

Maai (mā-ā'ī, **to be compassionate),** a son of the priests who blew trumpets at the dedication of the wall of Jerusalem (Neh. 12:36).

Maaleh-Acrabbim (mā'ā-lĕ-ā-krab'īm, **ascent of Akrabbim),** a section of the area assigned to the tribe of Judah (Josh. 15:3).

Maarath (mā'a-răth, **a place naked of trees),** a city of Judah, near Hebron (Josh. 15:59).

Maaseiah (mā'ā-sē'yā, **work of Jehovah).** 1. Levites appointed to play a psaltery in praise of God while the ark was brought up to Jerusalem (I Chron. 15:18, 20). 2. A captain who assisted Jehoiada to overthrow Athaliah (II Chron. 23:1). 3. An officer of Uzziah (II Chron. 26:11). 4. A son of Ahaz, king of Judah (II Chron. 28:7). 5. The governor of Jerusalem in Josiah's reign (II Chron. 34:8). 6. One of the priests who had married a foreign woman (Ezra 10:18). 7. A priest of the family of Harim who took a foreign wife (Ezra 10:21). 8 A priest of the family of Passhur who took a foreign wife (Ezra 10:22). 9. A man of Israel of the family of Pahath Moab who took a foreign wife (Ezra 10:30). 10. The father of Azariah, a man who worked on the wall of Jerusalem near his house (Neh. 3:23). 11. One of the men who stood on the right side of Ezra as he read the law to the people (Neh. 8:4). 12. One of the men who explained the law to the people (Neh. 8:7). 13. One of the chiefs of the people who sealed the covenant with Nehemiah (Neh. 10:25). May be the same as No. 12. 14. One of the descendants of the son of Baruch of Perez who dwelt in Jerusalem (Neh. 11:5). 15. A Benjamite whose descendants dwelt in Jerusalem (Neh. 11:7). 16. A priest, one of those who blew a trumpet at the dedication of the wall of Jerusalem (Neh. 12:41). 17. Another priest who took part in this dedication of the wall (Neh. 12:42). 18. A priest whose son Zephaniah was one of the two men whom Zedekiah, king of Judah, sent to Jeremiah to ask him to inquire of the Lord for him (Jer. 21:1; 37:3). 19. The father of Zedekiah, a false prophet whom Jeremiah condemned (Jer. 29:21). 20. Gatekeeper of the temple (Jer. 35:4). 21. An ancestor of Baruch (Jer. 32:12).

Maasiai (mā-ās'ī-ī, **work of Jehovah),** a priestly family which returned to Jerusalem from exile (I Chron. 9:12).

Maath (mā'ăth, **to be small),** an ancestor of Christ (Luke 3:26).

Maaz (mā'ăz, **wrath),** son of Ram, the first born son of Jerahmeel (I Chron. 2:27).

Maaziah (mā-ā-zī'ā). 1. Head of 24th course of priests (I Chron. 24:18). 2. Priest who sealed covenant with Nehemiah (Neh. 10:8).

Maccabees (măk'ā-bēs, **hammer?)** Hasmonean Jewish family of Modin that led revolt against Antiochus Epiphanes, king of Syria, and won freedom for the Jews. The family consisted of the father, Mattathias, an aged priest, and his five sons: Johanan, Simon, Judas, Eleazar, Jonathan. The name Maccabee was first given to Judas, perhaps because he inflicted sledge-

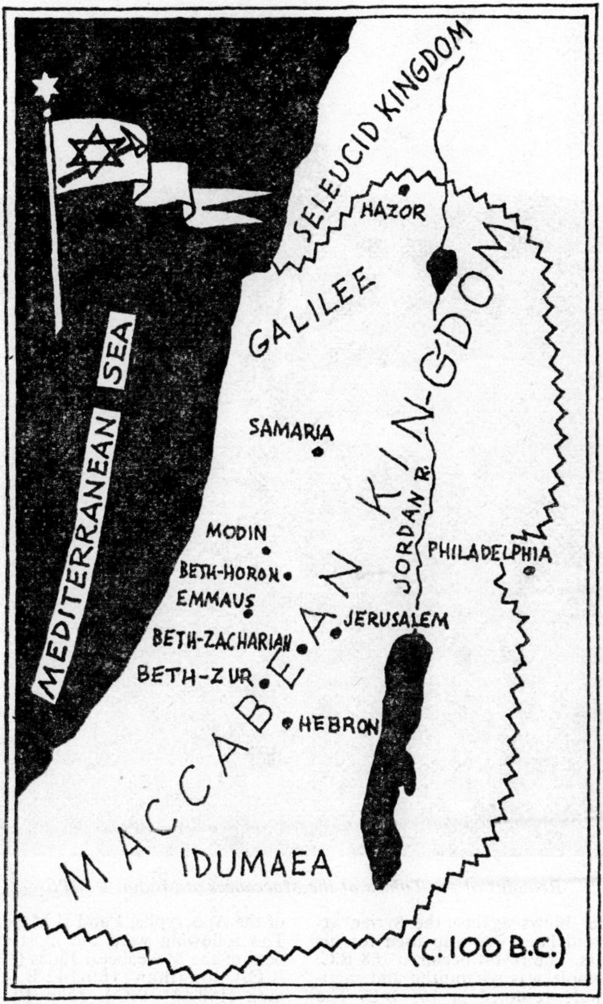

The Maccabean Kingdom. UANT

Remains of the Tombs of the Maccabees at Modin. © MPS

hammer blows against the Syrian armies, and later was also used for his brothers. The revolt began in 168 B.C. The temple was recaptured and sacrifices were resumed in 165 B.C. The cleansing of the temple and resumption of sacrifices have been celebrated annually ever since in the Feast of Dedication. The Maccabees served as both high priests and kings. The story of the Maccabees is told in two books of the Apocrypha, I and II Maccabees. The following were the most prominent of the Maccabees: Judas (166-160 B.C.), Jonathan (160-142 B.C.), Simon (142-134 B.C.), John Hyrcanus (134-104 B.C.), Aristobulus (104-103 B.C.), Alexander Jannaeus (103-76 B.C.), Alexandra (76-67 B.C.), Aristobulus II (66-63). In 63 B.C. the Romans took over when Pompey conquered the Israelites.

Macedonia (măs′ē-dō′nĭ-ȧ), country N of Greece in Balkan Peninsula first ruled by Philip (359-336 B.C.) and then by his son Alexander the Great (336-323 B.C.); became Roman province in 168 B.C.; often visited by Paul (Acts 16:9-12; 17:1-15; 20:1-6; Rom. 15:26; I Cor. 16:5; II Cor. 1:16; 2:13; 7:5; 8:1; 9:2; 11:9; Phil. 4:15; I Thess. 1:7; 4:10; I Tim. 1:3).

Machaerus (mă-kē′rŭs), Herod's southernmost stronghold E of the Dead Sea, built by Alexander Jannaeus (90 B.C.?) (Jos. **Ant.** 14.5.2). "The second citadel of Judaea" (Plin. H.N. 5.16). The fort was on the border of Peraea, the tetrarchy of Herod Antipas. Here John the Baptist died (Matt. 14:3ff).

Machbenah (măk-bē′nȧ, **bond),** a place in Judah in the genealogical list of Caleb (I Chron. 2:49).

Machbenai (măk′bȧ-nī, **clad with a cloak),** a Gadite who joined David's forces at Ziklag (I Chron. 12:13).

Machi (mā′kī), the father of Geuel, appointed from the tribe of Gad to be one of the 12 spies (Num. 13:15).

Machir (mā′kĭr, **sold).** 1. Eldest son of Manasseh, son of Joseph (Gen. 50:23; Num. 27:1; 32:39, 40); Machirites descended from him (Num. 26:29). 2. Man who brought provisions to David when he fled from Absalom (II Sam. 17:27).

Machnadebai (măk-năd′ē-bī), one of the men who married a foreign wife (Ezra 10:40).

Machpelah (măk-pē′lȧ, **a doubling),** a field near Hebron which Abraham purchased as a place of burial for Sarah (Gen. 23:19-20). Abraham (Gen. 25:9), Isaac, Rebekah, Leah, and Jacob (Gen. 50:13) were also buried there (Gen. 49:31).

Madai (măd′ā-ī, **Media),** a people descended from Japheth (Gen. 10:2; I Chron. 1:5). They occupied the same area which modern Iran does today and were called the Medes.

Madian (See Midian)

Madmannah (măd-măn′nȧ, **dunghill).** 1. A town in southern Judah about eight miles S of Kirjath-sepher (Josh. 15:31). 2. Grandson of Caleb (I Chron. 2:48, 49).

Madmenah (măd-mē′-nȧ, **dunghill),** a town of Benjamin, evidently a little N of Jerusalem (Isa. 10:31).

Madon (mā′dŏn, **contention),** a royal city of the Canaanites, whose king Johab was defeated by Joshua (Josh. 11:1; 12:19).

Magbish (măg′bĭsh, **congregating),** name of either a man, the head of a family which returned with Zerubbabel from exile, or of a place to which these people belonged. The list contains names of both towns and persons (Ezra 2:30).

Magdala (măg′dȧ-lȧ), a town on the NW shore of the Sea of Galilee, three miles N of Tiberias named only in the KJV rendering of Matthew 15:39. (ASV has more correct Magadan;

The village of Magdala and surrounding plain on the west coast of the Sea of Galilee. © MPS

The well of the Magi on the Bethlehem-Jerusalem Road. © *MPS*

Mark 8:10 the alternative Dalmanutha). Home of Mary Magdalene.

Magdalen, Magdalene (See Mary)

Magdiel (mag′dĭ-ĕl, **God is noble),** one of the chiefs of Edom (Gen. 36:43; I Chron. 1:54).

Magi (mā′jī), originally a religious caste among the Persians. Their devotion to astrology, divination, and the interpretation of dreams led to an extension in the meaning of the word, and by the first century the terms "magi" and "Chaldaean" were applied generally to fortune tellers and the exponents of esoteric religious cults throughout the Mediterranean world. Magus is, for example, the epithet of the charlatan Simon of Acts 8:9. The term is translated "sorcerer" in Acts 13:6, 8. "The wise men from the east" of the Nativity story (Matt. 2) are often referred to as "the Magi."

Magic, the science or art of the Magi, the Persian priestly caste, who, like the Levites, were devoted to the practice of religion. With the wide extension of the term "magus," the word magic, too, acquired broader significance. It came to mean all occult rituals or processes designed to influence or control the course of nature, to dominate men or circumstances by the alliance, aid, or use of supernatural powers, and generally to tap and to employ the forces of an unseen world. Divination, the art of forecasting the future with a view to avoiding its perils and pitfalls, might be included under the same classification (Exod. 22:18; Lev. 19:26; 20:27; Deut. 18:10, 11). Includes necromancy, exorcism, dreams, shaking arrows, inspecting entrails of animals, divination, sorcery, astrology, soothsaying, divining by rods, witchcraft (I Sam. 28:8; Ezek. 21:21; etc.).

References to magic practices are also found in the New Testament. The reference to the heathens' "vain repetitions" (Matt. 6:7; for example see I Kings 18:26 and Acts 19:28) may allude to the belief in the magic repetition of set formulae such as the Tibetan's meaningless **"om mani padme hum"** ("Hail to the jewel in the lotus flower"). Simon (Acts 8:9) and Elymas (Acts 13:8) are spoken of as practicing "curious arts." There is evidence that this tribe of charlatans was widespread, and often in origin Jewish (e.g. "the Sons of Sceva" in Ephesus, Acts 19:14). The story of the first Christian impact on the city of Ephesus reveals the tremendous influence of magic among the populace at large. The early Church, in general, did not dismiss magic as a delusion, but attributed its results to the work of malign and evil beings who were without power against a Christian. The Council of Ancyra (A.D. 315) first legislated against magic.

Magicians (See Magic)

Magistrate (măj′ĭs-trāt, **judge),** chief official in government of Roman colony (Acts 16:20, 22, 35, 36, 38).

Magnificat (măg-nĭf′ĭ-kăt), the song of praise by Mary recorded in Luke 1:46-55. Mary spoke this song in response to the assurance from Elizabeth that God would surely fulfill the words of the Angel Gabriel that she would be the woman chosen to bring the Son of God into the world.

Magog (mā′gŏg, **land of Gog?).** 1. Son of Japheth (Gen. 10:2; I Chron. 1:5). 2. Land of Gog; various identifications: Scythians, Lydians, Tartars of Russia. Used symbolically for forces of evil (Rev. 20:7-9).

Magor-Missabib (mā′gôr-mĭs′ȧ-bĭb, **terror on every side),** name which Jeremiah gave to Pashhur, who struck him (Jer. 20:3).

Magpiash (măg′pĭ-ăsh, **moth killer),** a chief who sealed the covenant with Nehemiah (Neh. 10:20).

Magus, Simon (See Simon)

Mahalah (mȧ-hā′lȧ, **disease),** a child, probably a son, of Hammolecheth, sister of Machir, son of Manasseh (I Chron. 7:18). ASV Mahlah.

Mahalaleel (mȧ-hā′lȧ-lē′ĕl, **praise of God),** the son of Kenan, who lived 895 years, and was the father of Jared (Gen. 5:12, 13, 15, 16, 17; I Chron. 1:2; Luke 3:37). ASV Mahalalel.

Mahalath (mā′hȧ-lăth, **sickness).** 1. A daughter of Ishmael and Esau's third wife (Gen. 28:9). 2. The first wife of Rehoboam; a granddaughter of David (II Chron. 11:18). 3. Musical term in the heading of Psalms 53 and 88.

Mahali (mā′hȧ-lī, **sick),** son of Merari, son of Levi (Exod. 6:19).

Mahanaim (mā′hȧ-nā′ĭm, **two hosts),** town in Gilead E of the Jordan on boundary between Gad and Manasseh; assigned to Levites (Josh. 21:38); angels met Jacob there (Gen. 32:2); David fled there from Absalom (II Sam. 17:24; 19:32); capital of Israel for a short time (II Sam. 2:8). Exact location uncertain.

Mahaneh-Dan (mā'hȧ-nĕ-dăn, **camp of Dan).** 1. A place where Samson grew up and first began to be moved by the Spirit of Jehovah, between Zorah and Eshtaol (Judg. 13:25 KJV). 2. A place behind Kiriath-jearim where 600 men of Dan encamped on their way to conquer Laish (Judg. 18:12).

Maharai (mȧ-hăr'ā-ī, **impetuous),** one of David's mighty men (II Sam. 23:28; I Chron. 11:30; 27:13).

Mahath (mȧ'hăth, **seizing).** 1. A Kohathite, an ancestor of Heman the singer (I Chron. 6:35). 2. One of the Levites who cleansed the temple in Hezekiah's reign (II Chron. 29:12; 31:13).

Mahavite (mā'hȧ-vīt), the family name of Eliel, one of David's warriors (I Chron. 11:46).

Mahazioth (mȧ-hā'zĭ-ŏth, **visions),** a son of Heman who praised God in the temple (I Chron. 25:4). He was given the 23rd lot to serve in song (I Chron. 25:30).

Maher-shalal-hash-baz (mā'hĕr-shăl'ăl-hăsh'băz, **the spoil speeds, the prey hastens).** This phrase was written down by Isaiah and officially recorded as a witness by God's direction. Later when the prophet's second son was born the Lord told Isaiah to give him this phrase as a name (Isa. 8:1, 3).

Mahlah (mȧ'lȧ, **disease).** 1. Eldest daughter of Zelophehad of the tribe of Manasseh. This man had no sons but seven daughters, who obtained permission to inherit land as if they were sons, provided they married within the tribe (Num. 26:33; 27:1ff; Chapter 36; Josh. 17:3ff). 2. Daughter of Hammolecheth, the sister of Machir, son of Manasseh (I Chron. 7:18).

Mahli (mȧh'lī, **sick).** 1. Son of Merari, son of Levi (Exod. 6:19 KJV, Mahli; Num. 3:20; Ezra 8:18). 2. Son of Mushi (I Chron. 6:47; 23:23; 24:30).

Mahlite (mȧh'līt), a descendant of Mahli, son of Merari (Num. 3:33; 26:58; I Chron. 23:22).

Mahlon (mȧ'lŏn, **sick),** son of Elimelech. Married Ruth in Moab, leaving her a widow about ten years later (Ruth 1:2, 5; 4:9, 10).

Mahol (mā'hŏl, **dance),** father of Calcol and Darda, men famous for their wisdom (I Kings 4:31).

Maid, Maiden. 1. **Female slave,** the property of her owners (Exod. 2:5; 21:20, 26), and often a bondmaid (Lev. 25:44). 2. **Virgin,** a girl secluded and separated from contact with men. Often used with this meaning (Exod. 22:16; Judg. 19:24; Pss. 78:63; 148:12). 3. **Girl, maiden** (Exod. 2:5; Ruth 2:8, 22, 23; 3:2 and often). 4. A girl of marriageable age, occurs only seven times (Gen. 24:43; Exod. 2:8; Ps. 68:25; S. of Sol. 1:3; 6:8; Prov. 30:19; Isa. 7:14). 5. Maid servant, a synonym of **amah,** maid (Gen. 16:2, 3, 5, 6, 8; 29:24, 29; 30:9, 10, 12, 18, etc.), bondmaid (Lev. 19:20), bond woman (Deut. 26:68; II Chron. 28:10; Esth. 7:4), hand maid (Gen. 16:1; 25:12; 29:24, 29 and often, maid servant (Gen. 12:16; 24:35; 30:43, etc.).

Mail, Coat of (See Armor)

Maimed (See Diseases)

Makaz (mā'kăz), a town near Beth Shemesh where Solomon's supply officer, Bendeker, was stationed (I Kings 4:9).

Makheloth (măk-hē'lŏth), encampment of Israel in the wilderness (Num. 33:25, 26).

Makkedah (măk-kē'dȧ, **a place of shepherds),** a town near Libnah and Azekah conquered by Joshua. Five kings hid in a cave in this town and were killed and buried there (Josh. 10:16ff; 15:41).

Maktesh (măk'tĕsh, **mortar** or **hollow place resembling a mortar),** the name of a place; location unknown (Zeph. 1:11).

Malachi (măl'ȧ-kī, **messenger of Jehovah** or **my messenger),** the name given to the last book of the OT, and the name of the prophet whose oracles the book contains. Nothing more is known about the author of this book.

The book of Malachi is believed to be one of the latest of the OT books. It was occasioned by the lack of zeal for the rebuilding of the temple, and a situation of moral and religious declension. The mixed marriages (2:10-12), failure to pay tithes (3:8-10) and offering of blemished sacrifices (1:6-14) are conditions not unlike those referred to in the times of Ezra and Nehemiah (Ezra 7-Neh. 13) and it would seem that Malachi's prophecy was given at about that time, or possibly shortly thereafter—about the middle or end of the fifth century B.C.

Analysis:

1. Title: 1:1.

2. An argument for the love of God towards Israel as shown in the contrasted experiences of Edom and Israel, 1:2-5.

3. A protest against the negligence of the priests in worship, 1:6-2:9.

4. A condemnation of those who divorce their wives and marry foreign women, 2:10-16.

5. An answer to those who complain that God is indifferent to injustice: a day of judgment is at hand, 2:17-3:5.

6. A rebuke for the neglect of tithes and offerings, 3:6-12.

7. A reply to doubters, and a promise to the faithful, 3:13-4:3.

8. A recall to the law and a prophecy of the coming of Elijah, 4:4-6.

Certain features are unique in this book:

1. The use of the rhetorical question and answer as a method of communication. This device begins most of the eight sections referred to above.

2. Malachi contains prophetic and priestly interests. It has been called "Prophecy within the law." Generally the prophets exhibit little interest in sacrifices and ceremonial laws, preferring to stress the more inward aspects of religious life. Malachi, however, sees the people's apostasy manifested by their carelessness in the sacrificial offerings (1:6-14), the priests' neglect of their duties (2:1-9), and the failure of the people to pay their tithes and other offerings (3:7-12). This book is thus an antidote to the view commonly held today that the prophets did not believe in the necessity of the ritual law.

3. The growing OT Messianic expectation is witnessed to in the announcement of God's "messenger of the covenant" by whose coming Israel will be purified and judged (3:1-5; cf. Matt. 11:10), and of the Prophet Elijah who will announce the day of the Lord (4:5, 6; cf. Matt. 17:9-13).

Malcham, Malcam (măl'kăm), either **Milcom,** an idol of the Moabites and Ammonites (Zeph. 1:5; Jer. 49:3) or their king (Amos 1:15; Jer. 49:1); maybe both.

Malchiah, Malchijah (măl-kī'ȧ, măl-kī'jȧ, **my king is Jehovah).** 1. A Gershonite, the ancestor of Asaph (I Chron. 6:40). 2. An ancestor of the priest Adaiah (I Chron. 9:12; Neh. 11:12). 3. A priest of David's time (I Chron. 24:9). 4. An Israelite who had married a foreign woman (Ezra 10:25). 5. Another who did the same (Ezra 10:25). 6. A member of the family of Harim who was guilty of the same practice (Ezra 10:31). 7. A son of Harim who worked on the wall (Neh. 3:11). 8. The son of Rechab (Neh. 3:14). 9. A goldsmith who worked on the wall (Neh. 3:31). 10. One of the men who stood beside Ezra as he read the law to the people (Neh. 8:4). 11. One of those who sealed the covenant with Nehemiah (Neh. 10:3). 12. A priest who took part in the dedication of the wall (Neh. 12:42). May be the same as No. 11. 13. Father of Pashur, messenger of the King Zedekiah to Jeremiah (Jer. 21:1) and who helped arrest the prophet (Jer. 38:1). 14. The son of King Zedekiah (Jer. 38:6).

Malchiel (măl'kĭ-ĕl, **God is my king),** son of Beriah (Gen. 46:17; Num. 26:45; I Chron. 7:31).

Malchijah (See Malchiah)

Malchiram (măl-kī-răm, **my king is high),** son of Jeconiah (I Chron. 3:18).

Malchi-shua (măl-kĭ-shōō'ȧ, **king of aid),** third son of King Saul (I Sam. 14:49; 31:2 [KJV Melchi-shua]; I Chron. 8:33; 9:39), killed by the Philistines (I Sam. 31:2; I Chron. 10:2).

Malchus (măl'kŭs), a servant of the high priest whose ear Peter cut off with a sword (John 18:10).

Malefactor (măl'ē-făk'têr, **evil doer),** the term by which the Jewish leaders described Christ to Pilate (John 18:30) and the designation of the two thieves who were crucified with Christ (Luke 23:32, 33, 39).

Maleleel (See Mahaleel)

Mallothi (măl'ō-thī, **I have uttered),** one of the sons of Heman, who with their father praised God with musical instruments (I Chron. 25:4, 26).

Mallow (See Plants)

Malluch (măl'lŭk, **counselor).** 1. Ancestor of Ethan (I Chron. 6:44). 2. Man who married a foreign woman (Ezra 10:29). 3. Son of Harim, another man who took a foreign wife (Ezra 10:32). 4. A priest who sealed the covenant (Neh. 10:4). 5. A chief of the people who sealed the covenant (Neh. 10:27).

Malta (See Melita)

Mammon (măm'ŭn, **riches),** the Aramaic word for "riches." Christ used it as a life-goal opposed to God (Matt. 6:24; Luke 16:13). Jesus also employed the word in the phrase "mammon of unrighteousness" (meaning "money") in His parable of the unjust steward (Luke 16:11, 13).

The ruins at Ramet el-Khalil (Mamre). These may date back and mark the site of the dwelling of Abraham when he lived under the oaks at Mamre. © MPS

Mamre (măm'rē, **strength**). 1. An Amorite who was with Abram (Gen. 14:13, 24). 2. A place a few miles N of Hebron where oak trees grew (Gen. 13:18; 18:1; 23:17, 19; 25:9; 35:27; 49:30; 50:13).

Man. Created by God in His image and likeness (Gen. 1:26, 27); has body, soul, spirit (Matt. 6:25; Gen. 2:7; 41:8); dependent upon God (Matt. 6:26-30); fell into sin (Gen. 3; Rom. 5); subject to death (Rom. 5:12, 17); saved through faith in Christ (Rom. 3:21, 22). New man denotes the regenerated individual (Eph. 2:15; 4:24); natural man, the unregenerated individual (I Cor. 2:14); inner man, the soul (Rom. 7:22; Eph. 3:16); outward man, the body (II Cor. 4:16).

Man of Sin (See Antichrist)

Man, Son of. This phrase was used once by the Lord in addressing Daniel (Dan. 8:17) and over 80 times in addressing Ezekiel.

Daniel used this phrase to describe a personage whom he saw in a night vision. He beheld one like unto "a son of man" who received an everlasting kingdom with great glory (Dan. 7:13, 14). The individual so described can only be Jesus Christ. The phrase "a son of man" means that this personage whom Daniel saw looked like a human being.

When the Son of God came down to earth as a man, mingling with people, He very significantly took this phrase as His designation of Himself.

Once this phrase occurs without the definite article simply "a son of man" (John 5:27 ASV). Jesus made the statement that He had been given authority to execute judgment because He was a son of man. That is, because of His experience as a man, living among men, He was qualified to judge man.

Manaen (măn'à-ĕn, **comforter**), a leader in the church at Antioch (Acts 13:1) and foster brother of Herod Antipas.

Manahath (măn'á-hăth, **resting place**). 1. An Edomite (Gen. 36:23; I Chron. 1:40). 2. A town in Edom (I Chron. 8:6).

Manahethites (mà-nā'hăth-īts). 1. Half of the Manahethites, (ASV has "half of the Menuhoth"), a Judean clan, descendants of Shobal, son of Caleb, the son of Hur (I Chron. 2:52). 2. Another group, "half of the Manhethites," descended from Salma, son of Caleb, the son of Hur (I Chron. 2:54). ASV Manahathites.

Manasseh (mă-năs'sĕ, **one who forgets**). 1. The elder son of Joseph and Aserath, born in Egypt (Gen. 41:51). Jacob claimed him and his younger brother Ephraim for his own sons, and when he blessed them he predicted Ephraim would be greater than Manasseh (Gen. 48:5, 19). 2. Priest named Moses whose name was changed to Manasseh because he dishonored God (Judg. 18:30). 3. 14th king of Judah; son and successor of Hezekiah; idolater (II Kings 21:7; 23:11); persecuted those faithful to Jehovah (II Kings 21:6); brought his country to ruin (Jer. 15:4); carried captive to Babylon (II

The prism of Esar-haddon, King of Assyria, which contains historical records, including mention of Manasseh's captivity and tribute. UMP

Chron. 33:11) and later allowed to return (II Chron. 33:10-13, 15-17). 4. One of those who married foreign wives (Ezra 10:30). 5. Another of those who married foreign wives (Ezra 10: 33).

Manasseh, Tribe of, the descendants of Joseph's son, Manasseh. This tribe contained 32,200 men of war, those over 20 years old (Num. 1:34) before the Israelites marched from Sinai. Forty years later the new generation in Manasseh numbered 52,700 men of war (Num. 26:34). Before the Israelites crossed over the Jordan River into Canaan, half the tribe of Manasseh along with the tribes of Reuben and Gad chose land E of the river and Moses assigned it to them (Num. 32:33-41; Deut. 3:13; Josh. 13:31). The rest of the tribe was given ten parts of land in Canaan including areas for Zelophehad's daughters (Josh. 17:1-6). This territory was situated between Ephraim on the S and Asher, Zebulon, and Issachar on the N. Its eastern border was the Jordan River and on the W was the Mediterranean Sea (Josh. 17: 7-10).

Manasseh joined David while he was a fugitive from Saul (I Chron. 12: 19-22). When David was made king at Hebron, W Manasseh furnished 18,000 soldiers, and E Manasseh with Reuben and Gad 120,000 (I Chron. 12:31, 37). People from W Manasseh and Ephraim joined with Judah in making a covenant to seek Jehovah during the reign of Asa, king of Judah (I Chron. 15:9-15). Certain pious souls from W Manasseh joined in the passover service during Hezekiah's reign (II Chron. 30:10-22).

Manasses (See Manasseh)

Manassites (mȧ-năs'īts, **forgetting),** descendants of the oldest son of Joseph (Gen. 41:51). Moses gave them a city of refuge in Bashan (Deut. 4:41-43). Because of evil under Jehu, God caused the Manassites to be cut off (II Kings 10:31-33).

Maneh (See Weights and Measures)

Manger, a stall or trough for cattle (Luke 2:7-16; 13:15). Luke alone gives it as the birthplace of Jesus. Justin Martyr wrote about A.D. 100 that the stall was in a cave adjoining an inn which was used for livestock.

Manna, a special food provided for the Hebrews during the exodus from Egypt. Just what it was has puzzled naturalists for ages. It came at night, resembling hoar frost, coming with the dew (Num. 11:9), and may have collected in dewdrops (Exod. 16:4). It was white, of delicious flavor, and resembled seed of the coriander, a plant of the eastern Mediterranean area which was both tasty and nourishing (Exod. 16:31). That it came by miraculous means is shown by its nature, its time of coming, and its preservation over the sabbaths (Exod. 16: 20-26; Deut. 8:3). Being seed-like in form it had to be ground (Num. 11: 7, 8). As soon as other food was available, the manna ceased (Josh. 5:12). The Bible makes it certain that manna came as a temporary provision for the chosen people.

Manoah (mȧ-nō'ȧ, **rest),** the father of Samson (Judg. 13; 14:1-11).

Mansions (an abiding place), an expression that occurs only in John 14: 2, where the plural is used. It is correctly rendered "abiding places," the plural form denoting the great extent of God's house as shown in Revelation 2:1.

Manslayer, a term used to describe a person who had killed another human being accidentally. Among the Israelites a manslayer could flee from an avenger of blood by taking asylum in a city of refuge (Num. 35:6, 12). There he was given a trial. If he was acquitted, he could stay in the city of refuge until the death of the high priest, after which he could return home (Num. 35:28). A deliberate murderer could find no protection in a city of refuge. If he tried it, he was immediately put to death (Exod. 21:14).

Mantle, usually a large, sleeveless, outer garment (I Kings 19:18, 19; II Kings 2:8, 13, 14), or such a garment with sleeves (Isa. 3:22).

Manuscripts, Dead Sea (See Dead Sea Scrolls)

Maoch (mā'ŏk, **a poor one),** father of Achish (I Sam. 27:2) who protected David (I Sam. 29:1-11).

Maon (mā'ŏn, **habitation).** 1. A descendant of Caleb (I Chron. 2:42-45). 2. A town on an elevated plain south of Hebron where David found refuge from Saul (I Sam. 23:24-28, marg.). It was the home of Nabal and Abigail (I Sam. 25:1-3).

Maonites (mā'ŏn-īts), enemies of Israel called Menuhim, probably from Arabian peninsula (Judg. 10:11, 12; Ezra 2:50).

Mara (mȧ'rȧ, **bitter),** a name adopted by Naomi instead of her own, which meant pleasant or delightful (Ruth 1:20, marg.).

A camel caravan pausing at the Springs of Moses (Ayoun Mousa), Biblical Marah (bitter water), where the Israelites stopped after crossing the Red Sea. © MPS

Marah (mā′rȧ, **bitterness**), a place where the Hebrews found bitter water. When they complained, God showed Moses a plant whose foliage sweetened the water (Exod. 15:23-26).

Maralah (măr′ȧ-lȧ), a city on the border of Zebulun's heritage (Josh. 19: 10, 11), about four miles from Nazareth.

Maranatha (mär'à-năth'à, **our Lord comes!**), an expression of greeting and encouragement as well as of triumphant faith, such as is shown in I Cor. 16:22 RSV margin. That is to say, "Our Lord comes, regardless of man's enmity!"

Marble (See Minerals)

Marcus (mär'kŭs), Roman name of John Mark, a kinsman of Barnabas. He deserted Paul (Acts 13:13) and later became a noted Christian worker (Acts 15:39; II Tim. 4:11).

Mareshah (mȧ-rē'shȧ, **a possession**). 1. The father of Hebron (I Chron. 2:42). 2. A grandson of Judah, more probably a town (I Chron. 4:21). 3. Important city of Judah between Hebrew and Gaza (Josh. 15:44); fortified by Rehoboam (II Chron. 11:5-12).

Mari, an ancient city of the Euphrates Valley, discovered in 1933. Excavations under the direction of André Parrot of the Louvre Museum resulted in rich finds, including some 20,000 cuneiform tablets, translation of which has opened up new vistas into ancient Syrian civilization. The Mari kingdom was contemporary with Hammurabi of Babylon and the Amorite tribes of Canaan, ancestors of the Hebrews. Falling a victim to the wiles of Hammurabi, the country was destroyed in the 32nd year of his reign.

Mark, a word with various meanings: a special sign or brand (Gen. 4:15; Gal. 6:17), a sign of ownership (Ezek. 9:4, 6; Rev. 7:2-8), signature (Job 31:35 RSV), a target (I Sam. 20:20), a form of tattooing banned by the Lord (Lev. 19:28), a goal to be attained (Phil. 3:14), a particular brand denoting the nature or rank of men (Rev. 13:16).

Mark, John (a large hammer; Jehovah is gracious), mentioned by name ten times in the New Testament. John was his Jewish name, Mark (Marcus) his Roman. In Acts he is twice (13:5, 13) referred to simply as John, once (15:39) as Mark, and three times (12:12, 25; 15:37) as "John, whose surname was Mark." In the epistles he is uniformly (four times) called simply Mark ("Marcus" three times in KJV).

The first allusion to John Mark may be in Mark 14:51, 52. The most reasonable explanation for the passing mention of this incident is that it was a vivid personal memory in the mind of the author of the second Gospel.

The first definite reference is Acts 12:12. Peter, when delivered from prison, went to the home of John Mark's mother, where many believers were praying for him. When Barnabas and Saul returned to Antioch from their famine visit at Jerusalem (Acts 11:27-30), they took along John Mark (Acts 12:25). This opened the opportunity for him to accompany them on their first missionary journey as an "attendant" (Acts 13:5, ASV). Paul distrusted him and refused to take him on the second journey (Acts 15:37, 38). The result was two missionary parties. Barnabas took Mark and revisited Cyprus, while Paul chose a new associate, Silas, and went overland to Asia Minor.

Mark next appears in Rome, where he is a fellow worker with Paul (Philem. 24). He is recommended by the apostle to the church at Colosse (Col. 4:10). That John Mark had fully reinstated himself with Paul is shown by the latter's statement in II Timothy 4:11: — "Take Mark, and bring him with thee; for he is useful to me for ministering." Peter refers to him as "Marcus my son" (I Pet. 5:13). This may be a mere expression of affection, or it may indicate that Mark was converted under Peter's ministry.

Mark, Gospel of, is the shortest of the four Gospels. Starting with the ministry of John the Baptist, it comes immediately to the public ministry of Christ, ending with His death and resurrection.

On two points the tradition of the early church is unanimous: the Second Gospel was written by Mark and presents the preaching of Peter. Most scholars today place the writing of Mark between A.D. 65 and A.D. 70, shortly before the destruction of Jerusalem in the latter year.

Mark's is the Gospel of action. Only one long message of Jesus is recorded, the Olivet Discourse (chap. 13). Mark includes 18 miracles of Jesus, about the same number as Matthew or Luke. In contrast he has only four of the parables, compared with 18 in Matthew and 19 in Luke.

The period of preparation (1:1-13) for Jesus' public ministry is described very briefly. It consists of three items: the ministry of John the Baptist (1:1-8), the baptism of Jesus (1:9-11), and the temptation of Jesus (1:12, 13). After only 13 verses of introduction—in contrast to 76 in Matthew and 183 in Luke—Mark plunges immediately into the public ministry of the Master.

First comes the great Galilean ministry (1:14-9:50). This is commonly thought to have lasted about a year and a half. It may be divided into three sections. The first period (1:4-3:12) was a time of great popularity. Jesus called four fishermen to follow Him — and later Levi — and engaged in a vigorous healing ministry. This was the time when large crowds thronged about Him.

In the second period (3:13-7:23) He appointed the 12 apostles and opposition began to show itself. The Pharisees clashed with Jesus over questions about sabbath observance and ceremonial cleansing. He healed the Gadarene demoniac and the woman with the issue of blood and raised Jairus' daughter. He sent out the twelve and fed the five thousand.

In the third period (7:24-9:50) Jesus gave more attention to His disciples. Three times He is described as withdrawing from the crowd to teach the disciples. After Peter's confession at Caesarea Philippi He began a new phase of teaching: predicting His passion.

The great Galilean ministry was followed by the briefer Perean ministry (10:1-52), and then by passion week (11:1-15:47) and the Resurrection (chap. 16).

Most scholars today favor the theory that Mark's Gospel was written first and was used by Matthew and Luke when they composed their Gospels. The fact is that about 95 per cent of Mark is found in Matthew and/or Luke. The freshness and vividness of Mark's language suggest it was written first. It should be noted, however, that this position is still being challenged.

Market, a place for trade. The term also means things traded, hence should be rendered in Ezekiel 27:13, 17, 19 as merchandise. Also used for recreation and fellowship, public business, courtroom, and forum (Matt. 11:16, 17; 20:3, 6; Mark 12:38; Acts 16:19; 17:17).

Maroth (mā'rŏth), a town probably in the plain W of Jerusalem (Mic. 1:12 RSV).

Marriage is an intimate personal union to which a man and woman consent, consummated and continuously nourished by sexual intercourse, and perfected in a life-long partnership of mutual love and commitment. It is also a social institution regulated by the Word of God and by the laws and customs which a society develops to safeguard its own continuity and welfare. The Creator made man and wo-

The busy marketplace, noisy with the shouts of buyers and sellers.
KC © FC

man, displaying His full image only as both man and woman. Each is made for the other, their essential natures being complementary, and brought into oneness in marriage (Gen. 12:26f; Matt. 19:4-6).

Marriage is the sacrament of human society. Husband and wife both share and perpetuate their happiness in having and rearing a family within the sphere of their own love. Thus marriage is more than an end in itself; it is the means to ends outside the married couple. The unity of husband and wife is of God's creative will, for from Him come the love and grace which enable them to grow together in life comradeship, to beget children, and to fulfill their responsibilities toward their children and to society as a family unit. Husband and wife become one in relation to the community, so that through marriage a new social unit emerges.

Scripture itself says little about the purpose of marriage. The earliest creation narrative suggests unitive purpose ("one flesh"), while the second creation narrative suggests procreative ("be fruitful and multiply"). The NT mentions the unitive and analogical purpose, but not expressly the procreative.

Distinctly Christian marriage is one in which husband and wife covenant together with God and publicly witness their commitment not only to each other but together to Him, to the end that they shall in unity fulfill His purposes throughout life (I Cor. 7:39; cf. II Cor. 6:14). Marriage is contracted "in the Lord," received as a divine vocation, acknowledged with humility and thanksgiving, and sanctified by the Word of God and prayer (I Tim. 4:4-5) Sex is holy, being the creation and gift of God. It is fulfilled only as regulated by the law of God in marriage. The exclusive sexual relation between husband and wife points to the exclusive commitment of total responsibility for each other. The sexual communion speaks of a pervading possessiveness, each partner offering a precious gift to the other which has been exclusively preserved for that one alone.

Paul comprehends marriage obligations for the husband under the principle of love, its highest standard being the love of Christ for His Church (Col. 3:19; Eph. 5:25, 28). Fidelity is required (I Cor. 6; I Thess. 4:3-7; Gal. 5:19; Heb. 13:4). Equality of the wife is indicated in the creation narrative where she is called a "helpmeet" (Gen. 2:18). Complete mutuality is taught in Eph. 5 and in I Cor. 7:3. Spiritual dignity is equal. The wife's duties, however, are summed up not under the principle of love, but of obedience (Eph. 5:22; Col. 3:18; I Pet. 3:1). This subordination is that of responsibility and subsequently of authority. It is not that of compulsion or of fear.

The total unity of persons in marriage, comprehended in the expression "one flesh," demands monogamy and indissolubility. One cannot relate in this way to more than one person at a time, nor with reserve as to the length of time. It is indissoluble as in the union between Christ and His Church. It is monogamous as is the relationship of Christ to His one bride, the Church. Monogamy is represented in the prophets as symbolic of the union of God with Israel (Hos. 2:19; Jer. 3:14; 31:32; Isa. 54:5). In the NT the bridegroom is God in Christ (Matt. 9:15), the bride the spiritual Israel elect out of every nation (II Cor. 11:2; Eph. 5: 23-32; Rev. 19:7).

The Lord's teaching on divorce (Matt. 5:31-32; 19:3-9; Mark 10:2-12; Luke 16:18) gives adultery as the sole reason a man may put away his wife. While Matthew suggests it is adultery on the wife's part only, Mark implies the same right belongs also to the woman. The Lord allowed, but did not make divorce mandatory. Throughout Scripture sin is characterized as spiritual adultery (Hos. 2:2; Jer. 3:9; 13:27).

Divorce was granted on a bill of divorcement in OT times according to the Law (Deut. 24:1-2). Remarriage was clearly acceptable. There was little else for a divorced woman to do. Jesus' statement in Matthew 5:31-32 that divorce is not to be allowed save for unchastity is not found in Mark. It does seem to indicate the principle that if a marriage is destroyed by unfaithfulness, it can not be further destroyed by divorce. Jesus was being put to the test by a group of hostile Jews who believed that only a woman could commit adultery, and Jesus there points out that a man can commit adultery too. He does not go further into the matter.

The Scriptures teach the higher law of forgiveness (Hosea) even for the repentant adulterer. Paul speaks in I Corinthians 7:10-15 of a specific case involving a mixed marriage. He states that should an unbelieving mate depart, the believer is not bound, the meaning of which is controversial. Some teach that Paul here allows for remarriage of the so-called innocent party.

Marrow, the heart of the bone (Job 21:24; Prov. 3:8; Heb. 4:12). Used figuratively of richness (Ps. 63:5) (fatness) and good things (Isa. 25:6).

Marsena (măr-sēn′ȧ), one of the counselors who advised King Ahasuerus to banish Queen Vashti (Esth. 1:10-14).

Mars Hill (Mill of Ares), a barren hill, 370 feet high, NW of the famous Acropolis in Athens, dedicated to Ares, the god of war. Paul was taken there to clarify his mysterious teachings (Acts 17:16-34).

Marsh, swamp lands near the mouths of some rivers and at various places along the banks of the Jordan and of the Dead Sea. Cf. Ezek. 47:11.

Martha (mâr′thȧ, **mistress),** sister of Lazarus and Mary of Bethany (Luke 10:38-41). The Scriptural narrative reveals Jesus was an intimate friend of Martha, Mary, and Lazarus. The sisters knew of His ability to work miracles (John 11:3, 5). He, no doubt, was a guest in their home during the last fateful days on earth (Matt. 21:17; Mark 11:1, 11). Martha was a careful hostess and was familiar enough with Jesus to complain to Him about her sister's conduct (Luke 10:38-42) and about His delay in coming when Lazarus was ill (John 11:1-3, 21).

Martyr (mâr′têr, **witness).** Because of its use in connection with Stephen (Acts 22:20; Rev. 17:6) and others who died for Christ, the word came to mean one who paid the extreme price for fidelity to Christ.

Mary (mâr′ĭ). Miriam in OT. 1. See **Mary, The Virgin.** 2. Mother of James and Joses (Matt. 27:56; Mark 15:40; Luke 24:10), probably the mother of Cleopas (John 19:25); witnessed crucifixion and visited grave on Easter morning (Matt. 27:56; 28:1). 3. Mary Magdalene; Jesus cast seven demons out of her (Mark 16:9; Luke 8:2); followed body of Jesus to grave (Matt. 27:61) and was first to learn of the resurrection (Matt. 28:1-8; Mark 16:9). 4. Mary of Bethany; sister of Lazarus and Martha; lived in Bethany (John 11:1); commended by Jesus (Luke 10:42); anointed feet of Jesus (John 12:3). 5. Mother of John Mark; sister of Barnabas (Col. 4:10); home in Jerusalem meeting place of Christians (Acts 12:12). 6. Christian at Rome (Rom. 16:6).

Mary, The Virgin, wife of Joseph (Matt. 1:18-25); kinswoman of Elizabeth, the mother of John the Baptist (Luke 1:36); of the seed of David (Acts 2:30; Rom. 1:3; II Tim. 2:8); mother of Jesus (Matt. 1:18, 20; Luke 2:1-20); attended to ceremonial purification (Luke 2:22-38); fled to Egypt with Joseph and Jesus (Matt. 2:13-15); lived in Nazareth (Matt. 2:19-23); took

Mars Hill at Athens. JFW

twelve-year-old Jesus to temple (Luke 2:41-50); at wedding in Cana of Galilee (John 2:1-11); concerned for Jesus' safety (Matt. 12:46; Mark 3:21, 31ff; Luke 8:19-21); at the cross of Jesus (John 19:25ff), where she was entrusted by Jesus to care of John (John 19:25-27); in the Upper Room (Acts 1:14). Distinctive Roman Catholic doctrines about Mary: Immaculate Conception (1854) and Assumption of Mary (1950).

Maschil (**màs'kīl, attentive, intelligent**), a Hebrew word found in the titles of Psalms 32; 42; 44; 45; 52; 53: 54: 55: 74; 78; 88; 89; 142. It is usually taken to mean an instructive or meditative ode.

Mash, a grandson of Shem (Gen. 10: 22, 23). Called "Meshech" in I Chron. 1:17.

Mashal (mā'shăl), a village in Asher (Josh. 19:26), assigned to the Gershonite Levites (Josh. 21:30). Called "Misheal" in Joshua 19:26, and "Mishal" in Joshua 21:30.

Mason (See Occupations and Professions)

Masrekah (măs'rē-kȧ, perhaps **vineyard**), the royal city of Samlah, son of Hadad (Gen. 36:31, 36; I Chron. 1: 47).

Massa (măs'ȧ, **burden**), a tribe descended from Ishmael (Gen. 25:14; I Chron. 1:30) which lived in the Arabian desert near the Persian Gulf.

Massah (măs'ȧ, **strife**), name given to the site of the rock in Horeb from which Moses drew water for the rebellious Hebrews (Exod. 17:1-7; Deut. 6:16; 9:22). The name is connected with Meribah (Deut. 33:8).

Master, word with a variety of meanings: ruler, lord, master of servant or slave (Gen. 24:9); prince, chief (I Chron. 15:27); owner (Exod. 22:8); teacher (Matt. 8:19); overseer (Luke 5:5); guide (Matt. 23:10); steersman (Acts 27:11).

Mathusala (See Methuselah)

Matred (mā'trĕd, **expulsion**), the mother of Mehetabel, wife of king Hadar of Edom (Gen. 36:39), called Hadad in I Chronicles 1:50).

Matri (**mā'trī, rainy**), head of a family of Benjamites from which Saul was chosen to be king of Israel (I Sam. 10:21).

Mattan (**măt'ăn, a gift**). 1. A priest of Baal among those who were slain under Jehoiada when Queen Athaliah had made Baal-worship supplant the worship of Jehovah (II Kings 11:1-18; II Chron. 23:16f). 2. Another man named Mattan was among the conspirators who cast Jeremiah into a filthy dungeon (Jer. 38:1-28).

Mattanah (**măt'ȧ-nȧ, a gift**), the name of one of the camps of Israel (Num. 21:18).

Mattaniah (măt'ȧ-nī'ȧ, **gift from Jehovah**). 1. Original name of King Zedekiah (II Kings 24:17). 2. Chief choir leader and watchman (Neh. 11:17; 12:8, 25). 3. Levite (II Chron. 20:14). 4. Son of Elam (Ezra 10:26). 5. Son of Zattu (10:27). 6. Son of Pahath-Moab (10:30). 7. Son of Bani (Ezra 10:37). 8. Grandfather of Hanan (Neh. 13:13). 9. Son of Heman; head musician (I Chron. 25:4, 5, 7, 16). 10. Levite who assisted Hezekiah (II Chron. 29:13).

Mattatha (See Mattathah)

Mattathah (măt'a-thȧ, **gift of Jehovah**), one who put away his pagan wife under Ezra (Ezra 10:33).

Mattathias (măt'ȧ-thī'ăs, **gift of Jehovah**). 1. One of those who stood at Ezra's right hand as he read the law (Neh. 8:4). 2. The name borne by two ancestors of Christ (Luke 3:25, 26). 3. A priest, founder of the Maccabee family (I Macc., ch. 2). 4. A captain in the army of Jonathan Maccabeus (I Macc. 11:70). 5. A son of Simon the high priest (I Macc. 16:14-16). 6. An envoy sent by Nicanor to Judas Maccabeus (II Macc. 14:19).

Mattenai (măt'ē-nā'ī, **a gift from Jehovah**). 1. A priest of the restoration who was among a special class called "heads of fathers" (Neh. 12:12-19). 2. Two priests under Ezra who put away alien wives (Ezra 10:33, 37).

Matthan (mătt'hăn, **gift of God**), grandfather of Joseph, Mary's husband (Matt. 1:15).

Matthat (măt'thăt, **gift of God**), two men in the ancestry of Jesus mentioned in the genealogy of Luke (Luke 3:24, 29).

Matthew (math'ū), son of Alphaeus (Mark 2:14), a tax collector (**telōnēs**), also called Levi (Mark 2:14; Luke 5: 27) whom Jesus met at the tax office and called to be one of His disciples (Matt. 9:9; Mark 2:14; Luke 5:27).

Matthew's background and talents would be of great value to Jesus. As a tax collector he was skilled at writing and keeping records. In addition, he must have been a man of deep spiritual convictions. This is revealed by his concern for his former col-

Matthew was a tax collector at Capernaum. © SPF

leagues whom he invited to a dinner at his own house (Luke's account alone [5:29-32] makes it clear that it was Matthew's house, not Jesus'), Jesus being the honored guest. No doubt Matthew's purpose was to win these men to Christ. Apart from the mention of Matthew in the lists of the Apostles (Matt. 10:3; Mark 3:18; Acts 1:13), no further notices of him are found in the NT.

Matthew, Gospel of, in the early Church Matthew was the most highly valued and widely read of the four Gospels. Among the reasons for this popularity two are particularly important:

1. The Gospel's apostolic authority. Matthew's name was associated with it from at least the early second century. 2. Its emphasis on Christ's teaching. A growing church needed the authoritative word of Christ both to instruct converts and to refute heresy.

Authorship. The First Gospel, as is the case with the other three, is anonymous. Nevertheless, the Church, from the early second century until the rise of modern critical studies, unanimously ascribed it to Matthew, one of the Twelve (Matt. 9:9; 10:3; Mark 3:18; Acts 1:13), also called Levi (Mark 2:14; Luke 5:27), a tax collector by occupation. There is good historical tradition that Matthew actually wrote Gospel material. This comes from Papias of Heirapolis as quoted by the church historian Eusebius: "Matthew wrote down the **Logia** in the Hebrew [i.e., Aramaic] language and everyone translated them as best he could" (**Church History,** III, xxxix, 16). The unanimous Christian tradition is that Matthew wrote it.

Thus, although certainty eludes us, there are cogent reasons for holding to the traditional view that Matthew, the Apostle and eyewitness to the events of Christ's life, wrote the First Gospel. If he used other sources, in particular Mark, he added his own apostolic witness to that of Peter's, and by so doing may have contributed to the alleviation of tensions between Gentile and Jewish Christianity.

Characteristics: 1. Matthew is **par excellence** the **teaching** Gospel. In this respect it greatly supplements Mark which is more interested in what Jesus **did** than in what He **said.**

2. Matthew is the Gospel of the **Church.** He is the only evangelist who uses the word church at all (16:18; **18:** 17).

3. Matthew is the Gospel of **fulfillment.** It is especially concerned with showing that Christianity is the fulfillment of the OT revelation. The many OT proof texts cited by the use of the formula "that it might be fulfilled," the emphasis on the Messiahship of Jesus, and the presentation of Christianity as a new "law" all reveal this basic concern of the author.

4. Matthew is the Gospel of the King. The genealogy of chapter one traces His lineage back to David; at His birth the magi come asking, "Where is he that is born King of the Jews?" (2:2); eight times the regal title "Son of David" is ascribed to Christ (1:1; 9:27; 12:23; 15:22; 20:30, 31; 21:9, 15); the triumphal entry clearly has kingly significance (21:1-11); in the Olivet Discourse Jesus prophesies His future kingly reign (25:31); Pilate asks, "Art thou the King of the Jews?" to which Jesus gives the tacit assent, "Thou sayest" (27:11); and over the cross the words are written, "This is Jesus the king of the Jews" (27:37).

Outline:

1. Prologue: the birth of the King (1, 2).

2. Narrative: the preparation of the King (3, 4).

3. First discourse: the law of the Kingdom (5-7).

4. Narrative: the power of the King (8, 9).

5. Second discourse: the proclamation of the Kingdom (10).

6. Narrative: the rejection of the King (11, 12).

7. Third discourse: the growth of the Kingdom (13).

8. Narrative: the mission of the King (14-17).

9. Fourth discourse: the fellowship of the Kingdom (18).

10. Narrative: the King goes to Jerusalem (19-23).

11. Fifth discourse: the consummation of the Kingdom (24, 25).

12. Narrative: the death and resurrection of the King (26:1-28:15).

13. Epilogue: the great challenge of the Kingdom (28:16-20).

Matthias (mă-thī'ăs, **gift of Jehovah),** the one chosen by lot after the death of Judas Iscariot to take his place among the twelve apostles (Acts 1: 15-26). He had been numbered among the followers of Christ (Acts 1:21, 22).

Mattithiah (măt'ĭ-thī'à, **gift of Jehovah).** 1. A Korahite Levite (I Chron. 9:31). 2. A Levite appointed by David to minister before the ark in music and thanksgiving (I Chron. 15:18, 21; 16:5; 25:3, 21). 3. Son of Nebo who, after the Exile, put away his Gentile wife (Ezra 10:43). 4. One who stood at the right hand of Ezra as he read the law to the people (Neh. 8:4).

Mattock (măt'ŭk), single-headed pickaxe with point on one side and broad edge on other side (I Sam. 13:20, 21; Isa. 7:25).

Maul, originally a hammer such as used by coppersmiths. Today it refers to any smashing weapon like those carried by most shepherds (Prov. 25: 18).

Maw, one of the stomachs of a ruminating animal. It was greatly prized by the ancients and with shoulder and cheeks became the priest's portion of the sacrificial victims (Deut. 18:3).

Mazzaroth (See Astronomy)

Meadow (mĕ'dō). 1. Place where reeds grow (Gen. 41:2, 18). 2. Pasture land (Judg. 20:33).

Meah (mē'à, **hundred),** a tower on the Jerusalem wall.

Meal, ground grain used for both food and sacrificial offerings (Gen. 18:6; Lev. 2:1).

Meal Offering (See Offerings)

Meals in the Bible periods varied greatly in time of eating, diet and table customs. Generally two meals were served daily, although three were not uncommon. The time of these meals was not set like ours today. The first meal of the day could be served at any time from early morning until noon (Prov. 31:15; John 21:12, 15). The rank and occupation of a person

Supper in the guest chamber of an Arab village in an area north of Jerusalem. © MPS

caused the time of the noon meal to vary. It came after the work of the morning was completed (Mark 7:4) or when the noonday heat made work too difficult (Ruth 2:14). The evening meal was not served at any set time but came when the day's work ended. This was usually the principal meal of the Hebrews (Ruth 3:7), while the Egyptians served their main meal at noon (Gen. 43:16). Jesus fed the multitudes at the end of the day (Matt. 14:15; Mark 6:35; Luke 9:12).

The food of the orientals generally may be classified into three groups, among them vegetables: wheat, barley, millet, spelt, lentils, beans, cucumbers, onions, leeks, garlic, salt-wort, pods of the carob tree referred to as "husks," and wild gourds. The corn referred to in the Bible was wheat. The grain was often picked in the field, rubbed in the hands to separate it from the chaff and eaten raw (Luke 6:1). Sometimes it was crushed with mortar and pestle and made into a porridge or cakes (Num. 11:8; Prov. 27:22).

No meal was considered complete without bread. Bread was both leavened and unleavened. Sometimes honey and oil were mixed into the dough as it was being made in the kneading-troughs or wooden bowls. It was usually eaten warm and seldom by itself, but was served with sour wine or meat gravy (John 13:26; 21:13).

Spices, used freely as flavors, consisted of cummin or dill, mustard or mint. Salt also became an important item in the diet of these people.

Fruits grew in great abundance in Palestine and consisted of grapes, figs, olives, mulberries (Sycamore), pomegranates, oranges, lemons, melons, dates, almonds and walnuts. Grapes were eaten as fresh food and dried as raisins. They were the chief source of the wines, which were used both sweet and fermented. Olives were eaten as food as well as used to make olive oil. There were two kinds of figs, early (Isa. 28:4) and late (Jer. 8:13). The late figs were dried and pressed into cakes. Dates were used both raw and dried.

The bulk of the meat came from sheep, lambs, kids and fatted calves. Swine were eaten, but not by the Hebrews. Some game such as the hart, gazelle, goat, antelope and deer as well as doves, turtle-dove and quail formed part of the meat diet. Some eggs were used for food (Isa. 10:14), locusts and fish. The Hebrews used milk from cattle and goats for drinking. From this they made cheese and butter. Arabs drank the milk from camels. The cheese was made from curdled milk and after being salted and formed into small units was placed in the sun to dry. Some of this was later mixed with water to make a sour but cooling drink.

Food was cooked in a variety of ways over a fire made from charcoal (Prov. 26:21), sticks (I Kings 17:10), thorns (Isa. 33:12), or grass (Luke 12:28). Archaeology is throwing light increasingly on the variety of utensils used in preparing food.

Mearah (mē-ā'rȧ, **cave**), a town or district in NE Palestine belonging to the Zidonians (Josh. 13:4).

Measure (See Weights and Measures)

Meat (See Food)

Meat Offering (See Offerings)

Mebunnai (mē-bŭn'ī, **well-built**), one of David's bodyguards (II Sam. 23:27) who slew a Philistine giant (II Sam. 21:18).

Mecerathite (mē-kē'răth-īt, **dweller in Mecharah**), a description of Hepher, one of David's mighty men (I Chron. 11:36).

Medad (mē'dăd, **affectionate**), one of the 70 elders appointed to assist Moses in the government of the people (Num. 11:24-30).

Medan (mē'dăn, **strife**), a son of Abraham by Keturah (Gen. 25:2; I Chron. 1:32).

Medeba (mĕd'ē-bȧ, **uncertain**), a city lying high in the grazing section of Moab E of the Jordan, and first referred to in Numbers 21:30. It is part of the section of land assigned to the tribe of Reuben (Josh. 13:9). The claim to this land was often disputed by the Reubenites, Ammonites and the Moabites. The Biblical records together with the testimony of the Moabite Stone shows that it was constantly changing hands (cf. I Chron. 19:7 with Isa. 15:2).

Medes, Media (mēdz, mē'dĭ-ȧ), the inhabitants of the land of Media.

The more than twenty references to these people or their land in the Scriptures show their importance. II Kings refers to their cities (II Kings 17:6; 18:11), Esther tells of the binding character of their laws (Esth. 1:19), Isaiah and Daniel tell of their power against Babylon (Isa. 13:17; Dan. 5:28). The last Scriptural reference to them is in

Acts 2:9 where representatives are in Jerusalem at the time of Pentecost.

Media (See Medes)

Mediation (See Mediator)

Mediator (mē'dĭ-ā'tēr, **middle man),** one who brings about friendly relations between two or more estranged people (I Sam. 2:25; Job. 33:23). Christ is the mediator of the new covenant between God and man (I Tim. 2:5; Heb. 8:6; 9:15; 12:24).

Medicine (See Diseases)

Mediterranean Sea (mĕd'ĭ-tĕ-rā'nē-ăn), referred to in Scripture as "the sea" (Num. 13:29), "the great sea" (Josh. 1:4), "the uttermost sea" (Deut. 11:24), "hinder sea" (Deut. 34:2 RSV), "Sea of the Philistines" (Exod. 23:31).

Crete and Cyprus made havens for shippers of ancient days. Paul was on both islands during his journeys (Acts 13:4; 27:7).

Two views of the Mediterranean shore. Above, the rugged coast of Phoenicia, showing the "Ladder of Tyre." Below, the beautiful beach at Alexandria. © MPS

The Mound of Megiddo (Tell El Mutesellim), as seen from the Plain of Esdraelon. © *MPS*

The modern village of Memphis. © *MPS*

Meekness, a fruit of the Spirit (Gal. 5:23). It is characteristic of Jesus (Matt. 11:29; II Cor. 10:1). Believers are commanded to be meek and to show a lowly spirit one to another (Eph. 4:2; Col. 3:12; Titus 3:2). A teacher should be meek (II Tim. 2:25). Meekness is a mark of true discipleship (I Pet. 3:15). The word does not imply a weak, vacillating or supine nature.

Megiddo (mĕ-gĭd′ō, **place of troops),** city on the Great Road linking Gaza and Damascus, connecting the coastal plain and the Plain of Esdraelon (Josh. 12:21; 17:11; Judg. 1:27; 5:19); fortified by Solomon (I Kings 9:15); wounded Ahaziah died there (II Kings 9:27); Josiah lost life there in battle with Pharaoh Necho (II Kings 23:29, 30; II Chron. 35:20-27). Large-scale excavations have revealed a great deal of material of great archaeological value.

Megiddon (See Megiddo)

Mehetabel (mĕ-hĕt′ȧ-bĕl, **God benefits).** 1. A daughter of Matred, wife of King Hadar (Gen. 36:39). 2. One who sought to betray Nehemiah (Neh. 6: 10-13).

Mehida (mē-hī′dȧ, **renowned),** ancestor and family name of some Nethinim (temple servants) who returned with Zerubbabel (Ezra 2:52; Neh. 7:54).

Mehir (mē′hîr, **price, hire),** son of Chelub (I Chron. 4:11).

Meholathite (mē-hō′lȧ-thīt), Gentile designation of Adriel to whom Saul married his daughter Merab (I Sam. 18:19; II Sam. 21:8). The place Abel-meholah was located in the Jordan valley near Beth-shan, the native place of Elisha (I Kings 19:16).

Mehujael (mē-hū′jā-ĕl), descendant of Cain and father of Methusael (Gen. 4:18).

Mehuman (mē-hū′măn), eunuch of Ahasuerus, king of Persia (Esth. 1:10).

Mejarkon (mē-jȧr′kŏn), a place in the tribe of Dan between Gath-rimmon and Rakkon (Josh 19:46).

Mekonah (mē-kō′nȧ), a town in the southern part of Judah near Ziklag (Neh. 11:28).

Melatiah (mĕl-ȧ-tī′ȧh), a Gibeonite who helped repair the walls of Jerusalem (Neh. 3:7).

Melchi (mĕl-kī), the name of two ancestors of Jesus through Mary, according to Luke's genealogy: (1) The son of Addi and father of Neri (Luke 3: 28); and (2) the son of Janna and father of Levi, fourth from Mary (Luke 3:24).

Melchiah (See Malchiah)

Melchisedec (See Melchizedek)

Melchi-shua (mĕl′kī-shōō′ȧ), a son of King Saul slain with his brothers on Mount Gilboa (I Sam. 31:2).

Melchizedek, Melchisedek (mĕl-kĭz′ĕ-dĕk, **king of righteousness),** priest and king of Salem (Jerusalem); blessed Abram in the name of Most High God and received tithes from him (Gen. 14:18-20); type of Christ, the Priest-King (Heb. 5:6-10; 6:20; 7).

Melea (mē′lē-ȧ), ancestor of Jesus (Luke 3:31).

Melech (mē′lĕk, **king),** a son of Micah, a grandson of Mephibosheth or Merib-baal, and a great grandson of Jonathan (I Chron. 8:35; 9:41).

Melicu (See Malluch)

Melita (mĕl′ĭ-tȧ), an island, now called Malta, situated in a strategically important position some 60 miles S of Sicily. Rome acquired the island in 218 B.C., but the Carthaginian language continued to be spoken. Hence Luke's phrase "the barbarous people" (Acts 28:2), "barbarous," of course, being used in the Greek sense of "foreign-speaking." Melita was the scene of Paul's shipwreck (Acts 27; 28).

Melody (See Music)

Melon (See Plants)

Melzar (mēl′zȧr, **overseer),** a man in whose care Daniel and his three companions were committed by the chief of the eunuchs of Nebuchadnezzar (Dan 1:11, 16).

Member, a word usually denoting any feature or part of the body (Job 17:7; James 3:5). "The members" is equivalent with "the body" (Ps. 139:16). The word is also used figuratively by the body of Christ (I Cor. 12:12-17; Eph. 4:16).

Memphis (mĕm′fĭs), the first capital of united Egypt (c. 3200 B.C.), situated on the W bank of the Nile, about 20 miles S of modern Cairo. The original name of the city was "The White Wall"; later it was called Men-nefer-Pepi, after the name of the pyramid of Pepi I of the Sixth Dynasty, and it is from this name that "Memphis" is derived. The chief god of M. was Ptah; also prominent at Memphis was the worship of the Apis bull, whose famous burial place, the Serapeum, is located just to the W, in the necropolis of Sakkarah. All of the Biblical references to M. are in the prophets (Hos. 9:6; cf. Jer. 41:16-18; 44:1; Isa. 19:13, Noph; Jer. 2:16; cf. Jer. 46:13, 19; Ezek. 30:13, 16), and spoke of coming distresses in that city.

Memucan (mē-mū′căn), one of the seven wise men at the Persian court who advised King Ahasuerus to punish Queen Vashti for her refusal to appear at the court festival (Esth. 1:13-22).

Menahem (mĕn′ȧ-hĕm, **comforted**), son of Gadi and king of Israel (II Kings 15:13-22) whose reign of ten years began by killing his predecessor Shallum. His son Pekahiah inherited the kingdom. "He did that which was evil in the sight of the Lord."

Menan (mē′năn), an ancestor of Jesus through Mary in Luke's genealogy (3: 31).

Mene, Mene, Tekel, Upharsin (mē′nē, mē′nē, tē′kĕl, ū-fȧr′sĭn), four Aramaic words of uncertain interpretation, but probably meaning "numbered, numbered, weighed, and found wanting," which suddenly appeared on the walls of Belshazzar's banquet hall (Dan, 5).

Meni (mē′nī, **fate, destiny**), probably Canaanite god of good luck or destiny (Isa. 65:11). Translated "number" in KJV.

Meonenim (mē-ŏn′ē-nĭm) plain near Shechem named for a diviner's tree (Judg. 9:37), exact site unknown.

Meonothai (mē-ŏn′ō-thī, **my dwelling**), a descendant of Judah through Caleb (I Chron. 4:13, 14).

Mephaath (mĕf′ā-ăth, **splendor**), a town in the territory of Reuben (Josh. 13:18) and given to the Levitical family of Merari (21:37).

Mephibosheth (mē′fĭb′ō-shĕth). Meribaal in I Chron. 8:34; 9:40. 1. Son of Saul and Rizpah (II Sam. 21:8). 2. Son of Jonathan; grandson of Saul; crippled in accident; honored and provided for by David (II Sam. 4:4; 9:6-13; 16:1-4; 19:24-30; 21:7).

Merab (mē′răb), daughter of King Saul (I Sam. 14:49; 18:17-19; II Sam. 21:8 where "Merab" should be read instead of "Michal").

Meraiah (mē-rā′yȧ, **rebellious**), a priest of Israel in the time of Joiakim (Neh. 12:12).

Meraioth (mē-rā′yŏth, **rebellious**). 1. A high priest of Israel in the seventh generation from Aaron (I Chron. 6:6, 7). 2. Another in the priestly line and ancestor of the great Hilkiah (I Chron. 9:11). 3. Ancestor of Helkai, a priest in the days of Joiakim the high priest (Neh. 12:15).

Merari (mē-rā′rī, **bitter**), the youngest son of Levi. The high priesthood descended through Aaron, and the other Levites assisted in the divine service. The "Merarites" had the responsibility for the woodwork of the tabernacle in its journeys (Num. 3:17, 33-37). Later, they had 12 cities in Reuben, Gad and Zebulun (Josh. 21:7, 34-40).

Merathaim (mĕr-ȧ-thā′ĭm, **repeated rebellion**), a symbolic name for Babylon (Jer. 50 and 51).

Merchandise, Merchant (See Commerce)

Mercurius (mẽr-kū′rĭ-ŭs), in English Mercury, according to Greek mythology the son of Zeus or Jupiter and Maia, the oldest of the Pleiades. As messenger of the gods he had wings on his feet and was notable also for eloquence. The people of Lystra called Paul "Mercury" because he was the chief speaker, and called Barnabas Jupiter (Acts 14:12).

Mercury (See Mercurius)

Mercy. 1. Forbearance from inflicting punishment upon an adversary or a law-breaker. 2. That compassion which causes one to help the weak, the sick or the poor. Showing mercy is one of the cardinal virtues of a true Christian (James 2:1-13) and is a part of the "fruit of the Spirit" (Gal. 5:22, 23).

Mercy Seat (See Tabernacle)

Mered (mē′rĕd, **rebellion**), a descendant of one of the Pharaohs (I Chron. 4:17, 18).

Meremoth (mĕr′ē-mŏth, **elevations**). 1. A priest who returned from Babylon with Zerubbabel (Neh. 12:3). 2. One who returned with Ezra 457 B.C. Son of Uriah, a priest of Israel (Ezra 8:33). He helped Nehemiah to rebuild the wall (Neh. 3:4, 21). (These may be two persons.) 3. One who had taken a foreign wife (Ezra 10:36). 4. A priest who signed the covenant (Neh. 10:5).

Meres (mē′rez, **worthy**), a Persian prince under Xerxes ("Ahasuerus") (Esth. 1:14).

Meribah (mĕr′ĭ-bȧ, **contention**). 1. A place near Sinai where Moses, at the command of Jehovah, struck the rock and water gushed out for the refreshment of the people (Exod. 17:1-7).

2. A place near Kadesh-barnea where the people again thirsted and where Jehovah commanded Moses to speak to the rock. Moses exceeded his instructions, and apparently wanting some of the credit for the miracle, he struck the rock, and water came forth (Num. 20:1-13). For this arrogance, Moses was forbidden to enter the Promised Land.

Merib-baal (mĕr′ĭb-bā′ăl, **Baal contends**), son of Jonathan, the son of

King Saul (I Chron. 8:34; 9:40). Possibly the same as Mephibosheth, **q.v.**

Meribah-kadesh (See Meribah)

Merodach (mē-rō′dăk), **Marduk,** a Babylonian god.

Merodach Baladan (mē-rō′dăk-băl′ȧ-dăn, **Marduk has given a son),** a king of Babylon called Berodach-baladan in II Kings 20:12. He was a strong, courageous leader of the Chaldeans, who lived in the marshes of southern Mesopotamia. In 722 B.C. he rebelled against the Assyrians, who had controlled Babylon for many years, and became king of Babylon. Sargon, king of Assyria, recognized him as Babylonian king in 721. He reigned 11 years. At about 712, Merodach Baladan sent an embassy to Hezekiah (II Kings 20:12-19; Isa. 39:1-8) to invite him to join in a confederacy with Babylon, Susiana, Phoenicia, Moab, Edom, Philistia and Egypt for a grand attack on the Assyrian empire. Sargon, getting wind of the plot, attacked and defeated his enemies individually. In 710 he took Babylon; in 709 Bit-Yakin (Merodach Baladan's home in southern Mesopotamia) fell and Merodach Baladan was captured. He managed to be reinstated in his princedom of Bit-Yakin. In 703 he briefly took Babylon and ruled there, but was again driven to Bit-Yakin by Sennacherib, Sargon's son and successor. Later he was obliged to flee the country and found refuge in Elam, while the Chaldeans were subjugated. Although Merodach Baladan had failed in his project to revive the power of the city of Babylon, the Chaldeans, whose chief he was, became from his days the dominant caste in Babylon (Dan. 2:2, 10; 5:7; Ezra 5:12).

Merom (mē′rŏm, **a high place),** a district near the head-waters of the Jordan river, N of the Sea of Galilee where Joshua defeated N. coalition (Josh. 11:5, 7). The men of the tribe of Dan, when searching for a more commodious land for the tribe (Judg. 18) passed through this region and described it as "very good" and "the land is large."

Meronothite (mē-rŏn′ȧ-thīt), an inhabitant of Meronoth, a region in Galilee which was given to the tribe of Naphtali. Its principal town was Shimron-meron which Joshua conquered (Josh. 11:1; 12:20).

Meroz (mē′roz), a place in Galilee not far from Nazareth; infamous because its inhabitants "came not to the help of Jehovah" when Deborah and Barak needed help against Jabin (Judg. 5:23).

Mesech (See Meshech)

Mesha (mē′shȧ). 1. A place in southern Arabia which marks a boundary of the habitations of the early Semitic Arabs (Gen. 10:30). 2. A Benjamite (I Chron. 8:9). 3. A descendant of Judah through Perez, Hezron and Caleb (I Chron. 2:42). 4. A king of Moab in the days of Ahab, and his two sons who succeeded him, Ahaziah and Jehoram (II Kings 3:4). He rebelled against Ahaziah. Jehoram, with the help of Jehoshaphat of Judah, attacked and defeated him (II Kings 3: 4-27).

Meshach (mē′shăk), the heathen name given to Mishael, one of the four princes of Judah taken by Nebuchadnezzar to be trained in his palace as counselors to the king (Dan. 1:3-7).

Meshech (mē′shěk, **tall).** 1. A son of Japheth (Gen. 10:2) associated with Magog and Tubal and thought by many to have been progenitors of Russians and other Slavic peoples. 2. The people descended from the preceding (Ezek. 27:13; 38, 39). 3. A grandson of Shem (I Chron. 1:17). 4. A tribe mentioned in Psalm 120:5 with (or probably contrasted with) the tents of Kedar. Probably the same as No. 2 above.

Meshelemiah (mē-shěl′ē-mī′ȧ), father of Zechariah (I Chron. 9:21; 26:1, 2, 9). Called "Shelemiah" in I Chronicles 26:14.

Meshezabeel (mē-shěz′ȧ-bēl, **God delivers).** 1. Ancestor of Meshullam (Neh. 3:4). 2. A covenanter with Nehemiah (Neh. 10:21). 3. A descendant of Judah through Zerah (Neh. 11:24).

Meshillemith (See Meshillemoth)

Meshillemoth (mē-shĭl′ē-mŏth **recompense).** 1. Father of Berechiah (II Chron. 28:12). 2. Priestly ancestor of Amashsai, who dwelt at Jerusalem in the Restoration (Neh. 11:13). Meshillemith (I Chron. 9:12) is another spelling of the same name.

Meshobab (mē-shō′băb, **restored),** a Simeonite in the days of Hezekiah (I Chron. 4:34).

Meshullam (mē-shŭl′ăm, **reconciled),** a very common name in the OT. 1. Grandfather of Shaphan, trusted scribe of Josiah (II Kings 22:3). 2. A son of Zerubbabel (I Chron. 3:19). 3. A leading Gadite under Jeroboam II (I

Chron. 5:13). 4. A chief Benjamite (I Chron. 8:17). 5. Father of Sallu (I Chron. 9:7). 6. Another Benjamite of Jerusalem (I Chron. 9:8). 7. A priest (I Chron. 9:11; Neh. 11:11). 8. Ancestor of another priest (I Chron. 9:12). 9. A Kohathite, overseer of repairing the temple (II Chron. 34:12). 10. A chief who returned with Ezra, 457 B.C. (Ezra 8:16). 11. One active in doing away with foreign marriages (Ezra 10:15). 12. One of the offenders in this matter (Ezra 10:29). 13. One who rebuilt two portions of the wall (Neh. 3:4, 30; 6:18). 14. Another repairer (Neh. 3:6). 15. One who stood with Ezra in the revival (Neh. 8:4). 16. A priest who signed the covenant (Neh. 10:7). 17. Another covenanter (Neh. 10:20). 18. A man of Benjamin (Neh. 11:7). 19. A priest c. 470 B.C. (Neh. 12:13). 20. Possibly the same man (Neh. 12:33). 21. Another priest c. 470 B.C. (Neh. 12:16). 22. A Levite gatekeeper at the time (Neh. 12:25).

Meshullemeth (mē-shŭl'ē-mĕth, fem. of **Meshullam),** daughter of Haruz of Jotbah, who married King Manasseh of Judah and was mother of Amon (II Kings 21:19).

Mesobaite (mē-sō'bȧ-īt), in ASV more correctly Mezobaite, a patronymic referring to a place otherwise unknown and unheard of (I Chron. 11:47).

Mesopotamia (mĕs'ō-pō-tā'mĭ-ȧ, **middle river),** the name applied in particular to the area between the Tigris and Euphrates rivers, a region which in the Hebrew is called Aram, Aram-Naharaim, or Padan-Aram, along with various other names for localities or peoples of this region. In present day application the term is used of a territory practically coextensive with modern Iraq (Gen. 24:10; Deut. 23:4; Judg. 3: 8-11; I Chron. 19:6; Acts 2:9; 7:2).

In the NT, the mention of Mesopotamia as one of the regions from which the Jews of the Diaspora had come to Jerusalem (Acts 2:9, "residents of Mesopotamia," RSV) probably has reference to that part of the Near East included in modern Iraq and may refer more particularly to the area near ancient Babylon. Stephen's allusion to the fact that the call of God came to Abraham, "while he was in Mesopotamia, before he lived in Haran" (Acts 7:2), definitely puts southern Iraq in Mesopotamia, for Abraham was then in the city of Ur (Gen. 11:31). The southern part of Mesopotamia, including Ur and a number of other city-states, was known as Sumer; the central section was called Akkad and later was named Babylonia, after the city of Babylon gained the ascendancy; the northern division, along with Tigris, was Assyria, the land of Asshur.

Mess, any dish of food, **sent** to the table (Gen. 43:34; II Sam. 11:8; Heb. 12:16).

Messiah (mĕ-sī'ȧ, **anointed one);** the basic meaning of the Heb. **mashiah** and the Gr. **Christos** is "anointed one." In the OT the word is used of prophets, priests, and kings who were consecrated to their office with oil. The expression "the Lord's anointed" and its equivalent is not used as a technical designation of the Messiah, but refers to the king of the line of David, ruling in Jerusalem, and anointed by the Lord through the priest. With the possible exception of Dan. 9:25, 26 the title "Messiah" as a reference to Israel's eschatological king does not occur in the OT. It appears in this sense later in the NT, where He is almost always called "the Christ." The OT pictures the Messiah as one who will put an end to sin and war and usher in universal righteousness and through His death will make vicarious atonement for the salvation of sinful men. The NT concept of the Messiah is developed directly from the teaching of the OT. Jesus of Nazareth is the Messiah; He claimed to be and the claim was acknowledged by His disciples (Luke 4:18, 19; Acts 4:27; 10:38).

Messias (See Messiah)

Metals (See Minerals of the Bible)

Meteyard (mēt'yȧrd), an archaic word for "measures of length" (Lev. 19:35).

Metheg-ammah (mē'thĕg-ăm'ȧ, **the bridle of the metropolis),** a town David took from the hands of the Philistines (II Sam. 8:1).

Methusael (mē-thū'sā'ĕl), father of Lamech (Gen. 4:18).

Methuselah (mē-thū'zĕ-lȧ, **man of the javelin),** antediluvial Sethite, died at 969 years of age, in the very year of the Flood (Gen. 5:22-27). He was the son of Enoch and the father of Lamech (Gen. 5:21-27).

Meunim (mē-ū'nĭm), people who lived in Arab city near Petra (I Chron. 4:41, translated "habitations"). "Menhunims" in II Chron. 26:7 KJV; "Mehunim" in Ezra 2:50, where they are counted among the "Nethinim" at the return.

Mezahab (mĕz'ā-hăb), grandfather of Mehetabel (Gen. 36:39; I Chron. 1:50).

Miamin (mī'ȧ-mĭn, **from the right hand** i.e. **fortunate).** 1. One who had taken a foreign wife (Ezra 10:25). 2. A priest who returned with Zerubbabel (Neh. 12:5). 3. "Mijamin" **q.v.** in I Chronicles 24:9 and Nehemiah 10:7 is the same word in Hebrew.

Mibhar (mĭb'hȧr, **choice),** one of David's mighty men (I Chron. 11:38).

Mibsam (mĭb'săm, **sweet odor,** related to **Balsam).** 1. One of the 12 Ishmaelite patriarchs (Gen. 25:13). 2. A grandson or great-grandson of Simeon (I Chron. 4:25).

Mibzar (mĭb'zȧr, **a fortress),** one of the 11 "sheikhs" or chiefs, not "dukes," descended from Esau (Gen. 36:42).

Micah (mī'kȧ), short form of the name **Micaiah** (or Michael), meaning "Who is like Jehovah (or God)?" The name is applied to seven individuals in the OT: 1. An Ephraimite (Judg. 18 and 19). 2. A Reubenite (I Chron. 5:5). 3. A grandson of Jonathan (I Chron. 8:34; 9:40). 4. A Levite (I Chron. 23:20). 5. The father of one of Josiah's officers (II Kings 22:12; II Chron. 34:20). 6. The canonical prophet Micah (Mic. 1:1 and Jer. 26:18). 7. The son of Imlah (II Chron. 18:14).

Micah, Book of, the fifth of the Minor Prophets, comes from the late 700's B.C. It predicts the fall of Samaria which occurred in 722, but concerns more especially the sins and dangers of Jerusalem in the days of Hezekiah around 700 B.C. As an outline will show, the message oscillates between condemnation for present sins and God's purpose of ultimate blessing for His people:

Outline:

I. Predicted desolation of Samaria and Jerusalem, 1:1-3:12.
II. Eventual blessings for Zion, 4:1-8.
III. Invasions and deliverance by the Davidic ruler, 4:9-5:15.
IV. Condemnation for sins, 6:1-7:6.
V. Eventual help from God, 7:7-20.

The condemnations of Section IV (6:1-7:6) include several references to the Pentateuch and other historical books (6:4; 6:5; 6:16. Cf. also 5:6 with Gen. 10:8, 9). The response of 6:8 is famous. Some have argued that it teaches salvation apart from sacrifice. Actually, it is an allusion to Deuteronomy 10:12 and involves Israel's duty to obey **all** the Mosaic injunctions. Christ probably alludes to this verse in His condemnation of the formalistic Pharisees (Matt. 23:23).

The book closes with the prophet's declaration of faith in the ultimate fulfilment of God's covenant of blessing for Abraham (7:20).

Micaiah (mī-kā'yȧ, **who is like Jehovah?),** prophet living in Samaria c. 900 B.C. who predicted the death of King Ahab (I Kings 22; II Chron. 18).

Micha (mī'cȧ, evidently, like Micah, an abb. of Micaiah, **Who is like Jehovah?).** 1. A grandson of Jonathan (II Sam. 9:12). 2. A Levite covenanter (Neh. 10:11). 3. Another Levite (Neh. 11:17). 4. Another (Neh. 11:22; Micah in I Chron. 9:15). These are uniformly Mica in ASV.

Michael (mī'kĕl, **who is like God?).** 1. Father of Sethur, a spy from the tribe of Asher (Num. 13:13). 2. Two Gadites in Bashan (I Chron. 5:13, 14). 3. Great-grandfather of Asaph, the singer (I Chron. 6:40). 4. A chief man of Issachar (I Chron. 7:3). 5. A Benjamite (I Chron. 8:16). 6. A captain of a thousand of Manasseh who joined David in Ziklag (I Chron. 12:20). 7. The father of one of David's mighty men (I Chron. 27:18). 8. A prince of Judah, son of Jehoshaphat and brother of Jehoram, kings of Judah (II Chron. 21:2). 9. Father of Zebadiah, a chief Jew who returned with Ezra (Ezra 8:8). 10. Last, and by far the most famous, the archangel whose chief responsibility seems to have been the care of the Jewish people. Michael had a dispute with Satan himself (Jude 9).

Michah (See Micah, Micha)

Michaiah (mī-kā'yȧ, **who is like Jehovah?).** 1. Father of Achbor, whom King Josiah sent with others to Huldah the prophetess to inquire about the prophecy which had been read to him (II Kings 22:12-14). 2. A daughter of Uriel of Gibeah (II Chron. 13:2). 3. A prince of Judah whom Jehoshaphat sent to teach the people (II Chron. 17:7). 4. Ancestor of a priest in Nehemiah's time, (Neh. 12:35). 5. A priest in Nehemiah's time (Neh. 12:41). 6. Grandson of Shaphan the scribe in Josiah's day who had brought the book of the law of the Lord to the king. In ASV the name is Micaiah.

Michal (mī'kăl, a contraction of **Michael),** the younger daughter of King Saul of Israel (I Sam. 14:49). Saul, insanely jealous of David, desired to kill him but found it impossible to do so by his own hands (I Sam. 18:11), so he tried trickery. He offered David his

The village of Michmash, site of historic battles in the history of Israel.

elder daughter Merab for his service against the Philistines, but changed his mind and gave her to another; then he learned that Michal loved David, so he offered her to David if he would give evidence of having slain 100 Philistines. He slew 200 and married Michal; but Saul hated him all the more. Once, when Saul sent to slay David, Michal helped him to escape (I Sam. 19:11-17), deceiving Saul's officers by putting an image in his bed, and thus giving him time to make good his escape. Though Michal truly loved David, she could not comprehend him, and scoffed at him for rejoicing before the Lord (II Sam. 6:16-23). As a result, she never had a child.

Michmas, Michmash (mĭk′măs, mĭk′mash, **a hidden place**), a place in the ancient tribe of Benjamin about eight miles NE of Jerusalem. A notable battle occurred there between Israel and the Philistines in the reign of Saul (I Sam. 13, 14; Neh. 7:31). Michmash lay in the pass which goes eastward from Bethel and Ai down to Jericho, and at one place the pass was contained between two rocks, "Bozez" and "Seneh" (I Sam. 14:4). There Jonathan and his armor-bearer clambered up and started the victory over the Philistines, and there the British forces under General Allenby used the same strategy and won a victory over the Turks.

Michmethah (mĭk′mē-thȧ), a landmark on the borders of Ephraim and Manasseh (Josh. 16:6 and 17:7), close to Shechem.

Michri (mĭk′rī), grandfather of Elah, a Benjamite in Jerusalem after the captivity (I Chron. 9:8).

Michtam (mĭk′tăm), a word of uncertain meaning found in the titles of six psalms of David (16, 56-60).

Middin (mĭd′ĭn), one of the six cities of Judah lying in the wilderness just W of the Dead Sea (Josh. 15:61).

Middle Wall, a term taken from Ephesians 2:14, probably a reference to the barrier which stood between the Court of the Gentiles and the Court of the Jews in the temple in Jerusalem. Gentiles were forbidden to cross it under pain of death. Paul uses it as a symbol of the legal partition between Gentile and Jew, removed by Christ.

Midian, Midianites (mĭd′ĭ-ăn, -īts). 1. A son of Abraham by Keturah (Gen. 25:1-6). 2. His descendants and the land which they claimed (Gen. 37:25, 36; Exod. 2:15-21).

Though nomads, they had in the time of Moses great wealth; all of which are mentioned in the booty taken by the men of Israel (Num. 31: 22, 32-34). The Midianites have long since disappeared from among mankind.

Migdal-el (mĭg′dăl-ĕl, **tower of God**), one of the 19 fortified cities of Naphtali (Josh. 19:38).

Migdal-gad (mĭg′dăl-găd, **tower of Gad**), a city of Judah when Joshua divided the land (Josh. 15:37). Now probably Mejdal about 24 miles W of Hebron.

Migdol (mĭg′dŏl). 1. A place just W of the former shallow bay at the N end of the Gulf of Suez, the westward arm of the Red Sea (Exod. 14:2; Num. 33:7). Close by, the Israelites made their last encampment in Egypt, and here Pharaoh thought that they were entrapped. 2. A place in the N of Egypt to which many Jews resorted in the days of Jeremiah, and where they even practiced idolatry in spite of the prophet's warnings (Jer. 44:1-14; 46: 14).

Migron (mĭg′rŏn, **precipice**), Benjamite town (I Sam. 14:2; Isa. 10:28).

Mijamin (mĭj′ȧ-mĭn, **from the right hand**). 1. A priest in David's time (I Chron. 24:9). 2. A priest who covenanted with Nehemiah (Neh. 10:7). 3. A priest who returned with Zerubbabel (Neh. 12:5, 7). 4. A man who put away his foreign wife (Ezra 10:25).

Mikloth (mĭk′lŏth, **rods**). 1. A Benjamite in Jerusalem after the Exile (I Chron. 8:32; 9:37, 38). 2. A ruler of 24,000 men under David (I Chron. 27: 4).

Mikneiah (mĭk-nē′yȧ), a Levite harp player in David's time (I Chron. 15: 18, 21).

Milalai (mĭ-ȧ-lā′ī), a priest with a musical instrument in Nehemiah's celebration (Neh. 12:36).

Milcah (mĭl′kȧ, **counsel**). 1. A daughter of Haran, Abram's eldest brother, who died at Ur of the Chaldees, and sister of Lot. She married her uncle Nahor and bore him eight children of whom one was Bethuel, father of Rebekah and Laban (Gen. 11:27-29; 22:20-23). 2. Daughter of Zelophehad, the Manassite (Num. 36:11).

Milcom (See Moloch)

Above, women grinding grain at a handmill. Below, a primitive wheat mill in Babylonia (Iraq), probably of the type that blinded Samson was forced to turn in the Philistine prison. © MPS

Mildew, a pale fungus growth which discolors and spoils grains and fruits in warm damp weather. In Scripture it is always associated with "blasting" (Deut. 28:22; I Kings 8:37; Amos 4:9; Hag. 2:17).

Mile (See Weights and Measures)

Miletus (mī-lē'tŭs), Ionian coastal city, 36 miles S of Ephesus; for centuries a great sea power; visited by Paul (Acts 20:15, 17; II Tim. 4:20, KJV has "Miletum").

Milk (See Food)

Mill, an apparatus used to grind any edible grain—wheat, barley, oats, rye, etc.—into flour. It consists of two circular stones, the lower one having a slightly convex upper surface to help the drifting of the broken grain toward the outer edge whence it drops. It is made of a hard stone, which after being shaped, is scratched with curved furrows so as to multiply the cutting and grinding effects (Exod. 11:5; Num. 11:7, 8; Deut. 24:6; Jer. 25:10; Matt. 24:41).

When the Philistines blinded Samson (Judg. 16:21) he had to grind in the prisonhouse, and this mill was probably a larger one ordinarily turned by a blinded ox or donkey. Abimelech, usurping "king" of Israel, was slain by a woman who dropped a millstone upon his head (Judg. 9:53) and our Lord prophesies that at His coming "two women shall be grinding at the mill: one shall be taken and the other is left" (Matt. 24:41). A millstone cast into the sea is a symbol of absolute destruction (Rev. 18:21).

Millennium, the Latin word for "thousand years." It comes from Revelation 20:1-15 where a certain period of a "thousand years" is mentioned six times. During this period (1) Satan is "bound" with a "great chain," "locked up" and "sealed" in "the abyss," so that he can not "deceive the nations"; (2) persons designated as "martyrs" who have been "beheaded," "live" and "reign with Christ" (I Cor. 15:23; Rom. 8:17-26; Acts. 3:20, 21).

The reigning of the saints with Christ after His second coming is several times predicted in the Lord's teachings. Those who look for Christ's visible return preceding His millennial kingdom, that is, premillennialists, adhere to the grammatico-historical method of exegesis, taking propositional truth in its simplest sense, understanding statements as "literal" unless there is sound reason to believe them to be intended figuratively. On the other hand, there has always been a tendency to "spiritualize" or "demythologize" whatever seems unfamiliar, and the "interpretations" of the millennium are numberless. Those called post-millennialists hold that Christ will return after the millennium. Amillennialists deny that there will be a millennial reign on earth.

The "blessed hope" of the church in all generations (Titus 2:13, cf. I Thess. 4:17) is the immanent, glorious return of Christ.

Millet (See Plants)

Millo (mĭl'ō, **fullness),** a mound or rampart built up with earth and stones. 1. An ancient fortification in or near Shechem (Judg. 9:6, 20). 2. Filled-in fortification just N of Mt. Zion (II Sam. 5:9; I Kings 9:15, 24; 11:27; I Chron. 11:8; II Chron. 32:5).

Mina (See Weights and Measures)

Mind, a word in Scripture that means **heart, soul;** the faculty of reflective consciousness, of moral thinking and knowing, **meditation, reflection.** None of these words is used with any precision of meaning. In the NT the word "mind" frequently occurs in an ethical sense, as in Colossians 2:18 and Romans 7:25.

Minerals of the Bible. The present science of mineralogy with its names and exact terminology is a young science coming later than physics, chemistry, astronomy, or mathematics. Mineralogy as a science certainly did not exist at the time the Bible was written. It is quite impossible to be certain in all cases that when a mineral name is used in the Bible, it is used with the same meaning as that attached in modern mineralogy. The gemstones or precious stones of the Bible are minerals with identities in a considerable state of uncertainty and confusion. There are of course a number of minerals that present no problems. Water is a mineral, the identity of which has always been certain. No one questions the meaning of gold, silver, and iron.

The minerals may be grouped as follows: A. Precious stones. B. Metals. C. Common minerals such as salt, sulfur, and water.

A. Precious Stones. As indicated in the introduction to the minerals, there is much uncertainty in the identification of specific minerals as precious stones of the Bible.

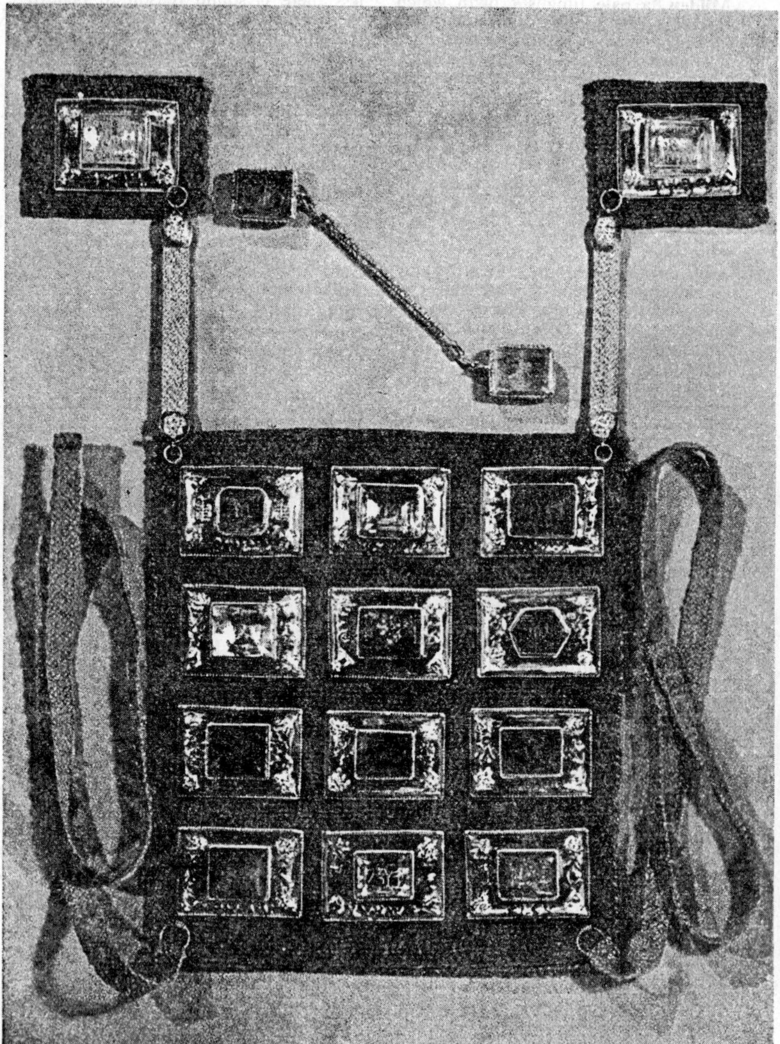

Replica of Aaron's Breastplate, with twelve precious stones. Courtesy American Baptist Assembly, Green Lake, Wisconsin. © *ABA*

There are four principal lists of minerals recorded in the Scriptures. They are as follows:

1. The 12 precious stones of Aaron's breastplate; each stone representing one of the tribes of Israel (Exod. 28: 17-20; 39:10-13).

2. The wisdom list of Job (Job 28: 16-19). Listed are the precious onyx, the sapphire, crystal, coral, pearls, rubies and topaz.

3. The gems of the king of Tyre (Ezek. 28:13). Listed are the sardius, topaz, diamond, beryl, onyx, jasper, sapphire, emerald, and carbuncle.

4. The Precious Stones of the Holy City (Rev. 21:18-21). There is a precious stone for each of twelve foundations.

The Precious Stone List: 1. Adamant (ăd'ȧ-mănt). (Also adamant stone). (Ezek. 3:9; Zech. 7:12). This is a reference to a very hard stone, "harder than flint." This could mean the hardest of all, diamond. But the ruby, the sapphire, or the less attractive forms of corundum would also be exceedingly hard stones. **2. Agate** (ăg'ăt). (Exod. 28:19; 39:12; Isa. 54: 12; Ezek. 27:16). Described under chalcedony. **3. Amber.** (Ezek. 1:4, 27; 8:2). It is such a mixture that it cannot properly be classified as a single mineral. It takes a high polish and has been valued for beads and other ornaments. **4. Amethyst** (ăm'ē-thyst). (Exod. 28:19; 39:12; Rev. 21:20). A purple to blue-violet form of quartz. **5. Bdellium** (dĕl'ĭ-ŭm). (Num. 11:7; Gen. 2:12). In Genesis it is something associated with gold and the onyx stone. From this association one could assume it to be a precious stone. In Numbers, "the manna was as coriander seed, and the color thereof as the color of bdellium." **6. Beryl** (bĕr'yl). (Exod. 28:20; 39:13; Ezek. 1:16; 10:9; Dan. 10:6; Rev. 21:20). Beryl, a beryllium aluminum silicate, is now mined and valued as a source of the light metal, beryllium, a metal not known until 1828. Beryl was the tenth stone of the breastplate and the eighth of the foundations of the Holy City. This stone has been variously considered as a blue, a green, a yellow, or a red stone, possibly other than beryl as we know it. **7. Carbuncle** (kär'bŭng-k'l) (Exod. 28:17; 39:10; Isa. 54:12; Ezek. 28:13). The third stone in the breastplate, the carbuncle, could have been any one of a series of red precious stones, perhaps garnet. **8. Carnelian** (See Sardius described under chalcedony). (Same as sard or sardius). This is the RSV translation of the first stone of the breastplate, and the sixth of the Holy City. **9. Chalcedony** (kăl-sĕd'ō-nĭ). (Rev. 21:19). (Agate in RSV). The following are some of the varieties of chalcedony: Agate, Carnelian, Chrysoprase, Flint, Jasper, Sardonyx. **10. Chrysolyte** (krĭs'ō-līt). (Rev. 21:20). The seventh foundation of the Holy City is chrysolite, a yellow to greenish-yellow form of olivine. **11. Coral** (Job 28:18; Ezek. 27:16). Coral has been used for various ornaments, such as beads and necklaces. Other factors such as vogue, symbology, and even superstition, may attach value at certain periods in history. In Ezekiel, coral is again associated with valued gems, sapphire and agate. **12. Chrysoprasus** (krĭs'ō-prāz). (Chrysoprase, RSV). (Rev. 21:20). The tenth foundation of the Holy City, chrysoprase may have been the apple-green form of chalcedony, sometimes called green jasper. **13. Crystal** (Job. 28:17; Ezek. 1:22; Rev. 4:6; 21:11; 22:1). The crystal of the Bible is something transparent and colorless, and valued as a gem stone. Clear quartz is the most logical choice for this. **14. Diamond** (Exod. 28:18; 39:11; Jer. 17:1; Ezek. 28:13). The sixth stone of the breastplate. **15. Emerald** (Exod. 28:18; 39:11; Ezek. 27:16; 28:13; Rev. 4:3; 21:19). The fourth gem of the breastplate and the fourth foundation of the Holy City. **16. Jacinth** (also hyacinth) (jā'sĭnth) (Rev. 9:17; 21:20). (Also Exod. 28:19; 39:12 RSV). The seventh stone of the breastplate in the KJV is ligure, translated jacinth in the RSV. **17. Jasper** (Exod. 28:20; 39:13; Ezek. 28:13; Rev. 4:3; 21:11, 18, 19). The last stone of the breastplate and the first in the foundation of the Holy City, jasper is described under chalcedony. **18. Ligure** (Jacinth RSV) (Exod. 28:19; 39:21). See Jacinth. **19. Onyx** (ŏn'ĭks) (Gen. 2:12; Exod. 25:7; 28:20; 39:13; Job 28:16; Ezek. 28:13). See chalcedony. This form of chalcedony was the 11th stone of the breastplate, and possibly the fifth foundation of the Holy City. **20. Pearls** (Job 28:18; Matt. 7:6; 13:45, 46; I Tim. 2:9; Rev. 17:4; 18: 12; 21:21). The references to pearls are found almost exclusively in the New Testament, and there is no reason to doubt the identity of this precious stone. **21. Ruby** (Job 28:18;

Gold helmet of a prince of Ur, about 2500 B.C., hammered from one piece of metal. UMP

Prov. 3:15; 8:11; 20:15; 31:10; Lam. 4:7). Corundum of a rich, clear red variety. **22. Sapphire** (săf'ĭr) (Exod. 24:10; 28:18; 39:11; Job 28:6, 16; Lam. 4:7; Isa. 54:11; Ezek. 1:26; 10: 10; 28:13; Rev. 21:19). Sapphires, like rubies, belong to the corundum or aluminum oxide family, with a hardness next to diamond. **23. Sardius** or sardine stone. Same as carnelian. (See carnelian and also varieties of chalcedony.) (Exod. 28:17; 39:10; Ezek. 28: 13; Rev. 4:3; 21:20). A red variety of chalcedony. The first stone of the breastplate, and the sixth of the Holy City. **24. Sardonyx** (Onyx in RSV) (Rev. 21:20). This stone is merely an onyx layered with red sard or carnelian. **25. Topaz** (Exod. 28:17; 39:10; Job 28:19; Ezek. 28:13; Rev. 21:20). The modern topaz is an aluminum fluoro hydroxy silicate harder than the quartz and chalcedony groups.

B. Metals. Of the 103 elements now known to man, 78 are metals.

1. Gold. Gold is named very early in the Bible (Gen. 2:11, 12). We are told that in the land of Havilah, in the vicinity of the Garden of Eden, there was gold, and further that the gold was good. Gold is also mentioned at the very end of the Bible (Rev. 21:15, 18, 21). Here the most precious of metals is envisioned as constituting the Holy City and its streets, gold transparent as glass. The reed used to measure the city was a golden reed. In between the beginning and the end of the Bible are so many references to gold that one must use an extensive concordance if he wishes to find all these references.

2. Silver. Many objects made of silver are referred to in the Scriptures. The cup that Joseph had secreted in Benjamin's sack of food was a silver cup (Gen. 44:2). Sockets, hooks, gods, chargers, bowls, trumpets, candlesticks, basins, cords, and images were made of silver. Demetrius, the silversmith of Ephesus, made silver shrines for Diana (Acts 19:24). Jesus was betrayed for 30 pieces of silver (Matt. 26:15). Silver is used also in a figurative or symbolic sense for something refined and pure, free from dross (Ps. 12:6).

3. Iron. The first reference to iron in the Bible is found in Gen. 4:22. Tubal-cain was a worker in brass and iron. In Deut. 4:20; I Kings 8:51, and Jer. 11:4 there is ample evidence that the Hebrews were familiar with furnaces for making iron. The smith with his forge was well known as shown in Isa. 44:12 and 54:16. The bedstead of Og was made of iron (Deut. 3:11). Og was a giant and needed a strong bed and a big one, about 15 feet long and 7 feet wide. The spearhead of Goliath weighed 600 shekels (roughly 20 pounds) of iron (I Sam. 17:7). There is ample evidence that many types of fetters and means of binding captives and slaves were made of iron. At times the term is, however, used in a figurative sense (Pss. 2:9; 107:10; 149:8; Jer. 28:13, 14).

4. Copper (Bronze). The earliest reference (KJV) to brass was that in Gen. 4:22. This was likely pure copper, though it may have been bronze. Whereas the 37th chapter of Exodus may be called the gold chapter, the 38th is the bronze and silver chapter. The KJV uses the words brass and brazen 15 times. Bronze is used to overlay many parts of the altar of burnt offering and the hangings of the court. Vessels, pots, shovels, fleshhooks, fire pans, grate, rings, and a laver are made of bronze. A partial list of copper or bronze objects includes the serpent made by Moses (Num. 21:9), the armor of Goliath consisting of helmet, coat of mail, greaves, and target (I Sam. 17:5, 6), fetters of bronze (II Kings 25:7), bronze cymbals (I Chron. 15:19), gates (Ps. 107:16; Isa. 54:2), and idols (Rev. 9:20).

5. Lead. References to lead in the Scriptures are as follows:

The high density of lead is noted in Exodus 15:10. In Numbers 31:22 lead is listed along with gold, silver, brass, iron and tin. Its use for lettering in rock is noted in Job 19:24. Bellows were used in a furnace with melting of lead (Jer. 6:29). Lead is listed with silver, brass, iron and tin as melted in a furnace (Ezek. 22:18, 20) and again with silver, iron, and tin as the riches traded in the fairs (Ezek. 27:12). See also Zechariah 5:7, 8.

6. Tin. The references to tin in the Bible are few. They are as follows: Numbers 31:22; Isaiah 1:25; Ezekiel 22:18, 20; 27:12.

7. Mercury (Quicksilver). The Hebrew word, **sig,** interpreted as dross, meaning the scum or refuse, usually thought of in connection with silver refining, is found in the following passages: Psalm 119:119; Proverbs 25:4, 5; 26:23; Isaiah 1:22, 25; Ezekiel 22:18, 19, 20. Even the references in Ezekiel suggest the molten or liquid character of mercury. The house of Israel has become brass, tin iron, and lead in the furnace; they have become dross. This could refer to their liquid character, while in the furnace.

C. The Common Minerals.

1. Alabaster (Matt. 26:7; Mark 14:3; Luke 7:37). All of these references include an alabaster box used to contain a precious ointment. Modern alabaster is a form of gypsum, hydrated calcium sulfate.

2. Brimstone (Sulfur) (Gen. 19:24; Deut. 29:23; Job 18:15; Ps. 11:6; Ezek. 38:22; Isa. 30:33; 34:9; Luke 17:29; Rev. 9:17, 18; 14:10; 19:20; 20:10; 21:8). It is generally agreed that the brimstone of the Bible is sulfur. In the Bible context brimstone is nearly always associated with fire and with punishment and devastation.

3. Marble (I Chron. 29:2; Esth. 1:6; S. of Sol. 5:15; Rev. 18:12). Marble is recrystallized limestone, which is capable of being given a high polish. There is no reason to think that the marble of the Bible was much different from the marble of modern times, except in the sense that marble from different quarries varies in color and texture.

4. Nitre (niter) (Prov. 25:20; Jer. 2:22). The usual interpretation of the Biblical niter is that the material is sodium carbonate.

5. Salt. Salt is extremely abundant; the evaporation of one cubic mile of sea water would leave approximately 140 million tons of salts most of which would be sodium chloride or common salt. The salt sea of the Bible was no doubt the Dead Sea. In most of the many references to salt, either the preservative property or else the savor it adds to food was the point of interest (Matt. 5:13).

6. Water. There are more references to this mineral than to any other in the Bible.

Mines, Mining, an ancient occupation of man, for we read in the description of Eden and its surroundings before the Flood of "the land of Havilah, where there is gold: and the gold of that land is good" (Gen. 2:11, 12); and in the account of the antediluvian Cainite patriarchs. Tubal-cain was "the forger of every cutting instrument of brass and iron" (Gen. 4:22). In Job 28:1-11 "a mine for silver and a place for gold is mentioned"; the statement that "iron is taken out of the earth and copper is molten out of the stone" is followed by a poetic account of a man digging a mine. The great development of metal working in Israel must have come between the time of King Saul and of Solomon. Compare I Samuel 13:19-22, where the Philistines are in the iron age which the Israelites had not yet reached with the accomplishments of Solomon's time (I Kings 7:13-50) only about a century later.

In the time of Moses, the Midianites had gold, silver, brass, iron, tin and lead (Neh. 31:22) and the Israelites knew how to cleanse them by fire; and Moses described the Promised Land as "a land whose stones are iron, and out of whose hills thou mayest dig brass (copper)" (Deut. 8:9).

Mingled People, in Exod. 12:38 the reference is to non-Israelite people who left Egypt with the Israelites. In Jer. 25:20 and 50:37 the term is used for the mixed blood of certain of Israel's enemies.

Miniamin (mĭn′yȧ-mĭn). 1. A Levite in Hezekiah's time (II Chron. 31:15). 2. Head of a family of priests (Neh. 12:17). 3. A priest (Neh. 12:41). See Miamin and Mijamin, which have the same meaning.

Minister. 1. Originally a servant, through distinguished from a slave who may work against his will, and a hireling, who works for wages. Joshua, as a young man, was minister to Moses (Exod. 24:13) though in rank he was a prince of the tribe of Ephraim (Num. 13:8). 2. One in the service of the state or God, like priests and Levites (Exod. 28:43; Num. 3:31) or Paul administering the gospel to the Gentiles (Rom. 15:16). 3. The representative and servant of a master; used especially for God's minister in the gospel (I Thess. 3:2; Eph. 6:21).

Minni (mĭn'ī), a kingdom associated with Ararat and Ashkenaz as instruments or agents for the destruction of the wicked Babylon. Later called Arminia.

Minnith (mĭn'ĭth), a city of the Ammonites which Jephthah smote while overcoming this nation (Judg. 11:33).

Minstrel, in the OT a player upon a stringed instrument; but in the NT a piper, or player upon a flute. David played his harp to quiet King Saul when the evil spirit was upon him (I Sam. 16:23). In Matthew 9:23 we read of "minstrels" (ASV "flute-players") at a funeral.

Mint (See Plants)

Miphkad (mĭf'kăd, RV Hammiphkad), the name of one of the gates of Jerusalem (Neh. 3:31).

Miracles. The word "miracle" literally means a marvelous event, or an event which causes wonder. The usage of "miracle" in Christian theology includes, but goes beyond, the meanings of the ancient words. A miracle is (1) an extraordinary event, inexplicable in terms of ordinary natural forces; (2) an event which causes the observers to postulate a super-human personal cause; (3) an event which constitutes evidence (a "sign") of implications much wider than the event itself.

Miracles are not simply works of providence. Miracles are further to be distinguished from the type of answers to prayer which do not constitute "signs," or demonstrative evidence for unbelievers. When Elijah prayed for fire on the altar of Jehovah (I Kings 18:17-46), God answered with a demonstrative miracle which convicted the priests of Baal.

Miracles of God should also be distinguished from works of magic. In magic, the wonder worker himself possesses a formula which causes the alleged result. The alleged supernatural power is controlled by the performer. Compare Exodus 7:11; 8:7. In miracles of God, the results depend wholly upon the divine will, and the one who works the miracle is simply an agent for the Lord.

Miracles of God must be distinguished from miracles of Satanic or demonic origin. Christ warned against such in His Olivet discourse (Matt. 24:24).

Miracles must also be distinguished from mere exotic occurrences. There are many events in nature which excite wonder, but such matters are evidences of nothing but oddity. Genuine miracles are always "signs" which teach a lesson. Every miracle of God is a part of God's great integrated system of revealed truth.

The majority of the miracles recorded in the Bible fall into three great epochs. First came the miracles of the Exodus: the burning bush, the ten plagues of Egypt, the numerous miracles between the parting of the Red Sea and the crossing of the Jordan, the fall of Jericho, and the battle of Gibeon. There followed, after the first epoch of miracles, a long period of decline under the judges, and then a revival of godly faith under David and Solomon. During all this time miracles were very few. God left not Himself without a witness, but the working of miracles was not His chosen method.

Then came a period of idolatrous compromise and "inclusive" religion. The names of Jehovah and Baal were hyphenated, and even the good King Jehoshaphat was badly mixed up with idolatrous Ahab (I Kings 21:25, 26; 22). So God gave the second great epoch of miracles centering in the ministry of Elijah and Elisha. By mighty "signs" and works of His grace, God restored and confirmed His pure worship.

The miracle of Jonah and two notable miracles at the time of Isaiah (II Kings 19:35; 20:9-11) were of outstanding significance, as were two or three special miracles in the experience of Daniel. But from the epoch of miracles in the time of Elijah and Elisha until the time of Christ and the apostles miracles were again very few.

The greatest epoch of miracles in all recorded history occurred in the ministry of Christ and His apostles. It was, in a way, a time of the lowest ebb of spirituality. At the Exodus

God's people had forgotten His name. At the time of Elijah and Elisha they had hyphenated His name with the name of Baal. But at the time of Christ and His apostles God's people had made the divinely prescribed system of worship an idolatrous object to such an extent that they were steeped in self-righteousness and hypocrisy. They were so "religious" in their pride that they crucified the Lord of glory. It was to this kind of world that God sent forth His Son.

Nearly 40 demonstrative "sign" miracles wrought by Christ are recorded in the Gospels; but these are selected by the writers from among a much larger number (John 20:30).

The ministry of the apostles after Christ's ascension began with the miracle of "languages" on the day of Pentecost. This miracle recurred until the church organization for this age was well established, and probably until the NT books were all put into circulation. There were numerous other demonstrative miracles (Heb. 2:3, 4).

From Bible history, and history since Bible times, the fact stands out that God does not choose to reveal Himself by demonstrative miracles at all times. On the contrary there have been long periods of history, even in Bible times, when God has not used miracles (except the "miracle of grace") in His dealings with His people.

Miracles are an absolutely essential element in Christianity. If Jesus Christ is not God manifest in the flesh, our faith is a silly myth. If He did not arise from the dead in bodily form, the grave being empty and His appearance being recognizable, then we are yet in our sins and of all men most miserable. If the miracle of grace is not verifiable, the transformation of the life of the one who puts his faith in Jesus as his Lord and Saviour, then our Christian Gospel is a miserable fraud. The purpose of miracles is revelation and edification (John 20:31). Miracles are recognized by faith as being from God. They are outside the operation of known laws (John 4:48; Acts 2:19; II Cor. 12:12).

Miriam (mĭr'ĭ-ăm), the daughter of Amram and Jochebed and the sister of Moses and Aaron (Num. 26:59; I Chron. 6:3; Exod. 2:4, 7-8). Miriam first appears by name in Exodus 15:20, where she is called a prophetess and is identified as the sister of Aaron. After the passage of the sea, she led the Israelite women in dancing and instrumental accompaniment while she sang the song of praise and victory (Exod. 15:20-21). In Numbers 12:1 M. and Aaron criticized Moses for his marriage to a Cushite woman. Because of this criticism, M. was punished by the Lord with leprosy (Num. 12:9), but upon the protest of Aaron (vs. 11) and the prayer of Moses (vs. 13), she was restored after a period of seven days, during which she was isolated from the camp and the march was delayed. Her case of leprosy is cited in Deuteronomy 24:9. M. died at Kadesh and was buried there (Num. 20:1).

Mirma (mûr'mȧ, **fraud**), a Benjamite (I Chron. 8:10).

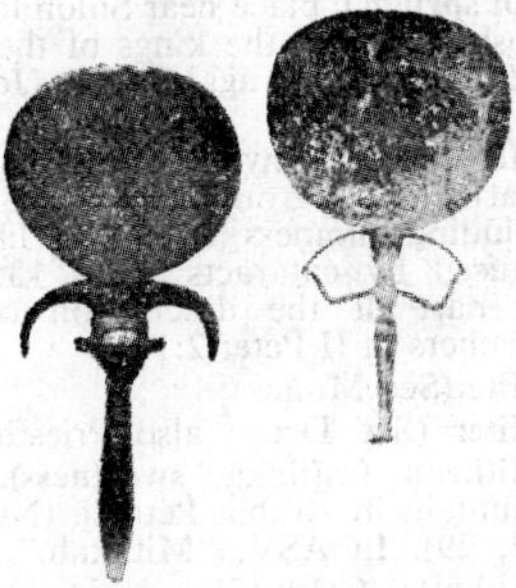

Ancient bronze mirrors, with sculptured handles, from Egypt, of the type that Israelite women took with them on the Exodus. © *BM*

Mirror, any smooth or polished surface as of glass or of metal that forms images by reflecting light. Were made of brass (Exod. 8:8). Paul reminds us (I Cor. 13:12) by saying that "now we see through a glass darkly." Paul does not mean that the mirror is transparent, but that the image is indistinct of the inadequacy of those ancient mirrors (James 1:23, 24).

Misgab (mĭs'găb, **a lofty place**), a town in the high hills of Moab (Jer. 48:1).

Mishael (mĭsh'ā-ĕl, **who is what God is?**). 1. A cousin of Moses and Aaron (Exod. 6:22; Lev. 10:4). 2. A man who stood with Ezra at the reading of the law (Neh. 8:4). 3. A prince of Judah, taken captive by Nebuchadnezzar (Dan. 3:19-30).

Mishal (mī'shăl), a Levitical city (Gershonite) in the tribe of Asher (Josh.

21:30); "Misheal" in Joshua 19:26 and "Mashal" in I Chronicles 6:74.

Misham (mī'shăm), a Benjamite (I Chron. 8:12).

Misheal (See Mishal)

Mishma (mĭsh'mȧ). 1. Son of Ishmael (Gen. 25:14; I Chron. 1:30). 2. Progenitor of a large family of Simeonites (I Chron. 4:25ff).

Mishmannah (mĭsh-măn'ȧ, **fatness),** a Gadite who joined David at Ziklag (I Chron. 12:10).

Mishraites (mĭsh'rā-īts), a family of Kiriath-jearim in Judah (I Chron. 2: 53).

Mispereth (mĭs'pē-reth), one who returned with Zerubbabel (Neh. 7:7); "Mispar" in Ezra 2:2.

Misrephoth-Maim (mĭs'rē-fŏth-mā'ĭm, **hot springs),** place near Sidon to which Joshua chased the kings of the North who had joined against him (Josh. 11: 8; 13:6).

Mist. 1. Steamy vapor rising from warm damp ground (Gen. 2:6). 2. A blinding dimness of vision like that caused by cataracts (Acts 13:11). 3. A part of the description of false teachers in II Peter 2:17.

Mite (See Money)

Miter (See Dress, also Priesthood)

Mithcah (mĭth'kȧ, **sweetness),** sweet fountain in Arabia Petraea (Num. 33: 28, 29). In ASV, "Mithkah."

Mithnite (mĭth-nīt), designation of Joshaphat, mighty man of David (I Chron. 11:43).

Mithraism, the cult of Mithras, a Persian sun-god, which reached Rome in or about A.D. 69 particularly appealed to military. December 25 was the chief feast of Mithras, and in fixing on that date for Christmas, the early Church sought to overlay both the Mithraic festival and the Saturnalia. Christianity triumphed over Mithraism because of its written records of a historic Christ, and its associated body of doctrine adapted for preaching, evangelism, and the needs of every day. Christianity, too, was universal, excluding neither woman, child, nor slave. It preached salvation by faith and demanded no stern ordeals.

Mithredath (mĭth'rē-dăth, **given by Mithras,** i.e., by the Sun), the Persian name of two men: 1. The treasurer of Cyrus (Ezra 1:8). 2. An enemy of the Jews in the days of "Artaxerxes," i.e., Cambyses, son of Cyrus (Ezra 4:7).

Mitylene (mĭt-ĭ-lē'nē). The name is more properly spelled Mytilene. It was the chief city of Lesbos, a splendid port with a double harbor (Acts 20:14), and a center of Greek culture.

Mixed Multitude. People who had been deeply impressed by the plagues and who realized the powerlessness of the gods of Egypt (Exod. 12:38). Though they joined Israel, their hearts were in Egypt as is seen in Numbers 11:4-6. In the revival after the return with Ezra and Nehemiah, Israel separated itself from a similar group of "camp-followers" (Neh. 13:3).

Mizar (mī'zȧr, **small),** a small peak near Mt. Hermon (Ps. 42:6). The word may be a common noun, "a little hill."

Mizpah (mĭz'pȧ, **watchtower, lookout-post).** Found in II Chron. 20:24 and Isa. 21:8 as a common noun. As a proper noun, it is used of: 1. An unidentified town in the territory of Judah (Josh. 15:38). 2. An unknown city in Moab (I Sam. 22:3), to which David went to confer with the king of Moab. 3. An unidentified region or valley mentioned in Joshua 11:3 and 11:8. 4. A city in Gilead (Judg. 11:29; cf. Ramoth-mizpeh, Josh. 13:26). 5. A town in Benjamin (Josh. 18:26).

Mizpar (mĭz'pȧr), a co-worker of Zerubbabel (Ezra 2:2). Mizpereth (ASV Mispereth) in Neh. 7:7.

Mizpeh (See Mizpah)

Mizraim (mĭz'rā-ĭm). 1. Son of Ham (Gen. 10:6, 13; I Chron. 1:8, 11); progenitor of Egyptians, people of N Africa, Hamitic people of Canaan. 2. Usual Hebrew word for "Egypt," always so translated in RSV.

Mizzah (mĭz'ȧ, **terror),** a grandson of Esau reckoned as one of the chiefs of Edom (Gen. 36:13, 17).

Mnason (nā'sŏn), a well-to-do Cypriot who had a house in Jerusalem, and who furnished hospitality for Paul and his party on their return from the third missionary journey (Acts 21:16).

Moab (mō'ăb, **seed).** 1. Grandson of Lot by incest with his elder daughter (Gen. 19:30-38). 2. People descended from Moab; also their land E of Jordan (Num. 21:13-15); refused Israel passage to Canaan (Judg. 11:17, 18); sent Balaam to curse Israel (Num. 22-24); subdued by David (II Sam. 8:2, 12; I Chron. 18:2, 11); denounced by prophets (Isa. 15-16; Jer. 9:26; Ezek. 25:8-11; Amos 2:1; Zeph. 2:8-11). Ruth was a Moabitess (Ruth 1:4).

Moabite Stone, The, an inscribed stone found in Moab and recording Moabite

Replica of the famous Moabite Stone in the Palestine government museum. It was a monument erected by Mesha, king of Moab, and dates back to about 850 B.C. © *MPS*

history. In 1868, F. A. Klein, a German missionary employed by the Church Missionary Society (Church of England), was informed by an Arab sheikh of a remarkable stone inscribed with writing, and lying at Dibon. The stone was bluish basalt, neatly cut into a monument about four by two feet with its upper end curved, and a raised rim enclosing an inscription. Mr. Klein informed the authorities of the Berlin Museum, and meanwhile M. Ganneau of the French Consulate at Jerusalem and a Capt. Warren had made "squeezes" and so had secured roughly the material of the inscription. While the French and the Germans were bargaining with the Turks for the stone, the Arabs, with Oriental acuteness, argued that if the stone as a whole was of value it would be far more valuable if cut to pieces, so they built a fire around it, poured cold water over it, and so well-nigh destroyed it. The fragments of the stone were purchased, pieced together and are now in the Louvre in Paris. The writing consisted of 34 lines, written in the Moabite language (practically a dialect of the Hebrew) by Mesha, king of the Moabites in the time of Ahaziah and Jehoram, the sons of Ahab, and giving his side of the story recorded in part in II Kings 3. Some have called the Moabite Stone "the earliest important Hebrew inscription" though written in Moabite. Since Moab and Jacob were both descendants of Terah, it is not strange that their tongues should resemble one another.

Moadiah (See Maadiah)

Moladah (mŏl'â-dȧ, **birth**), mentioned in Joshua 15 and 19 and lies about ten miles E of Beer-sheba (Neh. 11: 26).

Mole (See Animals)

Molid (mō'lid, **begetter**), an early member of the tribe of Judah (I Chron. 2:29).

Moloch, Molech (mō'lŏk, mō'lĕk), heathen god worshiped especially by Ammonites by sacrifice of children; worship forbidden the Israelites (Lev. 18: 21; 20:1-5); places of worship set up by Solomon for heathen wives (I Kings 11:7); sanctuary built in valley of Hinnom by Manasseh (II Chron. 33:6); abolished by Josiah (II Kings 23:10); denounced by prophets (Jer. 7:29-34; 19:1-13; Ezek. 20:26-39; Amos 5:26).

Molten Sea (See Tabernacle)

Money. There was no coined money in Israel until after the Exile. Before this time exchange of values took place by **bartering,** by trading one thing for another without the exchange of money. This method was followed by the weight system, later by minted coins. Wealth is first mentioned in the Bible in connection with Abraham (Gen. 12:5; 16, 20). The three main items of wealth in the ancient world are listed in Genesis 13:2, and Abraham had all three: "And Abram was very rich in **cattle,** in **silver,** and in **gold.**"

The Hebrews were not the first people to use minted coins. Except for a few brief periods of independence, they were compelled to use the coinage of their pagan conquerors. Thus in the Bible we find a wide variety of coins — mainly Greek, Roman, and Jewish — all used by the same people. Most historians believe that the earliest money pieces were struck about 700 B.C. in the small kingdom of Lydia in Asia Minor. These early Lydian "coins" were simply crude pieces of metal cut into small lumps of a standard weight and stamped with official marks to guarantee the value. After 330 B.C. the world-conquering Greeks developed the Persian and Babylonian coinage, and their own, into something of a fixed world system. Animals, natural objects, and the Greek gods were used as symbols on the coins. Each coin was made individually with hammer, punch, and die. The Greeks called these coins **drachmas (drachma** means "handful") of which there was a variety with about the same value. The "lost coin" (Luke 15:8) was a silver drachma equivalent to a Roman denarius, a day's wages. The coin Peter found in the fish's mouth was the Greek **statér** (Matt. 17:27). Since the temple tax was a half-shekel the stater would pay for two. In Exodus 21:32 we read that 30 shekels was the price of a slave.

The Greek **assárion** is mentioned twice in the NT (Matt. 10:29; Luke 12:6): "Are not two sparrows sold for a **farthing (assárion)?"** In the Roman Empire this Greek coin was both small in size and in value, and the English translators simply translated "farthing," in a similar small coin with which people in England would be familiar.

Lepton and Kodrantes (Widow's Mite). During pre-Roman times under the Maccabees (175-140 B.C.) the Jews for the first time were allowed to issue money of their own. One piece was the **leptón,** a tiny bronze or copper

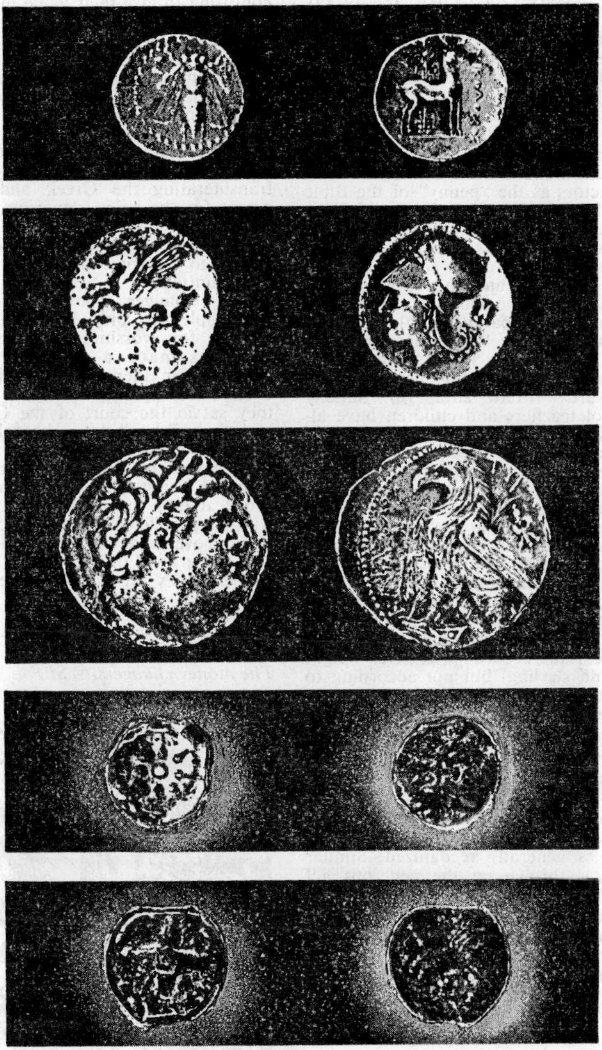

Coins of Bible times. Top: Tetradrachma of Ephesus. Second Row: Tridrachma of Corinth. Third Row: Greek Tetradrachma or Shekel of Tyre. Fourth Row: Widows Mite (Lepton). Fifth Row: Quadrans or Farthing. Coins from Schulz Memorial Library, Concordia Theological Seminary, Springfield, Illinois.

coin, which we know as the "widow's mite," (Mark 12:42; Luke 21:2; 12:59). **Leptón** was translated "mite" because it was the coin of least value among coins. Even the metal was inferior and deteriorated easily. This coin should really be the "penny" of the Bible, not the denarius. The **kodrántes** had twice the value of the **leptón.**

The most interesting coin of the Bible is the Roman **denarius,** known by collectors as the "penny" of the Bible because of this translation in the King James Version. This silver coin, which looks something like our dime, was the most common Roman coin during the days of Jesus and the apostles. The true value of the denarius may be seen in our Lord's parable of the laborers in the vineyard: "After agreeing with the laborers for a **penny** (Greek: **denárion)** a day he sent them into his vineyard" (Matt. 20:2, 10). Sunday school teachers and children have always wondered why any man would toil all day and receive only a penny. Even those who worked but one hour deserved more than that. Was it because wages were so low? But if one remembers that in the Roman world the denarius represented a day's pay, the dilemma is solved. Army pay was also a denarius a day. For this reason it is misleading today to state, as Bible margins often do, that the denarius is worth "eighteen or twenty cents"; this is the value according to silver weight (pound sterling) but not according to buying power, which is the important thing.

The denarius is mentioned in the miracle of feeding the five thousand (John 6). If one assumes that the treasury of the group contained 200 **denarii,** then Jesus and His disciples dispensed more money to the needy than is generally recognized. Similar light is thrown on the generous act of Mary who anointed Jesus with the precious spikenard. In John 12:5 Judas is quoted as saying, "Why was not this ointment sold for **three hundred pence (denarii),** and given to the poor?" Considering the value of a denarius in Jesus' day, Mary's gift was truly great. Few could afford it today. Perhaps Judas would not have grumbled over the $60.00 usually stipulated as the cost of this nard (20c x 300), but it was the 300 days' wages which evoked this cold comment from the lover of silver.

Regarding the value of the Bible coins, it is generally misleading and confusing to give their value in pound sterling. For example, to state that a denarius is worth 20 cents may give the value in silver weight, but not the value in purchasing power which gives the true or real value of the coin, just as people have learned during these days of inflation in America. Bible translators will do greater service and reduce confusion by simply transliterating the Greek and Latin names for the coins (denarius, shekel, assarion, etc.), which the new RSV has attempted to do, and allow the Bible reader to interpret the value of the coins himself.

Money Changer. The priests taught the people that only Jewish currency was fit for worship, so the money changers made a very profitable business for themselves. Having secured Jewish money from the priests, they sat in the court of the Gentiles and exchanged it (at a liberal profit for themselves) for the Roman money, then would make another exchange with the priests, no doubt making a profit at both ends. (See Matt. 21:12 with its parallel in Mark 11:15). Our Lord drove them out saying that they had made the Lord's house a den of robbers (KJV "a den of thieves").

The money changers. © *SPF*

The Hill of Moreh and the Plain of Jezreel (Esdraelon). © *MPS*

Monotheism (mŏn′ō-thē-ĭzm, **one god),** belief that there is but one God.

Monsters (See Animals)

Month (See Calendar, Time)

Moon (See Astronomy)

Morasthite (mō-rās′thīt), inhabitant of Moresheth, as Micah (Mic. 1:1; Jer. 26:18).

Mordecai (môr′dē-kī, from **Marduk,** chief god of Babylon). 1. A leader of the people of Judah during the return of Zerubbabel from exile (Ezra 2:2; Neh. 7:7). 2. The deliverer of the Jews in the book of Esther, a Benjamite who had been deported during the reign of Jehoiachin (Esth. 2:5, 6). He lived in Shushan (Susa) the Persian capital and brought up his cousin Esther, whose parents were dead (2:7). When Esther was taken into the royal harem, Mordecai forbade her to reveal her nationality (2:20); yet he remained in close contact with her. Mordecai discovered a plot against the king. By informing Esther of the plot, he secured the execution of the two eunuchs responsible (2:19-23). When Haman was made chief minister, Mordecai aroused his wrath by refusing to bow before him. To avenge the slight, Haman procured from the king a decree to destroy the Jews (3). Mordecai then sent Esther to the king to seek protection for her people (4). Haman meanwhile prepared a high gallows on which he planned to hang Mordecai (5). By a singular, almost humorous turn of events, Haman fell from favor and was hanged on the gallows he had prepared for Mordecai (7). Mordecai succeeded him as chief minister of the king (8). Thus the Persian officials everywhere assisted the Jews, who slew their enemies and instituted the feast of Purim to celebrate their deliverance (9). The book of Esther ends with an account of the fame and dignity of Mordecai (10).

Moreh, Hill of (mō′rĕ, **teacher).** Near this hill the Midianites were camped when Gideon attacked them (Judg. 7:1). Lies NW of the Plain of Jezreel, about eight miles NW of Mt. Gilboa and one mile S of Nain.

Moreh, Oak of (KJV, "Plain of Moreh"), a place near Shechem where Abraham camped and erected an altar to the Lord (Gen. 12:6). In Deut. 11:30 the Oak of Moreh is mentioned as a landmark near Ebal and Gerizim.

Moresheth-Gath (mō′rĕsh-ĕth-găth, **possession of Gath**), a town mentioned only in Micah 1:14, near Gath. It may be identified with Tel el-Judeideh, about five miles W of Gath in the Shephelah.

Moriah (mō-rī′ȧ), place where Abraham was told to offer up Isaac (Gen. 22:2). It was about a three days' journey from Beersheba where Abraham was living when given the command. According to II Chronicles 3:1 Solomon built the temple on Mt. Moriah, where God had appeared to David (I Chron. 21:15-22:1). Whether this is the same Mt. Moriah mentioned in the account of Abraham is not certain.

Morning Sacrifice (See Offerings)

Morsel, a meal (Heb. 12:16).

Mortal, Mortality. A mortal is a being subject to death (Rom. 8:11; I Cor. 15:53, 54).

Mortar. 1. Bowl-shaped vessel of stone in which grain and spices were crushed with a pestle (Num. 11:8). 2. Substance, like cement, used to bind bricks or stones together in a wall. Sometimes, mud, clay, or bitumen was used (Nah. 3:14; Ezek. 13:10, 11, 14, 15).

Mosaic, a picture or design made by setting tiny squares or cones of varicolored marble, limestone or semiprecious stones in some medium such as bitumen or plaster to tell a story or to form a decoration. Mosaics are one of the most durable parts of ancient structures and often are the only surviving vestige. Mosaics have survived from ancient Sumer from as early as 2900 B.C. They were widely used in the early Christian and Byzantine buildings in Palestine, and remaining examples throw considerable light on ancient Biblical customs, as well as affording insight into early Christian beliefs and symbols.

Moserah (mō-sē′rȧ, **bond**), in KJV Mosera, an encampment of the Israelites in the wilderness near Bene-jaakan (Deut. 10:6 RSV).

Moses, mō′zĕs, mō′zĭs, **drawn out, born**), the national hero who delivered the Israelites from Egyptian slavery, established them as an independent nation, and prepared them for entrance into Canaan. Exact dates for the life of Moses are dependent upon the date of the Exodus. On the basis of an early date for the Exodus, c. 1440 B.C., Moses was born about 1520 B.C. of Israelite parents in the land of Egypt. Not only were the Israelites enslaved, but a royal edict designed to keep them in subjection ordered the execution of all Israelite male children at birth. Hidden among the reeds near the river's bank, Moses was discovered by Pharaoh's daughter. So favorably was she disposed toward this Hebrew babe that she requested Moses' mother to nurse him until he was old enough to be taken to the royal court where he spent the first 40 years of his life. Little is narrated in the Book of Exodus regarding the early period of the life of Moses. Stephen in his address to the Sanhedren (Acts 7:22) asserts that Moses was not only instructed in the science and learning of the Egyptians but also was endowed with oratorical ability and distinctive leadership qualities.

Moses' first valiant attempt to aid his own people ended in failure. While trying to pacify two fellow Israelites he was reminded that he had killed an Egyptian. Fearing the vengeful hand of Pharaoh, Moses escaped to Midian where he spent a 40-year period in seclusion.

In the land of Midian Moses found favor in the home of a priest named Jethro (also known as **Reuel** in the Hebrew or **Reguel** in the Greek). In the course of time he married Jethro's daughter **Zipporah**. As shepherd of his father-in-law's flocks Moses gained a first-hand geographical knowledge of the territory surrounding the gulf of Aqaba. Little did he realize that through this area he would one day lead the great nation of Israel!

The call of Moses was indeed significant. Confronted with a bush afire he became conscious of a revelation of God, who commissioned him to deliver His people Israel from Egyptian bondage. Moses was assured not only of divine support (Gen. 15:12-21) but also of Aaron's support in his divine commission to deliver the Israelites from the powerful clutch of the Pharaoh. Accompanied by his wife Zipporah and their two sons, Moses returned to the land of Egypt.

In a series of ten plagues Moses and Aaron countered Pharaoh's attempt to retain Israel in bondage.

On the eve of Israel's dramatic departure the Passover feast was initially

The traditional Hill of the Burning Bush, near Sinai. © MPS

At the summit of Mt. Sinai (Jebel Mousa), showing part of Moses' Chapel, also sometimes called the Chapel of Elijah. © MPS

The famous statue of Moses by Michelangelo, in the church of St. Peter at Rome. RTHPL

observed (Exod. 12). Each family unit that followed the simple instructions of slaying a year-old male lamb or goat and applied the blood to the doorposts and lintel of their home was passed by in the execution of this divine judgment. Under divine direction Moses led Israel southward through the wilderness of Shur.

In this wilderness encampment Moses became the great law giver through whom Israel's religion was revealed. As a representative for his people Moses received the law from God. This law constituted God's covenant with His newly delivered nation. In turn the congregation ratified this covenant (Exod. 20:24), which included the ten commandments commonly known as the decalogue.

Relatively little is recorded about Moses' leadership during the 38 years of wilderness wanderings (Num. 15-20). Not only was the political leadership of Moses challenged by Dathan and Abiram but Korah and his supporters contested the ecclesiastical position of Aaron and his family. In the course of these rebellions 14,000 people perished in divine judgment.

The magnitude of Moses' character is clearly set forth in his farewell speeches to his beloved people as seen in Deuteronomy. Even though he himself was denied participation in the conquest and occupation of the land, he coveted the best for the Israelites as they entered Canaan.

At the close of Moses' career, Joshua, who had already been designated as Israel's leader, was ordained as successor to Moses. In a song (Deut. 32) Moses expressed his praise to God, recounting how God had delivered Israel and provided for them through the wilderness journey. Then, with the pronouncement of a blessing upon each tribe, Moses departed for Mount Nebo, where he was privileged to view the Promised Land before he died.

Moses, Assumption of, an anonymous Jewish apocalyptic book, probably written early in the first century A.D.

Moses, Law of (See Law)

Most High, a name applied to God (Gen. 14:18, 19, 20, 22; Ps. 7:17).

Mote, a particle of dust or chaff, or a splinter of wood that might enter the eye (Matt. 7:3-5; Luke 6:41, 42).

Moth (See Insects)

Mother (See Family, Marriage)

Mount, Mountain. Hill, mount and **mountain** are terms roughly synonymous in the English Bible. Much of Palestine is hilly or mountainous. These elevations are not dramatically high, but are old worn-down hills.

Many ancient peoples considered mountains as holy places. Mt. Sinai (Deut. 33:2; Judg. 5:4, 5) and Mt. Zion (Ps. 68:16) were specially revered by the Hebrews as the places of God's revelation and abode. Mountains in Scripture are symbolic of eternity (Gen. 49:26) and of strength and stability, but God is more strong and stable than they (Pss. 97:5; 121:1, 2 RSV; Isa. 40:12). They also portray the difficult obstacles of life, but God will overcome these mountains for His people (Isa. 49:11; Matt. 21:21).

Mount of Beatitudes, the site of the Sermon on the Mount (Matt. 5-7; Luke 6:20-49). Like many sites of Jesus' ministry, exact location is unknown.

Mount Ephraim (See Ephraim)

Mourn, Mourning. OT contains warnings against pagan mourning rites (Deut. 14:1, 2; Lev. 19:27, 28); Israelite priests not allowed to take part in mourning ceremonies (Lev. 21:1-4, 10, 11). Mourners rent clothes (II Sam. 1:2); sprinkled earth or ashes upon head (Josh. 7:6); wore sackcloth (Isa. 22:12); wore hair loose (Lev. 10:6). Professional mourners were hired (Jer. 9:17-22; Amos 5:16; Matt. 9:23); mourning lasted at least seven days (I Sam. 31:13).

Mouse (See Animals)

Mouth. Means "mouth," but also "language," "corner," "edge," "skirt," and any opening, such as of a well (Gen. 29:2), of a sack (Gen. 42:27), of a cave (Josh. 10:22), or of a grave (Ps. 141:7).

The way in which the Bible constantly uses the organ of speech in the sense of "language" is a good example of the employment of the concrete for the abstract. Silence is the laying of the hand upon the mouth (Job 40:4), freedom of speech is the enlarged mouth (Eph. 6:19). So to receive a message is to have words put into the mouth (Jer. 1:9). Humiliation is the mouth laid in the dust (Lam. 3:29).

Finally, the mouth is personified; it is an independent agent. It brings freewill offerings (Ps. 119:108), God sets a watch before it (Ps. 141:3), it selects food (Prov. 15:14), uses a rod (Prov. 14:3), and has a sword (Rev. 19:15). This personification helped to contribute to the Jewish idea of the Angel of the Lord, the voice of the Lord, and prepared the way for the "word made flesh" (John 1:14).

Mowing of the ripe grain was done in early Bible times with a short sickle made of pieces of sharp flint set in wood or even bone. Later sickles were made of metal—bronze, and then iron. The farmer grasped the grain with his left hand and lopped off the stalks fairly high up. They were then bound into sheaves and taken to the threshing floor. (See Agriculture).

Moza (mō'zȧ, **sunrise**). 1. A man of the house of Caleb (I Chron. 2:46). 2. A descendant of Jonathan (I Chron. 8:36, 37).

Mozah (mō'zȧ), a town of Benjamin (Josh. 18:26).

Muffler (See Dress)

Mulberry Tree (See Plants)

Mule (See Animals)

Mummification (See Embalm)

Muppim (mŭp'ĭm), a son or descendant of Benjamin (Gen. 46:21). He is also called Shupham (Num. 26:39) and Shuppim (I Chron. 7:12, 15). Possibly the Shephuphan of I Chronicles 8:5 is the same person.

Murder. From the days of Noah the Biblical penalty for murder was death (Gen. 9:6). Throughout OT times, the ancient Semitic custom of the avenger of blood was followed: a murdered man's nearest relative (the **goel)** had the duty to pursue the slayer and kill him (Num. 35:19). Since in the practice of avenging blood in this fashion men failed to distinguish between murder and manslaughter, and thus vicious blood feuds would frequently arise, the Mosaic law provided for cities of refuge (Num. 35). To these cities a man pursued by the avenger of blood could flee. He would be admitted and tried; if judged guilty of murder he would be turned over to the avenger; if judged innocent, he was afforded protection in this city from the avenger.

In a murder trial, the agreeing testimony of at least two persons was necessary for conviction (Num. 35:30; Deut. 17:6). An animal known to be vicious had to be confined, and if it caused the death of anyone, the animal was destroyed and the owner held guilty of murder (Exod. 21:29, 31).

The right of asylum in a holy place was not granted a murderer; he was dragged away even from the horns of the altar (Exod. 21:14; I Kings 2:28-34). No ransom could be accepted for a murderer (Num. 35:21).

Murrain (See Diseases)

Mushi, Mushites (mū'shī, mū'shīts), a Levite, son of Merari, and the founder of a tribal family or "house," called the Mushites (Exod. 6:19; Num. 3:20; 26:58; I Chron. 6:19, 47; 23:21, 23; 24:26, 30).

Music and Musical Instruments of the Bible, existed from earliest times (Gen. 4:21); used for varied occasions: feasts (II Sam. 19:35), weddings (Jer. 7:34), funerals (Matt. 9:23); David organized sacred Levitical choir (I Chron. 6:31-48; II Chron. 29:25), and this was continued by subsequent kings. Instruments: lyre (Gen. 4:21); pipe or flute (Job 21:12; 30:31; Ps. 150:4); tambourine or timbrel (Pss. 8:12; 149:3; 150:4); bell (Exod. 28:33-35), shofar (horn) (Josh. 6:20); trumpet (Num. 10:1, 2, 9, 10); harp (I Sam. 10:5); psaltery (Pss. 33:2; 144:9); oboe (I Kings 1:40); sistra or rattle, wrongly translated "cornets" (II Sam. 6:5); cymbals (I Chron. 15:16, 19, 28); organ (Gen. 4:21); **shalishim** a term of uncertain meaning (I Sam. 18:6); music and hymnody an important part of the Christian life (Eph. 5:19; Col. 3:16).

The history of Hebrew music, as well as the history of Israel's higher civilization in general and the organization of the musical service in the temple, began with King David's reign. To King David has been ascribed not only the creation and singing of the Psalms, but also the invention of musical instruments. II Chronicles 7:6 mentions "instruments of music of the Lord, which David the king had made to praise the Lord"; and according to I Chronicles 23:5, David himself said to the princes of Israel, to the priests and Levites, "four thousand praised the Lord with the instruments which I made to praise therewith."

King David chose the Levites to supply musicians for the Holy Temple. Out of the 30,000 who were employed at this time, the impressive number of 4,000 was selected for the musical service (I Chron. 15:16).

Years later, when King Solomon had finished all work for the temple and brought in all the things David his father had dedicated, the priest and the congregation of Israel assembled before the ark, and the musical service was begun by the Levites (I Chron. 25:6-7; II Chron. 5:12-14). When the king and the people had

Copper and silver trumpets of the Egyptian Pharaoh Tutankhamen. CM

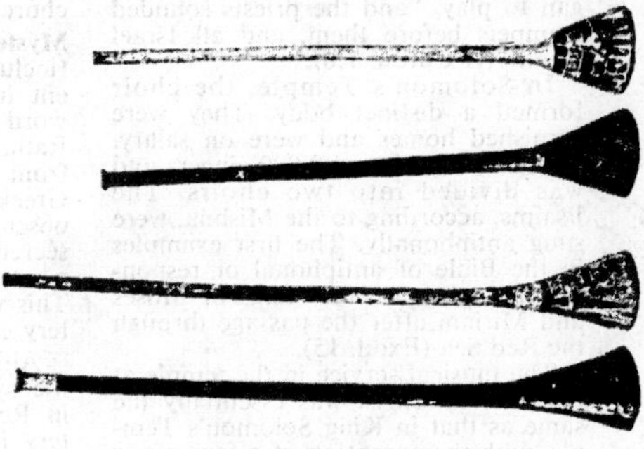

A Rabbi blowing the Shofar to announce the New Year celebration. The Shofar is also sounded every Friday evening at sunset to begin the Sabbath. © MPS

offered their sacrifices, the Levites began to play, "and the priests sounded trumpets before them, and all Israel stood" (II Chron. 7:6).

In Solomon's Temple, the choir formed a distinct body. They were furnished homes and were on salary. The choir numbered 2,000 singers and was divided into two choirs. The Psalms, according to the Mishna, were sung antiphonally. The first examples in the Bible of antiphonal or responsorial singing are the songs of Moses and Miriam after the passage through the Red Sea (Exod. 15).

The musical service in the temple at the time of Christ was essentially the same as that in King Solomon's Temple, with the exception of a few minor changes in certain forms of singing. There were two daily services in the temple—the morning and evening sacrifices. Music has been an integral part of Hebrew and Christian life since its inception.

Mustard (See Plants)

Muthlabben (mŭth′lăb′ĕn), an expression of doubtful meaning, occurring only in the title of Psalm 9. Probably it is the name of the tune to which the psalm was sung.

Muzzle. The Mosaic law forbade the muzzling of oxen when they were treading out the grain, i.e., threshing (Deut. 25:4). This was a simple, humane command, in accordance with the kindly spirit of much of the law.

Myra (mī′rȧ), now Dembre, one of the southernmost ports of Asia Minor, and once the chief haven of Lycia. Hither Paul came on the "ship of Adramyttium" (Acts 27:2), the seaport on the Aegean opposite Lesbos, and the likeliest vessel to put the party into the westward flowing stream of traffic from Asia.

Myrrh (See Plants)

Myrtle (See Plants)

Mysia (mĭsh′ĭ-ȧ), a district occupying the NW end of Asia Minor bounded (proceeding clockwise from the west) by the Aegean, the Hellespont (i.e. the Dardanelles), the Propontis (i.e. the Sea of Marmora), Bithynia, Phrygia, and Lydia.

From 280 B.C. Mysia formed part of the kingdom of Pergamum and fell to the Romans in 133 B.C. by the will and testament of Attalus III. It thereafter formed part of the province of Asia. The area was traversed by Paul on his second missionary journey (Acts 16:7, 8), but no work was done. There is, however, evidence of very early church foundations.

Mystery. Occurs 28 times in the NT (including I Cor. 2:1 where it is present in the better MSS). Neither the word nor the idea is found in the OT. Rather, they came into the NT world from Greek paganism. Among the Greeks **mystery** meant not something obscure or incomprehensible, but a secret imparted only to the initiated, what is unknown until it is revealed. This word is connected with the mystery religions of Hellenistic times.

Although occurring once in each of the synoptic Gospels and four times in Revelation, the chief use of mystery in the NT is by Paul. He knew well the thought world of the pagans and accepted this term to indicate the fact that "his gospel" had been revealed to him by the risen Christ. This face could best be made clear to his contemporaries by adopting the pagan term they all understood, pouring into it a special Christian meaning.

In a few passages, the term refers to a symbol, allegory or parable, which conceals its meaning from those who look only at the literal sense, but is the medium of revelation to those who have the key to its interpretation. So Revelation 1:20; 17:5, 7; Mark 4:11; and Ephesians 5:32 where marriage is a mystery or symbol of Christ and the Church.

The more common meaning of mystery in the NT, Paul's usual use of the word, is that of a divine truth once hidden, but now revealed in the Gospel (Rom. 16:25, 26; cf. Col. 1:26; Eph. 3:3-6). A mystery is thus now a revelation: Christian mysteries are revealed doctrines (Eph. 1:9; 3:3, 5, 10; 6:19; Col. 4:3, 4; Rom. 16:26; I Tim. 3:16). Christianity, therefore, has no secret doctrines, as did the ancient mystery religions. To the worldly wise and prudent the Gospel is foolishness (Matt. 11:25; I Cor. 2:6-9); it is not uncommunicated to them, but they do not have the capacity to understand it (II Cor. 4:2-4). The Christian mystery, then, is God's world-embracing purpose of redemption through Christ (Rom. 16:25).

Mystery Religions, a term applied in the Greek, the Hellenistic, and the Roman world, to the cult of certain deities which involved a private ceremonial of initiation, and a reserved and secret ritual. They were probably survivals of earlier religions.

–N–

Naam (nā'ăm, **pleasant**), a son of Caleb, and thus a descendant of Judah (I Chron. 4:15).

Naamah (nā'ă-mȧ, **pleasant**), feminine of Naam. 1. A daughter of Lamech and Zillah (Gen. 4:22). 2. Wife of Solomon, and mother of Rehoboam (I Kings 14:21, 31). 3. A town mentioned in Joshua 15:41 as an inheritance of Judah.

Naaman (nā'ȧ-măn, **pleasant**). 1. A son of Bela and grandson of Benjamin (Gen. 46:21). 2. The "commander of the army of the king of Syria" (II Kings 5:1-27), "but he was a leper." This was a most dreadful disease at that time and meant ostracism and an untimely death.

A young girl, who had been taken captive in one of the Syrian raids into

Remains of the house of Naaman the Leper in Damascus. © MPS

Israelitish territory, served Naaman's wife. One day she said to her mistress, "Would that my lord were with the prophet who is in Samaria! He would cure him of his leprosy" (5:3).

After a fruitless visit at the court of the king of Israel, Naaman finally goes to the prophet Elisha and is told to wash himself seven times in the River Jordan, a suggestion which is met with anger and contempt as Naaman recalls the clear waters of the rivers of Damascus which were "better than all the waters of Israel" (5:12).

Prevailed upon, however, by his servants to heed the prophet, Naaman "dipped himself seven times in the Jordan, according to the word of the man of God, and his flesh was restored like the flesh of a little child, and he was clean" (5:14), thus manifesting the power of God through his prophet. Naaman's cure led to his acceptance of the God of Israel as the only "God in all the earth."

In Luke 4:27 Jesus referred to this incident in "the time of the prophet Elisha" when he spoke in the synagogue at Nazareth.

Naahathite (nā'à-mȧ-thīt, **a dweller in Naaman),** a gentilic noun with an article, applied to Zophar, one of Job's friends (Job 2:11; 11:1; 20:1; 42:9).

Naamites (nā'à-mīts), patronymic name of a family descended from Naaman, Benjamin's grandson (Num. 26:40).

Naarah (nā'à-rȧ, **a girl).** 1. One of the wives of Ashhur, the father of Tekoa (I Chron. 4:5f). 2. A place on the border of Ephraim (Josh. 16:7).

Naari (nā'à-rī), the son of Ezbai (I Chron. 11:37), one of "the mighty men of the armies" in David's time.

Naaran (nā'à-răn), one of the towns in the possession of the sons of Ephraim (I Chron. 7:28). In Joshua 16:7 the place is called Naarah.

Naarath (See Naaran)

Naashon, Naasson (See Nahshon)

Nabal (nā'băl, **fool),** a rich sheepmaster of Maon in the southern highland of Judah. I Samuel 25:1-42 tells how he insulted David when the latter asked food for his men, who had protected Nabal's men and flocks; how his wife Abigail averted David's vengeance by her gifts and by wise words, and so won David's esteem. Abigail returned home to find Nabal feasting like a king. After he sobered, she told him, and his heart died within him, and he became as a stone, dying ten days later. Then David sought and won Abigail as his wife.

Nabatea, Nabateans (năb'à-tē'ăn), an Arabian tribe named in the Apocrypha but not in the Bible, and important to Bible history. Between the sixth and fourth centuries B.C. they moved to Edom and Moab (as alluded to in Mal. 1:1-7; Obad. 1-7). By NT times their territory stretched from the Mediterranean Sea S of Gaza, and the Red Sea, to the Euphrates, including Damascus. They lost Damascus when the Romans came to the aid of the Jews against them, but later recovered it, so that their king Aretas IV controlled it when Paul was there (II Cor. 11:32).

Nabonidas, Nabonidus (năb'ō-nī'dŭs), the last ruler of the Neo-Babylonian Empire, 556-539 B.C. His son Belshazzar (Dan. 5; 7:1; 8:1) was co-regent with him from the third year of his reign. His very existence was doubted until cuneiform tablets chronicling his reign were discovered and read.

Nabopolassar (năb'ō-pō-lăs'âr), first ruler of the Neo-Babylonian Empire, 626-605 B.C. Allied with Medes and Scythians he overthrew the Assyrian Empire, destroying Nineveh in 612 B.C., as prophesied by Zephaniah 2:13-15 and Nahum. When Pharaoh Necho came to aid the Assyrians, Josiah king of Judah opposed him and was killed at Megiddo (II Kings 23:29; II Chron. 35:20-27). Nabopolassar died in Babylon about the time his son Nebuchadnezzar II was engaged in the battle of Carchemish.

Naboth (nā'bŏth), the Israelite who owned a vineyard beside the palace of King Ahab in Jezreel. The king coveted this land for a garden, but Naboth refused to sell or exchange his inheritance, which made Ahab "heavy and displeased" (I Kings 21:4). His wife Jezebel undertook to get it for him by having Naboth falsely accused of blasphemy and stoned to death (I Kings 21:7-14). When Ahab went to take possession of the vineyard, Elijah met him and pronounced judgment on Ahab and his family. For a repentant mood, temporary stay was granted (I Kings 21:27-29), but after further warning by Micaiah the prophet, punishment fell on Ahab (I Kings 22:24-40) and on his son Joram and wife Jezebel (II Kings 9:25-37, where the vineyard is

In the land of the Nabateans. (Top) The rugged country around Petra. (Bottom) A closeup view of the temple Ed-Deir. © MPS

called "property, field, plot of ground," see KJV, ASV, RSV, showing that its use had been changed as Ahab purposed in I Kings 21:2).

Nachon, Nacon (nā'kŏn), a Benjamite at whose threshing floor Uzzah was smitten for touching the ark (II Sam. 6:6). Chidon in I Chronicles 13:9. Nacon in ASV, RSV.

Nachor (nā'kôr), ASV, RSV Nahor, the grandfather of Abraham (Luke 3:34).

Nadab (nā'dăb). 1. Son of Aaron (Exod. 6:23); accompanied Moses up Mt. Sinai (Exod. 24:1, 2, 9-15); priest (Exod. 28:1); he and brother Abihu offered strange fire on altar and were killed (Lev. 10:1-7; Num. 3:4, 26:61). 2. Great-grandson of Jerahmeel (I Chron. 2:26, 28, 30). 3. Benjamite (I Chron. 8:30; 9:36). 4. 2nd king of Israel; son and successor of Jeroboam; wicked; slain by Baasha, who succeeded him on throne (I Kings 14:20).

Naggai, Nagge (năg'ī, năg'ā-ī, năg'ē), an ancestor of Jesus Christ (Luke 3:25). KJV Nagge, ASV, RSV Naggai.

Nahalal, Nahallal, Nahalol (nā'hȧ-lăl, nā'hȧ-lŏl), a town in Zebulun whose inhabitants were not driven out but made tributary. In Joshua 19:15 KJV has Nahallal, ASV, RSV correctly Nahalal. All have Nahalal in Joshua 21:35, Nahalol in Judges 1:30.

Nahaliel (nȧ-hā'lĭ-ĕl, nȧ-hăl'ĭ-ĕl), a valley between Mattanah and Bamoth where the Israelites camped on their way from the Arnon to Jericho (Num. 21:19).

Naham (nā'hăm, **comfort),** a descendant of Judah through Caleb (I Chron. 4:19).

Nahamani (nā'hȧ-mā'nī, nȧ-hăm'ȧ-nī), leader who returned from captivity with Zerubbabel (Neh. 7:6, 7).

Naharai, Nahari (nā'hȧ-rī), Joab's armorbearer (II Sam. 23:37; I Chron. 11:39).

Nahash (nā'hăsh). 1. An Ammonite king whose harsh demands on the men of Jabesh-gilead led Saul to rally the Israelites against Nahash and to defeat him (I Sam. 11:1, 2; 12:12). 2. An Ammonite king whose son Hanun David befriended. Mistaking David's intentions, Hanun insulted David's messengers. David avenged the insult, and had no more trouble with the Ammonites (II Sam. 10; I Chron. 19). 3. Father of Abigail and Zeruiah (II Sam. 17:25).

Nahath (nā'hăth). 1. A son of Reul, son of Esau (Gen. 36:13, 17; I Chron. 1:37). 2. A descendant of Levi (I Chron. 6:26). 3. A Levite, overseer of offerings in the days of Hezekiah (II Chron. 31:13).

Nahbi (nȧ'bi), spy from Naphtali sent out by Moses (Num. 13:14).

Nahor (nā'hôr). 1. Son of Serug, father of Terah, grandfather of Abraham (Gen. 11:22-26; I Chron. 1:26, 27). 2. Son of Terah and brother of Abraham (Gen. 11:26-29; 22:20, 23; 24:15, 24, 47; 29:5; Josh. 24:2). The city of Nahor is in Mesopotamia (Gen. 24:10). The God of Nahor is the same God as the God of Abraham (Gen. 31:53). KJV has Nachor in Joshua 24:2 and Luke 3:34.

Nahshon (nȧ'shŏn), the son of Amminadab (I Chron. 2:10, 11); ancestor of David (Ruth 4:20); leader of the tribe of Judah in the wilderness (Num. 1:7; 2:3; 10:14). His sister Elisheba married Aaron (Exod. 6:23, KJV Naashon). He is named in the genealogies of Jesus Christ (Matt. 1:4; Luke 3:32, in both of which KJV has Naasson).

Nahum, the Elkoshite (nā'hŭm, **compassionate),** the name is a shortened form of **Nehemiah.** Of Nahum and his city of Elkosh nothing is known outside of the book that bears his name. See Nahum, Book of.

Nahum, Book of. The short book of Nahum is largely a poem, a literary masterpiece, predicting the downfall of Nineveh, the capital of Assyria. Nineveh was conquered by the Babylonians, Medes, and Scythians in 612 B.C. In Judah, the wicked Manasseh reigned until about 641, followed by Amon's two year reign and then the long reign of the good king Josiah (639-608). Perhaps it was in Josiah's days that Nahum prophesied the overthrow of the mighty nation that had so oppressed the Jews.

The book of Nahum is in two parts, first a poem concerning the greatness of God (1:2-15), then another and longer poem detailing the overthrow of Nineveh (2:1-3:19). The cruelty of the Assyrians is almost beyond belief. Their policy seems to have been one of calculated terror. Their own pictures show captives staked to the ground and being skinned alive! No wonder Nahum exulted at the overthrow of the proud, rich, cruel empire of Assyria.

The poem of Nineveh's doom (2:1-3:19) is really quite remarkable. The figures of speech are bold, and in staccato fashion the strokes of war are given. The glamour of the attack with whip and prancing horses and flashing swords suddenly gives way to the picture of the innumerable corpses that mark Nineveh's defeat (3:2, 3). If it was wrong for Nahum to rejoice at Nineveh's fall, what shall be said of the heavenly throng of Revelation 19: 1-6? Inveterate sin must at last bring condign punishment. The death-knell of all opposition to the Gospel is here: "Behold, I am against thee, saith the Lord of hosts" (Nah. 2:13; 3:5).

Nail. 1. **Finger-nail** (Deut. 21:12; Dan. 4:33; 7:19).

2. **Tent-pin** (Judg. 4:21, 22; 5:26); **a peg driven in the wall to hang things on** (Ezra 9:8; Isa. 22:23-25), or **tent-peg** (Zech. 10:4).

3. **Nails of iron** (I Chron. 22:3) **and gold** (II Chron. 3:9; Isa. 41:7; Jer. 10: 4) or either (Eccl. 12:11). Nails, pins and pegs were first of stone chips, wood, or bone, then copper or bronze, or in fine work, gold or silver.

Nain, modern Nein, a village of Galilee. Though unwalled, it had gates, near which Jesus raised a widow's son from death (Luke 7:11-17). The situation is beautiful, on the NW slope of the Hill of Moreh, known as Little Hermon.

Naioth (nā'ŏth, -ōth), a place in or near Ramah of Benjamin, not far N of Jerusalem, where David stayed with Samuel during an early flight from Saul (I Sam. 19:18-20:1). A band of prophets lived there.

Naked (nā'kĕd). The Heb. and Gr. words so translated mean: without any clothing (Gen. 2:25; 3:7-11; Isa. 20:2-4); poorly clad (Job. 22:6; I Cor. 4: 11; Matt. 25:36-44; James 2:15); without an outer garment (John 21:7). There are also figurative senses: uncovered, open (Heb. 4:13); without the body (I Cor. 15:37; II Cor. 5:3, 4); without preparation of the inner man (Rev. 3:17; 16:15).

Name. In Bible times the notion of "name" had a significance it does not have today, when it is usually an unmeaning personal label. A name was given only by a person in a position of authority (Gen. 2:19; II Kings 23:34), and signified that the person named was appointed to a particular position, function, or relationship (Gen. 35:18; II Sam. 12:25). The name given was often determined by some circumstance at the time of birth (Gen. 19:22); sometimes the name expressed a hope or prophecy (Isa. 8:1-4; Hosea 1:4). Where a person gave his own name to another, it signified the joining of the two in very close unity, as when God gave His name to Israel (Deut. 28:9, 10). To be baptized into someone's name therefore means to pass into new ownership (Matt. 28:19; Acts 8:16; I Cor. 1:13, 15). To forget God's name is to depart from Him (Jer. 23:27). The name, moreover, is the person as he has been revealed; for example, the "name of Jehovah" signifies Jehovah in the attributes He has manifested—holiness, power, love, etc. Often in the Bible the name signifies the presence of the person in the character revealed (I Kings 18:24). To be sent or to speak in someone's name signifies to carry his authority (Jer. 11:21; II Cor. 5:20). In later Jewish usage the name **Jehovah** was not pronounced in reading the Scriptures (cf. Wisdom 14:21), the name **Adhonai** ("my Lord") being substituted for it. To pray in the name of Jesus is to pray as His representatives on earth, in His Spirit and with His aim, and implies the closest union with Christ.

Names. By giving names, God enabled us to express relations of His creatures (Gen. 1:5, 8, 10; 2:11-14). Man named the beasts (Gen. 2:19, 20), and woman (Gen. 2:23) by derivation. Her personal name is from her function as mother of all living (human) beings (Gen. 3:20). Cain's name is a pun on two Heb. words (Gen. 4:1). Seth is a reminder that God "appointed" him instead of Abel (Gen. 4:25). "Men began to call upon the name of the Lord" (Gen. 4:26) when they began to recognize Him by His revealed name, Jehovah (Yahweh). God changed the name of Abram to Abraham in view of his destiny (Gen. 17:5).

Names compounded with El (God) or Jeho-, -iah (Jehovah) became common. Jacob (Gen. 32:24-32) received the name Israel, prince with God, for Jacob, supplanter, and recognized God without learning His secret name. Prophets gave their children symbolic names (Isa. 8:1-4; Hos. 1:4-11). Messiah was given significant names: Immanuel, God with us; Jesus, Saviour

(Isa. 7:14; Matt. 1:21, 23; Luke 1:31). In His name (Acts 3:16) miracles are wrought, as He promised (John 14:13, 14). When we act in Jesus' name we represent Him (Matt. 10:42). Patriarchal times saw names as indicators of character, function or destiny.

Nanner (nȧn′nȧr), the name given at Ur to the Babylonian moon-god Sin.

Naomi (nā′ō-mī, nā-ō′mĭ), wife of Elimelech of Bethlehem. Bereft of husband and sons, she returned from a sojourn in Moab with her Moabite daughter-in-law Ruth. She advised Ruth in the steps which led to Ruth's marriage to Boaz, and nursed Ruth's child (Ruth 1:1-4:22).

Naphish (nā′fĭsh), a son of Ishmael whose clan was subdued by Reuben, Gad, and Manasseh (Gen. 25:15; I Chron. 1:31; 5:19). His descendants, temple servants, returned with Zerubbabel from exile (Ezra 2:50; Neh. 7: 52; Nephisim, Nephushesim, etc.).

Naphtali (năf′tȧ-lī). 1. A son of Jacob. He had four sons (Gen. 46:24). Jacob's blessing for this son is brief and noncommittal (Gen. 49:21).

2. The Tribe of Naphtali. Naphtali appears in the lists of Numbers as a tribe of moderate size. It furnished 53,-400 soldiers at Kadesh Barnea (Num. 1:43) and 45,400 at the mustering of the troops across from Jericho (Num. 26:50). Naphtali's prince Ahira gave the last offering for the dedication of the altar (Num. 7:78). Naphtali received the next to last lot in the final division of the land (Josh. 19:32-39), but in many ways its inheritance was the best.

Naphtuhim (năf-tū′hĭm, năf′tū-hĭm), a "son" of Mizraim or (RSV) Egypt (Gen. 10:13; I Chron. 1:11). Naphtuhim being plural in form denotes a people.

Napkin (năp′kĭn), a cloth for wiping off perspiration. In the parable of the pounds one man kept his pound in a napkin (Luke 19:20). The face of Lazarus was covered with one when he came forth from the tomb (John 11: 44, RSV cloth). One had been on the head of Jesus when He was buried (John 20:7).

Narcissus (nȧr-cĭs′ŭs), a Roman whose household Paul greeted (Rom. 16:11).

Nard (See Plants, Spikenard)

Nathan (nā′thăn, **God has given).** 1. Prophet during the reigns of David and Solomon. David consulted him regarding the building of the temple (II Sam. 7; I Chron. 17). Nathan told David to leave temple-building to the son who should succeed him. David humbly obeyed, expressing gratitude to God for blessings bestowed and others promised. Later Nathan rebuked David for adultery with Bathsheba (II Sam. 12:1-25). David earnestly repented. Its title links Psalm 51 with this incident. When Adonijah sought to supplant his aged father David as king, Nathan intervened through Bathsheba to secure the succession for her son Solomon (I Kings 1:8-53). Nathan wrote chronicles of the reign of David (I Chron. 29:29) and shared in writing the history of the reign of Solomon (II Chron. 9:29). He was associated with David and Gad the seer in arranging the musical services for the house of God (II Chron. 29:25). 2. A son of David, born to him after he began to reign in Jerusalem (II Sam. 5:14; I Chron. 14:4). He is named in the genealogy of Jesus Christ as son of David and father of Mattatha (Luke 3:31). 3. Nathan of Zobah, father of Igal, one of David's mighty men (II Sam. 23:36). 4. The two Nathans mentioned in I Kings 4:5 as fathers of Azariah and Zabud may be the same man, and identified with No. 1, the prophet. If Zabad (I Chron. 2:36) is the same as Zabud, his father Nathan may also be the prophet. In that case we know that the prophet's father was Attai, a descendant of Jerahmeel (I Chron. 2:25). 5. One of the leading men among those who returned from exile (Ezra 8:16). 6. One of the returning exiles who put away a foreign wife (Ezra 10:39).

Nathanael (nȧ-thăn′ā-ĕl, **God has given),** one of the number of the 12 apostles introduced to Christ by Philip (John 1:45ff; 2:2), and presumably of Cana of Galilee. Evidently knowledge of the Scripture was considerable on the part of Nathanael, because of the rather amazing theological repartee, bordering on sacred pun, which was conducted between Christ and him (1: 51).

Nathan-Melech (nā′thăn-mē′lek, **king's gift),** an officer to whom King Josiah remanded the horses "sacred to the sun" after burning the chariots in the fire (II Kings 23:11).

Nations, usually means "Gentiles" and

"heathen" and, a few times, refers to the Israelites (Gen. 12:2; Deut. 32:28, etc.). The Gentiles were not sharply differentiated from the Israelites by the latter in OT times, but after the Babylonian exile, Gentiles were treated with scorn and hatred, undoubtedly because of the awful sufferings the Israelites endured from the Gentiles between the time of the Exile and the time of Christ.

Natural. 1. **Moist, full of sap,** and has reference to physical vigor (Deut. 34:7). 2. Animal, sensuous (I Cor. 15:44), unconverted (I Cor. 2:14), birth (James 1:23).

Nature, (James 3:6, "course of nature," meaning "the entire compass of one's life") and **the inherent character of a person or thing** (Rom. 1:26; 2:14; 11:21-24; I Cor. 11:14; Gal. 4:8), **by birth** (Rom. 2:27; Gal. 2:15; Eph. 2:3), **disposition** (II Pet. 1:4).

Naughtiness (See Sin)

Naum, Nahum (nā'ŭm, nā'hŭm), one of the ancestors of Christ (Luke 3:25).

Nave (nāv), the hub of a wheel (I Kings 7:33).

Navel (nā'vĕl). Following the LXX, a different reading has been suggested in Proverbs 3:8: **muscle, body.** In Ezekiel the reading "navel" has been retained in the sense of the umbilical cord not being cut (Ezek. 16:4).

Navy (See Ships)

Nazarene (năz'à-rēn), 1. Derived from Nazareth, the birthplace of Christ. Jesus was often called a Nazarene (Matt. 2:23). Used by His friends, it had a friendly meaning (Acts 2:22; 3:6; 10:38). Jesus applied the title to Himself (Acts 22:8). Used by His enemies, it was a title of scorn (Matt. 26:71; Mark 14:67). 2. In Acts 24:5 adherents of Christianity are called Nazarenes.

Nazareth (năz'à-rĕth), a town in lower Galilee belonging to the tribe of Zebulun, the home town of Mary and Joseph, the human parents of Jesus (Luke 1:26; 2:4). After the flight into Egypt to escape the ruthless hands of

A general view of Nazareth, as seen from the east. © MPS

Mount Nebo and the Springs of Moses. © MPS

Herod the Great (Matt. 2:13ff), the holy family contemplated returning to Bethlehem of Judea. Hearing that none too propitious a change had occurred in the government, they withdrew to Nazareth in Galilee.

Nazareth Decree, an inscription on a slab of white marble, dating c. A.D. 40 to 50, by Claudius Caesar, found in Nazareth, decreeing capital punishment for anyone disturbing graves and tombs.

Nazirite, Nazarite (năz′ĭ-rīt, năz′à-rīt, **dedicated** or **consecrated).** An Israelite who consecrated himself or herself and took a vow of separation and self-imposed abstinence for the purpose of some special service.

There were two different types of Nazaritism, the temporary and the perpetual, of which the first type was far more common. In fact, we know only of three of the last class: Samson, Samuel and John the Baptist.

The three principal marks which distinguished the Nazirite were: (1) a renunciation of wine and all products of the vine, including grapes; (2) prohibition of the use of the razor; (3) avoidance of contact with a dead body. John the Baptist, the forerunner of Christ, was a Nazirite from birth (Luke 1:15). The period of time for the vow was anywhere from 30 days to a lifetime (Num. 6:1-21; Judg. 13:5-7; Amos 2:11, 12).

Neah (nē′à), a town given by lot to the tribe of Zebulun (Josh. 19:13).

Neapolis (nē-ăp′ō-lĭs), a town on the N shore of the Aegean Sea; the seaport of Philippi to which Paul and party sailed after seeing the "Man of Macedonia" at Troas (Acts 16:11, 12).

Neariah (nē′à-rī′à). 1. A descendant of David (I Chron. 3:22). 2. A descendant of Simeon (I Chron. 4:42).

Nebai (nē′bī), one of the signers of the covenant in the days of Nehemiah (Neh. 10:19).

Nebaioth, Nebajoth (nē-bā′yŏth, nē-bā′jŏth). 1. Son of Ishmael, (Gen. 25:13; 28:9; 36:3; I Chron. 1:29). 2. A tribe (Isa. 60:7).

Neballat (nē-băl′ăt), a Benjamite town occupied after the Exile (Neh. 11:34) 4 miles NE of Lydda.

Nebat (nē′băt), the father of Jeroboam I, the first king of the northern confederacy (I Kings 12:16ff).

Nebo (nē′bō). 1. A god of Babylonian mythology. He receives mention by Isaiah (Isa. 46:1). Nebo was the god of science and learning. 2. The name of the mountain from which Moses beheld the Promised Land (Deut. 34:1ff). 3. A Moabite town near or on Mount Nebo (Num. 32:3). 4. A town mentioned immediately after Bethel and Ai (Ezra 2:29; Neh. 7:33).

Nebuchadnezzar, Nebuchadrezzar (nĕb′ū-kăd-nĕz′êr, nĕb′ū-kăd-rĕz′êr). 1. 4th Dynasty ruler of Old Babylonian Empire (c. 1140 B.C.). 2. Ruler of Neo-Babylonian empire (605-562 B.C.); son of Nabopolassar; conquered Pharaoh Necho at Carchemish (605

A brick from Babylon, 6th century B.C., inscribed with the name and titles of Nebuchadnezzar, recording his restoration of the temples of the gods Marduk, Nebo, etc. © BM

A view of Nebuchadnezzar's Babylon, restored according to Unger. OIUC

B.C.); destroyed Jerusalem and carried Jews into captivity (587 B.C.) (II Kings 25:1-21); succeeded by son Evil-Merodach. Often mentioned in OT (I Chron. 6:15; II Chron. 36; Ezra 1:7; 2:1; 5:12, 14; 6:5; Neh. 7:6; Esth. 2:6; Jer. 21:2; 52:4; Dan. 1-5).

Nebushasban (nĕb′ū-shăs′băn, **Nebo, save me),** an important officer in the army of Nebuchadnezzar at the time of the Babylonian siege of Jerusalem in 586 B.C. (Jer. 39:11-14).

Nebuzaradan (nĕb′ū-zȧr-ā′dăn, **Nebo has given seed),** Nebuchadnezzar's general when the Babylonians besieged Jerusalem (II Kings 25:8, 11, 12, 20; Jer. 52:12ff). The prophet Jeremiah was made the special charge and responsibility of Nebuzaradan (Jer. 39:11-14). After the fall of the city of Jerusalem in 586-85 B.C., Nebuzaradan was commissioned by Nebuchadnezzar to conduct the captives to Babylon. Nebuzaradan presented the option to Jeremiah to travel with him to Babylon or to remain in his own land (Jer. 40:1-6). The prophet chose to remain.

Necho, Nechoh, Necco (nē′kō), pharaoh of Egypt, 609-595 B.C.; defeated Josiah at battle of Megiddo (II Kings 23:29; II Chron. 35:20ff); defeated by Nebuchadnezzar at battle of Carchemish (II Kings 24:7).

Neck, a term often used in Scripture with literal and figurative meanings. The bowed neck is often used as a symbol of submission, while the unbowed or "stiff neck" represents insubordination and disobedience (Exod. 32:9; Deut. 9:13; Ps. 75:5; Ezek. 2:4; Acts 7:51). It was a military custom for the conqueror to place his foot upon the neck of the vanquished (Josh. 10:24; Ps. 110:1; Rom. 16:20). Sometimes portrays great emotional stress (Luke 15:20; Acts 20:37; Gen. 46:29).

Necklace, a chain worn as an ornament around the neck, and to which might be attached pendants (Isa. 3:19) or rings (Gen. 38:25).

Necromancer, Necromancy (nĕk′rō-măn-sẽr, nĕk′rō-măn-sē). Necromancy was a form of witchcraft, and was considered as one of the "black" or diabolical arts. Etymologically, the term signifies conversing with the dead for purposes of consultation or divination. The Mosaic law sternly forbade such a practice (Deut. 18:10, 11). The most familiar case in the Bible is that of King Saul and the witch of Endor (I Sam. 28:7-25).

Nedabaiah (nĕd′ȧ-bī′ȧ), a descendant of King David (I Chron. 3:18).

Needle's Eye, found only in Christ's statement in Matt. 19:24; Mark 10:25;

The Jaffa Gate in the wall of Jerusalem, showing the "Needle's Eye." Small doors such as this were common features of the gates of ancient cities; though humans could pass through easily, large animals, such as camels, had to be unloaded and kneel to get through. © *MPS*

Luke 18:25. Jesus probably intended to teach that it is utterly absurd for a man bound up in his riches to expect to enter the kingdom of God.

Needlework, the art of working in with the needle various kinds of colored threads in cloth. The coverings of the ancient tabernacle in the wilderness were so embroidered (Judg. 5:30; Ps. 45:14).

Neesing (nē′zĭng), Elizabethan English for "sneezing" or "snorting" (Job 41:18).

Negeb (nĕg′ĕb, **dry**), the desert region lying to the south of Judea, and hence the term has acquired the double meaning of the "South," because of its direction from Judah or the "desert" because of its aridity. It came to refer to a definite geographical region, as when we read concerning Abraham that he journeyed from the South to Bethel (Gen. 13:1). Numbers 13:22 represents the 12 spies as spying out the land by way of the South. In this territory Hagar encountered the angel when she fled from the face of her mistress, Sarah (Gen. 16:7, 14). Here both Isaac and Jacob dwelt (Gen. 24:62; 37:1). This territory was part of the original territory of the Amalekites (Num. 13:29). On the basis of Joshua 19:1-9, the Negeb was allotted to the tribe of Simeon. However, in Joshua 15:20-31, it was given to the tribe of Judah. Many of David's exploits are described as happening in the Negeb, centering around Ziklag (I Sam. 27:5f).

Neginah (See Music)

Nehelamite (nē-hĕl′ȧ-mīt). Shemaiah, a false prophet, an adversary of Jeremiah, is styled a Nehelamite (Jer. 29:24, 31, 32).

Nehemiah (nē′hē-mī′ȧ, **Jehovah has comforted**). 1. One of the leaders of the return under Zerubbabel (Ezra 2:2; Neh. 7:7). 2. The son of Azbuk, who helped repair the wall of Jerusalem (Neh. 3:16). 3. The son of Hachaliah and governor of the Persian province of Judah after 444 B.C. Of Nehemiah the son of Hachaliah little is known aside from what is in the book that bears his name.

Nehemiah was a "cupbearer" to King Artaxerxes (Neh. 1:11; 2:1).

Nehemiah was a man of ability, courage, and action. Arriving at Jerusalem, he first privately surveyed the scene of rubble (2:1-16), and encouraged the rulers at Jerusalem with his report of answered prayer and the granting of the king's new decree (2:18). Then he organized the community to carry out the effort of rebuilding the broken-down wall. Courageously and squarely he met the opposition of men like Sanballat, Tobiah, and Geshem (who are all now known from non-Biblical documents) and at last he saw the wall completed in the brief span of 52 days (6:15).

Nehemiah cooperated with Ezra in numerous reforms and especially in the public instruction in the law (chapter 8). However, he left for Persia, probably on official business, in 431 B.C. (13:6). Later he returned to Jerusalem, but for how long we do not know. Of the end of his life we know nothing.

Nehemiah, Book of. The Book of Nehemiah closes the history of the Biblical period. Closely allied to the Book of Ezra, it was attached to it in the old Jewish reckoning. It gives the history and reforms of Nehemiah the governor from 444 to about 420 B.C.

Outline:

I. Nehemiah returns to Jerusalem, 1:1-2:20.
II. Building despite opposition, 3:1-7:4.
III. Genealogy of the first returning exiles, 7:5-73 (=Ezra 2:2-70).
IV. The revival and covenant sealing, 8:1-10:39.
V. Dwellers at Jerusalem and genealogies, 11:1-12:26.
VI. Dedication of the walls, 12:27-47.
VII. Final reforms, 13:1-31.

Nehemiah's reform involved the teaching of Moses' law by Ezra and others at the feast of tabernacles (as commanded in Deut. 31:10). This led to the great prayer of confession of Nehemiah 9, redolent with quotations from and allusions to the Pentateuch. A covenant was solemnly sealed to walk in the law of the Lord as given by Moses (10:29).

Nehiloth (nē′hĭ-lŏth), a musical term found in the title to Psalm 5. May mean "wind instrument."

Nehum (nē′hŭm), one of the 12 heads of Judah returning with Zerubbabel, also called Rehum (Ezra 2:2; Neh. 7:7).

Nehushta (nē-hŭsh′tȧ), the mother of King Jehoiachin of Judah (II Kings

24:8). Exiled with her son to Babylon (II Kings 24:12; Jer. 29:2).

Nehushtan (nĕ-hŭsh'tăn), the name given to the serpent of brass surviving from the times of Moses, but destroyed by Hezekiah during his reforms because the Israelites had been making it an object of worship (II Kings 18:4).

Neiel (nē-ī'ĕl), a boundary town between Zebulun and Asher (Josh. 19: 27).

Neighbor. Commandments 6-10 deal with duties toward one's neighbor. In OT neighbor meant one who lived nearby, a fellow Israelite (Exod. 20: 16, 17); in the NT a neighbor referred to anyone for whom Christ died — all men (Luke 10:25-37). Both Testaments teach "Thou shalt love thy neighbor as thyself" (Lev. 19:18c; Matt. 19:19).

Nekeb (nē'kĕb), a town on the NW border of Naphtali (Josh. 19:33).

Nekoda (nē-kō'dȧ), the head of a family of Nethinim who could not prove their Israelitish descent at the return from Babylon (Neh. 7:60, 61; Ezra 2: 60).

Nemuel (nĕm'ū-ĕl). 1. Brother of Dathan and Abiram who led the insurrection against Moses and Aaron (Num. 26:9). 2. A son of Simeon (Gen. 46:10; Num. 26:12; I Chron. 4:24), where variant "Jemuel" is used.

Nepheg (nē'fĕg, **sprout, shoot**). 1. Son of Izhar, brother of Korah, Dathan, and Abiram (Exod. 6:21). 2. A son of David (II Sam. 5:15; I Chron. 3:7; 14: 6).

Nephew, a term found in the KJV four times, meaning grandson (Judg. 12:14), descendant (Job 18:19; Isa. 14:22), grandchild (I Tim. 5:4).

Nephilim (nĕf'ĭ-lĭm), a term rendered "giants" in the KJV, describing certain of the antediluvians (Gen. 6:4) and aboriginal dwellers in Canaan (Num. 13:32, 33), where they are identified with the Sons of Anak. Though no direct trace of a people of such abnormal stature has been discovered there is ample evidence as to the underlying tradition. Not angelic fallen beings (Deut. 1:28).

Nephish (See Naphish)

Nephishesim (nē-fĭsh'ĕ-sĭm), a family of Nethinim (Ezra 2:50; Neh. 7:52).

Nephthalim (See Naphtali)

Nephtoah (nĕf-tō'ȧ, **an opening**), a spring between Judah's and Benjamin's border (Josh. 15:9; 18:15) two miles NW of Jerusalem.

Nephusim (nĕ-fū'sĭm), a variant reading of Nephishesim, the head of a family of the Nethinim who returned from exile (Ezra 2:50).

Ner (nûr, **a lamp**). 1. Father of Abner (I Sam. 14:50; 26:14). 2. The grandfather of King Saul (I Chron. 8:33. See II Sam. 8:12; I Kings 2:5, 32).

Nereus (nē'rūs), a Roman Christian to whom the Apostle Paul extended greetings (Rom. 16:15).

Nergal (nār'gȧl), a Babylonian deity of destruction and disaster, associated with the planet Mars (II Kings 17:30).

Nergal-Sharezer (nār'găl-shȧ-rē'zêr, **may Nergal protect the prince**), the son-in-law of Nebuchadnezzar (Jer. 39: 3-13).

Neri (nē'rī), a name listed in the ancestry of Jesus Christ, the grandfather of Zerubbabel (Luke 3:27). See Neriah.

Neriah (nē-rī'ȧ, **whose lamp is Jehovah**), the father of Seraiah and Baruch, the latter being the scribe of Jeremiah (Jer. 32:12, 16; 36:4; 43:3).

Neriglissar (See Nergal-Sharezer)

Nero (nē'rō), the fifth Roman emperor, born A.D. 37, commenced reign 54, died June 9th, 68. Nero's father was Enaeus Domitus Ahenobarbus, a man given to viciousness and vice. His mother was Agrippina, who cared little for her son's morals but was interested only in his temporal advancement.

The first years of Nero's reign were quite pacific and gave promise of good things to come. Nero himself could

The Emperor Nero.

boast that not a single person had been unjustly executed throughout his extensive empire. During these "rational years" of Nero's administration, the Apostle Paul was brought before him as the regnant Caesar in compliance with his own expressed appeal (Acts 25:10, 11) c. A.D. 63. We can hardly do otherwise than infer that Paul was freed of all charges to continue his labors of evangelization.

Nero's marriage to Poppaea opened the second period of his reign. He killed his mother, his chief advisers Seneca and Burrus, and many of the nobility to secure their fortunes.

In A.D. 64 a large part of Rome was destroyed by fire. Whether or not Nero actually ordered the burning of the city is very controversial. However, justly or not, the finger of suspicion was pointed in Nero's direction. A scapegoat was provided in the Christians.

Conspiracies and plots dogged the latter years of Nero. He was advised to destroy himself, but could not find the courage to do so. Learning that the Senate had decreed his death, his last cruel act was to put many of them to death. He finally died by his own hand in the summer of 68. Thus perished the last of the line of Julius Caesar. Both Paul and Peter suffered martyrdom under Nero.

Nest. The nests of birds differ from species to species (Job 39:27; Jer. 49:16; Ps. 104:7). The first occurrence of the word **nest** in the Bible is in the parable of the prophet Balaam (Num. 24:21). In Deuteronomy 22:6, the law forbids one who happens to find a bird's nest with the mother and her brood from harming the mother bird. Isaiah compares the despoiling of Israel by the Assyrians to the robbing of a bird's nest (Isa. 10:14; Matt. 8:20; Luke 9:58).

Nethaneel (nē-thăn'ē-ĕl, **God has given)**, the name of ten OT men: 1. The prince of Issachar (Num. 1:8; 2:5, in ASV "Nethanel"). 2. Son of Jesse and older brother of David (I Chron. 2:14). 3. One of the priests who played trumpets before the ark (I Chron. 15:24). 4. A Levitical scribe whose son Shemaiah was a recorder under David (I Chron. 24:6). 5. Fifth son of Obed-edom, appointed as one of the doorkeepers of the Tabernacle (I Chron. 26:4). 6. A prince of Judah (II Chron. 17:7). 7. A wealthy Levite (II Chron. 35:9). 8. A priest (Ezra 10:22). 9. A priest and head of a household (Neh. 12:21). 10. A priestly musician (Neh. 12:36). Nathaniel of Cana of Galilee in the days of Jesus (John 1:45-49) had the same name, though in the Greek it is slightly changed.

Nethaniah (nĕth'ā-nī'a, **whom Jehovah gave).** 1. Father of Ishmael the assassin (Jer. 40:8-41:18). 2. A chief singer (I Chron. 25:2, 12). 3. A teaching Levite (II Chron. 17:8). 4. Father of Jehudi whom the princes sent to Baruch for Jeremiah's book (Jer. 36:14).

Nethinim (nĕth'ĭ-nĭm, **given ones),** large group of servants who performed menial tasks in the temple (I Chron. 9:2; Ezra 2:43-58; 8:17-20; Neh. 7:46-56); probably descended from Midianites (Num. 31:47), Gibeonites (Josh. 9:23), and other captives. They are usually listed with priests, Levites, singers, and porters (Ezra 2:70).

Netophah, Netophathites (nē-tō'fȧ, nē-tŏ'fȧ-thīt), a village of Judah and its inhabitants. About three miles S of Jerusalem and 3½ miles S of Bethlehem. The "villages of the Netophathites" (I Chron. 9:16; Neh. 12:28) were apparently given to, or inhabited by Levites. Several of David's men are named as from this place (II Sam. 23:28, 29; I Chron. 2:54).

Nettle (See Plants)

Network represents three distinct words in the Hebrew: 1. "Networks" (Isa. 19:9 KJV) is "white cloth," probably white linen as in ASV. 2. An ornamental carving upon the pillars of Solomon's temple (I Kings 7:18-42). 3. A grate for the great altar of burnt-offerings at the tabernacle (Exod. 27:4; 38:4).

New Birth, the beginning of spiritual life in a believer (John 3:3, 5, 6; II Cor. 5:17; I Pet. 1:23). See Regeneration.

New Moon (See Calendar, Feasts)

New Testament, a collection of 27 documents, the second part of the sacred Scriptures of the Christian Church, the first part being called by contrast the "Old Testament." In the name "New Testament," apparently first given to the collection in the second half of the second century, the word "testament" "settlement," "covenant," the last of these being on the whole the most satisfactory equivalent. The new covenant is the new order or dispensation inaugurated by the death of Jesus (compare His own reference to "the new covenant in my blood" in I Cor. 11:25); it was so called as fulfilling the promise made by God to His people in Jeremiah 31:31ff that He would "make a new covenant" with them whereby the desire and power to do His will would be implanted within them and all their past sins would be wiped out (cf. Heb. 8:6ff). By contrast with this covenant the earlier covenant established by God with Israel in Moses' day came to be known as the "old covenant" (cf. Heb. 8:13). The foundation documents of the new covenant inaugurated by Jesus are accordingly known as "the books of the new covenant (or testament)," the earlier Scriptures, which trace the history of the old dispensation, being known as "the books of the old covenant (or testament)."

The order in which the 27 documents appears in our present-day NT is an order of subject-matter rather than a chronological order. First come the four Gospels — or rather the four records of the one and only Gospel — which narrate Jesus' ministry, death and resurrection. These are followed by the Acts of the Apostles, which takes up the Gospel story with Jesus' resurrection and shows how, over the next 30 years, Christianity spread along the road from Jerusalem to Rome. This book was originally written as the continuation of one of the four Gospels — Luke's. These five constitute the narrative section of the NT.

The next 21 documents take the form of letters written to communities or individuals. Of these 13 bear the name of Paul as writer, two the name of Peter, one of James, one of Jude (Judas). The others are anonymous.

The last book of the NT, Revelation, bears some features of the epistolary style, in that it is introduced by seven covering letters, addressed to seven churches in the Roman province of Asia; but for the most part it belongs to the class of literature called "apocalyptic," in which the outworking of God's purpose on earth is presented in the form of symbolical visions.

While the four Gospels deal with events of the first 30 years of the Christian era, and the epistles belong to the remaining two-thirds of the first century, several of the epistles were in existence before even the earliest of the Gospels. With the possible exception of the Epistle of James, the earliest NT documents are those epistles which Paul wrote before his two years' detention in Rome (A.D. 60-62). This means that when one of the earlier Pauline epistles mentions an action or saying of Jesus, that mention is our earliest written account of it; thus, Paul's account of the institution of the Holy Communion (I Cor. 11:23ff) is earlier by some years than the account of it given in our oldest Gospel (Mark 14:22ff).

Jesus Himself wrote no book, but He gave His teaching to His disciples in a form which could be easily memorized, and enjoined them to teach others what they had learned from Him. And there is good reason to believe that one of the earliest Christian writings was a compilation of His teaching, arranged according to the chief subjects of which He treated, although this document has not been preserved in its original form but has been incorporated in some of the existing NT books. The apostles were conscious that they expressed the mind of Christ, under the guidance of His Spirit, and so their letters are full of teaching, imparted to their first readers by apostolic authority, which retains its validity to the present time, and has by divine providence been preserved for our instruction.

The Gospels began to appear about the end of the first generation after the death and resurrection of Jesus. By that time the eyewitnesses were beginning to be removed by death, and the time must come when none of them would be left. It was desirable, therefore, that their testimony should be placed on permanent record so that those who survived them would not be at a disadvantage as compared with first-generation Christians.

For some time these four evangelic records circulated independently and locally, being valued, no doubt, by those for whom they were primarily written. But by the beginning of the second century they were gathered together and began to circulate as a fourfold Gospel-record throughout the Christian world. When this happened, Acts was detached from Luke's Gospel, to which it formed the sequel, and commenced a separate, but not insignificant, career of its own.

Paul's letters were preserved at first

by the churches or individuals to whom they were sent; at least all that have come down to us were so preserved, for here and there in his surviving correspondence we find reference to a letter which was probably lost at a very early date (cf. I Cor. 5:9; Col. 4:16). But by the last decade of the first century there is evidence of a move to collect his available epistles and circulate them as a collection among the churches. Thus Clement of Rome, writing as secretary of his church to the church of Corinth about A.D. 95, can quote freely not only from Paul's Epistle to the Romans (which would naturally be available to him) but also from I Corinthians and possibly from one or two of his other epistles. What provided the stimulus for this move to collect Paul's letters, or who began to collect them, we can only speculate. Paul himself had encouraged some interchange of his letters (cf. Col. 4:16), and one or two of them were probably from the start general or circular letters, not intended for one single group of recipients.

By the early years of the second century, at any rate, a Pauline collection was in circulation — first a shorter collection of ten epistles, and then a larger collection of 13 (expanded by the inclusion of the three "Pastoral Epistles," those addressed to Timothy and Titus).

After generations of debate about the few "disputed" books in relation to the majority of "acknowledged" books, we find the 27 documents which make up our New Testament today listed by Athanasius of Alexandria in A. D. 367, and not long afterwards by Jerome and Augustine in the West. These scholars were not imposing decisions of their own, but stating what was generally recognized. It is unhistorical to represent the limits of the NT as being due to the verdict of any church council. When first a church council did make a pronouncement on this subject (A.D. 393), it did no more than record the general consensus of the Church in east and west.

The invention of the codex, or leaf-form of book, made it possible for the NT writings, or indeed the whole Bible, to be bound together in one volume, as had not been possible with the older roll-form of book. The earliest comprehensive codices known to us belong to the fourth century; but already in the third century, and possibly even in the second, it was practicable to collect groups of NT books together in smaller codices. The Chester Beatty Biblical papyri include one codex of the four Gospels and Acts and one of the Pauline epistles and Hebrews.

The essential authority of the NT derives from the authority of Christ, whether exercised in His own person or delegated to His apostles. The apostolic writings (whether penned directly by apostles or indirectly by "apostolic men") are available in the NT canon to serve as the Church's rule of faith and order — the criterion by which it may be determined whether doctrine or fellowship or anything else that claims to be apostolic really is so. And from those days to our own, it is the NT that, from time to time, has called Christians back to the ways of apostolic purity, to the truth as it is in Jesus. Reformation is not something that the Church needed once for all, in the 16th century; true "reformation according to the Word of God" is an abiding need of the Church. And where the NT is given its proper place in the Church's faith and life, true reformation goes on continually.

In all this we do not ignore the place of the OT as an integral part of the Christian Scriptures. For the two Testaments are so organically interwoven that the authority of the one carries with it the authority of the other. If the OT records the divine promise, the New records its fulfillment; if the OT tells how the world was prepared over many centuries for the coming of Christ, the New tells how He came and what His coming brought about. If even the OT writings are able to make the reader "wise unto salvation through faith which is in Christ Jesus" and equip him thoroughly for the service of God (II Tim. 3:15-17), how much more is this true of the NT writings! Our Lord's statement of the highest function of the former Scriptures applies with at least equal force to those of the NT: "these are they which bear witness of me" (John 5:39).

New Year (See Feasts, Feast of Trumpets)

Neziah (nē-zī'à, **sincere**), one of the Nethinim whose descendants returned from captivity (Ezra 2:54; Neh. 7:56).

Nezib (nē'zĭb), a village belonging to

Judah and lying about 10 miles NW of Hebron (Josh. 15:43).

Nibhaz (nĭb′hăz), a god in the form of a dog, worshiped by the Avites when the Samaritan race was being formed (II Kings 17:31).

Nibshan (nĭb′shăn), a town in the S of Judah between Beersheba and the Dead Sea (Josh. 15:62).

Nicanor (nī-kā′nôr), one of the seven chosen by the church at Jerusalem to administer alms (Acts 6:5).

Nicodemus (nĭk′ō-dē′mŭs, **victor over the people**), a leading Pharisee, "a ruler of the Jews" and a member of the Sanhedrin. Perhaps from curiosity, and possibly under conviction, but certainly led of God, he came to Jesus by night (John 3:1-14). He must have thought of himself as quite condescending to address Jesus, the young man from Galilee, as "Rabbi," but Jesus, instead of being puffed up by the recognition, quickly put Nicodemus in his place by announcing the necessity of a new birth in order "to see the kingdom of God." Nicodemus did not then understand, but was deeply touched, though he had not yet the courage to stand out for the Lord. Later, when at the Feast of Tabernacles (John 7:25-44) the Jewish leaders were planning to kill Jesus, Nicodemus spoke up, though mildly, in the Sanhedrin, suggesting their injustice in condemning a man without a fair trial. After the death of Jesus, however, Nicodemus came boldly with Joseph of Arimathea (John 19:38-42), provided a rich store of spices for the embalmment, and assisted in the burial of the body.

Nicolaitans (nĭk′ō-lā′ĭ-tănz), a group of persons whose works both the church at Ephesus and our Lord hated (Rev. 2:6) and whose doctrine was held by some in the Pergamene church (Rev. 2:15). Their doctrine was similar to that of Balaam through whose influence the Israelites ate things sacrificed to idols and committed fornication (Rev. 2:14, 15).

Nicolaus, Nicolas (nĭk′ō-lā′ŭs, nĭk′ō-lȧs, **conqueror of the people**), a "proselyte of Antioch" mentioned only in Acts 6:5 whom the church at Jerusalem very early chose to administer alms as one of the seven original "deacons."

Nicopolis (nī-cŏp′ō-lĭs, **city of victory**), an ancient city of Epirus situated on the Gulf of Actium, and founded by Augustus Caesar (Titus 3:12).

Niger (nī′jêr, **black**), a surname of Symeon, one of the five "prophets and teachers" of the church at Antioch who were led of the Lord to send forth Paul and Barnabas on the first missionary journey (Acts 13:1-3).

Night (See Time)

Night Hawk (See Birds)

Nile (nīl, meaning not certainly known), main river of Egypt and of Africa, 4,050 miles long; in the KJV

The Nile near the traditional spot where the daughter of Pharaoh is supposed to have found the baby Moses.

The Nile River at flood stage

usually called "The River," but never the "Nile," begins at Lake Victoria and flows northward to the Mediterranean; annual overflow deposits rich sediment which makes N Egypt one of the most fertile regions in the world. Moses was placed on the Nile in a basket of bulrushes; turning of the Nile into blood was one of the 10 plagues (Exod. 7:20, 21); on its bank grows the papyrus reed from which the famous papyrus writing material is made. Also called "Sihor" in KJV (Isa. 23:3).

Nimrah (nĭm′rȧ, **limpid** or **flowing water),** a city in Gilead, assigned by Moses to the tribe of Gad (Num. 32:3) and cf. vs. 36 where it is called "Beth-nimrah" i.e. "house of limpid water." It lies about ten miles NE of Jericho.

Nimrim (nĭm′rĭm), a place in Moab noted for its waters (Isa. 15:6; Jer. 48:34). Probably SE of the Dead Sea.

Nimrod (nĭm′rŏd), son of Cush; hunter, ruler, builder; founded Nineveh and kingdoms in Shinar (Gen. 10:8-12; I Chron. 1:10; Micah 5:6).

Excavations at Nippur, one of Nimrod's cities, where thousands of tablets with inscriptions were uncovered. Photo shows remains of excavated pillars. © MPS

The Mound of Nimrud, once the capital of Assyria. © *MPS*

Ruins of ancient Nineveh. OIUC

Nimrud (nĭm′rŭd), ancient Calah in Assyria, founded by Nimrod. See Calah.

Nimshi (nĭm′shī), the grandfather of Jehu whose coup-d'etat ended the rule of the house of Ahab (II Kings 9:2, 14). Elsewhere Jehu is called "son of Nimshi" (I Kings 19:16).

Nineveh, Nineve (nĭn′ĕ-vĕ), one of the most ancient cities of the world, founded by Nimrod (Gen. 10:11, 12), a great-grandson of Noah, and enduring till 612 B.C.

Jonah was sent of the Lord to warn the people of Nineveh, saying "Yet forty days and Nineveh shall be overthrown" (Jonah 3:4) but God gave Nineveh a respite for nearly 200 years: for many years capital of Assyrian empire; kings who strengthened and beautified it; Sennacherib, Esarhaddon, Ashurbanipal; destroyed in 612 B.C. by Babylonians, Scythians, and Medes; many treasures have been discovered in its ruins by archaeologists.

Nisan (See Calendar)

Nisroch (nĭs′rŏk), a god worshiped at Nineveh in whose temple Sennacherib was slain by his two. sons Adrammelech and Sharezer (Isa. 37:36-38 repeated in II Kings 19:35-37).

Niter (nī′têr). Not the same as our present niter, but an impure mixture of washing and baking sodas found in deposits around the alkali lakes of Egypt. Used to make soap. (Prov. 25: 20 "nitre," ASV "soda"). (Jer. 2:22, ASV, "lye").

No (nō, **the city of the god Amon**), capital of Upper Egypt, lying on both sides of the Nile at the great semicircular curve of the river about 400 miles S of Cairo. It was the capital of Egypt as early as the 11th century. Its tremendous ruins at Luxor and Karnak are among the world's wonders. Its fuller name was No-amon (Amon from a local god), but so similar to the Hebrew for "multitude" that the KJV mis-translates it. "The multitude of No" (Jer. 46:25) should be "Amon of No," as in ASV and "populous No" (Nah. 3:8) should be "No-amon." It was known to the classical writers under the name of Thebes.

Noadiah (nō′à-dī′à, **with whom Jehovah meets**). 1. Levite before whom the gold and silver vessels were weighed on the return to Jerusalem (Ezra 8:33). 2. A false prophetess who tried to terrorize Nehemiah (Neh. 6: 14).

Noah (nō′à, **rest**). 1. The son of Lamech and tenth in descent from Adam in the line of Seth (Gen. 5:28-29). He received this name because Lamech forsaw that through him God would comfort the race and partially alleviate the effects of the Edenic curse. Noah was uniquely righteous (6:8-9; 7:1; Ezek. 14:14) in a totally corrupt age (Gen. 6:1-13). When he was 480 years old, 120 years before the Flood (6:3), he was warned of God that the world would be destroyed by water (Heb. 11:7). He was then given exact instructions for building the Ark (Gen. 6:14-16). While engaged in this colossal task, he warned men of the coming catastrophe, as a "preacher of righteousness" (II Pet. 2:5), while God in longsuffering waited for men to repent (I Pet. 3:20). Noah's three sons, Shem, Ham, and Japheth, were not born until he was 500 years old (Gen. 5:32). One week before the Flood, God led Noah and his family into the Ark, and then, supernaturally directed, the animals "went in unto Noah into the ark, two and two of all flesh, wherein is the breath of life" (7:15). When all were safely inside, God shut the door (7:16).

The Flood came in Noah's 600th year, increased steadily for 40 days, maintained its mountain-covering depth for 110 more days, and then subsided sufficiently for Noah to disembark in the mountains of Ararat after another 221 days (see Flood or Deluge). To determine whether it was safe to disembark, Noah sent forth first a raven and then a dove at regular intervals (8:6-10). The freshly-plucked olive leaf proved to him that such sturdy plants had already begun to grow on the mountain heights. God commanded him to disembark, and Noah built an altar and offered clean beasts as burnt-offerings to God. The Lord then promised never to send another universal flood, confirming it with the rainbow sign (8:21-22; 9:9-17). God blessed Noah and his family and commanded them to multiply and fill the earth (9:1). Human government was instituted by the provision of capital punishment for murderers (9: 5-6). Among the things preserved in the Ark was sinful human nature. Noah became a husbandman, planted a vineyard, drank himself into a drunken stupor, and shamefully exposed himself in his tent (9:20-21).

Ham, presumably led by his son Canaan, made fun of Noah. For this foul deed, Canaan was cursed and Ham received no blessing (9:25-27). On the other hand, Shem and Japheth showed due respect to their father (9:23) and received rich blessings for their descendants. Noah lived 350 years after the Flood, dying at the age of 950 (9:29). 2. One of the five daughters of Zelophehad, of the tribe of Manasseh (Num. 26:33; 27:1; 36:11; Josh. 17:3).

Nob (nōb), a town of the priests in Benjamin just N of the city of Jerusalem (Isa. 10:32). In the time of King Saul the tabernacle stood here for a time, and David's visit to Ahimelech the priest (I Sam. 21) was the cause or at least the occasion for the complete destruction of the city by Saul (I Sam. 22:19). David, fleeing from Saul, asked for provision for his young men and for a sword, all of which the priest granted; but a mischief-maker, Doeg the Edomite, was a witness to the transaction and reported it to Saul, who in his insane hatred and jealousy of David, caused the priests to be slain and their city to be destroyed.

Nobah (nō'bȧ). 1. Manassite; took Kenath from Amorites (Num. 32:42). 2. Town near which Gideon defeated Midianites (Judg. 8:11).

Nobai (See Nebai)

Nobleman, one belonging to a king or well born (John 4:46-53; Luke 19:12-27).

Nod (nŏd, **wandering**), a district eastward from Eden to which Cain went in his wandering (Gen. 4:16).

Nodab (nō'dăb), a tribe of Arabs, probably Ishmaelites E of the Jordan, early conquered by the two and a half tribes (I Chron. 5:19).

Noe (See Noah)

Nogah (nō'gȧ, **brilliance**), a son of David born in Jerusalem (I Chron. 3:7; 14:6).

Nohah (nō'hȧ, **rest**), the fourth among the ten sons of Benjamin (I Chron. 8:2).

Non (See Nun)

Noon (See Time)

Noph (nŏf), better known as Memphis, a city on the W side of the Nile S of Cairo (Isa. 19:13; Jer. 2:16; 46:19).

Nophah (nō'fȧ), city of Moab (Num. 21:30).

North. The word often occurs merely as a point of the compass, but there are many passages, especially in the prophets, where it refers to a particular country, usually Assyria or Babylonia (Jer. 3:18; 46:6; Ezek. 26:7; 38:6; Zeph. 2:13).

Nose, Nostrils. Because the nostrils quiver in anger, the word for nostril is rendered "anger," almost akin to "snorting" in 171 places; and this is used not only of Jacob (Gen. 27:45) but of Moses "the meekest of men" (Exod. 32:19) and even of the Lord (Num. 11:1, 10). A long nose was counted an element of beauty (S. of Sol. 7:4), and the nose was often decorated with a ring (Ezek. 16:12 ASV, cf. Isa. 3:21). A hook in the nose however was a means of subjection (Isa. 37:29).

Nose Jewel (See Dress)

Novice (nŏv'ĭs, **newly-planted**), used only in I Timothy 3:6 concerning the requirements for being a bishop. Means a recent convert.

Numbers. The Hebrews in ancient times used the common decimal system as a method of counting. There is no evidence that they used figures to denote numbers. Before the Exile they spelled the numbers out in full, as is seen in the present text of the Hebrew Scriptures. After the Exile some of the Jews employed such signs as were used among the Egyptians, the Aramaeans, and the Phoenicians — an upright line for 1, two such lines for 2, three for 3, etc., and special signs for 10, 20, 100. Numbers were used conventionally and symbolically. Certain numbers and their multiples had sacred or symbolic significance: 3, 4, 7, 10, 12, 40, 70. For example, three expressed emphasis, as in "I will overturn, overturn, overturn it" (Ezek. 21:27). From early times seven was a sacred number among the Semites (Gen. 2:2; 4:24; 21:28). Ten was regarded as a complete number. Forty was often used as a round number (Exod. 24:18; I Kings 19:8; Jonah 3:4). Some of the higher numbers also seem sometimes to have been used as round numbers: 100 (Gen. 26:12; Lev. 26:8; II Sam. 24:3, etc.), 10,000 (Lev. 26:8; Deut. 32:30, etc.).

Numbers, Book of, 4th book of the Pentateuch; called **Numbers** because Israelite fighting force was twice numbered (1:2-46; 26:2-51). Hebrew title is **In the Wilderness** because the book describes the 40-year wilderness wandering of the Israelites after the arrival at Sinai (Exod. 19). Outline: 1. Additional legislation; organization of the host (1-10:11). 2. March from Sinai to Kadesh-Barnea (10:12-12:16). 3. Debacle at Kadesh (13:14). 4. Wanderings in wilderness (15-21:11). 5. Conquest of Trans-Jordan and preparations to enter Canaan (21:12-36:13).

Nun (nŭn), Ephraimite father of Joshua (Exod. 33:11; Neh. 8:17). His descent is given in I Chron. 7:25-27.

Nurse (See Occupations and Professions)

Nut (See Plants)

Nymphas (nĭm′făs), member of a church in Laodicea, or Colossae, which met in his house (Col. 4:15). Paul sent him greetings.

–O–

Oak (See Plants)

Oath (ōth), a solemn appeal to God, a person, or an object to witness the truth of a statement or of the binding character of a promise (Gen. 21:23; 42:15; Matt. 5:34). Some oaths were simple; some, elaborate. Various formulas and ceremonies were used (Gen. 14:22; 24:2; I Sam. 20:23; Jer. 34:18, 19). Christ condemned indiscriminate and light taking of oaths (Matt. 5:33-37). The apostles gave oaths (II Cor. 11:31; Gal. 1:20).

Obadiah (ō′bȧ-dī′ȧ, **servant of Jehovah).** 1. Governor of Ahab's household (I Kings 18:3-16). 2. Judahite (I Chron. 3:21). 3. Chief of Issachar (I Chron. 7:3). 4. Son of Azel (I Chron. 8:38). 5. Levite who returned from captivity (I Chron. 9:16) called "Abda" in Neh. 11:17. 6. Gadite soldier (I Chron. 12:9). 7. Father of Ishmaiah, prince of Zebulun (I Chron. 27:19). 8. Prince of Judah (II Chron. 17:7). 9. Merarite Levite (II Chron. 34:12). 10. Jew who returned from captivity (Ezra 8:9). **11.**

The Well of the Oath. © *MPS*

Priestly covenanter with Nehemiah (Neh. 10:5). 12. Gate-keeper in Jerusalem (Neh. 12:25). 13. Prophet who wrote Book of Obadiah.

Obadiah, Book of. 4th of the minor prophets. Subject — the destruction of Edom, which from time immemorial had been hostile to Israel. The book is undated, but a probable date is late in the 8th century B.C., during the reign of Ahaz of Judah, when Edom and the Philistines were associated in warfare against Judah (verse 19). Outline: 1. Judgment pronounced upon Edom (1-14). 2. Israel's restoration in the day of Jehovah (15-21).

Obal (ō'băl), an early Arab, son of Joktan (Gen. 10:28). Called Ebal in I Chron. 1:22.

Obed (ō'bĕd, **worshiper**), the name of five OT men: 1. An early man of Judah (I Chron. 2:37, 38). 2. One of David's mighty men (I Chron. 11:47). 3. A Levitical gate-keeper (I Chron. 26:7). 4. Father of captain who helped make Joash king (II Chron. 23:1). 5. Son of Boaz and Ruth and grandfather of David the king (Ruth 4:21, 22 copied in I Chron. 2:12; Matt. 1:5; and Luke 3:32).

Obed-Edom (ō'bĕd-ē'dŏm, **one who serves Edom**). 1. A man of Gath into whose house David had the ark of God carried (II Sam. 6:10-12; I Chron. 13: 9-13). Obed-edom and his family revered the ark and God blessed them greatly. 2. Levite musician (I Chron. 15:18-24). 3. A son of Jeduthun, and a door-keeper of the tabernacle (I Chron. 16:38). 4. Perhaps the same as No. 3, appointed with his sons over the treasury (I Chron. 26:15). 5. A descendant of No. 4 who kept the treasury in Amaziah's time (II Chron. 25: 24).

Obedience. Man normally comes under five principal authorities which require obedience: first, as a child, his parents (Col. 3:20); then, in school, his teachers (Prov. 5:12, 13); then in industry or business, his employers or masters (I Pet. 2:18); fourthly, the government (Rom. 13:1, 2) and lastly and principally, God (Gen. 26:5, etc.). The supreme test of faith in God is obedience (I Sam. 28:18). He who obeys because he loves God, is very wise. Throughout the Bible obedience is linked to faith (Gen. 22:18; Rom. 1:5; I Peter 1:14). Christ Himself obeyed the Father (Phil. 2:8), giving to us the supreme example of obedience. Christians are called "children of obedience" (I Pet. 1:14).

Obeisance (ō-bā'săns), the act of bowing low or of prostrating one's self; whether before (1) God (Mic. 6:6), (2) a god (II Kings 5:18), (3) an earthly ruler (Gen. 42:6), or (4) in courtesy toward one's equals (Gen. 23:12).

Obil (ō'bĭl, **camel driver**), Ishmaelite keeper of the king David's camels (I Chron. 27:30).

Oblation (See Offerings)

Oboth (ō'bŏth), a place E of Moab, where Israel encamped (Num. 21:10, 11; 33:43).

Occupations and Professions.

Apothecary, a compounder of drugs, oils and perfumes. More often the word could well be translated "perfumer." All large oriental towns had their perfumers' street. Their stock included anything fragrant in the form of loose powder, compressed cake, or essences in spirit, oil, or fat, as well as seeds, leaves and bark.

Perfumes were used in connection with the holy oil and incense of the tabernacle (Exod. 30:25, 35; 37:29; II Chron. 16:14; Neh. 3:8). The ritual of Baal-worshipers (Isa. 57:9), and the embalming of the dead and rites of burial (Gen. 1:12; 16:14; Lk. 23:56) all used the perfume. The apothecary compounded and sold these sweet spices and anointing oils. The frequent references in the OT to physicians and apothecaries indicate the high esteem in which the professions were held.

Artificer, a fabricator of any materials, as carpenter, smith, engraver, etc., (Gen. 4:22; Isa. 3:3). Especially workers skilled in metals, carving wood and plating it with gold, setting precious stones, and designing embroideries. Solomon procured many men of this class from Hiram, King of Tyre, when building the temple (I Chron. 29:5; II Chron. 34:11).

Author, the composer of a literary production. Agur and Lemuel are referred to as having recorded "words" in the form of prophecy and wisdom (Prov. 30:1; 31:1).

Bakers, occupied a special street in Jerusalem (Jer. 27:21). The baking of bread is one of the chief household duties. But in the towns and principal villages, the larger oven of the regular baker is required. In addition to the home baker and the public baker was the royal baker, who baked for the king (Gen. 40:2).

Bakers delivering bread in Oriental fashion.

The Hebrews made use of large stone jars, open at the mouth, about three feet high, with a fire inside for baking bread and cakes. As soon as the sides were sufficiently heated, the thin dough was applied to the outside, the opening at the top being closed. Sometimes wood was used for heating, but more often thorns and occasionally dry dung was used (Ezek. 4:12).

Kinds of ovens: **The bowl oven,** the simplest form of oven, was used by ancients, and was made of clay, with a movable lid. The bowl was placed inverted upon small stones, and thus heated with dry dung heaped over and around it. **The jar oven,** heated by grass or stubble, dry twigs or thorns. **The pit oven,** partly in the ground and partly built up of clay and plastered throughout, narrowing toward the top. The fire was kindled inside the oven.

Barber. The word barber occurs but once in the Scriptures (Ezek. 5:1). However, great attention was paid to the hair and beard among the ancients. The barber must have been a well-known tradesman. The instruments of his work were probably, the razor, the basin, the mirror, and perhaps the scissors. He usually plied his trade in the open, on the street.

Beggar, one who lives from the alms of others. It was his regular business to solicit alms publicly, and even to go from door to door. Beggars are numerous in the East. They are usually "maimed, lame or blind" (Luke 14:13). The commonest and most pathetic form of infirmity is blindness. Some of these blind beggars are led by children and have regular places to station themselves. Beggars are encouraged by a superstitious hope that alms given may atone for things obtained by cheating. Alms-giving has a high place among the religious virtues of the E.

Butler, an officer of considerable responsibility who attended Eastern monarchs. This officer is of very great antiquity, being mentioned in connection with the Egyptians, the Persians, the Assyrians and the Jewish rulers. The butler (also called cup-bearer) was required to taste of the foods and wines before serving them, as a pledge that they were not poisoned (Gen. 40:1; Neh. 1:11).

Carpenter, a worker in wood; a builder. Joseph, the legal or foster father of Jesus, was a carpenter (Matt. 13:55); so also was Jesus (Mark 6:3). The work of carpenters is frequently mentioned in the Bible (Gen. 6:14; Exod. 37; Isa. 44:13). David employed Phoenician carpenters in building his palace (II Sam. 5:11; I Chron. 14:1).

Some of the tools used by the ancient Egyptians were the adze, saw, square, awl, hammer and gluepot (Jer. 10:4; Exod. 21:6). The adze was their favorite implement. In ripping a board with the saw, the carpenter sat on the board and sawed away from himself (Isa. 44:13). In its broadest sense, carpentry included an artificer in stone and metal, as well as wood.

Chamberlain, an officer employed to look after the personal affairs of a sovereign. Potiphar seems to have had such an officer (Gen. 39:1). This officer was introduced into the court by Solomon, and was sometimes referred to as "steward" (I Kings 4:6; 16:9; 18:3) or "governor."

Clerk. The clerk or "town clerk" (Acts 19:35) was likely the city recorder. He was probably a magistrate of considerable authority and influence. He may have been mayor or the chief sovereign of the city. The clerk is often mentioned in Ephesian inscriptions.

Confectioner, a female perfumer or apothecary (I Sam. 8:13). When the orange-trees, violets and roses were in bloom, the women made scented waters which they kept in large, close-

A Jewish carpenter shop. KC © FC

ly-sealed bottles for use in the summer as cooling syrup-drinks.

Coppersmith, a worker in any kind of metals. It is likely that Alexander was given this title because copper was so common in his day (II Tim. 4:14). The coppersmiths had a particular way of smelting the copper and iron. Their smelters were located so as to face the wind currents, thus using the natural winds to fan their fires sufficiently for smelting (I Kings 7:45).

Counselor, an adviser in any matter, particularly the king's state adviser (II Sam. 15:12; I Chron. 27:33). Usually one of the chief men of the government (Job 3:14; 12:17). In the NT the name likely refers to a member of the Sanhedrin (Mark 15:43; Luke 23:50).

Doctor of the Law. Gamaliel was such a person (Acts 5:34, 40). He kept and handed down the Cabala, or sacred laws as received from Mount Sinai. May also have applied to the scribe in his practical administration of the law.

Diviner, one who obtains or seems to obtain secret knowledge, particularly of the future, and is a pagan counterpart of prophecy. Balaam was a heathen diviner but rose to the status of a bonafide prophet of the Lord, although he seems to have reverted back to paganism (Num. 22-24). Though the diviner is classed with the prophet, this does not mean an endorsement of divination.

Dyer. The practice of dying textiles was in existence even before the time of Abraham. Dying vats and clay looms that were used as weights have been found in Lachish. The dyer obtained his dye from various sources. The crimson was obtained from a worm or grub that feeds on the oak or other plants. Indigo was made from the rind of the pomegranate. The purple was made from the murex shellfish found on the beach. Luke tells of Lydia, "a seller of purple, of the city of Thyatira" (Acts 16:14). Excavations have revealed that "a guild of dyers" existed in the vicinity of Thyatira.

Farmer. Farming had its beginning with the first man, Adam. Cain tilled the soil, and Abel was a livestock farmer, perhaps a shepherd. The early farm implements were very crude. The plow was a very crude affair, made of wood and having an iron share, small and shaped like a sword. Asses and oxen were used to pull the light plow, which had only one handle, except in cases where human beings were used in place of oxen.

Fisher. The frequent allusions to the art of fishing are in connection with the Sea of Galilee. Several methods of fishing were practiced. 1. The casting-net, when the fisherman stood on the bank or waded breast-deep into the water, and skillfully threw the net which he had arranged on his arm into the water in front of him. It fell in the shape of a ring, and as the weights dragged it down, the net took the shape of a dome or cone and enclosed the fish. 2. The dragnet was used in herring and salmon fishing, with floats along the top of the weights to sink the net. 3. Hooks or angles were occasionally used. Fish were speared on the Mediterranean coast. Night fishing was very common, especially on Galilee.

Fuller, one who washed or bleached clothing (II Kings 18:17; Isa. 7:3; 36:2). One of the oldest arts. Both men and women engaged in cleaning clothes and other materials. The fuller may have been a sub-division of the dyers. However, it consisted chiefly in cleaning and bleaching garments. The cleansing was done by treading or stamping the garments with the feet or with rods or sticks in containers of water. Alkaline, potash, niter and herbs were employed in the washing and bleaching process.

The fullers discovered a singular art of bleaching cloth white by the aid of alkali, soap, putrid urine, fumes of sulpher and the ashes of certain desert plants. Therefore, the fuller's shop was

Fishermen mending their nets on the shores of the Sea of Galilee. © MPS

Fullers at work. This is the wool-bleaching industry at Mosul, on the Tigris, in Iraq. © *MPS*

usually located outside the city where offensive odors could be avoided, the cloth could be trampled clean in a running stream, and the fuller then have room to spread the cloth out for drying (Isa. 7:3).

Herdsman, a tender of oxen, sheep, goats and camels. The patriarchs were great herdsmen. The occupation was not inconsistent with state honors. David's herdsmen were among his chief officers of state (Gen. 13:7; 26:20; I Sam. 21:7; Amos 1:1; 7:14). In general, however, the herdsman was seldom the owner of the flock or herd which he tended.

Hunter. The hunter or fowler was one of the earliest occupations. It was originally a means of support, but later became a recreation. It was held in very high repute and was engaged in by all classes, but more frequently with royalty (Gen. 10:9; 27:3, 5; I Sam. 26:20; Job 38:39; Prov. 6:5). Three principal methods of hunting are mentioned in the Bible: 1. Shooting with the bow and arrows (Exod. 27:3). 2. Snaring by the spring net and cage, especially for birds, such as quail, partridge, and duck (Amos 3:5; Jer. 5: 27). 3. Pits were covered with a net

Herdsmen tending their flocks on the Shepherds Fields near Bethlehem. © MPS

and brushwood for deer, foxes, wolves, bears, lions, etc. (Ps. 35:7; Isa. 24:18; 42:22).

Judge. The head of the house was considered the judge over his own household, even with life and death (Gen. 35:24). This power quite naturally passed to the heads of tribes and clans. After Israel came into the wilderness beyond Sinai, Moses found the responsibility of handling all the judicial matters too great. Upon the advice of his father-in-law, Jethro, he chose "able men, such as feared God, men of truth, hating covetousness" to handle these matters. There were to be judges over thousands and judges over hundreds and judges over fifties (Exod. 18:19-26). The more difficult cases were referred to Moses, and he turned such cases over to a higher court, with its seat at the place of sanctuary, and it was handled by priests and judges, the high priest being the supreme judge.

Lawyer, one who is conversant with the law. There were court lawyers and the synagogue lawyers (Matt. 22: 35; Luke 7:30; 10:25; 11:45, 46, 52; 14:3; Titus 3:13). The scribe functioned in the capacity of a lawyer in the pronouncement of legal decisions. (See Doctor of the Law.)

Magician, one who practiced superstitious ceremonies. The Hebrews were forbidden to consult magicians (Gen. 41:8; Exod. 7:11, 22; Dan. 1:20; 2:2; 5:11; Acts 13:6, 8). Magic is of two kinds—natural or scientific and supernatural or spiritual.

There are many accounts of the use of magical art in the Scriptures. Before Israel left Egypt the magicians were called by Pharaoh to duplicate the works of God in converting the rod of Aaron into a serpent. They were sometimes classified with the "wise men." In the interpretation of dreams and visions the magicians and soothsayers were called.

Mason, a worker in stone. His equipment consisted of the plumbline, the measuring reed, the leveling line, the hammer with the toothed edge for shaping stones, and a small basket for carrying off earth.

Musician. Music was a prominent art in Biblical times and played an important part in the life of Israel. Hebrew music was primarily vocal, yet many of the Psalms have signs indicating that they were to be accompanied by musical instruments. The "chief musician" occurs in the titles of 54 of the Psalms. Asaph and his brothers were apparently the first to hold this position, and the office was probably hereditary in the family. Among the instruments used by the Hebrews were the cymbal, harp, organ, pipe, psaltery, sackbut and trumpets.

Nurse, one who looks after, tutors or guides another, as in a period of inexperience or sickness. In ancient times, the nurse was an honorable person (II Sam. 4:4; II Kings 11:2). Most patriarchal families had a nurse or nurses (Gen. 24:59; 35:8).

Physician. In the days of Moses there were midwives and regular physicians who attended the Israelites (Exod. 21:19). They brought some knowledge of medicine with them from Egypt, whose physicians were celebrated in all antiquity. In the early stages of medical practice, attention was more frequently confined to surgical aid and external applications. Even down to a comparatively late period, outward maladies appear to have been the chief subjects of medical treatment among the Hebrews, although they were not entirely without remedies for internal and even mental disorders. The medicines prescribed were salves, particular balms, plaster and poultices, oil-baths, mineral baths, etc. In Egypt the physicians aided in carrying out the elaborate preparations connected with embalming the body.

Plowman, one who used or held the plow, a farmer in general. The plow now used by Arabs in Palestine is lightly built, with the least possible skill or expense, and consists of two poles, which cross each other near the ground; the pole nearer the oxen is fastened to the yoke, while the other serves, the one end as the handle, the other as the plowshare. It is drawn by oxen, camels, cows or heifers. The operator of this instrument is a plowman.

Porter. The Biblical porter was a gate-keeper, not a burden-bearer (II Sam. 18:26; I Chron. 9:22). The Levites who had charge of the various entrances to the temple were called porters (I Chron. 9:17; 15:18; II Chron. 23:19). In some instances the same original word is rendered "doorkeeper" (I Chron. 15:23, 24; 23:5). A porter was stationed at the city gates, and among shepherds was responsible for keeping the doors of the sheepfold.

Potter. One of the first manufacturers. The potter found the right kind of clay, prepared it by removing stones and other rough substances, shaped and made it into the vessel desired, baked and marketed it. If the vessel became marred in the making it was "made over again another vessel." When one became broken after baking it was discarded, and thrown into "the potter's field."

Although regarded as an inferior trade, it supplied a universal need, and potters lived in settlements in the lower city of Jerusalem (Jer. 18:2-4), in the neighborhood of Hebron and Beit Jibrin, where clay was plentiful and the royal potteries probably were situated (I Chron. 4:23).

Preacher, one who heralds or proclaims, usually by delivering a discourse upon a text of Scripture. Noah is referred to as "a preacher of righteousness" (II Pet. 2:5). The temple, the synagogue and the church has been designed chiefly as a place where the profession of preaching has been practiced, by man becoming the human channel through which God sent His messages.

Priest, one who offers sacrifices, or presides over things relating to God. Previous to the Mosaic ritual, the offering of sacrifices pertained to private individuals. The father was the priest of his own family, and officiated at the domestic altar; being succeeded at death by his firstborn son. Possibly a more general priesthood existed, such as that exercised by Melchizedek. When the Mosaic dispensation was introduced, a particular order of men was appointed to that special service (Exod. 28), with a very solemn and imposing ceremony. From that time, the offering of sacrifices was restricted, in the main, to those who were duly invested with the priestly office (II Chron. 26:18). After the Captivity, those who could not prove their descent from Aaron lost their privileges as priests. The corruption of the priesthood, by making the office a means of amassing wealth and gaining political power, hastened the ruin of the Jewish nation. Christ is described in the NT as the firstborn king, the anointed, a priest after the order of Melchizedek (Heb. 7:8).

Phophet(-ess), a person who acts as the organ of divine communication with men, especially with regard to the future. The prophet differs from the priest in representing the divine side of this mediation, while the priest rather acts from the human side. The term "prophet" is an Anglicized Greek word, and literally denotes one who speaks for another or in another's name. Strictly speaking, a prophet is one to whom the knowledge of secret things is revealed, whether past (John 4:19), present (II Kings 5:26), or to come (Luke 1:76-79). Among the prophetesses mentioned in the Bible are Miriam, Deborah, Huldah, Noadiah, and Anna.

Publican, an under-collector of Roman revenue. Of these there appear to have been two classes: 1. The "chief of the publicans" of whom Zacchaeus is an example. 2. The ordinary publican, the lowest class of the servants engaged in the collecting of the revenue, and of whom we have an instance in Levi, who was afterwards the Apostle Matthew.

The publicans were hated as the instruments by which the subjection of the Jews to the Roman emperor was perpetuated. The publicans of the NT were regarded as traitors and apostates, defiled by their frequent intercourse with the heathen, and willing tools of the oppressor. Hence, they were classed with sinners, harlots and the heathen (Matt. 9:11; 21:31; 18:17).

Rabbi, a title given by the Jews to the teachers of their law. It was also applied to Christ by His disciples and others (Matt. 23:7, 8; John 1:38, 49; 3:2, 26; 6:25). The term Rabbi literally means "master" (John 1:38; 20:16).

Recorder, an officer of high rank in the Jewish state, exercising the functions, not simply of an annalist, but of chancellor or president of the privy council (Isa. 36:3, 22). He was not only the grand custodian of the public records, but kept the responsible registry of the current transactions of government (II Sam. 8:16; 20:24; II Kings 18:18).

Robber, one who engages in theft and plunder. Ishmael, the Bedouin, became a "wild man" and a robber of trade (Gen. 16:12).

Ruler, one who rules or governs, or who assists in carrying on a government. An honor often bestowed by kings on their subjects. Daniel was made ruler over the whole province of Babylon by Nebuchadnezzar for

The publicans were tax collectors and customs gatherers for the Romans.
KC © FC

interpreting a dream; and again made third ruler of the kingdom after interpreting the writing upon the wall at the time of Belshazzar's great feast (Dan. 2:10, 38; 5:7, 16, 29). There was the ruler of the synagogue, the ruler of the treasures, or the chief treasurer, and the high priest who was considered the "ruler of the house of God" (I Chron. 9:11).

Sailor, one whose occupation is navigation, or the operation of ships. Particularly one who manipulates a ship with sails. Those that trade by the sea (Rev. 18:17).

Saleswoman, a woman who sells merchandise, such as Lydia, the "seller of purple" (Acts 16:14, 15, 40).

Schoolmaster, one who exercised careful supervision over scholars, forming their manners, etc.

Scribe, persons employed to handle correspondence and to keep accounts.

The scribe came to be a student and interpreter of the law. In the time of Christ, the scribes had attained great influence and power as a class, and were regarded with great respect (Matt. 23:5; Luke 14:7).

Seer, one who is considered able to foresee things or events. A prophet (I Sam 9:9). Samuel identified himself as a seer (I Sam. 10:19). He is referred to as "the seer" who ordained David and Samuel (I Chron. 9:22).

Senators, the "elders of Israel" who formed one of the three classes represented in the Sanhedrin. The scribes and priests formed the other two classes (Acts 5:21). They were considered chief men or magistrates (Ps. 105:22). Also translated **elder.**

Sergeant, Roman officers who attended the chief magistrates when they appeared in public, and who inflicted the punishment that had been pronounced (Acts 16:35, 38).

Servant, sometimes applied to any one under the authority of another, and not necessarily a domestic or slave. In some passages of Scripture, the word properly means "young man" or "minister."

Servitor, one who ministers to, or serves, but not in a menial capacity (II Kings 4:43).

Sheepmaster, one who is both a shepherd and the owner of the sheep (II Kings 3:4).

Sheep-Shearer, one who shears the sheep. When the wool is long and ready to "harvest," a sheep-shearing time is announced, and it is a great time of rejoicing (Gen. 38:12; II Sam. 13:23, 24).

Shepherd, one employed in tending, feeding and guarding the sheep. Abel, Rachel and David were all keepers of sheep. The shepherd usually carried a sling to protect himself and the sheep against wild animals. He carried a rod (stick) about 30 inches long with a knob on one end and a staff that looked like our walking cane, usually with a crook on one end.

Silversmith, a worker in silver (Acts 19:24).

Singer, a trained or professional vocalist (II Sam. 19:35; I Kings 4:32).

Slave, a person held in bondage to another, having no freedom of action, his person and service being wholly under the control of his master or owner. Jewish slaves were of two classes—Hebrew and non-Hebrew—and both were protected by law. Hebrew slaves became such through poverty or debt, through theft and inability to repay, or in case of females, because they had been sold by their parents as maid-servants. Their slavery was the mildest form of bond-service. Christianity ultimately changed all this.

Smith, a workman in stone, wood or metal. The first Smith mentioned in Scripture is Tubal-cain. Removed from a vanquished nation to more certainly disable it (Isa. 44:12; 54:16; Jer. 24:1).

Soldier, one engaged in military service, and receiving pay for his services. In the earlier times, every man above the age of 20 was a soldier (Num. 1:3; 2:2; 10:14); and each tribe formed a regiment.

Sorcerer, one who practiced the arts of the magicians by which he pretended to foretell events with the supposed assistance of evil spirits (Isa. 47:9, 12; Acts 8:9, 11).

Spinner, a person who used the distaff and the spindle in the making of thread from wool, flax or cotton (Prov. 31:19; Matt. 6:28).

Steward, one to whose care is committed the management of the household (Gen. 43:19; Luke 16:1). The term is also applied to ministers (I Cor. 4:1) and to Christians (I Pet. 4:10).

Tanner, one who is skilled in dressing and preserving hides, or skins of animals. Among the ancient Jews, ceremonial uncleanness was attached to the occupation of the tanner, and hence he was obliged to pursue his calling outside the town (Acts 9:43; 10:6, 32).

Taskmaster, an overseer or bond master (Exod. 1:11; 3:7; 5:6, 10, 13, 14). Pharaoh appointed taskmasters over the Hebrews to make their work hard and wearisome.

Tax Collector, Taxgatherer, one who collected or gathered a certain tax or revenue for the government. The publicans of the Roman Empire were engaged in this profitable traffic. It has led to much oppression and injustice, and has fostered a feeling of hostility towards anything connected with the government. Zacchaeus was a tax collector (Luke 19:23).

Teacher, a well informed individual who imparts instruction, and com-

Tanners processing goatskins at a tannery at Hebron. © *MPS*

municates knowledge of religious truth or other matters. "Doctors" or teachers are mentioned among divine gifts in Ephesians 4:11.

Tent-maker, one skilled in making tents from hair or wool, or skins. The early patriarchs were largely tent-dwellers, and therefore had to have some knowledge in tent-making. Paul practiced this trade with Aquila at Corinth (Acts 18:1-3).

Tetrarch, a ruler of the fourth part of a kingdom or province. This title is applied in the Bible to any petty ruler in the Roman empire. His authority was similar to that of a king, and that title was often given to him (Matt. 14:9).

Tiller, the greatest occupation of the Hebrews; tilling the soil, or cultivating the soil. This word is used synonymously with **husbandman.** A useful

A native weaver at work on his loom at Kifi, in Iraq. © MPS

and honorable occupation (Gen. 9:20; Isa. 28:24-28).

Times, Observer of, persons who had a superstitious regard for days that were supposed to be lucky or unlucky, as decided by astrology. Such people were condemned (Deut. 18:9-14).

Town Clerk, a keeper of the public records, who presided over public gatherings, and performed the duties of the chief magistrate when he was away. An official of great importance (Acts 19:35).

Treasurer, important officer in Oriental courts, probably having charge of the receipts and disbursements of the public treasury (Ezra 1:8; 7:21; Isa. 22:15).

Watchman, one whose duty was to stand in the tower on the walls or at the gates of the city. They also patrolled the streets, and besides protecting the city and its inhabitants from violence, were required to call out the hours of the night (II Sam. 18:24-27; S. of Sol. 5:7; Isa. 21:11, 12).

Weaver, one who was skilled in the making of cloth or rugs from spun thread or string. For the most part in the hands of women, although there were also weavers among men. The stuffs woven were linen, flax, and wool (Exod. 35:35; Lev. 13:48; I Chron. 11:23; Isa. 38:12).

Wizard, a "knowing or wise one." Witch was the name given to the woman and wizard the name given to the man who practiced witchcraft. There was a pretended communication with demons and spirits of the dead by means of which future events were revealed, etc. It was severely denounced (Exod. 22:18; Lev. 20:6; II Kings 9:22; Gal. 5:20).

Writer. The knowledge of writing was possessed by the Hebrews at a very early period. The materials on which they wrote were of various kinds. Tables of stone, metal, plaster, wax-covered frames, skins, paper made from bulrushes and fine parchment were used. The prophets were often told to write, by the Lord, and may be considered writers (Rev. 1:11; 21:5).

Ochran, Ocran (ŏk'răn), prince of the tribe of Asher, appointed to assist in the first census of Israel (Num. 1:13; 7:72).

Oded (ō'dĕd, **he has restored,** or **prophet).** 1. The father of Azariah the prophet. 2. A prophet in Samaria in the days of Ahaz, king of Judah (II Chron. 28:9-15). Pekah, king of the northern tribes, had taken captive 200,000 Jews, after slaying 120,000 valiant men of Judah, and as the captives and the spoil were being brought into Samaria Oded rebuked them and persuaded them to feed and clothe the captives and to return them to Judah.

Odor (ō'dêr), that which affects the sense of smell. In ASV the word refers to a pleasant or sweet odor, while an unpleasant one is called "ill savour" or "stench." The Levital offerings which did not deal with sin were called offerings of sweet savor (Mal. 1:11). The prayers of the saints (figuratively) are offerings of a sweet savor to the Lord (Rev. 5:8).

Offense (ŏ-fĕns). Used in a variety of ways in Scripture, as it is in English: injury, hurt, damage, occasion of sin, a stumbling block, an infraction of law, sin, transgression, state of being offended. In the NT it is often used in the sense of stumbling-block (Matt. 5:30; 11:6; 18:6; I Cor. 8:13, etc.).

Offerings. Biblical prescriptions regarding the various kinds of offerings arose from the need for purification from sin or the desire of the worshiper to enter into fellowship with God. Offeings were derived from both animal and vegetable kingdoms. Types of offerings: sin offering—for acts of unconscious transgression, mistakes or other inadvertencies (Lev. 4:1-35; 6:24-30); trespass offering, or guilt offering, signified expiation and restitution, and availed for inadvertent offenses, false swearing and improper dealings with a neighbor; peace offering—symbolized right spiritual relations with God; meal offering, or meat offering; drink offering, or libation, accompanied many of the sacrifices (Exod. 29:40f); wave offering, heave offering (Exod. 29:24-28; Lev. 7:14).

Officer, a holder of an official position. (1) One who has been set up over others (I Kings 4:7, etc.); (2) A eunuch, such as Oriental kings set in charge of their women and also of much of the routine business of the court (Gen. 37:36, etc.); (3) A writer or clerk (Exod. 5:6; Deut. 20:9, etc.); (4) A police officer or bailiff (Luke 12:58); (5) Originally an assistant or under-ruler (Matt. 5:25).

Offscouring, a contemptuous word for sweepings, scrapings, filth, dung, etc. "Thou hast made us an offscouring and refuse" (Lam. 3:45); "the filth of the world, the offscouring of all things" (I Cor. 4:13).

Og (ŏg), Amorite king of Bashan (Deut. 31:4; Josh. 2:10; 13:21; I Kings 4:19). He held sway over 60 separate communities. Og's defeat before the invading Hebrews (Deut. 3:1-13) became proverbial, for it dispelled a legend of invincibility based upon the daunting appearance of some of the Canaanitish hoplites (Deut. 1:28). The tradition was long-lived (Pss. 135:11; 136:20). Og's territory was assigned in the partition of Palestine to Reuben, Gad, and the half-tribe Manasseh (Num. 32:33). The "bedstead of iron" preserved as a museum piece at Rabbah among the Amorites (Deut. 3:11) was possibly a sarcophagus cut from black basaltic rock.

Ohad (ō'hăd), son of Simeon (Gen. 46:10) and head of a clan in that tribe (Exod. 6:15).

Ohel (ō'hĕl, **tent),** a son of Zerubbabel, a descendant of King Jehoiakim (I Chron. 3:20).

Oholah, Oholibah (ō-hō'là, ō-hŏl'ĭ-bà), symbolic names for Samaria and for Jerusalem, pictured as harlots wandering from God (Ezek. 23).

Oil, in the Bible almost always olive oil, perhaps the only exception being Esther 2:12, where it is oil of myrrh. The olives were sometimes beaten (Lev. 24:2), sometimes trodden (Mic. 6:15), but generally crushed in a mill designed for that purpose. Not only a

Top: Arab peasants harvesting the olive crop.
Bottom: Crushing olives with a large stone roller, before extracting the olive oil. © *MPS*

prime article of food, the bread being dipped in it, but was used for cooking, for anointing, and for lighting. Oil was one of the principal ingredients in making soap (Jer. 2:22).

Anointing with oil was for three diverse purposes: wounded animals were anointed for the soothing and curative effects of the oil (Ps. 23:5); people anointed themselves with oil for its cosmetic value (Ps. 104:15); but most notably men were anointed as an official inauguration into high office. Priests (Exod. 28:41; 29:7), prophets and kings (I Kings 19:15, 16) were anointed and were called "messiahs" i.e., "anointed ones" (Lev. 4:3, 5, 16; I Sam. 2:10; I Chron. 16:22). Anointing the head of a guest with oil was a mark of high courtesy (Luke 7:46). Oil is used also as a symbol for the Holy Spirit. Our Lord's Messiahship was not bestowed with the use of literal oil, but was evidenced when the Holy Spirit came down upon Him in the form of a dove at His baptism (Luke 3:22, etc.). Oil was also the prime source of light in dwellings and in the tabernacle.

Oil Tree (See Plants)

Ointments and Perfumes. Originally used for ceremonial purposes, first religious then secular, and became a personal habit with the growing sophistication of society, and the need for deodorants in hot lands (Esth. 2:12; Prov. 7:17; 27:29; Isa. 57:9). So universal was the practice that its intermission was an accepted sign of mourning (Deut. 28:40; Ruth 3:3; II Sam. 14:2; Dan. 10:3; Amos 6:6; Mic. 6:15; etc.). The skin, as well as the hair, was thus perfumed and anointed (Ps. 104:15), and, especially on high occasions, the scented unguent was used with profusion (Ps. 133:2). Its use was also a courtesy to an honored guest (Luke 7: 46). The process of manufacture is not clear, and the account takes for granted that "the art of the apothecary" (more correctly "perfumer") is commonly familiar to the reader (Exod. 30:25, 35; Neh. 3:8; Eccl. 10: 1). The compound was based on the aromatic gum of Arabian plants and that the medium or base was some form of fat or oil (probably calves' fat and olive oil). In its later trade form the perfume was sometimes packed in alabaster boxes or flasks (Luke 7:37). Such ointment was heavily scented (John 12:3) and costly (John 12:5).

Old Gate, at the NW corner of the city of Jerusalem in Nehemiah's time, near the present site of the Holy Sepulchre (Neh. 3:6; 12:39).

Old Testament. The OT is composed of 39 books—5 of law, 12 of history, 5 of poetry, 5 of major prophets, and 12 of minor prophets. The classification of our present Hebrew Bibles is different—5 of law, 8 of prophets, and 11 of miscellaneous writings. These 24 in various combinations contain all of our 39 books. Neither of these classifications exhibits the fact that much of the Pentateuch is history, nor do they show the chronological relations of the books. A logical survey of the OT literature may approach the subject chronologically. All of these books were regarded by Israelites as Scripture, inspired and authoritative, before the 1st century A.D. They appeared over a period of c. 1000 years. The authors of many of them are unknown. For more detailed information about individual books, see entries elsewhere in this dictionary.

Malachi, the final book of the OT, was written around 400 B.C. It reveals the problems of the day caused by insincerity among some of the priests themselves. But it also, like so many of the other prophets, pointed forward to Messianic times. The OT closes with the annunciation of the rise of a new and greater prophet in the spirit and power of Elijah who would precede the Messiah of Israel.

Olive (See Plants)

Olives, Mount of, (called Olivet in two KJV contexts: II Sam. 15:30; Acts 1: 12). A ridge, c. 1 mile long, with four identifiable summits, E of Jerusalem, beyond the Valley of Jehoshaphat, through which flows the Kidron stream. Gethsemane, Bethphage, and Bethany are on its slopes (II Sam. 15: 30; Zech. 14:4; Matt. 21:1; 24:3; 26: 30; Mark 11:1; 13:3; 14:26; Luke 19: 29, 37; 22:39; John 8:1; Acts 1:12).

Olympas (ō-lĭm′păs), a Christian in Rome to whom Paul sent greetings (Rom. 16:15).

Omar (ō′mȧr), a grandson of Esau (Gen. 36:11, 15).

Omega (ō-mē′gȧ), literally, big "O," last letter of the Greek alphabet, long o. In three contexts (Rev. 1:8; 21:6; 22:13) it is employed as a symbol of inclusiveness: "... Alpha and Omega, the beginning and the end, the first and the last."

Omer (See Weights and Measures)

Omnipotence (ŏm-nĭp′ō-tĕns), the attribute of God which describes His ability to do whatever He wills. He cannot do anything contrary to His nature as God, such as to ignore sin, to sin, or to do something absurd or self-contradictory. God is not controlled by His power, but has complete control over it; otherwise He would not be a free being. Although the word "omnipotence" is not found in the Bible, the Scriptures clearly teach the omnipotence of God (Job 42:2; Jer. 32:17; Matt. 19:26; Luke 1:37; Rev. 19:6).

Omnipresence (ŏm′nĭ-prĕz′ĕns), the attribute of God by virtue of which He fills the universe in all its parts and is present everywhere at once. Not a part, but the whole of God is present in every place. The Bible teaches the omnipresence of God (Ps. 139:7-12; Jer. 23:23, 24; Acts 17:27, 28). This is true of all three members of the Trinity.

Omniscience (ŏm-nĭsh′ĕns), the attribute by which God perfectly and eternally knows all things which can be known, past, present, and future. God's omniscience is clearly taught in Scripture (Prov. 15:11; Ps. 147:5; Isa. 46:10).

Omri (ŏm′rē). 1. Sixth king of Israel (886 to 874 B.C.). An able if unscrupulous soldier, and founder of a dynasty, the first Hebrew monarch to be mentioned in non-Biblical records.

The brief but vivid account of Omri's somewhat sinister reign, and his military coup d'état, is told in I Kings 16:15-28. Omri was commander-in-chief under Elah, son of Baasha. When Elah was murdered by Zimri, Omri was proclaimed king by the army in

The ruins of Omri's Palace in Samaria. © MPS

the field, a pattern of events which was to become grimly familiar in the imperial history of Rome.

Omri is dismissed by the Hebrew historian as an evil influence (I Kings 16:25, 26), and indeed, his marriage of Ahab, his son, to Jezebel, princess of Tyre, to cement, no doubt, a trade alliance, was fraught with most disastrous consequences, continuation, though it was, of Solomon's and David's Tyrian policy. The calf-worship of Jeroboam (I Kings 12:32) was continued at Bethel throughout the reign, and 140 years after his death, Micah is found denouncing "the statutes of Omri" (6:16). 2. A Benjamite, family of Becher (I Chron. 7:8). 3. A man of Judah, family of Perez (I Chron. 9:4). 4. A prince of the tribe of Issachar in David's reign (I Chron. 27: 18).

On (ŏn). 1. A Delta city of Egypt, called by the Greeks Heliopolis (City of the Sun) and so rendered in the Septuagint (Gen. 41:45, 50; 46: 20). In Ezekiel 30:17 the name has been changed to "Aven" by misvocalization. "Aven" means "idolatry." It is called Bethshemesh in Jeremiah 43:13, a word of similar import. On is an Egyptian word signifying "light" or "sun," so the Greek and Hebrew names are fair translations. The priest of On, whose daughter Asenath became Joseph's wife, was a person of considerable importance. The worship of the Sun-god which was centered there had peculiar features which suggest Syrian influence. Ra was identified with Baal by Semites, and with Apollo by the Greeks. There must therefore have been a cosmopolitan element in the temple cult to match the atmosphere of a center of international trade. It is perhaps significant that On is named as the place of sojourn of the Holy Family after the flight into Egypt. 2. A Reubenite chief who took part in the rebellion of Korah (Num. 16:1).

Onam (ō'năm, **strong).** 1. Son of Shobal, son of Seir the Horite (Gen. 36: 23). 2. Great-great-grandson of Judah (I Chron. 2: 26, 28).

Onan (ō'năn, **strong),** second son of Judah by a Canaanite wife, daughter of Shua. He refused to consummate a levirate marriage with Tamar, and so Jehovah slew him too, leaving Tamar twice a widow (Gen. 38:4-10).

Onesimus (ō-nĕs'ĭ-mŭs, **profitable),** a slave of Philemon of Colossae who robbed his master, and made his way to Rome, the frequent goal of such fugitives, the "common cesspool of the world," as the aristocratic historian Sallust called the city (Cat. 37:5). Some Ephesian or Colossian in Rome, perhaps Aristarchus (Acts 27:2; Philem. 24; Col. 4:10-14), or Epaphras (Col. 1:7; 4:12, 13; Philem. 23) seems to have recognized the man and brought him to Paul in his captivity. Onesimus became a Christian and was persuaded to return to his master. From the incident came the exquisite letter of Paul to Philemon, which demonstrates so vividly the social solvent which Christianity had brought into the world. It would appear that Onesimus left Rome in company with Tychicus, carrying the letter to Philemon, and also the Pauline communications to the Ephesian and Colossian churches.

Onesiphorus (ŏn'ĕ-sĭf'ō-rŭs, **profit-bringer),** an Ephesian who ministered fearlessly to Paul at the time of the apostle's second captivity in Rome (II Tim. 1:16-18; 4:19). Paul's warm gratitude, and his care in the midst of his own distress to convey his greetings to the Ephesian family, is a light on his generous character, and further evidence of his capacity for commanding devotion.

Onions (See Plants)

Only-Begotten, a title applied to our Lord by John (John 1:14, 18; 3:16, 18; I John 4:9) and once in Hebrews (11:17) connected with the doctrine of the "eternal generation of the Son of God" (cf. Ps. 2:7 with Acts 13:33; Heb. 1:5; 5:5).

Ono (ō'nō, **strong),** town in Benjamin, c. 6 miles SE of Joppa (I Chron. 8:12; Neh. 6:2; 11:35).

Onycha (ŏn'ĭ-kȧ), an ingredient of the sweet-smelling incense which Moses was directed to make (Exod. 30:34). Made from a certain mussel found in India, which when burning emitted an odor resembling musk. Very costly. See Incense.

Onyx (See Minerals)

Ophel ō'fĕl, **hill),** properly a hill, but when used with the definite article in Hebrew, it is rendered "Ophel" and refers to a part of Jerusalem. In II Kings 5:24 the word is rendered "tower" in the KJV and "hill" in the ASV, but no one knows the exact location. In Micah 4:8 it is rendered "stronghold" in the KJV, but the ASV

The Hill of Ophel, at the southeast corner of Jerusalem city wall. Beyond this is the temple area. © MPS

has "the hill of the daughter of Zion," and probably refers to **the** Ophel of Jerusalem. In Isaiah 32:14, the KJV has "forts," but the ASV, more accurately, "hill," and probably refers to Ophel. Ophel lies outside the wall of modern Jerusalem just S of the Mosque "el Aksa" and above the junction of the valleys of the Kidron and of the "son of Hinnom."

Ophir (ō′fêr). 1. A son of Joktan (Gen. 10:29). The names in "the table of the nations" (Gen. 10) often indicate locations, and Ophir is placed between Sheba and Havilah, both of which were in southern Arabia. 2. The land occupied by the descendants of Ophir. In I Kings 9:28 it is mentioned as the source of much gold (cf. 2:11, 12). Ophir in Arabia was not only the source of gold, but it may have been a way-station for the "ships of Tarshish" coming westward from India, if the apes, ivory, and peacocks (I Kings 10:22), to say nothing of the almug trees (I Kings 10:11, 12), had to come from India. These large ships which made the round trip once in three years (I Kings 10:22) could have voyaged from the neighborhood of Goa on the west coast of India to Ophir, and thence up the Red Sea and the Gulf of Aqabah to Ezion-geber (I Kings 9:26), keeping in sight or nearly in sight of land all of the way. Ophir was famous for its gold from very early days (Job 22:24; 28:16).

Ophni (ŏf′nī), a city in the northern part of Benjamin, mentioned only in Joshua 18:24. About 2½ miles NW of Bethel on one of the two main roads northward from Jerusalem to Samaria.

Ophrah (ŏf′rȧ, **hind**). 1. A town in Benjamin (Josh. 18:23). It lies on a conical hill about three miles NE of Bethel and probably is the "Ephraim" of John 11:54. 2. A town in Manasseh (Judg. 6:24) pertaining to the Abiezrites, a family of that tribe. Here the Angel of Jehovah appeared, sitting under an oak tree, and talking with Gideon, commissioning him to deliver Israel from the Midianites. 3. A son of Meonothaia Judahite (I Chron. 4:14).

Oracle (ŏr'ȧ-k'l). 1. An utterance supposedly coming from a deity and generally through an inspired medium. 2. Utterance of prophecy, translated "burden" (Isa. 14:28; 15:1; Ezek. 12:10; Nah. 1:1). 3. Holy of Holies in the temple (I Kings 6:5f). 4. The OT was referred to as "living (KJV 'lively') oracles" (Acts 7:38), and in Hebrews 5:12 "the oracles of God" would include Christian teaching. Christians are told to speak as the oracles of God (I Pet. 4:11).

Orator. 1. Isaiah 3:3 (KJV) has "the eloquent orator," where ASV reads "the skilful enchanter" which is correct, for the word is derived from the verb for **charming serpents.** 2. A public speaker, especially an advocate (Acts 24:1). One was Tertullus whom the Jews employed to speak against Paul before Felix, not that they lacked eloquence, but because Tertullus, a Roman, could make the accusation in Latin, the language of the Roman courts.

Ordain, Ordination. In the KJV "to ordain" is the rendering of about 35 different Hebrew, Greek, and Latin words. The word has many shades of meaning, chiefly the following: (1) to set in order, arrange (Ps. 132:17; Isa. 30:33); (2) to bring into being (I Kings 12:32; Num. 28:6; Ps. 8:2, 3); (3) to decree (Esth. 9:27; Acts 16:4; Rom. 7:10); (4) to set apart for an office or duty (Mark 3:14; John 15:16; Acts 14:23). Ordination in the sense of setting aside officers of the Church for a certain work by the laying on of hands was practiced in apostolic times (I Tim. 4:14; II Tim. 1:6), but it is nowhere described or enjoined.

Oreb and Zeeb (ō'rĕb, zē'ĕb, **raven** and **wolf),** two princes of the Midianites in the days of Gideon. After Gideon's notable defeat of the Midianites, the Midianites who survived fled, and Gideon called upon the men of Manasseh to cut off the retreat at the crossings of the Jordan. Here they captured the two princes and beheaded them. The places of their deaths were named in their memory: Oreb died at the rock of Oreb and Zeeb at the wine-press of Zeeb (Judg. 7:24, 25).

Oreb, Rock of (See Oreb and Zeeb)

Oren (ō'rĕn, **cedar),** son of Jerahmeel (I Chron. 2:25).

Organ (See Musical Instruments)

Orion (See Astronomy)

Ornament (See Dress)

Ornan (ôr'năn), a Jebusite prince (called Araunah in II Sam. 24:16ff, etc.) whose threshing-floor was purchased by David (I Chron. 21:15-25).

Orontes (ō-rŏn'tēz), chief river in Sy-

At the mouth of the Orontes, chief river of Syria. © MPS

ria, almost 400 miles long, rises in Anti-Lebanon range, and flows N for most of its course.

Orpah (ôr′pȧ, **neck,** i.e. **stubbornness),** a Moabite woman whom Chilion, son of Elimelech and Naomi, married. She loved her mother-in-law, but remained in Moab, while Ruth, Naomi's other daughter-in-law, went with her (Ruth 1:1, 14; 4: 9, 10).

Osee (See Hosea)

Oshea (See Joshua)

Osnappar (See Ashurbanipal)

Ospray (See Birds)

Ossifrage (See Birds)

Ostia (ôs′tyȧ), the port of Rome, on the Tiber mouth, some 16 miles from the city. Ostia became a naval base and continued to grow in commercial importance until the end of the second century of the Christian era. Evidence for a Christian community in Ostia can be traced with certainty as far back as A.D. 200.

Ostraka (ŏs′trȧ-kȧ), inscribed fragments of pottery (sing., ostrakon). In the ancient world handy writing material was rare, but potsherds, or broken pieces of earthenware, were abundant, hence the habit of writing brief memoranda or communications on such ready material. The surface holds the inscription well and some important ancient documents have come down to us in this form (e.g. the Lachish Letters).

Ostrich (See Birds)

Othni (ŏth′nī, abbrev. of Othniel), son of Shemaiah, a doorkeeper of the tabernacle under David (I Chron. 26: 7).

Othniel (ŏth′nĭ-ĕl), son of Kenaz, the brother of Caleb, who with Joshua had brought back a good report of the land of Canaan after spying it out. Othniel took Debir and so acquired Caleb's daughter Achsah as wife (Josh. 15:13-19; Judg. 1:11-15). Within 15 years after the death of Joshua, Israel fell into apostasy and God delivered them into the hand of Chushan-rishathaim (Judg. 3:8-11), king of Mesopotamia. In their distress they prayed to the Lord, who raised up Othniel to deliver them. He was thus the first of the seven "judges" to deliver Israel from foreign oppression (I Chron. 4: 13).

Ouches (ouch′ĕz). 1. Settings for precious stones on the high-priest's ephod (Exod. 28:11). 2. A rich texture inwrought with gold thread of wire (Ps. 45:13).

Oven; ancient ovens were primitive — often a hole in the ground coated with clay and in which a fire was made. The dough was spread on the inside and baked. Sometimes ovens were made of stone, from which the fire is raked when the oven is very hot, and into which the unbaked loaves are placed (Hos. 7:4-7). See also Bread and Occupations and Professions (Baker).

Overseer, inspector, (Gen. 39:4, 5; II Chron. 34:12, 17); **foreman** (II Chron. 2:18; 34:13); **officer; bishop, overseer** (Acts 20:28).

Owl (See Birds)

Owner of a Ship. The phrase is found in Acts 27:11, "Nevertheless the centurion believed the master and the owner of the ship, more than those things which were spoken by Paul." A distinction is made between the master and the owner. The first refers to the steersman, or pilot; while the second refers to the sailing-master of a ship engaged in state service (although the word also means ship-owner). This was, however, a corn ship in the imperial service, and would not be privately owned.

Ox (See Animals, Cattle)

Ox Goad, a pointed stick used to urge the ox to further effort (Judg. 3:31). See Goad.

Ozem (ō′zĕm). 1. The sixth son of Jesse (I Chron. 2:15). 2. A son of Jerahmeel (I Chron. 2:25).

Ozias (See Uzziah)

Ozni (ŏz′nī), son of Gad and father of the Oznites (Num. 26:16).

Paarai (pāȧ-rī, **devotee of Peor),** one of David's mighty men (II Sam. 23: 35). He is called Naarai in I Chron. 11:37.

Padan-Aram (pā'dăn-ā'răm, **plain of Aram).** Originally signified a unit of measuring. It is the home of Jacob's exile (Gen. 31:18), the home of Laban, Haran of the upper Euphrates Valley. It is also sometimes translated as simply "Mesopotamia." In Genesis 48: 7, Padan only; RSV, Paddan-aram.

Padon (pā'dŏn, **redemption),** one of the Nethinim who returned with Zerubbabel from Babylon (Ezra 2:44; Neh. 7:47).

Pagiel (pā'gĭ-ĕl, **a meeting with God),** chief of Asher (Num. 7:72).

Pahath-Moab (pā'hăth-mō'ăb, **governor of Moab),** head of one of the chief houses of Judah. Part of the descendants of this man returned from Babylon with Zerubbabel (Ezra 2:6; Neh. 7:11) and another part returned with Ezra (Ezra 8:4).

Pai (See Pau)

Painting the Eyes (See Dress)

Palace, the dwelling place of an important official. Palaces are found all over the Biblical world. The science of archaeology has given much light on these ancient structures. Israel built many palaces and one finds frequent mention of them in the Scriptures. At Gezer the remains of a palace belonging to the period of Joshua's conquest have been found. It is thought to be the palace of Horam, king of Gezer, whom Joshua conquered (Josh. 10:33). Many of these old palaces were made of stone. This palace belongs to the group of palaces known as fortress palaces. They were sometimes the entrances to great tunnels. Some were constructed over important wells or springs of water which they controlled.

David had two palaces at different times in his ministry. The first was a simple one located at Hebron, but the second one was much more elaborate, built of cedar trees furnished by Hiram of Tyre and erected by workmen that Hiram supplied (II Sam. 5:11). Solomon's palace that came later was a much more lavish structure, judging from its description given in I Kings 7. It was about 150 feet by 75 feet in size, constructed mostly of cedar in the interior and of hand-hewn stones for the exterior. Some of the foundation stones were 15 feet long. Solomon's wealth together with the skilled Phoenician craftsmen must have produced a magnificent building. Nothing remains of this building today.

An ivory palace belonging to Ahab is mentioned in I Kings 22:39. For a long time scholars denied the truthfulness of this record, but the archaeologist has confirmed the report. It was

Ivory panels from King Ahab's palace. PAM

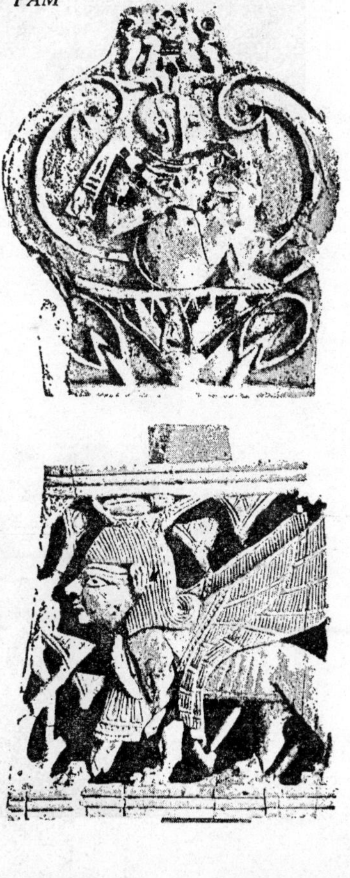

Above: The hill country around Nazareth and Mt. Tabor.
Below: The arid valley of the Arabah, mountains of Edom in the distance. © MPS

a large edifice 300 feet long from N to S. Many of its walls were faced with white marble. Wall paneling, plaques and furniture have been uncovered, made of or adorned with ivory.

Probably the most famous palace in the NT period was the one belonging to Herod the Great. Josephus informs us that this structure was built in Jerusalem. Its rooms were of a very great height and adorned with all kinds of costly furniture.

Palal (pā'lăl, **he judges),** son of Uzai who helped in repairing the Jerusalem walls (Neh. 3:25).

Palestine (păl'ĕs-tīn). The name is derived from Philistia, an area along the S seacoast occupied by the Philistines (Ps. 60:8); original name was Canaan (Gen. 12:5); after the conquest it came to be known as Israel (I Sam. 13:19), and in the Greco-Roman period, Judea. The land was c. 70 miles wide and 150 miles long, from the Lebanon mts. in the N to Beersheba in the S. The area W of the Jordan was 6,000 miles; E of the Jordan, 4,000 miles. In the N, from Acco to the Sea of Galilee, the distance is 28 miles. From Gaza to the Dead Sea in the S the distance is 54 miles. The land is divided into five parts: the Plain of Sharon and the Philistine Plain along the coast; adjoining it, the Shepheleh, or foothills region; then the central mt. range; after that the Jordan valley; and E of the Jordan the Transjordan plateau. The varied configuration of Palestine produces a great variety of climate. The Maritime Plain has an annual average temperature of 57 degrees at Joppa; Jerusalem averages 63 degrees; while Jericho and the Dead Sea area have a tropical climate. As a result, plants and animals of varied latitudes may be found. The winter season, from Nov. to April, is mild and rainy; the summer season, from May to October, is hot and dry. Before the conquest the land was inhabited by Canaanites, Amorites, Hittites, Horites, and Amalekites. These were conquered by Joshua, judges, and kings. The kingdom was split in 931 B.C.; the N kingdom was taken into captivity by the Assyrians in 722 B.C.; the S kingdom by the Babylonians in 587 B.C. From 587 B.C. to the time of the Maccabees the land was under foreign rule by the Babylonians, Persians, Alexander the Great, Egyptians, and Syrians. In 63 B.C. the Maccabees lost control of the land to the Romans, who held it until the time of Mohammed. In NT times Palestine W of the Jordan was divided into Galilee, Samaria, and Judea; and E of the Jordan into the Decapolis and Perea.

Pallu, Palluite (păl'ū, păl'ū-īt, **distinguished, a descendant of Pallu),** Reuben's second son (Gen. 46:9). (See also Exod. 6:14; Num. 26:5, 8; I Chron. 5:3). He was the founder of the Palluites (Num. 26:5).

Palmer Worm, means "caterpillar," but in the Heb. text probably a kind of locust (Joel 1:4; 2:25; Amos 4:9).

Palm Tree (See Plants)

Palmyra (See Tadmor)

Palsy (See Diseases)

Palti (păl'tī, **delivered).** 1. One of the 12 spies, from the tribe of Benjamin (Num. 13:9). Once Phalti in KJV (I Sam. 25:44). 2. The man to whom Saul gave Michal, David's wife (I Sam. 25:44).

Paltiel (păl'tĭ-ĕl, **God delivers).** 1. The son of Azzan from the tribe of Issachar (Num. 34:26). 2. Once Phaltiel in KJV (II Sam. 3:15), the same as Palti 2.

Paltite (păl'tīt, **delivered),** the Gentile name of Helez, one of David's valiant men. Called the Pelonite (I Chron. 11:27; 27:10). Same as Palti.

Pamphylia (păm-fĭl'ĭ-ȧ). A small Roman province of southern Asia Minor extending along the Mediterranean coast 75 miles and 30 miles inland to the Taurus Mountains, at the time of St. Paul. The tiny country is first mentioned in the NT in Acts 2:10 where it is said that some of the people at Pentecost were from Phrygia and Pamphylia. The Apostle Paul visited the territory on his first missionary journey when he preached at Perga, its chief city (Acts 13:13; 14:24). It is said that most of the inhabitants of Pamphylia were backward and illiterate. Christianity never flourished there as in other places of Asia Minor.

Pannag (păn'ăg), one of the articles of trade between Judah and Israel (Ezek. 27:17).

Pap (păp, **bulging),** obsolete English word, that has been replaced by the word "breast" (Luke 11:27; Rev. 1:13).

Paper (See Papyrus, Writing)

Paphos (pā'fŏs), the capital city of Roman Cyprus, located at the extreme W end of this large island. The Paphos of the Bible is really New Paphos, a Roman city rebuilt by Au-

Above: Bedouin women carrying bundles of payrus. © MPS
Below: Bedouin women weaving papyrus mats for tents or dwellings. © MPS

gustus; the old Greek city of Paphos, dedicated to the worship of Aphrodite, lay ten miles to the S. In New Paphos Paul and Barnabas encountered the wiles of the Jewish sorcerer Elymas in the court of Sergius Paulus, the Roman governor. Paul's miracle of blinding the magician led to the conversion of Paulus (Acts 13:6-13). Now known as Baffa.

Papyrus (på-pī'rŭs), a plant-like reed or rush which grows in swamps and along rivers or lakes, often to the height of 12 feet with beautiful flowers at the top. The stalk is triangular in shape, something like a giant celery stalk. In ancient times it was found mainly along the Nile in Egypt but was also known in Palestine. For commercial use the stalk was cut into sections about a foot long and these pieces were then sliced lengthwise into thin strips which were shaped and squared and laid edge to edge to form a larger piece.

The manufacture of papyrus was a flourishing business in Egypt, where baskets, sandals, boats and other articles were made of it. It was not unknown among the Hebrews (Job 8:11) and some believe that the ark of Moses was made of papyrus (Exod. 2:3). But the most common use of the product was for writing material, so much so that "papyrus" became the name for writing paper. The art of making papyrus goes back to 2,000 B.C. and it was the common writing material in the Greek and Roman worlds from 500 B.C. until A.D. 400, when vellum largely replaced it. There is little doubt that the New Testament books were written on papyrus (pl. **papyri**). The material was also called **chartes** in Greek and John no doubt wrote his Second Epistle on such paper (II John 12). For long books (rolls or scrolls) many pieces of papyrus were glued together and rolled up. Such a roll was called **biblos** or **biblion** from which our word Bible is derived (cf. II Tim. 4:13; Rev. 10:10; Ezek. 2:9-10). The width of the roll varied from three to twelve inches and sometimes the roll got to be as long as 25 feet. Luke's Gospel is estimated at 30 feet, but II Thessalonians may have been only 18 inches long and short letters like **Jude** or **Philemon** were perhaps written on a single small sheet. The writer wrote in columns evenly spaced along the length of the roll and the reader read one column at a time, unrolling with one hand and rolling up with the other.

Papyrus, however, becomes brittle with age and easily decays, especially when damp. This is why the autographs of the New Testament writings have perished. They may also have been literally read to pieces and during persecution were deliberately destroyed. But thousands of ancient papyri have been found in the dry sands of Egypt and elsewhere.

Parable (păr'å-b'l, **likeness),** a comparison of two objects for the purpose of teaching.

Although the word properly belongs to the NT, being found there 46 times, it does occur 15 times in the OT. Sometimes it is a proverbial saying or byword (I Sam. 10:12; 24:14). In Numbers it is seen more as a prophetic figurative discourse (Num. 23:7, 18, 24). Ezekiel employs the word much as one would today with the idea of similitude or parable (Ezek. 17:2; 21:5; 24:3). Several writers treat the word as a poem (Num. 21:27-30; I Kings 5:12; Pss. 49:5; 78:2). The writer of the Proverbs thinks of it as a sentence that contains ethical wisdom (Prov. 10:1; 25:1). Finally it is associated with the riddle or dark saying (Ps. 49:4; Ezek. 17:2; 20:4-9).

There are a number of English words similar in meaning to the parable, and probably no one has been more definite and clear in distinguishing between these than Trench. Trench summarizes thus: "The parable differs from the fable, moving as it does in a spiritual world, and never transgressing the actual order of things natural — from the mythus, there being in the latter an unconscious blending of the deeper meaning with the outward symbol, the two remaining separate and separable in the parable — from the proverb, inasmuch as it is longer carried out, and not merely accidentally and occasionally, but necessarily figurative — from the allegory comparing as it does one thing with another, at the same time preserving them apart as an inner and outer, not transferring, as does the allegory, the properties and qualities and relations of one **to the other.**

While Christ did not invent the

A scene illustrative of the parable of "The lost sheep." © *MPS*
Inset: The parable of the day laborers. © *SPF*

parable, it is significant that He is the only one who used them in the NT. At one time in His ministry it was His only method in speaking to the masses (Matt. 13:34). It is interesting to note when Christ began to use this methodology. So abrupt was the change in His form of teaching that His disciples asked Him why He did this (Matt. 13:10). In His reply one notes the value of this method of instruction. It was an effective method of revealing truth to the spiritual and ready mind and at the same time of concealing it from others (Matt. 13:11). Christ came as Israel's King and only after they had rejected Him did He employ this form of imparting spiritual truth. Those who had rejected Him were not to know the "mysteries of the kingdom of heaven" (Matt. 13:11).

The following classification of parables is adapted from A.B. Bruce, **The Parabolic Teaching of Christ,** London: 1904, pp. 8ff:

I. Didactic Parables

A. Nature and Development of the Kingdom:
1. The Sower (Matt. 13:3-8; Mark 4:4-8; Luke 8:5-8)
2. The Tares (Matt. 13:24-30)
3. The Mustard Seed (Matt. 13:31, 32; Mark 4:3-32; Luke 13:18, 19)
4. The Leaven (Matt. 13:33; Luke 13:20, 21)
5. The Hidden Treasure (Matt. 13:44)
6. The Pearl of Great Price (Matt. 13:45, 46)
7. The Drag Net (Matt. 13:47-50)
8. The Blade, the Ear, and the Full Corn (Mark 4:26-29)

B. Service and Rewards:
1. The Laborers in the Vineyard (Matt. 20:1-16)
2. The Talents (Matt. 25:14-30)
3. The Pounds (Luke 19:11-27)
4. The Unprofitable Servants (Luke 17:7-10)

C. Prayer:
1. The Friend at Midnight (Luke 11:5-8)
2. The Unjust Judge (Luke 18:1-8)

D. Love for Neighbor:
1. The Good Samaritan (Luke 10:30-37)

E. Humility:
1. The Lowest Seat at the Feast (Luke 14:7-11)
2. The Pharisee and the Publican (Luke 18:9-14)

F. Worldly Wealth:
1. The Unjust Steward (Luke 16:1-9)
2. The Rich Fool (Luke 12:16-21)
3. The Great Supper (Luke 14:15-24)

II. Evangelic Parables

A. God's Love for the Lost:
1. The Lost Sheep (Matt. 18:12-14; Luke 15:3-7)
2. The Lost Coin (Luke 15:8-10)
3. The Lost Son (Luke 15:11-32)

B. Gratitude of the Redeemed:
1. The Two Debtors (Luke 7:41-43)

III. Prophetic and Judicial Parables

A. Watchfulness for Christ's Return:
1. The Ten Virgins (Matt. 25:1-13)
2. The Faithful and Unfaithful Servants (Matt. 24:45-51; Luke 12:42-48)
3. The Watchful Porter (Mark 13:34-37)

B. Judgment on Israel and Within the Kingdom:
1. The Two Sons (Matt. 21:28-32)
2. The Wicked Husbandmen (Matt. 21:33-34; Mark 12:1-12; Luke 20:9-18)
3. The Barren Fig Tree (Luke 13:6-9)
4. The Marriage Feast of the King's Son (Matt. 22:1-14)
5. The Unforgiving Servant (Matt. 18:23-25)

Paraclete (păr'ȧ-klēt, **advocate),** one who pleads another's cause. It is used by Christ of the Holy Spirit in John's Gospel (14:16, 26; 15:26; 16:7) and of Christ in I John 2:1. The rendering of the word in ERV is **Comforter** in the Gospel, and **Advocate** in the Epistle.

Paradise (păr'ȧ-dīz, **park),** a word of Persian origin, found only three times in Scripture (Luke 23:43; II Cor. 12:4; Rev. 2:7), referring in each case to heaven. There was a similar word in the Hebrew OT, **parades,** translated **forest** or **orchard** (Neh. 2:8; Eccl. 2:5; S. of Sol. 4:13).

The LXX uses the word 46 times and there it is applied to quite a wide category of places: Adamic Eden (Gen. 2:15; 3:23); of the well watered plains of the Jordan that Lot envisioned (Gen. 13:10). Since it was used to describe gardens of beauty and splendor, one is not surprised to see the NT begin to use the term to refer to the place of spiritual bliss (Luke 23:43).

The exact location of paradise is uncertain. Paul uses it in II Cor. 12:4 and identifies it with the third heaven. Ecclesiasticus 44:16 identifies paradise with heaven into which Enoch was translated. Christ's single use of the term seems to establish its location best for the believer, for He uses it as comfort for the dying thief.

Parah (pā′rȧ, **heifer),** a city in Benjamin (Josh. 18:23) a short distance NE of Jerusalem.

Parallelism, a characteristic of OT Hebrew verse, which has neither rhyme nor meter, but parallelism—the repetition in successive phrases of similar or contrasting ideas. Four forms are most common: synonymous (Ps. 36:5), antithetic (Ps. 20:8), synthetic (Job. 11:18), and climactic (Ps. 29:1).

Paralysis (See Diseases)

Paralytic (See Diseases)

Paramour (păr′ȧ-mōōr, **a concubine),** a term used in Ezekiel 23:20 of a male lover, but rendered elsewhere by **concubine.**

Paran (pā′răn, **ornamental),** a wilderness area first refered to in Genesis 14:6 as "El-Paran." Its boundaries are uncertain; it lies in the central area of the Sinaitic Peninsula. It was the area in which Ishmael lived (Gen. 21:21). On two occasions after the Israelites left Mt. Sinai they camped in this wilderness (Num. 10:12; 12:16).

Parbar (pȧr′bȧr, **suburb),** a Persian word referring to some building on the W side of the temple area (I Chron. 26:18; II Kings 23:11).

Parched Ground, a phrase meaning **mirage** used only once in the Scriptures (Isa. 35:7).

Parchment (See Writing)

Pardon, distinctively an OT word and if all its forms are included it occurs only 20 times. However, it is so closely related to forgiveness and justification that the three are often taken together. The divine pardon offered to the sinner stands in sharp contrast to human pardon. God demands a righteous ground for His pardoning of the sinner, that can be found only in the atoning work of Christ at Calvary. Pardon is one aspect of salvation. Some sins could not be pardoned (I Sam. 15:25-26; II Kings 24:4), but for the one who met God's conditions pardon was offered in abundance (Isa. 55:7).

Parent, a distinctly NT word. Although our English word does not occur in the OT, there is much instruction there about the parent-child relation. Children were to honor their parents (Exod. 20:12) and obey and reverence them (Lev. 19:3; Deut. 5:16). The same high regard for parents is expected of children in the NT (Eph. 6:1; Col. 3:20). Parents were expected on the other hand to love their children, care and provide for them and not to provoke them to wrath (II Cor. 12:14; Eph. 6:4; Col. 3:21).

Parental Blessings, very important in OT times. Blessings from godly parents were prophetic of a child's future and assured him of success (Gen. 27:4, 12, 27-29).

Parmashta (pȧr-măsh′tȧ, **the very first),** son of Haman slain by the Jews (Esth. 9:9).

Parmenas (pȧr′mē-năs, **constant),** one of the seven chosen to care for the daily distribution to the poor (Acts 6:5).

Parnach (pȧr′năk), father of Elizaphan the prince of Zebulun (Num. 34:25).

Parosh (pā′rŏsh, **a flea),** one whose descendants returned to Babylon under Zerubbabel (Ezra 2:3; Neh. 7:8). **Pharosh** in KJV cf. Ezra 8:3.

Parousia (pă-rōō′sĭ-ȧ, **presence, coming),** a word most frequently used in the NT of our Lord's return, and describes both the rapture and the return of Christ to the earth (I Cor. 15:23; I Thess. 4:15; Matt. 24:3; I Thess. 3:13; II Pet. 1:16). Used by false cults to express the coming of a hidden divinity and, on the other hand, the official term for the visit of a person of high rank.

Parshandatha (pȧr′shăn-dā′thȧ, **inquisitive),** the eldest of Haman's sons (Esth. 9:7).

Parthians (pȧr′thĭ-ănz). Luke's geographical list of the people who were in Jerusalem on the day of Pentecost (Acts 2:9) is headed by "Parthians and Medes." By "Parthians" Luke no doubt meant all the Jews and proselytes who lived in the old Parthian Empire to the E, known today as Iran. The earliest dispersion of the ten tribes took place in the eastern countries. Later they were augmented by immigration and colonization so that by the first century A.D. the number of Jews in the eastern territories ran into millions. Known for their prowess in war, instead of the arts and sciences, they never developed a literature of their own. But it is certain that the apostles of our Lord preached the Gospel among them.

Partition, Middle Wall of. Christ has broken down the "middle wall of partition" (Eph. 2:14) which divided Jews and Gentiles, and has made of the two one new man. Paul probably has in mind a literal wall as a tangible symbol of the division between Jews and Gentiles—the wall in the temple area in Jerusalem separating the court of the Gentiles from the courts into which only Jews might enter. On this wall was a notice in Greek and Latin warning Gentiles to keep out on pain of death. Paul himself almost lost his life in the temple enclosure when at the end of his third missionary journey his Jewish enemies accused him of bringing Trophimus the Ephesian past this barrier in the temple (Acts 21:29)

Partridge (See Birds)

Paruah (pȧ-rōō′ȧ, **blooming),** father of Jehoshaphat employed by Solomon (I Kings 4:17).

Parvaim (pȧr-vā′ĭm), a place mentioned from which Solomon obtained gold for the temple (II Chron. 3:6).

Pasach (pā′săk, **to divide),** the son of Japhet who descended from Asher (I Chron. 7:33).

Pasdammim (păs′dăm′ĭm, **place of bloodshed),** a place in Judah of encounter between David and the Philistines (I Chron. 11:13). Called "Ephesdammim" in I Sam. 17:1.

Paseah (pȧ-sē′ȧ, **lame).** 1. A son of Eshton (I Chron. 4:12). 2. The head of a family of Nethinim (Ezra 2:49; Neh. 7:51), one of whose descendants helped in the resoration (Neh. 3:6).

Pashur (păsh′hêr). 1. A priest, the son of Immer (Jer. 20:1-6), the "chief governor" in the Lord's house. Angered at the prophecies of Jeremiah, he placed him in stocks located near the house of the Lord. 2. The priestly son of Melchiah who was one of the chief court princes during Zedekiah's reign and joined others in seeking to have Jeremiah put to death (Jer. 21:1; 38:1, 4). Probably the same person referred to in I Chron. 9:12; Ezra 2:38; Neh. 7:41; 10:3; and 11:12. 3. The father of Gedaliah mentioned in Jeremiah 38:1 who aided in Jeremiah's imprisonment.

Passage, may refer to the ford of a river (Gen. 32:23), a mountain pass (I Sam. 13:23), or a crossing (Josh. 22:11).

Passion of Christ (See Christ, Jesus)

Passover, Feast of (See Feasts)

Pastoral Epistles. A common title for I and II Timothy and Titus, which were written by the apostle Paul to his special envoys sent on specific missions in accordance with the needs of the hour. I Timothy was written to Timothy at Ephesus while Paul was still traveling in the coastal regions of the Aegean Sea; Titus was written to Titus in Crete, probably from Nicopolis or some other city in Macedonia; II Timothy, from Rome toward the end of the second imprisonment. The epistles concern church organization and discipline, including such matters as the appointment of bishops and deacons, the opposition of heretical or rebellious members, and the provision for maintenance of doctrinal purity.

The authorship of these epistles has been disputed because of differences in vocabulary and style from the other epistles ascribed to Paul, and because their references to his travels do not accord with the itineraries described in Acts. The differences though real, have been exaggerated, and can be explained on the basis of a change of time, subject-matter, and destination. These are letters written by an old man to his understudies and successors at the close of his career, and for churches that have passed the pioneering stage. The historical references can be fitted into Paul's biography if he were released from the first imprisonment mentioned in Acts, and if he resumed traveling before his final imprisonment and execution. There is no theological discrepancy between the Pastorals and the other epistles, for while these emphasize good works, they emphasize also salvation by faith (Titus 3:5).

Background: Released from the first imprisonment, Paul left Titus on Crete to organize the churches (Titus 1:5) and went to Ephesus, where he stationed Timothy (I Tim. 1:3, 4). Proceeding to Macedonia, he wrote to Timothy and Titus. Evidently Paul had visited the Ionian cities just before his last arrest, for he mentions Troas, Corinth, and Miletus (II Tim. 4:13, 20). He had been deserted by most of his friends (4:10, 11) and had already stood trial once (4:16).

Outlines: I Timothy: 1. Personal Testimony, 1:1-20; 2. Official Regulations, 2:1-4:5; 3. Administrative Coun-

On the Island of Patmos, a view from the monastery. © RTHPL

sel, 4:6-6:21. Titus: Church Administration, 1:1-16; 2. Individual Conduct, 2:1-3:8; Personal Advice, 3:9-15. II Timothy: 1. Memories of the Past, 1: 1-18; 2. Mandate for the Future, 2:1-26; 3. Menace of Apostasy, 3:1-17; 4. Memoranda for Action, 4:1-22.

Patara (păt'à-rà), an ancient seaport of Lycia near the mouth of the Xanthus. The trade of the river-valley and its position on the Asia Minor coast gave the port its importance. It was convenient for ships running E before the prevailing autumn wind for Phoenicia or Egypt. Paul made for Tyre in one stage from Patara (Acts 21:1, 2).

Pathros (păth'rŏs), mentioned five times in the OT prophets (Isa. 11:11; Jer. 44: 1 and 15; Ezek. 29:14; 30:14) in connection with the repatriation of Jewish remnants. Pathros was Upper Egypt, the Egyptian "Pteres" or "Southland," extending from S of Memphis to the First Cataract. The division corresponds to two ancient kingdoms.

Pathruism (păth-rōō'sĭm, **an inhabitant of Pathros**), Egyptians who, it is believed, came from Pathros, from which their name is derived. They are descended from Mizraim (Gen. 10:13f; I Chron. 1:11f).

Patience. Two Greek words are translated by our English word **patience,** but they are not exactly synonymous in meaning. One is the quality of endurance under trials. It is mainly an attitude of heart with respect to things. The other word, **longsuffering,** is an attitude with respect to people. Longsuffering is listed in Galatians 5:22 as a fruit of the Spirit. Patience is a virtue that God prizes highly in man and seems to be best developed under trials (James 1:3-4; 5:11). Both terms are used of God (Rom. 2:4; 15:5; I Pet. 3:20).

Patmos, a tiny wind-swept island of the Sporades group, lying off the coast of Asia Minor in the Aegean Sea about 28 miles S of Samos. Only 25 square miles in area, it was one of the many isolated places to which the Romans banished their exiles, and according to tradition the Emperor Domitian banished the Apostle John to this lonely place from Ephesus in A.D. 95 (Rev. 1:9). During the estimated 18 months spent there, he received the visions of the Lord now recorded in **The Revelation.**

Patriarchs, Patriarchal Age (patriárches, the father of a family, tribe, or **race)**, a name given in the NT to those who founded the Hebrew race and nation. In the NT it is applied to Abraham (Heb. 7:4), the sons of Jacob (Acts 7:8, 9), and David (Acts 2:29). The term is now commonly used to refer to the persons whose names appear in the genealogies and covenant-histories before the time of Moses (Gen. 5, 11, histories of Noah, Abraham, Isaac, Jacob, etc.). In the patriarchal system the government of a clan was the right of the eldest lineal male. The patriarchal head was the priest of his own household.

Patrobas (păt'rō-bàs), a Roman Christian to whom Paul sent greetings (Rom. 16:14).

Pau (pā'ū, **bleating**), the capital city of king Hadar of Edom (Gen. 36:39); written Pai in I Chron. 1:50.

Paul (pôl, **little**), the great apostle to the Gentiles. The main Biblical source for the life of Paul is The Acts of the Apostles, with important supplemental information from the Pauline Epistles. Allusions in the epistles make it clear that many events in his checkered and stirring career are unrecorded (cf. II Cor. 11:24-28).

His Hebrew name was Saul and he is always so designated in Acts until his clash with Bar-Jesus at Paphos, where Luke writes, "But Saul, who is also **called** Paul" (13:9). Thereafter in Acts he is always called Paul. As a Roman citizen he doubtless bore both names from youth. His double name is implied in Luke's statement, "Saul, the one also Paul" **(Saulos ho kai Paulos).** Three elements of the world's life of that day, Greek culture, Roman citizenship, and Hebrew religion met in the apostle to the Gentiles. Paul was born near the beginning of the first century in the busy Graeco-Roman city of Tarsus, located at the NE corner of the Mediterranean Sea. Proud of the distinction and advantages conferred on him, by his Roman citizenship, Paul knew how to use that citizenship as a shield against injustice from local magistrates and to enhance the status of the Christian faith. His Gentile connections greatly aided him in bridging the chasm between the Gentile and the Jew. But of central significance was his strong Jewish heritage, being fundamental to all he was and became. He was never ashamed to acknowledge himself a Jew (Acts 21:

39; 22:3), was justly proud of his Jewish background (II Cor. 11:22), and retained a deep and abiding love for his brethren according to the flesh (Rom. 9:1-2; 10:1). Becoming a Christian meant no conscious departure on his part from the religious hopes of his people as embodied in the OT Scriptures (Acts 24:14-16; 26:6-7). This racial affinity with the Jews enabled Paul with great profit to begin his missionary labors in each city in the synagogue, for there he had the best prepared audience.

Born of purest Jewish blood (Phil. 3:5), the son of a Pharisee (Acts 23:6), Saul was cradled in orthodox Judaism. At the proper age, perhaps 13, he was sent to Jerusalem and completed his studies under the famous Gamaliel (Acts 22:3; 26:4-5).

At his first appearance in Acts as "a young man" (7:58), probably at least 30 years old, he was already an acknowledged leader in Judaism. His active opposition to Christianity marked him as the natural leader of the persecution that arose upon the death of Stephen (7:58-8:3; 9:1-2). The persecutions described in 26:10-11 indicate his fanatical devotion to Judaism. He was convinced that Christians were heretics and that the honor of Jehovah demanded their extermination (26:9). He acted in undoubting unbelief (I Tim. 1:13). The spread of Christians to foreign cities only increased his fury against them, causing him to extend the scope of his activities. As the persecutor, armed with authority from the high priest, was approaching Damascus, the transforming crisis in his life occurred. Repeatedly in his epistles Paul refers to it as the work of divine grace and power, transforming him and commissioning him as Christ's messenger (I Cor. 9:16-17; 15:10; Gal. 1:15-16; Eph. 3:7-9; I Tim. 1:12-16). The three accounts in Acts of the conversion are controlled by the immediate purpose of the narrator and supplement each other. Luke's own account (chap. 9) is historical, relating the event objectively, while the two accounts by Paul (chaps. 22, 26) stress those aspects appropriate to his immediate endeavor.

When the supernatural Being arresting him identified Himself as "Jesus whom thou persecutest," Saul at once saw the error of his way and surrendered instantaneously and completely. The three days of fasting in blindness were days of agonizing heartsearching and further dealing with the Lord. The ministry of Ananias of Damascus consummated the conversion experience, unfolded to Saul the divine commission, and opened the door to him to the Christian fellowship at Damascus. Later in reviewing his former life Paul clearly recognized how God had been preparing him for his future work (Gal. 1:15-16).

The new convert at once proclaimed the deity and Messiahship of Jesus in the Jewish synagogues of Damascus, truths that had seized his soul (9:20-22). Since the purpose of his coming was no secret, this action caused consternation among the Jews. Paul's visit to Arabia, mentioned in Galatians 1:17, seems best placed between Acts 9:22 and 23. There is no hint that its purpose was to preach; rather it seems that he felt it necessary to retire to rethink his beliefs in the light of the new revelation that had come to him. The length of the stay is not certain, but Paul came out of Arabia with the essentials of his theology fixed.

Upon returning to Damascus, his aggressive preaching forced him to flee the murderous fury of the Jews (Acts 9:23-25; Gal. 1:17; II Cor. 11: 32-33). Three years after his conversion Saul returned to Jerusalem with the intention of becoming acquainted with Peter (Gal. 1:18). The Jerusalem believers regarded him with cold suspicion, but the good offices of Barnabas secured his acceptance among them (Acts 9:26-28). His bold witness to the Hellenistic Jews aroused bitter hostility and cut the visit to 15 days (Gal. 1:18). Instructed by the Lord in a vision to leave (Acts 22:17-21), he agreed to be sent home to Tarsus (Acts 9:30), where he remained in obscurity for some years. Galatians 1:21-23 implies that he did some evangelistic work there, but we have no further details. Some think that many of the events of II Corinthians 11:24-26 must be placed here.

The work of Gentile foreign missions was inaugurated by the church at Antioch under the direction of the Holy Spirit in the sending forth of "Barnabas and Saul" (13:1-3). **The first missionary journey,** begun apparently in the spring of A.D. 48, began with work among the Jews on Cyprus. Ef-

The house of Ananias, near Straight Street, in Damascus (Acts 9:11).

forts at Paphos to gain the attention of the proconsul, Sergius Paulus, encountered the determined opposition of the sorcerer Elymas. Saul publicly exposed his diabolical character and the swift judgment that fell upon Elymas caused the amazed proconsul to "believe" (13: 4-12). It was a signal victory of the Gospel.

After the events at Paphos Saul, henceforth called Paul in Acts, emerged as the recognized leader of the missionary party. Steps to carry the Gospel to untrodden regions were taken when the party sailed to Perga in Pamphylia on the southern shores of Asia Minor. Here their attendant, John Mark, cousin of Barnabas (Col. 4:10 A.S.V.), deserted them and returned to Jerusalem, an act which Paul regarded unjustified. Arriving at Pisidian Antioch, located in the province of Galatia, the missionaries found a ready opening in the Jewish synagogue. Jewish-inspired opposition forced the missionaries to depart for Iconium, SE of Antioch, where the results were duplicated and a flourishing church begun. Compelled to flee a threatened stoning at Iconium, the missionaries began work at Lystra, which was apparently without a synagogue. The healing of a congenital cripple caused a pagan attempt to offer sacrifices to the missionaries as gods in human form. Paul's horrified protest (14: 15-17), arresting the attempt, reveals his dealings with pagans who did not have the OT revelation. Timothy apparently was converted at this time. Fanatical agitators from Antioch and Iconium turned the disillusioned pagans against the missionaries and in the uproar Paul was stoned. Dragged out of the city, the unconscious apostle was left for dead, but as the disciples stood around him he regained consciousness, reentered the city, and the next day was able to make the trip to neighboring Derbe. After a fruitful and unmolested ministry there, the missionaries retraced their steps to instruct their converts and organize them into churches with responsible leaders (14:1-23). They returned to Syrian Antioch and reported how "God had opened a door of faith unto the Gentiles" (14:27). That is a summary of Paul's philosophy of Gentile missions, salvation solely through faith in Christ.

For the second missionary journey Paul and Barnabas separated because of their "sharp contention" concerning John Mark. Barnabas sailed to Cyprus with Mark, while Paul chose Silas and revisited the churches in Galatia (15: 36-41). At Lystra Paul added young Timothy to the missionary party, having circumcised him to remove obstacles for work among the Jews. Leaving Luke at Philippi, the missionaries next began an expository ministry in the synagogue at Thessalonica. With the synagogue soon closed to him, Paul apparently carried on a successful Gentile ministry there. A Jewish-instigated riot forced the missionaries to flee to Berea, where a fruitful ministry resulted among the "noble" Bereans. Later, in Athens, Paul preached in the synagogue and daily in the market. His appearing on "Mars' Hill" was not a formal trial. His memorable speech before the pagan philosophers (17:22-31) is a masterpiece of tact, insight, and condensation. The work at Corinth, a city of commerce, wealth, squalor and gross immorality, proved to be a definite success, lasting 18 months (18:1-17). After finding employment at his tent-making trade with Aquila and Priscilla, recently expelled from Rome, Paul preached in the Corinthian synagogue.

From Corinth Paul took Aquila and Priscilla with him as far as Ephesus, intending upon his return to continue the profitable partnership with them there. Refusing an invitation for further ministry in the Ephesian synagogue, Paul hurried to Judea. He apparently visited Jerusalem and then spent some time at Antioch (18:18-22).

Paul's departure from Antioch traditionally marks the beginning of the **third missionary journey.** It is convenient to retain the traditional designation, but it should be remembered that with the second journey Antioch ceased to be the center for Paul's activities.

Having strengthened the disciples in "the region of Galatia and Phrygia," Paul commenced a fruitful ministry at Ephesus, lasting nearly three years (19: 1-41; 20:31). While at Ephesus Paul inaugurated a collection among his Gentile churches for the saints in Judea (I Cor. 16:1-4). Since its delivery was to mark the close of his work in the E, Paul was making plans to visit Rome (Acts 19:21), intending from there to go to Spain (Rom. 15:22-29). First he took the collection to Jerusalem.

A tablet on Mars Hill, Athens, commemorating Paul's sermon there. LO

D. O. M.

The Mamertine Prison, in Rome, where both Paul and Peter were imprisoned. JFW

MAMERTINUM
LA PRIGIONE DEI SS. APOSTOLI
PIETRO E PAOLO
IL PIU ANTICO CARCERE DI ROMA
XXV SECOLI DI STORIA

A tablet in Latin marking the site of these events. JFW

Although cordially received at Jerusalem by James and the elders, Paul's presence created tension in the church because of reports that he taught Jews in the dispersion to forsake Moses. To neutralize these reports they suggested to Paul a plan to prove that he had no aversion to a voluntary keeping of the law. Always anxious to avoid offense, Paul agreed to their proposal. The act of conciliation apparently satisfied the Judean believers but was the cause of Paul's arrest. Certain Jews from Asia, seeing him in the temple, created a tumult by falsely charging him with defiling the temple. Rescued from death at the hands of the Jewish mob by the Roman chiliarch and some soldiers, Paul proved his love for the Jews by securing permission to address them from the castle steps. They gave silent attention until he mentioned his commission to the Gentiles, when the riot broke out anew. A scourging, ordered to force information out of him, was avoided by Paul's mention of his Roman citizenship. Efforts by the chiliarch the next day to gain further information about Paul before the Sanhedrin proved futile. That night the Lord appeared to the discouraged apostle, commended his efforts at witnessing, and assured him that he would go to Rome. Informed of a plot to murder Paul, the chiliarch sent Paul to Caesarea under a large protective guard (23:17-23:35). He appeared before Felix at Caesarea which made it clear that the charges against him were spurious but, unwilling to antagonize the Jews, Felix simply postponed a decision. Asked to expound the Christian faith before Felix and his Jewish wife, Drusilla, Paul courageously probed their consciences by preaching "of righteousness, and self-control, and the judgment to come" (24:1-27).

With the coming of the new governor, Festus, the Jewish leaders renewed their efforts to secure Paul's condemnation. When it became clear to Paul that he could not expect justice from the new governor, he used his right as a Roman citizen and appealed his case to Caesar, thereby removing it from the jurisdiction of the lower courts (25:1-12). When Herod Agrippa II and his sister Bernice came to visit the new governor, Festus, perplexed about Paul's case, presented the matter to Agrippa, an acknowledged expert in Jewish affairs. The next day before his royal audience Paul delivered a masterly exposition of his position and used the occasion to seek to win Agrippa to Christ. Uncomfortable under Paul's efforts, Agrippa terminated the meeting, but frankly declared Paul's innocence to the governor (25:13-26:32).

Paul was sent to Rome, perhaps in the autmun of A.D. 60, under the escort of a centurion named Julius. Luke and Aristarchus accompanied him. Luke's detailed account of the voyage has the minuteness, picturesqueness, and accuracy of an alert eye-witness. Adverse weather delayed the progress of the ship. At Myra they transferred to an Alexandrian grain ship bound for Italy. Futile efforts to reach commodious winter quarters at Phoenix caused the ship to be caught in a typhonic storm for 14 days, ending in total wreck on the island of Malta. After three months on Malta, the journey to Rome was completed in another Alexandrian grain ship. Paul's treatment in Rome was lenient; he lived in his own hired house with a soldier guarding him. Permitted to receive all who came, he was able to exercise an important ministry in Rome. The "Prison Epistles," Colossians, Philemon, Ephesians and Philippians, are abiding fruit of this period which afforded him opportunity to meditate and to write.

Acts leaves the question of Paul's release unanswered, but there is strong evidence for believing that he was released at the end of two years. After his release, perhaps in the spring of A.D. 63, Paul went east, visited Ephesus, stationing Timothy there when he left for Macedonia (I Tim. 1:3). He left Titus to complete missionary work on Crete, and in writing to him mentions plans to spend the winter at Nicopolis (1:5; 3:12). From Nicopolis he may have made the traditional visit to Spain, working there at the outbreak of the Neronian persecution in autumn of A.D. 64. II Timothy makes it clear that Paul is again a prisoner in Rome, kept in close confinement as a malefactor (1:16-17; 2:9). At his first appearing before the court he escaped immediate condemnation, but in writing to Timothy he has no hope of release (4:16-18, 6-8). He was executed at Rome in late A.D. 66 or early 67.

Physically, Paul did not present an imposing appearance, as is evident from II Corinthians 10:10. Tradition pictures him as being small of stature, having a decidedly Jewish physiognomy. That he possessed a rugged physical constitution seems plain from all the hardships and sufferings he underwent (II Cor. 11:23-27), as well as his ability, amid his spiritual anxieties, to earn his own living through manual labor. He endured more than most men could endure, yet he keenly felt his bodily frailty. Especially was he afflicted by "a thorn [or stake] in the flesh" (II Cor. 12:7). The exact nature of the affliction can only be conjectured; attempts at identification have varied widely. Whatever its precise nature, his feelings of weakness made him constantly dependent upon divine empowerment (II Chron. 12:10; Phil. 4:12-13).

Paulus, Sergius (pô'lŭs, sûr'jĭ-ŭs). When Paul and Barnabas visited Paphos, the capital of Cyprus, on their first missionary journey, they were called before Sergius Paulus, the Roman proconsul (AV, "deputy"), because this man of understanding "desired to hear the word of God" (Acts 13:4-13). When Elymas, his court magician, attempted to turn him against the Gospel, Paul through a miracle struck him with blindness. The incident so affected Sergius Paulus that he "believed, being astonished at the doctrine of the Lord" (Acts 13:12).

Pavement, The (paved with stones), the courtyard outside the Praetorium or palace in Jerusalem where Pilate passed public sentence on Jesus (John 19:13).

Pavilion (pȧ-vĭl'yŭn, [Ps. 27:5; Ps. 31:20], **booth, tent),** a covered place in which a person may be kept hid. It is used chiefly to symbolize God's favor and protection provided for His children (Ps. 18:11). To the eastern king's inner court or pavilion none has access except those to whom he gives permission.

Peace, a frequent word in both testaments used in a variety of ways. In the OT times it was the usual word of greeting (Gen. 29:6). It is used also throughout the Bible to indicate a spirit of tranquillity and freedom from either inward or outward disturbance (Num. 6:26; I Kings 4:24; Acts 9:31). When nations enjoyed this, it was regarded as a gift from God (Lev. 26:6; Ps. 29:11). Perhaps its most frequent use in both testaments is to denote that spiritual tranquillity which all can enjoy when through faith in Christ they are brought into a right relation with God (Rom. 5:1; Col. 1:20; Phil. 4:6-7). Christ came to provide peace on earth (Luke 2:14), but this will not be realized fully until He returns again to effect it in person (Isa. 9:6-7; 11:6-9; Mic. 4:3).

Peace Offering (See Offerings)

Peacock (See Birds)

Pearl. In the OT (Job 28:18, KJV), the RV and RSV have more correctly rendered the word "crystal." In the NT the word is used in several ways. It denotes the costly precious stone (I Tim. 2:9; Rev. 17:4). Pearls are accidental concretions formed within the bodies of certain mollusks, especially the **Avicula margaritifera** from the Indian Ocean and Persian Gulf.

The word has a figurative use in the NT (Matt. 7:6; 13:45-46).

Pedahel (pĕd'ȧ-hĕl, **God delivers),** a prince of Naphtali appointed by Moses to apportion Palestine (Num. 24:28).

Pedahzur (pē-dȧ'zêr, **the rock),** a prince of the tribe of Manasseh, "father of Gamaliel," appointed to aid in numbering the people (Num. 1:10; 2:20).

Pedaiah (pē-dā'yȧ, **Jehovah redeems).** 1. One from Rumah, father of Zedudah who was Josiah's wife and Jehoiakim's mother (II Kings 23:36). 2. Father of Zerubbabel, son of Jeconiah (I Chron. 3:18). 3. Ruler of western Manasseh under David (I Chron. 27:20). 4. One from the family of Parosh who aided in repairing the wall of Jerusalem (Neh. 3:25). 5. A Benjamite (Neh. 11:7). 6. Levite treasurer over the Lord's house (Neh. 13:13).

Peep (to chirp), the cry of a bird (Isa. 10:14) and the noise made by wizards uttering sounds that are supposed to come from the dead (Isa. 8:19).

Pekah (pē'kȧ, **to open),** the son of Remaliah the 18th king of Israel. In the 52nd year of Uzziah, he usurped the throne by murdering his predecessor, Pekahiah. He began to reign about 734 B.C. and reigned for 20 years (II Kings 15:27). He formed a league with the Gileadites to resist the encroachments of Assyria. To strengthen his position further, he allied himself with Rezin of Damascus against Jotham, king of Judah (II Kings 15:37-38). The godly character of Jotham (II Chron. 27) probably delayed the realization of this plot until Jotham's son, Ahaz, was on the throne. The details of this campaign are recorded in two places in the OT (II Kings 16; II Chron. 28).

Finally Pekah became subject to the Assyrian power (II Kings 15:28-29) and a short time later was murdered by Hoshea.

Pekahiah (pĕk'ȧ-hī'ȧ, Jehovah has opened), Israel's 17th king, the son of Menahem. Followed the practices of idolatry formulated by Jeroboam (II Kings 15:24). After a brief reign of but two years, he was brutally murdered by Pekah.

Pekod (pē'kŏd, **visitation),** a name applied to an Aramaean tribe living to the E and near the mouth of the Tigris (Jer. 50:21; Ezek. 23:23).

Pelaiah (pē-lā'yȧ, Jehovah is wonderful), Elioenai's son from Judah's royal house (I Chron. 3:24). This name was given also to the Levite who aided Ezra in explaining the law (Neh. 8:7) and later sealed the covenant with Nehemiah (Neh. 10:10).

Pelaliah (pĕl'ȧ-lī'ȧ, Jehovah has judged), priest, father of Jeroham and son of Amzi (Neh. 11:12).

Pelatiah (pĕl'ȧ-tī'ȧ, Jehovah has delivered). 1. Grandson of Zerubbabel (I Chron. 3:21). 2. Simeonite leader who helped Hezekiah (I Chron. 4:42). 3. One who sealed the covenant (Neh. 10:22). 4. Prince of Benaiah (Ezek. 11:1) who along wtih others devised iniquity and gave wicked counsel in Jerusalem (Ezek. 11:2). Ezekiel was instructed to prophesy against them and while he was doing so Pelatiah fell dead (Ezek. 11:13).

Peleg (pē'lĕg, **division),** one of the sons of Eber, brother of Joktan and the father of Rue (Gen. 10:25; 11:16-19; I Chron. 1:25). "In his days was the earth divided" (Gen. 10:25). This probably refers to the confounding of the language and the consequent scattering of the descendants of Noah (Gen. 11:1-9).

Pelet (pē'lĕt, **deliverance),** Jahdai's son (I Chron. 2:47); also one of Azmaveth's sons from the tribe of Benjamin who joined David at Ziklag (I Chron. 12:3).

Peleth (pē'lĕth, **swiftness).** 1. The father of On, who became a part of the conspiracy against Moses and Aaron (Num. 16:1). 2. A descendant of Jerahmeel through Onan (I Chron. 2:33).

Pelethites (pĕl'ē-thīts, **courier),** a group who along with the Cherethites formed David's bodyguard. Perhaps they were the ones who conveyed the king's messages to distant places.

Pelican (See Birds)

Pella (pĕl'ȧ), one of the towns of the district named Decapolis, or **Ten Cities,** by the Romans, which is mentioned in Matthew 4:25 and Mark 5:20; 7:31. Pella thus lay E of the Sea of Galilee in the mountains of Gilead.

Pelonite (pĕl'ō-nīt, **separates),** the title of two of David's mighty men, Helez and Ahijah (I Chron. 11:27, 36).

Pen (See Writing)

Pence (See Money)

Pendant (See Dress)

Peniel, Penuel (pē-nī'ĕl, pē-nū'ĕl, **face of God).** 1. The spot where Jacob wrestled with the angel of God (Gen. 32:24-32). 2. Hur's son, the father of Gedor (I Chron. 4:4). 3. One of Shashah's sons (I Chron. 8:25).

Peninnah (pē-nĭn'ȧ, **coral),** one of Elkanah's wives, who bore children and taunted Hannah (I Sam. 1:2-7) while she was childless.

Penknife, a small knife used to sharpen pens or writing reeds (Jer. 36:23).

Penny (See Money)

Pentateuch, The (pĕn'tȧ-tōōk, **law or teaching).** This is composed of five books: Genesis, Exodus, Leviticus, Numbers, and Deuteronomy. These books, whose canonicity has never been called into question by the Jews, Protestants, or Catholics head the list of the OT canon. As a literary unit they provide the background for the OT as well as the New.

Chronologically the Pentateuch covers the period of time from the creation to the end of the Mosaic era. Since the date for the creation of the universe is not given, it is impossible to ascertain the length of this entire era.

Genesis begins with an account of creation, but soon narrows its interest to the human race. Adam and Eve were entrusted with the responsibility of caring for the world about them, but forfeited their privilege through disobedience and sin. In subsequent generations all mankind became so wicked that the entire human race, except Noah and his family, was destroyed. When the new civilization degenerated, God chose to fulfill His promises of redemption through Abraham. From Adam to Abraham represents a long period of time for which the genealogical lists in Genesis 5 and 10 hardly serve as a time table.

The patriarchal era (Gen. 12-50), narrates the events of approximately four generations, namely those of

Abraham, Isaac, Jacob, and Joseph. After the opening verses of Exodus the rest of the Pentateuch is chonologically confined to the lifetime of Moses. Consequently the deliverance of Israel from Egypt and their preparation for entrance into the land of Canaan is the prevailing theme. The historical core of these books is briefly outlined as follows:

Exodus 1-19, From Egypt to Mount Sinai

Exodus 19-Numbers 10, Encampment at Mount Sinai (approximately 1 year)

Numbers 10-21, Wilderness Wanderings (approximately 38 years)

Numbers 22-Deuteronomy 34, Encampment before Canaan (approximately one year).

The Mosaic law was given at Mount Sinai. For nearly a year Israel was carefully instructed in the law and the covenant. Moses reviewed the law for the younger generation. This review, plus timely instructions for the occupation of Palestine, is summarized in the Book of Deuteronomy. For study purposes the Pentateuch lends itself to the following analysis:

- I. The era of beginnings, Genesis 1:1-11:32.
  - A. The account of creation, 1:1-2:25.
  - B. Man's fall and its consequences, 3:1-6:10.
  - C. The flood: God's judgment on man, 6:11-8:19.
  - D. Man's new beginning, 8:20-11:32.
- II. The patriarchal period, 12:1-50:26.
  - A. The life of Abraham, 12:1-25:18.
  - B. Isaac and Jacob, 25:19-36:43.
  - C. Joseph, 37:1-50:26.
- III. Emancipation of Israel, Exodus 1:1-19:2.
  - A. Israel freed from slavery, 1:1-13:19.
  - B. From Egypt to Mt. Sinai, 13:20-19:2.
- IV. The religion of Israel, Exodus 19:3-Leviticus 27:34.
  - A. God's covenant with Israel, Exodus 19:3-24:8.
  - B. The place of worship, 24:9-40:38.
  - C. Instructions for holy living, Leviticus 1:1-27:34.
    1. The Offerings, 1:1-7:38.
    2. The priesthood, 8:1-10:20.
    3. Laws of purification, 11:1-15:33.
    4. Day of atonement, 16:1-34.
    5. Heathen customs forbidden, 17:1-18:30.
    6. Laws of holiness, 19:1-22:33.
    7. Feasts and seasons, 23:1-25:55.
    8. Conditions of God's blessings, 26:1-27:34.
- V. Organization of Israel, Numbers 1:1-12:10.
  - A. The numbering of Israel, 1:1-4:49.
  - B. Camp regulations, 5:1-6:21.
  - C. Religious life of Israel, 6:22-9:14.
  - D. Provisions for guidance, 9:15-10:10.
- VI. Wilderness wanderings, Numbers 10:11-22:1.
  - A. From Mt. Sinai to Kadesh, 10:11-12:16.
  - B. The Kadesh crisis, 13:1-14:45.
  - C. The years of wandering, 15:1-19:22.
  - D. From Kadesh to the Plains of Moab, 20:1-22:1.
- VII. Instructions for entering Canaan, 22:2-36:13.
  - A. Preservation of God's chosen people, 22:2-25:18.
  - B. Preparation for conquest, 26:1-33:49.
  - C. Anticipation of occupation, 33:50-36:13.
- VIII. Retrospect and prospect, Deuteronomy 1:1-34:12.
  - A. History and its significance, 1:1-4:43.
  - B. The law and its significance, 4:44-28:68.
  - C. Final preparation and farewell, 29:1-34:12.

The Pentateuch itself supports the view that Moses is essentially responsible for its authorship. References throughout the rest of the OT as well as the NT point to Moses as the author. Being personally involved as the deliverer and lawgiver of Israel, Moses was familiar with the developments as recorded in the last four books of the Pentateuch. Very likely he had many scribes to assist him in keeping a record of all the details that pertain to organization, geography, and history. Naturally it would have been his concern to leave a written copy of the law and a history of this unique experience of the Israelites before his departure. Especially was this in accord with his desire that they should carefully conform to the law in order that they might continually enjoy God's favor.

Pentecost (pĕn′tē-kŏst). The word derives from the Greek for "the fiftieth day." It was the Jewish Feast of Weeks (Exod. 34:22; Deut. 16:9-11), variously called the Feast of Harvest (Exod. 23:16), or the Day of First-Fruits (Num. 28:26), which fell on the 50th day after the Feast of the Passover. The exact method by which the date was computed is a matter of some controversy.

Originally, the festival was the time when, with appropriate ritual and ceremony, the first-fruits of the corn-harvest, the last Palestinian crop to ripen, were formally dedicated. The festival cannot therefore have antedated the settlement in Palestine. Leviticus 23 prescribes the sacred nature of the holiday, and lists the appropriate sacrifices. Numbers 28 appears to be a supplementary list, prescribing offerings apart from those connected with the preservation of the ritual loaves. It was the events of Acts 2 which transformed the Jewish festival into a Christian one. Some have seen a symbolic connection between the first-fruits of the ancient festival, and the "first-fruits" of the Christian dispensation. "Whitsunday" is therefore the 50th day after Easter Sunday. The name derives from the white garments of those seeking baptism at this festival, a practice of very ancient origin.

Peor (pē′ôr, **opening**). 1. The name given to the mountain in Moab to the top of which King Balak led Balaam that he might see and curse Israel (Num. 23:28). 2. In Numbers 25:18; 31:16 and Joshua 22:17 Peor is used four times as a contraction for Baal-Peor. 3. Moses twice uses the term (Num. 25:18; 31:16) to refer to the god of Baal-Peor.

Peraea (pĕ-rē′ȧ), name given by Josephus to the region E of the Jordan; known in the Gospels as "beyond Jordan" (Matt. 4:15, 25; Mark 3:7, 8); the word "Peraea" does not occur in the Bible.

Perazim, Mount (pĕr′ȧ-zĭm, **mount of breaches),** usually identified with Baal-perazim, where David won a victory over the Philistines (II Sam. 5:20; I Chron. 14:11).

Perdition (pêr-dĭ′shun, **perishing, destruction).** In each of the eight uses of the English word in the NT (John 17:12; Phil. 1:28; II Thess. 2:3; I Tim. 6:9; Heb. 10:39; II Pet. 3:7; Rev. 17:8, 11), the final state of the wicked is referred to. In popular usage men make this word a synonym for hell and eternal punishment.

Perdition, Son of, a phrase used to designate two men of the NT. Christ uses it in referring to Judas Iscariot (John 17:12). Paul uses the same title in II Thessalonians 2:3, applying it to the "man of sin" who is the Antichrist. It is derived from the custom among the Hebrews of noting a certain trait or characteristic in a person and then referring to him as the son of that trait.

Perea (See Peraea)

Peres (pē′rĕs, **to split),** one of the words that was written by the hand on the wall for Belshazzar and interpreted by Daniel (Dan. 5:1-29).

Peresh (pē′rĕsh, **dung),** Machir's son by his concubine, Maachah, the Aramite (I Chron. 7:14, 16).

Perez (pē′rĕz, **breach),** one of Judah's twin sons by his daughter-in-law, Tamar (Gen. 38:29). Also called "Pharez" (Gen. 46:12; Num. 26:20, 21).

Perez-uzza (pē′rĕz-ŭz′ȧ, **beach of Uzzah),** name of place where Uzzah was struck dead for touching the ark of God (II Sam. 6:8).

Perfection, Perfect. Basic meaning is close to the fundamental and etymological sense of the English word, "complete" or "finished." It is used for the ritually clean victim of sacrifice (Exod. 12:5), and for uprightness of character (Gen. 6:9; 17:1; Ps. 119:1). It is applied to the Law, and to God Himself. The NT suggests that perfection is the attainment of the end or aim of being, and is therefore a relative term to be understood within its context. Absolute perfection can therefore be an attribute of God alone. Hence the explanation of such apparent contradictions as Philippians 3:12 and 15. So, too, Matthew 5:48, command though it is, involves no impossibility. The Christian is enjoined to fulfill the functions of his being as God fulfills His, and the sermon in which the precept is embedded explains the mode and manner of such attainment. The concept of perfection which has been taught by some theologians and preachers has erred in neglecting the relativity of the term and such clear teaching as that of John (I John 1:8), James (3:2) and Paul (Phil. 3:12).

Perfume (Prov. 27:9). There are many passages in the Bible that indicate the fondness for and use of perfume in the Oriental countries. Perfumes had many uses in the Orient. In connection with the tabernacle worship, God revealed a special divine formula which could not be copied for personal use by the Hebrews apart from punishment (Exod. 30:7, 8, 34-38). These perfumes were prepared by men known as "apothecaries" (Exod. 30:35; Eccl. 10: 1).

Moses mentions one perfume to be made of pure myrrh, sweet cinnamon, sweet calamus, cassia and olive oil. It was to be used only as a holy anointing oil. Anyone who duplicated it would be cut off from his people (Exod. 30:22-33).

Hebrews used perfumes for embalming their dead (John 19:38-40); for burning with the dead (II Chron. 16: 14); for preparing a virgin to appear before the Persian king (Esth. 2:12-14); for preparing women for marriage (S. of Sol. 1:12-14).

In the hot eastern countries perfumes became a sanitary necessity. They were used both to cover up bad odors which abounded in the Orient and to make life more enjoyable for all concerned.

Quite a large number of scents were used in the compounding of these perfumes. Perhaps the most frequently mentioned are frankincense (S. of Sol. 3:6) and myrrh (Ps. 45:8).

Perga (pûr′gȧ), the chief city of old Pamphylia of Asia Minor located about 12 miles from Attalia on the River Cestris which formed an inland port. Paul and Barnabas passed through the city twice on the first missionary journey, both going and returning (Acts 13:13-14; 14:24-25). Here John Mark left the party and returned to Jerusalem. During Greek times a celebrated temple of Artemis, or Diana, was located in the vicinity which perhaps was the reason Christianity never flourished there as in other cities of Asia Minor.

Pergamum, Pergamos (pûr′gȧ-mŭm, pûr′gȧ-mŏs), city of Mysia in Asia Minor (Rev. 1:11; 2:12-17). Modern Bergama.

Perida (pē-rī′dȧ, **divided),** one of Solomon's servants (Neh. 7:57). "Peruda" in Ezra 2:55.

Perizzite (pâr′ĭ-zīt). References in the Pentateuch, Joshua, and Judges make it clear that the Perizzites were a pre-Israelitish tribe or racial group of Palestine (Gen. 13:7; 34:30; Exod. 3:8, 17; 23:23; 33:2; 34:11; Deut. 20:17; Josh. 3:10; 24:11; Judg. 1:4). Apart from these well-defined Biblical references, the Perizzites seem to have left no other marks on history.

Perjury (pêr′jêr-ē), closely related to several Biblical words such as **oath** or **punishment.** Oaths consisted of a promise made and an appeal to God for the ratification of it. Such oaths were considered binding promises, so that to break an oath was regarded as perjury as well as using falsehood under oath (Lev. 19:12; Ezek. 16:59).

Persecution (pêr′sĕ-qū′shŭn). Daniel and Jeremiah were persecuted. Systematic persecution of the Christians began with the Roman imperial government. Notably tolerant towards alien religious beliefs in general, the Romans clashed with the Christians over the formalities of Caesar-worship. Nero must be regarded as the first persecutor. In A.D. 64 (Tacitus, **Annals** 15:38-44) this emperor used the small Christian community as scapegoats for a disastrous fire in Rome and the charge of incendiarism which was popularly leveled against him. Domitian's execution of Glabrio and Flavius Clemens in A.D. 95, and the exile of Domitilla for "atheism," and "going astray after the customs of the Jews" (Dio Cassius 67:44), was probably anti-Christian action, an incident which strikingly reveals the vertical spread of Christianity by the end of the first century. Marcus Aurelius was guilty of a sharp persecution at Lyons (A.D. 117). Diocletian continued a now established policy of toleration until A.D. 303 when, under the influence of Galerius, he initiated the last short but savage period of persecution.

Persepolis (pēr-sĕp′ō-lĭs), capital of Persia, it lay 30 miles NE of modern Shiraz. It was founded by Darius I (521-486 B.C.). The whole complex of palaces and public buildings was fortified. Alexander the Great took Persepolis, and burned and looted it as an act of warfare designed to break Persian resistance, in 331 B.C. Persepolis is mentioned in II Maccabees 9:2 in connection with an attempted raid by Antiochus Epiphanes (215-163 B.C.), an outrage defeated by strong local resistance. The reference suggests that Persepolis was still a rich and powerful city a century and a half after Alexander's vandalism.

Perseverance (pûr-sĕ-vēr'ăns); the word is found only in Eph. 6:18, where it is used in connection with prayer. The theological doctrine of the perseverance of the saints holds that the truly regenerated cannot ever fall away from Christ so as to lose their salvation. Both Calvinists and Arminians seek support for their view in the Scriptures, both sides often using the same passages, but interpreting them differently.

Persia (pûr'zhȧ), geographically, Persia comprised the Iranian plateau, bounded by the Tigris valley on the W and S, the Indus valley on the E, and by the Armenian ranges and the Caspian Sea to the N, comprising c. one million square miles. Cyrus founded the empire by defeating Media and Babylonia, and it dominated Asia from 539 to 331 B.C. Cyrus the Great permitted the Jews to return from the Babylonian captivity (II Chron. 36:22, 23; Ezra 1); Darius I authorized the rebuilding of the temple (Ezra 6); Xerxes I was probably the Ahasuerus of the book of Esther; and Artaxerxes I permitted additional exiles to return (Ezra 7:8; Neh. 2:1-8).

Persis (pûr'sĭs, **Persian),** a Christian woman at Rome greeted by Paul (Rom. 16:12).

Peruda (See Perida)

Peshitta (pĕ-shēt'tȧ), the ancient Syriac (Aramaic) translation of the Bible. The OT was translated before the Christian era, no doubt by Jews who spoke Aramaic and lived in the countries E of Palestine. Syriac Christians rendered the NT during the early centuries of the Church, the standard version being that of Rabbula, bishop of Edessa in the fifth century. The Syriac Bible played an important role in the Christian missionary thrust into the countries of the Far East, including India.

Pestilence (pĕs'tĭlĕns), a word frequently found in the OT to refer to any fatal epidemic often coming as the result of divine judgment (Exod. 5:3; Jer. 14:12). The word is used in the NT only by Christ (Matt. 24:7; Luke 21:11).

Pestle (pĕs''l, **lifted),** an instrument made either of wood or stone, rounded at the ends and used to grind in a mortar (Prov. 27:22).

Peter (pē'têr, **rock),** the most prominent of the 12 apostles in the Gospels and an outstanding leader in the early days of the Christian Church. His original name was Simon, a common Greek name, or more properly Symeon (Acts 15:14), a popular Hebrew name. A native of Bethsaida (John 1:44), the son of a certain John (John 1:42 ASV; 21:15-17 ASV; Matt. 16:17), he received a normal elementary education. As a native of "Galilee of the Gentiles" he was able to converse in Greek, while his native Aramaic was marked with provincialisms of pronunciation and diction (Matt. 26:73). The evaluation by the Sanhedrin of Peter and John as "unlearned and ignorant men" (Acts 4:13) simply meant that they were unschooled in the rabbinical lore and were laymen. With his brother Andrew he followed the hardy occupation of a fisherman on the Sea of Galilee, being partners with Zebedee's sons, James and John (Luke 5:7). He was a married man (Mark 1:30; I Cor. 9:5) and at the time of Christ's Galilean ministry lived in Capernaum (Mark 1:21, 29).

Gospel period. Of the second period of his life, from his first encounter with Jesus until the ascension, the Gospels give a vivid picture. Simon attended the preaching ministry of John the Baptist at the Jordan and, like Andrew, probably became a personal disciple of John. When he was personally introduced to Jesus by his brother Andrew, Jesus on seeing him with prophetic insight remarked, "Thou art Simon the son of Jona: thou shalt be called Cephas" (John 1:42). That John translated the Aramaic **Kēphās** into Greek **Petros,** both meaning **rock,** indicates that it was not a proper name but rather a descriptive title (cf. "sons of thunder," Mark 3:17). The designation, afterwards more fully explained in its prophetic import (Matt. 16:18; Mark 3:16), came to be regarded as his personal name. (No other man in the NT bears the name Peter.) After a period of companionship with Jesus during His early Judean ministry (John 1:42-4:43),

The courtyard of the house of Caiaphas, where a monk looks at a plaque representing a cock crowing, in remembrance of Peter's denial of his Lord. © MPS

Peter resumed his ordinary employment.

With the commencement of Christ's Galilean ministry, Peter and Andrew, with James and John, were called by Jesus to full time association with Him to be trained as "fishers of men" (Mark 1:16-20; Luke 5:1-11). With the growth of the work, Jesus selected 12 of His followers to be His nearest companions for special training (Mark 3:13-19; Luke 6:12-16). In the lists of these 12 designated apostles (Luke 6:13), Peter is always named first (Mark 3:16-19; Luke 6:14-16; Matt. 10:2-4; Acts 1:13-14). His eminence among them was due to his being among the first chosen as well as his native aggressiveness as a natural leader. But the other disciples did not concede to Peter any authority over them, as is evident from their repeated arguments about greatness (Matt. 20-20-28; Mark 9:33-34; Luke 22:24-27). While He was with them, Jesus alone was recognized as their leader.

The development of an inner circle among the disciples is first seen when Jesus took Peter, James, and John with Him into the house of Jaírus (Mark 5:37; Luke 8:51). The three were further privileged to witness the transfiguration (Matt. 17:1; Mark 9:2; Luke 9:28) and the agony in the garden (Matt. 26:37; Mark 14:33). Even in this inner circle Peter usually stands in the foreground, but the Fourth Gospel indicates that his position of eminence was not exclusive.

Peter was the natural spokesman of the 12. When Christ's sermon on the Bread of Life produced a general defection among His followers, Peter spoke for the 12 in asserting their loyalty to Him (John 6:66-69). Again, at Caesarea Philippi, when Jesus asked the 12 their view of Him, Peter promptly replied, "Thou art the Christ, the Son of the living God" (Matt. 16:16). His confession of the Messiahship and Deity of our Lord expressed a divinely-given insight higher than the current view which regarded the Messiah only as a man exalted to the Messianic office (cf. Matt. 22:41-46). His confession elicited Christ's prompt commendation and the further assertion, "Thou art Peter, and upon this rock I will build my church" (Matt. 16:18). By his believing confession Peter has identified himself with Christ the true Rock (I Cor. 3:11; Isa. 28:16; I Pet. 2:4-5), thus fulfilling Christ's prediction concerning him (John 1:42). He has thus become a rock **(petros),** and upon "this rock" **(petra),** composed of Peter and the other apostles joined by faith to Christ the chief corner stone (Eph. 2:20), Jesus announces that He will build His triumphant church.

The third period in Peter's life began with the ascension of Jesus. In the early days of the Church (Acts 1-12), Peter appeared as the spokesman of the apostolic group, but there is no hint that he assumed any authority not also exercised by the other apostles. He suggested the choice of another to fill the place of Judas (1:15-26), preached the Spirit-empowered sermon on Pentecost to the assembled Jews (2:14-40), and with John healed the lame man, the first apostolic miracle to arouse persecution (3:1-4:21). He was used to expose the sin of Ananias and Sapphira (5:1-12), was held in high esteem by the people during the miracle ministry in the church that followed (5:12-16), and spoke for the 12 when arraigned before the Sanhedrin (5:27-41). With John he was sent to Samaria where, through the laying on of hands, the Holy Spirit fell on the Samaritan believers and Peter exposed the unworthy motives of Simon (8:14-24). During the persecution of the Church by Agrippa I in A.D. 44, Peter escaped death by a miraculous deliverance from prison (21:1-19).

With the opening of the door to the Gentiles and the spread of Christianity, Peter receded into the background and Paul became prominent as the apostle to the Gentiles. In the Acts narrative Peter is last mentioned in connection with the Jerusalem conference, where he championed the liberty of the Gentiles (15:6-29). The remaining NT references to Peter are scanty. Nothing much further is heard of Peter until the writing of the two epistles that bear his name, apparently written from Rome. A final NT reference to the closing years of Peter's life is found in John 21:18-19. John's interpretation of Christ's prediction makes it clear that the reference is to Peter's violent martyr death. Beyond this the NT is silent about him.

The character of Peter is one of the most vividly drawn and charming in the NT. His sheer humanness has made him one of the most beloved and winsome members of the apostolic band.

The roof of the house of Simon the Tanner in Jaffa, ancient Joppa, where Peter saw his vision. © *MPS*

He was eager, impulsive, energetic, self-confident, aggressive, and daring, but also unstable, fickle, weak, and cowardly. He was guided more by quick impulse than logical reasoning, and readily swayed from one extreme to the other. He was preeminently a man of action. His story exhibits the defects of his qualities as well as the tremendous capacities for good which he possessed. He was naturally forward and often rash, liable to instability and inconsistency, but his love for and associations with Christ moulded him into a man of stability, humility and courageous service for God, becoming one of the noble pillars (Gal. 2:9) of the Church.

Peter, First Epistle of, the keynote of the First Epistle of Peter is suffering, and the Christian method of meeting it. The writer endeavored to convey a message of hope to Christians who had been undergoing persecution, and who were succumbing to discouragement because they could find no redress. It contains a hortatory presentation of Christian truth, calculated to strengthen believers.

The internal structure reflects Peter's mind and life. The first main paragraph, "Blessed be the God and Father of our Lord Jesus Christ, who hath begotten us again unto a living hope by the resurrection of Jesus Christ from the dead" (1:3) expresses the joy which Peter felt after the forgiveness bestowed on him by the risen Christ after the denial. The injunction to "feed (shepherd) the flock of God" (5:2) is almost identical in language with Jesus' commission to him at the lake of Galilee (John 21:16). "Gird yourselves with humility" may be a reminiscence of the last supper, when Jesus girded Himself with a towel and washed the disciples' feet (John 13: 4, 5).

There are also some remarkable agreements between the vocabulary of I Peter and the speeches of Peter in Acts (I Pet. 1:17; Acts 10:34; I Pet. 1: 21; Acts 2:32; 10:40, 41; the quotation I Pet. 2:7, 8 with Acts 4:10, 11).

The epistle was directed to members of the Dispersion located in the northern Roman provinces of Asia Minor which Paul did not visit, and which may have been evangelized by Peter between the Council of Jerusalem (A.D. 48) and Nero's persecution at Rome (A.D. 64). I Peter bears traces of the influence of Paul's Epistle to the Romans and to the Ephesians in its structure and thought (cf. I Pet. 2:13; Rom. 13:1-4; I Pet. 2:18; Eph. 6:5; I Pet. 3:9; Rom. 12:17; I Pet. 5:5; Eph. 5:21) which would imply that it was written after A.D. 60. Probably I Peter was written about the year 64 when the status of Christians in the empire was very uncertain, and when persecution had already begun in Rome.

In general arrangement I Peter resembles closely the Pauline epistles, with a salutation, body, and conclusion. Its main subject is the Christian's behavior under the pressure of suffering, its key is the salvation which is to be revealed at the last time (1:5). The epistle may be outlined as follows:

I. Introduction, 1:1, 2
II. The Nature of Salvation, 1:3-12
III. The Experience of Salvation, 1:13-25
IV. The Obligations of Salvation, 2:1-10
V. The Ethics of Salvation, 2:11-3:12
VI. The Confidence of Salvation, 3:13-4:11
VII. The Behavior of the Saved Under Suffering, 4:12-5:11
VIII. Concluding Salutations, 5:12-14

Peter, Second Epistle of, is a general treatise, written to warn its readers of threatening apostasy. It contains a definite allusion to a preceding letter (3:1).

The reference to a previous letter sent to the same group (3:1) connects this document with I Peter, which was written to the Christians of northern Asia Minor. Whereas the first epistle was an attempt to encourage a church threatened with official persecution and repression, the second epistle dealt with the peril of apostasy, which was even a greater threat. An influx of conscienceless agitators who repudiated the lordship of Christ (2:1) and whose attitude was haughty (2:10), licentious (2:13), adulterous (2:14), greedy (2:14), bombastic (2:18), and libertine (2:19) seemed imminent. Knowing that he would not be spared to keep control of the situation, Peter was writing to forestall this calamity and to warn the church of its danger.

The key to this epistle is the word "know" or "knowledge," which occurs 16 times in the three chapters, six of which refer to the knowledge of Christ. This knowledge is not primarily academic, but is spiritual, arising from a growing experience of Christ (3:18). It produces peace and grace (1:2), fruitfulness (1:8), is the secret of freedom from defilement (2:20) and is the sphere of Christian growth (3:18). It may be that the false teachers were Gnostics, who stressed knowledge as the means of salvation, and that Peter sought to counteract their falsehoods by a positive presentation of true knowledge.

II Peter teaches definitely the inspiration of Scripture (1:19-21) and stresses the doctrine of the personal return of Christ, which was ridiculed by the false teachers (3:1-7). It concludes with an appeal for holy living, and with the promise of the new heavens and the new earth.

The following is a brief outline of the Epistle:

I. Salutation, 1:1
II. The Character of Spiritual Knowledge, 1:2-21
III. The Nature and Perils of Apostasy, 2:1-22
IV. The Doom of the Ungodly, 3:1-7
V. The Hope of Believers, 3:8-13
VI. Concluding Exhortation, 3:14-18.

Pethahiah (pĕth′ȧ-hī′ȧ, **Jehovah opens up**). 1. Head of 19th course of priests during David's reign (I Chron. 24:16). 2. A disobedient Levite who, in the time of Ezra, had married a foreign wife (Ezra 10:23; Neh. 9:5). 3. Counselor for King Artaxerxes (Neh. 11:24).

Pethor (pē′thôr, **pethôr**), mentioned twice in connection with the hireling prophet Balaam (Num. 22:5; Deut. 23:4). Both passages place Pethor in Mesopotamia on the Euphrates.

Pethuel (pē-thū′ĕl, **God's opening**), the prophet Joel's father (Joel 1:1).

Petra (pē′trȧ, **rock, cliff**), capital city of the Nabataeans mentioned indirectly (Judg. 1:36; II Kings 14:7; Isa. 16:1).

Peulethai, Peulthai (pē-ŭl′ē-thī, pē-ŭl′thī, **Jehovah is a reward**), a Levite porter of the tabernacle in the time of David (I Chron. 26:5).

Phalec (fā′lĕk), a Greek form of the Hebrew **Peleg** (Luke 3:35).

Phallu (See Pallu)

Phalti (făl′tī, **delivered**). 1. The spy from Benjamin's tribe sent by Moses to search out Canaan (Num. 13:9). 2. Saul's son-in-law, who married Michal after her husband, David, had been driven away (I Sam. 25:44). "Phaltiel" in II Samuel 3:15, 16 KJV.

Phaltiel (făl′tĭ-ĕl, **God delivers**). 1. A prince of Issachar (Num. 34:26). 2. Saul's son-in-law called also "Phalti" (II Sam. 3:15).

Phanuel (fȧ-nū′ĕl, **face of God**), the father of Anna the prophetess (Luke 2:36).

Pharaoh (fâr′ō), title of Egyptian rulers. Twenty-six separate dynasties of pharaohs have been recorded, extending from Menes, 3400 B.C. to Psamtik III, deposed at the Persian conquest in 525 B.C. Individual names were given the pharaohs at birth: Pharaoh Neco, Pharaoh Hophra, etc. Pharaohs mentioned in OT contexts: 1. Contemporaries of Abraham (Gen. 12:10-20). 2. Pharaohs mentioned in connection with Joseph (Gen. 39:1; 40:2ff; 43; 45:16-21; 47:1-11). 3. Pharaohs who oppressed Israelites in Egypt (Exod. 1-15). 4. Daughter of the Pharaoh, whom Mered married (I Chron. 4:18). 5. Pharaoh Sheshonk I (945-924 B.C.) — reigned during Solomon's reign (I Kings 3:1; 9:16, 24; 11:1). 6. Pharaoh of Sennacherib's day (II Kings 19:21; Isa. 36:6). 7. Pharaoh Neco (II Kings 23:29-35). 8. Pharaoh Hophra (Ezek. 29:2-3).

Phares, Pharez (fā′rēz, **breach**), Judah's twin son by his daughter-in-law, Tamar (Gen. 38:29; I Chron. 2:4). He had a large number of descendants (Ruth 4:12; I Chron. 27:3; Neh. 11:4, 6). In a number of these passages he is called "Perez."

Pharisees (fâr′ĭ-sēz). Of the three prominent societies of Judaism at the time of Christ — Pharisees, Sadducees and Essenes — the Pharisees were by far the most influential. The origin of this most strict sect of the Jews (Acts 26:5) is obscure, but it is believed the organization came out of the Maccabean Revolt (165 B.C.). There was, however, a group of Jews resembling the Pharisees as far back as the Babylonian Captivity.

The name "Pharisee," which in its Semitic form means "the separated ones, separatists," first appears during the reign of John Hyrcanus (135 B.C.). Generally, the term is in the plural rather than in the singular. They were also known as **chasidim,** meaning "loved of God" or "loyal to God." They were found everywhere in Palestine, not only in Jerusalem, and even wore a distinguishing garb so as to be easily recognized. According to Josephus, their number at their zenith of popularity was more than 6,000. Because of the significant role the Pharisees played in the life of the Lord and the Apostles, knowledge of the character and teachings of this group is of great importance for the understanding of the NT. They are mentioned dozens of times, especially in the Gospels, and often form the foil and fabric of the works and words of Jesus.

They became a closely organized group, very loyal to the society and to each other, but separate from others, even their own people. They pledged themselves to obey all facets of the traditions to the minutest detail and were sticklers for ceremonial purity. They even vowed to pay tithes of everything they possessed in addition to the temple tax. They would not touch the carcass of a dead animal or those who had come into contact with such things. They had no association with people who had been defiled through sickness. In truth, they made life difficult for themselves and bitter for others. They despised those whom they did not consider their equals and were haughty and arrogant because they believed they were the only interpreters of God and His Word.

The doctrines of the Pharisees included predestination. They also laid much stress on the immortality of the soul and had a fundamental belief in spirit life, teachings which usually caused much controversy when they met the Sadducees who just as emphatically denied them (Acts 23:6-9). Being people of the Law they believed in final reward for good works and that the souls of the wicked were detained forever under the earth, while those of the virtuous rose again and even migrated into other bodies (Josephus, **Antiq.** 18:1, 3; Acts 23:8). They accepted the OT Scriptures and fostered the usual Jewish Messianic hope which they gave a material and nationalistic twist. It was inevitable, in view of these factors, that they bitterly opposed Jesus and His teachings. If they despised the Herods and the Romans, they hated Jesus' doctrine of equality and claims of messiahship with equal fervor (John 9:16, 22).

The picture of the Pharisees painted by the NT is almost entirely black, but the discriminating Bible student should bear in mind that not everything about every Pharisee was bad. It is perhaps not just to say all Pharisees were self-righteous and hypocritical. Many Pharisees actually tried to promote true piety. What we know as Pharisaism from the NT was to some degree a degeneration of Pharisaism. Jesus condemned especially their ostentation, their hypocrisy, their salvation by works, their impenitence and lovelessness, not always Pharisees as such. Some of the Pharisees were members of the Christian movement in the beginning (Acts 6:7). Some of the great men of the NT were Pharisees — Nicodemus (John 3:1), Gamaliel (Acts 5:34), and Paul (Acts 26:5; Phil. 3:5). Paul does not speak the name "Pharisee" with great reproach but as a title of honor, for the Pharisees were highly respected by the masses of the Jewish people. When Paul says he was "in the matter of the law, a 'Pharisee,'" (Phil. 3:5), he did not think of himself as a hypocrite but claims the highest degree of faithfulness to the law. In similar manner, church leaders today might say, "We are the Pharisees." Much of modern scholarship, however, has cast the Pharisees into too favorable a light; when one reads our Lord's heated denunciation of Pharisaism in Matthew, chapter 23, where He specifically lists their sins, one has not only a true but a dark picture of Pharisaism as it was at the time of Christ.

Pharosh (See Parosh)

Pharpar (fȧr′pȧr). The scornful Naaman contrasted the silt-laden waters of the Jordan with "Abanah and Pharpar, the rivers of Damascus" (II Kings 5:12). The river is not necessarily close to Damascus.

Pharzite (fȧr′zīt), a descendant of Pharez, son of Judah (Num. 26:20).

Phaseah (See Paseah)

Phaselis (fȧ-sē′lĭs), a Rhodian colony in Lycia (I Macc. 15:23).

Phaselus (fȧ-sĕl′ŭs), a Latinization of Phasael, alternatively Phasaelus, the son of Antipater the Idumaean, and brother of Herod I.

Phebe (See Phoebe)

Phenice, Phoenix (fē-nī′sē, fē′nĭks), a town and harbor on the S coast of Crete (Acts 27:12). It has been identified with Loutro, the only harbor W of Fair Havens large enough to accommodate a galley as large as the vessel in the story.

Phi-Beseth (fī′bē-sĕth, **house of the goddess Bast**), a city in Egypt (Ezek. 30:17). About 40 miles N of Memphis.

Phichol (fī′kōl), the army captain belonging to Abimelech, the Philistine king of Gerah (Gen. 21:22, 32; 26:26).

Philadelphia (fĭl'á-dĕl'fĭ-á, **brotherly love),** a Lydian city in Asia Minor, founded by Attalus II Philadelphus (159-138 B.C.). Philadelphia was an outpost of Hellenism in native Anatolia. The district is disastrously seismic, and the great earthquake of A.D. 17 ruined it completely. Placed right above the fault, Philadelphia was tormented by 20 years of recurrent quakes after the disaster of 17. Hence, says Ramsey, is derived the imagery of Revelation 3:12 ("a pillar," "go no more out," "a new name"). The "new name" is certainly a reference to the proposal to rename the city **Neocaesarea** in gratitude for Tiberius' generous earthquake relief. A Christian witness, in spite of Moslem invasion and pressure, was maintained in Philadelphia through medieval and into modern times.

Philemon, Epistle to, written by Paul during his 1st Roman imprisonment, and addressed to "Philemon . . . Apphia . . . Archippus, and the church in your house." It deals with Philemon's runaway slave, Onesimus, who was converted through Paul, established in the faith by him, and then sent back to Philemon with a plea that Onesimus be forgiven for the wrong done to his master. The slave had apparently absconded with some of his master's money, which he had squandered; and Paul suggests that Philemon not insist on getting his money back, and if he did then Paul would repay it.

Philetus (fĭ'lē'tŭs, **worthy of love).** Paul alone mentions him as a false teacher in the church of Ephesus, who together with Hymenaeus, held that "the resurrection is past already" (II Tim. 2:17), that is, he did not radically deny a doctrine of the resurrection but allegorized it into a spiritual awakening or conversion and not a bodily resurrection as St. Paul taught in I Corinthians 15.

Philip (See Herod)

Philip the Apostle (fĭl'ĭp, **lover of horses).** In the lists of the apostles (cf. Matt. 10:3) the fifth in the list is called simply Philip, but the church has always called him "the Apostle" to distinguish him from Philip the Evangelist or Philip the Deacon (Acts 6:8). His home town was Bethsaida of Galilee and no doubt he was a close friend of Andrew and Peter who lived in the same fishing village (John 1:44). Probably he was first a disciple of John the Baptist, because Jesus called him directly near Bethany beyond the Jordan, where John was preaching (John 1:43). He brought Nathanael to Jesus (John 1:45; 14:8-14). This no doubt is why Jesus asked him the unusual question to arouse and test his faith before feeding the five thousand: "How are we to buy bread so that this people may eat?" (John 6:5-6). He served as something of a contact man for the Greeks and is familiarly known for bringing Gentiles to Jesus (John 12:20-23). The last information regarding Philip in the NT is found in Acts 1:13 where we are told that he was among the number of disciples in the upper chamber before Pentecost.

Philip the Evangelist (fĭl'ĭp, **lover of horses).** Although the Church, beginning with the second century, often confused him with Philip the Apostle, this Philip's name does not occur in the Gospels, but his story is told in the Book of Acts. He was one of the famous seven deacons, said to be "men of good repute, full of the Spirit and of wisdom" (Acts 6:2). He is second in the list, following Stephen, the first Christian martyr (Acts 6:5). A Greek-speaking Jew, as a deacon he was to serve under the apostles (Acts 6:6) by taking care of the neglected Hellenist widows and of the poor in general in the Jerusalem church. But after the death of Stephen the persecutions scattered the Christians abroad and, due to the great need, the deacons became evangelists or Christian missionaries. They even performed signs and wonders among the people (Acts 8:39; 6:8). In Acts 8 it is said that Philip preached in Samaria with great success. He cast out devils and healed the paralytics and the lame just as the apostles did. Some of his converts were Simon the magician of Samaria (Acts 8:9-13) and the Ethiopian eunuch (Acts 8:26-40). Thus perhaps Philip was instrumental in introducing Christianity into Africa. Most of his labors seem to have been centered along the Mediterranean seaboard, where following the Lord's command, he preached to the Gentiles. It can easily be seen, therefore, why Paul dwelt at his home (Acts 21:8-9), since they had much in common. In Acts 21 it is said that Philip had four unmarried daughters who were prophets. Little else is known of his later life.

The ruins of ancient Philippi. JFW

Philippi (fĭ-lĭp′ī), a Macedonian city founded by Philip II, father of Alexander, in 358-7 B.C. The position dominated the road system of northern Greece; hence it became the center for the battle of 42 B.C. in which Anthony defeated the tyrannicides, Brutus and Cassius. After Actium (31 B.C.), Octavian (the future Augustus), constituted the place a Roman colony, housing partisans of Antony whose presence was undesirable in Italy. There was a school of medicine in Philippi connected with one of those guilds of physicians which the followers of early Greek medicine scattered through the Hellenistic world. This adds point to the suggestion that Luke was a Philippian. There is a touch of pride in Luke's description of Philippi, "a city of Macedonia, the first of the district" (Acts 16:12 ASV). Amphipolis was, in fact, the capital. Philippi was the first European city to hear a Christian missionary, as far as the records show. Paul's choice of the locality throws light on the strategy of his evangelism.

Philippians (fĭ-lĭp′ĭ-ănz), one of the most personal of all Paul's letters. The church at Philippi in ancient Macedonia was the first European church founded by Paul, and thus represents the first major penetration of the Gospel into Gentile territory (Acts 16: 9-40; cf. Phil. 4:14-15). It is not unusual, therefore, that Paul's first convert there was a merchant woman named Lydia, a seller of purple. Her whole household was baptized and became the nucleus of the new church (Acts 16:15). The remarkable conversion of the jailer with its accompanying miraculous events also took place in Philippi (Acts 16:25-34). There was, therefore, a very intimate relationship between the apostle and this church. No doubt this was true also because the congregation consisted mainly of Gentiles and Paul saw in them the real future of the church. They were poor, but the fruits of faith were abundant. On several occasions they collected funds for Paul and also aided him while in prison (Phil. 4:10-16).

The letter was occasioned by the gift of funds and clothing which Epaphroditus brought to Paul in prison. Paul took the opportunity to thank the Philippians for this and other favors. In doing so, as was his custom, Paul added practical Christian admonition to humility, joy and steadfastness, which a reading of the letter will reveal. The main emphasis is joy; the concept "rejoice" appears no less than 16 times in the letter. It also is a theological letter. The doctrines of the person and work of Christ, justification by faith, the second coming of Christ, etc., are found among the practical admonitions.

General outline of contents of the letter: **Chapter I:** Greetings and thanksgiving (1:1-11). Progress of the Gospel (1:12-20). On remaining in the world and working and suffering for Christ (1:21-30). **Chapter II:** Exhortation to humility based on the humiliation and exaltation of Christ (2:1-13). Exhortation to the Christian life (2: 14-18). Personal remarks involving Timothy and Epaphroditus (2:19-30). **Chapter III:** Warning against false teachers (3:1-3). Paul's mighty confession of his faith (3:4-14). The Christian's hope of heaven (3:15-21). **Chapter IV:** "Rejoice in the Lord alway!" (4:1-7). Admonition to Christian virtues (4:8-13). Paul's confidence in Divine Providence (4:14-19). Final greeting (4:20-22).

Philistines (fĭ-lĭs-tēnz); in KJV "Palestina" in Exod. 15:14; Isa 14:29, 31; "Palestine" in Joel 3:4. A people who inhabited the Philistine plain of Palestine during the greater part of OT times. Their country extended from Joppa to S of Gaza, and had five great cities; Ashdod, Gaza, Ashkelon, Gath, and Ekron (Josh. 13:3; I Sam. 6:17). They come from Caphtor (Jer. 47:4; Amos 9:7), which may be Crete or the islands of the Aegean. They were non-Semitic, perhaps Aryans, and came to Palestine in large numbers about the time of the judges. Eventually the whole land of Canaan was given the name of the small area along the coast where the Philistines lived. They brought with them a knowledge of metal working, which the Hebrews did not have until the time of David, and therefore they dominated the Israelites until the time of David (Judg. 13:1). Deliverance for Israel came through various deliverers: Shamgar (Judg. 3: 31), Samson (Judg. 13-16), Samuel (I Sam. 7:1-14); they were defeated by Jonathan (I Sam. 14) and subjugated by David (I Sam. 17; 18). During the divided monarchy they regained their power (I Kings 15:27; II Chron. 21:16; 28:18). Sargon (722-705 B.C.) deported some of them and set over them an Assyrian governor.

A panoramic view of the Plain of Sharon, the land of the Philistines, on the shore of the Mediterranean. © *MPS*

Philo Judaeus (fī'lō jōō-dē'ŭs), the Jewish scholar and philosopher, was born in Alexandria about 20 B.C. Alexandria had an old tradition of Jewish scholarship, and Philo sprang from a rich and priestly family. Few details are known of his life, save that in A.D. 39 he took part in an embassy to Rome to plead the case of the Jews whose religious privileges, previously wisely recognized by Rome, were menaced by the mad Caligula. The embassy is described by Philo in the **Legatio ad Caium.** Philo lived until A.D. 50 and was a prolific author. His writings include philosophical works, commentaries on the Pentateuch, and historical and apologetic works.

Philologus (fī-lŏl'ō-gŭs, **fond of learning),** a believer in Rome to whom Paul sent a salutation (Rom. 16:15).

Philosophy. "Philosophy" **(love of wisdom)** and "philosopher" each occurs only once in the Bible, and that in a derogatory sense. It is not genuine philosophy which Paul deprecates, but "philosophy and vain deceit, after the traditions of men, after the rudiments [i.e. idolatrous principles] of the world, and not after Christ" (Col. 2:8). The "philosophers of the Epicureans and of the Stoics" (Acts 17:18) who led Paul to the Areopagus and heard him only part way through, are not to be taken as worthy or even serious representatives of those philosophies. Their superficiality is indicated in vs. 21.

Phinehas (fĭn'ē-ăs, **mouth of brass).** 1. Son of Eleazar and grandson of Aaron (Exod. 6:25; I Chron. 6:4, 50; 9:20; Ezra 7:5; 8:2), who slew Zimri and Cozbi at God's command (Num. 25:6-13; Ps. 106:30). 2. A son of Eli, and an unfaithful priest (I Sam. 1:3; 2:12-17, 22-25, 27-36; 3:11-13). He and his brother Hophni brought the ark into the camp of Israel in hope of its presence bringing victory against the Philistines, but the ark was taken and Hophni and Phinehas slain (I Sam. 4). 3. Father of the Eleazar who returned from exile (Ezra 8:23-34).

Phlegon (flē'gŏn, flĕg'ŏn, **burning),** a believer in Rome to whom Paul sent a loving greeting (Rom. 16:14).

Phoebe, Phebe (fē'bē, **pure),** mentioned only in Rom. 16:1, 2, she was one of the first deaconesses, if not the first, of the Christian Church, and was highly recommended by the Apostle Paul. Paul entrusted her to carry the important epistle to the Roman Christians.

Phoenicia, Phenicia (fē-nĭsh'ĭ-ȧ), country along Mediterranean coast, c. 120 miles long, extending from Arvad or Arados to Dor, just S of Carmel. The Semitic name for the land was Canaan. The term Phoenicia is from a Greek word meaning "dark red," perhaps because the Phoenicians were the discoverers of the crimson-purple dye derived from the murex shell-fish. The people were Semites who came in a migration from the Mesopotamian region during the 2nd millennium B.C. They became great seafarers, establishing colonies at Carthage and Spain, and perhaps even reached England. They were famous shipbuilders (Ezek. 27:9) and carpenters (I Kings 5:6). Its most famous cities were Tyre and Sidon. Its religion was polytheistic and immoral, and was brought to Israel by Jezebel (I Kings 16:31; 18:19). Hiram, one of their kings was friendly with David and Solomon (II Sam. 5:11; I Kings 5:1-12; II Chron. 2:3-16), and another Hiram helped Solomon in the building of the temple in Jerusalem (I Kings 7:13-47; II Chron. 2:13, 14). Jesus healed a Syrophoenician woman's daughter in its regions (Mark 7: 24-30). Paul visited Christians there (Acts 15:3; 21:2-7).

Phrygia (frĭj'ĭ-ȧ), province in SW Asia Minor which once included the greater part of Asia Minor; obtained by Rome in 133 B.C. Paul preached there on his 2nd and 3rd missionary journeys (Acts 16:6; 18:23).

Phurah, Purah (fū'rȧ, **branch),** a servant of Gideon (Judg. 7:10, 11; ASV, RSV Purah).

Phut (fŭt), 3rd son of Ham (Gen. 10: 6; I Chron. 1:8); descendants lived in Africa between Ethiopia (Cush) and Egypt (Mizraim) (Gen. 10:6); many were mercenary soldiers (Ezek. 27:10; Jer. 46:9).

Phuvah, Pua, Puah (fū'vȧ, pū'ȧ). 1. The second son of Issachar (Gen. 46: 13; Num. 26:23; I Chron. 7:1). 2. The father of Tola who judged Israel after the death of Abimelech (Judg. 10:1).

Phygellus (fī-jĕl'ŭs). Paul mentions by name Phygellus and Hermogenes as being among those Christians of Asia (western province of Asia Minor) who had turned away from the apostle (II Tim. 1:15). From the context (II Tim. 1:13-14) it may be assumed that the apostasy included the repudiation of Paul's doctrine. Some scholars feel that Phygellus may also have been one

Phoenicia, now and then. Above: Modern Beirut, on St. George's Bay, with snow-clad Mount Sunnin in the distance. Below: Ruins at Byblos, ancient Gebal, on the Phoenician coast. © *MPS*

of the leaders of a group of wayward Christians in Rome (Phil. 1:15-16).

Phylactery (See Dress)

Physician (See Occupations & Professions)

Pi-beseth (pī-bē'sĕth), a city in the delta of Lower Egypt (Ezek. 30:17) near Aven (On or Heliopolis), on the western bank of the Pelusiae branch of the Nile. The names of Rameses II and Shishak, conqueror of Rehoboam, are inscribed on the ruins. See Phi-beseth.

Pictures (pĭk'tūrz), occurs three times in KJV. Numbers 33:52 ASV, RSV has "figured stones." Stone idols appear to be meant. In Proverbs 25:11 ASV has "network," RSV "setting." Pleasing inlaid work in gold and silver seems to be the sense. In Isaiah 2:16 another word from the same Heb. root is translated "imagery" in ASV; margin "watchtowers." RSV has "beautiful craft."

Piety (pī'ĕ-tē), means "religious duty." The phrase "show piety at home" refers primarily to reverence for parents; filial piety; but other uses of related Greek words broaden the sense to "godly behavior."

Pigeon (See Birds)

Pi-hahiroth (pī'hȧ-hī'rŏth), place in NE Egypt where the Israelites were overtaken by the Egyptians just before the Red Sea (Exod. 14:2, 9; Num. 33:7). Exact location unknown.

Pilate (pī'lȧt), the 5th procurator, or governmental representative, of imperial Rome in Palestine at the time of Christ (A.D. 26 to 36). To Christians he is known almost entirely for his cowardly weakness in the condemnation of Jesus to Roman crucifixion in A.D. 30. The four Gospels relate the sad but glorious story fully, especially the Gospel of John. Pilate is also mentioned in the Acts of the Apostles (3: 13; 4:27; 13:28) and in I Timothy 6: 13 where we are told that Jesus "before Pontius Pilate witnessed a good confession." His name **Pontius** was his family name, showing that he was descended from the Roman family or **gens** of **pontii,** while **Pilate** no doubt comes from the Latin **pilatus** meaning "one armed with a **pilum** or javelin."

Most procurators disliked being stationed in a distant, difficult, dry outpost such as Judea. Pilate, however, seemed to enjoy tormenting the Jews, although, as it turned out, he was seldom a match for them. He never really understood them, as his frequent rash and capricious acts reveal. The Jewish historian Josephus tells us that he immediately offended the Jews by bringing the "outrageous" Roman standards into the Holy City. At another time he hung golden shields inscribed with the names and images of Roman deities in the temple itself. Once he even appropriated some of the temple tax to build an aqueduct. To this must be added the horrible incident mentioned in Luke 13:1 about "the Galileans whose blood Pilate had mingled with their sacrifices," meaning no doubt that Roman soldiers slew these men while sacrificing in the Holy Place. These fearful events seem to disagree with the role Pilate played in the trial of Jesus where he was as clay in the hands of the Jews, but this may be explained by the fact that his fear of the Jews increased because of their frequent complaints to Rome.

After the Jews had condemned Jesus in their own courts, they brought Him to Pilate, no doubt residing in Herod's palace near the temple, early in the morning. It is surprising he gave them an ear so early in the day (John 18:28). From the beginning of the hearing he is torn between offending the Jews and condemning an innocent person, and he tries every device to set Jesus free apart from simply acquitting Him. He declares Jesus innocent after private interrogation; he sends Him to Herod; he has Jesus scourged, hoping this will suffice; finally he offers the Jews a choice between Jesus and a coarse insurrectionist. When he hears the words, "If thou let this man go, thou art not Caesar's friend," and "We have no king but Caesar!" he thinks of politics rather than justice and condemns an innocent man to crucifixion. Washing his hands only enhanced his guilt.

Scripture is silent regarding the end of Pilate but Eusebius says he ended a suicide.

Pildash (pĭl'dăsh), son of Nahor, Abraham's brother (Gen. 22:22).

Pileha (pĭl'ē-hȧ), one who sealed the covenant with Nehemiah (Neh. 10:24; ASV, RSV Pilha).

Pilgrim (pĭl'grĭm, **a sojourner in a strange place).** Hebrews 11:13-16 shows that the faithful sought a heavenly city and did not consider themselves permanently attached to earth. I Peter 2:11 exhorts Christians to purity because of this status.

Pilgrimage (pĭl′grĭ-mij). 1. Jews were expected to make pilgrimages to the temple in Jerusalem for the great feasts (Pss. 120-134; Acts 2:5-11). 2. The NT describes Christians as pilgrims (Heb. 11:13; I Peter 2:11).

Pillar (pĭl′ẽr). 1. Stone pillars were often set up as a memorial (Gen. 28: 18; 31:45; 35:20; II Sam. 18:18). 2. Pillars as supports of buildings (I Kings 10:12). 3. Pillar of cloud and fire which guided Israel in the wilderness (Exod. 13:21; 14:19-24). 4. In the NT the word occurs figuratively, of God (I Tim. 3:15); of men (Gal. 2:9; Rev. 3:12); and of an angel's legs (Rev. 10: 1).

Pillar of cloud and fire. God guided Israel out of Egypt and through the wilderness by a pillar of cloud by day. This became a pillar of fire by night that they might travel by night in escaping from the Egyptian army (Exod. 13:21-22). When the Egyptians overtook the Israelites, the angel of the Lord removed this cloudy, fiery pillar from before them and placed it behind them as an effective camouflage (Exod. 14:19, 20, 24). The pillar of cloud stood over the tent of meeting outside the camp, whenever the Lord met Moses there (Exod. 33:7-11). The Lord came down for judgment in the cloud (Num. 12). No natural phenomenon fits the Biblical description: the cloud and fire were divine manifestations, in a form sufficiently well-defined to be called a pillar.

Pillow (pĭl′ō), stone pillow for Jacob (Gen. 28:11, 18); bolster in I Sam. 19: 13; cushion for the head (Mark 4:38).

Pilot (pī′lŭt, **sailor, rope-puller),** one of the skilled craftsmen of Tyre (Ezek. 27:8, 27, 28, 29).

Piltai (pĭl′tī), a priest, head of his father's house of Moadiah in the days of Joiakim (Neh. 12:17).

Pim (See Weights and Measures)

Pin, a tent peg, usually of wood, sharpened at one end, shaped at the other for attaching the tent cord (Judg. 4: 21; 5:26, KJV nail, ASV tent pin, RSV tent peg). The pin of Judges 16:13, 14 was a stick used for beating up the woof in the loom. The tent peg (KJV, ASV nail) like the corner stone assures support (Zech. 10:4 RSV). **Crisping pins** (Isa. 3:22 KJV) were probably bags or purses (ASV satchels, RSV handbags).

Pine (See Plants)

Pinnacle (pĭn′ȧ-k'l, pĭn′ĭ-k'l), anything shaped like a wing; on a building, a turret, battlement, pointed roof or peak. The pinnacle of the temple (Matt. 4:5; Luke 4:9) is the spot to which the devil conveyed Jesus, and whence he invited Him to cast Himself down.

Pinon (pī′nŏn), a duke or chief of Edom, of the family of Esau (Gen. 36: 40, 41; I Chron. 1:52).

Piram (pī′răm), Canaanite king who joined Adoni-zedek against Gibeon, and who was killed there, either by Joshua or by hailstones (Josh. 10:1-11).

Pirathon (pĭr′ȧ-thŏn), a town of Ephraim in the hill country of the Amalekites, where Abdon, one of the judges, lived and was buried (Judg. 12:13-15). Benaiah also was from Pirathon (II Sam. 23:30; I Chron. 11:31; 27:14).

Pirathonite (See Pirathon)

Pisgah (pĭz′gȧ), mt. on NE shore of Dead Sea (Num. 21:20). Balak brought Balaam to the top of Pisgah (Num. 23:14), and Moses viewed the Land of Promise from the top of Pisgah (Deut. 3:17).

Pishon, Pison (pī-shŏn), KJV Pison, first of the four rivers of Eden, flowed around the whole land of Havilah. Conjectures as to its identification are almost as numerous as the rivers of southwestern Asia, and include the Persian Gulf thought of as a river, and even the Nile.

Pisidia (pĭ-sĭd′ĭ-ȧ), one of the small Roman provinces in southern Asia Minor just N of Pamphilia which lay along the coast. It was mountainous, but more densely populated than the rough coastal areas, especially because it contained the important city of Antioch. Paul visited the city twice. On his first journey (Acts 13:14-50) he preached a lengthy sermon in the synagogue, testifying of Christ. Then the jealous Jews stirred up both the honorable women and the chief men of the city (vs. 50) and Paul and Barnabas were forced out of this greatest Pisidian city. On his second journey Paul revisited Pisidia and Antioch, ". . . exhorting them to continue in the faith" (Acts 14:21-24).

Pison (See Pishon)

Pispa, Pispah (pĭs′pȧ), an Asherite, a son of Jether (I Chron. 7:38).

Pit (pĭt), represents several Heb. and two Greek words whose usages are not sharply distinguished. A pit may be a **bitumen deposit** (Gen. 14:10 so ASV margin; RSV); a **deep place,** natural or made by man (Matt. 12:11; Gen. 37:20-29; II Sam. 17:9; Exod. 21: 33, 34, etc.); often a **well** (Luke 14:5, so ASV, RSV) or **cistern** (Jer. 14:3 ASV, RSV; Isa. 30:14 ASV, RSV; Lev. 11:33 ASV, **earthen vessel;** RSV **cistern,** etc.). Pit stands also for **death,** the **grave,** or **Sheol** (Job 33:18; Isa. 14: 15; Num. 16:30, 33 ASV, RSV Sheol; Rev. 9:1, 2).

Pitch, either bitumen or a viscous inflammable liquid associated with it, which was found in Mesopotamia and around the Dead Sea (Gen. 14:10 RSV); used to make vessels watertight (Exod. 2:3). As a verb, **pitch** renders several Heb. words also translated "encamp, set up" (ASV, RSV) and refers to placing tents, or the tabernacle (Gen. 12:8; 31:25; Exod. 17:1; Num. 1:51; Josh. 8:11, etc.); or other objects (Josh 4:20).

Pitcher, an earthenware jar with one or two handles, ordinarily borne on the head or shoulder for carrying water (Gen. 24:14-20, 43-46 ASV, RSV **jar).** Jars empty of water once held lamps (Judg. 7:16-20 RSV, **jars).** To break one was so serious as to be a figure for death (Eccl. 12:6).

Pithom (pī′thŏm), a city in Egypt in the valley between the Nile and Lake Timsâh; perhaps Tell er-Retâbah; dedicated to the sun-god Atum; with Raamses to the N, one of the store-cities built by the slave-labor of the Israelites (Exod. 1:11). As a store-city on the frontier it held supplies of grain for military forces operating thence.

Pithon (pī′thŏn), a son of Micah and descendant of King Saul (I Chron. 8: 35; 9:41).

Pity (pĭ′tē), a tender, considerate feeling for others, ranging from judicial clemency (Deut. 7:16, etc.) through kindness (Prov. 19:17; 28:8; Job 6:14) and mercy (Matt. 18:33) to compassion (Lam. 4:10). Pity for one's children is of the essence of fatherhood, human or divine (Ps. 103:13); inherent in the redemptive activity of God (Isa. 63:9).

Plague (See Diseases)

Plagues of Egypt, ten in number, these were the means by which God induced Pharaoh to let the Israelites leave Egypt. A series chiefly of natural phenomena, unusual in their severity, in that all occur within one year, in their accurate timing, in that Goshen and its people are spared some of them, and in the evidence of God's control over them, overcame the opposition of Pharaoh, discredited the gods of Egypt (the Nile and the sun), and defiled their temples. Because many of them were natural phenomena, the Egyptians claimed to duplicate them.

1. **Water becomes blood** (Exod. 7: 14-25). When the Nile is at its lowest, in May, the water is sometimes red, not fit to drink, and fish die. The Egyptians had to dig wells, into which river water would filter through sand. 2. **Frogs** (Exod. 8:1-15). When the flood waters recede, frogs spawn in the marshes, and invade the dry land. God directed Moses to lift up his rod at such a time. 3. **Lice** (Exod. 8:16-19). So many pests abound in Egypt that people might not be discriminating in naming them. The magicians failed, by their own admission, to reproduce this plague, and recognized in it "the finger of God." 4. **Flies** (Exod. 8:20-31). The rod is no longer mentioned. Swarms of flies came over Egypt in unusual density, to feed on dead frogs. The Israelites, with higher notions of cleanliness, may have disposed of the dead frogs in their territory. Pharaoh tentatively offers to let the people go to sacrifice to their God, only in the land of Egypt (8:25). Moses insists that they must go three days' journey into the wilderness. Pharaoh assents, provided they do not go far, and the plague is stayed at the intercession of Moses. The plague removed, Pharaoh again refuses to let the people go. 5. **The plague (RSV) of murrain (KJV) upon cattle** (Exod. 9:1-7). This is announced with a set time (tomorrow) for its occurrence. There is no record of its removal: presumably it wore itself out. 6. **Boils (KJV), blains (ASV) or sores (RSV) upon man and beast** (Exod. 9: 8-12). The air over Egypt was filled with dust, and it became boils breaking out on man and beast. The magicians, still watching Moses, could not stand because of the boils. From the specific mention that the plague was upon "all the Egyptians" we may infer that the Israelites were not attacked. This plague was not recalled: presumably it wore itself out. 7. **Hail** (Exod. 9:13-35). God directs Moses to stretch forth his hand, and hail (which rarely occurs in Egypt) will descend in unusual violence. Only in Goshen there was no hail. The hand of God directed its

local incidence. The season must have been January or February, for the flax was in the ear and the barley in bud (RSV) or in bloom (ASV: 9:31, 32). 8. **Locusts** (Exod. 10:1-20). After seven plagues, even a frequently recurring one, such as locusts, is so dreaded that Pharaoh's servants use bold language in advising that the Israelites be let go (10:7). Goshen is not spared this visitation. Still Pharaoh is obdurate. 9. **Darkness** (Exod. 10:21-29). A sand storm, accentuated by the dust-bowl condition of the land, and borne on the west wind which drove off the locusts, brought a tawny, choking darkness. The patience of God is at an end: Pharaoh will see the face of Moses no more. Three days the darkness lasted, but the children of Israel had light in their dwellings. 10. **Death of the first-born** (Exod. 11:1-12:36). This final and convincing demonstration of God's power broke down the resistance of Pharaoh long enough for the Israelites to escape. The Israelites are directed how to protect their first-born with the blood of the passover lamb, that they may not be slain along with those of the Egyptians. They "borrow" valuables of the Egyptians, and amid the lamentations of the latter are allowed to leave. Egypt has had enough. The character of this plague is clearly that of divine judgment upon incurable obstinacy. The memory of the plagues was cultivated as a warning to Israel in later centuries (Pss. 78: 43-51: 105:26-36; 135:8, 9; Acts 7:36; 13:17; Heb. 11:28).

Plain, broad stretch of level land (Gen. 11:2; Ezek. 3:22).

Plaister (See Plaster)

Plaiting (See Dress)

Plane, a scraping tool used in shaping idol images (Isa. 44:13).

Plane Tree (See Plants)

Plants of the Bible. The following plants are mentioned in the Bible. Some of them are not identifiable. Algum tree (II Chron. 2:8; 11:9); almond (Exod. 25:33-36); almug tree probably identical with algum (I Kings 10:11, 12); aloes (Ps. 45:8; John 19:39); translated "odours"; amomum, (Rev. 18:13); anise (Matt. 23:23); apple (S. of Sol. 2:3),—many think that the apricot is meant; aspalathus (Ecclesiasticus 24:15); balm (Ezek. 27:17); barley (Hos. 3:2); bdellium (Num. 11:6, 7);

Left: First and second figs. Right: A fig tree laden with first figs. © *MPS*

"Lilies of the field" (Anemones) in the Jerusalem area. © *MPS*

The Mustard Tree. © *MPS*

Olive branches loaded with fruit. © *MPS*

Narcissus, possibly the "Rose of Sharon" of the Bible. © *MPS*

The shittah tree, or acacia, from which the Ark of the Tabernacle was built. © *MPS*

Stalks of wheat. © *MPS*

beans (Ezek. 4:9); box tree (Isa. 41:19; 60:13); bramble (Judg. 9:14, 15); brier (Ezek. 28:24); bulrush (Exod. 2:3); bush (burning bush) (Exod. 3:2, 3); camphire (S. of Sol. 1:14); cassia (Exod. 30:22-25); cedar of Lebanon (Ezek. 31:3, 5); chestnut (plane tree) (Gen. 30:37); cinnamon (Exod. 30:23); cockle (Job 31:40); coriander (Exod. 16:31); corn (wheat) (Deut. 8:8); cotton (Esth. 1:5, 6 RSV); cucumber (Num. 11:5); cummin (Isa. 28:26, 27); cypress (Isa. 44:14); desire (caper) (Eccl. 12:5); dove's dung (II Kings 6: 25); ebony (Ezek. 27:15); eelgrass (Jonah 2:5); elm (Hos. 4:13); flag (Exod. 2:3, 5); fig (Gen. 3:6, 7); fir (Isa. 60: 13); fitches (Isa. 28:25-27); flax, source of linen (Luke 23:52, 53); frankincense (Matt. 2:11); galbanum (Exod. 30:34-36); gall (Matt. 27:34); garlic (Num. 11:5); gourd (Jonah 4:5-7); grape (Gen. 40:10, 11); green bay tree (Ps. 37:35); hemlock (Hos. 10:4); herbs, bitter herbs (Exod. 12:8); hyssop (I Kings 4:33); juniper (I Kings 19:3, 4); leeks (Num. 11:5); lentil (Gen. 25:29, 30, 34); lilies (of the field) (Luke 12: 27); lily (S. of Sol. 5:13); locusts (Matt. 3:4); mallows (Job 30:1, 3, 4); mandrake (Gen. 30:14-16); melon (Num. 11:5); millet or "pannag" (Ezek. 4:9; 27:17); mint (Luke 11:42); mulberry tree (II Sam. 5:23, 24); mustard (Matt. 13:31, 32); myrrh (OT) (Gen. 37:25, 26, 27), (NT) (Matt. 2:11); myrtle (Zech. 1:7, 8); nettle (Job 30:7); nuts (walnut) (S. of Sol. 6:11); nuts (pistachio) (Gen. 43:11); oak (holly oak) (Gen. 35:8); oak (valonia oak) (Zech. 11:2); oil tree (Isa. 41:19); olive (Exod. 27:20); onion (Num. 11:5); onycha (Exod. 30:34, 35); palm (date) (Num. 33:9; pannag (millet) (Ezek. 4:9; 27: 17); parched corn (wheat, q.v.); pine tree (fir) (Isa. 60:13); plane tree (chestnut, q.v.); pomegranate (I Sam. 14:2); poplar (Gen. 30:37); pulse (II Sam. 17: 28); reed (Job 40:15, 20-22); rie, rye (spelt) (Exod. 9:32); rolling thing (rose of Jericho) (Isa. 17:13); rose (narcissus) (Isa. 35:1); rose of Sharon (S. of Sol. 2:1, 2); rue (Luke 11:42); rush (flag) (Exod. 2:3); saffron (S. of Sol. 4:14); shittah tree (Isa. 41:18; Exod. 25:10); spices (Gen. 43:11); spikenard (Mark 14:3); stacte (storax) (Exod. 30: 34); strange vine (vine, q.v.); sweet cane (sugar cane) (Isa. 43:24); sweet cane (calamus, sweet calamus) (Jer. 6: 20); sycamine (Luke 17:6); sycamore (Amos 7:14); tares (Matt. 13:25); teil (turpentine tree, q.v.); thistles (II Kings 14:9); thorns (crown of thorns) (Mark 15:17); thorns (Isa. 7:19); thyine wood (Rev. 18:12); turpentine tree (teil tree) (Isa. 6:13); vine (true) (Gen. 40:9-11); vine (wild vine, vine of Sodom, q.v.); vine of Sodom (Deut. 32:23),—it is uncertain what plant is intended; water lily (I Kings 7:19, 22, 26); weeds (eelgrass, q.v.); wheat (Gen. 41:22); wild gourd (II Kings 4:39); willow (aspen) (Ps. 137:2); willow "withes" (Judg. 16: 7-9); wormwood (Lam. 3:15, 19).

Plaster (plăs′têr). The Egyptians plastered their stone buildings, even the finest granite, inside and out, to make a smooth surface for decoration. The poor used a mixture of clay and straw. In Palestine and Syria, an outside clay coating would have to be renewed after the rainy season (Deut. 27:2, 4; Dan. 5:5; Lev. 14:42-48).

Plaster, Medicinal. In Isaiah 38:21 (KJV, ASV) a cake of figs applied (RSV) to a boil.

Pledge, personal property of a debtor held to secure a payment (Gen. 38:17-26). The law of Moses was concerned with protection of the poor. If the pledge was an outer garment, it must be restored at sunset for a bed covering (Exod. 22:25-27; Deut. 24:12, 13). The creditor was forbidden to enter his neighbor's house to take the pledge (Deut. 24:10, 11). A handmill or its upper millstone might not be taken (Deut. 24:6), nor a widow's clothing (Deut. 24:17, 18). Abuses of the pledge are censured (Job 22:6; 24:3, 9; Amos 2:8; Hab. 2:6 ASV, RSV; "thick clay" in KJV mistranslates the Heb.). He who goes surety for strangers ought himself to be taken in pledge (Prov. 20:16; 27:13). The pledge (ASV, RSV) in I Timothy 5:12 (KJV, ASV margin, faith) is the marriage troth.

Pleiades (See Astronomy)

Pliny (plĭn′ē), Caius Plinius Caecilius Secundus, called "the Younger," to distinguish him from his learned uncle, lived from A.D. 61 to about A.D. 114. Pliny was strongly influenced in all matters of literature and scholarship by his scientist uncle. Pliny passed through the ordered stages of the standard public career of a Roman aristocrat of the early Empire, but his claim to fame in the modern world is his collection of ten volumes of literary letters. The epistles, exquisitely written, cover all manner of subjects, from the eruption of Vesuvius to the famous description of the Christian Church in Bithynia, a province which Pliny governed in A.D. 112, just before his death. Trajan's replies to his requests for instruction survive, and are important evidence for the official attitude towards the Christians.

Plowman (See Occupations & Professions)

Plow, Plough, a farming tool used to break up the ground for sowing. An ancient plow scratched the surface, but did not turn over the soil. It consisted of a forked stick, the trunk hitched to the animals which drew it, the branch braced and terminating in the share, which was at first the sharpened end of the branch, later a metal point. It was ordinarily drawn by a yoke of oxen (Job 1:14; Amos 6:12). Plowing with an ox and an ass yoked together was forbidden (Deut. 22:10), but this prohibition is not observed today. A man guided the plow with his left hand, goading the oxen and from time to time cleaning the share with the goad in his right, keeping his eyes front in order to make the furrow straight (Luke 9:62). The plowman should plow in hope of a share of the crop (I Cor. 9:10). Elisha plowing with 12 yoke of oxen indicates his ability and the magnitude of his farming operations (I Kings 19:19). Samson calls the Philistines' badgering his betrothed to tell his riddle, "plowing with his heifer" (Judg. 14:18).

Plowshare (plou′shâr, **the blade of a plow),** to beat swords into plowshares was symbolic of an age of peace (Isa. 2:4; Mic. 4:3); to beat plowshares into swords portended coming war (Joel 3:10).

Plumb Line (plŭm līn), a cord with a stone or metal weight, the plummet, tied to one end; used in testing whether a wall is perpendicular. Plumb line and plummet are used figuratively of God's action in testing the uprightness of His people (Amos 7:7-9; II Kings 21:13; Isa. 28:17).

Pochereth (pŏk′ē-rĕth, pō′kĕ), a servant of Solomon whose descendants returned from exile with Zerubbabel (Ezra 2:57; Neh. 7:59).

Poet (pō′ĕt, a maker); Paul quotes from pagan poets in Acts 17:28; I Cor. 15:32; and Titus 1:12. A great deal of the OT is written in the form of poetry.

Poetry (pō′ĕt-rē).. We recognize as poetry literature which has regular, rhythmically-patterned form and imaginatively concrete, emotionally charged substance. If the substance is lacking to the form, we call it verse; if the form is lacking to the substance, we call it poetic prose. All these terms are elastic: there is a wide range between what is readily recognized as poetry and what is obviously prose. There has been a growing recognition that for God and His patriarchs, prophets, and apostles to speak in poetic language, even in poetic form, does not derogate from the authority of the Bible as the Word of God. The growth of this feeling is illustrated by the fact that while the KJV is all in prose, the ASV prints a number of passages as poetry, and the RSV so prints a great many more.

The most obivous feature of Hebrew poetic form is its parallelism. Many varieties have been distinguished, of which the three principal are: **synonymous,** in which the meaning of both members is similar, e.g., Pss. 15:1; 24: 1-3; I Sam. 18:7); **antithetic,** in which the meanings of the members are opposed (Ps. 37:9; Prov. 10:1; 11:3); **synthetic,** in which noun corresponds to noun, verb to verb, and member to member, and each member adds something new (e.g., Ps. 19:8, 9). Acrostic poems were favorites (e.g., Pss. 9; 10; 34; 37; Prov. 31:10-31; Lam. 1-4). In Psalm 119 all the verses of each stanza of eight verses begin with the same letter of the Heb. alphabet. Of the books always recognized as poetic, Psalms is a hymn book, containing songs suitable for public worship, and for private devotion; historical and other didactic poems. Proverbs is a collection of proverbs and other didactic poems. The Song of Solomon, at first glance appearing to be a secular love-cycle, has always been interpreted as an appropriate, rich and inspired expression of the love between the Messiah, Jesus Christ, and His Bride, the Church of OT and NT saints. Job is dramatic, though not technically a drama, and rises to ecstatic heights in God's address to Job (38-41). Didactic poetry and prose alternate in Ecclesiastes. Of the prophetic books, most of Isaiah is poetry; Jeremiah, except the historical sections; most of the minor prophets, except Haggai and Malachi. Of Jonah, only his prayer (2:2-9), and of Zechariah only 9:1-11:3, 17; 13:7-9 are printed as poetry in RSV. Lamentations is poetry, 1-4 being acrostic, while in chapter 5 the singer's emotion may have become too intense to be confined in this artificial form. In Daniel there are poetic sections: 2:20-23; 4:3; 4:34b, 35; 6:26, 27; 7:9, 10, 13, 14, 23-27, apocalyptic. In Ezekiel, prose alternates with poetry.

Short poems (so printed in RSV) are frequent in the historical books. The English reader and also the casual student of Hebrew will do well to content himself with appreciating the beauty of the poetic imagery in which so much of the OT is dressed, without trying to analyze the poetic form, for such analysis is a doubtful and uncertain work for experts, and has as little relation to appreciation and interpretation of the meaning, as botany has for the enjoyment of flowers. It is the thought within the form which edifies.

In the NT, easily recognizable poems are all in the Gospel according to Luke: the Magnificat of Mary (1:46b-55), adapted from Hannah's song (I Sam. 2:1-10); the prophecy of Zacharias (1:68-79); the angels' Gloria in Excelsis (2:14); and the Nunc Dimittis of Simeon (2:29-32). All these are echoes of Hebrew poetry, sung by Hebrews. Snatches of Christian hymns are thought to be found in the epistles (Eph. 5:14; I Tim. 1:17; 3:16; 6: 16; II Tim. 4:18). Paul rises to heights of poetic eloquence (e.g., Rom. 8; 11: 33-12:2; I Cor. 13; 15:25-27). James' letter is lyrical. The language of Jesus is poetic in the highest degree. The NT contains many quotations of OT poetry. But it is the elevated thought of the NT as of the OT and not the technical form, which gives us the feeling of poetry.

Poets, Pagan, Quotations from. NT quotations from pagan poets are confined to Paul. Acts 17:28 contains a quotation from Cleanthes. Titus 1:12 is a quotation from Epimenides. I Cor. 15:33 is a quotation from Menander.

Poison, a substance producing a deadly effect, like the venom of reptiles (Deut. 32:24, 33; Job 20:16; Ps. 58:4). Vegetable poisons were known in antiquity; hemlock (Hos. 10:4 RSV); wild gourd (II Kings 4:39, 40). A poisoned drink is referred to in Mark 16:18.

Pole (pōl), the standard (ASV) on which the brazen serpent was displayed (Num. 21:8, 9).

Politarch (pŏl'ĭ-tärk). The city magistrates of Thessalonica are referred to as "politarchs" (Acts 17:6 and 8). It was evidently a Macedonian term. It was Luke's general practice to use the term in commonest educated use. Hence he called the officials of Philippi "praetors," and an inscription has similarly established the fact that this was a courtesy title given to the magistrates of a Roman Colony.

Poll (pōl), **skull, head,** a **unit for counting persons,** as a noun (Num. 1:2-22 RSV, "head by head"; 3:47 RSV, "apiece"; I Chron. 23:3, 24 RSV omits poll). As a verb, **shear** (Mic. 1:16 ASV, RSV, "cut off hair") as sign of mourning; (II Sam. 14:26 ASV, RSV, "cut the hair") (Ezek. 44:20 ASV, **"cut off,"** RSV, **"trim the hair").**

Pollution (pŏ-lū′shŭn), may be from menstruation (Ezek. 22:10 ASV, RSV impurity); from food sacrificed to idols (Acts 15:20, 29); from the evil in the world (II Pet. 2:20 ASV, RSV defilements). Imperfect offerings, brought with a wrong motive were polluted (Mal. 1:7-9). An altar was to be of unhewn stone: to cut was to pollute it (Exod. 20:25 RSV profane). Several Heb. and Greek words translated "pollute" refer to ceremonial or moral defilement, profanation, and uncleanness.

Pollux (pŏl′lŭks), with Castor (Acts 28: 11 KJV), one of the Dioscuri or Twin Brothers (ASV, RSV), sons of Zeus and patrons of sailors.

Polygamy (See Marriage)

Pomegranate (See Plants)

Pommel (pŭm″l, **basin, bowl,** II Chron. 4:12, 13; I Kings 7:41, 42), the bowl- or globe-shaped part of the capitals of the temple pillars.

Pontius Pilate (See Pilate)

Pontus (pŏn′tŭs, **sea),** a large province of northern Asia Minor which lay along the Black Sea (Acts 2:9). Luke mentions in Acts 18:2 that a certain Christian Jew named Aquila was born in Pontus. So far as we know, Pontus and the other northern provinces were not evangelized by Paul. The Holy Spirit did not permit him to preach in Bithynia (Acts 16:7). However, the Apostle Peter addresses his first letter to "the strangers (Jewish Christians) scattered throughout Pontus, etc." lending credence to the tradition that Peter preached in N Asia Minor rather than in Rome after Pentecost.

Pool, a pocket of water, natural or artificial, refers to natural depressions; by the Nile (Exod. 7:19; 8:5); in the wilderness (Pss. 107:35; 114:8 ASV, RSV); desolated Babylon (Isa. 14:23); the restored wilderness (Isa. 35:7; 41: 18); dried up in judgment (Isa. 42:15); for the sluices and ponds of Isaiah 19: 10, ASV, RSV adopt entirely different readings of the text. An artificial pool to conserve water for irrigation or drinking was made by damming streams. Smaller ones were rectangular, wider than deep, to collect rain from the roofs or from the surface of the gound: similar to cylindrical pits or cisterns which served the same purpose. Water from springs was collected in masonry pools. Solomon made pools to water his forest nursery (Eccl. 2:6). Psalm 84:6 speaks of the rain filling pools (ASV has "blessings" here). Nineveh was of old like a pool (Nah. 2:8 KJV, ASV) or, being destroyed, like a pool whose waters have run out (RSV). In the NT, the pool of Bethesda (John 5:2, 4, 7); of Siloam (John 9: 7, 11).

Poor. God's love and care for the poor are central to His providence (Pss. 9: 18; 12:5; Eccl. 5:8, etc.). He enjoins like consideration on us (Exod. 22:23, etc.). The Mosaic law has specific provisions for the benefit of the poor (Exod. 22:25-27; 23:11; Lev. 19:9, 10, 13, 15; 25:6, 25-30, 39-42, 47-54; Deut. 14:28, 29; 15:12, 13; 16:11-14; 24:10-15, 17-22; 26:12, 13; Ruth 2:1-7; Neh. 8:10). Israel as a nation was born out of deep poverty (Exod. 1:8-14; 2:7-10), and was never allowed to forget it (e.g., I Kings 8:50-53). If Israel met the conditions of God's covenant, there would be no poor among them, but God knew this would never be realized (Deut. 15:4-11). The wrongs of the poor concern the prophets (e.g., Isa. 1:23; 10:1, 2; Ezek. 34; Amos 2:6; 5:7; 8:6; Mic. 2:1, 2; Hab. 3:14; Mal. 3:5).

At the outset of His ministry, Jesus presents as His first aim, "to preach the gospel to the poor" (Isa. 61:1, 2). That physical poverty is meant is shown by the contrasts in Luke 6:20-26. Matt. 5:3 speaks of spiritual poverty. Jesus moved among the poor and humble. He recognized the continuing obligation toward the poor, as well as appreciating a unique expression of love toward Himself (Mark 14:7). The early church moves amidst the poor, who are not too poor to be concerned for one another's welfare (II Cor. 8:2-5, 9-15), drawing inspiration from Christ's leaving heavenly riches for earthly poverty. The origin of the diaconate is linked with a special need (Acts 6:1-6). Those with property contributed to the common fund (Acts 2: 45; 4:32-37). The Jerusalem Council asked Paul and Barnabas to remember the poor (Gal. 2:10). James has some sharp words about the relations of rich and poor (James 1:9-11; 2:1-13; 5:1-6).

Poplar (See Plants)

Poratha (pō-rā′thȧ, pŏr′ȧ-thȧ), son of Haman who died with his brothers (Esth. 9:8).

Porch, an area with a roof supported by columns: vestibule (I Kings 7:6ff), colonnade (Judg. 3:23), place before a court (Mark 14:68), gateway (Matt. 26:71).

Porcius (See Festus)

Porter (See Occupations & Professions)

Portion (pôr′shŭn), a part, that is, less than the whole of anything; a share (Num. 31:30, 47; as of food served to one person (Neh. 8:10, 12; Dan. 1:5-16; 11:26; Jer. 51:33, 34; Deut. 18:8); of property acquired by gift (I Sam. 1:4, 5) or by inheritance (Gen. 31:14; Josh. 17:14); a plot of ground (II Kings 9:10, 36, 37, RSV territory); destiny (Ps. 142:5; Job 20:29; 31:2; Lam. 3:24).

Post (pōst), a doorway (I Kings 6:33). Anything strong (Ezek. 40:14, 16). One of the most common uses of the word post is its reference to anyone who conveyed a message speedily (Job 9:25). The first went by foot and later by horses. Royal messages were conveyed in this way (II Chron. 30:6, 10).

Pot. Utensils of metal or clay for holding liquids, and solid substances such as grain and ashes (II Kings 4:38; Jer. 1:13). There were a great variety of sizes and shapes. Their chief NT use was for water or wine (John 2:6; Mark 7:4).

Potentate (pō′tĕn-tāt, **mighty one),** a person with great power and authority (I Tim. 6:15).

Potiphar (pŏt′ĭ-fêr, **whom Re has given),** one of the pharaoh's officers mentioned in Genesis in connection with Joseph's sojourn in that land. He purchased Joseph from the Midianites, and made him head overseer over his house (Gen. 39:1-20).

Potipherah (pō-tĭf′êr-å, **the one given by the sun-god),** the Egyptian priest of On whose daughter, Asenath, was given to Joseph for a wife (Gen. 41:45, 50; 46:20).

Potsherd (pŏt′shûrd), a piece of earthenware. Job used a potsherd to scrape his body in his affliction (Job 2:8). Potsherds are referred to in other places in the Bible (Ps. 22:15; Prov. 26:23).

Pottage (pŏt′ĭj, **boiled),** thick broth made with vegetables and meat or suet. Jacob bought Esau's birthright for a mess of pottage (Gen. 25:29, 30, 34. See also II Kings 4:38-39).

Potter (See Occupations & Professions)

Potter's Field (pŏt′êrz fēld), the piece of ground which the priests bought with the money Judas received when he betrayed our Lord (Matt. 27:7; Acts 1:18). It was used by the Jews as a burial plot in which to bury strangers.

Potter's Gate, a gate in the wall of Jerusalem which is thought to be referred to by Jeremiah (Jer. 19:2).

Pottery, one of the oldest crafts in Bible lands. Place where potter's clay

The potter's shop. This Palestinian potter is using a foot-powered wheel, of the type used in Bible times. © MPS

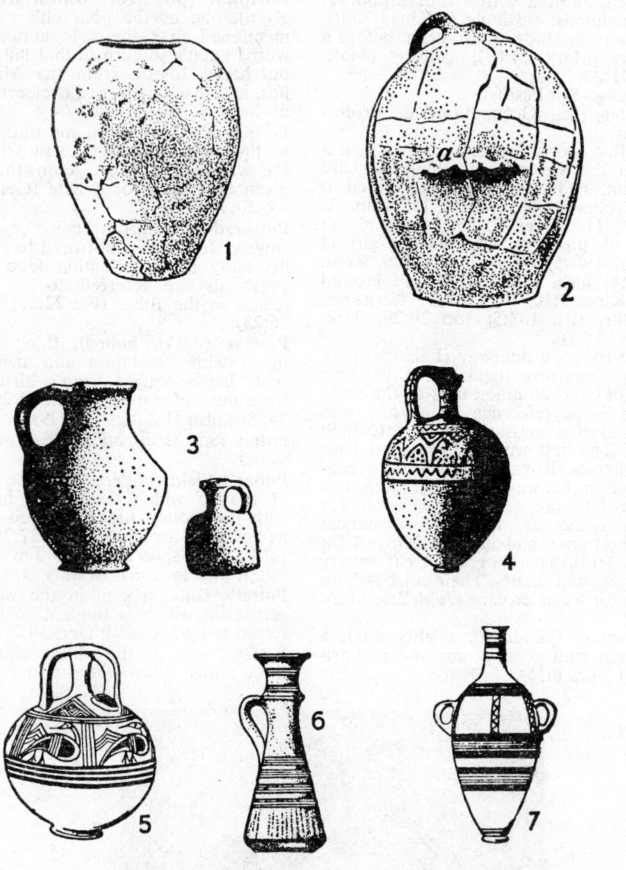

Pottery styles from Palestine. 1, 2. Large jars from Jericho. No. 2 has both loop and ledge handles, to facilitate balancing jar on the head. 3. Small jugs with handles from Megiddo. 4. Finely modeled egg-shaped jug, from Jericho. 5. Decorated Philistine jug from Gezer. 6. Vase ornamented with ridges, from Taanach, late Israelite. 7. Pitcher from Tell Zakariyeh (probably Azekah). DV

was dug was called "potter's field" (Matt. 27:7). Pottery was shaped by hand on a potter's wheel, powered by foot or by an apprentice (Jer. 18:3-6), then dried and baked in a kiln. Many different items were made: bowls, basins, and cups; cooking pots; jars; decanters, flasks, and juglets; lamps; ovens braziers; dishes. Thousands of objects have been found by the archaeologists. Careful study has been made of the historical development of pottery styles, so that experts can date and place pottery with considerable accuracy.

Pound (See Weights and Measures)

Power. Many kinds of power are referred to in the Bible: man's, Satan's, military, official, Christ's. The word is used in two senses: ability to act (Luke 1:35; 5:17) and the authority to act (Acts 5:4; Rom. 9:21).

Praetor (prē'tôr). Originally the highest Roman magistrate. Hence the adjective **praetorius** in such expressions as **praetorium** for a provincial seat of government, and the **cohors praetoria** for the imperial guard. When the praetors of earlier days became known as consuls, the term **praetor** was applied to officials elected to administer justice. With Rome's acquisition of overseas provinces, there was an enlargement of praetorial activity, and the number of the officers increased to four in 227 B.C. to cover the administration of Sicily and Sardinia, and to six in 197 B.C. to cover Spain. Hence a resumption of military functions, earlier held by the consuls only, and a narrowing of the margin of superior authority between consul and praetor. The praetors played a major part as officers of justice in developing the corpus of Roman law. With the principate the office, though nominally in existence, declined in prestige, power and functions, until eventually it was only honorary.

Praetorian Guard (prē-tō'rĭ-ăn). The term "Praetorian Guard" does not actually occur in the Scriptures, but has been implied in the statements of Paul about the Praetorium and Caesar's household (Phil. 1:13 and 4:22), which have been viewed as the emperor's army garrison or bodyguard in Rome. Recently, however, scholars have discovered that "Caesar's house" refers not only to soldiers but to all those in government service.

Praetorium (prē-tō'rĭ-ŭm). Originally it meant the general's tent in the camp of an army station. Sometimes it referred to the military headquarters in Rome itself or in the provincial capitals. It also meant the staff of men in such an establishment or even the session of a planning council. In the Gospels (Matt. 27:27; Mark 15:16; John 18:28, 33) it refers to the temporary palace or headquarters ("judgment hall") of the Roman governor or procurator while in Jerusalem, which was actually Herod's palace adjacent to the temple. Cf. Acts 23:35.

Praise, broad term for words or deeds which exalt or honor people, God, or gods (Prov. 27:21; Exod. 15:11; Judg. 16:24). Book of Psalms is filled with praise; Psalms 113-118 are called the Hallel, the praises. Praise for redemption dominates the NT (Luke 2:13, 14; Rev. 19:5-7).

Prayer. Created in the image of God, man is uncurably religious. And because religion is universal and ineradicable, prayer is the same. Recognizing their dependence upon some higher order of reality, people everywhere seek a propitious relationship with that higher order no matter what their understanding of it may be — primitive or sophisticated, gross or spiritual, anthropomorphic or impersonal. People never outgrow their need for prayer any more than their need for air and food. Living in a pecarious world, surrounded by the vast and terrifying forces of nature, inescapably death-shadowed, people in their weakness, anguish, and need pray spontaneously. Especially in times of crisis is the instinctive nature of prayer disclosed (cf. Ps. 107:23-28).

Yet though prayer is a universal phenomenon, it becomes unique and commanding in Biblical faith.

Luther remarks in his homely way: "As a shoemaker makes a shoe, and a tailor makes a coat, so ought a Christian to pray. Prayer is the daily business of a Christian." And Biblical prayer, let it be borne in mind, is here and now the focus of our concern.

Scripture nowhere offers any **apologia** for prayer: it simply assumes the necessity and effectiveness of man's communication with God, provided certain conditions are met. Loyal to the teaching of Scripture, so doughty a Calvinist as Charles Haddon Spurgeon could say, "Prayer is able to prevail with Heaven and bend omnipotence to its desire." Yet, according to the Bible prayer goes unanswered unless certain conditions are met. Nothing could show more plainly that prayer is the farthest removed from pious pretense; it is no matter of spiritual gymnastics possessing only a reflex value psychologically. Quite the reverse. Biblically considered, it is a force.

As a many-faceted phenomenon, prayer must not be reduced merely to supplication, as is sometimes done. The immense sweep of Biblical teaching with respect to this phenomenon can scarcely be compressed into the single and rather crass category of "getting things from God," to quote the title of a once popular book by Charles A. Blanchard. Prayer, essentially, is **communion,** a desire to enter into conscious and intimate relationship with the Thou who is our life (Ps. 63:1-8; Ps. 73:25-26; Luke 6:12; I John 1:3). And the astonishing corollary of this truth is that God hungers for man's fellowship (Rev. 3:20). Prayer is also **adoration,** the praise of God because of His greatness and goodness. The Book of Psalms is a collection of man's loving, awe-inspired praise as, contemplating his Creator and Saviour, he is lost in wonder and amazement at the purity, pity, and power of the perfect Person. Again, prayer is **thanksgiving,** the outpouring of gratitude to God because of His grace, mercy, and lovingkindness. Psalm 103 is a classic expression of the emotion aroused by unmerited blessing. The entire Psalter, indeed, is full of such hymns. Once more, prayer is **confession** as sinful man acknowledges his guilty disobedience. David's penitential candor in Psalm 51 voices the common experience of transgression followed by grief-stricken remorse before God. Inevitably this kind of prayer becomes petition as the offender beseeches cleansing, a plea for personal help. Under the pressure of need man begs God for some specific favor. The legitimacy of petition is guaranteed by the very prayer which our Lord taught us to pray, in which we ask not only for pardon but likewise for bread and deliverance (Matt. 6:9-15). Paul is following his Master when he directs his converts to ask quite literally for anything (Phil. 4:6). Prayer, yet again, is **intercession** which we may define as petition on behalf of one's neighbor, entreaty for his good, his beatitude. Consider Paul's burden for Israel (Rom. 9:1-2; 10:1) in which egocentric interests are completely obliterated. Prayer, finally, is **submission.** As man abandons his own desires, he surrenders his will to God's will. This is prayer at its highest level, the antithesis of primitive magic which thinks that the supernatural may be coerced, wheedled, shamed, or bribed into doing man's will.

The intensity, freedom and effectiveness of Biblical prayer may best be seen in the lives of its greatest personalities. Consider, for instance, the prayers of Moses (Exod. 32:11-13, 31, 32; 33:12-18; Num. 11:11-15; 14:13-19); Abraham (Gen. 18:22-23); Jacob (Gen. 32:24-30); Elijah (James 5:17-18); David (Pss. 3, 32, etc.); Solomon (II Chron. 1:7-12; 6:14-42); Hezekiah (II Kings 19:14-19; cf. Isa. 37:14-20); Ezra (9:5-15); Jeremiah (17:13-18; Lam. 5); Paul (Eph. 1:15-22; 3:14-19, etc.). In this area of spiritual experience as in every area of relationship with God, Jesus Christ has left an unsurpassed and perfect example (I Pet. 2:21). Prayer occupied a place of singular importance in His own life and teaching. In time of decision and crisis He gave Himself to prayer. Thus our Lord prayed when He was baptized (Luke 3:21-22); when He chose His twelve apostles (Luke 6:12-13); when He was transfigured (Luke 9:29); when He was engaging in sustained and exhausting service (Mark 1:35-39); when He called forth Lazarus from the grave (John 11:41-42); when He was burdened for Simon Peter (Luke 22:31-32); when He faced betrayal, execution, and divine abandonment (Mark 14:32-42); when He thought of His disciples and their future ministry (John 17); and when He died (Luke 23:46).

But our Lord also prayed in times of joy (Luke 10:21), even as He prayed gratefully when food was served (Luke 22:17; John 6:11). Prayer, indeed, was so evidently the habit of our Saviour's life that His example aroused within His followers a longing for the same power and blessing (Luke 11:1). Every kind of prayer may be found in the Gospel record — communion, adoration, thanksgiving, petition, intercession, and submission; yes, every kind but one — confession. With that ex-

Albrecht Durer's famous representation of prayer, "Praying Hands."

ception it may be said that our Lord's model prayer (Matt. 6:8-15), together with His parables and discourses on this subject, sprang from His own experience with the Father (Matt. 6:1-7; 18:21-33; Mark 11:22-26; Luke 7:3-4; 11:5-13; 18:1-8; John 14:13-14; 15:1-7; 16:24-26).

Now in His state of exaltation our Saviour functions as a Priest whose all-absorbing task is intercession (Heb. 7:25).

Undeniably, some of our requests are denied: fervent pleas do go unanswered — if we may ignore the contention that "No" and "Not yet" and "In some strange disguise" are divine answers equally as valid as "Yes." It is not merely that some of God's devoted servants have sessons when prayer seems to be unavailing (Ps. 88:13-14; Lam. 3:44; Hab. 1:2, 13); there are likewise cases where a repeated petition is refused for reasons which may be humanly opaque (II Chron. 12:7-9). Yet granting that some cases of unanswered prayer are at present inexplicable (I Cor. 13:12), there are other cases where the divine refusal can be accounted for by the suppliant's failure to obey the principles which govern effective intercession. The God-man relationship, we have previously asserted, is not that of automata; it is genuinely interpersonal. Hence, as in any I-Thou fellowship, certain conditions must be met. Assuming, then, that filial bond established by an acceptance of Jesus Christ as Saviour (Matt. 5:1-2; 6:8; Rom. 8:14-17; Gal. 3:23; cf. John 8:44), the following principles appear to be regulative. Prayer avails: 1. Only as it is made in faith (Heb. 11:6; Matt. 17:20; Mark 11:23-24; James 1:6). 2. Only as it is made in the Name of Jesus (John 14: 13; 15:16).. 3. Only as it is made in keeping with the will of God (I John 5:14-15). Hence sinful egocentricity precludes effectiveness in supplication (James 4:2-3). 4. Only as it is made under the direction and dynamic of the Holy Spirit (Jude 20; Matt. 20:22; John 4:10; Rom. 8:26-27). 5. Only as it is made by a suppliant who has confessed and renounced sin (Ps. 66:18; Prov. 28:9; Isa. 59:1-2). 6. Only as it is made by a forgiving heart (Matt. 6: 12-15; 18:21-35; Mark 11:25-26; cf. James 5:14-16). 7. Only as it is made in a context of harmonious relationships on the human level (Matt. 5:23-24; 18:19; I Pet. 3:1-7). 8. Only as it is made with importunity (Luke 11: 5-8; 18:1-8), for persistence evidences genuine care, compassion, and concern. 9. Only as it is made with concentration and intensity (James 5:16). This is one reason why our Lord teaches the need for detachment (Matt. 6:6; cf. Mark 1:35). This, too, is why He advises fasting (Mark 9:29; cf. Acts 13:1-3).

Under the pressure of emotional and physical suffering Job skeptically inquired, "What is the Almighty, that we should serve him? and what profit should we have, if we pray unto him?" (Job 21:15). But prayer, obviously, is of incalculable profit. From the standpoint of human responsibility, it is the major element in the outworking of God's redemptive program (I Tim. 2:1-4). Besides this, prayer is the source of vision, power, creativity, and blessing in personal experience. Consequently, because of its profit, we are enjoined to give this ministry unquestioned priority (Luke 18:1; Eph. 6:18; Phil. 4:6; I Tim. 2:1; I Thess. 5: 17). Neglect of prayer or indolence in prayer is nothing short of sin (I Sam. 12:23), since it impedes the operation of God's grace in man's life.

Preacher, Preaching (See Occupations & Professions)

Predestination (See Election)

Presbytery (prĕz′bĭ-têr-ē), the Christian elders who formally recognized Timothy's spiritual gift (I Tim. 4:14, RSV **the elders).** The same Greek word occurs in Luke 22:66 (KJV, ASV **the elders,** RSV **the assembly of the elders)** and Acts 22:5 (KJV, ASV **the estate of elders,** RSV **council of elders)** for the organized body of Jewish elders in Jerusalem.

Presidents (prĕz′ĭ-dĕnts, **chief).** Administrative officers placed by Darius over the 120 satraps in his kingdom. Daniel was one (Dan. 6:2-7).

Press (to crowd, a crowd), words used in Mark 2:4 and Luke 8:19.

Press Fat (prĕs′făt, **a trough),** vessel used to collect liquid from pressed grapes (Hag. 2:16).

Press (oil or wine), a rendering of several Hebrew and Greek words used to refer to a device used for extracting liquids from certain fruits from which wines and oils were made.

Prick (a thorn, a goad), any slender-pointed thing, like a thorn (Num. 33: 55). The spiritual goads of conviction against which Saul kicked before his conversion (Acts 9:5; 26:14).

Priest, Priesthood. The NT word for "priest" is related to a word meaning "holy," and indicates one who is consecrated to and engaged in holy matters. The Heb. word for priest is of uncertain origin, but seems originally to have meant a "seer," as well as one who has to do with divine things. A priest is a minister of any religion, whether heathen (Gen. 41:45; Acts 14: 13) or Biblical (Matt. 8:4; I Pet. 2:5, 9). Originally, individuals were priests (Gen. 4:3, 4); later, fathers of families (Gen. 12:7; 13:18); at Sinai God through Moses designated Aaron, his sons, and his descendants priests (Exod. 28:1). The Aaronic priests had to meet very rigid standards (Lev. 21: 16-24); in the sanctuary they ministered in special garments, and adhered to a definite ritual. They were divided into 24 courses, each serving a week at a time (I Chron. 24:1-19). They represented the people before God, offering sacrifices and praying in their behalf. The chief, or high, priest supervised the priests, offered a sin offering (Lev. 4) and sacrificed on the Day of Atonement (Lev. 16), and ascertained the will of God by the Urim and Thummim (Num. 27:21; Neh. 7:65). The Levites served as assistants to the Aaronic priests (Num. 3). In the NT Jesus Christ is described as a high priest after the order of Melchizedek (Heb. 6:10, 20-7:17). The Aaronic priesthood is abolished in Him (John 14:6; I Tim. 2:5, 6; Heb. 5:7-10). The sacrifice He offered was Himself, and it never needed to be repeated. By His death He made atonement for the sins of men once for all. The NT teaches the priesthood of all believers; they share in Christ's priestly activity, bringing the word to men and bringing men to Christ (Eph. 2:18; Heb. 10:19-25; 13:15; I Pet. 2:5, 9; Rev. 1:5, 6).

Prince, Princess (prĭns, prĭn′-sĕs). A leader, an exalted person clothed with authority; the daughter or wife of a chief or king. There are princes of various nations (Matt. 20:25 ASV, RSV rulers); of (part of) the land of Canaan (Gen. 34:2); of Ishmael's descendants (Gen. 17:20; 25:16); of the Hittites (Gen. 23:6); of Egypt (Gen. 12:15); of the Philistines (I Sam. 18: 30); of Persia (Esth. 1:3), called **satraps** in ASV, RSV of Daniel 3:2, etc.; of Babylon (Jer. 39:13 ASV, RSV **chief officers);** of Tyre (Ezek. 28:2); of the north (Ezek. 32:30); of Meshech and Tubal (Ezek. 38:2 ASV margin, **chief princes).** There were merchant princes in Tyre (Isa. 23:8). The heads of the tribes or of the congregation of Israel are princes (Num. 1:16 RSV **leaders;** Josh. 9:15 RSV **leaders).** David is called **prince** (I Kings 14:7 ASV margin, RSV **leader),** and he eulogizes Abner as a prince (II Sam. 3:38). The enemies of Jesus call Him Beelzebub, prince of the demons (Mark 3:22). The devil is the prince of this world (John 12:31 RSV ruler). Personal spiritual powers of evil are princes (I Cor. 2:6 ASV, RSV **rulers;** Eph. 2:2). Messiah is the prince (Dan. 9:25); of Peace (Isa. 9:6); of Life (Acts 3:15 ASV margin, RSV **Author);** of the kings of the earth (Rev. 1:5 ASV, RSV **ruler).** Bethlehem is called one of the princes of Judah (Matt. 2:6 RSV **rulers)** because the Davidic dynasty had its origin there.

Of princesses far less is said. Solomon had 700 princesses as wives, in contrast with 300 concubines (I Kings 11: 3). Jerusalem is apostrophized as a princess (Lam. 1:1). A king's daughter (Ps. 45:9-12) a prince's daughter (S. of Sol. 7:1 RSV **queenly maiden),** and a daughter of a prince of Midian (Num. 25:18) are mentioned. The new name of Abraham's wife, Sarah, means princess (Gen. 17:15 ASV margin).

Principalities (prĭn′sĭ-păl′ĭ-tēz). 1. Rule; ruler (Eph. 1:21; Titus 3:1). 2. Order of powerful angels and demons (Rom. 8:38; Eph. 6:12).

Print, the translation of two Hebrew words and one Greek word, meaning a mark made by pressure (Lev. 19:28; Job 13:27; John 20:25).

Prisca, Priscilla (prĭs′kȧ, prĭ-sĭl′ȧ). Priscilla (diminutive of **Prisca,** Rom. 16: 3) was the wife of the Jewish Christian, Aquila, with whom she is always mentioned in the NT. They were tentmakers whom Paul met in Corinth (Acts 18:2); they instructed Apollos in Ephesus (Acts 18:24-26); Paul sent them greetings in Rome (Rom. 16:3); and in I Corinthians 16:19 Paul speaks of them being in Ephesus again where they had a church in their house.

Prison (prĭz′′n), a place where persons suspected, accused, or convicted of crime are kept. Joseph was cast into a pit while his brothers decided how to dispose of him (Gen. 37:22-28), and into the Egyptian king's prison, in the house of the captain of the guard (Gen. 39:20-40:7). Samson was confined in a Philistine prison at Gaza (Judg. 16:21, 25). Prisoners taken in war were usually killed or enslaved (Num. 21:1 ASV, RSV captive; Isa. 20:4).

The pitiable state of those in prison is spoken of (Ps. 79:11; Isa. 14:17; 42: 22; Lam. 3:34; Zech. 9:11), and their hope in God (Pss. 69:33; 102:20; 142: 7; 146:7; Isa. 42:7). John the Baptist was imprisoned for criticizing a king's marriage (Matt. 4:12; 11:2; 14:3, 10 and parallels); Peter and John for preaching about Jesus (Acts 4:3; 5:18-25); Peter was delivered by an angel (Acts 12:3-19). Paul led Christians to prison (Acts 8:3; 22:4; 26:10) and was himself often in prison (II Cor. 11: 23); with Silas at Philippi (Acts 16:23-40); in Jerusalem (23:18); in Caesarea (25:27); on shipboard (27:1, 42); under house arrest in his own rented dwelling (28:16, 17, 30). He refers to his imprisonment as for the Lord (Eph. 3:1; 4:1; Phil. 1:14, 17; II Tim. 1:8; Philem. 9); to his fellow-prisoners (Rom. 16:7; Col. 4:10). Barabbas was released from prison in place of Jesus (Matt. 27:15, 16 and parallels). Jesus refers to imprisonment on civil process, as for debt (Matt. 5:25; 18:30; Luke 12:58); to visiting those in prison (Matt. 25:36, 39, 43, 44); and predicts that His followers will be put in prison during persecution (Luke 21:12; Rev. 2:10).

Prochorus (prŏk′ō-rŭs), one of the first deacons (Acts 6:5) who were elected to take care of the Greek-speaking widows.

Proconsul (prō′kŏn-sŭl), a Roman official, generally of praetorian or consular rank, who served as deputy consul in the Roman provinces. The term of office was usually one year. Sergius Paulus, Paul's famous convert (Acts 13:7), and Gallio (Acts 18:12) were such officials mentioned in the Bible. Often called "deputy" in the English Bible.

Procurator (prŏ′kū-rā′têr), governor of a Roman province. Pilate, Felix and Festus were such governors in Palestine with headquarters in Caesarea. Generally the procurators were appointed directly by the emperor to govern the Roman provinces and were often subject to the imperial legate of a larger political area.

Profane (prō-fān′), to descrate or defile. Such things as the altar, the sabbath, the sanctuary and God's name could all be profaned. Esau was called a profane person because he despised his birthright (Heb. 12:16). A godless or unholy person in the NT is called profane.

Promise (prŏm′ĭs). In the OT there is no Heb. word corresponding to **promise;** the words **word, speak,** and **say** being used instead. In the NT, however, the word **promise** is often used, usually in the technical sense of God's design to visit His people redemptively in the person of His Son. This promise is first given in the **proto-evangelium** (Gen. 3:15), is repeated to Abraham (Gen. 12:2, 7, etc.), and to David that his house would continue on his throne (II Sam. 7:12, 13, 28), and is found repeatedly in the OT (Isa. 2:2-5; 4:2; 55:5, etc.). In the NT all these promises are regarded as having their fulfillment in Christ and His disciples (II Cor. 1:20; Eph. 3:6). Jesus' promise of the Spirit was fulfilled at Pentecost. In the NT there are hundreds of promises to believers, among them the kingdom (James 2:5), eternal life (I Tim. 4:8), Christ's coming (II Pet. 3:9).

Prophecy, Prophets, a spokesman for God. OT prophets were not interpreters of God's will; they uttered the actual words which God gave them. Two aspects to their work: forthtelling and foretelling. There were schools of the prophets, but little is known of them (I Sam. 19:19, 20; II Kings 2: 3, 5; 4:38; 6:1). There were true and false prophets (Jer. 28:1ff). The prophets of the OT were of two kinds: the former, who wrote an interpretative history of the background of the period in which the great writing prophets lived and worked; the latter, also called writing prophets — Isaiah, Jeremiah, Ezekiel, Daniel and the Twelve Minor Prophets.

Prophetess, a woman who exercised the prophetic gift in ancient Israel or in the early Christian church. There are at least four women bearing this designation in the OT: (1) Miriam, sister of Moses (Exod. 15:20); (2) Deborah (Judg. 4:4); (3) Huldah, (II Kings 22:14); (4) the unnamed wife of Isaiah, who bore him children with prophetic names (Isa. 8:3). In the NT, Philip the evangelist is said to have had "four unmarried daughters who prophesied" (Acts 21:8, 9).

Propitiation (prō-pĭsh′ĭ-ā′shŭn, **to cover)** to appease the wrath of God so that His justice and holiness will be satisfied and He can forgive sin. Propitiation does not make God merciful; it makes divine forgiveness possible. For this, an atonement must be provided; in OT times, animal sacrifices; now, the death of Christ for man's sin. Through Christ's death propitiation is made for man's sin (Rom. 3: 25; I John 2:2; 4:10).

Proselyte (prŏs′ĕ-līt), a foreign resident, often rendered "stranger" (Exod. 20:10; Deut. 5:14). The word occurs only four times in the NT: 1. In Jesus' denunciatory discourse, Matt. 23:1-39, one of His serious charges against the "scribes and Pharisees, hypocrites!" is, "ye compass sea and land to make one proselyte, and when he is made, ye make him twofold more

CHRONOLOGICAL CHART OF THE PROPHETS

Northern Kingdom Prophet	Northern Kingdom King		Southern Kingdom Prophet		Southern Kingdom King	
	Jeroboam	933-912				
	Nadab	912-911				
	Baasha	911-888				
	Elah	888-887				
	Zimri	887				
	Tibni	887-863				
	Omri	887-877				
ELIJAH	Ahab	876-854			Jehoshaphat	873-849
	Ahaziah	854-853			Jehoram	849-842
ELISHA	Jehoram	853-842			Ahaziah	842
	Jehu	842-815			Athaliah	842-836
	Jehoahaz	814-798	JOEL?		Jehoash	836-797
	Jehoash	798-793			Amaziah	797-779
JONAH	Jeroboam II	793-743	ISAIAH		Uzziah	779-740
AMOS	Zachariah	743	MICAH			
HOSEA	Shallum	743	OBADIAH?			
	Menahem	743-737				
	Pekahiah	737-736			Jotham	740-736
	Pekah	736-730			Ahaz	736-728
	Hoshea	730-722			Hezekiah	727-699
Fall of the Northern Kingdom						
			NAHUM?		Manasseh	695-642
					Amon	642-640
			JEREMIAH		Josiah	640-609
			HABAKKUK?			
			ZEPHANIAH?			
		The Exile				
			DANIEL		Jehoiakim	609-597
					Jehoiachin	597
			EZEKIEL		Zedekiah	597-586
		The Restoration				
			ZECHARIAH	520		
			HAGGAI	520		
			MALACHI	432?		

the child of Gehenna than yourselves" (vs. 15).

The other three NT occurrences of the word "proselyte" are all in the book of Acts. 2. In the long list of places and people represented in Jerusalem on the day of Pentecost "Jews and proselytes" (Acts 2:10) are mentioned. Of the 3,000 who were swept into the Christian movement that day, and the hundreds more who soon joined them, the probability is that there were many hundreds of proselytes. 3. When it came to the selection of the first diaconate (Acts 6:1-6) one of the seven was "Nicolas, a proselyte from Antioch" (vs. 5).

4. After Paul's great sermon in the synagogue at Pisdian Antioch (Acts 13:14-41), we read that "many of the Jews and devout proselytes followed Paul and Barnabas" (vs. 43). From this point on in the record we cannot distinguish the proselytes. "The Gentiles" came in great crowds, and "the Jews" became jealous and hostile (vss. 44-52). A distinction was apparently made between uncircumcised proselytes, i.e., those who had not fully identified themselves with the Jewish nation and religion; and circumcised proselytes, those who identified themselves fully with Judaism.

Prostitute (prŏs'tĭ-tūt). The idea is usually conveyed by "harlot" (Gen. 34: 31; Matt. 21:31, 32; Luke 15:30) or in KJV "whore" (Lev. 21:7). A famous example is Rahab (Josh. 2:1; Heb. 11: 31; James 2:25). Israel, unfaithful to God, is called a harlot by the prophets (Isa. 1:21; Jer. 2:20; 3:1; Ezek. 16: 15, 16; Hos. 4:15). A special class of prostitutes performed sex acts in heathen worship.

Provender (prŏv'ĕn-dêr), **feed,** as grain or hay fed to cattle, horses and the like (Gen. 24:25, 26; 42:27; Judg. 19:19, 21).

Proverb (prŏv'ûrb), a pithy saying, comparison or question (I Kings 4:32; Proverbs 1:1, 6; Eccl. 12:9). A proverb may be a snatch of poetry, showing parallelism of structure; a sharp question; a pregnant sentence; a very brief story. Felicity of expression insures its long preservation and wide currency through oral transmission, even after it is fixed in literary, written form.

Proverbs, Book of. The best representative of the so-called Wisdom literature of ancient Israel, the Book of Proverbs comprises 31 chapters of pithy statements on moral matters. Its text is "The fear of the Lord is the beginning of wisdom" (Prov. 1:7).

The headings in 1:1 and 10:1 claim a Solomonic authorship for the bulk of the book, and this claim, though often denied in recent days, has no objective evidence against it. Chapters 25-29 are said to be by Solomon, "copied out" by the men of Hezekiah. This obscure reference may refer to later collecting or editing of other Solomonic material. Of the authors Agur (chap. 30) and King Lemuel (chap. 31) we know nothing. They may even be poetic references to Solomon himself. Proverbs is mentioned in the apocryphal book of Ecclesiasticus (47:17), written about 180 B.C. Although the canonicity of Proverbs, Ezekiel, and a few other books was questioned by individual rabbis as late as in the council of Jamnia, A.D. 90, still it had long been accepted as authoritative Scripture, as the quotation in the Zadokite Document shows (col. 11, 1.19ff). It is quoted and alluded to several times in the NT.

Outline:

I. Introduction, 1:1-1:9.
II. Sin and righteousness personified and contrasted, 1:10-9:18.
III. Single-verse contrasts of sin and righteousness, 10:1-22:16.
IV. Miscellaneous and longer contrasts, 22:17-29:27.
V. Righteousness in poems of climax, 30:1-31:31.

Providence (prŏv'ĭ-dĕns), the universal sovereign reign of God; God's preserving and governing all His creatures, and all their actions (Job 9:5, 6; 28: 25; Pss. 104:10-25; 145:15; 147:9; Matt. 4:4; 6:26-28; Luke 12:6, 7; Acts 17:25-28). General providence includes the government of the entire universe, especially the affairs of men. Special providence is God's particular care over the life and activity of the believer (Rom. 8:28).

Divine providence is presented as "upholding all things by his powerful word" (Heb. 1:3); ". . . he maketh his sun to rise upon the evil and the good, and sendeth rain on the just and on the unjust" (Matt. 5:45, see Ps. 68:9; Rom. 1:20; Acts 14:15-17. See Common Grace).

Although God's grace is always offered to all men (Acts 10:34, 35), yet the **main stream** of historical revelation and blessing for the world, through the instrumentality of Israel and the Church, is a principal theme of all Scripture (see Rom. 3:1, 2; 9:3-6; 11:1; I Tim. 3:15; Acts 7:1-60; 13:16-43). To this end God sometimes moves in unrecognized events and processes (Isa. 40:1-5; 44:28-45:4).

Not only is the general course of nature sustained by God's providence, but the moral order and its logical consequences as well: "Whatsoever a man soweth, that shall he also reap. He that soweth to the flesh shall of the flesh reap corruption. He that soweth to the Spirit shall of the Spirit reap life everlasting" (Gal. 6:7, 8). Divine providence sustaining the moral order is the principal theme of the book of Proverbs.

Province (prŏv'vĭns), unit of an empire, like those of the Roman empire. In Persia they were called satrapies. Rome's provinces were divided into two categories: imperial, those requiring a frontier army, and ruled by a legate appointed by the emperor; senatorial, those presenting no major problems, and ruled by someone appointed by the Senate—a proconsul (Acts 13: 7).

Provocation (prŏv'ō-kā'shŭn), any cause of God's anger at sin (I Kings 15:30; 21:22; II Kings 23:26; Ezek. 20:28; Job 17:2). In the prayer of repentance of the returned exiles (Neh. 9:18, 26) the provocation (RSV **great blasphemies)** consisted in making the molten calf. In Psalm 95:8 ASV, RSV transliterate instead of translating Heb.

Meribah, the geographical location named for the provocation when the Israelites demanded water, which Moses brought out of a rock (Exod. 17:1-7; Num. 20:13, 24; 27:14; Deut. 32:51; 33:8; Ps. 81:7), the waters of Meribah. The one NT passage which (in KJV) **provocation** occurs (Heb. 3:8, 15, 16 RSV **rebellion)** relates to this incident. The verb **provoke** occasionally has a good sense, **to stir up** (Heb. 10:24).

Pruning Hook, an agricultural tool used in the cultivation of the vine, with a sharp knife-like end for pruning (Isa. 2:4; Joel 3:10; Mic. 4:3).

Psalms, The Book of, follows "the law" and "the prophets" in Hebrew (Luke 24:44), inaugurating the final division of the OT, called "the writings." It is the longest book in the Bible. The majority of its chapters, moreover, are antedated only by Genesis-Ruth. But the basic reason why Psalms is more quoted by the NT and more revered by Christians than any other Old Testament book is found in its inspiring subject matter, for its 150 poems constitute the height of God-given literature.

The Hebrew designation of Psalms means "praises," a term that reflects much of the book's content (cf. Ps. 145, title).

The Psalms, naturally enough, make no attempt within their respective poetic framework to elaborate the circumstances of their composition. But, as might indeed be expected, many of them do prefix explanatory titles in prose, indicating their authorship and occasion for writing as well as poetic-type and musical direction (see below, Sections V and VI). Most commonly appears the phrase, Psalm of Moses (David, etc.). The Hebrew preposition rendered by the word "of" expresses authorship (cf. Hab. 3:1, "of Habakkuk the prophet") but also possession (Ps. 24:1a, "the Lord's") or dedication (Ps. 4, etc., RSV, "to the choirmaster"). But while "Psalm of David" has sometimes been interpreted to mean merely "of Davidic character," or, "belonging to a collection entitled, **David,"** its actual usage in Scripture clearly indicates Davidic authorship (cf. Pss. 7, 18). The book of Psalms thus assigns 73 of its chapters to David, two to Solomon (Pss. 72, 127), one each to the wise men Heman and Ethan (Pss. 88-89, cf. I Kings 4: 31), one to Moses (Ps. 90), and 23 to the Levitical singing-clans of Asaph (Pss. 50, 73-83) and Korah (Pss. 42 [including 43], 44-49, 84-85, 87-88) concerns compilation; see below, 49 remain anonymous.

David himself is known to have enjoyed musical and literary endowments (I Sam. 16:16-18, Amos 6:5; cf. his acknowledged composition of II Sam. 1:19-27, etc.), to have exercised leadership in the development of Israel's liturgy (II Sam. 6:5, 13; I Chron. 15-16, 25; II Chron. 7:6, 29:30), and to have realized Spirit-born empowerment as "the sweet psalmist of Israel" (II Sam. 23:1-2; Mark 12:36; Acts 1: 16, 2:30-31, 4:25; see DAVID). The NT repeatedly authenticates ascriptions to David: Pss. 16 (Acts 2:25), 32 (Rom. 4:6), 69 (Acts 1:16; Rom. 11:9), 110 (Luke 20:4-32; Acts 2:34). Certain of the anonymously-titled psalms are

"Thou anointest my head with oil." © MPS

also recognized as of Davidic composition Pss. 2 (Acts 4:25), 95 (Heb. 4:7, where "in David"—his person, not his book, as if Psalms were entirely his), 96, 105, and 106 (underlying David's words in I Chron. 16:8-36, though cf. HDB, IV, 148). But it is significant that no psalm which claims **other** authorship, or contains later historical allusions (as Ps. 137, exilic) is ever attributed in Scripture to him.

Psalms is organized into five books: 1-41, 42-72, 73-89, 90-106, and 107-150; and, since the same psalm appears in more than one collection—e.g., Pss. 14 and part of 40 (Book I) as 53 and 70 (Book II), and the latter halves of 57 and 60 (Book II) as 108 (Book V) —it seems likely that each compilation experienced independent existence. Furthermore, since the last psalm of each collection was composed with terminal ascriptions that were designed for the book as a whole (41:13; 72:18-20; 89:52; 106:48, and the entire 150th Psalm for Book V), it appears that the origins of these five concluding psalms provide clues for the compilation of their respective books. Psalm 41 was written by David; and, since the remaining psalms of Book I are also attributed to him (except for Ps. 1, which constitutes the book's introduction; Ps. 10, which combines with 9 to form one continuous acrostic; and Ps. 33, which has no title), it would appear that David himself brought together this first collection. He further composed Psalm 106 (cf. I Chron. 16:34-36); so that Book IV, with its liturgical nature (contrast the more personal character of Pss. 1-41), must likewise be traced to David's own hand, prior to his death in 970 B.C. Books II-III exhibit more of a national interest (cf. their stress upon Elohim, God transcendent, rather than upon the Lord's personal name, Jehovah). King Solomon (d. 930 B.C.), who was responsible for the doxology of 72:18-20, thus becomes the historical compiler of Book II (his reference to "the prayers of David," 72:20, seems to be due to his father's having composed over half of the chapters that make up Pss. 42-72). Book III, however, was completed and collected by unnamed Korahites soon after 586 B.C. (see above); for though the body of Psalms 88-89 was written by Solomon's Ezrahites, the title that is prefixed to both (cf. the inappropriateness of the description "song [joyful]" to Ps. 88 alone) designates the sons of Korah as its ultimate compilers. Finally Book V, which parallels David's Book IV in liturgical interest but includes several post-Exilic (as well as early Davidic) psalms, came into being shortly after 537 B.C. It then remained for a Spirit-led scribe to bring Books IV and V into union with I-III, adding his own inspired composition of Psalms 146-150 as a grand halleluia for the entire Psalter. Since this last writing occurred in 444 B.C. (Ps. 147:13) at the time of Ezra's proclamation of the written law and reform of temple worship (Neh. 8-10), it may well be that Ezra himself executed the final compilation of the book (cf. Ezra 7:10).

Each of the 150 psalms exhibits the formal character of Hebrew poetry. This consists, not primarily in rhyme, or even rhythmic balance, but rather in a parallelism of thought, whereby suceceeding phrases either repeat or in some way elaborate the previous line. The compilation embraces not simply the congregational hymnbook of Solomon's temple but also the devotional heart beat of men like David, who "strengthened himself [against the crowd] in Jehovah his God" (I Sam. 30:6 ARV). The richest blessings of the Psalms flow from its affirmations of personal faith, "The LORD is **my** shepherd; **I** shall not want" (23:1).

Psalms of Solomon. One of the pseudepigrapha, extant in Greek, consisting of 18 psalms in imitation of the canonical psalms, probably written between 64 and 46 B.C.

Psalmody (See Music)

Psalter (See Music, Psalms)

Psaltery (See Music, Psalms)

Pseudepigrapha (sū'dē-pĭg'rȧ-fȧ), books not in the Heb. canon or the Apocrypha, ascribed to earlier authors; including **The Ascension of Isaiah, Assumption of Moses, Book of Enoch, Book of Jubilees, Greek Apocalypse of Baruch, Letters of Aristeas, III and IV Maccabees, Psalms of Solomon, Secrets of Enoch, Sibylline Oracles, Syriac Apocalypse of Baruch, Epistle of Baruch,** and **Testament of the Twelve Patriarchs.** They are important for their disclosure of Jewish ideas in the intertestamental period.

Ptolemais (See Accho)

Ptolemy (tŏl'ĕ-mē), common name of the 15 Macedonian kings of Egypt whose dynasty extended from the

Ptolemy I reproduced from a silver tetradrachma of the period (323-283 B.C.).

death of Alexander the Great in 323 B.C. to the murder of Ptolemy XV, son of Julius Caesar and Cleopatra in 30 B.C.: Ptolemy I, Soter (323-285 B.C.); Ptolemy II, Philadelphus (285-246 B.C.); LXX translated, Golden Age of Ptolemaic Egypt; Ptolemy III (c. 246-222 B.C.); Ptolemy IV, Philopator (222-205 B.C.); Ptolemy V, Epiphanes (205-181 B.C.); Ptolemy VI, Philometor (181-145 B.C.); Ptolemy VII, Physcon (145-117 B.C.); Ptolemy XI was the last of the male line of Ptolemy I, killed by Alexandrians; Ptolemy XII (51-47 B.C.) fled to Rome; Ptolemy XIII had Cleopatra to wife.

Pua (pū'ȧ), member of the family clan of Tola, of the tribe of Issachar (Num. 26:23).

Puah, Puvah (pū'ȧ, pū'vȧ), the name of one of the Hebrew midwives who refused to obey the edict of the Pharaoh to destroy the infant sons born of Hebrew women (Exod. 1:15-20).

Publican (See Occupations and Professions)

Publius (pŭb'lĭ-ŭs), the chief person on the island of Malta (Melita) in the Mediterranean. He gave lodging and food to Paul and his companions after their shipwreck on the island's rocky coast (Acts 27:27-44; 28:7-10).

Pudens (pū'dĕnz, **modest**), a Roman Christian (II Tim. 4:21).

Puhites (pū'hīts, **simple**) family descended from Caleb (I Chron. 2:50, 53).

Pul (pŭl, pōōl). 1. A king of Assyria, Tiglath-pileser III, who invaded Israel in the days of Menahem and was bribed to depart (II Kings 15:19), though he carried off captives (I Chron. 5:26).

2. A tribe or place in Africa (Isa. 66:19).

Pulpit (pŭl'pit), a scaffolding, a platform, or a high object of any kind (Neh. 8:4), used primarily as a position from which to speak.

Pulse (See Plants)

Punishment (pŭn'ĭsh-mĕnt). Death was the punishment for striking or even reviling a parent (Exod. 21:15, 17); blasphemy (Lev. 24:14, 16, 23); sabbath breaking (Num. 15:32-36); witchcraft (Exod. 22:18); adultery (Lev. 20:10); rape (Deut. 22:25); incestuous or unnatural connection (Lev. 20:11, 14, 16); kidnaping (Exod. 21:16); idolatry (Lev. 20:2). Cutting off from the people is **ipso facto** excommunication or outlawry, forfeiture of the privileges of the covenant people (Lev. 18:19). The hand of God executed the sentence in some cases (Gen. 17:14; Lev. 23:30; 20:3; Num. 4:15, 18, 29). Capital punishment was by stoning (Deut. 22:24); burning (Lev. 20:14); the sword (Exod. 32:27); hanging (Gal. 3:13; II Sam 21:6, 9); strangulation (not in Scripture, but in rabbinical writings). Other punishments; sawing asunder (Heb. 11:37); cutting with iron harrows (II Sam. 12:31; RSV, labor with harrows, etc.); precipitation (Luke 4:29; II Chron. 25:12); stripes, only 40 allowed (Deut. 25:2, 3), therefore only 39 given (II Cor. 11:24); the convict stripped to the waist, received them from a three-thonged whip, either lying on the ground (Deut. 25:2), or in a bent position tied to a pillar. If the executioner exceeded the number he was punished. Punishment in kind **(lex talionis)** was a common principle (Exod. 21:23-25), also composition, restitution of the thing or its equivalent (Exod. 21:19, 30). Crucifixion was not practiced till Roman times. Punishment for sin is widely recognized in the Bible, and is in the hands of God (directly, Gen.

4:1-16; Lam. 3:37-39; 4:6; Zech. 14:19; indirectly, I Pet. 2:14; everlasting punishment (Matt. 25:46). See Prison.

Punishment, Everlasting. The fact of everlasting punishment, for those who reject God's love revealed in Christ, is plainly stated in Matthew 25:46 and is explicit in the OT in Daniel 12:2.

The final place of everlasting punishment is called the "lake of fire" (Rev. 19:20; 20:10, 14, 15). This is also called "the second death" (Rev. 2:11; 20:6, 14, 15). In this connection it should be remembered that "death" in Biblical usage **never** means extinction or non-existence. Always the word designates a relative state of existence. That "the second death" is a state of conscious existence is evident from Rev. 14:9-11; 20:10.

"Hell" is an Anglo-Saxon word the root meaning of which probably is "the hidden," "the unseen realm."

In the NT, however, **Hades,** translated "Hell," occurs five times in contexts in which it could not mean the physical grave, and there are none of the remaining five passages (Matt. 11:23, parallel to Luke 10:15, these two obviously figurative: Matt. 16:18; Rev. 1:18; 6:8, the last also figurative) in which the context demands any other meaning than "the unseen realm where the souls of all the dead are."

The **reason** for eternal punishment is rejecting the love of God in Christ (John 3:18). God has given men the free offer of the Gospel (John 3:16) and the convicting work of the Holy Spirit (John 16:8, 9). Jesus described the act of rejecting this work of the Holy Spirit as being "guilty of eternal sin" (Mark 3:29).

Punites (pū'nīts), descendants of Puvah, of the tribe of Issachar (Num. 26:23; Gen. 46:13; I Chron. 7:1).

Punon (pū'nŏn), a desert encampment of the Israelites marking the second stop after leaving Sinai (Num. 33:42, 43), E of Edom.

Pur (pūr, **lots),** a Jewish festival celebrated on the 14th and 15th of the month Adar (Feb.-Mar.) commemorating the deliverance of the Hebrews from the plots of the wicked Haman in the post-Exilic period (Esth. 3:7; 9:26).

Pura (See Phurah)

Purification (pūr'ĭ-fĭ-cā'shŭn). Religious purity was both ceremonial and ethical. Under the Mosaic law, ceremonial purification was required for four acts: (1) the birth of a child, removed through circumcision (if male) and the isolation of the mother for a varying period (Lev. 12:2ff); (2) contact with a corpse; the offering of the red heifer is prescribed for the sacrifice of purification (Num. 19:1-10); (3) certain diseases, as leprosy (Lev. 13:8); (4) uncleanness due to a running sore (Lev. 15). Family purity was guarded through strict relations concerning sex (Lev. 20:1-21; Deut. 22:20, 21). In the NT though there is a transference from the outward to the inner; there is no relaxing of the basic requirements for purity itself (Matt. 5:27f; 19:3-9; Mark 10:2-11; I Cor. 5:9-13; 6:18-20; 7:8ff).

Purple. (Exod. 25:4; 26:36; 28:15; 35:6; Judg. 8:26; II Chron. 2:14; 3:14; Esth. 1:6; 8:15; S. of Sol. 3:10; Mark 15:17, 20; Luke 16:19; Acts 16:4). Purple was a very costly dye extracted from the **marine mulex trunculus,** a marine mollusk, from which the Phoenicians were able to manufacture the dye. A crushed gland gave out a milk-like fluid that turned purple or scarlet upon contact with the air. Because of its extreme costliness, it became a mark of distinction to wear a robe of purple. In later times, ecclesiastical officials arrayed themselves in purple robes. In early times, royalty was so dressed.

Purse, a finely finished leather pouch or bag. In Matthew 10:9, refers to the Oriental girdle made of crude leather or woven camel's hair worn around the waist. Sometimes, these "girdles" were finely tooled, and contained "slots," in which gold and silver coins could be kept (cf. Luke 10:4; 12:34).

Purtenance (pŭr'tē-năns), rendered "inwards" or "entrails" by the more recent versions (Lev. 1:9; 3:3; etc).

Put (pŭt). 1. Son of Ham (Gen. 10:6). 2. Libya (Isa. 66:19; Ezek 27:10; 38:5; Nah. 3:9). Put has also been taken to signify Egypt.

Puteoli (pū-tē'ō-lē, **little wells** or **springs),** a well-known seaport of Italy located in the Bay of Naples; it was the nearest harbor to Rome. It was the natural landing place for travelers from the East to Rome. In Acts 28:13-14 Luke reports that Paul landed there with the other prisoners when he was taken to Rome for trial.

Putiel (pū'tĭ-ĕl), the father-in-law of Eliezer, Aaron's son (Exod. 6:25).

Puvah (See Phuvah)

Pygarg (See Animals)

Pyramids (pēēr'ȧ-mĭds), approximately 80 tombs with superstructures of pyramidal form still in existence from ancient Egypt. The Egyptian Old Kingdom, especially Dynasties 3-4 (about 2700 B.C.) was in a particular sense the Pyramid Age, for in that period it was customary for royalty to be interred in such a tomb.

Pyrrhus (pĭr'ŭs, fiery red), the father of Sopater (Acts 20:4).

The great pyramid of Cheops at Gizeh (Giza), near Cairo. © MPS

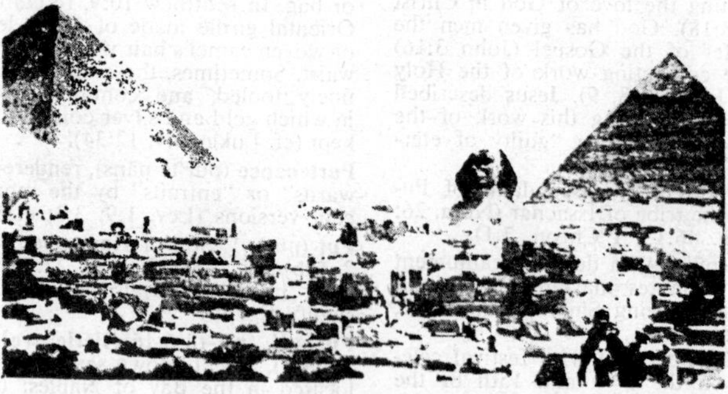

The excavated Sphinx amid the pyramids. © MPS

–Q–

Quail (See Birds)
Quarantania (kwŏr'ăn-tā'nĭ-à), the mountain where according to tradition Satan tempted Jesus to worship him (Matt. 4:8-10); Tell es-Sultân, a short distance W of OT Jericho.
Quarries (kwŏr'ēz, **graven images). In** Judges 3:19, 26, the marginal readings in KJV and ASV suggest "graven images," a rendering supported by the authority of the Septuagint and the Vulgate. The word "quarry" occurs in another disputed passage at I Kings 6:7. RSV says, probably correctly, that the stones were dressed "at the quarry."
Quartus (kwôr'tŭs), a Christian man of Corinth whose greetings Paul sends to the church at Rome (Rom. 16:23).
Quaternion (kwà-tĕr'nĭ-ŭn), a Roman guard of four men (Acts 12:4).
Queen. Dowager queens, or mothers of the monarch, are those who appear in the most influential roles in the Biblical records. 1. Jezebel, princess of Tyre who, during the 22 years of her husband Ahab's reign, and during the 13 years' rule of her sons Ahaziah and Joram, exercised a strong influence in favor of Phoenician pagan cults (I Kings 16:28-II Kings 9:37 **passim**). 2. Athaliah, daughter of Jezebel, and a similar character, was the wife of Jehoram of Judah, son of Jehoshaphat. 3. Bathsheba, mother of Solomon, widow of David (I Kings 1).

Foreign queens mentioned in the OT are: 1. Vashti, the deposed queen of Ahasuerus of Persia (Esth. 1). 2. Esther, the Jewess. 3. Balkis, legendary name of the Queen of Sheba (I Kings 10). 4. Neh. 2:6 and Dan. 5:10 refer to unnamed queens.

In the NT are: 1. Bernice, or Berenice, sister of Agrippa II, and wife of her uncle, Herod, king of Chalcis (Acts 25 and 26). 2. Drusilla, wife of Felix, procurator of Judaea.
Queen of Heaven, female deity to whom priestly Hebrew women made offerings (Jer. 7:18; 44:17-25). The most likely identification is with Ashtoreth, goddess of love and fertility, synonymous with the Assyrian and Babylonian Ishtar, and the Roman Venus.
Quicksands, sandbanks off shores of N Africa S of Crete; very treacherous (Acts 27:17).
Quirinius (kwĭ-rĭn'ĭ-ŭs), The reference to this Roman governor is in Luke 2:2. It is known that Quirinius ("Cyrenius" is an Anglicized form of the Greek rendering of the name) was governor of Syria A.D. 6-9, that Judaea was incorporated at the time, and a census taken which caused the rebellion of Judas (Acts 5:37).
Quotations from Pagan Poets (See Poets, Pagan)
Qurun Hattin (See Hattin, Horns of; Beatitudes, Mount of)

-R-

Ra (See Re)

Raamah (rā'ȧ-mȧ), fourth son of Cush and grandson of Ham (I Chron. 1:9); the father of Sheba and Dedan (Gen. 10:7; cf. I Chron. 1:9). One of the merchant tribes that traded in spices, gold and precious stones with Tyre (Ezek. 27:22).

Raamiah (rā'ȧ-mī'ȧ, **Jehovah has thundered),** one of the companions of Zerubbabel who returned with him to Jerusalem from the captivity (Neh. 7:7); Reelaiah (Ezra 2:2).

Raamses (rā-ăm'sēz). Raamses and Pithon are the names given in Exodus 1:11 for the two store cities the Israelites were forced to build for the Pharaoh of the Oppression. From Raamses the Israelites began their exodus from Egypt (Exod. 12:37; Num. 33:3, 5).

Rabbah, Rabbath (răb'ȧ, răb'ăth). 1. Town in Judah (Josh. 15:60); not now identifiable. 2. Capital of Ammon, represented today by Amman, capital of Jordan, 22 miles E of Jordan (Josh. 13: 25; II Sam. 11:1; 12:27-29; I Chron. 20:1; Jer. 49:2, 3). Subsequently captured by Ptolemy Philadelphus (285-247 B.C.), who changed its name to Philadelphia; became one of the cities of the Decapolis. Twice spelled "Rabbath" (Deut. 3:11; Ezek. 21:20).

Rabbath-Ammon (See Rabbah)

Rabbi (See Occupations and Professions)

Rabbith (răb'ĭth), a town in the tribe of Issachar (Josh. 19:20).

Rabboni (răb-bō'nī), a variant of **Rabbi,** the Heb. word for **Master** (John 21: 16).

Rab-mag (răb'măg), one of the Babylonian princes present at the capitulation of Jerusalem (Jer. 39:3). Same as Nergalsharezer (Jer. 39:3).

Rabsaris (răb'sȧ-rĭs), the title of a high Assyrian and Babylonian official usually taken to be "chief eunuch" (II Kings 18:17; 19:35-36).

Rabshakeh (răb'shȧ-kĕ), the title of an Assyrian official, with the meaning "chief cup-bearer" or "chief of the officers(?)" (II Kings 18:17, 19, 26-28, 37; 19:4, 8, and parallel, Isa. 36:2, 4, 11-13, 22; 37:4, 8). While Sennacherib was besieging Lachish, he sent his Rabshakeh to Jerusalem to deliver an ultimatum to that city.

Raca (rȧ'kȧ, **empty, vain,** or **worthless fellow),** a term of contempt or scorn (Matt. 5:22).

Race. The clearest refs. are I Cor. 9: 24; Heb. 12:1; II Tim. 4:7. Other passages may well allude to it (Rom. 9: 16; Gal. 5:7; Phil. 2:16). The Greek race was one of a series of highly competitive games.

Rachab (See Rahab)

Rachal (rā'căl), a place in the Negev of Judah where David and his men roamed as fugitives as they were pursued by the relentless Saul (I Sam. 30: 29).

Rachel (rā'chĕl, **ewe),** the wife of Jacob, the mother of Joseph and Benjamin (Gen. 29:6, 16, 18, 31; 30:1-9; cf. Jer. 31:15; Matt. 2:18). Rachel was the younger daughter of Laban, the Aramaean (AV. "Syrian"), the brother of Rebekah, Jacob's mother (Gen. 28: 2); thus Jacob and Rachel were full cousins. For some time, Rachel remained barren, bearing Jacob no children. The two children that Rachel bore to Jacob were Joseph (30:22), while yet in the house of Laban, and Benjamin after the return home. Rachel, however, died in childbirth with Benjamin (Gen. 35:16-19). This may partially show why Jacob favored the sons of his beloved Rachel above the sons of Leah. The character of Rachel varies between the very attractive and the unattractive. She partook of her family's traits of scheming and duplicity (Gen. 31:34). A believer in monotheism, she yet clung to the forms of polytheism. Jeremiah pictures her as rising from her grave to weep over the children who are being carried to Babylon, never to return (Jer. 31:15). The Apostle Matthew takes this as prophetic of the slaughter of the Innocents by Herod the great (Matt. 2: 18).

Raddai (răd'ā-ī), fifth of the seven sons of Jesse, father of David (I Chron. 2:14).

Ragau (rā'gô), the Greek form of Reu, an ancestor of Christ (Luke 3:35).

Raguel, Reuel (ră-gū'ĕl), the father-in-law of Moses (Num. 10:29), KJV Reuel (Exod. 2:18); a Midianite, also described as a Kenite (Judg. 4:11).

Rahab (rā'hăb, **broad).** 1. A woman best known for her prominent role in

The so-called Tomb of Rachel near Bethlehem. © *MPS*

the capture of Jericho during the days of Joshua (Josh. 2:1, etc. Matt. 1:5; Heb. 11:31; James 2:25). The spies sent by Joshua were received into the house of Rahab prior to the siege of the city by the army of Israel. Joshua and his men spared Rahab after they had captured the city (Josh. 6:17).

According to Matthew's genealogy, she is not only one of the four women mentioned in the family tree of the Saviour, but also the mother of Boaz, the husband of Ruth, and the great-grandmother of King David (Matt. 1:5; Ruth 4:18-21). The author of Hebrews speaks of her as a shining example of faith (Heb. 11:31). James shows his appreciation of her as a person in whom faith was not merely "theological" but practical as well (James 2:5).

2. A mythical monster of the deep (Job 9:13; Ps. 89:10; Isa. 51:9). Applied to Egypt (Isa. 30:7; Ps. 87:4).

Raham (rā'hăm, **pity, love**), son of Shema, father of Jorkeam (I Chron. 2:44).

Rahel (See Rachel)

Raiment (See Dress)

Raiment, Changes of (See Dress)

Rain. In Palestine the rainy season extends from October to April; the dry season, from May to October. The early rain occurs in October and November (Ps. 84:6; Isa. 30:23; Jer. 5:24); the latter rain in March and April (Job 29:23; Prov. 16:15; Jer. 3:3; 5:24; Zech. 10:1). Crops are therefore planted so that they will grow during the rainy season. "Rain" is often used in the OT in a figurative sense. Abundance of rain denotes the rich blessing of Jehovah upon His people (Deut. 28:12); lack of rain is a sign of God's displeasure (Deut. 28:23, 24). In Canaanite religion Baal was conceived as the god of rain, and was therefore ardently worshipped.

Rainbow. The Biblical interpretation of the rainbow is found in the story of Noah, with whom God entered into a covenant that never again would He send a universal deluge to destroy the whole inhabited earth (Gen. 9:8-17).

Raisins (See Food)

Rakkath (răk'ăth), one of the fortified cities assigned to the tribe of Naphtali (Josh. 19:35) probably near the Sea of Galilee on site of Tiberias.

Ram (See Animals, Sheep)

Rama, Ramah (rā'må, **height**). 1. Ra-

Er-Ram, probable site of Ramah, the birthplace of the prophet Samuel © *MPS*

mah-Arael, a city of Naphtali, probably to be identified with the modern er-Rama (Josh. 19:36). 2. Rhama-Ramah, a territory mentioned as forming the boundary of Asher (Josh. 19:25). 3. Ramah Iamah of Benjamin mentioned along with Gibeon and Beeroth; the headquarters of Deborah, judge of Israel during the days of the oppression of Sisera (Judg. 4:5). 4. Ramah-Aramathiam, the hometown of Elkanah and Hannah, and the birthplace of the Prophet Samuel (I Sam. 1:19; 2: 11). 5. Ramah-of-the-south, see Ramath-Lehi, below.

Ramath-Lehi (rā'măth-lē'hī, **the hill** or **height of Lehi)**, the place where Samson cast away the jawbone of an ass after the slaughter of the Philistines (Judg. 15:17).

Ramath-Mizpeh (rā'măth mĭz'pĕ, **the heights,** or **the watchtower)**, the northern boundary line of the tribe of Gad (Josh. 13:26; Gen. 31:46-48). It has the triple names of Mizpeh, Galeed and Jegar-Sahadutha.

Ramath (Ramah) of the South, a city in the southern sector of Judah which was allotted to the tribe of Simeon (Josh. 19:8 AV).

Ramathaim-Zophim (See Ramah)

Ramathite (See Ramah)

Ramesses (râ-ăm'sēz, various other spellings, e.g., Rameses, Ramses), name of 11 Egyptian pharaohs, of whom Ramesses II (c. 1301-1234 B.C.) was the most famous, many scholars holding that he was the pharaoh of the Exodus. Some of these pharaohs must have had at least indirect influence on Israelite life, but none of them is mentioned in the OT.

Ramiah (rȧ-mī'ȧ, **Jah is set on high)**, a descendant of Parosh, mentioned in the list of those who renounced their foreign wives (Ezra 10:25).

Ramoth (rā'mŏth, **height). 1. A** precious stone or uncertain variety (Job 28:18; Ezek. 26:16). 2. An Israelite who after the Exile divorced his Gentile wife (Ezra 10:29). 3. Cities of refuge in the tribe of Gad, elsewhere called Ramoth-Gilead (Josh. 20:8; 21: 38).

Rams' Horns (See Musical Instruments, Shofar)

Rams' Skins, the skins of the sheep tanned with oil used for outer clothing by the shepherds of the Near East. They were utilized as the exterior covering for the tabernacle (Exod. 25:5).

A stele of Rameses II, eight feet high, with inscriptions. UMP

Ransom (răn′sŭm), the price paid for the redemption of a slave (Lev. 19:20); a reparation paid for injury or damages (Exod. 22:10-12); a fee, fine, or heavy assessment laid upon a man as a substitute for his own life (Exod. 21:30). In the NT the term signifies that redemptive price offered by Christ upon the cross for the salvation of His people (Mark 10:45; I Tim. 2:5).

Rapha (rā′fȧ). 1. The last son of Benjamin (I Chron. 8:2). 2. A descendant of Saul (I Chron. 8:37).

Raphu (rā′fū), father of Palti, one of the spies sent in to Canaan (Num. 13:9).

Ras Shamra (rȧs shȧm′rȧ), modern name of mound marking the site of ancient city of Ugarit, located on Syrian coast opposite island of Cyprus; an impotrant commercial center; destroyed by Sea Peoples who overran the area in 15th-14th centuries B.C. Several hundred clay tablets forming part of scribal library were found from 1929 though 1936; personal and diplomatic correspondence; business, legal, and governmental records; veterinary texts, and, most important religious literature. These throw a great deal of light upon Canaanite religion, culture and Hebrew literary style; and show striking similarities between Canaanite and Hebrew systems of worship. They clarify our knowledge of the world in which Israel developed.

Aerial view of Ras Shamra, ancient Ugarit, on the Syrian coast. ASOR

Rasor, Razor (rā′zẽr). The earliest razors were made of flint. Later they were made of bronze, and finally of steel. Joseph is said to have shaved himself before he was liberated from prison to stand before Pharaoh (Gen. 41:14). The cutting of the beard by a priest of Israel was forbidden, presumably because of its affinity to pagan practices (Lev. 21:5). The Nazarite was likewise forbidden the use of the razor (Num. 6:5).

Raven (See Birds)

Re, Ra (rā), a masculine deity in the pantheon of the gods of Egypt, identified with the sun-god. In the mystery religions, he was designated as a **Soter-Theos,** a "savior-god," a deity who rescues his people from death. The center of the worship of Re was Heliopolis, the ancient On. The ninth plague was in reality a judgment on Re (Exod. 12:21-23). Joseph, after being made food administrator of the land, married the daughter of the priest of On of the cult of Re (Gen. 41:45).

Reaiah, Reaia (rē-ā′yȧ, **Jah hath seen).** 1. The eponym of a Calebite family (I Chron. 4:2). 2. A Reubenite (I Chron. 5:5). 3. The family name of a company of Nethinim (Ezra 2:47; Neh. 7:50).

Reaping. In ancient times, consisted in either pulling up the grain by the roots, or cutting it with a sickle. The stalks were then bound into bundles and taken to the threshing floor. Strict laws for reaping were imposed upon Israel (Lev. 19:9; 23:10; 25:11; Deut. 16:9). Samuel mentions that reaping will be a duty that the nation's newly-chosen king, Saul, will demand of them (I Sam. 8:12). The figurative usage of the term speaks of deeds that produce their own harvest (Prov. 22:8; Hos. 8:7; I Cor. 9;6; Gal. 6:7, 8).

Reba (rē′bȧ), Midian chieftain slain at the command of Moses (Num. 31:8; Josh. 13:21).

Rebekah, Rebecca (rĕ-bĕk′ȧ). She was the sister of Laban, the wife of Isaac, mother of Esau and Jacob, and first receives mention in the genealogy of Nahor, the brother of Abraham (Gen. 22:20-24). Though the object of her husband's love (Gen. 24:67), Rebekah bore him no children for 20 years. It was only after special intercession on the part of Isaac that God gave her the two famous children, Esau and Jacob. Although twins, Esau was reckoned as the firstborn and Jacob as the second. However, God told her "the elder shall serve the younger" (Gen. 25:23). Jacob became his mother's favorite, which led her to trick aged and blind Isaac. Disguised as his brother Esau, Jacob obtained the blessing (Gen. 27:5-17). When it became evident that Jacob and Esau could no longer live under the same roof, at her suggestion, Jacob fled from home to her relatives in Aram (Gen. 27:42-46). Rebekah never saw her son alive again. Outside of Genesis there is only one reference to her (Rom. 9:10-12).

Recah, Reca (rē′kȧ), an unknown place in the tribe of Judah (I Chron. 4:12).

Rechab (rē′kăb, **horseman).** 1. One of the assassins of Ishbosheth, a son of Saul. They expected to receive a reward, as the murder of Ishbosheth left David without a rival upon the throne of Israel. However, the reaction of the king was quite different from what they had anticipated, as he commanded them both to be executed (II Sam. 4:5-11). They were Benjamites from Beeroth (4:5). 2. Father of Jehonadab (II Kings 10:15; Jer. 35:6-19). 3. Father of Malchiah (Neh. 3:14).

Reconciliation (rĕk′ŏn-sĭl-ĭ-ā′shŭn), a change of relationship between God and man based on the changed status of man through the redemptive work of Christ. Three aspects of this change are suggested in the New Testament. 1. Reconciliation is God exercising grace toward man who is in enmity because of sin, establishing in Christ's redemptive work the basis of this changed relationship of persons (II Cor. 5:19).

This changed relationship, however, is possible only because of the changed status of man, not in God. God is never said to be reconciled to man, but man to God since it is man's sinfulness which creates the enmity (Col. 1:21; Rom. 8:7). 2. A reconciliation of **condition** so that all basis of the enmity-relationship is removed and a complete basis of fellowship is established (II Cor. 5:18-20; Eph. 2:16). The grace of God assures the reconciled man that the grace-basis replaces the sin-basis and that he is established before God in a new relationship. 3. A reconciliation arising out of the change in man **induced by the action of God.** Man is not reconciled merely because his relationship has changed, but because **God** has changed him through Christ so that he can be reconciled (Rom. 5:11; 11:15; II Cor. 5:18 and Eph. 2:5). Reconciliation arises therefore, out of God, through Christ, to man, so that not only may the barriers to fellowship existing in sinful man be removed, but the positive basis for fellowship may be established through the righteousness of Christ imputed to man. Even though the sufficient ground of reconciliation is established in the completed redemptive work of Christ, reconciliation is the basis upon which the continued fellowship is established, "for if, when we were enemies, we were reconciled to God by the death of his Son, much more, being reconciled, we shall be saved by his life" (Rom. 5:10).

Recorder (See Occupations & Professions)

Red, a blood-like or a blood-red color. The adjective "red" is applied to the following items: (1) the badger skins dyed red which formed the outward covering for the Tabernacle (Exod. 25:5; 26:14; 35:7; etc.); (2) the color of certain animals (Num. 19:2; Zech. 1:8; 6:2; Rev. 6:4; 12:13); (3) the color of the human skin (Gen. 25:25; I Sam. 16:12); (4) redness of eyes (Gen. 49: 12; Prov. 23:29); (5) red sores (Num. 12:10); (6) wine (Prov. 23:31; Isa. 27: 2 AV); (7) water (II Kings 3:22); (8) pavement (Esth. 1:6); (9) the color of sin (Isa. 1:18); (10) the advancing foe against the city of Nineveh is depicted as bearing red or scarlet shields before him.

Redeemed, Redeemer (See Redemption)

Redemption (rē-dĕmp′shŭn, to tear loose, a ransom). Rooted in the secular usage of the word, the NT doctrine of redemption draws its meaning from a parallel with the market-place concept "to buy back," and thus describes the specific means by which the larger salvation concepts may be gained.

Originally restricted to its commercial usage, the word is used in the NT to contain both the idea of deliverance and the price of that deliverance, or ransom. Both ideas are in Romans 3:24 where it is asserted that man is freely justified by grace "through redemption that is in Christ Jesus"; in I Corinthians 6:20 where redemption is viewed as being "bought with a price"; and in Galatians 3:13 where Christ is said to have redeemed us "from the curse of the law being made a curse for us" (Eph. 1:7; I Pet. 1:18, 19; Rev. 5:9).

Redemptiveness connotes deliverance from the enslavement of sin and release to a new freedom. This new freedom is presented in Scripture as always residing in Christ. Man is redeemed from sin to a new life in Christ (Rom. 6:4). The fundamental idea of the word is a dual one: redemption **from** and redemption **to.** Redemption is from the law; from the penalty of the law; from sin; from Satan and from all evil. Redemption is to a new freedom from sin, a new relationship to God, and a new life in Christ.

Redemption rests in Christ's satisfaction of the requirements for ransom. He took our sinful nature upon Himself in order that He might satisfy the demands of the Law by assuming our guilt. Voluntarily exercising His will so to do, He achieved the ransom within Himself in order that He might deliver us from the bondage of sin. "Christ also suffered for sins once, the righteous for the unrighteous, that he might bring us to God; being put to death in the flesh, but quickened in the spirit" I Peter 3:18.

Redemption of Land. In Hebrew society, any land which was forfeited through economic distress could be redeemed by the nearest of kin. If, however, there was no one to redeem it, the property still returned to its original owner in the year of Jubilee (Lev. 25:24-34).

Red Heifer. The ashes of the red heifer were used for the removal of certain types of ceremonial uncleanness (Num. 19:9; 20, 21).

Red Sea, 1,350 mile long oceanic gulf extending from Indian Ocean to Gulf of Suez. Has two arms: Gulf of Suez and Gulf of Aqabah. "Red Sea" may refer to either arm (Num. 33:10, 11; I Kings 9:26) or the entire Red Sea (Exod. 23:31), or the nearby lakes. The Red Sea of Exod. 13:17, 18 should be rendered "Reed Sea." It is improbable that the Red Sea is meant. More likely the reference is to a body of water near Goshen which the Egyptians themselves referred to as Reed Sea.

Reed (rēd). 1. Tall flags, rushes, grasses; sometimes used figuratively for fickleness (Matt. 11:7), weakness (Isa. 42:3), or uncertain support (II Kings 18:21). 2. A Hebrew unit of measurement, equal to six cubits (Ezek. 40:5).

Reelaiah (rē′ĕl-ā′yȧ), one of the 12 heads of families returning with Zerubbabel after the captivity (Ezra 2:2; Neh. 7:7). Nehemiah has "Raamiah."

Refine, Refiner (See Occupations: Coppersmith)

Refuge, Cities of, the six cities on either side of the Jordan which under the supervision of the Levites were set aside for the asylum of the accidental slayer. East of the Jordan, they were Bezer in the tribe of Benjamin, Ramoth-Gilead of Gad, Golan in Manasseh. West of the river, they were Hebron in Judah, Shechem in Ephraim, and Kedesh in Naphtali (Num. 35:6, 14; Josh. 20:7ff; 21:13; 27:32, 38). These cities of refuge were designated until the accused could stand fair trial.

Regem (rē′gĕm), a descendant of the house or clan of Caleb (I Chron. 2:47).

Regem-Melech (rēg′ĕm mĕlĕk), one of a delegation sent to inquire of Zechariah concerning the propriety of fasting (Zech. 7:2).

Regeneration (rē-jĕn-êr-ā′shun), "to be born again," or "to be restored." Though the word is actually used only twice in the NT (Matt. 19:28 and Titus 3:5), many synonymous passages suggest its basic meaning. Related terms are: born again (John 3:3, 5, 7); born of God (John 1:13; I John 3:9); quickened (Eph. 2:1, 5); and renewed (Titus 3:5 and Rom. 12:2).

Regeneration is, therefore, the spiritual change wrought in the heart of man by an act of God in which his inherently sinful nature is changed and by which he is enabled to respond to God in faith. Regeneration involves an illumination of the mind, a change in the will, and a renewed nature. It extends to the total nature of man, irrevocably altering his governing disposition, and restoring him to a true experiential knowledge in Christ (II Cor. 5:17; Rom. 6:4). It is a partaking of the divine nature (II Pet. 1:4), a principle of spiritual life implanted in the heart.

The efficient cause of regeneration is God (I John 3:9) acting in love through mercy (Eph. 2:4, 5) to secure the new life in man through the instrument of His Word (I Pet. 1:23).

In regeneration, the soul is both passive and active: passive while it is still in bondage to sin, and active when it is released. The regenerating work of the Holy Spirit is not con-

Moonlight on the Red Sea. © *MPS*

ditioned by a prior acquiescence of the soul, but when the soul is released from sin, regenerated, it voluntarily and spontaneously turns toward God in fellowship.

Rehabiah (rē′hă-bī′à), son of Eliezer, grandson of Moses (I Chron. 23:17; 24:21; 26:25).

Rehob (rē′hōb, **broad).** 1. The northern limit to which the spies came as they searched out the land (Num. 13:21; I Sam. 10:6). 2. Two separate towns belonging to the tribe of Asher (Josh. 19:28; 19:30). 3. The father of Hadadezer, king of Aram (II Sam. 8: 3, 12). 4. Levite co-signer of the covenant of Nehemiah (Neh. 10:11).

Rehoboam (rē′hō-bō′ăm), the son of Solomon and his successor on the throne of Israel. His mother was Naamah, an Ammonitess (I Kings 14:21). He was born about 975 B.C. and was 41 when he began to reign. The northern tribes turned to Jeroboam for leadership, to whom God had revealed that he was to rule ten of the tribes (I Kings 11:26-40). When the coronation had been set, Jeroboam was called home from Egypt, and through him an appeal was made to Rehoboam for easier taxes. The latter, however, heeding the advice of young men, refused with the result that Israel rebelled. When Adoram was sent to collect the tribute, he was slain and Rehoboam fled to Jerusalem (I Kings 12:16-19).

Rehoboam set to work to make his realm strong. Pagan high places were set up, and shrines throughout the land allowed abominable practices to be observed among the men (I Kings 14:22-24). Upon being dissuaded from attacking Israel, Rehoboam began to strengthen his land. He fortified Bethlehem, Gath, Lachish, Hebron and other cities, and made them ready to endure a siege by enemy forces. He gave refuge to priests and Levites whom Jeroboam had driven from Israel, and they brought wisdom and strength to his realm (II Chron. 11:5-17). The fortified cities were captured by King Shishak of Egypt (II Chron. 12:1-4).

Rehoboam seems to have inherited his father's love for luxury and show, for he gathered a goodly harem and reared a large family (II Chron. 11: 18-23).

Rehoboth (rē-hō′bŏth, **broad places).** 1. City in Assyria (Gen. 10:11). The home of Saul (Shaul in I Chron. 1: 48), a king of Edom prior to the coming of a Hebrew Monarch (Gen. 36: 31-37). 2. A well dug by Isaac in the Valley of Gerar after Abimelech had driven him from the land of the Philistines (Gen. 26:9-22).

Rehum (rē′hŭm, **beloved).** 1. A Hebrew who returned from captivity with Ezra (Ezra 2:2). 2. An officer of Artaxerxes' court (Ezra 4:7-24). 3. A son of Bani who helped repair the walls of Jerusalem (Neh. 3:17). 4. One who signed the covenant (Neh. 10:25). 5. A priest among the host that went to Palestine with Zerubbabel (Neh. 12:3, KJV margin, **Hamm).**

Rei (rē′ī, **friendly),** one who did not join Adonijah in his rebellion against David (I Kings 1:8).

Reins (rāns), a word used to designate the inward parts. The kidneys were thought by the Israelites to be the seat of the emotions (Pss. 7:9; 26:2; Jer. 17:10; Job 19:27).

Rekem (rē′kĕm, **friendship).** 1. A king of Midian (Num. 31:1-8). 2. A city belonging to Benjamin (Josh. 18:27). 3. A son of Hebron and father of Shammai (I Chron. 2:42-44).

Religion, man's recognition of his relation to God and the expression of that relation in faith, worship, and conduct; may be correct or not (Acts 26:5; James 1:26, 27). Biblical religion primarily a thing of heart and life rather than ritual.

Remaliah (rĕm′à-lī′à, **Jehovah adorns),** the father of King Pekah (II Kings 15:25).

Remeth (rĕ′mĕth, **height),** a city in the tribe of Issachar (Josh. 19:17-21); probably Ramoth of I Chron. 6:73 and Jarmuth of Joshua 21:29.

Remmon (See Rimmon)

Remnant. 1. People who survived political or military crises (Josh. 12:4; 13:12). 2. Spiritual kernel of Israel who would survive God's judgment and become the germ of the new people of God (Isa. 10:20-23; 11:11 12; Jer. 32:38, 39; Zeph. 3:13; Zech. 8:12).

Remon Methoar (rĕm′ŏn-mĕth′ō-âr), a town on the border of the heritage of Zebulun (Josh. 19:13). See Rimmon.

Remphan (rĕm′făn), a pagan deity worshiped by the Israelites in the wilderness (Acts 7:37-50).

Repentance (rē-pen′tans), that divinely wrought conviction of sin in the heart that the soul is guilty before God, and a resolute turning away from sin in which the sinner identifies himself with the gracious act of God in redeeming him. Repentance involves both a change of mind about sin, and a change of heart-attitude toward sin. It is at the time a renunciation of sin and an acceptance of the Holy Spirit's enablement to holy living. Repentance is necessary to salvation. Jesus asserted that it was a necessary condition (Matt. 3:2, 8; 4:17), while both Paul and Peter identified it with true salvation (Acts 20:21; II Pet. 3:9).

Rephael (rē′fā-ĕl, **God heals),** a Levite tabernacle gatekeeper (I Chron. 26:7-12).

Rephah (rē′fȧ, **a prop),** a grandson of Ephraim (I Chron. 7:23-25).

Rephaiah (rē-fā′yȧ, **Jehovah heals).** 1. Descendant of David (I Chron. 3:21, **Rhesa** of Luke 3:27). 2. Son of Ishi, who helped defeat the Amalekites (I Chron. 4:42-43). 3. Grandson of Issachar (7:2). 4. Descendant of Jonathan (I Chron. 9:40-43). 5. Son of Hur, a builder (Neh. 3:9).

Rephaim (rĕf′ā-ĭm, **mighty).** The name of a giant people who lived in Canaan even before the time of Abraham (Gen. 14:5; 15:20). They were like the Anakims in Deuteronomy 2:11, 20. Og, king of Bashan, was a descendant of the Rephaim (Josh. 12:4; 13:12; 17:15 marg.).

Rephaim, Valley of (rĕf′ā-ĭm, **vale of giants),** a fertile plain S of Jerusalem, three miles from Bethlehem. A productive area (Isa. 17:4, 5), was a prize for which the Philistines often fought. David twice defeated the Philistines in this valley (I Chron. 14:8-12; 14:16).

The Plain of Rephaim, south of Jerusalem, where David defeated the Philistines. © *MPS*

The luxurious palm grove at Wady Feiren, the Rephidim of the Israelite camp in the wilderness near Sinai. © MPS

Rephidim (rĕf'ĭ-dĭm, **plains),** a camping site of the Hebrews in the wilderness before they reached Sinai. There Moses struck a rock to secure water (Exod. 17:1-7; 19:2). At this place also occurred the battle with the Amalekites (Exod. 17:8-16).

Reprobate (rĕp'rō-bāt). The basic idea in reprobation is that of failing "to stand the test." When applied to man's relation to God it suggests moral corruption, unfitness, disqualification — all arising out of a lack of positive holiness. It is used in Romans 1:28 of a "reprobate (disapproved) mind"; in I Corinthians 9:27 of a "cast-away body," and II Corinthians 13:5-7 of a "sinful nature." Man in sin is reprobate, disqualified, disapproved, and rejected because he cannot "stand the test" of holiness. Only in Christ's righteousness may he be "approved."

Resen (rē'sĕn, **fortified place**), a town founded by Nimrod (Gen. 10:8-12) between Nineveh and Calah.

Reservoir, place where water is collected and kept for use when wanted, chiefly in large quantities. Because most of W Asia was subject to periodic droughts, and because of frequent sieges, reservoirs and cisterns were a necessity (II Chron. 26:10; 18:31; Eccl. 2:6).

Resheph (rē'shĕf, **a flame**), a descendant of Ephraim (I Chron. 7:25).

Rest, a word of frequent occurrence in the Bible. God commanded that the seventh day was to be one of rest (Exod. 16:23; 31:15) and that the land was to have its rest every seventh year (Lev. 25:4). God promised rest to the Israelites in the land of Canaan (Deut. 12:9). The word is sometimes used in the sense of trust and reliance (II Chron. 14:11). Christ offers rest of soul to those who come to Him (Matt. 11:28).

Resurrection (a raising), a return to life subsequent to death. To deny the resurrection is, in Biblical thought, to deny any immortality worthy of the character of our faith in God (Matt. 22:31, 32; Mark 12:26, 27; Luke 20:37, 38). It is not that the soul does not exist in a disembodied state (see Intermediate State) between death and resurrection; but in the Biblical view, man in the intermediate state is incomplete, and awaits "the redemption of the body" (Rom. 8:23. See II Cor. 5:3ff and Rev. 6:9-11).

In the Old Testament the most explicit passage on the resurrection is Daniel 12:2. The KJV reads, "Many of them that sleep in the dust of the earth shall awake; some to everlasting life, and some to shame and everlasting contempt."

A clearer translation is: "Many from among those who sleep in the dust of the earth will awake, these to everlasting life, but those [i.e. the rest of the dead, will awake] to shame and everlasting contempt." This clearer translation throws light on Revelation 20:4-15 and other NT passages in which the predicted resurrection of the dead is divided into two distinct phases.

Isaiah predicts the resurrection of the righteous dead in no uncertain terms: "Thy dead men shall live; together with my dead body shall they arise. Awake and sing, ye that dwell in dust; for thy dew is as the dew of herbs, and the earth shall cast out the dead" (Isa. 26:19).

Job's interest in the resurrection is evident from 14:13-15. In chapter 19 he is speaking of his resurrection when his Redeemer comes at the latter day to stand upon the earth. What Job literally said was, "Though, after my skin, [so diseased], they destroy this [body], yet from [the vantage point of] my flesh I shall see God." He then adds, in effect, "I myself shall see him with my very own eyes!"

Other OT references to resurrection are Psalm 16:9-11 (see Acts 2:25-28, 31; 13:35; Pss. 17:15; 49:15). There are also many passages in which faith in the resurrection must be assumed in the background.

The doctrine of resurrection is stated clearly in its simplest form in Paul's words before the Roman law court presided over by Felix: "there will be a resurrection both of the just and of the unjust" (Acts 24:15). The most detailed statement of the doctrine of twofold resurrection is found in Revelation 20:4-15.

In the words of Jesus the only clear allusion to a twofold resurrection is found in John 5:25, 28, 29. It must be remembered that John shares the cosmic perspective from which the eschatological complex began with the incarnation (see I John 2:18). In John 5:25 Jesus refers to the fact that He "now" exercises His power to raise the dead selectively, "they that hear will live." (Compare the resurrection of Lazarus, John 11, and of the son of the widow of Nain, Luke 7:11-17, as well as Matt. 27:50-53.) Verses 28 and 29 of John 5 refer to the future and allude to the distinction made in Dan. 12:2, which John explicates in Rev. 20:4-15.

Paul implies in I Thess. 4:16, 17 that the dead who are not "in Christ" will not be raised at the same time with the redeemed. This is made more clear in I Cor. 15:20-28. Verses 20-23 base the resurrection of the dead firmly upon the power of Christ as exhibited in His own resurrection (see Resurrection of Christ), and state the substance of the later pronouncement before Felix (Acts 24:15). By the power of Christ all the dead will be raised.

The nature of the redeemed in the resurrection is not described in great detail, yet the Scripture does not leave us totally ignorant. We shall be corporeally "like his [Christ's] glorious body" (Phil. 3:21. Cf. I John 3:2). It is enough to know that we shall be like our Lord.

It is essential to the Christian faith that Christ, like whom we shall be, arose from the dead "in the same body in which he suffered"; that the grave was empty and that His body of "flesh and bones" (Luke 24:39) was recognizable. Yet His body was "changed," "glorious," "spiritual," perfectly adapted as well for normal communications as for the free unencumbered activities of the spirit.

Our mortal body is "flesh and blood" (I Cor. 15:50) but not so the resurrection body. The marriage relationship in particular is a thing of the past for those who are raised from the dead as inheritors of the Kingdom (Luke 20:34-36; Cf. Mark 12:24, 25; Matt. 22:29, 30).

The resurrection saints will participate with Christ in the government of the world (Matt. 19:28; Luke 22:28, 29; I Cor. 6:2, 3. See Millennium).

Resurrection of Jesus Christ. The Easter miracle is the heart of Christian faith: the NT, if anything, is even more resurrection-oriented than it is cross-centered. Indeed, it is the resurrection which interprets the cross and which therefore shapes the Church's theology as well as its worship and life. Christian faith is resurrection-faith and Christian theism is resurrection-theism. The Christian God is not simply God, even the triune God: He is the God who raises the dead (Rom. 4:16-17; Eph. 1:19-20; I Pet. 1:21). Hence Christian faith **per se** is faith in the resurrection (Rom. 10:9), for the Easter miracle transforms the tragedy of the cross into Gospel (I Cor. 15:3-4).

In our Lord's own teaching, His resurrection is never divorced from His crucifixion. The atoning cross and the empty tomb form a redemptive complex (Matt. 16:21; Matt. 20:18-19; Mark 8:31; Mark 9:31; Mark 10:33-34; Luke 22:42; John 10:17-18). In the Book of Acts, the resurrection proves not only that the scandal of the cross is really God's saving deed, but also that Jesus is the true Messiah rather than a lying impostor (Acts 2:22-36; 3:12-18; 4:10; 5:29-32; 10:39-43; 13:19-37; 17:23-31). In all probability Peter's witness likewise forms the substance of the Marcan account. The testimony of the Johannine literature is somewhat limited but equally emphatic (John 11:25-26; 20-21; Rev. 1:18).

Paul frequently alludes to the resurrection (Cf., e.g., Acts 13:19-37; 17:23-31; 26:8; Rom. 1:4; 4:25; 6:4-11; 7:4; 8:11, 23; 14:9; I Cor. 15; II Cor. 1:9-10; 4:14; 5:14-15; 13:4; Gal. 1:4; Eph. 1:19-23; Phil. 3:10; Col. 1:18; 2:12; I Thess. 1:10; 4:14; 5:10; II Tim. 1:10; 2:8).

Christologically considered, the resurrection established Jesus as the Son of God with power (Rom. 1:4). By virtue of His resurrection, moreover, our Saviour entered upon His ministry as High Priest, presenting His own sacrificial blood to the Father, performing the functions of intercession (Rom. 8:34) and benediction. Though the Letter to the Hebrews contains only a single reference to the resurrection (13:20), the truth expressed in that single reference is nevertheless presupposed at every turn in the apostolic argument: the resurrected Christ is the Melchizedekian Priest. Again, by virtue of His resurrection, our Saviour was appointed Judge of the living and the dead (Acts 10:42; 17:31). In sum, by virtue of His resurrection, Jesus is now perfected Man, seated at the right hand of the Majesty on high, victorious and vindicated, the Destroyer of death, a life-giving Spirit, the Saviour, Head, and Priest of His people, the world's future King and Judge.

The resurrection is an integral part of the whole redemptive process. It is a guarantee that life continues after death (John 11:25, 26; 14:19), as well as a guarantee of judgment to come (Acts 17:31). It is not to be thought of as the survival of the soul of Jesus, or the continuation of the principles for which Jesus stood, but an actual historical event — the reappearance of Jesus in bodily, physical form, but with a body changed and incorruptible, not subject to disease and death.

A portion of the Garden Tomb enclosure showing Gordon's Calvary, traditional site of the crucifixion, in the background. © *MPS*

A closeup of the interior of the Garden Tomb. © *MPS*

Reu (rē′ū, **friendship**), the son of Peleg and a fifth generation son of Shem (Gen. 11:10-19). In Luke 3:35, Ragau.

Reuben (rōō′bĕn, **See a son!**), the eldest son of Jacob and Leah (Gen. 29:32). Nothing is known about his early life, except that he brought mandrakes (q.v.) to his mother which she used in getting Jacob to give her another son (Gen. 30:14f). Reuben committed incest at Eder (Gen. 35:22). Either because of this sin, or out of innate weakness (Gen. 49:4) his tribe never rose to power. He delivered Joseph from death by warning his brothers against the results of such an act (Gen. 37:19-22; 42:22) and later offered his sons a surety for Benjamin (42:37). He took four sons into Egypt (Gen. 46:9; Num. 1:21; 2:16). Reubenites made a covenant with Moses in order to occupy the rich grazing lands of Gilead (Num. 32:1-33). That they kept the covenant is attested by the monument to Bohan, a descendant of Reuben (Josh. 15:6). They sent 120,000 men to support King David (I Chron. 12:37). They were oppressed during Jehu's reign (II Kings 10:32, 33) and were taken into captivity by Tiglath-pileser of Assyria (I Chron. 5:25, 26).

Reubenites (rōō′bĕn-īts), descendants of Reuben, son of Jacob. When Moses took the census in Midian, Reuben numbered 43,730 men of military age (Num. 26:1-7). They supported David against the Philistines (I Chron. 11:42; 12:37).

Reuel (rōō′ĕl, **God is friend**). 1. A son of Esau (Gen. 36:4, 10). 2. A priest in Midian who gave Moses a daughter as wife (Exod. 2:16-22), probably the same as Jethro (Exod. 3:1). 3. The father of Eliasaph (called Deuel in Num. 1:14; 7:42, etc.; Num. 2:14). 4. A Benjamite (I Chron. 9:8).

Reumah (rōō′mȧ), a concubine of Nahor, brother of Abraham (Gen. 22:20-24).

Revelation (rĕv-ĕ-lā′shŭn), the doctrine of God's making Himself and relevant truths known to men. Revelation is of two kinds: general and special. General revelation is available to all men, and is communicated through nature, conscience, and history. Special revelation is revelation given to particular people at particular times (although it may be intended for others as well), and comes chiefly through the Bible and Jesus Christ.

Revelation, Book of the (an unveiling), sometimes called **The Apocalypse**, is the last book of the Bible and the only book of the NT that is exclusively prophetic in character. It belongs to the class of apocalyptic literature in which the divine message is conveyed by visions and dreams (see Apocalyptic Literature). The title which the book itself assumes (1:1) may mean either "the revelation which Christ possesses and imparts," or "the unveiling of the person of Christ."

Unlike many apocalyptic books which are either anonymous or published under a false name, Revelation is ascribed to John, evidently a well-known character among the churches of Asia Minor. He claimed to be a brother of those who were suffering persecution, and was called by one of the angels who imparted to him the vision of a "prophet." There are some positive likenesses to the accepted Johannine writings, such as the application of the term "Word of God" to Christ (19:13), the reference to the "water of life" (22:17), the concept of the "Lamb" (5:6). It is possible that John had the aid of an amanuensis in writing the Gospel and the Epistles, but that he was forced to transcribe immediately the visions that he had without the opportunity to reflect on them or to polish his expression.

The place of writing was the island of Patmos, where John had been exiled for his faith. Patmos was the site of a penal colony, where political prisoners were condemned to hard labor in the mines. Revelation was addressed to seven churches of the Roman province of Asia, which occupied the western third of what is now Turkey. The cities where these churches were located were on the main roads running N and S, so that a messenger carrying these letters could move in a direct circuit from one to the other. There were other churches in Asia at the time when Revelation was written, but these seem to have been selected because they were representative of various types of need and of Christian experience. They have been variously interpreted to represent successive periods in the life of the Church, or as seven aspects of the total character of the Church. Undoubtedly they were actual historical groups known to the author.

There are four main schools of interpretation. The **Preterist** holds that Revelation is simply a picture of the conditions prevalent in the Roman empire of the late first century, cast in the form of vision and prophecy to conceal its meaning from hostile pagans. The **Historical** view contends that the book represents in symbolic form the entire course of Church history from the time of its writing to the final consummation, and that the mystical figures and actions described therein can be identified with human events in history. The **Futurist,** on the basis of the threefold division given in Revelation 1:19, suggests that "the things which thou sawest" refer to the immediate environment of the seer and the vision of Christ (1:9-19), "the things which are" denote the churches of Asia, or the Church age, which they symbolize (2:1-3:22), and "the things which shall be hereafter" relate to those events which will attend the return of Christ and the establishment of the city of God. The **Idealist** or **Symbolic** school treats Revelation as purely a dramatic picture of the conflict of good and evil which persists in every age, but which cannot be applied exclusively to any particular historical period.

Revelation contains four great visions, each of which is introduced by the phrase "in the spirit" (1:10; 4:2; 17:3; 21:10). Each of these visions locates the seer in a different place, each contains a distinctive picture of Christ, and each advances the action significantly toward its goal.

Introduction: The Return of Christ 1:1-8
- I. Christ, the Critic of the Churches 1:9-3:22
- II. Christ, the Controller of Destiny 4:1-16:21
- III. Christ, the Conqueror of Evil 17:1-21:8
- IV. Christ, the Consummator of Hope 21:9-22:5

Epilogue: Appeal and Invitation 22:6-21

Revelling (orgy), a word used to designate any extreme intemperance and lustful indulgence, usually accompanying pagan worship (Gal. 5:21; I Pet. 4:3). The word is translated **riotous** in Romans 13:13 and **revel** in II Peter 2:13 (RSV).

Revile, Reviler, Reviling, a word meaning to address with opprobrious or contumelious language; to reproach (Exod. 21:17; Zeph. 2:8; Mark 15:32; I Cor. 6:10).

Revised Versions (See Bible, English version)

Reward, a word rendering at least a dozen different Hebrew and Greek words with very similar meanings. In modern English the word means something given in recognition of a good act. In the ERV, however, it generally refers to something given, whether for a good or a bad act (Ps. 91:8; Jer. 40:5; Mic. 7:3; I Tim. 5:18).

Rezeph (rē'zĕf, **stronghold),** an important caravan center in ancient times. It was ravaged by Assyria during Hezekiah's reign (II Kings 19:8-12; Isa. 37:12).

Rezia (rē-zī'ȧ), a descendant of Asher (I Chron. 7:39); also Rizia.

Rezin (rē'zĭn). 1. The last king of Syria to reign in Damascus. He was used to chasten Judah (II Kings 15:37). He restored Syrian cities (16:6), and the siege which he and Pekah undertook against Jerusalem led Isaiah to assure Judah by issuing the prophecy about the virgin birth of the Messiah (Isa. 7:4-16). To escape Rezin, Ahaz made an alliance with Tiglath-pileser, who invaded Israel, captured Damascus, slew Rezin and carried the Syrians into captivity (II Kings 16:9). 2. Founder of a family of Nethinims, or temple servants, mentioned in I Chron. 9:2; Ezra 2:43-48.

Rezon (rē'zŏn, **nobleman),** a citizen of Zobah, a small country NW of Damascus. He took advantage of an invasion of Zobah by David to lead a band of guerrillas to Damascus where he made himself king (I Kings 11:23-25). He must have been a wise ruler, for Syria soon became a strong nation. He made an alliance with Hadad of Edom and began to harass Israel whom he hated (vs. 25). He is almost certainly the same as Hezion mentioned in I Kings 15:18, although Hezion could have been his son. He founded a dynasty of strong Syrian rulers.

Rhegium (rē'jĭ-ŭm), a Greek colony on the toe of Italy, founded in 712 B.C. Opposite Messana in Sicily, where the strait is only six miles wide, Rhegium was an important strategic point. As such it was the special object of Rome's care, and in consequence a loyal ally. The port was also a haven in extremely difficult water (Acts 28: 13).

Rhesa (rē′sȧ), the son of Zerubbabel, and ancestor of Christ (Luke 3:27).

Rhoda (rō′dȧ, **rose),** servant girl who answered the door in the very human story of Acts 12:13. Probably a slave of Mary, John Mark's mother.

Rhodes (rōdz, **rose),** a large island off the mainland of Caria, some 420 square miles in extent. When Paul called on his way from Troas to Caesarea (Acts 21:1), Rhodes was only a station on the trade routes, a free city, but little more than a provincial town. Rhodes was the center of a sun-cult, the famous colossus being a statue of Helios. See Rodanim.

Ribai (rī′bī), a Benjamite of Gibeah, father of Ittai (II Sam. 23:29), a mighty man (I Chron. 11:26, 31).

Riblah (rĭb′lȧ). 1. City on boundary of Canaan and Israel, N of Sea of Galilee (Num. 34:11). 2. Important town on E bank of Orontes River 50 miles S of Hamath, in Assyrian province of Mansuate. In this place Pharaoh Necho (609 B.C.) put King Jehoahaz II of Judah in chains, and Nebuchadnezzar killed the sons of King Zedekiah of Judah (587 B.C.) and put out his eyes, and then carried him off in chains to Babylon (II Kings 25:6f; Jer. 39: 5-7). It is possible that the two Riblahs may be the same.

Riddle, (a hidden saying, a proverb). This is a form of language long used by man. The Queen of Sheba propounded to Solomon "hard questions," or riddles (I Kings 10:1; II Chron. 9: 1). A classic example of the riddle is that propounded by Samson to entrap his enemies (Judg. 14:14, RSV). Samson's noted retort to the Philistines is also a riddle (Judg. 14:18b). Solomon became famous as an author of proverbs and riddles (I Kings 4:32). To know dark sayings is a mark of wisdom (Prov. 1:6). Riddle also refers to words of indefinite meaning (Num. 12:8; Ps. 49:4; Dan. 5:12; Heb. 2:6). A NT riddle appears in Rev. 13: 18, and another in I Cor. 13:12, marg.

Righteousness (the quality of rightness or **justice).** In the most frequent and most important Biblical usage, righteousness is conceived as judged by the standard of God's holy law, which is derived from His holy character, and "summarily comprehended" in the decalogue (Exod. 20:1-17).

A 16th century artist's conception of the great Colossus of Rhodes, one of the seven wonders of the ancient world. Made of brass and more than 100 feet high, it spans the harbor entrance. Erected about 288 B.C., it was wrecked by an earthquake about 24 B.C. RTHPL

Throughout the Bible, mankind is considered to be corrupt and lacking in righteousness (Rom. 3:23, etc.) on account of the representative, self-corrupting act of our original progenitor (Rom. 5:12-21). Man is held to be totally incapable of making himself righteous (Rom. 3:19, 20).

Only through the atoning work of Christ can man be given righteousness. (Isa. 54:17, "Their righteousness is of me, saith the Lord.")

This imparting of righteousness is in two distinguishable but inseparable phases. In justification by faith man is forensically made right with the demands of the law by the atonement of Christ (II Cor. 5:21). In sanctification he is progressively made righteous in character and conduct (I John 1:7-9).

Rimmon (rĭm'ŏn, **pomegranate).** 1. A city near Edom in the S of Judah (Josh. 15:32). Nehemiah called it En-rimmon (11:29). 2. A noted rocky fortress not far from Gibeah was named Sela Rimmon, or Rimmon of the rocks (Judg. 20:45-47). 3. A Benjamite whose two sons slew Ishbosheth, Jonathan's son, and took his head to David who, in great anger, had them slain (II Sam. 4:2-12). 4. A Syrian god (II Kings 5: 15-19). 5. A village of Simeon listed next to Ain (I Chron. 4:32). 6. A city of Zebulun made a Levitical possession, going to the children of Merari (I Chron. 6:77).

Rimmon-Methoar (rĭm'ŏn-mĕ'thō-ȧr). It was part of the heritage of Judah in Zebulun (Josh. 19:13).

Rimmon Parez (See Rimmon-Perez)

Rimmon-Perez (rĭm'ŏn pĕ'rĕz, **Parez** in KJV). It was the fourth camp of Israel after Sinai (Num. 33:16-19). Rimmon was a common place name, due to the abundance of pomegranates at the time in the Near East. Parez means cleft, so this was, no doubt, a valley into which entrance was made between cliffs.

Rimmon, Rock of, a natural fortress to which 600 Benjamites fled after escaping slaughter (Judg. 20:45, 47; 21: 13).

Ring (See Dress)

Ring. This article of jewelry became the symbol of authority. The pharaoh gave one to Joseph (Gen. 41:42, 43). King Ahasuerus gave one to Haman, the enemy of the Jews (Esth. 3:10). The prodigal's father placed a ring on the hand of his son (Luke 15:22). This was more than an ornament; it restored the son to authority in the household. The ring early became very valuable, as is shown by Isaiah's plaint (3:18-23). Originally the signet was worn on a chain or wire about the neck, but the need to safeguard it led to its being put on the hand.

Ring-streaked, mottled of color, characterizing Laban's sheep (Gen. 30:35; 31:8, 12). Also ring-straked.

Rinnah (rĭn'ȧ), a son of Shimon of Judah (I Chron. 4:20).

Riot, to squander in evil ways (Prov. 23:20; 28:7); **waste** (Titus 1:6; I Pet. 4:4); **revelry** (Rom. 13:13); **luxury** (II Pet. 2:13).

Riphath (rī'făth), a son of Gomer (Gen. 10:3; I Chron. 1:6 see marg.).

Rissah (rĭs'ȧ, **ruins),** Israel's sixth camp after leaving Sinai (Num. 33:21), some 200 miles S of Jerusalem.

Rithmah (rĭth'mȧ, **juniper),** the third camp of Israel from Sinai (Num. 33: 18).

River, may refer to large streams (Gen. 2:10-14), the Nile (Gen. 41:1; II Kings 19:24), winter torrent the bed of which is dry in summer (Amos 6:14), fountain stream (Ps. 119:136). Used figuratively for abundance of good or evil (Job 20:17; Isa. 43:2).

River of Egypt, a brook **(RSV)** on the SW border of Palestine flowing into the Mediterranean Sea (Gen. 15:18; Num. 34:5). Now Wadi el Arish.

Rizpah (rĭz'pȧ, **hot stone),** a daughter of Aiah, a Horite (I Chron. 1:40, called Ajah in Gen. 36:24). Saul took her as a concubine (II Sam. 3:7a). Ishbosheth, a son of Saul, accused Abner, a cousin, of incest with her (II Sam. 3:7b).

Roads, may refer to paths or highways; hundreds of allusions to roads

An ancient Roman paved road near Antioch. © MPS

A winding road in the Ain Fara Gorge. © *MPS*

in Bible; road robbers quite common (Matt. 11:10; Luke 10:30); Romans built highways throughout empire, some of which are still in use; used by traders, travelers, and armies; Paul used Roman roads on his missionary journeys; the statement, "All roads lead to Rome," shows how well provided the Roman empire was with roads.

Robbery, illegal seizure of another's property. Early in Israel's history such a crime was forbidden by law (Lev. 19:13). In the days of the Judges it was unsafe to travel the highways because of robberies (Judg. 5:6) by highwaymen (Judg. 9:25). Houses were built to resist robbers, who were often base enough to seize the money of orphans and widows (Isa. 10:2). So depraved had Israel become by Hosea's day that companies of priests had turned to pillage (Hos. 6:9).

Among vices of God's people listed by Ezekiel is robbery (22:29). Nahum accused Nineveh of being a center of numerous robberies (Nah. 3:1). Withholding tithes and offerings from God's storehouse was robbery of this kind (Mal. 3:8).

The prevalence of robbery during NT times is attested by the story of the Good Samaritan (Luke 10:30-37). Jesus warned against robbers who will enter the Christian fold (John 10:1). Paul who knew his world as few men of his day knew it, was familiar with violent seizure by thieves (II Cor. 11:26).

Robe (See Dress)

Robinson's Arch, remains of ancient Jerusalem masonry, named for American archaeologist Edward Robinson, who discovered it in 1838. Giant stones, projecting from SW wall of Temple enclosure, are evidently part of an arch of a bridge or viaduct that in Herod's time connected Jerusalem's western hill with the eastern hill.

Roboam (See Rehoboam)

Rock, a natural fortress, as at Rimmon (Judg. 20:45, 47). Sometimes it was a mountain (I Sam. 23:25, 26). Both terms are used to refer to God: The Lord is my rock (II Sam. 22:2), and fortress (Pss. 18:2; 71:3). Moses smote rock for water (Exod. 17:6); sometimes used figuratively: referring to God (II Sam. 22:2), Peter (Matt. 16:18), believers (I Pet. 2:5).

Rod, originally a name given to a piece of tree limb used as a support or as a weapon. There is little difference between the word for rod and that for staff. The rod had varying uses in ancient times. Jacob used rods to change the color of Laban's goats and sheep (Gen. 30:37-41). Such rods became a symbol of authority (Jer. 48:17). Moses (Exod. 4:2, 17, 20; 7:9-20, etc.); Aaron (Exod. 8:16, 17). The rod, used at first as a weapon, came to be a sign of authority, hence a sceptre.

Rodanim (rŏd'ȧ-nĭm), a tribe descended from Javan, a son of Japheth (I Chron. 1:5, 7).

Roe, Roebuck (See Animals)

Rogelim (rō'gē-lĭm), a thrifty community near Mahanaim. Its citizens helped David (II Sam. 17:27, 29; 19: 31).

Rohgah (rō'gȧ), a descendant of Asher (I Chron. 7:34).

Roll, a scroll, a literary work on papyrus or parchment rolled around a core or spool. The decree of Cyrus to restore the temple was a roll (Ezra 1: 1), and Jeremiah wrote on such a roll (36:2). Books with pages did not come into use until the second century A.D. See Writing.

Roller, anything that turns or revolves. (Isa. 17:13).

Romamti-ezer (rō-măm'tĭ-ē'zēr, **highest help),** sons of Neman, temple musician (I Chron. 25:4, 31).

Roman Empire. City of Rome founded 753 B.C.; a monarchy until 509 B.C.; a republic from 509 to 31 B.C.; empire began in 31 B.C., fell in 5th cent. Rome extended hold over all Italy and eventually over whole Mediterranean world, Gaul, half of Britain, the Rhine-Danube rivers, and as far as Parthia. Augustus, the first Roman emperor, divided Roman provinces into senatorial,

The Pillar of the Tenth Roman Legion, in the old city of Jerusalem
© *MPS*

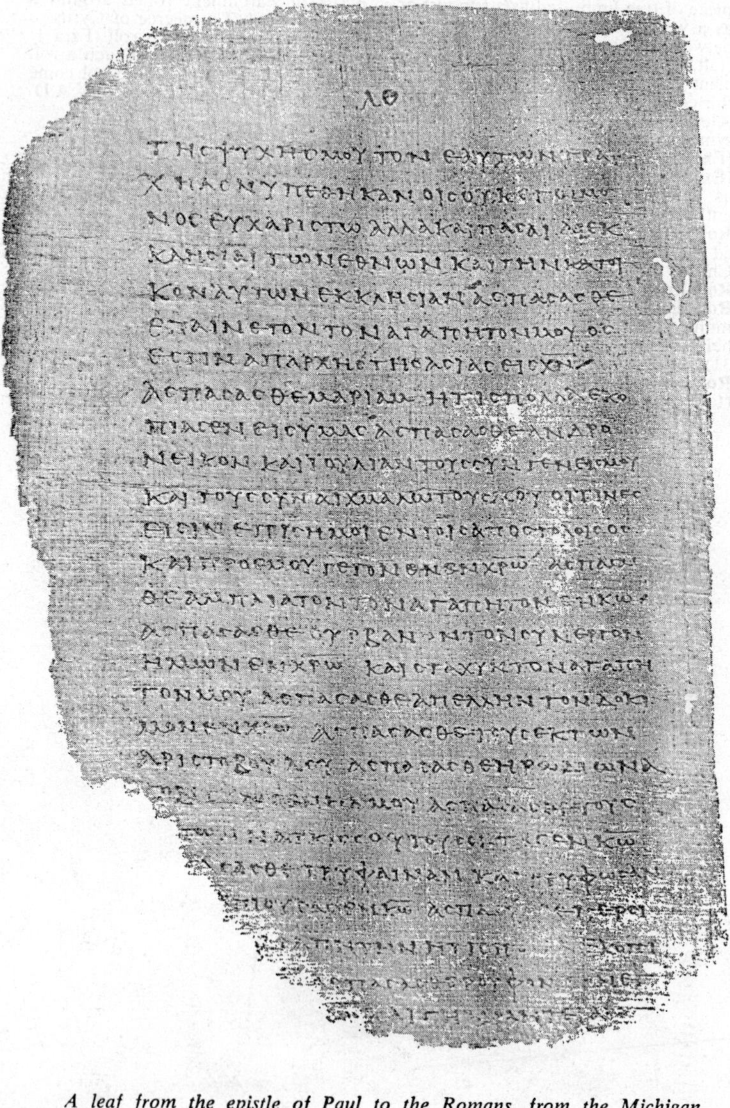

A leaf from the epistle of Paul to the Romans, from the Michigan Papyri P 46 (Beatty-Michigan MS.), in the University of Michigan Library. UML

which were ruled by proconsuls (Acts 13:7; 18:12; 19:38) and imperial, ruled by governors (Matt. 27:2; Luke 2:2; Acts 23:24). Moral corruption was responsible for the decline and fall of the Roman Empire. Roman reservoirs, aqueducts, roads, public buildings, statues survive. Many Roman officials are referred to in the NT, including the emperors Augustus (Luke 2:1), Tiberius (Luke 3:1), Claudius (Acts 11:28), Nero (Acts 25:11, 12).

Romans, Epistle to the. The genuineness of the Epistle has never been seriously questioned by competent critics familiar with first century history. Although other NT epistles have been wrongly attacked as forgeries not written by the alleged authors, this epistle stands with Galatians and I and II Corinthians as one of the unassailable documents of early church history.

There can be no doubt that the author, Paul, formerly Saul of Tarsus (Acts 13:9), was a highly intellectual, rabbinically educated Jew (Gal. 1:14; Acts 22:3) who had been intensely hostile to the Christian movement and had sought to destroy it (Gal. 1:13; I Cor. 15:9; Acts 8:1-3; 9:1, 2). Even the critics who reject the supernatural cannot deny the extraordinary nature of the fact that this able enemy became the greatest exponent of the Christian faith and wrote the most powerful statements of Christian doctrine.

This is a letter, not a treatise. It was not intended to be a formal literary product. In the midst of greetings from friends who were with the author as he wrote (16:21-23), Tertius, the scribe to whom the letter was dictated puts in his own personal greeting (16:22).

The main body of the letter ends at 16:20 with the words "The grace of our Lord Jesus Christ be with you. Amen." Verses 21 to 24 are intentionally a postscript. He has finished the personal greetings to people in Rome. Phebe, who is to take the letter to Rome, is nearly ready to begin her journey. Greetings from friends in Corinth, who may have assembled for a farewell, belong by themselves in a postscript, followed by another benediction (vs. 24). Then finally comes the exalted doxology (vss. 25-27).

The epistle clearly places itself in the three month period (Acts 20:3) which Paul spent in Corinth just before going to Jerusalem. According to the best authorities in NT chronology this three month period was about Dec. 56 to Feb. 57.

It has been said that if Galatians is the "Magna Charta" of the Gospel, Romans is the "Constitution." The theological substance of this epistle had to be presented to the NT church, whether addressed to Rome or not, but there were circumstances in Rome which made it appropriate for Paul, in a relatively calm frame of mind, with time for fuller elaboration, and without having become personally involved in local affairs, as he had in Galatia, to expand the central doctrine of the epistle to the Galatians. Thus he explained his purpose in coming to Rome and the main purpose of his life ministry and message. There was friction and misunderstanding between Jewish and Gentile Christians in the Roman church. We know from the personal greetings at the end that it was a mixed church. The problem is reflected in almost every section of the epistle, but especially in chapters three, four, nine, ten and eleven. Both sides were stubborn. There was a moment, probably brief, even after Paul had reached Rome, when Mark and a certain Jesus Justus were the only Christian Jews in Rome who would cooperate with Paul (Col. 4:10, 11). A clarification of the Gospel and its implications was needed.

The content and outline of this epistle must be understood from the point of view of Paul's total ministry and his particular travel plans. True, the **greatest** theme in the work is **justification by faith.** But this is **not an essay** on that subject. Much of the material simply does not fall under any sub-heading of that theme. This is a **letter** from the apostle to the Gentiles to the church in Rome, and the subject is **Why I Am Coming to Visit You.** Outlines which fail to see this viewpoint, and which seek to force the material into formal divisions as though this were an essay, are very likely to assign sub-topics and secondary subheadings which do not fit. Some outlines are almost like "zoning" laws, forbidding the reader to find in certain sections material which certainly is there.

The following very simple outline is suggested. (The great doctrinal

Scenes from ancient Rome.

Above, Ruins of the Forum, the Arch of Titus visible in the background at center. Below this are views of the Colosseum, exterior and interior. JFW and LO

themes are discussed in articles on doctrinal topics.)

I. The Apostle Paul to the Christians in Rome. I am entrusted with a message which I must deliver to you; i.e., the Gospel in all its implications (1:1-17).

II. (a) The Gentile world is wretchedly lost. (1:18:32). This is true in spite of God's justice toward attempted morality. (2:1-16).
(b) The Jewish world is equally lost, in spite of all their privileges. (2:17-3:20).

III. Justification by Faith is my great message. (3:21-5:21). There is no space for the wealth of sub-topics.

IV. Holy living in principle. (6:1-8:39).

V. God has not forgotten the Jews. (9:1-11:36).

VI. Details of Christian conduct. (12:1-15:13).

VII. (a) Travel plans. (15:14-33).
(b) Personal to people in Rome. (16:1-20).
(c) Personal from people in Corinth. (16:21-23).
(d) Doxology. (16:24-27).

Rome, like Babylon, became a symbol of organized paganism and opposition to Christianity in the Bible. In the lurid imagery of the document of protest which closes the canon of the NT, John mingles Empire and City in his symbolism of sin. The city appears once only in an historical context. Paul landed at Puteoli, probably traversed the Pontine Marshes by barge (Hor. **Sat.** 1:5:11-23), halted at Forum Appii (**ib.** 4), and pushed up the Appian Way through the village of Tres Tabernae, or Three Shops. Alerted by the little church of Puteoli members of Rome's Christian community met Paul at both stopping places. On the evidence of the Nazareth Decree, it appears that a group had been established in Rome since the principate of Claudius in the late forties of the century. Paul would enter by the Capena Gate. His "hired house" (Acts 28:30) would be in some block of flats, an "insula."

Capital of Roman Empire; founded in 753 B.C.; Paul imprisoned there twice (Acts 28; II Tim. 4).

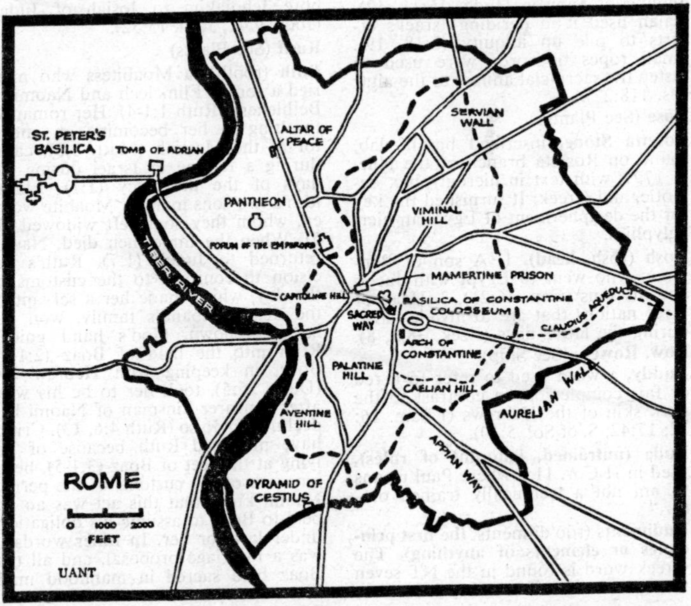

Room. 1. A chamber in a house (Acts 1:13). 2. In the KJV room is used in the sense of place or position in society (Matt. 23:6; Luke 14:7, 8; 20:46). This meaning is now obsolete.

Root, usually used in a figurative sense. Judah was promised new roots after the captivity (II Kings 19:30; Isa. 37:31; see Rom. 15:12). The **roots** of the wicked shall not endure (Isa. 5:24). Jesus was the root of David (Isa. 11:1, 10). The Messiah was to come from an unexpected **root** (Isa. 53:2). In the parable of the sower, the **roots** did not develop on or among stones (Matt. 13:20). The fig tree and its roots died (Mark 11:20). The source of spiritual life is in the **roots** (Rom. 11:17, 18), even as the love of money is the **root** of evil (I Tim. 6:10).

Rope (line or **cord, a woven band, a cable).** Hushai counseled Absalom to have Israel bring strong cables, with which to pull into the river the city where David might take refuge (II Sam. 17:7-13). Sackcloth upon the body and a woven band about the head were symbols of deep servility (I Kings 20:31, 32). Rahab used a rope to let the spies over the wall of Jericho (Josh. 2:1-16). Rope was used of the binding of Samson (Judg. 16:11, 12). Isaiah used it in deriding Israel's efforts to pile up iniquity (5:18, 19). Small ropes or cords were used to fasten the sacrificial animal to the altar (Ps. 118:27).

Rose (See Plants)

Rosetta Stone, inscribed basalt slab, found on Rosetta branch of the Nile, in 1799, with text in hieroglyphic, demotic, and Greek. It furnished the key for the decipherment of Egyptian hieroglyphics.

Rosh (rŏsh, **head).** 1. A son of Benjamin who went to Egypt with Jacob and his sons (Gen. 46:21). 2. Head of three nations that are to invade Israel during the latter days (Ezek. 38:2, 8).

Row, Rowers (See Ship)

Ruddy, a word used to refer to a red or fair complexion, in contrast to the dark skin of the Hebrews (I Sam. 16:12; 17:42; S. of Sol. 5:10).

Rude (untrained, ignorant of rules), used in II Cor. 11:6 where Paul means "I am not a technically trained orator."

Rudiments (rōō'di-mĕnts, **the first principles or elements of anything).** The Greek word is found in the NT seven times, and the KJV renders it in three different ways: Galatians 4:3, 9 and II Peter 3:10, 12 "elements"; Colossians 2:8, 20 "rudiments"; Hebrews 5:12 "first principles." In II Peter 3:10, 12 it probably means the physical elements of the world. In Hebrews 5:12 the KJV rendering is correct. In Galatians 4:3, 9 and Colossians 2:8, 20 the reference is to rudimentary religious teachings.

Rue (See Plants)

Rufus (rōō'fŭs). 1. Brother of Alexander and son of Simon of Cyrene who bore the cross (Mark 15:21). 2. Friend of Paul (Rom. 16:13).

Ruhamah (rōō-hă'mȧ, **to be pitied),** Hosea's daughter by Gomer (Hos. 2:1).

Ruler, a name used to translate several Hebrew and Greek words meaning **king, captain, exalted one, overlord, magistrate,** etc. (Gen. 45:8; Prov. 23:1; I Sam. 25:30; I Kings 1:35; Gen. 47:6; II Kings 11:4, 19; Ezra 9:2; Neh. 2:16 RSV marg). Other words occur in Daniel 3:2f; 5:29; in Deuteronomy 1:13; Isaiah 29:10; in II Samuel 6:21; Daniel 5:7; Acts 23:5; John 3:1; Mark 5:35; Eph. 6:12, etc.).

Rumah (rōō'mȧ, **tall place),** the home of Pedaiah, whose daughter, Zebudah, bore Jehoiakim to Josiah of Judah (Judg. 9:41; Josh. 15:52).

Rush (See Plants)

Ruth (rōōth), a Moabitess who married a son of Elimelech and Naomi of Bethlehem (Ruth 1:1-4). Her romance, resulting in her becoming an ancestor of the Messiah (Matt. 1:5), came during a famine in Israel during the days of the theocracy (1:1). Elimelech's two sons married Moabite women, whom they soon left widowed (1:5). When the three men died, Naomi returned to Judah (1:7). Ruth's decision to conform to the customs of the day, which made her a servant of the dead husband's family, won her lasting renown. God's hand guided Ruth into the field of Boaz (2:1-3). Boaz, in keeping with Hebrew law (Deut. 25:5), took her to be his wife, after a nearer kinsman of Naomi had declined to do so (Ruth 4:6, 13). Critics have maligned Ruth because of her lying at the feet of Boaz (3:1-5), being ignorant of the customs of the period. Naomi knew that this act was an appeal to Boaz to assume his obligations under law for her. In other words, it was a marriage proposal, and all that Boaz held sacred in manhood made him respond in honor.

Gleaners in the fields of Boaz, near Bethlehem, reminiscent of scenes in in the Book of Ruth. © *MPS*

Ruth, Book of. The primary purpose behind it was to present the link between Judah and the Gentile world in the ancestry of Jesus Christ (Matt. 1:5, 6). Some scholars think it was only a romance written to justify the marriage of Jews with alien women. The author is unknown, but he could have been a post-Exilic scholar who objected to Ezra's rigid elimination of alien wives from among the returning captives (Ezra 9, 10). Aside from its historical and genealogical contents, the book is of great merit because of its ethical teachings. Ruth's refusal to be free exalts the importance of safekeeping a moral obligation. She could not have known what would result from her decision. Her willingness to obey Naomi's instructions, as well as to be a menial laborer, emphasizes the message of the OT and of experience, that youth needs counsel from them who are more mature. Finally, the marriage ceremony shows that worthy people respect customs whose symbolism portrays basic commitments among men, e.g., the shoe as a sign of assuming another's obligations (4:7, 8. See Deut. 25:5-10).

Rye (See Plants)

–S–

Saba, Sabaeans (să'bȧ, să-bē'ănz). Mentioned in Gen. 10:7 and I Chron. 1:9 as a son of Cush. In Isa. 43:3 the name is coupled with Ethiopia, and in Ps. 72:10 with Sheba. In Isa. 45:14 God says to Israel, "The labour of Egypt, and merchandise of Ethiopia and of the Sabeans, men of stature, shall come over unto thee, and they shall be thine." "Sabeans from the wilderness" are referred to in Ezek. 23:42. Saba was situated between the Nile and the Atbara. It is a region about 400 miles long and 200 miles broad, and was known to the Hebrews as Cush. Strabo (xvi. 4, 8-10) says there was a harbor named Saba on the W coast of the Red Sea (Gen. 10:28; 25:3), was located in Arabia. The Queen of Sheba who visited Solomon came from there.

Sabachthani (sȧ-băkh'thȧ-nē), a word in the utterance of Jesus on the cross, "My God, my God, why hast Thou forsaken me?" (Matt. 27:46; Mark 15:34; see Ps. 22:1).

Sabaoth, the Lord of (săb'ā-ōth, **hosts**). Same as "Lord of hosts." The phrase is used in Romans 9:29 and in James 5:4. Its equivalent, the "Lord of hosts," is often found in the OT. The title expresses Jehovah's great power.

Sabbath (săb'ath, to **desist, cease, rest**), the weekly day of rest and worship of the Jews. The sabbath was instituted at creation. The story of creation (Gen. 1:1-2:3) closes with an account of God's hallowing of the seventh day, because on it He rested from His creative labors.

There is no express mention of the sabbath before Exodus 16:21-30. In the wilderness of Sin, before the Israelites reached Mount Sinai, God gave them manna, a double supply being given on the sixth day of the week, in order that the seventh day might be kept as a day of rest from labor. Forty years later, Moses reminded the Israelites of God's command to observe the sabbath and told them that they were under special obligation to keep it because God had delivered them from bondage in Egypt (Deut. 5:15). Among the Hebrews the sabbath was associated with the idea of rest, worship, and divine favor, not certain taboos.

With the development of the synagogue during the Exile, the sabbath became a day for worship and the study of the law, as well as a day of rest. There are not many references to the sabbath in the apocryphal books. Antiochus Epiphanes tried to abolish it, along with other distinctively Jewish institutions (168 B.C.).

During the period between Ezra and the Christian era the scribes formulated innumerable legal restrictions for the conduct of life under the law. Jesus had things like this in mind when He said, "Woe unto you also, ye lawyers! for ye lade men with burdens grievous to be borne, and ye yourselves touch not the burdens with one of your fingers" (Luke 11:46).

Jesus came into conflict with the religious leaders of the Jews especially on two points: His claim to be the Messiah, and on the matter of sabbath observance. The rabbis regarded the sabbath as an end in itself, whereas Jesus taught that the sabbath was made for man's benefit, and that man's needs must take precedence over the law of the sabbath (Matt. 12:1-14; Mark 2:23-3:6; Luke 6:1-11; John 5:1-18). He Himself regularly attended worship in the synagogue on the sabbath (Luke 4:16).

The early Christians, most of whom were Jews, kept the seventh day as a sabbath, but since the resurrection of their Lord was the most blessed day in their lives, they began very early also to meet for worship on the first day of the week (Acts 2:1), and designated it as the Lord's day. As the split between the Jews and Christians widened, the Christians came gradually to meet for worship only on the Lord's day and gave up the observance of the seventh day.

Sabbath, Covert for the, obscure expression found in II Kings 16:18; may refer to a colonnade in the temple compound.

Sabbath, Morrow After the, expression of uncertain meaning found in Lev. 23:11; may refer to the ordinary weekly sabbath or the first day of the Passover on whatever day of the week it might fall.

Sabbath, Second After the First, expression of uncertain meaning found in Luke 6:1. Many explanations have been suggested.

Sabbath Day's Journey. A journey of limited extent which the scribes thought a Jew might travel on the sabbath without breaking the Law (Acts 1:12). Such a journey was 2,000 cubits (3,000 feet) from one's house or domicile, a distance derived from the statement found in Joshua 3:4 that there was to be that much distance between the ark and the people on their march. The rabbis, however, devised a way of increasing this distance without infringing the Law by depositing some food at the 2,000-cubit limit, before the sabbath, and declaring that spot a temporary residence.

Sabbatical Year (See Feasts)

Sabbeus (să-bē'ŭs), in I Esdras 9:32, the same as "Shemaiah" in Ezra 10:31.

Sabta, Sabtah (săb'tȧ), the third son of Cush (Gen. 10:7; I Chron 1:9); perhaps also a place in South Arabia.

Sabtecha, Sabtechah (săb'tē-kȧ), the fifth-named of the sons of Cush in the genealogy of Genesis 10:5-7.

Sacar (sā'kȧr, **wages).** 1. Father of Ahiam, a follower of David (I Chron. 11:35). "Sharar" in II Sam. 23:33. 2. A son of Obed-edom (I Chron. 26:4).

Sackbut (See Music)

Sackcloth (săk'klōth), a coarse cloth, dark in color, usually made of goat's hair. It was worn by mourners (II Sam. 3:31; II Kings 19:1, 2), often by prophets (Isa. 20:2; Rev. 11:3), and by captives (I Kings 20:31).

Sacrament (săk'rȧ-mĕnt). Because of the absence of any defined sacramental concept in the early history of the church, the number of sacraments was not regarded as fixed. Baptism and the Lord's Supper were the chief. In the 12th century Hugo of St. Victor listed 30 sacraments that had been recognized by the church, while Gregory of Bergamo and Peter Lombard listed only seven: Baptism, Confirmation, the Eucharist, Penance, Extreme Unction, Orders, and Matrimony—a list adopted by Thomas Aquinas, and later by the Council of Trent. The number seven was supported by many fanciful arguments that seven is a sacred number. There is no NT authority for it, and it is a purely arbitrary figure. It is hard to see on what principle Baptism and the Lord's Supper, which were instituted by Christ, can be put in the same category with marriage, which is as old as the human race.

The Reformers saw in the NT sacraments three distinguishing marks: (1) they were instituted by Christ; (2) Christ commanded that they be observed by His followers; (3) they are visible symbols of divine acts. Since baptism and the Lord's Supper are the only rites for which such marks can be claimed, there can be only two sacraments. There is justification for classifying them under a common name because they are associated together in the NT (Acts 2:41, 42; I Cor. 10:1-4).

Sacrifice (săk'rĭ-fīs), a religious act belonging to worship in which offering is made to God of some material object belonging to the offerer—this offering being consumed in the ceremony, in order to attain, restore, maintain, or celebrate friendly relations with the

The High Priest in the Holy Place, before the Altar of Incense. At rear is the veil dividing the Holy Place from the Holy of Holies. At left is the seven branched candlestick and accessories. At right, the Table of Shewbread. DV

An altar rock for a heathen god at Baalbek, in Lebanon. JFW

The Altar of Burnt Offering in Solomon's Temple once stood on this Rock of Moriah, which is now in the center of the mosque called the Dome of the Rock in the old temple area at Jerusalem. © MPS

deity; expresses faith, repentance, and adoration; main purpose of the sacrifice is to please the deity and to secure His favor. Practiced from ancient times (Gen. 4:4f; 8:20f; 12:7, 8; 13:4, 18; 15:4f; 26:25; Job 1:5; 42:7-9). Before building of temple in Jerusalem sacrifices were offered by heads of families. Sacrifices have not been offered by Jews since the destruction of the temple by the Romans in A.D. 70. In Mosaic sacrifices only certain kinds of animals and fowl could be offered. Sacrifices were of two kinds, animal and vegetable. Animal sacrifices: Sin Offering (Lev. 4:1-35; 6:24-30), Guilt Offering (Lev. 5:14-6:7), Burnt Offering (Lev. 1), Peace Offering (Lev. 3). Vegetable sacrifices: Meat Offerings (Lev. 2:1-16; 6:14-18), Drink Offerings (Num. 6:17; 15:1-12). All OT sacrifices point forward to and are a type of the sacrifice of Jesus Christ (Heb. 9:10).

Sacrilege (săk′rĭ-lĕj), in Rom. 2:22 it means to rob temples.

Saddle (săd′l, **riding seat**), getting a beast ready for riding (Gen. 22:3; Num. 22:21; Judg. 19:10; II Sam. 16:1; 17:23). Asses were not ridden with saddles; when carrying heavy burdens they had a thick cushion on their back.

Sadducees (săd′yū-sēz), Jewish religious sect in the time of Christ. Beliefs: acceptance only of the Law and rejection of oral tradition; denial of resurrection, immortality of the soul, spirit world (Mark 12:18; Luke 20:27; Acts 23:8); suported Maccabeans; a relatively small group, but generally held the high priesthood; denounced by John the Baptist (Matt. 3:7, 8) and Jesus (Matt. 16:6, 11, 12); opposed Christ (Matt. 21:12f; Mark 11:15f; Luke 19:47) and the apostolic church (Acts 5:17, 33).

Sadoc (sā′dŏk). 1. An ancestor of Ezra (II Esdras 1:1). 2. A descendant of Zerubbabel and ancestor of Jesus (Matt. 1:14).

Saffron (See Plants)

Sail (See Ship)

Sailor (See Occupations and Professions)

Saint. 1. A member of God's covenant people Israel, whether a pious layman (II Chron. 6:41; Ps. 16:3) or someone like a priest who is consecrated to God (Ps. 106:16; I Peter 2:5). 2. A NT believer, belonging exclusively to God (Acts 9:13; I Cor. 16:1; II Cor. 1:1). The saints are the Church (I Cor. 1:2), people called out of the world to be God's own people. Throughout the Bible the saints are urged to live lives befitting their position (Eph. 4:1; Col. 1:10).

Sala, Salah, (sā′lȧ, **missile, petition**), a son of Arphaxad (Gen. 10:24; 11:13ff; I Chron. 1:18, 24; Luke 3:35-36).

Salamis (săl′ȧ-mĭs), a town on the E coast of Cyprus. It had a good harbor and was a populous and flourishing town in the Hellenic and Roman periods. Paul and Barnabas preached the Gospel there in the synagogues of the Jews (Acts 13:5), showing that there was a large Jewish community in Salamis.

Salathiel (sȧ-lā′thĭ-ĕl, **I have asked God**), the son of Jeconiah, king of Judah, and father of Zerubbabel, according to the genealogy in Matthew 1:12; while in the Lukan genealogy he appears as the father of Zerubbabel, indeed, but as the son of Neri (Luke 3:27). The apparent discrepancy in the genealogies is probably to be explained on the principle that Matthew gives the genealogy of Jesus according to the legal succession, while Luke gives it according to the actual succession or right of inheritance.

Salcah (săl′kȧ), a city on the extreme NE boundary of the kingdom of Bashan, near Edrei (Deut. 3:10; Josh. 12:5; 13:11). It is now known as Salkhad.

Salchah (sal′kȧ), another spelling of Salcah, q.v.

Salem (sā′lĕm, **peace**), the name of the city of which Melchizedek was king (Gen. 14:18; Heb. 7:1, 2). Jewish writers generally regarded it as a synonym of Jerusalem.

Salim (sā′lĭm), a place near Aenon, where John was baptizing (John 1:28; 3:23, 26; 10:40) shows that it must have been W of the Jordan, but its exact location is unknown.

Sallai (săl′ā-ī). 1. Benjamite chief (Neh. 11:8). 2. Priestly family (Neh. 12:20), called "Sallu" in verse 7.

Sallu (See Sallai)

Salma (săl′mȧ, **strength**), a son of Caleb, son of Hur, and father of Bethlehem (I Chron. 2:51; 2:54).

Salmon (săl′mŏn, **clothing**), the father of Boaz the husband of Ruth, and grandfather of Jesse, father of David (Ruth 4:20, 21; I Chron. 2:11; Matt. 1:4, 5; Luke 3:32).

Salmone (săl-mō′nē), a promontory forming the E extremity of the isle of Crete (Acts 27:7).

Salome (så-lō'mē, fem. of Solomon). 1. The wife of Zebedee, and mother of James and John (cf. Matt. 27:56 with Mark 15:40; 16:1). She was one of the women who companied with Jesus in Galilee to minister to Him (Mark 15:40, 41). She was present at the crucifixion of Jesus, and was among those who at Easter morning came to the tomb to anoint the dead body of their Lord (Mark 16:1). 2. The daughter of Herodias, and the grandniece of Herod Antipas, whose dancing before Herod pleased him so much that as a reward she obtained the head of John the Baptist (Matt. 14:3-11; Mark 6:17-28). Her name is not given in the Gospels.

Salt, used in ancient times for seasoning and preserving food (Job 6:6; Isa. 30:24 RSV; Matt. 5:13), as an antiseptic in medicine (Ezek. 16:4), and with offerings of all kinds (Lev. 2:13; Ezek. 43:24). Captured cities were sometimes destroyed and sown with salt (Judg. 9:5). Covenants were sometimes made with salt (Num. 18:19; II Chron. 13:5). Christ's disciples called "the salt of the earth" (Matt. 5:13; Mark 9:50; Luke 14:34).

Salt, City of, a city in the wilderness of Judah, not far from the Dead Sea, being between Nibshan and Engedi (Josh. 15:62), site uncertain.

Salt, Covenant of, a covenant confirmed with sacrificial meals at which salt was used (Lev. 2:13; Num. 18:19).

Salt Sea (See Dead Sea)

Salt, Valley of, a valley between Jerusalem and Edom in which great victories were won over the Edomites, first by the army of David (II Sam. 8:14), and later by Amaziah, king of Judah (II Kings 14:7; II Chron. 25:11).

Salu (sā'lū), the father of Zimri who was slain by Phinehas (Num. 25:14; I Macc. 2:26).

Salutation (săl-ū-tā'shŭn), a greeting given either orally (Luke 1:29, 41, 44) or in writing (I Cor. 16:21; Col. 4:18; II Thess. 3:17). Greetings in the Bible sometimes included acts as well as words: a profound obesiance or prostration, a kissing of the hand, kneeling, falling upon the neck of another, embracings. Every situation in life had its own salutation: the return of a friend from a journey, the birth of a son, a marriage, wearing new clothes, dining, the appeals of a beggar, etc. Because salutations were usually so time-consuming, when Jesus sent out the Seventy, He forbade salutations by the way (Luke 10:4). Salutations were given at partings as well as at meetings. "Go in peace," or "Farewell" (I Sam. 1:17; 20:42; II Sam. 15:9; Mark 5:34). Epistolary salutations were more brief and direct. The salutations of Paul's epistles are usually elaborate and of rich spiritual fulness.

Salvation (săl-vā'shŭn), not necessarily a technical theological term, but simply denotes "deliverance" from almost any kind of evil, whether material or spiritual. Theologically, however, it denotes (1) the whole process by which man is delivered from all that interferes with the enjoyment of God's highest blessings, (2) the actual enjoyment of those blessings. The root idea in salvation is **deliverance** from some danger or evil. This deliverance may be from defeat in battle (Exod. 15:2), trouble (Ps. 34:6), enemies (II Sam. 3:10), violence (II Sam. 22:3), reproach (Ps. 57:3), exile (Ps. 106:47), death (Ps. 6:4), sin (Ezek. 36:29). The outstanding instance of divine salvation in the early history of Israel was the deliverance from Egypt. Since it is God who provides the deliverance, He is often spoken of as Saviour (Isa. 43:3, 11; Jer. 14:8), a title which in the NT is usually applied to Jesus Christ. At first the conception of salvation is primarily national, but gradually the prophetic horizon broadens and salvation is seen to include Gentiles as well as Jews (Isa. 49:5, 6; 55:1-5). There is also increasing stress upon the individual. Salvation is not necessarily for the nation as a whole, but for the righteous remnant. It includes, moreover, deliverance from sin itself as well as from the various evils which are the consequence of sin (Ps. 51; Jer. 31:31-35; Ezek. 36:25-29). With the development of the Messianic idea the word salvation comes to be used in the technical theological sense of the deliverance, especially from sin, to be brought in with the Messianic age.

In the OT, complete trust in God was the most important of the human conditions for salvation. Next in importance, and following naturally from the first, was obedience to God's moral law as expressed in the various codes of law. God, however, was not satisfied with a mere legalistic fulfilment of the letter of the law. Forgiveness of sins was conditioned upon repentance. Most sins also required a ritual sacrifice as part of the act of repentance.

The central theme of the entire apostolic age is the salvation brought by Jesus. Salvation is represented primarily as deliverance from sin. The whole NT lays stress upon the sufferings and death of Christ as mediating salvation (Eph. 2:13-18). As in the teaching of Jesus (Matt. 9:22) salvation throughout the NT is regarded as a present experience, but it is eschatological as well. Indeed, the blessings of salvation the believer has now are only a foretaste of what are to be his in the coming age, after Christ comes. The salvation Christ brings is not merely deliverance from future punishment, but also from sin as a present power (Rom. 6). It includes all the redemptive blessings we have in Christ, chiefly conversion, regeneration, justification, adoption, sanctification, and glorification. It provides a solution for the whole problem of sin, in all its many aspects. In some sense, the doctrine of salvation extends beyond man so as to affect the universe. Eventually all things are to be subjected unto the Son (I Cor. 15:28), and all things in heaven and on earth will be summed up in Christ (Eph. 1:10).

Samaria (sȧ-mār'ĭ-ȧ, **watch tower). 1.** Another name for the N kingdom of Israel, founded when the 10 N tribes refused to acknowledge Rehoboam, the son of Solomon, as their king. It extended from Bethel to Dan, and

A first glimpse of the city of Samaria, from the Shechem road. © MPS

Two views of the land of Samaria. Top: The Plain of the Maidens, near Shiloh (Judges 21:19-21).
Below: Looking north from Mount Gerazim, looking toward ancient Shechem at left, Sychar in upper center and Jacob's Well at right, the scene of Christ's conversation with the woman of Samaria. © *MPS*

from the Mediterranean to Syria and Ammon. Important cities: Shechem, Samaria, Sychar, Shiloh, Bethel. 2. Capital of N kingdom built by Omri c. 5½ miles NW of Shechem; rebuked for luxury and corruption (I Kings 18: 3; 21; Isa. 7:9; Jer. 31:5; Ezek. 23:33; Hos. 8:5; Amos 3:1-22). Modern Sebastiyeh.

Samaritan Pentateuch (See Samaritans)

Samaritans (så-măr′ĭ-tăns). (1) The inhabitants of Samaria (the region rather than the town; e.g. II Kings 17:26; Matthew 10:5; Luke 9:52; 10:33; 17: 16; John 4:9, 30, 40; Acts 8:25); (2) the sect which derived its name from Samaria, a term of contempt with the Jews (John 8:48); (3) since the seventeenth century, "a good Samaritan" (Luke 10:33) has signified a generous benefactor.

Samgarnebo (săm′gȧr-nēb′bō), one of Nebuchadnezzar's chief army officers who entered Jerusalem (Jer. 39:3).

Samlah (săm′lȧ, **a garment**), one of the kings of Edom (Gen. 36:36, 37; I Chron. 1:47, 48).

Samos (sā′mŏs, **height**), an island off western Asia Minor colonized by Ionians in the 11th century B.C., notable for metal-work, woolen products, and probably utility pottery, though it is not certain that "Samian ware" necessarily implied a large native industry of this sort. Paul touched at Samos on his last voyage at Jerusalem (Acts 20: 15).

Samothrace (săm′ō-thrās, **Samos of Thrake**), an island in the NE Aegean, mountainous and rising to over 5,000 feet, lying between Troas and Neopolis. Paul called here on his first voyage to Europe (Acts 16:11).

Samson (săm′sŭn), one of the judges of Israel, perhaps the last before Samuel. The story of his life is told in Judges 3-16. He was an Israelite of the tribe of Dan, the son of Manoah. His birth was announced by the angel of the Lord beforehand to his mother, who was barren. The angel told her that she would have a son, that this son should be a Nazirite from his birth, and that the Lord should begin to use him to deliver Israel out of the hand of the Philistines. Nazirites were under special vow to God to restrain their carnal nature, thus showing the people generally that if they would receive God's blessing they must deny and govern themselves and be faithful to their vows of consecration as God's covenant people. The preternatural strength that Samson exhibited at various times in his career was not his because he was a natural giant, but because the Spirit of the Lord came upon him to accomplish great deeds. Almost from the beginning of his career he showed one conspicuous weakness, which was ultimately to wreck him: he was a slave to passion. He insisted, against the objections of his parents, on marrying a Philistine woman of Timnath. He went home without his wife, giving the impression that he had forsaken her. When, later, he returned to her, he found that her father had given her in marriage to someone else, and was offered her sister in her stead. In revenge, Samson caught 300 jackals, and sent them into the Philistine fields of corn in pairs with burning torches tied between their tails. The Philistines retaliated by burning his wife and her father.

This act of vengeance only provoked another and a greater from himself. He smote them hip and thigh with a great slaughter, and took up his abode on the top of a rock called Etam. The Philistines invaded Judah and demanded the surrender of their archenemy. Samson agreed to allow the Israelites to deliver him into the hands of the Philistines, but on the way he broke the cords that bound him, and seizing the jawbone of an ass he killed with it 1,000 men. With this great feat Samson clearly established his title to the position of a judge in Israel.

Samson next went down to Gaza, a Philistine stronghold, and yielded to the solicitations of a harlot. When it became known that he was in the city, the Philistines laid a trap for him; but at midnight Samson arose, took the doors of the gate of the city, and the two posts, and carried them a quarter of a mile to the top of the hill before Hebron. God in His mercy continued to give him supernatural strength notwithstanding his evil actions.

Continuing his life of vicious self-indulgence, Samson before long became enamored of another Philistine woman, Delilah, through whom he lost his physical power. The Philistine leaders bribed her with a large sum of money to betray him into their hands. By their direction she begged him to tell her in what his great strength lay. Three times he gave her deceitful answers, but at last he gave in to her importunities and revealed that if only his

The so-called Cave of Samson at the Rock Etam. © MPS

hair were cut he would be like other men. She lulled him into a profound sleep; his hair was cut; and when he awoke and heard her derisive cry, "The Philistines be upon thee Samson," he found that, not merely his strength, but also God had departed from him. Now at the mercy of his enemies, he was bound with chains, his eyes were put out, and he was sent to grind in the prisonhouse of Gaza.

How long Samson continued in this state of shameful bondage is unknown — perhaps some weeks or even months. On the occasion of a great feast to the god Dagon, his captors resolved to make sport of him by making him play the buffoon before the assembled multitude. The temple of Dagon was filled with people — with 3,000 on the roof to watch the sport. Meanwhile, his hair had grown again, and with his returning strength he longed to be avenged on his enemies for at least one of his two blinded eyes (Judg. 16:28). He asked the lad who attended him to allow him to rest between the two pillars on which the building was supported. Taking hold of them, he prayed that God would help him once more; and with a mighty effort he moved the pillars from their position and brought down the roof, burying with himself a large number of Philistines in its ruins. In this dying act he slew more than he had slain in his life.

Samuel (săm'ū-ĕl, **name of God,** or **God hears).** Samuel is often called the last of the judges (cf. I Sam. 7:6, 15-17) and the first of the prophets (3:20; Acts 3:24; 13:20). He was the son of Elkanah and Hannah. The account of the events associated with the birth of Samuel indicates that his parents were a devoted and devout couple. Hannah's childlessness led her to pour out her complaint and supplication to God in bitterness of heart; but she trusted God to provide the answer and promised to give to the Lord the son she had requested. When Samuel was born, she kept her promise; as soon as the child was weaned she took him to Shiloh and presented him to Eli. The Lord blessed Samuel and "let none of his words fall to the ground" (2:19), so that all Israel knew that Samuel was a prophet of the Lord. Eli died upon receiving the news of the death of his sons and the capture of the Ark of the Covenant in a Philistine victory over Israel. Some time after the return of the Ark to Israel, Samuel challenged the people to put away foreign gods and to serve the Lord only (7:3). When the Philistines threatened the Israelite gathering at Mizpah, Samuel interceded for Israel and the Lord answered with thunder against the enemy. The Philistines were routed and Samuel set up a memorial stone which he called Ebenezer ("Stone of help," 7:12).

Samuel, judge and priest, made his home at Ramah, where he administered justice and also built an altar. He went on circuit to Bethel, Gilgal, and Mizpah (7:15). In his old age he appointed his sons, Joel and Abijah (cf. I Chron. 6:28), as judges in Beersheba, but the people protested that his sons did not walk in his ways but took bribes and perverted justice. The people requested a king to rule them. God had revealed to Samuel that Saul was to come to see him; at the conclusion of this first meeting, Samuel secretly anointed Saul as king (10:1) and foretold some confirmatory signs, which came to pass as predicted (10:1-13). Samuel then called an assembly of Israel at Mizpah and the choice of Saul was confirmed. Samuel related to the people the rights and duties of a king and wrote these in a scroll which was placed in the sanctuary (lit., "before the Lord," 10:25). After Saul's victory over the Ammonites, Samuel again convened Israel and Saul's kingship was confirmed at Gilgal. Samuel was now advanced in years and retired from public life in favor of the king.

Samuel next appears in conflict with Saul; a national crisis had arisen with a Philistine threat and Saul summoned the people to Gilgal. When Samuel was late in coming to make offerings, Saul presumed to make them himself. Samuel accused Saul of foolishness and disobedience and said that Saul's kingdom would not continue. Samuel then went to Gibeah and Saul engaged in a victorious battle with the Philistines. After Saul's success, Samuel commissioned him to annihilate the Amalekites (chap. 15). In this expedition Saul again showed incomplete obedience; Samuel reminded him of the necessity of absolute obedience and told him God had rejected him to remain as king. This was the last official meeting of Samuel and Saul (15:35); Samuel returned to Ramah and grieved over Saul. The Lord appointed Samuel to serve again as "king-maker" and sent him to Bethlehem to anoint the young shepherd, David, as Saul's successor (cf. I Chron. 11:3).

Samuel's last message to Saul came upon the occasion of Saul's recourse to the spirit-medium of Endor on the eve of Saul's death on Mt. Gilboa. Samuel is mentioned in several other OT books and is recognized as a man of prayer. In Psalm 99:6 it is said that he was "among those who called on His name." The intercession of Samuel is cited in Jeremiah 15:1. In the NT he is referred to by Peter (Acts 3:24) as one who foretold the events of NT times; Paul mentions him in a sermon at Antioch of Pisidia (Acts 13:20). In Hebrews 11:32 he is listed among those whose faith pleased God.

Samuel, Books of. The books are named after Samuel, the outstanding figure of the early section. Originally there was only one book of Samuel, but the LXX divided it into two. There is little external or internal evidence as to the authorship of Samuel. Jewish tradition ascribes the work to the Prophet Samuel even though all of the events of I Samuel 25-31 and II Samuel occurred after Samuel's death.

Outline (after Pfeiffer). (1) Shiloh and Samuel, I Samuel 1:1-7:1; (2) Samuel and Saul, 7:2-15:35; (3) Saul and David, I Samuel 16-31; II Samuel

Fragments of a scroll of the book of Samuel found among the Dead Sea Scrolls. PAM

1; (4) David as king of Judah, II Samuel 2-4; (5) David as king of all Israel, II Samuel 5-24.

Sanballat (săn-băl'ăt, **the god Sin (moongod) has given life),** very influential Samaritan who tried unsuccessfully to defeat Nehemiah's plans for rebuilding the walls of Jerusalem (Neh. 4:1ff; 6:1-14; 13:28).

Sanctification (sănk-tĭ-fĭ-kā'shŭn, **separation, setting apart),** to separate from the world and consecrate unto God. To sanctify anything is to declare that it belongs to God. It may refer to persons, places, days and seasons, and objects used for worship (Exod. 13:2; 19:5, 6; 29:27, 44; Lev. 27:14, 16; Num. 3:12; Neh. 13:19-22). In an ethical sense it means the progressive conformation of the believer into the image of Christ, or the process by which the life is made morally holy. Sanctification is through the redemptive work of Christ and the work of the indwelling Holy Spirit. It begins at regeneration and is completed when we see Christ.

Sanctuary (săngk'tū-â-rē, **holy place),** refers almost exclusively to the tabernacle or temple. God's sanctuary was His established earthly abode, the place where He chose to dwell among His people (Ps. 114:2; Isa. 8:14; Ezek. 11:19). The word is used particularly of the holy of holies, whether of the tabernacle or temple. A sanctuary was also a place of asylum, the horns of the altar especially being regarded as inviolable (cf. I Kings 2:28f). In the NT the word is used only in the Epistle to the Hebrews (8:2; 9:1, 2; 13:11), where the author makes clear that the earthly sanctuary was only a type of the true sanctuary which is in heaven, of which Christ is the high priest, and in which He offers Himself as a sacrifice (Heb. 10:1-18).

Sand, loose grains of small size formed as the result of weathering and decomposition of various kinds of rocks. It is found in abundance in deserts, in the sea, and on the shores of large bodies of water. Symbolic (1) numberlessness, vastness, (2) weight, (3) instability (Gen. 22:17; Jer. 33:22; Rom. 9:27; Heb. 11:12; Josh. 11:4; Judg. 7:12; I Sam. 13:5). Joseph accumulated grain as the sand of the sea (Gen. 41:49). God gave to Solomon understanding and largeness of heart as the sand on the seashore (I Kings 4:29). Job says that if his grief were weighed it would be heavier than the sand of the sea (Job 6:3). A house built on sand symbolizes a life not built on the teachings on Jesus (Matt. 7:26).

Sandal (See Dress)

Sanhedrim, Sanhedrin (săn'hē-drĭm, săn'hē-drĭn, **a council),** the highest Jewish tribunal during the Greek and Roman periods. The origin of the Sanhedrin is unknown, and there is no historical evidence for its existence before the Greek period. During the reign of the Hellenistic kings Palestine was practically under home rule, and was governed by an aristocratic council of elders which was presided over by the hereditary high priest. This later developed into the Sanhedrin. During most of the Roman period the internal government of the country was practically in its hands, and its influence was recognized even in the Diaspora (Acts 9:2; 22:5; 26:12). After the death of Herod the Great, however, during the reign of Archelaus and the Roman procurators, the civil authority of the Sanhedrin was probably restricted to Judaea proper, which is very likely the reason why it had no judicial authority over our Lord so long as He remained in Galilee. The Sanhedrin was abolished after the destruction of Jerusalem (A.D. 70).

The Sanhedrin was composed of 70 members, plus the president, who was the high priest. Nothing is known as to the way in which vacancies were

A hearing before the Sanhedrin. © SPF

The tomb of Sarah in the Cave of Machpelah Mosque in Hebron.
© MPS

filled. The members of the Sanhedrin were drawn from the three classes named in Matthew 16:21; 27:41; Mark 8:31; 11:27; 14:43, 53; 15:1; Luke 9: 22; 22:26: "the chief priests, with the scribes and the elders." The Pharisees were more and more represented in the Sanhedrin as they grew in importance.

In the time of Christ the Sanhedrin exercised not only civil jurisdiction, according to Jewish law, but also, in some degree, criminal. It could deal with all those judicial matters and measures of an administrative character which could not be competently handled by lower courts, or which the Roman procurator had not specially reserved for himself. It was the final court of appeal for all questions connected with the Mosaic law. It could order arrests by its own officers of justice (Matt. 26:47; Mark 14:43; Acts 4:3; 5:17f; 9:2). It was also the final court of appeal from all inferior courts. It had the right of capital punishment until about 40 years before the destruction of Jerusalem. After that it could still pass, but it could not execute, a sentence of death without the confirmation of the Roman procurator. That is why our Lord had to be tried not only before the Sanhedrin but also before Pilate (John 18:31, 32). But for this, He would have been put to death in some other way than by crucifixion, for crucifixion was not a Jewish mode of punishment.

Sansannah (săn-săn'à, **a palm branch),** a town in the S of Judah (Josh. 15:31), identical with Hazar-susah, (Josh. 19: 5).

Saph (săf, **a basin, threshold),** a Philistine giant who was slain by one of David's heroes (II Sam. 21:18; I Chron. 20:4).

Saphir (sā'fẽr, **glittering),** one of a group of towns mentioned in Micah 1:10-15, most likely in SW Palestine.

Sapphira (să-fī'rà, **beautiful),** the wife of Ananias who with her husband was struck dead because they both lied to God (Acts 5:1-10).

Sapphire (See Minerals)

Sara, Sarah, Sarai (sâr'à, **princess).** 1. The wife of Abraham, first mentioned in Gen. 11:29. According to Genesis 20:12, she was Abraham's half-sister, the daughter of his father, but not of his mother. Her name was originally Sarai. She was about 65 years old when Abraham left Ur for Haran. Later, she accompanied Abraham into Egypt, and was there passed off by him as his sister because he feared the Egyptians might kill him if they knew she was his wife. Years later, Abraham did the same thing at the court of Abimelech, king of Gerar (Gen. 20: 1-18). In each instance grievous wrong was averted only by God's intervention, and Abraham was rebuked by the pagan rulers for his lack of candor. Still childless at the age of 75, she induced Abraham to take her handmaid Hagar as a concubine. According to the laws of the time, a son born of this woman would be regarded as the son and heir of Abraham and Sarah. When Hagar conceived, she treated her mistress with such insolence that Sarah drove her from the house. Hagar, however, returned at God's command, submitted herself to her mistress, and gave birth to Ishmael. Afterward, when Sarai was about 90, God promised her a son; her name was changed to Sarah; and a year later, Isaac, the child of promise, was born (Gen. 17:15-27). A few years later, at a great feast celebrating the weaning of Isaac, Sarah observed Ishmael mocking her son, and peremptorily demanded the expulsion of Hagar and Ishmael (Gen. 21). Abraham reluctantly acceded, after God had instructed him to do so. Sarah died at Kiriath-arba (Hebron) at the age of 127, and was buried in the cave of Machpelah, which Abraham purchased as a family sepulchre (Gen. 23: 1, 2). Sarah is mentioned again in the OT only in Isaiah 51:2, where she is referred to as the mother of the chosen race. In the NT she is mentioned in Romans 4:19; 9:9; Galatians 4:21-5:1; Hebrews 11:11; and I Peter 3:6. 2. The daughter of Raguel, the wife of Tobias (Tobit 3:7, 17).

Saraph (sā'răf, **noble one),** a descendant of Judah, at one time ruler in Moab (I Chron. 4:22).

Sardine (See Mineral)

Sardis (sàr'dĭs), the chief city of Lydia, famous for arts and crafts, and was the first center to mint gold and silver coinage (Rev. 1:11; 3:1-6).

Sardite (săr'dīt), a name given to the descendants of Sered (Gen. 46:14; Num. 26:26).

Sardius, Sardonyx (See Minerals)

Sarepta (sà-rĕp'tà), the name in Luke 4:26 (KJV) for the town of Zarephath, where Elijah lived with a widow and her son (I Kings 17:9, 10). RSV renders it Zarephath.

Sargon (sȧr′gŏn, **the constituted king).** 1. Sargon I, king and founder of early Babylonian empire (2400 B.C.). Not referred to in Bible. 2. Sargon II (722-705 B.C.), Assyrian king (Isa. 20:1); successor of Shalmaneser who captured Samaria (II Kings 17:1-6); defeated Egyptian ruler So (II Kings 17:4); destroyed Hittite empire; succeeded by his son Sennacherib.

Sarid (sā′rĭd, **survivor),** a village on the boundary of Zebulun (Josh. 19:10, 12).

Saron (See Sharon)

Sarsechim (sȧr′sē-kĭm), one of Nebuchadnezzar's princes who entered Jerusalem when it fell (Jer. 39:3).

Saruch (See Serug)

Satan (sā′tăn, **adversary).** 1. As a common noun: enemy or adversary (I Sam. 29:4; I Kings 5:4; 11:14; Pss. 38:20; 109:6). 2. As a proper noun: the chief of the fallen spirits, the grand adversary of God and man (Job 1:6, 12; 2:1; Zech. 3:1); hostile to everything good. Names and descriptive designations by which he is known: devil (Matt. 4:1; Luke 4:2), accuser of the brethren (Rev. 12:9, 10), adversary (I Pet. 5:8), Beelzebub (Matt. 12:24), Belial (II Cor. 6:15), deceiver of the whole world (Rev. 12:9), the great dragon (Rev. 12:9), the evil one (Matt. 13:19, 38), the father of lies (John 8:44), god of this world (II Cor. 4:4), murderer (John 8:44), the old serpent (Rev. 12:9), the prince of this world (John 12:31; 14:30), prince of the powers of the air (Eph. 2:2), the tempter (Matt. 4:5; I Thess. 3:5). Not an independent rival of God, but is able to go only as far as God permits (Job 1:12; 2:6; Luke 22:31); basically evil; story of his origin not told, but he was originally good; fell through pride (I Tim. 3:6); ruler of a powerful kingdom standing in opposition to God (Matt. 12:26; Luke 11:18); ever seeks to defeat the divine plans of grace toward mankind; defeated by Christ at Calvary; will some day be cast into the like of fire to be eternally doomed (Matt. 25:41; Rev. 20:1-3, 7-10).

Satrap (sā′trăp), the official title of the viceroy who in the Persian empire ruled several small provinces combined as one government. Each of these provinces had its own governor. In Ezra 8:36 and Esther 3:12 the term is translated **lieutenants** in KJV. In Daniel 3:2; 6:1, the KJV renders it **princes.**

Satyr (săt′êr) lascivious deity, half man and half goat, in Mediterranean mythology (Isa. 13:21; 34:14).

Saul (sôl, **asked of God).** 1. First king of Israel; son of Kish; Benjamite; anointed king by Samuel (I Sam. 8-10); chosen king by Israelites (I Sam. 10:17-27); defeated Israel's enemies: Ammonites, Philistines, Moabites, Amalekites (I Sam. 11-14); disobeyed God and was rejected by Him (I Sam. 13:1-14; 15); jealous of David because of his greater popularity and sought to kill him (I Sam. 16-26); ended his own life after being wounded in battle (I Sam. 31). 2. Hebrew name for Paul (Acts 13:9).

Saviour (sāv′yôr, **saviour, deliverer, preserver),** one who saves, delivers, or preserves from any evil or danger, whether physical or spiritual, temporal or eternal. A basic OT concept is that "God is the deliverer of His people"; it is emphatically declared that man cannot save himself and that Jehovah alone is the Saviour (Ps. 44:3, 7; Isa. 43:11; 45:21; 60:16; Jer. 14:8; Hos. 13:4). In the OT the term is not applied to the Messiah; He receives salvation from God (Pss. 28:8; 144:10; II Sam. 22:51), but He comes to offer salvation to all (Zech. 9:9; Isa. 49:6, 8; etc.). The term is also applied to men who are used as the instruments of God's deliverance (Judg. 3:9, 15 ASV; II Kings 13:5; Neh. 9:27; Obad. 21). In the NT it is never applied to a mere man. It is used of both God the Father and Christ the Son. God the Father is Saviour, for He is the author of our salvation which He provided through Christ (Luke 1:47; I Tim. 1:1; 2:3; 4:10; Titus 1:3; 2:10; 3:4; Jude 25). Saviour is pre-eminently the title of the Son (Titus 1:4; 2:13; 3:6; II Tim. 1:10; II Pet. 1:1, 11; 2:20; 3:2, 18; I John 4:10). At His birth the angel announced Him as "a Saviour, who is Christ the Lord" (Luke 2:11). His mission to save His people from their sins was announced before His birth (Matt. 1:21) and was stated by Jesus as the aim of His coming (Luke 19:10). The salvation which He wrought is for all mankind and He is "the Saviour of the world" (I John 4:14; John 4:42). He shall come again to consummate our salvation in the transformation of our bodies (Phil. 3:20).

Savor, Savour (sā′vôr), **taste** (Matt. 5:13; Luke 14:34) or **smell,** whether stench (Joel 2:20) or a pleasant smell. In the latter case it is in the OT usually qualified by the word sweet, and is used to refer to a sacrifice which God was pleased to accept (Gen. 8:21, cf. Num. 15:3). In the NT the word is used metaphorically to refer to the incense burnt in a victor's triumphal procession (II Cor. 2:14), to Christ's obedience to God (Eph. 5:2), or to the Christian's sacrifice of obedience to God (II Cor. 2:15; Phil. 4:18).

Savory Meat, the meals made by Jacob and Esau for their father Isaac prior to receiving his blessing (Gen. 27:4, 9, 14, 17, 31).

Saw. Probably the earliest saws were made of flint, with serrated edges, mounted in a frame. Other saws were like knives, of bronze or iron. Small handsaws were like ours today, but the teeth were shaped in the other direction, so that the worker did not shove, but pulled against the wood. Large western handsaws were unknown in Bible times. Palestinian carpenters probably sat on the floor and held the wood between their toes, which became as skillful as extra hands. Stone was sawed as well as wood (I Kings 7:9).

Scab (See Diseases, Skin)

Scaffold. Solomon knelt on a "brazen scaffold" (platform) when he dedicated the temple (II Chron. 6:13).

Scale. 1. Only fish having fins and scales were permitted as food for the Hebrews (Lev. 11:9-12). 2. Scales as an instrument for weighing are referred to in Isaiah 40:12 and Proverbs 16:11; 20:23 (balance, KJV).

Scall (See Diseases, Skin)

Scapegoat, the 2nd of two goats for which lots were cast on the Day of Atonement (Lev. 16:8, 10, 26). The first was sacrificed as a sin offering, but the second had the people's sins transferred to it by prayer and was then taken into the wilderness and released.

Scarlet. The color was probably a bright rich crimson. It was obtained from the eggs of the insect **(coccus ilicis)** called **kirmiz** by the Arabs, from which is derived the English word **crimson.** Scarlet cloth was used for the hangings of the tabernacle (Exod. 25:4; Num. 4:8) and for the high priest's vestments (Exod. 39:1). Scarlet stuff was used for the cleansing of the recovered leper (Lev. 14:4) and in other ceremonies of purification (Num. 19:6). Royal or expensive apparel was of scarlet (II Sam. 1:24; Prov. 31:21; Lam. 4:5; Matt. 27:28; Rev. 17:4; 18:12, 16). It appears to have been used to mark thread or rope (Gen. 38:28, 30; Josh. 2:18, 21), and the lips of the bride in Song of Solomon are likened to scarlet thread (4:3). Sins are "as scarlet" (Isa. 1:18).

Scarlet (See Plants)

Scepter (sĕp′têr), a rod held in the hands of kings as a token of authority (II Sam. 7:14), a shepherd's crook (Ps. 23:4), or the staff of a marshal (as RSV translates Judg. 5:14).

This staff-scepter might be used for protection (II Sam. 23:21; Ps. 23:4) or for punishment (Isa. 10:24; 30:31). When dying Jacob blessed his son Judah and promised him the royal leadership in words which Christians understand as a Messianic prediction, it was the scepter which denoted the royal prerogative (Gen. 49:10). God's kingship is also represented thus (Ps. 45:6).

Sceva (sē′vȧ), a Jew, who was a chief priest living in Ephesus, whose seven sons were exorcists (Acts 19:14-17).

Schism (sĭz′m, **rent** or **division),** a formal division inside a religious group (I Cor. 12:25).

School, place or institution devoted to teaching and learning. In the early history of Israel the home was the primary agency for religious training, which was imparted chiefly through conversation, example, and imitation. All teaching was religiously oriented.

A class in a synagogue school KC © FC

Samuel instituted a school of the prophets (I Sam. 19:19, 20). During the Babylonian captivity the synagogue had its origin. It was a place of teaching, never of sacrifice. Later an elementary school system was developed with the synagogue attendant (Luke 4:20) as the teacher. Memorization had a prominent place. Teachers had an important part in the work of the church (James 3:1; Rom. 12:7).

Science, (Dan. 1:4; I Tim. 6:20 **knowledge).** Daniel 1:4 is literally "understanding knowledge or thought." In I Timothy 6:20 the reference is to that professed knowledge which sets itself up in contradiction to the truth of the Gospel.

Scoff, to mock, deride (II Kings 2:23; Ezek. 22:5; Hab. 1:10).

Scoffer, one who scoffs or mocks, one playing with trifles, hence one who derides, mocks (II Pet. 3:3, "mocker" in ASV; so rendered in Jude 18).

Scorpion (skôr′pĭ-ŏn), an insect of the arachnid (spider-like) type, with claws that give it the appearance of a miniature lobster. Its tail bears a stinger with which it poisons its victim, and it is therefore described as a creature to be feared (Deut. 8:15; Ezek. 2:6; Luke 10:19; 11:12; Rev. 9:5, 10). The punishment with scorpions which King Rehoboam threatened (I Kings 12:11; II Chron. 10:11) likely referred to whips or scourges, q.v.

Scourge (skûrj, **to whip, lash),** a public punishment of the condemned, the act or the instrument used to inflict severe pain by beating. Scourging, well known in the East, was familiar to the Hebrews from Egypt. The Mosaic law authorized the beating of a culprit, apparently with a rod, but limited to 40 the strokes given the prostrate victim (Deut. 25:3). It was administered by local synagogue authorities (Matt. 10:17; Acts 22:19) or by the Sanhedrin (Acts 5:40). Among the Romans either rods were used (Acts 16:22; II Cor. 11:25) or whips, the thongs of which were weighted with jagged pieces of bone or metal to make the blow more effective (Matt. 27:26; Mark 15:15; John 19:1). It was used to wrest confessions and secrets from its victims (Acts 22:24). Scourge is used figuratively for "affliction" in Joshua 23:13; Job 5:21; 9:23; Isaiah 10:26; 28:15, 18.

Screech Owl (See Birds)

Scribes (See Occupations and Professions)

Scribes, Jewish, class of learned men who made the systematic study of the law and its exposition their professional occupation. Also called "lawyers" (Matt. 22:35), "doctors of the law" (Luke 5:17), "rabbis" (Matt. 23:8). They devoted themselves to the preservation, transcription, and exposition of the law. To safeguard the sanctity of the law they gradually developed an extensive and complicated system of teaching, known as "the tradition of the elders" (Matt. 15:2-6). All higher instruction was in their hands. They often served as judges in Jewish courts and were an important element in the membership of the Sanhedrin (Matt. 26:57). They were laymen, not priests. Most of them followed some trade, as they were not expected to receive money for their teaching. They fiercely opposed Jesus (Mark 2:16) and were denounced by Him (Matt. 23). They played an important part in His death (Matt. 26:57) and also persecuted the early church (Acts 4:5; 6:12).

Scrip (See Dress)

Scripts (See Writing)

Scripture (See Bible, Canon, Old Testament, New Testament)

Scroll, book made of papyrus or smoothed skins of animals sewn together to make a long strip which was wound around sticks at both ends (Isa. 34:4; Jer. 36; Ezek. 3:1-3; Rev. 5; 10:1-10). They varied in length from a few feet to 35 feet. The codex form of book was not used until the 2nd century A.D.

Scrolls, Dead Sea (See Dead Sea Scrolls).

Sculpture (See Art)

Scurvy (See Diseases, Skin)

Scythian (sĭth′ĭ-ăn), the name is used by classical writers as a general term for the barbarians of the steppes. In common parlance it was a term for the savage and uncivilized (Col. 3:11). Scythia was the name given by the Greeks to an ill-defined area between the Carpathians and the Don, the western portion of which included the black earth wheatlands of the modern Ukraine. Scythians appeared in upper Mesopotamia and Syria between 650 and 620 B.C. and another force reached the middle Danube. South Russia, to speak in modern geographical terms, was firmly occupied. The nomads were formidable soldiers, swift archer-cavalry versed in the tactics of desert warfare and mobile strategy.

An old Samaritan scroll on display in a synagogue. © MPS

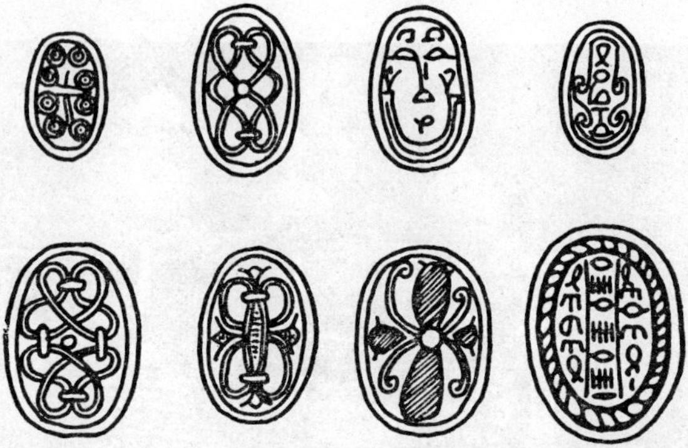

Scarabs of the 17th century BC, from Garstang, the story of Jericho.

Detail of seal

A typical seal on a jar handle, the seal impression of Eliakim, steward of King Jehoiakin, from Tell Beit-Mirsim, from about 587 B.C. © MPS

The Celts and Samaritans seem to have displaced the Scythians in the last three centuries before Christ.

Sea. In the Bible the term is used in several ways. 1. The ocean, the gathering of the waters at the creation, is called sea (Gen. 1:10; Pss. 8:8; 24:2). 2. Almost any body of water, salt or fresh, is called sea. The Mediterranean (Acts 10:6), the sea of Galilee (Matt. 4:18; Num. 34:11), the Dead Sea (Deut. 3:17), the Red Sea (Exod. 13:18; 14:2). Not all of these would be called seas by us. Galilee is a lake, being only about 12½ by 7½ miles in size, but it is often called a sea. 3. Even rivers may, in poetic language, be called a sea: the Nile (Isa. 18:2; 19; 5), and the Euphrates (Isa. 21:1). 4. The basin in Solomon's temple was called a sea (see Sea, Brazen).

Sea, Brazen, the great basin in Solomon's temple where the priests washed their hands and feet preparatory to temple ministry (I Kings 7:23-26; II Chron. 4:2-6). It was made of brass which David had taken in war (I Chron. 18:8).

Sea of Glass. In the vision of heaven in the Revelation, a glassy sea is seen before the throne of God (4:6; 15:2). It is translucent, "like unto crystal."

Sea of Jazer. No such sea is known. Jer. 48:32 is probably a scribal error, and the city of Jazer is meant (cf. RSV).

Sea Mew (See Birds, Cuckoo)

Sea Monster, any great fish of the sea (Gen. 1:21; Job 7:12; in KJV **whale).**

Seal, device bearing a design, name, or some other words so that it can impart an impression in relief upon a soft substance like clay or wax; used as a mark of authority and authenticity on letters, etc. (I Kings 21:8), to ratify a covenant (Jer. 32:11-14), to protect books and other documents (Jer. 32:14), to furnish proof of deputed authority and power (Gen. 41:42), to seal doors (Matt. 27:66) as an official mark of ownership.

Scripture often uses the term metaphorically to betoken authentication, confirmation, ownership, evidence, or security. God does not forget sin, but stores it up against the sinner, under a seal (Deut. 32:34; Job 14:17). Prophecies that are intended to be kept secret for a time or bound with a seal (Dan. 12:4, 9; Rev. 5:1ff; 10:4).

Season (See Time, Calendar)

Seat, a chair, stool (I Sam. 20:18; Judg. 3:20) or throne (Luke 1:52; Rev. 2:13; 4:4; 11:16; 13:2; 16:10). It is used also of the exalted position occupied by men of rank or influence (Matt. 23:2; Ps. 1:1). Jesus reproached some of the men of His day for preferring the chief seats in the synagogue (Matt. 23:6; Mark 12:39; Luke 11:43; 20:46).

Seba (sē'bȧ), a people descended from Cush (Gen. 10:7) who lived in southern Arabia. Same as Sheba.

Sebat (sē'băt), the 11th month of the Hebrew year (Zech. 1:7), spelled Shebat in RSV. It corresponded to our February. See Year.

Secacah (sē-kā'kȧ), a village in the wilderness of Judah (Josh. 15:61), location unknown.

Sechu (sē'kū) a village near Samuel's town of Ramah (I Sam. 19:22).

Second Coming of Christ, The, one of the most prominent doctrines in Scripture. In the NT alone it is referred to over 300 times. The night before His crucifixion Jesus told the apostles that He would come again (John 14:3), and at the time of His ascension two angels appeared to the apostles, saying that He would come back in the same manner as they had seen Him go (Acts 1:11). The NT shows that thenceforward His coming was the "blessed hope" of His people (Titus 2:13). There is a great difference of opinion as to what is meant by the Lord's return. Some regard it as the coming of the Holy Spirit on the day of Pentecost, or the coming of Christ into the heart at conversion, or Christ's coming in judgment at the destruction of Jerusalem in A.D. 70, or Christ's coming for the believer at death, or Christ's coming for the conversion of the world. Careful examination of the Scriptures referring to the second coming makes it clear, however, that His coming will be personal, bodily, and visible. For example, the coming of the Holy Spirit at Pentecost cannot be what is meant because the Acts and the Epistles show that long after the day of Pentecost the Church was still looking for the fulfillment of Christ's promise that He would come again. Christ Himself, moreover, clearly distinguished between death and His coming (John 21:23). The coming of Christ is the climax and culmination of His redemptive work, when the Church will be completed, and the Lord will usher in that Kingdom which will eventually result in God being all in all (Rom. 8:19-23; I Cor. 15:23-28; Eph. 1:14). See also Christ.

Sect (sĕkt, **sect, party, school)**, of schools of philosophy; in NT of religious parties: the Sadducees (Acts 5: 17), the Pharisees (15:5; 26:5), the Christians (24:5; 28:22). Also in 24:14 ASV ("heresy" in KJV).

Secundus (sē-kŭn'dŭs), a Thessalonian Christian, otherwise unknown, who with several others had preceded Paul to Troas (Acts 20:4).

Security, the theological teaching which maintains the certain continuation of the salvation of those who are saved; also known as the perseverance of the saints (John 10:28; Romans 8:38-39; Philippians 1:6; II Thessalonians 3:3; I Peter 1:5). These maintain that since salvation is God's work, the regenerate must be ultimately saved or God's purpose and work would come to naught, and that the very nature of eternal life forbids the thought of its not being eternal.

Seducer (sē-dūs'êr, **wailer, howler)**, a cheat, a false teacher, a deceiver, perhaps through the use of magical arts (II Tim. 3:13; "imposter" in ASV).

Seed. There is a threefold usage of this word in Scripture. 1. **Agricultural.** The farmer held his seed in his upturned garment, casting it out as he walked. Grain was sown in the early winter, after the first rains. Christ's parable of the sower is well known (Mark 4:1-20; Luke 8:5-15). 2. **Physiological.** "Seed of copulation" (RSV, "emission of semen") is a frequent expression in the Hebrew laws of cleanness (Lev. 15: 16ff). The NT speaks of Christians as having been begotten by God—"of incorruptible seed" (I Pet. 1:23; I John 3:9). 3. **Figurative.** Here seed means descendants (Gen. 13:16) or genealogy (Ezra 2:59; Neh. 7:61), or a class of people ("seed of evildoers," Isa. 1:4).

Seedtime (See Agriculture)

Seer (See Occupations)

Segub (sē'gŭb). 1. The younger son of Heil. He died when his father set up the gates of Jericho, which he was then building (I Kings 16:34). 2. Son of Hezron (I Chron. 2:21, 22).

Seir (sē'ēr). Seir the Horite (Gen. 36: 20; I Chron. 1:38) was the ancestor of the inhabitants of the land of Seir.

Seir, Land of and Mount (sē'êr) 1. The land of Seir and Mt. Seir are alternate names for the region occupied by the descendants of Edom or Esau. Originally called the land of Seir (Gen. 32: 3; 36:20, 21, 30; Num. 24:18), it was later called Edom. It is a mountainous and extremely rugged country, about 100 miles long, extending S from Moab on both sides of the Arabah or the great depression connecting the southern part of the Dead Sea with the Gulf of Akabah (Gen. 14:6; Deut. 2:1, 12; Josh. 15:1; Judg. 11:17, 18; I Kings 9:26). The summit of Mt. Seir rises about 3500 feet above the adjacent Arabah.

Esau made his home in Mt. Seir, and his descendants dispossessed the Horites (Deut. 2:12; Josh. 24:4), the original inhabitants (Gen. 14:6). A remnant of the Amalekites took refuge in these mountain fastnesses, but were finally destroyed by the Simeonites (I Chron. 4:42, 43). The term Seir is also used collectively for the people who lived in Mt. Seir (Ezek. 25:8). 2. Another region called Seir is a ridge on the border of the territory of Judah W of Kirjath-jearim (Josh. 15:10), generally identified with the rocky point on which the village of Saris stands, southwest of Kirjath-jearim.

Seirah, Seirath (sē-ī'rȧ, sē-ī'răth), a place in Mt. Ephraim, probably in the SE part, to which Ehud escaped after murdering Eglon (Judg. 3:26).

Sela (sē'lȧ), a place in Edom taken by King Ahaziah (II Kings 14:7). It is probably also referred to in II Chronicles 25:12; Isaiah 42:11 and Obadiah 3 where in each case the KJV translates "rock." The second reference the RSV translates "Sela." It seems to be the place made famous in Greek times by the name Petra, the capital of the Nabateans.

Selah (sē'lȧ, **to lift up)**, a term occurring 71 times in the Psalms, and also in Habakkuk 3:3, 9, 13, meaning unknown. It is generally believed that its usage was that of a musical or liturgical sign. The LXX seems to understand it as a direction to the orchestra—"lift up," i.e., play the instruments while the singers are silent. Jacob of Edessa (A.D. 640-708) compared it to the Amen sung by the Christians after the Gloria. Perhaps Selah was used in a similar way, as a signal for the singing of some sort of doxology or benediction after psalms or parts of psalms divided for liturgical use. It will be noted that the word

Seir, the land and the mount: Two views, top, the Wadi Sayyaga, with the Wadi Mousa torrent bed and the Khubta range in the distance. Below, the great rock El-Biyara, at Petra on which the Edomite capital stood. © *MPS*

usually occurs at a place where a very significant statement has been made, making that a good place for a break or pause.

Sela-Hammahlekoth (sē'lȧ-hă-mȧ'lē-kōth), a cliff in the wilderness of Maon. It was called Sela-hammahlekoth ("rock of divisions or escapes") because there David eluded Saul (I Sam. 23:28).

Seled (sē'lĕd), a man of Judah of the family of Jarahmeel (I Chron. 2:30).

Seleucia (sē-lū'shĭ-ȧ). The Seleucia of the NT was founded in 300 B.C. by Seleucus I Nicator, to provide a seaport for Syrian Antioch which lay some 16 miles inland. Near the mouth of the Orontes, it was a naval base in Roman imperial times. It was the port of departure for Paul and Barnabas on their first journey (Acts 13:14).

Seleucids (sĕ-lū'sĭds), a dynasty of rulers of the kingdom of Syria (included Babylonia, Bactria, Persia, Syria, and part of Asia Minor), descended from Seleucus I, general of Alexander the Great. It lasted from 312 to 64 B.C., when the Romans took it over. One of them, Antiochus Epiphanes, precipitated the Maccabean War by trying forcibly to Hellenize the Jews.

Selvedge (sĕl'vĕj), the edge of each of the two curtains (which were themselves each composed of five parts), which together covered the boards of the sanctuary of the tabernacle. They were coupled at the selvedge by 50 loops of blue connected by clasps with 50 others on the opposite side (Exod. 26:4; 36:11).

Sem (See Shem)

Semachiah (sĕm'ȧ-kī'ȧ, **Jehovah has sustained)**, a Levite, a descendant of Obed-edom (I Chron. 26:4).

Semei (sĕm'ē-ī). 1. One of those who put away their "strange wives" (I Esdras 9:33), probably the same as Shimei in Ezra 10:33. 2. The KJV form of Semein (Luke 3:26).

Semein (sĕm'ē-ĭn), an ancestor of Christ, who lived after the time of Zerubbabel (Luke 3:26).

Semites (sĕm'īts). Derived from Noah's son Shem (Gen. 9:18, 19; 10:21-31), the term is used to identify a diverse group of ancient peoples whose languages are related, belonging to the Semitic family of languages. The world of the Semites, in ancient historical times, was the Fertile Crescent, that green land which begins in southern Babylonia in the E, and includes Mesopotamia, Syria and Palestine, ending at the border of Egypt in the W. It is hemmed in by mountains, seas, and deserts. The principal Semitic peoples of ancient times were:

1. The Akkadians—The Babylonians and Assyrians who lived in Mesopotamia and spoke a common language. From c. 2350 B.C. to 538 B.C. these gifted, vigorous people dominated Mesopotamia. Several times they produced empires which ruled the ancient world.

2. The Arameans. Principally traders and catalysts of culture rather than its creators, the Aramean speaking people lived in Syria from c. 1700 B.C. to the time of Christ, although their political power ceased some centuries earlier. Damascus, Aleppo, Hama, and Zobah were their cities. Today there are still a few Aramaic speaking islands of culture in the Middle East.

3. The Canaanites. This term is used to designate a number of peoples who lived in southern Syria (including Palestine) in ancient times. Even the Hebrews can be considered a Canaanite group. The Hebrews seem to have borrowed the Canaanite language and culture, and made it their own.

4. The Arabs. Little is known about the inhabitants of Arabia prior to Mohammed.

5. The Ethiopians. Across the Red Sea from southern Arabia, the Ethiopians had a flourishing Semitic civilization from 500 B.C. to the time of Mohammed.

Senaah (sē-nā'ȧ), the descendants of Senaah (sometimes spelled Hassenaah, with the Hebrew definite article attached) were a part of the company returning from captivity under Zerubbabel (Ezra 2:35; Neh. 7:38). They rebuilt the fish gate of Jerusalem (Neh. 3:3).

Senate (sĕn'ăt, a council of elders), mentioned in Acts 5:21; not a body different from the "council" (Sanhedrin) but a more precise equivalent.

Senator (See Occupations and Professions)

Seneh (sē'nĕ). Jonathan and his armorbearer passed this crag on their way to surprise the Philistine garrison (I Sam. 14:4, 5). Located 3½ miles SE of Michmash.

Senir (sē'nĭr), the Amorite name of Mt. Hermon (Deut. 3:9; S. of Sol. 4:8), a source of fir timber (Ezek. 27:5). Twice spelled Shenir in KJV.

Sennacherib (sĕ-năk'êr-ĭb, **Sin** (moon-god) **multiplied brothers),** an Assyrian king (705-681 B.C.), the son and successor of Sargon II (722-705 B.C.) He restored the capital to Nineveh, on the E bank of the Tigris, opposite the present city of Mosul. Upon his succession to the throne he found it necessary to deal with revolts throughout the empire. Exasperated by the repeated intrigues of Babylon and its king, Merodach-baladan, he finally reduced the city to ruins in 689 B.C.

It was in the 14th year of Hezekiah that Sennacherib came against Judah and took all of its fortified cities. Hezekiah offered to pay tribute and had to strip the temple of its treasures to make payment. The Assyrian sent his officers to Jerusalem to deliver an ultimatum concerning capitulation. At this time Sennacherib was besieging Lachish, which he took, and then moved against Libnah. The reliefs of the palace of Sennacherib at Kuyunjik depicted the capture of Lachish. When Sennacherib heard that Tirhakah king of Judah was coming against him, he sent a second message to Hezekiah. Hezekiah made this a matter for prayer and the prophet Isaiah brought him God's assurance of deliverance. Tirhakah was involved in the coalition defeated by Sennacherib; Egypt of that period was correctly evaluated by the Assyrian spokesman as "a broken reed" (II Kings 18:21; Isa. 36:6). The Bible relates that Jerusalem was delivered by the Lord, who sent His angel to smite the Assyrian armies and thus forced Sennacherib to retire to his homeland (I Kings 19:35-36; II Chron. 32:21; Isa. 37:36-37).

Back in Nineveh, Sennacherib was assassinated by two of his sons in 681 B.C. (II Kings 19:37; Isa. 37:38) in an effort to upset the succession which he had decreed for Esarhaddon, but Esarhaddon was equal to the situation and gained the throne.

Sensual (sĕn'shū-ăl, **pertaining to the soul),** having the nature and characteristics of the soul, i.e., the natural life which men have in common with brutes; of the physical body (I Cor. 15:44); of one dominated by the self-life with its carnal desires (Jude 19; I

Stone relief from Nineveh showing Sennacherib, King of Assyria, sitting upon his throne, receiving spoils from the city of Lachish. BM

Cor. 2:14); of the sensual wisdom characterizing the unregenerated mind (James 3:15).

Senuah (See Hasenuah)

Seorim (sē-ō'rĭm), a descendant of Aaron; head of the 4th course of priests in the time of David (I Chron. 24:1-8).

Sephar (sē'fȧr), the eastern limit of the territory of the sons of Joktan (Gen. 10:30).

Sepharad (sē-fā'răd), the place of captivity by Sargon of certain people of Jerusalem (Obad. 20). Among the Jews of the post-Biblical period the term was used to refer to Spain.

Sepharvaim, Sepharvite (sĕf'ȧr-vā'ĭm, sē'fȧr-vīt), the place from which the Assyrians brought colonists to live in Samaria (II Kings 17:24, 31). The place is also referred to in the Rab-shakeh's threatening speech to Jerusalem (II Kings 18:34; 19:13) as a place conquered by the Assyrian armies. Probably located in the region of Hamath.

Septuagint (sĕp'tū-ȧ-jĭnt), the first and most important of a number of ancient translations of the Hebrew OT into Greek. The story of the origin of the Septuagint is told in the **letter of Aristeas,** a pseudepigraphical book written in the second half of the second century B.C. It states that Ptolemy II (called Philadelphus, the king of Egypt, 285-247 B.C.) wished to have a translation of the Jewish Law for his famous library in Alexandria. At his request, the high priest Eleazer of Jerusalem sent 72 men, six from each tribe, to Egypt with a scroll of the Law. In 72 days, they translated one section each from this scroll, and afterwards decided on the wording together. So the version was called Septuagint (the translation of the 70, abbreviated LXX). Later writers elaborated on this story to the effect that the 72 had translated the whole OT (not the Pentateuch only), each independently of the other, in seclusion. The exact agreement of the 72 copies proved the work's inspiration.

It seems most likely that the LXX originated not by the desire of Ptolemy II (although the project may have had his approval), but out of the need of the Alexandrian Jews. Alexandria of the third century B.C. was a large city with a great Jewish population. These Jews were Greek speaking, having long since forgotten their own language.

The early Christian Church, built largely on converts from the synagogues of the Greek-speaking world, took over the LXX as their Bible. Their use of it, to prove to the Jews that Jesus was the Messiah, caused a change in the Jews' attitude toward it. Soon after A.D. 100, the Jews completely gave up the LXX and it became a Christian book.

Our oldest copies of the LXX today are from the three great Greek MSS of the Bible from the fourth and fifth centuries A.D.—Sinaiticus, Vaticanus, and Alexandrinus. It is quite plain that these represent a LXX which has had a long textual history, and that it is now impossible to say to what extent these copies agree with the original translation made some 600 or 700 years before. Origen (died c. A.D. 250) sensed the problem of many divergent readings in the MSS in his day, and sought to produce a resultant text in his **Hexapla.** The textual criticism of the LXX is a difficult task, on which the last word remains to be said. In spite of these problems, it can be said that the LXX is an eloquent witness to the accuracy with which the OT has come down to us from ancient days.

Sepulchre (See Tomb)

Sepulchre, Church of the Holy, the church professedly covering the tomb where Jesus was buried. Constantine built an elaborate church on the site, dedicated in A.D. 335. The authenticity of the site is much disputed. The destruction of Jerusalem in A.D. 70 and its more complete devastation in A.D. 135 make the certainty of the identification questionable.

Serah (sē'rȧ), a daughter of Asher (Gen. 46:17; I Chron. 7:30). Once spelled Sarah (Num. 26:46).

Seraiah (sē-rā'yȧ). 1. A son of Kenaz (I Chron. 4:13). 2. A scribe under David (II Sam. 8:17). 3. A Simeonite, son of Asiel (I Chron. 4:35). 4. One of the men sent to arrest Jeremiah and Baruch (Jer. 36:26). 5. The high priest when Nebuchadnezzar captured Jerusalem. He was put to death by Nebuchadnezzar at Riblah (II Kings 25:18-21; Jer. 52:24-27). 6. The son of Neriah, a quartermaster (RSV), carried to Babylon when Jerusalem fell (Jer. 51:59-64). 7. The son of Tanhumeth (II Kings 25:23; Jer. 40:8). 8. A priest who returned from Babylon to Jerusalem with Zerubbabel (Ezra 2:2; Neh. 7:7, where he is called Azariah; 12:1). He became governor of the temple when it was rebuilt (Neh. 11:11). He is mentioned (as Azariah) also in I Chronicles 9:11.

Seraphim (sĕr′ȧ-fĭm, **burning ones**), celestial beings whom Isaiah saw standing before the enthroned Lord (Isa. 6:2, 3, 6, 7).

Serapis (sĕ-rā′pĭs), Graeco-Egyptian god widely worshipped in Mediterranean world; not mentioned in Bible.

Sered (sē′rĕd), a son of Zebulun (Gen. 46:14; Num. 26:26), and founder of a tribal family.

Sergeant (See Occupations and Professions)

Sergius Paulus (sûr′jĭ-ŭs pô′lŭs), the Roman proconsul (KJV "deputy") of Cyprus, a senatorial province from 22 B.C. He was "a prudent man," one possessed of intelligence and discretion; he "believed," which most naturally means that he became a Christian (Acts 13:7-12).

Sermon on the Mount, the first of six extended discourses of Jesus given in the Gospel of Matthew, covering chapters five, six and seven.

It is remarkable what unity and order of thought is evident in the sermon on the mount. There is no space for a detailed analytical outline, which

The traditional site of the Sermon on the Mount, the view from Jebel Hattin (Horns of Hattin), looking out over the Sea of Galilee. © MPS

the careful reader can profitably make for himself. Is the teaching of Jesus literally applicable to human beings in this world? The meek do not now inherit the earth (5:5) and public or national non-resistance leads to slavery.

If we take the teaching of Jesus in the same reasonably flexible way in which He obviously intended it, the way in which He interpreted the ten commandments (Matt. 12:4, 5, 11, 12, etc.), the way of the heart rather than of mere outward conduct (Matt. 5:22, 28), there is not a word which we need not heed today. We should be willing to take a slap in the face. This is not to say that we must stand by and see the innocent suffer lawless injury. Jesus did not contradict the principle that those responsible for law enforcement must bear "the sword" (Rom. 13:1-5) and that "not in vain." The sermon on the mount is Christ's instruction to us for godly living in the present world.

Serpent (See Animals, Reptiles)

Serug (sē'rŭg), a descendant of Shem; son of Reu and great-grandfather of Abraham (Gen. 11:20, 22f; I Chron. 1: 26). In KJV of Luke 3:35 he is called Saruch; ASV and RSV have Serug. He is thus in the Messianic line.

Servant, used of slave, wage servant. Israelites acquired slaves through purchase (Lev. 25:44, 45) and war (Num. 31:25-47). Israelites could become slaves through poverty (Exod. 21:1-11; Lev. 25:39, 47; II Kings 4:1), theft (Exod. 22:3), and birth (Exod. 21:4). Mosaic law protected servants (Exod. 20:10; Lev. 25:55). Slaves and servants often referred to in NT (Mark 1:20; John 18:10-18; Acts 12:13-15).

Servant of Jehovah, agent of the Lord like patriarchs (Exod. 32:13); Moses (Num. 12:7f), prophets (Zech. 1:6), and others. Chiefly used as a title for the Messiah in Isaiah 40:66. NT applies the Servant-passages to Christ (Isa. 42:1-4; Matt. 12:16-21).

Service, refers to all sorts of work from the most inferior and menial to the most honored and exalted (Lev. 23: 7f; Num. 3:6ff).

Servitor (See Occupations and Professions)

Seth (sĕth). 1. Adam's third son; father of Enos (Gen. 4:25f; 5:3-8). His name (meaning "appointed," i.e., "substituted") signifies that he was considered a "substitute" for Abel (4:25). 2. The Moabites (Num. 24:17). [Sheth, see ASV].

Sethur (sē'ther, **hidden),** a representative of Asher sent by Moses to spy out Canaan (Num. 13:2f, 13).

Seveneh (sē-vē'nĕ), mentioned in Ezekiel 29:10; 30:6. It is rendered Syene in the KJV. This is the Hebrew reading of an Egyptian town located on the first cataract of the Nile, known today as Aswan.

Seventy, The, Disciples of our Lord. The mission of the Seventy (mentioned only in Luke 10:1-20) probably represents a rehearsal of responsibilities and conditions that the disciples would meet after Christ's departure.

Seventy Weeks, The, name applied to period of time (probably 490 years) referred to in Dan. 9:24-27. It has been interpreted in many different ways.

Seven Words From the Cross. These words of Christ were probably uttered in the following order: (1) Before the darkness: "Father, forgive them," etc. (Luke 23:34); "Verily I say unto thee," etc. (Luke 23:43); "Woman, behold thy son," (John 19:26f). (2) During the darkness: "My God, my God," (Matt. 27:46; Mark 15:34). (3) After the darkness: "I thirst" (John 19:28, fulfilling Ps. 69:21); "It is finished" (John 19: 30); "Father, into thy hands" (Luke 23:46, quoting Ps. 31:5). Theologically, these words, in the order given above, illustrate (1) divine forgiveness; (2) assurance of immortality; (3) good works; (4) the awfulness of Christ's death; (5) the true humanity of Christ; (6) the perfection of Christ's atonement; (7) the divine complacency.

Shaalabbin (shā'à-lăb'ĭn), a town listed in Joshua 19:42 between Ir-shemesh and Aijalon as assigned to the Danites. See Shaalbim.

Shaalbim (shā-ăl'bĭm), a town won by the Danites from the Amorites with the help of the Ephraimites (Judg. 1: 35).

Shaalbonite (See Shaalbim)

Shaaph (shā'ăf). 1. Son of Jahdai (I Chron. 2:47). 2. A son of Caleb by Maachah, a concubine. This man became the progenitor of the inhabitants of Madmannah (I Chron. 2:49; cf. Josh. 15:31).

Shaaraim (shā'à-rā'ĭm). 1. A town belonging to Judah in the Shephelah or "low country" (Josh. 15:36); mentioned elsewhere only in I Sam. 17:52. 2. A town belonging to Simeon (I Chron. 4:31); listed as Sharuhen in

Joshua 19:6 and Shilhim in Joshua 15: 32.

Shaashgaz (shā-ăsh′găz), a chamberlain (or eunuch) in charge of "the second house" of concubines belonging to King Ahasuerus (Xerxes); Esther was entrusted to his care (Esth. 2:14).

Shabbethai (shăb′ē-thī, **Sabbath-born),** a Levite of Ezra's time who is mentioned as a participant in the foreign-wives controversy (Ezra 10:15, ASV; cf. mg.), as an interpreter of the Law (Neh. 8:7f), and as a chief Levite over the temple (Neh. 11:16).

Shachia (shȧ-kī′ȧ), a Benjamite (I Chron. 8:10).

Shaddai (shăd′ī), name (exact meaning unknown) for God often found in OT (Gen. 17:1; 28:3; 43:14; Num. 24:4, 16; Ps. 68:14).

Shadow, a word used literally, figuratively, and theologically. Literally, of a mountain (Judg. 9:36), tree (Dan. 4: 12; Hos. 4:13; Mark 4:32), dial (II Kings 20:9-11), booth (Jonah 4:5), gourd (Jonah 4:6), a person (Acts 5: 15); figuratively, of life's shortness (I Chron. 29:15; Job 8:9; Ps. 102:11), of protection (either good, as in Pss. 17:8; 36:7; 91:1; or evil, as in Isa. 30:3; Jer. 48:45), of the Messiah's blessings (Isa. 4:6; 32:2; 49:2; 51:16), of death (either physical, as in Job 10:21f; Pss. 23:4; 107:10, 14; or spiritual, as in Isa. 9:2; Matt. 4:16; Luke 1:79); and theologically as follows: of God's unchangeableness (James 1:17).

Shadrach (shā′drăk), the Babylonian name given to Hananiah, one of the three Hebrew youths (Dan. 1:3, 7).

Shaft, shank of the golden candelabrum (Exod. 25:31); used in Messianic sense in Isa. 49:2.

Shagee (shā′gē, **wandering),** a Hararite ("the mountaineer"), one of David's mighty men (I Chron. 11:34).

Shaharaim (shā′hȧ-rā′ĭm, **double dawn),** a Benjamite who, in the land of Moab, had three wives (Hushim, Baara, Hodesh) and nine sons, who became heads of families (I Chron. 8:8-11).

Shahazimah (shā′hȧ-zī′mȧ, **toward the heights),** a town in Issachar between Tabor and the Jordan (Josh. 19:22).

Shalem (shā′lĕm, **safe),** a place mentioned in Genesis 33:18 (KJV); however, most modern scholars take the Hebrew to express the manner of Jacob's return to Shechem.

Shalim, Land of (shā′lĭm, **district of foxes),** a region, probably near the N boundary of Benjamin's territory, traversed by Saul in search of his father's asses (I Sam. 9:4).

Shalishah (shȧ-lī′shȧ, **a third part),** a district near Mt. Ephraim through which Saul went in search of his father's asses (I Sam. 9:4).

Shallecheth, The Gate of (shăl′ĕ-kĕth), the name of the W gate of Solomon's Temple assigned by lots to Shuppim and Hosah, Levitical porters (I Chron. 26:13-16).

Shallum, Shallun (shăl′ŭm, shăl′ŭn, **recompense),** a name **(Shallum)** applied to all of the following except the last **(Shallun):** 1. The youngest son of Naphtali (I Chron. 7:13=Shillem in Gen. 46:24 and Num. 26:48f). 2. The son of Shaul and grandson of Simeon (I Chron. 4:25; cf. Gen. 46:10; Exod. 6:15; Num. 26:12f). 3. The son of Sisamai and father of Jekamiah (I Chron. 2:40f). 4. Son of Kore and chief of the gate-keepers (I Chron. 9:17, 19, 31; Ezra 2:42; 10:24; Neh. 7:45=Meshelemiah of I Chron. 26:1 and Shelemiah of I Chron. 26:14). 5. Son of Zadok and father of Hilkiah (I Chron. 6:12f); ancestor of Ezra (Ezra 7:1f)=Meshullam of I Chron. 9:11 and Neh. 11:11). 6. A king of Israel who, having slain Zechariah, reigned in his place for one month; then he himself was slain by Menahem (II Kings 15:10-15). 7. An Ephraimite chief (II Chron. 28:12). 8. Husband of the prophetess Huldah; custodian of the sacerdotal wardrobe (II Kings 22:14; II Chron. 34:22; perhaps=Jer. 32:7 [Jeremiah's uncle]; see 10 below). 9. A king of Judah, son of Josiah (I Chron. 3:15; Jer. 22:11; better known as Jehoahaz II (II Kings 23:30f, 34; II Chron. 36:1). 10. Uncle of Jeremiah (Jer. 32:7; see 8 above). 11. Father of Maaseiah (Jer. 35:4; cf. 52:24). 12. Levitical porter compelled to divorce his foreign wife (Ezra 10: 24). 13. A son of Bani who was compelled to divorce his foreign wife (Ezra 10:42). 14. The son of Hallohesh; a ruler who, with his daughters, helped to build the walls of Jerusalem (Neh. 3:12). 15. Shallun, a builder of the walls of Jerusalem (Neh. 3:15).

Shalmai (shăl′mī), ancestor of Nethinim that returned with Zerubbabel (Ezra 2:46; Neh. 7:48).

Shalman (shăl′măn), either contraction of Shalmaneser or the Moabite king Salmanu (Hos. 10:14).

Shalmaneser (shăl′măn-ē′zêr, **the god Shulman is chief),** title of five Assyrian kings, of whom one is mentioned in OT, another refers to an Israelitish king. 1. Shalmaneser III (859-824 B.C.); son of Ashurnasirpal; inscription left by him says that he opposed Benhadad of Damascus and Ahab of Israel, and made Israel tributary. 2. Shalmaneser V (726-722 B.C.), son of Tiglath-pileser; received tribute from Hoshea; besieged Samaria and carried N tribes into captivity (II Kings 17:3; 18:9), "Shalman" in Hos. 10:14.

Shama (shā'mȧ, **He [God] has heard),** one of David's mighty men (I Chron. 11:44).

Shamariah (See Shemariah)

Shambles, meat market (I Cor. 10:25).

Shame, Shamefacedness, shame is a feeling brought about by a sense of guilt (Ezra 9:7), impropriety (Exod. 32:25), or disillusionment through false confidence (Ps. 97:7); shamefacedness in I Tim. 2:9 denotes sexual modesty.

Shamed (shā'mĕd, **destruction:** however, many MSS. read **shāmer, watcher;** ASV has **Shemed),** the third-named son of Elpaal (I Chron. 8:12).

Shamer (shā'mêr, **guard).** 1. A descendant of Levi; father of Bani (I Chron. 6:46). 2. Son of Heber and head of an Asherite clan (I Chron. 7:32; Heb. **Shômer** [so KJV]; same as **Shamer** (Heb. **Shāmer)** in vs. 34. Numerous variations exist in Heb. MSS. See also Shemed (I Chron. 8:12) and Shemer (I Kings 16:24).

Shamgar (shăm'gȧr), son of Anath; slayer of 600 Philistines with an oxgoad (Judg. 3:31; cf. I Sam. 13:19-22). He thus prepared the way for the greater deliverance of Israel under Deborah and Barak.

Shamhuth (shăm'hŭth, **desolation), an** Izrahite; the fifth divisional commander in David's organization of his army (I Chron. 27:8, RSV).

Shamir (shā'mêr, **a sharp point).** 1. A town allotted to Judah (Josh. 15:48). 2. A town in Mount Ephraim; the residence and burial-place of Tola, one of the judges (Judg. 10:1f). 3. A Levite, son of Micah; a temple-attendant (I Chron. 24:24).

Shamma (shăm'ȧ, **astonishment or desolation),** one of the 11 sons of Zophah; a descendant of Asher (I Chron. 7:37).

Shammah (shăm'ȧ, **waste).** 1. Grandson of Esau (Gen. 36:13, 17; I Chron. 1:37). 2. Brother of David (I Sam. 16: 9; 17:13); also called Shimea (I Chron. 20:7), Shimeah (II Sam. 13:3, 32), and Shimei (II Sam. 21:21). 3. One of David's mighty men (II Sam. 23:11). "Shage" in I Chron. 11:34. 4. Another of David's mighty men (II Sam. 23: 33); also called Shammoth (I Chron. 11:27) and Shamhuth (I Chron. 27:8). May be same as 3.

Shammai (shăm'ā-ī, **Jehovah has heard),** the name of three descendants of Judah: 1. A son of Onam, who was the son of Jerahmeel by Atarah; father of Nadab and Abishur (I Chron. 2:28, 32). 2. A son of Redem and father of Maon (I Chron. 2:44f). 3. A descendant of Ezra (I Chron. 4:17f). The text here is extremely ambiguous and uncertain; probably, by a transposition, Shammai was the son of Mered by Bithiah, Pharaoh's daughter (I Chron. 4:18).

Shammoth (shăm'ōth, **desolation),** one of David's mighty men of war (I Chron. 11:27); apparently the same as Shammah (II Sam. 23:25) and Shamhuth (I Chron. 27:8).

Shammua (shă-mū'ȧ, **heard or renowned).** 1. A spy of Reuben, sent into the land of Canaan (Num. 13:4). 2. A son of David by Bath-sheba; brother of Solomon (II Sam. 5:14 [KJV has Shammuah]; I Chron. 14:4), or Shimea (I Chron. 3:5). 3. A Levite father of Abda (or Obadiah) (Neh. 11:17=Shemaiah in I Chron. 9:16). 4. The representative of the priestly family of Bilgah (I Chron. 24:14; Neh. 12:5, 18=Bilgai in Neh. 10:8); a priest, whose father returned with Zerubbabel (Neh. 12:1-12).

Shammuah (shă-mū'ȧ), son of David (II Sam. 5:14=Shammua in I Chron. 14:4 [KJV] and Shimea in I Chron. 3:5 (KJV]).

Shamsherai (shăm'shē-rī, **sunlike),** son of Jeroham; a Benjamite (I Chron. 8: 26).

Shapham (shā'făm), a Gadite who lived in Bashan, second in authority in the time of Jotham (I Chron. 5:12).

Shaphan (shā'făn, **hyrax** or **rock rabbit),** scribe during Josiah's reign (II Kings 22:3-20; II Chron. 34:8-28). The record cites four responsibilities that he faithfully performed: (1) his oversight of the finances of the repairs of the temple (II Chron. 34:8-13, 16f); (2) his transmission of the newly discovered law-book to Josiah (II Chron. 34:14f); (3) his reading of this book before Josiah (II Chron. 34: 18); (4) his mission, with others, to carry Josiah's message to the prophetess Huldah (II Chron. 34:20-28).

Shaphat (shā'făt, **he has judged).** 1. The son of Hori, who was chosen from the tribe of Simeon to spy out the land of Canaan (Num. 13:5). 2. The father of Elisha (I Kings 19:16, 19; II Kings 3:11; 6:31). 3. A Gadite chief (I Chron. 5:12). 4. The son of one of David's herdsmen (I Chron. 27:29). 5. The last named son of Shemaiah, a descendant of the royal line of David (I Chron. 3:22).

Shapher (shā'fer, **beauty),** the name of a mountain between Kehelathah and Haradah at which the Israelites encamped in their wilderness wanderings (Num. 33:23).

Shaphir (See Saphir)

Sharai (shȧ-rā'ī), a "son" of Bani; mentioned in a list of men who, at Ezra's command, divorced their foreign wives (Ezra 10:10, 40, 44).

Sharaim (shȧ-rā'ĭm, **two gates),** a town in Judah (Josh. 15:36, AV); see **Shaaraim.**

Sharar (shā'rêr, **firm),** the father of Ahiam the Hararite; one of David's mighty men (II Sam. 23:33=Sacar in I Chron. 11:35).

Share (plowshare), an agricultural instrument mentioned only in I Sam. 13:20.

Sharezer (shȧ-rē'zêr, **protect the king),** 1. A son of the Assyrian king Sennacherib, who, with his brother Adrammelech, slew his father (II Kings 19:37=Isa. 37:38). 2. A contemporary of Zechariah the prophet (Zech. 7:2 =**Sherezer** in KJV).

Sharon (shăr'ŭn, **plain).** 1. The coastal plain between Joppa and Mount Carmel, a place proverbial in ancient times for its fertility, pasturage and beauty (I Chron. 27:29; S. of Sol. 2: 1; Isa. 35:2); the location of such towns as Dor, Lydda (Acts 9:35), Joppa, Caesarea and Antipatris. 2. The suburbs (ASVm "pasture lands") of Sharon possessed by the tribe of Gad (I Chron. 5:16). 3. Lassharon q.v. (Josh. 12:18). 4. Figuratively, (a) of man's state of regeneracy — fruitfulness and glory (Isa. 35:2); (b) of man's eternal state — of peace for evermore (Isa. 65:10, 17).

Sharonite (shăr'ŭn-īt, **of Sharon),** a description applied to Shitrai, David's chief herdsman in the plain of Sharon (I Chron. 27:29).

Sharuhen (shȧ-rōō'hĕn), an ancient town in SW Palestine, S of Gaza and W of Beersheba; assigned to the tribe of Simeon within Judah's territory (Josh. 19:6; cf. Gen. 49:7).

Shashai (shā'shī, **whitish** or **noble),** a "son" of Bani; listed among those men who, at Ezra's command, divorced their foreign wives (Ezra 10:40).

Shashak (shā'shăk), a Benjamite, son of Beriah (I Chron. 8:14f); father of 11 sons (I Chron. 8:22-25).

Shaul, Shaulites (shā'ŭl, shā'ŭ-līts, **asked).** 1. The sixth in a list of eight kings that ruled over Edom (Gen. 36: 37f [Saul in AV]=I Chron. 1:48f). 2. A son of Simeon (Gen. 46:10; Exod. 6: 15; Num. 26:13; I Chron. 4:24). 3. A descendant of Levi; son of Uzziah; ancestor of Samuel (I Chron. 6:24= Joel in vs. 36).

Shaveh, Valley of (shā'vĕ, **a plain),** a place near Salem (i.e., Jerusalem [Ps. 76:2]), where, after rescuing his nephew Lot, Abraham met the king of Sodom (Gen. 14:17).

Shaveh-Kiriathaim (shā'vĕ-kĭr' yȧ-thā' ĭm, **the plain of Kiriathaim** [i.e., "twin cities"]), a plain where Chedorlaomer smote the Emim (Gen. 14:5), probably located on the E of the Dead Sea (cf. Num. 32:37).

Shaving. The priests (Lev. 21:5; Ezek. 44:20) and the Nazirites (Num. 6:5; cf. I Sam. 1:11) among the Israelites were prohibited from shaving; furthermore, the Hebrews as a people, in contrast to surrounding nations, generally accepted the beard as a sign of dignity (cf. II Sam. 10:4f). Shaving had these connotations: (1) an act of contrition (Job 1:20); (2) an accommodation to a custom (Gen. 41:14; cf. I Cor 11:5f); (3) an act of consecration for Levites (Num. 6:9; 8:7); (4) an act of cleansing for lepers (Lev. 14:8f; 13:32ff); (5) an act completing a vow (Num. 6:18; Acts 18:18; 21:24); (6) an act of commitment of a captive woman (Deut. 21: 12); (7) an act of conspiracy against a man's Nazirite vow (Judg. 16:19); (8) an act of contempt (II Sam. 10:4=I Chron. 19:4); (9) an act, fig. expressed, of cleansing a corrupt nation (Isa. 7: 20; cf. 1:16; 6:5; and II Kings 18:13ff).

Shavsha (shăv'shȧ), David's secretary of state (I Chron. 18:16=**Shisha** in I Kings 4:3=**Seraiah** in II Sam. 8:17 =**Sheva** in II Sam. 20:25).

Sheaf, a handful of grain left behind the reaper (Jer. 9:22, RSV), gathered and bound usually by children or women (Ruth 2:7, 15) in a joyous mood (Pss. 126:6; 129:7f). Thus stacked they became dry and inflammable (Zech. 12:6; cf. Judg. 15:1-5, ASV); but they were beautiful sights (S. of Sol. 7:2). A donkey (Neh. 13:15) or a heavily loaded cart (Amos 2:13) bore these bundles to the threshing-floor (Ruth 3:6f; Mic. 4:12). Some sheaves, however, were left behind for the poor (Deut. 24:19; cf. Ruth 2:7, 15; Job 24:10).

Sheal (shē'ăl, **asking),** a "son" of Bani; listed among those who divorced their foreign wives (Ezra 10:29).

Sheariah (shē'ȧ-rī'ȧ, **Jehovah esteems),** one of the sons of Azel; a descendant of Jonathan (I Chron. 8:38; 9:44).

Shearing House (bindinghouse of the shepherds), the place between Jezreel and Samaria where Jehu met and slaughtered 42 unsuspecting members of the royal house of Ahaziah, king of Judah, while they were on their way, apparently ignorant of Jehu's revolt, to Ahaziah, who was visiting Joram, the wounded king of Israel (II Kings 10:12-14). The corpses were cast into a pit (Heb. **bôr;** cf. its use in Gen. 37:24; Jer. 41:7, 9).

Shear-Jashub (shē'ȧr-jȧ'shŭb, **a remnant shall return),** the symbolic name of Isaiah's oldest son (Isa. 7:3; 8:18). The symbolism is reflected in the historic return from Babylon and is fulfilled in the spiritual return to the Lord at Messiah's advent (Isa. 1:9; 4:3f; 10:20-23; 65:8f; Rom. 11:5f, 16-29).

Shealtiel (shē'ăl'tĭ-ĕl, **I have asked God),** the father of Zerubbabel (Ezra 3:2, 8; 5:2; Neh. 12:1; Hag. 1:1, 12, 14; 2:2, 23=**Salathiel** in I Chron. 3:17; Matt. 1:12; Luke 3:27).

Sheba (shē'bȧ, **seven, an oath).** 1. A chief of a Gadite family (I Chron. 5:13). 2. A town allotted to Simeon (Josh. 19:2). 3. A Benjamite who led a short-lived insurrection against the kingship of David (II Sam. 20). 4. A son of Raamah, son of Cush (Gen. 10:7; I Chron. 1:9). 5. A son of Joktan; grandson of Eber (Gen. 10:28; I Chron. 1:22). 6. The oldest son of Jokshan, Abraham's son by Keturah (Gen. 25:3; I Chron. 1:32). It is probable that this man's descendants, by intermarriage or otherwise, finally became identified with the descendants of 4 and 5; together they constitute what is called the kingdom of Sheba or the Sabeans.

Shebah (shē'bȧ, **seven** or **oath),** the name of a well which the servants of Isaac dug. The town Beer-sheba, i.e. "well of the oath" is so-called from this well (Gen. 26:31-33, but cf. 21:28-31).

Shebam (shē'băm, **sweet smell),** a town in Reuben (Num. 32:3) called also "Shibmah" (Num. 32:38). ASV "Sebam" and "Sibmah" are more acceptable. E of the Dead Sea, but exact location unknown. Cf. Isaiah 16:8, 9.

Shebaniah (shĕb'ȧ-nī'ȧ, meaning uncertain). 1. One of seven priests appointed to blow trumpets before the ark of the covenant when it was brought to Jerusalem (I Chron. 15:24). 2. Levite who signed the covenant with Nehemiah (Neh. 9:4, 5; 10:10). 3. Another Levite who was among the covenanters (Neh. 10:12). 4. A priest who was among the covenanters (Neh. 10:4). 5. The head of a family of priests who served in the days of the high priest Joiakim (Neh. 12:14).

Shebarim (shĕb'ȧ-rĭm, **breaches,** or ASV margin **quarries),** a place to which the men of Ai chased the soldiers of Israel (Josh. 7:5).

Shebat (See Sebat)

Sheber (shē'bêr), son of Caleb (not the famous spy) by his concubine Maachah (I Chron. 2:48).

Shebna (shĕb'nȧ). 1. Steward of Hezekiah (Isa. 22:15-21). 2. A scribe, also in Hezekiah's time, who went out with others to face the Rabshakeh (Isa. 36:3-37:2; II Kings 18).

Shebuel (shē-bū'ĕl), 1. A chief Levite in the time of David, descended from Moses through his son Gershom (I Chron. 23:16; 26:24), placed over the treasures. In I Chronicles 24:20 "Shubael." 2. One of the sons of Heman, chief musician in David's service of praise (I Chron. 25:4).

Shecaniah, Shechaniah (shĕk-ă-nī'ȧ, **dweller with Jehovah).** 1. Head of the tenth course of priests in the days of David (I Chron. 24:11). 2. A Levite under Hezekiah (II Chron. 31:15). 3. A descendant of David in the time of the Restoration, and head of a house (I Chron. 3:21, 22). 4. A descendant of Parosh, whose descendant Zechariah returned with Ezra leading 150 men (Ezra 8:3). 5. A son of Jehaziel (Ezra 8:5) who led back 300 men. 6. A son of Jehiel, one of the sons of Elam, who first made confession to Ezra of having married foreign women, and who proposed that a covenant be made and that the foreign wives and children be put away (Ezra 10:2-4). 7. Keeper of the E gate of Jerusalem (Neh. 3:

29). 8. Son of Arah, and father-in-law to Tobiah, the notorious foe of Nehemiah at the time of the rebuilding of the walls of Jerusalem (Neh. 6:18). 9. One of the chiefs of the priests who returned with Zerubbabel (Neh. 12:3).

Shechem (shē′kĕm, **shoulder**). 1. Ancestor of Manassites (Num. 26:31). 2. Son of Shemidah; Gileadite (I Chron. 7:19). 3. City in hill country of Ephraim near S border of Manasseh, 41 miles N of Jerusalem, at E end of pass between Mts. Ebal and Gerizim; one of chief cities of Canaanites during most of 2nd millennium B.C.; first place visited by Abraham (Gen. 12:6); Jacob bought ground there (Gen. 33: 18-20); Joseph buried there (Josh. 24: 32); scene of Abimelech's abortive attempt to found a kingdom (Judg. 9); Jeroboam I established his first royal

A view from modern Shechem and Mount Gerizim. © MPS

A sheepfold built of rough stone walls. DV

residence there (I Kings 12:25). Site is Tell Balatah, just E of Nablus; archaeologists have excavated the ruins.

Shechinah (See Shekinah)

Shedeur (shĕd′ē-êr, **caster forth of light),** a Reubenite, the father of Elizur, prince of Reuben (Num. 1:5; 2:10; 7:30; 10:18).

Sheep (See Animals)

Sheepcote, Sheepfold, an enclosure intended for the protection of sheep and also to keep them from wandering out and getting lost. These folds were simple walled enclosures, usually without roofs, with the walls covered with thorns to keep out robbers.

Sheep Gate, a gate of Jerusalem mentioned in Neh. 3:32; 12:39.

Sheep Market, not mentioned in the Greek NT but possibly implied in John 5:2. The Greek simply means something that pertains to the sheep.

Sheepmaster (See Occupations & Professions)

Sheep-Shearer (See Occupations & Professions)

Sheerah (See Sherah)

Sheet, a large piece of linen (Acts 10:11; 11:15).

Shehariah (shē-hȧ-rī′ȧ), one of the sons of Jeroham, a Benjamite (I Chron. 8:26) listed among the early inhabitants of Jerusalem after the captivity.

Shekel (See Money)

Shekinah (shē-kī′nȧ, **dwelling of God),** the visible presence of Jehovah. It is alluded to in such places as Isa. 60:2 by the phrase "his glory" and in Rom. 9:4 by the phrase "the glory." Moses calls this the "cloud" in Exodus 14:19. (See Exod. 13:21; 14:19-20ff).

Shelah, Shelanite (shē′lȧ, **sprout).** 1. Son of Arpachshad and father of Eber among the early Semites (Gen. 10:24); written Salah in KJV, and Sala in Luke 3:55 KJV 2. The third son of Judah (Gen. 38:5-26). The Shelanites were named from him (Num. 26:20).

Shelemiah (shĕl-ē-mī′ȧ, **friend of Jehovah).** 1. Door-keeper at the E side of the house of God in David's time (I Chron. 26:14). In the previous verses of this chapter, he is called Meshelemiah. 2. The son of Cushi and grandfather of Jehudi (Jer. 36:14). 3. One of the three whom Jehoiakim sent to arrest Baruch and Jeremiah, the prophet (Jer. 36:26). 4. The father of Jehucal or Jucal whom Zedekiah sent to Jeremiah to ask his prayers (Jer. 37:3, cf. 38:1). 5. Son of Hananiah (Jer. 37:13). 6. Two men who divorced foreign wives (Ezra 10:39, 41). 7. Father of Hananiah, a repairer of the wall (Neh. 3:30). 8. A priestly treasurer (Neh. 13:13).

Sheleph (shē′lĕf), a son of Joktan and head of an Arab tribe (Gen. 10:26).

Shelesh (shē′lĕsh), son of Helem, an early descendant of Asher, son of Jacob (I Chron. 7:35).

Shelomi (shē-lō′mī, **at peace),** father of Ahihud, a prince of the tribe of Asher whom the Lord appointed to help divide the land (Num. 34:27).

Shelomith, Shelomoth (shē-lō′mĭth, shē-lō′mŏth). 1. Daughter of Dibri; her son was killed for blasphemy (Lev. 24:10-12, 23). 2. Cousin of Moses (I Chron. 23:18). 3. Gershonite Levite (I Chron. 23:9). 4. Descendant of Moses (I Chron. 26:25). 5. Child of Rehoboam (II Chron. 11:20). 6. Daughter of Zerubbabel (I Chron. 3:19). 7. Ancestor of a family that returned with Ezra (Ezra 8:10).

Shelumiel (shē-lū′mĭ-ĕl, **God is peace),** a Simeonite chief in the days of Moses who helped take the census (Num. 1:6; 7:36).

Shem (shĕm, **name, fame),** second son of Noah, and progenitor of the Semitic race, was born 98 years before the Flood (Gen. 11:10) and lived six hundred years, outliving his descendants for nine generations excepting Eber and Abraham.

Shema (shē'mȧ, **fame, rumor).** 1. A town in the southern part of Judah (Josh. 15:26). 2. Son of Hebron of the descendants of Caleb (I Chron. 2:44). 3. Son of Joel and father of Azaz in the genealogy of the Reubenites (I Chron. 5:8). 4. A Benjamite who put to flight the inhabitants of Gath (I Chron. 8:13). 5. One who stood at the right hand of Ezra (Neh. 8:4). 6. "Shema" is the Hebrew name for Deuteronomy 6:4, probably the most often quoted verse in the Bible, as every good Jew repeats it several times every day—"Hear, O Israel: the Lord our God is one Lord."

Shemaah (shē-mā'ȧ, **fame),** a man of Gibeah of Benjamin whose two sons helped David at Ziklag (I Chron. 12:3).

Shemaiah (shē-mā'yȧ, **Jehovah has heard).** 1. A prince of Simeon (I Chron. 4:37). 2. A Reubenite, son of Joel (I Chron. 5:4). 3. A chief Levite of the sons of Elizaphan (I Chron. 15: 8, 11). 4. A Levite scribe in the days of David (I Chron. 24:6). 5. Also in David's time, the first-born son of Obed-edom and father of mighty men among the door-keepers of the house of God (I Chron. 26:4, 6, 7). 6. A brave prophet of God who forbade Rehoboam, king of Judah, to go against the house of Israel in the N (I Kings 12:22-24). 7. A descendant of David, related to the Messianic line (I Chron. 3:22) 8. A Merarite Levite in the days of Nehemiah (I Chron. 9: 14; Neh. 12:18). 9. A Levite, son of Galal and a descendant of Elkanah, mentioned among the first inhabitants who returned from exile (I Chron. 9: 16). In Nehemiah 11:17 he is called "Shammua." 10. A Levite whom King Jehoshaphat sent to teach in the towns of Judah (II Chron. 17:8). 11. One of the Levites who cleansed the temple in the days of Hezekiah (II Chron. 29:14). 12. A Levite who was appointed to assist in the distribution of food to the cities of the priests in the days of Hezekiah (II Chron. 31:15). 13. A chief Levite in the days of Josiah (II Chron. 35:9). 14. A leader of the Levites who returned with Ezra (Ezra 8:13). 15. One whom Ezra sent back for ministers (Ezra 8:16), possibly the same as the preceding. 16. A son of the priests, who had married a foreign wife (Ezra 10:21). 17. Another, guilty of the same sin (Ezra 10:31). 18. Son of Shecaniah, keeper of the E gate of Jerusalem, who helped rebuild the wall (Neh. 3:29). 19. One who tried to intimidate Nehemiah (Neh. 6:10). 20. A priest who signed the covenant (Neh. 10:8). 21. A priest or Levite who returned with Zerubbabel (Neh. 12:6). 22. A musical priest in the days of Nehemiah (Neh. 12:36). 23. A priest who assisted in the celebration of the completing of the wall, possibly the same as the preceding (Neh. 12:42). 24. The father of Uriah the prophet, whom Jehoiakim, king of Judah slew for prophesying against the sins of Jerusalem (Jer. 26:20). 25. A false prophet who fought against Jeremiah (Jer. 29:24-32). 26. The father of Delaiah, one of the princes in the days of Jehoiakim, who heard the words of the prophet (Jer. 36:12).

Shemariah (shĕm-ȧ-rī'ȧ, **Jehovah keeps).** 1. One of the mighty men of Benjamin who joined David while he was at Ziklag (I Chron. 12:5). 2. A son of Rehoboam (II Chron. 11:19). 3. One of the family of Harim who married a foreign wife and was compelled to put her away (Ezra 10:32). 4. One of the sons of Bani who had been likewise guilty (Ezra 10:41). In KJV (II Chron. 11:19) sometimes spelled Shamariah.

Shemeber (shĕm-ē'bēr), king of Zeboiim, a city near the Dead Sea (Gen. 14: 2). He rebelled against Chedorlaomer of Elam.

Shemer (shē'mēr, **guard),** owner of a hill in central Palestine which Omri, king of Israel, bought and fortified and named after its former owner, Samaria (I Kings 16:24). Shamar in KJV of Chronicles.

Shemida, Shemidah (shē-mī'dȧ, an early member of the tribe of Manasseh through Gilead, and therefore inheriting land E of the Jordan (Num. 26:32; Josh. 17:2).

Shemidaites (shē-mī'dȧ-īts), the family descended from Shemida **q.v.** (Num. 26:32; Josh. 17:2), belonging to the half-tribe of Manasseh.

Sheminith (shĕm'ĭ-nĭth, **eighth,** i.e. the octave, and meaning the lower octave), a musical term. The harps tuned to the "sheminith" were to be used with men's voices (I Chron. 15:21, titles for Pss. 6 and 12).

Shemiramoth (shē-mĭr'ȧ-mŏth). 1. Second degree Levite musician under David (I Chron. 15:18, 20). 2. One of the teaching Levites appointed by King Jehoshaphat (II Chron. 17:8).

Shemuel (shĕ-mū'ĕl, **name of God),** the same as Samuel in Hebrew. 1. A Simeonite, divider of Canaan under Joshua (Num. 34:20). 2. Samuel, here spelled Shemuel in KJV (I Chron. 6: 33). 3. The head of a house in Issachar (I Chron. 7:2).

Shen (shĕn, **tooth** or **pointed rock),** a sharp rock a short distance W of Jerusalem near which Samuel set up the monument he called "Ebenezer" (I Sam. 7:12).

Shenazar (shē-năz'âr), a son of Jeconiah, i.e. Jehoiachin, son of Jehoiakim, born in captivity (I Chron. 3:18). ASV has Shenazzar.

Shenir (shē'nēr), the Amorite name for Mount Hermon, a place of fir trees (Ezek. 27:5), one of the limits of the half-tribe Manasseh (I Chron. 5:23). KJV, Deuteronomy 3:9 and Song of Solomon have "Shenir," but the Hebrew and ASV have uniformly "Senir."

Sheol (shē'ōl), the OT name for the place of departed souls, corresponding to the NT word "Hades." When translated "hell" it refers to the place of punishment, but when translated "grave" the reference is to the souls of good men. It often means the place or state of the soul between death and resurrection. The clearest indication of different conditions in Sheol is in Christ's parable of the rich man and Lazarus (Luke 16:19-31).

Shepham (shē'făm, **nakedness),** a place in the NE of Canaan, near the Sea of Galilee (Num. 34:10, 11).

Shephatiah (shĕf'á-tī'á, **Jehovah is Judge).** 1. The fifth son of David (II Sam. 3:4). 2. Son of Reuel and father of Meshullam (I Chron. 9:8). 3. One who joined David at Ziklag (I Chron. 12:5). 4. Son of Maacah, a Simeonite prince ruling his tribe in the days of David (I Chron. 27:16). 5. One of the seven sons of Jehoshaphat, king of Judah (II Chron. 21:2). 6. Founder of a family with 372 descendants who returned with Zerubbabel (Ezra 2:4). 7. One of the children of Solomon's servants whose descendants returned with Zerubbabel (Ezra 2:57). 8. One whose descendant Zebadiah returned with Ezra (Ezra 8:8). 9. Son of Mahalaleel whose descendant Athaiah dwelt at Jerusalem soon after the walls had been rebuilt (Neh. 11:4). 10. One of the men of Zedekiah who wanted Jeremiah to be put to death for prophesying (Jer. 38:1).

Shephelah, The (shē-fē'lá, **low country).** The undulating country between the mountains of Judah and the maritime plain S of the plain of Sharon, extending through the country of Philistia along the Mediterranean. In Joshua 12:8 it is one of the six geographical sections of the promised land W of Jordan. Samson's exploits took place there, and David hid there from Saul.

Shepher (See Shapher)

Shepherd (See Occupations and Professions)

Shephi, Shepho (shē'fī, shē'fō, **barrenness),** one of the early descendants of Seir, the Horite (Gen. 36:23; I Chron. 1:40). "Shepho" in Gen., "Shephi" in I Chron.

Shephuphan (shē-fū'făm), a grandson of Benjamin (I Chron. 8:5).

Sherah (shē'rá), a daughter or a granddaughter of Ephraim. Her descendants built or fortified three villages (I Chron. 7:24 cf. II Chron. 8:5).

Sherd (See Potsherd, Ostraka)

Sherebiah (shĕr-ē-bī'á). 1. One of the chief priests who was brought from Casiphia to join Ezra on his return to Jerusalem, to whom Ezra entrusted treasures for the temple (Ezra 8:9, 18, 24; 9:4). 2. A covenanter with Nehemiah (Neh. 10:12). 3. A Levite who returned with Zerubbabel (Neh. 12:8). 4. A chief Levite in the days of Eliashib (Neh. 12:24).

Sheresh (shē'rĕsh), a grandson of Manasseh (I Chron. 7:16) and the ancestor of Manassites living in Gilead.

Sherezer (shĕ-rē'zēr), a man sent from Bethel to Jerusalem to ask the priests whether the days of mourning should be continued (Zech. 7:2).

Sheshach (shē'shăk), perhaps a cryptogram for "Babel" or "Babylon" (Jer. 25:26; 51:41).

Sheshai (shē'shī), one of the sons of Anak, giants whom the spies feared (Num. 13:22), but whom Caleb drove out (Josh. 15:14; Judg. 1:10).

Sheshan (shē'shan), an early descendant of Judah through Perez, Hezron and Jerahmeel (I Chron. 2:31, 34) whose daughter married an Egyptian (I Chron. 2:35-41).

Sheshbazzar (shĕsh-băz'êr), a prince of the Jews when Cyrus made a decree permitting the Jews to go back to Jerusalem to rebuild the house of God. He was made governor, was given the sacred vessels of the temple which had been taken at the captivity, and helped lay the foundation of the temple (Ezra 1:8, 11; 5:14, 16). He may be the same as Zerubbabel.

Sheth (shĕth, **compensation).** 1. The name given by Eve to her third son (I Chron. 1:1). 2. An unknown race mentioned in Balaam's parable (Num. 24: 17).

Shethar (shē'thår), one of the seven princes of Persia and Media who "saw the king's face" in the days of Xerxes (Esth. 1:14).

Shethar-Bozenai, Shethar-Boznai (shē'thår-bŏz'ē-nī, shē'thår-bŏz'nī), a Persian official who tried to prevent the Jews from building the temple (Ezra 5:3, 6).

Sheva (shē'vå). 1. David's scribe or secretary (II Sam. 20:25), perhaps the same as "Seraiah" in 8:17). 2. Son of Caleb (probably not the famous spy) by his concubine Maacah (I Chron. 2:49).

Shewbread, Showbread (See Tabernacle)

Shibah (shī'bå), the well from which Beer-sheba was named (Gen. 26:33). In KJV "Shebah."

Shibboleth shĭb'bō-lĕth, **an ear of grain** or **a stream),** a word which was differently pronounced on the two sides of the Jordan, and so was used by the men of Gilead under Jephthah as a test to determine whether the speaker was of Ephraim or not (Judg. 12:5, 6).

Shibmah, Sibmah (shĭb'må), a city taken by the tribe of Reuben from the Moabites (Num. 32:38).

Shicron, Shikkeron (shĭk'rŏn), a town W of Jerusalem on the northern border of Judah (Josh. 15:11). ASV Shikkeron.

Shield (See Armor)

Shiggaion (shĭ-gā'yŏn), a musical term found in the heading of Psalm 7. It may refer to a dithyramb, or rhapsody.

Shigionoth (shĭg-ĭ-ō'nŏth), plural of Shiggaion. The heading of Habakkuk's lovely psalm (Hab. 3:1).

Shihon, Shion (shī'ŏn), a town on the border of Issachar (Josh. 19:19), near Nazareth. ASV Shion.

Shihor, Sihor (shī'hôr). At least three views have been held regarding Shihor (usually Sihor in KJV): (1) the Nile; (2) a stream which separated Egypt from Palestine; (3) a canal, with waters drawn from the Nile, on the border between Egypt and Palestine. See Josh. 13:3; I Chron. 13:5; Isa. 23:3; Jer. 2:18.

Shihor-Libnath (shī'hôr-lĭb'năth), a small stream flowing into the Mediterranean Sea on the southern border of Asher (Josh. 19:26).

Shikkeron (See Shicron)

Shilhi (shĭl'hī), father-in-law of Jehoshaphat, king of Judah (I Kings 22:42).

Shilhim (shĭl'hĭm), a town in the S of Judah (Josh. 15:32).

Shillem, Shillemite (shĭl'ĕm, shĭl'ĕm-īt), the fourth son of Naphtali (Gen. 46: 24) and the family descended from him (Num. 26:49). Shallum in I Chron. 7:13.

Shiloah (See Siloam)

Shiloh (shī'lō). 1. City in Ephraim, c. 12 miles N and E of Bethel where the tabernacle remained from the time of Joshua to the days of Samuel (Judg. 21:19; I Sam. 4:3); Benjamites kidnaped wives (Judg. 21:15-24); residence of Eli and Samuel (I Sam. 3); home of the prophet Ahijah (I Kings 14); a ruin in Jeremiah's time (Jer. 7: 12, 14). 2. Word of uncertain meaning regarded by many Jews and Christians as a reference to the Messiah (Gen. 49:10).

Shiloni, Shilonite (shĭ-lō'nī, shī'lō-nīt). 1. An inhabitant of Shiloh. The one most often mentioned is Ahijah, the Shilonite (I Kings 11:29; II Chron. 9: 29). 2. Ancestor of Maaseiah, one of the Jewish princes who dwelt in Jerusalem under Nehemiah (Neh. 11:5).

Shilshah (shĭl'shå), one of the 11 sons of Zophah, an early member of the tribe of Asher (I Chron. 7:37).

Shimea (shĭm'ē-å). 1. A brother of David whose son slew a giant of Gath (I Chron. 20:7). 2. Son of David and Bathsheba (I Chron. 3:5). 3. A Merarite Levite (I Chron. 6:30). 4. A Gershonite Levite, grandfather of Asaph who stood with Heman in the service of sacred song under David.

No. 1 is probably the same as "Shimma" (I Chron. 2:13 KJV), "Shamma" (I Sam. 16:9), "Shimeah" (II Sam. 21: 21 KJV), and "Shimei" **(ibid.** ASV). The name is spelled three ways in the Hebrew, five ways in the English.

Shimeah (shĭm'ē-å). 1. Brother of David (II Sam. 13:3). 2. A son of Mikloth a Benjamite (I Chron. 8:32). In 9:38 "Shimeam."

Shimeam (See Shimeah)

Shimeath (shĭm'ē-ăth, **fame),** an Ammonitess, whose son Zabad (II Chron. 24:26) or Jozacar (II Kings 12:21) helped to assassinate King Joash of Judah.

Shimeathites (shĭm'ē-ăth-īts), one of the three families of scribes that dwelt at Jabez in Judah (I Chron. 2:55). They were Kenites related to the Rechabites.

Shimei (shĭm'ē-ī, **famous).** 1. A son of Gershon and head of a Levite family, Shimi in KJV (Exod. 6:17). 2. A Gershonite Levite, head of one of the courses of Levites (I Chron. 23:7-10). 3. One of David's mighty men who remained faithful in Adonijah's attempted usurpation (I Kings 1:8). 4. One of Solomon's purveyors of food who was over Benjamin (I Kings 4:18). 5. The grandson of Jehoiachin, or, as he was later called, Jeconiah (I Chron. 3:19). 6. A Simeonite (I Chron. 4:26, 27). 7. An early Reubenite, son of Gog and father of Micah (I Chron. 5:4). 8. An early Merarite Levite (I Chron. 6: 29). 9. Judahite (I Chron. 8:21), Shimhi in KJV. 10. The head of one of the 24 courses of musical Levites, who with his 12 sons and brethren made up the tenth course (I Chron. 25:17). 11. A man of Ramah, whom David set over the vineyards (I Chron. 27:27). 12. One of the descendants of Heman, the singer, who helped in the housecleaning of the temple under Hezekiah (II Chron. 29:14). 13. A Levite, treasurer over the oblations and tithes in Hezekiah's time (II Chron. 31:12, 13). 14. One of the Levites who had married a foreign woman (Ezra 10:23). 15. One of the family of Hashum who had married a foreign woman (Ezra 10:33). 16. One of the family of Bani who had done the same (Ezra 10:38). 17. Son of Kish and grandfather of Mordecai the Jew who brought up Esther (Esth. 2: 5). 18. A Benjamite of the house of Saul, and son of Gera who cursed David in the day when he was fleeing from Absalom his son, and cast stones at David. David refused to let his cousin Abishai slay him (II Sam. 16: 5-14). When David was returning, victorious, Shimei prayed for forgiveness and David pardoned him (II Sam. 19: 16-23), but when Solomon sat upon the throne (I Kings 2:36-46) he first confined him to Jerusalem, then executed him for disobedience.

Shimeon (shĭm'ē-ŭn, **hearing),** one of the family of Harin who had married a foreign wife (Ezra 10:31).

Shimhi (See Shimei)

Shimi (See Shimei)

Shimite (shĭm'īt), a member of the family descended from Shimei (Num. 3:21 KJV; ASV Shimeites).

Shimma (shĭm'ȧ), the third son of Jesse (I Chron. 2:13 KJV), also Shammah (I Sam. 16:9).

Shimon (shī'mŏn), Judahite (I Chron. 4:20).

Shimrath (shĭm'răth, **watch),** one of the sons of Shimei in the tribe of Benjamin (I Chron. 8:21).

Shimri (shĭm'rī). 1. Son of Shemaiah and head of a father's house in the tribe of Simeon (I Chron. 4:37). 2. Father of two of David's mighty men (I Chron. 11:45). 3. A son of Hosah of the Merarite Levites, whom Hosah made chief of his 13 kinsmen. Simri in KJV (I Chron. 26:10). 4. A Levite who helped cleanse the temple (II Chron. 29:13).

Shimrith (shĭm'rĭth, **watchful),** mother of Jehozabad who heped to slay Joash, king of Judah (II Chron. 24:26); also called Shomer (II Kings 12:21).

Shimrom, Shimron (shĭm'rŏm, shĭm'rŏn, **a guard).** 1. Son of Issachar, son of Jacob (Gen. 46:13). In I Chron. 7:1 KJV has Shimrom. 2. A town in the northern part of Canaan whose king united with Jabin, king of Hazor, to fight against Joshua and the Israelites (Josh. 11:1ff).

Shimron-Meron (shĭm'rŏn-mē'rŏn), a town listed among the 34 victories of Joshua in the conquest of Canaan (Josh. 12:20).

Shimshai (shĭm'shī, **sunny),** a scribe who hindered the attempts to rebuild the temple (Ezra 4:8).

Shinab (shī'năb), king of Admah, one of the Canaanite cities, later destroyed with Sodom (Gen. 14:2).

Shinar (shī'nȧr), alluvial plain of Babylonia in which lay cities of Babel, Erech, Accad, and Calneh (Gen. 10: 10); tower of Babel built there (Gen. 11:1-9); Amraphel, king of Shinar, invaded Canaan (Gen. 14:1); Jews exiled to Shinar (Zech. 5:11); Nebuchadnezzar transported temple treasures to Shinar area (Dan. 1:2).

Shion (shī'ŏn, **overturning),** a town in Issachar (Josh. 19:19). KJV Shihon.

Shiphi (shī'fī), father of Ziza, a Simeonite prince (I Chron. 4:37).

Shiphmite (shĭf'mīt), the patronymic of Zabdi, vineyard overseer under David (I Chron. 27:27).

Shiphrah (shĭf'rȧ, **beauty),** one of the Hebrew midwives who risked their

A typical sailing and fishing boat of the Middle East. © *MPS*

lives to save the Hebrew boy babies (Exod. 1:15-21).

Shiphtan (shĭf'tăn, **judicial),** father of Kemuel, a prince of Ephraim, whom Joshua appointed to help divide the land (Num. 34:24).

Ships. The Israelites were an agricultural, not a sea-going, people because the coastline of Palestine was harborless. Small fishing boats and ferryboats were used on the Sea of Galilee and the Jordan (Matt. 4:21; 9:1; 14:22). Solomon had a fleet at Ezion-geber (I Kings 9:26-28), but it was composed of Phoenician ships and manned by Phoenician crews. Jehoshaphat's fleet was shipwrecked (II Chron. 20:35-37). Phoenicians were the great navigators of the ancient world, travelling as far as Cornwall for tin, and to the Canaries. Egyptian boats were often built of bundles of papyrus (Isa. 18:2). Romans used triremes and quinqueremes for warships, and large ships (up to 3250 tons burden) to transport grain from Egypt. Paul travelled on one of these ships that carried 276 people when it was shipwrecked (Acts 27). Travelling by ship on the Mediterranean in the fall of the year was very dangerous, as Paul's experience shows.

A portion of the relief of Pharaoh Shishak I, from the wall of the temple at Karnak, depicting conquered Palestinian captives. © MPS

Shisha (shī'shȧ), the father of two of Solomon's secretaries; Elihoreph and Ahijah (I Kings 4:3).

Shishak (shī'shăk), an Egyptian king, the founder of the 22nd or Libyan dynasty. He was from a Libyan family which for some generations had been situated at Herakleopolis in the Fayyum.

Earlier in his reign he had provided asylum to the Israelite Jeroboam, who had fled to Egypt to escape the wrath of Solomon (I Kings 11:40). With Jeroboam on the northern throne, Shishak showed no favoritism, but impartially overran both Judah and Israel. Jerusalem was a victim of this campaign and the temple was looted of its treasures (I Kings 14:25-26; II Chron. 12:1-9). Though his dynasty endured for roughly 200 years, internal conflict, stagnation, and incapability kept it at, or below, the level of mediocrity.

Shitrai (shĭt'rī), a Sharonite, placed by David over the flocks that fed in Sharon (I Chron. 27:29).

Shittah Tree (See Plants)

Shittim (shĭt'ĭm), the name of the wood which comes from the acacia tree, mentioned 26 times in connection with the tabernacle and its furniture (Exod. 25-38). The wood is hard, fine-grained, yellowish-brown in color but turns nearly black with age.

Shittim (place) a contraction of Abel-shittim, i.e. "meadow of acacias," the last stop of Israel in the wilderness before crossing the Jordan into the promised land (Num. 25:1; 33:49). There Balaam tried to curse Israel but had to bless instead, and there he told Balak how to seduce the men of Israel (Mic. 6:5; Num. 22:1; 25:3). From there Joshua sent the two spies to Jericho (Josh. 2:1) and thence Israel departed to cross the Jordon (Josh. 3:1).

Shiza (shī'zȧ), a man of Reuben, father of Adina, one of David's mighty men (I Chron. 11:42).

Shoa (shō'ȧ, **rich**), people mentioned in association with Babylonians, Chaldeans, and Assyrians (Ezek. 23:23). May be Sutu of Amarna letters.

Shobab (shō'bab). 1. A grandson of Hezron of Judah through Caleb (I Chron. 2:18). 2. A son of David (I Chron. 3:5).

Shobach (shō'bak), the general of the Syrian army under Hadarezer, king of Zobah, defeated by David (II Sam. 10: 16-18). In I Chron. 19:16, Shophach.

Shobai (shō'bī), a gatekeeper of the temple, some of whose descendants returned with Zerubbabel (Ezra 2:42; Neh. 7:45).

Shobal (shō'băl). 1. One of the sons of Seir the Horite, very early inhabitant of what was later Edom (Gen. 36: 20, 23). 2. An early Ephrathite of the sons of Caleb (not the spy), an ancestor or founder of Kiriath-jearim (I Chron. 2:50, 52; Josh. 15:9). 3. A grandson of Judah and father of Reaiah (I Chron. 4:1, 2).

Shobek (shō'bĕk), one of the 44 chiefs of the Jewish people who covenanted with Nehemiah to keep the law of Jehovah (Neh. 10:24).

Shobi (shō'bī), a prince of the Ammonites (II Sam. 17:27).

Shocho (shō'kō), a city in Judah, built by Rehoboam (II Chron. 11:7). ASV has Soco, KJV Shoco.

Shoe (See Dress)

Shoe Latchet (See Dress)

Shofar (See Music, Musical Instruments)

Shoham (shō'hăm), a Merarite Levite in the days of David (I Chron. 24:27).

Shomer (shō'mêr, **keeper, watcher).** 1. The father of Jehozabad, one of the conspirators against Joash of Judah (II Kings 12:20, 21; II Chron. 24:25, 26). 2. A great-grandson of Asher, through Beriah and Heber (I Chron. 7:32). In verse 34, Shemer (ASV) and Shamer (KJV).

Shophach (shō'făk), general of the Syrians, whom David slew (I Chron. 19:16, 18). In II Sam. 10:16, Shobach.

Shophan (shō'făn), the second half of the name of Atroth-shophan, a city of the tribe of Gad (Num. 32:35).

Shophar (See Music, Musical Instruments)

Shore, the land where it meets the sea (Josh. 15:2; Judg. 5:17; Matt. 13:2).

Shoshannim (shō-shăn'ĭm, **lilies),** found in the titles of Psalms 45, 69, 80 and in Ps. 60 in the singular. Perhaps lily-shaped musical instruments, perhaps the name of spring-songs.

Shoulder, a word often used in both a literal and figurative sense. When a man of Israel offered an ox or a sheep, the shoulder went to the officiating priest as a part of his portion (Deut. 18:8). The shoulder pieces of the ephod, the sacred garment of the high priest, were to bear onyx stones on which were graven the names of the tribes (Exod. 28:1-12), thus indicating that the priest bore a heavy responsibility for the people; and similarly, a ruler bears upon his shoulders the weight of the government (Isa. 9:6). Although in traveling, the sections of the tabernacle could be carried in wagons, the priests had to carry the sacred furniture upon their shoulders (Num. 7:6-9), much as Jehovah is pictued as bearing his beloved upon his shoulders (Deut. 33:12), and as the good shepherd bears the lost sheep when he finds it (Luke 15:5). "To pull away the shoulder" (Zech. 7:11) is to refuse to obey, and to "thrust with the shoulder" (Ezek. 34:21) is insolence.

Shoulder Piece. 1. That part of the ephod in which the front and the back were joined together so as to make the garment to be of one piece (Exod. 28:7, 8). 2. The piece of meat which is taken from the shoulder of the beast (Ezek. 24:4).

Shovel, a tool used for clearing out ashes, etc. from the altar (Exod. 27:3; II Chron. 4:11, etc.), for sanitary purposes (Deut. 23:13), or for winnowing (Isa. 30:24).

Showbread, Shewbread (See Tabernacle)

Shrine, a dwelling for a god (Acts 19:24).

Shroud, generally the dress for the dead, but also a bough (Ezek. 31:3) where KJV has "a shadowing shroud," but ASV has "a forest-like shade."

Shrub (See Plants)

Shua (shōō'a, **prosperity).** 1. A Canaanite whose daughter became Judah's wife (Gen. 38:2, 12). The KJV incorrectly spells this **Shuah.** 2. The daughter of Heber who was the grandson of Asher (I Chron. 7:32).

Shuah (shōō'ah, **depression).** 1. A son of Abraham by Keturah (Gen. 25:2; I Chron. 1:32). 2. (See Shua No. 1). 3. Chelub's brother (I Chron. 4:11).

Shual (shōō'al, **fox).** 1. One of the 11 sons of Zophar from the tribe of Asher (I Chron. 7:36). 2. I Samuel 13:17 refers to the "Land of Shual." It is named as one of the places invaded by one of the marauding tribes of Philistines. It probably lies a few miles NE of Bethel.

Shubael (shōō'bā-ĕl, **captive).** A name given to two Levites (I Chron. 24:20; 25:20). They are also referred to as Shebuel.

Shuham, Shuhamite (shōō'hăm, shōō'hăm-īt), the son of Dan (Num. 26:42; Gen. 46:23), called also "Hushim." Dan's descendants are called "Shuhamites."

Shuhite (shōō'hīt, **a native of Shuah),** a term describing one of Job's friends by the name of Bildad (Job 2:11; 8:1; 18:1; 25:1; 42:9). It is very likely that this term refers back to Abraham's son by Keturah named Shuah.

Shulamite (shōō'lăm-īt, **peaceful),** a title applied to a young woman in the Song of Solomon 6:13, probably native of Shunem. See Shunammite, Shunem.

Shumathites (shōō'măth-īts, **garlic),** a family of Kirjath-jearim (I Chron. 2:53).

Shunammite (shōō'năm-īt, **a native of Shunem).** 1. An unnamed woman whose son Elisha raised from the dead (II Kings 4:12; 8:1-6). 2. Applied also to David's nurse, Abishag (I Kings 1:3; 2:17-22).

Shunem (shōō'nĕm), a place belonging to the tribe of Issachar (Josh. 19:18). Here the Philistines encamped before they fought at Gilboa (I Sam. 28:4). Here lived David's nurse, Abishag (I Kings 1:3). Shunen was also the home of the woman who befriended Elisha whose son he restored (II Kings 4:8-37). It lies in a very rich section of Palestine a short distnce N of Jezreel at the foot of "Little Hermon."

Shuni, Shunite (shōō'nī, shōo'nīt), the son of Gad who founded a group known as Shunites (Gen. 46:16; Num. 26:15).

Shupham, Shuphamite (shōō'fam, shōō'făm-īt), a son of Benjamin and founder of the group known as "Shuphamites" (Num. 26:39). May be same as "Shephuphan" (I Chron. 8:5).

Shuppim (shŭ'pĭm). 1. A Benjamite (I Chron. 7:12, 15). 2. One of the two who had charge of the gate of the temple, Shallecheth (I Chron. 26:16), a Levite.

Shur (shōōr, **wall),** a locality S of Palestine and E of Egypt. It was in this region that the angel of the Lord found Hagar when she fled from Sarah (Gen. 16:7-14).

Shushan (shōō'shăn), a city of the Babylonians probably named from the lilies that grow in this region in large numbers. It was famous in Biblical history as one of the capitals of the Persian empire (Neh. 1:1; Esth. 1:2; Dan. 8:2) during the time of Darius the Great. Here also Persian kings came to reside for the winter, and Daniel

The village of Shunem (Sulem) on the edge of the Plain of Esdraelon. © *MPS*

had the vision mentioned in Daniel 8: 2. The Greeks called this place "Susa." It was located in the fertile valley on the left bank of the Choaspes River called Ulai in Daniel 8:2, 16. It enjoyed a very delightful climate. Many Jews lived here and became prominent in the affairs of the city as the Books of Esther and Nehemiah show. From this city was sent the group who replaced those removed from Samaria (Ezra 4:9).

Shushan-Eduth (shōō'shan-ē'dŭth, **a lily of testimony),** the title of Psalm 80. Meaning uncertain.

Shuthelah, Shuthalhite (shōō-thē'lȧ, shōō-thăl'hīt). 1. One of the three sons of Ephraim (Num. 26:35-36). His descendants are called "Shuthalhites" (I Chron. 7:20-21). 2. I Chronicles 7:21 mentions his father as Zabad and reveals that he is the father of Ezer and Elead.

Shuttle (shŭ'tl), a word used as a figure of the quick passing of life (Job 7:6).

Sia (sī'ȧ, **assembly),** a leader of the Nethinim whose descendants returned with Zerubbabel (Neh. 7:47). Siaha in Ezra 2:44.

Sibbecai, Sibbechai (sĭb′ē-kī, sĭb′ē-kī), a captain of several thousand men in David's army, usually designated as "The Hushathite" (II Sam. 21:18; I Chron. 11:29; 20:4; 27:11).

Sibboleth (See Shibboleth)

Sibmah (sĭb′mȧ), a town located on the E of the Jordan and belonging originally to Moab. It was finally taken by the Amorites led by King Sihon (Num. 21:26). Later it was captured by and given to the tribe of Reuben (Josh. 13:19).

Sibraim (sĭb-rā′ĭm), a point marking Palestine's N boundary between Damascus and Hamath (Ezek. 47:16).

Sichem (sī′kĕm), the same as Shechem.

Sicily (sĭs′ĭ-lē), the triangular island lying off the toe of Italy. Visited by Paul (Acts 28:12). See Syracuse.

Sick, Sickness (See Diseases)

Sickle (sĭk′l, **reaping hook).** The earlier sickles varied in size, shape, and in the material from which they were made. The earliest type seems to have been constructed of wood. It resembled our modern scythes, though smaller, and its cutting edge was made of flint. Later sickles were constructed of metal. These were used mostly for cutting grain, but on occasions they were used for pruning. Used figuratively of the instrument of God's judgment (Mark 4:29; Rev. 14:14, 16ff).

Siddim, Vale of (sĭd′ĭm, **the valley of the fields),** a place mentioned in Genesis 14:3-8 as the battleground where Chedorlaomer and his allies met the kings of Sodom and other nearby cities. Because of the wickedness of the inhabitants of this area, God judged the locality many years ago in the days of Abraham. Its cities were completely destroyed and probably much of this territory was inundated by the waters of the Dead Sea.

Sidon (sī′dŏn), a Phoenician city midway between Berytus (Beirut) and Tyre. Small offshore islands made an excellent port. In ancient times they seem to have been linked by moles. Sidon appears in the OT as the chief city of Phoenicia, and the name was applied frequently to the whole nation (Gen. 10:15; Judg. 10:12). The city seems to have been a center of trade and enterprise.

The art of glass blowing was discovered in the first century B.C. at Sidon, and the names of a number of Sidonian glass-blowers have been recovered from surviving samples of their art. Sidon shared fully in the seafaring, commercial, and colonizing enterprises of the Phoenician people. By and large, the history of Sidon followed the course of that of all Phoenicia. In common with the rest of the lands of the Middle East, Sidon fell under the power in turn of Assyria, Babylon, Persia, Greece, and Rome. Brief-lived patterns of alliance (Jer. 27:3), periods of independence, parley, subjection, ill-advised revolt, destruction, and renaissance, were the common lot of the smaller lands of the region amid the rise and fall of the great empires. Sidon had a bad name in Scripture as a hot-bed of Phoenician idolatry (Isa. 23; Ezek. 28), and of Gentile materialism (Matt. 11:21, 22). The neighborhood of Sidon, not more than 50 miles from Nazareth, was visited by Christ (Matt. 15:21; Mark 7:24-31), and Sidonians resorted to Him (Mark 3:8; Luke 6:17). Sidon was a residence of Christian disciples, and a port of call of Paul (Acts 27:3).

Siege (See War)

Sieve (sĭv, **netted, nāphāh, a sieve),** a utensil used by the eastern people to sift grains. Some of the Egyptian sieves were made of strings or reeds. Those constructed of string were used for finer work whereas those made from reeds were used for sifting coarser material. Used figuratively (Isa. 30:28; Amos 9:9).

Sign, (a signal, a miracle, an indication). In Scripture this word generally refers to something addressed to the senses to attest the existence of a divine power. Miracles in the Old Testament were often signs (Exod. 4:8; 8:23). Several specific things were given as signs, such as the rainbow (Gen. 9:12-13); some of the feasts (Exod. 13:9); the sabbath (Exod. 31:13); and circumcision (Rom. 4:11). Often extraordinary events were given as a sign to insure faith or demonstrate authority. When Moses would not believe God, his rod was turned into a serpent and his hand became leprous as signs of God's divine commission (Exod. 4:1-8). When Christ was born, the place of His birth and His dress were to be signs of His identity to the shepherds. When the Scribes and the Pharisees asked Jesus for a sign, He assured them that no sign was to be given them except the sign of Jonah, whose experience in the fish was to portray Christ's burial and resurrection.

Signet (See Seal)

Sihon (sī'hŏn), a king of the Amorites who became prominent chiefly because of his opposition to Israel on their journey from Egypt to Palestine. When he led the attack against Israel, he was killed and his forces scattered (Num. 21:21-24; Deut. 1:4, 20, 24-30). His capital was taken and the territory given to Israel. This episode is often referred to as a reminder to Israel of what God had done for them and became a source of encouragement to them (Deut. 3:2).

Sihor (sī'hôr, **turbid),** a body of water mentioned in connection with Egypt (Josh. 13:3; Isa. 23:3; Jer. 2:18). "Shihor" may be its correct spelling. It is the Nile River, or Brook of Egypt.

Silas (sī'lȧs, **asked),** a prominent member of the Jerusalem church (Acts 15:22, 32) and a Roman citizen (Acts 16:37), who was sent by the church with Paul and Barnabas to deliver the letter which was formulated by the Jerusalem council to the church at Antioch (Acts 15:22, 23). When Paul fell out with Barnabas, he turned for help on his so-called second missionary journey. He was with Paul at Philippi and shared both in the beating and imprisonment there. When Paul left Berea for Athens, Silas and Timothy were left behind. Apparently Timothy rejoined Paul only at Athens, while Silas stayed on in Macedonia. He, along with Timothy, who had returned to Thessalonica, rejoined Paul at Corinth (Acts 18:5). Although no further references to the name Silas occur in the NT, it is almost certain that Silvanus is the same person. He joins Paul in the salutation of both I and II Thessalonians (1:1), and is mentioned by Paul in his second letter to the Corinthians with reference to the preaching of Christ at Corinth (II Cor. 1:19). Silvanus also appears as the amanuensis of Peter (I Pet. 5:12).

Silk, imported from China by Phoenicians (Prov. 31:22; Ezek. 16:10, 13; Rev. 18:12).

Silla (sĭl'ȧ, **embankment),** an unknown place below Millo (II Kings 12:20).

Siloah, Shiloah (See Siloam)

Siloam (sĭ-lō'ăm), a reservoir located within the city walls of Jerusalem at the S end of the Tyropoean Valley constructed by Hezekiah (II Kings 20:

The Pool of Siloam at the southern end of Hezekiah's Tunnel, in the Kidron Valley. *© MPS*

20; II Chron. 32:30). The conduit leads from the intermittent Spring of Gihon (Jerusalem's most important water supply) through the rock Ophel to the reservoir called the Pool of Siloam.

The importance of the Siloam inscription discovered in 1880 can scarcely be overestimated. Not only does it give a fascinating account of the building of the tunnel, but as G. Ernest Wright says it "has for many years been the most important monumental piece of writing in Israelite Palestine, and other Hebrew inscriptions have been dated by comparing the shapes of letters with it" (**Biblical Archaeology,** Philadelphia: Westminster Press, 1957, p. 169).

In 1890 a vandal entered the tunnel and cut the inscription out of the rock. It was subsequently found in several pieces in the possession of a Greek in Jerusalem who claimed he had purchased it from an Arab. The Turkish officials seized the pieces and removed them to Istanbul where they are today.

The Siloam tunnel was not the only conduit which had been built to bring water from the Spring of Gihon into Jerusalem. At least two others preceded it, but neither was adequately protected against enemy attack. It was probably to one of these former conduits that Isaiah referred in the words, "the waters of Shiloah that flow gently" (Isa. 8:6). It was to the pool of Siloam that Jesus sent the blind man with the command, "Go, wash" (John 9:7). He obeyed, and came back seeing.

Siloam, Tower of (sĭ-lō′ăm), a tower which was probably part of the ancient system of fortifications on the walls of the city of Jerusalem near the pool of Siloam. The collapse of this tower and the resulting death of 18 persons is cited by Jesus (Luke 13:4). Apparently the accident was well known to His hearers, but is not mentioned elsewhere.

Siloam, Village of (sĭ-lō′ăm). There is no mention of a village by this name in the Bible. However, on the rocky slope across the valley E of the Spring Gihon (see **Siloam,** above) is a rocky slope on which is situated the modern village of Silwan (Siloam).

Silvanus (See Silas)

Silver (See Minerals)

Silversmith (See Artificer under Occupations and Professions)

Simeon (sĭm′ē-ŭn). 1. The second son of Jacob by Leah (Gen. 29:33). He and his brother Levi massacred the Hivites living in Shechem because of an injury done to their sister Dinah (Gen. 34:24-31). 2. The tribe of which Simeon, the son of Jacob, became the founder. 3. An ancestor of Jesus (Luke 3:30). 4. Devout Jew who took the infant Jesus into his arms and praised God (Luke 2:25, 34). 5. Simon Peter (Acts 15:14). See Peter. 6. One of the Christian leaders in the church at Antioch, surnamed Niger, who set apart Paul and Barnabas for their missionary work (Acts 13:1, 2).

Simeonite, a member of the tribe of Simeon; see above 2.

Similitude (sĭ-mĭl′ĭ-tūd, **likeness, pattern, resemblance).** The first word is found four times in the OT (Num. 12:8; Deut. 4:12, 15, 16), and some form of the divine manifestation seems to be intended. The second word is probably best translated by "pattern," as II Chronicles 4:3 reveals. The third word seems to convey a resemblance of that which it represents (Pss. 106:20; 144:12). The last has the idea of something that is like or similar to another thing (Rom. 5:14; Heb. 7:15; James 3:9).

Simon (sī′mŭn, **hearing).** 1. The son of Jonas, and brother of Andrew, a fisherman who became a disciple and apostle of Christ (Matt. 4:18; 16:17, 18, etc). See Peter. 2. Another disciple of Jesus called the "Cananaean," a member of the party later called "the Zealots" (Matt. 10:4; Mark 3:18). 3. A leper of Bethany in whose house Jesus' head was anointed (Matt. 26:6; Mark 14:3). 4. A brother of the Lord (Matt. 13:55; Mark 6:3). 5. A man from Cyrene, father of Alexander and Rufus, who was compelled to carry the cross of Jesus (Matt. 27:32; Mark 15:21; Luke 23:26). 6. A Pharisee in whose house Jesus' feet were anointed by the sinful woman (Luke 7:40, 43, 44). 7. Judas Iscariot's father (John 6:71; 12:4; 13:2, 26). 8. Simon Magus, a sorcerer at Samaria, with great power and influence among the people (Acts 8:9-13). When Simon saw that the Spirit was given by the laying on of hands he tried to buy this power for himself from the apostles. His request called forth a blistering rebuke by Peter (Acts 8:14-24). 9. A tanner at Joppa with whom Peter stayed "for many days" (Acts 9:43; 10:6, 17, 32).

Simon Maccabeus (sī'mŭn măk'à-bē-ŭs), Hasmonaean ruler in Palestine (143-134 B.C.).

Simon Magus (See Simon)

Simple. The basic idea of the word in the OT is "easily influenced" (Pss. 19:7; 119:130; Prov. 7:7). The two uses of the word in the NT (Rom. 16:18, 19) carry the idea of being harmless or guileless.

Simri (sĭm'rī), a son of the Levite, Hosah, David appointed him as doorkeeper in the temple and head of his tribe (I Chron. 26:10).

Sin, anything in the creature which does not express, or which is contrary to, the holy character of the Creator. The first sin in the universe was an act of free will in which the creature deliberately, responsibly, and with adequate understanding of the issues, chose to corrupt the holy, godly character with which God originally endowed His creation. Sin in the human race had its origin in Adam and Eve (Gen. 3), but sin in the universe had its origin in angelic beings who rebelled against the creator and whose nature, as a result, became fixed in evil (II Pet. 2:4; Jude 6). Adam and Eve were created with a holy, godly nature, in fellowship with God; as a result of their sin their nature became corrupt; they became hostile to God and guilty before Him; and they involved the whole human race in their corruption and guilt (Rom. 5:12f). The essence of sin is living independently of God. The solution to the problem of sin is found in Christ, in the redemption provided by Him (Rom. 3:21-8:39).

Sin (clay), an Egyptian city lying on the eastern arm of the Nile River. Ezekiel refers to it as "the stronghold of Egypt" (30:15). A wall was built on the S, and with the sea on the N and impassable swamps on the other sides the city was practically impregnable.

Sin, Wilderness of, a wilderness through which the Israelites passed between Elim and Mt. Sinai (Exod. 16:1; 17:1; Num. 33:11, 12).

Sin Offering (See Offerings)

Sina (See Sinai)

Sinai (sī'nī, meaning uncertain), a word used in three senses in the Old Testament: 1. It is applied to a peninsula which lay to the south of the Wilderness of Paran between the Gulf of Aqabah and Suez on the E and W respectively. This peninsula has a triangular shape and is 150 miles wide

A shepherd and his flock before the rugged slopes of Jebel Musa and Ras Safsaf, the traditional and most probable site of Mount Sinai, or Horeb. © MPS

at the N and 250 miles long. 2. It is applied to a wilderness, the "Wilderness of Sinai" (Exod. 19:1). It is the place where Israel came in the third month after they left Egypt. It may be used loosely as a synonym for the Sinaitic Peninsula but probably technically does not embrace as much territory 3. Finally, there is the mountain often referred to as Mount Sinai (Exod. 19:20), or Horeb. It was on this mountain that God met and talked with Moses and gave him the law (Exod. 19:3). Exact location disputed.

Sinew (sĭ'nū, **sinew**), the tendons and sinews of the body (Gen. 32:32; Job 40:17; Ezek 37:6-8). It is used once in a figurative sense (Isa. 48:4).

Singing (See Song; Music)

Single Eye, an eye that is clear, sound, and healthy, with the connotation **generous** (Matt. 6:22; Luke 11:34).

Sinim (sī'nĭm), remote, unknown area (Isa. 49:12); RSV reads Syene.

Sinites (sī'nīts), a tribe descended from Canaan (Gen. 10:17; I Chron. 1:15).

Sion, Mount (sī'ŭn, **lofty**), a designation for Mount Hermon (Deut. 4:48).

Siphmoth (sĭf'mŏth), a place in the southern part of Judah to which David often came (I Sam. 30:28). Site not positively identified.

Sippai (sĭp'ī), a man, known also as Saph, descended from the giants. Slain by Sibbechai (I Chron. 20:4).

Sirach, Son of (sī'răk), the supposed author of the Apocryphal book of Ecclesiasticus. He calls himself "Jesus, the Son of Sirach the Jerusalemite." He wrote about 190-170 B.C.

Sirah (sī'rȧ), a well (II Sam. 3:26), probably 'Ain Sarah, located about a mile N of old Hebron.

Sirion (sĭr'ĭ-ŏn, **coat of mail**), a name given to Mt. Hermon by the Zidonians (Deut. 3:9). Shirion in Ps. 29:6.

Sismai, Sisamai (sĭs'mī, sĭs'ȧ-mī), a son of Eleasah from the tribe of Judah. One who descended from Sheshan's daughter (I Chron. 2:40).

Sisera (sĭs'êr-ȧ). 1. A man employed by Jabin, king of Hazor, as the captain in his army. Sisera was a thorn in Israel's side for 20 years (Judg. 4:2-3). Finally, Deborah the prophetess, who judged Israel at that time, urged Barak under the direction of God to unite his forces and go against Sisera. These two armies met in battle on the plain at the foot of Mount Tabor (Judg. 4:14). The forces of Sisera were killed or scattered and Sisera fled on foot, taking refuge in the tent of Jael, the wife of Heber, the Kenite. Here he was killed by Jael while he slept in her tent. The remarkable victory was celebrated by the song of Deborah. 2. The name Sisera is found again in the names of the Nethinim (Ezra 2:53; Neh. 7:55) who returned from captivity under Zerubbabel's leadership. See Barak, Deborah.

Sister. 1. Full or half sister (Gen. 20:12; Deut. 27:22). 2. Wife (S. of Sol. 4:9). 3. Woman of same country or tribe (Num. 25:18). 4. Blood relatives (Matt. 13:56; Mark 6:3). 5. Female fellow Christian (Rom. 16:1; II John 13).

Sitnah (sĭt'nȧ, **hostility**), the name given to the second well dug by Isaac (Gen. 26:21), between Gerah and Rehoboth.

Sivan (sē-vȧn'), the name given to the third month of the Hebrew sacred year which is the ninth month of the civil year (Esth. 8:9). See Calendar.

Skin. Skins of animals were used as bottles both for water and for wine. They formed many useful articles of clothing. Various kinds formed the protection for the tabernacle in the wilderness. Ezekiel tells of shoes being made from skins (Ezek. 16:10). The word is also used figuratively in several places (Job 2:4; 19:20).

Skirt (See Dress)

Skull (See Golgotha)

Sky, a word found only in the plural in the Bible (Ps. 18:11; Isa. 45:8). The word refers sometimes to the clouds and other times to the firmament. At least once it is used figuratively (Deut. 33:26).

Slander, a malicious utterance designed to hurt or defame the person about whom it is uttered. The Scriptures frequently warn against it (Lev. 19:16; Ezek. 22:9; Eph. 4:31; Col. 3:8; James 4:11).

Slave, Slavery (bondslave, servant). While the Hebrew and Greek words are very common in the Bible, the English word **slave** is found but twice (Jer. 2:14; Rev. 18:13), and the word **slavery** does not occur at all in the KJV, because both the Hebrew and the Greek word involved are more often rendered "servant."

Sleep. 1. Physical rest (Ps. 4:8; John 11:13). 2. Death (I Cor. 11:30; I Thess. 4:13). 3. Spiritual indolence (Matt. 25:5; Rom. 13:11).

Slime, bitumen; used as cement for bricks and for waterproofing (Gen. 6:14; 11:3; Isa. 34:9; Exod. 2:3)

Slip, a cutting from a plant (Isa. 17: 10).

Slothful. (Indolent, lazy). The combined idea from these words is that of a person who is undependable because of his laziness.

Slow. Moses says he is slow of speech (Exod. 4:10). This does not refer to any particular defect but simply to the fact that his words did not come readily. "Long-suffering" would almost be a synonym (Neh. 9:17; Pss. 103:8; 145:8). It always has a reference to the passions in the OT. The Greek words are found only three times in the NT (Luke 24:25; Titus 1:12; James 1:19).

Sluggard (See Slothful)

Smith (See Occupations & Professions)

Smyrna (smîr′nȧ), a port on the W coast of Asia Minor at the head of the gulf into which the Hermus debouches, a well protected harbor, and the natural terminal of a great inland trade-route up the Hermus valley. Smyrna was famous for science, medicine, and the majesty of its buildings. Apollonius of Tyana refers to her "crown of porticoes," a circle of beautiful public buildings which ringed the summit of Mount Pagos like a diadem; hence John's reference (Rev. 2:10). Polycarp, Smyrna's martyred bishop of A.D. 155, had been a disciple of John.

Snare, a device for catching both birds (Ps. 124:7) and animals. The words are employed often in the Bible in a figurative sense (Pss. 91:3; 141:9).

Snout, the long, projecting nose of a beast, as of a pig (Prov. 11:22).

Snow, common in the hill country of Palestine. It never becomes very deep and it is not uncommon to have winters without any. The tops of the high mountains are covered with snow most of the year and this becomes the source of much of the water there. It is stored in caves in the mountains in the winter for cooling beverages and for refrigerating purposes in the summer. It is a symbol of the highest purity and stands for the condition of the redeemed soul (Isa. 1:18; Ps. 51:7); and the righteousness of the believer (Rev. 19:8). It symbolizes whiteness and purity (Matt. 28:3; Rev. 1:14).

Snuff, panting for wind (Jer. 14:6) or in a symbolic sense to express contempt for God's sacrifices (Mal. 1:13).

So, the king of Egypt, mentioned in II Kings 17:4 as king in the days of Ahaz, king of Judah, and Hoshea, king of Israel. Hoshea made an alliance with So, bringing down the wrath of Assyria upon Israel (II Kings 17:5). It is difficult to identify him.

Soap. Soap in a modern sense was unknown in OT times. Clothes, cooking utensils, and even the body were cleansed with the ashes of certain plants containing alkali (e.g., soapwort, glasswort, and saltwort). This cleansing material is referred to in Jer. 2:22 and Mal. 3:2.

Socho, Sococh, Socoh (sō′kō, **branches).** 1. Town in Judah (Josh. 15:35) NW of Adullam; identified with Khirbet Shuweikeh. 2. Another city by this name 10 miles SW of Hebron (Josh. 15:48). 3. Son of Heber (I Chron. 4: 18).

Socket (See Tabernacle)

Sodi (sō′dī), father of the Israelite spy representing the tribe of Zebulun (Num. 13:10).

Sodom (sŏd′ŭm), one of the so-called "Cities of the Plain," the others being Admah, Gomorrah, Zeboiim, and Zoar. Located on S portion of Dead Sea; probably water covers the remains. Lot lived there (Gen. 13:1-13); destroyed because of its wickedness (Gen. 19); symbol of vice, infamy, and judgment (Isa. 1:9, 10; 3:9; Jer. 23:14; Lam. 4:6; Ezek. 16:46; Matt. 10:15; Rev. 11:8). "Sodoma" in KJV Rom. 9:29. It was the theme of judgment on iniquity which was in the mind of the Jew or Christian who, some time before the eruption of A.D. 79, scribbled on a wall in Pompeii "Sodoma Gomorra."

Sodoma (See Sodom)

Sodomite (See Sodomy)

Sodomy (sŏd′ŭm-ē, **male temple prostitute),** unnatural sexual perversion for which Sodom became noted (Gen. 19, 5). Forbidden by Law (Deut. 23:17); fastened itself upon Israel (I Kings 14: 24) and ancient heathen world (Rom. 1:26f); practiced even in temple (II Kings 23:7).

Solder (sŏ′dêr, **joint),** a metallic substance used to join metals together (Isa. 41:7).

Soldier (See Occupations & Professions, also Warfare)

Solomon (sŏl′ō-mŭn, **peaceable),** the third and last king of united Israel. He built the kingdom to its greatest geographical extension and material prosperity. Though a very intelligent man, Solomon in his later years lost his spiritual discernment and for the sake of political advantage and voluptuous living succumbed to apostasy. He was the second son of David and Bathsheba, the former wife of Uriah the Hittite. When he was born, the Lord loved him, so that the child was also called Jedidiah, "beloved of the Lord" (II Sam. 12:24-25). He did not enter into the history of Israel until in David's advanced old age, when a conspiracy attempted to make Adonijah, the son of David and Haggith, king. Solomon had to deal harshly with Adonijah and his followers when they continued to plot against him. Adonijah and Joab were put to death and Abiathar the priest was expelled from the priesthood. Solomon made Benaiah head of the army and Zadok became priest in Abiathar's stead. David had also told Solomon to kill Shimei, who had cursed David at the time of Absalom's revolt; this was done by Solomon, after placing Shimei on a probation which Shimei violated.

Solomon now began a series of marriage alliances which were his eventual undoing. He married the daughter of the king of Egypt, who had sufficient power to capture Gezer and to present it as a dowry to his daughter. Early in his reign he loved the Lord; he sacrificed at the great high place of Gibeon, where the tabernacle was located; here he offered a thousand burnt offerings. That night at Gibeon the Lord appeared to him in a dream and told him to make a request of Him of whatever he desired. Solomon chose above all else understanding and discernment. God was pleased with this choice and granted his request and also gave him riches and honor.

Solomon was a wise and learned man; it is stated that his wisdom was greater than that of the wise men of the East and of Egypt. He was expert in botany and zoology; he was a writer, credited with 3,000 proverbs and 1,005 songs; he is named the author of the Song of Songs, his greatest song (Song of Solomon 1:1), the book of Proverbs (Prov. 1:1), Ecclesiastes (Eccl. 1:1, 12); and two Psalms (cf. titles, Pss. 72, 127). His fame was widespread and people came from afar to hear him. He made an alliance with Hiram king of Tyre, who had been a friend of David. This relationship was of great advantage to him in a tremendous building program, particularly that of the temple in Jerusalem on Mt. Moriah. He contracted with Hiram for the supply of cedar and cypress wood and arranged for Phoenician builders to supplement the Israelite corvée. A description of the temple is given in some detail (I Kings 6:2-36).

The temple was finished in seven years and Solomon's palace was 13 years in building. When the temple was completed, an impressive dedication service was held. The Ark of the Covenant was brought up from Zion by the priests and was placed in the Holy of Holies. Solomon blessed the people, and made a heartfelt prayer of dedication. Sacrifices were made and fire from heaven consumed them. Finally, a great feast was held. The Lord appeared to Solomon again, as at Gibeon; He had heard his supplication and now promised to establish his heirs as He had promised to do for David, if he and his descendants remained faithful to the Lord.

Solomon had 1400 chariots and 12,000 horsemen (II Chron. 1:14); he also had 4,000 stalls for horses (II Chron. 9:25). Stables for at least 450 horses were found at Megiddo: similar stables were excavated at Gezer, Taanach, Tell el Hesi, and Tell el Far'ah. He also engaged in a profitable trade in chariots and horses between Egypt and the Hittites. His commercial interests led him to the sea; since the Mediterranean coast afforded no good harborage in the area held by him, he made his port at Ezion-geber near Eloth on the Gulf of Akabah of the Red Sea. Again he was assisted by Hiram, who provided Phoenician seamen (II Chron. 8:18).

The rule of Solomon had been quite peaceful, but trouble was brewing. Hadad the Edomite, who as a child had survived a raid by David and had escaped to Egypt, now returned to plague him. In Syria Rezon was made king at Damascus and became an enemy of Israel. In Israel a capable young man, Jeroboam the son of Nebat, was informed by the Prophet Ahijah that he would become ruler of 10 tribes of Israel. Solomon attempted to kill Jeroboam, but Jeroboam took refuge in Egypt until the death of

Solomon. The signs of the impending division of the kingdom were evident; when he died in 930 B.C. and his son Rehoboam became king, the break soon became a reality. A great temporal ruler, possessing every natural advantage, almost inconceivably wealthy in material splendor, learning, and experience, Solomon was nevertheless a disappointment. Though he began so well, the tragedy of his gradual apostasy had more disastrous results than the infamous scandal of his father, who sincerely repented and was a man after the Lord's own heart.

Solomon, Song of, full title is "The song of songs which is Solomon's" (1:1); the last of the five OT poetic books in the English Bible. Also called Canticles, from Latin **Canticum Canticorum** (1:1). Authorship attributed by book itself and by tradition to Solomon. Outline: 1. The mutual admiration of the lovers (1:2-2:7). 2. Growth in love (2:8-3:5). 3. The marriage (3:6-5:1). 4. Longing of the wife for her absent husband (5:2-6:9). 5. The beauty of the Shulammite bride (6:10-8:4). 6. The wonder of love (8:5-8:14). There is great diversity and much overlapping among interpretations of the book. Various views are: 1. Allegorical, 2. Typical, 3. Literal, 4. Dramatic, 5. Erotic-literary, 6. Liturgical, and 7. Didactic-moral. Commonly held interpretation by Jews is that the bridegroom represents God; the Shulammite bride, the Jewish people. Many Christians hold that the bridegroom is Christ; the Shulammite bride, the Church.

Solomon's Pools, three pools near Jerusalem from which water was brought by means of aqueducts to Jerusalem (Eccl. 2:6). They are still in use.

Solomon's Pools, the finest of the three pools south of Jerusalem. © *MPS*

Solomon's Porch, colonnade built by Solomon on E side of the temple area (John 10:23; Acts 3:11; 5:12).

Solomon's Servants, slaves used by Solomon in his temple for menial tasks; their descendants returned from Babylon under Zerubbabel (Ezra 2:55, 58; Neh. 7:57, 60; 11:3).

Solomon's Temple (See Temple).

Son. 1. Any human offspring regardless of sex (Gen. 3:16). 2. Male descendant (II Kings 9:20; Mal. 3:6). 3. Member of a guild or profession (II Kings 2: 3, 5; Neh. 3:8). 4. Spiritual son (I Tim. 1:18). 5. Address to younger man (I Sam. 3:6). 6. Follower (Num. 21:29; Deut. 14:1). 7. Adopted son (Exod. 2: 10). 8. Native (Lam. 4:2). 9. Possessor of a quality (I Sam. 25:17; Luke 10: 6). 10. Used of Christ in a unique sense.

Son of God. The key text for a proper understanding of the words "Son of God," as applied to Jesus, is John 5: 18bff; The words "Son of God" were clearly understood in the Jewish setting as meaning "God," or "equal with God."

This fact doubtless stems from the Hebrew usage in which, when the context did not in any way indicate derivation of being, the words "son of . . ." meant "of the order of . . .," as the sons of the prophets, of the apothecaries, of the goldsmiths, of the singers (Neh. 3:8, 31; 12:28).

With this usage in mind, it is easy to see how Jesus' contemporaries in Palestine took His claim to be the Son of God as a claim to be of the order of God, that is, "equal with God," or "God."

It is suggested (contrary to common opinion) that "Son of God" as applied to Jesus **never** has reference to the derivation, or "eternal generation," of His being, but the words simply designate His eternal, co-equal and consubstantial deity.

The virgin birth is not the ground and reason of the title Son of God, but the supernatural protection of the Holy Spirit is the ground of the sinlessness, holiness, of the virgin birth.

There should be extensive and thorough research into the history of the doctrine of the "eternal generation of the Son." It arose in Christian theology to negate the Arian error that there ever was a time when the Son was not. Origen made "eternal generation" a kind of Platonic subordinationism. His views, and the pre-Nicene views of Eusebius were repudiated by the orthodox church. In Athanasian theology, "eternal generation" is simply a firm denial of Arianism and nothing more. Son of God, as a title of Jesus, refers exclusively to His co-equality, co-eternity, con-substantiality with the Father and the Spirit in the eternal Triune Godhead.

Son of Man. 1. A member of the order of humanity (Ezek. 2:1, 3, 8ff; Dan. 8: 17). 2. Used in a Messianic sense in Dan. 7:13, 14. Jesus applies the term to Himself many times in the Gospels (Matt. 8:20; 9:6; 10:23; 11:19; 12:8, etc.). Sometimes He uses it in connection with His earthly mission, but He also uses it when describing His final triumph as Redeemer and Judge (Matt. 16:27f; 19:28; 24:30; 25:31). He appears to identify Himself with the Son of Man of Dan. 7:13, 14.

Song. Singing played a prominent part in the worship and national life of the Hebrews (Gen. 4:23-24ff). It was not uncommon for the Jews to compose a song celebrating some special victory or religious experience that was significant (Exod. 15). The Psalter has been designated "The Song of Israel" and it contains many kinds of songs. Paul urges believers to sing (Eph. 5:19; Col. 3:16). The book of Revelation speaks often of heavenly singing (Rev. 5:9; 14:3).

Song of Degrees (See Music)

Song of Songs (See Solomon, Song of)

Song of the Three Hebrew Children, an addition to the book of Daniel found in the OT Apocrypha. It is a hymn of praise, and has practically nothing to do with the sufferings of the three young men.

Sons of God, Children of God. The words here discussed may refer metaphorically to any personal creatures of God. In Job 1:6; 2:1; 38:7; angelic beings are designated. In speaking of the inappropriateness of worshiping idols (Acts 17:28) Paul quotes Aratus, "we also are his offspring," thus applying the concept to the entire human race. Compare Luke 3:38; "Adam was the son of God."

The meaning of "sons of God" occurring twice in Genesis 6:1-4 is much disputed. The meaning of "giants" and of "mighty men . . . of renown" is involved in the question.

It is possible here only to summarize the opinion which is presented as preferable: 1. The term "mighty men . . . of renown" explains the word "giants." Neither term indicates anything demonic or mythological, but both should be understood in their simple literal meaning, even as in modern English. (See I Chron. 11:10, 24; Num. 13:33; and see "giant" in Webster's dictionary.) 2. The statement of Genesis 6:4, taken simply and literally, informs the reader that such giants of old, mighty men of renown, were born of normal human marriage. In other words, they were not demonic beings. 3. "Sons of God," here as often elsewhere, simply means human beings with special emphasis upon man's nature as created in the image of God. 4. There is nothing essentially wicked in men selecting beautiful wives. The words translated "of [literally, from among] all which they chose," do not properly suggest any excess or even polygamy, but rather discriminating selection, choice from among those who were eligible. 5. The fact that the context condemns gross universal wickedness (vss. 5-7 and possibly also vs. 3) does not prove that vss. 1, 2, 4 designate anything in itself wicked, or abnormal. In fact "mighty men of renown" is rather likely to point to outstanding good men among evil men.

It is reasonable therefore to hold that "sons of God" in Genesis 6:1-4 is a normal reference to men created in the image of God. The most important Scriptural use of "sons" or "children of God" is that which designates the regenerate as distinct from the unregenerate (Rom. 8:14-19; Col. 3:4; I John 3:2).

Sons of the Prophets, members of prophetic guilds or schools; gathered around great prophets like Samuel and Elijah for common worship, united prayer, religious fellowship, and instruction of the people (I Sam. 10:5, 10; II Kings 4:38, 40). In the times of Elijah and Elisha they lived together at Bethel, Jericho, and Gilgal (II Kings 2:3, 5; 4:38).

Soothsayer, Soothsaying, one claiming or thought to possess the power to foretell future events (Josh. 13:22; Jer. 27:9), interpret dreams (Dan. 4:7), and reveal secrets (Dan. 2:27).

Sop, a morsel of bread, a thin wafer used to dip food from a common platter (John 13:26; Ruth 2:14; Prov. 17:1).

Sopater (sō'pȧ-têr), Christian who accompanied the Apostle Paul on his last journey from Corinth to Jerusalem (Acts 20:4; Rom. 16:21).

Sophereth (sō'fē-rĕth), one of Solomon's servants who returned to Jerusalem with Zerubbabel (Ezra 2:55).

Sorcerer, Sorcery, one who claimed to have supernatural power or knowledge. He often used magic potions and was considered to be in league with evil forces. The practice of sorcery was widespread in ancient times (Exod. 7:11), and was regarded an evil practice for Israel (Isa. 47:9; Mal. 3:5). Practice of the occult arts was prevalent in NT days. Simon of Samaria used sorcery, but was converted under Philip (Acts 8:9-13). Paul and Barnabas found a sorcerer in Paphos (Acts 13:8-11).

Sore (See Diseases)

Sorek (sō'rĕk, **vineyard),** a valley which extends from near Jerusalem to the Mediterranean Sea about eight and one-half miles S of Joppa. It was in this valley that Samson found Delilah (Judg. 16:4). There the Philistines suffered a great defeat at the hands of the Israelites (I Sam. 7:3-14).

Sosipater (See Sopater)

Sosthenes (sŏs'thĕ-nēz). 1. Ruler of the synagogue at Corinth; beaten by crowd in presence of Gallio (Acts 18:17). 2. Christian friend of Paul (I Cor. 1:1). May be same as 1.

Sotai (sō'tī), one of the servants of Solomon who returned from captivity under Zerubbabel (Ezra 2:55; Neh. 7:57).

Soul, the word commonly used in the Bible to designate the non-material ego of man in its ordinary relationships with earthly and physical things, the immortal part of man (Matt. 10:28). It is one of a number of psychological nouns, all designating the same non-material self, but each in a different functional relationship. When the blessed dead in heaven are spoken of as having been put to a martyr's death, they are called "souls" (Rev. 6:9). When there is no reference to their former bodily experience, they are called "spirits" (Heb. 12:23). These functional names of the ego are not used with technical discrimination. They often overlap. The difference between man and beast is not that man has a soul or spirit (Gen. 1:20; 7:15;

Eccl. 3:21), but that man is created in the image of God, whereas the beast is not.

The above remarks assume dichotomy, that is, that there are only two substantive entities which make up the whole man (1) the body, which at death returns to dust, awaiting the resurrection, and (2) the non-material self which, if regenerate, goes to paradise or heaven; if not, to the abode of the wicked dead. There are many, however, who hold to a trichotomous view, arguing that "soul" and "spirit" are two distinct substantive entities, and the body, a third. They cite I Thessalonians 5:23; I Corinthians 15:44; Hebrews 4:12 for evidence.

South, refers primarily to an indefinite area lying between Palestine and Egypt. Abram journeyed toward the South (Gen. 12:9). He went to the South when returning from Egypt (Gen. 13:1). David conquered the South (I Sam. 27:8-12), and so did the Philistines (II Chron. 28:18, etc.). This region extended from the lower end of the Dead Sea SW to Kadesh-Barnea, thence NW along the River of Egypt to the Mediterranean, its boundaries being somewhat indefinite.

Sovereignty of God, the supreme authority of God. He is called "Almighty" (II Cor. 6:18 and nine times in Rev.); "the blessed and only Potentate, the King of Kings and Lord of Lords" (I Tim. 6:15). He "worketh all things after the counsel of his own will" (Eph. 1:11). His sovereignty follows logically from the doctrine that He is God, Creator and Ruler of the universe (Rom. 9:20, 21; See Isa. 45:9. Cf. Ps. 115:3; Dan. 4:35; and many similar passages). God is not subject to any power or any abstract rule or law which could be conceived as superior to or other than Himself.

Sower, Sowing (See Agriculture)

Spain, the westernmost peninsula of Europe. It was not until the time of Augustus that the peninsula was finally pacified and organized. It was rapidly Romanized. Trajan, Hadrian, and Theodosius I, among the emperors, were Spaniards; among men of letters, the two Senecas, Lucan, Columella, Quintilian, Martial, and Prudentius came from Spain. Paul's projected visit (Rom. 15:24) was clearly in line with his evident policy to capture for the Church the nodal points and principal bastions of empire.

Span (See Weights and Measures)

Sparrow (See Birds)

Speckled, mottled in color, a word used to denote varied colors of beasts (Gen. 30:25-43).

Spice, anything having a pleasant odor, usually herbs. The principal Heb. word refers to any aromatic vegetable compound, such as myrrh, cinnamon, cassia and so forth (Exod. 30:23, 24). Spices were often mixed with oil to make them more durable and easily applied (Exod. 30:25; 35:8). Spices played an important part in worship throughout the Near East (Exod. 25:1-6). Spices were used in preparing the body of Jesus for burial (John 19:40). Some were brought to the tomb after Jesus had risen (Mark 16:1).

Spies. The custom of sending secret agents to discover facts about an enemy is age-old. Joseph accused his brothers of being spies (Gen. 42). Joshua sent spies to Jericho (Josh. 6:23). David sent them to see if Saul was with his army at Hachilah (I Sam. 26:1-4). Absalom put secret agents throughout Israel to seize power when notified he had become king (II Sam. 15:7-10). Priests and scribes sent spies to entrap Jesus (Luke 20:20).

Spikenard (See Plants)

Spindle, an implement, 8 to 12 inches long, used in spinning. The rope of carded fiber or wool was attached to one end and the spindle rotated by hand. Thus the thread was twisted (Exod. 35:25; Prov. 31:19).

Spinning (See Occupations and Professions)

Spirit (breath, wind, spirit), one of the Biblical nouns (see list of such nouns, and also the trichotomist view, in the article on Soul) denoting the non-material ego in special relationships. The self is generally called "spirit" in contexts where its bodily, emotional, and intellectual aspects are not prominent, but where the direct relationship of the individual to God is the point of emphasis (Rom. 8:15b, 16).

The same Hebrew and Greek words translated "spirit" can also mean "wind" or "breath" (John 3:8).

Spirit, Holy (See Holy Spirit)

Spirits in Prison. Several opinions: 1. "Quickened by the Spirit" (I Pet. 3:18) refers to Christ's resurrection (Rom. 8:11), not to His disembodied state. 2. The time when Christ, in the Spirit, "went and preached" (vs. 19) was when the longsuffering of God waited in the days of Noah" (vs. 20. Cf. I Pet. 1:11; II Pet. 2:5). 3. The "spirits in prison" (vss. 19, 20) are those who, in the days of Noah, refused Noah's message (II Pet. 2:4) part of Hades. 4. I Peter 4:6 means "This is why the Gospel was preached [of old (cf. Gal. 3:8)] to [those who are now] dead, so that they might be judged as men [now] in the flesh [are to be judged], and might live according to God by the Spirit."

There is nowhere in Scripture any warrant for the doctrine of a chance to hear the Gospel after death.

Spiritual Gifts. Extraordinary gifts of the Spirit given to Christians to equip them for the service of the Church. Several lists of such gifts are given (Rom. 12:6-8; I Cor. 12:4-11, 28-30; cf. Eph. 4:7-12). They may be broadly divided into two categories, those connected with the ministry of the Word of God, and those connected with the ministry of practical service.

Spit, Spittle, Spitting. Spitting in the face indicated gross insult (Num. 12:14; Deut. 25:9). Jesus used spittle in curing blind eyes in Bethsaiada (Mark 8:23) and put spittle upon a mute tongue in Decapolis (Mark 7:33). Jesus was insulted during His trial by being spat upon (Matt. 26:67; Mark 14:65).

Spoil, plunder taken from the enemy in war; pillage; booty; loot. The spoils of war were divided equally between those who went into battle and those who were left behind in camp (Num. 31:27; Josh. 22:8; I Sam. 30:24).

Spokes, rods connecting the rim of a wheel with the hub. In the temple there were ten lavers or basins made of bronze (I Kings 7:27-33), apparently for the washing of sacrifices.

Sponge (See Animals)

Spot. The Heb. word denotes a blemish on the face (S. of Sol. 4:7; Job 11:15). It is also rendered "blemish" (Lev. 24:19f) and "blot" (Prov. 9:7). The Gr. word is used figuratively of a stain of sin (II Pet. 3:14; Jude 23).

Spouse (See Marriage)

Spread, Spreading, to scatter, strew, or disperse, as in "spread abroad" (Isa. 34:3; Matt. 21:8; Mark 1:28).

Sprinkling. Sprinkling of blood, water, and oil formed a very important part of the act of sacrifice (Exod. 24:6-8). When Aaron and his sons were consecrated, some blood was sprinkled on the altar and some on Aaron and his sons and on their garments. In the various offerings—burnt, peace, sin—blood was always sprinkled.

Stable, enclosure in which to lodge and feed animals (Ezek. 25:5).

Stachys, a Roman Christian to whom Paul sent a greeting (Rom. 16:9).

Stacte, a rare ointment used as an ingredient of the sacred perfume to be used in the tabernacle worship (Exod. 30:34, 38), probably myrrh.

Staff, Staves (See Rod)

Stairs, steps (probably of wood) leading to an upper chamber (I Kings 6:8; Mark 14:15; Acts 9:37). Stairs led up to the city of David (Neh. 12:37), to the porch of the gate to Jerusalem (Ezek. 40:6), and to the altar on its east side (Ezek. 43:17).

Stake, a tent-pin or tent-pole (Exod. 27:19; Isa. 33:20; 54:2).

Stall, a place for the care of livestock. One kind was not enclosed, often being a thatched or tented shelter, at times a fattening place (Amos 6:4; Mal. 4:2). Solomon's barns provided stalls for 4,000 horses (II Chron. 9:25, 40,000 in I Kings 4:26).

Star (See Astronomy)

Star of the Wise Men (See Astronomy)

Stature, God does not regard stature in size as a primary asset for leadership (I Sam. 16:7; Isa. 10:33). Jesus grew in stature (Luke 2:52). Zacchaeus was short of stature (Luke 19:3). One's height (stature) cannot be increased by wishing (Matt. 6:27; Luke 12:25).

Steel (See Minerals: Iron)

Stele (stē'lē, **an erect block or shaft).** The custom of erecting stone markers, usually upright narrow slabs, prevailed among ancient Egyptians. They were placed in tombs and public buildings where they honored people of high estate. The Grecian stele was the forerunner of modern gravestones.

Stephanas (stĕf'ȧ-năs, **crown),** a Christian at Corinth, whose household were Paul's first converts in Achaia (I Cor. 1:16; 16:15).

Stephen (stē'vĕn, **crown),** one of the seven deacons appointed to look after the daily distribution to the poor in the early church (Acts 6:1-6). Stephen, described as "a man full of faith and of the Holy Spirit" (Acts 6:5), and six others were elected by the church and consecrated by the apostles in order to insure an equitable distribution.

Stephen taught in the synagogue of the Libertines (i.e., freedmen) and there debated with **Diaspora** Jews

The Greek Orthodox chapel of St. Stephen, at the lower right hand corner of the picture, marks the traditional spot of the first Christian martyr (Acts 7:58, 59).

from Cyrene, Alexandria, Cilicia and Asia.

Acts 7 records Stephen's remarkable **apologia** before the council after he was accused of blasphemy. Stephen's exclamation at the close of his speech is particularly important to a proper understanding of it: "Behold, I see the heavens opened, and the Son of man standing on the right hand of God" (Acts 7:56). This is the only occurrence of the title "Son of Man" in the NT on the lips of anyone other than Jesus Himself. It reveals that **"Stephen grasped and asserted the more-than-Jewish-Messianic sense in which the office and significance of Jesus in religious history were to be understood.** . . . Whereas the Jewish nationalists were holding to the permanence of their national historical privilege, and even the 'Hebrew' Christians gathered around the Apostles were, with all of their new Messianic faith, idealizing the sacred institutions of the past, . . . Stephen saw that the Messiah was on the throne of the Universe. The Son of Man, spoken of by Daniel the prophet, had arrived in the presence of God, and had received from God 'dominion, and glory, and a kingdom, that all peoples, nations, and languages should serve him' " (William Manson, **The Epistle to the Hebrews,** London: Hodder and Stoughton, 1951, pp. 31, 32).

Such radical thinking was too much for the listening Sanhedrin. "They cried out with a loud voice and stopped their ears . . . and cast him out of the city, and stoned him," and the witnesses, whose responsibility it was to cast the first stones (cf. Deut. 17:7), laid their clothes at Saul's feet" (Acts 7:57, 58).

Steward (See Occupations and Professions)

Stocks. 1. The bole of a tree was a stock and was worshiped by apostate Israel (Isa. 44:19; Jer. 2:27; Hos. 4:12). 2. A family (Lev. 25:47; Isa. 40:24; Acts 13:26; Phil. 3:5). 3. An instrument of punishment by which the body was twisted into an unnatural position and thus made to endure excruciating agony (Jer. 20:2, 3). Madmen, posing as prophets, were put on the rack (Jer. 29:26). Paul and Silas were put in stocks to make sure they did not escape from prison in Philippi (Acts 16: 24).

Stoicism (stō'ĭ-sĭzm), school of philosophy founded by the Greek Zeno; system of pantheistic monism; regarded virtue as highest good; ethics were austere; unmoved by pleasure or pain (Acts 17:18).

Stone, abundant in Palestine; used for building (I Kings 5:17; Amos 5:11), landmarks (Josh. 15:6), walls of city, altars, memorials, weapons (I Sam. 17: 40), idols (Isa. 57:3-7). Often used figuratively (Exod. 15:5, 16; I Sam. 25: 37; Ezek. 11:19; Dan. 2:34; Matt. 21: 42).

Stones, Precious (See Minerals)

Stoning, the ordinary form of capital punishment prescribed by Hebrew law. Stoning was the penalty for blasphemy (Lev. 24:16), idolatry (Deut. 13:6-10), desecration of the sabbath (Num. 15: 32-36), human sacrifice (Lev. 20:2), and occultism (Lev. 20:27). Achan and his family were stoned (Josh. 7:16-26). Jesus rebuked Jerusalem for stoning the prophets (Matt. 23:37; Luke 13: 34). Stephen was stoned (Acts 7:58, 59). The execution took place outside the city (Lev. 24:14; I Kings 21:10, 13; Acts 7:58).

Stool, a three or four-legged seat. The Shunammite woman put one in Elisha's room (II Kings 4:10). A stool of peculiar form was used in Egypt for women in childbirth (Exod. 1:16).

Store Cities, supply depots for provisions and arms (I Kings 9:15-19; II Chron. 8:4-6).

Storehouse, a place for keeping treasures, supplies, and equipment (Deut. 28:8; Mal. 3:10). David built a storehouse and thus prepared an abundant supply of materials for the temple (I Chron. 29:16). The temple storehouse was a vital part of equipment needed in Hebrew worship (II Chron. 31:10).

Stork (See Birds)

Stove, in Palestine, usually made of clay. Some were small portable fireplaces, burning charcoal. Others were built outside the house and were heated with dry sticks, grass, and even dung. The hearth mentioned in Jer. 36: 22 was a bronze heater. Only the well-to-do could afford a brazier.

Straight Street, a name given to any route extending in a straight course across a city. Most streets were narrow and crooked. The avenue across Damascus, 100 feet wide with a walk along each side, was called Straight (Acts 9:11).

Strakes, Archaic word for "streaks" (Gen. 30:37; Lev. 14:37).

Stranger. 1. Foreigner who put himself under protection of Israel and Israel's God, who submitted to many requirements of the law of Israel, and who was therefore given certain privileges (Exod. 20:10; 22:21). 2. Foreigner who did not have cultus-fellowship with Israel (Ezek. 44:7-9). 3. People entirely different from, or even hostile to, Israel (Isa. 1:7; Ezek. 11:9).

Strangle, to deprive of life by choking, and so without bloodshed. Israelites were forbidden to eat flesh from strangled animals because it contained the blood (Lev. 17:12). At the Jerusalem council even Jewish Christians were forbidden to eat such meat, lest they offend the Jews (Acts 15:20).

Stream of Egypt (See River of Egypt)

Striker, a pugnacious person (I Tim. 3:3; Titus 1:7).

Stringed Instruments (See Music)

Stripes. Scourging by lashing was a common form of punishment in ancient times. The Jewish law authorized it for certain ecclesiastical offenses (Deut. 25:2, 3). Among the Jews a scourge consisting of three thongs was employed, and the number of stripes varied from a few up to 39. Roman scourges had pieces of metal or bones attached to the lashes. The victim was stripped to the waist and bound in a stooping position. The body was horribly lacerated so that often even the entrails were exposed.

Strong Drink (See Wine)

Stubble, stalks of grain left after reaping. Usually about half of the stem remained in the field (Exod. 5:10-14). The word became a simile for wayward Israel (Isa. 47:14).

Stumbling Block, anything that causes a person to trip or fall. Figuratively it means a cause of material or spiritual ruin. Israel's iniquity and idolatry were a stumbling block to her (Ezek. 14:3, 4; Jer. 18:15). Paul urged Christians not to put a stumbling block in the way of a brother (Rom. 14:13; I Cor. 8:9). Jesus, as preached by Paul (Rom. 9:32), was a stumbling block to the Jews (I Cor. 1:23).

Suah (sū'à), descendant of Asher (I Chron. 7:36).

Suburb, lands near cities used for pasturage of animals (Josh. 21:2, 42; Ezek. 45:2).

Succoth (sŭk'ŏth, **booths** or **huts).** 1. A place E of the Jordan at which Jacob built a house for himself and booths for his animals after his return from Mesopotamia (Judg. 8:4, 5; Gen. 32:22). It was in the valley of the Jordan, near Zarethan (I Kings 7:46), and was assigned to the Gadites (Josh. 13:27). Gideon punished the town severely for its refusal to assist him (Judg. 8:5-16). 2. The first station of the Hebrews on leaving Rameses (Exod. 12:37; 13:20; Num. 33:5).

Succoth Benoth (sŭk'ŏth bē'nŏth), a pagan god whose image was worshiped in Samaria after Assyria had captured it and put foreign rulers over it (II King 17:24-30).

Suchathites (sū'kăth-īts), a native or inhabitant of Sucah or Socah (I Chron. 2:55); site is unknown.

Suetonius (swē-tō'nĭ-ŭs), Roman writer (c. A.D. 69-140), famous for his **Lives of the Caesars.**

Sukkiim (sŭk'ĭ-ĭm), a tribe of people whose warriors joined Shishak of Egypt when he invaded Judah. Identity uncertain.

Sukkoth (See Feasts)

Sulphur (See Minerals)

Sumer (sū'mêr), one of the two political divisions, Sumer and Akkad, originally comprising Babylonia.

Sun. The beneficent nature of the sun was known among the Hebrews. Sun, moon and stars determine times and seasons (Gen. 1:14; Jer. 31:35; Job 38:33; Ps. 119:91). Night and day were caused by the sun (Gen. 1:5). Since the location of the sun determined the extent of heat and light, the day was divided accordingly. Mid-morning was when the sun grew hot (I Sam. 11:9); noon was when it was brightest (Gen. 43:16); beyond noon the heat waned and it was the cool of the day (Gen. 3:8). The sun determined directions. The rising of the sun became E (Isa. 45:6); the going down of the sun (Ps. 50:1) became W. The left hand or darker quarter was N, and the right hand or brighter quarter S (Gen. 13:14; Job 37:17; Ezek. 40:24). Poetic fancies arose about the sun. It is like a bridegroom (Ps. 19:4, 5), stands in his house (Hab. 3:11), is ever watchful (Ps. 19;6b), dependable (Ps. 72:5), and tells of God's continuing care (Ps. 84:11). The worship of the sun has found varied forms as far apart as the cult of Apollo in Greece and the religion of the Mayas and Incas in the American continent. Egypt, however, in the ancient world, was its special home.

The beautiful psalm to the sun written by the pharaoh bears striking resemblance to Psalm 104 of the Hebrew Psalter, and throws vivid light on a remarkable religious leader, and the most interesting religious movement in Egyptian history. (See Chapter XVIII in J. H. Breasted, **op. cit.)**

Sunday, first day of the week, commemorating the resurrection of Jesus (John 20:1-25) and the Day of Pentecost (Acts 2:1-41). For a time after the ascension of Jesus the Christians met on 7th and 1st days of the week, but as the Hebrew Christian churches declined in influence, the tendency to observe the Hebrew sabbath slowly passed. The disciples at Troas worshiped on the first day (Acts 20:7). Paul admonished the Corinthians to lay by in store as God had prospered them, doing it week by week on the first day (I Cor. 16:2). The term "Lord's Day" occurs in Rev. 1:10.

Superscription. 1. The wording on coins (Matt. 22:20; Mark 12:16; Luke 20:24). 2. The words painted on a board which was attached to the cross (Mark 15:26; Luke 23:38). The Roman custom was to have such a board, naming the crime of which the condemned man was accused, carried before him to the place of execution (John 19:19, 20; Matt. 27:37).

Superstitious (sū'pêr-stĭsh'ŭs). Used in Acts 17:22. Paul calls the Athenians **"very religious."** The Greek word is neutral and applies to any religion, good or bad.

Suph, Suphah (sōōf). KJV has "the Red Sea" for both names. Suph (Deut. 1:1 ASV, RSV) is the place in front of which Moses repeated the law to Israel. Suphah (Num. 21:14 ASV, RSV) is also E of Jordan. Neither can be identified.

Supper, Lord's (See Lord's Supper)

Supplication (See Prayer)

Surety, Suretyship (shōōr'tē, shōōr'ĕ-tē-shĭp). 1. One who makes himself responsible for the obligations of another is a surety (Prov. 6:1; 11:15; 17:18; 20:16). 2. Guarantee; security for payment (Gen. 44:32).

Surfeiting (sûr'fĕt-ĭng, **a drinking-bout),** over-indulgence of food or drink; intoxication; a drunken headache (Luke 21:34). **Dissipation** is a good rendering (RSV).

Susa (See Shushan)

Susanchites (sū-săn'kīts), colonists planted in Samaria by the Assyrians when they deported the Israelites (Ezra 4:9, 10),

Susanna (sū-zăn'ȧ, **lily).** One of the women who went with Jesus and the Twelve on their missionary journeys, and provided for them out of their means (Luke 8:1-3).

Susi (sū'sī), a Manassite, father of Gaddi, one of the 12 men sent to spy out the land (Num. 13:11).

Swaddling Band, bands of cloth in which a new born baby was wrapped. The child was placed diagonally on a square piece of cloth which was folded over the infant's feet and sides. Around this bundle swaddling bands were wound. Mary herself wrapped the baby Jesus in swaddling bands (Luke 2:7, 12). Used figuratively in Job 38:9.

Swallow (See Birds)

Swan (See Birds)

Swear (See Oath)

Sweat. After the Fall, God tells Adam that he will now have to work hard enough to cause sweat to get his food (Gen. 3:19). Priests in the future temple are not to wear anything that causes sweat (Ezek. 44:18). During Christ's agony in Gethsemane "his sweat became as it were great drops of blood . . ." (Luke 22:44).

Sweat, Bloody, a physical manifestation of the agony of Jesus in Gethsemane (Luke 22:44). Since Luke is believed to have been a physician, his language has been subjected to closest scrutiny. He does not say that the sweat became blood, but that it became "as it were" or "like" great drops of blood.

Swelling (swĕl'ĭng), usually translated "pride," but in Psalm 46:3 refers to the tumult of a stormy sea. Other references (Jer. 12:5; 49:19; 50:44).

Swine (See Animals)

Sycamine (See Plants)

Sycamore, Sycomore (See Plants)

Sychar (sī'kȧr), a village of Samaria located near Jacob's well, where Jesus met the Samaritan woman (John 4:5). It was situated on the main road that led from Jerusalem through Samaria to Galilee. Probably close to Shechem (with which it has often been incorrectly identified) and on the eastern slope of Mount Ebal. The site which by continuous tradition has been iden-

The village of Sychar, in Samaria, near Jacob's Well. In the background is Mt. Gerizim. © MPS

tified with Jacob's well lies about half a mile to the S. In Jesus' day Sychar was only a small village.

Sychem (See Shechem)

Syene (sī-ē'nē), an Egyptian city, identified as present-day Aswan, at the First Cataract of the Nile, on the E bank of the river, opposite the island of Elephantine. During much of the history of Egypt this area marked the effective southern boundary of Egypt. The name Syene appears but twice in the OT (Ezek. 29:10; 30:16), both times in prophecies against Egypt.

Symbol, that which stands for or represents something else; a visible sign or representation of an idea or quality or of another object. Symbolism in its religious application means that an object, animal, action, form or words or whatever else is involved has a deeper spiritual meaning than a simple literal interpretation might suggest. A symbol, unlike a type, is usually not prefigurative but rather represents something which already exists. The Passover, however, was both symbolical and typical, and the symbolic actions of the OT prophets were often predictive in nature.

It is evident that certain numbers in the Bible have symbolical significance. The following are particularly important: **Seven,** probably the most important number in Scripture (it occurs about 600 times), has been called the sacred number **par excellence.** In the literature of ancient Babylonia it is the number of totality or completeness. The Book of Revelation makes frequent use of the number seven. There are seven churches (1:4), spirits (1:4), candlesticks (1:12, 13), stars (1:16), lamps (4:5), seals (5:1; 8:1), horns and eyes (5:6), trumpets (8:2), thunders (10:3), heads of the great dragon (12:3), angels with plagues (15:1), vials (15:7), heads of the beast (13:1), mountains (17:9) and kings (17:10). **Four** in the Bible seems to stand for completeness, especially in relation to range or extent. Thus there are four winds (Jer. 49:36; Ezek. 37:9), four directions, four corners of a house (Job 1:19), of the land of Israel (Ezek. 7:2) and of the whole earth (Isa. 11:12). **Ten,** since it is the basis of the decimal system, is also a significant number. In the Bible it is often a round number of indefinite magnitude. **Twelve** seems to be the mystical number of the people of God. The twelve tribes, twelve apostles, and the twelve thousand times twelve thousand sealed in the Book of Revelation bear out this symbolical meaning. **Forty** is the round number for a generation and also appears to be symbolical of a period of judgment (cf. the forty days of the flood, the forty years of wilderness wandering, and the forty days and nights of Jesus' temptation).

Much care must be taken in seeking to assign symbolic meanings to colors. The following are suggestions: **White,** the color of light, is a symbol of purity, holiness and righteousness (Rev. 7:14). **Blue** is diffcult, but perhaps Terry is right when he says that "blue, as the color of the heaven, reflected in the sea, would naturally suggest that which is heavenly, holy and divine" **(op. cit.,** p. 393). **Scarlet,** since it was most often the dress of kings, is regarded as symbolic of royalty. **Black,** the opposite of white, would naturally be associated with evil, such as famine (Rev. 6:5, 6) or mourning (Jer. 14:2). **Red** is symbolic of bloodshed and war (Rev. 6:4; 12:3).

Symbolic Actions. Not only objects, names, numbers and colors are symbolic in Scripture, but actions too may be symbolic. Symbolic actions often are prefigurative and are especially associated with the Old Testament prophets. Such symbolical actions by the prophets are found as early as Samuel's day. When Saul took hold of Samuel's robe and tore it, this was understood by Samuel to be symbolic of the tearing away of Saul's kingdom (I Sam. 15:27, 28). By tearing his garment into 12 pieces Ahijah symbolized the break-up of the kingdom of Solomon (I Kings 11:29, 30; cf. also II Kings 13:14-19; 22:11).

Jesus also used symbolical actions to convey spiritual truth. While all the Gospels attest to our Lord's symbolical actions, the author of the fourth Gospel places special stress on them. He calls Jesus' miracles signs. When in the Fourth Gospel Jesus multiplies the loaves, this is symbolic of the fact that He is Himself the Bread of Life (John 6). The blind man healed is symbolic of Christ as the Light of the World (John 9), and Lazarus raised from the dead is symbolic of Jesus as the Resurrection and the Life (John 11).

Symeon (See Simeon)

Artist's restoration of the synagogue at Capernaum. UANT

Synagogue (sĭn′ȧ-gŏg, **place of assembly),** Jewish institution for the reading and exposition of the OT, which originated perhaps during the Babylonian exile (Ezra 8:15; Neh. 8:2; 9:1). It means both a community of persons organized for a religious purpose, and also the building in which gatherings for such purposes were held (Matt. 4: 23). Functions were: worship and instruction, provide place where adults and children could learn the Law, social center—for the discussion of community problems, funerals, legal transactions. There were synagogues all over the Mediterranean world. Synagogues had a reading platform with lectern, case for sacred books, seats for congregation, lamps and trumpets, and officers who were responsible for the services. The NT has many references to the synagogue. Services included prayer, reading of the Scriptures, sermon, and benediction. Synagogue officials were: ruler of the synagogue, responsible for the building, general oversight of the public worship, appointing of persons to read the Scriptures, pray, and address the congregation; the minister or attendant, who took care of the building, furniture, and rolls of Scripture (Luke 4:20). The congregation was divided, the men on one side and the women on the other. The more prominent members took the front seats. No single individual was appointed to do the preaching. Any competent worshiper might be invited by the ruler to bring the sermon for the day (Luke 4:16, 17; Acts 13:15). The form of worship of the synagogue was adopted by the Christian Church.

An artist's representation of a service in a synagogue of Bible times. The reader is reading from a scroll of the Scriptures. KC © FC

Synagogue, Men of the Great, a council of 120 men, supposedly originating at the time of Ezra, to which Jewish tradition attributed the origination and authoritative promulgation of many ordinances and regulations. Among the many functions ascribed to them were the completion of the collection of sacred books by the addition of Ezekiel, Daniel, Esther and the Twelve, minor alterations of the OT text, the authorization of the observance of the Feast of Purim and the days on which it was to be kept, and the setting up of the curriculum of study in the three main branches of Jewish learning.

Synoptic Problem (See Gospels)

Syntiche, Syntyche (sĭn'tĭ-chē, **fortunate),** a Christian woman at Philippi who was having a disagreement with a fellow lady Christian, Euodias. Paul, in his letter to that church, entreats these two women to "agree in the Lord" (Phil. 4:2).

Syracuse (sĭr'ȧ-kūs), a town on the E coast of Sicily. Syracuse was the most important and prosperous Greek city on the island. The Alexandrian ship in which Paul sailed from Malta to Puteoli put in at Syracuse for three days (Acts 28:12). Whether or not Paul went ashore during this time is not stated in the Acts account.

Syria (sĭr'ĭ-ȧ), abbreviation of "Assyria" or possibly from the Babylonian "Suri"; "Aram" in OT, after the Aramaeans who occupied the area in the 12th cent. B.C.; boundaries varied over the centuries, but generally included area S of Taurus Mts., N of Galilee and Bashan, W of Arabian desert, and E of the Mediterranean; chief cities: Damascus, Antioch, Byblos, Aleppo, Palmyra, and Carchemish; conquered by David (II Sam. 10:6-19), but became independent under Solomon (I Kings 11:23-25); often in conflict with Jews (I Kings 15:18-20; 20; 22; II Kings 6:8-33; 7; 9:14, 15; 10:32, 33; 13); Romans made it a province in 64 B.C.

Syria played a prominent part in the early Church. It was at Antioch that the followers of Jesus were first called Christians (Acts 11:26). Paul was converted in Syria on the road to Damascus (Acts 9:1-9) and was commissioned with Barnabas by the Antioch church to take the Gospel to the Gentiles (Acts 13:1-3).

Syria Maachah (See Maachah)

Syriac, the Syrian tongue or language, KJV uses "Aramaic" or the "Aramean language" (II Kings 18:26; Ezra 4:7; Isa. 36:11; Dan. 2:4). Syriac is Eastern Aramaic and the literary language of the Christian Syrians.

Syriac Versions (See Texts and Versions)

Syrian (sĭr'ĭ-ăn). 1. The language of Syria; Aramaic (II Kings 18:26; Ezra 4:7; Isa. 36:11; Dan. 2:4 KJV, Syriac). 2. The people of Syria (II Sam 8:5, etc.); in earlier times, broadly the Arameans (Gen. 25:20; 28:5; Deut. 26:5).

Syrophoenician (sī'rō-fē-nĭsh'ăn, sĭr'ō-), an inhabitant of the region near Tyre and Sidon, modern Lebanon. A Greek-speaking Canaanite woman, native of this region, though a Gentile, by persistence and humility won from Jesus healing for her daughter (Mark 7:26; cf. Matt. 5:22).

Syrtis (sûr'tĭs). The Syrtes (pl.) were the banks of quicksand off the coast of Libya (Acts 17:17).

Taanach (tā'ȧ-năk), a fortified city of Canaan, 5 miles SE of Megiddo, whose king was defeated by Joshua (Judg. 1: 27; 5:19; Josh. 12:21; 17:11; I Chron. 7:29).

Taanath-Shiloth (tā'ȧ-năth-shī'lō, **approach to Shiloh),** a town on the NE border of the heritage of Ephraim (Josh. 11:6). It was about ten miles E of Shechem and the same distance W of the Jordan River.

Tabbaoth (tă-bā'ŏth, **rings),** a family of temple servants who returned with Zerubbabel (Ezra 2:43; Neh. 7:46).

Tabbath (tăb'ăth), a place named in tracing the route of flight of the Midianites and their allies after Gideon's 300 defeated them (Judg. 7:22).

Tabeal, Tabeel (tā'bē-ăl, tā'bē-ĕl). 1. Father of one of the allied kings whom Rezin of Damascus and Pekah of Israel attempted to make their puppet king of Israel (Isa. 7:6 KJV Tabeal; ASV, RSV Tabeel). 2. An official in Samaria who complained to Artaxerxes about the Jews (Ezra 4:7, all versions Tabeel).

Taberah (tăb'ĕ-rȧ, **burning),** a place in the wilderness where the fire of the Lord burned some complainers (Num. 11:1-3; Deut. 9:22). Probably three days' journey from Sinai (Num. 10: 33); site unidentified.

Tabernacle (tăb'ĕr-năk-l, **tent),** portable sanctuary that served as a place of worship for the Israelites from the time of the wilderness wanderings until the building of the temple by Solomon; typified God dwelling with His people (Exod. 25:8); variously called (Exod. 25:9; 26:9; 33:7; 39:32; I Chron. 6:48; 9:23; 17:5; II Chron. 24:6); described in Exod. 25:10-27:19, 35-38; tabernacle stood in a court 150 feet long and 75 feet wide, the sides of which were covered with linen curtains, which were fastened to 60 supporting pillars of bronze. Within the court were the great altar of burnt offering (Exod. 27: 1-8) and the bronze laver used by the priests for ritual ablutions (Exod. 30: 17-21).

The tabernacle, which stood at the W end of the court, was a wooden structure 45 by 15 feet, divided by a heavy veil into two parts, a holy place and a most holy place. This was covered on the inside with embroidered linen tapestry and on the outside with double blankets of skin. The holy place contained the table of showbread, a golden candlestick, and the altar of incense. The most holy place, or Holy of Holies, had in it only the ark of covenant, a small box-like structure of wood covered with gold in which there were the tablets of the law, a pot of manna, and Aaron's rod (Exod. 25:16, 22; Heb. 9:4). The tabernacle was set up at Sinai the beginning of the second year after leaving Egypt (Exod. 40:2, 17); for 35 years it stood at Kadesh, and always preceded the Israelites when on the march (Num. 10:33-36). Later it was stationed at Gilgal (Josh. 4:19), Shiloh (Josh. 18:1), Nob (I Sam. 21:1), Gibeon (I Chron. 16:39; 21:29). David moved it to Jerusalem. It was superseded by the building of the temple. The old tabernacle was but a shadow of the true ideal (Heb. 8:5; 10:1).

Tabitha (tăb'ĭ-thȧ, **a gazelle),** the name of a Christian woman disciple who lived in Joppa and made clothing to give to poor widows. When she died, Peter was summoned and he raised her from death (Acts 9:36-43).

Table. 1. Table for food (Judg. 1:7; I Kings 2:7). 2. Lord's table — Lord's Supper (I Cor. 10:21). 3. "Serving tables" (Acts 6:2) refers to distribution of food, etc., to the Christian poor. 4. Tabernacle and Temple were provided with various tables. 5. Stone tablets on which Law was written (Exod. 24:12). 6. Tables were also tablets on which messages were written (Luke 1:63).

Table of Shewbread (See Tabernacle)

Tables of the Law, stone tablets on which Moses wrote the ten commandments (Exod. 24:3, 4a, 12; 31:18; Deut. 4:13; 5:22). When Moses came down from the mountain and saw the worship of the golden calf, he threw down the tablets, breaking them (Exod. 32: 15, 19; Deut. 9:9-17; 10:1-5). At God's command, Moses again went up the mountain with two new tablets, and wrote the law anew (Exod. 34:1-4, 27-29). Though God said "I will write," He also said to Moses, "Write these words." Moses put these tablets in the ark (Deut. 10:5) where they were in the time of Solomon (I Kings 8:9=

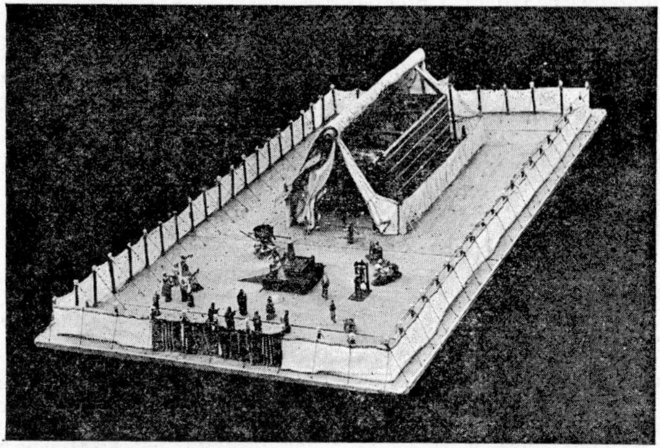

The Tabernacle in the wilderness as pictured in the model by Dr. Conrad Schick. © *MPS*

II Chron. 5:10). They are referred to in the NT (II Cor. 3:3; Heb. 9:4).

Tablet (See Dress)

Tabor (ta'bêr). 1. A mountain in Galilee where the borders of Issachar, Zebulun and Naphtali meet (Josh. 19:22). On its slopes Barak gathered 10,000 soldiers (Judg. 4:6, 12, 14; 5:18) to fight against Sisera and the Canaanite army at Megiddo. Here Zeba and Zalmunna, kings of Midian, killed Gideon's brothers (8:18, 19). Mt. Tabor is E of Nazareth, SW of the Sea of Galilee, NE of the plain of Esdraelon. 2. The plain of Tabor, or (ASV, RSV) oak of Tabor (I Sam. 10:3). Samuel told Saul he would meet men bearing gifts here, as a sign of God's favor (9:5-10:10). Probably in Benjamin. 3. A Levite city in Zebulun (I Chron. 6:77).

Tabret (See Musical Instruments)

Tabrimmon, Tabrimon (tăb-rĭm'ŏn), father of Benhadad, king of Syria (I Kings 15:18). Tabrimon in KJV.

Tache (tăch), a clasp of gold, to couple the cloth curtains of the tabernacle (Exod. 26:6; 36:13); of bronze, to couple the goat's hair curtains (26:11; 36:18).

Tachmonite, Tachemonite (tăk'mō-nīt), the family of David's chief captain (II Sam. 23:8) who sat in the gate; the same as Jashobeam, a Hachmonite (I Chron. 11:11).

Tackling, refers either to the hawsers (Isa. 33:23) or furniture (Acts 27:19) of a ship.

Tadmor (tăd'môr), a city in the desert NE of Damascus. In patriarchal times a much-traveled road ran through it from Damascus N to Haran. When Israel was in Egypt, a caravan route already ran eastward from Qatna to the Euphrates. Solomon either built a new city close by, or rebuilt the old, after his conquest of Hamath-zobah (II Chron. 8:4). The context (8:3-6) mentions Solomon's building projects in various parts of his dominion. In the parallel passage in I Kings 9:18 KJV, Tadmor is spoken of as "in the wilderness, in the land." ASV has Tamar, RSV "Tamir in the wilderness, in the land of Judah." Later called Palmyra and rich trade center.

Tahan, Tahanite (tā'hăn-īt). 1. A son of Ephraim and founder of a tribal family (Num. 26:35). 2. A descendant of the same family (I Chron. 7:25).

Tahapanes, Tahpanhes (tȧ-hăp'ȧ-nēz), a fortress city at the eastern edge of the Nile Delta, on the eastern border of Egypt. Jeremiah saw it as powerful enough to break "the crown" of Judah. Hither Jews fled after the fall of Jerusalem (Jer. 2:16 KJV Tahapanes, ASV, RSV Tahpanhes; 43:1-7). Here Jeremiah (43:8-11; 44:1; 46:14) prophesied its destruction; Ezekiel also (30:18, Tehaphnehes).

Tahash (tā'hăsh), a son of Reumah and Nahor, Abraham's brother (Gen. 22:24 KJV, Thahash).

Tahath (tā'hăth, **below**). 1. A Kohathite Levite, father of Uriel (I Chron. 6: 24, 37). 2. Son of Bered, grandson of Shuthelah the son of Ephraim (I Chron. 7:20). 3. Also the 24th station of Israel from Egypt, and the 11th from Sinai (Num. 33:26, 27).

Tahpenes (tȧ'pēn-ēz), Egyptian queen who brought up Genubath, the son of her sister and of Hadad, the Edomite adversary of David and Solomon (I Kings 11:14-22).

Tahrea (tȧ'rē-ȧ), a grandson of Mephibosheth, a descendant of Saul through Jonathan (I Chron. 9:41; Tarea in 8: 35).

Tahtim-Hodshi (tȧ'tĭm-hŏd'shī), a Hittite town at the northern limit of David's census (II Sam. 24:22).

Tale, a sigh (Ps. 90:9); number (Exod. 5:8, 18); count (I Chron. 9:28); slander (Ezek. 22:9); idle talk (Luke 24: 11).

Talebearing, slander, forbidden in the law (Lev. 19:16, see RSV); reproved in Proverbs 11:13; 20:9, RSV **gossiping).** A word meaning "whisperer" (so ASV, RSV) is used in Proverbs 18:8; 26:20, 22. (See also I Tim. 5:13.)

Talitha Cumi (tă-lĕ'thȧ kōō'mē), the Aramaic words which Jesus spoke when He raised Jairus' 12-year-old daughter from death (Mark 5:41) meaning "Damsel, arise."

Talmai (tăl'mī, -mā-ī,). 1. A son of Anak in Hebron (Num. 13:22; Josh. 15:14; Judg. 1:10). 2. A king of Geshur, whose daughter Maacah was one of David's wives and Absalom's mother (II Sam. 3:3; 13:37; I Chron. 3:2).

Talmon (tăl'mŏn), a Levite porter and founder of a tribal family, members of which returned with Zerubbabel (I Chron. 9:17; Ezra 2:42; Neh. 7:45; 11: 19; 12:25).

Talmud (tăl'mŭd), a collection of Jewish writings of the early Christian centuries. There is a Palestinian Talmud, and a later, more authoritative, much longer Babylonian Talmud.

Tamah (tā'mȧ), temple servant (Neh. 7:55; Ezra 2:53) whose family returned from exile with Zerubbabel. ASV, RSV Temah.

Tamar (tā'mêr, **palm tree).** 1. The wife of Er; then Levirate wife of Onan; by whom, after the death of Onan, her father-in-law Judah had twin sons, Perez and Zerah (Gen. 38). She is remembered in Ruth 4:12, in the genealogy in I Chronicles 2:4, and her name is recorded as that of one of the women in the ancestral line of Jesus (Matt. 1:3 KJV Thamar). 2. A daughter of David and sister of Absalom, whom her half-brother Amon violated (II Sam. 13:1-33). 3. The daughter of Absalom (II Sam. 14:27). 4. A place at the SE corner of the boundary of the future Holy Land (Ezek. 47:18, 19; 48:28). 5. A city in Syria, more commonly known as Tadmor, later Palmyra. See Tadmor.

Tamir (See Tadmor)

Tammuz (tăm'ŭz), a fertility god widely worshiped in Mesopotamia, Syria, and Palestine; equivalent to Osiris in Egypt and Adonis of the Greeks. His consort was the goddess Ishtar (Astarte or Ashtoreth). The only mention of him in the Bible occurs in connection with the custom of women mourning for him (Ezek. 8:14), which, being observed at the very gate of the temple of the true God, seemed to the prophet one of the most abominable idolatries.

Tanach (See Taanach)

Tanhumeth (tăn-hū'mĕth), a Netophathite (II Kings 25:23; Jer. 40:8).

Tanis (See Zoar)

Tanner, Tanning (See Occupations and Professions)

Taphath (tā'făth), Solomon's daughter, wife of the son of Abinadab (I Kings 4:11).

Tappuah (tă-pū'ȧ). 1. A city whose king Joshua conquered (Josh. 12:17) in the lowland of Judah (15:34). 2. A town on the boundary of Ephraim (Josh. 16:8; 17:8 RSV). Its spring, Entappuah, was on the boundary of Manasseh (17:7). Modern Sheikh Abū Zarad. 3. One of the sons or descendants of Hebron (I Chron. 2:43).

Tarah (tā'rȧ), a stage in Israel's march between Tahath and Mithcah (Num. 33:27, 28 ASV, RSV Terah).

Taralah (tăr'ȧ-lȧ), a city of Benjamin between Irpeel and Zelah (Josh. 18: 27).

Tarea (tā'rē-ȧ), a descendant of King Saul (I Chron. 8:35), Tahrea in I Chron. 9:41.

Tares (See Plants)

Tarpelites (tȧr'pĕl-īts), the people transported into Samaria as colonists (Ezra 4:10). KJV has "Asnapper." King was probably Esar-haddon of Assyria (Ezra 4:2) or a general under him.

Tarshish (tȧr'shĭsh). 1. A son of Javan,

great-grandson of Noah (Gen. 10:4). 2. A place, presumably in the western Mediterranean region, conjecturally identified by many with Tartessus, an ancient city located on the Atlantic coast of Spain but long lost. Jonah fled to it (Jonah 1:3). 3. "Ships of Tarshish" seems to refer to large ships of the kind and size that were used in the Tarshish trade (I Kings 10:22). 4. A great-grandson of Benjamin (I Chron. 7:10). 5. One of the seven princes of Persia and Media with Xerxes (Esth. 1:14).

Tarsus (tär′sŭs), a city of Cilicia, the capital of the province from A.D. 72, and the birthplace and early residence of the Apostle Paul (Acts 21:39). The city stood on the Cilician plain, a little above sea-level, and some ten miles inland. Tarsus was an ancient city, the seat of a provincial governor when Persia ruled, and, in the days of the Greek Syrian kings, the center of a lumbering and linen industry. Acts 18:3 probably refers to an associated skill, the manufacture of a rough goat-hair cloth.

Tarsus stood, like Alexandria, at a confluence of East and West. The wisdom of the Greeks and the world-order of Rome, mingled with the good and ill of Oriental mysticism, were deep in its consciousness. A keen-minded Jew, born and bred at Tarsus, would draw the best from more than one world as Paul probably did.

Tartak (tär′tăk), a god worshiped by the Avvites, a people of Assyria who were colonists in Samaria (II Kings 17:31).

Tartan (tär′tăn), a commander-in-chief of the Assyrian army (Isa. 20:1; II Kings 18:17). A title, not a proper name.

Taskmasters (See Occupations & Professions)

Tattenai, Tatnai (tăt′ē-nī, tăt′nī), a Persian governor ordered to assist the Jews in rebuilding the temple (Ezra 5:3, 6; 6:6, 13).

Tavern (See Inn)

Taverns, Three, the place where the Christian brethren of Rome met Paul (Acts 28:15), near or at Appii Forum, about 33 miles SE of Rome.

Taxes, charges imposed by governments, either political or ecclesiastical, upon the persons or the properties of their members or subjects. Hebrews did not pay taxes during nomadic period. Under the theocracy of Israel every man paid a half shekel for the support of tabernacle worship (Exod. 30:13; 38:25, 26). Under the kings heavy taxes were imposed, so that when Solomon died the N tribes rebelled (I Kings 12). The Ptolemies, Seleucidae, and the Romans farmed out the taxes (Matt. 17:24; 22:17).

Teacher, Teaching (See Occupations & Professions, School, Synagogue)

Tebah (tē′bȧ), a nephew of Abraham, born to Nahor by his concubine Reumah (Gen. 22:24).

Tebaliah (tēb-ȧ-lī′ȧ), a Merarite Levite (I Chron. 26:11).

Tebeth (See Calendar)

Teeth. Isaiah 41:15 tells of "a sharp threshing instrument having teeth," literally "possessor of sharp edges," a figure referring to Israel as God's instrument of judgment upon the nations. In Psalm 58:6 "great teeth," literally "biters," could refer either to teeth or jaws. In Proverbs 30:14 "jaw teeth as knives" is clearly figurative. In none of the preceding instances is the ordinary word for tooth used. Some of the more frequent uses of the common words are illustrated in the following passages: Gen. 49:12; Exod. 21:24; Job 16:9; Matt. 8:12; Lam. 2:16; Acts 7:54.

Tehinnah (tē-hĭn′ȧ, **entreaty),** son of Eshton of Judah, (I Chron. 4:12).

Teil Tree (See Plants)

Tekel (tĕ′kĕl), part of the curse of Belshazzar, who was "weighed" in the balances and found wanting (Dan. 5:25).

Tekoa, Tekoah, Tekoite (tē-kō′ȧ -īt), a city of Judah or an inhabitant thereof. Tekoa lay 12 miles S of Jerusalem and the same distance NE of Hebron. It was fortified by Rehoboam (II Chron. 11:6). Previous to this, Joab, David's cousin and general, had sent to Tekoa for a "wise woman" and intrigued with her to persuade David to bring back Absalom. The prophet Amos describes himself as "among the herdsmen of Tekoa" (Amos 1:1).

Tel-Abib (tĕl′ā′bĭb), a place by the river Chebar in Babylonia where Ezekiel visited and ministered to the Jewish exiles (Ezek. 3:15).

Telah (tē′lȧ, **fracture),** an early Ephraimite (I Chron. 7:25).

Telaim (tē-lā′ĭm, **lambs),** the place where Saul mustered his army against Amalek (I Sam. 15:4); may be same as Telem (Josh. 15:24) in Judah. See Telem.

Telassar (tē-lăs′er), a city in Mesopotamia, mentioned by the Rabshakeh of Assyria as inhabited by the children of Eden, whose gods could not deliver them from the Assyrian kings (Isa. 37:12). It has not been identified.

Telem (tē′lĕm). 1. A city of Judah near the border of Edom (Josh. 15:24). 2. A porter who divorced his foreign wife (Ezra 10:24).

Tel-Haresha, Tel-Harsa (tĕl′hȧ-rē′shȧ, tĕl′hȧr′sȧ), a place in Babylonia from which certain people returned with Zerubbabel (Ezra 2:59; Neh. 7:61).

Tell (Arabic, Heb. **tel),** a mound or heap of ruins which marks the site of an ancient city and is composed of accumulated occupational debris, usually covering a number of archeological or historical periods and showing numerous building levels or strata. In the Bible, the fact that a city had become only a mound is often regarded as a result of judgment. Deut. 13:16 prescribes that an apostatizing city should be destroyed and reduced to a tell. Joshua executed judgment upon Ai when he burned it (Josh. 18: 28, RSV). Jeremiah prophesied that Rabbah of Ammon would become "a desolate mound" (49:2, RSV). The term **tel** also appears as an element in place-names of living towns; see Ezekiel 3:15; Ezra 2:59; and Nehemiah 7:61.

Tel el Amarna (tĕl-ĕl-ȧ-mȧr′nȧ), city built as the capital of Egypt by Akhnaton (Amenhotep IV, c. 1387-1366 B. C.), as a result of his break with the priests of Amon at Thebes. Both the city and the religious innovations of the king did not long survive his reign. Of great historical importance are the clay tablets (more than 350) accidentally discovered here by a peasant woman in 1887. These tablets, written in cuneiform and addressed to Amenhotep III and Amenhotep IV, mainly represent the official correspondence from the petty rulers of Palestine- Syria.

Tel-Melah (tĕl-mē′lȧ, **hill of salt),** a Babylonian town, probably on the low salty district not far N of the Persian Gulf (Ezra 2:59; Neh. 7:61).

Tema (tē′mȧ). 1. One of the 12 sons of Ishmael (Gen. 25:12-16). 2. A place at the northern edge of the Arabian desert where the above tribe lived (Job 6:18-20; Isa. 21:14; Jer. 25:23).

Temah (See Tamah)

Teman (tē′măn, **on the right,** i.e. toward the south). 1. Grandson of Esau (Gen. 36:11, 15). 2. An Edomite chief (Gen. 36:42). 3. A city in northeastern Edom, noted at one time for the wisdom of its people (Jer. 49:7).

Temani (tĕm′ȧ-nī), an inhabitant of Teman (Gen. 36:34).

Temeni (tĕm′ĕ-nī), a son of Ashhur (I Chron. 4:6).

Temperance, self-control (Acts 24:25; Gal. 5:23; II Pet. 1:6; I Cor. 9:25). It is not limited to abstinence from liquor. In Acts 24:25 the reference is to chastity. In I Timothy 3:2, 11; Titus 2:2 the opposite of "drunken."

Temple, name given to complex of buildings in Jerusalem which was the center of the sacrificial cult for the Hebrews. Three temples stood successively on Mt. Moriah (II Chron. 3:1) in Jerusalem: Solomon's, Zerubbabel's, and Herod the Great's. Material for Solomon's collected by David (II Sam. 7; I Chron. 17; 28:12-19); built with help of Hiram, king of Tyre; consisted of three sections: porch through which temple proper was entered; Holy Place — 60 feet long, 30 feet wide, 45 feet high; Holy of Holies — a 30 foot cube; stone walls were covered with paneling of cedar overlaid with gold; Holy Place contained 10 golden lampstands (I Kings 7:49), 12 tables of shewbread, and an incense altar (I Kings 7:48); Holy of Holies contained two wooden cherubim overlaid with gold and the ark of the covenant, a box overlaid with gold, its lid called the mercy seat (Lev. 16:14, 15); on W, E, and S sides were three stories of rooms for officials and storage; on the N was a portico with two pillars called Jachin and Boaz; around the temple was an inner court for priests, and in it were the great altar for sacrifices and the laver used by priests for ceremonial washing; around the inner court was an outer court for Israel (I Kings 6, 7; II Chron. 3, 4). Solomon's temple was burned by the Babylonians (II Kings 25:8-17; Jer. 52:12-23). Temple of Zerubbabel was less magnificent (Ezra 6). This was later rebuilt and enlarged by Herod the Great. It had four courts: for priests, Jewish males, women, and Gentiles. Herod began the work 20 B.C. The temple was burned when Jerusalem fell to the Roman armies in A.D. 70.

The Dome of the Rock Mosque, which stands on the site of the Temples of Solomon and Herod. © *MPS*

Temptation. On the one hand, temptation signifies any attempt to entice into evil; on the other hand, temptation indicates a testing which aims at spiritual good. Unless these two meanings are kept in view, the positive as over against the negative aspect, confusion inevitably results.

In its negative significance, that of enticement to perpetrate evil, temptation in Biblical teaching is traceable to Satan, the malignant being who stands opposed to the divine purposes of any morality — Satan is the ultimate source of all desire and action contrary to the holy love of God. Designated the Tempter in Matthew 4:3 and I Thessalonians 3:5 (cf. I Cor. 7:5), his mode of operation is vividly described in Genesis 3. Employing the serpent as his tool, Satan skillfully undermines man's fidelity to God (I Tim. 2:14-15). These same stratagems were deployed against our Lord on the threshold of His ministry (Matt. 4:1-11). Triumphantly He ran the whole gamut of evil enticement. Hence the author of the Epistle to the Hebrews declares that our Saviour was "in all points tempted like as we are, yet without sin" (4:15). And that same author declares that, because of His triumph over temptation, Jesus "is able to succour them that are tempted" (2:18).

The positive significance of temptation is that of testing with the intent of creating spiritual good: it is **proving** with a view to **approving** or **improving** and occasionally **reproving.** Thus God, who as Holy Love can never be the source of evil in any form (James 1:13), tested Abraham (Gen. 22:1). Thus God tested Job, who exclaimed, "But he knoweth the way that I take; when he hath tried me, I shall come forth as gold" (Job 23:10). Thus God still tests His people (I Pet. 1:7; 4:12-13; James 1:2, 12). But He tests, even sometimes severely and painfully, only for purposes of reproving and improving (Deut. 8:2-3; 13:3; Judg. 2:20-23; I Cor. 11:32; Heb. 12:4-11) or for purposes of approving. The divine intention in testing is plainly stated in Deut. 8:16.

Tenons (tĕn′ŭn, **hand),** projections at the lower ends of the tabernacle boards to sink into sockets to hold the boards in place (Exod. 26:17, etc.).

Tent, a temporary dwelling of various shapes generally made of strong goat's-hair cloth stretched over poles and held in place by cords reaching out to stakes driven into the ground. The word tent is often used to refer to a habitation generally (Gen. 9:27; I Kings 8:66; Job 8:22; Ps. 84:10), and it is often used figuratively (Isa. 13:20; 54:2; Jer. 10:20).

Tent of Meeting (See Tabernacle)

Terah (tē′ră). 1. Son of Nahor (Gen. 11:24-32); father of Abraham, Nabor, Haran; lived at Ur of the Chaldees and was an idolater (Josh. 24:2). When

God called Abram out of Ur with its civilized idolatry, Terah went as far as Haran in Mesopotamia where he and his family remained till Terah died at 205 years of age. 2. A wilderness camp of the Israelites (Num. 33:27, 28).

Teraphim, a term used of a kind of household idol and means of divination. In Genesis 31:19 the teraphim of Laban were stolen by Rachel; these were small enough to be concealed in a camel-saddle (vss. 34-35). They were a valuable possession. Michal, by placing such an object in David's bed, deceived Saul's messengers into thinking that David was there but was too ill to receive visitors (I Sam. 19:13-16). This idol resembled a man sufficiently well to make the ruse temporarily effective. In the spiritual revival under King Josiah the teraphim and other "abominations" in Judah and Jerusalem were put away (II Kings 23:24). Zechariah asserted that "the teraphim utter nonsense" (Zech. 10:2, RSV). Hosea prophesied that "the children of Israel shall dwell many days without king or prince, without sacrifice or pillar, without ephod or teraphim" (Hosea 3:4, RSV). Ezekiel included the consultation of teraphim among the divination practices of the king of Babylon preceding the destruction of Jerusalem (Ezek. 21:21).

Teresh (tē′rĕsh), chamberlain of Xerxes ("Ahasuerus") of Persia who attempted to assassinate his master but was exposed by Mordecai (Esth. 2:21).

Terrace, steps which Solomon made of algum trees as an approach to the temple (II Chron. 9:11).

Terror, extreme fear or dread; or sometimes, the one who causes such agitation (Ps. 55:4; Gen. 35:5; II Cor. 5:11).

Tertius (tûr′shĭ-ŭs), the scribe or amanuensis of Paul, the writer, at the dictation of Romans (16:22).

Tertullus (têr-tŭl′ŭs), a diminutive of Tertius. It was the name borne by the professional advocate employed by the Jews to state their case against Paul before Felix, the procurator of Judaea (Acts 24:1).

Testament. More accurately rendered "covenant," a binding agreement or contract between man and man, or man and God. The earliest account of the institution of the Lord's Supper contains the words: "This cup is the new covenant (testament) in my blood" (I Cor. 11:25; Ex. 24:8). A new relation between God and man was thereby created. The imagery in Heb. 9:15-20 takes in the further notion of a testamentary disposition, operative only after the death of the testator. Hence the Revisers' preference in vss. 16, 17 for the word "testament."

Testaments of the Twelve Prophets, an apocryphal document that claims to report the last words of the 12 sons of Jacob. It is probably a second century production concocted of traditional material. Probably inspired by Jacob's commission to his sons from his deathbed (Gen. 49).

Testimony, generally "a solemn affirmation to establish some fact" and commonly, among Christians, the statement of one's Christian experience. In Scripture, it usually refers to that which was placed in the ark of the covenant (Exod. 25:21), or to the Word of God (Ps. 119:14, 88, 99, etc.). In Mark 6:11 shaking off the dust of the feet in leaving an unfriendly city was to be considered as a testimony against it.

Tetrarch (See Occupations & Professions).

Texts and Versions (Old Testament). The original manuscripts of the OT have all been destroyed; the oldest manuscripts that survive are the famous Dead Sea Scrolls found in 1947 and later in caves along the Dead Sea, dating from 250 B.C. to c. A.D. 70; all the OT books except Esther are represented, most of them in fragmentary form. The oldest versions of the OT are: (1) Greek, Septuagint (250-100 B.C.), versions made in the 2nd cent. A.D. by Aquila, Theodotion, and Symmachus, and a translation made by Origen c. A.D. 240; (2) Aramaic (1st to 9th cent. A.D.); (3) Syriac (2nd or 3rd cent. A.D.); (4) the Latin (3rd and 4th centuries A.D.); (5) Coptic, Ethiopic, Gothic, Armenian, Georgian, Slavonic, Arabic (2nd to 10th centuries).

Texts and Versions (New Testament). Greek manuscripts whether of a portion or of the whole of the NT total nearly 4700. Of these c. 70 are papyri, 250 uncials, 2500 minuscules, and 1800 lectionaries; the earliest is a fragment of the Gospel of John and dates c. A. D. 125. The oldest NT versions are (1) Latin (2nd to 4th centuries), (2) Syriac (2nd to 6th centuries), (3) Coptic (2nd and 3rd centuries), (4) Gothic, Armenian, Georgian, Ethiopic, Arabic, Persian, Slavonic (4th to 9th centuries). A great deal of evidence for the text of the NT is also found in the writings of the early Church Fathers, principally in Greek, Latin, and Syriac.

Thaddaeus (thă-dē′ŭs), one of the 12 apostles, mentioned only in two of the four lists (Matt. 10:3; Mark 3:18). The other two lists (Luke 6:14-16 and Acts 1:13) omit this name but insert instead Jude, son of or possibly brother of James. Nothing is certainly known beyond the first two references above.

Thahash (See Tahash)

Thamah (See Tamah)

Thamar (See Tamar)

Thank Offering (See Offerings)

Thara (See Terah)

Theater. Israel produced no drama, and had therefore no theaters. Word means "to view" or "look upon." The Greek theater, and the Roman theater which followed it, were therefore structures designed to seat the viewers at a dramatic presentation. Theaters were commonly used for public gatherings, since they were likely to provide the largest places of assembly in the city; hence the use of the only theater mentioned in the NT (Acts 19:29), that of Ephesus. The ruins of this theater, a most imposing structure, seating 25, 000 people, have been excavated.

Thebes (thēbz), capital of Egypt during 18th dynasty called "No" in the Bible; on E bank of Nile; famous for temples; cult center of god Amon (Jer. 46:25); denounced by prophets (Jer. 46:25; Ezek. 30:14-16).

Thebez (thē′bĕz), a city in the tribe of Ephraim approximately half-way from Beth-Shean to Shechem (Judg. 9:50; II Sam. 11:21). Abimelech, son of Gideon, had taken the city except for a central tower, from the top of which a woman dropped a millstone upon him, thus causing his death. Now called Tubas.

Thelasar (thē-lā′sêr), the spelling in II Kings 19:12 (KJV) for Telassar, **q.v.** Located in Mesopotamia.

Theocracy (thē-ŏk′rȧ-sē), a government in which God Himself is the ruler. The best and perhaps the only illustration among nations is Israel from the time that God redeemed them from the power of the pharaoh till the time that Samuel acceded to their demand, "Now make us a king to judge us like all the nations" (I Sam. 8:5). During this period, God ruled through Moses (Exod. 19-Deut. 34), then through Joshua and finally through "judges" whom He raised up from time to time to deliver His people. Such a government was possible only because of God's special revelation of Himself to the nation.

Theology, The New. The new (radical) theology is characterized chiefly by a departure from the neo-orthodoxy of Karl Barth and Emil Brunner which has dominated a segment of the theological scene during the past forty years. Three of the main expressions of this radicalism are: Paul Tillich, Rudolph Bultmann and some of the proponents of the "God is dead" movement.

Paul Tillich (1886-1965) constructed a philosophical-theological system by accumulating a mass of historical, biographical and speculative data and arranging it by means of his "method of correlation" — philosophy (reason) asks the questions and theology (faith) gives the answers. So massive in content and intricate in systemization is Tillich's theology, that all attempts to digest or summarize his thought should be viewed as pointers to rather than expressions of his thinking. A knowledge of his **Systematic Theology** (3 volumes) is essential for an understanding of his philosophy.

Rudolf Bultmann (1884-) is a German New Testament scholar who has developed a radical method of Biblical interpretation. For him, the gospel message has meaning only when it brings meaning as an event to the individual through a decision made in faith. When the Bible speaks in this way, it is **kerygma;** when it speaks merely as history, it is **mythos.**

New Testament scholars of a more conservative bend have judged that Bultmann's abandonment of determining the historical Jesus has also disqualified him from formulating a Biblical Christology — a fundamental doctrine with historic Christianity.

Both Tillich and Bultmann contributed to the radical theologians who now constitute the "death of God" movement. However, some of the latter statements of Dietrich Bonhoeffer (1906-1945) point more directly to this radical theology.

Bonhoeffer was willing to abandon the definition of God as an individual reality in behalf of God as the ground of all being (Tillich); he also was willing to promote a secular Christianity. This meant the displacement of the old religious symbols (miracles, the cross, etc.) for new, more meaningful ones, understandable to the people outside the church. Furthermore, he believed that God was active in the world (without the help of the church) and consequently the church should react to its smallness and move out where the action is.

Bonhoeffer and his disciples have influenced many radical thinkers including: Bishop John A. T. Robinson, **(Honest to God);** William Hamilton, **(The New Essence of Christianity);** Paul van Buren, **(The Secular Meaning of the Gospel);** Harvey Cox, **(The Secular City);** Thomas J. J. Altizer, **(Radical Theology and the Death of God);** and Gabriel Vahanian, **(The Death of God; The Culture of Our Post- Christian Era).**

Although the ground from which this radical theology has sprung is fundamentally that of neo-orthodoxy with its existential, dialectic dimensions, it may be that future critical evaluations of this movement will judge it as basically a revival of the rational liberalism of the pre-Barthian era. Especially is this likely if liberalism is viewed as a mentality rather than a system of doctrine.

Theophany, a visible appearance of God, generally in human form. In the early days of humanity, before men had the written Word, before the incarnation, and before the Holy Spirit had come to make His abode in human hearts, God sometimes appeared and talked with men (Gen. 3:8; 4; 5:24; 6:9).

Theophilus (thē-ŏf'ĭ-lŭs). It is reasonable to suppose that Theophilus, to whom Luke dedicated both his Gospel (1:3), and the Acts (1:1), was a real person. The title "most excellent" demands this, while the name and title together suggest a person of equestrain rank who became a Christian convert.

Thessalonians, Epistles to the. With the possible exception of Galatians, I and II Thessalonians are the earliest letters surviving from the correspondence of Paul. They were written to the church in Thessalonica which was founded by Paul on his second journey en route from Philippi to Achaia.

Paul's stay both in Thessalonica and in Athens was brief, and he probably arrived in Corinth about A.D. 50. According to the narrative in Acts, Paul had begun his ministry there while working at the tentmaker's trade with Aquila and Priscilla (Acts 18:1-3). When Silas and Timothy rejoined him after their stay in Macedonia they brought funds which enabled him to stop working and to devote his entire time to evangelism (Acts 18:5; II Cor. 11:9). Shortly afterward the Jewish opposition to Paul's preaching became so violent that he was forced out of the synagogue. About a year and a half later he was haled before the tribunal of Gallio, the Roman proconsul (18:12). Gallio had taken office only a short time previously, in A.D. 51 or 52. The first epistle, then, must have been written at Corinth about a year prior to that date in A.D. 50 or 51.

Timothy brought a report concerning the problems of the church, with which Paul dealt in this letter. Some of his Jewish enemies had attacked his character, putting him under obligation to defend himself (2:1-6, 10, 14-16). A few of the converts were still influenced by the lax morality of the paganism from which they had so recently emerged and in which they had to live (4:3-7). Some of the church members had died, causing the rest to worry whether their departed friends would share in the return of Christ (4:13). Still others, anticipating the Second Advent, had given up all regular employment and were idly waiting for the Lord to appear (4:9-12). The epistle was intended to encourage the Thessalonians' growth as Christians and to settle the questions that were troubling them.

Outline and Content, I Thessalonians

I. The Conversion of the Thessalonians 1:1-10
II. The Ministry of Paul 2:1-3:13
  A. In founding the Church 2:1-20
  B. In Concern for the Church 3:1-13
III. The Problems of the Church 4:1-13
  A. Moral Instruction 4:1-12
  B. The Lord's Coming 4:13-5:11
  C. Ethical Duties 5:12-22
IV. Conclusion 5:23-28

II Thessalonians

The two epistles deal with two different aspects of the same general subject, and bear so many resemblances to each other that they are clearly related. Early evidence for the acceptance of II Thessalonians is almost as full as for that of I Thessalonians. The second epistle was probably sent from Corinth in A.D. 51, not more than a few months after the first epistle.

Evidently the Thessalonian Christians had been disturbed by the arrival of an epistle purporting to come from Paul, which he had not authorized (II Thess. 2:2). Some of them were suffering harsh persecution (1:4, 5); others were apprehensive that the last day was about to arrive (2:2); and there were still a few who were idle and disorderly (3:6-12). The second epistle serves to clarify further the problems of the first epistle, and to confirm the confidence of the readers.

Outline and Content, II Thessalonians

I. Salutation 1:1, 2
II. Encouragement in Persecution 1:3-12
III. The Signs of the Day of Christ 2:1-17
 A. Warning of False Rumors 2:1, 2
 B. The Apostasy 2:3
 C. The Revelation of the Man of Sin 2:4-12
 D. The Preservation of God's People 2:13-17
IV. Spiritual Counsel 3:1-15
V. Conclusion 3:16-18

Whereas the first epistle heralded the resurrection of the righteous dead and the restoration of the living at the return of Christ, the second epistle described the apostasy preceding the coming of Christ to judgment. Paul exhorted the Thessalonians to retain their faith and to improve their conduct. He spoke even more vehemently to those who persisted in idleness (3:6-12), recommending that the Christians withdraw fellowship from them.

Thessalonica (thĕs′ȧ-lō-nī′kȧ), a Macedonian town founded by Cassander, Alexander's officer, who took control of Greece after Alexander's death in 332 B.C. It dominated the junction of the northern trade-route and the road from the Adriatic to Byzantium, which later became the Via Egnatia. Its comparatively sheltered roadstead made it the chief port of Macedonia. In 146 B.C. it became the capital of the Roman province and was Pompey's base a century later in the Civil War with Julius Caesar. The population included a large Roman element, and a Jewish colony. Paul visited Thessalonica after Philippi, and appears to have worked among a composite group, comprising the Jews of the synagogue and Greek proselytes. There was a high degree of emancipation among the women of Macedonia. In Acts 17:6 and 8, the officials of the town are called in the original "politarchs."

Theudas (thū′dȧs). Jew who led a considerable revolt against Rome (Acts 5:36, 37).

Thief, Thieves, anyone who appropriates someone else's property, including petty thieves and highwaymen (Luke 10:30; John 12:6). Under the law of Moses, thieves who were caught were expected to restore twice the amount stolen. The thieves with Jesus on their crosses must have been robbers or brigands, judging by the severity of the punishment and the fact that one of them acknowledged that the death penalty imposed upon them was just (Luke 23:41).

Thigh, the upper part of the leg in man; or of a rear leg in a quadruped. To put one's hand under the thigh of another, was to enhance the sacredness of an oath (Gen. 24:2, 9; 47:29). To "smite hip and thigh" (Judg. 15:8) implied not only slaughter but slaughter with extreme violence. To smite upon the thigh is a sign of amazement or of great shame (Jer. 31:9; Ezek. 21:12).

Thimnathah (thĭm′nȧ-thȧ), town on N boundary of Judah three miles SW of Bethshemesh (Josh. 19:43). Modern Tibnah.

Thistle (See Plants)

Thomas, one of the 12 apostles (Matt. 10:3), also called "Didymus" or "the Twin" (cf. John 11:16; 20:24; 21:2). When the other apostles tried to dissuade Jesus from going to Bethany to heal Lazarus because of the danger involved from hostile Jews, Thomas said to them, "Let us also go, that we may die with him" (John 11:16). Shortly before the Passion, Thomas asked, "Lord, we know not whither thou goest; how know we the way?" (John 14:1-6). Thomas was not with the other apostles when Jesus presented Himself to them on the evening of the Resurrection, and told them later that he could not believe in resurrection (John 20:24, 25). Eight days later he was with the apostles when Jesus appeared to them again, and he exclaimed "My Lord and my God" (John 20:26-29). He was with the six other disciples when Jesus appeared to them at the Sea of Galilee (John 21:1-8) and was with the rest of the apostles in the upper room at Jerusalem after the ascension (Acts 1:13).

Thomas, Gospel of, Gnostic gospel consisting entirely of supposed sayings of Jesus; dated c. A.D. 140; found at Naj Hamadi in Egypt in 1945.

Thorn (See Plants)

Thorn in the Flesh, Paul's description of a physical ailment which afflicted him and from which he prayed to be relieved (II Cor. 12:7). His affliction was apparently not only painful but disfiguring. The Galatians did not despise him for it, and would have plucked out their own eyes and given them to the apostle, were it possible (Gal. 4:13-15). He says he was unable to recognize the high priest (Acts 23:5). Thus it may have been opthalmia. Ramsay thought it was some form of recurring malarial fever.

Thousand, frequently used symbolically for a very large but indefinite number, or as the division of a tribe (Num. 31:5; Josh. 22:14).

Thousand Years (See Millennium)

Thrace (thrās), a kingdom and later a Roman province, in SE Europe, E of Macedonia.

Three Holy Children, Song of (See Apocrypha)

Three Taverns (See Taverns, Three)

Threshing, done in two ways: (1) by beating the sheaves with a rod or flail; (2) by trampling them under the feet of oxen that pulled a wooden sled around the threshing floor (Isa. 28:27). Threshing was done out-of-doors on a hard surface of ground. Also a figurative use (Isa. 21:10; 41:15; Mic. 4:12, 13; I Cor. 9:10). See Agriculture, Farming.

Threshing Floor, the place where grain was threshed. Usually clay soil was packed to a hard smooth surface. Sheaves of grain were spread on the floor and trampled by oxen (Deut. 25: 4; Isa. 28:27; I Cor. 9:9). Threshing floors were often on hills where the night winds could more easily blow away the chaff.

Threshold, piece of wood or stone which lies below the bottom of a door, and has to be crossed on entering a house. The sill of a doorway.

Throne, a chair of state occupied by one in authority or of high position, like a high priest, judge, governor, or king (Gen. 41:40; II Sam. 3:10; Neh. 3:7; Ps. 122:5; Jer. 1:15; Matt. 19:28).

Thumb, either the great toe of the foot or the thumb of the hand. (Exod. 29:20; Lev. 8:23; 14:14). To cut off these members was to handicap a victim and brand him. A son of Reuben was named Thumb (Josh. 15:6).

Thummim (See Urim and Thummim)

Thunder, the noise that follows a lightning discharge. In Palestine, a rare phenomenon during summer months, so if it did occur it was considered a sign of divine displeasure (I Sam. 12: 17). Hebrews considered thunder to be a revelation of God's power (Job 37: 2-5; 40:9; Pss. 18:13; 29:2-9; Isa. 30: 30), and it represented God's anger and chastening (I Sam. 2:10).

Thunder, Sons of, the title given James and John by Jesus (Mark 3:17) apparently because of their bold and sometimes rash natures (Luke 9:54; Matt. 20:20-23).

Thutmose (also Tuthmosis, Thotmes), does not appear in the Bible, but is a common personal name and one of the great royal names of Egypt, given to four kings of the eighteenth dynasty. The outstanding Thutmose was Thutmose III, one of the greatest military leaders and administrators of antiquity. Thutmose I made a military expedition beyond the Euphrates and also extended the southern boundary to the Third Cataract. Thutmose II married his half-sister, Hatshepsut, and their daughter became the wife of Thutmose III. Hatshepsut was regent for a period after the death of Thutmose II and even had herself proclaimed "king"; upon her death, Thutmose II burst from obscurity and attempted to eliminate all references to this aunt and mother-in-law. He began his 17 expeditions to Palestine-Syria with a brilliantly strategic victory over an Asiatic coalition at Megiddo. He reached beyond the Euphrates and set up a stele beside that left by his grandfather (Thutmose I). The records of his expeditions are preserved in his annals at Karnak. Thutmose IV, the son of Amenhotep II, is the last of the kings of this name. The Dream Stele, which still stands between the forelegs of the Sphinx at Giza, relates how he came to the throne.

Thyatira (thī'ȧ-tī'rȧ) a city in the province of Asia, on the boundary of Lydia and Mysia famous for weaving and dyeing. Lydia, whom Paul met in Philippi, was a Thyatiran seller of "turkey red," the product of the madder-root (Acts 16:14). It is curious to find another woman, nicknamed after the princess who sealed Ahab's trading partnership with the Phoenicians, leading a party of compromise in the Thyatiran church (Rev. 2:20, 21).

Tiamat (tī'ȧ-măt), a mythical monster in the Babylonian-Assyrian creation story.

Tiberias (tī-bē'rĭ-ăs), a city of Herod Antipas, built between the years A.D. 16 and 22 on the W shore of the Sea of Galilee, or the Sea of Tiberias, as John, writing for non-Jewish readers, calls the lake (John 6:1; 21:1). It was named, of course, after the reigning emperor, Tiberius, reflecting the pro-Roman policy consistently followed by the Herods. A famous health resort and after A.D. 70, a center of rabbinic learning.

Tiberias, Sea of (See Sea of Galilee)

Tiberius (tī-bēr'ĭ-ŭs). Tiberius Julius Caesar Augustus succeeded to the principate on the death of Augustus in A.D. 14, becoming thus the second Roman emperor. He was born in 42 B.C., son of the Empress Livia, wife of Augustus, by her first husband, Tiberius Claudius Nero. Tiberius died on March 16, A.D. 37. He was the reigning emperor at the time of Christ's death.

Tibhath (tĭb'hăth), a city in the kingdom of Zobah, E of the Anti-Lebanon Mountains. David captured it from Hadarezer, and sent its treasures to Jerusalem (I Chron. 18:7-9, Betah of II Sam. 8:8).

Tibni (tĭb'nī), a son of Ginath, unsuccessful competitor for the throne of Israel with Omri (I Kings 16:15-21).

Tidal (tī'dăl) an unidentified king, mentioned only in Gen. 14:1, 9, where he is called "king of Goiim" ("nations," KJV) and is allied with Chedorlaomer (see 14:5, 17).

Tiglath-Pileser (tĭg'lăth-pī-lē'zêr), famous Assyrian king (1114-1074 B.C.) whose campaigns extended northward to the vicinity of Lake Van and westward to the Mediterranean. His annals tell of his efforts to establish a world empire, but his reign was followed by several centuries in which Assyria was weak. In 745 a usurper took the Assyrian throne and assumed the name Tiglath-pileser. Tiglath-pileser III (745-727) injected new vigor into the Assyrian empire, which had suffered another decline after a resurgence of power in the ninth century. He engaged in campaigns to E and W and was recognized as king even in Babylon (II Kings 15:19 and I Chron. 5:26). His annals list Azariah of Judah among the kings from whom he received tribute. Menahem of Samaria who also bought him off (II Kings 15:19-20).

During the reign of the Judean king Ahaz, Pekah of Israel and Rezin of Syria moved against Judah. Ahaz secured the help of Tiglath-pileser (II Kings 16:5-8), who captured Damascus, deported its people, and killed Rezin. He took a number of Israelite cities and exiled the inhabitants to Assyria (II Kings 15:29). Ahaz also requested military aid from him because of invasions by Edomites and Philistines; he "gave tribute to the king of Assyria; but it did not help him" (II Chron. 28:20-21).

Tigris (tī'grĭs), one of the two great rivers of the Mesopotamian area. It originates in the Taurus Mountains of Armenia and is 1,150 miles long. In the Bible the Tigris is mentioned with the Euphrates and two other streams as rivers which watered the garden of Eden (Gen. 2:14). Daniel 10:4 states that it was while the prophet "was standing on the bank of the great river, that is, the Tigris" (RSV), that he saw the vision he subsequently recorded.

Tikvah (tĭk'vȧ). 1. The father-in-law of the prophetess Huldah, the wife of Shallum (II Kings 22:8-14). 2. During the reforms under Ezra a son of another Tikvah was a chief leader (Ezra 10:9-15).

Tikvath (See Tikvah)

Tile. Ancient writing was done with a stilus on blocks of soft clay (Ezek. 4:1-8). When a permanent record was desired the inscribed tile was baked in a furnace. So skilled were scribes of the day that many of their tiles remain in perfect condition after 3,000 years. Roofing tiles are mentioned in Luke 5:19 and Mark 2:4.

Tilgath-Pilneser (See Tiglath-Pileser)

Tiling, used only in Luke 5:19, where the reference is apparently to clay roofing—tiles with which the roof was covered. Clay tiles were not commonly used as roofing material for houses in Palestine.

Tilon (tī'lŏn), one of the sons of Shimon (I Chron. 4:1, 20), a descendant of Judah.

Timbrel (See Musical Instruments)

Time. In the early Biblical period time was marked by sunrise and sunset, phases of the moon, and location of a few constellations; but there were no names for days and months, and no accurate knowledge of years. Ancient people had no method of reckoning long periods of time. They dated from great and well-known events, like the founding of Rome (753 B.C.), the beginning of the Olympian games (766 B.C.), the founding of the Seleucid dynasty (312 B.C.), the Exodus, the Babylonian Exile, the earthquake (Amos 1:1). The starting point in the Maccabean age was the beginning of the Seleucid era (312 B.C.). The year was lunar (354 days, 8 hours, 38 seconds), divided into 12 lunar months, with seven intercalary months added over 19 years. The Hebrew month began with the new moon. Early Hebrews gave the months names; later they used numbers; and after the Exile they used Babylonian names. The sacred year began with Nisan (March-April); the secular year, with Tishri (September-October). Months were divided by the Jews into weeks of seven days, ending with the Sabbath (Exod. 20:11; Deut. 5:14, 15). Days were divided into 24 hours of 60 minutes of 60 seconds. The Roman day began at midnight and had 12 hours (John 11:9); the Hebrew day was reckoned from sunset. Night was divided into watches. At first the Hebrews had three watches; in the time of Christ there were four. Various kinds of clocks were used: sundials, shadow clocks, water clocks.

Times, Observer of, person who has a superstitious regard for days regarded as lucky or unlucky, as decided by astrology (Deut. 18:9-14).

Timeus, Timaeus (tī-mē'ŭs), the father of a blind man whose eyes Jesus opened (Mark 10:46-52), the name Bartemaeus meaning "son of Timaeus."

Timna (tĭm'nȧ, **holding in check).** 1. A concubine of Esau's son Eliphaz (Gen. 36:12). 2. Sister of Lotan, son of Seir (Gen. 36:22). 3. A chief or clan descended from Esau (Gen. 36:40, spelled Timnah). 4. A son of Eliphaz (I Chron. 1:36).

Timnah (tĭm'nȧ). In KJV eight times Timnath (Gen. 38:12-14; Judg. 14:1-5), once Thimnathah (Josh. 19:43). 1. A town on the border of Judah (Josh. 15:10), later given to the tribe of Dan (Josh. 19:43). Its site is at Tibnah, c. three miles SW of Beth-Shemesh. 2. A town in the hill country of Judah (Josh. 15:57), exact location uncertain. 3. Probably a town in Edom (Gen. 36:12, 22, 40; I Chron. 1:39, 51).

Timnath (See Timnah)

Timnath-Heres (See Timnath-Serah)

Timnath-Serah (tĭm'năth-sēr'ȧ), the same as Timnath-heres (Judg.2:9), a village in Ephraim which Joshua requested as an inheritance (Josh. 19:50), which he rebuilt, and where his remains were buried (Josh. 24:30).

Timnite (tĭm'nīt), a native of Timnah whose daughter was married to Samson (Judg. 15:3-6).

Timon (tī'mŏn), one of the seven deacons chosen by the church in Jerusalem (Acts 6:5).

Timotheus (See Timothy)

Timothy (tĭm'ō-thē, **honoring God),** Paul's spiritual child (I Tim. 1:2; II Tim. 1:2), later apostle's fellow-traveler and official representative. Paul loved Timothy and admired his outstanding personality-traits (Phil. 2:19-22). None of Paul's companions is mentioned as often and is with him as constantly as is Timothy (II Tim. 4:9, 21).

Timothy is first mentioned in Acts 16:1, from which passage it may be inferred that he was an inhabitant of Lystra (cf. Acts 20:4). He was the offspring of a mixed marriage: a Greek pagan father and a devout Jewish mother, Eunice (Acts 16:1; II Tim. 1:5). From the days of his childhood Timothy had been instructed in the sacred writings of the OT (II Tim. 3:15). In the manner of devout Israelites his grandmother Lois and mother Eunice had nurtured him (II Tim. 1:5). Then came Paul who taught this devout family that Jesus Christ is the fulfilment of the OT. First grandmother Lois and mother Eunice accepted the Christ, then, as a result of their cooperation with Paul, Timothy also did so (II Tim. 1:5). This took place on Paul's first missionary journey. When, on the second journey, Paul and Silas came to Derbe and Lystra, Timothy became an active member of the group. Paul took Timothy and circumcised him. In all probability it was also at this time that by the elders of the local church Timothy was ordained to his new task, Paul himself taking part in this solemn laying on of hands (I Tim. 4:14; II Tim. 1:6).

Timothy then accompanied the missionaries by crossing over into Europe: Philippi, Thessalonica. He also helped the others in the next place to which they came, Berea. Here he and Silas were left behind to give spiritual support to the infant church, while Paul himself went on to Athens (Acts 17:10-15). He was later sent back to Thessalonica for the purpose of strengthening the brothers there (I Thess. 3:1, 2). After Paul had left Athens and had begun his labors in Corinth, both Silas and Timothy rejoined the apostle (Acts 18:1, 5). At Corinth Timothy worked with Paul. On the third missionary journey Timothy was again with the apostle during the lengthy Ephesus ministry. From there he was sent to Macedonia and to Corinth (Acts 19:21, 22; I Cor. 4:17; 16:10). When Paul arrived in Macedonia, Timothy rejoined him (II Cor. 1:1). Afterward he accompanied the apostle to Corinth (Rom. 16:21), was with him on the return to Macedonia (Acts 20:3, 4), and was waiting for him at Troas (Acts 20:5). He was probably also with Paul in Jerusalem (I Cor. 16:3). During Paul's first imprisonment at Rome the two were again in close contact (Phil. 1:1; Col. 1:1; Philem. 1:1). When the apostle expected to be released shortly, he told the Philippians that he expected to send Timothy to them soon (Phil. 2:19).

Timothy is next found in Ephesus. Paul, on leaving, asked Timothy to remain at this place (I Tim. 1:3). While there, Timothy one day received a letter from Paul, the letter which we now call I Timothy. Later another letter arrived in which Paul, writing from Rome as a prisoner facing death, urged his friend to come to him before winter (II Tim. 4:9, 21). Whether the two ever actually saw each other's face again is not recorded. That Timothy tried to see the apostle is certain. See Titus.

Timothy, Epistles to (See Pastoral Epistles)

Tinkling, the sound of small bells worn by women on a chain fastened to anklets (Isa. 3:16). I Cor. 13:1 should be rendered "clanging cymbals."

Tiphsah (tĭf'sȧ). 1. An important city on the northern border of Solomon's kingdom (I Kings 4:24), on the Euphrates River where the caravan route from Egypt and Syria passed en route to countries to the East. 2. A town, apparently not far from Tirzah, the inhabitants of which were massacred by Menahem (II Kings 15:16).

Tiras (tī'răs), youngest son of Japheth (Gen. 10:2; I Chron. 1:5). He is not mentioned elsewhere.

Tirathite (tī'răth-īt) a family of scribes from Tirah in Jabeth (I Chron. 2:13, 50, 55).

Tire (headdress), an ornamental headdress (Ezek. 24:17, 23) worn by Aaron (Exod. 39:28; KJV bonnet), women (Isa. 3:20; KJV bonnet), and bridegrooms (Isa. 61:10; KJV ornaments).

Tirhakah (tûr'hȧ-kȧ), an Egyptian king, the third and last king of the twenty-fifth or Ethiopian dynasty. II Kings 19:9 and Isa. 37:9 state that Sennacherib, while besieging Judean cities, heard that Tirhakah was coming against him. Sennacherib was successful against Tirhakah, but the loss of his troops forced him back to Assyria (I Kings 19:35-36; Isa. 37:36-37). Becoming king about 689, Tirhakah enjoyed a respite from the Assyrian threat for some years, but was defeated by Esarhaddon and later by Assurbanipal.

Tirhanah (tûr'hȧ-nȧ), a son of Caleb by his concubine Maacah (I Chron. 2:48)

Tiria (tĭr'ĭ-ȧ), a son of Jehaleleel (I Chron. 4:16).

Tirshatha (tûr-shā'thȧ, **revered),** the Persian title of the governor of Judah under the Persians. Zerubbabel (Ezra 2:63; Neh. 7:65, 70), and Nehemiah (Neh. 8:9; 10:1) bore the title.

Tirzah (tûr'zȧ). 1. The youngest daughter of Zelophehad (Num. 26:33; Josh. 17:3). 2. A town six miles E of Samaria captured by Joshua (Josh. 12:24). With the division of the kingdom after the death of Solomon, it became the captital of the northern kingdom (I Kings 14:17) until Omri.

Tishbite (tĭsh'bīt). Elijah is mentioned as a Tishbite in I Kings 17:1. The RSV gives a good reading, "Elijah the Tishbite of Tishbeh in Gilead."

Tithe (tīth, **tenth),** 10th part of one's income set aside for a specific use, to the government or ecclesiastics. Its origin is unknown, but it goes back far beyond the time of Moses, and it was practiced in lands from Babylonia to Rome. Abraham gave tithes to Melchizedek (Gen. 14:20; Heb. 7:2, 6); Jacob promised tithes to God (Gen. 28:22); Mosaic law required tithing of all produce of land and herds (Lev. 27:30-33); used for support of Levites and priests (Num. 18:21-32); additional tithes may have been required at certain times (Deut. 12:5-18; 14:22-29); there were penalties for cheating in tithing (Lev. 27:31; Deut. 26:13-15). Pharisees tithed even herbs (Matt. 22: 23; Luke 11:42).

Tittle (tĭt′l, **a horn),** a small horn-shaped mark used to indicate accent in Hebrew (Matt. 5:18; Luke 16:17).

Titus (tī′tŭs), a convert, friend, and helper of Paul (Titus 1:4), in the NT mentioned only in Paul's epistles, especially in II Cor. He was a Greek, a son of Gentile parents (Gal. 2:3). After his conversion he accompanied Paul to Jerusalem, where Paul rejected the demand of the Judaists that Titus be circumcised. Hence, Titus became a person of significance for the principle of Gentile-admission to the Church solely on the basis of faith in Christ. During Paul's third missionary journey Titus was assigned missions to Corinth to solve its vexing problems (I Cor. 1-6; II Cor. 2:13; 7:5-16) and to encourage material assistance to the needy at Jerusalem (II Cor. 8). Much later Titus was in Crete, left behind there by Paul to organize its churches (Titus 1:4, 5). He was requested to meet Paul at Nicopolis (Titus 3:12). Titus was consecrated, courageous, resourceful.

Titus, Epistle to (See Pastoral Epistles)

Titus, Flavius Vespasianus (A.D. 39-81), the son of the future emperor Vespasian, Titus served in Germany and Britain before proceeding to Palestine as a legate on his father's staff. Titus captured Jerusalem in A.D. 70. Titus was a popular emperor during the two brief years of his principate. Titus was notorious for his liaison with Bernice, sister of Agrippa II, who listened to Paul's defense at Caesarea (Acts 15: 13).

Titus Justus (See Justus)

Tizite (tī′zīt), Toha, one of the valiant men of David's army (I Chron. 11:45).

Toah (tō′ȧ), an ancestor of Samuel (I Chron. 6:34, Nathan in vs. 26). **Tohu** in I Sam. 1:1.

Tob (tŏb) a fertile district in Syria, extending NE from Gilead. Jephtha, a mighty man of Gilead, took refuge in Tob (Judg. 11:1-3).

Tob-Adonijah (tŏb-ăd-ō-nī′jȧ, **Jehovah is good),** a Levite sent by Jehoshaphat to teach the law to Judah (II Chron. 17:7-9).

Tobiah, Tobajah (tō-bī′ȧ, tō-bī′jȧ, **Jehovah is good).** 1. One of the Levites whom Jehoshaphat sent to teach the law in Judah (II Chron. 17:7-9). 2. A family which returned to Jerusalem under Zerubbabel, who were not able to provide proofs of being Israelites (Ezra 2:59, 60; Neh. 7:61, 62). 3. An Ammonite, half Jew, who with Sanballat tried to hinder Nehemiah in repairing Jerusalem (Neh. 2:10, 19; 13: 4ff). 4. Exile who returned to Jerusalem (Zech. 6:9-15).

Tobit, Book of (See Apocrypha)

Tochen (tō′kĕn, **a measure),** a town in the heritage of Simeon (I Chron. 4:32).

Togarmah (tō-gȧr′mȧ), a man who appears in two genealogies (Gen. 10:3; I Chron. 1:6) as a son of Gomer, who is a descendant of Japheth.

Tohu, an ancestor of Samuel (I Sam. 1:1). See Nahath 2.

Toi (tō′ē), king of Hamath who congratulated David for his victory over Hadadezer (II Sam. 8:9-11).

Token, a word which in the OT is used practically synonymously with **sign** (Exod. 13:9, 16). In Num. 17:10 and Joshua 2:12 it means a memorial of something past. In the NT the word is self-explanatory (Mark 14:44; Phil. 1: 28; II Thess. 1:5; 3:17).

Tola (tō′lȧ). 1. One of Issachar's sons (Gen. 46:1-13). 2. Son of Puah, of the tribe of Issachar, who judged Israel 23 years (Judg. 10:1, 2).

Tolad (tō′lăd), a city occupied by sons of Simeon (I Chron. 4:29).

Tomb. It may mean a chamber, vault or crypt, either under ground or above. It may refer to a pretentious burying place on a special site. It may be a beehive stucture wherein many bodies can be placed. In general, any burying place is a tomb. Some kings were interred in a vault in Jerusalem, the "sepulchre of their fathers" or of David (II Sam. 2:32; Neh. 2:3). Just where this burial place was located has not been determined.

Tombs of NT times were either caves or else were dug into stone cliffs. Tombs carried no inscriptions, no paintings. Embalming, learned in Egypt (Gen. 50:2), was soon a lost art (John 11:39). A general opening gave access to vaults which opened upon ledges to provide support for the stone doors. The door to such a grave weighed from one to three tons, hence the miracle

A well-preserved tomb, with a rolling stone at the entrance, near Kirjath-jearim. © MPS

of its being rolled away (Luke 24:2; John 20:1).

Tongs, usually means snuffers, and is used with snuffdish (Exod. 25:38; Num. 4:9); in Isaiah 6:6 it is **tongs.**

Tongue. 1. An organ of the body, used by Gideon's men in drinking (Judg. 7:5; see also Zech. 14:12; Mark 7:33; Ps. 68:23; Rev. 16:10). 2. An organ of speech (Job 27:4; Ps. 35:28; Prov. 15:2; Mark 7:35). 3. A language or dialect (Gen. 10:5, 20; Deut. 28:49; Esth. 1:22, tr. language in the KJV, Dan. 1:4; Acts 1:19; 2:8; 10:46). 4. A people or race having a common language (Isa. 66:18; Dan. 3:4; Rev. 5:9; 10:11, note the repetition, "peoples, nations, tongues"). 5. Figurative uses: can be sharpened, i.e. made to utter caustic words (Pss. 64:3; 140:3); a sharp sword (Ps. 57:4). The tongue is little but can do great things (James 3:5, 8), etc.

Tongues, Confusion of. The Tower of Babel presents an answer to an otherwise insoluble mystery, and a revelation regarding God's anger against human vanity and disobedience. That there was originally a common language among men becomes more certain as linguistic research progresses. See Gen. 11:1-9, for He who designed the media of speech could have, in an instant, made such modifications in these media as to have caused the confusion a punishment for arrogance.

Tongues of Fire, one of the phenomena which occurred at the outpouring of the Holy Spirit on the day of Pentecost (Acts 2:3, ASV). The tongues of fire were symbolic of the Holy Spirit who came in power on the Church.

Tongues, Gift of, a spiritual gift mentioned in Mark 16:17; Acts 2:1-13; 10:44-46; 19:6; I Cor. 12, 14. The gift appeared on the day of Pentecost with the outpouring of the Holy Spirit on the assembled believers (Acts 2:1-13). The phenomenon appeared again in the home of Cornelius (Acts 10:44-11:17), at Ephesus (Acts 19:6), and in the church at Corinth (I Cor. 12, 14). Instruction regarding the use of tongues is given by Paul in I Cor. 12-14.

Tools. In the Bible a variety of tools used by the ancients are mentioned. These may be grouped into various categories: 1. **Cutting tools:** knife (Gen. 22:6, 10; Judg. 19:29); saw (Isa. 10:15); sickle (Joel 3:13); axe (Deut. 19:5; 20:19); reaping hook (Isa. 44:12); pruning hook (Isa. 2:4; 18:5). 2. **Boring tools:** the aul (Exod. 21:6; Deut. 15:17). 3. **Forks and shovels** (I Sam. 13:21; I Kings 7:40, 45); tongs (Exod. 25:38). 4. **Carpentry tools:** hammer (Judg. 5:26); plane (Isa. 44:13); plummet (Amos 7:8); level (II Kings 21:13). 5. **Drawing tools:** stylus (Isa. 44:13); compass (Isa. 44:13). 6. **Measuring tools:** line (I Kings 7:23; II Kings 21:13); measuring reed (Ezek. 40:3-8; Rev. 11:1). 7. **Tilling tools:** ploughshare (I Sam. 13:20, 21); mattock (I Sam. 13:20, 21). 8. **Metal-working tools:** anvil (Isa. 41:7); file (I Sam. 13:21). 9. **Stone-working tools:** chisel (Exod. 20:25); saw (I Kings 7:9).

Tooth. Human teeth are meant in Numbers 11:33, also in the following passages: in the law of retaliation, "a tooth for a tooth" (Exod. 21:24; Lev. 24:20; Deut. 19:21; Matt. 5:38; cf. Exod. 21:27); in the common expression: "gnashing of the teeth," in cruel hatred (Job 16:9; Pss. 35:16; 37:12; Lam. 2:16; Acts 7:54), or in anguish and despair (Ps. 112:10; Matt. 8:12; 13:42; 22:13; 24:15; 25:30; Luke 13:28); once gnashing the teeth is mentioned as due to epilepsy (Mark 9:18; ASV "grinding"); Prov. 10:26 refers to the effect of acid on teeth. A number of references mention the teeth of animals: of unspecified beasts (Deut. 32:24); of young lions (Job 4:10); of leviathan, probably a crocodile (Job 41:14); two prophetic visions reveal symbolic beasts with teeth: a bear (Dan. 7:5), a terrible beast (Dan. 7:7, 19), locusts with teeth like lions' (Rev. 9:8).

The teeth are used in a variety of figurative expressions: Jeremiah and Ezekiel cite a proverb of the people, "the fathers have eaten sour grapes and the children's teeth are set on edge" (Jer. 31:29; Ezek. 18:2). The Lord changed this proverb to read: "every man that eateth sour grapes, his teeth shall be set on edge" (Jer. 31:30); a prophetic passage mentions "teeth white with milk" as part of the description of abundant prosperity (Gen. 49:12); the teeth are used to depict evil people, the teeth standing for the person: the unrighteous (Job 29:17), enemies (Ps. 3:7), the wicked (Ps. 124:6), false prophets (Mic. 3:5), an oppressor (Zech. 9:7); escaped by the skin of his teeth meaning a narrow escape (Job 19:20); cleanness of teeth, meaning a famine (Amos 4:6).

Tophel (tō′phĕl, **lime, cement),** a place in the wilderness where Moses addressed the Israelites (Deut. 1:1).

Tophet, Topheth (tō′phĕt KJV, tō′phĕth ASV), area in the valley of Hinnom where human sacrifices were made to Molech (Jer. 7:31; II Kings 23:10). It is first mentioned by Isaiah who declared that a Topheth, a place of burning, was prepared by the Lord for the king of Assyria (30:33). Jeremiah predicted that the name of the place would be changed to the valley of slaughter because of the many people who would be killed there (Jer. 7:32, 33; 19:6). Josiah defiled this place so that it no longer could be used for idolatrous practices (II Kings 23:10).

Torah (tō′rȧ, **direction, instruction, law),** the common Hebrew word for "law," so rendered over 200 times in the OT. It is used for human instruction, but it usually expresses divine law. The entire Pentateuch became known as the Torah. This section of the OT is constantly referred to in the Scriptures as the "law of Moses" or "the law of the Lord." Torah even became the name of the entire Jewish Scriptures. Jesus cited Psalm 82:6 as part of the law (John 10:34).

Tormentor (torturer). This word occurs only in the NT (Matt. 18:34) where the unforgiving debtor is delivered to tormentors, probably meaning the jailers.

Tou (tō'ōō), king of Hamath who sent presents to David for conquering their common enemy Hadarezer (I Chron. 18:9, 10).

Tow, the coarse and broken part of flax ready for spinning (Judg. 16:9; Isa. 1:31).

Towel, linen cloth, towel), (John 13:4, 5) Jesus wrapped Himself in a towel and wiped the disciples' feet with it.

Tower, a lofty structure used for purposes of protection or attack: to defend a city wall, particularly at a gate or a corner in the wall (II Chron. 14:7; 26:9); to protect flocks and herds and to safeguard roads (II Kings 17:9; II Chron. 26:10; 27:4); to observe and to attack a city (Isa. 23:13); to protect a vineyard (Matt. 21:33).

Town, in ancient times large cities had towns or villages surrounding them for protection (Num. 21:25, 32; Josh. 15:45-47); sometimes it means an unwalled town (Deut. 3:5; I Sam. 16:4).

Trachonitis (trăk-ō-nī'tĭs, **rough region),** a volcanic region SE of Damascus, identified by inscriptions and mentioned in Luke 3:1 as a tetrarchy of Philip. The "Rough Region" is still known to the Arabs as "the Refuge" or "the fortress of Allah." It has been likened to "a tempest in stone," or a black, petrified sea.

Trade and Travel. Trade in the OT. Ur of the Chaldees a trading port; Egypt, from earliest times, a great trading nation (Gen. 37:25); first organized commerce of Hebrew people was under Solomon, who formed a partnership with the great mercantile cities of Tyre and Sidon (I Kings 9:27, 28; 10:11); after the death of Solomon Israel again became an agricultural nation. **Trade in the NT.** Jewish trade and commerce have small place in the Gospels. All through NT times trade, in the wider sense of the word, was in the hands of Rome and of Italy. **Travel.** Motives for travel: trade, colonization, exploration, migration, pilgrimage, preaching, courier service, exile. Travel had serious hazards (II Cor. 11:25-27; Acts 27, 28); was facilitated by wonderful Roman roads, some of which still are used. Regular passenger service by land or sea was unknown.

Trade Guilds, societies of tradesmen organized chiefly for purpose of social intercourse (Acts 19); not trade unions in the modern sense.

Tradition (trȧ-dĭ'shŭn, **a giving over,** by word of mouth or in writing). There are three types of tradition mentioned in the NT. The most common use is the kind of tradition handed down by the Jewish fathers or elders which constituted the oral law which the Pharisees tended to make of even greater authority than the Scriptures (Matt. 15:2f; Mark 7:3f). A classic example of their traditions is recorded in the Gospels (Matt. 15:2-6; Mark 7:1-13). The second type of tradition is mentioned in Col. 2:8. The emphasis seems to be upon the **human,** not necessarily Jewish, origin of these teachings. The third type is the gospel truths that the Apostle Paul taught. He uses the word three times (I Cor. 11:2 ASV [KJV "ordinances"]; II Thess. 2:15; 3:6). The meaning of this kind of tradition is "instruction."

Train. 1. Retinue of a monarch, as in the case of the Queen of Sheba (I Kings 10:2). 2. **Skirt** of a robe (Isa. 6:1). 3. **To train up** (Prov. 22:6) in rearing a child. 4. **To discipline** (Titus 2:4); translated in KJV "teach," changed in ASV to "train."

Trajan (trā'jăn). Marcus Ulpius Traianus held the principate from A.D. 98 to 117. Born in Spain in A.D. 53, Trajan was adopted by Nerva as his heir in A.D. 97, after a distinguished military career. During Trajan's principate the Roman Empire reached its widest extent.

Trance (a throwing of the mind out of its normal state), a mental state in which the senses are partially or wholly suspended and the person is unconscious of his environment while he contemplates some extraordinary object. Peter describes a trance (Acts 10:9-16). Paul relates how he fell into a trance while praying in the temple (Acts 22:17-21). There are other similar experiences recorded in the Scriptures which are not called trances but must have been such (Num. 24:4, 16; Isa. 6:1-13; Ezek. 8-11; 40-48; Rev. 4-22).

Transfiguration, the name given to that singular event (Matt. 17:1-8; Mark 9: 2-8; Luke 9:28-36) when Jesus was visibly glorified in the presence of three select disciples. The accounts portray the transformation as outwardly visible and consisting in an actual physical change in the body of Jesus: "the fashion of his countenance was altered" (Luke 9:29), "his face did shine as the sun" (Matt. 17:2), while "his garments became glistening, exceeding white" (Mark 9:3). The glory was not caused by the falling of a heavenly light upon Him from without but by the flashing forth of the radiant splendor within. It was witnessed by Peter, James, and John, and occurred while Jesus "was praying" (Luke 9:29). The natural simplicity of the accounts and their sober insistence upon its detailed features powerfully testify to the reality of the event. Its historical reality is attested by the Apostle Peter (II Pet. 1:16-18).

Transgression (trăns-grĕ′shŭn, **rebellion),** the breaking of a law (Prov. 17: 11; Rom. 4:15).

Transjordan, Trans-Jordan (trăns-jôr′dăn), large plateau E of Jordan, comprised in modern Hashemite Kingdom of Jordan; in NT times, the Peraea and the Decapolis; in OT times, Moab, Ammon, Gilead, and Bashan. Associated with Moses; Joshua; the tribes Reuben, Gad, and Manasseh; David; Nabataeans.

Translate (trăns′lāt, **to transfer, to remove from one place to another).** The Hebrew word is rendered once as "translate" (II Sam. 3:10 KJV, ASV has "transfer"). The Greek words occur in Hebrews 11:5. In Colossians 1: 13 the believer is described as passing from the kingdom of darkness into that of light.

Transportation (See Trade and Travel)

Travail (trăv′āl), pangs of childbirth (Gen. 35:16; 38:27; I Sam. 4:19), trouble (Isa. 23:4; 54:1), to be weak or sick (Jer. 4:31), weariness (Exod. 18:8).

Travel (See Trade and Travel)

Treasure, a collection of objects of value, including stores of provisions (e.g. Jer. 41:8, where RSV renders "stores"). See Ezek. 28:4, and Dan. 11: 43. The "treasure cities" of Exodus 1: 11 were arsenals and depots for provisions (cf. Gen. 41:48, 56). The metaphorical meaning of treasure is a more common figure of speech in the OT than in the NT (Exod. 19:5; Deut. 28: 12; Ps. 17:14; Matt. 13:44; Luke 12:21; II Cor. 4:7). The last reference is to practices such as those illustrated by the Dead Sea Scrolls, the preservation of precious possessions in earthenware jars, sealed for safety.

Treasurer (See Occuptians and Professions)

Tree. Palestine in ancient times must have been extensively wooded as there are over 300 references to trees and wood in the Bible. Also over 25 different kinds of trees have been identified as having grown in the Holy Land. Most of the wooded areas in Palestine have been cut down. Trees identified with holy places were permitted to flourish. Trees were venerated by heathen people who believed gods inhabited them (Deut. 12:2; I Kings 14:23, etc.). The Hebrews were forbidden to plant a tree near a sacred altar (Deut. 16:21). Trees identified places (Gen. 12:6; Deut. 11:30, etc.). Jesus used the fruit bearing of trees as an illustration of believers' fruit bearing (Matt. 7:16-19). See Plants.

Tree of Knowledge, a special tree in the garden of Eden, set apart by the Lord as an instrument to test the obedience of Adam and Eve (Gen. 2: 9, 17). Its fruit probably was not much different from that of the other trees from which they ate. The sin in eating its fruit did not lie in the tree but in the disobedience of the persons who ate.

Tree of Life, was another special tree in the garden of Eden (Gen. 2:9, 22, 25). This tree appears again in Rev. 22:2 as a fruit-bearing tree with leaves. It will have healing in its leaves (Rev. 22:2).

Trench, "rampart" and "intrenchment" (II Sam. 20:15; I Sam. 26:5, 7; 17:20).

Trespass, the violation of the rights of others, whether of God or of man. In Jewish law, acknowledged violation of a man's rights required restoration, plus one-fifth of the amount or value of the thing involved, and the presentation of a trespass offering.

Trespass Offering (See Offerings)

Tres Tabernae (See Three Taverns)

Trial of Jesus, betrayed by Judas into the hands of the Jewish religious leaders, Jesus was first brought before Annas, former high priest, and father-in-law of the current high priest Caiaphas, for a brief examination (John 18:13); then at cock-crowing time He appeared before the Sanhedrin in the palace of Caiaphas, where He was questioned and had indignities heaped upon Him (Mark 14:60-65; Luke 22:63-64); at dawn He appeared before the Sanhedrin again and was condemned to death (Luke 22:66-70); next He was brought by the Sanhedrin before Pilate, who after an examination pronounced Him innocent (John 18:33-38), but the Jews would not hear of His being released, and Pilate therefore sent Him to Herod Antipas, who was also present for the Passover, on the plea that He belonged to Herod's jurisdiction. Herod, however, merely mocked Jesus and returned Him to Pilate uncondemned (Luke 23:2-12); Pilate then gave the Jews the opportunity of choosing for release either Barabbas or Jesus, and the Jews chose Barabbas; another attempt by Pilate to have Jesus released met with failure, for the Jews threatened him if he did not carry out their wishes; after the Roman soldiers scourged and mocked Him, Jesus was crucified (Mark 15:16-20).

Tribe, Tribes. A tribal group comprised all the individuals descended from the same ancestor. In the case of the Hebrews, each tribe was made up of all the persons descended from one of the sons of the patriarch Jacob.

The 12 tribes of Israel (the name of Jacob [Gen. 32:28]) were first mentioned by Jacob in prophecy (Gen. 49:16, 28). While the Hebrews were in Egypt they were grouped according to their fathers' houses (Exod. 6:14). After they left Egypt the whole company was conceived of as the 12 tribes of Israel (Exod. 24:4). The 12 sons of Jacob were Reuben, Simeon, Levi, Judah, Zebulun, Issachar, Dan, Gad, Asher, Naphtali, Joseph (later divided into Ephraim and Manasseh) and Benjamin. Although they all had a common father, they had four mothers, Leah and Rachel, who were full wives, and Bilhah and Zilpah, who were concubines. The tribes were called by these names. On the breastplate of the high priest were 12 precious stones arranged in four rows; each stone had the name of a tribe engraved on it (Exod. 28:21, 29; 39:14).

When the Israelites were numbered to find out the number of the men of war in each group, the tribe of Levi was left out of this census because the Lord selected them to take care of the keeping and transporting of the tabernacle and its furniture (Num. 1). The whole encampment of Israelites at Sinai was organized and each tribe assigned its place in which to march and to camp (Num. 2).

The leadership of Judah among the tribes was prophesied by Jacob (Gen. 49:10), and this tribe was assigned first place in the order of marching (Num. 2:3; 10:14). Judah also was the first tribe to offer an oblation after the setting up of the tabernacle (Num. 7:12). Before the Israelites entered the Promised Land two tribes, Reuben and Gad, and half of Manasseh chose to settle on the E side of the Jordan (Num. 32:33). After the land of Canaan was subdued, the land was divided among the nine and a half tribes (Josh. chaps. 15-19).

During the period of the Judges in Israel the tribes were each one a law unto themselves. The Judges' leadership was sectional. When David became king over the whole land the 12 tribes were unified. Jerusalem was conquered and made the capital of the country. There Solomon built the temple. The Lord chose this city as the one place out of all the tribes of Israel where He would put His name (II Chron. 12:13). David appointed a captain over each tribe (I Chron. 27:16-22). He also took a census of the tribes (II Sam. 24:2). The unity of the tribes had a tendency to be disrupted into two factions. After the death of Saul, David reigned over only Judah at first (II Sam. 2:4), and did not become king of all the tribes until later (II Sam. 5:3). After the death of Solomon this same division occurred again, Judah and Benjamin became one nation, the kingdom of Judah, and all the area N of them became another nation, the kingdom of Israel (I Kings 12:20). This division continued until both kingdoms went into captivity, Israel in 721 B.C. to Assyria and Judah in 586 B.C. to Babylon. These catastrophes wiped out tribal distinctions. The tribes are not mentioned by name again except in the devotional literature of the Psalms and in prophecy.

Tribulation, Great Tribulation (trĭb-ū-lā'shŭn), trouble of a general sort (Job 28:33; Ps. 13:4; Matt. 13:21; John 16:33). Sometimes this suffering is just the natural part of one's life (Rom. 12:12; James 1:27), while at other times it is looked upon as a definite punishment or chastening from the Lord for misbehavior (Rom. 2:9).

The Great Tribulation is a definite

period of suffering sent from God upon the earth at the end. This period of suffering will be unlike any other period in the past or future (Dan. 12: 2; Matt. 24:21).

Tribute, enforced contributions to individuals, governments, or institutions — like the Temple: took the form of human labor (Exod. 5; Josh. 16:10) and enforced contributions of precious things, commodities, or slaves (I Kings 20:1-7; II Kings 17:1-6).

Trinity. The Biblical doctrine of the Trinity is most distinctly expressed in the words of Christ in the "Great Commission" (Matt. 28:18-20). There are many other clear indications of the Trinity (II Cor. 13:14). The doctrinal formalization of the Biblical data on the Trinity is satisfactorily worded in the Westminster Shorter Catechism: "There are three persons in the Godhead, the Father, the Son, and the Holy Ghost; and these three are one God, the same in substance, equal in power and glory." The unity of the Godhead is unanimously attested throughout the entire range of the Judeo-Christian sources (cf. Deut. 6: 4, 5; Isa. 44:6-8; 45:21-23; I Cor. 8:5, 6).

That the persons, Father, Son, and Holy Spirit are not merely modes of one Person, as Sabellians hold, is evidenced by the prayer life of Jesus (cf. John 17) in which He speaks objectively to the Father; by the Father's witness to the Son (Mark 1:11; 8:7 and parallels; John 12:28, 29); and by numerous objective references to the Holy Spirit (John 15:26; 16:7-15).

The data of revelation, then, established in the minds of NT Christians four convictions: 1. God is One. 2. Jesus is God. 3. The Holy Spirit is God. 4. The three Persons are Subject and Object, "I and Thou," each to the others.

Spiritual and philosophical values in the doctrine can only be mentioned. 1. Only in terms of the Trinity, including infinite Subject-Object relationships, can we conceive of the eternal existence of God before the creation of the finite universe. 2. Only in terms of the Trinity can we conceive of God's redemptive program: The Father gave the Son (John 3:16); the Son gave Himself (Gal. 2:20); "through the eternal Spirit" He "offered Himself" (Heb. 9:14). 3. The revelation of the Eternal Son illuminates our finite sonship in the "household" of God (Rom. 8:16, 29; I John 3:1, 2; 17:21, 22).

Triumph (to lead in triumph). In Roman times a triumph was a magnificent procession in honor of a victorious general, the highest military honor he could obtain. He entered the city in a chariot, preceded by the senate and magistrates, musicians, the spoils of his victory, and the captives in chains (II Cor. 2:14; Col. 2:15).

Troas (trō′ăs), a name applied both to a region and a city. 1. The region is the NW corner of Asia Minor, in the district of Mysia, and the Roman province of Asia on the Aegean coast. 2. The city was Alexandria Troas, some ten miles from the ruins of ancient Troy. Troas was a Roman colony in Augustus' day, and one of the most important cities of NW Asia (Acts 16:8; 20:5; II Cor. 2:12).

Trogyllium (trō-jĭl′ĭ-ŭm), a slender promontory thrusting SW from the Asian mainland N of Miletus, and overlapping the eastern extension of Samos (Acts 20:15).

Trophimus (trŏf′ĭ-mŭs, **nourishing),** a Gentile Christian of Ephesus (Acts 21: 29) and companion of Paul (II Tim. 4:20; II Cor. 8:19ff; Acts 20:4). In Jerusalem he was the innocent cause of the tumult resulting in Paul's imprisonment when hostile Asian Jews hastily **supposed** that Paul had illegally introduced him into the temple itself (Acts 21:29).

Truth, correspondence of the known facts of existence with the sum total of God's universe; may be known by general and special revelation — but only so much as God chooses to reveal. God has made known all that man needs to know for life and salvation. Truth is manifested supremely in Christ (John 1:14, 17; 14:6); those who turn away from Him choose to live in error.

Tryphena (trī-fē′nȧ, **dainty),** a Christian woman who lived in Rome and was known to Paul. He asked the Roman believers to greet her and Tryphosa, her close relative (Rom. 16: 12).

Tryphosa (See Tryphena)

Tubal (tū′-bȧl), a tribe descended from Japheth (Gen. 10:2; Isa. 66:19).

Tunic (See Dress)

Turban (See Dress)

Turtle (See Birds)

Turtledove (See Birds)

A general view of Tyre, with the entrance to its harbor, on the Mediterranean coast of ancient Phoenicia. © *MPS*

Twelve, The (See Apostles)

Tychicus (tĭk′ĭ-kŭs, **fortuitous**), an Asian Christian and close friend and valued helper of Paul (Acts 20:4; II Cor. 8:19ff; Titus 3:12). He was with Paul during the first Roman imprisonment and carried the letters to the Ephesians (Eph. 6:21) and the Colossians (Col. 4:7-9), being delegated to report to them concerning Paul. Onesimus, returning to his master, accompanied him (Col. 4:7-9; Philem.). Tychicus was with Paul during his second Roman imprisonment and was sent to Ephesus by him (II Tim. 4:12).

Tyrannus (tī-răn′ŭs, **tyrant**), Greek teacher in whose school Paul preached after he was expelled from the synagogue (Acts 19:9).

Tyre, Tyrus (tīr, tī′rŭs, **rock**), Phoenician port S of Sidon and N of Carmel; founded by Sidon (Isa. 23:2, 12); assigned to Asher, but never occupied (Josh. 19:29; II Sam. 24:7); first built on mainland, but later on a nearby island; David and Solomon in friendly alliance with its kings (I Kings 9:10-14; II Chron. 2:3-16); powerful merchant city (Isa. 23:8); famous especially for dyes, glassware, and metal works; Carthage founded by Tyrian colonists; denounced by prophets (Isa. 23:1-17; Jer. 27:3; Ezek. 26-28); Jesus visited region and was well received (Mark 7:24-31); Paul stayed there seven days (Acts 21:3-7).

Tyropeon Valley (See Jerusalem)

Ucal (ū'kăl), obscure word; usually taken as son or pupil of Agur (Prov. 30:1).

Uel (ū'ĕl), man who divorced foreign wife (Ezra 10:34).

Ugarit (ū'gȧ-rĭt), ancient city on N Syrian coast, 40 miles SW of Antioch; also called Ras Shamra; great commercial and religious center; hundreds of tablets known as "Ras Shamra Tablets" discovered there.

Uknaz (ŭk'năz), Jephunneh's son (I Chron. 4:15). KJV has "even Kenaz"; RV has "and Kenaz."

Ulai (ū'lī), a river which Daniel mentions twice (8:2, 16). It ran through the province of Elam, and flowed through Susa.

Ulam (ū'lăm). 1. A son of Sheresh from the tribe of Manasseh (I Chron. 7:16, 17). 2. A descendant of the Benjamite, Eshek (I Chron. 8:39-40).

Ulla (ŭ'lȧ), one of Asher's descendants who became the father of three distinguished men of the tribe (I Chron. 7:39).

Ummah (ŭm'ȧ, **association),** one of the cities belonging to the tribe of Asher (Josh. 19:30).

Uncial Letters (See Texts, Writing)

Uncircumcised (ŭn-sûr'kŭm-sīzd). 1. One who has not submitted to Jewish rite of circumcision. 2. Gentiles (Gen. 34:14; Judg. 14:3; Rom. 4:9). 3. One whose heart is not open to God (Jer. 4:4; 6:10; Acts 7:51).

Uncle. 1. Brother of one's father or mother (II Kings 24:17). 2. Any kinsman on father's side (Lev. 10:4; Amos 6:10).

Unclean, Uncleanness. 1. Two kinds of uncleanness: moral and ceremonial. 2. Foods regarded as unclean in OT: animals that did not chew the cud and part the hoof; animals and birds which eat blood or carrion; anything strangled or that died of itself (Lev. 11:1-8; 26-28); water creatures without scales and fins (Lev. 11:9-12); insects without hind legs for jumping (Lev. 11). 3. Other forms of ceremonial uncleanness: contact with the dead (Lev. 11: 24-40; 17:15; Num. 19:16-22); leprosy (Lev. 13; 14; Num. 5:2); sexual discharge (Lev. 15:16-33); childbirth (Lev 12:6-8). In Christianity uncleanness is moral, not ceremonial.

Unction (ŭngk'shŭn, **anointing),** the act of anointing, in the KJV found only in I John 2:20. In I John 2:27 the Greek is translated "anointing."

Undefiled, any person or thing not tainted with moral evil (Ps. 119:1; Heb. 7:26; 13:4; I Pet. 1:4).

Undersetters, supports of the layer in Solomon's temple (I Kings 7:30, 34).

Unicorn (ū'nĭ-kôrn), fabulous animal; horned; strong; wild; difficult to catch; may be wild ox (Num. 23:22; 24:8; Deut. 33:17; Job 39:9f; Ps. 29:6). See Animals.

Unity, togetherness of persons (Gen. 13:6); fellowship (Judg. 19:6); praise (Ps. 34:3); or of animals (Isa. 11:6-7). The NT word bespeaks the unity of faith that binds together the people of God (Eph. 4:13).

Unknown God. On Mars Hill Paul began his message to the philosophers by saying, "I found an altar with this inscription, **To the unknown God"** (Acts 17:23). This was probably a votive altar erected by some worshiper who did not know what god to thank for some benefit he had received. Using this as a starting point, Paul preached the true God unto them.

Unknown Tongue, the charismatic gift of speaking in tongues (I Cor. 14:2, 4, 13, 14, 19, 27).

Unlearned, illiterate (Acts 4:13; II Pet. 3:16); non-professional (I Cor. 14:16, 23f).

Unleavened. When used literally, it refers to bread unmixed with leaven or to the Passover Feast, when only unleavened bread could be used. When used figuratively it means "unmixed" (I Cor. 5:7, 8).

Unleavened Bread, bread made without any fermented dough, eaten at the Passover (Exod. 12:8).

Unleavened Bread, Feast Of (See Feasts)

Unni (un'ī). 1. One of the Levite musicians whom David appointed (I Chron. 15:18, 20). 2. Another Levite employed in the music service of the temple (Neh. 12:9). "Unno" is the corrected spelling.

Unpardonable Sin, not a phrase used in the Bible, but the usual way of referring to the blasphemy against the Holy Spirit (Matt. 12:31-32; Mark 3: 28-29; Luke 12:10). There is much difference of opinion as to the meaning of this sin, but it probably refers to the sin of decisively and finally rejecting the testimony of the Holy Spirit regarding the person and work of Jesus Christ.

Untempered Mortar, mortar made of clay instead of slaked lime. It was smeared on the walls of houses made of small stones or mud bricks so as to prolong the life of the building.

Upharsin (ū-fȧr'sĭn), one of the words found written on the wall at Belshazzar's feast (Dan. 5:24-28). It probably means "divisions" or "divided." See Mene, Mene, Tekel, Upharsin.

Uphaz (ū'făz), a gold-producing region mentioned in Jer. 10:9 and Dan. 10:5. Its location is still unknown. Perhaps "Ophir" or "and fine gold" should be read instead.

Upper Chamber, Upper Room, a room frequently built on the roofs of houses and used in summer because it was cooler than the regular living quarters (Mark 14:15; Luke 22:12; Acts 1:13; 20:8). One of these was the scene of our Lord's last supper (Luke 22:12).

Ur (ûr, **flame),** the father of Eliphal, one of David's mighty men (I Chron. 11:35).

Ur of the Chaldees, the early home of Abraham, mentioned in Gen. 11:28, 31; 15:7; I Chron. 11:35; and in Neh. 9:7. Located in southern Mesopotamia, about 140 miles SE of the site of old Babylon.

Education was well developed at Ur, for a school was found there with its array of clay tablets. Further studies have revealed the fact that commerce was well developed and that ships came into Ur from the Persian Gulf bringing diorite and alabaster used in statue making, copper ore, ivory, gold and hard woods.

Urbane (ûr'bān, **polite),** a Roman Christian to whom Paul sent greetings (Rom. 16:9).

Uri (ū'rī, **fiery).** 1. The father of Bezaleel (Exod. 31:2; 35:30; 38:22; I Chron. 2:20; II Chron. 1:5). 2. The father of Geber, one of the 12 provision officers of Solomon (I Kings 4:19). 3. A porter of the temple who put away his foreign wife (Ezra 10:24).

Uriah, Urias (ū-rī'ȧ, ū-rī'ăs, **Jehovah is light).** 1. A Hittite, the husband of Bathsheba (II Sam. 11:3). After David had committed adultery with Bathsheba, he recalled Uriah from the battle and sent him to his house, trying thus to hide his sin. When Uriah refused to do violence to his religion, David sent him back to the war with special instructions for Joab to place him in the thick of the fight that he might die. When he was finally killed, David took Bathsheba for his own wife. 2. High priest during reign of Ahaz of Judah, for whom he built a pagan altar in the temple (II Kings 16:10-16). 3. Priest who aided Ezra (Neh. 8:4). 4. Father of Meremoth (Ezra 8:33; Neh. 3:4). 5. Son of Shemaiah, a prophet of Kirjath-jearim (Jer. 26:20-23).

Uriel (ū'rī-ĕl, **God is light).** 1. Kohathite Levite (I Chron. 6:24). 2. Chief of Kohathites who assisted in bringing the ark from house of Obed-Edom (I Chron. 15:5, 11). 3. Father of Michaiah, wife of Rehoboam (II Chron. 13: 2).

Urijah (ū-rī'jȧ, **Jehovah is light).** 1. A prophet, the son of Shemaiah of Kirjath-jearim, who predicted the destruction of Judah (Jer. 26:20). The king, angry at his predictions, had him killed (Jer. 26:21-23). 2. See Uriah numbers 2 and 3.

Urim and Thummim (ū'rĭm and thŭm'ĭm, **lights and perfections),** objects not specifically described, perhaps stones, placed in the breastplate of the high priest: by which he ascertained the will of God in any important matter affecting the nation (Exod. 28:30; Lev. 8:8). One theory is that they were used as the lot and cast like dice, the manner of their fall somehow revealing the Lord's will (I Sam. 10:19-22; 14: 37-42). Another theory is that they served as a symbol of the high priest's authority to seek counsel of Jehovah, God's will being revealed to him through inner illumination (Exod 28: 30; Num. 20:28; Neh. 7:65).

Usury, charging of interest on money loaned; law forbade loaning of money to a brother Jew for interest (Exod. 22:25; Deut. 23:19), but permitted lending money to a stranger with interest (Deut. 23:20). Jesus did not condemn receiving reasonable rates of interest for money loaned (Matt. 25: 27; Luke 19:23).

Uthai (ū'thī). 1. A descendant of Judah who lived in Jerusalem after the Babylonian captivity (I Chron. 9:4). 2. One who returned with Ezra (Ezra 8:14).

Uz (ŭz). 1. One of Nahor's sons by Milcah (Gen. 22:21). KJV has "Huz." 2. Son of Aram (Gen. 10:23), the grandson of Shem (I Chron. 1:17). 3. Son of Dishan (Gen. 36:28). 4. The country in which Job lived (Job 1:1), site uncertain. This country is referred to also twice by Jeremiah (Jer. 25: 20; Lam. 4:21).

Uzai (ū'zī), father of Palal who aided Nehemiah in rebuilding the walls of Jerusalem (Neh. 3:25).

Uzal (ū'zăl), a Shemite, the sixth son of Joktan (Gen. 10:27; I Chron. 1:21). He founded Uzal, the capital of Yemen.

Uzza (ŭz'ȧ, **strength).** 1. The son of Shimei who became the father of Shimea (I Chron. 6:29). 2. The eldest son of Ehud (I Chron. 8:7). 3. Caretaker, owner of a garden in which Manasseh and his son, Amon, were buried (II Kings 21:18, 26). 4. One whose children returned under Zerubbabel (Ezra 2:49; Neh. 7:51).

Uzza, Garden of, mentioned in II Kings 21:18, 26. Manasseh and his son Amon were buried here.

Uzzah (ŭz'ȧ, **strength).** Son of Abinadab who accompanied the ark of the Lord when it was being brought from Kirjath-jearim to Jerusalem. The ark was being drawn on a cart pulled by oxen and when something happened causing the ark to shake, Uzzah took hold of it, thus displeasing the Lord. As a result, he met instant death (II Sam. 6:3-8; I Chron. 13:6-11).

Uzzen-Sherah (ŭz'ĕn-shē'ē-rȧ, **plat of Sherah),** a town built by Ephraim's daughter Sheerah (I Chron. 7:24).

Uzzi (ŭz'ī, **strong).** 1. One of Aaron's descendants who became the father of Zerahiah (I Chron. 6:5, 51; Ezra 7:4). 2. Grandson of Issachar (I Chron. 7:2, 3). 3. Bela's son from the tribe of Benjamin (I Chron. 7:7). 4. Another Benjamite, the father of Elah (I Chron. 9:8). 5. An overseer of the Levites (Neh. 11:22). 6. A priest in the family of Jedaiah (Neh. 12:19)

Uzzia (ŭ-zī'ȧ, **strength),** one of David's mighty men who was from Ashtaroth (I Chron. 11:24).

Uzziah (ŭ-zī'ȧ, **Jehovah is strength).** 1. Uzziah, also called Azariah, the son of Amaiah. At the age of 16 he became Judah's 11th king (II Kings 14:21), and ruled 52 years. He undertook, very early in his career, an expedition against his father's enemies, and won battles against the Edomites, Philistines, Arabians, and the Mehunims (II Kings 14:22; II Chron. 26: 1-7). He strengthened his kingdom (II Chron. 26:2), and made many improvements on his home front (II Chron. 26:9-10). He possessed real ability at organization (II Chron. 26: 11-15). The report of his strength spread as far as Egypt (II Chron. 26: 8). In spite of these successes, he strayed far from the Lord at the end of his life. Apparently as long as the Prophet Zechariah lived, his influence was great on the king and "as long as he sought the Lord, God made him to prosper" (II Chron. 26:5). However, when he became strong, pride filled his heart, and going into the temple he determined to burn incense unto the Lord, a duty to be performed only by the priest. The chief priest, Azariah, with 80 priests went into the temple to reason with him, but he would not listen. Because of his self will, God struck him with leprosy which stayed with him until his death (II Chron. 26:16-21). 2. A Levite descended from Kohath (I Chron. 6:24). 3. The father of a certain Jehonathan in David's time (I Chron. 27:25). 4. One of the sons of Harim who put away his foreign wife (Ezra 10:16-21). 5. The father of Athaiah who returned to Jerusalem (Neh. 11:4).

Uzziel, Uzzielite (ŭ-zī'ĕl, ŭ-zī'ĕl-īt, **God is strength).** 1. A Levite, son of Kohath (Exod. 6:18, 22; Lev. 10:4; Num. 3: 19, 30; I Chron. 6:2, 18). 2. A Simeonite captain under Hezekiah (I Chron. 4:42). 3. Head of a Benjamite family (I Chron. 7:7). 4. One of David's musicians (I Chron. 25:4). 5. One of the sons of Jeduthun, a Levite, who assisted in cleansing the temple (II Chron. 29:14-19). 6. The son of Harhaiah, a goldsmith, who aided Nehemiah in repairing the walls of Jerusalem (Neh. 3:8). Anyone who descended from Uzziel, the Levite, was known as a Uzzielite. This group is referred to in several places (Num. 3:27; I Chron. 15:9; 26:23; 15:10).

–V–

Vagabond (to wander), a word used in the curse pronounced upon Cain (Gen. 4:12, 14). The plural form is found in the imprecatory prayer in Psalm 109:10. The sorcerers mentioned in Acts 19:13 as "vagabond Jews" were professional exorcists.

Vajezatha (vȧ-jĕz′ȧ-thȧ, **son of the atmosphere),** one of the ten sons of Haman (Esth. 9:9).

Vale, Valley. 1. The place of Moses' burial (Deut. 34:6), the valley of Hinnom (Josh. 15:8; 18:16; II Kings 23:10; Jer. 7:31), a valley of salt (II Sam. 8:13; I Chron. 18:12; II Chron. 25:11), the valley of Hamon-gog (Ezek. 39:11, 15), and the great valley formed when Christ returns to the earth to rule (Zech. 14:4-5). 2. A valley that is the bed of a brook or river which can be filled quickly by rain, which often happens in the climate of Palestine (Gen. 26:19; Num. 13:23; Josh. 12:1). 3. A number of places such as: Valley of Achor (Josh. 7:24); Valley of Ajalon (Josh. 10:12); of Gibeon (Isa. 28:21); of Hebron (Gen. 37:14); of Jehoshaphat (Joel 3:2); of Jezreel (Josh. 17:16). 4. A plain between two hills or mountains and in that sense a valley (Deut. 11:11; 34:3; Josh. 11:17). 5. Not a valley, but the low lying hills that stretch from Israel's coast up to the mountains (Josh. 10:40; Jer. 32:44). 6. A ravine (Luke 3:5).

Valley Gate (gate of the Gai), a gate mentioned in Neh. 2:13; 3:13; 12:31, 38.

Vaniah (vȧ-nī′ȧ), a son of Bani who gave up his Gentile wife (Ezra 10:36).

Vanity, emptiness, evanescence, worthlessness, futility, unprofitableness (Job 7:3; Ps. 39:5, 6; I Sam. 12:21; II Kings 17:15; Eph. 4:17; II Pet. 2:18); never used in KJV in sense of conceit or undue self-esteem.

Vashni (văsh′nī, **weak),** eldest son of Samuel (I Chron. 6:28); in I Sam. 8:2 Joel is named as Samuel's first-born. The Hebrew text is probably corrupt here.

Vashti (văsh′tī, **beautiful woman),** Xerxes' queen whom he divorced because of her refusal to show herself to the king's guests at a feast and whose place was taken by Esther (Esth. 1:11).

Veil (See Dress, Temple)

Vein (source), Job 28:1 KJV has "a vein for the silver." The RV "mine" probably conveys the meaning of the Hebrew more accurately (Num. 30:12; Deut. 8:3; Ps. 19:6).

Vengeance, any punishment meted out in the sense of retribution. The word is used in both a bad sense (Judg. 15:7) and a good sense (Jer. 11:20; 20:12). NT uses (Acts 23:4; Luke 18:7; Matt. 3:7, etc.).

Venison (game of any kind), properly the flesh of the deer, but as used in Gen. 25:28 and 27:5ff it could mean any game taken in hunting.

Vermilion, a red pigment used for painting walls of palaces (Jer. 22:14) and for coloring the exotic clothing of the Chaldeans (Ezek. 23:14).

Versions of the Scriptures (See Bible, also Texts and Versions)

Vessel, any material thing or object which may be used for any purpose, whether it be a tool, implement, weapon, or receptable. Hosea 13:15 has "pleasant vessels" in the KJV; this is more correctly rendered by "precious thing" in the RSV. In Rom. 9:20-24 and II Tim. 2:20, 21 the term is applied to persons, and in II Cor. 4:7 it means the person as an instrument of God's will. In I Thess. 4:4 "vessel" is used figuratively for either a man's own body or for his wife, more likely the latter.

Vestry, a place where royal or ceremonial vestments were kept (II Kings 10:22).

Vesture, archaic word for garments (Gen. 41:42; Deut. 22:12; Ps. 22:18). Sometimes used metaphorically (Ps. 102:26; Heb. 1:12).

Via Dolorosa, "the sorrowful way," the traditional route which our Lord traveled on the day of His crucifixion from the judgment seat of Pilate (Matt. 27:26, 31; Mark 15:20; Luke 22:25; John 19:16) to the place of His crucifixion on Mount Calvary (Matt. 27:33; Mark 15:22; Luke 23:33; John 19:18).

Vial, a flask or bottle (I Sam. 10:1), rendered "box" in II Kings 9:1, 3 KJV, but "vial" in ASV. In Rev. 5:8; 21:9, a shallow bowl or basin.

Victual (See Food)

Village. Villages were usually grouped around a fortified town to which the people could flee in time of war (II Chron. 28:18). The usual OT word signifies an enclosure (Josh. 13:23, 28) and is frequently compounded to name a particular village e.g. Hazar-addar (Num. 34:4).

Vine (See Plants)

Vinegar, a sour fluid obtained by fermentation of cider, but in Bible times from wine. The Nazirite was to abstain from drinking it (Num. 6:3), and it was used as a condiment on bread (Ruth 2:14). Its action on the teeth (Prov. 10:26) and its fizzing with soda (Prov. 25:20) are mentioned by Solomon. Our Lord, upon the cross, was offered vinegar (ASV "wine") mixed with gall or with myrrh (Matt. 27:34, cf. Mark 15:23) in fulfillment of Ps. 69:21, but He refused it. Later He was offered on a sponge a mixture of water and vinegar (Matt. 27:48), a drink very popular among the poor and used by Roman soldiers when in camp.

Vineyard. Soil of Palestine has always been very favorable to the cultivation of grapes (Num. 13:20, 24); vineyards usually surrounded with a protecting wall to keep out animals and thieves (Num. 22:24); also had tower for watchman (Mark 12:1), winepress hollowed out of a flat rock, and a vat into which the wine flowed from the winepress (Isa. 1:8; 5:1-7; Matt. 21:33-41); gleanings left to the poor (Lev. 19:10); wine stored in new goatskin bags (Matt. 9:17) or in large pottery jars. Grapes were eaten fresh, made into jelly, dried into raisins or cakes for future eating (I Sam. 25:18), and made into wine. Pulp was placed in vat with water and allowed to ferment to make vinegar or poor grade of wine (Ps. 69:21; Matt. 27:48). Every seventh year the vines were allowed to lie fallow (Exod. 23:11; Lev. 25:3). Figuratively, the vine symbolized prosperity and peace (I Kings 4:25; Mic. 4:4; Zech. 3:10) and the chosen people Israel.

Vineyards, Plain of the, a village of the Ammonites E of the Jordan (Judg. 11:33).

Viper (See Animals)

Virgin. 1. A young unmarried woman (Gen. 24:16; Exod. 22:16f; II Sam. 13:2). It is also used figuratively to personify a city or a state (Isa. 23:12;

An Arab girl picking grapes in a vineyard of Ephraim. © MPS

47:1; Amos 5:2. 2. A young woman of marriageable age, whether married or not (Gen. 24:43; S. of Sol. 1:3; 6:8; Isa. 7:14, etc.). Only the context can give it the force "virgin."

Virgin Birth. Christendom in the Apostles' Creed confesses that its Lord and Saviour was "conceived by the Holy Ghost, born of the Virgin Mary." This formulation of faith, going back to the second century, is based upon two NT passages, Matthew 1:18-25 and Luke 1:26-2:7.

The Virgin Birth means that Jesus Christ entered into the stream of human life without the mediation of an earthly father, born not as a result of sexual intercourse but as a result of supernatural "overshadowing" of the Holy Spirit.

From a strictly theological perspective, the Virgin Birth has weighty significance. For one thing, it attests the omnipotent grace and creative freedom of God. Again, the Virgin Birth signifies and establishes an organic connection with mankind, on the one hand, and a radical discontinuity with it, on the other. How else could the double requirement of soteriology, simultaneous connection and discontinuity, be achieved? Once more, the Virgin Birth reveals the heavenly origin and unique status of the Messiah's Person. Orr, for example, vigorously contends that the sinlessness of Jesus, His pre-existence, and his role as the Second Adam require the Virgin Birth: Jesus was a spiritual miracle whose entrance into the human race necessitated a physical miracle **(The Virgin Birth of Christ,** pp. 200ff).

Faith in the miracle of the Virgin Birth still serves as a convenient touchstone of faith in the mystery of God enfleshed.

Virtue (strength, ability, often involving moral worth; any excellence of a person or a thing; **power, influence).** The phrase, "a virtuous woman" (Ruth 3:11; Prov. 12:4; 31:10, 29), is literally "a woman of ability." Sometimes the word is used in its Old English sense of "power" (Mark 5:30; Luke 6:19; 8:46) and "strength" (II Cor. 12:9; Heb. 11:11).

Vision, sight presented to the mind through a dream, vision, or other nonobjective stimulus. Most visions in Scripture convey revelations from God. Biblical visions concerned both immediate situations (Gen. 15:1f; Acts 12:7) and more distant ones connected with the development of the kingdom of God, as may be seen in the writings of Isaiah, Ezekiel, Hosea, Micah, Daniel, and John. In the OT false prophets feigned visions and were denounced by Jeremiah (14:14; 23:16) and Ezekiel (13:7).

Visitation, a divine visit for the purpose of rewarding or punishing people for their deeds (Jer. 10:15; Luke 19:44; I Pet. 2:12).

Vophsi (vŏf'sī), a spy from Naphtali (Num. 13:14).

Vow, a voluntary promise to God to perform some service or do something pleasing to Him, in return for some hoped for benefits (Gen. 28:20-22; Lev. 27:2, 8; Num. 30; Judg. 11:30); or to abstain from certain things (Num. 30:3). A vow had to be uttered to be binding (Deut. 23:23). In the NT Jesus mentions vows only to condemn the abuse of them (Matt. 15:4-6; Mark 7:10-13). Paul's vow in Acts 18:18 was probably a temporary Nazirite vow.

Vulgate (See Texts and Versions)

Vulture (See Birds)

Wadi (wä'dē), a valley which forms the bed of a stream during the winter, but which dries up in the hot season (Gen. 26:19). The word is Arabic, and does not appear in the Bible.

Wafers, thin cakes (Exod. 16:31; 29:2). The same word is rendered "cakes" in I Chron. 23:29 KJV.

Wages, pay given for labor, generally reckoned by the day, and distinguished from fees paid for professional service or salaries which may be paid by the month or the year; withholding wages condemned (Jer. 22:13; Mal. 3:5; James 5:4). The earliest mention of wages is in the bargaining between Laban and his nephew Jacob (Gen. 29). It is implicit in the narrative that he must also have received his living during those 14 years: then he labored for another six years, receiving as his wages considerable herds and flocks (Gen. 29, 30). Pharaoh's daughter promised wages to the mother of Moses to act as his nurse (Exod. 2: 5-9). In the Mosaic law, a hired servant must be paid at the end of the day (Lev. 19:13; Deut. 24:14, 15). The same sort of poverty is in the parable of the 11th hour laborers (Matt. 20: 1-16). Mercenary soldiers were advised by John the Baptist to "be content with your wages" (Luke 3:14). The idea of wages is spiritualized in "the wages of sin is death" (Rom. 6: 23), where it is contrasted with "the gift of God—eternal life in Christ Jesus our Lord." Paul speaks of his gifts from churches at Philippi as "wages" (II Cor. 11:8; cf. Phil. 4:15-18), and though he earned his living with his hands, he teaches the right of the laborer to his hire (I Tim. 5:18).

Wagon, a vehicle with wheels (usually two) used for carrying goods as well as persons. Ancient wagons were crude, with wheels made of wood. Wagons are first mentioned in Gen. 45:19-46:5.

Wail. In ancient funeral processions wailing relatives, often accompanied by hired female (sometimes male) mourners and musicians, preceded the body to the grave (Jer. 9:16f; Amos 5: 16; Matt. 9:23).

Walk, used hundreds of times, generally literally but often figuratively (Ps. 1:1). In the NT epistles the word is used uniformly in the figurative sense and refers to the whole manner of life and conduct (Eph. 2:2, 10; 5:2, 8, 15) and the observance of laws or customs (Acts 21:21).

Wall. All over the East the walls of houses were built of sun-baked mud brick; stone little used; every ancient city had enormous walls surrounding it. Symbol of truth and strength (Jer. 15:20), protection (Zech. 2:5), salvation (Isa. 26:1).

War. For Israelites war had a religious significance; priests often accompanied Israel's armies into battle; battles were begun with sacrificial rites (I Sam. 7:8-10; 13:9), and after consulting the divine oracle (Judg. 20: 18ff; I Sam. 14:37); blowing of trumpet throughout land announced call to arms (Judg. 3:27). Weapons included slings, spears, javelins, bows and arrows, swords, and battering-rams. Strategical movements included ambush (Josh. 8:3ff), feint (Judg. 20:20ff), flank movement (II Sam. 5:22f), surprise attack (Josh. 11:1f), raid (I Chron. 14:9), foray (II Sam. 3:22), foraging to secure supplies (II Sam. 23: 11). Wars sometimes settled by single combat (I Kings 11:15). Prisoners sold into slavery or killed (Deut. 20:16-18; Amos 1:6, 9); booty equally divided (I Sam. 30:24, 25).

Washing. Frequent bathing was necessary in the warm climate of the East. In Egypt, Syria, and Palestine people washed the dust from their feet when they entered a house (Gen. 18:4; John 13:10). Ceremonial defilement was removed by bathing the body and washing the raiment (Lev. 14:8; Num. 19: 7-8). The priests washed their hands and feet before entering the sanctuary or offering a sacrifice (Exod. 30:19-21). In the time of Christ the Jews did much ceremonial washing of hands before eating (Mark 7:3, 4).

Watch, a man or group of men set to guard a city. Nehemiah, when building the walls of Jerusalem, set a watch day and night against his enemies (4: 9) and after the walls were completed, he set watches near the gate (7:3). Even today, when the crops are ripening in the fields and vineyards in the East, one may see watchmen on guard day and night.

Watches of the Night, the divisions into which the 12 hours of the night were divided. The Jews had a threefold division (Judg. 7:19), while the Romans had four watches (Mark 6:48).

Watchman, one who guards a city or the headquarters of an army (I Sam. 14:16; II Sam. 18:24-27). Such watchmen were set on city walls or on hilltops (Jer. 31:6).

Water. Because of its scarcity in Palestine, it is much appreciated; absence of water very serious (I Kings 17:1ff; Jer. 14:3); rivers mostly small; people dependent upon springs and fountains; cisterns a necessity; drinking water carried in goatskins and often sold in streets. Water used for ceremonial washings (Lev. 11:32; 16:4; Num. 19:7). Used as symbol of cleansing of the soul from sin (Ezek. 16:4, 9; 36:25; John 3:5).

Water of Bitterness (Num. 5:12-31), water, mingled with dust from the floor of the sanctuary, which a woman suspected of carnal sin was asked to drink —a sort of "trial by ordeal" but ordered of the Lord. If she were guilty, her body would swell and her "thigh fall away," a statement possibly meaning dire disorder of the generative organs. If she were innocent, the water had no effect.

Water of Jealousy (See Water of Bitterness)

Water of Separation. Water for the removal of impurity (Num. 19:9, 13, 20, 21; 31:23).

Waterpot, earthen jars for carrying or holding water, either for drinking (John 4:28) or for purifying purposes (John 2:6f).

Waterspout. Ps. 42:7 ASV has "waterfall." It is used of a large rush of water sent by God, perhaps great floods of rain.

Wave Offering (See Offerings)

Way. There are about 25 Heb. and Gr. words rendered "way" in the Bible. It is often used metaphorically to describe the conduct or manner of life, whether of God or of man (Exod. 32:8; Deut. 5:33; Job 16:22). In the NT, God's plan of salvation is called "the way of the Lord" (Matt. 3:3, etc.). The term is also used to mean Christianity or Judaism (Acts 9:2; 19:9; 22:4).

Wayfaring Man, a traveler (Judg. 19:17; II Sam. 12:4; Isa. 33:8; 35:8).

Wealth, abundance of possessions whether material, social or spiritual. Among early Hebrews, wealth consisted largely of flocks and herds, silver and gold, brass, iron and clothing (Josh. 22:8). In the days of Job, his sons had houses, but their wealth consisted largely of camels, asses, flocks and herds and "a very great household" (Job 1:3), no doubt implying many servants. From the beginning of Israel, God taught His people that He was the giver of their wealth (Deut. 8:16) and He taught them to be liberal (Prov. 11:24). Jesus did not condemn wealth, but stressed the handicap of wealth to one wanting to enter the kingdom of God (Matt. 19:24; Luke 16:19-31).

Wean, Weaning. To wean is to accustom a child to depend upon other food than its mother's milk; often deferred for as much as three years (I Sam. 1:22; 2:11). The weaning of a child was celebrated by a feast (Gen. 21:8) and with an offering (I Sam. 1:24).

Weasel (See Animals)

Weapon (See Arms, Armor)

Weather. There is no Hebrew word corresponding to "weather," but the Israelites were keenly aware of weather phenomena. The great topographical diversity of Palestine assures a variety of weather on a given day: on the top of Mt. Hermon (9,000 feet above sea level) there is snow on the ground the year round; while at Jericho in summer (1,300 feet below sea level) the heat is very oppressive, and the region around the Dead Sea (3,000 feet below sea level) is intolerable. On the coast even the hottest summer day is made bearable by refreshing breezes from the Mediterranean.

Weaving, known in very early times; Jabal, an antediluvian, is called "the father of such as dwell in tents and have cattle" (Gen. 4:20), implying that the weaving of cloth for tents was then known; cloth made into garments, tents, curtains for shrines, etc.; Paul, Aquilla, and Priscilla did weaving (Acts 18:2, 3); guilds of weavers existed in NT times; materials used for weaving included sheep's wool, goats' hair, camels' hair, flax, hemp, and ramie.

Wedding. Marriage customs in the Bible center around the two events of betrothal and wedding. The wedding itself did not include a religious ceremony, although it is probable that the betrothal was ratified by an oath (Ezek. 16:8; Mal. 2:14); and after the Exile written contracts were drawn up and sealed. On the day of the wedding (Gen. 24:65; Isa. 61:10) the bride-

A wedding procession of Bible times. © SPF

groom, attended by friends and accompanied by musicians and singers, went to the bride's house (Matt. 25:7); and then after receiving her from her parents with their blessing he conducted the whole party back to his own house. On the way other friends of the bride and groom joined the party, and there was much music and dancing (Ps. 45:15). A feast was held at the bridegroom's house. Later in the evening the bride's parents escorted her to the nuptial chamber (Gen. 29:23), while he was led there by his friends or the brides' parents. The next day the festivities were resumed and continued for one or two weeks (Gen. 29:27; Judg. 14:12). The wedding festivities included much music and joking.

Wedge, literally "tongue" (Josh. 7:21, 24). Occurrence of word in Isa. 13:12 is an error. ASV properly renders "golden wedge" as "pure gold."

Weeds (See Plants)

Week (See Calendar)

Weeks, Feast of (See Feasts)

Weights and Measures. Balances were used for scales (Lev. 19:36; Prov. 16:

11) and stones for weights (Lev. 19: 36). Some Biblical measures: 1. **Liquid. Log** equals 2/3 pint; **hin** equals 12 logs, or one gallon; **bath** equals six **hins,** or six gallons; **cor** equals 10 **baths,** or 60 gallons. 2. **Dry. Cab** equals two plus pints; **omer** equals 1-4/5 **cabs,** or four pints; **seah** equals 3-1/3 **omers,** or 1/5 bushel; **ephah** equals three **seahs,** or 3/5 bushel; **homer** equals 10 ephahs, or 6-1/4 bushels. 3. **Length. Finger** equals 3/4 inches; **palm** equals four **fingers,** or three inches; **span** equals three **palms,** or nine inches; **cubit** equals two **spans,** or 18 inches; **fathom** equals four **cubits,** or six feet. 4. **Weights. Gerah** equals nine grains; **beqa** equals 10 **gerahs,** or 88 grains; **shekel** equals two **beqas,** or .4 ounce; **maneh** equals 50 **shekels,** or 20 ounces; **talent** equals 60 **manehs,** or 75.5 pounds.

SOME BIBLICAL MEASURES

Liquid

Hebrew term	**equals**	**US liquid measures**
log		2/3 pint
hin	12 logs	1 gal.
bath	6 hins	6 gals.
cor	10 baths	60 gals.

6 gals.=ephah
60 gals.=homer

Dry

Hebrew term	**equals**	**US dry measures**
cab		2+ pints
omer	1 4/5 cabs	4 pints
se'â	3 1/3 omers	1/5 bushel
ephah	3 **se'âs**	3/5 bushel
homer	10 ephahs or 100 omers	6 1/4 bushels

The Common Shekel

Name	**Comparative value**	**Value Today**
talent	60 minehs	75.5 lbs.
mineh	50 shekels	20 oz.
shekel	2 beqa's	.4 oz.
beqa	10 gerahs	88 gr.
gerah		9 gr.

Few weights are mentioned in the NT. **Talent** and **pound** in Luke 19:13-25 are sums of money. **Pound** in John 12:3 and 19:39 represents another Greek word, **litra,** a weight of some 7/10 pound avoirdupois.

Well, a pit or hole dug in the earth down to the water-table, i.e., the level at which the ground is permanently saturated with water. For purposes of safety as well as permanence the well is generally surrounded by a wall of stone (John 4). A well is generally to be distinguished from a cistern (Jer. 2: 13), which is merely for storing water, a spring, which is found at the surface of the ground, and a fountain, from which the water is actively flowing (Josh. 15:9).

West, used figuratively with "east" to denote great distance (Ps. 103:12).

Whale. 1. Any large sea animal (Gen. 1:21; Ezek. 32:2). 2. Sea monster (Matt. 12:40). Great fish in Jonah 1:17. See Animals.

Wheat, most commonly used for flour, but other grains used in emergency or by the poor (Ezek. 4:9, 10); ground between stones.

Wheel, probably at first just a disk of wood cut from a log, but quite early developed into something resembling the modern device (Exod. 14:24, 25). In I Kings 7:30-33, reference is made to wheels with their axle-trees, their naves, spokes and felloes, showing that by Solomon's time (c. 1000 B.C.) the wheel was quite developed and was similar to modern wagonwheels. The word for "potter's wheel" means literally "two stones" (Jer. 18:3). In ancient times two circular stone disks were joined by a short shaft, and so spun.

Whelp, the young of a dog or a beast of prey; a cub. In the Bible the term is always used figuratively (Gen. 49:9; Deut. 33:22; Jer. 51:38; Nah. 2:11, 12).

Whip, generally a lash attached to a handle; figurative use (I Kings 12:14).

Whirlwind, any violent wind, not necessarily a whirling one (Ezek. 1:4; Hos. 8:7; James 3:4); figurative use (Prov. 1:27; Isa. 5:28; Jer. 4:13).

Whore, a woman who habitually commits adultery or fornication, especially for hire; a prostitute, harlot. It is noteworthy that in a very large proportion of cases, the word is used for idolatry. The two words "adultery" and "idolatry" can be identically defined as "taking the love which belongs to one and giving it to another." The practice of selling daughters into whoredom was not unknown in Israel (Lev. 19:29), but was forbidden of the Lord. Whoredom was a capital crime (Gen. 38:24).

Widow, under God's special care (Pss. 68:5; 146:9; Prov. 15:25). From early times they wore a distinctive garb. The Hebrews were commanded to treat them with special consideration and they were punished if they did otherwise (Exod. 22:22; Deut. 14:29; Isa. 1:17; Jer. 7:6). The church looked after poor widows in apostolic times (Acts 6:1; James 1:27). Paul gives instructions to Timothy about the care of widows by the church (I Tim. 5:4).

Wife (See Family, Marriage)

Wild Vine or Grape (See Plants, Vine)

Wilderness. Either to a barren desert or to an uncultivated region suitable for pasturage and occupied by nomads. (1) **A place for the driving of cattle** (Num. 14:33; Judg. 1:16; Deut. 2:8). The word may refer to grassy pastures (Ps. 65:12; Joel 2:22) or a waste of rock and sand (Deut. 32:10; Job 38: 26); (2) **A dry or riverless region** (Isa. 43:19, 20); (3) **Arid, barren** (Isa. 33:9; 51:3) when used with the definite article denotes the plain of the Jordan and Dead Sea (Ezek. 47:8; II Sam. 2: 29); (4) **Land of drought** (Hos. 2:3); (5) **Empty waste** (Job 6:18; 12:24; Ps. 107:40).

Willow (See Plants)

Willows, Brook of the, a brook on the boundary of Moab (Isa. 15:7).

Wills, or testaments, are statements, oral or written in form, to which law courts give effect, by which property may be disposed of after death. The only distinct Bible reference to a will is in Heb. 9:16, 17.

Window (See House)

Winds are important in the Bible, both literally and figuratively. God causes them, He created them (Gen. 8:1; Exod. 13:10; Num. 11:31; Pss. 107:25; 135:7; 147:18; Jer. 10:13=51: 16; Jonah 1:4). The four winds are limits of distance or direction (Jer. 49: 36; Ezek. 37:9; Dan. 7:2; 8:8; 11:4; Zech. 2:6; Matt. 24:31=Mark 13:27; Rev. 7:1). Of the cardinal directions, the east wind is most frequently mentioned (Exod. 10:13; 14:21; Job 15:2; Ps. 48:7; Isa. 27:8; Jer. 18:17; Ezek. 17:10; 19:12; 27:26; Hos. 12:1; 13:15; Jonah 4:8; Gen. 41:6, 23, 27; Job 27: 21; 38:14; Ps. 78:26; Hab. 1:9). It is stormy, wrecks ships, withers growing things. The north wind brings rain (Prov. 25:23), is refreshing (S. of Sol. 4:16) or stormy (Ezek. 1:4). The south wind is gentle, helps growth (S. of Sol. 4:16; Ps. 78:26; Job 37:17). The west wind blew away the plague of locusts (Exod. 10:19). Whirlwinds are mentioned several times. Wind blows chaff (Pss. 1:4; 35:5; 83:13; Isa. 17:14; 41:16; Jer. 13:24; Dan. 2:35; Job 21:18); fulfils God's commands (Pss. 148:8; 104: 4 RSV); reveals weakness, transitoriness, worthlessness (Job 7:7; 15:2; 30: 15, 22; 6:26; 8:2; Pss. 18:42; 78:39; 103: 16; Prov. 11:29; 25:14; 27:16; 30:4; Eccl. 5:16; 11:4; Isa. 7:2; 26:18; 41:8; 57:13; 64:6; Jer. 5:11; 22:22; 49:32); clears the sky (Job 37:21); drives ships (James 3:4). Elisha promises water not brought by wind (II Kings 3:17). God rides on the wings of the wind (II Sam. 22:11=Pss. 18:10; 104:3). Wind has a drying effect (Isa. 11:15; Jer. 4:11, 12). Princes are to be a hiding place from the wind (Isa. 32:2). Believers are warned against evil winds of false doctrine (Eph. 4:4; Jude 12).

Wine, priests forbidden to drink wine on duty (Lev. 10:9); Nazirites could not touch it (Num. 6:3, 20); abuse of wine condemned (Prov. 4:17; 31:4, 5). In OT times wine not diluted; in NT times mixed with much water. Used as medicine (I Tim. 5:23). Over-indulgence warned against (I Tim. 3:8; Titus 2:3). Jesus made water into wine at Cana (John 2:2-11); "fruit of the vine" used in Last Supper (Matt. 26:29).

Winepress, a trough, usually of stone, cement-lined, from which juice flowed through a hole near the bottom into a vat (Judg. 6:11; Neh. 13:15; Isa. 63: 2, 3; Matt. 21:33). The grapes were pressed by men treading them, holding to ropes suspended overhead. The process is compared to the execution of the wrath of God (Lam. 1:15; Rev. 14:19, 20; 19:15).

Wineskin (See Bottles)

Wing. Birds (Lev. 1:17); cherubim (I Kings 6:24) or "living creatures" (Ezek. 16; 10:5; Rev. 4:8) have wings. Migration is suggested in Job 39:26. The most significant Bible uses of wings are figurative (Pss. 18:10; 55:6; 17:8; 91:4); used for renewed strength (Isa. 40:31); compassion (Matt. 23:37). Note two symbolic women (Zech. 5: 9; cf. Rev. 12:4).

Winnowing, separating kernels of threshed grain from chaff; done by shaking bunches of grain into breeze-stirred air so that the kernels fall to the ground, while the chaff is blown away by the wind (Ruth 3:2; Isa. 30: 24).

Winter, in Palestine is usually short and mild, but in higher regions brings snow and hail (Gen. 8:22; Ps. 74:17; Zech. 14:8).

Winterhouse. The wealthy had separate residences for hot and cold seasons (Amos 3:15).

Wisdom, attribute of God (Prov. 3: 19); in Hebrew thought characterized by such virtues as industry, honesty, sobriety, chastity, concern for good reputation; includes technical skill

(Exod. 28:3), military prowess (Isa. 10: 13), shrewdness (I Kings 2:6); given to men through fear of the Lord (Ps. 111:10; Job 28:28); personified (Prov. 8; Matt. 11:19); Jesus is wisdom (I Cor. 1:30; Col. 2:2, 3); wisdom of believers contrasted with wisdom of world (I Cor. 1:19-26).

Wisdom of Jesus, Son of Sirach (See Apocrypha)

Wisdom of Solomon (See Apocrypha)

Wise Men. 1. Men of understanding and skill in ordinary affairs (Prov. 1:5; Job 15:2; Ps. 49:10); came to be recognized as a distinct class, listed with priests and prophets in Jer. 18:18, and also found outside Palestine (Gen. 41: 8; Exod. 7:11; Dan. 2:12-5:15). 2. The magi (Matt. 2:1ff); astrologers; came from East; number and names are legendary.

Witch, one (usually a woman) in league with evil spirits who practices the black art of witchcraft; condemned by law (Exod. 22:18; Deut. 18:9-14; I Sam. 28:3, 9; II Kings 23:24; Isa. 8:19; Acts 19:18, 19).

Withe (wĭth, wīth, **bowstring, cord),** a strong, flexible willow or other twig. The "green withes" with which Samson was bound (Judg. 16:7-9) were probably new (ASV margin) or fresh (RSV) bowstrings.

Withered Hand (See Diseases)

Witness, one who may be called to testify to an event at which he was present. Things may be witnesses; a heap of stones (Gen. 31:44-52), as a sign that God witnessed Jacob and Laban's covenant; a song (Deut. 31:19-21); the Law (Deut. 31:26); an altar (Josh. 22:

A camel caravan nearing Bethlehem from the East, reminiscent of the visit of the wisemen. © MPS

27-34); a stone which has "heard" God speak (Josh. 24:27); an altar and a pillar on the border of Egypt (Isa. 19:20). Bearing false witness is condemned (Exod. 20:16; 23:2; Deut. 5:20) and punished as for the crime of which one accused another (Deut. 19:16-18). True and false witnesses are contrasted (Prov. 14:5). Two or three witnesses were required in legal proceedings (Deut. 19:15; Matt. 18:16; II Cor. 13: 1; I Tim. 5:19; Heb. 10:28). Jeremiah (32:6-25, 44) describes the use of witnesses in a conveyance of real property. God is called upon as a witness (Gen. 31:50; Job 16:19; Jer. 29:23; 42: 5; Mic. 1:2; Mal. 3:5; Rom. 1:9; I Thess. 2:5, 10). God called His people His witnesses (Isa. 43:10, 12; 44:8; Luke 24:48; Acts 1:8) and the apostles acknowledged themselves to be such (Acts 2:32; 3:15; 5:32; 10:39, 41; I Thess. 2:10). Peter thought that Judas must be replaced as a witness (Acts 1: 22). Paul had a special appointment as witness (Acts 22:15; 26:16). He reminds Timothy of many witnesses (I Tim. 6:12; II Tim. 2:2). John calls Jesus Christ the "faithful witness" (Rev. 1:5; 3:14).

Witness of the Spirit. "When we cry, 'Abba! Father!' it is the Spirit himself bearing witness with our spirit that we are children of God" (Rom. 8:15b, 16). The origin of this witness in the work of Christ, and its operation in the believer, is further spelled out in I John 5:6-13. The content of the witness of the Spirit appears in John 14: 16, 17, 26; 15:26; 16:7-15; Rom. 5:5; I Cor. 2 and wherever the work of the Holy Spirit in relation to the believer is spoken of. The Spirit witnesses through Scripture (Heb. 10:15-18), sometimes expressly on particular subjects (I Tim. 4:1; Acts 20:23). The witness of the Spirit, though direct, immediate and personal, is always in harmony with the written Word: we are to test the spirits, for many spirits other than the Spirit of God seek to get our attention (I John 4:1-6). The Holy Spirit talks about Jesus, not about Himself (John 16:13-15).

Wizard (wĭz'êrd, **one who knows**), a male or female magician or sorcerer; one acquainted with the secrets of the unseen world (Lev. 19:31; 20:6, 27; Deut. 18:11; I Sam. 28:3, 9; II Kings 21:6; 23:24; II Chron. 33:6; Isa. 8:19; 19:3).

Wolf (See Animals)

Woman. Genesis (1:26, 27) asserts the full humanity of woman. The special account of her creation (Gen. 2:18-24) emphasizes woman's superiority to all lower animals; man's need for her as helper; her intimate relationship to him as part of his inmost being; and the indissoluble nature of marriage. Though many OT women were shadowy, subordinate figures, the patriarchal wives Sarah, Rebekah and Rachel were outstanding; likewise Moses' sister Miriam (Exod. 2:1-9; 15:21; Num. 12). In the period of the Judges Deborah exercised unusual leadership (Judg. 4, 5) and the Moabitess Ruth became a chaste blessing to Israel. Hannah (I Sam. 1:1-2:11) illustrates both the despair of a childless woman and the grace of godly motherhood. Queens good and bad, and evil women of lesser degree are frankly portrayed in the Bible. The ancient world was a man's world: such prominence as women attained was achieved by force of character; sometimes, as in the case of Esther, aided by circumstances not of her seeking. The teaching of Jesus stressed the original nature of marriage; the obligation of purity toward women (Matt. 5:27-32). His example in healing (Matt. 9:18-26) and social intercourse (Luke 10:38-42) reinforced His words. The Gospel of Luke is full of evidence of Jesus' understanding of and sympathy with women, which set a pattern for normal Christian living. Godly women were influential in Jesus' background: Elizabeth, mother of His forerunner (Luke 1); the Virgin Mary; Anna (Luke 2:36-38); the sinner of Luke 7:36-40: Mary Magdalene; Martha and Mary of Bethany; the women who accompanied the disciples on missionary journeys and who provided for them out of their means (Luke 8:3 RSV). Women remained at the crucifixion until the burial,, and were first at the empty tomb. Between the Ascension and Pentecost women joined the men in prayer (Acts 1:14). The disciples met in the house of Mary, mother of John Mark in Jerusalem (Acts 12:12). Women were the first converts in Europe, including the prosperous business woman Lydia at Philippi (Acts 16:13-15). Phoebe, a deaconess, and many other women are greeted in Romans 16. Paul (I Cor. 11:2-16; 14: 34, 35) urges subordination for women, in the immoral atmosphere of Corinth, but exalts her as a type of the Church, the Bride of Christ (Eph. 5:21-33).

He sets high standards for the wives of church officers, and for women in official position (I Tim. 3:11; Titus 2: 3-5). I Peter 3:1-6 urges a subordinate but noble role for married women.

Wool, the fleece of sheep and some other animals. Israelites were forbidden to wear mixed woolen and linen stuff (Deut. 22:11). It symbolizes purity (Isa. 1:18). It was used principally for the outside garments. Snow is compared to it (Ps. 147:16).

Word, Word of the Lord. Lógos is used of Jesus as the Revelation of God (John 1:1; I John 1:1; Rev. 19:13; Heb. 1:2). He is the supreme and definitive Word or Revelation of God. Before He came into the world, the Word of God came to men through patriarchs (Gen. 15:1), through the lawgiver Moses (Exod. 4:30; 20:1), and through prophets (Num. 22:38; II Kings 7:1; Isa. 1:10; Jer. 1:2). The Word of the Lord is creative (Ps. 33: 6; Gen. 1:3, 6, 9, 11, 14, 20, 24, 26; Heb. 11:3). The Word of God is sure (Ps. 119:89; Isa. 40:8), forever, and cannot be broken (John 10:35). Words are distinguished from power (I Cor. 4:20; I Thess. 1:5) and from deeds (Mal. 2:17; I Cor. 4:20; I John 3:18), for the Word of God is to be done as well as heard and talked about (James 1:22-25).

World. 1. Universe (John 1:10). 2. Human race (Pss. 9:8; 96:13; Acts 17: 31). 3. Unregenerate humanity (John 15:18; I John 2:15). 4. Roman Empire (Luke 2:1).

Worm (See Insects)

Wormwood (See Plants)

Worship (bow down, to prostrate, do obeisance to), the honor, reverence, and homage paid to superior beings or powers, whether men, angels, or God; used especially of divine honors paid to a deity; when given to God, involves acknowledgement of divine perfections; may be private or public, involving a cultus. Four stages of development in Bible: patriarchs worshipped by building altars and sacrificing (Gen. 12:7, 8; 13:4); organized worship in Temple ritual, with complex ritual and system of sacrifices; synagogue, which began during Exile; Christian, consisting of preaching (Acts 20:7), reading of Scripture (James 1:22), prayer (I Tim. 2:8), singing (Eph. 5:19), baptism and Lord's Supper (Acts 2:41; I Cor. 11:18-34), and almsgiving (I Cor. 16:1, 2).

Wrath. 1. Anger of men (Gen. 30:2; I Sam. 17:28); may be evil (II Cor. 12: 20) or reaction to evil (I Sam. 20:34); work of the flesh (Gal. 5:20). 2. Anger of God—reaction of righteous God against sinful people and evil in all forms (Deut. 9:7; Isa. 13:9; Rom. 1:18; Eph. 5:6; Rev. 14:10, 19).

Wrestle, three basic meanings: 1. "Twist" (Gen. 30:8); Rachel's wrestling (emotional and vocal rather than literal) with Leah, which led Rachel to name her handmaid's son Naphtali, **my wrestlings.** 2. **Get dusty, wrestle** (Gen. 32:24, 25), Jacob's wrestling with the angel (physical effect, the dislocation of Jacob's thigh). 3. Later any kind of fighting. The Christian's spiritual conflict with the powers of evil (Eph. 6:12).

Writing, invented in Mesopotamia, probably by Sumerians, at least as early as 2500 B.C.; they had a primitive, nonalphabetic linear writing, not phonetic but pictographic, ideas being recorded by means of pictures or sense-symbols, rather than by sound-symbols. The next stage in the history of writing was the introduction of the phonogram, or the type of sign which indicates a sound, and afterward came alphabetic scripts. Egyptians first developed an alphabetic system of writing. Hebrews derived their alphabet from Phoenicians. Semitic writing dating between 1900 and 1500 B.C. has been found at Serabit el-Khadim in Sinai. Greeks received their alphabet from Phoenicians and Aramaeans. Writing first mentioned in Bible in Exod. 17:14. Ten Commandments written with finger of God (Exod. 31: 18; 32:15, 16). Ancient writing materials: clay, wax, wood, metal, plaster (Deut. 27:2, 3; Josh. 8:32; Luke 1:63); later, parchment (II Tim. 4:13) and papyrus (II John 12). Instruments of writing: reed, on papyrus and parchment; stylus, on hard material (Exod. 32:4).

–X–

Detail of crown prince Xerxes standing behind his father, King Darius, on the throne. OIUC

Xerxes (zûrk'sēz), king of the Persian Empire from 486-465 B.C. He is the same as Ahasuerus, mentioned in the books of Ezra, Esther, and Daniel. The main support for this identification is to be found in the linguistic equivalence of the names, and a close similarity has been noted between the character of Xerxes and the character of the king of the Persians portrayed in the book of Esther. There are also historical correlations. Thus, the feast which was held in the third year of the reign of Ahasuerus at Shushan (Esth. 1:3) corresponds to an assembly held by Xerxes in his third year in preparation for the invasion of Greece. Herodotus states that Xerxes, following his defeat at Salamis and Plataea, consoled himself in his seventh year with the pleasures of the harem (Herodotus IX, 108). This parallels the Biblical account which relates that Ahasuerus replaced Vashti by marrying Esther in his seventh year (Esth. 2:16) after gathering all the fair young virgins to Shushan.

–Y–

Yahweh (See God, also YHWH below)

Yarmuk, Wadi el. One of the three important streams to the SE of the Sea of Galilee. Located six miles to the SE of this sea, it contributes large quantities of water to the Jordan. It marked the southern boundary of the ancient kingdom of Bashan.

Yarn (yărn), the KJV translation of the Hebrew word which occurs in I Kings 10:29 and II Chron. 1:16. In each of these cases "linen yarn" seems to convey the wrong meaning. It is correctly rendered in the RSV by the proper name "Kue," the old Assyrian name given to Cilicia, the land located in the southeastern portion of Asia Minor.

Year (See Calendar)

Yhwh. The "tetragrammaton," the four consonants standing for the ancient Hebrew name for God commonly referred to as "Jehovah" or "Yahweh." YHWH was considered too sacred to pronounce; so **'adonai (my Lord)** was substituted in reading. When eventually a vowel system was invented, since the Hebrews had forgotten how to pronounce YHWH, they substituted the vowels for **'adonai,** making "Jehovah," a form first attested at the beginning of the 12th century A.D.

Yodh (yōd), 10th letter of Hebrew alphabet, pronounced much like English "y."

Yoke, wooden frame for joining two draft animals; a wooden bar held on neck by thongs around neck (Num. 19:2; Deut. 21:3). Yoke of oxen is a pair (I Sam. 14:14; Luke 14:19). Often used figuratively to denote subjection (I Kings 12:4, 9-11; Isa. 9:4); removal of yoke denotes deliverance (Gen. 27:40; Jer. 2:20; Matt. 11:29, 30).

Yokefellow (yoked together), a common word among Greek writers referring to those united by close bonds, as in marriage, labor, etc. It is found only once in the NT (Phil. 4:3).

Yom Kippur, Hebrew for "Day of Atonement." (See Feasts)

-Z-

Zaanaim (zā'à-nā'ĭm), a word found only in Judges 4:11, but it is probably the same place referred to as Zaanannim in Joshua 19:33. This place was located on Naphtali's southern border near to the spot where Sisera lost his life at the hands of Heber the Kenite.

Zaanan (zā'à-năn) a place mentioned by Micah (1:11) in the Shephelah of Judah.

Zaanannim (See Zaanaim)

Zaavan (zā'à-văn, **not quiet),** son of Ezer (Gen. 36:27; I Chron. 1:42).

Zabad (zā'băd, **Jehovah has given).** 1. Son of Nathan (I Chron. 2:36). 2. Son of Shimeath; conspired against King Joash; killed by Amaziah (II Chron. 24:26). 3. Ephraimite (I Chron. 7:21). 4-6. Three Israelites who put away foreign wives (Ezra 10:27, 33, 43).

Zabbai (zăb'ā-ī). 1. Son of Bebai who put away his foreign wife (Ezra 10:28). 2. Father of Baruch (Neh. 3:20).

Zabbud (zăb'ŭd, **given),** the son of Bigvai who accompanied Ezra to Jerusalem from Babylon (Ezra 8:14).

Zabdi (zăb'dī, **he (God) has given).** 1. Achan's grandfather (Josh. 7:1, 17). 2. Son of Shimei from the tribe of Benjamin (I Chron. 8:19). 3. One of the officers of David listed as having charge of the wine cellars (I Chron. 27:27). 4. Ancestor of Mattaniah, who aided in worship in the days of Nehemiah (Neh. 11:17).

Zabdiel (zăb'dĭ-ĕl, **God has given).** 1. The father of Jashobeam (I Chron. 27:2). 2. A temple overseer (Neh. 11:14). 3. An Arabian who, after beheading Alexander Balas, sent his head to Ptolemy (I Macc. 11:17).

Zabud (zā'bŭd, **bestowed),** the son of Nathan; a principal officer of Solomon and his best friend (I Kings 4:5).

Zabulon (See Zebulun)

Zaccai (zăk'ā-ī), the ancestral head of a post-Exilic family whose 760 descendants returned to Jerusalem with Zerubbabel (Neh. 7:14 and Ezra 2:9).

Zacchaeus (ză-kē'ŭs, **pure),** a publican, referred to only in Luke, who resided at Jericho. He is described as a "chief" publican, and therefore had charge of collecting taxes. When Jesus was passing through Jericho on one occasion, Zacchaeus climbed a tree to see Him. Jesus paused in His journey beneath this very tree and, looking up, urged Zacchaeus to come down, for He had decided to abide at his house (Luke 19:5). With joy he came down. He became a disciple (Luke 19:8).

Zaccur (zăk'ûr, **remembered).** 1. The father of the Reubenite spy, Shammua (Num. 13:4). 2. The son of Hamuel, a Simeonite (I Chron. 4:26), Zacchur in AV. 3. Son of Merari (I Chron. 24:27). 4. Son of Asaph set apart by David for musical service (I Chron. 25:1-2; Neh. 12:35). 5. The son of Imri who aided in rebuilding the wall of Jerusalem (Neh. 3:2). 6. One of those who sealed the covenant (Neh. 10:12). 7. One of the treasurers, father of Hanan (Neh. 13:13).

Zacchur (See Zaccur)

Zachariah (zăk'à-rī'à, **Jehovah has remembered),** the 14th king of Israel, the son of Jeroboam II. In fulfillment of II Kings 10:30, he was the last of the house of Jehu. After a brief reign of six months, he was slain by Shallum, his successor (II Kings 15:8-10).

Zacharias (zăk'à-rī'ăs, **Jehovah has remembered).** 1. The name of the father of John the Baptist (Luke 1:5). He was a priest and childless in his old age. Both he and his wife were righteous, and while Zacharias was performing his services in the temple, an angel appeared and reported to him that he was to have a son whom he was to name John. Because of doubt, he was stricken dumb until his son was named, at which time his speech was restored (Luke 1:67-69). 2. The son of Barachias, mentioned in Matt. 23:35 and in Luke 11:51, by Christ as having been slain between the altar and the temple.

Zacher (zā'kêr, **memorial),** one of Jehiel's sons (I Chron. 8:31; 9:37).

Zadok (zā'dŏk, **righteous),** 1. Son of Ahitub; priest who helped David (II Sam. 8:17; I Chron. 12:28); helped bring ark to Jerusalem (I Chron. 15:11-13); supported David against Absalom (II Sam. 15:24-36; 17:15); made high priest by Solomon (I Kings 2:35). 2. Father of Shallum (I Chron. 6:12). 3. Father of Jerusha (II Kings 15:33; II Chron. 27:1). 4. Man who aided in constructing walls of Jerusalem (Neh. 3:4; 10:1). 5. Son of Immer; also aided in rebuildling walls (Neh. 3:29). 6. Scribe (Neh. 13:13). May be same as 5 or 6.

Zaham (zā'hăm, **odious fool),** Rehoboam's youngest son (II Chron. 11:19).

Zair (zā'ĭr, **small),** a village E of the Dead Sea in Idumea, where Joram smote the Edomites (II Kings 8:21).

Zalaph (zā'lăf), the father of Hanun who aided Nehemiah in repairing the Jerusalem walls (Neh. 3:30).

Zalmon (zăl'mōn, **dark).** 1. A Benjamite who was one of David's mighty men (II Sam. 23:28). He is also called "Ilai" (I Chron. 11:29), and in both passages "The Ahohite." 2. A forest near Shechem (Judg. 9:48).

Zalmonah (zăl-mō'nȧ, **gloomy),** one of the places in the wilderness where Israel camped.

Zalmunna (zăl-mŭn'ȧ, **deprived of shade),** one of the two kings of Midian whom Gideon captured and killed (Judg. 8:4-21; Ps. 83:11).

Zamzummim (zăm-zŭm'ĭm, **murmurers**). It is used of the race of giants (Deut. 2:20) called Rephaim (II Sam. 5:18, 22), who lived in a spot E of the Jordan. Later on the Ammonites captured them and occupied their land. They may be the same as the Zuzims (Gen. 14:5).

Zanoah (zȧ-nō'ȧ, **rejected).** 1. A town located in the low-lying hills of Judah (Josh. 15:34). After the Babylonian captivity some Jews returned to live there (Neh. 11:30), and assisted in the rebuilding of the walls of Jerusalem (Neh. 3:13). 2. A town located in the mountains of Judah (Josh. 15:56) 10 or 12 miles SW of Hebron. It was built or rebuilt by Jekuthiel who is called its "father" (I Chron. 4:18).

Zaphenath-Paneah (zăf'ē-năth-pȧ-nē'ȧ, **the one who furnishes the sustenance of the land),** the name given to Joseph by the pharaoh on the occasion of his promotion (Gen. 41:45).

Zaphon (zā'fŏn, **north),** a territory E of the Jordan allotted by Moses to Gad (Josh. 13:27). It is the modern Amateh.

Zara (zā'rȧ), the Greek for the Hebrew Zerah, in the ancestry of Christ (Matt. 1:3).

Zareah (See Zorah)

Zareathite (See Zorah)

Zared (See Zered)

Zareda (See Zarethan)

Zarephath (zăr'ĕ-făth, **refinement),** an OT town remembered chiefly because Elijah resided here during the latter half of the famine caused by the drought (I Kings 17:9ff). Its Greek equivalent "Sarepta" is mentioned in Luke 4:26. Here God miraculously sustained the prophet through the widow. Ruins of the ancient town survive S of the modern village of Sarafand, about 8 miles S of Sidon, 14 miles N of Tyre.

The town of Sarafand, ancient Zarephath (Sarepta) on the Mediterranean coast. SHH

Zarethan (zăr′ĕ-thăn), a place near Beth-shean and Adam mentioned in connection with Israel's crossing of the Jordan (Josh. 3:16); Zaretan in KJV. Exact site has not been ascertained.

Zareth-Shahar (zā′rĕth-shā′hȧr, **the glory of dawn),** a city located in the land belonging to Reuben "in the mount of the valley" (Josh. 13:19).

Zarhites, The (zȧr′hīts, **those who shine),** members of the tribe of Judah descended from Judah's son, Zerah (Num. 26:13, 20; Josh. 7:17; I Chron. 27:11, 13).

Zartanah (zȧr-tā′nȧ), a place referred to only in I Kings 4:12 as a means of locating Bethshean.

Zarthan (zȧr′thăn). 1. A place between Succoth and Zarthan where Hiram cast the copper vessels of the temple which he gave to King Solomon (I Kings 7:46). "Zeredathah" in II Chron. 4:17. 2. Another place by this name is cited in connection with the passage of the children of Israel across the Jordan (Josh. 3:16).

Zatthu (See Zattu)

Zattu (ză′tū), head of a large family (Ezra 2:8; Neh. 7:13) who returned with Zerubbabel to Jerusalem from the Babylonian captivity and signed the covenant with Nehemiah (Neh. 10:14).

Zavan (See Zaavan)

Zaza (zā′zȧ), a Jerahmelite (I Chron. 2:33).

Zealot (zĕl′ŭt, **zealous one),** a member of a Jewish patriotic party started in the time of Cyrenius to resist Roman aggression. According to Josephus (BJ, IV, iii, 9; v, 1; VII, viii, 1), the Zealots resorted to violence and assassination in their hatred of the Romans. Simon the Zealot was distinguished from Simon Peter by this epithet (Luke 6:15; Acts 1:13).

Zebadiah (zĕb′ȧ-dī′ȧ, **Jehovah has bestowed).** 1. A. descendant of Benjamin (I Chron. 8:15). 2. Another Benjamite descending from the line of Elpaal (I Chron. 8:17). 3. Ambidextrous Benjamite who joined David at Ziklag. He descended through Jeroham of Gedor (I Chron. 12:1-7). 4. Korahite door keeper of David's time (I Chron. 26:2). 5. Officer of David's army, son of Joab's brother, Asahel (I Chron. 27:7). 6. A Levite sent by King Jehoshaphat to teach the law to the residents of Judah (II Chron. 17:8). 7. Ishmael's son; head of King Jehoshaphat's affairs (II Chron. 19:11). 8. One who returned with Ezra from Babylon to Jerusalem with 80 men. He was the son of Michael (Ezra 8:8). 9. A priest who divorced a foreign wife. He was a son of Immer (Ezra 10:20).

Zebah (zē′bȧ, **sacrifice),** one of the two kings of Midian whom Gideon overthrew (Judg. 8:10, 12; Ps. 83:11) and killed.

Zebaim (zē-bā′ĭm, **gazelles),** the native dwelling place of Solomon's slaves, "sons of Pochereth" who returned with Zerubbabel (Ezra 2:57; Neh. 7:59).

Zebedee (zĕb′ĕ-dē), a fisherman on the Sea of Galilee (Mark 1:20), the father of James and John (Matt. 4:21; Mark 1:19). He was the husband of Salome and in all probability lived in the vicinity of Bethsaida (Matt. 27:46; Mark 15:40). Because of Mark's reference to his hired servants, one would judge him to be a man of means and influence (Mark 1:20).

Zebina (zē-bī′nȧ, **purchased),** a descendent of Nebo who put away his strange wife after the captivity (Ezra 10:43).

Zeboiim, Zeboim (zē-boi′ĭm, zēbō′ĭm, **gazelles, hyena).** 1. One of the five cities in the vale of Siddim that God destroyed with Sodom and Gomorrah (Gen. 10:19; 14:2, 8; Deut. 29:23; Hos. 11:8). 2. A ravine in Benjamin not far from Michmash (I Sam. 13:18; Neh. 11:34).

Zeboim, Valley of (zē-bō′ĭm), see above.

Zebudah (zē-bū′dȧ, **given),** Josiah's wife, the daughter of Pedaiah, the mother of Jehoiakim the king (II Kings 23:36).

Zebul (zē′bŭl, **dwelling),** one who, under Abimelech, ruled the city of Shechem (Judg. 9:26-48).

Zebulonite (See Zebulun)

Zebulun (zĕb′ū-lŭn, **habitation).** 1. Son of Leah and Jacob (Gen. 30:19-20). Three sons were born to him in the land belonging to Reuben "in the land of his birth (Gen. 46:14). 2. One of the 12 tribes of Israel springing from Zebulun. When God asked Moses to number the able-bodied men at Sinai, the tribe of Zebulun had 57,400 (Num. 1:31). The place assigned to this tribe at this period was on the E side of the tabernacle with the standard of Judah (Num. 2:7); its portion lay between the Sea of Galilee and the Mediterranean. This area included many points at which Christ later carried on His ministry, and Matthew records that He thus fulfilled the ancient prophecy of Isaiah (Isa. 9:1-2; Matt. 4:12-16). 3. City between Bethdagon and the valley of Jiphthahel (Josh. 19:27).

Zebulunite (See Zebulun)

Zechariah (zĕk'ȧ-rī'ȧ, **Jehovah remembers**). 1. A Reubenite chief (I Chron. 5:7). 2. A Korhite, son of Meshelemiah (I Chron. 9:21; 26:2, 24). 3. A Benjamite, son of Jehiel, brother of Kish (I Chron. 9:37). 4. A Levitical doorkeeper in the time of David (I Chron. 15:17-18). 5. One of the Davidic priests who was used as a trumpeter to help in bringing the ark from the house of Obededom back to Jerusalem (I Chron. 15:24). 6. A Levite from Uzziel (I Chron. 24:25). 7. A Merarite Levite (II Chron. 26:11). 8. A Manassite chief and the father of Iddo (I Chron. 27:21). 9. One of the princes whom Jehoshaphat sent to teach in the cities of Judah (II Chron. 17:7). 10. The father of the Prophet Jahaziel, son of Benaiah (II Chron. 20:14). 11. The third son of Jehoshaphat whom Jehoram killed (II Chron. 21:2-4). 12. A son of Jehoiada, the high priest who lived in the days of King Joash of Judah. A conspiracy was formed against him and, on the king's orders, he was stoned (II Chron. 24:20-22). 13. A prophet whose good influence on King Uzziah was outstanding (II Chron. 26:5). 14. The father of Abijah (II Chron. 29:1). 15. A Levite, the son of Asaph (II Chron. 29:13). 16. A Kohathite who faithfully assisted in the repair of the temple in the days of King Josiah (II Chron. 34:12). 17. One of the temple rulers in the time of King Josiah (II Chron. 35:8). 18. One "of the sons of Parosh" who returned to Jerusalem with Ezra (Ezra 8:3). 19. The son of Bebai who returned with Ezra (Ezra 8:11). 20. One of those who stood by Ezra as he read the law to the people (Neh. 8:4). 21. A son of Elam who divorced his Gentile wife (Ezra 10:26). 22. A son of Amariah (Neh. 11:4). 23. "The son of Shilonite" dwelling at Jerusalem (Neh. 11:5). 24. The son of Pashhur, who aided in the work at Jerusalem after the captivity (Neh. 11:12). 25. Son of Iddo, one of the priests in the days of Joiakim (Neh. 12:8, 16). 26. A priest, the son of Jonathan, one of the trumpeters at the dedication of the wall at Jerusalem (Neh. 12:35, 41). 27. The son of Jeberechiah, contemporary of Isaiah (Isa. 8:1-2). 28. The next to the last of the 12 minor prophets. He came from a line of priests, being the son of Berechiah and grandson of Iddo (Zech. 1:1). He was a prophet as well as a priest (Zech. 1:7). He returned from the Babylonian captivity to Jerusalem under the leadership of Zerubbabel (Zech. 1:1). He was contemporary with Haggai.

Zechariah, Book of. 1. Historical Background. Zechariah was the grandson of Iddo, the head of one of the priestly families that returned from the Exile (Neh. 12:4, 16). Twenty years after the return, the temple still lay a blackened ruin, and the discouraged people did not see how it could be restored. At this critical moment God raised up the prophets Haggai and Zechariah to encourage the Jews to rebuild the temple. The prophecies of the two men were delivered almost at the same time. Haggai appeared first, in August 520 B.C., and within a month after his appeal was made the foundation of the temple was laid. Soon after, Zechariah uttered his first prophecy (Zech. 1:1-6). Haggai finished his recorded prophecies the same year. The following year Zechariah gave a message consisting of eight symbolic visions, with an appendix (1:7-6:15). Two years later he gave a third message in answer to an inquiry by the men of Bethel regarding the observance of a fast. The two prophecies found in chapters 9-14 are not dated, and were probably given at a much later period.

2. Contents. I. Chapters 1-8. Messages delivered on three separate occasions.

A. 1:1-6. A general introduction.

B. A series of eight symbolic night-visions, followed by a coronation scene. 1:7-6:15. These visions were intended to encourage the Israelites to complete the temple.

These visions are followed by a scene in which a party of Jews have just come from Babylon with silver and gold for the temple. Zechariah is instructed to take part of it and make a crown for the high priest, a type of the Messiah-Branch who is to be both Priest and King to His people.

C. Chapters 7 and 8 were spoken two years later than the series of visions described above, and represent Zechariah's answer to questions put to him by certain visitors as to whether the fasts observed in memory of the destruction of Jerusalem should still be kept. The reply is No; for God demands not fasts, but observance of moral laws.

11. Chapters 9:14. This is made up of two distinct prophecies, without dates.

A. Chaps. 9-11. God will visit the nations in judgment and His people in mercy, but He will be rejected, and they will consequently again experience suffering .

B. Chaps. 12-14. A prophecy describing the victories of the new age and the coming day of the Lord. Three apocalyptic pictures are presented. 1. Jerusalem will be saved from a siege by her enemies by the intervention of Jehovah. 2. A remnant of Israel shall be saved. 3. The nations will come to Jerusalem to share in the joyous Feast of Tabernacles, and all will enjoy the blessings of God's kingdom.

Zedad (zē'dăd, **a siding),** a city located on the N boundary of Palestine (Num. 34:8; Ezek. 47:15).

Zedekiah (zĕd'ĕ-kī'ȧ, **Jehovah is righteous).** 1. The son of Chanaanah, the leader of the 400 false prophets whom Ahab consulted to learn the outcome of his proposed expedition against Ramoth-gilead. In reply to Ahab's question, Zedekiah said that Ahab would be successful in winning a victory over the Syrians (I Kings 22:7). When the true prophet was finally called and asked as to the outcome of this planned battle, he revealed the truth and was consquently struck by Zedekiah (I Kings 22:19-24; II Chron. 18: 10). 2. The last king of Judah, son of Josiah and Hamutal (I Kings 24:18). Because of the wickedness of Judah, God finally brought on the predicted Babylonian captivity. Nebuchadnezzar came to Jerusalem, took Judah's king, Jehoiachin, to Babylon and made Mattaniah, whose name he changed to Zedekiah, king in his stead (Ezek. 17: 11-14). Zedekiah, however, rebelled against the king of Babylon, and as a result, he was taken by Nebuchadnezzar and bound. His sons were killed before his eyes and his own eyes put out. He was then taken to Babylon where he died (II Kings 24, 25). 3. The son of Jeconiah (I Chron. 3:16). 4. The son of Maaseiah. He was a false prophet who carried on his ruinous work among those who had been deported to Babylon. His death by being "roasted in the fire" was foretold by Jeremiah as a warning to the rest (Jer. 29:21-23). 5. The son of Hananiah; prince of Israel in the reign of Jehoiakim (Jer. 36:12). 6. A high official who sealed the renewed covenant (Neh. 10:1).

Zeeb (zē'ĕb, **wolf),** one of the two princes of Midian slain by Gideon's men (Judg. 7:25ff).

Zelah (zē'lȧ), a town in Benjamin probably close to Jerusalem (Josh. 18:28); the family sepulchre of Saul (II Sam. 21:14).

Zelek (zē'lĕk, **a fissure),** an Ammonite, one of David's mighty men (II Sam. 23:37; I Chron. 11:39).

Zelophehad (zē-lō'fĕ-hăd), a Manassite who died in the wilderness leaving five daughters but no sons; and in the division of the land, they begged a share in the inheritance (Num. 27:1-11). When their tribesmen feared that their property might be alienated from the tribe by mariage (Num. 36:1-12) God commanded that they should marry only within their tribe, and this became a general law regarding heiresses.

Zelotes (See Zealot)

Zelzah (zĕl'zȧ), a town in the southern border of Benjamin near Rachel's tomb (Gen. 35:19, 20; 48:7; I Sam. 10: 2).

Zemaraim (zĕm'ȧ-rā'ĭm). 1. An ancient town allotted to the tribe of Benjamin, about four miles N of Jericho in the Arabah (Josh. 18:22). 2. A mountain in the hill country of Ephraim upon which King Abijah stood and rebuked Jeroboam and Israel for their rebellion against Judah and for their idolatry (II Chron. 13:4ff).

Zemarites (zĕm'ȧ-rīts), a tribe of Canaanites mentioned in the "table of the nations" (Gen. 10:18) in the Hamite list between the Arvadites and the Hamathites.

Zemira (zē-mī'rȧ), a grandson of Benjamin through his son Becher (I Chron. 7:8).

Zenan (zē'năn), a place in the lowland of Judah (Josh. 15:37), the same as Zaanan **q.v.** See Micah 1:11.

Zenas (zē'nȧs), a Christian lawyer in Crete whom Paul asked to be sent to him (Titus 3:13).

Zephaniah (zĕf'ȧ-nī'ȧ, **hidden of Jehovah).** 1. Ancestor of the prophet Samuel (I Chron. 6:36).

2. Author of the book of Zephaniah and very likely of royal descent as follows (Zeph. 1:1): Amariah and King Manasseh were brothers, Gedaliah and King Amon were cousins, Cushi and King Josiah were second cousins, and Zephaniah was third cousin of the

three kings Jehoahaz, Jehoiakim and Zechariah; thus putting the prophet into familiar relationship with the court, to which his message seems to be specially directed (e.g. 1:8). 3. A priest, son of Maaseiah, whom Zedekiah sent to inquire of Jeremiah (II Kings 25:18-21; Jer. 21:1). Nebuchadnezzar had him slain. 4. Father of a Josiah in the days of Darius to whom God sent the Prophet Zechariah with a message of comfort and encouragement (Zech. 6:9-15).

Zephaniah, Book of, the ninth of the Minor Prophets and the last before the Seventy Years' Captivity of Judah. The prophecy is dated in 1:1 in the reign of Josiah, that is, between 639 and 608 B.C.

The books divides naturally into 14 paragraphs (12 in ASV) as follows: 1. Title, author, and date (1:1). 2. Apostates to be destroyed (1:2-6), including the idolatrous priests. 3. Announcement of the great "Day of Jehovah" (1:7-13). 4. The Day of Jehovah described (1:14-18). 5. A plea for repentance (2:1-3). 6. Philistia to be destroyed (2:4, 5). 7. The Philistine coast will some day belong to Israel (2:6, 7). 8. Moab and the Ammonites denounced for their pride (2:8-11). 9. Ruin predicted from Ethiopia to Assyria (2:12-15). 10. Woe also to rebellious Jerusalem (3:1-7). 11. The judgment of the nations (3:8). 12. Restoration of Israel promised (3:9-11). 13. A remnant to be blessed (3:12, 13). 14. Jehovah in the midst of Zion (3:14-20).

Zephath (zē′făth, **watch-tower),** a Canaanite city about 22 miles SW of the southern end of the Dead Sea. It was utterly destroyed by the tribes of Judah and Simeon and renamed "Hormah," i.e. "devoted to God" in the sense of being laid waste (Judg. 1:17). Cf. "Hormah" in Numbers 21:3 for the use of the word.

Zephathah (zĕf′ȧ-thȧ, **watch-tower),** a valley near Mareshah in the western part of Judah, where King Asa met the hosts of Zerah the Ethiopian, and where, in answer to prayer, God gave a great victory to Judah (II Chron. 14: 9-12).

Zephi (zē′fī, **watchtower),** a grandson of Esau through Eliphaz (I Chron. 1: 36); in Genesis 36:11, 15, "Zepho."

Zepho (See Zephi)

Zephon (zē′fŏn, **watching),** a Gadite from whom the family of Zephonites descended (Num. 26:15). In Genesis 46:16 "Ziphion."

Zephonites (See Zepho)

Zer (zêr), a fenced city, NW of the Lake of Galilee, given to the tribe of Naphtali (Josh. 19:35).

Zerah (zē′rȧ, **rising).** 1. One of twin sons born to Judah (Gen. 38:30). Of him came the Zarhite family of Numbers 26:20 (ASV "Zerahites"). He was great-grandfather of Achan, "the Troubler of Israel" (Josh. 7). 2. A cousin of the preceding; son of Simeon (Num. 26:13) and head of another Zarhite family. 3. A Gershonite Levite of the sixth generation (I Chron. 6:21). 4. Another Gershonite Levite, but later (I Chron. 6:41). 5. A grandson of Esau through Reuel, son of Basemath (Gen. 36:13). He was a chief (Gen. 36:17 in KJV "duke"). 6. Father of Jobab, the second of the early kings of Edom (Gen. 36:33). 7. A king of Ethiopia (II Chron. 14:9) who invaded Judah during the reign of Asa, but Asa prayed and the Lord gave Asa victory.

Zerahiah (zĕr-ȧ-hī′ȧ, **Jehovah is risen).** 1. A Levite in the ancestry of Ezra (I Chron. 6:6, 51). 2. A leader of 200 men who returned with Ezra (Ezra 8:4).

Zered (zē′rĕd), a valley running northwestward on the border between Moab and Edom; also the brook which follows the valley. A camping place of Israel at the end of their long wanderings (Num. 21:12, KJV Zared; Deut. 2:13, 14).

Zereda (zĕr-ē′dȧ), the birthplace of Jeroboam of Ephraim (I Kings 11:26). ASV properly has Zeredah. Metal work for the temple was cast there.

Zeredathah (See Zarthan)

Zererath (zĕr′ĕ-răth), a part of the valley of Jezreel to which the Midianites fled from Gideon (Judg. 7:22).

Zeresh (zē′rĕsh, **golden),** the wife of Haman the Agagite, who advised him to build a gallows for Mordecai, but later saw her error (Esth. 5:10, 14; 6:13).

Zereth (zē′rĕth), an early descendant of Judah through Helah, second wife of Ashhur (I Chron. 4:7).

Zeri (zē′rī), one of the sons of Jeduthun in the days of David, who with harp and voice praised the Lord (I Chron. 25:3).

Zeror (zē′rôr), a Benjamite, great-grandfather of King Saul (I Sam. 9:1).

Zerqa (zêr′kȧ), a wadi running westward to the Jordan and corresponding to the ancient river Jabbok. Also "Zerka."

Zeruah (zê-rōō'å, **leprous),** the widow of Nebat, father of Jeroboam of Israel (I Kings 11:26).

Zerubbabel (zĕ-rŭb'å-bĕl, **shoot of Babylon),** the son of Shealtiel and the grandson of King Jehoiachin (Ezra 3:2; Hag. 1:1; Matt. 1:12). He was heir to the throne of Judah (I Chron. 3:17-19) and is listed in the genealogy of our Lord (Matt. 1:13; Luke 3:27).

When Cyrus allowed the Jews to return to their own land, he appointed Zerubbabel governor of the colony (Ezra 1:8, 11; 5:14). When he reached Jerusalem, he first set up the altar of burnt offerings, then proceeded to lay the foundation of the new temple. Soon, however, opposition arose. The adversaries of the Jews made an apparently friendly offer of assistance (Ezra 4), but Zerubbabel and the other leaders rebuffed them; whereupon they wrote to the king and succeeded in stopping the work during the reigns of Cambyses (the "Ahasuerus" of Ezra 4:6) and the pseudo-Smerdis (the "Artaxerxes" of Ezra 4:7ff). In 520 B.C. the work was resumed and completed four years later. A great celebration was held at the dedication of the new temple (Zech. 6:16-22), and so far as the record tells, the work of Zerubbabel was complete.

Zeruiah (zêr'ōō-ī'å) sister of David and mother of Joab, Abishai and Asahel. She was probably not a daughter of Jesse, but a daughter of David's mother by an earlier marriage with Nahash (II Sam. 17:25).

Zetham (zē'thăm, **olive tree),** a Gershonite Levite in David's time. He was son of Ladan (I Chron. 23:8).

Zethan (zē'thăn, **olive tree),** a Benjamite, son of Jediael (I Chron. 7:10).

Zethar (zē'thår), one of the seven chamberlains of Xerxes (Ahasuerus, Esth. 1:10).

Zeus (zūs), the chief of the Olympian gods, corresponding to the Roman Jupiter (see Acts 14:12, 13; 19:35). One of the crowning insults which Antiochus Epiphanes, king of Syria 176-164 B.C., offered to the Jews was his dedication of the temple at Jerusalem to Zeus (II Macc. 6).

Zia (zī'å), early Gadite (I Chron. 5:13).

Ziba (zī'bå, **plant),** member of Saul's household staff (II Sam. 9:2); appointed by David to work for Mephibosheth; slandered Mephibosheth (II Sam. 19:24-30).

Zibeon (zĭb'ē-ŭn, **hyena),** a Hivite, grandfather of Oholibama, a wife of Esau (Gen. 36:2, 14).

Zibia (zĭb'ĭ-å, **gazelle),** an early descendant of Benjamin (I Chron. 8:9).

Zibiah (zĭb'ĭ-å, **gazelle),** a woman of Beersheba who married King Ahaziah and was mother of Joash, king of Judah (II Kings 12:1; II Chron. 24:1).

Ziddim (zĭd'ĭm, **sides),** a fortified city in Naphtali (Josh. 19:35), c. one-half mile N of the Horns of Hattin, W of the Sea of Galilee.

Zidkijah (See Zedekiah)

Zidon (zī'dŏn, **fishery),** in KJV usually Zidon in OT, and always Sidon in NT; Canaanite city 22 miles N of Tyre (Gen. 10:15, 19); chief gods were Baal and Ashtoreth (I Kings 11:5, 33; II Kings 23:13); father of Jezebel a king of Zidon (I Kings 16:31); modern Saida.

Zidonians (See Zidon)

Zif (zĭf), the second month of the old Hebrew calendar, corresponding to Iyyar in the later Jewish calendar (I Kings 6:1, 37).

Ziggurate (zĭg'ōō-răt). A temple tower of the Babylonians, consisting of a lofty structure in the form of a pyramid, built in successive stages, with staircases on the outside, and a shrine at the top. The tower of Babel was a ziggurat (Gen. 11:1-9).

Ziha (zī'hå). 1. Head of a family of temple servants, "Nethinim," who returned to Jerusalem with Zerubbabel (Ezra 2:43; Neh. 7:46). 2. A ruler of the Nethinim in Ophel in the days of Nehemiah (Neh. 11:21).

Ziklag (zĭk'lăg), a city in the south of Palestine, given to Judah in Joshua's day (Josh. 15:31) but subsequently given to or shared by Simeon (Josh. 19:5). Later it was ruled by the Philistines; Achish, king of Gath, assigned it to David and his men who were fleeing from Saul (I Sam. 27:1-7). Later Ziklag became the property of the kings of Judah till the captivity.

Zikri (zĭk'rī). 1. Levite; cousin of Aaron and Moses (Exod. 6:21). 2. Benjamite; son of Shashak (I Chron. 8:23). 3. Benjamite of family of Shemei or Shema (KJV "Shimhi") (I Chron. 8:19). 4. Benjamite; son of Jeroham (I Chron. 8:27). 5. Ancestor of Mattaniah who returned from captivity (I Chron. 9:15); "Zabdi" in Neh. 11:17. 6. Descendant of Eliezer (I Chron. 26:25). 7. Father of Eliezer, Reubenite (I Chron. 17:16). 8. Father of Amasiah; soldier (II Chron. 17:16). 9. Father of

Atop the walls, or ramparts, of Zion, adjoining the temple area at Jerusalem. © *MPS*

Elishaphat (II Chron. 23:1). 10. Ephraimite; killed son of Ahaz (II Chron. 28:7). 11. Father of Joel, the overseer of Benjamites (Neh. 11:9). 12. Descendant of Abijah; priest (Neh. 12:17).

Zillah (zĭl'à, **shadow),** one of the two wives of the Cainite Lamech, the first known polygamist; and mother of Tubal-cain the patriarch of all workers in brass and iron (Gen. 4:19-22).

Zilpah (zĭl'pȧ), handmaid of Leah, given to her by her father Laban, and later through Jacob, the mother of Gad and Asher (Gen. 29:24; 30:9-13).

Zilthai (zĭl'thī, **shadow of Jehovah). 1.** An early Benjamite, and descended from Shema (I Chron. 8:20; in ASV Zillethai). 2. Captain of a thousand of the tribe of Manasseh who joined David at Ziklag (I Chron. 12:20).

Zimmah (zĭm'ȧ), a Gershonite Levite (I Chron. 6:20, 42, 43).

Zimran (zĭm'răn), a son of Abraham and Keturah (Gen. 25:2; I Chron. 2:32).

Zimri (zĭm'rī). 1. Prince of Simeon; slain by Phinehas, grandson of Aaron, for committing adultery with Midianite woman (Num. 25:14). 2. 5th king of N kingdom; murdered King Elah; ruled seven days (c. 876 B.C.); overthrown by Omri (I Kings 16:8-20). 3. Son of Zerah; grandson of Judah (I Chron. 2:6). 4. Benjamite; father of Moza (I Chron. 8:36; 9:42). 5. Unknown tribe in East (Jer. 25:25).

Zin (zĭn), a wilderness the Israelites traversed on their way to Canaan. It was close to the borders of Canaan (Num. 13:21) and included Kadesh-barnea within its bounds (Num. 20:1; 27:14; 33:36). Edom bordered it on the E, Judah on the SE (Josh. 15:1-3), and the wilderness of Paran on the S.

Zina (zī'nȧ), a Levite of the family of Gershom (I Chron.23:10). The correct spelling is Zizah, as in verse 11.

Zion (zī'ŭn), one of the hills on which Jerusalem stood. It is first mentioned in the OT as a Jebusite fortress (II Sam. 5:6-9). David captured it and called it the city of David. Archeological remains show that it was inhabited long before David's time; and certain Bible references (I Kings 8:1; II Chron. 5:2; 32:30; 33:14) indicate that this was the original Zion. David brought the Ark to Zion, and the hill henceforth became sacred (II Sam. 6:10-12). When Solomon later removed the Ark to the temple on nearby Mount Moriah, the name Zion was extended to take in the temple (Isa. 8:18; 18:7; 24:23; Joel 3:17; Micah 4:7). Zion came to be used for the whole of Jerusalem (II Kings 19:21; Pss. 48; 69:35; 133:3; Isa. 1:8, etc). The name is frequently used figuratively for the Jewish Church and polity (Pss. 126:1; 129:5; Isa. 33:14; 34:8; 49:14; 52:8) and for heaven (Heb. 12:22; cf. Rev. 14:1).

Zior (zī'ôr, **smallness),** a town in S Judah (Josh. 15:54). It was probably near Hebron.

Ziph (zĭf). 1. A city in the Negeb "toward the border of Edom" given to the tribe of Judah in Joshua's division of the land. Probably about four miles S by E from Hebron. 2. The wilderness named from No. 1 which was S of Jeshimon, and where David hid from Saul till the Ziphites betrayed him (I Sam. 23:14-24; 26:1, 2). 3. A city in the W part of Judah which Rehoboam fortified (II Chron. 11:8). 4. Possibly the same as No. 1 though mentioned separately in Josh. 15:55. 5. A Calebite family name (I Chron. 2:42). 6. A son of Jehallelel of the tribe of Judah (I Chron. 4:16). In KJV his father is Jehaleleel.

Ziphah (zī'fȧ, fem. of **ziph),** one of the sons of Jahaleleel (I Chron. 4:16).

Ziphims (See Ziphites)

Ziphion (See Zephon)

Ziphites (zĭf'īts), the inhabitants of Ziph, whether the town or the wilderness surrounding it (I Sam. 23:14-23; 26:1-5). Twice, apparently, David, being pursued by King Saul, hid in their vicinity and each time the Ziphites, though of David's tribe, told Saul of his location. They seemed to think it best to support the reigning king than to be kind to David, whom they considered a rebel.

Ziphron (zĭf'rŏn), a place on the northern border of the land of Canaan, between Zedad and Hazar-enan, probably not far from the city of Homs (Num. 34:9; Ezek. 47:15-17).

Zippor (zĭp'ôr, **bird),** the father of Balak, king of Moab, and apparently of the Midianites (Num. 22:3, 4).

Zipporah (zĭ-pō'rȧ, **bird,** fem. of **Zippor),** daughter of Jethro or Reuel, the priest of Midian, who became the first wife of Moses (Exod. 2:21). She was the mother of Gershom and of Eliezer (Exod. 18:1-6). Apparently Moses sent her back to her father during the stirring times connected with the Exodus, though she had at least started to

Egypt with him (cf. Exod. 4:20; 18:2).

Zithri (zĭth'rī, **my protection**), a Kohathite Levite, first cousin of Aaron and Moses (Exod. 6:22). Sithri in ASV.

Ziv (See Zif)

Ziz (zĭz, **shining**), a cliff mentioned only in II Chron. 20:16, which stood near the W side of the Red Sea on the way from Engedi to Tekoa.

Ziza (zī'zȧ, **abundance**). 1. Son of Shiphi (KJV "Ziphi") a Simeonite who with others, in the days of King Hezekiah, drove out the ancient inhabitants of Gedor, SW of Bethlehem, and took their land for pasture (I Chron. 4:37-41). 2. A son of Rehoboam and brother of Abijah, kings of Judah (II Chron. 11:20).

Zizah (zī'zȧ), second son of Shimei, a leading Gershonite Levite in the days of David (I Chron. 23:11). Called Zina in the preceding verse.

Zoan (zō'ăn), an ancient Egyptian city, built seven years later than Hebron (Num. 13:22) on the E part of the Delta. The first kings of Dynasty XII made it their capital; the Hyksos fortified it and changed the name to Avaris. When the Hyksos were driven out, the city was neglected, but it was reestablished by Sethi I. The Egyptian god Seth had a center of worship there. Moses met the pharaoh at Zoan (Ps. 78:12, 43). Isaiah and Ezekiel refer to it as an important city (Isa. 19: 11, 13; Ezek. 30:14). For a time the Assyrians were in control of it. The Greeks called it "Tanis." Eventually it was superseded by the new city of Alexandria.

Zoar (zō'êr, **little**), an ancient Canaanite city, now probably under the waters of the bay at the SE part of the Dead Sea. Formerly called "Bela" (Gen. 14: 2), it was saved from immediate destruction with Sodom and Gomorrah in answer to the prayer of Lot, "is it not a little one?" (Gen. 19:20-22).

Zoba, Zobah (zō'bȧ), a region in central Syria between Hamoth and Damascus, sometimes under one king (II Sam. 8:3), but in its first occurrence (I Sam 14:7) we read that Saul of Israel fought against the kings of Zobah, which may indicate more than one kingdom, or possibly successive kings. The kings of Zobah were persistent enemies of Israel, not only fighting against Saul, but against David (II Sam. 8) and Solomon (II Chron. 8:3).

Zobebah (zō-bē'bȧ), a Judahite name referring either to a place, person, or a clan (I Chron. 4:8).

Zohar (zō'hȧr). 1. A noble Hittite, father of Ephron from whom Abraham purchased the field of Machpelah where he buried the body of Sarah in a cave (Gen. 23:8; 25:9). 2. A son of Simeon, second son of Jacob (Gen. 46: 10; Exod. 6:15), "Zerah" in Num. 26: 13 and I Chron. 4:24. 3. A man of Judah (I Chron. 4:7).

Zoheleth (zō'hē-lĕth, **serpent**) a stone beside En-rogel where Adonijah, fourth son of David, and older than Solomon, gathered his conspirators before David's death, slaying sheep and oxen, in order to make himself king at or before the death of his father. The plot was revealed to David, who caused Solomon to be anointed and thus the plot was foiled (I Kings 1, esp. vs. 9).

Zoheth (zō'hĕth), son of Ishi, a Judahite (I Chron. 2:20).

Zophah (zō'fȧ), an Asherite, son of Helem (I Chron. 7:35, 36).

Zophai (zō'fī), an ancestor of Samuel the prophet (I Chron. 6:26; called "Zuph" in vs. 35).

Zophar (zō'fêr), one of Job's friends who came to comfort him in his affliction (Job 2:11).

Zophim (zō'fĭm, **watchers**), a field near the top of Pisgah (Num. 23:14).

Zorah (zō'ra), a city about 15 miles W of Jerusalem on the borders of Judah and Dan (Josh. 15:33; 19:41), the home of Manoah, father of Samson (Judg. 13:2). Samson was buried near there (Judg. 16:31). From Zorah the Danites sent spies to seek a new home for their tribe (Judg. 18:2).

Zorathites (zō'ră-thīts), the inhabitants of Zorah (I Chron. 2:53—KJV has Zoreathites; 4:2).

Zoreah (See Zorah)

Zorites (zō'rīts). In I Chron. 2:54 "Zorathites" should probably be read; otherwise the reference is to a man of some unknown place.

Zorobabel (See Zerubbabel)

Zuar (zū'êr, **small**), the father of Nethaneel of the tribe of Issachar, who was a prince of his tribe (Num. 1:8; 2:5).

Zuph (zŭf, **honeycomb**). 1. An ancestor of the Prophet Samuel. He was a Levite descended from Kohath (I Chron. 6:35). Called "Zophai" in I Chronicles 6:26. 2. A district in Benjamin, near its northern border (I Sam. 9:5).

Zur (zûr, **rock**). 1. One of the five kings of the Midianites slain by Israel

At Zorah, the home of Samson, overlooking the Plain of Sharon, the area of Samson's exploits. © MPS

(Num. 25:15; 31:8). Cozbi, his daughter, was slain by Phinehas, grandson of Aaron. 2. An inhabitant of Gibeon in Benjamin; son of Jeiel (I Chron. 8:30, 33).

Zuriel (zū'rĭ-ĕl, **whose rock is God**), son of Abihail, prince of the Merarite Levites in the wilderness (Num. 3:35).

Zurishaddai (zū'rĭ-shăd'ī, **whose rock is the Almighty**), father of Shelumiel, head of the tribe of Simeon in the wilderness (Num. 1:6; 2:12; 7:36, 41; 10:19).

Zuzim (zū'zĭm), a primitive race of giants, smitten by Chedorlaomer and his allies at an unknown place called Ham, E of the Jordan, in the days of Abraham (Gen. 14:5); erroneously called "Zuzims" in the KJV.

MAPS

Map Index

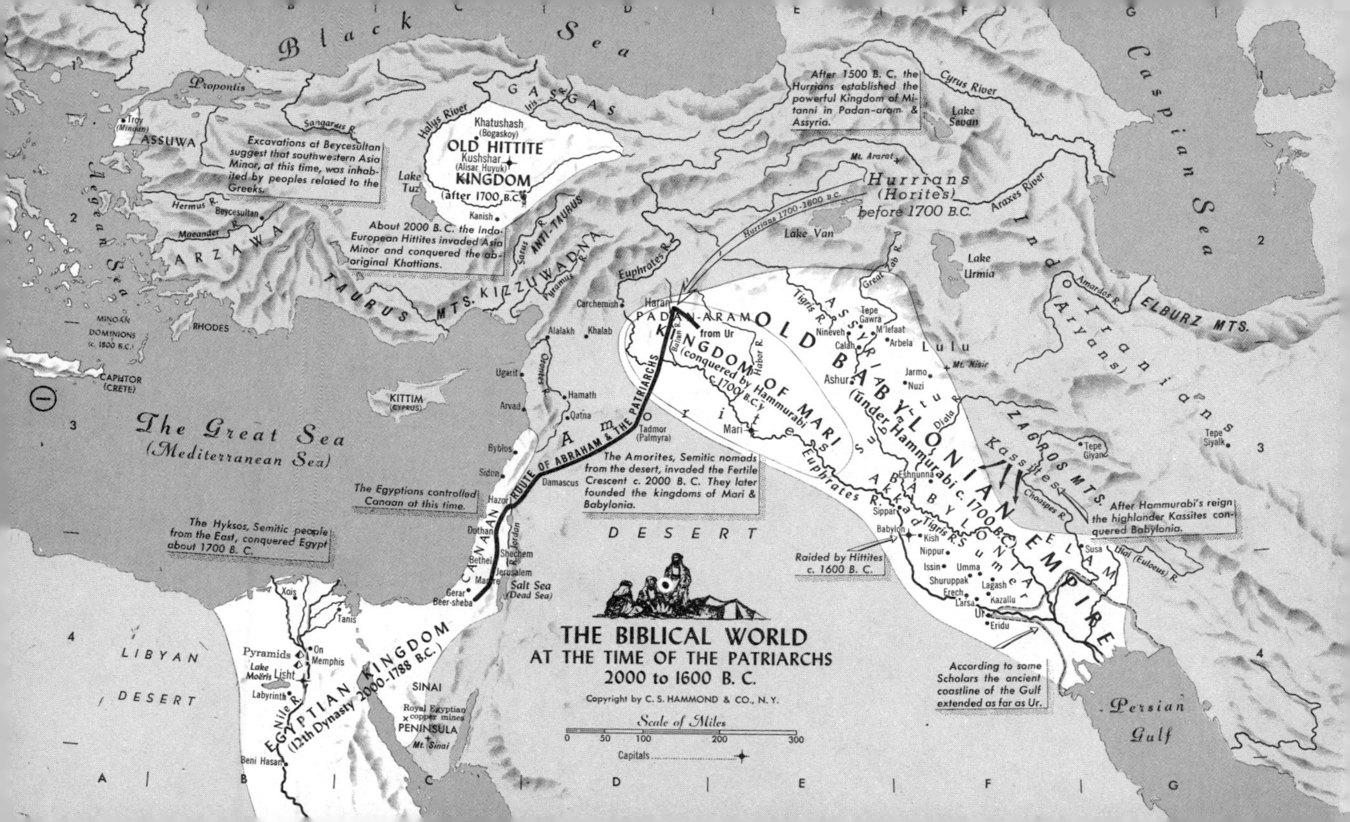
THE BIBLICAL WORLD
AT THE TIME OF THE PATRIARCHS
2000 to 1600 B. C.
Copyright by C. S. HAMMOND & CO., N. Y.
Scale of Miles
0 50 100 200 300
Capitals
Black Sea
Caspian Sea
Propontis
Aegean Sea
The Great Sea
(Mediterranean Sea)
Persian Gulf
Troy (Minoan)
ASSUWA
Sangarius R.
Excavations at Beycesultan suggest that southwestern Asia Minor, at this time, was inhabited by peoples related to the Greeks.
Hermus R.
Beycesultan
Maeander R.
ARZAWA
MINOAN DOMINIONS (c. 1500 B.C.)
RHODES
CAPHTOR (CRETE)
KITTIM (CYPRUS)
Halys River
Khatushash (Bogaskoy)
OLD HITTITE KINGDOM
Kushshar (Alisar Huyuk)
(after 1700 B.C.)
Lake Tuz
Kanish
About 2000 B.C. the Indo-European Hittites invaded Asia Minor and conquered the aboriginal Khattians.
GASGAS
Iris R.
TAURUS MTS.
KIZZUWADNA
ANTI-TAURUS
Sarus R.
Pyramus R.
Euphrates R.
Carchemish
Alalakh
Khalab
Ugarit
Orontes R.
Hamath
Arvad
Qatna
Byblos
Sidon
Damascus
Hazor
Dothan
Bethel
Shechem
Jordan
Jerusalem
Mamre
Salt Sea (Dead Sea)
Gerar
Beer-sheba
CANAAN
The Egyptians controlled Canaan at this time.
The Hyksos, Semitic people from the East, conquered Egypt about 1700 B. C.
ROUTE OF ABRAHAM & THE PATRIARCHS
Amorites
Tadmor (Palmyra)
The Amorites, Semitic nomads from the desert, invaded the Fertile Crescent c. 2000 B. C. They later founded the kingdoms of Mari & Babylonia.
DESERT
Haran
PADAN-ARAM
from Ur
Balikh R.
Habor R.
KINGDOM OF MARI
(conquered by Hammurabi c. 1700 B.C.)
Mari
OLD BABYLONIAN EMPIRE
(under Hammurabi c. 1700 B.C.)
ASSYRIA
Tigris R.
Nineveh
Tepe Gawra
M'lefaat
Calah
Arbela
Ashur
Jarmo
Nuzi
Lulu
Mt. Nisir
Great Zab R.
Diala R.
Eshnunna
AKKAD
BABYLONIA
SUMER
Euphrates R.
Sippar
Babylon
Kish
Tigris R.
Nippur
Issin
Umma
Shuruppak
Lagash
Erech
Larsa
Kazallu
Ur
Eridu
Raided by Hittites c. 1600 B. C.
According to some Scholars the ancient coastline of the Gulf extended as far as Ur.
ELAM
Susa
Ulai (Euloeus) R.
Choaspes R.
Kassites
ZAGROS MTS.
After Hammurabi's reign the highlander Kassites conquered Babylonia.
Tepe Giyan
Tepe Siyalk
Indo-Iranians (Aryans)
Amardos R.
ELBURZ MTS.
Lake Urmia
Lake Van
Hurrians (Horites) before 1700 B.C.
Hurrians 1700-1600 B.C.
Mt. Ararat
Araxes River
Lake Sevan
Cyrus River
After 1500 B.C. the Hurrians established the powerful Kingdom of Mitanni in Padan-aram & Assyria.
Xois
Tanis
On
Memphis
Pyramids
Lake Moeris
Lisht
Labyrinth
Nile R.
Beni Hasan
EGYPTIAN KINGDOM
(12th Dynasty 2000-1788 B.C.)
SINAI
Royal Egyptian copper mines
PENINSULA
Mt. Sinai
LIBYAN DESERT
A B C D E F G
1 2 3 4

CANAAN BEFORE THE CONQUEST
Copyright by C. S. HAMMOND & CO., N. Y.
Scale of Miles
0 5 10 20 30 40
Perennial Rivers
Seasonal Rivers & Streams
Capitals
The Great Sea
(Mediterranean Sea)
Phoenicians from the cities of Sidon and Tyre traded throughout the Mediterranean.
Canaan at this time was an Egyptian province organized on a city - state system. The local kings were only required to pay tribute and to furnish labor for Egyptian royal projects.
The 13th and 12th century kingdoms of Bashan, Ammon, Moab and Edom displaced the Rephaim, Zuzim, Emim and Horites respectively.
The destroyed cities of Sodom and Gomorrah are believed to be beneath the shallow waters of the Dead Sea which now cover the Vale of Siddim (shaded portion).
HITTITE EMPIRE
Ubi
Damascus
Sidonians (Phoenicians)
MOUNT LEBANON
Leontes R.
MT. HERMON
Sidon
Zarephath
Tyre
Kanah
Laish (Dan)
Kedesh
Misrephoth-maim
Achzib
Hazor
Merom
BASHAN (KINGDOM OF OG)
Karnaim
Ashtaroth
Accho
Achshaph
Chinnereth
Madon
Sea of Chinnereth (Galilee)
MT. CARMEL
Kishon R.
Shimron
Mt. Tabor
Jokneam
Yarmuk R.
Edrei
Dor
Megiddo
Taanach
Canaanites
Ibleam
Beth-shan
Pella
Jabesh-gilead
Ham
Ramoth-gilead
Gileadites
Dothan
Mahanaim
Plain of Sharon
Sochoh
Tirzah?
Mt. Ebal
Shechem
Jacob's Well
Mt. Gerizim
Jordan
Succoth
Jabbok R.
Penuel (Peniel)
Aphek
Tappuah
Adam
Joppa
Ono
Lod
Hivites
River
Amorites
KINGDOM OF SIHON
Jazer
Rabbath-ammon
AMMON
Bethel
Ai
Beeroth
Gezer
Gibeon
Jericho
Ekron
Chephirah
Jebusites
Gilgal
Plains of Moab
Heshbon
Kirjath-jearim
Mt. Nebo (Pisgah)
Jebus (Jerusalem)
Beth-shemesh
Ashdod
Medeba
Jarmuth
Bethlehem
Libnah
Adullam
Ashkelon
Jahaz
Gath
Lachish
Shephelah
Mamre
Gaza (Azzah)
Eglon
Hebron (Kirjath-arba)
Kiriathaim
Dibon
Aroer
Kirjath-sepher (Debir)
En-gedi
Salt Sea (Dead Sea)
Arnon R.
Gerar
Hittites
Raphia
Sharuhen
Beer-sheba
Arad
Ar?
Besor
Hormah
Kir-moab (Kir-hareseth)
Kenites
MOAB
Amalekites
Rehoboth
Zoar
Hazezon-tamar?
Ascent of Akrabbim
River of Egypt
Wilderness of Zin
Arabah
MT. SEIR
Brook Zered
Bozrah
Oboth
EDOM
Kadesh-barnea (En-mishpat)
Punon
A B C D E
1 2 3 4 5 6 7

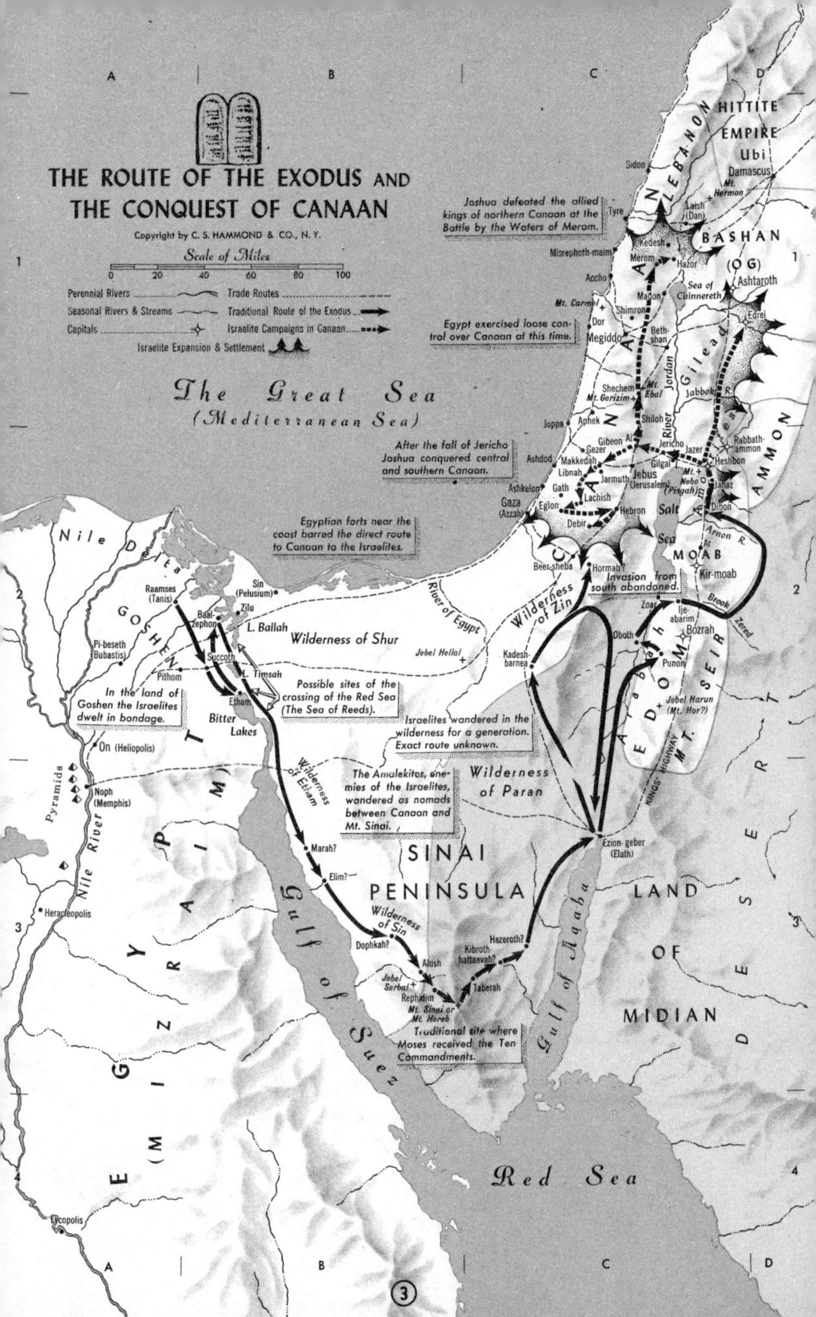
THE ROUTE OF THE EXODUS AND THE CONQUEST OF CANAAN
Copyright by C. S. HAMMOND & CO., N. Y.
Scale of Miles
0 20 40 60 80 100
Perennial Rivers
Seasonal Rivers & Streams
Capitals
Trade Routes
Traditional Route of the Exodus
Israelite Campaigns in Canaan
Israelite Expansion & Settlement
The Great Sea
(Mediterranean Sea)
Joshua defeated the allied kings of northern Canaan at the Battle by the Waters of Merom.
Egypt exercised loose control over Canaan at this time.
After the fall of Jericho Joshua conquered central and southern Canaan.
Egyptian forts near the coast barred the direct route to Canaan to the Israelites.
Invasion from south abandoned.
In the land of Goshen the Israelites dwelt in bondage.
Possible sites of the crossing of the Red Sea (The Sea of Reeds).
Israelites wandered in the wilderness for a generation. Exact route unknown.
The Amalekites, enemies of the Israelites, wandered as nomads between Canaan and Mt. Sinai.
Traditional site where Moses received the Ten Commandments.
HITTITE EMPIRE
Ubi
Damascus
Mt. Hermon
Sidon
LEBANON
Tyre
Laish (Dan)
Kedesh
Merom
Hazor
BASHAN
(OG)
Ashtaroth
Misrephoth-maim
Accho
Sea of Chinnereth
Madon
Mt. Carmel
Shimron
Dor
Edrei
Megiddo
Beth-shan
CANAAN
Jordan
Gilead
Shechem
Mt. Ebal
Mt. Gerizim
Jabbok R.
Joppa
Aphek
Shiloh
River
Gibeon
Ai
Jericho
Jazer
Rabbath-ammon
AMMON
Gezer
Ashdod
Makkedah
Gilgal
Heshbon
Libnah
Jebus (Jerusalem)
Mt. Nebo (Pisgah)
Jarmuth
Jahaz
Ashkelon
Gath
Lachish
Gaza (Azzah)
Eglon
Hebron
Salt Sea
Dibon
Debir
Arnon R.
Ar
MOAB
Beer-sheba
Hormah?
Kir-moab
Wilderness of Zin
Zoar
Brook Zered
Ije-abarim
Oboth
Bozrah
Kadesh-barnea
Punon
Arabah
EDOM
MT. SEIR
Jebel Harun (Mt. Hor?)
KINGS HIGHWAY
Nile Delta
Raamses (Tanis)
Sin (Pelusium)
GOSHEN
Baal-zephon
Zilu
L. Ballah
Wilderness of Shur
River of Egypt
Jebel Hellal
Pi-beseth (Bubastis)
Succoth
Pithom
L. Timsah
Etham
Bitter Lakes
On (Heliopolis)
Pyramids
Noph (Memphis)
Wilderness of Etham
Wilderness of Paran
Ezion-geber (Elath)
Marah?
Elim?
SINAI PENINSULA
LAND OF MIDIAN
Nile River
Heracleopolis
Wilderness of Sin
Dophkah?
Hazeroth?
Kibroth-hattaavah?
Alush
Jebel Serbal
Taberah
Rephidim
Mt. Sinai or Mt. Horeb
Gulf of Suez
Gulf of Aqaba
EGYPT (MIZRAIM)
DESERT
Red Sea
Lycopolis
A B C D
1 2 3 4

CANAAN AS DIVIDED AMONG THE TWELVE TRIBES
c. 1200-1020 B. C.
Copyright by C. S. HAMMOND & CO., N. Y.
Scale of Miles
0 5 10 20 30 40
Perennial Rivers
Seasonal Rivers & Streams
The tribal divisions marked on this map are only approximate since boundary lists are incomplete.
The Israelites were unable to capture the fortified towns of the plains during the early period of settlement.
The Israelites were under repeated attack from Philistine invaders who occupied the coastal area about 1200 B.C.
The cities assigned to Simeon were also a part of the inheritance of Judah. Simeon as a tribe was later absorbed by Judah.
Part of the tribe of Dan, unable to secure its inheritance, migrated north and captured Laish, renaming it Dan.
Although all of Bashan was assigned to the half tribe of Manasseh, it is doubtful that settlement reached beyond the Yarmuk Valley.
During the period of Judges, invading Ammonites, Moabites and Midianites were repulsed by the Israelites.
The priestly tribe of Levi did not receive a definite territory but instead was allotted 48 cities distributed over the tribal areas.
The Great Sea
(Mediterranean Sea)
Sidonians (Phoenicians)
MOUNT LEBANON
Leontes R.
MT. HERMON
Abana
Damascus
R.
Sidon
Zarephath
Tyre
Kanah
Abel-beth-maachah
DAN
Laish or Leshem (Dan)
ASHER
NAPHTALI
Bashan
MANASSEH
Hammon
Misrephoth-maim
Achzib
Abdon
Beth-emek
Accho
Achshaph
Cabul
Aphek
En-hazor
Kedesh
Iron
Hazor
Ramah
Hukkok
Chinnereth
Karnaim
Sea of Chinnereth
Geshur
Ashtaroth
Argob
Madon
Rimmon
Hannathon
Aphek
Golan?
MT. CARMEL
Kishon
ZEBULUN
Hammath
Gath-hepher
Shimron
Harosheth
Jokneam
Chesulloth
Mt. Tabor
Jabneel
Sarid
En-dor
Yarmuk R.
Dor
Plain of Jezreel
Shunem
Ophrah
Havoth-jair
Edrei
ISSACHAR
Camon
Megiddo
Jezreel
Ramoth-gilead
Harod (Spring)
Shihor-libnath
Taanach
Mt. Gilboa
Beth-shan
Ibleam
Pella
GILEAD
Dothan
Jabesh-gilead
Plain of Sharon
Bezek
Mahanaim
MANASSEH
Thebez
Abel-meholah
Tirzah?
River Jordan
AMMON
Mt. Ebal
Shechem
Zaphon
Mt. Gerizim
Succoth
Jabbok R.
Pirathon
Taanath-shiloh
Penuel
Kanah
Mizpeh
Janohah
GAD
Gath-rimmon?
Aphek
Tappuah
Shiloh
Adam
Joppa (Japho)
Bene-berak
Lebonah
Ataroth
Jogbehah
Ono
EPHRAIM
Timnath-serah
Jazer
Rabbath-ammon
Ophrah
Naarath
Betonim
Lod
Aijalon
Bethel
Ai
Beth-horon
Mizpah?
Beth-nimrah
DAN
Gezer
Jabneel
Ekron
Gibeon
Ramah
Geba
Jericho
Gilgal
Sorek
Gibbethon
Kirjath-jearim
BENJAMIN
Abel-shittim
Elealeh
Elteke
Gibeah
Beth-hoglah
Heshbon
Zorah
Chesalon
Beth-jeshimoth
Ashdod
Timnah
Jebus (Jerusalem)
Mt. Nebo
Beth-shemesh
Makkedah
Jarmuth
Medeba
Libnah
Etam
Bethlehem
Baal-meon
Azekah
Adullam
Ashkelon
Jahaz
Tekoa
Gath
Mareshah
Keilah
Beth-zur
REUBEN
Philistines
JUDAH
Eglon
Lachish
Salt Sea (Dead Sea)
Gaza
Hebron
Ataroth
Kiriathaim
Dibon
Debir
Ziph
En-gedi
Arnon R.
Aroer
Caleb
Juttah
Carmel
Gerar
Ziklag
Anab
Eshtemoh
Maon
Madmannah
Jattir
Raphia
Cherethites
Sharuhen
Arad
Beer-sheba
Moladah
Kenites
Ar?
MOAB
Hormah
Kir-moab (Kir-hareseth)
Beth-palet?
Aroer
SIMEON
Rehoboth
Ascent of Akrabbim
Brook Zered
Wilderness of Zin
EDOM
A
B
C
D
E
1
2
3
4
5
6
7

THE KINGDOM OF SAUL
c. 1020-1000 B. C.
Copyright by C. S. HAMMOND & CO., N.Y.
Scale of Miles
0 5 10 20 30 40
Perennial Rivers
Seasonal Rivers & Streams
Capitals
Israelite Forces
Enemies of the Israelites
Kingdom of Saul at its greatest extent
The Great Sea
(Mediterranean Sea)
The Philistines invaded Israel through the Plain of Jezreel. The Israelites were defeated and Saul slain at Mt. Gilboa.
Saul defeated the Ammonites besieging Jabesh-gilead. For his triumph Saul was proclaimed king of all Israel.
Home of Samuel. Saul anointed here.
Jonathan's exploits at Michmash routed the Philistines.
Encounter of David and Goliath.
David, driven into exile by Saul, finally took refuge among the Philistines and settled in Ziklag.
Saul secured the southern border of Judah by defeating the Amalekites.
Phoenicians
MOUNT LEBANON
ZOBAH
MT. HERMON
SYRIAN STATES
Aramaeans
MAACHAH
GESHUR
Bashan
TOB
Havoth-jair
GILEAD
AMMON
MOAB
EDOM
JUDAH
PHILISTIA
Canaanites
Cherethites
Kenites
Amalekites
Wilderness of Judah
Salt Sea (Dead Sea)
Sea of Chinnereth
Plain of Sharon
Plain of Jezreel
MT. CARMEL
MT. GILBOA
Mt. Tabor
Mt. Ebal
Mt. Gerizim
Mt. Nebo
Kishon R.
Leontes R.
Abana R.
Yarmuk R.
Jabbok R.
River Jordan
Arnon R.
Brook Zered
Besor
Elah
Sidon
Zarephath
Tyre
Achzib
Accho
Damascus
Ijon
Abel-beth-maachah
Dan
Kanah
Kedesh
Hazor
Cabul
Aphek
Chinnereth
Karnaim
Ashtaroth
Rimmon
Hammath
Shimron
En-dor
Shunem
Jezreel
Dor
Megiddo
Taanach
Ibleam
Dothan
Beth-shan
Edrei
Camon
Ramoth-gilead
Jabesh-gilead
Mahanaim
Bezek
Thebez
Shechem
Succoth
Penuel
Adamah
Shiloh
Joppa
Ramathaim-zophim
Lod
Ophrah
Rabbath-ammon
Bethel
Beth-horon
Mizpah?
Geba
Michmash
Gibeon
Ramah
Gilgal
Jabneel
Gezer
Ekron
Kirjath-jearim
Gibeah
Nob
Heshbon
Ashdod
Timnah
Beth-shemesh
Jebus (Jerusalem)
Bethlehem
Medeba
Azekah
Socoh
Ashkelon
Adullam
Tekoa
Keilah
Gath
Eglon
Lachish
Hebron
Gaza
Ziph
En-gedi
Dibon
Aroer
Carmel
Maon
Gerar
Ziklag
Raphia
Jattir
Ar?
Beer-sheba
Hormah
Aroer
Kir-moab (Kir-hareseth)

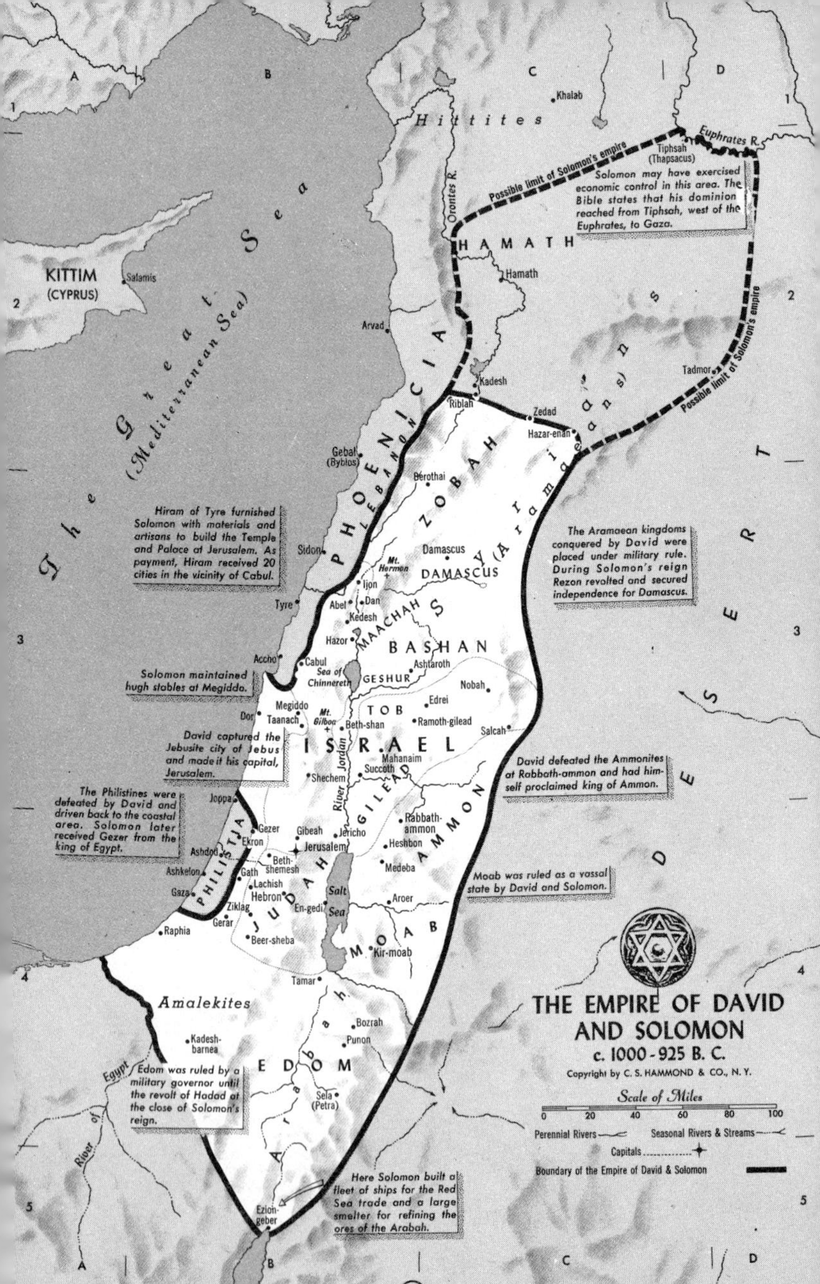
THE EMPIRE OF DAVID AND SOLOMON
c. 1000 - 925 B. C.
Copyright by C. S. HAMMOND & CO., N. Y.
Scale of Miles
0 20 40 60 80 100
Perennial Rivers
Seasonal Rivers & Streams
Capitals
Boundary of the Empire of David & Solomon
Solomon may have exercised economic control in this area. The Bible states that his dominion reached from Tiphsah, west of the Euphrates, to Gaza.
Hiram of Tyre furnished Solomon with materials and artisans to build the Temple and Palace at Jerusalem. As payment, Hiram received 20 cities in the vicinity of Cabul.
The Aramaean kingdoms conquered by David were placed under military rule. During Solomon's reign Rezon revolted and secured independence for Damascus.
Solomon maintained hugh stables at Megiddo.
David captured the Jebusite city of Jebus and made it his capital, Jerusalem.
The Philistines were defeated by David and driven back to the coastal area. Solomon later received Gezer from the king of Egypt.
David defeated the Ammonites at Rabbath-ammon and had himself proclaimed king of Ammon.
Moab was ruled as a vassal state by David and Solomon.
Edom was ruled by a military governor until the revolt of Hadad at the close of Solomon's reign.
Here Solomon built a fleet of ships for the Red Sea trade and a large smelter for refining the ores of the Arabah.
Possible limit of Solomon's empire
Possible limit of Solomon's empire
The Great Sea (Mediterranean Sea)
KITTIM (CYPRUS)
Salamis
Hittites
Khalab
Euphrates R.
Tiphsah (Thapsacus)
Orontes R.
HAMATH
Hamath
Arvad
Kadesh
Riblah
Zedad
Hazar-enan
Tadmor
Syrian Desert
(Aramaeans)
PHOENICIA
LEBANON
Gebal (Byblos)
Berothai
ZOBAH
Sidon
Damascus
DAMASCUS
SYRIA (Aramaeans)
Mt. Hermon
Ijon
Dan
Tyre
Abel
Kedesh
MAACHAH
Hazor
BASHAN
Accho
Cabul
Sea of Chinnereth
GESHUR
Ashtaroth
Nobah
Megiddo
TOB
Edrei
Dor
Taanach
Mt. Gilboa
Beth-shan
Ramoth-gilead
Salcah
ISRAEL
Mahanaim
Succoth
Shechem
GILEAD
River Jordan
Joppa
AMMON
Rabbath-ammon
Gezer
Gibeah
Jericho
Ekron
Jerusalem
Heshbon
Ashdod
PHILISTIA
Beth-shemesh
Medeba
Ashkelon
Gath
Lachish
Gaza
Hebron
Salt Sea
JUDAH
Aroer
En-gedi
Ziklag
Gerar
MOAB
Raphia
Beer-sheba
Kir-moab
Tamar
Amalekites
Bozrah
Kadesh-barnea
Punon
EDOM
Arabah
Sela (Petra)
River of Egypt
Ezion-geber
A B C D
1 2 3 4 5

THE KINGDOMS OF ISRAEL AND JUDAH
c. 925-842 B.C.
Copyright by C. S. HAMMOND & CO., N. Y.
Scale of Miles
0 5 10 20 30 40
Perennial Rivers
Seasonal Rivers & Streams
Capitals
Egyptian & Syrian Attacks
The Great Sea
(Mediterranean Sea)
Elijah took refuge in Zarephath and brought back to life the widow's son.
In the reign of Baasha the cities of northern Israel were raided by the king of Damascus in league with Asa, king of Judah.
The Syrians waged almost constant war against Israel. They were held in check by Ahab until his death in battle at Ramoth-gilead.
Elijah challenged the prophets of Baal at Mt. Carmel.
The introduction of Phoenician cults following the marriage of Ahab with Jezebel caused violent reactions in Israel that eventually wiped out the house of Omri.
Samaria, fortress capital of Israel was built by Omri c. 870 B. C.
Moab was ruled as a vassal kingdom under Omri and Ahab. The Moabite Stone commemorates the victory of Mesha, king of Moab, over Israel and the return of Moabite independence.
Shishak, Egyptian pharaoh, raided the divided kingdoms, plundering Jerusalem in the reign of Rehoboam.
During the reign of Jehoshaphat, Judah regained control over Edom.
PHOENICIA
MOUNT LEBANON
MT. HERMON
ARAMEANS
Syrians
GESHUR
Bashan
Havoth-jair
GILEAD
AMMON
MOAB
EDOM
ISRAEL
JUDAH
PHILISTIA
Plain of Sharon
Plain of Jezreel
Wilderness of Judah
Salt Sea (Dead Sea)
Sea of Chinnereth
Sidon
Zarephath
Tyre
Damascus
Abana R.
Leontes R.
Ijon
Dan
Abel-beth-maachah
Kedesh
Hazor
Accho
Cabul
Chinnereth
Karnaim
Ashtaroth
Aphek
Yarmuk R.
Hammath
Mt. Tabor
MT. CARMEL
Kishon R.
Dor
Shunem
Megiddo
Jezreel
Edrei
Ramoth-gilead
Taanach
Beth-shan
Ibleam
Dothan
Jabesh-gilead
Tishbe
Mahanaim
Sochoh
Abel-meholah
Samaria
Mt. Ebal
Tirzah?
Shechem
Mt. Gerizim
Jordan River
Succoth
Penuel
Jabbok R.
Janohah
Aphek
Joppa
Shiloh
Zeredah
Jeshanah
Lod
Zemaraim
Bethel
Beth-horon
Jabneel
Gezer
Aijalon
Mizpah?
Geba
Jericho
Ramah
Rabbath-ammon
Ekron
Gibbethon
Cherith
Gilgal
Elealeh
Heshbon
Zorah
Jerusalem
Ashdod
Timnah
Beth-shemesh
Mt. Nebo
Azekah
Bethlehem
Medeba
Ashkelon
Socoh
Etam
Baal-meon
Adullam
Tekoa
Gath
Mareshah
Beth-zur
Ataroth
Lachish
Hebron
Gaza
Adoraim
Dibon
Debir
Ziph
Aroer
En-gedi
Arnon R.
Gerar
Ziklag
Raphia
Ar?
Beer-sheba
Kir-moab
(Kir-hareseth)
Valley of Salt
Brook Zered
7

THE ASSYRIAN EMPIRE
824 to 625 B. C.
Copyright by C. S. HAMMOND & CO., N.Y.
Scale of Miles
0 50 100 200 300
Capitals
Assyrian Empire – 824 B. C.
Assyrian Empire – 671 B. C.
The Medes & Babylonians destroyed the Assyrian Empire in 612 B. C.
Greek colonization of the Mediterranean world began in this period.
Site of Assyrian trading post 1850 B. C.
Sargon II destroyed the Kingdom of Israel in 721 B. C.
Shalmaneser III's victory over Ahab 854 B. C.
Sennacherib's great capital
Early Assyrian capital
Destroyed by Sennacherib 689 B. C.
Home of Assyrian colonists of Samaria
The Assyrians held Egypt from 671 B. C. to 652 B. C.
Destroyed by Ashurbanipal 663 B. C.
The Great Sea
(Mediterranean Sea)
Black Sea
Caspian Sea
Red Sea
Persian Gulf
Thracians
Macedonians
Scythians
(Ashkenaz)
Cimmerians
(Gomer)
KINGDOM OF URARTU
(before 712 B.C.)
PHRYGIAN KINGDOM
LYDIAN KINGDOM
GREEK CITY STATES
CAPPADOCIA
CILICIA
ASSYRIAN EMPIRE
ASSYRIA
AKKAD
BABYLONIA
Sumer
Chaldea
ELLIP
ELAM
Medes
Cadusii
Amardi
ELBURZ MTS.
ZAGROS MTS.
TAURUS MTS.
ANTI-TAURUS
Tubal
Aegean Sea
ARABIAN DESERT
Aribi
(Arabs)
Kedar
Libyans
LIBYAN DESERT
EGYPTIAN KINGDOM
(before 671 B.C.)
Sinai Peninsula
PHOENICIA
SYRIA (ARAM)
JUDAH (trib. to Assyria)
AMMON
MOAB
EDOM
Salt Sea (Dead Sea)
Jordan R.
Orontes R.
Euphrates R.
Tigris
Tigris River
Habor R.
Great Zab R.
Araxes River
Cyrus R.
Halys R.
Sangarius R.
Hermus R.
Maeander R.
Nile R.
L. Sevan
L. Van
Lake Urmia
L. Tuz
L. Moëris
Mt. Ararat
Propontis
Thasos
Byzantium
Chalcedon
Cyzicus
Astacus
Abydos
Tieum (Greek)
Sinope (Greek)
Trapezus (Greek)
Ancyra
Gordium
Sardis
Celaenae
Miletus
LESBOS
CHIOS
SAMOS
EUBOEA
Athens
Corinth
Sparta
RHODES
CRETE
Phaselis (Greek)
CYPRUS
Salamis
Paphos
Kanish
Cilician Gates
Tarsus
Marqash
Samal
Arpad
Carchemish
Til Barsip
Haran
Gozan
Nisibis
Tushpa (Turushpa)
Musasir
Dur Sharrukin
Arbela
Nineveh
Calah
Ashur
Arrapakha
Ecbatana
Karkar
Hamath
Arvad
Byblos
Sidon
Tyre
Damascus
Tadmor
Anatho
Opis
Sippar
Babylon
Borsippa
Cuthah
Kish
Nippur
Erech
Ur
Susa (Shushan)
Samaria
Elteke
Jerusalem
Ashkelon
Raphia
Sela
Dumah
Cyrene (Greek)
Ammonium
Sais
Tanis
Pelusium
Bubastis
Memphis
On
Heracleopolis
Akhetaton (Tell el Amarna)
Siut
Abydos
Thebes
Jeb (Elephantine I.)

THE RESTORATION OF JUDAH
c. 445 B.C.
Copyright by C. S. HAMMOND & CO., N. Y.
Scale of Miles
0 5 10 20 30 40
Perennial Rivers
Seasonal Rivers & Streams
Route of the Returning Exiles
Judah was a small province in the Fifth Persian Satrapy (pink area), which extended from the border of Cilicia to the border of Egypt and included all Phoenicia, Palestine and Syria.
Lod, Ono and Hadid were Jewish cities outside the province of Judah.
The Edomites were driven north from their land into the southern half of the old territory of Judah by the Arabs.
After Cyrus the Persian issued a decree permitting the exiles to return to their homeland in 538 B. C., many exiles took the long journey back to Judah.
In 458 B. C. (398 B. C.?) Ezra led a group of the exiles back to Judah to reform conditions there according to the laws of God.
In 445 B. C. Nehemiah led a group of exiles back to Judah to rebuild the walls and gates of Jerusalem.
After the reformation in Judah, the priests became the dominating power and influence among the Jews. They kept the Jews a distinct race by forbidding marriage with other tribes and peoples.
Sheshbazzar, who brought with him from Babylon the sacred vessels carried away by Nebuchadnezzar, started the rebuilding of the Temple in Jerusalem. The Temple was completed by Zerubbabel in 515 B. C.
The Great Sea
(Mediterranean Sea)
Phoenicians
SIDON
MOUNT LEBANON
MT. HERMON
From Babylonia
Aramaeans
Sidon
Tyre
Leontes R.
Dan
Damascus
Kedesh
Hazor
Accho
GALILEE
Bashan
KARNAIM
Karnaim
Sea of Galilee
Yarmuk R.
MT. CARMEL
Kishon R.
Mt. Tabor
Megiddo
Dor
Edrei
Jezreel
Ramoth-gilead
Beth-shan
Pella
GILEAD
DOR
Plain of Sharon
SAMARIA
River Jordan
Samaria
Shechem
Mt. Gerizim
Jabbok R.
Joppa
Ono
Lod
Neballat
Hadid
Bethel
Mizpah?
Ai
Michmash
Jericho
Beth-horon
Gibeon
Geba
Gilgal
Gezer
Ekron
Emmaus
Chephirah
Ramah
Anathoth
Nob
Jerusalem
Zareah
Kirjath-jearim
Beth-haccherem
Ashdod
Zanoah
Azekah
Jarmuth
JUDAH
Bethlehem
Ashkelon
Adullam
Keilah
Tekoa
Lachish
Beth-zur
Gaza
Hebron
Philistines
ASHDOD
Edomites
En-gedi
Salt Sea
(Dead Sea)
Tyrus
Rabbath-ammon
AMMON
Heshbon
Medeba
Dibon
Arnon R.
MOAB
Kir-moab
(Kir-hareseth)
Gerar
Ziklag
En-rimmon
Raphia
Jeshua
Moladah
Beer-sheba
Beth-phelet?
Brook Zered
Arabs
A B C D E
1 2 3 4 5 6 7

THE DOMINIONS OF HEROD THE GREAT
37 to 4 B.C.
Copyright by C. S. HAMMOND & CO., N. Y.
Scale of Miles
0 5 10 20 30 40
Perennial Rivers
Seasonal Rivers & Streams
Capitals
Cities of the Decapolis
The Great Sea (Mediterranean Sea)
PHOENICIA
SYRIA
MOUNT LEBANON
ABILENE
Abila
Damascus
Abana R.
Pharpar R.
Leontes R.
ITURAEA
MT. HERMON
Sidon
Tyre
PANIAS
Paneas
Ulatha and Panias were placed under Herod's control in 20 B.C.
ULATHA
Jordan
Cadasa
Lake Semechonitis
Gischala
Ecdippa
Herod's first territory was Galilee, given to him by his father, Antipater.
Ptolemais
GALILEE
GAULANITIS
BATANAEA
TRACHONITIS
Raphana
Tarichaea (Magdala)
Arbela
Sea of Galilee
Gamala
Sepphoris
Hippos
Dion
Kanatha
MT. CARMEL
Gaba
Nazareth
Philoteria
Yarmuk R.
Abila
AURANITIS
Gadara
Plain of Esdraelon
Dora
Edrei
Hippos and Gadara were cities of the Decapolis given to Herod by Augustus.
Caesarea (Strato's Tower)
City and port were built by Herod.
Bostra (Bosora)
Scythopolis
SAMARIA
Pella
DECAPOLIS
Herod rebuilt Samaria, giving it the new name of Sebaste.
The Decapolis was a league of neighboring city districts united for mutual protection against marauding tribes. It was not a compact geographical or political unit with definite boundaries.
Plain of Sharon
River Jordan
Gerasa
Sebaste (Samaria)
Amathus
Apollonia
Sychem
Mt. Gerizim
Cleopatra for several years held many towns including Jericho and much of the coast.
Jabbok R.
PERAEA
Antipatris
Alexandrium
Joppa
Thamna
Phasaelis
Gophna
Lydda
Modin
Philadelphia
Bethel
AMMON
NABATAEA
Bethennabris
Jamnia
Ekron
Gazara
Beth-horon
Jericho
Emmaus
Herod gained control of Jerusalem in 37 B.C., defeating Antigonus, and began to rule Judaea as king.
Jerusalem
Mt. of Olives
Khirbet Qumrân
Livias (Beth-haran)
Essebon
Azotus
Hyrcanium
Ascalon
Birthplace of Herod.
Bethlehem
JUDAEA
Herodium
Beth-gubrin
Marisa
Callirhoë
Machaerus
Bethsura
Anthedon (Agrippium)
Hebron
Gaza
En-gedi
Salt Sea (Dead Sea)
Dibon
Arnon R.
IDUMAEA
Masada
Bersabee
MOABITIS
Kir-moab
Elusa
NABATAEANS
Brook Zered

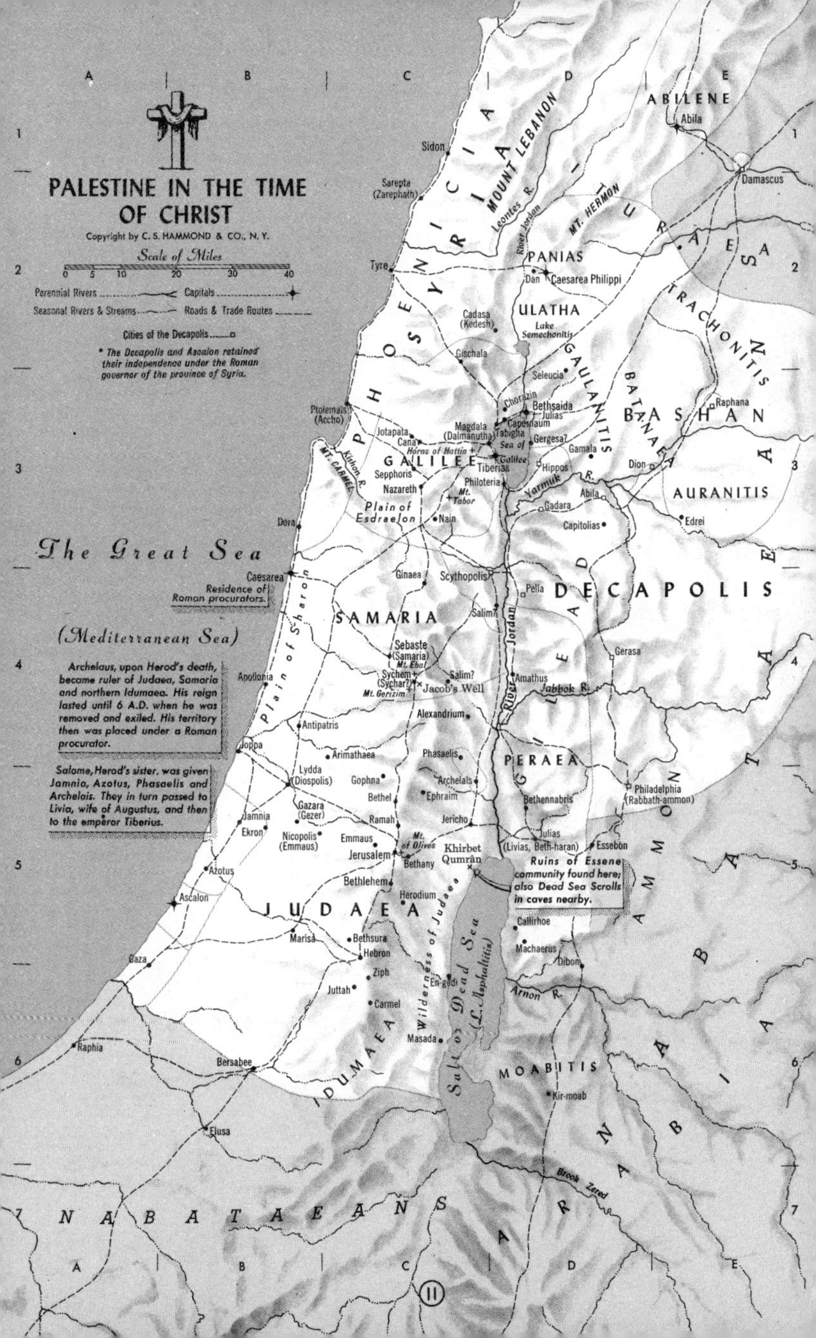
PALESTINE IN THE TIME OF CHRIST
Copyright by C. S. HAMMOND & CO., N. Y.
Scale of Miles
0 5 10 20 30 40
Perennial Rivers
Capitals
Seasonal Rivers & Streams
Roads & Trade Routes
Cities of the Decapolis
* The Decapolis and Ascalon retained their independence under the Roman governor of the province of Syria.
The Great Sea
(Mediterranean Sea)
Residence of Roman procurators.
Archelaus, upon Herod's death, became ruler of Judaea, Samaria and northern Idumaea. His reign lasted until 6 A.D. when he was removed and exiled. His territory then was placed under a Roman procurator.
Salome, Herod's sister, was given Jamnia, Azotus, Phasaelis and Archelais. They in turn passed to Livia, wife of Augustus, and then to the emperor Tiberius.
Ruins of Essene community found here; also Dead Sea Scrolls in caves nearby.
PHOENICIA
SYRIA
MOUNT LEBANON
MT. HERMON
ITURAEA
ABILENE
Abila
Damascus
Sidon
Sarepta (Zarephath)
Leontes R.
River Jordan
PANIAS
Tyre
Dan
Caesarea Philippi
ULATHA
Cadasa (Kedesh)
Lake Semechonitis
Gischala
GAULANITIS
TRACHONITIS
BATANAEA
BASHAN
Raphana
Seleucia
Chorazin
Bethsaida Julias
Capernaum
Magdala (Dalmanutha)
Tabigha
Sea of Galilee
Gergesa?
Gamala
Hippos
Dion
Ptolemais (Accho)
Jotapata
Cana
Horns of Hattin
GALILEE
Tiberias
MT. CARMEL
Kishon R.
Sepphoris
Nazareth
Philoteria
Yarmuk R.
Abila
AURANITIS
Mt. Tabor
Gadara
Plain of Esdraelon
Nain
Capitolias
Edrei
Dora
Caesarea
Ginaea
Scythopolis
Pella
DECAPOLIS
GILEAD
Plain of Sharon
SAMARIA
Salim
Jordan
Sebaste (Samaria)
Mt. Ebal
Gerasa
Sychem (Sychar?)
Mt. Gerizim
Salim?
Jacob's Well
Amathus
Apollonia
Jabbok R.
Alexandrium
Antipatris
Joppa
Arimathaea
Phasaelis
PERAEA
Lydda (Diospolis)
Gophna
Archelais
Ephraim
Bethel
Philadelphia (Rabbath-ammon)
Bethennabris
Jamnia
Gazara (Gezer)
Ramah
Jericho
Ekron
Nicopolis (Emmaus)
Emmaus
Mt. of Olives
Julias (Livias, Beth-haran)
Essebon
Jerusalem
Bethany
Khirbet Qumrân
Azotus
Bethlehem
Herodium
Ascalon
JUDAEA
Wilderness of Judaea
Salt or Dead Sea (L. Asphaltitis)
AMMON
Callirhoe
Marisa
Bethsura
Hebron
Machaerus
Gaza
Ziph
Dibon
Juttah
En-gedi
Arnon R.
Carmel
IDUMAEA
Masada
Raphia
Bersabee
MOABITIS
Kir-moab
ARABIA
Elusa
Brook Zered
NABATAEANS
ARABIA PETRAEA
A B C D E
1 2 3 4 5 6 7

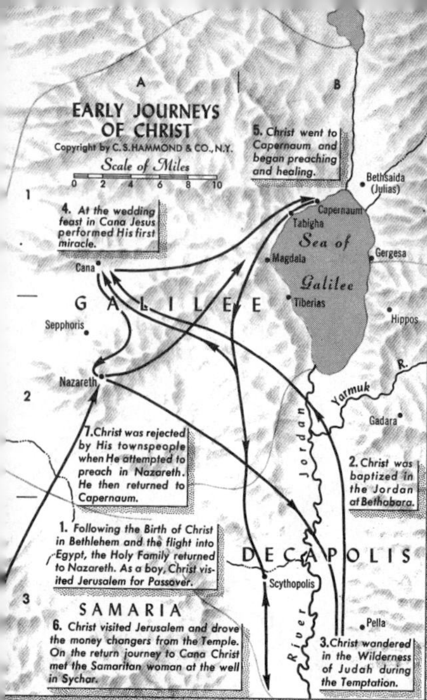
EARLY JOURNEYS OF CHRIST
Copyright by C. S. HAMMOND & CO., N.Y.
Scale of Miles
0 2 4 6 8 10
1. Following the Birth of Christ in Bethlehem and the flight into Egypt, the Holy Family returned to Nazareth. As a boy, Christ visited Jerusalem for Passover.
2. Christ was baptized in the Jordan at Bethobara.
3. Christ wandered in the Wilderness of Judah during the Temptation.
4. At the wedding feast in Cana Jesus performed His first miracle.
5. Christ went to Capernaum and began preaching and healing.
6. Christ visited Jerusalem and drove the money changers from the Temple. On the return journey to Cana Christ met the Samaritan woman at the well in Sychar.
7. Christ was rejected by His townspeople when He attempted to preach in Nazareth. He then returned to Capernaum.
GALILEE
DECAPOLIS
SAMARIA
Sea of Galilee
Capernaum
Tabigha
Bethsaida (Julias)
Magdala
Gergesa
Tiberias
Hippos
Cana
Sepphoris
Nazareth
Gadara
Yarmuk R.
River Jordan
Scythopolis
Pella

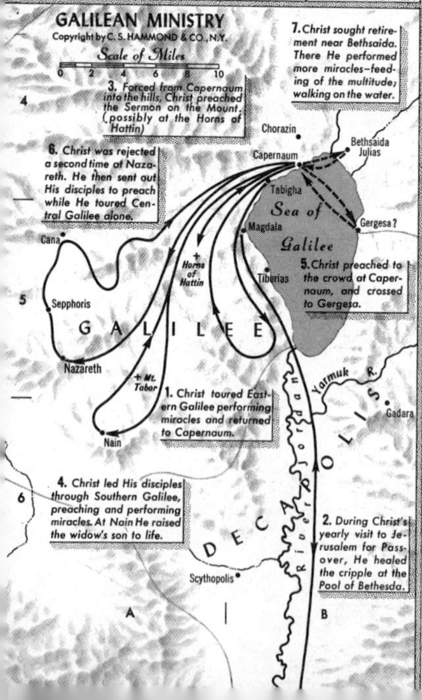
GALILEAN MINISTRY
Copyright by C. S. HAMMOND & CO., N.Y.
Scale of Miles
0 2 4 6 8 10
1. Christ toured Eastern Galilee performing miracles and returned to Capernaum.
2. During Christ's yearly visit to Jerusalem for Passover, He healed the cripple at the Pool of Bethesda.
3. Forced from Capernaum into the hills, Christ preached the Sermon on the Mount. (possibly at the Horns of Hattin)
4. Christ led His disciples through Southern Galilee, preaching and performing miracles. At Nain He raised the widow's son to life.
5. Christ preached to the crowd at Capernaum, and crossed to Gergesa.
6. Christ was rejected a second time at Nazareth. He then sent out His disciples to preach while He toured Central Galilee alone.
7. Christ sought retirement near Bethsaida. There He performed more miracles—feeding of the multitude; walking on the water.
Chorazin
Capernaum
Bethsaida Julias
Tabigha
Sea of Galilee
Gergesa ?
Magdala
Tiberias
Cana
Horns of Hattin
Sepphoris
GALILEE
Nazareth
Mt. Tabor
Nain
Yarmuk R.
Gadara
River Jordan
DECAPOLIS
Scythopolis

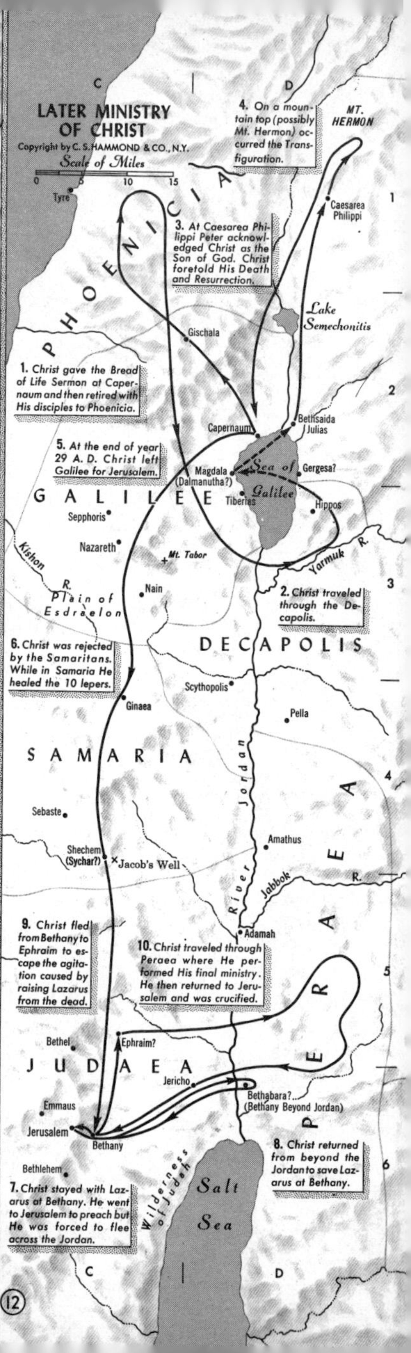
LATER MINISTRY OF CHRIST
Copyright by C. S. HAMMOND & CO., N.Y.
Scale of Miles
0 5 10 15
1. Christ gave the Bread of Life Sermon at Capernaum and then retired with His disciples to Phoenicia.
2. Christ traveled through the Decapolis.
3. At Caesarea Philippi Peter acknowledged Christ as the Son of God. Christ foretold His Death and Resurrection.
4. On a mountain top (possibly Mt. Hermon) occurred the Transfiguration.
5. At the end of year 29 A. D. Christ left Galilee for Jerusalem.
6. Christ was rejected by the Samaritans. While in Samaria He healed the 10 lepers.
7. Christ stayed with Lazarus at Bethany. He went to Jerusalem to preach but He was forced to flee across the Jordan.
8. Christ returned from beyond the Jordan to save Lazarus at Bethany.
9. Christ fled from Bethany to Ephraim to escape the agitation caused by raising Lazarus from the dead.
10. Christ traveled through Peraea where He performed His final ministry. He then returned to Jerusalem and was crucified.
MT. HERMON
Tyre
PHOENICIA
Caesarea Philippi
Lake Semechonitis
Gischala
Capernaum
Bethsaida Julias
Magdala (Dalmanutha?)
Sea of Galilee
Gergesa?
Tiberias
Hippos
GALILEE
Sepphoris
Nazareth
Mt. Tabor
Kishon R.
Plain of Esdraelon
Nain
Yarmuk R.
DECAPOLIS
Scythopolis
Ginaea
Pella
SAMARIA
Sebaste
Shechem (Sychar?)
Jacob's Well
Amathus
Jabbok R.
River Jordan
Adamah
PERAEA
Bethel
Ephraim?
JUDAEA
Jericho
Bethabara? (Bethany Beyond Jordan)
Emmaus
Jerusalem
Bethany
Bethlehem
Wilderness of Judah
Salt Sea

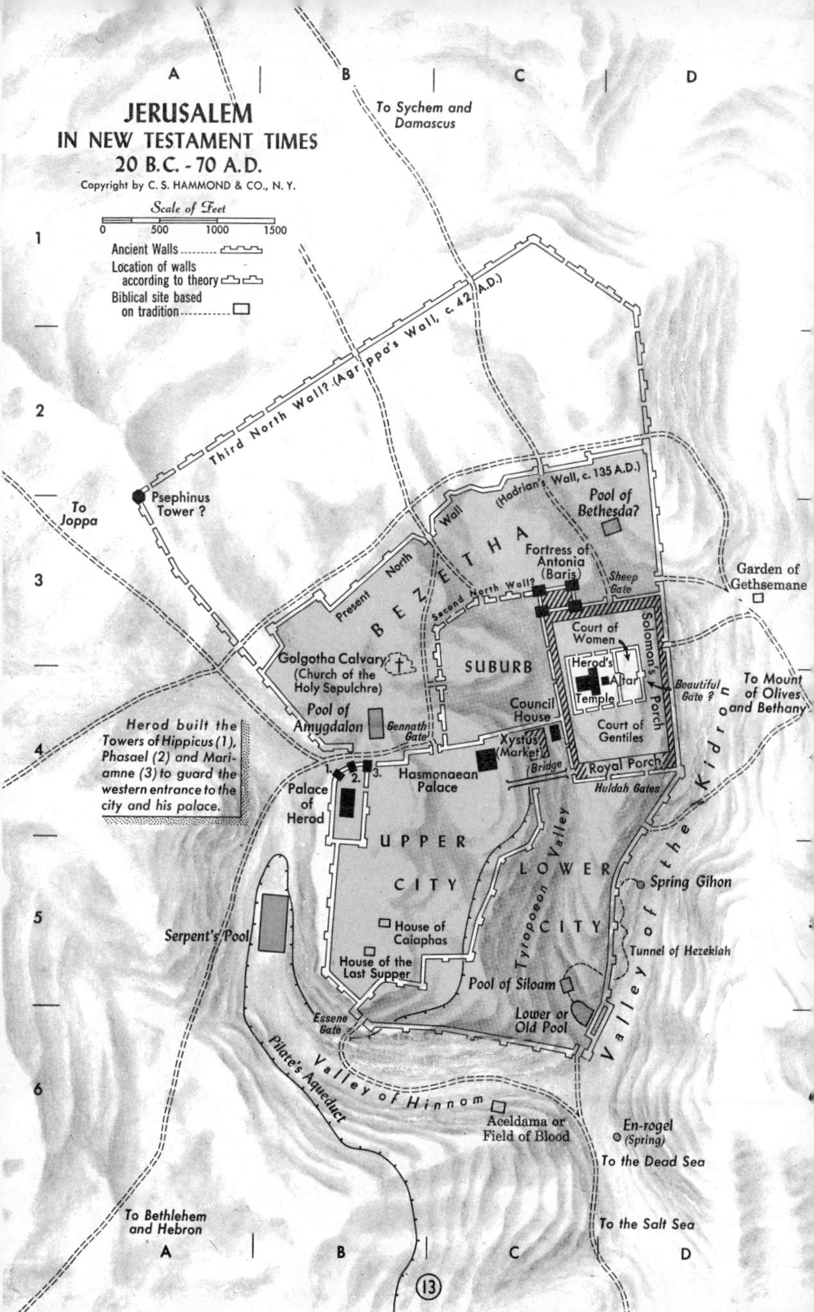
JERUSALEM
IN NEW TESTAMENT TIMES
20 B.C. - 70 A.D.
Copyright by C. S. HAMMOND & CO., N. Y.
Scale of Feet
0 500 1000 1500
Ancient Walls
Location of walls according to theory
Biblical site based on tradition
A
B
C
D
1
2
3
4
5
6
To Sychem and Damascus
Third North Wall? (Agrippa's Wall, c. 42 A.D.)
Psephinus Tower ?
To Joppa
Present North Wall (Hadrian's Wall, c. 135 A.D.)
Pool of Bethesda?
B E Z E T H A
Fortress of Antonia (Baris)
Sheep Gate
Second North Wall?
Garden of Gethsemane
Court of Women
Herod's Temple
Altar
Solomon's Porch
Beautiful Gate ?
To Mount of Olives and Bethany
Golgotha Calvary (Church of the Holy Sepulchre)
SUBURB
Council House
Court of Gentiles
Pool of Amygdalon
Gennath Gate
Xystus (Market)
Bridge
Royal Porch
Huldah Gates
Herod built the Towers of Hippicus (1), Phasael (2) and Mariamne (3) to guard the western entrance to the city and his palace.
1.
2.
3.
Hasmonaean Palace
Palace of Herod
UPPER CITY
Tyropoeon Valley
LOWER CITY
Spring Gihon
Tunnel of Hezekiah
Valley of the Kidron
Serpent's Pool
House of Caiaphas
House of the Last Supper
Pool of Siloam
Lower or Old Pool
Essene Gate
Pilate's Aqueduct
Valley of Hinnom
Aceldama or Field of Blood
En-rogel (Spring)
To the Dead Sea
To Bethlehem and Hebron
To the Salt Sea

ST. PAUL'S FIRST AND SECOND JOURNEYS
Copyright by C. S. HAMMOND & CO., N. Y.
Scale of Miles
0 50 100 200 300
First Journey
Second Journey
Rome
Ortona
Three Taverns
Appii Forum
Beneventum
Neapolis
Puteoli
ITALY
Brundisium
Buxentum
Tarentum
Anxa
Croton
Tyrrhenian Sea
Messana
Rhegium
SICILY
Agrigentum
Syracuse
MELITA (MALTA)
ILLYRICUM (DALMATIA)
Scodra
Dyrrhachium
Adria
MOESIA
MACEDONIA
Epirus
Corcyra
Nicopolis
ACHAIA
Berea
Larisa
Amphipolis
Philippi
Neapolis
Apollonia
Thessalonica
Hebrus R.
THRACE
Mesembria
Byzantium
SAMOTHRACE
Propontis
Aegean Sea
Corinth
Athens
Cenchrea
(GREECE)
Sparta
CYCLADES
Troas
Mysia
Assos
Adramyttium
LESBOS
Mitylene
CHIOS
Pergamum
Thyatira
Sardis
Smyrna
Lydia
Ephesus
SAMOS
Trogyllium
Miletus
Caria
COOS
Cnidus
RHODES
Patara
Xanthus
LYCIA
Myra
Philadelphia
Hierapolis
Laodicea
Colossae
Phrygia
ASIA
Dorylaeum
Pontus Euxinus (Black Sea)
Heraclea Pontica
Nicomedia
Nicaea
BITHYNIA & PONTUS
Sinope
Amisus
Paphlagonia
Germanicopolis
Sangarius R.
Ancyra
Halys R.
Pessinus
GALATIA
MINOR
Amasia
Zela
Tavium
Sebastia
KDM. OF POLEMON
Caesarea Mazaca
L. Tatta
CAPPADOCIA
Antioch
Lycaonia
Iconium
Lystra
Derbe
Tyana
Pisidia
Perga
Attalia
PAMPHYLIA
Selinus
CILICIA
Tarsus
Starting point of 1st & 2nd journeys
Seleucia
Antioch
SYRIA
CYPRUS
Salamis
Paphos
Cydonia
Cnossus
Phoenix
CRETE
Lasea
C. Salmone
CLAUDA
Fair Havens
The Great Sea (Mediterranean Sea)
Phoenicia
Damascus
Sidon
Tyre
Ptolemais
Galilee
Caesarea
Joppa
Jerusalem
Judaea
Gaza
Limit of Roman Empire
ARABIA
Pelusium
EGYPT
PHAROS
Alexandria
Heliopolis
Memphis
Nile R.
Catabathmus
Paraetonium
CYRENAICA (Libya)
B
C
D
E
F
1
2
3
14

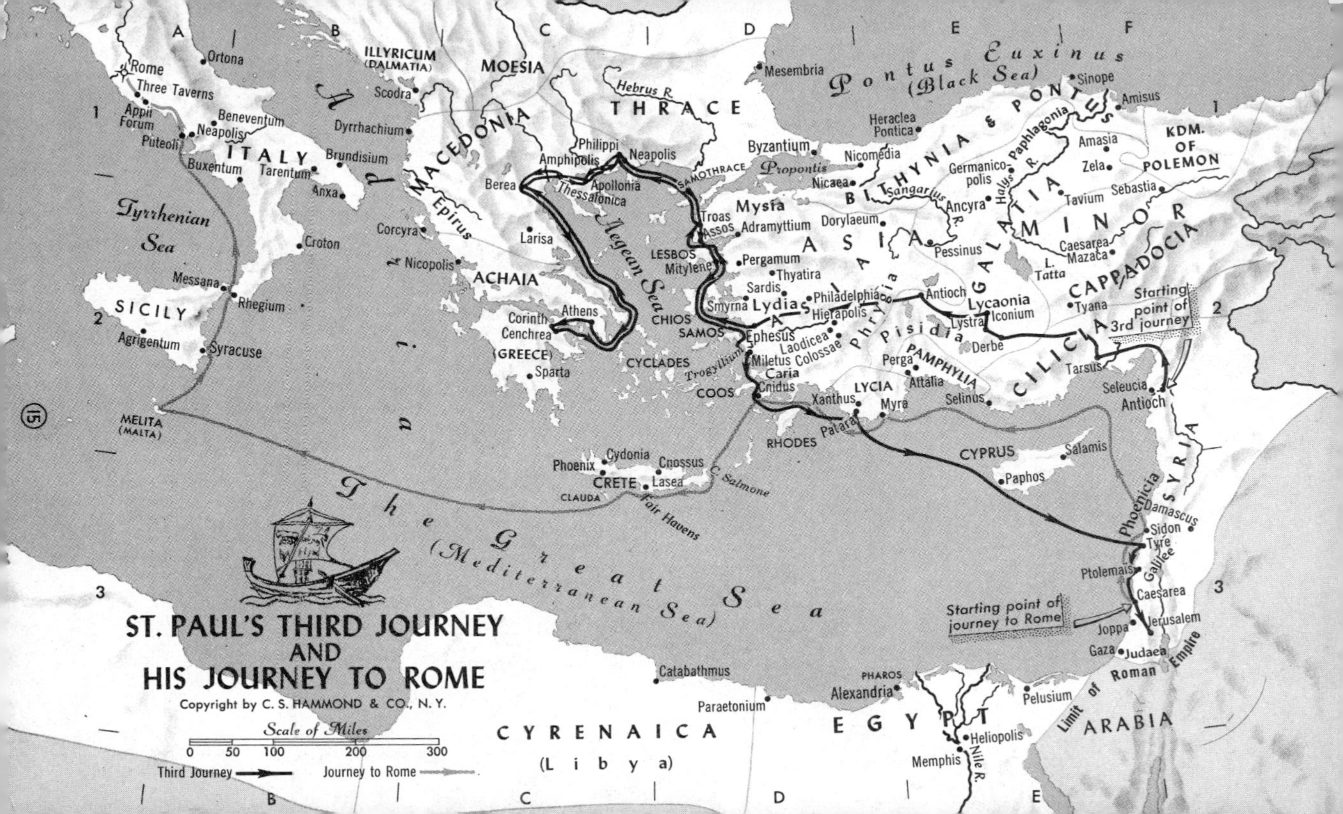
ST. PAUL'S THIRD JOURNEY
AND
HIS JOURNEY TO ROME
Copyright by C. S. HAMMOND & CO., N. Y.
Scale of Miles
0 50 100 200 300
Third Journey
Journey to Rome
Starting point of 3rd journey
Starting point of journey to Rome
Pontus Euxinus (Black Sea)
The Great Sea (Mediterranean Sea)
Aegean Sea
Tyrrhenian Sea
Adria
ITALY
SICILY
ILLYRICUM (DALMATIA)
MOESIA
MACEDONIA
THRACE
Epirus
ACHAIA
(GREECE)
BITHYNIA & PONTUS
KDM. OF POLEMON
GALATIA
MINOR
ASIA
CAPPADOCIA
CILICIA
Mysia
Lydia
Phrygia
Pisidia
Lycaonia
PAMPHYLIA
LYCIA
Caria
SYRIA
Phoenicia
Galilee
Judaea
ARABIA
EGYPT
CYRENAICA (Libya)
Limit of Roman Empire
CYPRUS
CRETE
RHODES
CLAUDA
MELITA (MALTA)
LESBOS
CHIOS
SAMOS
COOS
CYCLADES
SAMOTHRACE
PHAROS
Propontis
Rome
Three Taverns
Appii Forum
Puteoli
Neapolis
Beneventum
Ortona
Buxentum
Tarentum
Brundisium
Anxa
Croton
Rhegium
Messana
Syracuse
Agrigentum
Scodra
Dyrrhachium
Corcyra
Nicopolis
Berea
Larisa
Thessalonica
Apollonia
Amphipolis
Philippi
Neapolis
Hebrus R.
Athens
Corinth
Cenchrea
Sparta
Mesembria
Byzantium
Nicomedia
Nicaea
Heraclea Pontica
Sinope
Amisus
Amasia
Zela
Sebastia
Tavium
Germanicopolis
Paphlagonia
Halys R.
Sangarius R.
Ancyra
Pessinus
Dorylaeum
Caesarea Mazaca
L. Tatta
Tyana
Troas
Assos
Adramyttium
Pergamum
Mitylene
Thyatira
Sardis
Smyrna
Philadelphia
Hierapolis
Laodicea
Colossae
Ephesus
Trogyllium
Miletus
Cnidus
Antioch
Iconium
Lystra
Derbe
Perga
Attalia
Selinus
Tarsus
Seleucia
Antioch
Xanthus
Patara
Myra
Salamis
Paphos
Cydonia
Cnossus
Phoenix
Lasea
Fair Havens
C. Salmone
Damascus
Sidon
Tyre
Ptolemais
Caesarea
Jerusalem
Joppa
Gaza
Pelusium
Heliopolis
Memphis
Nile R.
Alexandria
Paraetonium
Catabathmus
15

THE ROMAN EMPIRE
AT ITS GREATEST EXTENT
c. 117 A. D.
Copyright by C. S. HAMMOND & CO., N.Y.
Scale of Miles
0 100 200 400 600
Capital
Maximum extent of Roman control in the time of Trajan, 98-117 A. D.
Roman walls
The Germanic tribes exerted constant pressure on the Rhine-Danube frontier, placing the Empire on the defensive. The western provinces and Italy were overrun by Germanic invaders in the fifth century.
Trajan's conquests east of the Euphrates were abandoned by Hadrian in 118 A. D.
In 395 A. D. the Roman world was divided into separate eastern and western empires.
Atlantic Ocean
North Sea (Oceanus Germanicus)
Baltic Sea
Black Sea (Pontus Euxinus)
Caspian Sea (Mare Hyrcanium)
Mediterranean Sea (Mare Internum)
Adriatic Sea
Tyrrhenian Sea
Ionian Sea
Aegean Sea
Red Sea (Sinus Arabicus)
Persian Gulf
English Channel
Hibernia
BRITAIN
GAUL
SPAIN
ITALY
AFRICA
EGYPT
Sarmatia
Germania
Arabia
SAHARA
PARTHIAN EMPIRE
16